Criminological Theory

Third Edition

Stephen G. Tibbetts dedicates this book to his daughter, Rian Sage, who has been really cool to hang out with watching SpongeBob over the past decade; Rian has been the best daughter anyone could ask for.

Craig Hemmens dedicates this book, all the books in this series, and everything of value he has ever done to his father, George Hemmens, who showed him the way; James Marquart and Rolando del Carmen, who taught him how; and Mary and Emily, for giving him something he loves even more than his work.

Criminological Theory

A Text/Reader

Third Edition

Stephen G. Tibbetts
California State University, San Bernardino

Craig Hemmens
Washington State University

Los Angeles | London | New Delhi
Singapore | Washington DC | Melbourne

FOR INFORMATION:

SAGE Publications, Inc.
2455 Teller Road
Thousand Oaks, California 91320
E-mail: order@sagepub.com

SAGE Publications Ltd.
1 Oliver's Yard
55 City Road
London EC1Y 1SP
United Kingdom

SAGE Publications India Pvt. Ltd.
B 1/I 1 Mohan Cooperative Industrial Area
Mathura Road, New Delhi 110 044
India

SAGE Publications Asia-Pacific Pte. Ltd.
3 Church Street
#10-04 Samsung Hub
Singapore 049483

Acquisitions Editor: Jessica Miller
Editorial Assistant: Rebecca Lee
Production Editor: Laureen Gleason
Copy Editor: Megan Markanich
Typesetter: C&M Digitals (P) Ltd.
Proofreader: Scott Oney
Indexer: Michael Ferreira
Cover Designer: Janet Kiesel
Marketing Manager: Jillian Oelsen

Printed in the United States of America

Library of Congress Cataloging-in-Publication Data

Names: Tibbetts, Stephen G., author. | Hemmens, Craig, author.

Title: Criminological theory : a text/reader / Stephen G. Tibbetts, California State University, San Bernardino, Craig T. Hemmens, Washington State University.

Description: Third edition. | Los Angeles : SAGE, [2019] | Includes bibliographical references and index.

Identifiers: LCCN 2017041106 | ISBN 9781506367828 (pbk. : alk. paper)

Subjects: LCSH: Criminology. | Crime.

Classification: LCC HV6018 .T53 2019 | DDC 364.01—dc23
LC record available at https://lccn.loc.gov/2017041106

This book is printed on acid-free paper.

SFI label applies to text stock

18 19 20 21 22 10 9 8 7 6 5 4 3 2

Brief Contents

Detailed Contents

Foreword

You hold in your hands a book that we think is a different approach to this subject matter and to student learning. It is billed a "text/reader." What that means is that we have blended the two most commonly used types of books, the textbook and the reader, in a way that will appeal to both students and faculty.

Our experience as teachers and scholars has been that textbooks for the core classes in criminal justice (or any other social science discipline) leave many students and professors cold. The textbooks are huge and crammed with photographs, charts, highlighted material, and all sorts of pedagogical devices intended to increase student interest. Too often, however, these books end up creating a sort of sensory overload for students and suffer from their focus on "bells and whistles," such as fancy graphics, at the expense of coverage of the most significant and current research on the subject matter. And, in the end, isn't that what matters most? We study crime and justice to better understand why crime happens and how society processes it, and it is research—not pretty pictures—that inform this process. Our students deserve more than a nicely packaged recitation of boring facts; they need to understand what the research says, and this research needs to be presented in a fashion that does not scare them off.

Readers, on the other hand, are typically composed of recent and classic research articles on the subject matter. They generally suffer, however, from an absence of meaningful explanatory material. Articles are simply lined up and presented to the students with little or no context or explanation. Students, particularly undergraduate students, are often confused and overwhelmed by the jargon and detailed statistical analyses presented in the articles. It is unrealistic to expect students to fully grasp criminal justice research if this research is not placed in context and presented in a manner suited to their knowledge level.

This text/reader represents our attempt to take the best of both textbook and reader approaches. The book includes a combination of previously published articles on criminological theory and of textual material introducing the articles and providing structure and context. The text/reader is intended to serve either as a supplement to a core undergraduate textbook or as a stand-alone text.

The book is divided into a number of sections. The sections of the book track the typical content and structure of a textbook on the subject. Each section of the book has an introductory chapter that introduces, explains, and provides context for the readings that follow. The readings are a selection of the best recent research from academic journals as well as some classic readings where appropriate. The articles are edited as necessary to make them accessible to students. This variety of research and perspectives will provide the student with a grasp of the development of research as well as an understanding of the current status of research in the subject area. The approach gives the student the opportunity to learn the basics (in the introductory portion of each section) and to read some of the most interesting research on the subject.

There is also a preface and an introductory chapter. The preface explains the organization and content of the book, and the introductory chapter provides a framework for the material that follows and introduces relevant themes, issues, and concepts to assist the student in understanding the articles.

Each section concludes with a summary of the material covered as well as a set of discussion questions. Discussion questions also appear at the end of each reading. These summaries and discussion questions should facilitate student thought and class discussion of the material.

Ancillary materials, such as PowerPoint slides, a test bank, and lecture outlines, are available to help assist the instructor in moving from a standard textbook to this hybrid approach.

We acknowledge that this approach may be viewed by some as more challenging than the traditional textbook. To that we say, "Yes! It is!" But we believe that if we raise the bar our students will rise to the challenge. Research shows that students and faculty often find textbooks boring to read. It is our belief that many criminal justice instructors welcome the opportunity to teach without having to rely on a "standard" textbook that covers only the most basic information and that lacks both depth of coverage and an attention to current research. This book provides an alternative for instructors who want more than a basic textbook aimed at the lowest common denominator and filled with flashy but often useless features that merely drive up its cost. This book is intended for instructors who want their students to be exposed to more than the ordinary, basic coverage of criminal justice.

We also believe students will find this approach more interesting. They are given the opportunity to read current, cutting-edge research on the subject while also being provided with background and context for this research. In addition to including the most topical and relevant research, we have included a short guide: "How to Read a Research Article." The purpose of this entry, placed toward the beginning of the book, is to provide students with an overview of the components of a research article. It helps walk them through the process of reading a research article, lessening their trepidation and increasing their ability to comprehend the material presented therein. Many students will be unfamiliar with reading and deciphering research articles; we hope this feature will help them do so.

In addition, we provide a student study site on the Internet with supplemental research articles, study questions, practice quizzes, and other pedagogical material to assist the student in learning the material. We chose to put these pedagogical tools on a companion study site rather than in the text to allow instructors to focus on the material, while still offering students the opportunity to learn more.

To date, there have been 13 books published in the text/reader series. Many of them have gone into (or are in the process of going into) multiple editions. The feedback we have received from early adopters has been overwhelmingly positive. Instructors have successfully used these books in community colleges and universities at both the undergraduate and graduate levels. Faculty tell us they find the books more interesting to use and teach from, and that students appreciate the different approach.

We hope that this unconventional approach will be more interesting to students and faculty alike and thus make learning and teaching more fun. Criminal justice is a fascinating subject, and the topic deserves to be presented in an interesting manner. We hope you will agree.

Craig Hemmens, JD, PhD, Series Editor

Department of Criminal Justice and Criminology
Washington State University

Preface

A number of excellent criminology theory textbooks and readers are available to students and professors, so why this one? The reason is that stand-alone textbooks and readers (often assigned as an expensive addition to a textbook) have a pedagogical fault that we seek to rectify with the present book. Textbooks provide a broad overview of the topic but lack depth and a focus on current research, whereas readers often feature in-depth articles about a single topic but give little or no text to describe the history of each model or the context in which it was proposed, little text to unify the readings, and little in the way of pedagogy. This book, especially in its third edition, provides more in the way of text and pedagogy and uses recent research-based articles to help students understand criminological theory. This book is unique in that it is a hybrid text/reader, offering the best of both worlds. It includes a collection of articles on criminological theory that have previously appeared in a number of leading criminology journals along with original text that explains and synthesizes the readings. We have selected some of the best recent research and literature reviews and assembled them into this text/reader for an undergraduate or graduate theory class.

Journal articles and book chapters have been chosen based primarily on how they add to and complement the text and on how interesting we perceive them to be for students. Although seminal theoretical pieces are included among the previously published works, we have emphasized contemporary empirical studies that actually test the theories in each respective section. We believe this focus on recent empirical studies and scholarly works regarding the various major theoretical models in criminology, most from leading criminology journals, is a distinguishing feature of this text/reader as compared to other books on criminological theory. In our opinion, these articles are the best contemporary work on the issues they address. For example, in this third edition, we are including more than a dozen new readings that are either far more recent or seen as more relevant for applying the theoretical models and concepts presented in the text.

Furthermore, of the 13 new readings in this new edition, all were published after 2012 (with most since 2014), and most of them were published by authors or using samples from places outside of the United States. These international readings include South Africa, the Netherlands, Brazil, Canada, the West Indies, Korea, Ukraine, and Australia. This was done for purposes of integrating a more global view of incorporating criminological research and theory across nations and continents. After all, there is much validity in how such established theories are unified by their empirical support and validity, as well as policy applications, across societies and cultures around the world.

However, journal articles are written for professional audiences, not for students, and thus often contain quantitative material that students are not expected to understand. They also often contain concepts and hair-splitting arguments that tend to turn students glassy-eyed. Mindful of this, we have carefully and meticulously edited the articles contained in this text/reader to make them as student friendly as possible. We have done this without doing injustice to the core points raised by the authors or detracting from the authors' key findings and conclusions. Those wishing to read these articles (and others) in their entirety can do so by accessing the SAGE website provided for users of this book. Research-based quantitative articles are balanced by review or overview essay-type articles and qualitative articles providing subjective insight into criminal behavior from the points of view of offenders.

This book can serve as a supplemental reader or the primary text for an undergraduate course in criminological theory or as the primary text for a graduate course. In a graduate course, it would serve as both an introduction to the extant literature and a sourcebook for additional reading as well as a springboard for enhanced class discussion. When used in an undergraduate course, this book can serve to provide greater depth than the standard textbook. It is important to note that the readings and the introductory texts provide a comprehensive survey of the existing scientific literature in virtually all areas of criminological theory as well as giving a history of how we got to this point regarding each theoretical model and each topic.

Structure of the Book

We use a rather typical outline for criminological theory textbook topics, or sections, beginning with an introduction of the definitions of crime and criminology and measuring crime as well as what such measures of crime reveal regarding the various characteristics that are most associated with higher offending rates. This is a very important aspect of the book, because each theory or model must be judged by how well it explains the distribution of crime rates among these various characteristics.

This text/reader is divided into 12 sections that mirror the sections in a typical criminology textbook, each dealing with a particular subject in criminology, with the exception that we very notably have a separate section regarding feminist perspectives of crime, which we are very proud to present. These sections are as follows:

I. Introduction to the Book: An Overview of Issues in Criminological Theory

We first provide an introductory section that deals with what criminological theory is as well as examining the concepts of crime and the criteria used to determine whether a theory is adequate for explaining behavior. This section introduces the facts and criteria by which all of the theoretical models presented in the following sections will be evaluated. We also include a discussion of the criteria involved in determining whether a given factor or variable actually causes criminal behavior.

II. Preclassical and Classical Theories of Crime

In this section, we examine the types of theories that were dominant before logical theories of crime were presented, namely supernatural or demonic theories of crime. Then we examine how the Age of Enlightenment led to more rational approaches to explaining criminal behavior, such as that of the Classical School and neoclassical theory. We also discuss at length the major model that evolved from the Classical School: deterrence theory. We describe studies that have empirically tested deterrence theory.

III. Modern Applications of the Classical Perspective: Deterrence, Rational Choice, and Routine Activities or Lifestyle Theories of Crime

In this section, we review more contemporary theoretical models and empirical findings regarding explanations of crime that focus on deterrence and other recent perspectives—such as rational choice theory, routine activities theory, and the lifestyle perspective—that are based on the assumption that individuals rationally choose their behavior or targets. Some of these perspectives focus more on the perceived costs or benefits of a given act to the individual who carries it out, whereas other models focus on the types of locations that people choose to commit crime or the daily activities or lifestyles that predispose them to certain criminal behavior.

IV. Early Positive School Perspectives of Criminality

This section will examine the early development of theoretical models proposing that certain individuals or groups are predisposed to criminal offending. The earliest theories in the 19th century proposed that certain physical traits are associated with criminal behavior, whereas perspectives in the early 20th century proposed that such criminality is due to level of intelligence. This section also examines body-type theory, which proposes that the physical body type of an individual has an effect on criminality. We will also examine modern applications of this perspective and review the empirical support such theoretical models have received in modern times.

V. Modern Biosocial Perspectives of Criminal Behavior

In this section, we will review the various forms of modern studies that investigate the link between physiology and criminality, including family studies, twin and adoption studies, cytogenetic studies, and studies on hormones and neurotransmitters. We will examine some of the primary methods used to explore this link as well as discuss the findings of more rational and recent empirical studies, which show a relatively consistent link between physiological factors and criminal behavior.

VI. Early Social Structure and Strain Theories of Crime

This section reviews the development of the social structure perspective, which originated in the 19th century and culminated with Robert Merton's theory of strain in the early 20th century. A variety of perspectives based on Merton's strain theory will be examined, but all of these models have a primary emphasis on how the social structure produces criminal behavior. We examine the many empirical studies that have tested the validity of these early social structure theories, as well as discussing policy implications that these models suggested.

VII. The Chicago School and Cultural and Subcultural Theories of Crime

In this section, we examine the evolution and propositions of the scholars at the University of Chicago, the most advanced form of criminological theorizing of the early 20th century. In addition to discussing the evolution of the Chicago School and its application of ecological theory to criminal behavior, we examine the more modern applications of this theoretical framework for explaining criminal behavior among residents of certain neighborhoods. Finally, we discuss several theoretical models that examine cultural or subcultural groups that differ drastically from conventional norms.

VIII. Social Process and Learning Theories of Crime

This section examines the many perspectives that have proposed that criminal behavior is the result of being taught by significant others to commit crime. When these theories were first presented, they were considered quite novel. We examine the evolution of various theories of social learning, starting with the earliest, which were based on somewhat outdated forms of learning theory, and then progressing to more modern theories that incorporate contemporary learning models. We also examine the most recent versions of this theoretical perspective, which incorporates all forms of social learning in explaining criminal behavior.

IX. Social Reaction and Critical Models of Crime

In this section, we examine a large range of theories, with the common assumption that the reason for criminal behavior is factors outside of the traditional criminal justice system. Many social reaction theories, for example, are based on labeling theory, which proposes that it is not the individual offender who is to blame but rather the societal reaction to such early antisocial behavior. Furthermore, this section examines the critical perspective, which blames the existing legal and economical structure for the "criminal" label that is used against most offenders.

X. Feminist Models of Crime

This section examines the various theoretical feminist perspectives of crime. Feminist criminology evolved when various assumptions and stereotypes about women in criminal justice were being questioned. Such questions included women as both offenders and victims. We discuss the importance of research regarding female offending, which was largely neglected in nearly all previous research before the late 19th century, and then discuss the extant literature that has been produced in recent years. This section discusses how important it is to examine the research that has been done on female offending and how key it is to understanding why women are so much less likely to commit serious violent offenses than males—and perhaps to using that understanding to reduce male chronic offending in society.

XI. Life-Course Perspectives of Criminality

This section examines the various theoretical perspectives that emphasize the predisposition and influences present among individuals who begin committing crime at early versus later ages. We also examine the various stages of life that tend to have a high influence on an individual's state of criminality (e.g., marriage) as well as the empirical studies that have examined these types of transitions in life. Finally, we examine the various types of offenders and the kinds of transitions and trajectories that tend to influence their future behavior along with various policy implications that can be suggested by such models of criminality.

XII. Integrated Theoretical Models and New Perspectives of Crime

In this section, we present the general theoretical framework for integrated models. Then we introduce criticisms of such integration of traditional theoretical models. In addition, we present several integrated models of criminality, some of which are based on micro-level factors and others that are based on macro-level factors. Finally, we examine the weaknesses and strengths of these various models based on empirical studies that have tested their validity.

New to This Edition

- Nearly half of the journal articles have been updated and cover important topics such as media consumption and support for capital punishment, gender differences in delinquency, bias and police stops, and the effectiveness of reintegrative shaming and restorative justice.
- Integrating a more global view of criminological research and theory across nations and continents, several of the new readings were published by authors or using samples from places outside of the United States. These international readings include South Africa, the Netherlands, Brazil, Canada, the West Indies, Korea, Ukraine, and Australia.
- A new section dedicated entirely to feminist perspectives (Section X) examines the feminist models of crime and underscores the importance of examining research related to female offending.
- Case studies that examine offender motives help students apply the theories discussed.
- Coverage of policy is now further integrated into each section as opposed to having a stand-alone section on this topic.

- Coverage of critical topics, such as the influence of employment on criminal behavior, and the success of school programs to reduce delinquent behavior have been expanded throughout.
- Statistics, graphs, and tables have all been updated to demonstrate the most recent trends in criminology.

Digital Resources

To enhance the use of this text/reader and to assist those using this book as a core text, we have developed high-quality digital resources for instructors and students.

Instructor's Resource Site. A variety of instructor's materials are available. For each chapter, these include summaries, PowerPoint slides, chapter activities, web resources, and a complete set of test questions.

Student Study Site. A comprehensive student study site features chapter outlines students can print for class, flash cards, self quizzes, web exercises, links to journal articles, online videos, links to *Frontline* videos, links to NPR and PBS program archives, and more.

Acknowledgments

We would first of all like to thank executive editor Jessica Miller. Jessica's faith in and commitment to the project is greatly appreciated, and she has provided excellent guidance in making this new edition much better than the previous versions of this text. We also owe much gratitude to our very able production editor, Laureen Gleason. They kept up a most useful three-way dialogue among authors, publisher, and a parade of excellent reviewers, making this text the best that it could possibly be. We would also like to thank Erin Conley, who wrote the guide "How to Read a Research Article." Our copy editor, Megan Markanich, spotted every errant comma, dangling participle, and missing reference in the manuscript, for which we are truly thankful. Thank you one and all. We would like to express our great appreciation for Jerry Westby, the editor for the first two editions of this text. Jerry showed the initiative to start this series with Craig and took a chance on Steve coming on board when he had never been involved in such a large book project before. Jerry remains a very close friend with both authors. Jerry, we wish you well in the next stage of your life!

Stephen Tibbetts also would like to thank the various individuals who helped him complete this book. First, he would like to thank the professors he had as an undergraduate at the University of Florida, who first exposed him to criminological theory. These professors include Ronald Akers and Lonn Lanza-Kaduce, with a special thanks to Donna Bishop, who was the instructor in his first criminological theory course. He also would like to thank the influential professors he had at the University of Maryland, including Denise Gottfredson, Colin Loftin, David McDowell, Lawrence Sherman, and Charles Wellford. He gives a very special acknowledgment to Raymond Paternoster, who was his primary mentor and adviser and exerted an influence words can't describe. Ray and his wife, Ronet Bachman, provided rare support as surrogate parents when Tibbetts was in graduate school. Ray also introduced him to the passion for criminological theory that he hopes is reflected in this book.

Tibbetts would like to thank Alex Piquero, also at the University of Maryland, with whom he had the great luck of sharing a graduate student office in the mid-1990s and who is now a professor at the university. Without the many collaborations and discussions about theory that he had with Alex, this book would be quite different and would likely not exist. Alex and his wife, Nicole Leeper Piquero, have consistently been key influences on Tibbetts's perspective on and understanding of theories of crimes, especially contemporary models (and the works of both of the Piqueros are represented in this book).

In addition, Tibbetts would like to thank several colleagues who have helped him subsequent to his education. First, he would like to thank John Paul Wright at the University of Cincinnati and Chris Gibson at the University of

Florida for inspiring him to further explore biosocial and developmental areas of criminality. Also, he would like to thank Donna Derbish and Matthew Logan at California State University, San Bernardino (CSUSB), who provided much help in the compilation and discussion of materials for this book. In addition, he would like to especially thank Pamela Schram and Larry Gaines, fellow professors at CSUSB, who have provided the highest possible level of support and guidance during his career. Furthermore, it should be noted that Pamela Schram provided key insights and materials that aided in the writing of several sections of this book. Finally, he would like to thank Jose Rivera, an award-winning lecturer at CSUSB, for sharing his experiences in his more than eight years of being a prisoner in California state prisons and providing material for this and other books and articles; he is a true friend and colleague.

My mother and father, Jane and Steve Tibbetts Sr., have been the key to all of my accomplishments. We don't get to choose our parents, but I won the lottery by having them to guide me through life.

Tibbetts owes the most gratitude to his wife, Kim, who has patiently put up with him typing away for the past few years while working on various versions of this book. Her constant support and companionship are what keeps him going; she is the most supportive companion anyone could ask for.

Both authors are grateful to the many reviewers who spent considerable time reading early drafts of their work and who provided helpful suggestions for improving both the textual material and the edited readings. Trying to please so many individuals is a challenge but one that is ultimately satisfying and undoubtedly made the book better than it would otherwise have been. Heartfelt thanks go to the following experts:

Stuart Agnew, University of Suffolk

Shannon Barton-Bellessa, Indiana State University

Deborah Baskin, Loyola University–Chicago

Michael L. Benson, University of Cincinnati

Robert Brame, University of South Carolina

Tammy Castle, University of West Florida

James Chriss, Cleveland State University

Ellen G. Cohn, Florida International University

Toni DuPont-Morales, Pennsylvania State University

Joshua D. Freilich, John Jay College

Randy Gainey, Old Dominion University

Julie L. Globokar, Kent State University

Evan Gorelick, Germanna Community College

Robert Hanser, Kaplan University

Jay Healey, Simon Fraser University

Heath Hoffman, College of Charleston

Thomas Holt, University of North Carolina at Charlotte

Rebecca Katz, Morehead State University

Dennis Longmire, Sam Houston State University

Gina Luby, DePaul University

Michael J. Lynch, University of South Florida

J. Mitchell Miller, University of Texas at San Antonio

Michelle Hughes Miller, Southern Illinois University Carbondale

Jake Phillips, Sheffield Hallam University

Travis Pratt, Arizona State University

Lois Presser, University of Tennessee

Aqeel Saeid, Humber Institute of Technology and Advanced Learning

Robert Sarver, University of Texas at Arlington

Martin S. Schwartz, Ohio University

Joseph Scimecca, George Mason University

Victoria Silverwood, Cardiff University

Ira Sommers, California State University, Los Angeles

Amy Thistlethwaite, Northern Kentucky University

Kimberly Tobin, Westfield State College

Adam Trahan, University of North Texas

Michael Turner, University of North Carolina at Charlotte

Scott Vollum, James Madison University

Courtney Waid, North Dakota State University

Barbara Warner, Georgia State University

Mary G. Wilson, Kent State University Trumbull Campus

James Windle, University of East London

Sarah Yercich, Northern Arizona University

SECTION I

Introduction to the Book

An Overview of Issues in Criminological Theory

Welcome to the world of criminological theory! It is an exciting and complex endeavor that explains why certain individuals and groups commit crimes and why other people do not. This book will explore the conceptual history of this endeavor as well as current theories. Most of us can relate directly to many of these theories; we may know friends or family members who fit dominant models of criminal behavior.

This introduction begins by describing what criminology is; what distinguishes it from other perspectives of crime, such as religion, journalism, and philosophy; and how definitions of crime vary across time and place. Then it examines some of the major issues used to classify different theories of criminology. After exploring the various paradigms and categories of criminological theory, we discuss what characteristics help to make a theory a good one—in criminology or in any scientific field. In addition, we review the specific criteria for proving causality—for showing which predictors or variables actually cause criminal behavior. We also explain why—for logistic and ethical reasons—few theories in criminology will ever meet the strict criteria required to prove that key factors actually cause criminal behavior. Finally, we look at the strengths and weaknesses of the various measures of crime, which are used to test the validity of all criminological theories, and what those measures reveal about how crime is distributed across various individuals and groups. Although the discussion of crime distribution, as shown by various measures of criminality, may seem removed from our primary discussion regarding theories of why certain individuals and groups commit more crime than others, nothing could be further from the truth. Ultimately, all theories of criminal behavior will be judged based on how much each theory can explain the observed rates of crime shown by the measures of criminality among individuals and groups.

What Is Criminology, and How Does It Differ from Other Examinations of Crime?

Criminology is the scientific study of crime—and especially of why people commit crime. Although many textbooks have more complex definitions of crime, the word *scientific* separates our definition from other perspectives and examinations of crime.[1] Philosophical and legal examinations of crime are based on logic and deductive reasoning, for example, by developing propositions for what makes logical sense. Journalists play a vital role in

[1]Stephen Brown, Finn Esbensen, and Gilbert Geis, *Criminology*, 8th ed. (Cincinnati, OH: Anderson, 2013).

examinations of crime by exploring what is happening in criminal justice and revealing injustices and new forms of crime; however, they tend to examine anecdotes or examples of crime as opposed to objective measures of criminality.

Taken together, philosophical, legal, and journalistic perspectives of crime are not scientific because they do not involve the use of the **scientific method**. Specifically, they do not develop specific predictions, known scientifically as **hypotheses**, which are based on prior knowledge and studies, and then go out and test these predictions through observation. Criminology is based on this scientific method, whereas other examinations of crime are not.

Instead, philosophers and journalists tend to examine a specific case, make conclusions based on that one example of a crime incident, and then leave it at that. Experts in these nonscientific disciplines do not typically examine a multitude of stories similar to the one they are considering, nor do they apply the elements of their story to an existing theoretical framework that offers specific predictions or hypotheses. Further, they do not test those predictions by observation. The method of testing predictions through observation and then applying the findings to a larger body of knowledge, as established by theoretical models, is solely the domain of criminologists, and it separates criminology from other fields. The use of the scientific method is a distinguishing criterion for many studies of human behavior, such as psychology, economics, sociology, and anthropology, which is why these disciplines are generally classified as **social sciences**; criminology is one of them.

To look at another perspective on crime, religious accounts are almost entirely based on dogmatic, authoritarian, or reasoning principles, meaning that they are typically based on what some authority (e.g., the Pope or the Bible, the Torah, or the Koran) has to say about the primary causes of crime and the best ways to deal with such violations. These ideas are not based on observations. A science like criminology is based not on authority or anecdotes but on empirical research—even if that research is conducted by a 15-year-old who performs a methodologically sound study. In other words, the authority of the scientist performing the study does not matter; rather, the observed evidence and the soundness of the methodology—how the study was performed—are of utmost importance. Criminology is based on science, and its work is accomplished through direct observation and testing of hypotheses, even if those findings do not fit neatly into logical principles or the general feelings of the public.

What Is Theory?

Theory can be defined as a set of concepts linked together by a series of statements to explain why an event or phenomenon occurs. A simple way of thinking about theories is that they provide explanations of why the world works the way it does. In other words, a theory is a model of the phenomenon that is being discussed, which in this case is criminal behavior. Sometimes, perhaps quite often, theories are simply wrong, even if the predictions they give are highly accurate.

For example, in the early Middle Ages, most people, including expert scientists, believed Earth was the center of the universe because everything seemed to rotate and revolve around our home planet. If we wake up day after day and see the sun (or moon) rise and set in close to the same place, it appears that these celestial bodies are revolving around Earth, especially considering the fact that we don't feel the world around us moving. Furthermore, calendars predicting the change of seasons, as well as the location and phases of these celestial bodies (such as the moon), were quite accurate. However, although the experts were able to predict the movements of celestial objects quite well and develop extremely accurate calendars, they had absolutely no understanding of what was actually happening. Later, when some individuals tried to convince the majority that they were wrong, specifically that Earth was not the center of the universe, they were condemned as heretics and persecuted, even though their theoretical models were correct.

The same type of argument could be made about Earth being flat; at one time, observations and all existing models seemed to claim it as proven and true. Some disagreed and decided to test their own predictions, which is how America was discovered by European explorers. Still, many who believed Earth was round were persecuted or cast out of mainstream society in Europe at the time.

Two things should be clear: Theories can be erroneous, and accurate predictions can be made (e.g., early calendars and moon and star charts) using them, even though there is no true understanding of what is actually happening. One way to address both of these issues is to base knowledge and theories on scientific observation and testing. All respected theories of crime in the modern era are based on science; thus, we try to avoid buying into and applying theories that are inaccurate, and we continuously refine and improve our theories (based on findings from scientific testing) to gain a better understanding of what causes people to commit crime. Criminology, as a science, always allows and even welcomes criticism of its existing theoretical models. There is no emphasis on authority but rather on the scientific method and the quality of the observations that take place in testing the predictions. All scientific theories can be improved, and they are improved only through observation and empirical testing.

▲ **Image 1.1** Earth seen from the surface of the moon. Theories of Earth as the center of the universe were dominant for many centuries, and scientists who proposed that Earth was not the center of the universe were often persecuted. Over time, the theory was proved false.

SOURCE: © istockphoto.com / RomoloTavani

Case Study: Burke and Hare

During the 1820s, Edinburgh, Scotland, was a major center for those pursuing an education in medicine. Almost 60 years prior to Jack the Ripper, the first serial murderers, William Burke and William Hare, captured media attention. During a 12-month period, Burke and Hare killed 16 people in Edinburgh before being arrested in November 1828. What made these killings so sordid was that Burke and Hare committed them for the sole purpose of selling the cadavers to medical schools for dissection and medical research. They were assisted by Burke's companion, Helen M'Dougal, and Hare's wife, Margaret. Burke and Hare would lure their victims with alcohol. Then, they would suffocate their inebriated victims by lying on their chests and holding their mouths and nostrils closed. Subsequently, Burke and Hare would sell these cadavers, "no questions asked," to Dr. Robert Knox, a promising anatomist.

What made these killings so sordid was that Burke and Hare committed them for the sole purpose of selling the cadavers to medical schools for dissection and medical research.

(Continued)

(Continued)

During the trial, Hare was granted immunity in return for testifying against Burke. Burke was found guilty and sentenced to death by hanging. He was hanged on January 28, 1829. Ironically, the next day, Burke's cadaver was donated to the University of Edinburgh, where Professor Alexander Monro conducted the dissection in the anatomical theater.[2] In fact, the University of Edinburgh Anatomical Museum has an exhibit of William Burke's skeletal remains. A description of the exhibit ends with a 19th-century children's rhyme:

Up the close and down the stair

In the house with Burke and Hare

Burke's the butcher

Hare's the thief

Knox the boy who buys the beef.[3]

In January 2016, Arthur and Elizabeth Rathburn from Grosse Pointe Park, Michigan (6 miles outside of Detroit), were indicted for running a black-market body part business. The Rathburns obtained most of the cadavers from two Chicago-area body donation labs. Many of the families who donated the bodies of their loved ones did so with the belief that they would go to science. A number of these cadavers were infected with HIV, hepatitis B, and other diseases. The Rathburns would use chainsaws, band saws, and reciprocating saws to butcher these cadavers for body parts. The Rathburns stored body parts from more than 1,000 people inside a warehouse. Subsequently, they would sell these butchered body parts to medical and dental trainees. However, they sometimes did not disclose to their customers that these body parts were infected with disease.[4]

More than 180 years separate these two cases; the technological expertise needed to carry out these crimes significantly changed during this time. However, one consistent theme that links these two cases is motive—monetary gain. This is one of the most fascinating aspects to studying crime—although technology may have changed how crimes are committed (e.g., Internet fraud), have the explanations changed? Studying motives and factors (e.g., poverty, peer influences, low self-control) that cause such motives is the primary topic of this book.

What Is Crime?

Definitions of crime vary drastically. For example, some take a **legalistic approach** to defining crime, including only acts that are specifically prohibited in the legal codes of a given jurisdiction. The problem with such a definition is that what is a crime in one jurisdiction is not necessarily a crime in other jurisdictions. To clarify, some

[2]Lisa Rosner, *Anatomy Murders: Being the True and Spectacular History of Edinburgh's Notorious Burke and Hare and of the Man of Science Who Abetted Them in the Commission of Their Most Heinous Crimes* (Philadelphia: University of Pennsylvania Press, 2011), 240–244.

[3]The University of Edinburgh, Biomedical-Sciences/Anatomy, "William Burke," March 22, 2016, http://www.ed.ac.uk/biomedical-sciences/anatomy/anatomymuseum/exhibits/burke.

[4]Meg Wagner, "Detroit Couple Accused of Hacking Donated Corpses with Chainsaw, Selling Diseased Body Parts to Unwitting Medical Students," *New York Daily News*, January 30, 2016, http://www.nydailynews.com/news/crime/body-part-dealer-rented-infected-cadavers-students-article-1.2514657.

acts, such as murder and armed robbery, are against the law in virtually all countries and all regions of the United States, across time and culture. These are known as acts of ***mala in se***, literally meaning *evil in itself*.[5] Typically, these crimes involve serious violence and shock the society in which they occur.

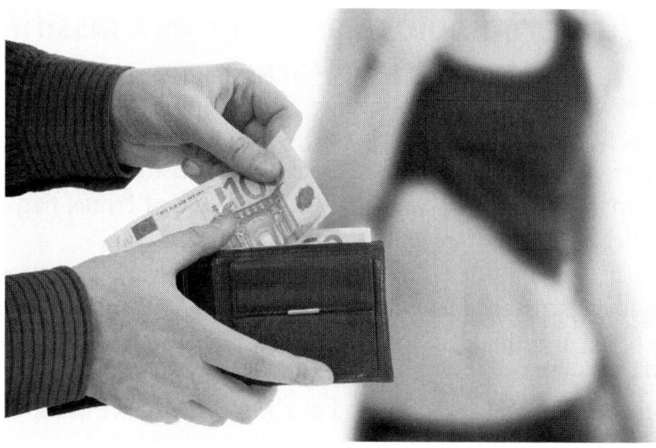

▲ **Image 1.2** Prostitution is considered a *mala prohibita* offense because it is not inherently evil and is even legal in many jurisdictions around the world.

SOURCE: © istockphoto.com / stevanovicigor

Other crimes are known as acts of ***mala prohibita***, which has the literal meaning of *evil because prohibited.* This term acknowledges that these crimes are not inherently evil acts; they are bad only because the law says so.[6] A good example is prostitution, which is illegal in most of the United States but is quite legal and even licensed in most counties of Nevada. The same can be said about gambling and drug possession or use. These are just examples of acts that are criminal only in certain places or at certain times and thus are not agreed upon by most members of a given community.

This book examines both *mala in se* and *mala prohibita* types of offenses, as well as other acts of **deviance**, which are not against the law in many places but are statistically atypical and may be considered more immoral than illegal. For example, in Nevada in the 1990s, a young man watched his friend (who was later criminally prosecuted) kill a young girl in the bathroom at a casino, but he told no one. Although most people would claim that this was highly immoral, at that time, the Nevada state laws did not require people who witnessed a killing to report it to authorities. (Note: As a result of this event, Nevada made withholding such information a criminal act.) Therefore, this act was deviant because most people would find it immoral, but it was not criminal because it was not technically against the laws in the jurisdiction at that time.

Other acts of deviance are not necessarily immoral but are certainly statistically unusual and violate social norms, such as purposely "passing gas" at a formal dinner. Such activities are relevant for our discussion, even if they are not defined as criminal by the law, because they show a disposition toward antisocial behavior, which is often found in individuals who are likely to become criminal offenders. Furthermore, some acts are moving from deviant to illegal all the time, such as using cell phones while driving or smoking cigarettes in public; many jurisdictions are moving to have these behaviors made illegal and have been quite successful to date, especially in New York and California.

Most *mala in se* activities (e.g., murder) are highly deviant, too, meaning they are not typically found in society, but many, if not most, *mala prohibita* acts are not deviant because they are committed by most people at some point. Speeding on a highway is a good example of a *mala prohibita* act that is illegal but not deviant. This book will examine theories for all of these types of activities, even those that do not violate the law in a given jurisdiction at the present time.

---

[5]Brown, Esbensen, and Geis, *Criminology*.

[6]Ibid.

How Are Criminological Theories Classified? The Major Theoretical Paradigms

Scientific theories of crime can be categorized based on several important concepts, assumptions, and characteristics. To begin, most criminological theories are classified by the paradigm they emphasize. **Paradigms** are distinctive theoretical models or perspectives; in the case of crime, they vary based largely on opposing assumptions of human behavior. There are four major paradigms.[7]

The first of these, deterrence or rational choice theories, commonly referred to as the **Classical School** perspective, will be discussed at length later in this book. It assumes that individuals have free will and choose to commit crimes based on rational, hedonistic decisions; they weigh out the potential costs and benefits of offending and then choose what will maximize their pleasure and minimize their pain. The distinguishing characteristic of these theories is that they emphasize the free choice individuals have in committing crime. The other paradigms are based on the influence of factors other than free will or rational decision making—for example, biology, culture, parenting, and economics.

Another category of theories is positivism, which is somewhat the opposite of rational choice theories. These theories argue that individuals do not have free will or rationality in making decisions to commit crime. Rather, the **Positive School** perspective assumes that individuals are passive subjects of determinism, which means that people do not freely choose their behavior. Instead, their behavior is determined by factors outside of their free will, such as genetics, IQ, education, employment, peer influences, parenting, and economics.[8] Most of the highly respected and scientifically validated criminological theories of the modern era fall into this category.[9]

Another group of criminological theories belongs to the conflict or critical perspective, which emphasizes the use of law as a reaction or tool to enforce restraint on others by those in power or authority; it also involves how society reacts when a person (often a juvenile) is caught doing something wrong. These theories emphasize group behavior over individual behavior: Groups that are in power use the criminal codes as a tool in keeping people who have limited power restrained or confined.

Finally, over the past few decades, a new category has emerged, namely the integrated theoretical models, which attempt to combine the best aspects of explanatory models into a single, better theoretical framework for understanding crime. These models tend to suffer from the logical inconsistencies inherent in integrating theoretical models that have opposing assumptions or propositions. All of these categories will become clearer as we progress through this book.

Additional Ways to Classify Criminological Theories

Although the major paradigms are the primary way criminological theories are classified, there are several other ways that they can be categorized. Specifically, theoretical models can be classified based on whether they focus on individuals or groups as their primary units of examination. For instance, some theories emphasize why certain individuals do or do not commit crime. This level of investigation, in which the focus is on the individual, is often referred to as the **micro level of analysis**, much as microeconomics is the study of economics on the individual (person) level. When your instructors score each student on an exam, this is a micro-level analysis.

On the other hand, many theories emphasize primarily the group or **macro level of analysis**, much as macroeconomics is the study of economic principles at the aggregate or group level. In this book, some sections are

---

[7]Thomas J. Bernard, Jeffrey B. Snipes, and Alexander L. Gerould, *Vold's Theoretical Criminology*, 6th ed. (Oxford: Oxford University Press, 2010).

[8]Ibid.

[9]Lee Ellis and Anthony Walsh, "Criminologists' Opinions about Causes and Theories of Crime and Delinquency," *The Criminologist* 24 (1999): 1–4.

separated by whether the individual or the group level of analysis is emphasized. For example, social process theories tend to be more micro-level oriented, whereas social structure theories are more macro-level oriented. Here's a good example: If instructors compare the mean score (or average) of one class to the mean score of another, this is a comparison of group rates, regardless of the performance of any individual in either class. Ultimately, a great theory would explain both the micro and macro levels of analysis, but we will see that very few attempt to explain or account for both levels.

Criminological theories can also be classified by their general perspective on how laws are made. Some theories assume that laws are made to define acts as criminal to the extent that they violate rights of individuals, and thus, virtually everyone agrees that such acts are immoral. This type of perspective is considered a **consensual perspective** (or nonconflict model). On the other hand, many modern forms of criminological theories fall into an opposite category, commonly known as the **conflict theories**, which assume that different groups disagree about the fairness of laws and that laws are used as a tool by those in power to keep down other, lower-power groups. There are many forms of both consensual and conflict theoretical models, and both will be specifically noted as we progress through the book.

A final, but perhaps most important, way to classify theories is in terms of their assumptions regarding human nature. Some theories assume that people are born good (giving, benevolent, etc.) and are corrupted by social or other developmental influences that lead them to crime. A good example is strain theory, which claims that people are born innocent and with good intentions but that society causes them to commit crime. On the other hand, many of the most popular current theories claim that virtually all individuals are born with a disposition toward being bad (selfish, greedy, etc.) and must be socialized or restrained from following their inherent propensities for engaging in crime.[10] A good example of this is control theory, which assumes that all individuals have a predisposition to be greedy, selfish, violent, and so on (i.e., they are criminally disposed) and therefore that people need to be controlled or prevented from acting on their natural, inherent disposition toward selfish and aggressive behaviors.

A variation of these theories is often referred to as *tabula rasa*, literally translated as blank slate. This assumes that people are born with no leaning toward good or bad but are simply influenced by the balance of positive or negative influences that are introduced socially during their development. A good example of this perspective is differential association or reinforcement theory, which assumes that all individuals are born with a blank slate and that they learn whether to be good or bad based on what they experience.

Although the dominant assumption tends to vary across these three models from time to time, the most popular theories today (which are self- and social-control theories) seem to imply the second option, specifically that people are born selfish and greedy and must be socialized and trained to be good and conforming.[11] There are other ways that criminological theories can be classified, but the various characteristics we have discussed in this section summarize the most important factors.

Characteristics of Good Theories

Respected scientific theories in any field, whether it be chemistry, physics, or criminology, tend to have the same characteristics. After all, the same scientific review process (i.e., blind peer review by experts) is used in all sciences to determine which studies and theoretical works are of high quality. The criteria that characterize a good theory in chemistry are the same as those used to judge a criminological theory. Such characteristics include parsimony,

[10] Ibid.

[11] Ibid.

scope, logical consistency, testability, empirical validity, and policy implications.[12] Each of these characteristics is examined here. (It should be noted that our discussion and many of the examples provided for the characteristics are taken from Akers and Sellers, 2012.[13])

Parsimony is achieved by explaining a given phenomenon—in our case criminal activity—in the simplest way possible. Other characteristics being equal, the simpler a theory, the better. The problem with criminal behavior is that it is highly complex. However, that has not stopped some criminologists from attempting to explain this convoluted phenomenon in highly simple ways. For example, one of the most recent and most popular theories (as indicated by the amount of related research and by which theories the experts believe are most important) is the theory of low self-control (which we discuss later in this book). This very simple model holds that one personality factor—low self-control—is responsible for all criminal activity. The originators of this theory, Michael Gottfredson and Travis Hirschi, asserted that every single act of crime and deviance is caused by this same factor: low self-control.[14] Everything from speeding, smoking tobacco, not wearing a seat belt while driving, and having numerous sex partners to committing serious crimes such as murder and armed robbery are caused by low self-control.

Although this theory has been disputed by much of the subsequent research on this model, it remains one of the most popular and accepted models of the modern era.[15] Furthermore, despite the criticisms of this theory, many notable criminologists still believe that this is the best single model of offending that has been presented to date. In addition, there is little doubt that this model has become the most researched theoretical model over the last two decades.[16]

Perhaps the most important reason why so much attention has been given to this theory is its simplicity, putting all of the focus on a single factor. Virtually all other theoretical models have proposed multiple factors that may play major parts in determining why individuals commit crime. After all, how can low self-control explain white-collar crime? Some self-control is required to obtain a white-collar position of employment. It is true that a simple theory is better than a more complex one, as long as other characteristics are equivalent. However, given a complex behavior like criminal behavior, it is unlikely that a simple explanation, such as naming one factor to account for everything, will prove adequate.

Scope, the next characteristic of a theory, indicates how much of a given phenomenon the theory seeks to explain. This is somewhat related to parsimony in the sense that some theories, like the theory of low self-control, seek to explain all crimes and all deviant acts as well. Thus, the theory of low self-control has a very wide scope. Other theories of crime, such as some versions of strain theory, may seek to explain only property crime or drug use. However, the wider the scope of what a theory can explain, the better the theory, assuming other characteristics are equal.

Logical consistency is the extent to which a theory makes sense in terms of its concepts and propositions. It is easier to show what we mean by logical consistency if we give examples of what does not fit this criterion. Some theories simply don't make sense because of the face value of their propositions. For example, Cesare Lombroso, called the father of criminology, claimed that the most serious offenders are "born criminals," biological throwbacks to an earlier stage of evolutionary development who can be identified by their physical features.[17] Lombroso, who is discussed at more length later in this book, claimed that tattoos were one of the physical features that identified these born criminals. This doesn't make sense, however, because tattoos are not biological physical features—no

---

[12]Ronald Akers and Christine Sellers, *Criminological Theories*, 6th ed. (Oxford: Oxford University Press, 2012).

[13]Ibid., 4–19.

[14]Michael Gottfredson and Travis Hirschi, *A General Theory of Crime* (Palo Alto, CA: Stanford University Press, 1990).

[15]Ellis and Walsh, "Criminologists' Opinions," 3–4.

[16]Anthony Walsh and Lee Ellis, "Political Ideology and American Criminologists' Explanations for Criminal Behavior," *The Criminologist* 24 (1999): 1, 14.

[17]Cesare Lombroso, *The Criminal Man* (Milan: Hoepli, 1876).

baby has ever been born with a tattoo. This criticism will make even more sense when we discuss the criteria for determining causality later in this section.

Another prominent example of theories that lack logical consistency is the work of early feminist theorists, such as Freda Adler, who argued that, as females gain educational and employment opportunities, their rates of crime will be more likely to converge with those of males.[18] Such hypotheses were logically inconsistent with the data available at the time they were presented and are even more inconsistent with the data available today; the facts show that females who are given the most opportunities commit the fewest crimes, while females who have not been given these benefits commit the most crimes.

These are just two examples of how past theories were logically inconsistent with the data available at the time they were created, not to mention inconsistent with future research findings, which have completely dismissed their hypotheses.

Testability is the extent to which a theory can be put to empirical, scientific testing. Some theories simply cannot be tested. A good example is Sigmund Freud's theory of the psyche. Freud described three domains of the psyche—the conscious ego, the subconscious id, and the superego—but none of these domains can be observed or tested.[19] Although some theories can be quite influential without being testable (as was Freud's theory), other things being equal, it is a considerable disadvantage for a theoretical model to be untestable and unobservable. Fortunately, most established criminological theories can be examined through empirical testing.

Empirical validity is the extent to which a theoretical model is supported by scientific research. Obviously, this is highly related to the previous characteristic of testability. However, while virtually all accepted modern criminological theories are testable, that does not mean they are equal in terms of empirical validity. Although some integrated models (meaning two or more traditional theories that have been merged together; these will be examined later in this book) have gained a large amount of empirical validity, these models "cheat" because they merge the best of two or more models, even when the assumptions of these models are not compatible. The independent theoretical model that has garnered the most empirical validity is differential reinforcement theory, which has been strongly supported for various crime types (from tobacco usage to violence) among a wide variety of populations (from young children to elderly subjects).[20]

Ultimately, empirical validity is perhaps one of the most important characteristics used in determining how good a theory is at explaining a given phenomenon or behavior. If a theory has good empirical validity, it is an accurate explanation of behavior; if it does not have good empirical validity, it should be revised or dismissed because it is simply not true.

Policy implications refer to the extent to which a theory can create realistic and useful guidance for changing the way society deals with a given phenomenon. In our case, this means providing a useful model for informing authorities of how to deal with crime. An example is the broken windows theory, which says that to reduce serious crimes, authorities should focus on the minor incivilities that occur in a given area. This theory has been used successfully by many police agencies (most notably by New York City police, who reduced their homicide rate by more than 75% in the past decade). Other theories may not be as useful in terms of reducing crime because they are

---

[18]Freda Adler, *Sisters in Crime* (New York: McGraw-Hill, 1975).

[19]See Stephen G. Tibbetts, *Criminological Theory: The Essentials* (Thousand Oaks, CA: Sage, 2015), 8.

[20]See Ronald Akers and Gang Lee, "A Longitudinal Test of Social Learning Theory: Adolescent Smoking," *Journal of Drug Issues* 26 (1996): 317–43; Ronald Akers and Gang Lee, "Age, Social Learning, and Social Bonding in Adolescent Substance Abuse," *Deviant Behavior* 19 (1999): 1–25; Ronald Akers and Anthony J. La Greca, "Alcohol Use among the Elderly: Social Learning, Community Context, and Life Events," in *Society, Culture, and Drinking Patterns Re-examined*, ed. David J. Pittman and Helene Raskin White (New Brunswick, NJ: Rutgers Center of Alcohol Studies, 1991), 242–62; Sunghyun Hwang, *Substance Use in a Sample of South Korean Adolescents: A Test of Alternative Theories* (Ann Arbor, MI: University Microfilms, 2000); and Sunghyun Hwang and Ronald Akers, "Adolescent Substance Use in South Korea: A Cross-Cultural Test of Three Theories," in *Social Learning Theory and the Explanation of Crime: A Guide for the New Century*, ed. Ronald Akers and Gary F. Jensen (New Brunswick, NJ: Transaction, 2003).

too abstract or propose changes that are far too costly or impossible to implement, such as theories that emphasize changing family structure or the chromosomal makeup of individuals. So, other things being equal, a theory that has readily available policy implications would be more advantageous than theories that do not.

Criteria for Determining Causality

There are several criteria for determining whether a certain variable causes another variable to change—in other words, causality. For this discussion, we will be using standard scientific notation to designate an independent or predictor variable (*X*) that results in a dependent or explanatory variable (*Y*). Such criteria are used for all scientific disciplines, whether chemistry, physics, biology, or criminology. In this book, we are discussing crime, so we will concentrate on examples that relate to this goal, but some examples will be given that are not crime related. Unfortunately, we will also see that, given the nature of our field, there are important problems with determining causality, largely because we are dealing with human beings as opposed to a chemical element or biological molecule.

The three criteria that are needed to show causality are (1) temporal ordering; (2) correlation, or covariation; and (3) accounting for spuriousness.

Temporal ordering requires that the predictor variable (*X*) precede the explanatory variable (*Y*) if we are to determine that *X* causes *Y*. Although this seems like a no-brainer, it is sometimes violated in criminological theories. For example, you'll remember that Lombroso claimed born criminals could be identified by tattoos, which obviously goes against this principle.

A more recent scientific debate has focused on whether delinquency is an outcome variable (*Y*) due to associations with delinquent peers and associates (*X*) or whether delinquency (*X*) causes associations with delinquent peers and associates (*Y*), which then leads to even more delinquency. This can be seen as the argument of which came first, the chicken or the egg. Studies show that both processes are often taking place, meaning that delinquency and associations with delinquent peers are likely to be both predictor and explanatory variables in most cases, and this forms a reciprocal or feedback loop that encourages both causal paths.[21] Thus, temporal ordering is an important question, and often it is quite complex and must be examined fully before causal order can be understood.

▲ **Image 1.3** Early theories identified criminals by whether they had tattoos; at that time, this might have been true. In contemporary times, many individuals have tattoos, so this would not apply.

SOURCE: © istockphoto.com / Rawpixel Ltd

Correlation, or **covariation**, is the extent to which a change in the predictor (*X*) is associated with a change (either higher or lower) in the explanatory variable (*Y*). In other words, a change in *X* leads to a change in *Y*. For example, a rise in unemployment (*X*) in a given location is likely to lead to a rise in crime rates (Y) in the same area; this would be a positive association because both

[21] Terence Thornberry, "Toward an Interactional Theory of Delinquency," *Criminology* 25 (1987): 863–87.

increased. Similarly, an increase in employment (*X*) is likely to lead to a decrease in crime rates (*Y*) in that area; this would be a negative, or inverse, association, because one decreased and the other increased. The criterion of covariance is not met when a change in *X* does not produce any change in *Y*. That is, if a statistically significant change in *X* does not lead to a statistically significant change in *Y*, then this criterion is not met.

However, correlation alone does not mean that *X* causes *Y*. For example, if ice cream sales (*X*) tend to be highly associated with crime rates (*Y*), this does not mean that ice cream sales cause higher crime rates. Rather, other factors—in this case, warm weather—lead to increases in both sales of ice cream and the number of people who are outdoors in public areas and interacting, which naturally leads to greater opportunities and tendencies to engage in criminal activity. This brings us to the final criterion for determining causality.

Accounting for **spuriousness** is a complicated way of saying that, to determine that *X* causes *Y*, other factors (typically called *Z* factors) that could be causing the observed association must be accounted for before we can be sure that it is actually *X* that is causing *Y*. In other words, it is often a third factor (*Z*) that causes two events to occur together in time and place. A good example of a spurious association would be the observation that a greater number of firefighters at the scene of a fire is correlated with more damage. If only the first two criteria of causality were followed, this would lead to the conclusion that an increased number of fire officers (*X*) causes the heavier fire damage (*Y*). This conclusion meets the temporal ordering and covariance criteria. However, a third *Z* variable or factor is causing both *X* and *Y* to appear together. This *Z* variable is the size of the fire, which is causing more officers to show up and also causing more damage. Once this *Z* factor is accounted for, the effect of *X* on *Y* becomes nonexistent.

Using the Lombroso example, tattoos may have predicted criminality at the time he wrote (although criminals weren't born with them). However, Lombroso did not account for an important *Z* factor—namely, associates or friends who also had tattoos. This *Z* factor caused the simultaneous occurrence of both other factors. To clarify, individuals who had friends or associates with tattoos tended to get tattoos, and (especially at that time in the 1800s) friends or associates who had tattoos also tended to commit more crime. In that era, pirates and incarcerated individuals were most likely to get tattoos. Therefore, had Lombroso controlled for the number of tattooed associates of the criminals he studied, he likely would have found no causal effect on crime from body art.

Ultimately, researchers in criminology are fairly good at determining the first two criteria of causality: temporal ordering and covariance or correlation. Most scientists can perform classical experiments that randomly assign subjects either to receive or not to receive the experimental manipulation to examine the effect on outcomes. However, the dilemma for criminologists is that the factors that appear to be important (according to police officers, parole agents, and corrections officers) are family variables, personality traits, employment variables, intelligence, and other similar characteristics that cannot be experimentally manipulated to control for possible *Z* factors. After all, how can we randomly assign certain people or groups to bad parents or bad educations, no jobs, low IQs, bad genetics, or delinquent peers? Even if we could manage such manipulations, ethical constraints would prohibit them.

Thus, as criminologists, we may never be able to meet all the criteria of causality, so we are essentially stuck with building a case for the factors we think are causing crime by amassing as much support as we can in terms of temporal ordering and covariance or correlation, and perhaps accounting for other factors in advanced statistical models. Ultimately, social science, especially criminology, is a difficult field in terms of establishing causality, and we shall see that the empirical validity of various criminological theories is hindered by such issues.

Measures of Crime

Crime can be measured in an infinite number of ways. To some extent, readers have measured crime by observing what has been happening in their own neighborhoods or reading or watching the news every day. However, some measures of crime go beyond these anecdotal or personal experiences, and these more exacting measures are what criminologists commonly use to gauge rates of crime across time and place.

Specifically, three major categories of crime measures are used by social scientists to examine crime. The first and most used measure is the **Uniform Crime Report (UCR)**. Police send reports about certain crimes and arrests to the Federal Bureau of Investigation (FBI), which combines the many thousands of reports they receive from across the nation and publishes the UCR annually.

The second measure is the **National Crime Victimization Survey** (**NCVS**; prior to the early 1990s, it was known as the National Crime Survey [NCS]). Like the UCR, this report is issued by the U.S. Department of Justice (DOJ), but the data are collected in an entirely different way. Specifically, interviews are conducted with a large, random sample of U.S. households, asking how much crime they have experienced in half-year intervals. The NCVS is collected by the research branch of the DOJ, called the Bureau of Justice Statistics (BJS), in conjunction with the U.S. Census Bureau, which was one of the earliest agencies to collect information about citizens and thus is the most experienced at such endeavors.

The third measure, which is perhaps the most important for purposes of this book, is **self-report data (SRD)**, which are primarily collected by independent academic scientists or think tank agencies, such as the RAND Corporation. Participating in surveys or interviews, individuals report crimes against themselves or crimes they have committed. This measure is the most important for the purposes of this book because the UCR and NCVS do not provide in-depth information on the offenders or the victims, such as personality, biology or physiology, family life, and economic information. These factors are of the utmost importance for our purposes because there is a broad consensus that they cause people to commit crime, yet they are missing from the most commonly used measures of crime. SRD are the best, and in most cases the only, measure for figuring out why some people offend and others do not. However, like the other measures, self-reports have numerous weaknesses as well as strengths.

Each of these three measures is briefly examined here. Although the measures are not the primary emphasis of this book, it is important to understand their strengths and weaknesses.

▲ **Image 1.4** The annual UCRs are produced by the FBI. Local, county, and state criminal justice agencies send their annual crime data to the J. Edgar Hoover Building in Washington, DC. UCR data are, by their nature, incomplete, as many crimes are never reported to the police at all. This dark figure of crime might be as high as 90% of all crime incidents.

SOURCE: © istockphoto.com / mixmotive

The Uniform Crime Report

The UCR is the oldest and most used measure of crime rates in the United States for purposes of examining trends and distribution of crime. It was first published in the early 1930s, and although changes have been made along the way, it is relatively stable in terms of comparing various years and decades. As mentioned before, the data are collected by many thousands of independent police agencies at federal, state, and local levels. These thousands of agencies send their reports of crimes and arrests to their respective state capitals, which then forward their synthesized reports to FBI headquarters, where all reports are combined to provide an overview of crime in the nation.

FBI definitions of crimes often differ from state categorizations, and how crimes are differentiated will be important in future discussions in this section. The FBI concentrates on eight (four violent and four property) **index offenses**, or Part I offenses. The four violent crimes are murder and nonnegligent manslaughter, forcible (not statutory) rape, robbery, and aggravated assault (which involves intentions of serious injury to the victim). The four property offenses are burglary (which includes a breaking and entering or trespass), motor vehicle theft, larceny (which does not involve a trespass; e.g., shoplifting), and arson (which was added to the crime index count in the late 1970s). All reports to police for these eight offenses are included in the crime index, whether or not they resulted in an arrest. This information is often referred to as crimes known to police (CKP).

The UCR also includes about two dozen other offenses known as **nonindex offenses**, or Part II offenses, which are reported only if an arrest is made. These offenses range from violent crimes (such as simple assault), to embezzlement and fraud, to offenses that are considered violations of the law only if an individual is under 18 years of age (such as running away from home). The major problem with the estimates of these nonindex offenses is that the likelihood of arresting someone for such crimes is less than 10% of the actual occurrence, so the data regarding nonindex offenses are highly inaccurate. The official count from the FBI is missing at least 90% of the actual offenses that take place in the United States. Therefore, we will primarily concentrate on index offenses for the purposes of our discussion.

Even the count of index offenses has numerous problems. The most important and chronic problem with using the UCR as a measure of crime is that, most of the time, victims fail to report crimes—yes, even aggravated assault, forcible rape, robbery, burglary, and larceny. Recent studies estimate that about 70% to 80% of these serious crimes are not reported to police. Criminologists call this missing amount of crime the **dark figure** because it never shows up in the police reports that get sent to the FBI.

There are many reasons why victims do not report these serious crimes to the police. One of the most important is that they consider it a personal matter. Many times, the offense is committed by a family member, a close friend, or an acquaintance. For instance, police are rarely informed about aggravated assaults among siblings. Rape victims are often assaulted on a date or by someone they know; they may feel that they contributed to their attack by choosing to go out with the offender, or they may believe that police won't take such a claim seriously. Regardless of the reason, many crime victims prefer to handle it informally and not involve the police.

Another major reason why police are not called is that victims don't feel the crime is important enough to report. For example, a thief may steal a small item that the victim won't miss, so she or he may not see the need to report what the police or FBI would consider a serious crime. This is likely related to another major reason why people do not report crime to the police: They have no confidence that reporting the case to law enforcement will do any good. Many people, often residents of neighborhoods that are the most crime-ridden, are likely to feel that the police are not competent or will not seriously investigate their charges.

There are many other reasons why people do not report their victimizations to police. Some may fear retaliation, for example, in cases involving gang activity; many cities, especially those with many gangs, have seen this occur even more in recent years. The victims may also fail to report a crime for fear that their own illegal activities will be exposed; an example is a prostitute who has been brutally beaten by her pimp. In U.S. society, much crime is committed against businesses, but those businesses may be very reluctant to report crimes because they don't want a reputation for being a hot spot for criminal activity. Sometimes when victims do call the police or 911, they leave the scene if the police fail to show up in a reasonable amount of time. This has become a chronic problem despite efforts by police departments to prioritize calls.

Perhaps the most chronic, most important reason for failure to report crimes—but one that is often ignored—can be traced to U.S. school systems. Most studies of crime and victimization in schools show that many and maybe even most juvenile crimes occur in schools, but these offenses almost never get reported to police, even when school resource officers (SROs) are assigned to the school. Schools—and especially private schools—have a vested interest in not reporting crimes that occur on their premises to the police. After all, no school (or school system) wants to become known as crime-ridden.

Schools are predisposed to being crime-ridden because the most likely offenders and the most likely victims—young people—interact there in close quarters for most of the day. The school is much happier, however, if teachers and administrators deal informally with the parties involved in an on-campus fight; the school doesn't want these activities reported to and by the media. In addition, the student parties involved in the fight don't want to be formally arrested and charged with the offense, so they are also happy with the case being handled informally. Finally, the parents of the students are also generally pleased with the informal process because they don't want their children involved in a formal legal case.

Even universities and colleges follow this model of not reporting crimes when they occur on campus. A good example can be seen on the websites of most major colleges, which are required by federal law to report crimes on campus. Official reports of crimes, ranging from rapes to liquor law violations, are often in the single digits each year for campuses housing many thousands of students. Of course, some crimes may not be reported to the school, and others may be dealt with administratively rather than by calling police. The absence of school data is a big weakness of the UCR.

Besides the dark figure, there are many other criticisms of the UCR as a measure of crime. For example, the way that crimes are counted can be misleading. Specifically, the UCR counts only the most serious crime that is committed in a given incident. For example, if a person or persons rob, rape, and murder a victim, only the murder will show up in the UCR; the robbery and rape will not be recorded. Furthermore, there are inconsistencies in how the UCR counts the incidents; for example, if a person walks into a bar and assaults eight people there, it is counted as eight assaults, but if the same person walks into the bar and robs every person of wallets and purses, it is counted as one robbery. This makes little sense, but it is the official count policy used by the UCR.

Other, more important criticisms of the UCR involve political considerations, such as the fact that many police departments (such as in Philadelphia and New York City) have systematically altered the way that crimes are defined, for example, by manipulating the way that classifications and counts of crimes are recorded (e.g., aggravated assault [an index crime] vs. simple assault [a nonindex crime]). Thus, official estimates can make it seem as if major crimes have decreased in the city when in fact they may have actually increased.

It is also important to note the strengths of the UCR. First, it was introduced in 1930, making it the longest-lasting systematic measure of crime in the United States. This is a very important advantage when we want to examine trends in crime over most of the 20th century. We will see later that there have been extremely high crime rates at certain times (such as during the 1930s and the 1970s to 1980) and very low crime rates at other times (such as the early 1940s and recent years [late 1990s to the present]). Other measures, such as the NCVS and national SRD, did not come into use until much later, so the UCR is important for the fact that it started so early.

Another important strength of this measure is that two of the offenses that the UCR concentrates on are almost always reported and therefore overcome the weakness of the dark figure, or lack of reporting to police. These two offenses are murder or nonnegligent manslaughter and motor vehicle theft. Murder is almost always reported because a dead body is found; very few murders go unreported to authorities. Although a few may elude official recording—for example, if the body is transported elsewhere or carefully hidden—almost all murders are recorded. Similarly, motor vehicle thefts, a property crime, are almost always reported because any insurance claims must provide a police report. Most cars are worth thousands (or at least many hundreds) of dollars, so victims tend to report when their vehicle(s) have been stolen; this provides a rather valid estimate of property crime in specific areas. The rest of the offenses (yes, even the other index crimes) counted by the UCR are far less reliable. If someone is doing a study on homicide or motor vehicle theft, the UCR is likely the best source of data, but for any other crime, researchers should probably look elsewhere.

This is even further advised for studies examining nonindex offenses, which the UCR counts only when someone is arrested for a given offense. The vast majority of nonindex offenses do not result in an arrest. To shed some light on how much actual nonindex crime is not reported to police, it is useful to examine the **clearance rate** of the index offenses in the UCR, our best indicator of solving crimes. Even for the crimes that the FBI considers most serious, the clearance rate is about 21% of crimes reported to police ("reported to police" meaning that police made a report of the crime). Of course, the more violent offenses have higher clearance rates because (outside of murder) they inherently have a witness, namely the victim, and because police place a higher priority on solving violent crimes. However, for some of the index crimes, especially serious property offenses, the clearance rates are very low. Furthermore, it should be noted that the clearance rate of serious index crimes has not improved at all over the past few decades despite much more advanced resources and technology, such as DNA testing, fingerprints, and faster cars. These data on the clearance rates are only for the most serious, or index, crimes; thus, the reporting of the UCR regarding nonindex crimes is even more inaccurate because there is even less reporting (i.e., the dark figure) and less clearance of these less serious offenses. In other words, the data provided by the UCR regarding nonindex offenses are totally invalid and thus for the most part completely worthless.

Ultimately, the UCR is good for (a) measuring the overall crime rate in the United States over time, (b) examining what crime was like prior to the 1970s, and (c) investigating murder and motor vehicle theft. Outside of these offenses, the UCR has serious problems, and fortunately, we have better measures for examining crime rates in the United States.

The National Crime Victimization Survey

Another commonly used measure of crime is the NCVS (the NCS until the early 1990s), which is distinguished from other key measures of crime because it concentrates on the victims of crime, whereas other measures tend to emphasize the offenders. In fact, that is the key reason why this measure was started in 1973 after several years of preparation and pretesting. To clarify, one of the key recommendations of Lyndon Johnson's President's Commission on Law Enforcement and Administration of Justice in the late 1960s was to learn more about the characteristics of victims of crime; at that time, virtually no studies had been done on the subject, whereas much research had been done on criminal offenders. The efforts of this commission set into motion the creation of the NCVS.

Since it began, the NCVS has been designed and collected by two agencies: the U.S. Census Bureau and the BJS, which is one of the key research branches of the DOJ. The NCVS is collected in a completely different way from the other commonly used measures of crimes; the researchers select tens of thousands of U.S. households, and each member of the household who is over 12 years of age is interviewed every 6 months about crime that occurred in the previous 6-month period (each selected household remains in the survey for 3 years, resulting in seven collection periods, including the initial interview). Although the selection of households is to some extent random, the way the sampling is designed guarantees that a certain proportion of the selected households have certain characteristics. For example, before the households are selected, they are first categorized according to factors such as region of the country, type of area (urban, suburban, rural), income level, and racial or ethnic composition. This type of sampling, called a multistage, stratified cluster sampling design, ensures that enough households are included in the survey to permit conclusions regarding these important characteristics. As you will see later in this section, some of the most victimized groups (by rate) in the United States do not make up a large portion of the population or households. So, if the sampling design were not set up to select a certain number of people from certain groups, it is quite likely the researchers would not obtain enough cases to draw conclusions about them.

The data gathered from this sample are then adjusted, and statistical estimates are made about crime across the United States, with the NCVS estimates showing about 3 times more crime than the UCR rates. Some may doubt the ability of this selected sample to represent crime in the nation, but most studies find that its estimates are far more accurate than those provided by the UCR (with the exception of homicide and maybe motor vehicle theft). This is largely due to the expertise and professionalism of the agencies that collect and analyze the data, as well as the carefully thought out and well-administered survey design, as indicated by interview completion rates (which are typically more than 90% higher than those of virtually all other crime and victimization surveys).

One of the biggest strengths of the NCVS is that it directly addresses the worst problem with the previously discussed measure, the UCR. Specifically, the greatest weakness of the UCR is the dark figure, or the crimes that victims fail to report, which happens most of the time (except in cases of homicide or motor vehicle theft). The NCVS interviews victims about crimes that happened to them, even those that were not reported to police. Thus, the NCVS captures far more crime events than the UCR, especially crimes that are highly personal (such as rape). The extent to which the NCVS captures much of this dark figure of crime is its greatest strength.

Despite this important strength, the NCVS, like the other measures of crime, has numerous weaknesses. Probably the biggest problem is that two of the most victimized groups in U.S. society are systematically not included in the NCVS. Specifically, homeless people are completely left out because they do not have a home and the participants are contacted through households, yet they remain one of the most victimized groups per capita in our society. Another highly victimized group in our society that is systematically not included in the NCVS is young children. Studies consistently show that the younger a person is, the more likely she or he is to be victimized. Infants in particular, especially in their first hours or days of life, face great risk of death and other sorts of victimization, typically from parents or caregivers. This is not very surprising, especially in light of the fact that very young children cannot defend themselves or run away. They can't even tell anyone until they are old enough to speak, and then most are too afraid to do so or are not given an opportunity. Although, to some extent, it is understandable to exempt young children from such sensitive questions, the loss of this group is huge in terms of estimating victimization in the United States.

The NCVS also misses the crimes suffered by American businesses, which cumulatively constitute an enormous amount of crime. In the early years of the NCVS, businesses were also sampled, but that practice was discontinued in the late 1970s. Had it continued, it would have provided invaluable information for social scientists and policy makers, not to mention the businesses that are losing billions of dollars each year as a result of crimes committed against them.

Many find it surprising that the NCVS does not collect data on homicide, which most people and agencies consider the most serious and important crime. Researchers studying murder cannot get information from the NCVS but must rely on the UCR, which is most accurate in its reporting for this crime type.

The NCVS also has issues with people accurately reporting the victimization that has occurred to them in the previous 6 months. However, studies show that their reports are surprisingly accurate most of the time. Often when participants report incidents inaccurately, they make unknowing mistakes rather than intentionally lying. Obviously, victims sometimes forget incidents that have occurred, probably because, most of the time, they know or are related to the person committing the offense against them, so they never think of it as a crime per se but rather as a personal disagreement. When asked if they were victims of theft, they may not think to report the time that a brother or uncle borrowed a tool without asking and never returned it.

Although NCVS researchers go to great lengths to prevent it, a common phenomenon known as **telescoping** tends to occur, which leads to overreporting of incidents. Telescoping is the human tendency to perceive events as having occurred more recently than they actually did. This is one of the key reasons why NCVS researchers interview household subjects every 6 months, but telescoping still happens. For instance, a larceny may have occurred 8 months ago, but it seems as if it happened just a few months ago to the participant, so it is reported to the researchers as occurring in the past 6 months when it really didn't. Telescoping thus inflates national crime rate estimates for a given interval.

As mentioned before, an additional weakness is that the NCVS did not start until 1973, so it cannot provide any estimates of victimization prior to that time. A study of national crime rates prior to the 1970s has little choice but to use the UCR. Still, for most crimes, the NCVS has provided a more accurate estimate over the past three decades. Since the NCVS was created, the crime trends it has revealed have tended to be highly consistent with those shown by the UCR. For example, both measures show violent crime rates peaking at the same time (about 1980), and both agree on when the rates increased (the 1970s) and decreased (the late 1990s to the present) most. This is very good, because if they did not agree, that would mean at least one of them was wrong. Before we discuss the national trends in crime rates, however, we will examine the strengths and weaknesses of a third measure of crime.

Self-Report Studies of Crime

The final measure of crime consists of various self-report studies of crime, in which individuals report (in either a written survey or an interview) the extent of their own past criminal offending or victimization and other information. There is no one systematic study providing a yearly estimate of crime in the United States; rather, self-report studies tend to be conducted by independent researchers or institutes. Even when they do involve a national sample (such as the National Youth Survey [NYS]), they almost never use such data to make estimates of the extent of crime or victimization across the nation.

This lack of a long-term, systematic study that can be used to estimate national crime rates may be the greatest weakness of self-report studies; however, this very weakness—not having a universal consistency in collection—is also its greatest strength. To clarify, researchers can develop their questionnaires to best fit the exact purposes of their study. For example, if researchers are doing a study on the relationship between a given personality trait (e.g., narcissism) and criminal offending, they can simply give participants a questionnaire that contains a narcissism scale and items that ask about past criminal behavior. Of course, these scales and items must be checked for their reliability and validity, but this is a relatively easy way to directly measure and test the hypotheses the researcher is most concerned about.

Some question the accuracy of SRD because they believe participants typically lie, but most studies have concluded that participants generally tell the truth. Specifically, researchers have compared self-reported offenses to lie detector machine results, readministered the same survey to the same individuals to see if they answer the same way each time (called test–retest reliability), and cross-checked self-reported arrests with police arrest data. All of these methods have shown that most people tend to be quite truthful when answering surveys.[22]

The most important aspect of self-report surveys is that they are the only available source of data for determining the social and psychological reasons people commit crime. The UCR and NCVS have virtually no data on the personality, family life, biological development, or other characteristics of criminal offenders, which are generally considered key factors in the development of criminality. Therefore, although we examine the findings of all three measures in the next section, the vast majority of the content we cover in this book will be based on findings from self-report studies.

What Do the Measures of Crime Show regarding the Distribution of Crime?

It is important to examine the most aggregated trends of crime, namely the ups and downs of overall crime rates in the United States across different decades. We will start with crime in the early 1900s—largely because the best data started being collected during this era and also because the 20th century (especially the most recent decades) is most relevant to our understanding of the reasons for our current crime rates. However, most experts believe that the U.S. crime rate, whether in terms of violence or property offending, used to be far higher prior to the 20th century; historians have arrived at this conclusion based on sporadic, poorly recorded documentation from the 18th and 19th centuries. By virtually all accounts, crime per capita (especially homicide) was far higher in the 1700s and 1800s than at any point after 1900, which is likely due to many factors but perhaps most importantly because formal agencies of justice, such as police and corrections (i.e., prisons, parole), did not exist in most of the United States until the middle or end of the 1800s. Up to that time, it was up to individual communities or vigilantes to deal with offenders.

---

[22]Michael Hindelang, Travis Hirschi, and J. Weis, *Measuring Delinquency* (Beverly Hills, CA: Sage, 1981).

▲ **Image 1.5** Group portrait of a police department liquor squad posing with cases of confiscated alcohol and distilling equipment during Prohibition.

SOURCE: © Getty Images / Archive Photos / Archive Photos

Therefore, there was little ability to investigate or apprehend criminals and no means to imprison them. But, as industrialization increased, the need to establish formal police agencies and correctional facilities evolved as a way to deal with people who offended in modern cities. By 1900, most existing states had formed police and prison systems, which is where our discussion will begin. See Figure 1.1.

The level of crime in the United States, particularly homicide, was relatively low at the beginning of the 20th century, perhaps because of the formal justice agencies that had been created during the 19th century. For example, the first metropolitan U.S. police departments were formed in Boston and then New York during the 1830s; in the same decade but a bit earlier, the first state police department, the Texas Rangers, had been established, and the U.S. Marshals Service had

Figure 1.1 • Homicide rates in the United States

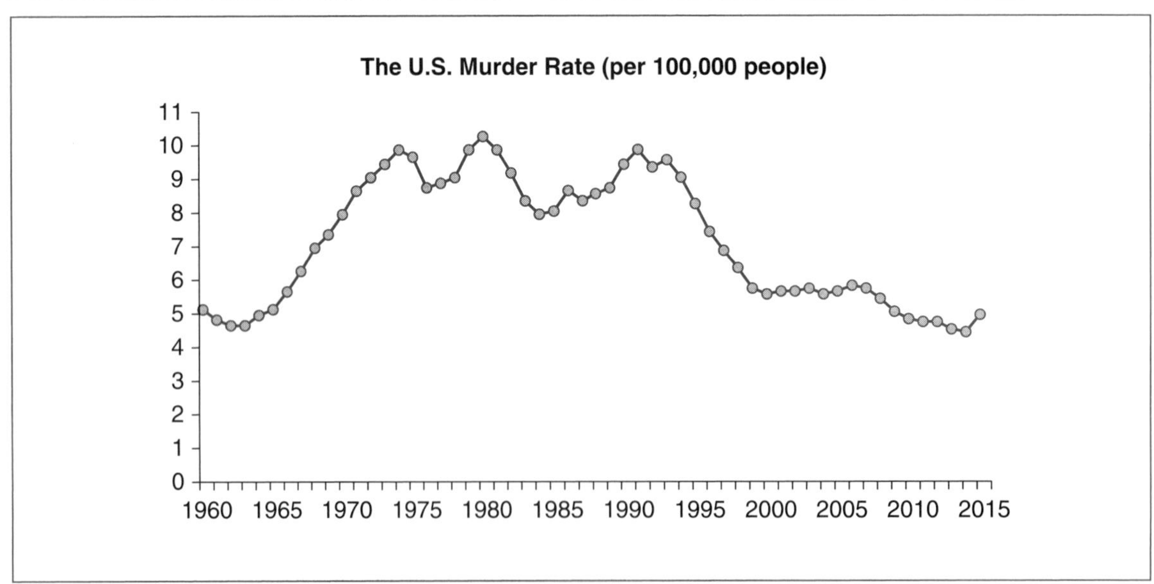

NOTE: The 2001 rate includes deaths attributed to the 9/11 terrorist attacks.

SOURCE: FBI.

been founded still earlier. Although prisons started in the late 1790s, they did not begin to resemble their modern form or proliferate rapidly until the mid-1800s. The first juvenile court was formed in the Chicago area in 1899. The development of these formal law enforcement and justice agencies may have contributed to the low levels of crime and homicide in the very early 1900s. (Note: Our discussion of the crime rate in the early 1900s will primarily deal with homicide, because murder records constitute the only valid records of crime from that time; the UCR did not start until the 1930s. Most people consider homicide the most serious crime, and its frequency typically reflects the overall crime rate.)

The effects of the creation of these formal agencies did not persist long into the 20th century. Looking at the level of homicides that occurred in the United States, it is obvious that large increases took place between 1910 and 1920, likely because of extremely high increases in industrialization as the U.S. economy moved from an agricultural to an industrial emphasis. More important, population growth was rapid as a result of urbanization. Whenever high numbers of people move into an area (in this case, cities) and form a far more dense population (think of New York City at that time or Las Vegas in current times), it creates a crime problem. This is likely due to there being more opportunities to commit crimes against others; after all, when people are crammed together, it creates a situation in which there are far more potential offenders in close proximity to far more potential victims. A good modern example of this is high schools, which studies show have higher crime rates than city subways or other crime-ridden areas, largely because they densely pack people together, and in such conditions, opportunities for crime are readily available. Thus, the rapid industrialization and urbanization of the early 1900s is probably the most important reason for the increase in homicide and crime in general in the United States at that time.

The largest increases in U.S. homicide in the early 1900s occurred during the 1920s and early 1930s, with the peak level of homicide coming in the early 1930s. Criminologists and historians have concluded that this huge increase in the homicide rate was primarily due to two factors beyond the industrialization and urbanization that explained the increase prior to the 1920s. First, the U.S. Congress passed a constitutional amendment that banned the distribution and consumption of alcohol beginning in 1920. The period that followed is known as Prohibition. This legal action proved to be a disaster, at least in terms of crime, and Congress later agreed—but not until the 1930s—by passing another amendment to do away with the previous amendment that banned alcohol. For about 14 years, which notably recorded the highest U.S. rates of homicide and crime before 1950, the government attempted to stop people from drinking.

Prior to Prohibition, gangsters had been relatively passive and had not held much power. However, the ban on alcohol gave the black market a lot of potential in terms of monetary profit and reasons for killing off competition. Some of the greatest massacres of rival gangs of organized crime syndicates (e.g., the Italian Mafia) occurred during the Prohibition era. The impact on crime was likely only one of the many problems with Prohibition, but it was a very important and deadly one for our purposes. Once Prohibition ended in the early 1930s, homicide and crime rates decreased significantly, which may have implications for modern drug policies. According to studies, many banned substances today are less violence producing than alcohol, which studies show is the most violence-causing substance. For example, most criminologists believe that the current war on drugs may actually be causing far more crime than it seeks to prevent (even if it may be lowering the number of drug addicts) due to the black market it creates for drugs that are in demand, much like the case with alcohol during Prohibition.

Another major reason why the homicide rate and overall crime levels increased so much during the early 1930s was the Great Depression, which sent the United States into an unprecedented state of economic upheaval. Most historians and criminologists agree that the stock market crash of the late 1920s was a primary contributor to the large numbers of homicides in the early 1930s. We will return to this subject later when we examine the strain theory of crime, which emphasizes economic structure and poverty as the primary causes of crime.

Although the homicide and crime rate experienced a significant drop after Prohibition was eliminated, another reason for this decrease was likely the social policies of the New Deal, which was implemented by President Franklin D. Roosevelt. Such policies included those that created new jobs for people hit hardest by the Depression through programs such as Job Corps and the Tennessee Valley Authority, both of which still exist today. Although such programs likely aided economic (and thus crime) recovery in the United States, world events of the early 1940s provided the greatest reasons for the huge decreases that were seen at that time.

The entry of the United States into World War II was probably the biggest contributor to decreasing U.S. crime in the early 20th century. As you will notice, homicides decreased dramatically during the 4 years (1941–1945) that hundreds of thousands of young men (the most likely offenders and victims) were sent overseas to fight on two fronts, Europe and the South Pacific. Anytime a society loses a huge portion of the most common offenders, namely young (teenage to 20s) males, it can expect a drop in crime like the one the United States experienced in the 1940s. However, at the end of 1945, most of these men returned and began making babies, which triggered the greatest increase in babies that U.S. society had ever seen. This generation of babies started what historians call the baby boom, which would have the greatest impact on crime levels that has ever been recorded in U.S. history.

Although crime rates increased after soldiers returned home from overseas in the late 1940s, they did not rise to anywhere near the levels present during Prohibition and the Great Depression. Alcohol was legal, and the economy was doing relatively well after World War II. During the 1950s, the crime level remained relatively low and stable until the early 1960s, when the impact of the baby boom emerged in terms of the crime rate. If a very large share of the population is made up of young people, particularly teenage or early-20s males, the crime rate will almost inevitably go up. This is exactly what occurred in the United States, starting in the early 1960s, and it led to the largest 10-year increase in crime that the country has ever seen.

The Baby Boom Effect

The UCR shows that the greatest single-decade increase in the crime rate occurred between 1965 and 1975. In that time, the overall crime rate more than doubled, an unprecedented increase. Notably, this increase occurred during the War on Poverty, which was set into motion by President Lyndon B. Johnson in a program he termed the Great Society; the crime increase thus turned many people and policy makers against having the government address economic issues to better society. However, the demographic factor that these individuals did not take into account was that this was the era in which most people in society belonged to young age groups, which predisposed the nation to the high crime rates experienced at this time. In contrast, the following generation, called Generation X, which includes those individuals born between 1965 and 1978, had a very low birth rate, which may have contributed to the low crime rates observed in recent years.

The high numbers of young people in society were not the only societal trend going on during the late 1960s and early 1970s that would lead to higher crime rates. For example, a large number of people were being arrested as a result of their participation in the civil rights movement, the women's rights movement, and anti–Vietnam War activities. Perhaps most important, the 1970s showed the highest levels of drug usage and favorable attitudes toward drugs since accurate national studies had first been conducted. Virtually all measures of drug usage peaked during the 1970s or early 1980s.

So, ultimately, many things came together between the mid-1960s and the late 1970s to usher in the greatest increase in the crime rate that the United States has ever seen, culminating in the peak of crime and homicide in 1980. All of our measures agree that crime, especially homicide, reached its highest level about that year. Although other periods, such as the early 1990s, showed similar increases in crime, largely due to juvenile offending, no other period showed higher rates than the 1980 period, most likely due to the coming of age of many baby boomers and their high drug usage.

Crime levels declined somewhat in the early 1980s and then rose again in the late 1980s and early 1990s, but the crime and homicide rate never exceeded the 1980 peak. Furthermore, after 1994, the crime rate decreased drastically every year for about a decade, to the point that it dropped as low as it had been in the early 1960s. The U.S. crime rate is currently around where it was about 50 years ago.

There are many reasons for this huge decrease over the past two decades. One of the biggest reasons is that the population has a relatively smaller proportion of young people than it did during the 1960s and 1970s, but obviously there is more to the picture. Drug usage, as well as favorable attitudes toward drugs, has dropped a lot in recent years. Furthermore, the incarceration rate of prisoners is about 400% to 500% of what it was in the early 1970s. Although many experts have claimed that locking up criminals does not reduce crime levels in a society, it is hard to deny that imprisoning 5 times more people will not result in catching many, if not most, of the habitual offenders. It makes sense: By rate, the United States currently locks up more citizens in prison than virtually any other developed country.

Almost all crime tends to be nonrandom. Consistent with this, the crime measures show a number of trends in which crime occurs among certain types of people, in certain places, at certain times, and so on. We turn to an examination of such concentrations of crime, starting with large, macro differences in crime rates across regions of the United States.

Rates of Crime

Regional and City Differences

Crime tends to be higher in certain regions of the country. According to the UCR, the United States is separated into four regions: Northeast, Midwest, South, and West. For the past few decades, crime rates (based on crime per capita) have been significantly higher in two of these regions: the South and the West. These two regions consistently have higher rates than the other regions, with one or the other having the highest rates for violence or property offenses or both each year. Some studies have found that, when poverty levels are accounted for, much of the regional difference is explained away. Although this is a very simple conclusion, the studies seem to be consistent in tying regional differences to variations in social factors, notably socioeconomic levels.

Regardless of the region, there seems to be extreme variation from high to low crime rates across states and cities within each of these large regions. For example, crime measures consistently show that certain U.S. states and jurisdictions have consistently high crime rates. The two standouts are Louisiana and the District of Columbia, with the latter having an extremely high rate—typically more than 8 times the national average for homicide. It is quite ironic that arguably the most powerful city in the world has an extremely serious crime problem, certainly one of the worst in our nation.

Another question is why crime rates in states or jurisdictions, or in cities and counties, vary drastically from one region to the next. For instance, Camden, New Jersey, one of the cities in the lower-rate Northeast region according to the UCR, had the highest rate of crime among all U.S. cities in the years 2004 and 2005. Detroit, Michigan, was second worst for both of these years; it used to be number one before Camden outdid it. At the same time, however, New Jersey had some of the safest cities in the nation for these years—2 of the 10 safest cities are in New Jersey, which shows how much crime can vary from place to place, even those in relatively close proximity. Notably, in the most recent estimates from the FBI, the cities of St. Louis and New Orleans exhibited the highest rates of serious violent crimes in 2006 and 2007, respectively. An important factor for New Orleans was the devastation of the city's infrastructure after Hurricane Katrina, which essentially wiped out the city's criminal justice system and resources.

Crime has also been found to cluster within a given city, whether the overall city is relatively low crime or high crime. Virtually every area (whether urban, suburban, or rural) has what are known as **hot spots**, or places that have high levels of crime activity. Such places are often bars or liquor stores or other types of businesses, such as bus stops and depots, convenience stores, shopping malls, motels and hotels, fast-food restaurants, check-cashing businesses, tattoo parlors, or discount stores (such as dollar stores). However, hot spots can also be residential places, such as homes that police are constantly called to for domestic violence or apartment complexes that are crime-ridden—something often seen in subsidized housing areas.

Even the nicest of cities and areas have hot spots, and even the worst cities and areas also tend to have most of their police calls coming from specific addresses or businesses. This is one of the best examples of how crime does not tend to be random. Many police agencies have begun using spatial software on computer systems to analyze where the hot spots in a given city are and to predict where certain crimes are likely to occur in the future. This allows more preventive patrols and proactive strategies in such zones. One criminological theory, routine activities theory, is largely based on explaining why hot spots exist.

Rates of Crime according to Time of Day and Time of Year

Another way that crime is known to cluster is by time of day. This varies greatly depending on the type of group being examined. For example, juvenile delinquency and victimization, especially for violence, tends to peak sharply at 3:00 p.m. on school days (about half of the days of the year for children), which is the time that youths are most likely to lack supervision (i.e., children are let out of school and are often not supervised by adults until they get home). On the other hand, adult crime and victimization, especially for violence, tends to peak much later on, at about 11:00 p.m. on almost all days, which is a sharp contrast to the juvenile peak in midafternoon. These estimates are primarily based on FBI and UCR data.

To some extent, the peak hour for juveniles is misleading; other non-police-based estimates show that just as much crime is going on during school, but schools tend not to report it. As stated previously, this widespread lack of reporting by schools occurs because none of the parties involved wants a formal police report taken. Typically, the youth doesn't want to be arrested; the child's parents don't want their daughter or son to be formally processed by police; and most important, no school wants to become known as a dangerous place. Thus, the police are typically called only in extreme cases—for example, if a student pulls a gun on another student or actually uses a weapon.

This underreporting also occurs in colleges and universities, because such institutions depend largely on tuition for funding, and this goes down if enrollment levels decline. After all, no parents want to send their teenagers to a college that is high in crime. Federal law now requires virtually all colleges to report their crime levels to the public, so there is a lot at stake if police take formal reports on crime events. Thus, most colleges, like K–12 school systems, have an informal process in place so that even violent crimes can often be handled informally.

Crimes tend to peak significantly during the summer. Studies show that criminals tend to be highly opportunistic, meaning that they happen to be going about their normal activities when they see an opportunity to commit a crime, as compared to a more hydraulic model, in which an offender actually goes out looking to commit a crime. Because criminals are like everyone else in most ways, they tend to be out and about more in the summer, so they are more likely to see opportunities at that time. Furthermore, youths are typically out of school during the summer, so they are often bored and not supervised by adults as much as during the traditional school year. Burglary tends to rise 300% during the summer, an increase that may be linked to the fact that people go on vacation and leave their homes vacant for weeks or months at a time. All of these factors come together to produce much higher rates in the summer than in any other season.

A couple of crimes, such as murder and robbery, tend to have a second peak in the winter, which most experts believe is due to high emotions during the holidays, additional social interaction (and often the drinking of alcohol) during the holidays, and an increase in wanting money or goods for gift giving, which would explain robbery increases at that time. These offenses are the exception, however, not the rule. Most offenses, including murder and robbery, tend to have their highest peaks during warmer summer months.

Rates of Crime according to Age and Gender

Age is perhaps the most important way that crime and victimization tend to cluster in certain groups. Almost no individual gets arrested before the age of 10; if one does, it is a huge predictor that the child is likely to become a habitual, chronic offender. However, between the ages of 10 and 17, the offending rate for all serious street crimes (i.e., FBI index crimes) goes up drastically, peaking at an average age of 17. Then the offending rates begin decreasing significantly, such that by the time people reach the age of 20, the likelihood of being arrested has fallen in half as compared to the midteenage years. This offending level continues to decline throughout life for all of the serious index crimes, although other crimes, such as white-collar crimes, tax evasion, and gambling, are likely to be committed more often at later ages.

The extraordinarily high levels of offending in the teenage years have implications for how we prevent and deal with juvenile delinquency and help explain why we are so bad at preventing habitual offenders from committing so many crimes. We are often good at predicting who the most chronic, serious offenders are by the time they are in their 20s, but that does little good because most offenders have committed most of their crimes before they hit 20 years old.

Another characteristic important in the way crime clusters is gender. In every society, at every time in recorded history, males have committed far more serious street crimes (both violent and property) than females. It appears there is almost no closing of this gap in offending—at least for FBI index crimes. Even in the most recent years, males have been the offenders in 80% to 98% of all serious violent crimes (murder, robbery, aggravated assault, forcible rape) and have made up the vast majority of offenders in property index crimes (burglary, motor vehicle theft, arson, and larceny). The fact that the last offense is committed more frequently by males often surprises people because the most common type of larceny is shoplifting, which people often perceive as being done mostly by women. All studies show that men commit most of the larcenies in the United States. It is important to realize that males in all societies throughout the world commit the vast majority of offenses, and the more violent and serious the crimes are, the more men are represented.

However, there are a few nonindex crimes that females commit as much as, or more than, males. Specifically, in terms of property crimes, embezzlement and fraud are two offenses that females commit at rates comparable to those for men, which likely has to do with enhanced opportunities to commit such crimes. Most of the workforce is now female, which wasn't true in past decades, and many women work in banking and other businesses that tempt employees by having large amounts of money available for embezzling. In terms of public disorder, prostitution arrests tend to be mostly female, which is not too surprising.

The only other offense in which females are well represented is running away from home, which is a status offense (illegal for juveniles only). However, virtually all sources and studies of offending rates (e.g., self-report studies) show that male juveniles run away far more than females, but because of societal norms and values, females get arrested far more than males. Feminist theories of the patriarchal model (in short, men are in charge and dominate or control females) and the chivalry model (females are treated differently because they are seen as more innocent) argue that females are protected as a type of property. This may be important in light of the opposing findings regarding female and male rates of running away versus female and male rates of being arrested for running away. The bottom line is that families are more likely to report missing girls than missing boys and more likely to press law enforcement agencies to pursue girls who have run away than boys who have done so. We will explore explanations for such differences in later sections, particularly in the section in which we cover conflict and feminist theories of crime.

Rates of Crime according to Population Density

Victimization and offending rates are also clustered according to the density of a given area. All sources of crime data show that rates of offending and victimization are far higher per capita in urban areas than in suburban and rural regions. Furthermore, this trend is linear: The more rural an area, the lower the rates for crime and victimization. To clarify, urban areas have, by far, the highest rates for offending, followed by suburban areas; the least amount of crime and victimization is found in rural (e.g., farming) areas. This trend has been shown for many decades and is undisputed. Keep in mind that such rates are based on population in such areas, so this trend holds true even per capita for citizens in a given region. This is likely due to enhanced opportunities to commit crime in urban and even suburban areas, as well as the fact that rural communities tend to have stronger **informal controls**, such as family, church, and community ties. Studies consistently show that informal controls are far more effective in preventing and solving crimes than are the **formal controls** of justice, which include all official aspects of law enforcement and justice, such as police, courts, and corrections (i.e., prisons, probation, parole).

A good example of the effectiveness of informal sanctions can be seen in the early formation of the U.S. colonies, such as the Massachusetts Bay Colony. In the early 1600s, crime per capita was at an all-time low in what would become the United States. It may surprise many that police and prisons did not exist then; rather, the low crime rate was due to high levels of informal controls: When people committed crimes, they were banished from the society or were shunned.

As in Nathaniel Hawthorne's novel *The Scarlet Letter*, even for what would now be considered a relatively minor offense (adultery), people were forced to wear a large letter (such as an *A* for adultery or a *T* for theft), and they were shunned by all others in their social world. Such punishments were (and still are) highly effective deterrents for offenders, but they work only in communities with high levels of informal controls. Studies have shown that, in such societies, crime tends to be extremely low—in fact, so low that such communities may "invent" serious crimes so that they can have an identifiable group on which to blame societal problems. We saw this occur in the Massachusetts Bay Colony with the creation of a new offense, witchcraft, for which hundreds of people were put on trial and many were executed.

Such issues will be raised again later when we discuss the sociological theories of Émile Durkheim. Nevertheless, it is interesting to note that some judges and communities have gone back to public-shaming punishments, such as making people carry signs of their offenses or putting the names of offenders in local newspapers. But the conclusion at this point is that rural communities tend to have far higher informal controls, which keep their crime rates low. On the other hand, urban (especially inner-city) areas tend to have very low levels of informal controls, which lead to few attempts by the community to police itself.

Crime also tends to cluster according to social class, with the lower classes experiencing far more violent offending and victimization. This is now undisputed and consistently shown across all sources of data regarding criminal offending. Interestingly, the characteristics associated with offending tend to be a mirror image of those associated with victimization. To clarify, young, poor urban males tend to have the highest rates of criminal offending—and this group also has the highest rates of victimization as a result of violent offending. This mirror image phenomenon is often referred to as the **equivalency hypothesis**. However, the equivalency hypothesis does not characterize the relationship between social class and property crimes. Specifically, members of middle- to upper-class households tend to experience just as much and often more victimization for property crimes than do lower-class households, but the most likely offenders in most property crimes are from the lower class. This makes sense; offenders will tend to steal from the people and places that have the most property or money to steal. This tendency has been found since criminological data were first collected, even back to the early 1800s, and it is often found in present times, although it is not consistently shown each year (e.g., in NCVS data). Nevertheless, the equivalency hypothesis holds true for violent crimes: Lower-class individuals, especially those who are young, inner-city males, commit more violent crimes, and they are victimized more as a result of such violent crimes.

Rates of Crime according to Race or Ethnicity

Another important way crimes are clustered in U.S. society is by race or ethnicity. In terms of violent crimes, the most victimized group by far in the United States is Native Americans or American Indians. According to NCVS data, Native Americans are victimized at almost twice the rate of any other racial or ethnic group. This is likely due to the extreme levels of poverty, unemployment, and so on that exist on virtually all American Indian reservations.

Although some Indian tribes have recently gained profits from operating gaming casinos on their lands, the vast majority of tribes in most states are not involved in such endeavors, so deprivation and poverty are still the norm.

Although there is little offending data for this group (the UCR does not adequately measure this group in its arrest data), it is generally assumed that Native Americans have the highest rates of offending as well. This is a fairly safe assumption, because research has clearly shown that the vast majority of criminal offending and victimization are **intraracial**. This means that crime tends to occur within a race or ethnicity (e.g., Whites offending against Whites) as opposed to being **interracial** or across races or ethnicities (e.g., Whites offending against Blacks).

▲ **Image 1.6** Offenders being forced to hold signs as part of their punishment is becoming a more popular informal sanction that shames individuals in their communities.

SOURCE: © Joe Amon / Denver Post / Getty Images

Another major group that experiences an extremely high rate of victimization, particularly for homicide, is Blacks. (The term *Black* is used here, as opposed to *African American*, because this is what most measures [e.g., the UCR and NCVS] use and because many African Americans are not Black [e.g., many citizens from Egypt or South Africa]). According to UCR data for homicide, which the NCVS does not report, Blacks have by far the highest rates of victimization and offending. Again, this is likely due to the extreme levels of poverty experienced by this group as well as the high levels of single-headed households among this population (which likely explains much of the poverty).

A good example of the high levels of homicide rates among Blacks, in terms of both offending and victimization, can be seen in certain U.S. cities. Washington, DC, New Orleans, St. Louis, and Detroit have some of the highest murder rates among U.S. cities. They also have some of the highest proportions of Black residents as compared to other U.S. cities. Notably, studies have shown that when researchers control for poverty rates and single-headed households, the racial and ethnicity effects seem to disappear.

For example, data show that Washington, DC, and the state of Louisiana are the top two jurisdictions for high rates of poverty, with most of the poor being children or teenagers, the latter of whom are most prone to committing crimes, especially violent offenses (such as murder). Thus, the two racial and ethnic groups rated highest for violent crime, both as victims and offenders—Native Americans and Blacks—also tend to have the highest rates in the nation for poverty and broken families. It should be noted that Hispanics, a common ethnic group in the United States, also have relatively high offending and victimization rates as compared to Whites and other minorities, such as Asians, who tend to experience low rates.

Policy Implications

One of the key elements of a good theory is that it can help inform policy makers in making decisions about how to reduce crime. This theme will be reviewed at the end of each section in this book. After all, a criminological theory is only truly useful in the real world if it helps to reduce criminal offending. Many theories have been used as the basis of such changes in policy, and we will present examples of how the theories of crime discussed in each section have guided policy making. We will also examine empirical evidence for such policies, specifically to determine whether or not such policies have been successful (and many have not).

Conclusion

Although there are numerous other ways that crime tends to be clustered in our society, we have covered most of the major variables in this section. The rest of this book will examine the various theories of why crime tends to occur in such groups and individuals, and the way that we determine the accuracy of these theories will directly relate to how well they explain the high rates of crime in the groups that we have discussed.

SECTION SUMMARY

- Criminology is the scientific study of crime. It involves the use of the scientific method and testing hypotheses, which distinguishes it from other perspectives of crime (e.g., journalistic, religious, legal) because these fields are not based on science.
- Criminological theory seeks to do more than simply predict criminal behavior; rather, the goal is to more fully understand the reasons why certain individuals offend and others do not.
- Definitions of crime vary drastically across time and place; most criminologists tend to focus on deviant behaviors whether or not they violate criminal codes.
- There are various paradigms, or unique perspectives, pertaining to crime, which have contrasting assumptions and propositions. The Classical School of criminological theory assumes free will and choice among individuals, whereas the Positive School focuses on biological, social, and psychological factors that negate the notion of choice among criminal offenders. Other theoretical paradigms, such as conflict, critical, and integrated models of offending, also exist.
- Criminological theories can be classified by their fundamental assumptions as well as other factors, such as the unit of measure on which they focus—the individual or the group (micro or macro, respectively)—or the assumptions they make regarding basic human nature: good, bad, or blank slate.
- There are more than a handful of characteristics that good criminological theories should have and that bad criminological theories do not have.
- Three criteria are required for determining causality and thus are essential in determining whether or not an independent (predictive) variable (*X*) actually affects a dependent (consequent) variable (*Y*).
- This introduction also discussed the primary measures that are used for estimating the crime committed in the United States; these primary measures are police reports (e.g., the UCR), victimization surveys (e.g., the NCVS), and offenders' self-reports of the crimes they have committed.
- We also discussed in this section what the measures of crime have shown regarding the distribution of criminal offending according to region, race and ethnicity, time of day, time of year, age, gender, socioeconomic status, and period of history. It is important to note that various theories presented in this book will be tested on the extent to which they can explain the clustering of crime among certain individuals and groups.

KEY TERMS

Classical School 6

clearance rate 14

conflict theories 7

consensual perspective 7

correlation, or covariation 10

criminology 1

dark figure 13

deviance 5

empirical validity 9

equivalency hypothesis 24

formal controls 24

hot spots 21

hypotheses 2

index offenses 13

informal controls 24

interracial 25

intraracial 25

legalistic approach 4

logical consistency 8

macro level of analysis 6

mala in se 5

mala prohibita 5

micro level of analysis 6

National Crime Victimization Survey (NCVS) 12

nonindex offenses 13

paradigms 6

parsimony 8

policy implications 9

Positive School 6

scientific method 2

scope 8

self-report data (SRD) 12

social sciences 2

spuriousness 11

telescoping 16

temporal ordering 10

testability 9

theory 2

Uniform Crime Report (UCR) 12

DISCUSSION QUESTIONS

1. How does criminology differ from other perspectives of crime?
2. How does a good theoretical explanation of crime go beyond simply predicting crime?
3. Should criminologists emphasize only crimes made illegal by law, or should they also study acts that are deviant but not illegal? Explain why you feel this way.
4. Even though you haven't been exposed to all the theories in this book, do you favor classical or positive assumptions regarding criminal behavior? Explain why.
5. Which types of theories do you think are most important: those that explain individual behavior (micro) or those that explain criminality among groups (macro)? Explain your decision.
6. Do you tend to favor the idea that human beings are born bad, good, or a blank slate? Discuss your decision, and provide an example.
7. Which characteristics of a good theory do you find most important? Which are least important? Make sure to explain why you feel that way.

8. Of the three criteria for determining causality between a predictor variable and a consequent variable, which do you think is easiest to show, and which is hardest to show? Why?
9. Which of the measures of crime do you think is the best estimate of crime in the United States? Why? Also, which measure is the best for determining associations between crime and personality traits? Why?
10. Looking at what the measures of crime show, which finding surprises you the most? Explain why.
11. What types of policies do you feel reduce crime the most? Which do you think have little or no effect in reducing crime?

WEB RESOURCES

Measures of Crime

http://criminal-justice.iresearchnet.com/criminology/theories
https://ucr.fbi.gov/crime-in-the-u.s/2015/crime-in-the-u.s.-2015
http://www.bjs.gov/index.cfm?ty=dcdetail&iid=245

How to Read a Research Article

As you travel through your criminal justice and criminology studies, you will soon learn that some of the best-known and emerging explanations of crime and criminal behavior come from research articles in academic journals. This book is full of research articles, and you may be asking yourself, "How do I read a research article?" It is my hope to answer this question with a quick summary of the key elements of any research article, followed by the questions you should be answering as you read through the assigned sections.

Every research article published in a social science journal will have the following elements: (a) introduction, (b) literature review, (c) methodology, (d) results, and (e) discussion or conclusion.

In the introduction, you will find an overview of the purpose of the research. Within the introduction, you will also find the hypothesis or hypotheses. A hypothesis is most easily defined as an educated statement or guess. In most hypotheses, you will find that the format usually followed is "If *X* happens, then *Y* will occur." For example, a simple hypothesis might be "If the price of gas increases, more people will ride bikes." This is a testable statement that the researcher wants to address in her or his study. Usually authors will state the hypothesis directly, but not always. Therefore, you must be aware of what the author is actually testing in the research project. If you are unable to find the hypothesis, ask yourself what is being tested or manipulated and then the expected results.

The next section of the research article is the literature review. At times, the literature review will be separated from the text in its own section, and at other times it will be found within the introduction. In any case, the literature review is an examination of what other researchers have already produced in terms of the research question or hypothesis. For example, returning to my hypothesis on the relationship between gas prices and bike riding, we may find that five researchers have previously conducted studies on the increase in gas prices. In the literature review, the author will discuss her or his findings and then discuss what the study will add to the existing research. The literature review may also be used as a platform of support for the hypothesis. For example, one researcher may have already determined that an increase in gas prices causes more people to roller-skate to work. The author can use this study as evidence to support her or his hypothesis that increased gas prices will lead to more bike riding.

The methods used in the research design are found in the next section of the research article. In the methodology section, you will find the following: who or what was studied, how many subjects were studied, the research tool (e.g., interview, survey, observation), how long the subjects were studied, and how the data that were collected were processed. The methods section is usually very concise, with every step of the research project recorded. This is important because a major goal of the researcher is reliability; describing exactly how the research was done allows it to be repeated. Reliability is determined by whether the results are the same.

The results section is an analysis of the researcher's findings. If the researcher conducted a quantitative study, using numbers or statistics to explain the research, you will find statistical tables and analyses that explain whether or not the researcher's hypothesis is supported. If the researcher conducted a qualitative study, nonnumerical research for the purpose of theory construction, the results will usually be displayed as a theoretical analysis or interpretation of the research question.

The research article will conclude with a discussion and summary of the study. In the discussion, you will find that the hypothesis is usually restated, and there may be a small discussion of why this was the hypothesis. You will also find a brief overview of the methodology and results. Finally, the discussion section looks at the implications of the research and what future research is still needed.

Now that you know the key elements of a research article, let us examine a sample article from your text: "The Use and Usefulness of Criminology, 1751–2005: Enlightened Justice and Its Failures" by Lawrence W. Sherman.

1. What is the thesis or main idea from this article?

   - The thesis or main idea is found in the introductory paragraph of this article. Although Sherman does not point out the main idea directly, you may read the introduction and summarize the main idea in your own words. For example, the thesis or main idea is that criminology should move away from strict analysis and toward scientific experimentation to improve the criminal justice system and crime control practices.

2. What is the hypothesis?

   - The hypothesis is found in the introduction of this article. It is first stated in the beginning paragraph: "As experimental criminology provides more comprehensive evidence about responses to crime, the prospects for better basic science—and better policy—will improve accordingly." The hypothesis is also restated in the middle of the second section of the article. Here, Sherman actually distinguishes the hypothesis by stating, "The history of criminology . . . provides an experimental test of this hypothesis about analytic versus experimental social science: *that social science has been most useful, if not most used, when it has been most experimental, with visibly demonstrable benefits (or harm avoidance) from new inventions.*"

3. Is there any prior literature related to the hypothesis?

   - As you may have noticed, this article does not have a separate section for a literature review. However, you will see that Sherman devotes attention to prior literature under the heading "Enlightenment, Criminology, and Justice." Here, he offers literature regarding the analytical and experimental history of criminology. This brief overview helps the reader understand the prior research, which explains why social science became primarily analytic.

4. What methods are used to support the hypothesis?

   - Sherman's methodology is known as a historical analysis. In other words, rather than conducting his own experiment, Sherman is using evidence from history to support his hypothesis regarding analytic and experimental criminology. When conducting a historical analysis, most researchers use archival material from books, newspapers, journals, and so on. Although Sherman does not directly state his source of information, we can see that he is basing his argument on historical essays and books, beginning with Henry Fielding's *An Enquiry into the Causes of the Late Increase of Robbers* (1751) and continuing through the social experiments of the 1980s by the National Institute of Justice. Throughout his methodology, Sherman continues to emphasize his hypothesis about the usefulness of experimental criminology, along with how experiments have also been hidden in the shadows of analytic criminology throughout history.

5. Is this a qualitative study or a quantitative study?

   - To determine whether a study is qualitative or quantitative, you must look at the results. Is Sherman using numbers to support his hypothesis (quantitative), or is he developing a nonnumerical theoretical argument (qualitative)? Because Sherman does not use statistics in this study, we can safely conclude that this is a qualitative study.

6. What are the results, and how does the author present the results?

   - Because this is a qualitative study, as we earlier determined, Sherman offers the results as a discussion of his findings from the historical analysis. The results may be found in the section titled "Criminology: Analytic, Useful, and Used." Here, Sherman explains that "*the vast majority of published criminology remains analytic and nonexperimental.*" He goes on to say that although experimental criminology has been shown to be useful, it has not always been used or used correctly. Because of the misuse of experimental criminology, criminologists have steered toward the safety of analysis rather than experimentation. Therefore, Sherman concludes that "analytic social science still dominates field experiments by 100 to 1 or better in criminology. . . . Future success of the field may depend upon a growing public image based on experimental results."

7. Do you believe that the author(s) provided a persuasive argument? Why or why not?

   - This answer is ultimately up to the reader, but looking at this article, I believe that it is safe to assume that readers will agree that Sherman offered a persuasive argument. Let us return to his major premise: The advancement of theory may depend on better experimental evidence, but as history has illustrated, the vast majority of criminology remains analytical. Sherman supports this proposition with a historical analysis of the great thinkers of criminology and the absence of experimental research throughout a major portion of history.

8. Who is the intended audience of this article?

   - A final question that will be useful for the reader deals with the intended audience. As you read the article, ask yourself to whom the author is wanting to speak. After you read this article, you will see that Sherman is writing for students, professors, criminologists, historians, and criminal justice personnel. The target audience may most easily be identified if you ask yourself, "Who will benefit from reading this article?"

9. What does the article add to your knowledge of the subject?

   - This answer is best left up to the reader because the question is asking how the article improved your knowledge. However, one answer to this question is as follows: This article helps the reader to understand that criminology is not just about theoretical construction. Criminology is both an analytical and an experimental social science, and to improve the criminal justice system as well as criminal justice policies, more attention needs to be given to the usefulness of experimental criminology.

10. What are the implications for criminal justice policy that can be derived from this article?

    - Implications for criminal justice policy are most likely to be found in the conclusion or the discussion sections of the article. This article, however, emphasizes the implications throughout. From this article, we are able to conclude that crime prevention programs will improve greatly if they are embedded in well-funded, experiment-driven data rather than strictly analytical data. Therefore, it is in the hands of policy makers to fund criminological research and apply the findings in a productive manner to criminal justice policy.

Now that we have gone through the elements of a research article, it is your turn to continue through your text, reading the various articles and answering the same questions. You may find that some articles are easier to follow than others, but do not be dissuaded. Remember that each article will follow the same format: introduction, literature review, methods, results, and discussion. If you have any problems, refer to this introduction for guidance.

READING /// 1

In this selection, Lawrence Sherman provides an excellent review of the policies that have resulted from the very early stages of classical theories, through the early positivist era, and into modern times. Sherman's primary point is that experimental research is highly important in determining the policies that should be used with offenders and potential offenders. Although many important factors can never be experimentally manipulated—bad parents, poor schooling, negative peer influences—there are, as Sherman asserts, numerous types of variables that can be experimentally manipulated by criminological researchers. The resulting findings can help guide policy makers in pushing forward more efficient and effective policies regarding the prevention of and reaction to various forms of criminal offending. There is no better scholar to present such an argument and support for it; Sherman is perhaps the best-known scholar who has applied the experimental method to criminological research, given his experience with studies regarding domestic violence and other criminal offenses.

While reading this entry, readers are encouraged to consider the following:

- The "pioneers" and studies that led the way in showing a way to experimentally examine the effectiveness of various approaches to reducing crime
- Other variables or aspects of crime that can be examined via experimental forms of research
- The vast number of variables that are important causes of crime or delinquency but could never be experimentally manipulated for logistic or ethical reasons
- The conclusion and policy implications stated by Joan McCord in the final words of her address to the American Society of Criminology in 2003

The Use and Usefulness of Criminology, 1751–2005

Enlightened Justice and Its Failures

Lawrence W. Sherman

Criminology was born in a crime wave, raised on a crusade against torture and execution, and then hibernated for two centuries of speculation. Awakened by the rising crime rates of the latter twentieth century, most of its scholars chose to pursue analysis over experiment. The twenty-first century now offers more policy-relevant science than ever, even if basic science still occupies center stage. Its prospects for integrating basic and "clinical" science are growing, with more scholars using multiple tools rather than pursuing single-method work. Criminology contributes only a few drops of science in an ocean of decision making, but the number of drops is growing steadily. As experimental criminology provides more comprehensive evidence about responses

SOURCE: Lawrence Sherman, "The Use and Usefulness of Criminology, 1751–2005," *ANNALS of the American Academy of Political and Social Science* 600, no. 1 (2005): 115–35. The selection here is taken from A. Walsh and C. Hemmens, *Introduction to Criminology: A Text/Reader* (Thousand Oaks, CA: SAGE, 2008), 24–32.

to crime, the prospects for better basic science—and better policy—will improve accordingly.

Enlightenment, Criminology, and Justice

The entire history of social science has been shaped by key choices scholars made in that transformative era, choices that are still made today. For criminology more than most disciplines, those Enlightenment choices have had enormous consequences for the use and usefulness of its social science. The most important of these consequences is that justice still remains largely un-Enlightened by empirical evidence about the effects of its actions on public safety and public trust.

Historians may despair at defining a coherent intellectual or philosophical content in the Age of Enlightenment, but one idea seems paramount: "that we understand nature and man best through the use of our natural faculties" (May 1976, xiv) by systematic empirical methods, rather than through ideology, abstract reasoning, common sense, or claims of divine principles made by competing religious authorities. Kant, in contrast, stressed the receiving end of empirical science in his definition of Enlightenment: the time when human beings regained the courage to "use one's own mind without another's guidance" (Gay 1969, 384).

Rather than becoming *experimental* in method, social science became primarily *analytic*. This distinction between experimental manipulation of some aspect of social behavior versus detached (if systematic) observation of behavioral patterns is crucial to all social science (even though not all questions for social science offer a realistic potential for experiment). The decision to cast social science primarily in the role of critic, rather than of inventor, has had lasting consequences for the enterprise, especially for the credibility of its conclusions. There may be nothing so practical as a good theory, but it is hard to visibly—or convincingly—demonstrate the benefits of social analysis for the reduction of human misery. The absence of "show-and-tell" benefits of analytic social science blurred its boundaries with ideology, philosophy, and even emotion. This problem has plagued analytic social science ever since, with the possible exception of times (like the Progressive Era and the 1960s) when the social order itself was in crisis. As sociologist E. Digby Baltzell (1979) suggested about cities and other social institutions, "as the twig is bent, so grows the tree." Social science may have been forged in the same kind of salon discussions as natural science, but without some kind of empirical reports from factories, clinics, or farm fields. Social science has thus famously "smelled too much of the lamp" of the library (Gay 1969). Even when analytic social science has been most often used, it is rarely praised as useful.

That is not to say that theories (with or without evidence) have lacked influence in criminology, or in any social science. The theory of deterrent effects of sanctions was widely used to reduce the severity of punishment long before the theory could be tested with any evidence. The theories of "anomie" and "differential association" were used to plan the 1960s "War on Poverty" without any clear evidence that opportunity structures could be changed. Psychological theories of personality transformation were used to develop rehabilitation programs in prisons long before any of them were subject to empirical evaluation. Similarly, evidence (without theory) of a high concentration of crime among a small proportion of criminal offenders was used to justify more severe punishment for repeat offenders, also without empirical testing of those policies.

The criminologists' general preference for analysis over experiment has not been universal in social science. Enlightenment political science was, in an important—if revolutionary—sense, experimental, developing and testing new forms of government soon after they were suggested in print. The Federalist Papers, for example, led directly to the "experiment" of the Bill of Rights.

Perhaps the clearest exception to the dominance of analytic social science was within criminology itself in its very first work during the Enlightenment. The fact that criminologists do not remember it this way says more about its subsequent dominance by analytic methods than about the true history of the field. Criminology was born twice in the eighteenth century, first (and forgotten) as an experimental science and then (remembered) as an analytic one. And though experimental criminology in the Enlightenment had an enormous impact on institutions of justice, it was analytic criminology that was preserved by law professors and twentieth-century scholars as the foundation of the field.

The history of criminology thus provides an experimental test of this hypothesis about analytic versus experimental social science: *that social science has been most useful, if not most used, when it has been most experimental, with visibly demonstrable benefits (or harm avoidance) from new inventions.* The evidence for this claim in eighteenth-century criminology is echoed by the facts of criminology in the twentieth century. In both centuries, the fraternal twins of analysis and experiment pursued different pathways through life, while communicating closely with each other. One twin was critical, the other imaginative; one systematically observational, the other actively experimental; one detached with its integrity intact, the other engaged with its integrity under threat. Both twins needed each other to advance their mutual field of inquiry. But it has been experiments in every age that made criminology most useful, as measured by unbiased estimates of the effects of various responses to crime.

The greatest disappointment across these centuries has been the limited usefulness of experimental criminology in achieving "geometric precision" (Beccaria 1764/1964) in the pursuit of "Enlightened Justice," defined as "the administration of sanctions under criminal law guided by (1) inviolate principles protecting human rights of suspects and convicts while seeking (2) consequences reducing human misery, through means known from (3) unbiased empirical evidence of what works best" (Sherman 2005). While some progress has been made, most justice remains unencumbered by empirical evidence on its effects. To understand why this disappointment persists amid great success, we must begin with the Enlightenment itself.

Inventing Criminology: Fielding, Beccaria, and Bentham

The standard account of the origin of criminology locates it as a branch of moral philosophy: part of an aristocratic crusade against torture, the death penalty, and arbitrary punishment, fought with reason, rhetoric, and analysis. This account is true but incomplete. Criminology's forgotten beginnings preceded Cesare Beccaria's famous 1764 essay in the form of Henry Fielding's 1753 experiments with justice in London. Inventing the modern institutions of a salaried police force and prosecutors, of crime reporting, crime records, employee background investigations, liquor licensing, and social welfare policies as crime prevention strategies, Fielding provided the viable preventive alternatives to the cruel excesses of retribution that Beccaria denounced—before Beccaria ever published a word.

The standard account hails a treatise on "the science of justice" (Gay 1969, 440) that was based on Beccaria's occasional visits to courts and prisons, followed by many discussions in a salon. The present alternative account cites a far less famous treatise based on more than a thousand days of Fielding conducting trials and sentencing convicts in the world's (then) largest city, supplemented by his on-site inspections of tenements, gin joints, brothels, and public hangings. The standard account thus chooses a criminology of analytic detachment over a criminology of clinical engagement.

The standard account in twentieth-century criminology textbooks traced the origin of the field to this "classical school" of criminal law and criminology, with Cesare Beccaria's (1738–1794) treatise *On Crimes and Punishments* (1764) as the first treatise in scientific criminology. (Beccaria is also given credit [incorrectly], even by Enlightenment scholars, for first proposing that utility be measured by "the greatest happiness divided among the greatest number"—which Frances Hutcheson, a mentor to Adam Smith, had published in Glasgow in 1725 before Beccaria was born [Buchan 2003, 68–71]). Beccaria, and later Bentham, contributed the central claims of the deterrence hypothesis on which almost all systems of criminal law now rely: that punishment is more likely to prevent future crime to the extent that it is certain, swift, and proportionate to the offense (Beccaria) or more costly than the benefit derived from the offense (Bentham).

Fielding

This standard account of Beccaria as the *first* criminologist is, on the evidence, simply wrong. Criminology did not begin in a Milanese salon among the group of aristocrats who helped Beccaria formulate and publish his epigrams but more than a decade earlier in a London magistrate's courtroom full of gin-soaked robbery defendants. The first social scientist of crime to publish in the English—and perhaps any—language was Henry Fielding, Esq. (1707–1754). Fielding was appointed by the government as magistrate at the Bow Street Court in London. His years on that bench, supplemented by his visits to the homes of London labor and London poor, provided him with ample qualitative data for his 1751 treatise titled *An Enquiry Into the Causes of the Late Increase of Robbers.*

Fielding's treatise is a remarkable analysis of what would today be called the "environmental criminology" of robbery. Focused on the reasons for a crime wave and the policy alternatives to hanging as the only means of combating crime, Fielding singles out the wave of "that poison called gin" that hit mid-century London like crack hit New York in the 1980s. He theorizes that a drastic price increase (or tax) would make gin too expensive for most people to consume, thereby reducing violent crime. He also proposes more regulation of gambling, based on his interviews with arrested robbers who said they had to rob to pay their gambling debts. Observing the large numbers of poor and homeless people committing crime, he suggests a wider "safety net" of free housing and food. His emphasis is clearly on prevention without punishment as the best policy approach to crime reduction.

Fielding then goes on to document the failures of punishment in three ways. First, the system of compulsory "voluntary policing" by each citizen imposed after the Norman Conquest had become useless: "what is the business of every man is the business of no man." Second, the contemporary system of requiring crime victims to prosecute their own cases (or hire a lawyer at their own expense) was failing to bring many identified offenders to justice. Third, witnesses were intimidated and often unwilling to provide evidence needed for conviction. All this leads him to hint at, but not spell out, a modern system of "socialized" justice in which the state, rather than crime victims, pays for police to investigate and catch criminals, prosecutors to bring evidence to court, and even support for witnesses and crime victims.

His chance to present his new "invention" to the government came two years after he published his treatise on robbery. In August 1753, five different robbery-murders were committed in London in one week. An impatient cabinet secretary summoned Fielding twice from his sickbed and asked him to propose a plan for stopping the murders. In four days, Fielding submitted a "grant proposal" for an experiment in policing that would cost £600 (about £70,000 or $140,000 in current value). The purpose of the money was to retain, on salary, the band of detectives Fielding worked with, and to pay a reward to informants who would provide evidence against the murderers.

Within two weeks, the robberies stopped, and for two months not one murder or robbery was reported in Westminster (Fielding 1755/1964, 191–193). Fielding managed to obtain a "no-cost extension" to the grant, which kept the detectives on salary for several years. After Henry's death, his brother John obtained new funding, so that the small team of "Bow Street Runners" stayed in operation until the foundation of the much larger—and uniformed—Metropolitan Police in 1829.

The birth of the Bow Street Runners was a turning point in the English paradigm of justice. The crime wave accompanying the penny-a-quart gin epidemic of the mid-eighteenth century had demonstrated the failure of relying solely on the *severity* of punishment, so excessive that many juries refused to convict people who were clearly guilty of offenses punishable by death—such as shoplifting. As Bentham would later write, there was good reason to think that the *certainty* of punishment was too low for crime to be deterrable. As Fielding said in his treatise on robbery, "The utmost severity to offenders [will not] be justifiable unless we take every possible method of preventing the offence." Fielding was not the only inventor to propose the idea of a salaried police force to patrol and arrest criminals, but he was the first to conduct an *experiment* testing that invention. While Fielding's police experiment would take decades to be judged successful (seventy-six years for the "Bobbies" to be founded at Scotland Yard in 1829), the role of experimental evidence proved central to changing the paradigm of practice.

Beccaria

In sharp contrast, Beccaria had no clinical practice with offenders, nor was he ever asked to stop a crime wave. Instead, he took aim at a wave of torture and execution that characterized European justice. Arguing the same ideology of prevention as Fielding (whose treatise he did not cite), Beccaria urged abolition of torture, the death penalty, and secret trials. Within two centuries, almost all Europe had adopted his proposals. While many other causes of that result can be cited, there is clear evidence of Beccaria's 1764 treatise creating a "tipping point" of public opinion on justice.

What Beccaria did not do, however, was to supply a shred of scientific evidence in support of his theories of the deterrent effects of non-capital penalties proportionate to the severity of the offense. Nor did he state his theories in a clearly falsifiable way, as Fielding had done. In his method, Beccaria varies little from law professors or judges (then and now) who argue a blend of opinion and factual assumptions they find reasonable, deeming it enlightened truth *ipse dixit* ("because I say so myself"). What he lacked by the light of systematic analysis of data, he made up for by eloquence and "stickiness" of his aphorisms. Criminology by slogan may be more readily communicated than criminology by experiment in terms of fame. But it is worth noting that the founding of the British police appears much more directly linked to Fielding's experiments than the steady abolition of the death penalty was linked to Beccaria's book.

Bentham

Beccaria the moral-empirical theorist stands in sharp contrast to his fellow Utilitarian Jeremy Bentham, who devoted twelve years of his life (and some £10,000) to an invention in prison administration. Working from a book he wrote on a "Panopticon" design for punishment by incarceration (rather than hanging), Bentham successfully lobbied for a 1794 law authorizing such a prison to be built. He was later promised a contract to build and manage such a prison, but landed interests opposed his use of the site he had selected. We can classify Bentham as an experimentalist on the grounds that he invested much of his life in "trying" as well as thinking. Even though he did not build the prison he designed, similar prisons (for better or worse) were built in the United States and elsewhere. Prison design may justifiably be classified as a form of invention and experimental criminology, as distinct from the analytic social science approach Bentham used in his writings—thereby making him as "integrated" as Fielding in terms of theory and practice. The demise of Bentham's plans during the Napoleonic Wars marked the end of an era in criminology, just as the Enlightenment itself went into retreat after the French Revolution and the rise of Napoleon. By 1815, experimentalism in criminology was in hibernation, along with most of criminology itself, not to stir until the 1920s or spring fully to life until the 1960s.

Two Torpid Centuries—With Exceptions

Analytic criminology continued to develop slowly even while experimental criminology slumbered deeply, but neither had any demonstrable utility to the societies that fostered them. One major development was the idea of involuntary causes of crime "determined" by either social (Quetelet 1835/2004) or biological (Lombroso 1876/1918) factors that called into question the legal doctrines of criminal responsibility. The empirical evidence for these claims, however, was weak (and in Lombroso's case, wrong), leaving the theoretical approach to criminology largely unused until President Johnson's War on Poverty in the 1960s.

Cambridge-Somerville

The first fully randomized controlled trial in American criminology appears to have been the Cambridge-Somerville experiment, launched in Massachusetts in the 1930s by Dr. Richard Clark Cabot. This project offered high-risk young males "friendly guidance and social support, healthful activities after school, tutoring when necessary, and medical assistance as needed" (McCord 2001). It also included a long-term "big brother" mentoring relationship that was abruptly terminated in most cases during World War II. While the long-term effects of the program would not be known until the 1970s, the critical importance of the experimental design was recognized at the outset. It was for that reason that the outcomes test could reach its startling conclusion: "The results showed that as compared with members of the control group, those who had been in the treatment program were more likely to have been convicted for crimes indexed by the Federal Bureau of Investigation as serious street crimes; they had died an average of five years younger; and they were more likely to have received a medical diagnosis as alcoholic, schizophrenic, or manic-depressive" (McCord 2001, 188). In short, the boys offered the program would have been far better off if they had been "deprived" of the program services in the randomly assigned control group.

No study in the history of criminology has ever demonstrated such clear, unintended, criminogenic effects of a program intended to prevent crime. To this day, it is "exhibit A" in discussions with legislators, students, and others skeptical of the value of evaluating government programs of any sort, let alone crime prevention programs. Its early reports in the 1950s also set the stage for a renaissance in experimental criminology, independently of the growth of analytic criminology.

Renaissance: 1950–1982

Amidst growing concern about juvenile delinquency, the Eisenhower administration provided the first federal funding for research on delinquency prevention. Many of the studies funded in that era, with both federal and nonfederal support, adopted experimental designs. What follows is merely a highlighting of the renaissance of experimental criminology in the long twilight of the FDR coalition prior to the advent of the Reagan revolution.

Martinson and Wilson

While experimental evidence was on the rise in policing, it was on the decline in corrections. The comprehensive review of rehabilitation strategies undertaken by Lipton, Martinson, and Wilks (1975) initially focused on the internal validity of the research designs in rehabilitation experiments within prisons. Concluding that these designs were too weak to offer unbiased estimates of treatment effects, the authors essentially said "we don't know" what works to rehabilitate criminals. In a series of less scientific and more popular publications, the summary of the study was transformed into saying that there is no evidence that criminals can be rehabilitated. Even the title "What Works" was widely repeated in 1975 by word of mouth as "nothing works."

The Martinson review soon became the basis for a major change in correctional policies. While the per capita rates of incarceration had been dropping throughout the 1960s and early 1970s, the trend was rapidly reversed after 1975 (Ruth and Reitz 2003). Coinciding with the publication of Wilson's (1975) first edition of *Thinking About Crime*, the Martinson review arguably helped fuel a sea change from treating criminals as victims of society to treating society as the victim of criminals. That, in turn, may have helped to feed a three-decade increase in prisoners (Laub 2004) to more than 2.2 million, the highest incarceration rate in the world.

Warp Speed: 1982–2005

Stewart

In September 1982, a former Oakland Police captain named James K. Stewart was appointed director of the National Institute of Justice (NIJ). Formerly a White House Fellow who had attended a National Academy of Sciences discussion of the work of NIJ, Stewart had been convinced by James Q. Wilson and others that NIJ needed to invest more of its budget in experimental criminology. He acted immediately by canceling existing plans to award many research grants for analytic criminology, transferring the funds to support experimental work. This work included experiments in policing, probation, drug market disruption, drunk-driving sentences, investigative practices, and shoplifting arrests.

Schools

The 1980s also witnessed the expansion of experimental criminology into the many school-based prevention programs. Extensive experimental and quasi-experimental evidence on their effects—good and bad—has now been published. In one test, for example, a popular peer guidance group that was found effective as an alternative to incarceration was found to increase crime in a high school setting. Gottfredson (1987) found that high-risk students who were not grouped with other high-risk students in high school group discussions did better than those who were.

Drug Courts

The advent of (diversion from prosecution to medically supervised treatments administered by) "drug courts" during the rapid increase in experimental criminology has led to a large and growing volume of tests of drug court effects on recidivism. Perhaps no other innovation in criminal justice has had so many controlled field tests conducted by so many different independent researchers. The compilations of these findings into meta-analyses will shed increasing light on the questions of when, and how, to divert drug-abusing offenders from prison.

Boot Camps

Much the same can be said about boot camps. The major difference is that boot camp evaluations started off as primarily quasi-experimental in their designs (with matched comparisons or worse), but increasing numbers of fully randomized tests have been conducted in recent years (Mitchell, MacKenzie, and Perez 2005). Many states persist in using boot camps for thousands of offenders, despite fairly consistent evidence that they are no more effective than regular correctional programs.

Child Raising

Criminology has also claimed a major experiment in child raising as one of its own. Beginning at the start of the "warp speed" era, the program of nurse home visits to at-risk first mothers designed by Dr. David Olds and his colleagues (1986) has now been found to have long-term crime prevention effects. Both mothers and children show these effects, which may be linked to lower levels of child abuse or better anger management practices in child raising.

Criminology: Analytic, Useful, and Used

This recitation of a selected list of experiments in criminology must be labeled with a consumer warning: *the vast majority of published criminology remains analytic and nonexperimental.* While criminology was attracting funding and students during the period of rising crime of the 1960s to 1990s, criminologists put most of their efforts into the basic science of crime patterns and theories of criminality. Studies of the natural life course of crime among cohorts of males became the central focus of the field, as measured by citation patterns (Wolfgang, Figlio, and Thornberry 1978). Despite standing concerns that criminology would be "captured" by governments to become a tool for developing repressive policies, the evidence suggests that the greatest (or largest) generation of criminologists in history captured the field away from policymakers.

The renaissance in experimental criminology therefore addressed very intense debates over many key issues in crime and justice, providing the first unbiased empirical guidance available to inform those debates. That much made criminology increasingly useful, at least potentially. Usefulness alone, of course, does not guarantee that the information will be *used.* Police agencies today do make extensive use of the research on concentrating patrols in crime hot spots, yet they have few repeat offender units, despite two successful tests of the "invention." Correctional agencies make increasing use of the "what works" literature in the United States and United Kingdom, yet prison populations are still fed by people returned to prison on the unevaluated policy of incarcerating "technical" violators of the conditions of their release (who have not committed new crimes). Good evidence alone is not enough to change policy in any context. Yet absent good evidence, there is a far greater danger that bad policies will win out. Analytic criminology—well or badly done—poses fewer risks for society than badly done experimental criminology. It is not clear that another descriptive test of differential association theory will have any effect on policy making, unless it is embedded in a program evaluation. But misleading or biased evidence from poor-quality research designs—or even unreplicated experiments—may well cause the adoption of policies that ultimately prove harmful.

This danger is, in turn, reduced by the lack of influence criminology usually has on policy making or operational decisions. That, in turn, is linked to the absence of clear conclusions about the vast majority of criminal justice policies and decisions. Until experimental criminology can develop a more comprehensive basis of evidence for guiding operations, practitioners are unlikely to develop the habit of checking the literature before making a decision. The possibility of improving the quality of both primary evidence and systematic reviews offers hope for a future in which criminology itself may entail less risk of causing harm.

This is by no means a suggestion that analytic criminology be abandoned; the strength of experimental criminology may depend heavily on the continued advancement of basic (analytic) criminology. Yet the full partnership between the two has yet to be realized. Analytic social science still dominates field experiments by 100 to 1 or better in criminology, just as in any other field of research on human behavior. Future success of the field may depend upon a growing public image based on experimental results, just as advances in treatment attract funding for basic science in medicine.

Conclusion

Theoretical criminology will hold center stage for many years to come. But as Farrington (2000) has argued, the advancement of theory may depend on better experimental evidence. And that, in turn, may depend on a revival in the federal funding that has recently dropped to its lowest level in four decades. Such a revival may well depend on exciting public interest in the practical value of research, as perhaps only experiments can do.

"Show and tell" is hard to do while it is happening. Yet it is not impossible. Whether anyone ever sees a crime prevention program delivered, it is at least possible to embed an experimental design into every long-term analytic study of crime in the life course. As Joan McCord (2003) said in her final words to the American Society of Criminology, the era of purely observational criminology should come to an end. Given what we now know about the basic life-course patterns, McCord suggested, "all longitudinal studies should now have experiments embedded within them."

Doing what McCord proposed would become an experiment *in* social science as well as *of* social science. That experiment is already under way, in a larger sense. Criminology is rapidly becoming more multi-method, as well as multi-level and multi-theoretical. Criminology may soon resemble medicine more than economics, with analysts closely integrated with clinical researchers to develop basic science as well as treatment. The integration of diverse forms and levels of knowledge in "consilience" with each other, rather than a hegemony of any one approach, is within our grasp. It awaits only a generation of broadly educated criminologists prepared to do many things, or at least prepared to work in collaboration with other people who bring diverse talents to science.

References

Baltzell, D. (1979). *Puritan Boston and Quaker Philadelphia: Two Protestant ethics and the spirit of class authority and leadership.* New York: Free Press.

Beccaria, C. (1964). *On crimes and punishments* (J. Grigson, Trans.). Milan, Italy: Oxford University Press. (Original work published 1764)

Buchan, J. (2003). *Crowded with genius: The Scottish Enlightenment: Edinburgh's moment of the mind.* New York: HarperCollins.

Farrington, D. (2000). Explaining and preventing crime: The globalization of knowledge. The American Society of Criminology 1999 Presidential Address. *Criminology, 38,* 1–24.

Fielding, H. (1964). *The journal of a voyage to Lisbon.* London: Dent. (Original work published 1755)

Gay, P. (1969). *The Enlightenment: An interpretation. Vol. 2, The science of freedom.* New York: Knopf.

Gottfredson, G. (1987). Peer group interventions to reduce the risk of delinquent behavior: A selective review and a new evaluation. *Criminology, 25,* 671–714.

Laub, J. (2004). The life course of criminology in the United States: The American Society of Criminology 2003 Presidential Address. *Criminology, 42,* 1–26.

Lipton, D., Martinson, R., & Wilks, J. (1975). *The effectiveness of correctional treatment: A survey of treatment evaluation studies.* New York: Praeger.

Lombroso, C. (1918). *Crime, its causes and remedies.* Boston: Little, Brown. (Original work published 1876)

May, H. (1976). *The Enlightenment in America.* New York: Oxford University Press.

McCord, J. (2001). *Crime prevention: A cautionary tale.* Proceedings of the Third International, Interdisciplinary Evidence-Based Policies and Indicator Systems Conference, University of Durham. Retrieved April 22, 2005, from http://cem.dur.ac.uk

McCord, J. (2003). *Discussing age, crime, and human development. The future of life-course criminology.* Denver, CO: American Society of Criminology.

Mitchell, O., MacKenzie, D., & Perez, D. (2005). A randomized evaluation of the Maryland correctional boot camp for adults: Effects on offender anti-social attitudes and cognitions. *Journal of Offender Rehabilitation, 40*(4).

Olds, D., Henderson, C., Chamberlin, R., & Tatelbaum, R. (1986). Preventing child abuse and neglect: A randomized trial of nurse home visitation. *Pediatrics, 78,* 65–78.

Quetelet, A. (2004). A treatise on man. As cited in F. Adler, G. O. W. Mueller, and W. S. Laufer, *Criminology and the criminal justice system* (5th ed., p. N-6). New York: McGraw-Hill. (Original work published 1835)

Ruth, H., & Reitz, K. (2003). *The challenge of crime: Rethinking our response.* Cambridge, MA: Harvard University Press.

Sherman, L. (2005). *Enlightened justice: Consequentialism and empiricism from Beccaria to Braithwaite.* Address to the 14th World Congress of Criminology, International Society of Criminology, Philadelphia, August 8.

Wilson, J. (1975). *Thinking about crime.* New York: Basic Books.

Wolfgang, M., Figlio, R., & Thornberry, T. (1978). *Evaluating criminology.* New York: Elsevier.

REVIEW QUESTIONS

1. According to Sherman, what part did Henry Fielding's research play in the early stages of research on crime and the influence it had on stopping robberies in London? Explain in detail. What implications can be drawn about using resources (i.e., money) to stop a given crime in a certain location?
2. What does Sherman have to say about what Beccaria and Bentham contributed to policies regarding crime? Do you agree with Sherman's assessment?
3. What does Sherman have to say about Martinson's review of rehabilitation programs and its impact on policy?
4. What does Sherman have to say about criminological research regarding schools, drug courts, boot camps, and child raising? Which recent programs does he claim had success? Which recent programs or designs does he suggest do not work?
5. How do Joan McCord's final words in her address to the American Society of Criminology have both theoretical and policy implications for the study of causes of crime?

SECTION II

Preclassical and Classical Theories of Crime

This section will examine the earliest logical theories of rule breaking—namely, explanations of criminal conduct that emphasize free will and the ability of individuals to make rational decisions regarding the consequences of their behavior. The natural capabilities of human beings to make decisions based on expected costs and benefits were acknowledged during the **Age of Enlightenment** in the 17th and 18th centuries. This understanding of human capabilities led to what is considered the first rational theory of criminal activity, **deterrence theory**. This theory has had a more profound impact on justice systems in the United States than any other perspective to date. Furthermore, virtually all criminal justice systems (e.g., policing, courts, corrections) are based on this theoretical model even today.

Such theories of human rationality were in stark contrast to the theories focusing on religious or supernatural causes of crime, which had prevailed through most of human civilization up to the Age of Enlightenment. In addition, the Classical School theories of crime are distinguished from theories in subsequent sections of this book by their emphasis on the free will and rational decision making of individuals, which modern theories of crime tend to ignore. The theoretical perspectives discussed in this section all focus on the ability of human beings to choose their own behavior and destinies, whereas paradigms that existed before and after this period tend to emphasize the inability of individuals to control their behavior due to external factors. Therefore, the Classical School is perhaps the paradigm best suited for analysis of what types of calculations are going on in someone's head before he or she commits a crime.

The different Classical School theories presented in this section vary in many ways, most notably in what they propose as the primary constructs and processes individuals use to determine whether they are going to commit a crime. For example, some Classical School theories emphasize the potential negative consequences of their actions, whereas others focus on the possible benefits of such activity. Still others concentrate on the opportunities and existing situations that predispose people to engage in criminal activity. Regardless of their differences, all of the theories examined in this section emphasize a common theme: Individuals commit crime because they identify certain situations and acts as beneficial due to the perceived lack of punishment and the perceived likelihood of profits, such as money or peer status. In other words, the potential offender weighs out the possible costs and pleasures of committing a given act and then behaves in a rational way based on this analysis.

The most important distinction of these Classical School theories, as opposed to those discussed in future sections, is that they emphasize individuals making their own decisions regardless of extraneous influences, such as the economy or bonding with society. Although many extraneous factors may influence the ability of an individual to rationally consider offending situations, the Classical School assumes that the individual takes all these influences into account when making the decision about whether or not to engage in criminal behavior. Given the focus placed on individual responsibility, it is not surprising that Classical School theories are used as the basis for U.S. policies on punishment for criminal activity. The Classical School theories are highly compatible and consistent with the conservative, get-tough movement that has existed since the mid-1970s. Thus, the Classical School still retains the highest importance in terms of policy and pragmatic punishment in the United States as well as throughout all countries in the Western world.

As you will see, the Classical School theoretical paradigm was presented as early as the mid-1700s, and its prominence as a model of offending behavior in criminal justice systems is still dominant. Scientific and academic circles, however, have dismissed many of the claims of this perspective. For reasons we shall explore in this section, the assumptions and primary propositions of Classical School theories have been neglected by most recent theoretical models of criminologists. This dismissal is likely premature, given the impact that this perspective has had on understanding human nature, as well as the profound influence it has had on most criminal justice systems, especially in the United States.

Preclassical Perspectives of Crime and Punishment

Over the long course of human civilization, people have mostly believed that criminal activity is caused by supernatural causes or religious factors. It has been documented that some primitive societies believed that crime increased during major thunderstorms or major droughts. Most primitive cultures believed that when a person engaged in behavior that violated the tribe's or clan's rules, the devil or evil spirits were making him or her do it.[1] For example, in many societies, if someone committed criminal activity, it was common to perform exorcisms or primitive surgery, such as breaking open the skull of the perpetrator to allow the demons to leave his or her head. Of course, this almost always resulted in the death of the accused person, but it was seen as a liberating experience for the offender.

This was just one form of dealing with criminal behavior, but it epitomizes how primitive cultures understood the causes of crime. As the movie *The Exorcist* revealed, exorcisms were still being performed on offenders by representatives of a number of religions, including Catholicism, in the 21st century to get the devil out of them. In June 2005, a Romanian monk and four nuns acknowledged engaging in an exorcism that led to the death of the victim, who was crucified, a towel stuffed in her mouth, and left without food for many days.[2] When the monk and nuns were asked to explain why they did this, they defiantly said they were trying to take the devils out of the 23-year-old woman. Although they were prosecuted by Romanian authorities, many governments might not have done so because many societies around the world still believe in and condone such practices.

Readers may be surprised to learn that the Roman Catholic Church still authorizes college-level courses on how to perform exorcisms. Specifically, news reports revealed that a Vatican-recognized university was offering a course in exorcism and demonic possession for a second year because of its concern about the "devil's lure."[3] In fact, Pope Benedict XVI welcomed a large group of Italian exorcists who visited the Vatican in September 2005 and

---

[1]Stephen E. Brown, Finn-Aage Esbensen, and Gilbert Geis, *Criminology: Explaining Crime and Its Context*, 8th ed. (Cincinnati, OH: Anderson, 2012).

[2]Associated Press, "Romanian Priest Jailed for Killing Young Nun Who Was Crucified during Botched Exorcism Ritual," *Daily Mail*, June 24, 2005, http://www.dailymail.co.uk/news/article-2692892/Romanian-priest-jailed-killing-young-nun-CRUCIFIED-botched-exorcism-ritual.html.

[3]Associated Press, "University Offering Course on Exorcism," *Telegraph*, July 9, 2005, http://www.telegraph.co.uk/news/worldnews/europe/italy/1480798/Vatican-offers-course-in-Satanism-and-exorcism.html.

encouraged them to carry on their work for the Catholic Church.[4] Furthermore, in 1999, the Roman Catholic Church issued revised guidelines for conducting exorcisms, which recommend consulting physicians when exorcisms are performed; it also provides an 84-page description of the language (in Latin) to be used in such rituals. It should be noted that the use of such exorcisms is quite rare, especially in more developed nations. However, U.S. Catholic bishops recently (in November 2010) cited the need for more trained exorcists and even held a conference in Baltimore, Maryland, on how to conduct exorcisms. This two-day training session instructed clergy on evaluating evil possession as well as reviewing the rituals that comprise an exorcism. More than 50 bishops and 60 priests attended this training session, despite the tendency for exorcists in U.S. dioceses to keep a very low profile.[5]

▲ **Image 2.1** Although more common in ancient times, exorcisms are still approved and carried out by certain groups in attempts to remove evil spirits from individuals.

SOURCE: © iStockphoto.com/KatarzynaBialasiewicz

One of the most common supernatural beliefs in primitive cultures was that the full moon caused criminal activity. Then, as now, there was much truth to the full-moon theory. In primitive times, people believed that crime was related to the influence of higher powers, including the destructive influence of the moon itself. Modern studies have shown, however, that the increase in crime is primarily due to a Classical School theoretical model: There are simply more opportunities to commit crime when the moon is full because there is more light at night, which results in more people being out on the streets. In any case, nighttime is well established as a high-risk period for adult crimes, such as sexual assault.

Although some primitive theories had some validity in determining when crime would be more common, virtually none of them accurately predicted who would commit the offenses. During the Middle Ages, just about everyone was from the lower classes, and only a minority of that group engaged in offending against the normative society. So, for most of human civilization, there was virtually no rational theoretical understanding of why individuals violate the laws of society; instead, people believed crime was caused by supernatural or religious factors of the devil-made-me-do-it variety.

Consistent with these views, the punishments related to offending during this period were quite harsh by modern standards. Given the assumption that evil spirits drove the motivations for criminal activity, the punishments for criminal acts—especially those deemed particularly offensive to the norms of a given society—were often quite inhumane. Common punishments at that time were being beheaded; being tortured; being burned alive at the stake; and being drowned, stoned, or quartered. Good discussions of such harsh examples of punishment, such as quartering, can be found in Brown et al.'s discussion of punishment.[6]

---

[4]Reuters, "Pope Benedict XVI Warmly Greets Exorcist Convention," September 17, 2005. https://www.usatoday.com/story/news/world/2013/05/21/pope-francis-exorcism/2347197.

[5]Rachel Zoll, "Catholic Bishops: More Exorcists Needed," *Seattle Times,* November 12, 2010.

[6]Brown et al., *Criminology*, 170–184.

Although many would find the primitive forms of punishment and execution to be quite barbaric, some modern societies still practice them. For example, Islamic court systems, as well as other religious and ethnic cultures, are often allowed to carry out executions and other forms of corporal punishment. Fifteen individuals were whipped with a cane for gambling in Aceh, Indonesia, a highly conservative Muslim region. The caning was held in public and outside a mosque.[7] In the United States, gambling is a relatively minor crime—when it is not totally legal, as in many places in the United States. It is interesting to note, however, that a relatively recent Gallup poll regarding the use of caning (i.e., public whipping) of convicted individuals was supported by most of the American public.[8]

▲ **Image 2.2** A woman protesting the frequent use of stoning to punish individuals, in this case a woman in Iran who was convicted of adultery. Public stoning and caning are still used as punishment by certain societies around the world.

SOURCE: © Getty Images / Sean Gallup / Staff

Compared to U.S. standards, the more extreme forms of corporal punishment, particularly public executions carried out by many religious courts and countries, are drawn out and very painful. An example is stoning, in which people are buried up to the waist and local citizens throw small stones at them until they die (large stones are not allowed because they would lead to death too quickly). In most of the Western world, such brutal forms of punishment and execution were done away with in the 1700s due to the impact of the Age of Enlightenment.

The Age of Enlightenment

In the midst of the extremely draconian times of the mid-1600s, Thomas Hobbes, in his book *Leviathan* (1651), proposed a rational theory of why people are motivated to form democratic states of governance.[9] Hobbes started with the basic framework that all individuals are in a constant state of warfare with all other individuals. He used the extreme examples of primitive tribes and sects. He argued that the primitive state of man is selfish and greedy, so people live in a constant state of fear of everyone else. However, Hobbes also proclaimed that people are also rational, so they will rationally organize sound forms of governance, which can create rules to avoid this constant state of fear. Interestingly, once a government is created, the state of warfare mutates from one waged among individuals or families to one waged between nations. This can be seen in modern times; after all, it is quite rare that a person or family declares war against another (although gangs may be an exception), but we often hear of governments declaring war.

Hobbes stated that the primitive state of fear—of constant warfare of everyone against everyone else—was the motivation for entering into a contract with others to create a common authority. At the same time, Hobbes specified that it was this exact emotion—fear—that was needed to make citizens conform to the given rules or laws in

[7] Irwan Firdaus, "15 Caned in Muslim Indonesia for Gaming," *StarNews*, June 25, 2005.

[8] Philip Shenon, "U.S. Youth in Singapore Loses Appeal on Flogging," *New York Times*, April 1, 1994.

[9] Thomas Hobbes, *Leviathan* (1651; repr. New York: Library of Liberal Arts, 1958).

society. Strangely, it appears that the very emotion that inspires people to enter into an agreement to form a government is the same emotion that inspires these same individuals to follow the rules of the government that is created. It is ironic, but it is quite true.

Given the social conditions during the 1600s, this model appears somewhat accurate; there was little sense of community in terms of working toward progress as a group. It had not been that long since the Middle Ages, when one third of the world's population had died from sickness, and many cultures were severely deprived or in an extreme state of poverty. Prior to the 1600s, the feudal system had been the dominant model of governance in most of the Western world. During this feudal era, a very small group of aristocrats (less than 1% of the population) owned and operated the largely agricultural economy that existed. Virtually no rights were afforded to individuals in the Middle Ages or at the time Hobbes wrote his book. Most people had no individual rights in terms of criminal justice, let alone a say in the existing governments of the time. Hobbes's book clearly took issue with this lack of say in the government, which had profound implications for the justice systems of that time.

Hobbes clearly stated that until the citizens were entitled to a certain degree of respect from their governing bodies as well as their justice systems they would never fully buy into the authority of government or the system of justice. Hobbes proposed a number of extraordinary ideas that came to define the Age of Enlightenment. He presented a drastic paradigm shift for social structure, which had extreme implications for justice systems throughout the world.

Hobbes explicitly declared that people are rational beings who choose their destinies by creating societies. Hobbes further proposed that individuals in such societies democratically create rules of conduct that all members of that society must follow. These rules, which all citizens decide upon, become laws, and the result of not following the laws is punishment determined by the democratically instituted government. It is clear from Hobbes's statements that the government, as instructed by the citizens, not only has the authority to punish individuals who violate the rules of the society but, more important, has a duty to punish them. When such an authority fails to fulfill this duty, breakdown in the social order can quickly result.

The arrangement of citizens promising to abide by the rules or laws set forth by a given society in return for protection is commonly referred to as the **social contract**. Hobbes introduced this idea, but it was also emphasized by all other Enlightenment theorists after him, such as Jean-Jacques Rousseau, John Locke, Voltaire, and Baron Charles Montesquieu. The idea of the social contract is an extraordinarily important part of Enlightenment philosophy. Although Enlightenment philosophers had significant differences in what they believed, the one thing they had in common was the belief in the social contract: the idea that people invest in the laws of their society with the guarantee that they will be protected from others who violate such rules.

Another shared belief among Enlightenment philosophers was that the people should be given a say in the government, especially the justice system. All of them emphasized fairness in determining who was guilty as well as appropriate punishments or sentences. During the time in which Enlightenment philosophers wrote, individuals who stole a loaf of bread to feed their families were sentenced to death, whereas upper-class individuals who stole large sums of money or committed murder were pardoned. This goes against common sense; moreover, it violates the social contract. If citizens observe people being excused for violating the law, then their belief in the social contract breaks down. This same feeling can be applied to modern times. When the Los Angeles police officers who were filmed beating suspect Rodney King were acquitted of criminal charges in 1992, a massive riot erupted among the citizens of the community. This is a good example of the social contract breaking down when people realize that the government is failing to punish members of the community (in this case, ironically, and significantly, police officers) who have violated its rules.[10]

The concept of the social contract was likely the most important contribution of Enlightenment philosophers, but there were others. Another key concept of Enlightenment philosophers focused on democracy, emphasizing that

---

[10]Ruben Castaneda, "Rodney King Rewind: L.A. Riots, Crips, Armed Koreans and Two Heroes," *Baltimore Post-Examiner*, May 1, 2012, http://baltimore postexaminer.com/rodney-king-rewind-l-a-riots-crips-armed-koreans-and-two-heroes/2012/05/01.

every person in society should have a say via the government; specifically, they promoted the ideal of "one person, one vote." Granted, at the time they wrote, this meant one vote for each White, landowning male, and not for women, minorities, or the poor, but it was a step in the right direction. Until then, no individuals outside of the aristocracy had had any say in government or the justice system.

The Enlightenment philosophers also talked about each individual's right to life, liberty, and the pursuit of happiness. This probably sounds familiar because it is contained in the U.S. Declaration of Independence. Until the Enlightenment, individuals were not considered to have these rights; rather, they were seen as instruments for serving totalitarian governments. Although most citizens of the Western world take these rights for granted, they did not exist prior to the Age of Enlightenment.

Perhaps the most relevant concept that Enlightenment philosophers emphasized, as mentioned previously, was the idea that human beings are rational and therefore have free will. The philosophers of this age focused on the ability of individuals to consider the consequences of their actions, and they assumed that people freely choose their behavior (or lack thereof), especially in regard to criminal activity. Beccaria, the father of criminal justice, made this assumption in his formulation of what is considered to be the first bona fide theory of why people commit crime, described next.

The Classical School of Criminology

The foundation of the Classical School of criminological theorizing is typically traced to the Enlightenment philosophers, but the specific origin of the Classical School is considered to be the 1764 publication of *On Crimes and Punishments* by Italian scholar Cesare Bonesana, Marchese Beccaria (1738–1794), commonly known as Cesare Beccaria. Amazingly, he wrote this book at the age of 26 and published it anonymously, but its almost instant popularity persuaded him to come forward as the author. Due to this significant work, most experts consider Beccaria the father of criminal justice and the father of the Classical School of criminology but perhaps most importantly, the father of deterrence theory. This section provides a comprehensive survey of the ideas and impact of Cesare Beccaria and the Classical School.

Influences on Beccaria and His Writings

The Enlightenment philosophers had a profound impact on the social and political climate of the late 1600s and 1700s. Growing up in this time period, Beccaria was a child of the Enlightenment, and as such, he was highly influenced by the concepts and propositions that these great thinkers proposed. The Enlightenment philosophy is readily evident in Beccaria's essay, and he incorporates many of its assumptions into his work. As a student of law, Beccaria had a good background for determining what was and was not rational in legal policy. But his loyalty to the Enlightenment ideal was ever present throughout his work.

Beccaria emphasized the concept of the social contract and incorporated the idea that citizens give up certain rights in exchange for the state's or government's protection. He also asserted that acts or punishments by the government that violate the overall sense of unity will not be accepted by the populace, largely due to the need for the social contract to be a fair deal. Beccaria explicitly stated that laws are compacts of free individuals in a society. In addition, he specifically noted his appeal to the ideal of the greatest happiness shared by the greatest number, which is otherwise known as **utilitarianism**. This, too, was a focus of Enlightenment philosophers. Finally, the emphasis on free will and individual choice is key to his propositions and theorizing. Indeed, as we shall see, Enlightenment philosophy is present in virtually all of his propositions; he directly cited Hobbes, Montesquieu, and other Enlightenment thinkers in his work.[11]

[11]Hobbes, *Leviathan*; Charles Louis de Secondat, Baron de la Brède et de Montesquieu, *The Spirit of the Laws* (1748; New York: Library of Liberal Arts, 1949).

Beccaria's Proposed Reforms and Ideas of Justice

When Beccaria wrote, authoritarian governments ruled the justice systems, which were actually quite unjust during that time. For example, it was not uncommon for a person who stole a loaf of bread in order to feed his or her family to be imprisoned for life or executed. A good example of this is seen in the story of Victor Hugo's *Les Misérables*: The protagonist, Jean Valjean, gets a lengthy prison sentence for stealing food for his starving loved ones. On the other hand, a judge might excuse a person who had committed several murders because the confessed killer was from a prominent family.

Beccaria sought to rid the justice system of such arbitrary acts on the part of individual judges. Specifically, Beccaria claimed in his essay that "only laws can decree punishments for crimes . . . judges in criminal cases cannot have the authority to interpret laws."[12] Rather, he believed that legislatures, elected by the citizens, must define crimes and the specific punishment for each criminal offense. One of his main goals was to prevent a single person from assigning an overly harsh sentence to a defendant and allowing another defendant in a similar case to walk free for the same criminal act, which was quite common at that time. Thus, Beccaria's writings call for a set punishment for a given offense without consideration of the presiding judge's personal attitudes or the defendant's background.

▲ **Image 2.3** Cesare Beccaria (1738–1794).

SOURCE: © Kean Collection/Archive Photos/Getty Images

Beccaria believed that "the true measure of crimes is namely the harm done to society."[13] Thus, anyone at all who committed a given act against the society should face the same consequence. He was very clear that the law should impose a specific punishment for a given act, regardless of the circumstances. One aspect of this principle was that it ignored the intent the offender had in committing the crime. Obviously, this principle is not followed in most modern justice systems; intent often plays a key role in the charges and sentencing of defendants in many types of crimes. Most notably, the different degrees of homicide in most U.S. jurisdictions include first-degree murder, which requires proof of planning or *malice aforethought*; second-degree murder, which typically involves no evidence of planning but rather a spontaneous act of killing; and various degrees of manslaughter, which generally include some level of provocation on the part of the victim. This is just one example of the importance of intent, legally known as ***mens rea*** (literally, guilty mind), in most modern justice systems. Many types of offending are graded by degree of intent as opposed to being categorized based only on the act itself, known legally as ***actus reus*** (literally, guilty act). Beccaria's propositions focus on only the *actus reus* because he claimed that an act against society was just as harmful, regardless of the intent, or *mens rea*. Despite his recommendations, most societies factor in the intent of the offender in criminal activity. Still, his proposal that *a given act should always receive the same punishment* certainly seemed to represent a significant improvement over the arbitrary punishments handed out by the regimes and justice systems of the 1700s.

---

[12]Cesare Beccaria, *On Crimes and Punishments*, trans. Henry Paolucci (New York: MacMillan, 1963), 14.

[13]Ibid., 64.

Another important reform that Beccaria proposed was to do away with practices that were common in "justice" systems of the time (the word *justice* is in quotation marks because they were largely systems of injustice). Specifically, Beccaria claimed that secret accusations should not be permitted; rather, defendants should be able to confront and cross-examine witnesses. Writing about secret accusations, he said, "Their customary use makes men false and deceptive"; he asked, "Who can defend himself against calumny when it comes armed with tyranny's strongest shield, *secrecy*?"[14] Although some modern countries still accept and use secret accusations and disallow the cross-examination of witnesses, Beccaria set the standard in guaranteeing such rights to defendants in the United States and most Western societies.

In addition, Beccaria argued that torture should not be used against defendants:

> A cruelty consecrated by the practice of most nations is torture of the accused . . . either to make him confess the crime or to clear up contradictory statements, or to discover accomplices . . . to discover other crimes of which he might be guilty but of which he is not accused.[15]

Although some countries, such as Israel and Mexico, currently allow the use of torture for eliciting information or confessions, most countries abstain from the practice. There has been wide discussion about a memo, written by former U.S. attorney general Alberto Gonzales when he was President George W. Bush's lead counsel at the White House, claiming that the U.S. military could use torture against terrorist suspects. However, at least in terms of domestic criminal defendants, the United States has traditionally agreed with Beccaria, who believed that any information or oaths obtained under torture are relatively worthless. Beccaria's belief in the worthlessness of torture is further seen in his statement that "it is useless to reveal the author of a crime that lies deeply buried in darkness."[16]

It is likely that Beccaria believed the use of torture was one of the worst aspects of the criminal justice systems of his time and a horrible manifestation of the barbarousness common in the Middle Ages. This is seen in his further elaboration of torture:

> This infamous crucible of truth is a still-standing memorial of the ancient and barbarous legislation of a time when trials by fire and by boiling water, as well as the uncertain outcomes of duels, were called "judgments of God."[17]

Beccaria also expressed his doubt of the relevance of any information received via torture:

> Thus the impression of pain may become so great that, filling the entire sensory capacity of the tortured person, it leaves him free only to choose what for the moment is the shortest way of escape from pain.[18]

As Beccaria saw it, the policy implications from such use of torture are that "of two men, equally innocent or equally guilty, the strong and courageous will be acquitted, the weak and timid condemned."[19]

---

[14]Ibid., 25–26.

[15]Ibid., 30.

[16]Ibid., 30–31.

[17]Ibid., 31.

[18]Ibid., 32.

[19]Ibid., 32.

Beccaria also claimed that defendants should be tried by fellow citizens or peers, not by judges:

> I consider an excellent law that which assigns popular jurors, taken by lot, to assist the chief judge . . . each man ought to be judged by his peers.[20]

It is clear that Beccaria felt that the responsibility of determining the facts of a case should be placed in the hands of more than one person, a belief driven by his Enlightenment beliefs about democratic philosophy—namely, that citizens of the society should have a voice in judging the facts and deciding the verdicts of criminal cases. This proposition is representative of Beccaria's overall leaning toward fairness and democratic processes, which Enlightenment philosophers shared.

Today, U.S. citizens often take for granted the right to have a trial by a jury of their peers. It may surprise some readers to know that some modern, developed countries have not provided this right. For example, in the 1990s, Russia held jury trials for the first time in 85 years. When Vladimir Lenin was in charge of Russia, he had banished jury trials. Over the course of several decades, the bench trials in Russia produced a 99.6% rate of convictions. This means that virtually every person in Russia who was accused of a crime was found guilty. Given the relatively high percentage of defendants found to be innocent of crimes in the United States—not to mention the numerous people who have been released from death row after DNA analysis showed that they were not guilty—it is rather frightening to think of how many falsely accused individuals have been convicted and unjustly sentenced in Russia over the past century.

Another important aspect of Beccaria's reforms involved making the justice system, particularly its laws and decisions, more public and better understood. This fits the Enlightenment assumption that individuals are rational: If people know the consequences of their actions, they will act accordingly. Beccaria stated that "when the number of those who can understand the sacred code of laws and hold it in their hands increases, the frequency of crimes will be found to decrease."[21] At the time, the laws were often unknown to the populace, in part because of widespread illiteracy but perhaps more as a result of the failure to publicly declare what the laws were. Even when laws were posted, they were often in languages that the citizens did not read or speak (e.g., Latin). Thus, Beccaria stressed the need for society to ensure that its citizens be educated about what the laws are; he believed that this alone would lead to a significant decrease in law violations.

Furthermore, Beccaria believed that the important stages and decision-making processes of any justice system should be made public knowledge rather than being held in secret or carried out behind closed doors. He stated, "Punishment . . . must be essentially public."[22] This has a highly democratic and Enlightenment ring to it, in the sense that citizens of a society are assumed to have the right to know what vital judgments are being made. After all, in a democratic society, citizens give the government the profound responsibility of distributing punishment for crimes against the society. The citizens are entitled to know what decisions their government officials are making, particularly regarding justice. Besides providing knowledge and understanding of what is going on, this sets in place a form of checks and balances on what is happening. Furthermore, the public nature of trials and punishments inherently produces a form of deterrence for those individuals who may be considering criminal activity.

One of Beccaria's most profound and important proposed reforms is one of the least noted. Beccaria said, "The surest but most difficult way to prevent crimes is by perfecting education."[23] We know of no other review of his work that notes this hypothesis, which is quite amazing, because most of the reviews are done for an educational audience. Furthermore, this emphasis on education makes sense, given Beccaria's focus on knowledge of laws and consequences of criminal activity as well as his focus on deterrence.

---

[20]Ibid., 21.

[21]Ibid., 17.

[22]Ibid., 99.

[23]Ibid., 98.

Beccaria's Ideas regarding the Death Penalty

Another primary area of Beccaria's reforms dealt with the use—and, in his day, the abuse—of the death penalty. First, let it be said that Beccaria was against the use of capital punishment. (Interestingly, he was not against corporal punishment, which he explicitly stated was appropriate for violent offenders.) Perhaps this was due to the times in which he wrote, in which a large number of people were put to death, often by harsh methods. Still, Beccaria had several rational reasons for why he felt the death penalty was not an efficient and effective punishment.

First, Beccaria argued that the use of capital punishment inherently violated the social contract:

> Is it conceivable that the least sacrifice of each person's liberty should include sacrifice of the greatest of all goods, life? . . . The punishment of death, therefore, is not a right, for I have demonstrated that it cannot be such; but it is the war of a nation against a citizen whose destruction it judges to be necessary or useful.[24]

The second reason that Beccaria felt that the death penalty was an inappropriate form of punishment was along the same lines: If the government endorsed the death of a citizen, it would provide a negative example to the rest of society. He said, "The death penalty cannot be useful, because of the example of barbarity it gives men."[25] Although some studies show some evidence that use of the death penalty in the United States deters crime,[26] most studies show no effect or even a positive effect on homicides.[27] Researchers have called this increase of homicides after executions the **brutalization effect**, and a similar phenomenon can be seen at numerous sporting events (boxing matches, hockey games, soccer or football games, etc.) when violence breaks out among spectators. There have even been incidents in recent years at youth sporting events.

To further complicate the possibly contradictory effects of capital punishment, some analyses show that both deterrence and brutalization occur at the same time for different types of murder or crime, depending on the level of planning or spontaneity of a given act. For example, a sophisticated analysis of homicide data from California examined the effects of a high-profile execution in 1992, largely because it was the first one in the state in 25 years.[28]

---

[24]Ibid., 45.

[25]Ibid., 50.

[26]For a review and analysis, respectively, showing deterrent effects of capital punishment, see Charles F. Manski and John V. Pepper, "Deterrence and the Death Penalty: Partial Identification Analysis Using Repeated Cross Sections," *Journal of Quantitative Criminology* 29 (2013): 123–41; and Steven Stack, "The Effect of Publicized Executions on Homicides in California," *Journal of Crime and Justice* 21 (1998): 1–16. See also Isaac Ehrlich, "Capital Punishment and Deterrence," *Journal of Political Economy* 85 (1977): 741–88; Isaac Ehrlich, "The Deterrent Effect of Capital Punishment: A Question of Life and Death," *American Economic Review* 65 (1975): 397–417; Stephen K. Layson, "Homicide and Deterrence: A Reexamination of United States Time-Series Evidence," *Southern Economic Journal* 52 (1985): 68–89; David P. Phillips, "The Deterrent Effect of Capital Punishment: Evidence on an Old Controversy," *American Journal of Sociology* 86 (1980): 139–48; Steven Stack, "Execution Publicity and Homicide in South Carolina," *Sociological Quarterly* 31 (1990): 599–611; Steven Stack, "The Impact of Publicized Executions on Homicide," *Criminal Justice and Behavior* 22 (1995): 172–86; and Steven Stack, "Publicized Executions and Homicide, 1950–1980," *American Sociological Review* 52 (1987): 532–40.

[27]William C. Bailey, "The Deterrent Effect of the Death Penalty for Murder in California," *Southern California Law Review* 52 (1979): 743–64; William C. Bailey and Ruth D. Peterson, "Murder and Capital Punishment: A Monthly Time Series Analysis of Execution Publicity," *American Sociological Review* 54 (1989): 722–43; William J. Bowers, "The Effect of Execution Is Brutalization, Not Deterrence," *Capital Punishment: Legal and Social Science Approaches*, ed. Kenneth C. Haas and James A. Inciardi (Newbury Park, CA: Sage, 1988), 49–89; John K. Cochran, Mitchell Chamlin, and Mark Seth, "Deterrence or Brutalization? An Impact Assessment of Oklahoma's Return to Capital Punishment," *Criminology* 32 (1994): 107–34; James A. Fox and Michael L. Radelet, "Persistent Flaws in Econometric Studies of the Deterrent Effect of the Death Penalty," *Loyola of Los Angeles Law Review* 23 (1990): 29–44; David Lester, "The Deterrent Effect of Execution on Homicide," *Psychological Reports* 64 (1989): 306–14. For a review, see William C. Bailey and Ruth D. Peterson, "Capital Punishment, Homicide, and Deterrence: An Assessment of the Evidence," in *Studying and Preventing Homicide*, ed. M. Dwayne Smith and Margaret A. Zahn (Thousand Oaks, CA: Sage, 1999), 223–45.

[28]John K. Cochran and Mitchell B. Chamlin, "Deterrence and Brutalization: The Dual Effects of Executions," *Justice Quarterly* (2000): 685–706; Eric G. Lambert et al., "The Impact of Information on Death Penalty Support, Revisited," *Crime and Delinquency* 57 (2011): 572–99.

As predicted, the authors found that nonstranger felony murders, which typically involve some planning, significantly decreased after the high-profile execution, whereas the level of argument-based, stranger murders, which are typically more spontaneous, significantly increased during the same period. Thus, both deterrence and brutalization effects were observed at the same time and location following a given execution.

Another primary reason that Beccaria was against the use of capital punishment was that he believed it was an ineffective deterrent. Specifically, he thought that a punishment that was quick, such as the death penalty, could not be as effective a deterrent as a drawn-out penalty. He stated, "It is not the intensity of punishment that has the greatest effect on the human spirit, but its duration."[29] It is likely that many readers can relate to this type of argument, not that they necessarily agree with it; the idea of spending the rest of one's life in a cell is a very scary concept to most people. To many people, such a concept is more frightening than death, which supports Beccaria's idea that the duration of the punishment may be more of a deterrent than the short, albeit extremely intense, punishment of execution.

Beccaria's Concept of Deterrence and the Three Key Elements of Punishment

Beccaria is generally considered the father of deterrence theory for good reason. Beccaria was the first known scholar to write a work that summarized such extravagant ideas regarding the direction of human behavior toward choice as opposed to fate or destiny. Prior to his work, the common wisdom on the issue of human destiny was that it was chosen by the gods or God. At that time, governments and societies generally believed that people are born either good or bad. Beccaria, as a child of the Enlightenment, defied this belief in proclaiming that people freely choose their destinies and thus their decisions to commit or not commit criminal behavior.

Beccaria suggested three characteristics of punishment that make a significant difference in whether an individual decides to commit a criminal act: celerity (swiftness), certainty, and severity.

Swiftness

The first of these characteristics was celerity, which we will refer to as **swiftness of punishment**. Beccaria saw two reasons why swiftness of punishment is important. At the time he wrote, some defendants were spending many years awaiting trial. Often, this was a longer time than they would have been locked up as punishment for their alleged offenses, even if the maximum penalty had been imposed. As Beccaria stated, "The more promptly and the more closely punishment follows upon the commission of a crime, the more just and useful will it be."[30] Thus, the first reason that Beccaria recommended swiftness of punishment was to reform a system that was slow to respond to offenders.

The second reason that Beccaria emphasized swift sentencing was related to the deterrence aspect of punishment. A swift trial and swift punishment were important, Beccaria said, "because of privation of liberty, being itself a punishment, should not precede the sentence."[31] He felt that this "privation of liberty" was not only unjust, in the sense that some of these defendants would not have been incarcerated for such a long period even if they had been convicted and sentenced to the maximum for the charges they were accused of committing, but also detrimental because the individual would not link the sanction with the violation(s) committed. Specifically, Beccaria believed that people build an association between the pains of punishment and their criminal acts. He asserted the following:

---

[29]Beccaria, *Crimes and Punishments*, 46–47.

[30]Ibid., 55.

[31]Ibid., 55.

> Promptness of punishments is more useful because when the length of time that passes between the punishment and the misdeed is less, so much the stronger and more lasting in the human mind is the association of these two ideas, crime and punishment; they then come insensibly to be considered, one as the cause, the other as the necessary inevitable effect. It has been demonstrated that the association of ideas is the cement that forms the entire fabric of the human intellect.[32]

An analogy can be made to training animals or children; you have to catch them in the act, or soon after, or the punishment doesn't matter because the offender doesn't know why he or she is being punished. Ultimately, Beccaria argued that, for both reform and deterrence reasons, punishment should occur quickly after the act. Despite the commonsense aspects of making punishments swift, this has not been examined by modern empirical research and therefore is the most neglected of the three elements of punishment Beccaria emphasized.

Case Study: Deborah Jeane Palfrey

▲ **Image 2.4** Deborah Jeane Palfrey, known as the "DC Madam," committed suicide in jail before being sentenced. Her case reveals the potentially powerful effects of formal sanctions on individuals' decision making.

SOURCE: © Jacquelyn Martin / ASSOCIATED PRESS

Deborah Jeane Palfrey, known as the "DC Madam," was brought up on charges of racketeering and money laundering related to running a prostitution ring in Washington, DC, and surrounding suburbs in Maryland and Virginia. The clientele of this prostitution ring included some notable politicians, such as state senators and other elected officials. Palfrey faced a maximum of 55 years in prison but likely would have received far less time had she not committed suicide before her sentencing. Her body was found in a storage facility at her mother's home in Tarpon Springs, Florida.

News reports revealed that she had served time before (for prostitution). Author Dan Moldea told *Time* magazine that she had contacted him for a book he was working on and told him "she had done time once before . . . and it damned near killed her. She said there was enormous stress—it made her sick, she couldn't take it, and she wasn't going to let that happen again."[33] The situation could have been worsened by the heightened media attention this case received; while most prostitution cases are handled by local or state courts, this one was handled by federal courts because it concerned Washington, DC.

---

[32] Ibid., 56.

[33] Adam Zagorin, "D.C. Madam: Suicide before Prison," *Time*, May 1, 2008, http://www.time.com/time/nation/article/0,8599,1736687,00.html.

> ***"She had done time once before . . . and it damned near killed her. She said there was enormous stress—it made her sick, she couldn't take it, and she wasn't going to let that happen again."***

It is quite likely that the impending maximum prison sentence led her to take her own life, given what she had said to Moldea. This shows the type of deterrent effect that jail or prison can have on an individual—in this case, possibly leading her to choose death over serving time. Ironically, Palfrey had commented to the press, after the suicide of a former employee in her prostitution network—Brandy Britton, who hanged herself before going to trial—"I guess I'm made of something that Brandy Britton wasn't made of."[34] It seems that Palfrey had the same concerns as Britton, and she ended up contradicting her bold statement when she ended her own life.

This case study provides an example of the profound effects legal sanctions can have on individuals. Legal sanctions are not meant to inspire offenders to end their lives, but this case does illustrate the potential deterrent effects of facing punishment from the legal system. We can see this on a smaller scale when a speeding driver's heart rate increases at the sight of a highway patrol or other police vehicle (which studies show happens to most drivers). Even though this offense would result in only a fine, it is a good example of deterrence in our everyday lives. We will revisit the Palfrey case at the conclusion of this section, after you have had a chance to review some of the theoretical propositions and concepts that make up deterrence theory.

On a related note, a special report from the U.S. Department of Justice (DOJ), Bureau of Justice Statistics (BJS), concludes that the suicide rate has been far higher among jail inmates than among prison inmates.[35] Specifically, suicides in jails have tended over the past few decades to occur 300% (or 3 times) more often than among prison inmates.

A likely reason for this phenomenon is that many persons arrested and/or awaiting trial (which is generally the status of those in jail) have more to lose, such as their relationships with family, friends, and employers, than do the typical chronic offenders that end up in prison. Specifically, many of the individuals picked up for prostitution and other relatively minor, albeit embarrassing, offenses are of the middle- and upper-class mentality and, thus, are ill equipped to face the real-world consequences of their arrest. The good news is, this same DOJ report showed that suicides in both jails and prisons have decreased during the past few decades, likely due to better policies in correctional settings regarding persons considered at "high risk" for suicide.

Think About It

1. Do you think that some of the clientele (e.g., notable politicians) should have also been charged for a criminal offense?
2. Do you think it made a difference that this case was handled by federal courts rather than local or state courts?
3. Do you think prostitution should be legal?

---

[34] Ibid.

[35] Christopher J. Mumola, *Suicide and Homicide in State Prisons and Local Jails* (Washington, DC: U.S. Department of Justice, Office of Justice Programs, August 2005). http://bjs.gov/content/pub/pdf/shsplj.pdf.

Certainty

The second characteristic that Beccaria felt was vital to the effectiveness of deterrence was **certainty of punishment**. Beccaria considered this the most important quality of punishment: "Even the least of evils, when they are certain, always terrify men's minds."[36] He also said, "The certainty of punishment, even if it be moderate, will always make a stronger impression than the fear of another which is more terrible but combined with the hope of impunity."[37] As scientific studies later showed, Beccaria was accurate in his assumption that perceived certainty or risk of punishment was the most important aspect of deterrence.[38]

It is interesting to note that certainty is the least likely characteristic of punishment to be enhanced in modern criminal justice policy. Over the past few decades, the likelihood that criminals will be caught and arrested has not increased. Law enforcement officials have been able to clear only about 21% of known felonies. Such clearance rates are based on the rate at which known suspects are apprehended for crimes reported to police. Law enforcement officials are no better at solving serious crimes known to police (CKP) than they were in past decades, despite increased knowledge and resources put toward solving such crimes.

Severity

The third characteristic that Beccaria emphasized was **severity of punishment**. Specifically, Beccaria claimed that, for a punishment to be effective, the possible penalty must outweigh the potential benefits (e.g., financial payoff) of a given crime. However, this criterion came with a caveat. This aspect of punishment was perhaps the most complicated part of Beccaria's philosophy, primarily because he thought that too much severity would lead to more crime, but the punishment must exceed any benefits expected from the crime. Beccaria said the following:

> For a punishment to attain its end, the evil which it inflicts has only to exceed the advantage derivable from the crime; in this excess of evil one should include the . . . loss of the good which the crime might have produced. All beyond this is superfluous and for that reason tyrannical.[39]

Beccaria made clear in this statement that punishments should equal or outweigh any benefits of a crime to deter individuals from engaging in such acts. However, he also explicitly stated that any punishments that largely exceed the reasonable punishment for a given crime are inhumane and may lead to further criminality.

A modern example of how punishments can be taken to an extreme and thereby cause more crime rather than deter it is the current three-strikes-you're-out approach to sentencing. Such laws have become common in many states, such as California. In such jurisdictions, individuals who have committed two prior felonies can be sentenced to life imprisonment for committing a crime, even a nonviolent crime, that the state statutes consider a *serious felony*. Such laws have been known to drive some relatively minor property offenders to become violent when they know that they will be incarcerated for life when they are caught. A number of offenders have even wounded or killed people to avoid apprehension, knowing that they would face life imprisonment even for a relatively minor property offense. In a recent study, the authors analyzed the impact of three-strikes laws in 188 large cities in the 25 states

---

[36]Beccaria, *Crimes and Punishments*, 58.

[37]Ibid., 58.

[38]For a good recent review, see Bruce Jacobs and Alex R. Piquero, "Boundary-Crossing in Perceptual Deterrence: Investigating the Linkages between Sanction Severity, Sanction Certainty, and Offending," *International Journal of Offender Therapy & Comparative Criminology* 57 (2013): 792–812.

[39]Beccaria, *Crimes and Punishments*, 43.

that have such laws and concluded that there was no significant reduction in crime rates as a result. Furthermore, the areas with three-strikes laws typically had higher rates of homicide.[40]

Ultimately, Beccaria's philosophy on the three characteristics of good punishment in terms of deterrence—swiftness, certainty, and severity—is still highly respected and followed in most Western criminal justice systems. Despite its contemporary flaws and caveats, perhaps no other traditional framework is so widely adopted. With only one exception—namely, his proposal that a given act should always be punished in exactly the same way (see the next section)—Beccaria's concepts and propositions are still considered the ideal in virtually all Western criminal justice systems.

Beccaria's Conceptualization of Specific and General Deterrence

Beccaria also defined two identifiable forms of deterrence: specific and general. Although these two forms of deterrence tend to overlap in most sentences given by judges, they can be distinguished in terms of the intended target of the punishment. Sometimes the emphasis is clearly on one or the other, as Beccaria noted in his work.

Although Beccaria did not coin the terms ***specific deterrence*** and ***general deterrence***, he clearly made the case that both are important. Regarding punishment, he said, "The purpose can only be to prevent the criminal from inflicting new injuries on its citizens and to deter others from similar acts."[41] The first portion of this statement—preventing the criminal from reoffending—focuses on the defendant and the defendant alone, regardless of any possible offending by others. Punishments that focus primarily on the individual are considered specific deterrence, also referred to as special or individual deterrence. This concept is appropriately labeled because the emphasis is on the specific individual who offended. On the other hand, the latter portion of Beccaria's quotation emphasizes the deterrence of others, regardless of whether the individual criminal is deterred. Punishments that focus primarily on other potential criminals and not on the actual criminal are referred to as general deterrence.

Readers may wonder how a punishment would not be inherently both a specific and general deterrent. After all, in today's society, virtually all criminal punishments given to individuals (i.e., specific deterrence) are prescribed in court, a public venue, so people are somewhat aware of the sanctions (i.e., general deterrence). However, when Beccaria wrote in the 18th century, much if not most sentencing was done behind closed doors and was not known to the public and had no way to deter other potential offenders. Therefore, Beccaria saw much utility in letting the public know what punishments were handed out for given crimes. This fulfilled the goal of general deterrence, which was essentially scaring others into not committing such criminal acts, while it also furthered his reforms by letting the public know whether fair and balanced justice was being administered.

Despite the obvious overlap, there are identifiable distinctions between specific and general deterrence seen in modern sentencing strategy. For example, some judges have chosen to hand out punishments to defendants in which they are obligated, as a condition of their probation or parole, to walk along their towns' main streets while wearing signs that say "Convicted Child Molester" or "Convicted Shoplifter." Other cities have implemented policies in which pictures and identifying information of those individuals who are arrested, such as prostitutes or men who solicit them, are put in newspapers or placed on billboards.

These punishment strategies are not likely to be much of a specific deterrent. Having now been labeled, these individuals may actually be psychologically encouraged to engage in doing what the public expects them to do. The specific deterrent effect may not be particularly strong. However, authorities are hoping for a strong general

---

[40]Tomislav V. Kovandzic, John J. Sloan III, and Lynne M. Vieraitis, "'Striking Out' as Crime Reduction Policy: The Impact of 'Three-Strikes' Laws on Crime Rates in the U.S. Cities," *Justice Quarterly* 21 (2004): 207–40. See also Steven N. Durlauf and Daniel S. Nagin, "Imprisonment and Crime: Can Both Be Reduced?," *Criminology and Public Policy* 10 (2011): 13–54.

[41]Ibid., 42.

deterrent effect in most of these cases. They expect that many of the people who see these sign-laden individuals on the streets or in public pictures are going to be frightened away from engaging in similar activity.

There are also numerous diversion programs, particularly for juvenile, first-time, and minor offenders, which seek to punish offenders without engaging them in public hearings or trials. The goal of such programs is to hold the individuals accountable and have them fulfill certain obligations without having them dragged through the system, which is often public. Thus, the goal is obviously to instill specific deterrence without using the person as a poster child for the public, which obviously negates any aspects of general deterrence.

Although most judges invoke both specific and general deterrence in many of the criminal sentences that they hand out, there are notable cases in which either specific or general deterrence is emphasized, sometimes exclusively. Ultimately, Beccaria seemed to emphasize general deterrence and overall crime prevention, as suggested by his statement that "it is better to prevent crimes than to punish them. This is the ultimate end of every good legislation."[42] This claim implies that it is better to deter potential offenders before they offend rather than imposing sanctions on already convicted criminals. Beccaria's emphasis on prevention (over reaction) and general deterrence is also evident in his claim that education is likely the best way to reduce crime. After all, the more educated an individual is regarding the law and potential punishments, as well as public cases in which offenders have been punished, the less likely he or she will be to engage in such activity. Beccaria's identification of the differential emphases in terms of punishment was a key element in his work that continues to be important in modern times.

A Summary of Beccaria's Ideas and His Influence on Policy

Ultimately, Beccaria summarized his ideas on reforms and deterrence with this statement:

> In order for punishment not to be, in every instance, an act of violence of one or of many against a private citizen, it must be essentially public, prompt, necessary, the least possible in the given circumstances, proportionate to the crimes, dictated by the laws.[43]

In this statement, Beccaria is saying that the processing and punishment administered by justice systems must be known to the public, which delegates to the state the authority to make such decisions. Furthermore, he asserted that the punishment must be appropriately swift, certain (i.e., necessary), and appropriately severe, which fits his concept of deterrence. Finally, he reiterated the need to administer the same punishment every time for a given criminal act, as opposed to having arbitrary punishments imposed by one judge. These are just some of many ideas that Beccaria proposed, but he apparently saw these points as being the most important.

Although we, as U.S. citizens, take for granted the rights proposed by Beccaria, they were quite unique concepts during the 18th century. In fact, the ideas proposed by Beccaria were so unusual and revolutionary then that he published his book anonymously. It is obvious that Beccaria was considerably worried about being accused of blasphemy by the church and of being persecuted by governments for his views.

Regarding the first claim, Beccaria was right; the Roman Catholic Church excommunicated Beccaria when it became known that he wrote the book. In fact, his book remained on the list of condemned works until relatively recently (the 1960s). On the other hand, government officials of the time surprisingly embraced his work. The Italian government and most European and other world officials, particularly dictators, embraced his work as well. Beccaria was invited to visit many other country capitals, even those of the most authoritarian states at that time, to help reform their criminal justice systems. For example, Beccaria was invited to meet with Catherine the Great, the czarina of Russia, during the late 1700s, to help revise and improve Russia's justice system. Most historical records

[42]Beccaria, *Crimes and Punishments*, 93.

[43]Ibid., 99.

suggest that Beccaria was not a great diplomat or representative of his ideas, largely because he was not physically or socially adequate for such endeavors. However, his ideas were strong and stood on their own merit.

Dictators and authoritarian governments may have liked Beccaria's reform framework so much because it explicitly stated that treason was the most serious crime. He said this:

> The first class of crime, which are the gravest because most injurious, are those known as crimes of *lese majesty* [high treason]. . . . Every crime . . . injures society, but it is not every crime that aims at its immediate destruction.[44]

According to Enlightenment philosophy, violations of law are criminal acts not only against the direct victims but also against the entire society because they break the social contract. As Beccaria stated, the most heinous criminal acts are those that directly violate the social contract, which would be treason and espionage. In Beccaria's reform proposals, dictators may have seen a chance to pacify revolutionary citizens who might be aiming to overthrow their governments. In many cases, reforms were only a temporary solution. After all, the American Revolution occurred in the 1770s, the French Revolution occurred in the 1780s, and other revolutions occurred soon after this period.

Governments that tried to apply Beccaria's ideas to the letter experienced problems, but generally, most European (and American) societies that incorporated his ideas had fairer and more democratic justice systems than they'd had before Beccaria. This is why, to this day, he is considered the father of criminal justice.

The Impact of Beccaria's Work on Other Theorists

Beccaria's work had an immediate impact on the political and philosophical state of affairs in the late 18th century. He was invited to many other countries to reform their justice systems, and his propositions and theoretical model of deterrence were incorporated into many of the new constitutions of countries, most of them formed after major revolutions. The most notable of these was the Constitution and Bill of Rights of the United States.

It is quite obvious that the many founding documents constructed before and during the American Revolution in the late 1700s were heavily influenced by Beccaria and other Enlightenment philosophers. Specifically, the concept that the U.S. government is "of the people, by the people, and for the people" makes it clear that the Enlightenment idea of democracy and voice in government is of utmost importance. Another clear example is the emphasis on due process and individual rights in the U.S. Bill of Rights. Among the important concepts derived from Beccaria's work are the right to trial by jury, the right to confront and cross-examine witnesses, the right to a speedy trial, and the right to be informed about decisions of the justice system (charges, pleas, trials, verdicts, sentences, etc.).

The impact of Beccaria's ideas on the working ideology of our system of justice cannot be overstated. The public nature of our justice system comes from Beccaria, as does the emphasis on deterrence. The United States, as well as virtually all Western countries, incorporates in its justice system the certainty and severity of punishment to reduce crime. This system of deterrence remains the dominant model in criminal justice: The goal is to deter potential and previous offenders from committing crime by enforcing punishments that will make them reconsider the next time they think about engaging in such activity. This model assumes a rationally thinking human being, as described by Enlightenment philosophy, who can learn from past experiences or from seeing others punished for offenses that he or she is rationally thinking about committing. Thus, Beccaria's work has had a profound impact on the existing philosophy and workings of most justice systems throughout the world.

Beyond this, Beccaria also had a large impact on further theorizing about human decision making related to committing criminal behavior. One of the more notable theorists inspired by Beccaria's ideas was Jeremy Bentham (1748–1832) of England, who has become a well-known classical theorist in his own right,

---

[44]Ibid., 68.

▲ **Image 2.5** Jeremy Bentham, often credited as the founder of University College London, insisted that his body be put on display there after his death. You can visit a replica of it today.

SOURCE: © Popperfoto / Popperfoto / Getty Images

perhaps because he helped spread the Enlightenment/Beccarian philosophy to Britain. His influence in the development of classical theorizing is debated, and a number of major texts do not cover his writings at all.[45] Although he did not add a significant amount of theorizing beyond Beccaria's propositions regarding reform and deterrence, Bentham did further refine the ideas presented by previous theorists, and his legacy is well known.

One of the more important contributions of Bentham was the concept of *hedonistic calculus*, which is essentially the weighing of pleasure versus pain. This, of course, is strongly based on the Enlightenment/Beccarian concept of rational choice and utility. After all, if the expected pain outweighs the expected benefit of doing a given act, the rational individual is far less likely to do it. On the other hand, if the expected pleasure outweighs the expected pain, a rational person will engage in the act. Bentham listed a set of criteria that he thought would go into the decision making of a rational individual. An analogy would be an imagined two-sided balance scale on which the pros and cons of crimes are considered, and then the individual makes a rational decision about whether to commit the crime.

Beyond the idea of hedonistic calculus, Bentham's contributions to the overall assumptions of classical theorizing did not significantly revise the theoretical model. Perhaps the most important contribution he made to the Classical School was helping to popularize the framework in Britain. In fact, Bentham became better known for his design of a prison structure, known as the *panopticon*, which was used in several countries and in early Pennsylvania penitentiaries. This model of prisons used a type of wagon wheel design, in which a post at the center allowed 360-degree visual observation of the various "spokes"—that is, hallways that contained all of the inmate cells.

The Neoclassical School of Criminology

A number of governments, including the newly formed United States, incorporated Beccaria's concepts and propositions in the development of their justice systems. The government that most strictly applied Beccaria's ideas—France after the French Revolution of the late 1780s—found that it worked pretty well except for one concept. Beccaria believed that every individual who committed a certain act against the law should be punished the same way. Although equality in punishment sounds like a good philosophy, the French realized very quickly that not every one should be punished equally for a certain act.

The French system found that giving a first-time offender the same sentence as a repeat offender did not make much sense, especially when the first-time offender was a juvenile. Furthermore, there were many circumstances in which a defendant appeared to be unmalicious in doing an act, such as when he or she had limited mental capacity or acted out of necessity. Perhaps most important, Beccaria's framework specifically dismissed the intent (i.e., *mens rea*) of criminal offenders while focusing only on the harm done to society by a given act (i.e., *actus reus*). French society, as well as most modern societies such as the United States, deviated from Beccaria's framework in taking the

---

[45]See, for example, Thomas J. Bernard, Jeffrey B. Snipes, and Alexander L. Gerould, *Vold's Theoretical Criminology*, 6th ed. (Oxford: Oxford University Press, 2009).

intent of offenders into account, often in a very important way, such as in determining what type of charges should be filed against those accused of homicide. Therefore, a new school of thought regarding the classical or deterrence model developed, which became known as the **Neoclassical School** of criminology.

The only significant difference between the Neoclassical School and the Classical School of criminology is that the Neoclassical (*neo* means "new") School takes into account contextual circumstances of the individual or situation, allowing for increases or decreases in the punishment. For example, would a society want to punish a 12-year-old first-time offender the same way they would punish a 35-year-old who shoplifted the same item a second time? Does a society want to punish a mentally challenged person for stealing a car once as much as they would punish a person without disabilities who has been convicted of stealing more than a dozen cars? The answer is probably not—or at least, that is what most modern criminal justice authorities have decided, including those in the United States.

▲ **Image 2.6** Charles Darwin (1809–1882), author of evolutionary theory.

SOURCE: © Getty Images / Hulton Archive / Stringer

This was also the conclusion of French society, which quickly realized that, in this respect, Beccaria's system was neither fair nor effective in terms of deterrence. They came to acknowledge that circumstantial factors play an important part in how malicious or guilty a certain defendant is in committing a given crime. The French revised their laws to take into account both mitigating and aggravating circumstances. This neoclassical concept became the standard in all Western justice systems.

The United States also followed this model and considers contextual factors in virtually all of its charges and sentencing decisions. For example, juvenile defendants are actually processed in completely different courts. Furthermore, defendants who are first-time offenders are generally given options for diversion programs or probation as long as their offenses are not serious.

While the Neoclassical School added an important caveat to the previously important Classical School, it assumes virtually all other concepts and propositions of the Classical School: The social contract, due process rights, and the idea that rational beings will be deterred by the certainty, swiftness, and severity of punishment. This neoclassical framework had, and continues to have, an extremely important impact on the world.

Loss of Dominance of Classical and Neoclassical Theory

For about 100 years after Beccaria wrote his book, the Classical and Neoclassical Schools were dominant in criminological theorizing. During this time, most governments—especially those in the Western world—shifted their justice frameworks toward the neoclassical model. This has not changed even in modern times. For example, when officials attempt to reduce certain illegal behaviors, they increase the punishments or put more effort into catching relevant offenders.

However, the classical and neoclassical frameworks lost dominance among academics and scientists in the 19th century and especially after Darwin's publication in 1859 of *The Origin of Species*, which introduced the concept of evolution and natural selection. This perspective shed new light on other influences on human behavior beyond free will and rational choice (e.g., genetics, psychological deficits). Despite this shift in emphasis among academic and scientific circles, the actual workings of the justice systems of most Western societies still retain the framework of classical and neoclassical models as their model of justice.

Three-strikes laws are an example; others include police department gang units and injunctions that condemn any observed loitering by or gathering among gang members in a specified region. Furthermore, some jurisdictions, such as California, have created gang enhancements for sentencing; after the jury decides whether the defendant is guilty of a given crime, it then considers whether the person is a gang member. If a jury in California decides that the defendant is a gang member, which is usually determined by evidence provided by local police gang units, it automatically adds more time to any sentence the judge gives. These are just some examples of how Western justice systems still rely primarily on deterrence of criminal activity through increased enforcement and enhanced sentencing. The bottom line is that modern justice systems still base most of their policies on classical or neoclassical theoretical frameworks that fell out of favor among scientists and philosophers in the late 1800s.

Policy Implications

Many policies are based on deterrence theory: the premise that increasing the certainty and/or severity of sanctions will deter crime.[46] This is seen throughout our system of law enforcement, courts, and corrections. This is rather interesting, given the fact that classical deterrence theory has not been the dominant explanatory model among criminologists for decades. In fact, a recent poll of close to 400 criminologists in the nation ranked classical theory 22nd out of 24 theories in terms of being the most valid explanation of serious and persistent offending.[47] Still, given the dominance of classical deterrence theory in most criminal justice policies, it is very important to discuss the most common strategies, as well as those that do not appear to be effective, or in some cases are detrimental.

First, the death penalty is used as a general deterrent for committing crime in most U.S. state jurisdictions. As the father of deterrence theory predicted, most studies show that capital punishment has a negligible effect on criminality. A recent review of the extant literature concluded that "the death penalty does not deter crime."[48] In fact, some studies show evidence for a brutalization effect, an increase in homicides after a high-profile execution.[49] Although the evidence is somewhat mixed, it is safe to say that the death penalty is not a consistent deterrent.

Another policy flowing from classical and neoclassical models is adding more police officers to deter crime in a given area. A recent review of the existing literature concluded that simply "adding more police officers will not reduce crime."[50] Rather, it is generally up to communities to police themselves via informal factors of control (family, church, community ties, etc.). However, this same review did find that police engagement in problem-solving activities at a specific location can sometimes reduce crime, but at that point the strategy is not based on deterrence.[51] Furthermore, a recent report concluded that proactive arrests for drunk driving have consistently been found to reduce such behavior, as does arresting offenders for domestic violence, but only if these measures are employed consistently.[52]

---

[46]Stephen G. Tibbetts, *Criminological Theory: The Essentials* (Thousand Oaks, CA: Sage, 2012), 46–48.

[47]Lee Ellis, Jonathan Cooper, and Anthony Walsh, "Criminologists' Opinions about Causes and Theories of Crime and Delinquency: A Follow-up," *The Criminologist* 33 (2008): 23–26.

[48]Samuel Walker, *Sense and Nonsense about Crime and Drugs*, 7th ed. (Stamford, CT: Cengage, 2010).

[49]Bowers, "Effect of Execution."

[50]Walker, *Sense and Nonsense.*

[51]Ibid.

[52]Lawrence Sherman et al., *Preventing Crime: What Works, What Doesn't, What's Promising: A Report to the United States Congress* (Washington, DC: U.S. Department of Justice, 1997).

One example of court and correctional strategies is the "scared straight" approach that became popular several decades ago.[53] These programs essentially sought to scare or deter juvenile offenders into going "straight" by showing them the harshness and realities of prison life. However, nearly all evaluations of these programs showed that they were ineffective, and some evaluations indicated that these programs led to higher rates of recidivism.[54] There seem to be few successful deterrent policies in the court and corrections components of the criminal justice system. One recent review found that one of the court-mandated policies that seems promising is the provision of protection orders for battered women.[55] Another review in 2017 by David Weisburd, David Farrington, and Charlotte Gill of the systematic reviews and meta-analyses in the extant literature on the effects of court-imposed sanctions concluded that some of the programs showing effectiveness included mental health courts, as well as noncustodial sentences or interventions (such as ignition interlock devices for preventing drunk driving). However, this review concluded that interventions relating to the severity of the sentence and general deterrence had no evidence of effectiveness, and that studies have consistently shown that scared straight programs for juvenile offenders "did more harm than good."[56]

The policies, programs, and strategies based on classical deterrence theory will be examined more thoroughly in the final section of this book. To sum up, however, most of these strategies don't seem to work consistently to deter. This is because such a model assumes that people are rational and think carefully before choosing their behavior, whereas most research findings suggest that people often carry out behaviors that they know are irrational or without engaging in rational decision making,[57] which criminologists often refer to as *bounded rationality.*[58] Therefore, it is not surprising that many attempts by police and other criminal justice authorities to deter potential offenders do not seem to have much effect in preventing crime. This explanation will be more fully discussed in the final section of the book.

Conclusion

This section examined the earliest period of theorizing about criminological theory. The Classical School of criminology evolved out of ideas from the Enlightenment era in the mid- to late 18th century. This school of thought emphasized free will and rational choices that individuals make, from the perspective that people make choices regarding criminal behavior based on the potential costs and benefits that could result from such behavior. This section also explored the concepts and propositions of the father of the Classical School, which built the framework on which deterrence theory is based. We also discussed the various reforms that Beccaria proposed, many of which were adopted in the formation of the U.S. Constitution and Bill of Rights. The significance of the Classical School in both theorizing about crime and the actual administration of justice in the United States cannot be overestimated. The Classical and Neoclassical Schools of criminology remain to this day the primary framework within which

[53]For a review of these programs and evaluations of them, see Richard Lundman, *Prevention and Control of Juvenile Delinquency*, 3rd ed. (Oxford: Oxford University Press, 2001).

[54]Ibid. Also see David Weisburd, David P. Farrington, and Charlotte Gill, "What Works in Crime Prevention and Rehabilitation: An Assessment of Systematic Reviews," *Criminology & Public Policy* 16 (2017): 415–49.

[55]Sherman et al., *Preventing Crime.*

[56]Weisburd et al., "What Works in Crime Prevention," 424.

[57]For a review of the extant research on this topic, see Alex Piquero and Stephen Tibbetts, *Rational Choice and Criminal Behavior* (New York: Routledge, 2002).

[58]For a more recent discussion on the complexity of developing policies based on deterrence and rational choice models, see Travis Pratt, "Rational Choice Theory, Crime Control Policy, and Criminological Relevance," *Criminology and Public Policy* 7 (2008): 43–52.

justice is administered, despite the fact that scientific researchers and academics have, for the most part, moved past this perspective to consider social and economic factors.

SECTION SUMMARY

- The dominant theory of criminal behavior for most of the history of human civilization used demonic, supernatural, or other metaphysical explanations of behavior.
- The Age of Enlightenment was important because it brought a new logic and rationality to understanding human behavior, especially regarding the ability of individual human beings to think for themselves. Hobbes and Rousseau were two of the more important Enlightenment philosophers, and both stressed the importance of the social contract.
- Cesare Beccaria, who is generally considered the father of criminal justice, laid out a series of recommendations for reforming the brutal justice systems that existed throughout the world in the 1700s.
- Beccaria is also widely considered the father of the Classical School or deterrence theory; he based virtually all of his theoretical framework on the work of Enlightenment philosophers, especially their emphasis on humans as rational beings who consider perceived risks and benefits before committing criminal behaviors. This is the fundamental assumption of deterrence models of crime reduction.
- Beccaria discussed three key elements that punishments should have to be effective deterrents: celerity (swiftness), certainty, and severity.
- Specific deterrence involves sanctioning an individual to deter that particular individual from offending in the future. General deterrence involves sanctioning an individual to deter other potential offenders by making an example out of the individual being punished.
- The Neoclassical School was formed because societies found it nearly impossible to punish offenders equally for a given offense. The significant difference between the Classical and Neoclassical Schools is that the neoclassical model takes aggravating and mitigating circumstances into account when an individual is sentenced.
- Jeremy Bentham helped reinforce and popularize Beccaria's ideas in the English-speaking world, and he further developed the theory by proposing the hedonistic calculus, a formula for understanding criminal behavior.
- Despite falling out of favor among most criminologists in the late 1800s, the classical and neoclassical frameworks still constitute the dominant models and philosophies of all modern Western justice systems.

KEY TERMS

actus reus 47

Age of Enlightenment 41

brutalization effect 50

certainty of punishment 54

deterrence theory 41

general deterrence 55

mens rea 47

Neoclassical School 59

severity of punishment 54

social contract 45

specific deterrence 55

swiftness of punishment 51

utilitarianism 46

DISCUSSION QUESTIONS

1. Do you see any validity to the supernatural or religious explanations of criminal behavior? Provide examples of why you feel the way you do. Is your position supported by scientific research?
2. Which portions of Enlightenment thought do you believe are most valid in modern times? Which portions do you find least valid?
3. Of all of Beccaria's reforms, which do you think made the most significant improvement to modern criminal justice systems and why? Which do you think had the least impact and why?
4. Of the three elements of deterrence that Beccaria described, which do you think has the most important impact on deterring individuals from committing crime? Which of the three do you think has the least impact on deterring potential criminals? Back up your selections with personal experience.
5. Between general and specific deterrence, which do you think is more important for a judge to consider when sentencing a convicted individual? Why do you feel that way?
6. Provide examples of general and specific deterrence in your local community or state. Use the Internet if you can't find examples from your local community. Do you think such deterrence is effective?
7. Given the modern interpretation by the U.S. government of the definition of torture in context with what Beccaria thought about this issue, do you think that the father of criminal justice and deterrence would agree with the interrogation policies of the Bush administration during the Iraq War, which indisputably violated the guidelines set by the Geneva Conventions? Explain your position.
8. Regarding the use of the death penalty, list and explain at least three reasons why the father of criminal justice and deterrence theory felt the way he did. Which of these arguments do you agree with the most? Which argument do you disagree with the most? Ultimately, are you more strongly for or against the death penalty after reading the arguments of Beccaria?
9. Regarding the Neoclassical School, which mitigating factors do you think should reduce the punishment of a criminal defendant the most? Which aggravating circumstances do you think should increase the sentence of a criminal defendant the most? Do you believe that all persons who commit the same act should be punished exactly the same, regardless of age, experience, or gender?
10. What types of policy strategies based on classical and deterrence theory do you support? Which don't you support? Why?

WEB RESOURCES

Age of Enlightenment

http://history-world.org/age_of_enlightenment.htm

Cesare Beccaria

http://www.constitution.org/cb/beccaria_bio.htm

Demonic Theories of Crime

http://www.ucs.mun.ca/~skenney/courses/3290/3290class4.pdf
http://www.salemweb.com/memorial

Deterrence

http://www.sentencingproject.org/publications/deterrence-in-criminal-justice-evaluating-certainty-vs-severity-of-punishment
http://www.deathpenaltyinfo.org/article.php?scid=12&did=167

Jean-Jacques Rousseau

http://www.philosophypages.com/ph/rous.htm

Jeremy Bentham

http://www.ucl.ac.uk/Bentham-Project/who
http://www.utilitarianism.com/bentham.htm

Neoclassical School

http://study.com/academy/lesson/neoclassical-criminology-school-theory.html

Thomas Hobbes

http://www.philosophypages.com/hy/3x.htm

READING /// 2

This entry, passages from Cesare Beccaria's *On Crimes and Punishments* (originally published in 1764), is perhaps the most important in the entire book because it provides the framework on which all societies in the Western world have based their criminal justice systems. This is the model presented by the father of criminal justice, Cesare Beccaria, who published his work anonymously at first and then, once it became a widespread success, came forward as the author.

Beccaria is widely considered the father of the Classical School and the father of deterrence theory because he was the first to be recognized as emphasizing the importance of individuals' free will and rationale in choosing to engage in criminal behavior after considering the perceived costs and benefits. Although it is likely that he was not the first person to come to this realization, he was the first to get credit for explicitly stating this rational decision-making process in individuals before they commit criminal acts and for identifying the three elements that make a punishment a good deterrent.

While reading this entry, readers should pay special attention to the following:

- Beccaria's primary reasons for why a government/state has the right to punish offenders of the law
- The various reasons why Beccaria claims that punishment should be swift as well as how severe a punishment should be given the offense an individual committed
- The overall conclusions of the author, with each element being quite important and emphasized

On Crimes and Punishments

Cesare Beccaria

I. Origin of Punishments

Laws are the conditions by which independent and isolated men, tired of living in a constant state of war and of enjoying a freedom made useless by the uncertainty of keeping it, unite in society.[1] They sacrifice a portion of this liberty in order to enjoy the remainder in security and tranquility. The sum of all these portions of liberty sacrificed for the good of everyone constitutes the sovereignty of a nation, and the sovereign is its legitimate depository and administrator. The mere formation of this deposit, however, was not sufficient; it had to be defended against the private usurpations of each particular individual, for everyone always seeks to withdraw not only his own share of liberty from the common store, but to expropriate the portions of other men besides. Tangible motives were required sufficient to dissuade the despotic spirit of each man from plunging the laws of society back into the original chaos. These tangible motives are the punishments established for lawbreakers. I say "tangible motives," since

SOURCE: Cesare Beccaria, *On Crimes and Punishments*, with notes and introduction by David Young (Indianapolis: Hackett, 1985). The selection here has been abridged from the original.

experience has shown that the common crowd does not adopt stable principles of conduct, and the universal principle of dissolution which we see in the physical and the moral world cannot be avoided except by motives that have a direct impact on the senses and appear continually to the mind to counterbalance the strong impressions of individual passions opposed to the general good. Neither eloquence nor declamations nor even the sublime truths have sufficed for long to check the emotions aroused by the vivid impressions of immediately present objects.[2]

II. The Right to Punish

Every punishment which does not derive from absolute necessity, says the great Montesquieu, is tyrannical.[3] The proposition may be made general thus: every act of authority between one man and another that does not derive from absolute necessity is tyrannical. Here, then, is the foundation of the sovereign's right to punish crimes: the necessity of defending the depository of the public welfare against the usurpations of private individuals. Further, the more just punishments are, the more sacred and inviolable is personal security, and the greater is the liberty that the sovereign preserves for his subjects. Let us consult the human heart, and there we shall find the fundamental principles of the sovereign's right to punish crimes, for no lasting advantage is to be expected from political morality if it is not founded upon man's immutable sentiments. Any law that deviates from them will always encounter a resistance that will overpower it sooner or later, just as a continually applied force, however slight, eventually overcomes any violent movement communicated to a physical body.

No man freely gave up a part of his own liberty for the sake of the public good; such an illusion exists only in romances. If it were possible, each of us would wish that the agreements binding on others were not binding on himself. Every man thinks of himself as the center of all the world's affairs.

The increase in the numbers of mankind, slight in itself but too much for the means that sterile and uncultivated nature offered to satisfy increasingly interrelated needs, led the first savages to unite. These initial groups necessarily created others to resist the former, and thus the state of war was transposed from individuals to nations.[4]

It was necessity, then, that constrained men to give up part of their personal liberty; hence, it is certain that each man wanted to put only the least possible portion into the public deposit, only as much as necessary to induce others to defend it.[5] The aggregate of these smallest possible portions of individual liberty constitutes the right to punish; everything beyond that is an abuse and not justice, a fact but scarcely a right. Note that the word "right" is not a contradiction of the word "force"; the former is, rather, a modification of the latter—namely, the modification most useful to the greatest number. By "justice," moreover, I do not mean anything but the bond necessary to hold private interests together. Without it, they would dissolve into the earlier state of incompatibility. All punishments that exceed what is necessary to preserve this bond are unjust by their very nature. One must beware of attaching the idea of something real to this word "justice," as though it were a physical force or a being that actually exists. It is simply a human manner of conceiving things, a manner that has an infinite influence on the happiness of everybody.[6] Most certainly I am not speaking of the other sort of justice that comes from God and that is directly related to the rewards and punishments of the life to come.

XIX. Promptness of Punishment

The more prompt the punishment is and the sooner it follows the crime, the more just and useful it will be. I say more just, because it spares the criminal the useless and cruel torments of uncertainty, which grow with the vigor of one's imagination and the sense of one's own weakness; more just, because being deprived of one's liberty is a punishment, and this cannot precede the sentence except when necessity demands it. Imprisonment, then, simply means taking someone into custody until he is found guilty, and, as such custody is essentially punitive, it should last as short a time as possible and be as lenient as possible. The duration of imprisonment should be determined both by the time necessary for the trial and by the right of those who have been detained the longest to be tried first. The rigor of detention must not exceed what is necessary to forestall escape or the concealment of evidence. The trial itself must be completed in the shortest possible time. Can there be a more cruel contrast than the one between the indolence of a judge and the anguish of someone accused of a crime—between the comforts and pleasures of an unfeeling magistrate on the one hand, and, on the other, the tears and squalid condition of a prisoner? In general, the burden of a punishment and the consequence of a crime should have the greatest impact on others and yet be as mild as possible for the person who suffers it; for one cannot call any society "legitimate" if it does not recognize as an indisputable principle that men have wanted to subject themselves only to the least possible evils.

I have said that promptness of punishment is more useful, for the less time that passes between the misdeed and its chastisement, the stronger and more permanent is the human mind's association of the two ideas of *crime* and *punishment*, so that imperceptibly the one will come to be considered as the cause and the other as the necessary and inevitable result. It is well established that the association of ideas is the cement that shapes the whole structure of the human intellect; without it, pleasure and pain would be isolated feelings with no consequences. The farther removed men are from general ideas and universal principles—in other words, the more uneducated men are—the more they act on the basis of immediate and very familiar associations, neglecting the more remote and complicated ones. The latter are useful only to men strongly impassioned for the object after which they are striving. The light of their attention illuminates this one object only, leaving all others in darkness. Such remote and complicated associations are likewise useful to more lofty minds, for they have acquired the habit of rapidly surveying many objects at once, and they have the ability to contrast many partial sentiments with one another, so that the outcome, which is action, is less dangerous and uncertain.

The temporal proximity of crime and punishment, then, is of the utmost importance if one desires to arouse in crude and uneducated minds the idea of punishment in association with the seductive image of a certain advantageous crime. Long delay only serves to disconnect those two ideas, and whatever impression the chastisement of a crime may make, that impression will be made more as a spectacle than a punishment. Further, the impression will come only after the horror of a given crime, which ought to reinforce the feeling of punishment, has grown weak in the minds of the spectators.

Another principle serves admirably to tighten even further the connection between the misdeed and its punishment, namely, that the latter should conform as closely as possible to the nature of the crime. This analogy marvelously facilitates the contrast that should exist between the motive for a crime and the consequent impact of punishment, so that the latter draws the mind away and leads it to quite a different end than the one toward which the seductive idea of breaking the law seeks to direct it.

XXVII. Mildness of Punishments

But my train of thought has taken me away from my subject, and I hasten to return in order to clarify it. One of the greatest checks on crime is not the cruelty of punishments but their inevitability. Consequently, in order to be effective, virtues, magisterial vigilance and inexorable judicial severity must be accompanied by mild legislation. The certainty of a chastisement, even if it be moderate, will always make a greater impression than the fear of a more terrible punishment that is united with the hope of impunity; for, when they are certain, even the least of evils always terrifies men's minds, while hope, that heavenly gift that often fills us completely, always removes from us the idea of worse punishments, especially if that hope is reinforced by the examples of impunity which weakness and greed frequently accord. The very savagery of a punishment makes the criminal all the bolder in taking risks to avoid it precisely because the evil with which he is threatened is so great, so much so that he commits several crimes in order to escape the punishment for a single one of them. The countries and ages in which punishments have been most atrocious have always been the scene of the bloodiest and most inhuman actions, for the same spirit of ferocity that guided the hand of the legislator governed the hand of the parricide and the assassin. Seated on the throne, this spirit dictated iron laws for savage and slavish souls to obey; in private darkness, it moved men to destroy one tyrant in order to create another.[7]

To the degree that punishments become more cruel, men's souls become hardened, just as fluids always seek the level of surrounding objects, and the constantly active force of the passions leads to this: after a hundred years of cruel punishments, breaking on the wheel[8] occasions no more fright than imprisonment did at first. In order for a penalty to achieve its objective all that is required is that the harm of the punishment should exceed the benefit resulting from the crime. Further, the inevitability of the punishment and the loss of the anticipated advantage of the crime should enter into this calculation of the excess of harm.[9] Everything more than this is thus superfluous and therefore tyrannical. Men regulate their conduct by the repeated experience of evils which they know, not by those of which they are ignorant. Let us imagine two nations, each having a scale of punishments proportional to crimes; in one, the maximum penalty is perpetual slavery, and, in the other, breaking on the wheel. I maintain that the first nation will have as much fear of its greatest punishment as the second.[10] If for some reason the first of these nations were to adopt the more severe penalties of the second, the same reason might lead the latter to increase its punishments, passing gradually from breaking on the wheel to slower and more deliberate torments, and finally to the ultimate refinements of that science that tyrants know all too well.

Cruelty of punishments leads to two other ruinous consequences that are contrary to the very purpose of preventing crimes. The first is that it is far from easy to maintain the essential proportion between crime and punishment, for no matter how much industrious cruelty may have multiplied the forms of chastisement, they still cannot exceed the limit that the human physique and sensory capacity can endure.[11] Once this limit has been reached, it would not be possible to devise greater punishments for more harmful and atrocious crimes, and yet such punishments would be required to deter them. The second consequence is that impunity itself arises from the barbarity of punishments. There are limits to human capacities both for good and for evil, and a spectacle that is too brutal for humanity can only be a passing frenzy, never a permanent system such as the law must be. If the laws are indeed cruel, either they are changed or else fatal impunity results from the laws themselves.

Who would not tremble with horror when he reads in history books of the barbarous and useless torments that were devised and carried out in cold blood by men who were deemed wise? Who would not shudder to the depths of his being at the sight of thousands of poor wretches forced into a desperate return to the original state of nature by a misery that the law—which has always favored the few and trampled on the many—has either willed or permitted? Or at the spectacle of people accused of impossible crimes fabricated by timid ignorance? Or at the sight of persons whose only crime has been their fidelity to their own principles lacerated with deliberate formality and slow torture by men endowed with the same senses and hence with the same passions, providing a diverting show for a fanatical crowd?

XLVII. Conclusion

I conclude with the reflection that the magnitude of punishment ought to be relative to the condition of the nation itself. Stronger and more obvious impressions are required for the hardened spirits of a people who have scarcely emerged from a savage state. A thunderbolt is needed to fell a ferocious lion who is merely angered by a gun shot. But, to the extent that human spirits are made gentle by the social state, sensibility increases; as it increases, the severity of punishment must diminish if one wishes to maintain a constant relationship between object and feeling.[12]

From all that has been seen hitherto, one can deduce a very useful theorem, but one that scarcely conforms to custom, the usual lawgiver of nations. It is this: *In order that any punishment should not be an act of violence committed by one person or many against a private citizen, it is essential that it should be public, prompt, necessary, the minimum possible under the given circumstances, proportionate to the crimes, and established by law.*

Notes

1. The idea of laws as conditions of the social contract was fundamental to Rousseau. Jean-Jacques Rousseau, *Du contrat social*, in Jean-Jacques Rousseau, *Oeuvres complètes*, ed. Brenard Gagnebin and Marcel Raymond, vol. 3 (Paris, 1964), bk. 2, chap. 6, pp. 378–380.

2. This view of human nature as motivated chiefly by self-interest was common among eighteenth-century utilitarians. Helvétius had declared that all men seek to become despots and that tangible motives are necessary to check this tendency. Helvétius, *D l'esprit*, disc. 3, chap. 17, pp. 284–289. Beccaria frankly admitted that he owed a large part of his ideas to Helvétius. Beccaria to Morellet, 26 Jan. 1766, in *Opere* (Romangnoli ed.), 2:865. Kant and Hegel, of course, vehemently objected to such a theory of punishment, and it must be noted that it was not always typical of Beccaria. Immanuel Kant, *The*

Metaphysical Elements of Justice. Part I of the Metaphysics of Morals, ed. and trans. John Ladd (Indianapolis, 1965), p. 100; G. W. Hegel, *Hegel's Philosophy of Right*, ed. and trans. T. M. Knox (London, 1967), p. 246.

3. Montesquieu had held that excessive and unnecessary penalties are suitable only for a despotic government. Montesquieu, *De l'esprit des lois* (Caillois ed.), bk. 6, chap. 9, 2:318–319.

4. This account of the formation of societies closely parallels the one which Montesquieu gave in his *De l'esprit des lois* (Caillois ed.), bk 1, chap. 3, 2:236–238.

5. Beccaria's account of the social contract is quite unlike the total surrender of rights of which Rousseau spoke. Rousseau, *Du contrat social* (Gagnebin and Raymond ed.), bk. 1, chap. 6, 3:360–362. It is, rather, much closer to Locke's idea that the sovereign is purely fiduciary and that the people forming a state make only a minimal surrender of their liberty. John Locke, *The Second Treatise of Government*, ed. Thomas P. Peardon (Indianapolis, 1952), chap. 3, para. 21, p. 14; chap. 8, paras. 95–101, pp. 54–57.

6. Beccaria's utilitarian view of justice appears very similar to the ideas expounded by Helvétius. Helvétius, *D l'esprit*, disc. 2, chap. 5, pp. 55–57; chap. 8, pp. 69–74; chap. 12, pp. 89–97.

7. On several occasions, Montesquieu remarked that cruel punishments are suitable only in a despotic state, which is based upon fear, and that excessive penalties are most likely to be found in such a regime. Montesquieu, *Lettres persanes* (Callois ed.), vol. 1 (Paris, 1949) letter 80, pp. 252–253, Montesquieu, *De l'esprit des lois* (Callois ed.), bk. 12, chap. 4, 2:433–435.

8. Breaking on the wheel was a common form of execution in the eighteenth century. An English traveler in France described such an execution: "On the scaffold was erected a large cross exactly in the form of that commonly represented for Saint Andrew's. The executioner and his assistants then placed the prisoner on it, in such a manner that his arms and legs were extended exactly agreeable to the form of the cross, and strongly tied down; under each arm, leg, etc., was cut a notch in the wood, as a mark where the executioner might strike, and break the bone with greater facility. He held in his hand a large iron bar . . . and in the first place broke his arms, then in a moment after both his thighs; it was a melancholy, shocking sight, to see him heave his body up and down in extreme agony, and hideous to behold the terrible distortions of his face; it was a considerable time before he expired. . . ." Sacheverell Stevens, *Miscellaneous Remarks Made on . . . France, Italy, Germany, and Holland* (London, 1756) as cited in Jerry Kaplow, *The Names of Kings: The Parisian Laboring Poor in the Eighteenth Century* (New York, 1972), p. 135.

9. Bentham later elaborated on the calculation of the excess of harm over the profit of the crime, citing Beccaria in the process. Bentham, *Principles* (Burns and Hart ed.), chap. 14, pp. 165–174, esp. sec. 8, n.

10. Montesquieu had made precisely this point as early as 1721. Montesquieu, *Lettres persanes* (Callois ed.), letter 80, 1:252–253.

11. The point Beccaria is making here is based on the psychology of Helvétius, Helvétius, *D l'esprit* (1759 ed.), disc. 1, pp. 1–32; disc. 3, chaps. 1–3, pp. 187–202.

12. Hegel fully agreed with Beccaria on this score, arguing that punishments can and should vary according to the degree of a society's refinement or barbarism. "A penal code, then," concluded Hegel, "is primarily the child of its age and the state of civil society at the time." Hegel, *Philosophy of Right* (Knox ed.), p. 140. For a modern view substantially like Beccaria's, see Jan Gorecki, *Capital Punishment: Criminal Law and Social Evolution* (New York, 1983), esp. pp. 31–80.

REVIEW QUESTIONS

1. What are Beccaria's primary reasons for why a government or state is given the right to punish? How does this relate to the idea of the "social contract" presented in the text of this section?
2. What two reasons did Beccaria have for arguing that punishments should be prompt or swift? Which of these relates to deterrence theory (whereas the other is a reform for fairness and due process)?
3. Do you agree with all of the statements in Beccaria's conclusion? If not, which ones do you disagree with and why?

READING /// 3

In this empirical study, Sarah Britto and Krystal Noga-Styron examine the influence of various types of media on individuals' attitudes regarding the use of the death penalty. The forms of media asked about in the survey included watching different types of television shows, reading newspapers, listening to the radio, and interacting with the Internet. The study not only examines general support for capital punishment but also the alternative option that provides for the availability of life without parole, which makes the study more robust than many previous studies that only provided the options of death penalty or life imprisonment with possible parole.

While reading this article, one should consider the following topics:

- The extent to which the "Marshall hypothesis" is supported by current trends in citizen attitudes and current changes in death penalty policy in the United States
- The type of demographic and perceptual variables that have been found by previous studies to influence public support for capital punishment and theoretical reasons why such factors are believed to affect such attitudes
- The extent to which the findings of the current study support the authors' four hypotheses as well as the ways that the results vary for general support for the death penalty versus when the option of life without parole is provided
- The results of this study regarding which types of media seem to have the most influence on attitudes toward capital punishment

Media Consumption and Support for Capital Punishment

Sarah Britto and Krystal E. Noga-Styron

Introduction

In recent years, both Garland (2001) and Simon (2007) argue that several significant historical changes have resulted in a culture of fear that has heightened the public's sensitivity to risk and led to support for increasingly punitive policies. Scholars tend to agree that the majority of the public's knowledge about crime and the criminal justice system come from the consumption of such a media-rich diet (Surrette, 2010; Tonry, 1999). As a result, it is essential to understand how the media influences public attitudes, particularly on the criminal justice system's ultimate punishment—the death penalty. Understanding the media's influence in shaping such attitudes is important because some believe that perceptions play a role in policy decisions regarding capital punishment (Vollum, Longmire, & Buffington-Vollum, 2004).

SOURCE: Sarah Britto and Krystal E. Noga-Styron, "Media Consumption and Support for Capital Punishment," *Criminal Justice Review* 39, no. 1 (2014): 81–100.

Literature Review

The Media and Public Policy

Garland (2001) and Simon (2007) both argue that the United States' punitive turn in the 1970s was a result of many factors, including increasing crime rates, an economic recession, an increasing economic inequality gap, suburbanization, and the media's blurring of the lines between entertainment and news. These arguments were consistent with the work of media theorist George Gerbner (1970) who asserted that the perceptions cultivated by television have consequences not only for people's personal and social relationships but also for social policy and social control. Furthermore, media coverage of crime expanded during this time period as a result of 24-hr news, cable programming with a crime focus, and the popularity of police-reality programming and crime dramas (Roman & Chaflin, 2008; Surrette, 2010).

Similarly, Altheide (2009) contends that fear is the driving emotion behind shifts in crime control and government intervention efforts. Research that looks directly at the political effects of the public's fear in response to crime "waves" indicates that such fears can promote political shifts (Doyle, 2006). "The media suggests that the 'problem' can be changed, that mechanisms exist to change it, and that we (as a society) already have an agent and process in place to fix the problem, usually the government" (Kort-Butler & Hartshorn, 2011, p. 40). Kort-Butler and Hartshorn (2011) argue that the more individuals consume media, the less supportive they are of the criminal justice system's ability to deal with crime, which translates to them being more supportive of punitive measures, like longer sentences and increased use of capital punishment.

Sotirovic (2001) suggests that the mass media may affect criminal justice policy preferences with both the structure and presentation of its content. Specifically, she finds that the use of complex media content (content that provides a variety of different perspectives on an issue) is related to more complex thinking about crime, and thus a preference for preventive criminal justice policies (Sotirovic, 2001). In line with this argument, Baumgartner, DeBoef, and Boydstury (2008), in the book *The Decline of the Death Penalty and the Discovery of Innocence*, suggest that the news media's recent focus on innocence cases has led to reduced support of the death penalty on the grounds of fairness. On the other hand, exposure and attention to the simple, infotainment formats of various reality-based pseudo news, talk, and crime drama shows is related to lower levels of complex thinking, and therefore a preference for punitive criminal justice policies (Sotirovic, 2001).

Sotirovic's findings are echoed in the research conducted by Demker, Towns, Duus-Otterstrom, and Sebring (2008) in Sweden. Demker et al. found a correlation between tabloid consumption and punitiveness, in which regular tabloid readers were more clearly in favor of introducing the death penalty in Sweden than nontabloid readers or those who seldom read tabloids. This was particularly true among males (Demker et al., 2008). Holbert, Shah, and Kwak (2004) studied three genres of crime-related television viewing, including police-reality shows, television news, and crime dramas, and found that all three types of television viewing correlate to sentiments in favor of capital punishment. Furthermore, Holbert et al. found that viewing police reality and crime dramas has a significant direct correlation with attitudes on capital punishment, whereas viewing television news is negatively related to the endorsement of capital punishment. Oliver and Armstrong (1995) find that regular viewing of reality-based crime programs and increased enjoyment of these programs is correlated with punitive attitudes, but contrary to Holbert et al. viewing fictional crime shows is not.

In a study of media use by young adults, Brady (2007) found an association between hours spent viewing violent movies and television and favorable attitudes toward military preparedness and defense among young men. Brady also found that increased time spent viewing violent movies and television was associated with more favorable attitudes toward interpersonal violence and punitive criminal justice policies among women.

Kort-Butler and Hartshorn (2011) studied television news, network crime dramas, and police-reality shows, and integrated a fourth type of media known as nonfictional documentary-style programs. The nonfictional documentary-style programs included shows such as American Broadcasting Company's "Primetime," A&E's "The First 48," and Discovery's "The New Detectives." Their results support the notion that program type does matter. Viewing crime dramas predicted support for the death penalty, but other program types did not (Kort-Butler & Hartshorn, 2011). In contrast, Grabe and Drew (2007) found little evidence that any form of media was consistently related to perceptions and opinions about crime and justice.

It is also quite possible, as many media scholars have pointed out, that individuals with certain characteristics and attitudes will seek out media channels and genres that show individuals like themselves in a positive light and that reinforce their preexisting attitudes (Eschholz, Blackwell, Gertz, & Chiricos, 2002; Holbert et al., 2004; Oliver & Armstrong, 1995; Reith, 1999; Surrette, 2010). For example, in terms of television news viewing, Holbert et al. (2004) indicate that age, race, and religion are consistently significant predictors of television news viewing. Specifically, television news appeals to older persons, and those who consider themselves religious, but is least appealing to Caucasians as a source of public affairs information (Holbert et al., 2004). In reference to viewing police-reality programs, females, older persons, Caucasians, and the more educated are less likely to view this type of programming. Yet, frequency of hunting activity is predictive of this type of viewing. As for crime drama viewing, age and race were positively related, with Caucasians viewing this type of programming the least (Holbert et al., 2004).

Support for Capital Punishment and Support for Life Without Parole

Public support has an influence on the death penalty's use as a legitimate form of state-sanctioned punishment (Bohm & Vogel, 2004). In his concurring opinion in *Furman v. Georgia* (1972), Justice Thurgood Marshall—in what is known as the Marshall hypothesis—postulated that support for the death penalty is contingent upon the degree to which the public is informed about the realities surrounding the administration of capital punishment. Justice Marshall emphasized, "it is imperative for constitutional purposes to attempt to discern the probable opinion of an informed electorate" (p. 362, fn. 145). Justice Marshall assumed that with information, "the great mass of citizens would conclude . . . that the death penalty is immoral and therefore unconstitutional" (p. 363). This is consistent with Baumgartner et al.'s (2008) hypothesis that the recent reduction in support for the death penalty and changes in death penalty policy in the United States is in large part a result of the news media coverage of innocence cases.

However, Marshall stated that if retribution was the underlying basis for support for the death penalty, then information would have little to no effect. The research of Bohm, Clark, and Aveni (1991) supports Marshall's view that, to the degree that retribution is the basis for support of the death penalty, knowledge about how it is administered has little effect on public attitudes. This may be one reason why studies that include an alternative measure of support for capital punishment that include the option of life without parole (LWOP) find much lower levels of support for capital punishment (Bohm & Vogel, 2004; Bowers, Vandiver, & Dugan, 1994; Sandys & McGarrell, 1994; Vollum et al., 2004), but that a sizable group continues to support capital punishment.

The media may be one of the major sources of information about crime and the death penalty (Graber, 1980; Roman & Chaflin, 2008; Tonry, 1999), but the veracity of the content presented is likely not consistent across media forms/channels and genres, and much crime-related programming focuses on sensational crimes and espouses a get tough on crime message (Surrette, 2010), rather than providing information about the use of capital punishment. Several studies have supported the hypothesis that if the public had a better understanding of the realities of the death penalty and how the system operates, fewer people would support it as a form of punishment (Bohm, Clark, & Aveni, 1991; Bowers et al., 1994; Longmire, 1996; Sandys & McGarrell, 1994; Sarat & Vidmar, 1976), but the information discussed in these studies often comes from an academic class on the topic, rather than the media. Based on past research, simple media messages about crime would likely lend support for capital punishment, while more complex media messages might reduce support for capital punishment, especially when using a general measure of support for capital punishment.

Research also indicates that many of the previously reviewed relationships may be conditioned by demographic variables. Vollum, Longmire, and Buffington-Vollum (2004) found that males were less supportive of a moratorium and more staunch supporters of the death penalty than were females and that older respondents were more likely to be staunch supporters of the death penalty than younger respondents. The study also found distinct class-related differences, in which low-income households were less confident in the death penalty system than those in high-income households (Vollum et al., 2004). The same was true with level of education, where those with less than a high school education were significantly more likely to support a moratorium than those with greater levels of education (Vollum et al., 2004). Research by Bohm (1991) determined that "Whites, wealthier people, males, Republicans, and westerners have tended to support the death penalty more than Blacks, poorer people, females, Democrats, and Southerners" (p. 135).

Similar to previous research (Bohm et al., 1991), the findings of Unnever and Cullen (2007a) show a racial divide in support for the death penalty, regardless of the control variables introduced into the models. Vollum et al. (2004) found that Blacks reflected the lowest levels of confidence in access to counsel and appeals, in the equitable administration of the death penalty, and in safeguards against the execution of the innocent. Hispanics had slightly more confidence in criminal justice issues and innocence concerns, than in issues concerning class and race equity (Vollum et al., 2004). Conversely, Whites expressed the highest level of confidence in all aspects of capital punishment.

Mallicoat and Brown (2008) find that the rationale for death penalty support among Hispanic/Latino and Asian American populations differs compared to Blacks and Whites. In fact, in reference to the Marshall hypothesis, Mallicoat and Brown's research concludes that "a lack of knowledge appears to have the strongest significant effects on the mutability of opinion for Asian Americans" (pp. 274–275). Overall, it seems that while Whites, as a whole, are most supportive of the death penalty, support among other racial groups is significantly lower with Asians being more supportive than Hispanics/Latinos, and Blacks being the least supportive (Houston Chronicle Article, 2001; Urbina, 2003).

Perceptual Control Variables

Many criminologists have suggested that perceptual variables like attitudes toward the police (ATP), fear of crime, collective efficacy, economic insecurity, and justice concerns all help shape attitudes toward capital punishment and are important control variables in these models. Additionally, these variables may interact with media variables to influence attitudes toward capital punishment (Kort-Butler & Hartshorn, 2011). Dowler (2003) finds that a favorable view of policing and police effectiveness is, at least in part, the result of law enforcement's public relations strategy. Researchers suggest that the police and the news media have a codependent relationship; the media are dependent on the police as a regular source of information, while the police are dependent on the media to maintain a positive public image (Ericson, Baranek, & Chan, 1987). Holbert et al. (2004) find that the propolice sentiments, and support for police authority, that are generated from viewing police-reality programs are highly predictive of positive attitudes toward capital punishment.

One of the more interesting elements in the study of fear and crime is the fact that public fear of crime has not waned despite decreasing crime rates since the 1990s (Gallup, 2012; U.S. Department of Justice, 2012). Despite the downward trend in crime, the increased salience of crime has contributed to a number of diffuse anxieties in both the United States and the United Kingdom (Garland, 2001). According to Garland (2001), these diffuse anxieties, which include concerns regarding the state of the economy, big government, welfare, union-led inflation, and affirmative action, can translate into fear of crime and support for punitive policies.

Additionally, politicians chose to manage and downplay these social and economic problems by linking them to crime and, thus, putting the focus on crime control. According to Costelloe, Chiricos, and Gertz (2009), crime control policies were promoted as a way to manage the social and economic risks created by the undeserving poor. Holloway and Jefferson (1997) agree that social and economic uncertainties are expressed as fear of crime. Therefore, fear of crime may translate, on a societal level, into punitive policies, restrictions on civil liberties, concentration of criminal activities in vulnerable communities, and institutional racism (Clear, 2007; Garland, 2001; Simon, 2007).

Research by Costelloe et al. (2009) and Hogan, Chiricos, and Gertz (2005) found a relationship between fear of crime and punitive attitudes and that this relationship is most pronounced for Whites. Dowler (2003) finds that the variables of race, education, income, marital status, and fear of crime are related to punitive attitudes. Kort-Butler and Hartshorn's (2011) results indicate that fear mediates the relationship between viewing nonfictional documentary-style programs and a lack of support for the criminal justice system (Kort-Butler & Hartshorn, 2011). On the other hand, viewing crime dramas predicted support for the death penalty, but the relationship was not mediated by fear (Kort-Butler & Hartshorn, 2011). Finally, their research indicates that viewing television news was unrelated to either fear or attitudes (Kort-Butler & Hartshorn, 2011).

In reference to economic anxieties, Simon (2007) adds that the fear of downward mobility has lent itself to public support of politicians who claim that social and economic issues can be managed and alleviated with lengthier and more punitive criminal sentences. According to Lyons and Scheingold (2000), "the anxieties associated with unwelcome social, economic, and cultural transformations generate anger, and punishment becomes a vehicle for that anger" (p. 127). A study by Hogan et al. (2005) indicates that the influence of economic insecurity and blame on punitive attitudes depends on the sex and race of respondents, finding the strongest association for White males.

Costelloe et al. (2009) found that when economic insecurity is analyzed in terms of the expectation that one's financial circumstances will not improve, or will remain stagnant in the coming year, there is little consequence for punitiveness. However, support for punitive criminal measures is consistently elevated for those who anticipate that their financial circumstances will get worse in the coming year (Costelloe et al., 2009), and the results are strongest for lower income White males.

Collective efficacy has also been hypothesized to both increase and decrease punitive sentiments. On one hand, individuals who trust and regularly interact with their neighbors and community members may be more open to rehabilitative methods (Clear, Hamilton, & Cadora, 2003); on the other hand, defying this community trust by committing murder may be seen as the ultimate betrayal and capital punishment may serve a boundary maintenance function (Erikson, 1966). Greer and Jewkes's (2005) analysis of British media found an overarching message, particularly in the conservative press, that people commit crimes because *they* are not like the rest of *us*. In other words, one of the common characteristics found in media explanations of crime is that the media plays into fears of "otherness." In the United Kingdom, Greer and Jewkes found that the conservative press focused almost exclusively on an individual's "otherness," often ignoring other possible explanations, as the sole cause of their deviance.

Finally, some researchers have included measures of a just world (belief that the world is a just place) in models of capital punishment attitudes. These studies show that individuals who feel that the world is a fair place generally believe that offenders should get the punishment they deserve (Freeman, 2006; O'Quin & Vogler, 1989). On the other side, individuals who are concerned with the lack of fairness and justice in the world are less likely to support punitive policies (Rosenberger & Callanan, 2011).

Current Study

This study will specifically test three separate but related media hypotheses derived from the literature review, while including sociodemographic and perceptual controls in the model.

1. Media consumption is related to support for capital punishment. Gerbner's (1970) cultivation hypothesis would predict that all media content is positively related to support for capital punishment.

2. Some media forms and genres influence support for capital punishment while others do not. Sotirovic's (2001) distinction between simple and complex media content would predict only simple media would increase support for capital punishment.

3. A positive relationship between media and support for capital punishment is predicted for crime dramas and police-reality programs (simple media), but not for television news, newspaper, and talk radio (complex media), which could produce relationships in either direction (supportive or against capital punishment).

4. Media consumption effects should be stronger for general support for capital punishment than for support for capital punishment with the LWOP option. General support for capital punishment is more likely to be influenced by simple media messages. The support for the LWOP question involves

more cognitive processing and is therefore more likely not to be influenced by simple media messages. It is also possible that media consumers may receive complex and contradictory messages about the death penalty, which could either increase or decrease support for capital punishment with the LWOP option.

Method

The data for this study were collected during the winter of 2010. Four hundred and seventy-seven individuals completed the survey, with 409 of the respondents residing in the State of Washington. A convenience sample was utilized, where 25 student researchers in a research methods in criminal justice class provided the e-mail contacts for 50 individuals they considered acquaintances. The students and the professor collectively decided on this sampling strategy because of its low cost, the ability to reach a sample that was not primarily students, the ability to collect data in a short time frame, and it allowed for a large enough sample size to test theoretical hypotheses. The number 50 was selected for each student because upon review of their various contact lists (social media, work, clubs, etc.) most students had at least this many noncollege peer connections. The students attended a midsize state institution located in a rural area, but the majority of students were from suburban or urban settings. Individuals were contacted with an introductory e-mail describing the study, a second e-mail containing a link to the study in Survey Monkey, and a follow-up thank-you/reminder e-mail. The survey took approximately 10–12 minutes to complete. An altruistic appeal was made to respondents to help assist students in learning how to conduct research and to advance the state of knowledge about crime-related public perceptions, but no incentives were offered. The survey began with an information page and a check box for consent, which was required for an individual to proceed to the survey. The survey concluded with contact information for the primary investigator and the Institutional Review Board office if there were any questions or concerns regarding the survey. The response rate for the survey was 38%, which is comparable to the response rates for most Internet surveys (Sheehan, 2001).

Table 1 shows some basic demographics of the sample as compared to available census data for residents of Washington State. The sample overrepresents younger individuals, slightly overrepresents women, and slightly underrepresents Asians, Blacks, and Hispanics (although this may be a function of race and ethnicity being a combined measure in this study). Although these deviations from the population are not uncommon in surveys (Tuckel & O'Neill, 2002; Lavrakas, 1987), they were also somewhat expected given the type of sample used in this

Table 1 • Sample Demographics Compared to the Demographics of Washington State

Variable	Sample	Washington State
Sex	57.2% Female	50.1% Female
Race/ethnicity	81.3% White	80.5% White
	0.7% Black	3.4% Black
	3.6% Asian	6.5% Asian
	15.9% Other	9.6% Other
	2.0% Hispanic	9.5% Hispanic
Age	Median = 27, M = 33.1	Median = 37.1
Education	33.8% Bachelors	30.5% Bachelors
Income	Median US$15,000–US$30,000	Median US$29,927

study. The lack of a probability sample necessitates taking caution with generalizations to a larger population. Nonetheless, the data are useful and appropriate for exploratory theory testing (Piquero & Bouffard, 2007) especially given the size of the sample.

Dependent Variables

Measurement of the support for capital punishment has garnered much debate over the years. There are general measures of support for capital punishment (Bohm, 1991) and a variety of specific measures of support for capital punishment for specific crimes or when the alternative of LWOP is also presented in the question (Bohm & Vogel, 2004; Bowers et al., 1994; Sandys & McGarrell, 1994; Vollum et al., 2004). Two measures of support for capital punishment were used in this study. On a 5-point scale, where 1 equals *strongly agree* and 5 equals *strongly disagree*, how much do you agree with the following statements:

1. General Measure: I favor the death penalty for people convicted of murder (reverse coded to consistently reflect high numbers support the death penalty and low numbers oppose the death penalty).
2. LWOP Measure: If I knew a murderer would stay in prison for the rest of their lives, I would not support the death penalty.

The General Measure of support for capital punishment was reverse coded, so that support for (agreement with) the death penalty increased with the numerical value of the response. The LWOP Measure was stated in the negative ("I would not support the death penalty") so higher numerical values also indicate increased support for (agreement with) the death penalty. Because the literature shows that perceptions of the death penalty change quite dramatically based on the way the variable is measured (Bohm & Vogel, 2004; Bowers et al., 1994; Sandys & McGarrell, 1994; Vollum et al., 2004), a separate analysis will be run for each operationalization of the variable. It is also possible that the relationship between the media and alternative measures of the dependent variable may be different because assessments of general support for the death penalty and support for the death penalty when the LWOP option is available may activate different cognitive processes for respondents when selecting a response (Sotirovic, 2001). Table 2 shows the frequency distribution of each of these measures.

Sixty-three percent of the respondents support (*agree* or *strongly agree*) the use of capital punishment with someone convicted of murder, compared to 47% of respondents who support the use of capital punishment when there is a LWOP option. A difference of means test finds these two measurements are statistically significant at $p < .001$ level ($\bar{x} = 3.7$ for General Capital Punishment Support Measure and $\bar{x} = 3.2$ for LWOP Measure). Because binary logistic regression is utilized in the analysis, both of these variables were dummy coded with *strongly disagree, disagree*, and *neutral* being coded as "0" and *agree* and *strongly agree* being coded as "1" and representing support for the death penalty.

Table 2 • Frequency Distributions of Support for Capital Punishment Measures

	General Support (%)	Support With LWOP Option (%)
Strongly disagree	8.7	14.4
Disagree	11.0	21.7
Neutral	17.2	17.2
Agree	25.7	26.6
Strongly agree	37.4	20.1

NOTE: LWOP = life without parole.

Independent Variables

Media consumption. Historically, media research focused on general measures of total media consumption (Eschholz, Chiricos, & Gertz, 2003; Gerbner, 1970; Gerbner, Gross, Morgan, & Signorielli, 1980), but media and capital punishment or punitive attitude studies have focused on television consumption, specifying the genre of programs watched, or tabloid news consumption (Brady, 2007; Demker et al., 2008; Oliver & Armstrong, 1995; Reith, 1999; Sotirovic, 2001). Few studies have included measures of newspaper, talk radio, or Internet consumption in models predicting attitudes toward capital punishment. This study includes the variables Newspaper, Radio (talk radio and radio news), Internet, TV (crime-related television content including police-reality programs, crime dramas, local news, national news, and newsmagazine programs), and specific measures of television genre Police TV (police-reality programs), News TV (local news, national news, and news magazines), and Crime Dramas TV. The television variables were all measured by asking how much time an individual spends watching these types of programs in a given week. The responses available were divided into 30-min units. The newspaper, radio, and Internet variables were measured by asking how much time an individual spends consuming these types of media in a given day.

Control Variables

Demographic controls. Based on past research, numerous demographic controls were included in support for capital punishment models. Sex was dummy coded (*female* = 1, *males* = 0) and was predicted to have an inverse relationship with support for capital punishment (Longmire, 1996). Race was also dummy coded (1 = *White*, 0 = *other*). While one of the most consistent findings in the capital punishment literature is that African Americans hold lower support of capital punishment than Whites (Bohm et al., 1991; Unnever & Cullen, 2007b; Urbina, 2003; Vollum et al., 2004), the demographics of Washington State coupled with the nonprobability nature of the sample did not yield a subsample of African Americans large enough to make meaningful comparisons. Similarly, the subsamples of Hispanics, Asians, and other groups were also not large enough to compare each group. Interestingly, the largest non-White racial category in the sample self-identified as mixed race and or ethnicity. Therefore, we divided race into two categories, White and other, but do not predict a direction of the relationship given the composition of our sample.

Education was measured on a 6-item scale from less than high school to graduate or professional degree and was predicted to have an inverse relationship with support for capital punishment (Dowler, 2003). Two dummy-coded variables were used to measure political party preference: Republican (coded 1 = *Republican*, 0 = *other*) and Independent (coded 1 = *Independent*, 0 =*other*) were both predicted to be positively associated with support for capital punishment (Bohm, 1991; Cochran & Chamblin, 2006). For each of these dummy codes, Democratic political party preference was the reference category. Residence was dummy coded into two variables: Suburban area (1 = *suburb*, 0 = *other*) and Rural area (coded 1 = *rural*, 0 = *other*), with urban areas being the reference category. Residents in both suburban and rural areas were predicted to have higher support for capital punishment. Age, measured by asking the respondent the year they were born, and Income, measured on a 6-point scale from less than US$15,000 to over US$100,000, were also both included in the models, but a direction is not specified because results have produced mixed findings (Rosenberger & Callanan, 2011).

Perceptual controls. Five perceptual variables, which are theoretically important in models of support for capital punishment, were included. Collective efficacy was measured on a 5-point scale, from *strongly disagree* to *strongly agree*, how much do you agree with the following statements? I interact regularly with my neighbors. I trust my neighbors. I participate in community activities (such as crime watch, community meetings, religious activities, etc.). The people in my neighborhood do not share the same values (reverse coded).

Perception of police performance measures the strength of formal social control operating in a neighborhood. Additionally, support for the police is often a predictor of punitive attitudes (Holber et al., 2004). Attitudes toward police were measured using a scale from 1 (*not at all satisfied*) to 10 (*very satisfied*), how satisfied are you in your local police department's ability to do the following: prevent crime, work with people in the community to solve neighborhood problems, enforce the law, maintain public order, and treat all members of the community equally regardless of sex, race, or religion. Factor-weighted scores were used to create a 5-item ATP index.

Following Ferraro and LaGrange (1987) and Ferraro's (1995) model, respondents were asked: "using a scale of 1 (*not at all fearful*) to 10 (*extremely fearful*), how much do you fear being a victim of a mugging; a home break in while you are there; rape or sexual assault; attack with knife, gun or club; or murder." Factor-weighted scores were used to create a 5-item index. Fear was predicted to be positively correlated with support for capital punishment (Costelloe et al., 2009).

Economic insecurity is measured using a 3-item index combining the questions: How concerned are you with the following issues, with 1 indicating *not at all concerned* and 10 indicating *extremely concerned*: the chance of losing your job because of the current economic situation; the chance of advancing in your career because of the current economic situation; and the effect that the decline in the value of stock will have on your retirement?

Finally, three questions on the survey assessed whether respondents felt there were fundamental fairness issues with the way the death penalty is carried out in the United States. Concern over these justice issues (JUSTICE) was measured using 3 items: On a 5-point scale, where 1 equals *strongly agree* and 5 equals *strongly disagree*, how much do you agree with the following statements. The poor are more likely to receive the death penalty than the middle class or rich. Minorities are more likely to receive the death penalty than Whites. Scientific evidence, such as DNA tests, should be required before a jury sentences someone to the death penalty (reverse coded for consistency).

Analysis

In an effort to understand the possible ways that demographic and perceptual variables may be related to media consumption, separate independent sample *t*-tests were run to compare nonmedia consumers with media consumers of newspaper, radio, Internet, TV police-reality programs, TV news, and TV crime dramas. Men, Whites, older individuals, and Republicans were significantly more likely to read the newspaper. Those with high fear levels and high justice concern levels were less likely to read the newspaper. Whites, those with higher education levels, older individuals, and Republicans were more likely to listen to the news on the radio. There was only one significant difference between Internet users and nonusers, with women being significantly less likely to use the Internet. Men, Whites, those with less education, and Republicans were significantly more likely to watch police-reality programs. Whites, older individuals, and Republicans were more likely to watch television news programs. And finally, women and minorities were more likely to watch television crime dramas. Surprisingly, except for Newspaper readership, there were no significant differences between media consumers and nonconsumers on any of the perceptual measures in this study.

Findings

In Model 1, education, Republican party preference, Independent party preference, living in the suburbs, and justice concerns all show significant relationships with support for capital punishment in the predicted direction. As expected, men, Whites, older individuals, individuals living in rural areas, those most supportive of the police, those with high fear of violent crime and those who are economically insecure are more supportive of the death penalty, but these results were not statistically significant. Income and collective efficacy showed a positive relationship with support for the death penalty, but these relationships were insignificant. Model 2 tests the first hypothesis of this study: Media consumption is related to support for capital punishment. The lack of consistent media effects does not support Gerbner's cultivation hypothesis, but does provide some support for the second hypothesis in this study. Both radio and TV consumption increased support for capital punishment, but there was no relationship for newspaper and Internet consumption. This suggests that radio and television consumption have a relatively small, but significant effect on attitudes toward the death penalty. The more one listens to radio news and watches television the more likely one is to support the use of capital punishment.

The results of these models indicate that radio, police TV, news TV, and Crime Dramas TV all increase support for capital punishment, but newspaper and Internet do not. It appears that radio news and television content regardless of the genre contributes to acceptance of the death penalty as a just response to murder, but that other media forms do not significantly alter support for capital punishment.

The only control variables that were significant predictors of support for capital punishment with the LWOP option were sex and justice. Interesting, but insignificant statistically, non-Whites, those with higher income, those in urban areas rather than suburban areas, those with less support for the police, lower fear of violent crime, and less economic insecurity were more supportive of the death penalty with the LWOP option. No media variables are significantly related to support for capital punishment with the LWOP option.

Hypothesis 2 predicting some media forms and genre would be related to support for the death penalty, while others would not. Only news TV is positively and significantly related to support for capital punishment with the LWOP option. Police TV and crime dramas TV do not appear to influence this dependent variable. This finding was surprising, given our previous classification of television news as a more complex media form than CDRAMA and POLICE TV.

The third hypothesis that media consumption effects should be stronger for general support for capital punishment than for support for capital punishment with the LWOP option. General support for capital punishment is more likely to be influenced by simple media messages. The support for the LWOP question involves more cognitive processing and is therefore more likely not to be influenced by simple media messages. In general, the results support this hypothesis with one caveat. There are more and stronger media effects in the general support for the death penalty model, but the one media variable that was related to support for capital punishment with the option of LWOP was TV News, which we had categorized as a complex form of media coverage. No negative media relationships were observed in either model.

Of considerable interest was the fact that the support for the capital punishment with the option of LWOP model had considerably less explanatory power than the general support for the death penalty model. This is consistent with the findings of Bowers, Vandiver, and Dugan (1994), Sandys and McGarrell (1994), and Bohm and Vogel (2004). A number of variables that were significant in the general support model (such as education, Republican party preference, Independent party preference, living in the suburbs or a rural area, and attitudes toward police) dropped out of the LWOP model. Additionally, sex was one of the strongest predictors in the LWOP model but was not significant in the general support model. It appears that additional contextual information (options available for alternative, yet severe punishment) is important in terms of deciding support or opposition to the death penalty. This is particularly the case for women.

Discussion and Conclusion

The combined results of this study indicate that the media is a predictor of general support for capital punishment, and plays a limited, but still statistically significant, role in support for capital punishment with the LWOP option. With that being said, not all media content is the same, although when there are media effects they are consistently found in the positive direction.

Television and talk radio consumption predicted general support for capital punishment, while only television consumption predicted support for capital punishment with the LWOP option. When focusing on specific television genres, police-reality programs, news programs, and crime dramas all were associated with higher levels of general support for capital punishment, but only news programs were associated with higher levels of support for capital punishment with the LWOP option. These findings run counter to the argument offered by Baumgartner et al. (2008) that linked recent reductions in support for capital punishment with the media using the innocence issue to frame much recent coverage of the death penalty. This may be a result of the cross-sectional nature of the current study not allowing for the capture of changes over time, or there could be alternative variables (e.g., social media measures or sociodemographic variables) that explain these changes.

The findings of this study are consistent with past research in noting that attitudes toward capital punishment are complex, and vary depending on both how media consumption and support for capital punishment are measured (Paternoster, Brame, & Bacon, 2008). General support measures a global attitude that likely does not involve complex thinking to provide a response, whereas support with the LWOP option requires the respondent to think about capital punishment in a more nuanced way. Another way to think about this is the difference between supporting the death penalty in principle compared to supporting the death penalty in practice (del Carmen, Vollum, Cheeseman, Frantzen, & Miguel, 2005). The dramatic differences between significant control variables in these two models is also indicative of very different processes going on when deciding support for the death penalty in these two circumstances.

These findings further support the Marshall hypothesis that support for the death penalty is dependent upon the general public's knowledge, and the availability of information, regarding both the administration of the death penalty and available alternatives (Bohm et al., 1991; Bowers et al., 1994; Sandys & McGarrell, 1994; Sarat & Vidmar, 1976). In fact, Bowers et al. (1994) and Sandys and McGarrell (1994) found that the number of people who supported the death penalty decreased when they were presented with the option of LWOP. Overall, studies suggest that death penalty attitudes are highly value expressive (Bohm et al., 1991; Bowers et al., 1994; Sandys & McGarrell, 1994; Sarat & Vidmar, 1976; Vollum et al., 2004) and the wording of death penalty questions can change the magnitude of death penalty support dramatically.

While the findings do not completely support Sotirovic's (2001) hypothesis that simple media content, or content with a consistent message, is more likely to drive affective decision making, whereas complex media content is more likely to inform cognitive processes that involve weighing multiple perspectives to make a decision, there was some support. Although television crime news was historically seen as presenting balanced perspectives on issues (Tetlock, 1989), many now see television news as becoming more simplistic and mirroring infotainment programs that attempt to capture news audiences by presenting factual information about specific cases in very stylized ways (Gamson, 1994; Surrette, 2010).

Surrette (2010) finds that television programming overemphasizes crimes of violence and offers stereotypical portrayals of offenders. For example, on television, less common crimes of murder and robbery overshadow more common property crimes (Surrette, 2010). According to Surrette (2010), offenders are portrayed as psychopaths who prey on the weak, helpless, and vulnerable, or as shrewd, ruthless, and violent businessmen or professionals. Other scholars agree that the media often presents offenders as evil and the criminal justice system as an effective and moral authority (Eschholz et al., 2003). Similarly, crime dramas emphasize that while the world may be a complex and confusing place, punitiveness is the simple and straightforward answer (Lyons & Scheingold, 2000).

Newspapers and Internet consumption (depending on the specific choice of sources) would theoretically offer a more balanced perspective and allow consumers to sift through information and activate more cognitive thought processes about the issues. These patterns were consistent with the findings that viewing television news, crime dramas, and police-reality programs were all consistently related to general support for the death penalty, while newspaper and Internet consumption were not. The positive relationship between talk and news radio consumption and general support for the death penalty was somewhat unexpected, but a closer look at a report in Talkers.com (2012) on The Top Talk Radio Audiences provides some clarification. Nine of the top 12 talk radio audiences were for conservative talk radio programs (i.e., Rush Limbaugh and Glenn Beck), which tend to present arguments supportive of punitive policies, including the death penalty. It should also be noted that news programs on public radio (not ranked on the Talk Radio list) are also quite popular and most likely offer more diverse perspectives on capital punishment. Future research should make sure to differentiate between the different types of talk/news radio that the respondent is consuming. Additionally, more content analysis studies of popular media content that focus on coverage of the death penalty are needed to assess current media messages about the death penalty.

The lack of media effects for the LWOP model, with the exception of TV news, was also generally consistent with Sotirovic's (2001) argument that media content would be less important for complex decision making. Similarly, the lack of effects for newspaper, radio, and Internet (arguably more complex media forms) may be a result of audiences weeding through various perspectives and arguments, combined with their own experience to reach a practice preference on using the death penalty when LWOP is an option.

Finally, we cannot ignore the fact that some of these results may be an artifact of individuals with specific characteristics selecting media content that is consistent with their own perspectives. In line with this possibility, Republicans were more likely to listen to talk radio, watch police-reality programs, and television news and they were also more supportive of the death penalty. Similarly, less educated individuals are more likely to watch police-reality programs and to support capital punishment. There were other media and demographic variable relationships that were not consistent with the patterns that were found in the support for capital punishment models. For example, those with a higher education are more likely to listen to talk radio, while education and support for capital punishment are negatively correlated.

There were several limitations to the current study. To begin, the convenience sample that was utilized does not allow for specific generalizations to be made to the general population. The sample also lacked enough minority group representations to make meaningful comparisons between African Americans, Asians, Hispanics, and Whites. The cross-sectional data did not allow for adequate tests of the time order between media consumption patterns, support for capital punishment, and a number of perceptual variables. Although the two measures of support for capital punishment are frequently used in the death penalty literature, they are single-item measures. Finally, several media and fear of crime studies have highlighted the importance of disaggregating samples by characteristics such as race, sex, and neighborhood characteristics to control for the possibility that the same media message may differentially impact audience members with different characteristics (Callanan & Rosenberger, 2011; Chiricos et al., 1997; Dowler, 2002; Eschholz et al., 2003). Unfortunately, the size of the current sample made multiple subdivisions of the sample impractical.

More work is needed on both theoretical models of media effects on capital punishment that include nonrecursive relationships and on developing longitudinal data sets that include media consumption and punitive attitude variables. Future research in this area should include measures of complexity of thinking about crime and attitudes toward capital punishment indexes, to help further clarify the relationship between media consumption patterns, and support for capital punishment. Additionally, future research should utilize a probability sampling technique so that generalizations to the general population can be made with greater confidence. It will also be important to separate measures of race from ethnicity, so that differences between and within these groups can be explored in greater detail.

References

Altheide, D. L. (2009). The Columbine shooting and the discourse of fear. *American Behavioral Scientist, 52*, 1354–1370.

Anderson, C. A., Berkowitz, L., Donnerstein, E., Huesmann, L. R., Johnson, J. D., Linz, D., . . . Wartella, E. (2003). The influence of media violence on youth. *Psychological Science Public Interest, 4*, 81–110.

Baumgartner, F., DeBoef, S., & Boydstun, A. (2008). *The decline of the death penalty and the discovery of innocence.* New York, NY: Cambridge University Press.

Bohm, R. (1991). *Death penalty in America: Current research.* Cincinnati, OH: Anderson.

Bohm, R. M., Clark, L. J., & Aveni, A. A. F. (1991). Knowledge and death penalty opinion: A test of the Marshall hypothesis. *Journal of Research in Crime and Delinquency, 28*, 360–387.

Bohm, R. M., & Vogel, B. L. (2004). More than ten years after: The long-term stability of informed death penalty opinions. *Journal of Criminal Justice, 32*, 307–327.

Bowers, W. J., Vandiver, M., & Dugan, P. H. (1994). A new look at public opinion on capital punishment: What citizens and legislators prefer. *American Journal of Criminal Law, 22*, 77–150.

Brady, S. (2007). Young adults' media use and attitudes toward interpersonal and institutional forms of aggression. *Aggressive Behavior, 33*, 519–525.

Callanan, V. J., & Rosenberger, J. S. (2011). Media and public perceptions of the police: Examining the impact of race and personal experience. *Policing and Society, 21*, 167–189.

Chiricos, T., Eschholz, S., & Gertz, M. (1997). Crime news and fear of crime: Toward an identification of audience effects. *Social Problems, 44*, 342–357.

Clear, T. R. (2007). *Imprisoning communities.* New York, NY: Oxford University Press.

Clear, T. R., Hamilton, J. R., & Cadora, E. (2003). *Community justice.* New York, NY: Routledge.

Cochran, J. K., & Chamlin, M. B. (2006). The enduring racial divide in death penalty support. *Journal of Criminal Justice, 34*, 85–99.

Cook, D. E., Kestenbaum, C., Honaker, L. M., & Anderson, E. R. (2000). *Joint statement on the impact of entertainment violence on children: Congressional Public Health Summit, July 26, 2000.* Retrieved from http:// www.aap.org/advocacy/releases/jstmtevc.htm

Costelloe, M. T., Chiricos, T., & Gertz, M. (2009). Punitive attitudes towards criminals: Exploring the relevance of crime salience and economic insecurity. *Punishment and Society, 11*, 25–49.

del Carmen, R. V., Vollum, S., Cheeseman, K., Frantzen, D., & San Miguel, C. (2005). *The death penalty*. New York, NY: Anderson Publishing.

Demker, M., Towns, A., Duus-Otterstrom, G., & Sebring, J. (2008). Fear and punishment in Sweden: Exploring penal attitudes. *Punishment & Society, 10*, 319–332.

Dowler, K. (2002). Media influence on citizen attitudes toward police effectiveness. *Policing and Society, 12*, 75–78.

Dowler, K. (2003). Media consumption and public attitudes toward crime and justice: The relationship between fear of crime, punitive attitudes, and perceived police effectiveness. *Journal of Criminal Justice and Popular Culture, 10*, 109–126.

Doyle, A. (2006). How not to think about crime in the media. *Canadian Journal of Criminology and Criminal Justice, 48*, 867–885.

Erikson, K. (1966). *Wayward puritans*. New York, NY: MacMillan.

Ericson, R., Baranek, P., & Chan, J. (1987). *Visualizing deviance*. Toronto, Canada: University of Toronto Press.

Eschholz, S., Blackwell, B. S., Gertz, M., & Chiricos, T. (2002). Race and attitudes toward the police: Assessing the effects of watching "reality" police programs. *Journal of Criminal Justice, 30*, 327–341.

Eschholz, S., Chiricos, T., & Gertz, M. (2003). Television and fear of crime: Program types, audience traits, and the mediating effect of perceived neighborhood composition. *Social Problems, 50*, 395–415.

Ferraro, K. F. (1995). *Fear of crime: Interpreting victimization risk*. Albany: State University of New York Press.

Ferraro, K. F., & LaGrange, R. (1987). The measurement of fear of crime. *Sociological Inquiry, 57*, 70–101.

Freeman, N. J. (2006). Socioeconomic status and belief in a just world: Sentencing of criminal defendants. *Journal of Applied Social Psychology, 36*, 2379–2394.

Gallup. (2012). *Crime*. Retrieved July 30, 2012, from http://www.gallup.com/poll/150464/americans-believe-crime-worsening.aspx

Gamson, J. (1994). Incredible news. *The American Prospect, 19*, 28–36.

Garland, D. (2001). *The culture of control: Crime and social order in contemporary society*. Chicago, IL: The University of Chicago Press.

Gerbner, G. (1970). Cultural indicators: The case of violence in television drama. *Annals of the American Academy of Political and Social Sciences, 388*, 69–81.

Gerbner, G., Gross, L., Eleey, M., Jackson-Beeck, M., Jeffries-Fox, S., & Signorielli, N. (1977). TV violence profile no. 8: The highlights. *Journal of Communications, 2*, 171–180.

Gerbner, G., Gross, L., Morgan, M., & Signorielli, N. (1980). The mainstreaming of America: Violence profile no. 11. *Journal of Communications, 30*, 10–29.

Grabe, M. E., & Drew, D. G. (2007). Crime cultivation: Comparisons across media genres and channels. *Journal of Broadcasting and Electronic Media, 51*, 147–171.

Graber, D. A. (1980). *Crime news and the public*. New York, NY: Praeger.

Greer, C., & Jewkes, Y. (2005). Extremes of otherness: Media images of social exclusion. *Social Justice, 32*, 20–31.

Hogan, M., Chiricos, T., & Gertz, M. (2005). Economic insecurity, blame, and punitive attitudes. *Justice Quarterly, 22*, 393–412.

Holbert, L., Shah, D. V., & Kwak, N. (2004). Fear, authority, and justice: Crime-related TV viewing and endorsements of capital punishment and gun ownership. *Journalism & Mass Communication Quarterly, 81*, 343–363.

Holloway, W., & Jefferson, T. (1997). The risk society in an age of anxiety: Situating fear of crime. *British Journal of Sociology, 48*, 255–266.

Houston Chronicle. (2001, February 5). Support for the death penalty under various circumstances. Retrieved July 30, 2012, from http://www.chron.com/content/chronicle/special/01/penalty/racialdiff.pdf

Johnston, L., & Sabin, K. (2010). Sampling hard-to-reach populations with respondent driven sampling. *Methodological Innovations Online, 5*, 38–48.

Kort-Butler, L. A., & Hartshorn, K. J. S. (2011). Watching the detectives: Crime programming, fear of crime, and attitudes about the criminal justice system. *The Sociological Quarterly, 52*, 36–55.

Lavrakas, P. (1987). *Telephone survey methods: Sampling, selection and supervision*. Newbury Park, CA: Sage.

Longmire, D. R. (1996). American's attitudes about the ultimate weapon: Capital punishment. In T. J. Flanagan & D. R. Longmire (Eds.), *Americans view crime and justice: A national public opinion survey* (pp. 93–108). Thousand Oaks, CA: Sage.

Lyons, W., & Scheingold, S. (2000). The politics of crime and punishment. In G. LaFree (Ed.), *The nature of crime: Continuity and change, criminal justice* (pp. 103–49). Washington, DC: U.S. Department of Justice.

Mallicoat, S. L., & Brown, G. C. (2008). The impact of race and ethnicity on student opinion of capital punishment. *Journal of Ethnicity in Criminal Justice, 6*, 255–280.

Oliver, M. B., & Armstrong, B. G. (1995). Predictors of viewing and enjoyment of reality-based and fictional crime shows. *Journalism and Mass Communication Quarterly, 72*, 559–570.

O'Quin, K., & Bogler, C. C. (1989). Effects of just world beliefs on perceptions of crime perpetrators and victims. *Social Justice Research, 15*, 85–98.

Paternoster, R., Brame, R., & Bacon, S. (2008). *The death penalty: America's experience with capital punishment*. New York, NY: Oxford University Press.

Piquero, A., & Bouffard, J. (2007). Something old, something new: A preliminary investigation of Hirschi's redefined self-control. *Justice Quarterly, 24*, 1–27.

Reith, M. (1999). Viewing of crime drama and authoritarian aggression: An investigation of the relationship between crime viewing, fear, and aggression. *Journal of Broadcasting & Electronic Media, 43,* 211–221.

Roman, J. K., & Chaflin, A. (2008). Has demand for crime increased? The prevalence of personal media devices and the robbery spike in 2005 and 2006. *American Criminal Law Review, 45,* 1149–1215.

Rosenberger, J. S., & Callanan, V. (2011). The influence of media on penal attitudes. *Criminal Justice Review, 36,* 435–455.

Sandys, M., & McGarrell, E. F. (1994). Attitudes toward capital punishment among Indiana legislators: Diminished support in light of alternative sentencing options. *Justice Quarterly, 11,* 651–677.

Sarat, A., & Vidmar, N. (1976). Public opinion, the death penalty, and the Eighth Amendment: Testing the Marshall hypothesis. *Wisconsin Law Review, 1,* 171–197.

Simon, J. (2007). *Governing through crime: How the war on crime transformed American democracy and created a culture of fear.* New York, NY: Oxford University Press.

Sheehan, K. B. (2001). E-mail response rates: A review. *Journal of Computer Mediated Communication,* 6. doi:10.1111/j.1083-6101.2001.tb00117x. Retrieved from http://onlinelibrary.wiley.com/doi/10.1111/j.1083-6101.2001.tb00117.x/full

Sotirovic, M. (2001). Affective and cognitive processes as mediators of media influence on crime-policy preferences. *Mass Communication & Society, 4,* 311–329.

Stinchcombe, A. L., Adams, R., Heimer, C. A., Scheppele, K. L., Smith, T. W., & Taylor, D. G. (1980). *Crime and punishment: Changing attitudes in America.* San Francisco, CA: Jossey-Bass.

Surrette, R. (2010). *Media, crime, and criminal justice: Images and realities* (4th ed.). New York, NY: Wadsworth Publishing.

Talkers.com. (2012). The top talk radio audiences. Retrieved from www.talkers.com

Tetlock, P. E. (1989). Structure and function in political belief systems. In A. R. Pratkanis, S. J. Brechler, & A.G. Greenwald (Eds.), *Attitude structure and function* (pp. 129–151). Hillsdale, NJ: Lawrence Erlbaum.

Tonry, M. (1999). Why are the U.S. incarceration rates so high? *Crime & Delinquency, 45,* 419–437.

Tuckel, P., & O'Neill, H. (2002). The vanishing respondent in telephone surveys. *Journal of Advertising Research, 42,* 26–48.

Unnever, J., & Cullen, F. (2007a). Reassessing the racial divide in support for capital punishment: The continuing significance of race. *Journal of Research in Crime and Delinquency, 44,* 124–158.

Unnever, J., & Cullen, F. (2007b). The racial divide in support for the death penalty: Does White racism matter? *Social Forces, 85,* 1281–1301.

Urbina, M. G. (2003). *Capital punishment and Latino offenders, racial and ethnic differences in death sentences.* New York, NY: LFB Scholarly Publishing.

U.S. Department of Justice. (2012). *Crime in the United States: 2011.* Federal Bureau of Investigation. Retrieved July 30, 2012, from http://www.fbi.gov/about-us/cjis/ucr/crime-in-the-u.s/2011/preliminary-annualucr-jan-dec-2011

Vollum, S., Longmire, D., & Buffington-Vollum, J. (2004). Confidence in the death penalty and support for its use: Exploring the value-expressive dimension of death penalty attitudes. *Justice Quarterly, 21,* 521–545.

Wiecko, F. (2010). Research note: Assessing the validity of college samples: Are students really that different? *Journal of Criminal Justice, 38,* 1186–1190.

REVIEW QUESTIONS

1. What type of punishment philosophy, when used as the primary basis for support for capital punishment, did Justice Marshall claim was most important?

2. In the current study, what specific demographic and perceptual control variables appear to have the most significant influence on public support for the death penalty?

3. Which types of media seem to have the most influence regarding support for capital punishment? To what extent do the findings of this study support the authors' four hypotheses?

SECTION III

Modern Applications of the Classical Perspective

Deterrence, Rational Choice, and Routine Activities or Lifestyle Theories of Crime

This section will discuss the early aggregate studies of deterrence in the late 1960s, then the perceptual studies of the 1970s, and finally the longitudinal and scenario studies of the 1980s and 1990s to the present. Other policy applications, such as increased penalties for drunk driving, white-collar crime, and so on, will also be examined. This section will also discuss the development of rational choice theory in economics and its later application to crime. Finally, it will examine the use of routine activities theory or lifestyle theory as a framework for modern research and applications for reducing criminal activity.

In Section II, we discussed the early development of the Classical and Neoclassical Schools of criminological thought. This theoretical perspective has been the dominant framework used by judges and practitioners in the practice of administering justice and punishment even in current times, but beginning in the late 19th century, criminological researchers dismissed the classical and neoclassical frameworks. Rather, criminological research and theorizing began emphasizing factors other than free will and deterrence. Instead, an emphasis was placed on social, biological, or other factors that go beyond free will and deterrence theory. These theories will be discussed in later sections, but first we will examine the recent rebirth of classical and neoclassical theory and deterrence.

The Rebirth of Deterrence Theory and Contemporary Research

As just discussed in Section II, the Classical and Neoclassical School frameworks fell out of favor among scientists and philosophers in the late 19th century, largely due to the introduction of Charles Darwin's ideas about evolution and natural selection. However, virtually all Western criminal systems retained the classical and neoclassical frameworks for their model of justice, particularly the United States. Nevertheless, the ideology of Beccaria's work was largely dismissed by academics and theorists after the presentation of Darwin's theory of evolution in the 1860s. Therefore, the Classical and Neoclassical Schools fell out of favor in terms of criminological theorizing for about 100 years. However, in the 1960s, the Beccarian model of offending experienced a rebirth.

In the late 1960s, several studies using aggregate measures of crime and punishment were published that used a deterrence model for explaining why individuals engage in criminal behavior. These studies revealed a new interest in the deterrent aspects of criminal behavior and further supported the importance of certainty and severity of punishment in deterring individuals from committing crime, particularly homicide. In particular, evidence was presented that showed that increased risk or certainty of punishment was associated with less crime for most serious offenses. Plus, it is a fact that most offenders who are arrested once never get arrested again, which provides some basic support for deterrence.

Many of these studies used statistical formulas to measure the degree of certainty and severity of punishment in given jurisdictions. One measure used the ratio between crimes reported to police and number of arrests in a given jurisdiction. Another measure of certainty of punishment was the ratio of arrests to convictions, or findings of guilt, in criminal cases. Other measures were also employed. Most of the studies showed the same result: The higher the rate of arrest compared to reports of crime, or the higher the conviction rate compared to the arrest rate, the lower the crime rate in the jurisdiction. On the other hand, the scientific evidence for severity, which such studies generally indicated by the lengths of sentences for comparable crimes or similar measures, did not show much impact on crime.

Additional aggregate studies examined the prevalence and influence of capital punishment on the crime rate in given states.[1] The evidence showed that the states with death penalty statutes also had higher murder rates than non-death-penalty states. Furthermore, the studies showed that murderers in death penalty states who were not executed actually served less time than murderers in non-death-penalty states. Thus, the evidence regarding increased sanctions, including capital punishment, was mixed. Still, a review of the early deterrence studies by the National Academy of Sciences concluded that, overall, there was more evidence for a deterrent effect than against it, although the finding was reported in a tone that lacked confidence, perhaps cautious of what future studies would show.[2]

It was not long before critics noted that studies incorporating aggregate (i.e., macro-level) statistics are not adequate indicators or valid measures of the deterrence theoretical framework, largely because the model emphasizes the perceptions of individuals. Using aggregate or group statistics is flawed because different regions may have higher or lower crime rates than others, thereby creating bias in the ratios for certainty or severity of punishment. Furthermore, the group measures produced by these studies provide virtually no information on the degree to which individuals in those regions perceive sanctions as being certain, severe, or swift. Therefore, the emphasis on the unit of analysis in deterrence research shifted from the aggregate level to a more micro, individual level.

The following phase of deterrence research focused on individual perceptions of certainty and severity of sanctions, primarily drawn at one point in time, known as **cross-sectional studies**. A number of cross-sectional studies of individual perceptions of deterrence showed that perceptions of the risk or certainty of punishment were strongly associated with intentions to commit future crimes, but individual perceptions of the severity of punishments were mixed. Furthermore, it readily became evident that it was not clear whether perceptions were causing changes in behavior or whether behavior was causing changes in perception. This led to the next wave of research—longitudinal studies of individual perceptions and deterrence—which measured behavior as well as perceptions of risk and severity over time.[3]

---

[1]Daniel Glaser and Max S. Zeigler, "Use of the Death Penalty v. Outrage at Murder," *Crime and Delinquency* 20 (1974): 333–38; Charles Tittle, Franklin E. Zimring, and Gordon J. Hawkins, *Deterrence: The Legal Threat in Crime Control* (Chicago: University of Chicago Press, 1973); Johannes Andenaes, *Punishment and Deterrence* (Ann Arbor: University of Michigan Press, 1974); Jack P. Gibbs, *Crime, Punishment and Deterrence* (New York: Elsevier, 1975).

[2]Alfred Blumstein, Jacqueline Cohen, and Daniel Nagin, eds., *Deterrence and Incapacitation: Estimating the Effects of Criminal Sanctions on Crime Rates* (Washington, DC: National Academy of Sciences, 1978).

[3]Raymond Paternoster et al., "Perceived Risk and Social Control: Do Sanctions Really Deter?," *Law and Society Review* 17 (1983): 457–80; Raymond Paternoster, "The Deterrent Effect of the Perceived Certainty and Severity of Punishment: A Review of the Evidence and Issues," *Justice Quarterly* 4 (1987): 173–217; Charles F. Manski and John V. Pepper, "Deterrence and the Death Penalty: Partial Identification Analysis Using Repeated Cross Sections," *Journal of Quantitative Criminology* 29 (2013): 123–44.

One of the primary concepts revealed by longitudinal research was that behavior was influencing perceptions of the risk and severity of punishment more than perceptions were influencing behavior. This was referred to as the **experiential effect**, which is appropriately named because people's previous experience highly influences their expectations regarding their chances of being caught and suffering the resulting penalties.

A common example is that of people who drive under the influence of alcohol (or other substances). Studies show that if you ask people who have never driven drunk how likely they would be to get caught if they drove home drunk, most predict an unrealistically high chance of getting caught. However, if you ask people who have been arrested for driving drunk—even those who have been arrested several times for this offense—they typically predict that the chance is very low. The reason for this is that these chronic drunk drivers have typically been driving under the influence for many years, mostly without being caught. It is estimated that more than 1 million miles are driven collectively by drunk drivers before one person is arrested.[4] If anything, this is likely a conservative estimate. Thus, people who drive drunk—some of whom do so every day—are not likely to be deterred even when they are arrested more than once because they have done so for years. In fact, perhaps the most notable experts on the deterrence of drunk drivers, H. L. Ross and his colleagues, have concluded that drunk drivers who "perceive a severe punishment if caught, but a near-zero chance of being caught, are being rational in ignoring the threat."[5] Thus, even the most respected scholars in this area admit that sanctions against drunk driving are nowhere near certain enough, even if they are growing in severity.

Another common example is seen with white-collar criminals. Some researchers have theorized that being caught by authorities for violating government rules enforced by the U.S. Securities and Exchange Commission (SEC) will make these organizations less likely to commit future offenses.[6] However, business organizations have been in violation of established practices for years by the time they get caught, so it is likely that they will continue to ignore the rules in the future more than organizations that have never violated the rules. Thus, the certainty of punishment for white-collar violations is so low—and many would argue that the severity is also quite low—that it is quite rational for businesses and business professionals to take the risk of engaging in white-collar crime.

It is interesting to note that white-collar criminals and drunk drivers are two types of offenders who are considered more likely to be deterred because they are mostly of the middle- to upper-level socioeconomic class. The extant research on deterrence has shown that individuals who have something to lose are the most likely to be deterred by sanctions. This makes sense: Those who are unemployed or poor or both do not have much to lose, and for them, as well as for some minorities, incarceration may not present a significant departure from the deprived lives that they lead.

The fact that official sanctions have limitations in deterring individuals from drunk driving and white-collar crime is not a good indication of the effectiveness of deterrence-based policies. Their usefulness becomes even more questionable when other populations are considered, particularly the offenders in most predatory street crimes (robbery, burglary, etc.), in which offenders typically have nothing to lose because they come from poverty-stricken

---

[4]Benjamin Hansen, "Punishment and Deterrence: Evidence from Drunk Driving" (paper presented at the 7th Annual Conference on Empirical Legal Studies, Stanford University, Stanford, CA, April 2013); H. Laurence Ross, *Deterring the Drunk Driver: Legal Policy and Social Control* (Lexington, KY: Lexington Books, 1982); H. Laurence Ross, *Confronting Drunk Driving: Social Policy for Saving Lives* (New Haven, CT: Yale University Press, 1992); H. Laurence Ross, "Sobriety Checkpoints, American Style," *Journal of Criminal Justice* 22 (1994): 437–44; H. Laurence Ross, Richard McCleary, and Gary LaFree, "Can Mandatory Jail Laws Deter Drunk Driving? The Arizona Case," *Journal of Criminal Law and Criminology* 81 (1990): 156–70.

[5]Ross, "Sobriety Checkpoints," 164.

[6]See the review in Sally Simpson and Christopher S. Koper, "Deterring Corporate Crime," *Criminology* 30 (1992): 347–76.

areas and are often unemployed. One recent study showed that being arrested had little effect on perceptions of the certainty of punishment; offending actually corresponded with decreases in such perceptions.[7]

Some people don't see incarceration as that much of a step down in life, given the three meals a day, shelter, and relative stability provided by such punishment. This fact epitomizes one of the most notable paradoxes we have in criminology: The individuals we most want to deter are the least likely to be deterred, primarily because they have nothing to fear. In early Enlightenment thought, Thomas Hobbes asserted that, although fear was the tool used to enforce the social contract, people who weren't afraid of punishment could not effectively be deterred. That remains true in modern days.

Along the same lines, studies have consistently shown that for young male offenders—at higher risk, with low emotional or moral inhibitions, low self-control, and high impulsivity—official deterrence is highly ineffective in preventing crimes with immediate payoffs.[8] Thus, many factors go into the extent to which official sanctions can deter. As we have seen, even among those offenders who are in theory the most deterrable, official sanctions have little impact because their experience of not being caught weakens the value of deterrence.

The identification and understanding of the experiential effect had a profound influence on the interpretation of evidence regarding the impact of deterrence. Researchers saw that, to account for such an experiential effect, any estimation of the influence of perceived certainty or severity of punishment must control for previous experiences of engaging in unlawful behavior. The identification of the experiential effect was the primary contribution of the longitudinal studies of deterrence, but such studies faced even further criticism.

Longitudinal studies of deterrence provided a significant improvement over the cross-sectional studies that preceded this advanced methodology. However, such longitudinal studies typically involved designs in which measures of perceptions of certainty and severity of punishment were collected at points in time that were separated by up to a year, including long stretches between when the crime was committed and when the offenders were asked about their perceptions of punishment. Psychological studies have clearly established that perceptions of the likelihood and severity of sanctions vary significantly from day to day, not to mention month to month and year to year.[9] Therefore, in the late 1980s and early 1990s, a new wave of deterrence research evolved, which asked study participants to estimate their likelihood of committing a criminal act in a given situation as well as their immediate

---

[7]Greg Pogarsky, KiDeuk Kim, and Raymond Paternoster, "Perceptual Change in the National Youth Survey: Lessons for Deterrence Theory and Offender Decision-Making," *Justice Quarterly* 22 (2005): 1–29.

[8]For reviews, see Stephen Brown, Finn Esbensen, and Gilbert Geis, *Criminology*, 8th ed. (Cincinnati, OH: Anderson, 2012); Nancy Finley and Harold Grasmick, "Gender Roles and Social Control," *Sociological Spectrum* 5 (1985): 317–30; Harold Grasmick, Robert Bursik, and Karla Kinsey, "Shame and Embarrassment as Deterrents to Noncompliance with the Law: The Case of an Antilittering Campaign," *Environment and Behavior* 23 (1991): 233–51; Harold Grasmick, Brenda Sims Blackwell, and Robert Bursik, "Changes in the Sex Patterning of Perceived Threats of Sanctions," *Law and Society Review* 27 (1993): 679–705; Pamela Richards and Charles Tittle, "Gender and Perceived Chances of Arrest," *Social Forces* 59 (1981): 1182–99; George Loewenstein, Daniel Nagin, and Raymond Paternoster, "The Effect of Sexual Arousal on Expectations of Sexual Forcefulness," *Journal of Research in Crime and Delinquency* 34 (1997): 209–28; Toni Makkai and John Braithwaite, "The Dialects of Corporate Deterrence," *Journal of Research in Crime and Delinquency* 31 (1994): 347–73; Daniel Nagin and Raymond Paternoster, "Enduring Individual Differences and Rational Choice Theories of Crime," *Law and Society Review* 27 (1993): 467–96; Alex Piquero and Stephen Tibbetts, "Specifying the Direct and Indirect Effects of Low Self-Control and Situational Factors in Offenders' Decision Making: Toward a More Complete Model of Rational Offending," *Justice Quarterly* 13 (1996): 481–510; Raymond Paternoster and Sally Simpson, "Sanction Threats and Appeals to Morality: Testing a Rational Choice Model of Corporate Crime," *Law and Society Review* 30 (1996): 549–83; Daniel Nagin and Greg Pogarsky, "Integrating Celerity, Impulsivity, and Extralegal Sanction Threats into a Model of General Deterrence: Theory and Evidence," *Criminology* 39 (2001): 404–30; and Alex Piquero and Greg Pogarsky, "Beyond Stanford and Warr's Reconceptualization of Deterrence: Personal and Vicarious Experiences, Impulsivity, and Offending Behavior," *Journal of Research in Crime and Delinquency* 39 (2002): 153–86. For a recent review and a different explanation of these conclusions, see Greg Pogarsky, "Identifying 'Deterrable' Offenders: Implications for Research on Deterrence," *Justice Quarterly* 19 (2002): 431–52.

[9]Icek Ajzen and Martin Fishbein, *Understanding Attitudes and Predicting Social Behavior* (Englewood Cliffs, NJ: Prentice Hall, 1980); Martin Fishbein and Icek Ajzen, *Belief, Attitude, Intention, and Behavior* (Reading, MA: Addison-Wesley, 1975); Icek Ajzen and Martin Fishbein, "Attitude–Behavior Relations: A Theoretical Analysis and Review of Empirical Research," *Psychological Bulletin* 84 (1977): 888–918. For a recent review, see Pogarsky et al., "Perceptual Change."

perceptions of the certainty and severity of punishment in the same situation. This wave of research was known as **scenario (vignette) research.**[10]

Scenario research (i.e., vignette design) was created to deal with the limitations of previous methodological strategies for studying the effects of deterrence on criminal offending—specifically, the criticism that individuals' perceptions of the certainty and severity of punishment change drastically from time to time and across different situations. The scenario method dealt with this criticism directly by providing a specific, realistic (albeit hypothetical) situation in which a person engages in a criminal act. Participants in the study are then asked to estimate the chance that they would engage in such activity in the given circumstances and to respond to questions regarding their perceptions of the risk of getting caught (i.e., certainty of punishment) and the degree of severity of punishment they expect.

Another important and valuable aspect of scenario research was that it promoted contemporaneous (i.e., instantaneous) responses about perceptions of risk and the severity of perceived sanctions. In comparison, previous studies (e.g., aggregate, cross-sectional, longitudinal) had always relied on either group or individual measures of perceptions over long periods of time. While some argue that intentions to commit a crime given a hypothetical situation are not accurate measures of what people would do in reality, studies have shown an extremely high correlation between what people report doing in a given scenario and what they would do in real life.[11] A recent review of criticisms of this research method showed that one weakness was that it did not allow respondents to offer their own perceptions of the risk and costs associated with each offense.[12] Despite such criticisms, the scenario method appears to be the most accurate that we have to date to estimate the effects of individuals' perceptions on the likelihood of their engaging in given criminal activity at a given point in time. This is something that the previous waves of deterrence research—aggregate, cross-sectional, and longitudinal studies—could not estimate.

Ultimately, the studies using the scenario method showed that participants were more affected by perceptions of certainty and less so, albeit sometimes significantly, by perceptions of severity. These findings supported previous methods of estimating the effects of *formal* or *official deterrence*, meaning the deterrent effects of three general groups: law enforcement, courts, and corrections (i.e., prisons and probation or parole). Thus, the overall conclusion regarding the effects of official sanctions on individual decision making remained unaltered. However, one of the more interesting aspects of the scenario research method is that it helped solidify the importance of extralegal variables in deterring criminal behavior, variables that had been neglected by previous methods.

---

[10]Loewenstein et al., "The Effect of Sexual Arousal"; Nagin and Paternoster, "Enduring Individual Differences"; Piquero and Tibbetts, "Specifying the Direct"; Paternoster and Simpson, "Sanction Threats"; Stephen G. Tibbetts, "Traits and States of Self-Conscious Emotions in Criminal Decision Making," in *Affect and Cognition in Criminal Decision Making*, ed. Jean-Louis Van Gelder, Henk Elffers, Danielle Reynald, and Daniel Nagin (London: Routledge, 2014), 221–38; Ronet Bachman, Raymond Paternoster, and Sally Ward, "The Rationality of Sexual Offending: Testing a Deterrence/Rational Choice Conception of Sexual Assault," *Law and Society Review* 26 (1992): 343–72; Harold Grasmick and Robert Bursik, "Conscience, Significant Others, and Rational Choice: Extending the Deterrence Model," *Law and Society Review* 24 (1990): 837–61; Harold Grasmick and Donald E. Green, "Legal Punishment, Social Disapproval, and Internalization as Inhibitors of Illegal Behavior," *Journal of Criminal Law and Criminology* 71 (1980): 325–35; Stephen Klepper and Daniel Nagin, "The Deterrent Effects of Perceived Certainty and Severity of Punishment Revisited, *Criminology* 27 (1989): 721–46; Stephen Tibbetts and Denise Herz, "Gender Differences in Students' Rational Decisions to Cheat," *Deviant Behavior* 18 (1996): 393–414; Stephen Tibbetts and David Myers, "Low Self-Control, Rational Choice, and Student Test Cheating," *American Journal of Criminal Justice* 23 (1999): 179–200; Stephen Tibbetts, "Shame and Rational Choice in Offending Decisions," *Criminal Justice and Behavior* 24 (1997): 234–55.

[11]Ajzen and Fishbein, *Understanding Attitudes*; Donald Green, "Measures of Illegal Behavior in Individual Behavior in Individual-Level Deterrence Research," *Journal of Research in Crime and Delinquency* 26 (1989): 253–75; Icek Ajzen, "From Intentions to Actions: A Theory of Planned Behavior," in *Action-Control: From Cognition to Behavior*, ed. Julius Kuhl and Jurgen Beckmann (New York: Springer, 1985), 11–39; Icek Ajzen and Martin Fishbein, "The Prediction of Behavioral Intentions in a Choice Situation," *Journal of Experimental Psychology* 5 (1969): 400–416.

[12]Jeffrey A. Bouffard, "Methodological and Theoretical Implications of Using Subject-Generated Consequences in Tests of Rational Choice Theory," *Justice Quarterly* 19 (2002): 747–71.

These extralegal or informal deterrence variables, which include any factors beyond the formal sanctions of police, courts, and corrections—such as employment, family, friends, or community—are typically known as informal or unofficial sanctions. The scenario research studies helped show that these informal sanctions provided most of the deterrent effect—if there was any. These findings coincided with the advent of a new model of deterrence, which became commonly known as *rational choice theory*.

Rational Choice Theory

Rational choice theory is a perspective that criminologists adapted from economists, who used it to explain a variety of individual decisions regarding a variety of behaviors. This framework emphasizes all the important factors that go into a person's decision to engage or not engage in a particular act. In terms of criminological research, the rational choice model emphasized both official or formal forms of deterrence and also the informal factors that influence individual decisions regarding criminal behavior. This represented a profound advance in the understanding of human behavior. After all, as studies showed, most individuals are more affected by informal factors than they are by official or formal factors.

Although there were several previous attempts to apply the rational choice model to the understanding of criminal activity, the most significant work, which brought rational choice theory into the mainstream of criminological research, was Derek Cornish and Ron Clarke's *The Reasoning Criminal: Rational Choice Perspectives on Offending* in 1986.[13] Furthermore, in 1988, Jack Katz published his work *Seductions of Crime*, which, for the first time, placed an emphasis on the benefits (mostly the inherent physiological pleasure) of committing crime.[14] Before Katz's publication, virtually no attention had been paid to the benefits of offending, let alone the fun that people feel when they engage in criminal behavior. A recent study showed that the publication of Cornish and Clarke's book, as well as the timing of other publications such as Katz's, led to an influx of criminological studies in the late 1980s to mid-1990s based on the rational choice model.[15]

These studies on rational choice showed that while official or formal sanctions tend to have some effect on individuals' decisions to commit crime, they almost always are relatively unimportant compared to extralegal or informal factors.[16] The effects of people's perceptions of how much shame or loss of self-esteem they would experience, even if no one else found out that they committed the crime, was one of the most important variables in determining whether or not they would do so.[17] Additional evidence indicated that females were more influenced by the effects of shame and moral beliefs in this regard than were males.[18] Recent studies have shown that differing

[13]Derek Cornish and Ron Clarke, *The Reasoning Criminal: Rational Choice Perspectives on Offending* (New York: Springer-Verlag, 1986).

[14]Jack Katz, *Seductions of Crime* (New York: Basic Books, 1988).

[15]Stephen Tibbetts and Chris Gibson, "Individual Propensities and Rational Decision-Making: Recent Findings and Promising Approaches," in *Rational Choice and Criminal Behavior*, ed. Alex Piquero and Stephen Tibbetts (New York: Routledge, 2002), 3–24. See recent review by Jean-Louis Van Gelder et al. (eds.), *Affect and Cognition in Criminal Decision Making* (London: Routledge, 2014).

[16]For a recent review, see Pamela Schram and Stephen Tibbetts, *Introduction to Criminology: Why Do They Do It?*, 2nd ed. (Thousand Oaks, CA: Sage, 2018), 96–100.

[17]Grasmick and Bursik, "Conscience"; Pogarsky, "Identifying 'Deterrable' Offenders"; Tibbetts, "Shame and Rational Choice"; Nagin and Paternoster, "Enduring Individual Differences"; Tibbetts and Herz, "Gender Differences"; Tibbetts and Myers, "Low Self-Control"; Harold Grasmick, Brenda Sims Blackwell, and Robert Bursik, "Changes over Time in Gender Differences in Perceived Risk of Sanctions," *Law and Society Review* 27 (1993): 679–705; Harold Grasmick, Robert Bursik, and Bruce Arneklev, "Reduction in Drunk Driving as a Response to Increased Threats of Shame, Embarrassment, and Legal Sanctions," *Criminology* 31 (1993): 41–67; Stephen Tibbetts, "Self-Conscious Emotions and Criminal Offending," *Psychological Reports* 93 (2004): 101–31.

[18]Tibbetts and Herz, "Gender Differences"; Grasmick et al., "Changes in the Sex Patterning"; Finley and Grasmick, "Gender Roles"; Pogarsky et al., "Perceptual Change"; Stephen Tibbetts, "Gender Differences in Students' Rational Decisions to Cheat," *Deviant Behavior* 18 (1997): 393–414.

▲ **Image 3.1** There are both formal and informal elements of deterrence that influence decisions of whether or not to commit criminal behavior.

SOURCE: © istockphoto.com / kali9; © istockphoto.com / JackF; © istockphoto.com / IPGGutenbergUKLtd; © istockphoto.com / shironosov; © istockphoto.com / f8grapher; © istockphoto.com / Rklfoto

levels of certain personality traits, especially self-control and empathy, are likely the reason why males and females differ so much in engaging in criminal activity.[19] Finally, the influence of peers has a profound impact on individual perceptions of the pros and cons of offending, because seeing friends get away with crimes significantly decreases the perceived risk of punishment.[20]

Another area of rational choice research dealt with the influence that an individual's behavior would have on those around her or him. A recent review and test of perceived social disapproval showed that this was one of the most important variables in decisions to commit crime.[21] In addition to self-sanctions, such as feelings of shame and embarrassment, the perception of how loved ones, friends, and employers would respond is perhaps the most important factor that goes into a person's decision to engage in criminal activity. These are the people we deal with every day, and some of them are the source of our livelihoods, so it should not be too surprising that our perceptions of how they will react strongly affect how we behave.

Perhaps the most important finding of rational choice research was that the expected benefits—in particular, the pleasure offenders would get from offending—had one of the most significant effects on their decisions to offend. Many other conclusions have been made regarding the influence of extralegal or informal factors on criminal offending, but the ultimate conclusion that can be made is that these informal deterrent variables typically hold more influence on individual decision making regarding deviant activity than the official or formal factors that were emphasized by traditional Classical School models of behavior.

---

[19]Nagin and Paternoster, "Enduring Individual Differences"; Grasmick et al., "Changes over Time"; Tibbetts, "Self-Conscious Emotions"; Tibbetts, "Traits and States."

[20]Pogarsky et al., "Perceptual Change."

[21]Pogarsky, "Identifying 'Deterrable' Offenders."

The rational choice model of criminal offending became the modern framework of deterrence. Official authorities acknowledged the influence of extralegal or informal factors, as seen in modern efforts to incorporate the family, employment, and community in rehabilitation efforts. Such efforts are highly consistent with the current understanding of the Classical School and rational choice frameworks—namely, that individuals are more deterred by the perceived impact of their actions on informal aspects of their lives than they are by the formal punishments they might face if they carry out illegal acts.

Routine Activities Theory

Routine activities theory, or **lifestyle theory**, is another contemporary form of the Classical School framework in the sense that it assumes an offender who makes rational decisions. The general model of routine activities theory was originally presented by Lawrence Cohen and Marcus Felson in 1979.[22] This theoretical framework emphasized the presence of three factors that come together in time and place to create a high likelihood of crime and victimization. These three factors are motivated offender(s), suitable target(s), and lack of guardianship. Overall, the theory is appropriately named in the sense that it assumes that most crime occurs in the daily routine of people who happen to see—and then seize—tempting opportunities to commit crime. Studies tend to support this idea, as opposed to the idea that most offenders leave their home knowing they are going to commit a crime; the latter offenders are called hydraulic and are relatively rare compared to the opportunistic type.

▲ **Image 3.2** Marcus Felson (1947–), Rutgers University, author of routine activities theory.

SOURCE: Courtesy of Marcus Felson

Regarding the first factor noted as being important for increasing the likelihood of criminal activity—a motivated offender—routine activities theory does not provide much insight. Rather, the model simply assumes that some individuals tend to be motivated and leaves it at that. Fortunately, we have many other theories that can fill this notable absence. The strength of routine activities theory lies in its elaboration of the other two aspects of a crime-prone environment: suitable targets and lack of guardianship.

Suitable targets can include a variety of situations. For example, a very suitable target can be a vacant house in the suburbs, which the family has left for summer vacation. Data clearly show that burglaries more than double in the summer when many families are on vacation. Other forms of suitable targets range from an unlocked car to a female alone at a shopping mall carrying a lot of cash and credit cards or purchased goods. Other likely targets are bars or other places that serve alcohol. Offenders have traditionally targeted drunk persons because they are less likely to be able to defend themselves, as illustrated by a history of lawbreakers rolling drunks for their wallets that extends back to the early part of the 20th century. This is only a short list of the many types of suitable targets that are available to motivated offenders in everyday life.

The third and final aspect of the routine activities model for increased likelihood of criminal activity is the lack of guardianship. Guardianship is often thought of as a police officer or security guard, which is often the case. There are many other forms of guardianship, however, such as

[22]Lawrence Cohen and Marcus Felson, "Social Change and Crime Rates: A Routine Activities Approach," *American Sociological Review* 44 (1979): 214–41.

owning a dog to protect a house, which studies demonstrate can be quite effective. Just having a car or house alarm constitutes a form of guardianship. Furthermore, the presence of an adult, neighbor, or teacher can effectively guard an area against crime. In fact, recent studies show that increased lighting in the area can prevent a significant amount of crime, with one study showing a 20% reduction in overall crime in areas randomly chosen to receive improved lighting as compared to control areas that did not.[23] Regardless of the type of guardianship, it is the absence of adequate guardianship that sets the stage for crime; on the other hand, each step taken toward protecting a place or person is likely to deter offenders from choosing the target in relation to others. Locations that have a high convergence of motivated offenders, suitable targets, and lack of guardianship are typically referred to as *hot spots.*[24]

Case Study: The Green River Killer

Gary Leon Ridgway was convicted and sentenced in 2003 after many decades of acting as the Green River Killer; he had stabbed his first victim at age 16 in 1965. He confessed to killing 71 victims (although he was convicted of only 48), virtually all of them women. He appeared to live separate lives. In one aspect of his life in the Seattle area, he was the father of a son and husband to his third wife. The other side involved picking up women, mostly prostitutes and strippers, who were willing to engage in sexual activity with him in remote locations.

▲ **Image 3.3** Gary Leon Ridgway, who was a serial killer, confessed to murdering at least 71 victims.

SOURCE: King County Sheriff's Office, via Wikimedia Commons

He claimed that he would hide or bury the bodies of the victims he really "liked" because he knew he would want to go back and have sex with them later, which he did on occasion. He would also place various objects, such as a fish, bottle, or sausage, at the crime scene to throw off authorities, because these objects didn't match the modus operandi they were expecting to help link the crimes together. So he did appear to plan his crimes, at least in terms of manipulating the crime scenes (whether the primary scene, where the killing took place, or the secondary scene, where the body was dumped).

He also notably said, "I would choke them . . . and I was really good at it." But when asked by an investigator in an official interview where he ranked on a scale of evil from 1 to 5, he said he was a 3. So there appears to be a disconnect between the way he thinks and the way society at large thinks.

Ridgway was caught after DNA from crime scenes was matched to a saliva test he had taken years before, when authorities had suspected him but didn't have enough evidence to make an arrest. So he continued his killing spree for many years, until they finally obtained further evidence linking him to some of the murders. Ridgway

(Continued)

[23]David P. Farrington and Brandon C. Welsh, "Improved Street Lighting and Crime Prevention," *Justice Quarterly* 19 (2002): 313–43; Spiros Kitsinelisa and Georges Zissisa, "A Short Review on Lighting and Security," *Journal of Applied Security Research* 7 (2012): 341–353.

[24]For further discussion and more recent studies, see Schram and Tibbetts, "*Introduction to Criminology*," 100–105.

(Continued)

is now serving 480 years in prison for 48 life sentences, due to a bargain that got him out of the death penalty.

> ***. . . When asked by an investigator in an official interview where he ranked on a scale of evil from 1 to 5, he said he was a 3.***

But why did he do it? Obviously, he has some psychological issues. But he passed the psychological test to determine readiness to stand trial, so he was not ruled legally insane. Virtually all his victims easily fit within his lifestyle, as he traveled around in his truck and picked up women in essentially the same area where he worked and lived. He never went far out of his way. In fact, none of his victims seemed to come from outside the Seattle area. And he would almost always dump or bury the bodies within a relatively limited radius in that region—hence his label, "the Green River Killer."

In one notable instance, he claimed that his son was with him in the truck when he picked up a woman. He had his son stay in the truck while he took the woman a distance away and killed her. But we know that he tended to pick up and kill these women as part of his daily routine, which included working at a truck-painting factory. Thus, this case applies to the routine activities theory and lifestyles perspective covered in this section. Also keep in mind that even at the time when he was apprehended for these murders, he had a relatively stable marriage, which is not atypical for serial killers. They often lead separate lives, and both lives can seem fairly routine despite extreme contradictions.

1. What was the Green River Killer's typical method of operation (MO), or how he carried out most of his killings?
2. How is the Green River Killer's case a good example of routine activities theory?

SOURCE: Jeff Jensen and Jonathan Case, *Green River Killer: A True Detective Story* (Milwaukie, OR: Dark Horse Books, 2011).

Perhaps the most supportive evidence for routine activities theory and hot spots was the study of 911 calls for service in Minneapolis, Minnesota.[25] This study examined all serious calls (as well as total calls) to police for a 1-year period. Half of the top 10 places from which police were called were bars or locations where alcohol was served. As mentioned previously, establishments that serve alcohol are often targeted by motivated offenders because of their high proportion of suitable targets. Furthermore, a number of bars tend to have a low level of guardianship in relation to the number of people they serve. Readers of this book may well relate to this situation. Most college towns and cities have certain drinking establishments that are known as being hot spots for crime.

Still, the Minneapolis hot spot study showed other types of establishments that made the top 10 rankings. These included places such as bus depots, convenience stores, run-down motels and hotels, downtown malls, and strip malls. The common theme linking these locations and the bars was the convergence of the three aspects described by routine activities theory as being predictive of criminal activity. Specifically, these places attracted motivated offenders, largely because they have a lot of vulnerable targets and lack sufficient levels of security or guardianship.

---

[25]Lawrence Sherman, Patrick R. Gartin, and Michael Buerger, "Hot Spots of Predatory Crime: Routine Activities and the Criminology of Place," *Criminology* 27 (1989): 27–56.

Figure 3.1 • Routine activities theory

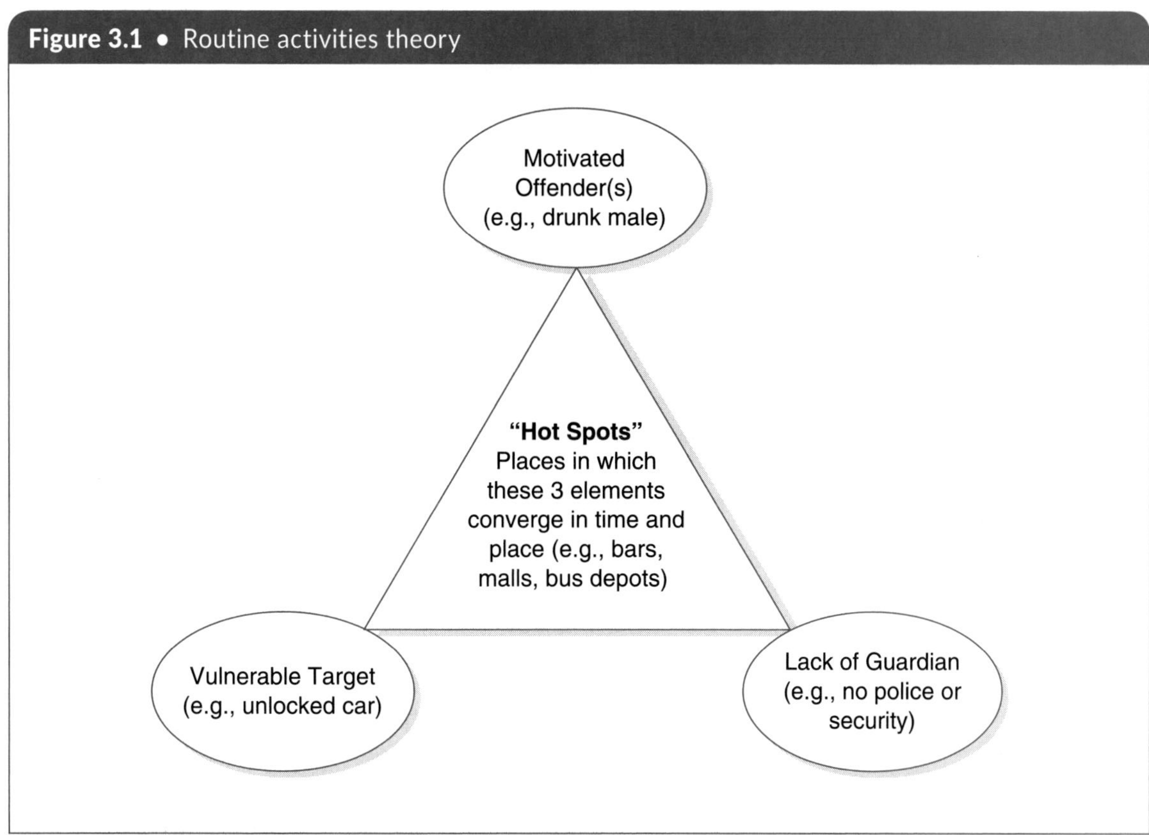

The routine activities framework has been applied in many contexts and places, many of them international.[26] Modern applications of routine activities theory include geographic profiling, which uses satellite positioning systems in perhaps the most attractive and marketable aspect of criminological research in contemporary times. Essentially, such research incorporates computer software for a Global Positioning System (GPS) to identify the exact location of every crime that takes place in a given jurisdiction. Such information has been used to solve or predict various crimes, to the point where serial killers have been caught by triangulating the sites where the victims were found to show the most likely place where the killer lived.

---

[26]Anthony A. Braga, Andrew V. Papachristos, and David M. Hureau, "The Effects of Hot Spots Policing on Crime: An Updated Systematic Review and Meta-Analysis," *Justice Quarterly* 29 (2012): 1–31; Jon Gunnar Bernburg and Thorolfur Thorlindsson, "Routine Activities in Social Context: A Closer Look at the Role of Opportunity in Deviant Behavior," *Justice Quarterly* 18 (2001): 543–67. See also Richard Bennett, "Routine Activity: A Cross-National Assessment of a Criminological Perspective," *Social Forces* 70 (1991): 147–63; James Hawdon, "Deviant Lifestyles: The Social Control of Routine Activities," *Youth and Society* 28 (1996): 162–88; James L. Massey, Marvin Krohn, and Lisa Bonati, "Property Crime and the Routine Activities of Individuals," *Journal of Research in Crime and Delinquency* 26 (1989): 378–400; Terrance Miethe, Mark Stafford, and J. Scott Long, "Social Differences in Criminological Victimization: A Test of Routine Activities/Lifestyles Theories," *American Sociological Review* 52 (1987): 184–94; Elizabeth Mustaine and Richard Tewksbury, "Predicting Risks of Larceny Theft Victimization: A Routine Activity Analysis Using Refined Lifestyle Measures," *Criminology* 36 (1998): 829–57; D. Wayne Osgood et al., "Routine Activities and Individual Deviant Behavior," *American Sociological Review* 61 (1996): 635–55; Dennis Roncek and Pamela Maier, "Bars, Blocks, and Crimes Revisited: Linking the Theory of Routine Activities to the Empiricism of Hot Spots," *Criminology* 29 (1991): 725–53; and Robert Sampson and John Wooldredge, "Linking the Micro- and Macro-Level Dimensions of Lifestyle-Routine Activity and Opportunity Models of Predatory Victimization," *Journal of Quantitative Criminology* 3 (1987): 371–93.

▲ **Image 3.4** Crimes tend to be concentrated in certain places and certain times and thus are not typically random events. The places that have a high concentration of crimes are referred to as hot spots.

SOURCE: © istockphoto.com / mrtom-uk

Some theorists have proposed a theoretical model based on individuals' lifestyles, which has a large overlap with routine activities theory, as shown in studies previously reviewed.[27] It only makes sense that a person who lives a more risky lifestyle, for example, by frequenting bars or living in a high-crime area, will be at more risk because she or he is close to various hot spots as identified by routine activities theory. Although some criminologists label this phenomenon a lifestyle perspective, it is virtually synonymous with the routine activities model because such lifestyles incorporate the same conceptual and causal factors in routine activities.

Policy Implications

There are numerous policy implications that can be derived from the theories and scientific findings in this section. Here, we will concentrate on some of the most important policies. First, we look at the policy of broken windows, which has many assumptions similar to those of the routine activities and rational choice theories. The broken windows perspective emphasizes the need for police to crack down on minor offenses to reduce major crimes.[28] Although many cities (e.g., New York and Los Angeles) have claimed reductions in serious crimes by using this theory, crime was reduced by the same amount across most U.S. cities during the same time (the late 1990s to mid-2000s).

Relatedly, regarding the effectiveness of targeting hot spots of crime—which is based primarily on routine activities theory—according to a 2017 article by David Weisburd, David Farrington, and Charlotte Gill, the most recent systematic reviews and meta-analyses studies have concluded that policing strategies that place focused emphasis on hot spots appear to be effective in reducing crime in those areas.[29] It is also notable that this same extensive recent review of the extant literature found little evidence for displacement of crime out of areas when they are targeted by focused policing efforts.[30] Thus, there appears to be strong support for police strategies in focusing on problematic hot spots in communities. Research by Cory Haberman in 2017 has promoted advancing the examination of spatial crime areas by examining the overlapping nature of hot spots of different crime types.[31]

---

[27]Hawdon, "Deviant Lifestyles"; Sampson and Wooldredge, "Linking the Micro"; Brown et al., *Criminology.*

[28]James Q. Wilson and George Kelling, "Broken Windows: The Police and Neighborhood Safety," *Atlantic Monthly* (March 1982): 29–38.

[29]David Weisburd, David P. Farrington, and Charlotte Gill, "What Works in Crime Prevention and Rehabilitation: An Assessment of Systematic Reviews," *Criminology & Public Policy* 16 (2017): 415–49.

[30]Ibid.

[31]Cory R. Haberman, "Overlapping Hot Spots? Examination of the Spatial Heterogeneity of Hot Spots of Different Crime Types," *Criminology & Public Policy* 16 (2017): 633–60.

Additionally, a study by Robert Apel and Julie Horney in 2017, based on a routine activities theoretical framework, examined the influence of employment and criminal behavior among a national sample of 717 males.[32] The findings of this study indicated that employment significantly reduced criminal behavior but only when individuals reported a strong level of commitment to their jobs. The authors concluded that for such individuals who had high levels of commitment to their job, their employment reduced the unstructured leisure time that would offer offenders the situational inducements or opportunities to commit crime. This certainly supports the routine activities theoretical framework; when individuals are not simply wandering about, but rather are at work, they are less likely to offend because they are not presented with attractive opportunities to commit street crimes.

Other policies derived from the theories in this section include the *three strikes, you're out* policy, which assumes that offenders will make a rational choice not to commit future offenses because they could go to prison for life if they commit three felonies; the negatives certainly outweigh the expected benefits for the third crime. Remember Beccaria's view that for deterrence to be extremely effective, punishment must be swift, certain, and severe. Where does the three-strikes policy fall in this equation? The bottom line is that it is much more severe than it is swift or certain. Given Beccaria's philosophy (see Section II), this policy will probably not work because it is not certain or swift. However, it is severe in the sense that a person can be sentenced to life if she or he commits three felony offenses over time.

A controversial three-strikes law was passed by voter initiative in California, and other states have adopted similar types of laws.[33] It sends third-time felons to prison for the rest of their lives regardless of the nature of that third felony. California first requires convictions for two *strikeable* felonies: crimes like murder, rape, aggravated assault, burglary, drug offenses, and so on. Then, any third felony can trigger a life sentence. The stories about people going to prison for the rest of their lives for stealing pieces of pizza or shoplifting DVDs, while rare, are quite true.

The question we are concerned with here is, does the three-strikes policy work? As a specific deterrent, the answer is clearly yes; offenders who are in prison for the rest of their lives cannot commit more crimes on the streets. In that regard, three-strikes works very well. Some people feel, however, that laws like three-strikes need to have a general deterrent effect to be considered successful, meaning that this law should deter everyone from engaging in multiple crimes. So is three-strikes a general deterrent? Unfortunately, there are no easy answers to this question because laws vary from state to state, the laws are used at different rates across the counties in a given state, and so forth.

There is at least some consensus in the literature, however. One study from California suggests that three-strikes has reduced crime,[34] but the remaining studies show that three-strikes either has had no effect on crime or has actually increased crime.[35] How could three-strikes increase crime? The authors attributed the increase in homicide following the enactment of three-strikes laws to the possibility that third-strikers have an incentive to kill victims and any witnesses in an effort to avoid apprehension. Although this argument is tentative, it may be true.[36]

---

[32]Robert Apel and Julie Horney, "How and Why Does Work Matter? Employment Conditions, Routine Activities, and Crime among Adult Male Offenders," *Criminology* 55 (2017): 307–43.

[33]David Shichor and Dale K. Sechrest, eds., *Three Strikes and You're Out: Vengeance as Social Policy* (Thousand Oaks, CA: Sage, 1996).

[34]Joanna M. Shepherd, "Fear of the First Strike: The Full Deterrent Effect of California's Two- and Three-Strikes Legislation," *Journal of Legal Studies* 31 (2002): 159–201.

[35]See Lisa Stolzenberg and Stewart J. D'Alessio, "Three Strikes and You're Out: The Impact of California's New Mandatory Sentencing Law on Serious Crime Rates," *Crime and Delinquency* 43 (1997): 457–69; Mike Males and Dan Macallair, "Striking Out: The Failure of California's 'Three-Strikes and You're Out' Law," *Stanford Law and Policy Review* 11 (1999): 65–72.

[36]Steven N. Durlauf and Daniel S. Nagin, "Imprisonment and Crime: Can Both Be Reduced?," *Criminology and Public Policy* 10 (2011): 13–54; Thomas B. Marvell and Carlisle E. Moody, "The Lethal Effects of Three-Strikes Laws," *Journal of Legal Studies* 30 (2001): 89–106. See also Tomislav Kovandzic, John J. Sloan III, and Lynne M. Vieraitis, "Unintended Consequences of Politically Popular Sentencing Policy: The Homicide-Promoting Effects of 'Three Strikes' in U.S. Cities (1980–1999)," *Criminology and Public Policy* 1 (2002): 399–424. For a review of empirical evaluations of three-strikes laws, see John Worrall, "The Effect of Three-Strikes Legislation on Serious Crime in California," *Journal of Criminal Justice* 32 (2004): 283–96.

This is just one of the many policy implications that can be derived from this section. We expect that readers of this book will come up with many more policy implications, but it is vital to examine the empirical literature to determine these policies' usefulness in reducing criminal activity. Other policy implications of the theories and findings described in this section will be discussed in the final section of this book.

In a strategy that is also strongly based on the rational choice model, a number of judges have started using shaming strategies to deter offenders from recidivating.[37] They have ordered everything from publicly posting pictures of men arrested for soliciting prostitutes to forcing offenders to walk down main streets of towns wearing signs that announce that they've committed crimes. These are just two examples of an increasing trend that emphasizes the informal or community factors required to deter crime. Unfortunately, to date, there have been virtually no empirical evaluations of the effectiveness of such shaming penalties, although studies of expected shame for doing an act consistently show a deterrent effect.[38]

Conclusion

This section reviewed the more recent forms of classical and deterrence theory, such as rational choice theory, which emphasizes the effects of informal sanctions (e.g., family, friends, employment) and the benefits and costs of offending, and a framework called routine activities theory, which explains why victimization tends to occur far more often in certain locations (i.e., hot spots) due to the convergence of three key elements in time and place—motivated offender(s), vulnerable target(s), and lack of guardianship—which create attractive opportunities for crime as individuals go about their everyday activities. The common element across all of these perspectives is the underlying assumption that individuals are rational beings who have free will and thus choose their behavior based on assessment of a given situation, such as by weighing possible risks versus potential payoffs. Although the studies examined in this section lend support to many of the assumptions and propositions of the classical framework, it is also clear that there is a lot more involved in explaining criminal human behavior than the individual decision making that goes on before a person engages in rule violation. After all, human beings, especially chronic offenders, are often not rational and often do things spontaneously without considering the potential risks beforehand. So, despite the use of the classical and neoclassical models in most systems of justice in the modern world, such theoretical models of criminal activity largely fell out of favor among experts in the mid-19th century, when an entirely new paradigm of human behavior became dominant. This new perspective became known as the Positive School, and we will discuss the origin and development of this paradigm in the following section.

/// SECTION SUMMARY

- After 100 years of neglect by criminologists, the classical and deterrence models experienced a rebirth in the late 1960s.
- The seminal studies in the late 1960s and early 1970s were largely based on aggregate and group rates of crime as well as group rates of certainty and severity of punishment, which showed that levels of actual punishment and especially certainty of punishment were associated with lower levels of crime.

---

[37] Alex Piquero and Stephen Tibbetts, eds., *Rational Choice and Criminal Behavior* (New York: Routledge, 2002).

[38] Tibbetts, "Gender Differences."

- A subsequent wave of deterrence research, cross-sectional surveys, which were collected at one time, supported previous findings that perceptions of certainty of punishment had a strong, inverse association with offending, whereas findings regarding severity were mixed.
- Longitudinal studies showed that much of the observed association between perceived levels of punishment and offending could be explained by the experiential effect, which is the phenomenon whereby behavior, rather than deterrence, affects perceptions (i.e., as opposed to perceptions affecting behavior).
- Scenario studies addressed the experiential effect by supplying a specific context—that is, through presenting a detailed vignette and then asking what subjects would do in that specific circumstance and what their perceptions of the event were.
- Rational choice theory emphasizes not only the formal and official aspects of criminal sanctions but also the informal or unofficial aspects, such as family and community.
- Whereas traditional classical deterrence theory ignored the benefits of offending, rational choice theory emphasizes them, such as the thrill offending produces, as well as the social benefits of committing crime.
- Routine activities theory provides a theoretical model that explains why certain places have far more crime than others and why some locations have hundreds of calls to police each year, whereas others have none.
- Lifestyle theories of crime reveal that the way people live may predispose them to both crime and victimization.
- Routine activities theory and the lifestyle perspective are becoming key in one of the most modern approaches to predicting and reducing crime and victimization. Specifically, GPS and other forms of geographical mapping of crime events have contributed to an elevated level of research and attention given to these theoretical models, due to their importance in specifically documenting where crime occurs and, in some cases, predicting where future crimes will occur.
- All of the theoretical models and studies reviewed in this section were based on classical and deterrence models, which assume that individuals consider the potential benefits and costs of punishment and then make their decisions about whether or not to engage in a criminal act.

KEY TERMS

cross-sectional studies 86

experiential effect 87

rational choice theory 90

routine activities theory (lifestyle theory) 92

scenario (vignette) research 89

DISCUSSION QUESTIONS

1. Do you think it was good that the deterrence model was reborn, or do you think it should have been left for dead? Explain why you feel this way.
2. Considering the aggregate level of research in deterrence studies, do you find such studies valid? Explain why or why not.
3. In comparing longitudinal studies to scenario (vignette) studies, which do you think offers the most valid method for examining individual perceptions regarding the costs and benefits of committing offenses? Explain why you feel this way.

4. Can you relate to the experiential effect? If you can't, do you know someone whose behavior seems to resemble that which results from this phenomenon? Make sure to articulate what the experiential effect is.
5. With rational choice theory in mind, consider whether you would rather be subject to formal sanctions if none of your family, friends, or employers found out that you had engaged in shoplifting, or face the informal sanctions but receive no formal punishment (other than being arrested) for such a crime. Explain your decision.
6. As a teenager, did you or family or friends get a rush out of doing things that were deviant or wrong? If so, did that feeling seem to outweigh any legal or informal consequences that might have deterred you or people you knew?
7. With routine activities theory in mind, consider which places, residences, or areas of your hometown fit the idea that certain places have more crime than others (i.e., are hot spots)? Explain how you, friends, or others (including police) in your community deal with such areas. Does it work?
8. Which of the three elements of routine activities theory do you feel is the most important to address in efforts to reduce crime in the hot spots?
9. What lifestyle characteristics lead to the highest offending or victimizing rates? List at least five factors that lead to such propensities.
10. Find at least one study that uses mapping and geographical (GPS) data, and report the conclusions of that study. Do the findings and conclusions fit the routine activities theoretical framework? Why or why not?
11. What types of policy strategies derived from rational choice and routine activities theories do you think would be most effective? Least effective?

WEB RESOURCES

Modern Testing of Deterrence

http://politics.oxfordre.com/view/10.1093/acrefore/9780190228637.001.0001/acrefore-9780190228637-e-313
https://marisluste.files.wordpress.com/2010/11/deterrence-theory.pdf

Rational Choice Theory

http://www.academia.edu/12541099/An_Evaluation_of_the_Rational_Choice_Theory_in_Criminology
http://www.answers.com/topic/rational-choice-theory-criminology

Routine Activities and Lifestyle Theory

http://www.popcenter.org/learning/pam/help/theory.cfm

READING /// 4

In this reading, Anthony Braga and David Weisburd present a review and analysis of various programs that emphasized reducing crime activity in the following areas: gang- or group-involved violence, repeat offenders, and the drug market. They carried out a systematic review to examine the evidence found from such strategies of focused deterrence, applying an advanced form of statistical analysis, called a meta-analysis, to combine the findings from numerous studies. Their findings contribute to our knowledge of the effectiveness of focused deterrence strategies for dealing with crime, especially in certain situations.

- What do the authors mean by "focused deterrence" strategies?
- What was the overall finding of this study regarding these strategies for reducing crime?
- What are some of the concerns or issues with some of the studies used in this meta-analysis?

The Effects of Focused Deterrence Strategies on Crime

A Systematic Review and Meta-Analysis of the Empirical Evidence

Anthony A. Braga and David L. Weisburd

Introduction

Deterrence theory posits that crimes can be prevented when the costs of committing the crime are perceived by the offender to outweigh the benefits (Gibbs 1975; Zimring and Hawkins 1973). Most discussions of the deterrence mechanism distinguish between "general" and "special" deterrence (Cook 1980). General deterrence is the idea that the general population is dissuaded from committing crime when it sees that punishment necessarily follows the commission of a crime. Special deterrence involves punishment administered to criminals with the intent to discourage them from committing crimes in the future. Much of the literature evaluating deterrence focuses on the effect of changing certainty, swiftness, and severity of punishment associated with certain acts on the

SOURCE: Anthony A. Braga and David L. Weisburd, "The Effects of Focused Deterrence Strategies on Crime: A Systematic Review and Meta-analysis of the Empirical Evidence," *Journal of Research in Crime and Delinquency* 49 (2012): 323–58.

prevalence of those crimes (see, e.g., Apel and Nagin 2011; Blumstein, Cohen, and Nagin 1978; Cook 1980; Nagin 1998; Paternoster 1987).

In recent years, scholars have begun to argue that police interventions provide an effective approach for gaining both special and general deterrence against crime. A series of experimental and quasi-experimental studies has shown that the police can be effective in preventing crime (Braga 2001, 2005; Skogan and Frydl 2004; Weisburd and Eck 2004) and that such crime prevention benefits are not offset by displacement of crime to areas near to police interventions (Braga 2001; Weisburd et al. 2006). Durlauf and Nagin have drawn from this literature to argue that "(i)ncreasing the visibility of the police by hiring more officers and by allocating existing officers in ways that heighten the perceived risk of apprehension consistently seem to have substantial marginal deterrent effects" (2011:14). Indeed, they conclude that crime prevention in the United States would be improved by "shifting resources from imprisonment to policing" (2011:9–10).

A recent innovation in policing that capitalizes on the growing evidence of the effectiveness of police deterrence strategies is the "focused deterrence" framework, often referred to as "pulling-levers policing" (Kennedy 1997, 2008). Pioneered in Boston as a problem-oriented policing project to halt serious gang violence during the 1990s (Kennedy, Piehl, and Braga 1996), the focused deterrence framework has been applied in many U.S. cities through federally sponsored violence prevention programs such as the Strategic Alternatives to Community Safety Initiative and Project Safe Neighborhoods (Dalton 2002). Focused deterrence strategies honor core deterrence ideas, such as increasing risks faced by offenders, while finding new and creative ways of deploying traditional and nontraditional law enforcement tools to do so, such as directly communicating incentives and disincentives to targeted offenders (Kennedy 1997, 2008). The basic principles of the focused deterrence approach have also been applied to overt drug market problems (Kennedy 2009) and repeat offending by substance-abusing probationers (Hawken and Kleiman 2009) with positive crime control gains reported.

The evaluation of the best-known focused deterrence strategy, Boston's Operation Ceasefire (Braga et al. 2001; Piehl et al. 2003), has been greeted with both a healthy dose of skepticism (Fagan 2002; Rosenfeld, Fornango, and Baumer 2005) and some support (Cook and Ludwig 2006; Morgan and Winship 2007). The National Academy of Sciences' recent report on firearms data and research concluded that the Ceasefire quasi-experimental evaluation was "compelling" in associating the intervention with a 63 percent reduction in youth homicide in Boston (Wellford, Pepper, and Petrie 2005:10); however, the report also stated that the lack of a randomized controlled trial left some doubt over how much of the decline was due to Ceasefire relative to other rival causal factors.

Method

Our examination of the effects of focused deterrence strategies on crime followed the systematic review protocols and conventions of the Campbell Collaboration. It is important to note here that, given limited space, this article focuses on our examination of the crime reduction benefits associated with focused deterrence strategies. We encourage readers interested in a broader range of program operation and evaluation issues to consult our Campbell review (Braga and Weisburd 2011).

Meta-analysis is a method of systematic reviewing and was designed to synthesize empirical relationships across studies, such as the effects of a specific crime prevention intervention on criminal offending behavior (Wilson 2001). Meta-analysis uses specialized statistical methods to analyze the relationships between findings and study features (Lipsey and Wilson 1993; Wilson 2001). The "effect size statistic" is the index used to represent the findings of each study in the overall meta-analysis of study findings and represents the strength and direction (positive or negative) of the relationship observed in a particular study (e.g., the size of the treatment effect found). The "mean effect size" represents the average effect of treatment on the outcome of interest across all eligible studies in a particular area and is estimated by calculating a mean that is weighted by the precision of the effect size for each individual study.

Criteria for Inclusion and Exclusion of Studies in the Review

To be eligible for this review, interventions had to be considered a focused deterrence strategy as described above. Only studies that used comparison group designs involving before and after measures were eligible for the main analyses of this review. The comparison group study had to be either a randomized controlled trial or a quasi-experimental evaluation with comparison groups (Campbell and Stanley 1966; Cook and Campbell 1979). The units of analysis could be areas, such as cities, neighborhoods, or police beats, or individuals. Eligible studies had to measure the effects of the focused deterrence intervention on officially recorded levels of crime at places or crime by individuals. Appropriate crime measures included crime incident reports, citizen emergency calls for service, and arrest data. Particular attention was paid to studies that measured crime displacement effects and diffusion of crime control benefit effects (Clarke and Weisburd 1994; Reppetto 1976). The review considered all forms of displacement and diffusion reported by the studies.

Search Strategies for Identification of Studies

Several strategies were used to perform an exhaustive search for literature fitting the eligibility criteria. First, a keyword search[1] was performed on 15 online abstract databases.[2] Second, we reviewed the bibliographies of past narrative and empirical reviews of literature that examined the effectiveness of focused deterrence programs (Kennedy 2008; Skogan and Frydl 2004; Wellford et al. 2005). Third, we performed forward searches for works that have cited seminal focused deterrence studies (Braga et al. 2001; Kennedy et al. 1996; McGarrell et al. 2006). Fourth, we searched bibliographies of narrative reviews of police crime prevention efforts (Braga 2008a; Sherman 2002; Weisburd and Eck 2004) and past completed Campbell systematic reviews of police crime prevention efforts (Braga 2007; Mazerolle, Soole, and Rombouts 2007; Weisburd et al. 2008). Fifth, we performed hand searches of leading journals in the field.[3] These searches were all completed between May 2010 and September 2010.

After finishing the above searches and reviewing the studies as described later, we e-mailed the list of studies meeting our eligibility criteria in September 2010 to leading criminology and criminal justice scholars knowledgeable in the area of focused deterrence strategies. These 90 scholars were defined as those who authored at least one study that appeared on our inclusion list, anyone involved with the National Academy of Sciences reviews of police research (Skogan and Frydl 2004) and firearms research (Wellford et al. 2005), and other leading scholars identified by the authors (available upon request). This helped us identify unpublished studies that did not appear in conventional databases or other reviews. Finally, we consulted with an information retrieval specialist at the outset of our review and at points along the way in order to ensure that we used appropriate search strategies to identify the studies meeting the criteria of this review.[4]

Statistical Procedures and Conventions

As a preliminary examination of the effects of focused deterrence strategies on crime, we used a vote counting procedure. In this rudimentary approach, each study metaphorically casts a vote for or against the effectiveness of treatment. In our closer examination of program effects, meta-analyses were used to determine the size, direction, and statistical significance of the overall impact of focused deterrence strategies on crime by weighting program effect sizes based on the variance of the effect size and the study sample size (Lipsey and Wilson 2001). We used the standardized mean difference effect size (also known as Cohen's *d*; see Cohen 1988; Rosenthal 1994) and employed the Effect Size Calculator, developed by David B. Wilson and available on the Campbell Collaboration's Web site, to calculate standardized mean difference effect sizes for reported outcomes in each study. We then used Biostat's Comprehensive Meta Analysis Version 2.2 to conduct the meta-analysis of effect sizes.

One problem in conducting meta-analyses in crime and justice is that investigators often do not prioritize outcomes examined. This is common in studies in the social sciences in which authors view good practice as demanding that all relevant outcomes be reported. However, the lack of prioritization of outcomes in a study raises the question of how to derive an overall effect of treatment. For example, the reporting of one significant result may reflect a type of "creaming" in which the authors focus on one significant finding and ignore the less positive results of other outcomes. But authors commonly view the presentation of multiple findings as a method for identifying the specific contexts in which the treatment is effective. When the number of such comparisons is small and therefore unlikely to affect the error rates for specific comparisons such an approach is often valid.

We analyze the studies using three approaches. The first is conservative in the sense that it combines all reported outcomes reported into an overall average effect size statistic. The second represents the largest effect reported in the studies and gives an upper bound to our findings. It is important to note that in some of the studies with more than one outcome reported, the largest outcome reflected what authors thought would be the most direct program effect. Finally, we present the smallest effect size for each study. This approach is the most conservative and likely underestimates the effect of focused deterrence on crime. We use it here primarily to provide a lower bound to our findings.

Findings

Search strategies in the systematic review process generate a large number of citations and abstracts for potentially relevant studies that must be closely screened to determine whether the studies meet the eligibility criteria (Farrington and Petrosino 2001). The screening process yields a much smaller pool of eligible studies for inclusion in the review. The four search strategies produced 2,473 distinct abstracts. The contents of these abstracts were reviewed for any suggestion of an evaluation of focused deterrence interventions. About 93 distinct abstracts were selected for closer review and the full-text reports, journal articles, and books for these abstracts were acquired and carefully assessed to determine whether the interventions involved focused deterrence strategies and whether the studies used randomized controlled trial designs or non-randomized quasi-experimental designs. Eleven eligible studies were identified and included in this review:

1. Operation Ceasefire in Boston, Massachusetts (Braga et al. 2001)
2. Indianapolis Violence Reduction Partnership in Indianapolis, Indiana (McGarrell et al. 2006)
3. Operation Peacekeeper in Stockton, California (Braga 2008b)
4. Project Safe Neighborhoods in Lowell, Massachusetts (Braga et al. 2008)
5. Cincinnati Initiative to Reduce Violence in Cincinnati, Ohio (Engel, Corsaro, and Skubak Tillyer 2010)
6. Operation Ceasefire in Newark, New Jersey (Boyle et al. 2010)
7. Operation Ceasefire in Los Angeles, California (Tita et al. 2004)
8. Project Safe Neighborhoods in Chicago, Illinois (Papachristos, Meares, and Fagan 2007)
9. Drug Market Intervention in Nashville, Tennessee (Corsaro and McGarrell 2009)
10. Drug Market Intervention in Rockford, Illinois (Corsaro, Brunson, and McGarrell Forthcoming)
11. Hawaii Opportunity with Probation Enforcement in Honolulu, Hawaii (Hawken and Kleiman 2009)

The 11 selected studies examined focused deterrence interventions that were implemented in small, medium, and large U.S. cities. Four of the eligible evaluations (Cincinnati, Honolulu, Nashville, and Newark) were not published at the time the review of abstracts was completed.[5] All 11 evaluations were released after 2000 and 8 were completed after 2007. Six studies evaluated the crime reduction effects of focused deterrence strategies on serious violence generated by street gangs or criminally active street groups (Boston, Cincinnati, Indianapolis, Los Angeles, Lowell, and Stockton). Two studies evaluated strategies focused on reducing crime driven by street-level drug markets (Nashville and Rockford), and three evaluated crime reduction strategies that were focused on individual repeat offenders (Chicago, Honolulu, and Newark).

Ten eligible studies used quasi-experimental designs to analyze the impact of focused deterrence strategies on crime. Seven evaluations used quasi-experimental designs with nonequivalent comparison groups (Boston, Cincinnati, Indianapolis, Lowell, Nashville, Rockford, and Stockton). The comparison units used in these evaluations were selected based on naturally occurring conditions, such as other cities or within-city areas that did not receive treatment, rather than through careful matching or randomization procedures to ensure comparability with treatment units. Two evaluations used quasi-experimental designs with near-equivalent comparison groups created through matching techniques (Chicago and Newark). The Los Angeles evaluation used a quasi-experimental design that included both nonequivalent and near-equivalent comparison groups; for the Los Angeles study, we included only the effects from the more rigorous matched comparison group analysis in our meta-analysis. Only one randomized controlled trial, the evaluation of the HOPE program in Honolulu, was identified.

Three studies examined possible immediate spatial crime displacement and diffusion of crime control benefits that may have been generated by the focused deterrence interventions (Los Angeles, Nashville, and Newark). The Los Angeles study also examined the criminal behavior of rival gangs socially connected to the targeted gang. Only one study noted potential threats to the integrity of the treatment. Tita et al. (2004) reported that the Los Angeles intervention was not fully implemented as planned. The implementation of the Ceasefire program in the Boyle Heights neighborhood of Los Angeles was negatively affected by the well-known Ramparts LAPD police corruption scandal and a lack of ownership of the intervention by the participating agencies.

The basic findings of our review are very positive. Of the 11 eligible studies, 10 reported strong and statistically significant crime reductions associated with the approach. Nonetheless, we are concerned with the lack of rigorous randomized experimental evaluations of this promising approach. While the biases in quasi-experimental research are not clear (e.g., Campbell and Boruch 1975; Wilkinson and Task Force on Statistical Inference 1999), recent reviews in crime and justice suggest that weaker research designs often lead to more positive outcomes (e.g., see Weisburd, Lum, and Petrosino 2001; Welsh et al. 2011). This does not mean that nonexperimental studies cannot be of high quality, but only that there is evidence that nonexperimental designs in crime and justice are likely to overstate outcomes as contrasted with randomized experiments. In his review of situational crime prevention evaluations, Guerette (2009) finds that the conclusions of randomized evaluations were generally consistent with the majority conclusion of the nonrandomized evaluations. While our vote counting review is consistent with Guerette's (2009) conclusion, our calculated effect sizes reveal that less rigorous focused deterrence evaluation designs were associated with stronger reported effects. As such, we think that caution should be used in drawing conclusions regarding population effect sizes for the pulling levers intervention.

At the same time, the effects observed in the studies reviewed were often very large, and such effect sizes are evidenced as well in those studies using strong comparison groups (e.g., Papachristos et al. 2007) and in the sole randomized controlled trial (Hawken and Kleiman 2009). Our review provides strong empirical evidence for the crime prevention effectiveness of focused deterrence strategies. Even if we assume that the effects observed contain some degree of upward bias, it appears that the overall impact of such programs is noteworthy. These findings are certainly encouraging and point to the promises of this approach.

We certainly believe that the positive outcomes of the present studies indicate that additional experimental evaluations, however difficult and costly, are warranted. The potential barriers are real, especially in regard to identifying valid treatment and comparison areas. But existing evidence is strong enough to warrant a large investment in multisite experiments (Weisburd and Taxman 2000). Such experiments could solve the problem of small numbers of places in single jurisdictions and would also allow for examination of variation in effectiveness across contexts.

Despite our concerns over the lack of randomized experiments, we believe that the findings of eligible focused deterrence evaluations fit well within existing research suggesting that deterrence-based strategies, if applied correctly, can reduce crime (Apel and Nagin 2011). The focused deterrence approach seems to have the desirable characteristic of altering offenders' perceptions of sanction risk. Our findings are also supported by the growing body of scientific evidence that suggests police departments, and their partners, can be effective in controlling specific crime problems when they engage a variety of partners, and tailor an array of tactics to address underlying criminogenic conditions and dynamics (Braga 2008a; Weisburd and Eck 2004). Indeed, our study suggests that Durlauf and Nagin (2011) are correct in their conclusion that imprisonment and crime can both be reduced through the noteworthy marginal deterrent effects generated by allocating police officers, and their criminal justice partners, in ways that heighten the perceived risk of apprehension.

While the results of this review are very supportive of deterrence principles, we believe that other complementary crime control mechanisms are at work in the focused deterrence strategies described here that need to be highlighted and better understood (see Weisburd 2011). In Durlauf and Nagin's (2011) article, the focus is on the possibilities for increasing perceived risk and deterrence by increasing police presence. Although this conclusion is warranted by the data and represents an important component of the causal mechanisms that have increased the effectiveness of focused deterrence strategies, we believe it misses an important part of the story. In the focused deterrence approach, the emphasis is not only on increasing the risk of offending but also on decreasing opportunity structures for violence, deflecting offenders away from crime, increasing the collective efficacy of communities, and increasing the legitimacy of police actions. Indeed, we suspect that the large effects we observe come precisely from the multifaceted ways in which this program influences criminals.

In closing, we think it is important to recognize that focused deterrence strategies are a very recent addition to the existing scholarly literature on crime control and prevention strategies. While the evaluation evidence needs to be strengthened and the theoretical underpinnings of the approach need further refinement, we believe that jurisdictions suffering from gang violence, overt drug markets, and repeat offender problems should add focused deterrence strategies to their existing portfolio of prevention and control interventions. The existing evidence suggests these new approaches to crime prevention and control generate noteworthy crime reductions.

Notes

1. The following search terms were used: focused deterrence, deterring violent offenders, pulling levers AND police, problem-oriented policing, police AND repeat offenders, police AND gangs, police AND guns, gang violence prevention, strategic gang enforcement, crackdowns AND gangs, enforcement swamping, and drug market intervention.

2. The following 15 databases were searched: Criminal Justice Periodical Index, Sociological Abstracts, Social Science Abstracts (SocialSciAbs), Social Science Citation Index, Arts and Humanities Search (AHSearch), Criminal Justice Abstracts, National Criminal Justice Reference Service (NCJRS) Abstracts, Educational Resources Information Clearinghouse (ERIC), Legal Resource Index, Dissertation Abstracts, Government Publications Office, Monthly Catalog (GPO Monthly), Google Scholar, Online Computer Library Center (OCLC) SearchFirst, CINCH data search, and C2 SPECTR (The Campbell Collaboration Social, Psychological, Educational and Criminological Trials Register).

3. These journals were: *Criminology*, *Criminology & Public Policy*, *Justice Quarterly*, *Journal of Research in Crime and Delinquency*, *Journal of Criminal Justice*, *Police Quarterly*, *Policing*, *Police Practice and Research*, *British Journal of Criminology*, *Journal of Quantitative Criminology*, *Crime & Delinquency*, *Journal of Criminal Law and Criminology*, and *Policing and Society*. Hand searches covered 1979 to 2010.

4. Ms. Phyllis Schultze of the Gottfredson Library at the Rutgers University School of Criminal Justice executed the initial abstract search and was consulted throughout on our search strategies.

5. During the development of this report, the Newark study was accepted for publication at *Justice Research and Policy* and the Nashville study was accepted for publication at *Evaluation Review*.

References

Apel, R. and D. Nagin. 2011. "General Deterrence: A Review of Recent Evidence." Pp. 411–36 in *Crime and Public Policy*, edited by J. Q. Wilson and J. Petersilia. New York: Oxford University Press.

Blalock, H. 1979. *Social Statistics*. Rev. 2nd ed. New York: McGraw-Hill

Blumstein, A., J. Cohen, and D. Nagin, eds. 1978. *Deterrence and Incapacitation: Estimating the Effects of Criminal Sanctions on Crime Rates*. Washington, DC: National Academy of Sciences.

Boyle, D. J., J. L. Lanterman, J. E. Pascarella, and C.-C. Cheng. 2010. *The Impact of Newark's Operation Ceasefire on Trauma Center Gunshot Wound Admissions*. Newark, NJ: Violence Institute of New Jersey, University of Medicine and Dentistry of New Jersey.

Boyum, D. A., J. P. Caulkins, and M. A. R. Kleiman. 2011. "Drugs, Crime, and Public Policy." Pp. 368–410 in *Crime and Public Policy*, edited by J. Q. Wilson and J. Petersilia. New York: Oxford University Press.

Braga, A. A. 2001. "The Effects of Hot Spots Policing on Crime." *Annals of the American Academy of Political and Social Science* 578:104–25.

Braga, A. A. 2005. "Hot Spots Policing and Crime Prevention: A Systematic Review of Randomized Controlled Trials." *Journal of Experimental Criminology* 1:317–42.

Braga, A. A. 2007. "The Effects of Hot Spots Policing on Crime." *Campbell Systematic Reviews*. DOI:10.4073/csr.2007.1.

Braga, A. A. 2008a. *Problem-Oriented Policing and Crime Prevention*. 2nd ed. Boulder, CO: Lynne Rienner.

Braga, A. A. 2008b. "Pulling Levers Focused Deterrence Strategies and the Prevention of Gun Homicide." *Journal of Criminal Justice* 36:332–43.

Braga, A. A. and D. M. Kennedy. 2012. "Linking Situational Crime Prevention and Focused Deterrence Strategies." Pp. 51–65 in *The Reasoning Criminologist: Essays in Honour of Ronald V. Clarke*, edited by G. Farrell and N. Tilley. London: Taylor and Francis.

Braga, A. A., D. M. Kennedy, E. J. Waring, and A. M. Piehl. 2001. "Problem-Oriented Policing, Deterrence, and Youth Violence: An Evaluation of Boston's Operation Ceasefire." *Journal of Research in Crime and Delinquency* 38:195–225.

Braga, A.A., G. L. Pierce, J. McDevitt, B. J. Bond, and S. Cronin. 2008. "The Strategic Prevention of Gun Violence Among Gang-Involved Offenders." *Justice Quarterly* 25:132–62.

Braga, A. A. and D. L. Weisburd. 2011. *Systematic Review of the Effects of Focused Deterrence Strategies on Crime.* Report submitted to the Campbell Collaboration Crime and Justice Group (available upon request from author).

Campbell, D. T. and R. F. Boruch. 1975. "Making the Case for Randomized Assignment to Treatment by Considering the Alternatives." Pp. 195–296 in *Evaluation and Experiments: Some Critical Issues in Assessing Social Programs*, edited by C. Bennett and A. Lumsdaine. New York: Academic Press.

Campbell, D. T. and J. Stanley. 1966. *Experimental and Quasi-Experimental Designs for Research.* Chicago, IL: Rand McNally.

Clarke, R. V. and D. L. Weisburd. 1994. "Diffusion of Crime Control Benefits: Observations on the Reverse of Displacement." *Crime Prevention Studies* 2:165–84.

Cohen, J. 1988. *Statistical Power Analysis for the Behavioral Sciences.* 2nd ed. Hillsdale, NJ: Lawrence Erlbaum.

Cook, P. J. 1980. "Research in Criminal Deterrence: Laying the Groundwork for the Second Decade." Pp. 211–68 in *Crime and Justice: An Annual Review of Research.* Vol. 2, edited by Norval Morris and Michael Tonry. Chicago, IL: University of Chicago Press.

Cook, P. J. and J. Ludwig. 2006. "Aiming for Evidence-Based Gun Policy." *Journal of Policy Analysis and Management* 48: 691–735.

Cook, T. and D. T. Campbell. 1979. *Quasi-Experimentation: Design and Analysis Issues for Field Settings.* Boston, MA: Houghton Mifflin.

Corsaro, N., R. Brunson, and E. McGarrell. Forthcoming. "Problem-Oriented Policing and Open-Air Drug Markets: Examining the Rockford Pulling Levers Strategy." *Crime & Delinquency.*

Corsaro, N. and E. McGarrell. 2010. *An Evaluation of the Nashville Drug Market Initiative (DMI) Pulling Levers Strategy.* East Lansing, MI: Michigan State University, School of Criminal Justice.

Dalton, E. 2002. "Targeted Crime Reduction Efforts in Ten Communities: Lessons for the Project Safe Neighborhoods Initiative." *U.S. Attorney's Bulletin* 50:16–25.

Durlauf, S. and D. Nagin. 2011. "Imprisonment and Crime: Can Both Be Reduced?" *Criminology & Public Policy* 10:13–54.

Duval, S. and R. Tweedie. 2000. "A Nonparametric 'Trim and Fill' Method of Accounting for Publication Bias in Meta-analysis." *Journal of the American Statistical Association* 95:89–98.

Engel, R. S., N. Corsaro, and M. Skubak Tillyer. 2010. *Evaluation of the Cincinnati Initiative to Reduce Violence (CIRV).* Cincinnati, OH: University of Cincinnati Policing Institute.

Fagan, J. 2002. "Policing Guns and Youth Violence." *The Future of Children* 12:133–51.

Fagan, J., T. Meares, A. V. Papachristos, and D. Wallace. 2008. "Desistance and Legitimacy: Effect Heterogeneity in a Field Experiment with High-Risk Offenders." Paper presented at the annual meeting of the American Society of Criminology, November, St. Louis, MO.

Farrington, D. and A. Petrosino. 2001. "The Campbell Collaboration Crime and Justice Group." *Annals of the American Academy of Political and Social Science* 578:35–49.

Gibbs, J. P. 1975. *Crime, Punishment, and Deterrence.* New York: Elsevier.

Guerette, R. T. 2009. "The Pull, Push, and Expansion of Situation Crime Prevention Evaluation: An Appraisal of Thirty-Seven Years of Research." Pp. 29–58 in *Evaluation Crime Reduction Initiatives, Crime Prevention Studies.* Vol. 24, edited by J. Knutsson and N. Tilley. Monsey, NY: Criminal Justice Press.

Hawken, A. and M. A. R. Kleiman. 2009. *Managing Drug Involved Probationers with Swift and Certain Sanctions: Evaluating Hawaii's HOPE.* Final report submitted to the National Institute of Justice, U.S. Department of Justice.

Horney, J. and I. H. Marshall. 1992. "Risk Perceptions Among Serious Offenders: The Role of Crime and Punishment." *Criminology* 30:575–94.

Kennedy, D. M. 1997. "Pulling Levers: Chronic Offenders, High-Crime Settings, and a Theory of Prevention." *Valparaiso University Law Review* 31:449–84.

Kennedy, D. M. 2008. *Deterrence and Crime Prevention: Reconsidering the Prospect of Sanction.* London: Routledge.

Kennedy, D. M. 2009. "Drugs, Race, and Common Ground: Reflections on the High Point Intervention." *National Institute of Justice Journal* 262:12–17.

Kennedy, D. M., A. M. Piehl, and A. A. Braga. 1996. "Youth Violence in Boston: Gun Markets, Serious Youth Offenders, and a Use-Reduction Strategy." *Law and Contemporary Problems* 59:147–96.

Kleiman, M. A. R. and K. D. Smith. 1990. "State and Local Drug Enforcement: In Search of a Strategy." Pp. 69–108 in *Drugs and Crime, Crime and Justice: A Review of Research.* Vol. 13, edited by M. Tonry and J. Q. Wilson. Chicago, IL: University of Chicago Press.

Lipsey, M. 2000. "Statistical Conclusion Validity for Intervention Research: A Significant ($p<.05$) Problem." Pp. 101–20 in *Validity and Social Experimentation: Donald Campbell's Legacy.* Vol. 1, edited by L. Bickman. Thousand Oaks, CA: Sage.

Lipsey, M. 2003. "Those Confounded Moderators in Meta-Analysis: Good, Bad, and Ugly." *Annals of the American Academy of Political and Social Science* 587:69–81.

Lipsey, M. and D. B. Wilson. 2001. *Practical Meta-analysis.* Applied Social Research Methods Series. Vol. 49. Thousand Oaks, CA: Sage.

MacKenzie, D. L. and L. Hickman. 1998. *What Works in Corrections?* Report to the State of Washington Joint Audit and Review Committee. College Park, MD: University of Maryland, Department of Criminology and Criminal Justice.

Mazerolle, L., D. W. Soole, and S. Rombouts. 2007. "Street Level Drug Law Enforcement: A Meta-analytic Review." *Campbell Systematic Reviews.* DOI: 10.4073/csr.2007.2.

McGarrell, E., S. Chermak, J. Wilson, and N. Corsaro. 2006. "Reducing Homicide through a 'Lever-Pulling' Strategy." *Justice Quarterly* 23:214–29.

Morgan, S. L. and C. Winship. 2007. *Counterfactuals and Causal Inference: Methods and Principals for Social Research.* New York: Cambridge University Press.

Nagin, D. 1998. "Criminal Deterrence Research at the Outset of the Twenty-First Century." Pp. 1–42 in *Crime and Justice: A Review of Research.* Vol. 23, edited by M. Tonry. Chicago, IL: University of Chicago Press.

Papachristos, A. V., T. Meares, and J. Fagan. 2007. "Attention Felons: Evaluating Project Safe Neighborhoods in Chicago." *Journal of Empirical Legal Studies* 4:223–72.

Paternoster, R. 1987. "The Deterrent Effect of the Perceived Certainty and Severity of Punishment: A Review of the Evidence and Issues." *Justice Quarterly* 4:173–217.

Paternoster, R., R. Brame, R. Bachman, and L. Sherman. 1997. "Do Fair Procedures Matter? The Effect of Procedural Justice on Spouse Assault." *Law & Society Review* 31:163–204.

Piehl, A. M., S. J. Cooper, A. A. Braga, and D. M. Kennedy. 2003. "Testing for Structural Breaks in the Evaluation of Programs." *Review of Economics and Statistics* 85:550–8.

Reppetto, T. 1976. "Crime Prevention and the Displacement Phenomenon." *Crime & Delinquency* 22:166–77.

Rosenfeld, R., R. Fornango, and E. Baumer. 2005. "Did Ceasefire, Compstat, and Exile Reduce Homicide?" *Criminology & Public Policy* 4:419–50.

Rosenthal, R. 1994. "Parametric Measures of Effect Size." Pp. 231–44 in *The Handbook of Research Synthesis*, edited by H. Cooper and L. Hedges. New York, NY: Russell Sage.

Rothstein, H. R. 2008. "Publication Bias as a Threat to the Validity of Meta-analytic Results." *Journal of Experimental Criminology* 4:61–81.

Sampson, R., S. Raudenbush, and F. Earls. 1997. "Neighborhoods and Violent Crime." *Science* 277:918–24.

Sherman, L. 2002. "Fair and Effective Policing." Pp. 383–412 in *Crime: Public Policies for Crime Control*, edited by J. Q. Wilson and J. Petersilia. Oakland, CA: ICS.

Skogan, W. and K. Frydl, eds. 2004. *Fairness and Effectiveness in Policing: The Evidence.* Committee to Review Research on Police Policy and Practices. Washington, DC: The National Academies Press.

Skubak Tillyer, M. and D. M. Kennedy. 2008. "Locating Focused Deterrence Approaches within a Situational Crime Prevention Framework." *Crime Prevention and Community Safety* 10:75–84.

St. Jean, P. K. B. 2007. *Pockets of Crime: Broken Windows, Collective Efficacy, and the Criminal Point of View.* Chicago, IL: University of Chicago Press.

Tyler, T. R. 1990. *Why People Obey the Law: Procedural Justice, Legitimacy, and Compliance.* New Haven, CT: Yale University Press.

Tyler, T. R. 2004. "Enhancing Police Legitimacy." *Annals of the American Academy of Political and Social Science* 593: 84–99.

Tita, G., K. J. Riley, G. Ridgeway, C. Grammich, A. Abrahamse, and P. Greenwood. 2004. *Reducing Gun Violence: Results from an Intervention in East Los Angeles.* Santa Monica, CA: RAND Corporation.

Weisburd, D. L. 1993. "Design Sensitivity in Criminal Justice Experiments." Pp. 337–79 in *Crime and Justice: A Review of Research.* Vol. 17, edited by Michael Tonry. Chicago, IL: University of Chicago Press.

Weisburd, D. L. 2011. "Shifting Crime and Justice Resources from Prisons to Police: Shifting Police from People to Places." *Criminology & Public Policy* 10:153–64.

Weisburd, D. L. and J. E. Eck. 2004. "What Can Police Do to Reduce Crime, Disorder and Fear?" *Annals of the American Academy of Political and Social Science* 593:42–65.

Weisburd, D. L., C. Lum, and A. Petrosino. 2001. "Does Research Design Affect Study Outcomes in Criminal Justice?" *The Annals of the American Academy of Social and Political Sciences* 578:50–70.

Weisburd, D. L. and F. Taxman. 2000. "Developing a Multi-Center Randomized Trial in Criminology: The Case of HIDTA." *Journal of Quantitative Criminology* 16:315–39.

Weisburd, D. L., C. Telep, J. Hinkle, and J. E. Eck. 2008. "The Effects of Problem-Oriented Policing on Crime and Disorder." *Campbell Systematic Reviews.* DOI:10.4073/csr.2008.14.

Weisburd, D. L., L. Wyckoff, J. Ready, J. Eck, J. Hinkle, and F. Gajewski. 2006. "Does Crime Just Move Around the Corner? A Controlled Study of Spatial Displacement and Diffusion of Crime Control Benefits." *Criminology* 44:549–92.

Wellford, C. F., J. V. Pepper, and C. V. Petrie, eds. 2005. *Firearms and Violence: A Critical Review.* Committee to Improve Research Information and Data on Firearms. Washington, DC: The National Academies Press.

Welsh, B. C. and D. P. Farrington. 2009. *Making Public Places Safer: Surveillance and Crime Prevention.* New York: Oxford University Press.

Welsh, B. C., M. E. Peel, D. P. Farrington, H. Elffers, and A. A. Braga. 2011. "Research Design Influence on Study Outcomes in Crime and Justice: A Partial Replication with Public Area Surveillance." *Journal of Experimental Criminology* 7:183–98.

Wilkinson, L. and Task Force on Statistical Inference. 1999. "Statistical Methods in Psychology Journals: Guidelines and Expectations." *American Psychologist* 54:594–604.

Wilson, D. B. 2001. "Meta-Analytical Methods for Criminology." *Annals of the American Academy of Political and Social Science* 578:71–89.

Wilson, J. Q. and G. L. Kelling. 1982. "Broken Windows: The Police and Neighborhood Safety." *Atlantic Monthly*, March, 29–38.

Zimring, F. and G. Hawkins. 1973. *Deterrence: The Legal Threat in Crime Control*. Chicago, IL: University of Chicago Press.

/// REVIEW QUESTIONS

1. What do the authors mean by "focused deterrence" strategies?
2. What was the overall finding of this study regarding these strategies for reducing crime?
3. What are some of the concerns or issues with some of the studies used in this meta-analysis?

READING /// 5

This article uses the scenario design or vignettes to test the compatibility of rational choice theory with what has become the most researched and discussed theory of the past two decades: low self-control theory. Briefly mentioned in the introduction to this section, low self-control theory is a rather simple model that assumes (like other control theories, which we will cover in Section VIII) that all individuals are born with a propensity for crime and that children develop self-control through socialization and discipline. However, some children's parents do not do a good job at monitoring or training their children, so these children never develop self-control and, thus, engage in crime when opportunities present themselves. Alex Piquero and Stephen Tibbetts review other studies that have successfully merged rational choice theory with the low self-control model and then present a test of individuals' perceptions regarding two offenses that most college students are familiar with: drunk driving and shoplifting.

While reading this study, readers should consider the following points:

- The key elements of the low self-control personality and the part they play in rational decision making of individuals in criminality
- The key concepts of the rational choice framework that go beyond traditional deterrence concepts
- The findings for both traditional deterrence variables and more informal and personal or emotional sanctioning factors
- The findings that the authors claim are the "most interesting"

SOURCE: Alex R. Piquero and Stephen G. Tibbetts, "Specifying the Direct and Indirect Effects of Low Self-Control and Situational Factors in Decision Making: Toward a More Complete Model of Rational Offending," *Justice Quarterly* 13 (3): 481–510.

Specifying the Direct and Indirect Effects of Low Self-Control and Situational Factors in Offenders' Decision Making

Toward a More Complete Model of Rational Offending

Alex R. Piquero and Stephen G. Tibbetts

It has been argued that criminology is in a state of theoretical paralysis (Wellford 1989:119) and that its theoretical developments have stagnated (Gibbs 1987). Recently, however, theorizing in criminology has undergone two important advances. One of these was proposed by Michael Gottfredson and Travis Hirschi (1990) in *A General Theory of Crime*. Their theory concerns individual differences, or propensities, that predispose an individual toward offending; their central concept is that of low self-control. The other theoretical advancement is the rational choice perspective (Cornish and Clarke 1986, 1987). This framework emphasizes the contextual and situational factors involved in decisions to offend, as well as the "choice-structuring" properties of offenses (Cornish and Clarke 1987:935).

Low self-control is established early and remains relatively stable throughout life. This is a characteristic of individuals who are more likely than others to engage in imprudent behaviors such as smoking, drinking, or gambling and commit criminal offenses such as shoplifting or assault. Gottfredson and Hirschi (1990:89) characterize low self-control as composed of elements such as immediate gratification, risk taking, orientation to the present, acts involving little skill or planning, and self-centeredness.

The rational choice framework focuses on situational inducements and impediments to offending (Cornish and Clarke 1986, 1987; Nagin and Paternoster 1993) such as the perceived costs (e.g., threat of sanctions) and benefits (e.g., pleasure) of crime. The rational choice model is consistent with a deterrence framework, especially in its focus on the perceived costs associated with committing an offense. It also includes the importance of examining an offender's perception of the benefits of offending and of informal and/or internal threats of sanction, which is absent from the traditional deterrence framework (Piliavin et al. 1986). Therefore the rational choice framework provides one way of looking at the influence of situational factors on offending. By the same token, this perspective is not confined to the situational determinants of (perceived) opportunity. Rational choice also examines how motivation is conditioned by situational influences and opportunities to commit crime.

Rational choice emphasizes would-be offenders' subjective perceptions of the expected rewards and costs associated with offending. From this perspective, a crime-specific focus is necessary because the costs and benefits of one crime may be quite different from those of another. This point suggests the importance of examining the choice-structuring properties of particular offenses (Cornish and Clarke 1987:935). Furthermore, the rational choice perspective suggests explanations in terms of those characteristics which promote or hinder gratification of needs, such as low self-control, shame, moral beliefs, threat of formal sanctions, or the pleasure of offending.

Situational factors and individual propensities are related to each other in a way suggested by Harold Grasmick and his colleagues. Grasmick et al. (1993b) noted that situational circumstances and individual characteristics may influence the extent to which low self-control affects criminal behavior. Thus the effect of low self-control depends on the situation; that is, low self-control may condition criminal behavior. Nagin and Paternoster (1993) have examined the compatibility of these perspectives. Using scenario data from a sample of college undergraduates, they found support for the underlying propensity (low self-control) argument advocated by Gottfredson and Hirschi, as well as some support for the effect of situational factors. Attractiveness of the crime target, ease of committing the crime with minimal risk, and perceptions of the costs and benefits of committing the crime were all related significantly to offending decisions. Their analysis, however, consisted solely of examining the direct effects of exogenous variables on the dependent variable (intentions to deviate).

Our analysis builds on Nagin and Paternoster's (1993) paper. We focus on specifying low self-control in an explicit causal model while taking into account the situational factors associated with offending decisions. We believe that low self-control has a direct effect on intentions to deviate, but we also argue that low self-control has indirect effects on these intentions, which operate through a variety of situational factors. These indirect effects are an important step in understanding criminals' decision-making processes.

Whereas Gottfredson and Hirschi distinguish between crime and criminality, Birkbeck and LaFree (1993) argue that theories of crime (situational explanations) should be united with theories of criminality (stable propensities). In this paper, following suggestions emanating from the work of Birkbeck and LaFree (1993) and Nagin and Paternoster (1993), we merge theories of crime (situational factors measured by subjective perceptions) and theories of criminality (low self-control) into a more highly specified causal model of rational offending. We argue that offenders are rational decision makers who are affected by various factors. These factors include not only an individual propensity to offend (i.e., low self-control) but also situational inducements (such as the pleasure of committing the crime) and situational impediments to crime (e.g., sanction threats, shame).

Previous Research

Perceived Sanction Threats and Perceived Pleasure

Deterrence concepts have been modified and expanded (Cornish and Clarke 1986, 1987; Paternoster 1989; Piliavin et al. 1986; Stafford and Warr 1993; Williams and Hawkins 1986), and recent research conducted within the rational choice framework (Bachman, Paternoster, and Ward 1992; Klepper and Nagin 1989b; Nagin and Paternoster 1993), using factorial vignette surveys, has found support for perceptions of certainty and its negative effect on delinquent behavior. Given the consistency with which sanctions may deter certain individuals who commit certain crimes (Bachman et al. 1992; Klepper and Nagin 1989b; Nagin and Paternoster 1993; Smith and Gartin 1989), we contend that these factors are quite important in a general model of rational offending.

The rational choice framework has focused strongly on the pleasure of offending (Bachman et al. 1992; Nagin and Paternoster 1993; Piliavin et al. 1986). Most researchers have found that the perceived benefits of criminal offending are important in a would-be offender's calculations, perhaps even more important than the estimated costs (Nagin and Paternoster 1993:482). The anticipated rewards or gains from offending may be more important than the potential costs to these individuals because the former are more immediate and more characteristic of risk taking and short-term gratification (Gottfredson and Hirschi 1990). Jack Katz (1988) argues that there are "seductions of crime," which result from the thrills and pleasures provided by committing criminal acts. Other research, however, suggests that seductions are influenced by several background factors including age, gender, and the strain associated with inadequate economic opportunities (McCarthy 1995). Almost all previous empirical tests of deterrence models neglected this beneficial dimension of offending; the few studies that have examined this construct find support for perceived pleasure (Nagin and Paternoster 1993; Piliavin et al. 1986).[1]

Shame

Thomas Scheff (1988) labeled shame as an important factor for social control. Scheff's work was followed closely by John Braithwaite's (1989) *Crime, Shame, and Reintegration,* which caused an immediate increase in the attention given to shame in criminology. Early theorizing on shame, however, tended to focus on acts of shaming by others (e.g., disintegrative/reintegrative shaming) rather than on the internal emotion of shame felt by the individual. Therefore those theorists implied that to experience shame, one must be shamed by a social audience. This assumption is not supported by the psychological literature on shame; in fact, the early researchers in this area acknowledged that most experiences of shame are not preceded by an act of shaming (H. Lewis 1971; Piers and Singer 1953). Experiences of shame are the result of a global, internal evaluation of the self in which the actor temporarily loses some of his or her self-esteem (M. Lewis 1992). Although acts of shaming by others may elicit shame in an individual, such an act need not occur to cause the person to feel that emotion (M. Lewis 1992; Piers and Singer 1953). In other words, individuals can be shamed without the presence of an audience (see Grasmick and Bursik 1990).

Despite the lack of criminological theory on the phenomenological nature of shame, researchers recently have attempted to measure the subjective experiences of shame within a rational choice framework. In these studies (Grasmick and Bursik 1990; Grasmick, Bursik, and Kinsey 1991; Grasmick et al. 1993b; Nagin and Paternoster 1993) respondents have been asked to describe the shame they felt, or would feel, if they had committed, or intended to commit, specific criminal offenses such as drunk driving, littering, date rape, tax evasion, or petty theft. Shame was found to have a strong inhibitory effect on the commission of all these offenses. Furthermore, for some of the offenses, shame had the strongest effect of all the variables specified in the model, including formal sanctions (Grasmick and Bursik 1990). Thus, a deterrent effect of shame seems to be strongly evident in the criminological literature.

Low Self-Control

Gottfredson and Hirschi (1990:90) contend that individuals with low self-control will tend to engage in criminal and analogous acts. Their ideas, which have met with some opposition (Akers 1991; Barlow 1991; Polk 1991), have generated a number of empirical studies (Benson and Moore 1992; Brownfield and Sorenson 1993; Gibbs and Giever 1995; Grasmick et al. 1993b; Keane, Maxim, and Teevan 1993; Nagin and Paternoster 1993; Polakowski 1994; Wood, Pfefferbaum, and Arneklev 1993). Although these studies generally support low self-control, some examination of this work is necessary. First, Grasmick et al. (1993b) developed a psychometric scale that measured low self-control, based on the criteria outlined by Gottfredson and Hirschi. The findings of their study, which examined only direct effects, indicated that low self-control was related strongly to offending (force and fraud). Keane et al. (1993) examined the relationship between low self-control and drinking and driving. Employing a behavioral measure of self-control (use of seat belts), they found that for both males and females, low self-control was an important predictor of driving under the influence of alcohol.

Gottfredson and Hirschi (1990:90) also believe that low self-control may manifest itself in various imprudent behaviors such as smoking, drinking, and gambling. Using the same data and measures as found in Grasmick et al. (1993b), Arneklev et al. (1993) tested this proposition. The results were mixed; on one hand, the low self-control index had a direct effect on an individual's participation in various imprudent behaviors. Yet one component of that index (risk taking) was more strongly predictive than the scale as a whole. Furthermore, smoking appeared to be unaffected by low self-control.[2] Similarly, Wood et al. (1993) argued that although low self-control was a significant predictor of imprudent behaviors and some forms of delinquency, their results suggested that the low self-control measure, as well as the different dependent variables, should be disaggregated.

Gibbs and Giever (1995) examined the manifestations of low self-control on a sample of college undergraduates by creating an attitudinal measure of low self-control and examining its impact on two noncriminal behaviors, cutting class and alcohol consumption. They found that low self-control was the strongest predictor of these behaviors. Their study, however, did not include factors other than self-control, such as moral beliefs or perceived threat of sanctions.

Moral Beliefs and Prior Offending

In addition to the variables discussed above, we included two other variables in the model specification: moral beliefs and prior offending. Moral beliefs are necessary in the study of any rational choice framework because such beliefs impede criminal behavior; theorists have stressed the importance of internalized moral constraints (Bachman et al. 1992; Bishop 1984; Grasmick and Bursik 1990; Paternoster et al. 1983; Tittle 1977, 1980). We also included prior offending as a control variable because it could capture the influence of other sources of stable criminality (Nagin and Paternoster 1991, 1993).

Proposed Model

The proposed model assumes that a rational human actor with low self-control encounters situational factors which push him or her toward crime (pleasure of the offense) and/or away from crime (moral beliefs, perceived risk of sanctions, and situational shame). When the push toward crime is greater than the push away from crime, an individual is more likely to choose crime. This idea is summarized by Gottfredson and Hirschi (1990:89) when they observe that a major characteristic of those with low self-control is the tendency to respond to tangible stimuli in the immediate environment and to have a concrete "here and now" orientation (also see Hirschi and Gottfredson 1993).

Although our theoretical model relies heavily on the most recent statement of control theory outlined by Gottfredson and Hirschi, it is not meant to downplay the importance of earlier control theorists, particularly Walter Reckless (1961; also see Toby 1957). In his seminal piece, Reckless noted that inner containment consists mainly of self-control, while outer containment represents the structural buffer in the person's immediate social world which is able to hold him or her within bounds (Reckless 1961:44–45). Expanding upon the idea of outer containment, one could easily infer that sanctions, pleasure, and shame are structural buffers in an individual's immediate social world. Moreover, Block and Flynn (1956:61) state that "there are many variables in the personality of the delinquent and the delinquency-producing situation itself which the investigators may not readily discern and which themselves may constitute the critical factors involved in the delinquent act." Conceivably, then, one could argue that our theoretical model is a refinement, an extension, and an empirical test of Reckless's theory and of Block and Flynn's assertions (also see A. Cohen 1955).

Methods

We collected data through a self-administered questionnaire that presented respondents with a realistic scenario describing in detail the conditions in which an actor commits a crime. The respondents were told only that the actor committed the act, not whether he or she approved of the act. Thus we focus not on the hypothetical actor's perceptions or approval of the act, but rather on the respondent's perceptions and approval. The questions were designed to measure respondents' perceptions of the costs and benefits of committing the offense described in the scenario, to estimate the probability that they would commit that offense, and to estimate the chance that their committing the offense would result in arrest and in exposure without arrest.

The scenario method differs from conventional data collection in perceptual social control/deterrence research in that it uses hypothetical, third-person scenarios of offending to elicit the dependent variable. This strategy has been used successfully in recent research on rational choice (Bachman et al. 1992; Klepper and Nagin 1989a, 1989b; Nagin and Paternoster 1993). The primary weakness of this approach is that an expressed intention to offend is not synonymous with actual offending. Fishbein and Ajzen (1975), however, argue that a person's intention to perform a particular behavior should be highly correlated with the actual performance of that behavior.[3] This proposition is supported empirically by Green (1989), whose two-wave panel design revealed a high correlation ($r = .85$) between intentions and actual performance of deviant behavior. In addition, Kim and Hunter's (1993) recent meta-analysis produced a strong relationship between attitude, intention, and behavior. In all, the scenario method is the best approach available because of its advantages, its realistic nature, and the specificity of the scenarios.[4]

The realistic and specific nature of the scenarios allows us to examine the effect of situational factors on both the intentions to offend and the anticipated risks and rewards of these behaviors. Without these contextual specifications, the respondents would impute their own details; such a situation would "undoubtedly vary across respondents and affect their responses" (Nagin and Paternoster 1993:474). Also, individuals may vary in their definition of illegal behavior. If these differences in definition vary systematically with responses measuring variables of interest, analysis of the effects of such variables on actual behavior may be misrepresented (Nagin and Paternoster 1993).

Another, perhaps more important advantage of the scenario method is its capacity to capture the "instantaneous" relationship between independent variables and the respondent's intentions to offend (Grasmick and Bursik 1990). Previous cross-sectional and panel studies on deterrence used measures of past behavior or behavior within waves to measure the dependent variable (e.g., Bishop 1984). Because perceptions of risk are unstable over time, however, this lagged type of measurement is not appropriate. These designs would tend to find lagged effects for independent variables that remained stable over time, such as moral beliefs, but no lagged effects for independent variables that are not stable, such as perceived threats of sanction (Grasmick and Bursik 1990). Therefore, because the scenario method permits the examination of "instantaneous" relationships, it is preferable to traditional designs.[5]

Sample and Scenario Design

Respondents were undergraduates at a major East Coast university, enrolled in several large introductory criminal justice courses in the fall 1993 semester. A total of 349 males and 293 females (642 in all) completed the questionnaire. Although participation was voluntary, only 4 percent of potential respondents refused to participate; given this small amount, analysis and conclusions appear not to be threatened by response bias. The respondents ranged in age from 17 to 35; the median age was 19. Because we selected introductory classes that fulfill general core requirements for the university curriculum, a substantial majority of students (69 percent) were not criminal justice majors and were currently in their freshman and sophomore years. In addition, questionnaires were administered during the second week of the semester. Therefore it is very unlikely that responses were biased by students' knowledge of deterrence or correctional concerns.[6] Listwise deletion of missing cases resulted in a sample of 604.

The Scenarios

Under an adaptation of the factorial survey methodology developed by Rossi and Anderson (1982), each student was given two scenarios—drunk driving and shoplifting—to which to respond. All of the scenarios were framed in settings familiar to these college student respondents. Selected scenario conditions were varied experimentally across persons. Respondents were asked to estimate the probability that they would commit the act specified in the scenario, to predict the chance that their commission of the offense would result in arrest, and to answer questions designed to measure their perceptions of the costs and benefits of committing the offense described in the scenario. In the present analysis, then, all respondents receive the opportunity to commit the same crimes in the same setting.[7]

Measurement of Variables

Intentions to Deviate

Separate models are estimated for each type of offense. The dependent variable is the respondent's estimate of the chance that he or she will do what the character did in the scenario. We measured intentions to offend on a scale from 0 (no chance at all) to 10 (100 percent chance). Responses were solicited for both the drunk driving (INTENTDD) and the shoplifting (INTENTSH) scenarios.

Shame

Shame is measured by two items following each scenario, which ask the respondent (1) "what is the chance" and (2) "how much of a problem" would loss of self-esteem be if he or she were to do what the actor in the scenario did, even if no one else found out. Responses to both of these items were measured on an 11-point scale (0 = no chance/no problem to 10 = 100 percent chance/very big problem). We computed shame (SHAME) by multiplying the responses of the two items; higher scores reflect a higher likelihood that the individual would feel shame if he or she were to commit the specified act.

Low Self-Control

We operationalized low self-control with a psychometric scale borrowed from Grasmick et al. (1993b), which includes 24 items intended to measure the six elements of low self-control.[8] We coded these items on a five-point Likert-type scale (1 = never to 5 = very often) and created a composite measure of self-control (SELFCONT) by summing the responses across 24 items. High scores on the scale indicate low self-control. This instrument was used in two previous studies (Grasmick et al. 1993b; Nagin and Paternoster 1993), both of which provided strong reliability and validity support for the scale. The high estimated reliability coefficient (α = .84) gave us confidence in the internal consistency of the scale. Furthermore, the factor loadings provided by a principal-components factor analysis were comparable to those reported by Grasmick et al. (1993b).

Perceived External Sanctions

Respondents were asked to estimate the chance of arrest (*Pf:* risk of formal discovery) and the chance that others would find out if they were not arrested (*Pi:* risk of informal discovery). To measure the perceptions of the implications of discovery, we asked respondents to estimate the probability that discovery by arrest or informal exposure would result in dismissal from the university (*Pdf, Pdi*), loss of respect by close friends (*Pff, Pfi*), loss of respect by parents and relatives (*Ppf, Ppi*), and diminished job prospects (*Pjf, Pji*). Each of these perceptual measures is intended to measure the risks of informal sanctions that may threaten an individual's "stake in conformity," or bonding to the moral order. To measure the perceived risk of formal sanctions, we asked respondents to estimate the risk of jail (*Pjaf*). The drunk-driving scenario was followed by an additional item measuring the perceived chance of losing one's driver's license (*Plf*) if an arrest was made. All responses were measured on an 11-point scale (0 = no chance at all to 10 = 100 percent chance).

These measures of risk probably would have little effect on intentions unless associated with perceptions of some cost (Grasmick and Bursik 1990). Thus we asked respondents to estimate the perceived severity of each sanction. Specifically, we asked each subject to estimate "how much of a problem" each sanction would pose for them. All responses were measured on an 11-point scale (0 = no problem at all to 10 = a very big problem). To create the composite scale of perceived external sanctions, we multiplied each risk-perception response by the corresponding severity-perception response. Then we summed these separately for drunk driving and for shoplifting (PEREXSAN); higher scores on the scale correspond to a high degree of perceived risk and cost of performing the act in question for that individual. We used the following formula:

$$\text{PEREXSAN} = \text{Pi}\,[(\text{Pdi})\,(\text{Sd}) + (\text{Pfi})\,(\text{Sf}) + (\text{Ppi})\,(\text{Sp}) + (\text{Pji})\,(\text{Sj})] + \text{Pf}\,[(\text{Pdf})\,(\text{Sd}) + (\text{Pff})\,(\text{Sf}) + (\text{Ppf})\,(\text{Sp}) + (\text{Pjf})\,(\text{Sj}) + (\text{Plf})\,(\text{SI}) + (\text{Pjaf})\,(\text{Sja})]$$

where *Sd* equals the perceived severity of sanction *d* (dismissal from university) and all other variables are as defined previously.

Moral Beliefs

To measure the perceived immorality of the behavior, we asked respondents to estimate how morally wrong they thought the incident would be if they were to commit drunk driving and shoplifting (MORALS). Response options varied on an 11-point scale (0 = not morally wrong at all to 10 = very morally wrong). Although some may contend that our respondents may not regard the behaviors under study as criminal or morally wrong, the mean moral value was 7.80 against drunk driving and 7.57 against shoplifting. These findings indicate that most of our respondents perceive even these behaviors as morally wrong.

Perceived Pleasure

To measure perceived pleasure, a single item asked respondents to estimate "how much fun or kick" it would be to commit drunk driving and shoplifting under the conditions specified in the scenarios (PLEASURE). Responses varied on an 11-point scale (0 = no fun or kick at all to 10 = a great deal of fun or kick).

Prior Offending

In addition to the variables discussed above, we included prior offending as a control in the model. We did so to capture the influence of sources of stable criminality extraneous to that of persistent individual differences due to personality traits included in the model (such as low self-control). To measure prior offending (PRIOROFF), we included two items (one for each scenario offense) that asked the respondents how many times in the past year they had driven while drunk and how many times they had shoplifted.[9]

Hypotheses

In this paper we postulate and examine three hypotheses:

> H_1: Low self-control has both direct and indirect effects via situational factors on intentions to deviate;

H_2: Situational characteristics have both direct and indirect effects on intentions to deviate and on other situational variables;

H_3: The model uniting the effects of low self-control and situational characteristics of crime will provide a good fit to the data.[10]

Analysis of Shoplifting

According to Hypothesis 1, low self-control will have a direct effect on intentions to deviate and indirect effects on intentions to deviate through situational factors. Significant maximum-likelihood estimates for shoplifting may be found in Table 1 and Figure 1. Of the four paths estimated for low self-control, three are significant. Low self-control has a direct positive effect (b = .153, t = 4.438) on intentions to shoplift and a direct positive effect (b = .178, t = 4.502) on perceived pleasure, an indication that the higher one scores on the low self-control scale, the more likely one is to intend to shoplift and to perceive pleasure from shoplifting. Low self-control has a direct negative effect (b = –.102, t = –2.889) on shame, indicating that the higher one scores on the low self-control scale, the less likely one is to experience shame due to shoplifting. The only insignificant effect is the effect of low self-control on perceived risk of sanctions.

Therefore, low self-control not only has a direct effect on intentions to shoplift; it also indirectly affects intentions to shoplift through situational variables (pleasure and shame). These results are consistent with Gottfredson and Hirschi's (1990:95) idea that individuals with low self-control will be less likely to consider the consequences of offending.

Hypothesis 2 indicates that situational characteristics should have direct effects on intentions to shoplift and indirect effects on intentions to shoplift which operate through other situational factors. With the exception of perceived sanctions, both shame (b = –.214, t = –5.372) and perceived pleasure (b = .220, t = 6.270) have the expected effects on intentions to shoplift. The null results for perceived sanctions are not surprising: Shoplifting is a very common crime and one that can be committed with relative impunity; thus an individual's perception of being caught would likely not be salient.

As for the other effects, shame (b = .434, t = 9.745) has a positive effect on perceived sanctions, indicating that the more likely one is to perceive shame, the more likely one is to perceive the threat of sanctions as salient. Even though perceived sanctions do not affect intentions to shoplift, they affect perceived pleasure in a rather interesting manner: Perceived sanctions have a positive effect (b = .153, t = 3.398) on perceived pleasure, in keeping with Katz's (1988) notion of "sneaky thrills." It appears that among our respondents, the more one perceives the risk of sanctions as high, the more pleasure one perceives

Table 1 • Significant Full-Information Maximum-Likelihood Estimates for Intentions to Shoplift (N = 604)

	Independent Variables					
Dependent Variables	**Shame**	**Perceived Sanctions**	**Perceived Pleasure**	**Moral Beliefs**	**Prior Offending**	**Low Self-Control**
Intentions to Shoplift	–.214	a	.220	–.186	.176	.153
Shame	—[b]	—	–.173	.483	—[a]	–.102
Perceived Sanctions	.434	—	—[b]	.117	—[a]	—[a]
Perceived Pleasure	—[b]	.153	—[b]	-.267	.169	.178

NOTE: LISREL shows the effects of columns on rows.

a. Path estimated but not significant.

b. Path not established.

Figure 1

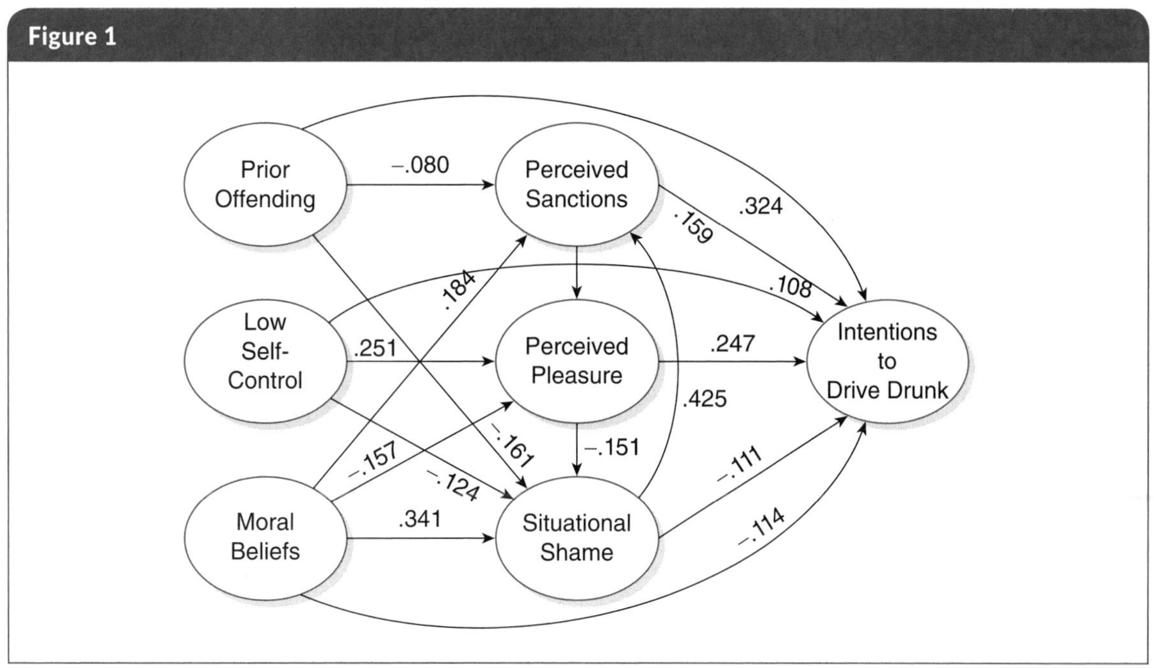

from shoplifting. Finally, perceived pleasure has a negative effect on shame ($b = -.173$, $t = -4.468$): The more one perceives pleasure from shoplifting, the less likely one is to feel shame.

Other effects include those of the other two exogenous variables, prior offending and moral beliefs. Prior offending has positive effects on intentions to shoplift ($b = .176$, $t = 5.322$) and on perceived pleasure ($b = .169$, $t = 4.421$), indicating that the more times respondents have shoplifted in the past, the more likely they are to intend to shoplift and to perceive pleasure from shoplifting. Prior behavior does not exert an effect on perceived sanctions. Moral beliefs are the only exogenous variable to be significant and consistent with all effects as predicted. Moral beliefs have the predicted negative effects on intentions to shoplift ($b = -.186$, $t = -4.669$) and on perceived pleasure ($b = -.267$, $t = -6.287$), indicating that the stronger one's moral beliefs against shoplifting, the less likely one is to intend to shoplift or to perceive pleasure from shoplifting. Likewise, moral beliefs have the predicted positive effects on shame ($b = .483$, $t = 13.599$) and on perceived sanctions ($b = .117$, $t = 2.691$), indicating that the stronger one's moral beliefs, the more likely one is to perceive shame and sanctions as important.

To test the third hypothesis, we constructed a model that united the effects of low self-control and of situational characteristics. To determine whether the proposed model fit the data adequately, we examined the chi-square statistic of the model. Because chi-square is sensitive to sample size and to departures from normality in the data, there are alternative methods for assessing the goodness of fit of a model; one such method is the ratio of chi-square to degrees of freedom. Smith and Patterson (1985) suggest that values of 5 or less indicate an adequate fit. For this model the value is 1.01 (4.05/4), indicating an adequate fit to the data.

Analysis of Drunk Driving

The significant maximum-likelihood estimates for drunk driving are shown in Table 2 and Figure 2. For low self-control, three of the four effects are significant. Low self-control has direct positive effects on intentions to drive drunk ($b = .108$, $t = 3.167$) and on perceived pleasure ($b = .251$, $t = 6.308$), indicating that the higher one scores on the low self-control scale, the more likely one is to intend to drive drunk and to perceive pleasure from drunk driving. Low self-control exerts a negative effect on shame (b = –.124, t = –3.257), indicating that persons with low self-control are less likely to feel shame. As in the analysis of shoplifting, the effect of low self-control on perceived sanctions is insignificant.

All three situational factors have the expected effects on intentions to drive drunk. Shame (b = –.111, t = –2.796) and perceived sanctions (b = –.159, t = –4.219) exert the expected negative effects on intentions to drink and drive, indicating that the more one perceives sanction threats and shame as important, the less likely one is to intend to drive drunk.[11] Perceived

Table 2 • Significant Full-Information Maximum-Likelihood Estimate for Intention to Drive Drunk (N = 604)

	Independent Variables					
Dependent Variables	**Shame**	**Perceived Sanctions**	**Perceived Pleasure**	**Moral Beliefs**	**Prior Offending**	**Low Self-Control**
Intentions to Drive Drunk	–.111	–.159	.247	–.114	.324	.108
Shame	—[b]	—[b]	–.151	.341	–.161	–.124
Perceived Sanctions	.425	—[b]	—[b]	.184	–.080	—[a]
Perceived Pleasure	—[b]	—[a]	—[b]	–.157	—[a]	.251

NOTE: LISREL shows the effects of columns on rows.

a. Path estimated but not significant.

b. Path not established.

Figure 2

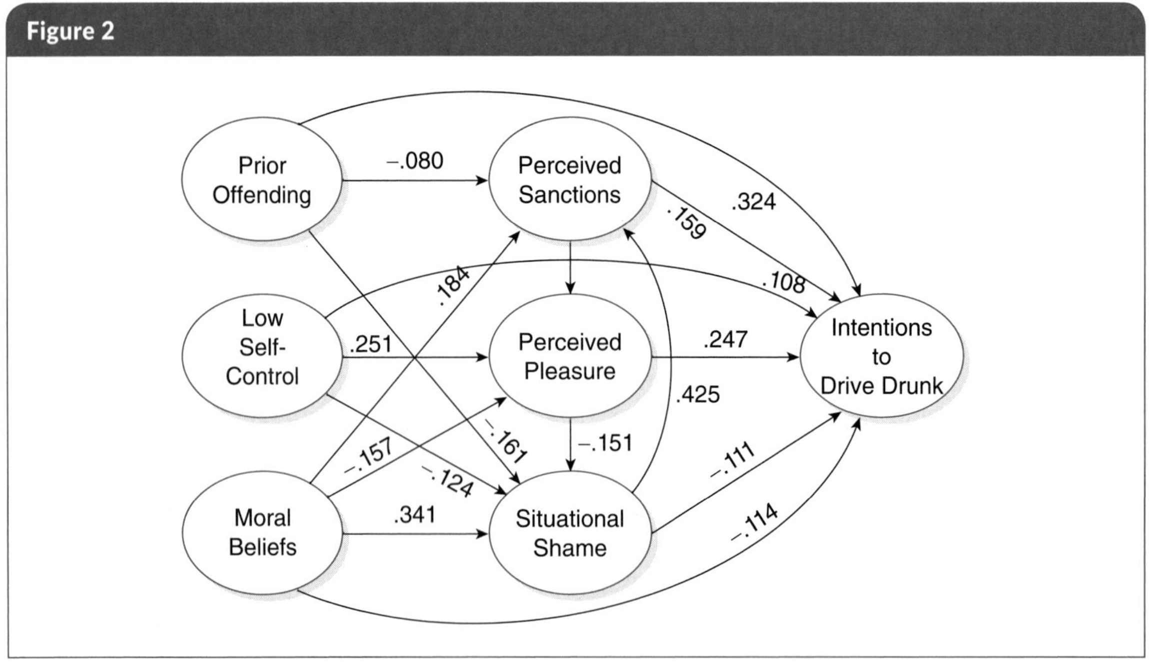

pleasure has the expected positive effect (b = .247, t = 7.313) on intentions to drive drunk, indicating that the more pleasure one perceives from drunk driving, the more likely one is to intend to drive drunk. Other effects for perceived pleasure include a negative effect on shame (b = –.151, t = –4.057), indicating that the more pleasure one obtains from drinking and driving, the less likely one is to lose self-esteem. Shame has a positive effect (b = .425, t = 11.123) on perceived sanctions, indicating that the more one perceives shame as salient, the more likely one is to perceive sanction threats as also important.

Effects of the other two exogenous variables (prior offending and moral beliefs) are largely as expected. Prior offending has a negative effect on shame (b = –.161, t = –4.498) and on perceived sanctions (b = –.080, t = –2.295), indicating that the more one has driven drunk in the past, the less likely one is to feel shame and to perceive sanctions as important. In addition, prior offending has a positive effect on intentions to drive drunk (b = .324, t = 9.946), which indicates that the more one has driven drunk in the past, the more likely one is to intend to drive drunk. Prior offending has no effect on the perceived pleasure of drunk driving.

All four moral belief effects are significant. Moral beliefs have negative effects on intentions to drink and drive (b = –.114, t = –3.177) and on perceived pleasure (b = –.157, t = –3.959), indicating that the stronger one's moral beliefs are against drunk driving, the less likely one is to intend to drive drunk and the less likely one is to derive pleasure from drinking and driving. Moral beliefs also have positive effects on shame (b = .341, t = 9.269) and on perceived sanctions (b = .184, t = 4.925), indicating that the stronger one's moral beliefs are, the more likely one is to experience shame and to perceive sanctions as important.

Results concerning Hypothesis 3 in regard to drinking and driving are similar to those for shoplifting. To determine whether the model constructed for drunk driving fit the data adequately, we performed the same two tests as we conducted for shoplifting. The first test examined the ratio of chi-square to degrees of freedom. Values of less than 5 indicate an adequate fit to the data: our value was .33 (1.00/3).

Conclusion

Building on the early work of Nagin and Paternoster (1993), we set out here to combine two different paths in theoretical criminology into a more complete model of offending. One path attributes crime to individual differences that are established early in life, specifically in low self-control. According to the second path, crime is the result of situational factors associated with criminal offending, such as the perceived costs and benefits of crime. As observed by Nagin and Paternoster (1993:489), these two paths have been explored separately rather than in conjunction. On the basis of our analysis, we find support for a model that integrates these two paths. The model holds after controlling for several important factors and performs well in two different tests designed to measure the fit of the model to the data.

Aside from delineating and testing a more complete model of rational offending, this paper represents the first attempt to examine the indirect effects of low self-control. This attempt is especially important because previous research in low self-control examined only the direct effects of low self-control and rational choice characteristics (Grasmick et al. 1993b; Nagin and Paternoster 1993). Of all our findings, the indirect effects of low self-control were the most interesting. In fact, these effects were more complex than we had imagined originally. We found that low self-control had similar effects on shame and perceived pleasure across offenses, but exerted no effect on perceived sanctions in either scenario. Modeling indirect effects of low self-control is a difficult task, which we undertook with almost no previous theoretical guidance. Such effects probably depend on the offense, but currently we have too little information about the indirect effects of low self-control on offending. Additional theoretical work and further modeling of the total effects are priorities in self-control research.

The model we have presented here may be extended in the following ways. First, we would like to see future studies examine a wide array of criminal and deviant behaviors, such as drug use, sexual assault, burglary, and robbery. Insofar as Gottfredson and Hirschi are correct, low self-control should be related to all types of criminal and deviant behaviors. Second, many variables could be interchanged with and/or added to our list of situational variables. We contend that because different offenses require different situational characteristics and circumstances, these mediating factors may change in type—but they will be situational factors nonetheless. For example, an examination of marijuana use may require inclusion of a situational variable such as the ease of obtaining marijuana, whereas an examination of breaking and entering would require situational characteristics such as the lack of capable guardians, lack of a security system, and the time of day or night. Still other examples of situational variables would include peer delinquency and peer associations. Because delinquency is overwhelmingly a group phenomenon (Reiss 1986), inclusion of such a measure has the potential to enhance the predictability of our model. This discussion should make apparent that although situational characteristics may vary in type depending on the crime, the framework of the model will remain the same: Time-stable variables such as low self-control will always precede and influence the situational variables.

Notes

1. Some may argue that the pleasure associated with offending is only part of the story, and that often the more important situational factors are the amount of time and energy saved (as in drunk driving) and the value of goods stolen (as in shoplifting). Because of the lack of significant findings from Nagin and Paternoster's (1993) vignettes of these conditions, we did not vary these situational characteristics.

2. This result may be due to the average age of the sample (46.5 years). It could be that these individuals began to smoke before the effects of smoking were known to be undesirable (Arneklev et al. 1993).

3. Fishbein and Ajzen (1975) identify three criteria for maximizing the correspondence between intentions and actual behavior. The first of these criteria is the degree to which the intentions are measured with the same specificity as the behavior that is being predicted. The scenarios presented here include highly specific circumstances. The second criterion is the stability of the expressed intention. In view of the realistic and specific conditions of the scenarios, there is no compelling reason to question the stability of these intentions. The final criterion is the degree to which the respondent can willfully carry out the intention.

4. Our scenarios were designed after those used by Nagin and Paternoster (1993) in regard to detail and contextual specificity. We achieved specificity by presenting details of the circumstance of the offense, such as naming the bar where the actor is drinking or the type of item the actor is shoplifting. The scenario approach has been used as well in research on death penalty juries (Bohm 1991).

5. We systematically varied the location of the intention questions for both the drunk driving and the shoplifting scenarios. In approximately half of these scenarios, the dependent variable item was placed directly after the scenario; other perceptual items (e.g., moral beliefs, perceived certainty) followed (this position was coded 0). In the other half, the dependent variable was located at the end of the battery of perceptual items (this position was coded 1). We adopted this procedure to examine for possible differences due to responses on the dependent variable item affecting the responses on the subsequent perceptual items. For instance, if the dependent variable item is placed directly after the scenario, the respondents may base their perceptions on their previous response to the dependent variable item. In contrast if the dependent variable item is placed after the perceptual items, respondents may respond differently on the dependent variable item if they have thought carefully about their perceptions regarding the offense. Bivariate correlations showed that the location of the dependent variable item did not have a significant effect on respondents' intentions to commit drunk driving or to shoplift (r = .06 and –.05, respectively). Therefore, we did not include this variable in the multivariate analyses.

6. The use of convenience samples in deterrence research is questionable and has drawn some criticism (Jensen, Erickson, and Gibbs 1978; Williams and Hawkins 1986). The major objection is that of representativeness. Large public universities, however, contain a moderate number of marginal offenders (Matza 1964), particularly for the kinds of offenses that are the focus of this study. In our data, 44 percent of respondents admit to having committed drunk driving in the past year (17 percent committed shoplifting in the past year). Furthermore, a Bureau of Justice Statistics Report (R. Cohen 1992) reveals that the rate of arrest for driving while under the influence of alcohol (DUI) is highest for persons between ages 21 and 24. Those in the 18–20 age range have the second-highest arrest rate for DUI. Also, a survey of 1,287 university students conducted in 1991 revealed that almost one-half were regular users of alcohol; 45 percent of these reported consuming four or more drinks at a time, and more than half reported driving within an hour after consuming their last drink (Kuhn 1992). When subjects in our sample were asked the likelihood of drinking and driving under the conditions of the scenario presented to them, only 33 percent reported "no chance." Shoplifting also has been shown to be quite common among young adults (Empey and Stafford 1991); self-reports show that shoplifting is about as common as drinking (Elliott et al. 1983; Hindelang, Hirschi, and Weis 1981). When subjects in our sample were asked the likelihood of committing shoplifting under the conditions of the scenario presented to them, only 37 percent reported "no chance." In addition, arrests for theft reported by the university police department totaled 1,267 for 1992; an overwhelming number of these crimes were committed by students. Given this information, one can conclude that

college student populations contain frequent offenders in situations involving drunk driving and shoplifting; thus college samples are appealing for studies such as this.

7. We varied the level of risk of exposure (informal and formal) in both the shoplifting and the drunk driving scenarios. Preliminary analysis revealed no effect for these scenario-varied conditions; as a result, they were not estimated in the LISREL equations. Furthermore, we used gender as a control variable in preliminary analyses. After controlling for low self-control, the effect of gender was not significant in predicting intentions to either shoplift or drive drunk. In addition, gender had no significant effect on the other exogenous variables. Thus we did not examine gender in the LISREL models. These results confirm Gottfredson and Hirschi's (1990:144–49) predictions concerning gender, low self-control, and crime and they are consistent with previous research regarding similarity between males and females in offending behavior regarding shoplifting and drunk driving (Grasmick, Bursik, and Arneklev 1993a; Hindelang et al. 1981; Keane et al. 1993; Nagin and Paternoster 1993; Yu, Essex, and Williford 1992).

8. Persons interested in obtaining a copy of the low self-control scale can write to us or consult Grasmick et al. (1993b) or Nagin and Paternoster (1993).

9. In the models that follow, when we investigate intentions to drive drunk, we use a past behavior measure: the number of times in the past year the respondent has driven drunk. Similarly, when we examine intentions to shoplift, we use a past behavior measure of respondent's previous shoplifting. An anonymous reviewer observed correctly that a situational variable from the perspective of rational choice theory may be a dispositional variable from the perspective of self-control theory, such that one can use the drunk driving (past behavior) variables to predict shoplifting and can use the shoplifting (past behavior) variables to predict drunk driving. Insofar as dispositions rather than situations are at work, the results should be largely the same in either case. For the sake of brevity and because it is not the focus of the present analysis, we did not examine this issue here. We plan on assessing this issue, however, in future work with these data.

10. To examine the validity of this hypothesis, the LISREL computer program provides a chi-square statistic that estimates the goodness of fit of the model.

11. This is the only effect for perceived sanctions and differs from the results for shoplifting. The sanction effects for drunk driving appear to be direct—not indirect, as they were for shoplifting—perhaps because of recent moral campaigns targeting drunk driving and because of the harshness of penalties that are reported by the media. This result is consistent with recent research concerning perceived sanctions on drunk driving (Grasmick et al. 1993a; Nagin and Paternoster 1993).

References

Akers, R. 1991. "Self-Control as a General Theory of Crime." *Journal of Quantitative Criminology* 7:201–11.

Arneklev, B., H. Grasmick, C. Tittle, and R. Bursik, Jr. 1993. "Low Self-Control and Imprudent Behavior." *Journal of Quantitative Criminology* 9:225–47.

Bachman, R., R. Paternoster, and S. Ward. 1992. "The Rationality of Sexual Offending: Testing a Deterrence/Rational Choice Conception of Sexual Assault." *Law and Society Review* 26:343–72.

Barlow, H. 1991. "Explaining Crimes and Analogous Acts, or The Unrestrained Will Grab at Pleasure Whenever They Can." *Journal of Criminal Law and Criminology* 82:229–42.

Benson, M. and E. Moore. 1992. "Are White Collar and Common Offenders the Same?" *Journal of Research in Crime and Delinquency* 29:251–72.

Birkbeck, C. and G. LaFree. 1993. "The Situational Analysis of Crime and Deviance." *Annual Review of Sociology* 19:113–37.

Bishop, D. 1984. "Legal and Extralegal Barriers to Delinquency." *Criminology* 22:403–19.

Block, H. and F. Flynn. 1956. *Delinquency: The Juvenile Offender in America Today.* New York: Random House.

Bohm, R. 1991. *Death Penalty in America: Current Research.* Cincinnati: Anderson.

Braithwaite, J. 1989. *Crime, Shame, and Reintegration.* New York: Cambridge University Press.

Brownfield, D. and A. Sorenson. 1993. "Self-Control and Juvenile Delinquency: Theoretical Issues and an Empirical Assessment of Selected Elements of a General Theory of Crime." *Deviant Behavior* 14:243–64.

Cohen, A. 1955. *Delinquent Boys.* New York: Free Press.

Cohen, R. 1992. *Drunk Driving.* Washington, DC: U.S. Department of Justice.

Cornish, D. and R. Clarke. 1986. *The Reasoning Criminal: Rational Choice Perspectives in Offending.* New York: Springer-Verlag.

———. 1987. "Understanding Crime Displacement: An Application of Rational Choice Theory." *Criminology* 25:933–47.

Elliot, D., S. Ageton, D. Huizinga, W. Knowles, and R. Canter. 1983. *The Prevalence and Incidence of Delinquent Behavior: 1976–1980.* Boulder: University of Colorado.

Empey, L. and M. Stafford. 1991. *American Delinquency: Its Meanings and Construction.* 3rd ed. Belmont, CA: Wadsworth.

Fishbein, M. and I. Ajzen. 1975. *Belief, Attitudes, Intention, and Behavior.* Reading, MA: Addison-Wesley.

Gibbs, J. 1987. "The State of Criminological Theory." *Criminology* 25:821–24.

Gibbs, J. and D. Giever. 1995. "Self-Control and Its Manifestations among University Students: An Empirical Test of Gottfredson and Hirschi's General Theory." *Justice Quarterly* 12:231–55.

Gottfredson, M. and T. Hirschi. 1990. *A General Theory of Crime.* Stanford: Stanford University Press.

Grasmick, H. and R. Bursik, Jr. 1990. "Conscience, Significant Others, and Rational Choice: Extending the Deterrence Model." *Law and Society Review* 24:837–61.

Grasmick, H., R. Bursik, Jr., and B. Arneklev. 1993a. "Reduction in Drunk Driving as a Response to Increased Threats of Shame, Embarrassment, and Legal Sanctions." *Criminology* 31:41–67.

Grasmick, H., R. Bursik, Jr., and K. Kinsey. 1991. "Shame and Embarrassment as Deterrents to Noncompliance with the Law." *Environment and Behavior* 23:233–51.

Grasmick, H., C. Tittle, R. Bursik, Jr., and B. Arneklev. 1993. "Testing the Core Implications of Gottfredson and Hirschi's General Theory of Crime." *Journal of Research in Crime and Delinquency* 30:5–29.

Green, D. 1988. "Measures of Illegal Behavior in Individual-Level Deterrence Research." *Journal of Research in Crime and Delinquency* 26:253–75.

Hindelang, M., T. Hirschi, and J. Weis. 1981. *Measuring Delinquency*. Beverly Hills: Sage.

Hirschi, T. and M. Gottfredson. 1993. "Commentary: Testing the General Theory of Crime." *Journal of Research in Crime and Delinquency* 30:47–54.

Jensen, G., M. Erickson, and J. Gibbs. 1978. "Perceived Risk of Punishment and Self-Reported Delinquency." *Social Forces* 57:57–78.

Katz, J. 1988. *Seductions of Crime*. New York: Basic Books.

Keane, C., P. Maxim, and J. Teevan. 1993. "Drinking and Driving, Self-Control and Gender: Testing a General Theory of Crime." *Journal of Research in Crime and Delinquency* 30:30–46.

Kim, M. and J. Hunter. 1993. "Relationships among Attitudes, Behavioral Intentions, and Behavior: A Meta-Analysis of Past Research. Part 2." *Communications Research* 20:331–64.

Klepper, S. and D. Nagin. 1989a. "Tax Compliance and Perceptions of the Risks of Detection and Criminal Prosecution." *Law and Society Review* 23:209–40.

———. 1989b. "The Deterrent Effect of Perceived Certainty and Severity of Punishment Revisited." *Criminology* 27:721–46.

Kuhn, R. 1992. "1991 Student Drug Survey." College Park: University of Maryland, President's Committee on Alcohol and Drug Policy.

Lewis, H. 1971. *Shame and Guilt in Neurosis*. New York: International Universities Press.

Lewis, M. 1992. *Shame: The Exposed Self*. New York: Macmillan.

Matza, D. 1964. *Delinquency and Drift*. New York: Wiley.

McCarthy, B. 1995. "Not Just 'For the Thrill of It': An Instrumentalist Elaboration of Katz's Explanation of Sneaky Thrill Property Crimes." *Criminology* 33:519–38.

Nagin, D. and R. Paternoster. 1991. "On the Relationship of Past and Future Participation in Delinquency." *Criminology* 29:163–89.

———. 1993. "Enduring Individual Differences and Rational Choice Theories of Crime." *Law and Society Review* 27: 467–96.

Paternoster, R. 1989. "Absolute and Restrictive Deterrence in a Panel of Youth: Explaining the Onset, Persistence/Desistence and Frequency of Delinquent Offending." *Social Problems* 36: 289–309.

Paternoster, R., L. Saltzman, T. Chiricos, and G. Waldo. 1983. "Estimating Perceptual Stability and Deterrent Effects: The Role of Perceived Legal Punishment in the Inhibition of Criminal Involvement." *Journal of Criminal Law and Criminology* 74:270–97.

Piers, G. and M. Singer. 1953. *Shame and Guilt*. New York: Norton.

Piliavin, I., R. Gartner, C. Thornton, and R. Matsueda. 1986. "Crime Deterrence and Rational Choice." *American Sociological Review* 51:101–19.

Polakowski, M. 1994. "Linking Self-Control and Social Control with Deviance: Illuminating the Structure Underlying a General Theory of Crime and Its Relation to Deviant Activity." *Journal of Quantitative Criminology* 10:41–78.

Polk, K. 1991. "Review of a General Theory of Crime." *Crime and Delinquency* 37:575–81.

Reckless, W. 1961. "A New Theory of Delinquency and Crime." *Federal Probation* 25:42–46.

Reiss, A. 1986. "Co-Offender Influences on Criminal Careers." Pp. 121–60 in *Criminal Careers and "Career Criminals,"* edited by A. Blumstein, J. Cohen, J. Roth, and C. Visher. Washington, DC: National Academy Press.

Rossi, P. and A. Anderson. 1982. "The Factorial Survey Approach: An Introduction." Pp. 15–67 in *Measuring Social Judgments*, edited by P. Rossi and S. Nock. Beverly Hills, CA: Sage.

Scheff, T. 1988. "Shame and Conformity: The Deference-Emotion System." *American Sociological Review* 53:395–406.

Smith, D. and P. Gartin. 1989. "Specifying Specific Deterrence: The Influence of Arrest on Future Criminal Activity." *American Sociological Review* 54:94–105.

Smith, D. and B. Patterson. 1985. "Latent-Variable Models in Criminological Research: Applications and a Generalization of Joreskog's LISREL Model." *Journal of Quantitative Criminology* 1:127–58.

Stafford, M. and M. Warr. 1993. "A Reconceptualization of General and Specific Deterrence." *Journal of Research in Crime and Delinquency* 30:123–35.

Tittle, C. 1977. "Sanction Fear and the Maintenance of the Social Order." *Social Forces* 55:579–96.

———. 1980. *Sanctions and Social Deviance*. New York: Praeger.

Toby, J. 1957. "Social Disorganization and Stake in Conformity: Complimentary Factors in the Predatory Behavior of Hoodlums." *Journal of Criminal Law, Criminology and Police Science* 48:12–17.

Wellford, C. 1989. "Towards an Integrated Theory of Criminal Behavior." Pp. 119–28 in *Theoretical Integration in the Study of Deviance and Crime: Problems and Prospects*, edited by S. Messner, M. Krohn, and A. Liska. Albany: SUNY Press.

Williams, K. and R. Hawkins. 1986. "Perceptual Research on General Deterrence: A Critical Review." *Law and Society Review* 20:545–72.

Wood, P., B. Pfefferbaum, and B. Arneklev. 1993. "Risk-Taking and Self-Control: Social Psychological Correlates of Delinquency." *Journal of Crime and Justice* 16:111–30.

Yu, J., D. Essex, and W. Williford. 1992. "DWI/DWAI Offenders and Recidivism by Gender in the Eighties: A Changing Trend?" *International Journal of the Addictions* 27:637–47.

/// REVIEW QUESTIONS

1. What are some of the elements of the low self-control personality?
2. What do Piquero and Tibbetts say are some of the key concepts of the rational choice framework that go beyond traditional deterrence concepts? Which of these concepts were most supported by their own findings?
3. What finding do Piquero and Tibbetts claim is the "most interesting"?

READING /// 6

Previous studies on the spatial distribution of victimization have shown the importance of examining the geographic areas where crime is concentrated. This study by Jordana K. Gallison and Martin A. Andresen provides another example in their analysis of crime along the "O-Train" system in Ottawa, the capital city of Canada. The primary focus of their examination is to determine whether the train system is influencing the level of crime in the areas near its route.

While reading this article, one should consider the following topics:

- In addition to routine activities theory, the theoretical perspectives of Burgess, as well Shaw and McKay, which are introduced here as part of the framework for the current study, and will be discussed at length in a later section (Section VII)
- Findings from previous studies regarding journey-to-crime characteristics, crime displacement, and negative perceptions or fear related to public transit
- Findings of the current study regarding why certain stations seemed to be correlated with crime clustering, and why others are not
- The results regarding which independent variables appear to have consistent or varying influence in predicting commercial burglary, robbery, and/or vehicle theft

SOURCE: Crime and Public Transportation: A Case Study of Ottowa's O-Train System, Jordana K. Gallison and Martin A. Andersen. *Canadian Journal of Criminology and Criminal Justice*, Vol. 59, No. 1, January 2017. Reprinted with permission from University of Toronto Press (www .utpjournals.com).

Crime and Public Transportation

A Case Study of Ottawa's O-Train System

Jordana K. Gallison and Martin A. Andresen

A critical aspect of the built environment to consider in relation to crime is the role of public transportation. Public transportation systems play a pivotal role in the development and sustainability of crime throughout large metropolitan cities. Complex networks of stations, trains, and platforms provide both targets and opportunities for motivated offenders to seize. Common types of crime committed in transit systems include, but are not limited to, vandalism, graffiti, theft, robbery, physical assault, and sexual assault (Smith and Clarke 2000). Such crimes can take place at boarding points; walking to, from, and between transit stations; and on board different modes of transport (Kruger and Landman 2007).

It has been argued that mass forms of public transit systems tend to attract and generate crime due to their standardized spatial and temporal settings (Brantingham, Brantingham, and Wong 1991). Offenders are drawn to commit crime based on a system's ability to triangulate opportunities and targets with little to no security and/or passenger intervention. This notion reflects the theoretical argument of Cohen and Felson's (1979) routine activity theory. Their argument, that crime occurs based on the convergence of a motivated offender, a suitable target, and a lack of a capable guardian, provides strong support that transit systems act as both crime generators and crime attractors (Cohen and Felson 1979).

Public transit systems cluster a substantially large number of people together, providing an opportunity structure for offenders to take advantage of. Predictable commuting times can give offenders a framework for offending. Offenders can become aware of departure and arrival times at busy stations (Brantingham et al. 1991). As passengers board buses and trains at set time intervals and stations, there is an influx of targets to choose from (Smith and Cornish 2006). However, the volume and frequency of such offences may vary among mode of transport (i.e., bus or train), location of the station (urban centre versus suburban station), and time and day of week (weekday versus weekend). Furthermore, most passengers on transit systems represent an ideal target for motivated offenders to victimize. Passengers tend to be tired and preoccupied, and they carry an assortment of bags that contain a large variety of valuable objects (Myhre and Rosso 1996).

It is important to recognize that transit-related crime is not limited to a transit station alone. Transit-generated crime can exceed the physical boundaries of a station and extend to the nearby environment. Neighbouring residential homes and commercial businesses may become vulnerable to an increase in crime due to the opening of a transit route. Many studies have begun to recognize the need to examine nearby transit surroundings in relation to crime (Plano 1993; Poister 1996; Loukaitou-Sideris, Liggett, and Iseki 2002; Billings, Leland, and Swindell 2011; Sedelmaier 2014). Some studies have suggested that a transit station can generate crime up to 750 metres away (Robinson and Giordano 2012; Gallison 2014).

It is critical to examine the nearby land use of a major transportation route to fully understand the potential risks of crime occurring in surrounding neighbourhoods. Public transport systems reflect two elements of land use: first, the nature of the land use, which indicates where activities are taking place, and second, the density of that land use, which indicates its intensity and concentration (Rodrigue, Comtois, and Slack 2009). Central areas of cities have higher levels of land-use density and mixed land use than peripheral areas. Thus, it can be argued that central areas will display higher levels of crime.

Early studies on the spatial distribution of crime have demonstrated the importance of considering the areas in which crime concentrates. The theoretical work of Burgess (1925) and, later, Shaw and McKay (1942) demonstrated attempts to study spatial patterns of crime at an urban level. Their work characterized neighbourhoods with higher levels of crime as places that have high residential turnover, high rates of social assistance, low rental rates, and low rates of home ownership. Further, central business districts (CBDs) have higher levels of recorded crime compared to their suburban counterparts farther away. Moreover, the location of major forms of mass transportation systems is dictated by the level of concentration of human activity, and in CBDs, the concentration is higher than in residential areas. Stations may be placed in areas that experience high traffic volume because they help boost the local economy while facilitating a network for people to travel along within a city, but stations may also be established first, with land development following. Thus, transit crime can be created and exacerbated where it interacts with pre-existing conditions that make crime ideal, such as the aforementioned socio-demographic factors: high residential turnover, high rates of social assistance, low rental rates, low rates of home ownership, and so forth.

The works of Burgess (1925) and Shaw and McKay (1942) are vital to consider in relation to the study of transit crime as they can help provide a greater understanding of why major transportation systems are vulnerable to crime and/or an increase in crime. Despite some land uses that can generate crime and disorder, even among highly facilitative land use types, some will have combinations of location characteristics that will be more attractive to potential offenders (Kinney et al. 2008). The importance of location indicates that, within a city, there will be a mixture of both high- and low-crime areas (Knight and Trygg 1977; Kinney et al. 2008; Andresen and Linning 2012). The immediate surroundings of a transit station tend to encourage a high concentration of commercial businesses, such as liquor stores, convenience stores, ATMs, and restaurants, to boost profits. Therefore, there will be some land uses that have higher crime rates, but not all units in that category will experience crime. It is best to view land uses as a selection filter that helps make the patterning of crime in an urban context more understandable (Kinney et al. 2008). Thus, it is important to recognize that not all high-risk land uses will facilitate crime; a combination of land-use types as well as other factors such as public transportation may be more detrimental, thus producing crime.

In addition, land use may help provide clues as to why offenders seek out particular transit stations to commit crime compared to other stations found along the same route. Transit stations and hubs have the ability to accumulate a high concentration of individuals who use public transit to travel. Offenders can seize this opportunity to commit crime as a population of potential targets is brought together in both time and space. Instead of searching for targets individually at different hunting grounds, offenders can select a target from those that inadvertently gather at a transit station, thus providing a "one-stop shop." Land use can also help us understand how individuals may use public transportation systems to travel to commit crime, searching for vulnerable areas that may have fewer protective factors in place to prevent crime from occurring.

Journey-to-crime literature suggests that crime trips tend to be short (Brantingham and Brantingham 1981; Snook 2004; Townsley and Sidebottom 2010; Andresen, Frank, and Felson 2014). Motivated offenders may seek out ways to commit crime by choosing targets close to an anchor point, most commonly their home and place of employment (Rengert 2004). The notion of an offender choosing targets close to their anchor points reflects Zipf's (1965) theory of least effort. Zipf (1965) stated that people would naturally choose the path of least resistance (effort). By providing a new means to travel in a short time, offenders may be drawn to commit crime in and near transit stations as it allows them to exert little effort to seize such opportunities. New routes can lead offenders to seek out more alluring targets as they become more familiar with the local area (Sedelmaier 2003). Belanger (1999) found that most repeat offenders committed crimes within 10 stops of their home, suggesting that public transit time can be as important a factor as distance in the journey to commit crime. Therefore, a transit system may become a new tactic of connecting an offender with a victim by allowing the offender to travel substantial distances in little time (Billings et al. 2011; Sedelmaier 2014).

Crime displacement is the relocation of crime from one place, time, target, offence, or tactic to another as a result of some crime-prevention initiative. Crime displacement is often viewed as a negative consequence of crime prevention efforts as it may increase crime in other areas and/or transfer risk to other groups. Anti-transit critics frequently state that inner-city crime will be displaced to suburban neighbourhoods if a public transit route is located there. However, Rengert (2004) found the opposite in the study of journeys to crime: offenders were more likely to travel away from a suburb to a city centre to commit crime. To date, there is a lack of research to empirically support the claim that public transportation can displace crime to suburban neighbourhoods (Billings et al. 2011; Gallison 2014). Adverse perceptions of public transit and crime have created both fear and resentment among the general public. Negative perceptions of mass transit systems can threaten the long-term viability of a metropolitan city (Poister 1996). Such perceptions and fears can adversely impact the economy, the environment, and the social welfare of a population. Thus, it is important to undertake spatial analysis of transit crime to more fully understand the spatial patterns of transit crime. In this paper, we ask whether the presence of an O-Train station predicts crime in the surrounding area. And, if so, which crime? And how much can be done to prevent and/or mitigate this effect?

The O-Train

The O-Train is a recent development in the expansion of Ottawa's public transportation system; it accommodates passengers travelling to various parts of downtown Ottawa. The light rail transit system travels northbound and southbound, mostly isolated from road traffic.

However, the O-Train shares the railway track with other trains (OC Transpo 2015). Legally, the O-Train is considered a mainline railway despite being used for local public transport purposes. Many argue that the services provided by the O-Train are more like those of an urban railway than a metro or tramway (ibid.).

The O-Train was implemented in 2001, a significant milestone serving as the city's first form of light rail transit (OC Transpo 2015), using a pre-existing rail corridor for the new rapid transit route. The O-Train operates along eight kilometres of track, helping commuting passengers cross the many waterways (such as the Ottawa River, Dow's Lake, and Rideau Canal) found within the city (ibid.). The line hosts five stations: Bayview (terminus), Carling, Carleton (university), Confederation, and Greenboro (terminus). For the average commuter, travel time is approximately 12 minutes from Bayview to Greenboro stations (ibid.). Both terminus stations also serve as transfer points to Ottawa's bus system. In the first quarter of 2013, it was reported that average weekday ridership was approximately 14,300 passengers (ibid.).

Data and Methods

The current research focuses on each station of the O-Train light rail transit system. Based on previous literature exploring the criminogenic effect of public transportation on local levels of crime, it was hypothesized that a similar criminogenic effect may be present in neighbourhoods surrounding the O-Train. The following discussion examines local levels of crime using a spatial perspective to determine whether the O-Train system can influence the number of crimes reported to the police in the city of Ottawa. Spatial analysis offers a new perspective in determining the effect that public transit systems can have on different types, counts, and rates of crime (Poister 1996; Loukaitou-Sideris et al. 2002; Sedelmaier 2003).

Ottawa is the capital city of Canada and located along the Ottawa River in southeastern Ontario. Ottawa is on the border of Ontario and Quebec, 192 kilometres west of Montreal and 352 kilometres northeast of Toronto. According to Statistics Canada's 2006 community profiles, Ottawa is the fourth-largest city in the country, based on population; in 2006, Ottawa had a population of approximately 812,000 persons, an increase of almost 5% over the previous census of 2001 (Statistics Canada 2007). The Ottawa census metropolitan area (CMA), which excludes the portion of Ottawa-Gatineau in the province of Quebec, is considered the sixth-largest metropolitan area in Canada, based on population: 926,000 in 2009, an increase of almost 6% over 2005 (Gannon 2006; Dauvergne and Turner 2010).

Total crime in the Ottawa CMA has steadily decreased, from 6,326 per 100,000 persons in 2003 to 5,775 per 100,000 persons in 2006 and 4,558 per 100,000 persons in 2009 (Wallace 2004; Silver 2007; Dauvergne and Turner 2010). As of 2006, the crime rate in the Ottawa CMA was greater than the crime rate in the Toronto CMA (5,020 per 100,000 persons), less than the crime rate in the Montreal CMA (6,912 per 100,000 persons), and approximately one half of the crime rate in the Vancouver CMA (10,609 per 100,000 persons) (Silver 2007).

In addition to being the political centre of Canada and the home of the federal Parliament Buildings, Ottawa has two major universities: the University of Ottawa and Carleton University. The University of Ottawa is located in downtown Ottawa, whereas Carleton University is located just south of downtown, among Dow's Lake, the Rideau River, and Bronson Avenue.

Crime and Socio-economic Data

The aim of the current research was to determine whether the O-Train is related to the level of crime in the neighbourhoods near its route. Neighbourhoods were measured using dissemination areas, defined by Statistics Canada. Dissemination areas are geographically smaller than census tracts, equivalent in size to a census block group in the U.S. census, approximately 400 to 700 persons, and composed of one or more blocks; before the 2001 census, these census boundaries were called enumeration areas. There are 1,275 dissemination areas in the city of Ottawa.

Crime-incident data were obtained from the Ottawa Police Service and covered a time period from January 2006 to December 2006—the most recent corresponding census data available. Data for three types of crime were publicly available: commercial break and enter (commercial burglary), robbery, and theft of vehicle. Data were geocoded to the street network for Ottawa and then aggregated to the dissemination-area level. The geocoding for these data generated a success rate of 96%. This is well above the minimum acceptable success rate of 85% set by Ratcliffe (2004), although the analyses in that paper were performed with little concern for spatial bias.

Census data were obtained from Statistics Canada and provided the boundaries of each dissemination area located in Ottawa. Data were also obtained from the city of Ottawa: the x-y coordinates of the O-Train stations as well as the location of the route. Together, the data helped us visually identify which dissemination areas in Ottawa were displaying higher levels of crime as well as determine whether the dissemination areas with higher levels of reported crime were located near an O-Train station. The study used 11 independent variables from the Canadian census to empirically test whether crime could be attributed to something other than the presence of the O-Train in Ottawa: residential population, young males, never married, single parents, renter-occupied dwellings, residential mobility, unemployment, education, visible minorities (a measure of ethnic heterogeneity), average income, and average value of dwelling. We also used three variables related to our study: University of Ottawa, Carleton University, and last, the presence of an O-Train station.

These socio-economic variables are often employed in studies of the geography of crime in the context of social disorganization theory and routine activity theory (Shaw and McKay 1931, 1942; Cohen and Felson 1979; Felson and Cohen 1980, 1981). Generally speaking, these 11 variables can be classified as population characteristics, socio-economic status, and dwelling characteristics. We measured population characteristics using the percentage of the population that was young (males aged 15 to 24), persons never married, lone-parent families, visible minorities, and people who had recently moved (within the past five years). We measured socio-economic status using the percentage of the population aged 20 years and older who had obtained a post-secondary education (completed certificate, diploma, or degree), the unemployment rate for those 15 and older participating in the labour force, and the average household income in thousands of dollars. And finally, we assessed the dwelling characteristics of a dissemination area by considering renter-occupied dwellings and average dwelling value.

Previous research has shown that being located within a central business district and distance from a CBD affect crime (Schmid 1960a, 1960b; Brown 1982). Because of this fact, we included a variable (distance to downtown) that identified the dissemination areas within the Ottawa CBD and distance from the CBD, measured in kilometres and calculated using the Euclidean distance between the centroid of the downtown area and the centroids of all dissemination areas. Descriptive statistics and correlations for the independent variables are presented in Tables 1 and 2.

Statistical Analyses

The analyses below begin by calculating the local Moran's *I* to demonstrate the spatial relationship between crime rates and public transportation. It is also known as a LISA, or local indicator of spatial association (Anselin 1995). Local Moran's *I* assesses the local variation of spatial autocorrelation (Fox et al. 2012). In other words, this technique determines whether spatial clustering occurs at the local level for each spatial unit under analysis. Local Moran's *I* can indicate in a statistical manner which regions have similar and dissimilar values surrounding them (Chainey and Ratcliffe 2005). This is a beneficial technique to use in crime mapping as it can add robustness to determining whether certain areas can be defined as hot spots. Values for local Moran's *I* range from −1 (perfect negative spatial autocorrelation) to +1 (perfect positive spatial autocorrelation).

Table 1 • Descriptive statistics for independent variables at the dissemination-area level

	Minimum	Maximum	*M*	*SD*
Commercial burglary count	0.00	42	3.01	4.40
Robbery count	0.00	20	0.56	1.53
Theft of vehicle count	0.00	62	2.09	4.44
Population	207	8,157	638.29	460.28
Young males, %	0.99	32.79	10.19	3.62
Never married, %	9.57	77.00	29.61	11.32
Single parents, %	0.00	23.90	4.26	3.23
Renter-occupied dwellings, %	0.00	100.00	27.31	30.97
Residential mobility, %	0.00	99.25	37.09	17.27
Unemployment rate	0.00	18.76	3.18	2.40
Education, % post-secondary	0.00	79.85	51.26	9.59
Visible minorities, %	0.00	100.00	17.55	14.95
Average income, $ (2006)	0.00	167,398	43,147	16,449
Average value of dwelling, $ (2006)	0.00	1,449,152	280,586	120,460
Distance to downtown, km	0.10	42.00	11.54	7.84

From these values, four types of local clusters can be identified: High–High, Low–Low, Low–High, and High–Low. High–High and Low–Low represent local positive spatial autocorrelation—that is, high-crime-rate areas that are contiguous with other high-crime-rate areas and low-crime-rate areas that are contiguous with other low-crime-rate areas, respectively. Low–High and High–Low represent local negative spatial autocorrelation: low-crime-rate areas that are contiguous with high-crime-rate areas and high-crime-rate areas that are contiguous with low-crime-rate areas, respectively. There are also other areas that are classified as having neither positive nor negative local spatial autocorrelation. These various forms of local spatial clusters can then be used in a modelling framework (Andresen 2011) as the outcome variable.

Results

The results demonstrated that local spatial autocorrelation existed in the current research. Results for LISA examining commercial burglary demonstrated that three of the O-Train stations were located in areas considered High–High. One possible reason is that the O-Train stations are situated in areas with commercial land use and are more likely to experience higher levels of reported burglary. However, caution should be exercised in this interpretation because we do not have longitudinal data. The O-Train route travels through downtown Ottawa, where many people live and travel into and out of to go to work and school. The High–High classification could also be attributed to the mixed land

Table 2 • Correlations for independent variables

Population											
Young males, %	–.00										
Never married, %	–.06*	.71**									
Single parents, %	.01	.16**	.21**								
Renter-occupied dwellings, %	.06*	.48**	.74**	.38**							
Residential mobility, %	.24**	.35**	.51**	.16**	.59**						
Unemployment rate	.02	.29**	.31**	.21**	.33**	.23**					
Education, % post-secondary	–.02	.09*	.12**	–.19**	–.11**	.23**	.05				
Visible minorities, %	.21**	.24**	.19**	.38**	.38**	.35**	.23**	–.15**			
Average income, $ (2006)	.01	–.30**	–.36**	–.34**	–.44**	–.19**	–.17**	.33**	–.29**		
Average dwelling value, $ (2006)	–.00	–.19**	–.20**	–.31**	–.29**	–.15**	–.09*	.25**	–.25**	.73**	
Distance to down-town, km	.06*	–.22**	–.57*	–.24**	–.54**	–.32**	–.18**	.07*	–.28**	.11**	–.01
	X1	X2	X3	X4	X5	X6	X7	X8	X9	X10	X11

* Correlation is significant at the 0.05 level (2-tailed).

** Correlation is significant at the 0.01 level (2-tailed).

X1 = Population; X2 = Young Males; X3 = Never Married; X4 = Single Parents; X5 = Renter-Occupied Dwellings; X6 = Residential Mobility; X7 = Unemployment; X8 = Education; X9 = Visible Minorities; X10 = Average Income; X11 = Average Dwelling Value.

use that the downtown portion of Ottawa exhibits. The role of land use has been known to impact crime patterns (see Kinney et al. [2008] for a further discussion of land use), and thus further analysis should be conducted to determine whether the O-Train is the sole factor causing the higher levels of break and enters shown in the areas under analysis. This is undertaken in Figure 1 below in an inferential context.

The results for LISA examining robbery illustrated varying results in regard to the spatial autocorrelation, but there were no local crime clusters associated with robbery along the O-Train system. Bayview is located close to areas with High–High and Low–High local crime clusters, but nothing that could be attributed to the O-Train. All O-Train stations are located in areas classified as statistically insignificant. This is somewhat surprising due to the fact that the Carleton station is located at Carleton University, where there are many students who use public transportation while attending school and who carry a variety of small but valuable items while travelling. Further analyses should be conducted to determine why robbery does not appear to be a significant issue at this station, such as the presence of numerous capable guardians or the type of station design.

The lack of statistically significant local clustering at Confederation and Greenboro stations is also surprising if public transportation is considered a generator or attractor of criminal activity. Both stations are located at or near the end of the O-Train route and are transfer points to other parts of Ottawa's public transportation system; therefore, they are potentially rife with opportunities for robbery because of all the transferring transit patrons. Both Confederation and Greenboro connect to Ottawa's

Figure 1 • LISA output, commercial burglary

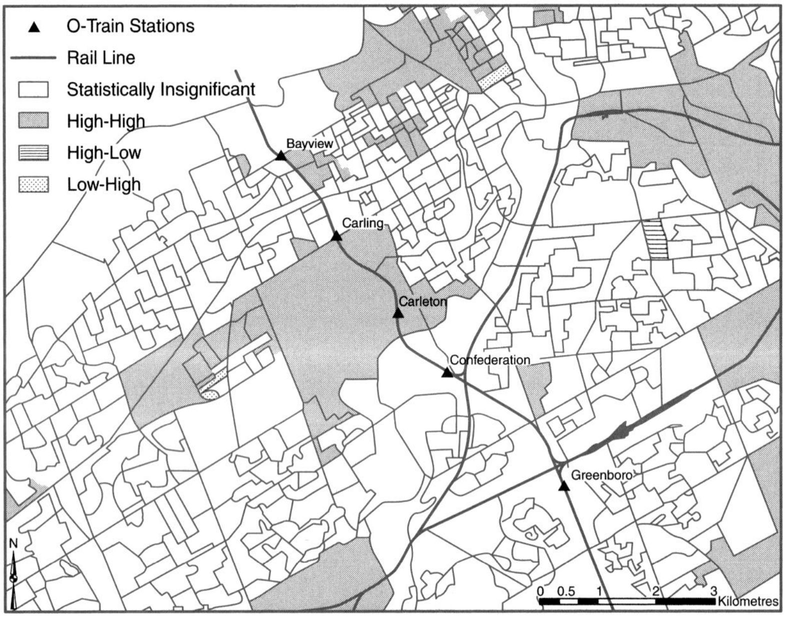

▲ O-Train Stations
Rail Line
Statistically Insignificant
High-High
High-Low
Low-High
Bayview
Carling
Carleton
Confederation
Greenboro
N
0 0.5 1 2 3 Kilometres

Figure 2 • LISA output, robbery

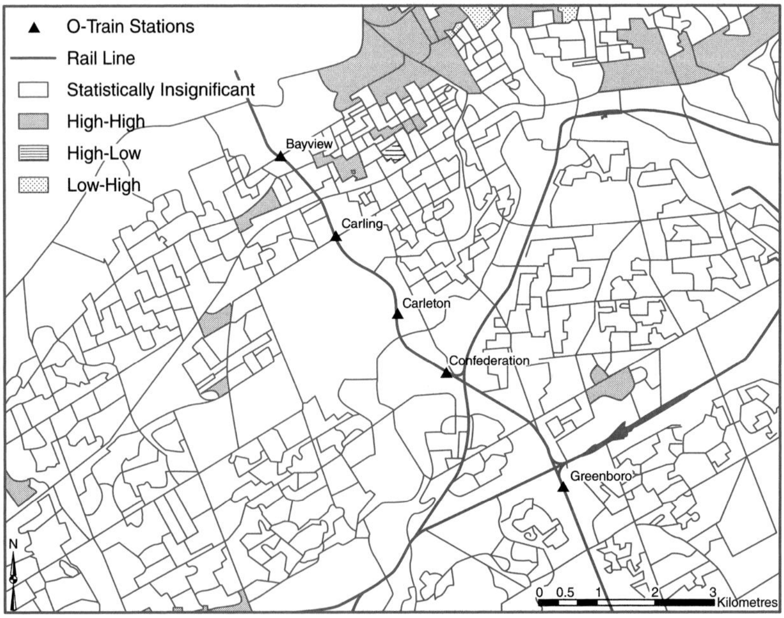

▲ O-Train Stations
Rail Line
Statistically Insignificant
High-High
High-Low
Low-High
Bayview
Carling
Carleton
Confederation
Greenboro
N
0 0.5 1 2 3 Kilometres

Figure 3 • LISA output, theft of vehicle

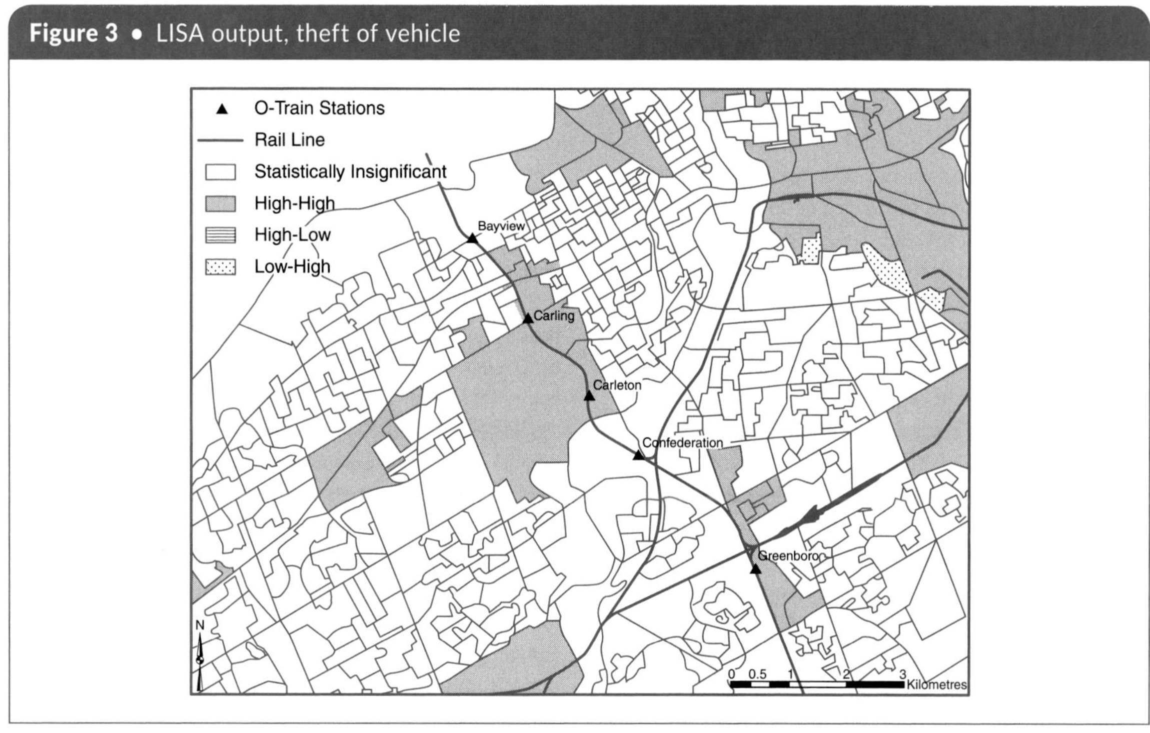

bus service, and offenders may be more tempted to commit robbery at these stations because it is easier for them to travel to other parts of the city without being apprehended. (See Figure 2.)

The results for LISA examining theft of vehicle show that almost all stations on the O-Train system are located in areas or close to areas classified as High–High. Bayview station was found not to be significant; however, three stations (Carling, Carleton, and Greenboro) are located in statistically significant local crime clusters. This is not particularly surprising given that these stations host park-and-ride lots and are located in downtown Ottawa, so there would be a wide variety of vehicles for an offender to choose from. (See Figure 3.)

Overall, the results demonstrate that the O-Train may play a role in the amount of crime reported in the dissemination areas located in Ottawa. Despite the route having only five stations, the dissemination areas that are within the city's geographical boundaries are more likely to experience higher levels of crime; this indicates that the O-Train may serve as either a crime generator or a crime attractor, particularly for commercial burglary and theft of vehicle. Moreover, based on the fact that the O-Train stations are not always located in local crime clusters (High–High, for example), depending on the crime type under analysis, it is possible that these stations attract particular types of crime. Such a claim, however, can only be substantiated with longitudinal data, which were not available.

Although the LISA results are instructive for the identification of local crime clusters in and around the O-Train stations, particularly when local crime clusters are not present, further inferential analyses are necessary to identify the factors that lead to local crime clusters, particularly High–High (a Low–Low local crime cluster is not considered to be problematic). To better identify the factors that lead to the development of High–High local crime clusters, the discussion will now turn to the results of the logistic regressions. We discuss only the variables remaining after statistical testing. Moreover, statistically insignificant variables were removed from the analyses.

The results for commercial burglary show that six of the independent variables remained in the final model: average income, distance from the CBD, average dwelling value, never married, rentals, and University of Ottawa. Average income was found to have a negative estimated parameter, as would be expected by theory (particularly social disorganization theory), but the magnitude of this parameter was rather small and is the equivalent of a statistically insignificant relationship. Distance from the CBD also had a negative estimated parameter, as would be expected, but the magnitude of this estimated parameter was greater. Average dwelling value had a statistical significance level that was marginal and a positive estimated parameter indicating the importance of target attractiveness for commercial burglary; however, as with average income, the magnitude of this relationship was effectively zero.

Never married, representing places with more people who are likely to have routine activities away from the home, had a small, positive impact on the probability of a High–High local crime cluster, and rentals had a very small and negative impact on the probability of a High–High local crime cluster. The largest-magnitude impact on the probability of a High–High local crime cluster was the presence of the University of Ottawa, with a 4.39 times greater probability. However, this is likely due to the fact that the University of Ottawa is mostly located in the CBD of Ottawa, whose estimated parameter, although statistically insignificant, is similar in magnitude to the estimated parameter for the University of Ottawa. Most notable, in the context of the current research, is that the O-Train is not a statistically significant predictor of High–High local crime clusters in the context of commercial burglary.

The results for robbery, are similar to those for commercial burglary in that the O-Train was not a statistically significant predictor of High–High local crime clusters. However, this should come as no surprise given that none of the O-Train stations were located in any of the High–High local crime clusters. Angel (1968) expected that robberies would occur in places that had a moderate level of pedestrian traffic: high enough to have targets, but not too many to have people who may intervene in a criminal event. Clarke, Belanger, and Eastmanx (1996), however, found that more robberies occurred at places with lower levels of population density. Thus, although one may suspect that the presence of an O-Train station in an area would increase robbery, our result is consistent with previous research.

The final model for robbery also retained six independent variables after individual and joint statistical significance testing. Distance from the CBD had its expected negative estimated parameter, but average dwelling value was also negative and statistically significant. This indicates that commercial burglary and robbery local crime clusters are located in different areas of the city, also evident from the maps of the LISA output. The presence of single parents increases the probability of a High–High local crime cluster, as does the increased presence of never-married persons and visible minorities. The presence of young males, however, decreases the probability of a High–High local crime cluster. Aside from the negative result for young males, these results all match expectations, particularly those of social disorganization theory—young males are the most criminogenic subpopulation and are expected to be positively associated with criminal activity (Hirschi and Gottfredson 1983; Boyd 2000).

The results for theft of vehicle are more interesting in the context of the O-Train. Average income, distance from the CBD, and visible minorities have expected negative estimated parameters. The magnitudes of the odds ratios for average income and visible minorities are rather low, similar to the results for robbery, but the impact of the distance from the CBD is of a much greater magnitude. This latter result, for this and the other crime types, is indicative of the fact that crime is so highly concentrated in the city of Ottawa (Andresen and Linning 2012; LaRue and Andresen 2015). Of most interest here, however, is the statistically significant result for the O-Train in the context of theft of vehicle. This estimated parameter is not only statistically significant and positive, but it is of a high magnitude, considering the odds ratio. The presence of an O-Train station increases the probability of a High–High local theft of vehicle crime cluster by almost seven times. This result is most obvious for the Carleton and Greenboro O-Train stations. Carleton station is located at Carleton University, which has car parks for faculty staff and students, all of which present many opportunities for vehicle-based crime. Greenboro, as mentioned above, is a transfer station that provides access to other parts of Ottawa's public transportation system, and the presence of automobiles represents opportunities similar to those for Carleton station.

Discussion and Conclusions

The aim of the current study was to determine whether neighbourhoods around the O-Train stations in the city of Ottawa, measured using dissemination areas, demonstrated higher levels of reported crime after controlling for several socio-economic and socio-demographic factors. Exploration of Ottawa's five O-Train stations across two offence types (commercial burglary and theft of vehicle) showed high levels of crime clustering in those areas with an O-Train station located within it or nearby. The findings of the current research highlight the importance of considering the criminal implications of the presence and operation of mass public transit systems. Strategic planning must be included in preparation for handling mass populations of commuters, which include both victims and offenders. More policing must be deployed routinely to patrol O-Train stations and nearby areas to deter motivated offenders from seeking out vulnerable targets, such as vehicles left for the day by individuals commuting to work or school using the O-Train. Such suggestions should be incorporated into the Ottawa Police Service's strategy to combat crime in and around mass forms of public transportation in the city (e.g., O-Train, bus loops, train stations, and so on).

However, as shown in the LISA output maps and the regression results, the impact is not the same across all crime types. After considering their High–High local crime clusters, robbery, in particular, was not a problem for the O-Train, and commercial burglary was not statistically related to the O-Train stations; however, theft of vehicle High–High local crime clusters were statistically related to O-Train stations, and with a high magnitude.

By employing geo-spatial measures to study the relationship between public transportation and crime, a greater understanding emerges that would not be apparent if other statistical measures were used. In the current research, local Moran's I (LISA) was the most appropriate geospatial measure used to understand the phenomenon of crime along the O-Train route. Unlike the other techniques used, LISA gave a visual representation of spatial autocorrelation, and it demonstrated the effect that the O-Train could have on particular crime types located near the stations and in nearby neighbourhoods.

There are some limitations associated with the current research. Like many studies of crime, this study includes only criminal incidents reported to the police. The dark figure of crime, which describes the amount of crime that occurs but is not reported, could alter the results. More crime may have taken place within the parameters of the study but not reported. Consequently, crime that was reported but was deemed not to have occurred might also be excluded. This exclusion reflects the discretion used by the police to determine whether a criminal offence took place or not.

Further, the study used three types of offences and excluded other, more common types of crime associated with public transportation systems. Including more offence categories may have yielded a different outcome. However, our results show that a public transportation system does not necessarily have to be positively related to crime. Thus, we are able to show the importance of not aggregating individual crime types when investigating the relationship between crime and public transportation. Future studies on the relationship between crime and public transportation should include a wide array of offence categories to gain more insight into the phenomenon of transit crime. Last, future studies should use longitudinal data to best witness changes over an extended period rather than the shorter time frame that a cross-sectional study provides.

Mass transit exists in a complex environment of temporal and spatial patterns. In a criminological context, the transit environment contains a multitude of targets that are stationary and unguarded, providing ample opportunities for motivated offenders (Smith and Clarke 2000). However, the risk of victimization could decrease if key stakeholders developed an effective plan to prevent and reduce crime from occurring in such environments using some form of patrol (Barclay et al. 1996) or environmental design (La Vigne 1996).

Local police must take precautionary measures to deal with established and potential criminal hot spots. If a station is placed in a pre-existing or potential hot spot, local police must take responsibility for securing and patrolling it and its surroundings to disrupt the opportunity structure for committing crime. The Ottawa Police Service could consider adopting a specialized police force to handle transit crime and disorder. For example, the city of Vancouver has established such a police force, Transit Police, that aims to deter potential criminals from committing crime by routinely patrolling SkyTrain stations (TransLink 2014). The presence of a uniformed officer can help ease commuters' fears of and concerns about crime, deter offenders, and provide on-site support for problems. City officials may also need to revise the procedures for allocating land use and issuing permits and licences to help prevent crime from occurring as a result of the potential negative interaction between some land use types and mass forms of public transportation. In addition, mixed land use, consisting of commercial businesses and residential homes, should be promoted to help enable legitimate activities to occur in the vicinity of a transit route.

As demonstrated in previous literature, there is a continual need to study the relationship between offender mobility and mass forms of public transportation. Various land uses, general crime rates, and strategic planning need to be taken into consideration when implementing routes for commuters travelling to and from work, school, and home. By employing geographic measures, one can understand the movement of mobile populations and the opportunities that arise from transit environments at a macro-, meso-, and micro-level.

References

Ackerman, William V. 1998 Socioeconomic correlates of increasing crime rates in smaller communities. Professional Geographer 50 (3): 372–87. http://dx.doi.org/10.1111/0033-0124.00127.

Andresen, Martin A. 2006a Crime measures and the spatial analysis of criminal activity. British Journal of Criminology 46 (2): 258–85. http://dx.doi.org/10.1093/bjc/azi054.

Andresen, Martin A. 2006b A spatial analysis of crime in Vancouver, British Columbia: A synthesis of social disorganization and routine activity theory. Canadian Geographer 50 (4): 487–502. http://dx.doi.org/10.1111/j.1541 0064.2006.00159.x.

Andresen, Martin A. 2007 Location quotients, ambient populations, and the spatial analysis of crime in Vancouver, Canada. Environment & Planning A 39 (10): 2423–44. http://dx.doi .org/10.1068/a38187.

Andresen, Martin A. 2011 Estimating the probability of local crime clusters: The impact of immediate spatial neighbors. Journal of Criminal Justice 39 (5): 394–404. http://dx.doi.org/10.1016/j .jcrimjus.2011.05.005.

Andresen, Martin A., Richard Frank, and Marcus Felson 2014 Age and the distance to crime. Criminology & Criminal Justice 14 (3): 314–33. http://dx.doi.org/10.1177/1748895813494870.

Andresen, Martin A. and Shannon J. Linning 2012 The (in)appropriateness of aggregating across crime types. Applied Geography (Sevenoaks, England) 35 (1–2): 275–82. http://dx.doi .org/10.1016/j.apgeog.2012.07.007.

Angel, Schlomo 1968 Discouraging crime through city planning. Working paper no. 75. Berkeley, CA: Center for Planning and Development Research.

Anselin, Luc 1995 Local indicators of spatial association – LISA. Geographical Analysis 27 (2): 93–115. http://dx.doi .org/10.1111/j.1538-4632.1995.tb00338.x.

Barclay, Paul, Jennifer Buckley, Paul J. Brantingham, Patricia L. Brantingham, and Terry Whinn-Yates 1996 Preventing auto theft in suburban Vancouver commuter lots: Effects of a bike patrol. Crime Prevention Studies 6: 133–61.

Belanger, M. 1999 Crime Mobility and Public Transport: The Case of the New York City Subway. PhD diss., School of Criminal Justice, Rutgers University, NJ.

Billings, Stephen B., Suzanne Leland, and David Swindell 2011 The effects of the announcement and opening of light rail transit stations on neighbourhood crime. Journal of Urban Affairs 33 (5): 549–66. http://dx.doi.org/10.1111/j.1467-9906.2011.005 64.x.

Boyd, Neil 2000 The Beast Within: Why Men Are Violent. Vancouver: Greystone.

Brantingham, Patricia L. and Paul J. Brantingham, eds. 1981 Environmental Criminology. Beverly Hills, CA: Sage.

Brantingham, Patricia L., Paul J. Brantingham, and Paul S. Wong 1991 How public transit feeds private crime: Notes on the Vancouver "Skytrain" experiences. Security Journal 2: 91–95.

Brown, Marilyn A. 1982 Modelling the spatial distribution of suburban crime. Economic Geography 58 (3): 247–61. http://dx.doi .org/10.2307/143513.

Burgess, Ernest 1925 The Urban Community: Selected Papers from the Proceedings of the American Sociological Society. New York: Greenwood.

Cahill, Meagan E. and Gordon F. Mulligan 2003 The determinants of crime in Tucson, Arizona. Urban Geography 24 (7): 582–610. http://dx.doi.org/10.2747/0272-3638.24.7.582.

Chainey, Spencer and Jerry H. Ratcliffe 2005 GIS and Crime Mapping. Chichester, UK: John Wiley & Sons. http://dx.doi .org/10.1002/9781118685181.

Clarke, Ronald V., Mathieu Belanger, and James A. Eastmanx 1996 Where Angel fears to tread: A test in the New York City subway of the robbery/density hypothesis. Crime Prevention Studies 6: 217–35.

Cohen, Lawrence E. and David Cantor 1980 The determinants of larceny: An empirical and theoretical study. Journal of Research in Crime and Delinquency 17 (2): 140–59. http://dx.doi .org/10.1177/002242788001700202.

Cohen, Lawrence E. and M. Felson 1979 Social change and crime rate trends: A routine activity approach. American Sociological Review 44 (4): 588–608. http://dx.doi.org/10.2307/2094589.

Cohen, Lawrence E., James R. Kluegel, and Kenneth C. Land 1981 Social inequality and predatory criminal victimization: An exposition and test of a formal theory. American Sociological Review 46 (5): 505–24. http://dx.doi.org/10.2307/2094935.

Dauvergne, Mia and John Turner 2010 Police-Reported Crime Statistics in Canada, 2009. Ottawa: Statistics Canada, Canadian Centre for Justice Statistics.

Felson, Marcus and Lawrence E. Cohen 1980 Human ecology and crime: A routine activity approach. Human Ecology 8 (4): 389–405. http://dx.doi.org/10.1007/BF01561001.

Felson, Marcus and Lawrence E. Cohen 1981 Modeling crime trends: A criminal opportunity perspective. Journal of Research in Crime and Delinquency 18 (1): 138–64. http://dx.doi.org/10.1177/002242788101800109.

Fox, Eric, Shivanand Balram, Suzana Dragicevic, and Arthur Roberts 2012 Spatial analysis of high resolution aerial photographs to analyze the spread of mountain pine beetle infestations. Journal of Sustainable Development 5 (9): 106–129. http://dx.doi.org/10.5539/jsd.v5n9p106.

Gallison, Jordana K. 2014 The line of crime: Dismantling fears and concerns of crime along Vancouver SkyTrain's Canada Line. Security Journal. Advance online publication 20 January, doi:10.1057/sj.2013.42.

Gannon, Maire 2006 Crime Statistics in Canada, 2005. Ottawa: Statistics Canada, Canadian Centre for Justice Statistics.

Harries, Keith D. 1974 The Geography of Crime and Justice. New York: McGraw-Hill.

Harries, Keith D. 1995 The ecology of homicide and assault: Baltimore City and County, 1989–91. Studies on Crime and Crime Prevention 4: 44–60.

Hirschi, Travis and Michael Gottfredson 1983 Age and the explanation of crime. American Journal of Sociology 89 (3): 552–84. http://dx.doi.org/10.1086/227905.

Kelling, George and Catherine M. Coles 1998 Fixing Broken Windows: Restoring Order and Reducing Crime in Our Communities. New York: Touchstone.

Kinney, J. Bryan, Patricia L. Brantingham, Kathryn Wuschke, Michael G. Kirk, and Paul J. Brantingham 2008 Crime attractors, generators and detractors: Land use and urban crime opportunities. Built Environment 34 (1): 62–74. http://dx.doi.org/10.2148/benv.34.1.62.

Knight, Robert L. and Lisa L. Trygg 1977 Evidence of land use impacts of rapid transit systems. Transportation 6 (3): 231–47. http://dx.doi.org/10.1007/BF00177453.

Kruger, T. and K. Landman 2007 Crime and public transport: Designing a safer journey. Proceedings of the 26th Southern African Transport Conference (SATC). Document Transformation Technologies: Pretoria, South Africa.

LaRue, Elise and Martin A. Andresen 2015 Spatial patterns of crime in Ottawa: The role of universities. Canadian Journal of Criminology and Criminal Justice 57 (2): 189–214. http://dx.doi.org/10.3138/CJCCJ.2013.E47.

La Vigne, Nancy G. 1996 Safe transport: Security by design on the Washington Metro. Crime Prevention Studies 6: 163–97.

Loukaitou-Sideris, Anastasia, Robin Liggett, and Hiroyuki Iseki 2002 The geography of transit crime: Documentation and evaluation of crime incidence on and around the Green Line stations in Los Angeles. Journal of Planning Education and Research 22 (2): 135–51. http://dx.doi.org/10.1177/0739456X02238443.

Morenoff, Jeffrey D., Robert J. Sampson, and Stephen W. Raudenbush 2001 Neighbourhood inequality, collective efficacy and the spatial dynamics of urban violence. Research report no. 00–451. Population Studies Centre, Institute for Social Research, University of Michigan.

Myhre, Marina L. and Fabien Rosso 1996 Designing for security in Météor: A projected new metro line in Paris. Crime Prevention Studies 6: 199–216.

OC Transpo 2015 O-Train: Light rail rapid transit. Accessed 15 April 2015. http://www.octranspo1.com/routes/o-train.

Plano, Stephen L. 1993 Transit-generated crime: Perception versus reality—a sociographic study of neighborhoods adjacent to Section B of Baltimore Metro. Transportation Research Record 1402 (1): 59–62.

Poister, Theodore H. 1996 Transit related crime in suburban areas. Journal of Urban Affairs 18 (1): 63–75. http://dx.doi.org/10.1111/j.1467-9906.1996.tb00366.x.

Ratcliffe, Jerry H. 2004 Geocoding crime and a first estimate of a minimum acceptable hit rate. International Journal of Geographical Information Science 18 (1): 61–72. http://dx.doi.org/10.1080/13658810310001596076.

Rengert, George F. 2004 The journey to crime. In Punishment, Places and Perpetrators: Developments in Criminology and Criminal Justice Research, ed. Gerben Bruinsma, Henk Elffers, and Jan De Keijser, 169–81. Collompton, UK: Willan.

Robinson, Jennifer B. and Lauren M. Giordano 2012 Spatial interplay: Interaction of land uses in relation to crime incidents around transit stations. In Patterns, Prevention and Geometry of Crime, ed. Martin A. Andresen and J.B. Kinney, 137–47. New York: Routledge.

Rodrigue, Jean-Paul, Claude Comtois, and Brian Slack 2009 The Geography of Transport Systems. Milton Park, UK: Routledge.

Sampson, Robert J. 1997 The embeddedness of child and adolescent development: A community-level perspective on urban violence. In Violence and Childhood in the Inner City, ed. Joan McCord, 31–77. Cambridge: Cambridge University Press. http://dx.doi.org/10.1017/CBO9780511571015.003.

Sampson, Robert J. and W. Byron Groves 1989 Community structure and crime: Testing social-disorganization theory. American Journal of Sociology 94 (4): 774–802. http://dx.doi.org/10.1086/229068.

Sampson, Robert J., Stephen W. Raudenbush, and Felton Earls 1997 Neighbourhoods and violent crime: A multilevel study of collective efficacy. Science 277 (5328): 918–24. http://dx.doi.org/10.1126/science.277.5328.918.

Schmid, Calvin F. 1960a Urban crime areas: Part I. American Sociological Review 25 (4): 527–42. http://dx.doi.org/10.2307/2092937.

Schmid, Calvin F. 1960b Urban crime areas: Part II. American Sociological Review 25 (5): 655–78. http://dx.doi.org/10.2307/2090139.

Sedelmaier, Christopher M. 2003 Railroaded: The Effects of a New Public Transport System upon Local Crime Patterns. PhD diss., Rutgers University, NJ.

Sedelmaier, Christopher M. 2014 Offender-target redistribution on a new public transport system. Security Journal 27 (S2): 164–79. http://dx.doi.org/10.1057/sj.2014.4.

Shaw, Clifford R. and Henry D. McKay 1931 Social Factors in Juvenile Delinquency. Washington, DC: U.S. Government Printing Office.

Shaw, Clifford R. and Henry D. McKay 1942 Juvenile Delinquency and Urban Areas: A Study of Rates of Delinquency in Relation to Differential Characteristics of Local Communities in American Cities. Chicago, IL: University of Chicago Press.

Silver, Warren 2007 Crime Statistics in Canada, 2006. Ottawa: Statistics Canada, Canadian Centre for Justice Statistics.

Smith, Martha J. and Ronald V. Clarke 2000 Crime and public transport. In Crime and Justice. Vol. 27, A Review of Research, 169–233. http://dx.doi.org/10.1086/652200.

Smith, Martha J. and Derek Cornish 2006 Secure and Tranquil Travel: Preventing Crime and Disorder on Public Transport. London: Jill Dando Institute of Crime Science, University College London.

Snook, Brent 2004 Individual differences in distance traveled by serial burglars. Journal of Investigative Psychology and Offender Profiling 1 (1): 53–66. http://dx.doi.org/10.1002/jip.3.

Statistics Canada 2007 2006 Community Profiles. Ottawa: Statistics Canada.

Townsley, Michael and Aiden Sidebottom 2010 All offenders are equal, but some are more equal than others: Variations in journeys to crime between offenders. Criminology 48 (3): 897–917. http://dx.doi.org/10.1111/j.1745-9125.2010.00205.x.

Translink 2014 Safety and Security. Accessed 1 November 2014. http://www.TransLink.ca/en/Rider-Guide/Safety-and-Security.aspx.

Tseloni, Andromachi, Denise R. Osborn, Alan Trickett, and Ken Pease 2002 Modelling property crime using the British Crime Survey: What have we learnt? British Journal of Criminology 42 (1): 109–28. http://dx.doi.org/10.1093/bjc/42.1.109.

Wallace, Marnie 2004 Crime Statistics in Canada, 2003. Ottawa: Statistics Canada, Canadian Centre for Justice Statistics.

Zipf, George K. 1965 Human behaviour and the principle of least effort: An introduction to human ecology. New York: Hafner.

/// REVIEW QUESTIONS

1. What are some specific reasons why public transit offers a good case study of routine activities theory? If you were to design such a study, which elements would you look for that this study did not?
2. In this study, what are some of the characteristics that may explain why the Confederation and Greenboro stations had different results than the other hubs or stations?
3. Which independent variables had the most influence on predicting crime clustering? Which independent factors contributed most to crime being concentrated in certain locations or stations?

SECTION IV

Early Positive School Perspectives of Criminality

In this section, we will discuss the dramatic differences in assumptions between the Classical and Positive Schools of criminological thought. We will also touch on the pre-Darwinian perspectives of human behavior (e.g., phrenology) as well as the influence that Charles Darwin had on the perspectives of all social sciences, particularly criminology. Finally, we will discuss the theories and methods used by early positivists, particularly Cesare Lombroso, IQ theorists, and body type researchers, with an emphasis on the criticisms of these perspectives, methodologies, and resulting policies.

After many decades of dominance by the Classical School (see Sections II and III), academics and scientists were becoming aware that the deterrence framework did not explain the distribution of crime. Their restlessness led to new explanatory models of crime and behavior. Most of these perspectives focused on the fact that certain individuals or groups tend to offend more than others and the idea that such "inferior" individuals should be controlled or even eliminated. This ideological framework fit a more general stance toward **eugenics**, the study of and policies related to the improvement of the human race via control over reproduction, which as we will see was explicitly mandated for certain groups. Thus, the conclusion was that there must be notable variations across individuals and groups that can help determine who is most at risk of offending.

So, in the early to mid-1800s, several perspectives were offered regarding how to determine which individuals or groups were most likely to commit crime. Many of these theoretical frameworks were made to distinguish the more "superior" individuals or groups from the "inferior" individuals or groups. Such intentions were likely related to the increased use of slavery in the world during the 1800s as well as imperialism's fight to quell rebellions at that time. For example, slavery was at its peak in the United States during this period, and many European countries controlled many dozens of colonies, which they were trying to retain for profit and domain.

Perhaps the first example of this belief was represented by **craniometry**. Craniometry was the belief that the size of the brain or skull represents the superiority or inferiority of certain individuals or ethnic or racial groups.[1] The size of the brain and the skull were considered because, at that time, it was believed that a person's skull perfectly conformed to brain structure; thus, the size of the skull was believed to reflect the size of the brain. Modern science has challenged this assumption, but there actually is a significant correlation between the size of the skull

[1]For a review, see Nicole Rafter, "The Murderous Dutch Fiddler," *Theoretical Criminology* 9, no. 1 (2005): 65–96.

and the size of the brain. Still, even according to the assumptions of the craniometrists, it is unlikely that much can be gathered about an individual's intelligence from the overall size of the brain, and certainly the skull, from simple measurements of mass.

The scientists who studied this model, if they were dealing with living subjects, would measure the various sizes or circumferences of the skulls. If they were dealing with recently dead subjects, then they would actually measure the brain weight or volume of the participants. When dealing with subjects who had died long before, craniometrists would measure the volume of skulls by pouring seeds inside and then pouring those that fit into graduated cylinders. Later, when these scientists realized that seeds were not a valid measure of volume, they moved toward using buckshot or ball bearings.

Most studies by the craniometrists tended to show that subjects of White or Western European descent were superior to those of other ethnic groups in terms of brain volume or skull size. Furthermore, the front portion of the brain (i.e., the genu) was thought to be larger in superior individuals or groups, and the hind portion of the brain or skull (i.e., the splenium) was predicted to be larger in inferior individuals or groups. Notably, these researchers typically knew which brains or skulls belonged to which ethnic or racial group before measurements were taken, making for an unethical and improper methodology. Such biased measurements continued throughout the 19th century and into the early 1900s.[2] These examinations were largely done with the intention of furthering the assumptions of eugenics, which aimed to prove under the banner of science that certain individuals and ethnic or racial groups are inferior to others. The fact that this was their intent is underscored by subsequent tests using the same subjects but performed without knowledge of which skulls or brains were from certain ethnic or racial groups; these later studies showed only a small correlation between size of the skull or brain and certain behaviors or personalities.[3]

Furthermore, once some of the early practitioners of craniometry died, their brains were found to have volumes that were less than average or average. The brain of K. F. Gauss, for example, was relatively small but more convoluted, with more gyri and fissures. Craniometrists then switched their postulates to say that more convoluted or complex brain structures, with more fissures and gyri, indicated superior brains.[4] However, this argument was even more tentative and more vague than the former hypotheses of craniometrists and thus did not last long. The same was true of craniometry in general, thanks to its noticeable lack of validity. However, it is important to note that modern studies show that people who have significantly larger brains tend to score higher on intelligence tests.[5]

Despite the failure of craniometry to explain the difference between criminals and noncriminals, scientists were not ready to give up the assumption that criminal behavior could be explained by visual differences in the skull (or brain), and they certainly weren't ready to give up the assumption that certain ethnic or racial groups were superior or inferior to others. Therefore, the experts of the time created **phrenology**. Phrenology was the science of determining human dispositions based on distinctions (e.g., bumps) in the skull, which were believed to conform to the shape of the brain.[6] Readers should keep in mind that much of the theorizing by the phrenologists still aimed

---

[2]For example, compare Robert Bean, "Some Racial Peculiarities of the Negro Brain," *American Journal of Anatomy* 5 (1906): 353–432, which showed a distinct difference in the brains across race when brains were identified by race before comparison, to Franklin P. Mall, "On Several Anatomical Characters of the Human Brain, Said to Vary According to Race and Sex, with Especial Reference to the Weight of the Frontal Lobe," *American Journal of Anatomy* 9 (1909): 1–32, which showed virtually no differences among the same brains when comparisons were made without knowledge of the races of the brains prior to comparison. See discussion in Stephen Jay Gould, *The Mismeasure of Man*, 2nd ed. (New York: Norton, 1996).

[3]See Mall, "On Several Anatomical Characters"; much of the discussion in this section is taken from Gould, *Mismeasure of Man*.

[4]Edward A. Spitska, "A Study of the Brains of Six Eminent Scientists and Scholars Belonging to the Anthropological Society, Together with a Description of the Skull of Professor E. D. Cope," *Transactions of the American Philosophical Society* 21 (1907): 175–308.

[5]Stanley Coren, *The Left-Hander Syndrome* (New York: Vintage, 1993); James Kalat, *Biological Psychology*, 8th ed. (New York: Wadsworth, 2004).

[6]Orson S. Fowler, *Fowler's Practical Phrenology: Giving a Concise Elementary View of Phrenology* (New York: O. S. Fowler, 1842).

to support the assumptions of eugenics and show that certain individuals and groups of people are inferior or superior to others.

It is important to keep in mind that, like the craniometrists, phrenologists assumed that the shape of the skull conformed to the shape of the brain. Thus, a bump or other abnormality on the skull directly related to an abnormality in the brain at that spot. Such assumptions have been refuted by modern scientific evidence, so it is not surprising that phrenology fell out of favor in criminological thought rather quickly.

Like its predecessor, however, phrenology got some things right. Certain parts of the brain are indeed responsible for specific tasks. For example, in the original phrenological map, destructiveness was indicated by abnormalities above the left ear. Modern scientific studies show that the most vital part of the brain in terms of criminality associated with trauma is the left temporal lobe, the area above the left ear.[7] Also, most readers know that specific portions of the brain govern the operation of different physical activities; one area governs the action of our hands, whereas other areas govern our arms, legs, and so on. So, the phrenologists had a few things right, but they were completely wrong about the extent to which bumps on the skull could indicate who would be most disposed to criminal behavior.

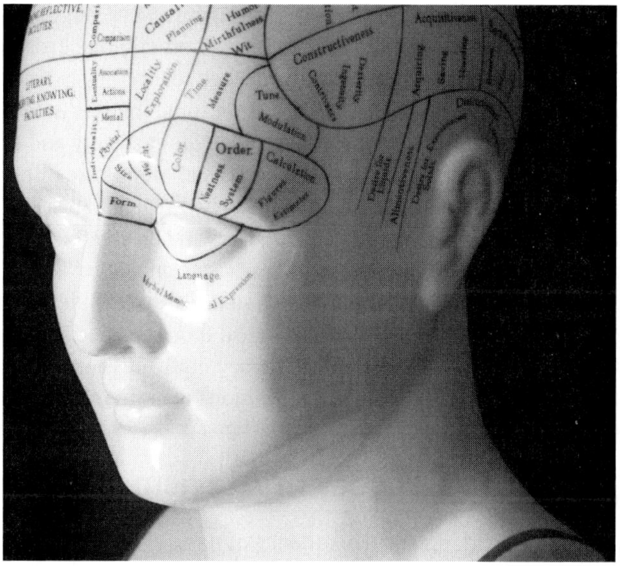

▲ **Image 4.1** Nineteenth-century phrenologists believed that each section of the brain was responsible for a particular human personality trait. If a section was enlarged or shrunken, the personality was assumed to be likewise abnormal. Doctors, particularly those doing entry examinations at American prisons, would examine each new inmate's head for bumps or cavities to develop a criminal profile. For example, if the section of the brain responsible for acquisitiveness was enlarged, the offender was probably a thief. Lombroso and his school combined phrenology with other models that included external physical traits to single out criminals from the general population.

SOURCE: © istockphoto.com / scotspencer

Once phrenology fell out of favor among scientists, researchers and society in general did not want to depart from the assumption that certain individuals or ethnic groups are inferior to others. Therefore, another discipline, known as **physiognomy**, became popular in the mid-1800s. Physiognomy is the study of facial and other bodily aspects to indicate developmental problems, such as criminality. Not surprisingly, the early physiognomy studies focused on contrasting various racial or ethnic groups to prove that some were superior or inferior to others.[8]

Given modern understandings of science, it is not surprising that physiognomy did not last long as a respected scientific perspective of criminality. At any time other than the late 1800s, their ideas would not have been accepted for long, if at all. However, the theory emerged at an auspicious time. Specifically, Darwin published his work *The Origin of Species* in the late 1800s and made a huge impact on societal views regarding the rank order of groups in societies.

---

[7]For reviews, see Adrian Raine, *The Anatomy of Violence: The Biological Roots of Crime* (New York: Pantheon, 2013), and Adrian Raine, *The Psychopathology of Crime* (San Diego: Academic Press, 1993).

[8]Josiah C. Nott and George R. Gliddon, *Types of Mankind* (Philadelphia: Lippincott/Grambo, 1854); Josiah C. Nott and George R. Gliddon, *Indigenous Races on Earth* (Philadelphia: Lippincott, 1868).

Darwin's model outlined a vague framework suggesting that humans had evolved from more primitive beings and that the human species (like all others) had evolved from a number of adaptations preferred by natural selection. In other words, some species are selected by their ability to adapt to the environment, whereas others do not adapt as well and die off or at least become inferior in terms of dominance. This assumption of Darwin's work, which was quickly and widely accepted by both society and scientists throughout the world, falsely led to an inclination to believe that certain ethnic or racial groups are inferior or superior to other groups. Despite a backlash by many religious authorities, who were likely threatened by the popularity of a theory that promoted natural design as opposed to a higher being or creator, Darwin had created a scientific snowball that spread like wildfire across virtually all scientific disciplines, particularly criminology.

Darwin was not a criminologist, so he is not considered a father or theorist in the field. However, he did set the stage for what followed in criminological thought. Specifically, Darwin's theory laid the groundwork for what would become the first major scientific theory of crime, namely, Lombroso's theory of born criminals, which also tied together the assumptions and propositions of craniometry, phrenology, and physiognomy.

Lombroso's Theory of Atavism and Born Criminals

Basing his work on Darwin's theory of natural selection, Cesare Lombroso (1835–1909) created what is widely considered the first attempt toward scientific theory in criminological thought. Most previous theorists were not scientists; Cesare Beccaria, for example, was trained in law and never tested his propositions. Unlike the craniometrists and phrenologists, Beccaria did not seek to explain levels of criminality. However, Lombroso was trained in medical science, and he aimed to document his observations and use scientific methodology. Furthermore, timing was on his side in the sense that Darwin's theory was published 15 years prior to Lombroso's major work, and in that time, the idea of evolution had become immensely popular with both scientists and the public.

Lombroso's Theory of Crime

The first edition of Lombroso's *The Criminal Man* was published in 1876 and created an immediate response in most Western societies, influencing both their ideas and policies related to crime and justice.[9] In this work, Lombroso outlined a theory of crime that largely brought together the pre-Darwinian theories of craniometry, phrenology, and physiognomy. Furthermore, Lombroso thought that certain groups and individuals were atavistic, and that they likely were born to commit crime. **Atavism** refers to the idea that a person or feature of an individual is a throwback to an earlier stage of evolutionary development. In other words, Lombroso thought serious criminals were lower forms of humanity in terms of evolutionary progression. For example, Lombroso would probably have suggested that chronic offenders are more like earlier stages of humankind—that is, like *missing links*—than they are like modern humans.

Lombroso noted other types of offenders, such as the mentally ill and *criminaloids*, who committed minor offenses due to external or environmental circumstances, but he argued that the *born criminals* should be the target in addressing crime, insisting that they were the most serious and violent criminals in any society. These are what most criminologists now refer to as *chronic offenders*. Furthermore, Lombroso claimed that born criminals cannot be stopped from their natural tendencies to be antisocial.

On the other hand, Lombroso claimed that, although it was their nature to commit crime, born criminals could be stopped, or at least partially deterred, by society. According to Lombroso, societies could identify born criminals,

[9]Cesare Lombroso, *The Criminal Man* (L'uomo Delinquente), 1st ed. (Milan: Hoepli, 1876), 2nd ed. (Turin: Bocca, 1878).

even early in life, through their **stigmata**. Stigmata were physical manifestations of the atavism of an individual—that is, features indicating a prior evolutionary stage of development.

▲ **Image 4.2** Cesare Lombroso (1837–1909).

SOURCE: Reproduced in "Rassenkunde des jüdischen Volkes" by Hans F. K. Günther 1929, J. F. Lehmanns Verlag, München, via Wikimedia Commons

Lombroso's List of Stigmata

According to Lombroso, more than five stigmata indicate that an individual is atavistic and inevitably will be a born criminal. Understandably, readers may be wondering what these stigmata are, given their importance. This is a great question, but the answer varies. In the beginning, this list was largely based on Lombroso's work as a physician; it included features such as large eyes and large ears. Lombroso changed this list as he went along, however, even in the last edition of his book published well into the 1900s, which might be considered poor science.

For the most part, stigmata consisted of facial and bodily features that deviated from the norm, which is almost anything that went outside the bell curve of normal human physical development—in other words, abnormally small or large noses, abnormally small or large ears, abnormally small or large eyes, abnormally small or large jaws. Lombroso also threw in some extraphysiological features, such as tattoos and a family history of epilepsy and other disorders.[10] Although tattoos may be somewhat correlated to crime and delinquency, is it likely that they cause antisocial behavior? Given Lombroso's model that people are born criminal, it is quite unlikely that such factors are causally linked to criminality. How many babies are born with tattoos? Ignoring the illogical nature of many of the stigmata, Lombroso professed that people who had more than five of these physical features were born criminals and that something should be done to prevent their inevitable future offending career.

As a physician working for the Italian army, Lombroso examined the bodies of war criminals who had been captured and brought in for analysis. According to Lombroso, he first came to the realization of the nature of criminals when a particular individual was brought in for him to examine:

> This was not merely an idea, but a flash of inspiration. At the sight of that skull, I seemed to see all of a sudden, lighted up as a vast plain under a flaming sky, the problem of the nature of the criminal—an atavistic being who reproduces in his person the ferocious instincts of primitive humanity and the inferior animals.[11]

This was Lombroso's first exposure to such a criminal, and this account of it was his first acknowledgment of the theory that he created. He expanded on this theory by specifying some of the physical features he observed in this individual:

---

[10]Gould, *Mismeasure of Man*, 153.

[11]Lombroso, *Criminal Man*, as cited and discussed by Ian Taylor, Paul Walton, and Jock Young, *The New Criminology: For a Social Theory of Deviance* (London: Routledge, 1973), 41.

> Thus were explained anatomically the enormous jaws, high cheek bones . . . solitary lines in the palms, extreme size of the orbits, handle-shaped ears found in criminals, savages and apes, insensibility to pain, extremely acute sight, tattooing, excessive idleness, love of orgies, and the irresponsible craving of evil for its own sake, the desire not only to extinguish life in the victim, but to mutilate the corpse, tear its flesh and drink its blood.[12]

Although most people may now laugh at his words, at the time he wrote this description, it would have rung true to most readers, which is likely why his book was the dominant text for many decades in the criminological field. In this description, Lombroso incorporates many of the core principles of his theory, including the idea that criminals are atavistic or biological throwbacks from evolution as well as the premise that they can be identified by "stigmata."

A good example of the popular acceptance of Lombroso's "scientific" stigmata was Bram Stoker's use of them in the 1896 novel *Dracula*, which featured a character based on Lombrosian traits of a villain, such as a high-bridged, thin nose; arched nostrils; massive eyebrows; and pointed ears. This novel was published in the late 1800s, when Lombroso's theory was highly dominant in society and in science. Lombroso's ideas became quite popular among academics, scientists, philosophers, fiction writers, and those responsible for criminal justice policy.

Beyond identifying born criminals by their stigmata, Lombroso said he could associate the stigmata with certain types of criminals—anarchists, burglars, murderers, shoplifters, and so on. Of course, his work is quite invalid by modern research standards.

Lombroso as the Father of Criminology and the Father of the Positive School

Lombroso's theory came a decade and a half after Darwin's work had been published and had spread rapidly throughout the Western world. Also, Lombroso's model supported what were then the Western world's views on slavery, deportation, and so on. Due to this timing and the fact that Lombroso became known as the first individual who actually tested his hypotheses through observation, Lombroso is widely considered the father of criminology. This title does not indicate respect for his theory, which has been largely rejected, or for his methods, which are considered highly invalid by modern standards. It is deserved, however, in the sense that he was the first person to gain recognition by testing his theoretical propositions. Furthermore, his theory coincided with political movements that became popular at that time: the Fascism and Nazism of the early 1900s.

Beyond being considered the father of criminology, Lombroso is also considered the father of the Positive School of criminology because he was the first to gain prominence in identifying factors beyond free will and free choice, which the Classical School said were the sole cause of crime. Although previous theorists, such as craniometrists and phrenologists, had presented perspectives that went beyond free will, Lombroso was the first to gain widespread attention. Lombroso's perspective gained almost immediate support in all developed countries of that time, which is the most likely reason why Lombroso is considered the father of the Positive School of criminology.

It is important to understand the assumptions of *positivism*, which most experts consider somewhat synonymous with the term ***determinism***. Determinism is the assumption that most human behavior is determined by factors beyond free will and free choice. In other words, determinism (i.e., the Positive School) assumes that human beings do not decide how they will act by logically thinking through the costs and benefits of a given situation. Rather, the Positive School attributes all kinds of behavior, especially crime, to biological, psychological, and sociological variables.

---

[12]Taylor et al., *New Criminology*, 41–42.

Many readers probably feel they chose their career paths and made most other key decisions in their lives. However, scientific evidence shows otherwise. For example, studies clearly show that far more than 90% of the world's population has adopted the religious affiliation (e.g., Baptist, Buddhist, Catholic, Judaist) of their parents or caretakers. Therefore, what most people consider to be an extremely important decision—the choice of beliefs regarding a higher being or force—is almost completely determined by the environment in which they were brought up. Almost no one sits down and studies various religions before deciding which one suits him or her the best. Rather, in almost all cases, religion is determined by culture, and this finding goes against the Classical School's assumption that free will rules. The same type of argument can be made about the clothes we wear, the food we prefer, and the activities that give us pleasure.

Another way to distinguish positivism and determinism from the Classical School lies in the way scientists view human behavior, which can be seen best in an analogy with chemistry. Specifically, a chemist assumes that, if a certain element is subjected to certain temperatures, pressures, or mixtures with other elements, a predicted response will result. In a highly comparable way, a positivist assumes that, when human beings are subjected to poverty, delinquent peers, low intelligence, or other factors, they will react and behave in predictable ways. Therefore, there is virtually no difference in how a chemist feels about particles and elements and how a positivistic scientist feels about how humans react when exposed to biological and social factors.

In Lombroso's case, the deterministic factor was the biological makeup of the individual. However, we shall see in the next several sections that positivistic theories focus on a large range of variables, from biology to psychology to social aspects. For example, many readers may believe that bad parenting, poverty, and associating with delinquent peers are some of the most important factors in predicting criminality. If you believe that such variables have a significant influence on decisions to commit crime, then you are likely a positive theorist; you believe that crime is caused by factors above and beyond free choice or free will.

Lombroso's Policy Implications

Beyond the theoretical aspects of Lombroso's theory of criminality, it is important to realize that his perspective had profound consequences for policy. Lombroso was called to testify in numerous criminal processes and trials to determine the guilt or innocence of suspects. Under the banner of science (comparable to what we consider DNA or fingerprint analysis in modern times), Lombroso was asked to specify whether or not a suspect had committed a crime.[13] Lombroso based such judgments on the visual stigmata that he could see among suspects.[14] Lombroso documented many of his experiences as an expert witness at criminal trials. Here is one example: "[One suspect] was, in fact, the most perfect type of the born criminal: enormous jaws, frontal sinuses, and zygomata, thin upper lip, huge incisors, unusually large head. . . . [H]e was convicted."[15]

When Lombroso was not available for such "scientific" determinations of the guilty persons, his colleagues or students (often referred to as lieutenants) were often sent. Some of these students, such as Enrico Ferri and Raphael Garrofalo, became quite active in the Fascist regime of Italy in the early 1900s. This model of government, like that of the Nazi Party of Germany, sought to remove the "inferior" groups from society.

Another policy implication in some parts of the world was the identification of young children on the basis of observed stigmata, which often become noticeable in the first 5 to 10 years of life. This led to tracking or isolating of certain children, largely based on physiological features. Although many readers may consider such policies

[13]See Gould, *Mismeasure of Man.*

[14]For a review of such identifications, see Gould, *Mismeasure of Man.*

[15]Cesare Lombroso, *Crime: Its Causes and Remedies* (Boston: Little, Brown, 1911), 436.

ridiculous, modern medicine has supported the identification, documentation, and importance of what are termed ***minor physical anomalies (MPAs)***, which it holds may indicate high risk of developmental problems. Some of these MPAs include the following:

- Head circumference out of the normal range
- Fine, "electric" hair
- More than one hair whorl
- Epicanthus, which is observed as a fold of skin extending from the lower eyelids to the nose and appears as droopy eyelids
- Hypertelorism (orbital), which represents an increased interorbital distance
- Malformed ears
- Low-set ears
- Excessively large gap between the first and second toes
- Webbing between toes or fingers
- No earlobes
- Curved fifth finger
- Third toe longer than the second toe
- Asymmetrical ears
- Furrowed tongue
- Simian crease[16]

Given that such visible physical aspects are still correlated with developmental problems, including criminality, it is obvious that Lombroso's model of stigmata for predicting antisocial problems has implications to the present day. Such implications are more accepted by modern medical science than they are in the criminological literature. Furthermore, some modern scientific studies have shown that being unattractive predicts criminal offending, which somewhat supports Lombroso's theory of crime.[17]

About three decades after Lombroso's original work was published, and after a long period of dominance, criminologists began to question his theory of atavism and stigmata. Furthermore, it became clear that more was involved in criminality than just the way people looked, such as psychological aspects of individuals. However, scientists and societies were not ready to depart from theories like Lombroso's, which assumed that certain people or groups of people were inferior to others, so they simply chose another factor to emphasize: intelligence or IQ.

---

[16]Taken from Mary Waldrop and Charles Halverson, "Minor Physical Anomalies and Hyperactive Behavior in Young Children," in *Exceptional Infant: Studies in Abnormalities*, ed. Jerome Hellmuth (New York: Brunner/Mazel, 1971), 343–81, as cited and reviewed by Diana Fishbein, *Biobehavioral Perspectives on Criminology* (Belmont, CA: Wadsworth, 2001).

[17]Robert Agnew, "Appearance and Delinquency," *Criminology* 22 (1984): 421–40.

Case Study: Carlton "Stocking Strangler" Gary

Carlton Gary was a significantly violent offender, who was nicknamed "the Stocking Strangler" because he would break into women's homes in Columbus, Georgia, then beat them up, rape them, and use a stocking or scarf to strangle them. He is believed to have killed seven white women aged fifty-five to ninety using this same consistent method.

Gary was a rather handsome man who even worked on local television as a model, and was dating a female deputy sheriff during the time he was committing some of these murders.

One interesting fact is that Gary was a rather handsome man who even worked on local television as a model, and was dating a female deputy sheriff during the time he was committing some of these murders. Additionally, he was a loyal caregiver for his elderly aunt. However, he was not only a murderer but also a drug dealer and pimp.

Gary was clearly sly, perhaps even intelligent, which was how he managed to escape from a prison in Onondaga County, New York, by sawing through bars of his cell; even though he broke his ankle in his jump from the prison wall, he still got away by stealing a bicycle. He also escaped from a South Carolina prison, and in Georgia successfully prolonged his killing career by falsely (and convincingly) accusing another man for one of his murders.

So Gary was a chronic offender who had been in and out of trouble since he was a child. But he also had a high IQ and showed near genius-like levels in his creative attempts to escape authorities numerous times. What explains the offending by this individual?

According to Dr. Adrian Raine at University of Pennsylvania, one of the leading experts on biosocial factors in criminality, many of Gary's problems relate to various biological and social risk factors coming together and creating a type of perfect storm. Specifically, he points out that Carlton Gary never really knew his father, having met him only once when he was twelve. His mother (and her boyfriends) were physically abusive to him when he was very young, and then his mother essentially abandoned him at an early age, so he was passed around to various relatives and acquaintances at least fifteen times before his first arrest as a youth. Gary resorted to living on the streets and, often malnourished, eating out of garbage cans. Beyond the malnutrition, another physiological risk factor was that he was knocked unconscious during school recess at a young age, and was diagnosed with minimal brain dysfunction. Additionally, he had at least five or more minor physical anomalies, such as adherent ear lobes and webbing of his fingers. According to Dr. Raine, the culmination and, more importantly, the interaction among all of these biological and social/environmental factors is very likely the reason why Carlton Gary became such a persistent, predatory killer.

SOURCE: Adrian Raine, *The Anatomy of Violence: The Biological Roots of Crime* (New York: Pantheon, 2013).

The IQ Testing Era

Despite the evidence that was presented against Lombroso, his theorizing remained dominant until the early 1900s, when criminologists realized that stigmata and the idea of born criminals were not valid. However, even at that time, theorists and researchers were not ready to give up on the eugenics assumption that certain ethnic or racial groups were superior or inferior to others. Thus, a new theory emerged based on a more quantified measure that was originated, with benevolent intentions, by Alfred Binet in France. This new measure was IQ, short for *intelligence quotient*. At that time, IQ was calculated as chronological age divided by mental age, which was then multiplied by 100, with the average score being 100. This scale has changed enormously over time, but the basic premise was that the test could be used to determine whether someone was above or below average intelligence (100).

As mentioned previously, Binet had good intentions: He created IQ scores to identify youths who were not performing up to par on academic skills. Binet was explicit in stating that IQ could be changed; the reason he proposed a score to identify slow learners was so that they could be trained to increase their IQs.[18] However, when Binet's work was brought over to the United States, his basic assumptions and propositions were twisted. One of the most prominent individuals who used Binet's IQ test in the United States for purposes of deporting, incapacitating, sterilizing, and otherwise ridding society of low-IQ individuals was H. H. Goddard.

Goddard is generally considered the leading authority on the use and interpretation of IQ testing in the United States.[19] He adapted Binet's model to examine immigrants who were coming into the United States from foreign lands. It is important to note that Goddard proposed quite different assumptions regarding intelligence or IQ than did Binet. Goddard asserted that IQ was static or innate, meaning that such levels could not be changed, even with training. His assumption was that intelligence was inherited from parents and passed from generation to generation.

Goddard labeled low IQ **feeblemindedness**, which in the 1900s actually became a technical, scientific term characterizing those who had significantly below-average levels of intelligence. Of course, being a scientist, Goddard specified certain levels of feeblemindedness, which were ranked based on the degree to which scores were below average. Ranking from the highest to the lowest intelligence, the first group were the *morons*, the second-lowest group were the *imbeciles*, and the lowest-intelligence group were the *idiots*.

▲ **Image 4.3** H. H. Goddard (1866–1957).

SOURCE: © Getty Images / Heritage Images / Contributor

According to Goddard, from a eugenics point of view, the biggest threat to the progress of humanity was not the idiots but the morons. In Goddard's words, "The idiot is not our greatest problem. . . . He does not continue the race with a line of children like himself. . . . It is the moron type that makes for us our great problem."[20] That is, the moron is the one group out of the three categories of feebleminded who is smart enough to slip through the cracks and reproduce.

Goddard received many grants to fund his research to identify the feebleminded. Goddard took his research team to the major immigration center at Ellis Island in the early 1900s to identify the feebleminded as they attempted to enter the United States. Many members of his team were women, who he felt were better at distinguishing the feebleminded by sight:

> The people who are best at this work, and who I believe should do this work, are women. Women seem to have closer observation than men. It was quite impossible for others to see how . . . women could pick out the feeble-minded without the aid of the Binet test at all.[21]

Goddard was proud of the increase in the deportation of potential immigrants to the United States, enthusiastically reporting that deportations for the reason of mental deficiency increased by 350% in 1913

[18]Gould, *Mismeasure of Man*.

[19]Again, most of this discussion is taken from Gould, *Mismeasure of Man*, because his review is perhaps the best known in the current literature.

[20]Henry H. Goddard, *The Kallikak Family, a Study of the Heredity of Feeble-Mindedness* (New York: MacMillan, 1912).

[21]Henry H. Goddard, "The Binet Tests in Relation to Immigration," *Journal of Psycho-Asthenics* 18 (1913): 105–7; quote taken from page 106, as cited in Gould, *Mismeasure of Man*.

and 570% in 1914 over the averages of the preceding five years.[22] However, over time, Goddard realized that his policy recommendations of deportation, incarceration, and sterilization were not based on accurate science.

▲ **Image 4.4** Ellis Island.

SOURCE: © iStockphoto.com / tarabird

After consistently validating his IQ test on immigrants and mental patients, Goddard finally tested his intelligence scale on a relatively representative cross-section of American citizens, namely draftees for military service during World War I. The results showed that many of these recruits would score as feebleminded (i.e., as having a mental age of less than 12) on the IQ test. Therefore, Goddard lowered the criterion for determining feeblemindedness from the mental age of 12 to that of age 8. Although this appears to be a clear admission that his scientific method was inaccurate, Goddard continued to promote his model of the feebleminded for many years, and societies used his ideas.

However, toward the end of his career, Goddard admitted that intelligence could be improved, despite his earlier assumptions that it was innate and static.[23] In fact, Goddard actually claimed that he had "gone over to the enemy."[24] However, despite Goddard's admission that his assumptions and testing were not determinant of individuals' intelligence levels, the snowball had been rolling for too long and had gathered too much strength to fight even the most notable theorists' admonishments.

Sterilization of individuals, mostly females, continued in the United States based on scores of intelligence tests. Often the justification was not a person's own intelligence scores but those of his or her mother or father. Goddard had proclaimed that the *germ-plasm* determining feeblemindedness was passed on from one generation to the next, so it inevitably resulted in offspring being feebleminded as well. Thus, the U.S. government typically sterilized individuals, typically women, based on the IQ scores of their parents.

The case of *Buck v. Bell*, brought to the U.S. Supreme Court in 1927, dealt with the issue of sterilizing individuals who had scored, or whose parents had scored, as mentally deficient on intelligence scales. The majority opinion, written by one of the court's most respected jurists, Oliver Wendell Holmes Jr., stated:

> We have seen more than once that the public welfare may call upon the best citizens for their lives. It would be strange if it could not call upon those who already sap the strength of the state for these lesser sacrifices. . . . Three generations of imbeciles are enough.[25]

---

[22]Gould, *Mismeasure of Man*, 198.

[23]Henry H. Goddard, "Feeblemindedness: A Question of Definition," *Journal of Psycho-Asthenics* 33 (1928): 219–27, as discussed in Gould, *Mismeasure of Man*.

[24]Ibid., 224.

[25]As quoted in Gould, *Mismeasure of Man*, 365.

Thus, the highest court in the United States upheld the use of sterilization for the purposes of limiting reproduction among individuals who were deemed feebleminded according to an IQ score. Such sterilizations continued until the 1970s, when the practice was finally halted. Governors of many states, such as North Carolina, Virginia, and California, have given public apologies for what was done. For example, in 2002, the governor of California, Gray Davis, apologized for the state law passed almost a century earlier that had resulted in the sterilization of about 19,000 women in California.

Although this aspect of U.S. history is often hidden from the public, it did occur, and it is important to acknowledge this blot on our nation's history, especially at a time when we were fighting abuses of civil rights by the Nazis and other regimes. Ultimately, the sterilizations, deportations, and incarcerations based on IQ testing are an embarrassing episode in the history of the United States.

For decades, the issue of IQ was not researched or discussed much in the literature. However, in the 1970s, a very important study was published in which Travis Hirschi and Michael Hindelang examined the effect of intelligence on youths' behaviors.[26] Hirschi and Hindelang found that, among youths of the same race and social class, intelligence had a significant effect on delinquency and criminality among individuals. This study, as well as others, showed that the IQ of delinquents or criminals is about 10 points lower than that of noncriminals.[27]

This study led to a rebirth in research regarding intelligence testing within the criminological perspective. A number of recent studies have shown that certain types of intelligence are more important than others. For example, several studies have shown that having low verbal intelligence has the most significant impact on predicting delinquent and criminal behavior.[28]

This tendency makes sense, because verbal skills are important for virtually all aspects of life, from everyday interactions with significant others to filling out forms at work to dealing with people via employment. In contrast, most people do not require advanced math or quantitative skills at their jobs or in day-to-day experiences, let alone spatial and other forms of intelligence that are more abstract. Thus, the fact that low verbal IQ is the type of intelligence that represents the most direct prediction for criminality is most likely due to the general need for verbal skills in routine daily activities. After all, people who lack communication skills will likely find it hard to obtain or retain employment or deal with family and social problems.

This rebirth in studies regarding the link between intelligence and criminality seemed to reach a peak with the publication of Richard Herrnstein and Charles Murray's *The Bell Curve* in 1994.[29] Although this publication changed the terms *moron*, *imbecile*, and *idiot* to relatively benign terms (e.g., *cognitively disadvantaged*), their argument was consistent with that of the feeblemindedness researchers of the early 20th century. Herrnstein and Murray argued that people with low IQ scores are somewhat destined to be unsuccessful in school, become unemployed, produce illegitimate children, and commit crime. They also suggest that IQ or intelligence is primarily innate, or genetically determined, and that there is little chance of improving it. These authors also noted that African Americans tended to score lowest, whereas Asians and Jewish people tended to score highest, and they

---

[26]Travis Hirschi and Michael Hindelang, "Intelligence and Delinquency: A Revisionist Review," *American Sociological Review* 42 (1977): 571–87.

[27]For a review, see Raymond Paternoster and Ronet Bachman, *Explaining Criminals and Crime* (Los Angeles: Roxbury, 2001). Also see Raine, *Psychopathology*.

[28]See Joshua Isen, "A Meta-Analytic Assessment of Wechsler's P > V Sign in Antisocial Populations," *Clinical Psychology Review* 30 (2010): 423–35; and Chris L. Gibson, Alex R. Piquero, and Stephen G. Tibbetts, "The Contribution of Family Adversity and Verbal IQ to Criminal Behavior," *International Journal of Offender Therapy and Comparative Criminology* 45 (2001): 574–92. See also Hirschi and Hindelang, "Intelligence and Delinquency"; Terrie Moffitt, "The Neuropsychology of Delinquency: A Critical Review of Theory and Research," in *Crime and Justice: An Annual Review of Research*, Vol. 12, ed. Michael Tonry and Norval Morris (Chicago: University of Chicago Press, 1990), 99–169; Terrie Moffitt and Bill Henry, "Neuropsychological Studies of Juvenile Delinquency and Juvenile Violence," in *The Neuropsychology of Aggression*, ed. Joel S. Milner (Boston: Kluwer, 1991), 67–91; and the conclusion by Paternoster and Bachman in *Explaining Criminals*, 51.

[29]Richard J. Herrnstein and Charles Murray, *The Bell Curve: Intelligence and Class Structure in the United States* (New York: Free Press, 1994).

offered results from social indicators supporting their argument that the intelligence levels of the latter resulted in relative success in life in terms of group-level statistics.

This book produced a public outcry, resulting in symposiums at major universities and other venues in which the authors' postulates were largely condemned. As noted by other reviews of the impact of this work, some professors at public institutions were sued in court because they used this book in their classes.[30] The book received blistering reviews from fellow scientists.[31] However, none of these scientific critics has fully addressed the undisputed fact that African Americans consistently score low on intelligence tests and that Asians and Jews score higher on these examinations. Furthermore, none has adequately addressed the issue that—even within these populations—low IQ scores (especially on verbal tests) predict criminality. For example, in samples of African Americans, the group that scores lowest on verbal intelligence consistently commits more crime and is more likely to become delinquent or criminal. So, despite the harsh criticism of *The Bell Curve*, it is apparent that there is some validity to the authors' arguments.

With the popularity of intelligence testing and IQ scores in the early 20th century, it is not surprising that this was also the period when other psychological models of deviance and criminality became popular. However, one of the most popular involved body type theories.

Body Type Theory: Sheldon's Model of Somatotyping

Although there were numerous theories based on body types in the late 1800s and early 1900s, such as Lombroso's and those of others who called themselves criminal anthropologists, none of these perspectives had a more enduring impact than that of William Sheldon. In the mid-1940s, a new theoretical perspective was proposed that merged the concepts of biology and psychology. Sheldon claimed that, in the embryonic and fetal stages of development, individuals tend to have an emphasis on certain tissue layers.[32] According to Sheldon, these varying degrees of emphasis are largely due to heredity and lead to the development of certain body types and temperaments or personalities. This became the best-known body type theory, also known as **somatotyping**.

According to Sheldon, all embryos must develop three distinct tissue layers, and this much is still acknowledged by perinatal medical researchers. The first layer of tissue is the **endoderm**, which is the inner layer of tissues and includes the internal organs, such as the stomach, large intestine, and small intestine. The middle layer of tissue, called the **mesoderm**, includes the muscles, bones, ligaments, and tendons. The **ectoderm** is the outer layer of tissue, which includes the skin, capillaries, and much of the nervous system's sensors.

Sheldon used these medical facts regarding various tissue layers to propose that certain individuals tend to emphasize certain tissue layers relative to others, typically due to inherited dispositions. In turn, Sheldon believed that such emphases lead to certain body types in an individual, such that people who have a focus on their endoderms in embryonic development will inevitably become **endomorphic**, or obese (see Image 4.5a). According to this theory, individuals who have an emphasis on the middle layer of tissue will typically become **mesomorphic**, or of an athletic or muscular build (see Image 4.5b), while individuals who have an emphasis on the outer layer will end up with an **ectomorphic** build, or thin (see Image 4.5c).

---

[30]See Stephen E. Brown, Finn-Aage Esbensen, and Gilbert Geis, *Criminology: Explaining Crime and Its Context*, 8th ed. (Cincinnati, OH: Anderson, 2012), 260 (see chap. 2).

[31]J. Blaine Hudson, "Scientific Racism: The Politics of Tests, Race, and Genes," *Black Scholar* 25 (1995): 1–10; David Perkins, *Outsmarting IQ: The Emerging Science of Learnable Intelligence* (New York: Free Press, 1995); Francis Cullen et al., "Crime and the Bell Curve: Lessons from Intelligent Criminology," *Crime and Delinquency* 43 (1997): 387–411; Robert Hauser, "Review of the Bell Curve," *Contemporary Sociology* 24 (1995): 149–53; Howard Taylor, "Book Review, *The Bell Curve*," *Contemporary Sociology* 24 (1995): 153–58; Gould, *Mismeasure of Man*, 367–90.

[32]William Sheldon, E. M. Hartl, and E. McDermott, *Varieties of Delinquent Youth* (New York: Harper, 1949).

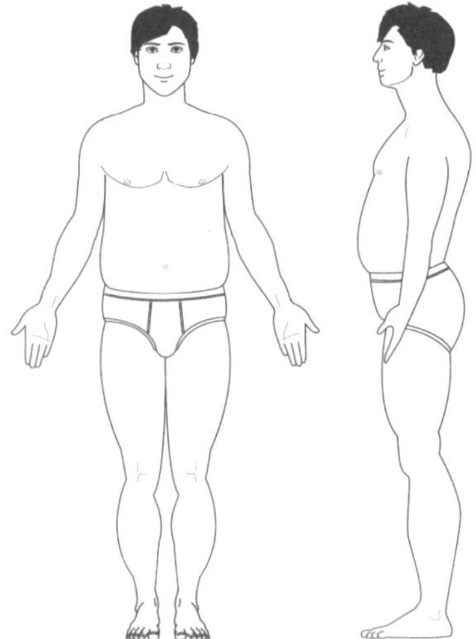

▲ **Image 4.5a** Endomorph. Physical traits: soft body, underdeveloped muscles, round shape, overdeveloped digestive system. Associated personality traits: love of food, tolerance, evenness of emotions, love of comfort, sociability, good humor, relaxed mood, need for affection.

SOURCE: © 2012 Encyclopaedia Britannica, Inc.

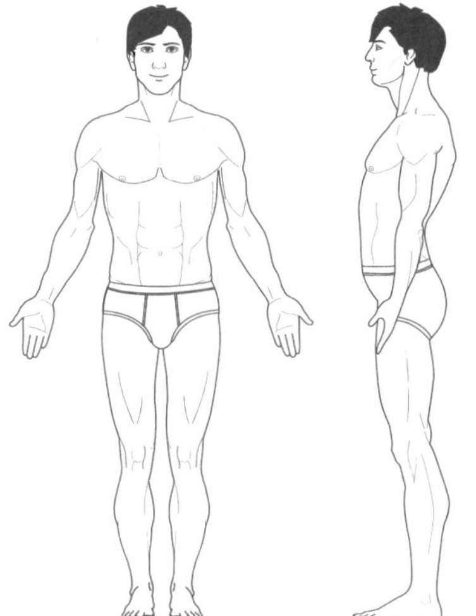

▲ **Image 4.5b** Mesomorph. Physical traits: hard, muscular body; overly mature appearance; rectangular shape; thick skin; upright posture. Associated personality traits: love of adventure, desire for power and dominance, courage, indifference to what others think or want, assertive mien, boldness, zest for physical activity, competitive nature, love of risk and chance.

SOURCE: © 2012 Encyclopaedia Britannica, Inc.

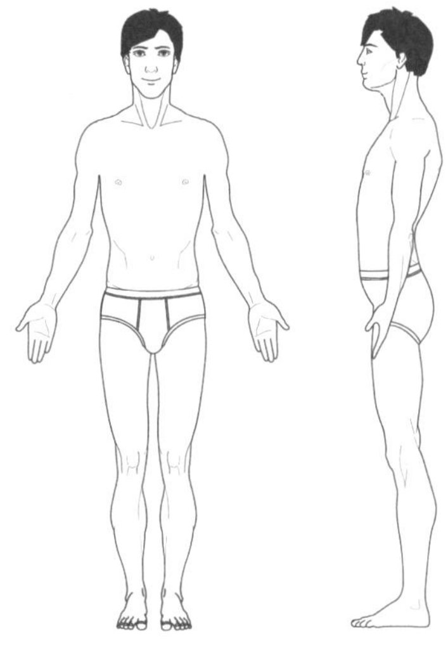

▲ **Image 4.5c** Ectomorph. Physical traits: thin, flat chest; delicate build; young appearance; light muscling; stooped shoulders; large brain. Associated personality traits: self-consciousness, preference for privacy, introversion, inhibition, social anxiety, artistic inclination, mental intensity, emotional restraint.

SOURCE: © 2012 Encyclopaedia Britannica, Inc.

Sheldon and his research team graded each subject on three dimensions corresponding to these body types. Each body type was measured on a scale of 1 to 7, with 7 being the highest score. Obviously, no one could score a 0 for any body type because all tissue layers are needed for survival; we all need our internal organs, bone and muscular structure, and outer systems (skin, capillaries, etc.).

Each somatotype always had the following order: endomorphy, mesomorphy, ectomorphy. Thus, the scores on a typical somatotype might be 3-6-2, which would indicate that this person scored a 3 (a little lower than average) on endomorphy, a 6 (high) on mesomorphy, and a 2 (relatively low) on ectomorphy. According to Sheldon's theory, this hypothetical subject would be a likely candidate for criminality because of the relatively high score on mesomorphy. In fact, the results from his data, as well as all studies that have examined the association of body types with delinquency or criminality, would support this prediction.

Perhaps most important, Sheldon proposed that these body types matched personality traits or temperaments. Individuals who were endomorphic (obese), Sheldon claimed, tended to be more jolly or lazy. The technical term for this temperament is **viscerotonic**. In contrast, people who were mesomorphic (muscular) typically had risk-taking and aggressive temperaments, called **somotonic**. Last, individuals who were ectomorphic (thin) tended to have introverted or shy personalities, which is referred to as **cerebrotonic**. According to Sheldon, members of the middle group, the mesomorphs, obviously had the highest propensity toward criminality because they were disposed toward a risk-taking and aggressive personality.

Interestingly, many politicians were subjects in Sheldon's research. Most entering freshmen at Ivy League schools, especially Harvard, were asked to pose for photos for Sheldon's studies. The Smithsonian Institution still retains a collection of nude photos of George W. Bush, Hillary Rodham Clinton, and many other notable figures.[33]

Sheldon used poor methodology to test his theory. He based his measures of subjects' body types on what he subjectively judged from viewing three perspectives of each subject and often from only three pictures taken of each subject in the three poses. He also had his trained staff view many of the photos and make their determinations of how these individuals scored on each category of body type. The reliability among these scorings has been shown to be weak, meaning that the trained staff did not tend to agree with Sheldon or among themselves on the somatotypes for each participant.

This is not surprising, given the high level of variation in body types and the fact that Sheldon and his colleagues did not employ the technology that is used today, such as caliper tests and submersion in water tanks, which provide the information for which he was searching. People may alter their weights, going from an ectomorphic or mesomorphic build to a more endomorphic form, or vice versa. Presented with the argument that individuals often alter their body types via diet or exercise, Sheldon responded that he could tell what the "natural" body type of each individual was from the three pictures that were taken. Obviously, this position is not a strong one, as demonstrated by the poor interrater reliability shown by his staff. Therefore, Sheldon's methodology is questionable, which casts doubt on the entire theoretical framework.

Despite the problems in his methodology, Sheldon clearly showed that mesomorphs, or individuals who had muscular builds and tended to take more risks, were more delinquent and criminal than individuals who had other body types or temperaments.[34] Furthermore, other researchers, even those who despised Sheldon's theory, found the same associations between mesomorphy and criminality as well as related temperaments (i.e., somotonic) and criminality.[35] Subsequent studies showed that mesomorphic boys were far more likely to have personality traits that predicted criminality, such as aggression, short temper, self-centeredness, and impulsivity.

Recent theorists have also noted the link between an athletic, muscular build and the highly extroverted, aggressive personality that is often associated with this body type.[36] In fact, some recent theorists have gone so far as to claim that chronic offenders, both male and female, can be identified early in life by their relatively V-shaped pelvic structure as opposed to a U-shaped pelvic structure.[37] The V-shaped pelvis is said to indicate relatively high levels of androgens (male hormones, like testosterone) in the system, which predisposes individuals toward crime. On the other hand, a more U-shaped pelvis indicates relatively low levels of such androgens and therefore lower propensity toward aggression and criminality. Using this logic, it may be true that more hair on an individual's arms (whether that person be male or female) is predictive of a high likelihood for committing crime. However, no research exists regarding this factor.

Regarding the use of body types and characteristics in explaining crime, many of the hard-line sociologists who have attempted to examine or replicate Sheldon's results have never been able to refute the association between mesomorphs and delinquency or criminality, nor the association between mesomorphy and the somotonic

---

[33]See discussion in Brown et al., *Criminology*, 246.

[34]Sheldon et al., *Varieties*.

[35]Sheldon Glueck and Eleanor Glueck, *Physique and Delinquency* (New York: Harper & Row, 1956). See also Emil Hartl, *Physique and Delinquent Behavior* (New York: Academic Press, 1982); and Juan Cortes, *Delinquency and Crime* (New York: Seminar Press, 1972). For the most recent applications, see Hans J. Eysenck and G. H. Gudjonsson, *The Causes and Cures of Criminality* (New York: Plenum, 1989).

[36]James Q. Wilson and Richard Herrnstein, *Crime and Human Nature* (New York: Simon & Schuster, 1985).

[37]Eysenck and Gudjonsson, *Causes and Cures*; Raine, *Psychopathology*.

characteristics of risk-taking and aggression.[38] Thus, the association between being muscular or athletically built and engaging in criminal activities is now undisputed and assumed to be true.

Still, sociologists have taken issue with the reasons for this association. Whereas Sheldon claimed it was due to inherited traits for a certain body type, sociologists argue that this association is due to societal expectations: Muscular male youths would be encouraged to engage in risk-taking and aggressive behavior. For example, a young male with an athletic build would be encouraged to join sports teams and engage in high-risk behaviors by peers. Who would gangs most desire as members? More muscular, athletic individuals would be better at fighting and performing acts that require a certain degree of physical strength and stamina.

Ultimately, it is now established that mesomorphs are more likely to commit crime.[39] Furthermore, the personality traits linked to having an athletic or muscular build are dispositions toward risk-taking and aggressiveness, and few scientists dispute this correlation. No matter which theoretical model is adopted—whether the biopsychologists' or the sociologists'—the fact is that mesomorphs are indeed more likely to be risk-taking and aggressive and, thus, to commit more crime than individuals of other body types.

However, whether the cause is biological or sociological is a debate that shows the importance of theory in criminological research. After all, the link between mesomorphy and criminality is now undisputed; the explanation of why this link exists has become a theoretical debate. Readers may make their own determination—if not now, then later.

Our position is that both biology and social environment are likely to interact with one another in explaining this link. Thus, it is most likely that both nature and nurture are at play in this association between mesomorphy and crime, and both Sheldon and his critics may be correct. A middle ground can often be found in theorizing on criminality. It is important to keep in mind that theories in criminology, as a science, are always considered subject to falsification and criticism and can always be improved. Therefore, our stance on the validity and influence of this theory, as well as others, should not be surprising.

Policy Implications

Many policy implications can be derived from the theories presented in this section. First, one could propose more thorough medical screening at birth and in early childhood, especially regarding minor physical anomalies (MPAs). The studies reviewed in this section obviously implicate numerous MPAs in developmental problems (most of them arising in the womb). These MPAs are a red flag signaling problems, especially in cognitive abilities, which are likely to have a significant impact on propensity for criminal behavior.[40] Recent reviews of such MPAs have been found to be very important in identifying red flags for higher likelihood for criminal behavior, even in children as young as age 3.[41] Furthermore, recent studies have found that a high number of MPAs interact with other social factors.[42] Specifically, MPAs have been found to interact with environmental risk factors, such as family disorder or adversity, consistently in prediction of antisocial or criminal adults.[43]

Other policy implications derived from the theories and findings of this section involve having same-sex classes for children in school because they focus on deficiencies that have been shown for both young boys and girls. Numerous school districts now have policies that specify same-sex math courses for female children.

---

[38]Cortes, *Delinquency and Crime*; Glueck and Glueck, *Physique and Delinquency*. For a review, see Eysenck and Gudjonsson, *Causes and Cures*.

[39]For a review, see Lee Ellis and Anthony Walsh, *Criminology: A Global Perspective* (Minot: Pyramid Press, 2000), supplemental tables and references.

[40]Fishbein, *Biobehavioral Perspectives*.

[41]Raine, *Anatomy of Violence*, 192–94.

[42]Ibid.

[43]Ibid.

This same strategy might be considered for male children in English or literature courses because males have a biological disposition for a lower aptitude than females in this area of study. Furthermore, far more screening should be done to determine IQ and aptitude levels of young children in order to identify which children require extra attention because studies show that such early intervention can make a big difference in improving their IQ and aptitude.[44]

A recent report that reviewed the extant literature regarding what types of programs work best for reducing crime noted the importance of diagnosing early head trauma and further concluded that one of the most consistently supported programs for such at-risk children are those that involve weekly infant home visitation.[45] Another obvious policy implication derived from biosocial theory is mandatory health insurance for pregnant mothers and children, which is quite likely the most efficient way to reduce crime in the long term.[46] Finally, all youths should be screened for abnormal levels of hormones, neurotransmitters, and toxins (especially lead).[47]

Conclusion

In this section, we discussed the development of the early Positive School of criminology. The Positive School can be seen as the opposite of the Classical School perspective, which we covered in Sections II and III, because positivism assumes that individuals have virtually no free will; rather, criminal behavior is considered to be the result of determinism, which means that factors other than rational decision making, such as poverty, intelligence, bad parenting, and unemployment, influence us and determine our behavior.

The earliest positivist theories, such as craniometry and phrenology, were developed in the early 1800s but did not become popular outside of scientific circles, likely because they were presented prior to Charles Darwin's theory of evolution. In the 1860s, Darwin's theory became widely accepted, which set the stage for the father of criminology, Lombroso, to propose his theory of born criminals. Lombroso's theory was based on Darwin's theory of evolution and argued that the worst criminals are born that way, being biological throwbacks to an earlier stage of evolution. Unfortunately, Lombroso's theory led to numerous policies that fit the philosophy and politics of Fascism, which found useful a theory proposing that certain people were inferior to others. However, Lombroso and many of his contemporaries became aware that the field should shift to a more multifactorial approach, such as one emphasizing how environment and social factors interact with physiological influences.

We also discussed theories regarding low IQ scores, traditionally known as feeblemindedness. Although most recent studies show that there is a correlation between crime and low IQ, this association is not quite as strong as thought in the early 1900s. Modern studies show consistent evidence that low verbal IQ is related with criminality,[48] especially when coupled with sociological factors, such as weak family structure. This is the state of the criminological field today, and it will be discussed in the next section.

Finally, we explored the theories and evidence regarding body types in predisposing an individual toward criminality. Studies have shown that the more athletic or mesomorphic an individual is, the higher the probability that this individual will be involved in criminality. This relationship is likely based on hormonal levels, and this type of association will be explored in the next section.

---

[44]John P. Wright, Stephen Tibbetts, and Leah Daigle, *Criminals in the Making: Criminality across the Life Course* (Thousand Oaks, CA: Sage, 2015).

[45]Lawrence Sherman et al., *Preventing Crime: What Works, What Doesn't, What's Promising: A Report to the United States Congress* (Washington, DC: U.S. Department of Justice, 1997) (see chap. 2).

[46]Wright et al., *Criminals in the Making.*

[47]Ibid., 258–63.

[48]Gibson et al., "Contribution of Family Adversity."

Ultimately, we have examined a variety of physiological and psychological factors that predict criminal offending according to empirical research. Still, the existence of such influence is largely conditional—that is, based on environmental and social factors.

SECTION SUMMARY

- The Positive School of criminology assumes the opposite of the Classical School. Whereas the Classical School assumes that individuals commit crime because they freely choose to act after rationally considering the expected costs and benefits of the behavior, the Positive School assumes that individuals have virtually no free will or choice in the matter; rather, their behavior is determined by factors outside of free will, such as poverty, low intelligence, bad child rearing, and unemployment.
- The earliest positive theories, such as craniometry and phrenology, emphasized measuring the size and shape of the skull and brain. These perspectives did not become very popular because they preceded Darwin's theory of evolution.
- Lombroso, the father of criminology, presented a theoretical model that assumed that the worst criminals are born that way. Highly influenced by Darwin, Lombroso claimed that born criminals are evolutionary throwbacks who are not as highly developed as most people.
- Lombroso claimed that these born criminals could be identified by physical features called stigmata. This led to numerous policy implications that fit with the societal beliefs at that time, such as Fascism.
- In the early 1900s, the IQ test was invented in France and was quickly used by American researchers in their quest to identify the feebleminded. This led to massive numbers of deportations, sterilizations, and institutionalizations across the United States and elsewhere.
- Modern studies support a link between low verbal IQ and criminality, even within a given race, social class, or gender.
- Merging elements of the early physiological and psychological perspectives are body type theories. The best known of these is somatotyping, which was proposed by William Sheldon. Sheldon found that an athletic or muscular build (i.e., mesomorphy) is linked to an aggressive, risk-taking personality, which in turn is associated with higher levels of crime.
- Despite the methodological problems with Sheldon's body type theory, many propositions and associations of the perspective hold true in modern studies.
- The early Positive School theories set the stage for most of the other theories we will be covering in this book because they emphasize use of the scientific method for studying and explaining criminal activity.

KEY TERMS

atavism 140
cerebrotonic 150
craniometry 137
determinism 142
ectoderm 149
ectomorphic 149
endoderm 149
endomorphic 149
eugenics 137
feeblemindedness 146
mesoderm 149
mesomorphic 149

minor physical anomalies (MPAs) 144

phrenology 138

physiognomy 139

somatotyping 149

somotonic 150

stigmata 141

viscerotonic 150

DISCUSSION QUESTIONS

1. What characteristics distinguish the Positive School from the Classical School regarding criminal thought? Which of these schools do you lean toward in your own perspective of crime and why?
2. Name and describe the various early schools of positivistic theories that existed in the early to mid-1800s (pre-Darwin) as well as the influence that they had on later schools of thought regarding criminality. Do you see any validity in these approaches (as modern medical science does)? Why or why not?
3. What were the significant reasons that these early schools of positivistic theories did not gain much momentum in societal popularity? Does this lack of popularity relate to the neglect of biological perspectives of crime in modern times?
4. What portion of Lombroso's theory of criminality do you find least valid? Which do you find most valid?
5. Most readers have taken the equivalent of an IQ test (e.g., SAT or ACT tests). Do you believe that this score is a fair representation of your knowledge as compared to that of others? Why or why not? Do your feelings reflect the criticisms of experts regarding the use of IQ (e.g., as in feeblemindedness theory) in identifying potential offenders?
6. In light of scientific findings that show that verbal IQ is a consistent predictor of criminality among virtually all populations and samples, can you provide evidence from your personal experience for why this occurs?
7. What portion of Sheldon's body type theory do you find most valid? What do you find least valid?
8. If you had to give yourself a somatotype (e.g., 3-6-2), what would it be? Explain why your score would be the one you provide, and note whether this would make you likely to be a criminal in Sheldon's model.
9. Provide somatotypes of five of your family members or best friends. Do the somatotypes have any correlation with criminality according to Sheldon's predictions? Either way, describe your findings.
10. Ultimately, do you believe that some of the positive theoretical perspectives presented in this section are valid, or do you think they should be entirely dismissed in terms of understanding or predicting crime? Either way, state your case.
11. What types of policies would you implement if you were in charge, given the theories and findings in this section?

WEB RESOURCES

Body Type Theories/Somatotyping

http://www.innerexplorations.com/psytext/shel.htm
http://www.teachpe.com/gcse_health/somatotypes.php

IQ Testing/Feeblemindedness

http://www.eugenicsarchive.org/html/eugenics/static/themes/12.html

Cesare Lombroso

http://www.historyextra.com/article/feature/born-criminal-lombroso-origins-modern-criminology

Phrenology/Craniometry

http://www.phrenology.org/index.html
http://skepdic.com/cranial.html

READING /// 7

Cesare Lombroso is generally considered the father of criminology as well as the father of the Positive School, primarily because he was the first to get credit for testing his theoretical propositions through observation. He emphasized using the scientific method in examining criminal behavior. This selection includes some of the key portions of his evolution-influenced theory of criminals, particularly those he referred to as "born criminals." He also reviews many examples of stigmata, or physical manifestations he believed were signs of evolutionary inferiority.

As you read this selection, it would be useful to pay close attention to the following points:

- The characteristics of the face of habitual murderers, according to Lombroso, as well as thieves, rapists, and other offenders
- Key characteristics that Lombroso claims are unique to female criminals, and how these differ from male criminals
- The types of tattoos that Lombroso observed on criminals and how these tattoos relate to the emotions of criminals

The Criminal Man (L'uomo delinquente)

Cesare Lombroso (as translated by Mary Gibson and Nicole H. Rafter)

2. Anthropometry and Physiognomy of 832 Criminals

To many, my attempt to conclude anything at all about the cranial dimensions of the criminal man from a few measurements of cadavers will seem futile and rash. Fortunately, however, I have been able to compare these measurements with those taken from 832 live specimens of criminals, thanks to the help of colleagues who are prison directors and prison physicians.

In terms of height, criminals reproduce their regional types. In Italy, they are very tall in the Veneto (1.69 meters), fairly tall in Umbria and Lombardy (1.66 m), less tall in Emilia, Calabria, and Piedmont (1.63 m), slightly shorter in Naples, Sicily, and the Marehes, and shortest of all in Sardinia (1.59 m).[1] Compared with healthy men in the army, criminals appear to be taller than the average Italian, especially in the Veneto, Umbria, Lombardy, Sicily, and Calabria. In the Marehes, Naples, and Piedmont, criminals are the same height as healthy men.

These findings, however, are skewed by the preponderance of robbers and murderers in my sample, and thus they conflict with the conclusions of Thomson and Wilson.[2] Robbers and murderers are taller than rapists, forgers, and especially thieves.[3] As for weight, we can compare the findings on 1,331 soldiers, studied by me and Dr. Franchini, with the average for criminals from each region. In the Veneto, healthy men weighed an average of

SOURCE: Cesare Lombroso, "Anthropometry and Physiognomy of 832 Criminals" (chap. 2), "Tattoos" (chap. 3), and "Emotions of Criminals" (chap. 4), in *Criminal Man* (L'uomo delinquente), ed. and trans. Mary Gibson and Nicole Rafter (Durham, NC: Duke University Press), 50–69. Footnotes are part of the original text.

68 kilograms, while criminals weighed 62.5kg.[4] But in most other regions, most notably Naples, Sicily, and Piedmont, criminals' average weight exceeded that of healthy men.

There are many erroneous ideas in circulation about the physiognomy, or facial expressions, of criminals. Novelists turn them into frightening-looking men with beards that go right up to their eyes, penetrating ferocious gazes, and hawklike noses. More serious observers, such as Casper, err on the other extreme, finding no differences between criminals and normal men.[5] Both are wrong. It is certainly true that there are criminals with notably large cranial capacity and beautifully formed skulls, just as there are those with perfectly regular physiognomy, particularly among adroit swindlers and gang leaders. Lavater and Polli wrote about a murderer whose face resembled one of the angels painted by Guido (*Saggio di Fisiognomia*, 1837).[6] But criminals whose handsome features make a strong impression can be misleading precisely because they contradict our expectations. They are usually individuals of uncommon intelligence, a trait associated with gracefulness of form.

When, on the other hand, one ignores those rare individuals who form the oligarchy of the criminal world to study the entire spectrum of these wretches, as I have done in various prisons, one has to conclude that while offenders may not look fierce, there is nearly always something strange about their appearance. It can even be said that each type of crime is committed by men with particular physiognomic characteristics, such as lack of a beard or an abundance of hair; this may explain why the overall appearance is neither delicate nor pleasant.

In general, thieves are notable for their expressive faces and manual dexterity, small wandering eyes that are often oblique in form, thick and close eyebrows, distorted or squashed noses, thin beards and hair, and sloping foreheads. Like rapists, they often have jug ears. Rapists, however, nearly always have sparkling eyes, delicate features, and swollen lips and eyelids. Most of them are frail; some are hunchbacked. Pederasts are often distinguished by a feminine elegance of the hair and feminine clothing, which they insist on wearing even under their prison uniforms.

Habitual murderers have a cold, glassy stare and eyes that are sometimes bloodshot and filmy; the nose is often hawklike and always large; the jaw is strong, the cheekbones broad; and their hair is dark, abundant, and crisply textured. Their beards are scanty, their canine teeth very developed, and their lips thin. Often their faces contract, exposing the teeth. Among nearly all arsonists, I have observed a softness of skin, an almost childlike appearance, and an abundance of thick straight hair that is almost feminine. One extremely curious example from Pesaro, known as "the woman," was truly feminine in appearance and behavior.

Nearly all criminals have jug ears, thick hair, thin beards, pronounced sinuses, protruding chins, and broad cheekbones. Dumollard, a rapist and murderer, had a deformed upper lip and very thick black hair.[7] The rapist Mingrat had a low forehead, jug ears, and an enormous square jaw. Archaeologists have established that the cruelest of the Caesars—Commodius, Nero, and Tiberius—had jug ears and swollen temples.

But anthropology needs numbers, not isolated, generic descriptions, especially for use in forensic medicine. Thus I will provide statistics on 390 criminals from the regions of Emilia, the Marehes, and southern Italy. Table 1 compares the hair color of these 390 criminals with that of 868 Italian soldiers from the same regions and 90 insane from Pavia. These figures show that hair color of criminals replicates typical regional characteristics, but only up to a certain point.

Jug ears are found on 28 percent of criminals, but the proportion varies by region: 47 percent of Sicilian criminals have jug ears, as do 33 percent from Piedmont, 11 percent from Naples, 33 percent from the Romagna, 9 percent from Sardinia, and 36 percent from Lombardy. Nine percent of all criminals have very long ears, although that proportion rises to 10 percent in Lombardy and the Romagna and 18 percent in Sicily and Piedmont.

It is difficult to determine the muscular force of criminals even with the best dynamometers because the subjects are completely out of condition after long periods of detention and inertia.[8] The problem is often compounded by the malignant spirit that characterizes prisoners' whole existence. They pretend to be weaker than they really are and do not put much effort into pushing the dynamometer. In this regard, it is noteworthy that, as I was able to verify in the penitentiary of Ancona, prisoners are more energetic when they work continuously than in institutions that permit them to be idle. Rapists, brigands, and arsonists are the strongest and thieves and

Table 1 • Hair Color of Soldiers and Criminals

	Brown (percent)		Black (percent)		Blond (percent)		Red (percent)	
Region	Soldiers	Criminals	Soldiers	Criminals	Soldiers	Criminals	Soldiers	Criminals
Sicily	51	41	25	54	17	0	0	3
Calabria	39	50	20	33	15	0	0	0
Naples	50	50	28	40	22	5	0.3	0
Central Italy	56	66	20	33	21	5	1	5
Piedmont	47	35	13	35	34	29	0	0
Lombardy	38	33	16	33	32	33	0	0
Insane from Pavia	83	–	12	–	4	–	0	–

NOTE: The last category, the insane from Pavia, is not consistent with Lombroso's regional categories but seems to be an attempt to compare the insane with soldiers (normal men) and criminals.

forgers the weakest, based on measurements of traction. Murderers and pickpockets differ in strength only by a slight fraction.

Criminal Women

At this point little can be said about female criminals because I have been allowed to examine only twenty-one of them and did so with much less ease than in the case of men. But this does not pose a complete obstacle because, first, I do not have enough information on normal women to make a comparison with criminal women; and, second, Parent-Duchatelet offers us numerous and reliable statistics on prostitutes, a class of women almost identical to criminal women in moral terms.[9] In addition, the esteemed Dr. Soresina has provided me with measurements on fifty-four prostitutes who were patients in the Milan lock hospital for venereal disease.[10]

The average cranial capacity of the twenty-one female criminals in my sample was 1,442 cc, slightly less than that of twenty insane women without dementia (1,468 cc), and above that of nineteen idiots with dementia (1,393 cc).

Table 2 presents these differences more clearly. Female criminals, and especially prostitutes, have oversized heads, but these are found only in a fraction of insane women. The rate of microcephaly, or a cranial circumference of forty-eight centimeters, among prostitutes is four times greater among the insane, who in turn have a rate double that of criminal women.

The only conclusion about the physiognomy of criminal women that I can draw from my sample is that female criminals tend to be masculine. (Among prostitutes even the voice often seems virile.) The only exception was a poisoner. Two out of twenty-one criminal women closely resembled the insane with their protruding and asymmetrical ears. Where criminal women differ most markedly from the insane is in the rich luxuriance of their hair. Not a single woman in my sample was bald, and only one showed precociously graying hair. Thomson, too, has noted rich manes of hair among female criminals.

Summing up in a few words that which scientific exigencies oblige me to express with arid numbers,[11] I conclude:

— The criminal is taller than the normal individual and even more so than the insane, with a broader chest, darker hair and (with the exception of Venetians) greater weight.

— In head volume, the criminal presents a series of submicrocephalic craniums, double the number for normal men, but fewer than in the case of the insane.

Table 2 • Cranial Circumference of Insane Women, Prostitutes, and Criminal Women

Cranial Circumference (cm.)	Insane Women (86)		Prostitutes (54)		Criminal Women (21)	
	Total	Percent	Total	Percent	Total	Percent
48	2	0.01	8	4.3		–
49	16	1.04	9	4.8	1	0.2
50	23	1.09	8	4.8	2	0.2
51	20	1.07	15	8.1	4	0.8
52	20	1.07		–	7	1.4
53	3	0.02	3	1.6	6	1.2
54	1	0.05	1	0.5	1	0.2
55			2	1.0		–
56			2	1.0		–

NOTE: The number of insane women in the second column adds to 85 rather than 86; the total number of prostitutes adds to 48 rather than 54. The percentage columns have no relationship to the other data in the table, illustrating Lombroso's statistical ineptitude or general carelessness with detail.

— Criminals, especially forgers, also exceed the insane in large-volume heads. But the average head size of criminals never reaches the size of healthy men.

— The cephalic index, or shape of the criminal skull, varies with ethnicity but tends to be brachycephalic, or short-headed, particularly among robbers.[12] Criminal skulls present frequent asymmetry, although less often than among the insane.

— Compared to the insane, criminals have more traumatic lesions of the head and oblique eyes. But they less frequently display degeneration of the temple arteries, abnormalities of the ear, thin beards, tics, virility of appearance (if they are female), dilated pupils, and, still less often, graying hair and baldness.

— Criminals and the insane show equal rates of prognathism, unequally sized pupils, distorted noses, and receding foreheads.

— Measured on the dynamometer, criminals reveal greater weakness than normal men, though they are not as weak as the insane.

— More often than in the healthy population, criminals have brown or dark eyes and thick black hair. Such hair is most frequently found among robbers.

— Hunchbacks are extremely rare among murderers but are more common among rapists, forgers, and arsonists.

— Arsonists, and even more so thieves, tend to have gray irises; members of both groups are always shorter, lighter, weaker, and smaller in cranial capacity than pickpockets, who are in turn shorter, lighter, and weaker than murderers.

Among criminal women, one thing that can be said with certainty is that, like their male counterparts, they are taller than the insane. Yet they are shorter, and, perhaps with the exception of prostitutes, lighter than healthy women. All three female groups are identical in their average cranial circumference. Prostitutes show both a greater than average number of large heads and more microcephaly. In prostitutes, extremely small heads are four times more common than among the mad, and the rates among the mad are twice as high as those of the criminal. Prostitutes have dark, thick hair, and in

Lombardy, but not in France, they frequently have dark irises. Female criminals are weaker than the insane and more often masculine looking.

Prognathism, thick and crisp hair, thin beards, dark skin, pointed skulls, oblique eyes, small craniums, overdeveloped jaws, receding foreheads, large ears, similarity between the sexes, muscular weakness—all these characteristics confirm the findings from autopsies to demonstrate that European criminals bear a strong racial resemblance to Australian aborigines and Mongols.

3. Tattoos

One of the most singular characteristics of primitive men and those who still live in a state of nature is the frequency with which they undergo tattooing. This operation, which has both its surgical and aesthetic aspects, derives its name from an Oceanic language. In Italy, the practice is known as *marea* [mark], *nzito, segno* [sign], and *devozione* [devotion]. It occurs only among the lower classes—peasants, sailors, workers, shepherds, soldiers, and even more frequently among criminals. Because of its common occurrence among criminals, tattooing has assumed a new and special anatomico-legal significance that calls for close and careful study. But first we must examine its frequency among normal individuals for the sake of comparison.

To do this, I will use data on 7,114 individuals: 4,380 were soldiers and 2,734 criminals, prostitutes, and criminal soldiers. For this information, I have to thank that valiant student of forensic medicine, Tarehini Bonfanti, as well as the illustrious Dr. Baroffio, Cavaliere Alborghetti of Bergamo, Professor Gamba of Turin, Dr. Soresina of Milan, and Professor De Amicis of Naples. Table 3 summarizes the results of the survey.

In Italy, as among savages, tattooing is infrequent among women. Among noncriminal men, the use of tattoos is decreasing, with rates ten times lower in 1873 than in 1863. On the other hand, the custom persists and indeed reaches enormous proportions among the criminal population, both military and nonmilitary, where among 1,432 individuals examined, 115 or 7.9 percent sported tattoos. The most common place for tattoos is the smooth part of the forearm, followed by the shoulder, the chest (sailors), and the fingers (miners), on

Table 3 • Tattoos in Soldiers, Criminals, and Prostitutes

Year	Group (total number)	Medical Examiner	Percentage With Tattoos
1863	Soldiers (1,147)	Dr. Lombroso	11.6
1873	Soldiers (2,739)	Dr. Baroffio	1.4
	Criminal soldiers (150)	Dr. Baroffio	8.6
1872	Criminals (500)	Dr. Lombroso	6.0
1873	Criminals (134)	Dr. Alborghetti	15.0
	Criminals (650)	Dr. Tarehini	7.0
	Criminal women (300)	Dr. Gamba	1.6
1866–1873	Prostitutes (1,000)	Dr. Soresina	–
1871	Prostitutes (small number)	–	a few
1874	Prostitutes (small number)	De Amicis	a few

NOTE: In this eclectic table, Lombroso has combined studies covering different parts of Italy and different years.

which they take the form of a ring. Only men who had been to Oceania or were in prison had tattoos on their backs or pubic regions.

The symbols and meanings of tattoos are generally divisible into the categories of love, religion, war, and profession. Tattoos are external signs of beliefs and passions predominant among working-class men. After a careful study of the designs chosen by 102 criminals, I found that several not only appear frequently but also carry a particular significance. In 2 out of the 102 cases, tattoos marvelously reveal a nature that is violent, vindictive, or divided by conflicting intentions. For example, an old Piedmontese sailor, who had been a swindler and committed murder as part of a vendetta, had inscribed on his chest between two fists the sad phrase "I swear to revenge myself." A Venetian thief who was a recidivist bore the following lugubrious words on his chest: "I will come to a miserable end." It is said that criminals know their own fate and engrave it on their skin.

Other tattoos are obscene, either from their design or the region of the body where they appear. Only a few soldiers, mostly deserters released from prison, had obscene tattoos in the genital region. More significant results are obtained from my direct study of 102 tattooed criminals, of whom four had obscene tattoos.[13] One had a figure of a nude woman traced over the length of his penis. A second had the face of a woman drawn on the glans, in such a way that the woman's mouth was the penis's orifice; higher up on the penis was the Savoyard flag. A third had the initials of his lover on his penis; a fourth had a bouquet of flowers. All of this reveals not only a shamelessness but also insensitivity, given that the sexual organs are extremely sensitive to pain. Even savages avoid tattooing these areas.

The study of tattoos sometimes helps us track individuals to criminal organizations. Many members of the Camorra, a Neapolitan criminal organization, have tarantulas drawn on their arms; and three young arsonists from Milan sported tattoos with the same initials. Even tattoos that do not seem to have anything criminal about them and resemble those of farmers, shepherds, and sailors from the same region can be useful to the legal system and forensic medicine: they may reveal an individual's identity, his origins, and the important events of his life. Criminals, too, are aware of the advantages to the legal system offered by these involuntary revelations; thus the cleverest of them avoid tattoos or try to remove those they already have.

It would be interesting for anthropologists to ponder why such an apparently disadvantageous custom is maintained, given the discomfort and damage it causes. Here are some hypotheses:

— Religion, which tends to preserve ancient habits and customs, certainly perpetuates the practice of tattooing. Those who are devoted to particular saints believe that having their name inscribed on their flesh signifies their devotion and affection.

— A second reason is imitation.[14] Proof of this curious influence is the fact that members of an entire regiment will often sport the same design, such as a heart.

— Laziness also plays a part. For this reason tattoos are often found on deserters, prisoners, and sailors. In one prison, I found that twenty-five out of forty-one inmates had obtained their tattoos while in custody. Idleness is more painful than pain itself.

— Equally if not more influential is vanity. Even those who are not psychiatrists are aware of the way this powerful sentiment, found at all social levels and possibly even among animals, can prompt the most bizarre and damaging behavior. This is why savages who walk around naked have designs on their chests, while those who wear clothes choose to have tattoos in places that are visible or easily revealed, such as the forearm, and more often on the right forearm than on the left.

— Also influential is the sense of camaraderie, and perhaps even, as the initials of those Milanese arsonists suggest, a sense of "sect." I would not be surprised if some *camorristi* adopted, in addition to tattoos of frogs or tarantulas, other primitive ornamentations to distinguish their sect, such as wearing rings, pins, little chains, or sporting a certain style of whiskers. African tribes distinguish themselves by scarring their faces.

— Up to a certain point, noble human passions are also involved. The rites of the paternal village, the image of the patron saint, scenes of infancy, and depictions of distant friends—naturally one does not want to forget these things. Tattoos bring memories to life in the poor soldier's mind; the "prick of remembrance" overcomes distance, deprivations, and dangers.

— The passion of love, or rather, eroticism, is also important, as indicated by the obscene figures (4 out of 102 cases) or the initials of lovers (10 out of 102 cases) found on our criminals, and similar images on lesbians and prostitutes. Tribal women tattoo themselves to show they are unmarried. In men, too, tattoos often indicate virility. As Darwin puts it somewhat exaggeratedly, tattoos are both a sign and a means of sexual selection.[15]

Among Europeans, the most important reason for tattooing is atavism and that other form of atavism called traditionalism both of which characterize primitive men and men living in a state of nature. There is not a single primitive tribe that does not use tattooing. It is only natural that a custom widespread among savages and prehistoric peoples would reappear among certain lower-class groups. One such group is sailors, who display the same temperament as savages with their violent passions, blunted sensitivity, puerile vanity, and extreme laziness. Sailors even adopt the habits, superstitions, and songs of primitive peoples. In their nudity, prostitutes, too, recall savage customs.

The foregoing should suffice to demonstrate to judges and practitioners of forensic medicine that tattoos can signify a previous incarceration. Criminals' predilection for this custom is sufficient to distinguish them from the insane. Both groups experience forced internment, strong emotion, and long periods of boredom. Although madmen resort to such strange pastimes as rolling stones, snipping their clothes and even their flesh, scribbling on walls, and filling entire reams of paper, they very rarely make designs on their skin. This is yet another proof of the influence of atavism on tattooing because madness is almost never a congenital illness and rarely atavistic.

Forensic medicine should recognize that in the case of the criminal man, who is in constant struggle against society, tattoos—like scars—are professional characteristics.

4. Emotions of Criminals

The unusual predilection of criminals for something as painful as tattooing suggests that they have less sensitivity to pain than ordinary men, a phenomenon that can also be observed in the insane, especially those with dementia. Except in cases of idiocy, what appears as insensitivity to pain is actually the dominance of certain passions. Thus lesbian prostitutes, to reach their lovers in hospital, use red-hot irons to give themselves blisters that resemble pustular eruptions. I once saw two murderers who had for a long time hated one another throw themselves at each other during exercise hour, remaining embroiled for some minutes, one biting the other's lip, the other tearing out the hair of his adversary. When they were finally separated, they were more concerned about their unfinished brawl than their wounds, which became seriously infected.

More generally, criminals exhibit a certain moral insensitivity. It is not so much that they lack all feelings, as bad novelists have led us to believe. But certainly the emotions that are most intense in ordinary men's hearts seem in the criminal man to be almost silent, especially after puberty. The first feeling to disappear is sympathy for the misfortunes of others, an emotion that is, according to some psychologists, profoundly rooted in human nature. The murderer Lacenaire confessed that he had never felt the slightest sense of regret seeing any cadaver except that of his cat: "The sight of agony has no effect on me whatsoever. I would kill a man as easily I would drink a glass of water."[16] Complete indifference to their victims and to the bloody traces of their crimes is a constant characteristic of all true criminals, one that distinguishes them from normal men.

An executioner, Pantoni, told me that nearly all robbers and murderers go to their death laughing. A thief from Voghera, shortly before his execution, ordered a boiled chicken and ate it with gusto. Another inmate wanted to choose his favorite among the three executioners and called him his "professor." While being taken to the gallows, the assassin Valle from Alessandria, who had killed two or three of his companions out of pure caprice, loudly sang the well-known song "It's Not True That Death Is the Worst of All Evils."

The criminal's insensitivity is further proved by the frequency with which an assassin's accomplices will return to murdering people just after he is put to death. Also instructive are the joking words that in criminal jargon are used to name the executioner and his instruments, as well as the tales that are told in prison, where hanging is the favorite theme.[17] This provides one of the strongest arguments for the abolition of the death penalty, which clearly dissuades only a very small number of these wretches from committing crimes. Instead, it may encourage crime thanks to that law of imitation that so dominates among the vulgar classes and to the horrendous prestige that accrues to the person of the condemned. His criminal companions are made envious by the lugubrious and solemn ritual of execution before a crowd of spectators.[18]

Insensitivity to their own and others' pain explains why some criminals can commit acts that seem to be extraordinarily courageous. Thus Holland, Doincau, Mottino, Fieschi, and Saint-Clair had previously won medals for valor on the battlefield. Coppa threw himself into the midst of a battalion firing his gun and came out unharmed. These apparent acts of courage are really only the effect of criminals' insensitivity and infantile impetuousness, which prevent them from recognizing even certain danger. It makes them blind when they have a goal or a passion to satisfy.

Insensitivity combined with precipitous passions explains the lack of logic in crimes and the disjuncture between the gravity of a deed and the motive. For example, a prisoner killed a fellow inmate because he snored too loudly and would not or could not stop (Lauvergne, p. 108). Another, from Alessandria, killed his fellow inmate because he would not polish his shoes. Such moral insensitivity among criminals explains a paradox: the frequent cruelty of criminals who at other times seem capable of kindness.

Criminals' feelings are not always completely gone; some may survive while others disappear. Troppman, a killer of women and children, cried on hearing the name of his mother. D'Avanzo, who roasted and ate a man's calf muscles, later, wrote poetry. Immediately after committing murder, Feron ran to his girlfriend's children and gave them sweets. Holland confessed to a murder committed because he wanted to obtain money for his family, saying, "I did it for my poor child."

Parent-Duchatelet shows that while many prostitutes lose all ties to their own family, others use their ill-gotten gains to provide for their children, their parents, and even friends. They are excessively passionate about their lovers, so much so that even violence does not detach them. One unfortunate prostitute, after breaking her leg trying to escape her pimp's beatings, returned to him. Assaulted once again, she suffered a broken arm but lost nothing of her intense affection.

In most criminals, the nobler sentiments tend to be abnormal, excessive, and unstable. Mabille, to entertain a friend he had made one night in a restaurant, committed a murder. A certain Maggin said to me, "The cause of my crimes is that I fall into friendships too easily; I cannot see a companion offended without putting a hand on my dagger to revenge him."

A few tenacious passions dominate criminals in place of their absent or unstable social and family feelings. First among these is pride, or rather, an excessive sense of self-worth, which seems to grow in inverse proportion to merit. It is almost as if the psyche is dominated by the same law that governs reflex reactions, which grow stronger as the nervous system weakens. But in the case of criminals, this disequilibrium reaches gigantic proportions. The vanity of criminals exceeds that of artists, the literati, and flirtatious women. A death sentence did not worry Lacenaire nearly as much as criticism of his dreadful poetry and fear of public ridicule. As he put it, "I do not mind being hated, but do mind being mocked" for verses like the following:

The storm leaves a track

While the humble flower passes without a trace.

The most common motive for modern crimes is vanity, the need to shine in society, which is sadly known as "cutting a fine figure." At the Pallanza prison, a criminal told me, "I killed my sister-in-law because our family was too big, and it was thus difficult to make a show in the world." Denaud killed his wife, and his lover killed her husband, so that they could marry and save their reputation. When an infamous thief adopted a certain type of waistcoat and tie, his fellows imitated him, dressing themselves in the same style. Thus Inspector Vidocq found, among twenty-two thieves caught in one single day, twenty who wore the same color waistcoat.[19] They were vain about their strength, their looks, their courage, their ill-gotten and short-lived gains, and, most distressing of all, their ability to commit crimes.

Criminals resemble prostitutes, who always believe they belong to the highest grade of their profession. To prostitutes, the phrase "you are a one-lira woman" is a deep offense. Male inmates who have stolen thousands of lire laugh at petty thieves; and murderers consider themselves superior to thieves and swindlers.

The excessive vanity of criminals explains why they discuss their crimes before and after committing them, showing incredible lack of foresight and providing the justice system with the best possible weapon for finding and sentencing them. Shortly before killing his father, the patricide Marcellino said, "When my father returns from the fields, he will remain here forever." Berard, before going to commit the last of his crimes—the murder of three rich women—was heard to say: "I want to be connected to something big; oh, how I will be talked about!" But the clearest and most curious example of criminals' incredible vanity is a photograph discovered by the police in Ravenna showing three villains who, after having killed a companion, had themselves portrayed in the positions they had assumed while striking their blows. They felt the need to immortalize this strange moment at the risk of being reported and apprehended, which in fact happened.

A natural consequence of criminals' limitless vanity and inordinate sense of self is an inclination toward revenge for even the pettiest motives, as in the example of the inmate who killed someone for refusing to polish his shoes. Prostitutes exhibit the same tendency. "They frequently become enraged for the smallest reason, for a comment about being ugly, for example. In this regard they are more childish than their own children. Prostitutes would consider themselves dishonored if they did not react" (Parent-Duchatelet, p. 152). Such violent passions also lie behind the ferocity of ancient and savage peoples, although today they are so rare as to appear monstrous.

Once criminals have experienced the terrible pleasure of blood, violence becomes an uncontrollable addiction. Strangely, criminals are not ashamed of their bloodlust, but treat it with a sort of pride. Thus while he lay dying, Spadolino lamented having killed ninety-nine men instead of reaching a hundred.

Everyone agrees that the few violent women far exceed men in their ferocity and cruelty. The brigand women of southern Italy and the female revolutionaries of Paris invented unspeakable tortures. It was women who sold the flesh of policemen; who forced a man to eat his own roasted penis; and who threaded human bodies on a pike. Thus Shakespeare depicts Lady Macbeth as more cruel and cold than her male accomplice.

After the delights of taking revenge and satisfying his vanity, the criminal finds no greater pleasures than those offered by drinking and gambling. However, the passion for alcohol is very complex, being both a cause and an effect of crime. Indeed, alcohol is a triple cause of crime. First, the children of alcoholics often become criminals, and second, inebriation gives cowards the courage to undertake their dreadful deeds, as well as providing them with a future justification for their crimes. Furthermore, precocious drinking seduces the young into crime.[20] Third, the tavern is a common gathering place for accomplices, where they hatch their plots and upend the proceeds. For many it is their only home. The innkeeper is their banker, with whom criminals deposit their ill-gotten gains.

Few criminals fail to feel a lively passion for gambling, which explains a continual contradiction in the life of the malefactor: he greatly desires the belongings of others but at the same time squanders the money he has stolen, possibly because it was so easily acquired. Love of gambling also explains why most criminals end up poor despite possessing at times enormous sums.

Rarely does a male criminal feel true love for women. His is a carnal love, which almost always takes place in brothels (especially in London, where two-thirds of these are dens of criminals) and which develops at a very young age.[21] Prostitutes experience lesbian love, which distinguishes them from normal women, and they are passionate about flowers, dancing, and dining.

But the pleasures of gambling, eating, sex, and even revenge are nothing but intermediate steps to criminals' predominate passion, that of the orgy. Even though criminals shy away from regular society, they crave a kind of social life all their own, veritable orgies in which they enjoy the jubilant, tumultuous, riotous, and sensuous companionship of other offenders and even police spies.

I will not discuss criminals' many other passions, which vary according to their habits and intelligence. These range from the most terrible, such as pederasty, to the most noble, such as music; collecting books, paintings, and medals; and the enjoyment of flowers—a particular enthusiasm of the prostitute. One can find unusual emotions among criminals as among healthy people; what distinguishes criminal passions is instability, impetuousness, and often violence. In the quest to satisfy themselves, they give no thought to the consequences.

In many of these characteristics, criminals resemble the insane, who also exhibit not only violent and unstable passions but also insensitivity to pain, an exaggerated egotism, and (less frequently) a craving for alcohol. But the insane rarely show a predilection for gambling and orgies, and more than criminals, they will suddenly start to hate those who have hitherto been dearest to them. While the criminal cannot live without his companions and seeks them out even at his peril, the mad prefer to be alone, fleeing from every association with others. Plotting is as rare in the mental hospital as it is common in the prison.

In their emotional intensity, criminals closely resemble not the insane but savages. All travelers know that among the Negroes and savages of America, sensitivity to pain is so limited that the former laugh as they mutilate their hands to escape work, while the latter sing their tribe's praises while being burned alive. During puberty initiations, the young savages of America submit without complaint to cruel tortures that would kill a European. For example, they hang themselves upside down on butchers' hooks over dense columns of smoke. Such insensitivity encourages painful tattooing—something few Europeans can bear—and customs like cutting the lips and the fingers or pulling out teeth during funeral ceremonies.

Even moral sensitivity is weak or nonexistent among savages. The Caesars of the yellow races, called Tamerlanes, made their monuments out of pyramids of dried human heads. The emperor Nero was infamous for his barbarity, but even it paled in comparison to the cruel rites of the Chinese. Savages and criminals are further alike in the impetuosity and instability of their passions. Savages, as Lubbock tells us, have quick and violent emotions; while their strength and passions are those of adults, in character they are children. Similarly, Schaffhausen reports that "in many respects savages are like children: they feel strongly and think little; they love games, dancing and ornaments; and they are sometimes curious and timid. They are unaware of danger, but deep down they are cowards, vengeful and cruel in their vendettas."[22] A Cacique, returning from a failed hunting expedition, was greeted by his young son, who ran between his legs; to vent his rage, the father picked him up by the leg and dashed him against some rocks.

Notes

1. These heights in meters are equivalent to 5 feet 4.4 inches; 5 feet 3.6 inches; 5 feet 2.8 inches; 5 feet 2.5 inches; and 5 feet 1.8 inches, respectively.

2. James Bruce Thomson (1810–73), chief physician at Scotland's Perth Prison, published influential articles based on degenerationist theory and arguing that many criminals are born criminals; these included "The Psychology of Criminals" in the 1870 issue of the *Journal of Mental Science*. Lombroso was fascinated by Thomson's work and cited it as evidence for his own theory. The Wilson to whom Lombroso refers was probably the British craniometrist George Wilson. The work of both men is discussed in Davie 2004, 2005.

3. Thomson found an average weight of 151 pounds among 423 Scottish criminals, 106 pounds among 147 Irish criminals, and 149 pounds among 55 English criminals. The average height was 5 feet 6.9 inches for the Scottish criminals, 5 feet 6.2 inches for the English, and 5 feet 6.6 inches for the Irish.

4. These weights in kilograms are equivalent to 150 pounds and 138 pounds, respectively.

5. Johann Ludwig Casper (1787–1853) was a prominent professor of forensic pathology in Berlin.

6. Johann Kasper Lavater (1741–1801) attempted to turn physiognomy, or the reading of character from facial expressions, into a science. In the early nineteenth century, physiognomy flowed into phrenology, and later in the century, phrenology flowed into criminal anthropology. The Guido to whom Lombroso here refers was probably the Italian baroque painter Guido Reni (1575–1642).

7. The French criminal Martin Dumollard, famous for drinking his victims' blood, was executed in 1862.

8. The dynamometer, or strength-testing machine, used by Lombroso was oval in shape with a dial to record results. Subjects had to compress the oval to test "compressive strength" and pull at the oval to test "tractive strength."

9. Alexandre J. B. Parent-Duchatelet (1805–59) was the first European to conduct a large-scale study of prostitution, *De la prostitution dans la ville de Paris* (*Prostitution in the City of Paris*, 1836). Lombroso relied on Parent-Duchatelet's work for most of his early data on female crime. In this first edition of *Criminal Man*, Lombroso begins to establish his theory that prostitution—that is sexual deviancy—constitutes the typical and most widespread form of female crime.

10. Lock hospitals (or *sifilicomi* in Italian) were nineteenth-century institutions for the internment of prostitutes with venereal disease. Although hospitals in name, they resembled prisons to which prostitutes were admitted forcibly by police. Lock hospitals provided criminologists like Lombroso with a captive female population for physical and psychological examinations.

11. In this summary of his conclusions on the anthropometry and physiognomy of criminals, Lombroso is referring (with only a few exceptions) to men. Some of his conclusions are based on material that we cut from this chapter.

12. The cephalic index was an important tool for nineteenth-century criminal anthropologists in their attempts to categorize races and identify born criminals. They obtained the cephalic index by multiplying the width of the skull by one hundred and dividing the result by the length of the skull. The resulting numbers enabled them to classify skulls into various categories including brachycephalic (or short-headed) and dolichocephalic (or long-headed). Born criminals fell into both categories; Lombroso considered their cephalic indices to be abnormal when the numbers deviated from the norm for their geographical region.

13. Tardieu has written about a coach driver and an iron smith who had boots tattooed on their penises.

14. Imitation became an important criminological concept in the late nineteenth century, especially in explanations of crowd behavior. The French jurist Gabriel Tarde (1843–1904) is best known for applying the concept of imitation to the etiology of crime in his 1890 book *La philosophie pénale* (*Penal Philosophy*). In this first edition of *Criminal Man*, Lombroso anticipates Tarde as well as later criminological debates over imitation. See Barrows 1981.

15. Charles Darwin (1809–82), the British naturalist, elaborated the theory of evolution in his famous work, *The Origin of Species* (1859). For Lombroso, Darwin's theory confirmed his intuition that criminals were atavistic or throwbacks on the evolutionary scale. In the third edition of *Criminal Man*, Lombroso aspires to do for criminals what Darwin had done for plant and animal species.

16. The French thief and poet Pierre-François Lancenair (1800–36) both shocked and fascinated public opinion with his murder of the widow Chardon and her son in 1835. The following year, he was executed by guillotine for his crime.

17. Fregier. *Des classes dangéreuses*, 1841, p. 111. In German slang, to be hanged is Heimgangen, going back home. In Italian there are various terms for being hanged, including "to grimace" or "to squint."

18. Lombroso was ambivalent about the death penalty, but in general he went from opposition to grudging acceptance of it as a means of social defense against recidivist born criminals and particularly violent members of organized crime like *mafiosi* and brigands. Yet he muffled his support of capital punishment in deference to the opposition of the majority of his positivist colleagues and the public in general. In 1889, Italy abolished the death penalty in its new criminal code.

19. The notorious French criminal Eugène François Vidocq (1775–1857) turned informer and finally became head of the French urban police force in 1811. He is the model for both Jean Valjean and Inspector Javert in Victor Hugo's novel *Les Misérables* (1862).

20. Lombroso often employs the word *precocity* to mean the premature development of physical or psychological characteristics or early indulgence in adult behaviors. In all cases, precocity signals abnormality for Lombroso.

21. Of 3,287 homicides and assaults in Italy, 299 were caused by sexual jealousy and 47 for prostitution and loose behavior. Of 41,454 crimes, 1,499 involved illicit loves. In England, of 10,000 persons sentenced, 3,608 were prostitutes; in Italy, of 383 women sentenced, 12 were prostitutes. Of 208 crimes committed for reasons of love according to Descruret, 91 were for adultery, 96 for concubinage, and 13 for jealousy. Of 10,000 crimes of violence in France and England, 1,477 were for reasons of love (Guerry). Of 10,899 suicides in France, 981 were for love.

22. *Uber den Zustand der Wilden*, 1868.

/// REVIEW QUESTIONS

1. What are some of the characteristics of the face of habitual murderers, according to Lombroso? What about thieves? Rapists?
2. What does Lombroso claim are key characteristics of female criminals? Do these differ from male criminals?
3. Review some of the tattoos that Lombroso observed on criminals. How do these tattoos relate to the emotions of criminals?

READING /// 8

In this empirical study, Ilhong Yun and Julak Lee examine the degree to which police arrest is affected by suspects' level of verbal intelligence. Using a national longitudinal study of youth, the researchers also examine whether the level of neighborhood disadvantage where the offender resides moderates the influence of verbal intelligence on arrest.

While reading this article, one should consider the following topics:

- The theoretical rationale for the IQ-delinquency causation hypothesis, and also the competing hypotheses for the consistently observed link between IQ and crime
- The reasons for why it is verbal IQ that is believed to be particularly important in terms of criminality, especially relative to other forms of IQ
- Findings of the current study regarding whether suspects' verbal IQ does indeed have an influence on police decisions to arrest, as well as theoretical reasons for the results
- The theoretical reasons, and this study's findings, regarding the possible conditioning effect of suspects who live in disadvantaged neighborhoods

IQ and Delinquency

The Differential Detection Hypothesis Revisited

Ilhong Yun and Julak Lee

A long line of research in clinical psychology and neuroscience indicates that self-control, which is a part of a larger executive function housed in the prefrontal cortex of the brain, is closely linked to verbal intelligence (Beaver, DeLisi, Vaughn, Wright, & Boutwell, 2008; Beaver & Wright, 2007; Luria, 1961; Moffitt, Caspi, Silva, & Stouthamer-Loeber, 1995). Based on this literature, we hypothesize that offenders' verbal intelligence also plays a statistically meaningful role in shaping police officers' decision to arrest. Thus, in the present study we examine the extent to which police arrest is influenced by offenders' level of verbal intelligence. Concomitantly, we examine whether the type of neighborhood in which the offender resides moderates the effect of an offender's verbal intelligence on arrest.

Intelligence and Delinquency

Intelligence means dozens of different things to different people (Nisbett et al., 2012). Further, the checkered history of biases and cruel criminal justice policies that were associated with the concept of intelligence (Dugdale, 1877; Goddard, 1914) advise criminologists to remain vigilant for the misuse of it. Nevertheless, intelligence when measured through common IQ tests is a reasonably strong correlate and predictor of a range of outcomes.[1] For

SOURCE: Ilhon Yun and Julak Lee, "IQ and Delinquency: The Differential Detection Hypothesis Revisited," *Youth Violence and Juvenile Justice* 11, no. 3 (2013): 196–211.

instance, the correlation between IQ scores and school grades is about .5, meaning that about 25% of the variance of school performance is explained by IQ scores (Neisser et al., 1996). Intelligence is also correlated with years of education ($r = .55$), job performance ($r = .54$), and other various aspects of successes and failures in life (Neisser et al., 1996).

IQ scores are also linked to delinquency, although the magnitude of the correlation is relatively weak compared to other aforementioned outcomes. Nonetheless, it is as strong as the effect of social class, and the IQ-delinquency relation holds up even after social class and race are controlled for (Hirschi & Hindelang, 1977). The IQ differences found between delinquents and nondelinquents are typically about eight points or half a standard deviation ([*SD*] Hirschi & Hindelang, 1977; Neisser et al., 1996). Contrary to some researchers' argument that the low IQ scores of delinquents merely reflect the lack of test motivation typical of delinquent youths (Tarnopol, 1970), the IQ-delinquency relation survives a statistical control of test motivation (Lynam, Moffitt, & Stouthamer-Loeber, 1993). Several studies also showed that the causal sequence flows from IQ to delinquency, and not vice versa (Lynam et al., 1993; Moffitt et al., 1995).

There has been a heated scholarly debate on why such a relationship exists. Herrnstein and Murray (1994), in their widely debated *The Bell Curve*, went so far as to suggest that IQ scores are *the* primary cause of delinquency while excluding all other salient sociological variables, a claim that was later repeatedly refuted as being pseudoscientific and politically oriented (Cullen, Gendreau, Jarjoura, & Wright, 1997). One hypothesis that has garnered most empirical support thus far is the school performance-mediation hypothesis. This hypothesis posits that intelligence and crime are related as a consequence of school performance, where low intelligence leads to poor school performance, which, in turn, induces frustration and retards the growth of social bonds to conventional institutions that may inhibit deviance (Hirschi & Hindelang, 1977; Ward & Tittle, 1994). Research that tested this hypothesis has consistently revealed evidence in support of this position while disputing other competing hypotheses (McGloin & Pratt, 2003; McGloin, Pratt, & Maahs, 2004; Moffitt & Silva, 1988).

IQ scores encompass varying dimensions, but it is worth noting that IQ deficits of delinquents are concentrated in the verbal dimension. In contrast, youths' abilities in visual, spatial, and motor domains are generally less associated with delinquency. For instance, Moffitt et al. (1995), employing the Dunedin Longitudinal Study, a prospective study of a cohort of 1,037 children born in New Zealand, shows that verbal skills and verbal memory far outweighs other dimensions of intelligence, such as visual–spatial, visual–motor integration, and mental flexibility in their predictive ability of delinquency. Youths with low verbal IQ scores are also at risk for a range of other maladaptive developmental outcomes such as problems understanding and communicating emotions accurately, self-regulation, and difficulties in social problem-solving skills and decision making (Dionne, 2005; Moffitt et al., 1995). These findings indicate that deficits in verbal capacity are also linked to deficits in the "executive function" of the brain that regulates planning, decision making, and moderation of social behaviors of humans. Impulsive violent offenders are often found to have deficient executive functions as well as low verbal IQ scores (Lynam et al., 1993; Moffitt et al., 1995).

Self-Control, Verbal Skills, and the Differential Detection Hypothesis

The IQ-delinquency causation hypothesis has its fair share of competing hypotheses. One of the competing hypotheses is what has been called the differential detection hypothesis. According to this, the relationship between intelligence and delinquency is essentially spurious, and the one half a "standard deviation" IQ score differential between delinquents and nondelinquents merely reflects the fact that less intelligent delinquents are more likely to be detected and arrested by the police, while their intellectually advantaged counterparts are somehow better at avoiding detection (Moffitt & Silva, 1988; Stark, 1975). Thus, insofar as official measures of delinquency are employed, the differential detection hypothesis considers the inverse correlation between IQ scores and delinquency as being spurious. Simply put, this hypothesis suggests that IQ scores of officially detected delinquents are not representative of the IQ scores of delinquents at large (Moffitt & Silva, 1988).

To ward off the differential detection confound that may be present in studies using official measures of delinquency, self-report studies have subsequently been conducted. Contrary to the expectation that the IQ difference between delinquents and nondelinquents would be eliminated in self-report studies, the results of these studies have also manifested a statistically significant negative correlation between IQ scores and delinquency. Most of the studies, however, revealed a substantially attenuated correlation compared to studies using an official measure of delinquency (see Hirschi & Hindelang, 1977). Because a significant inverse association still remains even in self-report studies, most researchers appear to have dropped the differential detection hypothesis in their research agenda.

However, we suggest that the fact that both official and self-report studies exhibit a negative correlation between delinquency and IQ scores does not necessarily provide a definitive conclusion that police officers are no more likely to arrest low IQ delinquents than they are to arrest high IQ delinquents. Individuals evoke different reactions from their social environment depending on their genetic propensities, personality traits, and behaviors (Scarr & McCartney, 1983). For instance, children in the same family evoke different reactions from their parents. A child who is genetically predisposed to be irritable and oppositional will likely elicit cold and negative responses from their parents, when compared to a child who is of agreeable and affable disposition. In a similar vein, we hypothesize that verbally deficient delinquents are more likely to elicit more punitive reactions from police officers as did delinquents with low self-control, as noted by Beaver et al.'s study (2009). Such a hypothesis is quite plausible considering the recent empirical and theoretical research into the association between language development and self-control.

Research has consistently shown that language/verbal skills are related to a wide range of adverse behavioral outcomes. Impaired language skills of children lead to delinquency, school failure, and physical aggression, while proper language development fosters emotional control and impulse regulation (Dionne, 2005; Moffitt et al., 1995). Note that the characteristics of these outcomes are quite similar to those of self-control described by Gottfredson and Hirschi (1990). In fact, a long line of research indicates that language development is closely related to self-control. Summing up the research results, Gallagher (1999, p. 5) stated that

> One of the most important functions of language is intrapersonal emotional and behavioral regulation. Children's language comprehension and expression skills are critical to their understanding, encoding, organization, and retrieval of rules that enable them to effect appropriate levels of self-control and emotional regulation.

Despite the close nexus, the precise mechanism surrounding language and self-control has not always been clear. Dionne (2005) summarizes two different perspectives that may account for the association. The first perspective—termed the shared etiology explanation—is that language skills and self-control are caused by the same but unknown factors. The causal factors could be environmental, genetic, or a combination of both factors. The second perspective—termed the causal effect explanation—is that self-control is caused by language skills. Gottfredson and Hirschi (1990) argued that self-control in children is instilled by continuous parental correction of their offspring's misbehavior. The process of correcting a child's misbehavior necessitates a minimum level of language skills on the part of the child, through which the child understands parents' commands, directions, and statements. Without the child's language skills, self-control thus would not develop. On a related note, Luria (1961; Luria & Hamskaya, 1964) posited that a child's neuronal pathways in the frontal lobes can develop properly only when the child learns to abide by parental verbal instructions and commands. Given that self-control is part of the executive function, housed in the frontal lobes of the brain (Beaver et al., 2008), it appears reasonable to assume that language skills contribute to proper development of self-control.

A recent study by Beaver and colleagues (2008) examined empirical viability of these two different perspectives using the subsample of twins from the Early Childhood Longitudinal Survey, Kindergarten Class of 1998–1999 (ECLS-K). Their findings shed some light on the research questions of the present study. First, language skills were robustly associated with self-control. The association held true both cross sectionally and longitudinally. Second, the covariation between language skills and self-control was largely accounted for by genetic factors, supporting the shared etiology explanation. Finally, their quantitative genetics model showed that, controlling for genetic effects and shared environmental effects, language skills were a significant predictor of self-control, supporting the causal effect explanation. In other words, analyses of ECLS-K data offer evidence supporting both perspectives.

Given the close connection between self-control and language skills, delinquent youths with verbal deficits may be more likely to end up resorting to quick physical or otherwise disrespectful reactions than verbally adroit youths. A plethora of studies show that officers are more likely to arrest youthful offenders who they perceive as belligerent, obdurate, disobedient, and disrespectful (Black, 1976; Piliavin & Briar, 1964; Terrill & Reisig, 2003). Piliavin and Briar (1964, pp. 210–211) note, in their classic study of police officers:

> The cues used by police to assess demeanor were fairly simple. Juveniles who were contrite about their infractions, respectful to officers, and fearful of the sanction that might be employed against them tended to be viewed by patrolmen as basically law-abiding or at least 'salvageable . . .' [I]n contrast, youthful offenders who were fractious, obdurate, or who appeared nonchalant in their encounters with patrolmen were likely to be viewed as 'would-be tough guys' or 'punks' who fully deserved the most severe sanction: arrest.

Given the close linkage between self-control and verbal capacity, differential detection contingent upon verbal IQ scores appears to be a plausible hypothesis. To our knowledge, however, there is only one study that has ever delved into this issue.

Utilizing the Dunedin Longitudinal Study, Moffitt and Silva (1988) compared the verbal IQ scores of the delinquents who were detected by the police according to official police records and the verbal IQ scores of delinquents who were not detected according to self-reports. They failed to find a significant difference in verbal IQ scores between the two groups of delinquents. Although methodologically sound, this study used a non-American sample; thus, whether the findings can be generalizable to an American sample is an empirical matter. In addition, no study has examined the possibility that the effect of verbal IQ may interact with other salient factors associated with police behavior, such as neighborhood disadvantage.

Neighborhood Disadvantage and Police Arrest

Donald Black (1976) posits that the application of punishment (e.g., arrest) by legal agents can also be explained by social space in which the subjects of control are placed. He further suggests that the police employ more punitive action toward offenders with low socioeconomic background or marginal cultural status, such as minorities, the poor, or those from disadvantaged communities (1976). In support of Black's argument, research following the Chicago School's tradition of neighborhood ecology reveals that police coercive actions are not evenly distributed across communities (Terrill & Reisig, 2003; Warner & Coomer, 2003; Werthman & Piliavin, 1967). It appears that officers develop a kind of cognitive script based on their prior experiences through which they believe individuals in poorer communities commit more crimes than in wealthier areas. Such cognitive scripts can induce officers to behave differently depending on the type of geographical areas in which the police–suspect encounter takes place. In a similar vein, Werthman and Piliavin (1967) in their classic study of patrol officers' behaviors found that patrol officers come to associate neighborhoods with the frequency with which they encountered suspicious persons. Officers not only define certain people as suspicious based on their behaviors and demeanors but also define geographical areas as suspicious. Further, the police tend to attach moral liability to the suspects they encounter in the suspicious neighborhoods irrespective of their individual behavioral manifestations. Likewise, Bayley and Mendelsohn (1969) also noted that the police behave more aggressively and make more arrests in lower class and high crime neighborhoods due to a perceived greater social distance between the police and the residents.

Empirical support for this position, however, is not unequivocal. A sizable number of police researchers are in fact reluctant to endorse the notion that officers behave more aggressively and vigorously in communities marked by structural disadvantages. For example, in his study of officers in one disadvantaged community, Goldstein (1960) observed that officers took rather a lukewarm approach to serious assault cases: they rarely arrested the assaulters, much less taking an official report. In support of this finding, Klinger (1997) and Skolnick (1966) argue that police activities in high crime communities are in reality less vigorous, thus leading to fewer arrests and less coercive actions, partly due to heavy workloads and resource constraints. Sherman also notes that police agencies in high-crime districts direct their limited resources only to major crimes, not being able to respond to all criminal acts with equal vigor (1990). Police often view criminal victims in such neighborhoods undeserving of police protection because they either precipitate their victimization or they themselves are criminals in other contexts. Officers become quite cynical, believing that, no matter what they do, crime rates will remain always high. Officers' cynicism and perceived victim undeservedness also contribute to less vigorous police actions (Klinger, 1997; Niederhoffer, 1967).

In view of such conflicting claims and empirical findings, more research is clearly needed to provide informed answers as to whether police are indeed more likely to arrest delinquents in disadvantaged communities. Given our discussion on the possible predictive effect of verbal intelligence on police arrest, one potentially fruitful area of research is to explore the extent to which the effect of verbal intelligence is conditioned by (or interacts with) the level of neighborhood disadvantage. It is illuminating to note that McCluskey, Reisig, Mastrofski, and Terrill's (1999) finding that disrespectfulness displayed by suspects was conditioned by the level of neighborhood disadvantage; that is, suspects were significantly more likely to exhibit disrespect toward officers when the police–suspect encounter occurred in neighborhoods characterized by concentrated disadvantage. Based on the argument that displays of disrespectful demeanors may be associated with low verbal IQs, we hypothesize that the neighborhoods' level of disadvantage moderates the effect of verbal IQs on arrest. To our knowledge, this issue has never been empirically examined.

The Present Study

The purpose of this study is to examine the degree to which police arrest is influenced by offenders' level of verbal intelligence. Concomitantly, we examine whether the level of concentrated disadvantage of the offender's neighborhood moderates the effect of verbal intelligence on arrest. To accomplish this, we examine the extent to which delinquent youths' self-reported arrests are significantly related to their verbal IQ scores and, further, to the interaction of verbal IQ scores and neighborhood disadvantage net of a set of theoretically relevant control variables.

Data Sources and Sample

Data for the present study comes from the National Longitudinal Study of Adolescent Health (Add Health), a longitudinal and nationally representative sample of American youths (Udry, 2003). Although four waves of data have been collected so far, only the first three waves of data are utilized in the present study. Initial data collection began in 1994–1995, when the respondents were enrolled in 7th through 12th grades. A total of one hundred thirty-two schools across the nation were sampled through multistage stratified sampling techniques. In the beginning, an in-school questionnaire was administered to students attending these schools, and more than 90,000 students completed the survey instrument.

To obtain more detailed information from the respondents, a stratified subsample was selected and reinterviewed at their home. In all, 20,745 adolescents and 17,700 of their primary caregivers were interviewed in this in-home survey. Adolescents were queried on involvement in delinquent behaviors, police contacts, and a plethora of other items pertaining to adolescent development in general (Harris et al., 2003). The second wave of data was collected from 14,738 of the respondents in 1996. Because the lapse of time between Wave I and Wave II was relatively short, most of the items in Wave I were also included in Wave II interviews. The third wave of data was collected in 2001–2002, when most participants reached the age of 18 and 26. As a consequence, the items in the survey instruments were redesigned to include more age-appropriate questions, such as their lifetime contact with the criminal justice system and marital status, along with other items pertaining to young adults. Overall, 15,197 participants were interviewed successfully.

To examine the research questions of the current study, we culled an analytical sample from the entire Add Health sample using two criteria. Considering the goal of the present study, the first step involved selecting adolescents who reported having engaged in a delinquent act in any of the three waves that could have resulted in an arrest. The Add Health data contain a range of items measuring delinquent acts that, if detected by the police, could lead to an arrest. For instance, youths were asked at Wave I to self-report how many times in the past 12 months they had hurt someone badly enough to need medical attention, deliberately damaged property, sold drugs, taken something from a store without paying, painted graffiti on someone else's property, driven other's car without permission, and gotten into a physical fight. Response categories were scored as 0 = never, 1 = once or twice, 2 = 3 or 4 times, and 3 = 5 or more times. Delinquency items at Wave II are quite similar because most participants were attending schools and were still in their adolescence at the time of Wave II. At Wave III, however, most respondents had reached young adulthood. Some of the questions were dropped accordingly and others were added to reflect age-appropriate topics. For example, respondents were asked whether they had deliberately written a bad check or used someone else's credit card without permission instead of the items on joyriding and painting graffiti. Delinquency scales were computed for each wave: Wave I and II delinquency scales consisted of 14 items, while delinquency III scale consisted of 11 items. Based on the three delinquency scales, we initially selected the adolescents who scored at least 1 on any of the scales.

Second, the current study's aim is to examine whether low verbal intelligence increases the odds of arrest via manifesting itself in the form of adverse attitudes or behaviors toward police officers after a delinquent act. Thus, the analytical sample should be confined to the delinquents who had had an encounter with the police. At Wave III, adolescents were asked whether they had ever been stopped or questioned by the police for any reason other than a traffic violation. Those who responded affirmatively to this question among the delinquents selected by the first selection criterion constitute the final analytical sample of the current study (N = 2,810).

Dependent Variable

The dependent variable of this study is whether a delinquent who had an encounter with a police officer has been arrested. To measure whether delinquents in our sample have ever been arrested by the police, a single item at Wave III—Have you ever been arrested or taken into custody by the police?—was used. Out of the 2,810 delinquents who had an encounter with the police, 57% reported that they had been arrested or taken into custody.

Independent Variables

Verbal intelligence. Verbal intelligence is measured using the Peabody Picture Vocabulary Test–Revised (PPVT-R). The PPVT is among the most well-established indicators of verbal intelligence (Baker, Keck, Mott, & Quinlan, 1993). Furthermore, the PPVT-R has been regarded as a sufficient proxy for other generalized tests of intelligence, such as the Wechsler Preschool and Primary Scale of Intelligence for young children (Vance, West, & Kutsick, 1989). Add Health respondents were administered an abridged version of a 78-item PPVT-R test at Wave I and Wave III, respectively. Every other item in the original PPVT-R was selected for use, and basal and ceiling rules were modified to take into account the smaller number of items. As in standard PPVT administration, the respondents were to select one picture among four illustrations that best illustrated the meaning of the word that was read by an interviewer. The raw scores were age-standardized and converted to the IQ metric, with a mean of 100 and a standard deviation of 15 by the Add Health research team. We conducted an exploratory iterated principal factor analysis on Wave I and Wave III PPVT scores to create a single measure of verbal intelligence for Add Health respondents. The two scores loaded heavily on a single latent factor (Wave I = 0.72 and Wave III = 0.72, respectively). Thus, extracted factor scores were used as a measure of verbal intelligence.

Neighborhood disadvantage. A neighborhood disadvantage scale was constructed by using items drawn from Add Health's Wave I contextual data file. This file included information on neighborhood structural disadvantages at the block level from the 1990 Census. The 5 items used for the neighborhood disadvantage scale are proportion of single parent-headed households, proportion of households with income less than $15,000, proportion of households receiving public assistance, proportion of African Americans, and the unemployment rate in the neighborhood. Because of potential collinearity, the items were factor analyzed, all of which loaded on a single factor. Factor scores were used to construct the neighborhood disadvantage scale. This scale is similar to the ones used by other researchers analyzing neighborhood-level conditions (Cleveland, 2003; Sampson, Raudenbush, & Earls, 1997). Higher values on this scale indicated greater levels of neighborhood disadvantage.

Control Variables

The control variables are age (in years), Black (0 = non-Blacks, 1 = Blacks), non-Black minority (0 = Whites/Blacks, 1 = non-Black minority), sex (0 = female, 1 = male), and household income. Household income was created by a parent's report of the total household income in 1994. In addition, we included two theoretically and empirically relevant control variables—self-control and delinquency at Wave I—to help ensure that any relationships revealed were not the result of spuriousness.

Self-control. Research shows that low self-control, a potentially robust precursor to delinquency and other analogous behaviors, is linked to low verbal intelligence (Beaver et al., 2008; Luria, 1961; Moffitt, 1990), indicating a common deficit in executive function in the brain (Beaver & Wright, 2007; Moffitt, 1990). Thus, when confronting the police, not only the low self-control delinquents but also the verbally deficient delinquents are likely to display, or be perceived by officers as displaying, disrespect to the police. Thus, given the conceptual overlap between self-control and verbal intelligence, a statistical control of self-control allows a conservative estimate of the effect of verbal intelligence.

Gottfredson and Hirschi (1990) argued that self-control is characterized by variations in factors such as impulsivity, a preference for simple tasks, an avoidance of mental activities, a preference for physical activities, and self-centeredness. We employed a 5-item additive scale to measure the degree of self-control of Add Health participants. Adolescents at Wave I responded on a 5-point Likert-type scale to the following statements: Have they had problems or trouble "keeping their mind on what they were doing," "getting their homework done," "paying attention in school," and "getting along with their teachers." These items tap into preference for simple tasks and physical activities, impulsivity, and temper components of self-control. In order to tap the self-centeredness component, respondents were asked whether they felt they were "doing everything just about right." Responses to these items were summed to form a low self-control scale. The same measure of self-control has been used by previous researchers analyzing the Add Health data (Beaver, 2010; Perrone, Sullivan, Pratt, & Margaryan, 2004). The self-control scale was coded in a way that high scores indicated lower levels of self-control.

Delinquency at Wave I. The analytical sample of the current study includes delinquents only. Yet, it is reasonable to assume that variation in the frequency of delinquency even among the delinquents affects the probability of arrest. To take into account this possibility, delinquency at Wave I was included as a statistical control. The Wave I delinquency scale consists of the same 14 delinquency items that were used to cull the analytical sample of this study. Table 1 includes the descriptive statistics for the variables and scales used in the analyses.

Plan of Analysis

The analyses for the current study proceeded in two related steps. First, a multivariate logit equation was estimated with the arrest measure (no arrest = 0 and ever been arrested = 1) as the dependent variable. We included verbal IQ scores, neighborhood disadvantage, and control variables as covariates. This model provided initial evidence of the association between verbal intelligence and the probability of arrest, while controlling for neighborhood disadvantage and other controls. The second step entailed examining the interaction between verbal intelligence and neighborhood disadvantage in the odds of arrest. An interface of research from two separate areas suggests that verbal intelligence may be more strongly associated with the likelihood of arrest when it is paired with concentrated neighborhood disadvantage (Moffitt et al., 1995; Terrill & Reisig, 2003; Werthman & Piliavin, 1967; Wilson & Herrnstein, 1985). In light of these findings, we hypothesized that verbal intelligence effects are more pronounced in the presence of concentrated neighborhood disadvantage, thereby leading to a higher likelihood of arrest of low verbal IQ delinquents.

Table 1 • Descriptive Statistics (N = 2,810)

Variable	Mean	SD	Minimum	Maximum
Dependent variable Arrest	.57	.49	0	1
Independent variables				
Verbal intelligence	.08	.70	−3.68	1.62
Neighborhood disadvantage	−.09	.91	−1.35	4.82
Control variables				
Age	15.89	1.75	12	21
Black	.20	.40	0	1
Non-Black minority	.15	.35	0	1
Sex	.73	.44	0	1
Household income	48.27	46.91	1	999
Low self-control	7.26	3.26	0	20
Wave I delinquency	6.90	6.90	1	45

We converted the neighborhood disadvantage scale into a dichotomous variable based on the mean score. Delinquents that lived in a neighborhood whose neighborhood disadvantage score was at or higher than the mean were called the disadvantaged neighborhood sample, while those who lived in neighborhoods whose score was below the mean were called the adequate neighborhood sample. We hypothesized that verbal intelligence would be significantly related to arrest in the disadvantaged neighborhood sample but not in the adequate neighborhood sample.

Results

The analysis began by estimating a multivariate logit regression equation, where the dichotomous arrest variable was used as the dependent variable. This model included verbal intelligence as measured by PPVT-R score, neighborhood disadvantage, and six control variables as covariates. As an initial step, we estimated the model on the full sample. Verbal intelligence maintains a statistically significant and negative association with arrest, indicating that delinquents with low verbal IQ scores are more likely to be arrested by the police. The significance of verbal intelligence was obtained by controlling for Wave I delinquency. To further test the robustness of the findings, we ran additional models controlling for Wave II delinquency and Wave III delinquency, respectively. A quite similar pattern was revealed, showing the significance of the association between verbal intelligence and arrest in both of the models. Yet, neighborhood disadvantage did not exhibit any statistically meaningful association with arrest. Nonetheless, in order to examine possible interaction between verbal intelligence and neighborhood disadvantage, we estimated split-sample models. The full sample was split at the mean of the neighborhood disadvantage scale. An interaction would be detected if verbal intelligence was associated with arrest in one sample but not in the other.

The first model estimated a logit equation for the adequate neighborhood sample, while the other model estimated for the disadvantaged sample. In both models, three of the covariates—non-Black minority, being male, and Wave I delinquency—increased the odds of arrest. Age was significant only in the adequate neighborhood sample, while low self-control was significant only in the disadvantaged neighborhood sample. Verbal intelligence, the key variable in this study exhibited a statistically significant negative association with arrest in the first equation. Yet, such an association did not hold true in the second model. These findings counter our hypothesis in that verbally deficient delinquents are more likely to be arrested *in adequate neighborhoods* but not in disadvantaged neighborhoods. Nevertheless, the findings do suggest that verbal intelligence interacts with neighborhood disadvantage in the likelihood of being arrested.

We calculated predicted probabilities of arrest against the verbal intelligence score for the two separate groups, while holding all other variables at their respective means. Figure 1 is the graphical representation of the calculated probabilities for the two groups. As shown, while both groups exhibit a decrease in the probability of arrest as verbal intelligence score increases, the decrease is more pronounced for the adequate neighborhood group than for the disadvantaged group.

Discussion

Beaver et al.'s (2009) recent research suggested that offenders' level of self-control influences the decisions of law enforcement and court officials. Given prior theorizing and empirical research showing that self-control is linked to verbal intelligence, we examined whether delinquents' verbal intelligence was also associated with the

Figure 1 • Predicted probability of arrest by verbal intelligence: adequate versus disadvantaged neighborhood

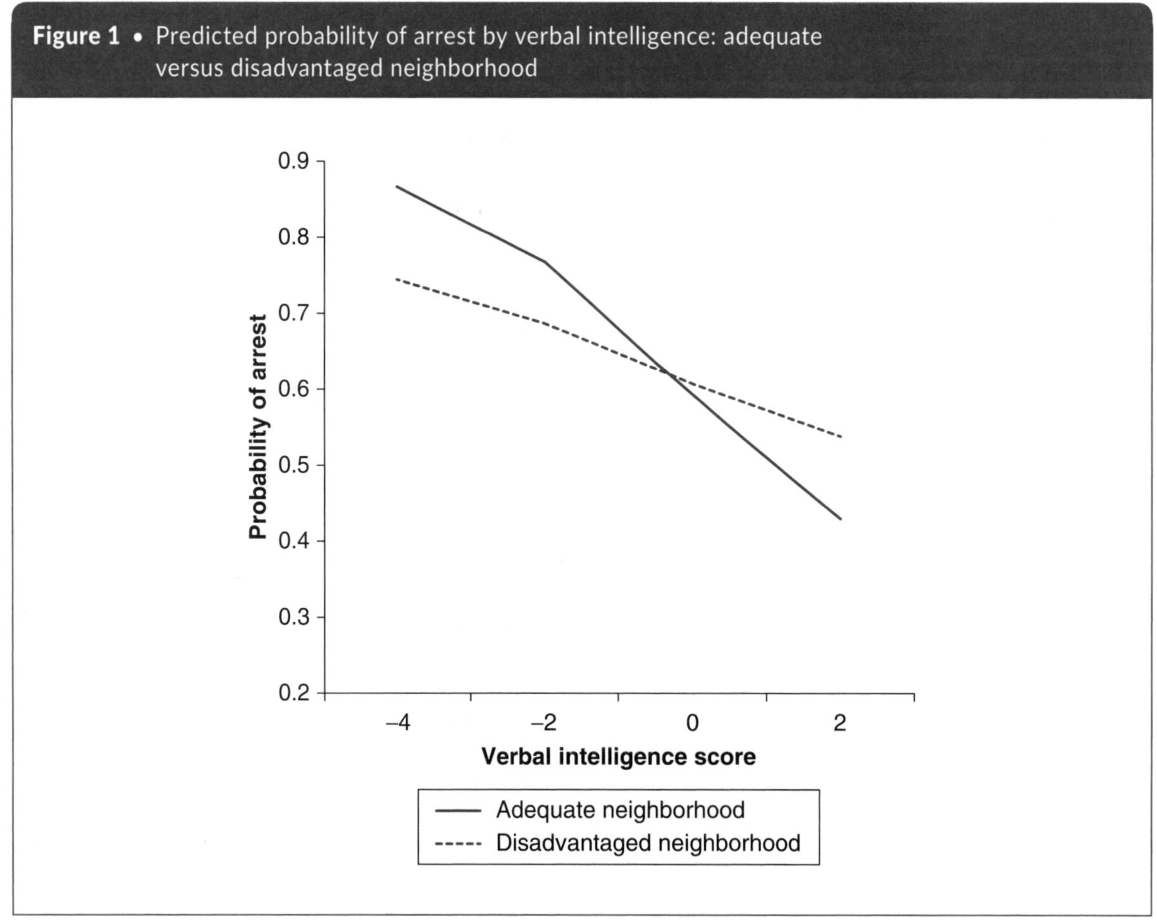

likelihood of arrest. Encapsulated as the "differential detection hypothesis," the link between intelligence and the probability of arrest had been previously studied, but quite limitedly, by early scholars (Cullen et al., 1997; Moffitt & Silva, 1988). Although these studies had produced contradicting findings, research interest in this issue has been considerably abated among later scholars, since they increasingly endorsed the position that IQ does not influence the probability of arrest. Our analyses, focusing only on the verbal dimension of intelligence, revealed a different picture: verbal intelligence, as measured by the PPVT-R, did have a bearing on whether an offender was more likely to be arrested.

Specifically, our study showed that lower verbal intelligence predicted a greater likelihood of arrest. The effect of verbal intelligence on arrest withstood a set of controls including delinquency frequencies, which indicated that the observed effect was net of any effect verbal intelligence might have on delinquency involvement. Such an effect also held up even with the control of self-control. This is to say that low verbal intelligence explains arrest over and beyond what is explained by low self-control. Regarding the causal mechanism surrounding language skills, self-control, and arrest, our results do not support the position that language skills cause self-control.

Our findings have implications on the differential detection debate in particular and the intelligence–crime linkage research in general. The general approach of prior researchers on differential detection hypothesis was choosing a right answer between two mutually exclusive options—either low intelligence individuals commit more crime or they are merely more arrested by police even though they do not particularly commit more crime than their normal intelligence counterparts. We argue that this either-or position does not reflect what actually occurs in the real world. Low intelligence does have a causal relationship with crime, whether it is indirect or direct, as numerous empirical studies have consistently revealed (Hirschi & Hindelang, 1977; Lynam et al., 1993; Moffitt et al., 1995; Nisbett et al., 2012). At the same time, low intelligence offenders are more likely to get arrested by the police, as our research indicates. That is to say that these two phenomena are not mutually exclusive but occur concomitantly.

Importantly, our analyses also showed that variations in neighborhood disadvantage across physical spaces conditioned the effect of verbal intelligence on arrest. However, the findings were not in the hypothesized direction, revealing that verbal IQ was a significant predictor of arrest only in adequate neighborhoods but not in disadvantaged neighborhoods.

At first flush, this unexpected finding seems counterintuitive, but it may in fact be consistent with empirical reality. Consider McCluskey et al.'s (1999) finding that suspects behaved in a more disrespectful manner toward officers when the encounter occurred in disadvantaged communities. Also consider the research findings that demonstrated that police acted less vigorously in disadvantaged, high crime areas due to workloads, resource concerns, and cynicism (Goldstein, 1960; Klinger, 1997; Skolnick, 1966; Niederhoffer, 1967). Then, even if verbally deficient delinquents are rightfully or wrongfully perceived by officers as disrespectful and obdurate, officers will encounter such delinquents more frequently in the disadvantaged neighborhoods. Saddled with workloads, high crime rates, and successive encounters with ostensibly disrespectful suspects, officers in such communities may react to another disrespectful delinquent with less vigor and be less inclined to arrest her or him. In such contexts, legal factors (e.g., severity of delinquent act) may play a far more dominant role in determining whether a delinquent will be arrested or not. In contrast, consider an officer responding to a verbally inept and disrespectful offender in an adequate neighborhood. In this neighborhood, the officer will typically encounter disrespectful suspects far less frequently and less crime is considered as normal. To the officers who have more time on their hands and are less cynical about the crime rates of the neighborhood, the seemingly disrespectful and unremorseful demeanor of a verbally inept delinquent may appear "out of context," less salvageable, or symptomatic of a "would-be-tough guy," thus deserving of an official sanction.

In summary, our research suggests that officers may take less vigorous and assertive actions against verbally deficient suspects in structurally disadvantaged neighborhoods than they would in advantaged neighborhoods. In regard to variation in police behaviors across physical space, then, our study partly supports the notions of Goldstein (1960), Klinger (1997), and Skolnick (1966), while countering the views of Terrill & Reisig (2003) and Werthman & Piliavin (1967). Admittedly, our interpretation is at best ad hoc in nature. Nevertheless, our findings hint at potential benefits that can accrue to future researchers of differential detection hypothesis if they include in their research schema the context in which police–delinquent encounters take place. Scientists typically seek parsimony, but they also need to be cautious about using simple models that do not consider context. Since the environment can influence human behavior, it behooves scholars to consider the environment.

Although our results were obtained through a large nationally representative sample that allowed for the inclusion of important statistical controls, we would be remiss if we did not mention the limitations of our study. First, the Add Health data are derived from a school-based sample. It is possible that adolescents who had low verbal skills and police arrest records were disproportionately likely to miss school or simply drop out (see Hirschi, 1969). These youths missing from the analyses may have influenced the research results in some unpredictable ways. Second, we construed, based on the theoretical linkage between self-control and verbal intelligence, that deficits in verbal intelligence would induce delinquents to behave in a manner that attracts punitive responses more from law enforcement agents. Yet, the Add Health data did not contain any information on the actual demeanors of delinquents during police encounters. Nor did it contain information on whether youths with low verbal intelligence recklessly engaged in delinquency regardless of high likelihood of detection by the police. This means that we were not able to examine whether verbal intelligence in fact influenced the manner in which youths engaged in offenses or they interacted with the police. Future research with qualitative components can elucidate these connections in detail. Third, our analyses could not incorporate detailed information regarding the circumstances of the police–delinquent encounter, such as victim requests or presence of witnesses. These factors could certainly moderate the effect of verbal intelligence on arrest. Finally, both measures of delinquency and arrest in this study were derived from self-reported data, which means the degree to which the validity and reliability of the responses may have been influenced by forgetfulness or dishonesty of the subjects is unknown. Multiple sources of delinquency and arrest would have made this study stronger in this regard. Despite these shortcomings, the present study examined an issue that the research community has been relatively slow to evaluate. Thus far, only one study has examined the effects of verbal intelligence on police arrests, and there is none that has tested an interactive effect of verbal intelligence and neighborhood context. In this regard, our study meaningfully contributes to the field by showing the existence of verbal intelligence–arrest association employing a nationally representative sample of adolescents. It also illustrates the importance of examining the interactions between verbal intelligence and neighborhood context.

Note

1. Technically speaking, intelligence and IQ scores are not the same. Intelligence is a theoretical construct that is associated with the general ability to reason, solve problems, and understand the world around us, while IQ is a score on an intelligence test. However, these two terms have been used interchangeably in the literature often for the ease of readers' understanding. Since distinguishing them overly technically did not seem to fit the goal of the current study, we also took the liberty of using them interchangeably.

References

Ai, C., & Norton, E. C. (2003). Interaction terms in logit and probit models. *Economics Letters, 80*, 123–129.

Baker, P., Keck, C., Mott, F., & Quinlan, S. (1993). *NLSY child handbook*. Columbus, OH: Center for Human Resource Research.

Bayley, D., & Mendelsohn, H. (1969). *Minorities and the police: Confrontation in America*. New York, NY: Free Press.

Beaver, K. (2010). The effects of genetics, the environment, and low self-control on perceived maternal and paternal socialization: Results from a longitudinal sample of twins. *Journal of Quantitative Criminology, 27*, 85–105.

Beaver, K., DeLisi, M., Mears, D., & Stewart, E. (2009). Low self-control and contact with the criminal justice system in a nationally representative sample of males. *Justice Quarterly, 26*, 695–715.

Beaver, K., DeLisi, M., Vaughn, M., & Boutwell, B. (2008). The relationship between self-control and language: Evidence of a shared etiological pathway. *Criminology, 46*, 939–970.

Beaver, K., Gibson, C., DeLisi, M., Vaughn, M., & Wright, J. (2011). The interaction between neighborhood disadvantage and genetic factors in the prediction of antisocial outcomes. *Youth Violence and Juvenile Justice, 10*, 25–40.

Beaver, K., & Wright, J. (2007). The stability of low self-control from kindergarten through first grade. *Journal of Crime & Justice, 30*, 63–86.

Beaver, K., Wright, J., & DeLisi, M. (2008). Delinquent peer group formation: Evidence of a gene x environment correlation. *The Journal of Genetic Psychology, 169*, 227–244.

Black, D. (1976). *The behavior of law.* New York, NY: Academic Press.

Cleveland, H. (2003). Disadvantaged neighborhoods and adolescent aggression: Behavioral genetic evidence of contextual effects. *Journal of Research on Adolescence, 13,* 211–238.

Cullen, F., Gendreau, P., Jarjoura, G., & Wright, J. (1997). Crime and the bell curve: Lessons from intelligent criminology. *Crime & Delinquency, 43,* 387–411.

Dionne, G. (2005). Language development and aggressive behavior. In R. Tremblay, W. Hartup, & J. Archer (Eds.), *Developmental origins of aggression* (pp. 330–352). New York, NY: Guilford Press.

Dugdale, R. (1877). *"The Jukes": A study in crime, pauperism, disease, and heredity: Also further studies of criminals.* New York, NY: G. P. Putnam's Sons.

Gallagher, T. (1999). Interrelationships among children's language, behavior, and emotional problems. *Topics in Language Disorders, 19,* 1–15.

Goddard, H. (1914). *Feeble-mindedness.* New York: Macmillan.

Goldstein, J. (1960). Police discretion not to invoke the criminal process: Low-visibility decisions in the administration of justice. *Yale Law Journal, 69*(4), 543–594.

Gottfredson, M., & Hirschi, T. (1990). A *general theory of crime.* Stanford, CA: Stanford University Press.

Harris, K., Florey, F., Tabor, J., Bearman, P., Jones, J., & Udry, J. (2003). *The national longitudinal study of adolescent health: Research design.* Retrieved June 29, 2009, from http://www.cpc.unc.edu/projects/addhealth/design

Herrnstein, R., & Murray, C. (1994). *The bell curve: Intelligence and class structure in American life.* New York, NY: Free Press.

Hirschi, T. (1969). *Causes of delinquency.* Berkeley, CA: University of California Press.

Hirschi, T., & Hindelang, M. (1977). Intelligence and delinquency: A revisionist review. *American Sociological Review, 42,* 571–587.

Klinger, D. (1997). Negotiating order in patrol work: An ecological theory of police response to deviance. *Criminology, 35,* 277–306.

Luria, A. (1961). *The role of speech in the regulation of normal and abnormal behavior.* New York, NY: Basic Books.

Luria, A., & Homskaya, E. (1964). Disturbance in the regulative role of speech with frontal lobe lesions. In J. M. Warren & K. Akert (Eds.), *The frontal granular cortex and behavior* (pp. 353–371). New York, NY: McGraw-Hill.

Lynam, D., Moffitt, T., & Stouthamer-Loeber, M. (1993). Explaining the relation between IQ and delinquency: Class, race, test motivation, school failure, or self-control? *Journal of Abnormal Psychology, 102,* 187–196.

McCluskey, J., Reisig, M., Mastrofski, S., & Terrill, W. (1999). Nasty as they wanna be? An investigation of suspect aggression during police encounters. Presented at the 51st Annual Meeting of the American Society of Criminology, November. Toronto, Canada.

McGloin, J., & Pratt, T. (2003). Cognitive ability and delinquent behavior among inner-city youth: A life-course analysis of main, mediating, and interaction effects. *International Journal of Offender Therapy and Comparative Criminology, 47,* 253–271.

McGloin, J., Pratt, T., & Maahs, J. (2004). Rethinking the IQ-delinquency relationship: A longitudinal analysis of multiple theoretical models. *Justice Quarterly, 21,* 603–635.

Moffitt, T. (1990). Juvenile delinquency and attention deficit disorder: Boys' developmental trajectories from age 3 to age 15. *Child Development, 61,* 893–910.

Moffitt, T., Caspi, A., Silva, P., & Stouthamer-Loeber, M. (1995). Individual differences in personality and intelligence are linked to crime: Cross-context evidence from nations, neighborhoods, genders, races, and age-cohorts. In J. Hagan (Ed.), *Current perspectives on aging and the life cycle: Vol. 4. Delinquency and disrepute in the life course.* Greenwich, CT: JAI Press.

Moffitt, T., & Silva, P. (1988). IQ and delinquency: A direct test of the differential detection hypothesis. *Journal of Abnormal Psychology, 97,* 330–333.

Neisser, U., Boodoo, G., Bouchard, T., Jr., Boykin, A., Brody, N., Ceci, S., . . . Halpern, D. (1996). Intelligence: Knowns and unknowns. *American Psychologist, 51,* 77–101.

Niederhoffer, A. (1967). *Behind the shield: The police in urban society.* Garden City, NY: Doubleday.

Nisbett, R., Aronson, J., Blair, C., Dickens, W., Flynn, J., Halpern, D., & Turkheimer, E. (2012). Intelligence: New findings and theoretical developments. *The American Psychologist, 67,* 130–159.

Paternoster, R., Brame, R., Mazerolle, P., & Piquero, A. (1998). Using the correct statistical test for the equality of regression coefficients. *Criminology, 36,* 859–866.

Perrone, D., Sullivan, C., Pratt, T., & Margaryan, S. (2004). Parental efficacy, self-control, and delinquency: A test of a general theory of crime on a nationally representative sample of youth. *International Journal of Offender Therapy and Comparative Criminology, 48,* 298–312.

Piliavin, I., & Briar, S. (1964). Police encounters with juveniles. *American Journal of Sociology, 70,* 206–214.

Sampson, R., Raudenbush, S., & Earls, F. (1997). Neighborhoods and violent crime: A multilevel study of collective efficacy. *Science, 277,* 918–924.

Scarr, S., & McCartney, K. (1983). How people make their own environments: A theory of genotype environment effects. *Child Development, 54,* 424–435.

Sherman, L. (1990). Police crackdowns: Initial and residual deterrence. In M. Tonry & N. Morris (Eds.), *Crime and justice: A review of research, Vol. 12* (pp. 1–48). Chicago, IL: University of Chicago Press.

Skolnick, J. (1966). *Justice without trial.* New York, NY: John Wiley & Sons.

Stark, R. (1975). *Social problems.* New York, NY: Random House.

Tarnopol, L. (1970). Delinquency and minimal brain dysfunction. *Journal of Learning Disabilities, 3,* 200–208.

Terrill, W., & Reisig, M. (2003). Neighborhood context and police use of force. *Journal of Research in Crime and Delinquency, 40,* 291–321.

Turner, M., Hartman, J., & Bishop, D. (2007). The effects of prenatal problems, family functioning, and neighborhood disadvantage in predicting life-course-persistent offending. *Criminal Justice and Behavior, 34,* 1241–1261.

Udry, J. (1998). *The national longitudinal sample of adolescent health.* Chapel Hill, NC: Carolina Population Center, University of North Carolina.

Udry, J. (2003). *The national longitudinal study of adolescent health (Add Health), Waves I and II, 1994–1996; Wave III, 2001–2002 [Machine-readable data file and documentation].* Chapel Hill, NC: Carolina Population Center, University of North Carolina.

Vance, B., West, R., & Kutsick, K. (1989). Prediction of Wechsler Preschool and Primary Scale of Intelligence IQ scores for preschool children using the Peabody Picture Vocabulary Test-R and the Expressive One Word Picture Vocabulary Test. *Journal of Clinical Psychology, 45,* 642–644.

Ward, D., & Tittle, C. (1994). IQ and delinquency: A test of two competing explanations. *Journal of Quantitative Criminology, 10,* 189–212.

Warner, B., & Coomer, B. (2003). Neighborhood drug arrest rates: Are they a meaningful indicator of drug activity? A research note. *Journal of Research in Crime and Delinquency, 40,* 123–138.

Werthman, C., & Piliavin, I. (1967). Gang members and the police. In D. Bordua (Ed.), *The police: Six sociological essays* (pp. 56–98). New York, NY: John Wiley.

White, H. (1980). A heteroskedasticity-consistent covariance matrix estimator and a direct test for heteroskedasticity. *Econometrica, 48,* 817–838.

Wilson, J., & Herrnstein, R. (1985). *Crime and human nature.* New York, NY: Simon & Schuster.

Worden, R. (1989). Situational and attitudinal explanations of police behavior: A theoretical reappraisal and empirical assessment. *Law Society Review, 23,* 667–711.

REVIEW QUESTIONS

1. What are some theoretical explanations for why verbal IQ is the form of intelligence that has been implicated most in previous studies?
2. Do the findings of the current study support the authors' hypothesis that suspects' verbal IQ scores will be inversely correlated with police decisions to arrest?
3. How does suspects' level of neighborhood disadvantage influence police decisions to arrest, especially when suspects have a low verbal IQ? What do the results of this study suggest is the nature of this complex relationship?

SECTION V

Modern Biosocial Perspectives of Criminal Behavior

This section will discuss the more modern biological studies of the 20th century. We will begin with studies from the early 1900s—particularly those that sought to emphasize the influence of biological factors on criminality. Virtually all of these studies have shown a significant biological effect in the development of criminal propensities. Then we will examine the influence of a variety of physiological factors, including chromosomal mutations, hormones, neurotransmitters, brain trauma, and other dispositional aspects of individuals' nervous systems. A special emphasis will be placed on showing the consistent evidence that has been found for the interaction between physiological and environmental factors (i.e., biosocial factors).

This section will examine a variety of perspectives that deal with interactions between physiological and environmental factors, which is currently the dominant model explaining criminal behavior. First, we will discuss the early studies that attempted to emphasize the biological aspects of offending: family, twin, and adoption studies. All of these studies show that biological influences are more important than social and environmental factors, and most also conclude that when both negative biological and disadvantaged environmental variables are combined, these individuals are by far the most likely to offend in the future, which fully supports the interaction between nature and nurture factors.

Later in this section, we will examine other physiological factors, such as hormones and neurotransmitters. We will see that chronic, violent offenders tend to have significantly different levels of hormones and other chemicals in their bodies than do other individuals. Furthermore, we will examine brain trauma and activity among violent offenders, and we will see that habitual violent criminals tend to have slower brain wave patterns and lower anxiety levels than other persons. Ultimately, we will see that numerous physiological distinctions can be made between chronic violent offenders and others but that these differences are most evident when physical factors are combined with being raised in poor, disadvantaged environments.

Nature versus Nurture: Studies Examining the Influence of Genetics and Environment

At the same time that Freud was developing his perspective of psychological deviance, other researchers were busy testing the influence of heredity versus environment to see which of these two components had the strongest effect on predicting criminality. This type of testing produced four waves of research: (1) family studies; (2) twin studies;

(3) adoption studies; and, in recent years, (4) studies of identical twins separated at birth. Each of these waves of research contributed to our understanding of how much criminality is inherited from our parents (or other ancestors) versus how much is due to cultural norms, such as family or community. Ultimately, all of the studies have shown that the interaction between these two aspects—genetics and environment—is what causes crime among individuals and groups in society.

Family Studies

The most notable **family studies** were done in the early 1900s by Richard Dugdale in his study of the Jukes family and the previously discussed researcher Henry Goddard, who studied the Kallikak family.[1] These studies were supposed to test the proposition that criminality is more likely to be found in certain families, which would indicate that crime is inherited. Due to the similarity of the results, we will focus here on Goddard's work on the Kallikak family.

This study showed that a much higher proportion of children from the Kallikak family became criminal. Furthermore, Goddard thought that many of the individuals (often children) from the Kallikak family actually looked like criminals, which fit Cesare Lombroso's theory of stigmata. In fact, Goddard had photographs made of many members of this family to back up these claims. However, follow-up investigations of Goddard's research have shown that many of these photographs were actually altered to make the subjects appear more sinister or evil (fitting Lombroso's stigmata) by altering their facial features—most notably their eyes.[2]

Despite the despicable methodological problems with Goddard's data and subsequent findings, two important conclusions can be made from the family studies that were done in the early 1900s. The first is that criminality is indeed more common in some families; in fact, no study has ever shown otherwise. However, this tendency cannot be shown to be a product of heredity or genetics. After all, individuals from the same family are also products of a similar environment—often a bad one—so this conclusion from the family studies does little to advance knowledge regarding the relative influence of nature versus nurture in terms of predicting criminality.

The second conclusion of family studies was more insightful and interesting. Specifically, they showed that criminality by the mother (or head female caretaker) had a much stronger influence on the future criminality of the children than did the father's criminality. This is likely due to two factors. The first is that the father is often absent most of the time while the children are being raised. Perhaps more important is that it takes much more for a woman to transgress social norms and become a convicted offender, which indicates that the mother is highly antisocial; this gives some (albeit limited) credence to the argument that criminality is somewhat inherited. Despite this conclusion, it should be apparent from the weaknesses in the methodology of family studies that this finding did not hold much weight in the nature versus nurture debate. Thus, a new wave of research soon emerged that did a better job of measuring the influence of genetics versus environment, which was twin studies.

Twin Studies

After family studies, the next wave of tests done to determine the relative influence on criminality between nature and nurture involved **twin studies**, the examination of identical twin pairs versus fraternal twin pairs. Identical twins are also known as **monozygotic (MZ) twins** because they come from a single (hence *mono*) egg (*zygote*). Such twins share 100% of their genotype, meaning they are identical in terms of genetic makeup. Keep in mind that everyone shares approximately 99% of the human genetic makeup, leaving about 1% that can vary over the entire species. On the other hand, fraternal twins are typically referred to as **dizygotic (DZ) twins** because they come

[1]Stephen Jay Gould, *The Mismeasure of Man*, 2nd ed. (New York: Norton, 1996) (see chap. 4, n. 2).

[2]Ibid., 198–204, for an excellent discussion of the alteration of Goddard's photographs.

from two (hence *di*) separate eggs. Such DZ twins share 50% of genes that can vary, which is the same amount that any siblings from the same two parents share. DZ twins can be of different genders and may look and behave quite differently, as many readers have probably observed.

▲ **Image 5.1** Identical twins.

SOURCE: © istockphoto.com / Image Source

The goal of the twin studies was to examine the **concordance rates** between MZ twin pairs and DZ twin pairs regarding delinquency. Concordance is a count based on whether two people (or a twin pair) share a certain trait (or lack of the trait); for our purposes, the trait is criminal offending. Regarding a count of concordance, if one twin is an offender, then we look to see if the other is also an offender. If that person is, then we say there is concordance given the fact that the first twin was a criminal offender. Also, if neither of the twins is an offender, that also is concordant because they both lack the trait. However, if one twin is a criminal offender and the other twin of the pair is not an offender, then this would be discordant in the sense that one has a trait that the other does not.

Thus, the twin studies focused on comparing the concordance rates of MZ twin pairs versus those of DZ twin pairs with the assumption that any significant difference in concordance could be attributed to the similarity of the genetic makeup of the MZ twins (which is 100%) versus the DZ twins (which is significantly less—that is, 50%). If genetics plays a major role in determining the criminality of individuals, then it would be expected that MZ twins would have a significantly higher concordance rate for being criminal offenders than would DZ twins. In these studies, it was assumed that each twin in each MZ or DZ twin pair had been raised in more or less the same environment as the other twin since each pair had been brought up in the same family at the same time.

A number of studies were performed in the early and mid-1900s that examined the concordance rates between MZ and DZ twin pairs. These studies clearly showed that identical twins had far higher concordance rates than did fraternal twins; most studies showed twice as much concordance or more for MZ twins—even for serious criminality.[3]

However, the studies regarding the comparisons between the twins were strongly criticized for reasons that many readers readily see. Specifically, identical twins, who look almost exactly alike, are typically dressed the same by their parents and treated the same by the public. In addition, they are generally expected to behave the same way. However, this is not true for fraternal twins, who often look very different and quite often are of different genders. Thus, the foundation for criticism of the twin studies was the very valid argument that the higher rate of concordance among MZ twins could have been due to the extremely similar way they were treated or expected to behave

[3]See reviews in Adrian Raine, *The Anatomy of Violence* (New York: Pantheon, 2013); Adrian Raine, *The Psychopathology of Crime* (San Diego: Academic Press, 1993); and John P. Wright, Stephen G. Tibbetts, and Leah Daigle, *Criminals in the Making: Criminality across the Life Course*, 2nd ed. (Thousand Oaks, CA: Sage, 2015) (see chap. 4). See also Juan B. Cortes, *Delinquency and Crime* (New York: Seminar Press, 1972); and Karl O. Christiansen, "Seriousness of Criminality and Concordance among Danish Twins," in *Crime, Criminology, and Public Policy*, ed. Roger Hood (New York: Free Press, 1974).

by society. Another criticism of the early twin studies had to do with the questionable accuracy of determinations of whether twins were fraternal or identical, which was often done by sight in the early tests.[4] Although these criticisms were seemingly valid, the most recent meta-analysis, which examined virtually all of the twin studies done up to the 1990s, concluded that the twin studies showed evidence of a significant hereditary basis for criminality.[5] Still, the criticisms of such studies were quite valid; therefore, in the early to mid-1900s, researchers involved in the nature versus nurture debate attempted to address these valid criticisms by moving on to another methodological approach to examining this debate: adoption studies.

Adoption Studies

Due to the valid criticisms leveled at twin studies in determining the relative influence of nature (biological) or nurture (environmental), researchers in this area moved on to **adoption studies**, which examined the predictive influence of the biological parents versus that of the adoptive parents who raised the children from infancy to adulthood. It is important to realize that, in such studies, the adoptees were typically given up for adoption prior to 6 months of age, meaning that the biological parents had relatively no interaction with their natural children; rather, they were almost completely raised from infancy by the adoptive parents.

Perhaps the most notable of the adoption studies was done by Sarnoff Mednick and his colleagues in which they examined male children born in Copenhagen between 1927 and 1941 who had been adopted early in life.[6] In this study and virtually all others that have examined adoptees in this light, by far the highest predictability for future criminality was found for adopted youths who had *both* a biological parent and an adoptive parent who were convicted criminals. However, the Mednick study also showed that the criminality of biological parent(s) had a far greater predictive effect on future criminality of offspring than did the criminality of adoptive parents. Still, the adopted children who were least likely to become criminal had no parent with a criminal background. In light of this last conclusion, these findings support the major contentions of this book's authors in the sense that they fully back up the nature *via* nurture argument as opposed to the nature *versus* nurture argument. They support the idea that both biological *and* environmental factors contribute to the future criminality of youths.

Unfortunately, the researchers who performed these studies focused on the other two groups of youths—those who had either only criminal biological parents or only criminal adoptive parents. Thus, these adoption studies found that the adoptees who had only biological parents who were criminal had a much higher likelihood of becoming criminal compared to the youths who had only adoptive parents who were criminal. Obviously, this finding supports the idea that genetic influence predisposes people toward criminality. However, this methodology was subject to criticism.

Perhaps the most notable criticism of adoption studies was that adoption agencies typically incorporated a policy of **selective placement** in which adoptees were placed with adoptive families similar in terms of demographics and background to their biological parents. Such selective placement could bias the results of adoption studies. However, recent analyses have examined the impact of such bias, concluding that, even after accounting for the influence of selective placement, the ultimate findings of the adoption studies are still somewhat valid.[7] Children's

---

[4]Raine, *Psychopathology of Crime.*

[5]Glenn Walters, "A Meta-Analysis of the Gene–Crime Relationship," *Criminology* 30 (1992): 595–613.

[6]Barry Hutchings and Sarnoff A. Mednick, "Criminality in Adoptees and Their Adoptive and Biological Parents: A Pilot Study," in *Biosocial Bases of Criminal Behavior*, ed. Sarnoff Mednick and Karl O. Christiansen (New York: Gardner Press, 1977), 127–41. See recent review and study by Randi Hjalmarsson and Matthew J. Lindquist, "The Origins of Intergenerational Associations in Crime: Lessons from Swedish Adoption Data," *Labour Economics* 20 (2013): 68–81.

[7]See James Q. Wilson and Richard J. Herrnstein, *Crime and Human Nature* (New York: Simon & Schuster, 1985); and Walters, "Gene–Crime Relationship."

biological parents likely have more influence on their future criminality than the adoptive parents who raise them from infancy to adulthood. Still, the criticism of selective placement was strong enough to encourage a fourth wave of research in the nature versus nurture debate, which became studies on identical twins separated at birth.

Twins Separated at Birth

Until recently, studies of identical twins separated at birth were virtually impossible because it was so difficult to get a high number of identical twins who had indeed been separated early. But since the early 1990s, **twins-separated-at-birth studies** have been possible. Readers should keep in mind that, in many of the identical twin pairs studied for these investigations, the individuals did not even know they had a twin. Furthermore, the environments in which they were raised were often extremely different; one twin might be raised by a very poor family in an urban environment while the other twin was raised by a middle- to upper-class family in a rural environment.

These studies—the most notable having been done at the University of Minnesota—found that the twin pairs often showed extremely similar tendencies for criminality, sometimes more similar than those seen in concordance rates for identical twins raised together.[8] This finding obviously supports the profound influence of genetics and heredity, which is not surprising to most well-read scientists, who now acknowledge the extreme importance of inheritance of physiological and psychological aspects to human behavior. Perhaps more surprising was why separated identical twins, who had never known that they had a twin and were often raised in extremely different circumstances, had just as high or even higher concordance rates than identical twins who were raised together.

The leading theory for this phenomenon is that identical twins who are raised together actually go out of their way to deviate from their natural tendencies to form an identity separate from their identical twin with whom they have spent their entire lives. As for criticisms of this methodology, none have been presented in the scientific literature. Thus, it is somewhat undisputed at this point that the identical-twins-separated-at-birth studies have shown that genetics has a significant impact on human behavior, especially regarding criminal activity.

Ultimately, taking all of the nature versus nurture methodological approaches and subsequent findings together, the best conclusion that can be made is that genetics and heredity both have significant impacts on criminality. Environment simply cannot account for all of the consistent results seen in the comparisons between identical twins and fraternal twins, those of identical twins separated at birth, and those of adoptees with criminal biological parents versus those who did not have such parents. Despite the taboo nature of and controversial response to the findings of such studies, it is quite clear that when nature and nurture are compared, biological rather than environmental factors tend to have the most influence on the criminality of individuals. Still, the authors of this book hope that readers will emphasize the importance of the interaction between nature and nurture (better stated as nature *via* nurture). Ultimately, we hope that we have shown quite convincingly through scientific study that it is the interplay between biology and the environment that is most important in determining human behavior.

Perhaps in response to this nature versus nurture debate, a new theoretical perspective was offered in the mid-1900s that merged biological and psychological factors in explaining criminality. Although it leaned more toward the nature side of the debate, critics would use this same perspective to promote the nurture side, so this framework was useful in promoting the interaction between biology and sociological factors.

Cytogenetic Studies: The XYY Factor

Beyond the body type theories, another model was proposed in the early 1900s regarding biological conditions that predispose individuals toward crime: **cytogenetic studies**. Cytogenetic studies of crime focus on the

---

[8]Thomas J. Bouchard et al., "Sources of Human Psychological Differences: The Minnesota Study of Twins Reared Apart," *Science* 250 (1990): 223–28. Also see the review in Wright et al., *Criminals in the Making* (chap. 4).

genetic makeup of individuals, with a specific focus on abnormalities in chromosomal makeup, and specifically chromosomal abnormalities that occur randomly in the population. Many of the chromosomal mutations that have been studied (such as XYY) typically result not from heredity but from random mutations in chromosomal formation.

The normal chromosomal makeup for women is XX, which represents an X from the mother and an X from the father. The normal chromosomal makeup for men is XY, which represents an X from the mother and a Y from the father. However, as in many species of animals, there are often genetic mutations, which we see in human beings. Consistent with evolutionary theory, virtually all possible variations of chromosomes that are possible have been found in the human population, such as XXY, XYY, and many others. We will focus our discussion on the chromosomal mutations that have been most strongly linked to criminality.

One of the first chromosomal mutations recognized as a predictor of criminal activity was XYY. In 1965, the first major study showed that this mutation was far more common in a Scottish male population of mental patients than in the general population.[9] Specifically, in the general population, XYY occurs in about 1 of every 1,000 males. The first major study that examined the influence of XYY sampled about 200 men in the mental hospital; one occurrence would have been predicted, assuming what was known about the general population. The study, however, found 13 individuals who were XYY, which suggested that individuals who have mental disorders are more likely to have XYY than those who do not. Males who have XYY have at least 13 times the likelihood (or a 1,300% chance) of having behavioral disorders compared with those who do not have this chromosomal abnormality. Subsequent studies have not been able to dismiss the effect of XYY on criminality, but they have concluded that this mutation is more often linked with property crime than with violent crime.[10]

Would knowing this relationship help in policies regarding crime? Probably not, considering the fact that 90% of the male mental patients were not XYY. Still, this study showed the importance of looking at chromosomal mutations as a predictor of criminal behavior.

Such mutations include numerous chromosomal abnormalities, such as XYY, which is a male who is given an extra Y chromosome, making him more "malelike." These individuals are often very tall but slow in terms of social and intelligence skills. Another type of mutation is XXY, which is otherwise known as Klinefelter's syndrome; it results in more feminine males (homosexuality has been linked to this mutation). Many other types of mutations have been observed, but it is the XYY mutation that has been the primary focus of studies, which is largely due to the higher levels of testosterone produced by this chromosomal mutation (see Figure 5.1).

One study examined the relative criminality and deviance of a group of individuals in each of these groups of chromosomal mutations (see Figure 5.1).[11] This study found that the higher the level of male hormones produced by the chromosomal mutation, the greater the likelihood that people with the mutation would commit criminal and deviant acts. On the other hand, the higher the level of feminine hormones produced by the chromosomal mutation, the lower the likelihood that the individuals would commit criminal activity. Ultimately, all of these variations in chromosomes show that there is a continuum of femaleness and maleness and that the more malelike the individual is in terms of chromosomes, the more likely he is to commit criminal behavior.

Ultimately, the cytogenetic studies showed that somewhat random abnormalities in an individual's genetic makeup can have a profound influence on her or his level of criminality. Whether or not this can or should be used in policy related to crime is another matter, but the point is that genetics does indeed contribute to a disposition to

---

[9]Patricia A. Jacobs et al., "Aggressive Behavior, Mental Sub-normality, and the XYY Male," *Nature* 208 (1965): 1351–52.

[10]See review in Raymond Paternoster and Ronet Bachman, *Explaining Criminals and Crime* (Los Angeles: Roxbury, 2001), 53.

[11]Anthony Walsh, "Genetic and Cytogenetic Intersex Anomalies: Can They Help Us to Understand Gender Differences in Deviant Behavior?" *International Journal of Offender Therapy and Comparative Criminology* 39 (1995): 151–66. See also Kristine Stochholm et al., "Criminality in Men with Klinefelter's Syndrome and XYY Syndrome: A Cohort Study," *British Medical Journal Open* 2 (2012).

Figure 5.1 • Hypothetical scattergram relating masculinity/androgen level (designated by karyotype) to deviance

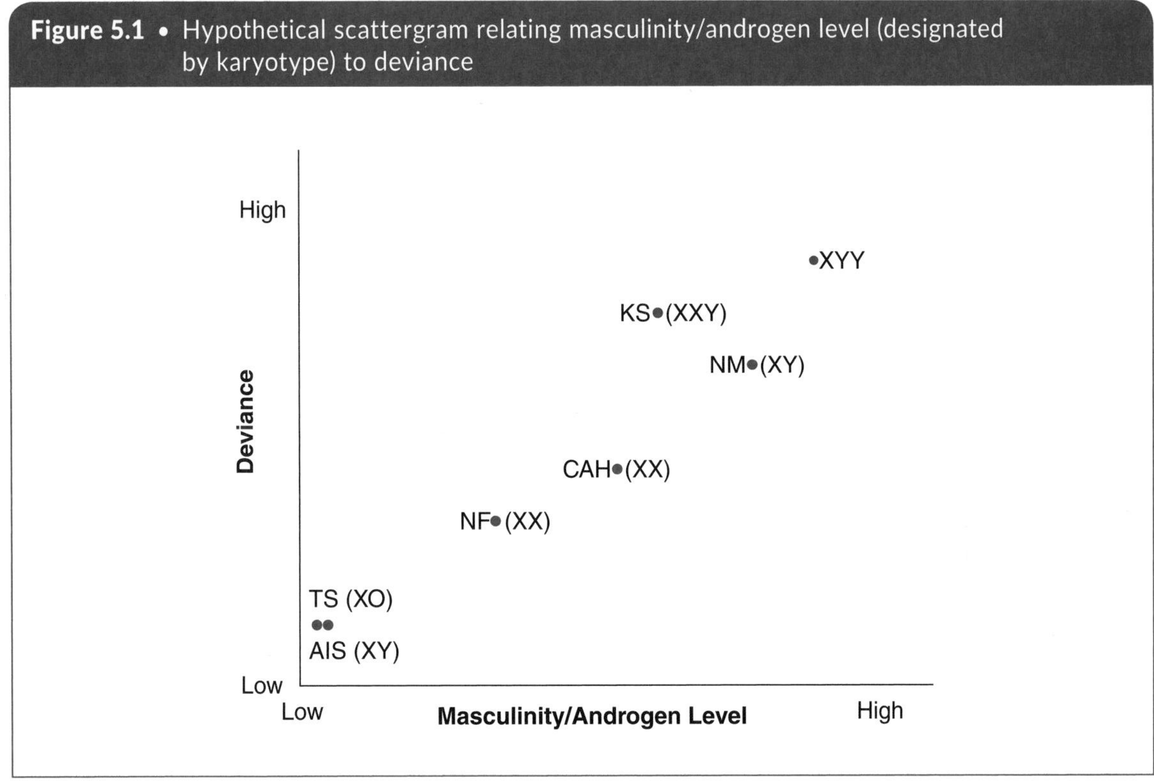

NOTE: TS = Turner's syndrome; AIS = androgen insensitivity syndrome; NF = normal female; KS = Klinefelter's syndrome; CAH = congenital adrenal hyperplasia; NM = normal male; XYY = Jacob's (supermale) syndrome.

SOURCE: Anthony Walsh, "Genetic and Cytogenetic Intersex Anomalies: Can They Help Us to Understand Gender Differences in Deviant Behavior?" *International Journal of Offender Therapy and Comparative Criminology* 39 (1995): 151–66. Copyright © 1995 SAGE Publications, Inc. Reprinted by permission of SAGE Publications, Inc.

commit criminal acts. The extent to which male hormones or androgens are increased by the mutation is an important predictor of criminal traits.

Hormones and Neurotransmitters: Chemicals That Determine Criminal Behavior

Various chemicals in the brain and the rest of the body determine how we think, perceive, and react to various stimuli. Hormones, such as testosterone and estrogen, carry chemical signals to the body as they are released from certain glands and structures. Some studies have shown that a relatively excessive amount of testosterone in the body is consistently linked to criminal or aggressive behavior; most studies show a moderate relationship.[12] This

[12]Alan Booth and D. Wayne Osgood, "The Influence of Testosterone on Deviance in Adulthood: Assessing and Explaining the Relationship," *Criminology* 31 (1993): 93–117; Richard Ronay and William von Hippel, "Power, Testosterone, and Risk-Taking," *Journal of Behavioral Decision Making* 23 (2010): 473–82; Hosanna Soler, P. Vinayak, and David Quadagno, "Biosocial Aspects of Domestic Violence," *Psychoneuroendocrinology* 25 (2000): 721–73. For a review, see Lee Ellis and Anthony Walsh, *Criminology: A Global Perspective* (Boston: Allyn & Bacon, 2000). See also Raine, *Anatomy of Violence.*

relationship is seen even in the early years of life.[13] On the other side of the coin, studies have also shown that hormonal changes in females can cause criminal behavior. Specifically, studies have shown that a high proportion of the women in prison for violent crimes committed their crimes during their premenstrual cycle at which time women experience a high level of hormones that make them more malelike due to relatively low levels of estrogen compared to progesterone.[14]

Anyone who doubts the impact of hormones on behavior should examine the scientific literature regarding performance on intelligence tests at different times of day. Virtually everyone performs better on spatial and mathematical tests early in the day, when people have relatively higher levels of testosterone and other male hormones in their bodies; on the other hand, virtually everyone performs better on verbal tasks in the afternoon or evening, when people have relatively higher levels of estrogen or other female hormones in their systems.[15] Furthermore, studies have shown that individuals who are given shots of androgens (male hormones) before math tests tend to do significantly better on spatial and mathematics tests than they would do otherwise. Scientific studies show that the same is true for people who are given shots of female hormones prior to verbal or reading tests.

It is important to realize that this process of differential levels of hormones begins at a very early age, specifically at about the fifth week after conception. At that time, the Y chromosome of the male tells the developing fetus that it is a male and stimulates production of higher levels of testosterone. So, even during the first few months of gestation, the genes on the Y chromosome significantly alter the course of genital and thus hormonal development.[16]

This level of testosterone alters the genitals of the fetus during gestation as well as prompting later changes in the genital area and produces profound increases in testosterone in the teenage and early adult years. This produces not only physical differences but also huge personality and behavioral alterations.[17] High levels of testosterone and other androgens tend to "masculinize" the brain toward risk-taking behavior, whereas the lower levels typically found in females tend to result in the default feminine model.[18] High levels of testosterone have numerous consequences, such as lowered sensitivity to pain, enhanced seeking of sensory stimulation, and a right hemisphere shift in brain dominance, which has been linked to higher levels of spatial aptitude but lower levels of verbal reasoning and empathy. These consequences have profound implications for criminal activity and are more likely to occur in males than females.[19]

Ultimately, hormones have a profound effect on how individuals think and perceive their environments. All criminal behavior comes down to cognitive decisions in our 3-pound brains. So, it should not be surprising that hormones play a highly active role in this decision-making process. Nevertheless, hormones are probably secondary compared to levels of **neurotransmitters**, which are chemicals in the brain and body that help transmit electric signals from one neuron to another.

Neurotransmitters can be distinguished from hormones in the sense that hormones carry a signal that is not electric, whereas the signals that neurotransmitters carry are indeed electric. Neurotransmitters are chemicals that

---

[13]Jose R. Sanchez-Martin et al., "Relating Testosterone Levels and Free Play Social Behavior in Male and Female Preschool Children," *Psychoneuroendocrinology* 25 (2000): 773–83.

[14]Diane Halpern, *Sex Differences in Cognitive Abilities* (Mahwah, NJ: Lawrence Erlbaum, 2000).

[15]Ibid.

[16]Lee Ellis, "A Theory Explaining Biological Correlates of Criminality," *European Journal of Criminality* 2 (2005): 287–315.

[17]Ibid.

[18]Chandler Burr, "Homosexuality and Biology," *Atlantic Monthly* 271 (1993): 47–65; Lee Ellis and M. Ashley Ames, "Neurohormonal Functioning and Sexual Orientation: A Theory of Homosexuality-Heterosexuality," *Psychological Bulletin* 101 (1987): 233–58; Ellis, "A Theory."

[19]Martin Reite et al., "Neuropsychological Test Performance and MEG-based Brain Lateralization: Sex Differences," *Brain Research Bulletin* 32 (1993): 325–28; Jorge Moll et al., "The Neural Correlates of Moral Sensitivity: A Functional Magnetic Resonance Imaging Investigation of Basic and Moral Emotions," *Journal of Neuroscience* 22 (2002): 2730–36; Kimberly Badger, Rebecca Simpson Craft, and Larry Jensen, "Age and Gender Differences in Value Orientation among American Adolescents," *Adolescence* 33 (1998): 591–96.

are released when a neuron, the basic unit of the nervous system, wants to send an electric message to one or more neighboring neurons. Sending such a message requires the creation of neural pathways, which means that neurotransmitters must be activated in processing the signal. At any given moment, healthy levels of various neurotransmitters are needed to pass messages from one neuron to the next across gaps between them, called synapses.

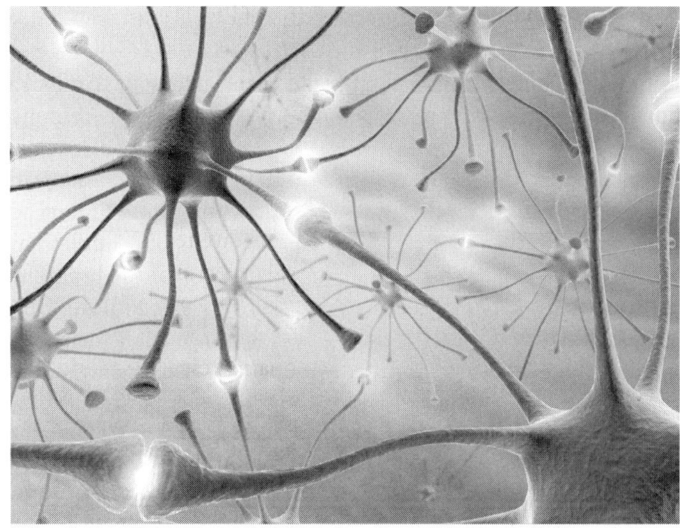

▲ **Image 5.2** Neurons are the basic cells in our nervous system, and they communicate via chemicals called neurotransmitters that aid in sending electric messages across gaps between neurons called synapses.

SOURCE: © istockphoto.com / ktsimage

Although there are many types of neurotransmitters, the most studied in relation to criminal activity are **dopamine** and **serotonin**. Dopamine is most commonly linked to feeling good. For example, dopamine is the chemical that tells us when we are experiencing good sensations, such as good food, sex, and so on. Most illicit drugs elicit a pleasurable sensation by enhancing the levels of dopamine in our systems. Cocaine and methamphetamine, for example, tell the body to produce more dopamine and inhibit the enzymes that typically mop up the dopamine in our systems after it is used.

Although a number of studies show that low levels of dopamine are linked to high rates of criminality, other studies show no association with—or even a positive link to—criminal behavior.[20] However, the relationship between dopamine and criminal behavior is probably curvilinear, such that both extremely high and extremely low levels of dopamine are associated with deviance. Unfortunately, no conclusion can be made at this point due to the lack of scientific evidence regarding this chemical.

On the other hand, a clear conclusion can be made about the other major neurotransmitter that has been implicated in criminal offending: serotonin. Studies have consistently shown that low levels of serotonin are linked with criminal offending.[21] Serotonin is important in virtually all information processing, whether it be learning or emotional; thus, it is vital in most aspects of interacting with the environment. Those who have low levels of serotonin are likely to have problems in everyday communication and life in general. Therefore, it is not surprising that low levels of serotonin are strongly linked to criminal activity.

---

[20]For reviews, see Kevin Beaver, *Biosocial Criminology: A Primer* (Dubuque, IA: Kendall/Hunt, 2008); Raine, *Anatomy of Violence*; and Diana H. Fishbein, *Biobehavioral Perspectives in Criminology* (Belmont, CA: Wadsworth/Thomson Learning, 2001).

[21]For a review, see Ellis, "A Theory." See also Rachel Blumensohn et al., "Reduction in Serotonin 5HT Receptor Binding on Platelets of Delinquent Adolescents," *Psychopharmacology* 118 (1995): 354–56; Emil F. Coccaro et al., "Central Serotonin Activity and Aggression," *American Journal of Psychiatry* 154 (1997): 1430–35; Mairead Dolan et al., "Serotonergic and Cognitive Impairment in Impulsive Aggressive Personality Disordered Offenders: Are There Implications for Treatment?" *Psychological Medicine* 32 (2002): 105–17; and Richard J. Davidson, Katherine M. Putnam, and Christine L. Larson, "Dysfunction in the Neural Circuitry of Emotion Regulation: A Possible Prelude to Violence," *Science* 289 (2000): 591–94.

Brain Injuries

Another area of physiological problems associated with criminal activity is that of trauma to the brain. As mentioned before, the brain weighs only 3 pounds, but it is responsible for every criminal act that an individual commits, so any problems related to this structure have profound implications regarding behavior, especially deviance and criminal activity.

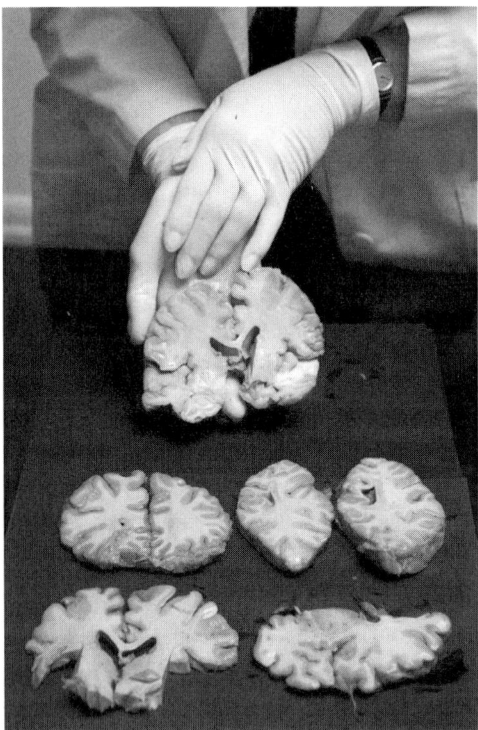

▲ **Image 5.3** Harking back to the 19th century, when postmortem examinations of the brains of criminals were a frequent phenomenon, researchers dissected the brain of serial killer John Wayne Gacy after his execution. The attempt to locate an organic explanation for his monstrous behavior was unsuccessful.

SOURCE: © AP Photo/M. Spencer Green

Studies have consistently shown that damage to any part of the brain increases the risk of crime by that individual in the future. However, trauma to certain portions of the brain tends to have more serious consequences than injury to other areas. Specifically, damage to the frontal or **temporal lobes** (particularly those on the left side) appears to have the most consistent associations with criminal offending.[22] These findings make sense primarily because the **frontal lobes** (which include the prefrontal cortex) are the areas of the brain where the realm of higher-level problem solving and "executive" functioning takes place.[23] Thus, the frontal lobes, especially on the left side, process what we are thinking and inhibit us from doing what we are emotionally charged to do. Thus, any moral reasoning relies on this executive area of the brain because it is the region that considers long-term consequences.[24] If people suffer damage to their frontal lobes, they will be far more inclined to act on their emotional urges because they are not receiving any logical inhibitions from this specialized region.

In a similar vein, the temporal lobe region is highly related to memory and emotion. To clarify, the temporal lobes cover and communicate almost directly with certain structures of our brain's limbic systems. Certain limbic structures govern our memories (the hippocampus) and emotions (the amygdala). Any damage to the temporal lobe, which is generally located above the ear, is likely to damage these structures or the effective communication of these structures to other portions of the brain. Therefore, it is understandable why trauma to the temporal region of the brain is linked to future criminality.

---

[22]For reviews, see Raine, *Anatomy of Violence*, 80–89; and Raine, *Psychopathology of Crime*, 129–54. See also Joseph M. Tonkonogy, "Violence and Temporal Lobe Lesion: Head CT and MRI Data," *Journal of Neuropsychiatry* 3 (1991): 189–96; and Percy Wright et al., "Brain Density and Symmetry in Pedophilic and Sexually Aggressive Offenders," *Annals of Sex Research* 3 (1990): 319–28.

[23]Ellis, "A Theory," 294. See also Diana Fishbein, "Neuropsychological and Emotional Regulatory Processes in Antisocial Behavior," in *Biosocial Criminology: Challenging Environmentalism's Supremacy*, ed. Anthony Walsh and Lee Ellis (New York: Nova Science, 2003), 185–208.

[24]Bobbi Jo Anderson, Malcolm D. Holmes, and Erik Ostresch, "Male and Female Delinquents' Attachments and Effects of Attachments on Severity of Self-Reported Delinquency," *Criminal Justice and Behavior* 26 (1999): 435–52.

Case Study: Charles Whitman

Charles Whitman's shooting spree is legendary and notorious for many reasons. He killed 15 people and injured 28 others from a landmark university tower at the University of Texas at Austin (UT Austin; the UT flagship campus). But what is almost more fascinating is his life story up until that fateful day.

▲ **Image 5.4** Charles Whitman shot 43 people from the university clock tower at University of Texas at Austin (UT Austin), killing 15.

SOURCE: ©iStockphoto.com/Gregg Mack

Whitman was, by most accounts, a great person and a good soldier. He was one of the youngest Eagle Scouts ever to earn the honor. He graduated near the top of his class in high school and then went on to become a stellar member of the U.S. Marine Corps, earning the rating of sharpshooter. He used this skill when he went on his shooting rampage on August 1, 1966. It should be noted that the day before, he killed his wife and mother and left some letters (which will come up later). Then he planned out his attack on the university for the following day.

The day after Whitman killed his wife and mother, he proceeded to the main tower at UT Austin, killed the receptionist, ascended the tower, and waited for classes to break; he then opened fire on the crowd of students. It is notable that he had taken with him a variety of materials that imply he was in it for the long haul. These items included toilet paper, spray deodorant, water canteens, gasoline, rope, and binoculars as well as a variety of weapons, such as a machete, a hatchet, a .357 Magnum revolver, a 12-gauge sawed-off shotgun, two rifles (one with a telescopic sight), 700 rounds of ammunition, and other weapons.

Whitman was shooting people on the run and in places only a trained sharpshooter could hit. He shot a pregnant woman, who later gave birth to a stillborn baby. He also shot a person crossing a street 500 yards away. This is the type of shot glorified in *Full Metal Jacket*, a Stanley Kubrick film that examined the Marine boot camps of the late 1960s. There is no doubt that Whitman was an expert sharpshooter and that the Marine Corps trained him well. Unfortunately, in this case his training was used against innocent targets. Whitman continued his mass killing for a couple of hours until several police officers were able to find a way through ground tunnels and then up to the top of the tower, where they shot and killed Whitman.

But why did he do it?The best guess we have, which directly relates to this section, began with one of his last letters. He wrote, "After my death, I wish an autopsy on me to be performed to see if there is any mental disorder." An autopsy was performed, and as Whitman sort of predicted, he did not simply have a mental disorder but a large brain tumor (about the size of a golf ball). As we examine how vulnerable our brain functioning can be to trauma, imagine the likely effects of a large tumor on thinking and processing skills.

But why did he do it?

Think About It

1. Do you believe Whitman was insane? Give your reasons why you believe so or not.
2. Given how much planning went into his attack, how much of an effect do you believe his tumor had on him at the time of the attack?

SOURCES: Ronald M. Holmes and Stephen T. Holmes, *Mass Murders in the United States* (Upper Saddle River, NJ: Prentice Hall, 2000); Jo Durden Smith, *100 Most Infamous Criminals* (New York: MetroBooks, 2003).

Central and Autonomic Nervous System Activity

The brain is a key player in two different types of neurological systems that have been linked to criminal activity. The first is the **central nervous system (CNS)**, which involves our brains and spinal columns and governs our voluntary motor activities. For example, the fact that you are reading this sentence means that you are in control of this brain-processing activity. Empirical studies of the influence of CNS functioning on criminality have traditionally focused on brain wave patterns with most using electroencephalograms (EEGs). Although EEGs do not do a good job of describing which areas of the brain are active or inactive, they do reveal how much the brain as an entire organ is performing at certain times.

Studies have compared brain wave patterns of known chronic offenders (e.g., psychopaths, repeat violent offenders) to those of "normal" people (i.e., those who have never been charged with a crime).[25] These studies consistently show that the brain wave patterns of chronic offenders are abnormal compared to those of the normal population with most studies showing slower brain wave patterns in psychopaths.[26] Four types of brain wave patterns are found, from slowest to fastest: delta, theta, alpha, and beta.[27] Delta waves are often seen when people sleep, whereas theta waves are typically observed in lower levels of wakefulness, such as drowsiness. Alpha waves (which tend to be divided into slow and fast wave patterns, as are beta waves) are usually related to a more relaxed wakefulness, and beta waves are observed with high levels of wakefulness, such as in times of extreme alertness and particularly in times of excited activity.

The studies that have compared brain wave patterns among chronic offenders and normals have shown significant differences. Psychopaths tend to have more activity in the theta (and sometimes slow alpha) patterns, whereas normals tend to show more activity in the fast alpha or beta waves. These consistent findings reveal that the cortical arousal of chronic offenders tends to be significantly slower than that of people who do not typically commit crimes. Thus, it is likely that chronic offenders typically do not have the mental functioning that would dispose them toward accurate assessments regarding the consequences of committing criminal behavior.

The second area of the nervous system that has been most linked to criminal behavior is the **autonomic nervous system (ANS)**, which is primarily responsible for involuntary motor activities, such as heart rate, dilation of pupils, and electric conductivity in the skin. This is the type of physiological activity that is measured by polygraph measures, or lie detector tests. Such measures capitalize on the inability of individuals to control physiological responses to anxiety, which occurs in most normal persons when they lie, especially regarding illegal behavior. However, such measures are not infallible because the individuals who are most at risk of being serious, violent offenders are the most likely to pass such tests even when they are lying. See Figure 5.2.

---

[25]Adrian Raine and Peter H. Venables, "Enhanced P3 Evoked Potentials and Longer P3 Recovery Times in Psychopaths," *Psychophysiology* 25 (1988): 30–38; Lance O. Bauer and Victor M. Hesselbrock, "Frontal P300 Decrements, Childhood Conduct Disorder, Family History, and the Prediction of Relapse among Abstinent Cocaine Abusers," *Drug and Alcohol Dependence* 44 (1997): 1–10. For a review, see Ellis, "A Theory."

[26]For a review, see Raine, *Psychopathology of Crime*, 174–78. See also Robert D. Hare, *Psychopathy: Theory and Practice* (New York: Wiley, 1970); Jan Volavka, "Electroencephalogram among Criminals," in *The Causes of Crime: New Biological Approaches*, ed. Sarnoff A. Mednick, Terrie E. Moffitt, and Susan Stack (Cambridge: Cambridge University Press, 1987), 137–45; Peter H. Venables, "Psychophysiology and Crime: Theory and Data," in *Biological Contributions to Crime Causation*, ed. Terrie E. Moffitt and Sarnoff A. Mednick (Dordrecht: Martinus Nijhoff, 1988); and Peter H. Venables and Adrian Raine, "Biological Theory," in *Applying Psychology to Imprisonment: Theory and Practice*, ed. Barry McGurk, David Thornton, and Mark Williams (London: Her Majesty's Stationery Office, 1987), 3–28.

[27]For further discussion and explanation, see Raine, *Psychopathology of Crime*, 174–77.

Figure 5.2 • Central nervous system and autonomic nervous system

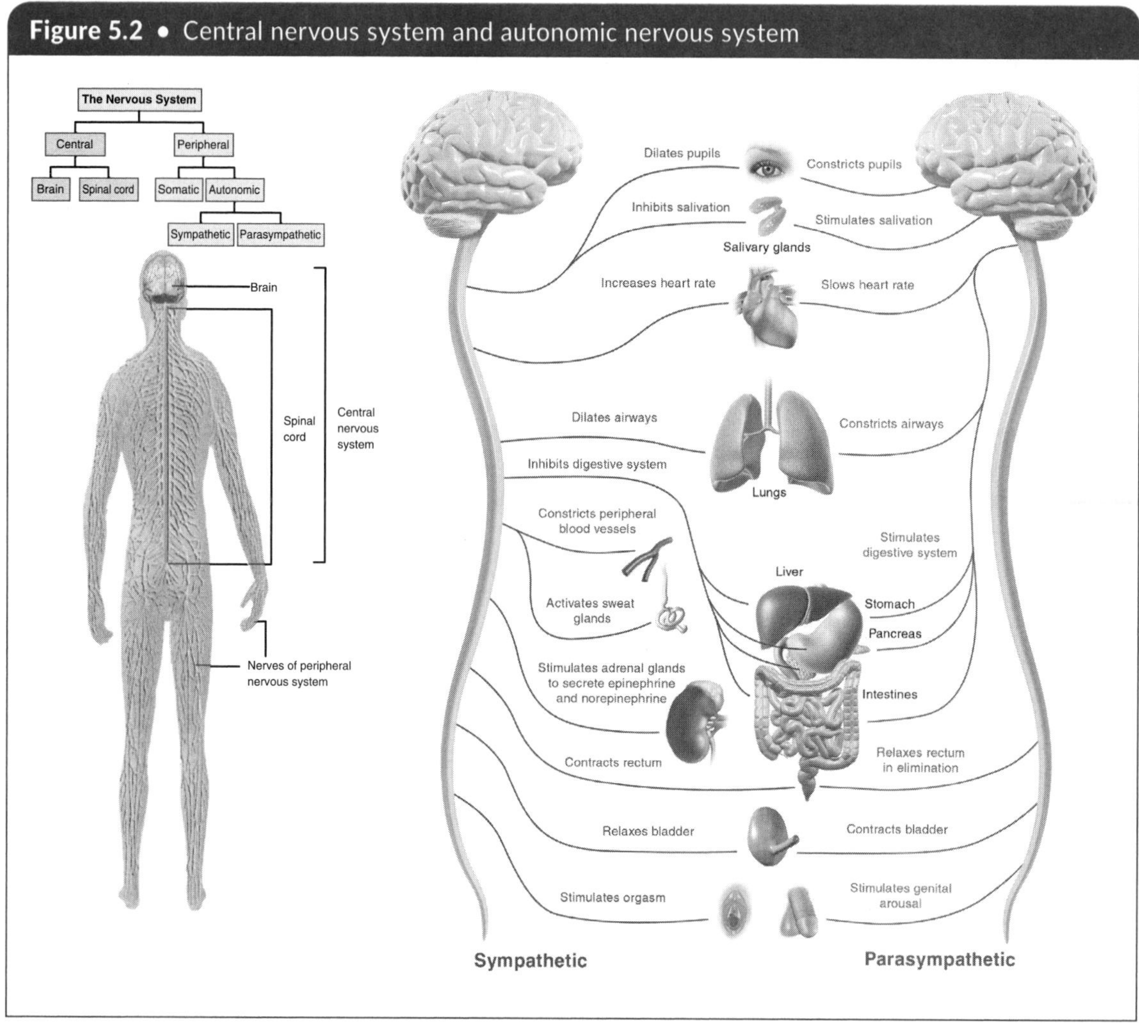

SOURCE: Bob Garrett, *Brain and Behavior: An Introduction to Biological Psychology*. Copyright © SAGE Publications, Inc. Reprinted by permission of SAGE Publications, Inc.

Consistent with the findings regarding CNS arousal levels, studies have consistently shown that individuals who have significantly low levels of ANS functioning are far more likely to commit criminal acts.[28] For example, studies consistently show that chronic violent offenders tend to have much slower resting heartbeats than normal people;

[28]For a review, see Raine, *Psychopathology of Crime*, 159–73. See also the following reviews and studies: Peter H. Venables, "Childhood Markers for Adult Disorders," *Journal of Child Psychology and Psychiatry and Allied Disciplines* 30 (1989): 347–64; Adrian Raine and Peter H. Venables, "Skin Conductance Responsivity in Psychopaths to Orienting, Defensive, and Consonant-Vowel Stimuli," *Journal of Psychophysiology* 2 (1988): 221–25; and Traci Bice, "Cognitive and Psychophysiological Differences in Proactive and Reactive Aggressive Boys" (doctoral dissertation, Department of Psychology, University of Southern California, 1993).

a number of studies estimate this difference to be as much as 10 beats per minute slower for the offenders.[29] This is a highly significant gap that cannot be explained away by alternative theories—for example, the explanation that offenders are just less excited in laboratory tests.

Furthermore, people who have such low levels of ANS arousal tend to experience what is known in the psychological literature as *stimulus hunger.* Stimulus hunger means that individuals with such a low level of ANS arousal may constantly seek out experiences and stimuli that are risky and thus often illegal. Readers may recall children they have known who can never seem to get enough attention, with some even seeming to enjoy being spanked or other forms of harsh punishment. In addition, people with a low level of ANS arousal may feel no anxiety about punishment, even corporal punishment, and thus they may not adequately learn right from wrong through normal forms of discipline. This is perhaps one of the reasons why children who are diagnosed with attention deficit hyperactivity disorder (ADHD) have a higher likelihood of becoming criminals than their peers.

Because people who are accurately diagnosed with ADHD have a neurological abnormality—a significantly low functioning ANS level of arousal—doctors prescribe stimulants (e.g., Ritalin) for such youths. It may seem counterintuitive to prescribe a hyperactive person a stimulant; however, the medication boosts the individual's ANS functioning to a normal level of arousal. This makes such individuals experience a healthy level of anxiety, which they would not normally experience from wrongdoing. Assuming that the medication is properly prescribed and at the correct dosage, children who are treated tend to become more attuned to the discipline that they face if they engage in rule violation.

Children who do not fear punishment at all—in fact, some of them do not feel anxiety even when being physically punished (e.g., spanking)—are likely to have lower-than-average levels of ANS functioning. Such individuals are likely to become chronic offenders if this disorder is not addressed, because they will not respond to discipline or consider the long-term consequences of their risky behavior. If people don't fear punishment or negative consequences from their behavior, they may be more likely to engage in selfish, greedy behavior. Thus, it is important to address this issue when it becomes evident. On the other hand, children will be children, and ADHD and other disorders have been overly diagnosed in recent years. A well-trained physician should investigate thoroughly to decide whether an individual has such a low level of ANS functioning that medication or therapy is required to curb deviant behavior.

Individuals who have significantly lower ANS arousal are likely to pass lie detector tests because they feel virtually no or little anxiety when they lie; many of them lie all the time. Thus, it is ironic, but the very people whom lie-detecting measures are meant to capture are the most likely to pass such tests, which is probably why they are typically not allowed to be used in court. Only through medication or cognitive behavioral therapy can such individuals learn to consider the long-term consequences of the decisions they make regarding their behavior.

Individuals with low levels of ANS functioning are not always destined to become chronic offenders. Some evidence has shown that people with low ANS arousal often become successful corporate executives, decorated military soldiers, world-champion athletes, and high-level politicians. Most of these occupations require people who constantly seek out exciting, risky behaviors, and others require constant and convincing forms of lying to others. So there are many legal outlets and productive ways for people with low levels of ANS functioning to use their natural tendencies. These individuals could perhaps be steered toward such occupations and opportunities when they present themselves. This is clearly a better option than committing antisocial acts against others in society.

---

[29]See Enrico Mezzacappa et al., "Anxiety, Antisocial Behavior, and Heart Rate Regulation in Adolescent Males," *Journal of Psychiatry* 38 (1997): 457–69; Graham A. Rogeness et al., "Differences in Heart Rate and Blood Pressure in Children with Conduct Disorder, Major Depression, and Separation Anxiety," *Psychiatry Research* 33 (1990): 199–206; and Daniel J. Kindlon et al., "Longitudinal Patterns of Heart Rate and Fighting Behavior in 9- through 12-Year-Old Boys," *Journal of the American Academy of Child and Adolescent Psychiatry* 34 (1995): 371–77.

Ultimately, low levels of cortical arousal in both the CNS and ANS are clearly linked to a predisposition toward criminal activity. However, modern medical research and societal opportunities exist to help such individuals divert their tendencies toward more prosocial outlets.

Biosocial Approaches to Explaining Criminal Behavior

Perhaps the most important and most recent perspective of how criminality is formed is that of biosocial approaches to explaining crime. Specifically, if there is any conclusion that can be made regarding the previous theories and research in this section, it is that both genetics and environment influence behavior, particularly the interaction between the two. Even the most fundamental aspects of life can be explained by these two groups of factors.

For example, if we look at the height of individuals, we can predict with a great amount of accuracy how tall a person will be by looking at the individual's parents and other ancestors because much of height is determined by a person's genotype. However, even for something as physiological as height, the environment plays a large role. As many readers will observe, individuals who are raised in poor, underdeveloped areas (e.g., Mexico, Asia) are shorter than children raised in the United States. However, individuals who descend from parents and relatives in these underdeveloped areas but are raised in the United States tend to be just as tall (if not taller) than children born here. This is largely due to diet, which obviously is an environmental factor.

In other words, our genotype provides a certain range or window that determines the height of an individual based on ancestral factors. But the extent to which individuals grow to the maximum or minimum, or somewhere in between, is largely dependent on what occurs in the environment as they develop. This is why biologists make a distinction between genotype, which is directly due to genetics, and **phenotype**, which is a manifestation of genetics interacting with the environment. The same type of biosocial effect is seen for criminal behavior.

Furthermore, over the past decades, a number of empirical investigations have examined the extent to which physiological variables interact with environmental variables, and the findings of these studies have shown consistent predictions regarding criminality. Such studies have been more accurate than those that rely on either physiological and genetic variables or environmental factors separately. For example, findings from a cohort study in Philadelphia showed that individuals who had low birth weights were more likely to commit crime, but that was true primarily if they were raised in a lower-income family or a family with a weak social structure.[30] Those who were raised in a relatively high-income household or a strong family structure were unlikely to become criminals. It was the coupling of both a physiological deficiency (i.e., low birth weight) and an environmental deficit (i.e., weak family structure or income) that had a profound effect on propensity for criminal behavior.

In addition, recent studies have shown that when incarcerated juveniles were assigned to diets with limited levels of simple carbohydrates (e.g., sugars), their reported levels of violations during incarceration declined by almost half (45%).[31] Furthermore, other studies have reported that various food additives and dyes, such as those commonly found in processed foods, can also have a significant influence on criminal behavior. Thus, the old saying "you are what you eat" appears to have some scientific weight behind it—at least regarding criminal behavior. Additional studies have found that high levels of certain toxins, particularly lead and manganese, can have profound effects on behavior, including criminality. Recent studies have found a consistent, strong effect of high lead levels in predicting criminal behavior. Unfortunately, medical studies have also found many subtle sources of high lead levels, such as the fake jewelry that many children wear as toys. Also unfortunate is that the individuals who are most vulnerable to high levels of lead (like virtually every other toxin) are children, yet they are the most likely to

---

[30]Stephen Tibbetts and Alex Piquero, "The Influence of Gender, Low Birth Weight, and Disadvantaged Environment in Predicting Early Onset of Offending: A Test of Moffitt's Interactional Hypothesis," *Criminology* 37 (1999): 843–78.

[31]Stephen J. Shoenthaler, *Improve Your Child's IQ and Behavior* (London: BBC Books, 1991).

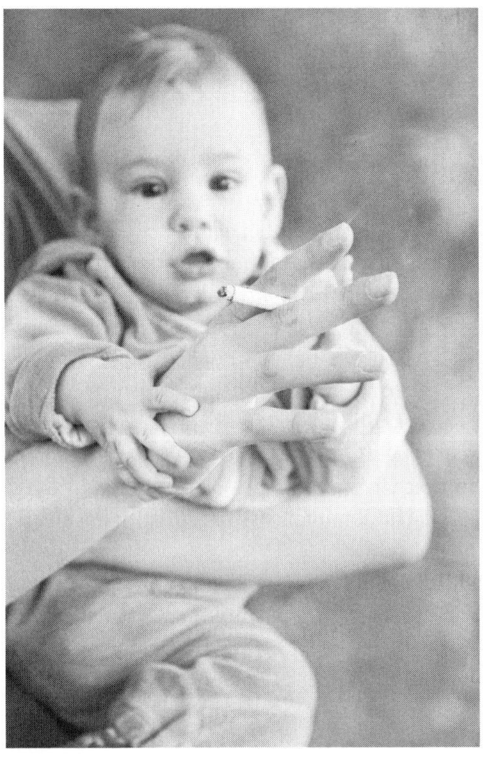

▲ **Image 5.5** Young children are particularly vulnerable when exposed to dangerous toxins.

SOURCE: © Photospower / iStock

be exposed. Even more unfortunate is that the populations most susceptible to biosocial interactions (e.g., poor, urban) are most likely to experience high levels of lead, largely due to old paint, which often contains lead, and other household products that contain dangerous toxins.[32]

Consistently, other studies have shown that prenatal and perinatal problems alone do not predict violence very well. However, when such perinatal problems are considered along with environmental deficits, such as weak family structure, this biosocial relationship often predicts violent rather than property crime.[33] Other studies have shown the effects on criminality of a biosocial interaction between the impact of physiological factors within the first minute of life, called Apgar scores, and environmental factors, including exposure to nicotine.[34] Additional studies have also found that the interaction between maternal cigarette smoking and the father's absence from the household is associated with criminal behavior, especially early in life, which is one of the biggest predictors of chronic offending in the future.[35] One of the most revealing studies showed that, although only 4% of a sample of 4,269 individuals had both birth complications and maternal rejection, this relatively small group of people accounted for more than 18% of the total violent crimes committed by the whole sample.[36] To quote a recent review of literature, Adrian Raine stated, "Almost wherever you go in the world, you find the same effect. The combination of birth complications and adverse home environments appears to be a useful biosocial key that can open the lock on the causes of violence." So studies have clearly shown that the interaction between biological factors and environmental deficiencies has the most consistent effect on future criminality.

Policy Implications

The theories in this section have plenty of policy implications; a few of the primary interventions are discussed here. First, there should be universal, funded preschool for all children. This early life stage is important not only for developing academic skills but also for fostering healthy social and disciplinary skills, which children who do

[32]Wright et al., *Criminals in the Making.*

[33]Alex Piquero and Stephen Tibbetts, "The Impact of Pre/Perinatal Disturbances and Disadvantaged Familial Environment in Predicting Criminal Offending," *Studies on Crime and Crime Prevention* 8 (1999): 52–71.

[34]For example, Chris Gibson and Stephen Tibbetts, "Interaction between Maternal Cigarette Smoking and Apgar Scores in Predicting Offending," *Psychological Reports* 83 (1998): 579–86. For a review, see Stephen G. Tibbetts, "Birth Complications and the Development of Criminality: A Biosocial Perspective," in Kevin Beaver and Anthony Walsh, *The Ashgate Research Companion to Biosocial Theories of Crime* (Burlington, VT: Ashgate, 2012), 273–90.

[35]Chris Gibson and Stephen Tibbetts, "A Biosocial Interaction in Predicting Early Onset of Offending," *Psychological Reports* 86 (2000): 509–18.

[36]Adrian Raine, Pauline A. Brennan, and Sarnoff A. Mednick, "Birth Complications Combined with Early Maternal Rejection at Age 1 Year Predispose to Violent Crime at Age 18 Years," *Archives of General Psychiatry* 51 (1994): 984–88.

not attend preschool often fail to develop.[37] In addition, there should be funded mental health and drug counseling for all young children and adolescents who exhibit symptoms of mental disorders or drug problems.[38] There should also be universal funding for health care for all expectant mothers, especially those who have risk factors (poverty, inner-city residence, etc.).

Perhaps most important, there should be far more thorough examinations of children's physiological makeup in terms of hormones, neurotransmitters, brain formation and functioning, and genetic design so that earlier interventions can take place. It has been shown empirically that the earlier that interventions take place, the better the outcomes.[39] A review of the extant literature, hereafter referred to as the Maryland Report (because all key authors of the report were professors at the University of Maryland), emphasized the importance of identifying and quickly treating any head and bodily trauma early in development among infants and toddlers, concluding that some of the most consistently supported early intervention programs for such physiological problems are those that involve weekly infant home visitation, typically by nurses or neonatal experts.[40]

Conclusion

This section has examined a large range of explanations of criminal behavior that place most of the blame on biological and psychological factors, which are typically intertwined. These types of explanations were primarily popular in the early years of the development of criminology as a science, but they have also been shown in recent years to be quite valid as significant factors in individual decisions to commit crime. This section examined the influence of genetics and environment in family studies, twin studies, adoption studies, and studies of identical twins separated at birth. These studies have ultimately shown the consistent influence of inheritance and genetics in predisposing individuals toward criminal activity. This is supported by the influence of hormones (e.g., testosterone) in human behavior as well as the influence of variations in chromosomal mutations (e.g., XYY). Recent research has supported both of these theories in showing that people with high levels of male androgens are far more likely to commit crimes than those who do not have high levels of these hormones.

The link between brain trauma and crime was also discussed, emphasizing the consistent association between damage to the left or frontal parts of the brain. We also examined theories regarding variations in levels of CNS and ANS functioning; nearly all empirical studies have shown that low levels of functioning of these systems have links to criminality. Finally, we explored the extent to which the interaction between physiological factors and environmental variables contributes to the most consistent prediction of criminal offending. Ultimately, it is interesting that the very theories that were key in the early years of the development of criminology as a science are now showing strong support in studies for being primary influences on criminal behavior.

Ultimately, despite the neglect that biosocial models of crime receive in terms of both recognition and policy implications, there is no doubt that this area is crucial if we hope to advance our understanding and create more efficient policies regarding criminal behavior. It is time that all criminologists recognize the degree to which human behavior results from physiological disorders. We all have brains, each about 3 pounds in weight, that determine the choices we make. Criminologists must acknowledge the influence of biological or physiological factors that influence this vital organ, or the discipline will be behind the curve in terms of understanding why people commit (or do not commit) criminal offenses.

---

[37] Wright et al., *Criminals in the Making.*

[38] Ibid.

[39] Samuel S. Wu et al., "Risk Factors for Infant Maltreatment: A Population-Based Study," *Child Abuse and Neglect* 28 (2004): 1253–64.

[40] Lawrence Sherman et al., *Preventing Crime: What Works, What Doesn't, What's Promising: A Report to the United States Congress* (Washington, DC: U.S. Department of Justice, 1997) (see chap. 2).

SECTION SUMMARY

- Early studies that examined the influence of biology focused on case studies of certain families. These studies showed that criminality was indeed clustered among certain families, but such studies did not separate biology from environment.
- The next stage of studies examined the concordance rates of identical twins versus nonidentical twins. These studies led to the conclusion that genetic makeup was very important, but critics called these conclusions into question.
- The following stage of research examined adoptees to determine which parents (biological or adoptive) had more influence in their future criminal behavior. These studies revealed that biological parents (whom the adoptees never knew) had far more influence than the adoptive parents who raised them. However, there were criticisms of these studies, so the findings were questioned.
- The final stage of the biology versus environment debate was that of identical twins separated at birth as compared to identical twins raised together. These studies showed that the twins who were separated at birth were just as similar, if not more so, than the twins who were reared together. To date, there are no criticisms of this method of study. Thus, it appears that all four waves of study are consistent in showing that biological influences are vitally important in explaining the criminality of individuals.
- This section also examined chromosomal mutations, such as the XYY mutation, which has consistently shown associations with criminality. Much, if not most, of this link is believed to be due to the increased male androgens (e.g., testosterone) produced by individuals who have the XYY chromosomal mutation.
- Studies have consistently shown that individuals with higher levels of testosterone and other androgens are more disposed toward criminality; for example, normal males are far more likely than normal females to engage in violent crimes.
- This section reviewed findings from studies that show that people with abnormal levels of certain neurotransmitters, such as serotonin, are far more likely to engage in crime than those who have normal levels of these chemicals in their brains or bodies.
- Studies show that criminality is more likely among individuals who have experienced brain trauma or have lower levels of brain functioning, especially in certain regions of the brain, such as the frontal and temporal lobes, which are the regions that largely govern higher-level, problem-solving functions.
- This section also reviewed the dispositions of individuals regarding two aspects of the nervous system, specifically the CNS and ANS. Those who have significantly slower brain waves and lower anxiety levels are far more likely to commit crimes.

KEY TERMS

adoption studies 184

autonomic nervous system (ANS) 192

central nervous system (CNS) 192

concordance rates 183

cytogenetic studies 185

dizygotic (DZ) twins 182

dopamine 189

family studies 182

frontal lobes 190

monozygotic (MZ) twins 182

neurotransmitters 188

DISCUSSION QUESTIONS

1. Is there any validity to family studies in determining the role of genetics in criminal behavior? Explain why or why not.
2. Explain the rationale of studies that compare the concordance rates of identical twins and fraternal twins who are raised together. What do most of these studies show regarding the influence of genetics on criminal behavior? What are the criticisms of these studies?
3. Explain the rationale of studies that examine the biological and adoptive parents of adopted children. What do most of these studies show regarding the influence of genetics on criminal behavior? What are the criticisms of these studies?
4. What are the general findings in identical twins who are separated at birth? What implications do these findings have for the importance of genetics or heritability regarding criminal behavior? Can you find a criticism for such findings?
5. Explain what cytogenetic disorders are, and describe the related disorder that is most linked to criminal behavior. What characteristics of this type of disorder seem to drive the higher propensity for criminal behavior?
6. What types of hormones have been shown by scientific studies to be linked to criminal activity? Give specific examples that show this link to be true.
7. Explain what neurotransmitters are, and describe which neurotransmitters are key in predicting criminal offending. Provide support from previous scientific studies.
8. Which areas of the brain, given trauma, have shown the greatest vulnerability regarding criminal offending? Does the lack of healthy functioning in these areas make sense? Why?
9. How do brain wave patterns differ between chronic, violent criminals and "normal" people? Does this make sense in biosocial models of criminality?
10. How does the ANS differ between chronic, violent criminals and "normal" people? Does this make sense in biosocial models of criminality?
11. What types of policy implications would you support based on the information provided by empirical studies reviewed in this section?

WEB RESOURCES

Autonomic Nervous System and Central Nervous System

http://www.merckmanuals.com/home/brain,-spinal-cord,-and-nerve-disorders/autonomic-nervous-system-disorders/overview-of-the-autonomic-nervous-system
https://www.ncbi.nlm.nih.gov/pubmedhealth/PMHT0024762/http://www.emedicinehealth.com/anatomy_of_the_central_nervous_system/article_em.htm

Brain Trauma and Crime

http://www.traumaticbraininjury.net/does-brain-injury-contribute-to-criminal-behavior
https://www.ncbi.nlm.nih.gov/pubmed/19996251

Cytogenetic Studies

http://www.jcdr.net/articles/PDF/615/771.pdf
https://www.ncbi.nlm.nih.gov/pmc/articles/PMC3356148
http://bmjopen.bmj.com/content/2/1/e000650

Family, Twin, or Adoption Studies

http://www.bookrags.com/research/twin-studies-wog
http://law.jrank.org/pages/784/Crime-Causation-Biological-Theories-Genetic-epidemiological-studies.html

Hormones and Neurotransmitters

http://serendip.brynmawr.edu/biology/b103/f02/web1/kamlin.html
http://www.gender.org.uk/about/06encrn/63faggrs.htm
https://www.ncbi.nlm.nih.gov/pmc/articles/PMC2612120

READING /// 9

In Lee Ellis's piece, we see an attempt at integrating many of the factors that we have explored in this section, as well as in Section III, into an explanatory model of offending. In this selection, we will see elements of evolution, early developmental problems, neurology, androgens, nervous systems, IQ or intelligence, emotions, and other factors as leading to various deviant or offending behaviors. This is one of the most comprehensive examples of a synthesis and use of the existing biosocial literature in developing a theoretical model of criminality.

While reading this entry, consider the following points:

- The name Ellis gives for the theoretical model he presents in this piece and reasons why this name is appropriate
- The 12 biological correlates of crime that Ellis reviews and which seem to be the most important or valid in predicting criminal behavior
- The three effects on brain functioning that are predicted by Ellis's theory and which seem to appear most important in predicting criminality

A Theory Explaining Biological Correlates of Criminality

Lee Ellis

Despite growing evidence that biology plays an important role in human behavior, most theories of criminal behavior continue to focus on learning and social environmental variables. This article proposes a biosocial theory of criminality that leads one to expect variables such as age, gender and social status will be associated with offending in very specific ways. According to the theory, androgens (male sex hormones) have the ability to affect the brain in ways that increase the probability of what is termed competitive/victimizing behavior (CVB). This behavior is hypothesized to exist along a continuum, with "crude" (criminal) forms at one end and "sophisticated" (commercial) forms at the other. Theoretically, individuals whose brains receive a great deal of androgen exposure will be prone toward CVB. However, if they have normal or high capabilities to learn and plan, they will transition rapidly from criminal to non-criminal forms of the behavior following the onset of puberty. Individuals with high androgen exposure and poor learning and planning capabilities, on the other hand, often continue to exhibit criminality for decades following the onset of puberty.

The Evolutionary Neuroandrogenic Theory of Criminal Behavior

The theory to be presented is called the evolutionary neuroandrogenic theory (ENA). The main types of offenses it attempts to explain are those that harm others, either by injuring them physically or by depriving them of their

SOURCE: Lee Ellis, "A Theory Explaining Biological Correlates of Criminality," *European Journal of Criminology* 2, no. 3 (2005): 287–315.

property. Two main propositions lie at the heart of ENA theory. The first addresses evolutionary issues by asserting that the commission of victimful crimes evolved as an aspect of human reproduction, especially among males. The second is concerned with identifying the neurochemistry responsible for increasing the probability of criminality among males relative to females. The theory maintains that sex hormones alter male brain functioning in ways that promote CVB, which is hypothesized to include the commission of violent and property crimes.

The concept of CVB is illustrated in Table 1. At one end of the continuum are acts that intentionally and directly either injure others or dispossess them of their property. In all societies with written laws, these obviously harmful acts are criminalized. At the other end of the CVB continuum are acts that make no profits on the sale of goods or services, although those who administer and maintain the organizations under which they operate usually receive much higher wages than do those who provide most of the day-to-day labor. In a purely socialist economy, the latter type of minimally competitive activities is all that is allowed; all other forms are criminalized. A capitalist economy, on the other hand, will permit profit-making commerce and often even tolerate commerce that involves significant degrees of deception. With the concept of CVB in mind, the two propositions upon which the theory rests can now be described.

The Evolutionary Proposition

Throughout the world, males engage in victimful crimes (especially those involving violence) to a greater extent than do females. To explain why, ENA theory maintains that female mating preferences play a pivotal role. The nature of this mating preference is that females consider social status criteria much more than males do in making mate choices, a pattern that has been documented throughout the world (Ellis, 2001). From an evolutionary standpoint, this female preference has served to increase the chances of females mating with males who are reliable provisioners of resources, allowing females to focus more of their time and energy on bearing offspring. Another consequence has been that female choice has made it possible for males who are status strivers to pass on their genes at higher rates than males who are not. Such female preferences are found in other mammals, as evidenced by their mating more with dominant males than with subordinate males.

According to ENA theory, female preferences for status-striving males have caused most males to devote considerable time and energy to competing for resources, an endeavor that often victimizes others. In other words, natural selection pressure on females to prefer status-striving mates has resulted in males with an inclination toward CVB. ENA theory maintains that the brains of males have been selected for exhibiting competitive/victimizing behavior to a greater extent than the brains of females, and that one of the manifestations of this evolved sex difference is that males are more prone than females toward victimful criminality.

Theoretically, the same natural selection pressure that has resulted in the evolution of CVB has also favored males who flaunt and even exaggerate their resource-procuring capabilities. More unpleasant consequences of the female bias for resource provisioning mates are male tendencies to seek opportunities to circumvent female caution in mating by using deceptive and even forceful copulation tactics. This implies that rape will always be more prevalent among males than among females. ENA theory also leads one to expect complex social systems to

Table 1 • Continuum of Victimizing Behavior (Reflecting Competitive/Victimizing Tendencies)

The Continuum	**very crude** ______	**intermediate** ______		**very sophisticated**	
Probability of Being Criminalized	**virtually certain** ______	**intermediate** ______		**exceedingly unlikely**	
Examples	Violent and property offenses ("street crime")	Embezzlement, fraud ("white collar crime")	Deceptive business practices, price gouging	Profit-making commerce	Nonprofit-making commerce

develop in order to prevent crime victimization. In evolutionary terms, these systems are known as *counter-strategies*. An example of a counter-strategy to crude forms of CVB is the evolution of the criminal justice system.

As with any theory founded on neo-Darwinian thinking, ENA theory assumes that genes are responsible for substantial proportions of the variation in the traits being investigated. In the present context, the average male is assumed to have a greater genetic propensity toward CVB than is true for the average female. However, this assumption must be compromised with the fact that males and females share nearly all of their genes. Consequently, the only possible way for the theory to be correct is for some of the genes that promote criminality (along with other forms of CVB) to be located on the one chromosome that males and females do not share—the Y-chromosome.

The Neuroandrogenic Proposition

The second proposition of ENA theory asserts that three different aspects of brain functioning affect an individual's chances of criminal offending by promoting CVB. Two additional neurological factors help to inhibit offending by speeding up the acquisition of sophisticated forms of CVB. Testosterone's ability to affect brain functioning in ways that promote CVB is not simple, but most of the complexities will not be considered here. The main point to keep in mind is that testosterone production occurs in two distinct phases: the organizational (or perinatal) phase and the activational (or postpubertal) phase. Most of the permanent effects of testosterone occur perinatally. If levels of testosterone are high, the brain will be masculinized; if they are low, the brain will remain in its default feminine mode.

ENA theory asserts that androgens increase the probability of CVB by decreasing an individual's sensitivity to adverse environmental consequences resulting from exhibiting CVB. This lowered sensitivity is accomplished by inclining the brain to be *suboptimally aroused*. Suboptimal arousal manifests itself in terms of individuals seeking elevated levels of sensory stimulation and having diminished sensitivity to pain.

The second way androgens promote CVB according to ENA theory is by inclining the limbic system to seizure more readily, especially under stressful conditions. At the extreme, these seizures include such clinical conditions as epilepsy and Tourette's syndrome. Less extreme manifestations of limbic seizuring are known as *episodic dyscontrol* and *limbic psychotic trigger*. These latter patterns include sudden bursts of rage and other negative emotions, which often trigger forceful actions against a perceived provocateur.

Third, ENA theory asserts that androgen exposure causes neocortical functioning to be less concentrated in the left (language-dominated) hemisphere and to shift more toward a right hemispheric focus. As a result of this so-called *rightward shift in neocortical functioning*, males rely less on language-based reasoning, emphasizing instead reasoning which involves spatial and temporal calculations of risk and reward probabilities. Coinciding with this evidence are intriguing new research findings based on functional magnetic resonance imaging (fMRI), which suggest that empathy-based moral reasoning occurs primarily in the left hemisphere. Predictably, empathy-based moral reasoning seems to be less pronounced in males than in females. Such evidence suggests that empathy-based moral reasoning is more likely to prevent victimful criminality than so-called justice-based moral reasoning.

Theoretically, the three androgen-enhanced brain processes just described have evolved in males more than in females because these processes contribute to CVB. Furthermore, competitive/victimizing behavior has evolved in males more than in females because it facilitates male reproductive success more than it facilitates female reproductive success.

Inhibiting Criminal Forms of Competitive/Victimizing Behavior

Regarding the inhibiting aspects of brain functioning, two factors are theoretically involved. One has to do with learning ability and the other entails foresight and planning ability. According to ENA theory, the ability to learn will correlate with the rapidity of male transitioning from crude to sophisticated forms of CVB. This means that intelligence and other measures of learning ability should be inversely associated with persistent involvement in criminal behavior. Likewise, neurological underpinnings of intelligence such as brain size and neural efficiency should also correlate negatively with persistent offending. These predictions apply only to persistent victimful offending, with a much weaker link to occasional delinquency and possibly none with victimless criminality.

The frontal lobes, especially their prefrontal regions, play a vital role in coordinating complex sequences of actions intended to accomplish long-term goals. These prefrontal regions tend to keenly monitor the brain's limbic region, where most emotions reside. Then the prefrontal regions devise plans for either maximizing pleasant emotions or minimizing unpleasant ones. In other words, for the brain to integrate experiences into well-coordinated and feedback-contingent strategies for reaching long-term goals, the frontal lobes perform what has come to be called *executive cognitive functioning.* Moral reasoning often draws heavily on executive cognitive functioning since it often requires anticipating the long-term consequences of one's actions.

Factors that can impact executive cognitive functioning include genetics, prenatal complications, and various types of physical and chemical trauma throughout life. According to ENA theory, inefficient executive cognitive functioning contributes to criminal behavior. Similar conclusions have been put forth in recent years by several other researchers.

To summarize, ENA theory asserts that three aspects of brain functioning promote competitive/victimizing behavior, the crudest forms of which are victimful crimes. At least partially counterbalancing these androgen-promoted tendencies are high intelligence and efficient executive cognitive functioning. These latter two factors affect the speed with which individuals quickly learn to express their competitive/victimizing tendencies in sophisticated rather than crude ways. Sophisticated expressions are less likely to elicit retaliation by victims, their relatives, and the criminal justice system than are crude ones. Males with low intelligence and/or with the least efficient executive cognitive functioning will therefore exhibit the highest rates of victimful criminal behavior.

Correlates of Criminal Behavior

Twelve biological correlates of crime with special relevance to ENA theory (testosterone, mesomorphy, maternal smoking during pregnancy, hypoglycemia, epilepsy, heart rate, skin conductivity, cortisol, serotonin, monoamine oxidase, slow brainwave patterns, and P300 amplitude) are discussed below.

Testosterone. ENA theory predicts that correlations will be found between testosterone and CVB. However, the nature of these correlations will not involve a simple one-to-one correspondence between an individual's crime probability and the amount of testosterone in his/her brain at any given point in time. Earlier, a distinction was made between the organizational and activational effects of testosterone on brain functioning, and that the most permanent and irreversible effects of testosterone occur perinatally. For this reason alone, testosterone levels circulating in the blood stream or in saliva following puberty may have little direct correlation with neurological levels, especially within each sex. Therefore, one should not expect to find a strong correlation between blood or saliva levels of testosterone among, say, 20-year-old males and the number of offenses they have committed even though testosterone levels in the brain at various stages in development are quite influential on offending probabilities.

Numerous studies have investigated the possible relationship between blood levels or saliva levels of testosterone and involvement in criminal behavior, and most have found modest positive correlations (Maras et al., 2003). Additional evidence of a connection between testosterone and aggressive forms of criminality involves a recent study of domestic violence, where offending males had higher levels of saliva testosterone than did males with no history of such violence (Soler, Vinayak, & Quadagno, 2000).

Overall, it is safe to generalize that circulating testosterone levels exhibit a modest positive association with male offending probabilities, particularly in the case of adult violent offenses. According to ENA theory, males are more violent than females, not because of cultural expectations or sex role training, but mainly because of their brains being exposed to much higher levels of testosterone than the brains of females.

Mesomorphy. Body types exist in three extreme forms. These are sometimes represented with a bulging triangle. Most people are located in the center of the triangle, exhibiting what is termed a basically balanced body type. At one corner of the triangle are persons who are extremely muscular, especially in the upper body, called mesomorphs. Ectomorphs occupy a second corner. Individuals with this body type are unusually slender and non-muscular. In the third corner, one finds endomorphs, individuals who are overweight and have little muscularity.

Studies have consistently revealed that offending probabilities are higher among individuals who exhibit a mesomorphic body type than either of the two other extreme body types (e.g., Blackson & Tarter, 1994). ENA theory explains this relationship by noting that testosterone affects more than the brain; it also enhances muscle tissue, especially in the upper part of the body.

Maternal Smoking During Pregnancy. There is considerable evidence that maternal smoking may lead to an elevated probability of offspring becoming delinquent (e.g., Räsänes et al., 1999). ENA theory assumes that fetal exposure to carbon monoxide and other neurotoxins found in cigarette smoke disrupt brain development in ways that adversely affect IQ or executive cognitive functioning, thereby making it more difficult for offspring to maintain their behavior within prescribed legal boundaries. However, it is possible that genes contributing to nicotine addiction may also contribute to criminal behavior. In fact, a recent study reported that the link between childhood conduct disorders (a frequent precursor to later criminality) and maternal smoking was mainly the result of mutual genetic influences (Maughan, Taylor, Caspi, & Moffitt, 2004).

Hypoglycemia. Glucose, a type of natural sugar, is the main fuel used by the brain. The production of glucose is largely regulated by the pancreas in response to chemical messages from a portion of the brain called the hypothalamus. When the hypothalamus senses that glucose levels are becoming too high or too low, it sends chemical instructions to the pancreas to either curtail or increase production of glucose by regulating the amount of insulin released into the blood system. In most people, this feedback regulatory process helps to maintain brain glucose at remarkably stable levels. For a variety of reasons, some people have difficulty stabilizing brain glucose levels. These people are said to be hypoglycemic. Dramatic fluctuations in brain glucose can cause temporary disturbances in thoughts and moods, with the most common symptoms being confusion, difficulty concentrating, and irritability.

Studies have indicated that hypoglycemia is associated with an elevated probability of crime, especially of a violent nature (e.g., Virkkunen, 1986). To explain such a connection, ENA theory draws attention to the importance of maintaining communication between the various parts of the brain in order to control emotionality. In particular, if the frontal lobes receive distorted signals from the limbic system, bizarre types of behavioral responses sometimes result, including responses that are violent and antisocial.

Epilepsy. Epilepsy is a neurological disorder typified by seizures. These seizures are tantamount to "electrical storms" in the brain. While people vary in genetic susceptibilities, seizures are usually induced by environmental factors such as physical injuries to the brain, viral infections, birth trauma, and exposure to various chemicals.

The main behavioral symptoms of epilepsy are known as *convulsions* (or *fits*), although not all epileptics have full-blown convulsive episodes. Mild epileptic episodes may manifest themselves as little more than a momentary pause in an on-going activity accompanied by a glazed stare. Seizures that have little to no noticeable debilitating effects on coordinated movement are called *subconvulsive* (or *subclinical*) *seizures*. Studies of human populations have shown that epilepsy affects only about one in every 150 to 200 persons. In prison populations, however, the prevalence of epilepsy is around one in 50, at least three times higher than in the general population (e.g., Mendez, Doss, & Taylor, 1993).

ENA theory can explain the links between epilepsy and offending by noting that very basic and primitive emotional responses sometimes emanate from the limbic region of the brain. While seizures in motor control centers are most likely to receive a diagnosis of epilepsy, seizures in the limbic region could provoke very basic survival instincts.

Resting Heart and Pulse Rates. Heart and pulse rates rise in response to strenuous exercise along with stressful and frightening experiences. Studies have shown that on average, the resting heart rate and pulse rate of convicted offenders are lower than those of persons in general (e.g., Mezzacappa et al., 1997:463). ENA theory would account for these relationships by stipulating that both low heart and low pulse rates are physiological indicators of suboptimal arousal. Such arousal levels should incline individuals to seek more intense stimulation and to tolerate unpleasant environmental feedback to a greater extent than individuals with normal or superoptimal arousal under most circumstances.

Skin Conductivity (Galvanic Skin Response). Sweat contains high concentrations of sodium, which is a good electrical conductor. A device called a Galvanic Skin Response (GSR) meter was developed nearly a century ago to monitor palm sweat. The GSR works by measuring electrical impulses passing through our bodies from one electrode to another. Thus, by putting one's fingers on two unconnected electrodes of a GSR device, one completes an electrical circuit through which imperceptible amounts of electricity flow. Temperature obviously affects how much people sweat, but so too do emotions. The more intense one's emotions become (especially those of fear and anger), the more one will sweat, and thus the stronger will be the readings on the GSR meter.

Numerous studies have examined the possibility that persons with the greatest propensities toward criminal behavior have distinctive skin conductivity patterns. These studies suggest that offenders exhibit lower skin conductivity under standard testing conditions than do people in general (e.g., Buikhuisen, Eurelings-Bontekoe, & Host, 1989; Raine, Venables, & Williams, 1996). As in the case of heart and pulse rates, ENA theory can account for such findings by hypothesizing that low GSR readings, especially under stressful testing conditions, are another indication of suboptimal arousal.

Cortisol. So-called stress hormones are secreted mainly by the adrenal glands during times of anxiety, stress, and fear. The stress hormone that has been investigated most in connection with criminality is cortisol. Most of these studies have suggested that offenders have below normal levels (e.g., Lindman, Aromaki, & Eriksson, 1997). As with heart rates and skin conductivity, one could anticipate a low cortisol–high criminality relationship by assuming that low cortisol production even in the face of stress is another indicator of suboptimal arousal. This would suggest that offenders are less intimidated by threatening aspects of their environments than are persons in general.

Serotonin. Serotonin is an important neurotransmitter. When serotonin is relatively active in the synaptic regions connecting adjacent nerve cells, people typically report feeling a sense of contentment and calm. Several drugs that have been designed to treat depression and anxiety disorders operate by either prolonging the presence of serotonin in the synaptic gaps between neurons or by facilitating the ability of receptor sites on the dendrites to bond to the serotonin that is available. Low serotonin activity has been linked to crime by numerous studies, especially impulsive crimes (e.g., Virkkunen, Eggert, Rawlings, & Linnoila, 1996; Matykiewicz, La Grange, Vance, Wang, & Reyes, 1997). Explaining the link between serotonin and criminality from the perspective of ENA theory draws attention to serotonin pathways connecting the brain's prefrontal areas with the emotion-control centers in the limbic system. Serotonin may facilitate the sort of executive cognitive functioning required to restrain impulsive behavior, especially regarding rage and persistent frustration.

Monoamine Oxidase. Monoamine oxidase (MAO) is an enzyme found throughout the body. Within the brain, MAO helps to break down and clear away neurotransmitter molecules (including serotonin), portions of which often linger in the synaptic gap after activating adjacent nerve cells. Studies indicate that MAO activity is unusually low among offenders (e.g., Alm et al., 1996; Klinteberg, 1996). ENA draws attention to the fact that low MAO activity seems to be related to high levels of testosterone. Furthermore, low MAO brain activity may interfere with the brain's ability to manufacture or utilize serotonin.

Brain Waves and Low P300 Amplitude. Brain waves are measured using electrodes placed on the scalp. These electrodes can detect electrical activity occurring close to the surface of the brain fairly clearly. Despite their complexity, brain waves can be roughly classified in terms of ranging from being rapid and regular (alpha brain waves) to being slow and irregular (delta brain waves). Most studies based on electroencephalographic (EEG) readings have found that offenders have slower brain waves than do persons in general (e.g., Petersen, Matousek, Mednick, Volovka, & Pollock, 1982).

Unlike traditional brain wave measurement, modern computerized brain wave detection is able to average responses to dozens of identical stimuli presented to subjects at random intervals. This reveals a distinctive brain wave pattern or "signature" for each individual. Nearly everyone exhibits a noticeable spike in electrical voltage, interrupted by a "dip" approximately one-third of a second following presentation of test stimuli. This is called the P300 amplitude of an event-related evoked potential. From a cognitive standpoint, the P300 amplitude is thought to reflect neurological events central to attention and memory.

While research has been equivocal thus far in the case of criminality, several studies have found a greater dip in P300 responses by individuals diagnosed with antisocial personality disorder than is true for general populations (see Costa et al., 2000). ENA theory can account for slower EEG patterns among offenders and a P300 decrement among persons with antisocial behavior by again focusing on suboptimal arousal. From a neurological standpoint, both slow brain waves and a tendency toward a greater than normal P300 decrement can be considered symptomatic of suboptimal arousal. If ENA theory is correct, both of these conditions will be found associated with elevated brain exposure to testosterone.

Summary and Conclusions

Unlike social environmental theories, the evolutionary neuroandrogenic (ENA) theory can account for statistical associations between biological variables and criminal behavior. Furthermore, ENA theory predicts the universal concentration of offending among males between the ages of 13 and 30, patterns that strictly environmental theories have always had difficulty explaining. As its name implies, ENA theory rests on two over-arching assumptions. The first assumption is an extension of Darwin's theory of evolution by natural selection. It maintains that males on average exhibit CVB more than females because females who prefer to mate with such males increase their chances of having mates who are competent provisioners of resources. These female biases have evolved because females who have had the assistance of competent provisioners have left more offspring in subsequent generations than other females. No comparable reproductive advantage comes to males who select mates based on resource procurement capabilities.

Some forms of CVB are crude in the sense of requiring little learning, nearly all of which are either assaultive or confiscatory in nature. Other forms are sophisticated in the sense that they require complex learning and involve much more subtle types of "victimization." A major expression of sophisticated competitive/victimizing behavior involves profitable business ventures and/or the management of large organizations. In most societies, these expressions are tolerated and even encouraged. However, the vast majority of people in all societies condemn the crudest expressions of CVB, and, in all literate societies, the criminal justice system has evolved to punish such behavior.

The theory's second assumption is that genes on the Y-chromosome have evolved which cause male brains to exhibit higher rates of competitive/victimizing behavior than female brains. These genes operate in part by causing would-be ovaries to develop instead into testes early in fetal development. Once differentiated, the testes produce testosterone and other sex hormones, which have three hypothesized effects upon brain functioning, all of which promote CVB. The three effects are termed *suboptimal arousal, seizuring proneness,* and *a rightward shift in neocortical functioning.* Furthermore, two neurological processes are hypothesized to help individuals shift from crude to sophisticated forms of competitive/victimizing behavior. These are learning ability (or intelligence) and executive cognitive functioning (or planning ability). The better one's learning ability or executive functioning, the quicker he/she will transition from crude to sophisticated forms of the behavior.

References

Alm, P. O., af Klinteberg, B., Humble, K., Leppert, J., Sorensen, S., Thorell, L. H., et al. (1996). Psychopathy, platelet MAO activity and criminality among former juvenile delinquents. *Acta Psychiatrica Scandinavica, 94,* 105–111.

Blackson, T. C., & Tarter, R. E. (1994). Individual, family, and peer affiliation factors predisposing to early-age onset of alcohol and drug use. *Alcoholism: Clinical and Experimental Research, 18,* 813–821.

Buikhuisen, W., Eurelings-Bontekoe, E. H. M., & Host, K. B. (1989). Crime and recovery time: Mednick revisited. *International Journal of Law and Psychiatry, 12,* 29–40.

Costa, L., Bauer, L., Kuperman, S., Porjesz, B., O'Connor, S., & Hesselbrock, V. M. (2000). Frontal P300 decrements, alcohol dependence, and antisocial personality disorder. *Biological Psychiatry, 47,* 1064–1071.

Ellis, L. (2001). The biosocial female choice theory of social stratification. *Social Biology, 48,* 297–319.

Klinteberg, A. (1996). Biology, norms, and personality: A developmental perspective: Psychobiology of sensation seeking. *Neuropsychobiology, 34*(3), 146–154.

Lindman, R. E., Aromaki, A. S., & Eriksson, C. J. P. (1997). Sober-state cortisol as a predictor of drunken violence. *Alcohol and Alcoholism, 32,* 621–626.

Maras, A., Laucht, M., Gerdes, D., Wilhelm, C., Lewicka, S., Haack, D., et al. (2003). Association of testosterone and dihydrotestosterone with externalizing behavior in adolescent boys and girls. *Psychoneuroendocrinology, 28,* 932–940.

Matykiewicz, L., La Grange, L., Vance, P., Wang, M., & Reyes, E. (1997). Adjudicated adolescent males: Measures of urinary 5-hydroxyindoleacetic acid and reactive hypoglycemia. *Personality and Individual Differences, 22,* 327–332.

Maughan, B., Taylor, A., Caspi, A., & Moffitt, T. E. (2004). Prenatal smoking and early childhood conduct problems: Testing genetic and environmental explanations of the association. *Archives of General Psychiatry, 61,* 836.

Mendez, M. F., Doss, R. C., & Taylor, J. (1993). Interictal violence in epilepsy: Relationship to behavior and seizure variables. *The Journal of Nervous and Mental Disease, 181,* 566–569.

Mezzacappa, E., Tremblay, R. E., Kindlon, D., Saul, J. P., Arseneault, L., Seguin, J., et al. (1997). Anxiety, antisocial behavior, and heart rate regulation in adolescent males. *Journal of Psychiatry, 38,* 457–469.

Petersen, K. G. I., Matousek, M., Mednick, S. A., Volovka, J., & Pollock, V. (1982). EEG antecedents of thievery. *Acta Psychiatrica Scandinavica, 65,* 331–338.

Raine, A., Venables, P. H., & Williams, M. (1996). Better autonomic conditioning and faster electrodermal half-recovery time at age 15 years as possible protective factors against crime at age 29 years. *Developmental Psychology, 32,* 624–630.

Rasanes, P., Hakko, H., Isohanni, M., Hodgins, S., Jarvelin, M.-R., & Tiihonen, J. (1999). Maternal smoking during pregnancy and risk of criminal behavior among adult male offspring in the Northern Finland 1966 birth cohort. *American Journal of Psychiatry, 156,* 857–862.

Soler, H., Vinayak, P., & Quadagno, D. (2000). Biosocial aspects of domestic violence. *Psychoneuroendocrinology, 25,* 721–739.

Virkkunen, M. (1986). Reactive hypoglycemic tendency among habitually violent offenders. *Nutrition Reviews, 44*(Supplement), 94–103.

Virkkunen, M., Eggert, M., Rawlings, R., & Linnoila, M. (1996). A prospective follow-up study of alcoholic violent offenders and fire setters. *Archives of General Psychiatry, 53,* 523–529.

/// REVIEW QUESTIONS

1. What does Ellis call the theoretical model he presents in this piece? Explain why this name is appropriate, given the primary propositions of the theory?
2. Of the 12 biological correlates of crime that Ellis reviews, which three do you feel are the most important or valid? Which three do you feel are least important or valid?
3. What three effects on brain functioning are predicted by Ellis's theory? Do you agree with all three? Which do you think is most important or valid in predicting most criminal behavior?

READING /// 10

In this theoretical piece, Laura C. Wilson and Angela Scarpa present a strong case for the field of criminology to make a stronger effort to include biological influences in future research. The authors primarily base their case on the fact that recent biosocial models that include both biological and environmental factors appear to be more theoretically robust and empirically valid than models that focus on only one of these categories.

While reading this article, one should consider the following topics:

- What the "social push" hypothesis states, and how it is used as an argument for including biological variables in criminological research

- Findings regarding heart rate, as used as a measure of autonomic arousal, particularly what the meta-analyses, which look at the results of many studies, conclude
- The use of "sensation seeking" theory as an explanation for studies finding consistent support for biological factors, such as skin conductance, implicated in aggression
- In terms of neurobiology, the distinction between functional and structural brain differences as well as the findings of previous studies on both areas of research
- In the area of neuroendocrine functioning, the difference between the hypothalamus-pituitary-adrenal system and the hypothalamus-pituitary-gonadal system

Criminal Behavior

The Need for an Integrative Approach That Incorporates Biological Influences

Laura C. Wilson and Angela Scarpa

The field of criminology addresses phenomena that contribute to criminal behavior and patterns of recidivism. For example, deviant peer relations (Warr, 2002), limited access to educational opportunities (Ulmer, 2001), and unemployment (Bahr, Harris, Fisher, & Armstrong, 2010) are frequently examined risk factors in the field of criminology. Due to the nature of this field, criminologists are informed by numerous disciplines, including sociology, psychology, anthropology, and law. Although criminology recognizes the influence of numerous factors in predicting and understanding criminal behavior, historically, the field has primarily focused on social factors.

Criminal behavior is a costly, pervasive, and persistent societal problem. According to the Bureau of Justice Statistics, in 2007, the financial cost for survivors of violent crimes was US$2 billion and for survivors of property crime was US$16 billion (Matson, 2010). In terms of the frequency of crime, 22,879,720 victimizations were reported in 2007 spanning all types of crimes. With these statistics in mind, it is troubling to examine findings related to recidivism. Of the 300,000 prisoners that were released in 1994 in 15 states, 67.5% were rearrested within a three year period (Langan & Levin, 2002). Although research suggests that interventions with criminals can reduce recidivism (e.g., McGuire, 2004), the continually demonstrated high rates of recidivism suggest that further gains in this area are needed. Because aggression and antisocial tendencies are resistant to change, understanding the biological mechanisms underlying these difficulties may inform intervention and prevention work and help criminologists better understand and predict criminal behavior.

Physiological measures of criminal behavior have received considerable attention over the past 50 years, particularly in the field of psychology. The motivation in

SOURCE: Laura C. Wilson and Angela Scarpa, "Criminal Behavior: The Need for an Integrative Approach That Incorporates Biological Influences," *Journal of Contemporary Criminal Justice* 28, no. 3 (2012): 366–81.

physiological research is the impression that these measures may provide unbiased and objective assessment of antisocial behavior and criminal tendencies that are not possible with self-report measures of psychosocial factors (Lorber, 2004). Furthermore, many researchers suggest that these psychophysiological mechanisms are key risk factors that need to be examined to fully capture the origins of aggression and psychopathy (Raine, 2002). Because of this, using theories that do not incorporate the biological influences of criminal behavior in some fashion would be misguided. A growing number of criminologists acknowledge that biological mechanisms, such as autonomic arousal, play a role in criminal behavior. In addition to appreciating the value of examining biological influences, they strive to include these variables in their research. At the same time, however, a large number of theories and research studies in the field fail to incorporate biological influence. Thus, the purpose of the current article is to provide an overview of psychophysiological research and findings related to criminal behavior in the hopes of emphasizing the plethora of knowledge in this domain that is relevant to criminologists and assisting in the merger of these two fields.

Physiology

At the most basic level, physiology and biological correlates provide a way of assessing bodily reactions and functions that directly relate to how people experience the world (Cacioppo, Tassinary, & Bernston, 2000, 2007). By physiology, the authors are referring to any measure that reflects biological measurement of bodily functions, such as heart rate or hormone levels. Throughout this article, other terms that will be used to refer to physiology include psychophysiology and biology. It should be noted that there are differences in the definitions of physiology, biology, and psychophysiology in the literature. Physiology and biology refer strictly to bodily functions, whereas psychophysiology incorporates the environmental context and psychological phenomena associated with bodily responses (Cacioppo, Tassinary, & Bernston, 2000, 2007). For the purposes of this article, these terms will be used interchangeably because of the diversity of research reviewed. It should also be noted that although genetics are largely ignored in this article, the physiological mechanisms discussed here are largely thought to be heritable in nature and therefore these influences may explain how genetic predispositions to criminal behavior are in fact expressed (Raine, 2005).

Social Push Perspective

In theory, encouraging criminologists to include both sociological and physiological factors sounds promising and worthwhile; however, one of the main obstacles is the logistics of theoretically and empirically merging these two domains of influences. Researchers that have successfully examined both sociological and physiological factors have uncovered an interesting interaction effect. That is, the relationship between physiological factors and antisocial behaviors is stronger in individuals who do not have sociological risk factors (Raine, 2005). For example, Raine and Venables (1984) demonstrated that antisocial individuals tended to have lower resting heart rates than nonantisocial individuals; however, this relationship was especially strong for antisocial individuals with higher socioeconomic status. This finding has also been demonstrated in other studies suggesting that low resting heart rate as a risk factor of antisocial behavior is particularly strong in individuals who do not have sociological risk factors (e.g., Maliphant, Hume, & Furnham, 1990; Raine, Venables, & Mednick, 1997; Scarpa & Ollendick, 2003).

One proposed explanation for this interaction effect is the social push hypothesis (Mednick, 1977; Raine & Venables, 1981). Based on this hypothesis, if an antisocial individual is not exposed to social risk factors that would "push" him or her towards antisocial behavior, then physiological influences will likely better account for his/her antisocial tendencies. Conversely, if a person is exposed to social criminogenic risk factors, then those influences will likely be more meaningful when predicting antisocial behaviors. In these circumstances, the biological mechanisms, though still present, may not be as obvious because the sociological risk factors overshadow the impact of physiology. Based on this theory, criminologists would be amiss to exclude physiological influences because, although sociological factors often provide sufficient information to predict criminal behavior, a subset of criminals may be more heavily influenced by physiological factors (whether alone or in combination with social factors).

Comprehensive Model of Biosocial Influences on Violence

The social push hypothesis, as described above, provides insight into the interplay between physiological and sociological influences. However, to truly promote comprehensive work related to criminal behavior, a full biosocial model is necessary. Raine, Brennan, and Farrington (1997) proposed a biosocial model of violence that appears particularly relevant to the purposes of this article (Raine, 2002). At the basis of this model, biological and social influences are identified as risk and protective factors that either increase or decrease the chances of an individual becoming violent. Genes and environment factors are thought to influence both the biological and social influences, and biological and social influences can in turn impact genes and environment. For example, a social risk factor may exaggerate the influence of a genetic predisposition, or a genetic predisposition may alter the experience of a social risk factor. Thus there is bidirectionality among factors. Additionally, the biological and social risk factors may also have reciprocal relationships. For example, a biological risk factor may exaggerate the experience of a social risk factor, and vice versa. Although many of these influences likely have complex interrelations, the model also specifies that either biological or social risk factors may directly determine the expression of violence, independent of each other. As detailed in the social push hypothesis, the model also recognizes that interactional or combined effect of biological and social factors, which is often referred to as biosocial interactions. A key part of the model is that either biological or social protective factors can overpower all other influences and reduce the chances of an individual engaging in violence. Finally, the outcome of violence can produce new risk factors, which restarts the model.

The literature reviewed in this article will be limited to psychophysiological findings since criminologists are well versed in social factors that have historically been the focus of this discipline. The purpose of the review is to inform readers of the general trends observed in psychophysiological research related to criminal behavior in order to encourage the incorporation of these predictors in future criminological research. The literature presented here is in no way exhaustive and is simply meant to offer a sample of physiological influences that appear to be related to criminal behavior.

Autonomic Arousal

Autonomic arousal is a frequently examined biological correlate of psychopathy, aggression, and criminal behavior. Specifically, heart rate and skin conductance are two of the most popular measures of psychophysiology (Lorber, 2004). Heart rate is influenced by the sympathetic (SNS) and parasympathetic (PNS) branches of the autonomic nervous system. Conversely, skin conductance is thought to be exclusively influenced by the SNS branch of the autonomic nervous system. There is some debate regarding whether or not changes in heart rate and skin conductance can serve as "autonomic signatures" for specific emotions or simply reflect global emotional responding that can only be differentiated in terms of positive versus negative affect (Kreibig, 2010). Regardless, many findings do reflect differences in autonomic arousal and therefore suggest that these individual differences are valuables pieces of information when understanding behavioral tendencies.

Heart Rate

Numerous studies have found that low resting heart rate is a risk factor for criminal behavior, aggression, psychopathy, and conduct problems. Of the psychophysiological correlates that have been examined in relation to aggression, low resting heart rate is the most consistently replicated in child, adolescent, and adult samples (Ortiz & Raine, 2004). Additionally, this psychobiological marker has been replicated in studies including both men and women, and in six different countries, including England, Germany, New Zealand, Mauritius, Canada and the United States (Ortiz & Raine, 2004; Raine, 2002). Five prospective research studies (i.e., Farrington, 1997; Moffitt & Caspi, 2001; Raine, Venables, et al., 1997; Raine, Venables, & Williams, 1990; Wadsworth, 1976) support that low resting heart rate predicts future aggression, rather than being a consequence of aggression. Low resting heart rate has even been found to be characteristic of aggressive and dominant behaviors in animals, including rabbits, macaques, baboons, and tree-shrews (Eisermann, 1992).

In a meta-analysis of 45 independent effect sizes from studies including children and adolescents (total sample of 5,868), Ortiz and Raine (2004) found a significant negative effect size of $d = -.44$ demonstrating a relationship between resting heart rate and antisocial behavior. This effect size suggests that low resting heart rate is associated with greater levels of antisocial behavior. The findings also suggested that factors such as gender, measurement of heart rate, research design, and recruitment source did not moderate the relationship.

In a meta-analysis of 95 studies, Lorber (2004) attempted to further elucidate the role of low resting heart rate in this domain of the literature by differentially examining aggression, psychopathy, and conduct problems. Significant effect sizes were demonstrated for aggression ($d = -.38$) and conduct problem ($d = -.33$), but not psychopathy ($d = .06$). The findings suggested that across studies, lower resting heart rate was associated with greater levels of aggression and conduct problems, but unrelated to psychopathy. These findings support aggression and psychopathy as two distinct constructs by demonstrating different psychophysiologic profiles and highlight the value of psychophysiological measures as tools to differentiate these related, but discrete constructs.

Both Ortiz and Raine (2004) and Lorber (2004) examined heart rate during task in their meta-analyses. Ortiz and Raine (2004) found a significant effect size of $d = -.76$ for the relationship between heart rate during task and antisocial behavior. Conversely, Lorber (2004) failed to find significant effect sizes for the relationships between heart rate during task and aggression, psychopathy, and conduct problems. Moderator analyses demonstrated that the type of task used in the study likely impacted the direction and magnitude of the relationship found. Therefore, findings related to heart rate during task and measures of criminal behavior are mixed and need further evaluation.

Directly related to criminality, Brennan and colleagues (1997) found that high heart rate reactivity and skin conductance were protective factors in men with criminal fathers. Specifically, the findings support higher heart rate reactivity and skin conductance in noncriminal men with criminal fathers compared to criminal men with and without criminal fathers, and noncriminal men with noncriminal fathers. This study is particularly interesting because it considered the role of a biological protective factor in conjunction with a social risk factor (i.e., criminal father). Raine, Venables, and Williams (1995) also found higher autonomic arousal to serve as a protective factor in a criminal population. Therefore, low autonomic arousal evidenced by low resting heart rate and reactivity, and skin conductance are not only risk factors, but higher autonomic arousal may actually serve as a protective factor.

Scarpa, Tanaka, and Haden (2008) examined both social and psychophysiological factors in relation to proactive and reactive aggression in children. Their findings suggest that exposure to community violence was associated with an increase in proactive aggression in children who evidenced low resting heart rates. Conversely, community violence exposure was related to a decrease in proactive aggression in children with high levels of resting heart rate. Witnessing community violence was associated with an increase in reactive aggression in children who evidenced greater heart rate variability. Conversely, witnessing community violence was associated with a decrease in reactive aggression in children with lower heart rate variability. Of note, the main effects of community violence exposure and autonomic nervous system functioning were not statistically significant. This finding provides support for the importance of examining the interaction between social and psychophysiological factors in relation to aggression since the results suggest it is not simply an additive effect of these two domains of influences.

These strong empirical findings related to resting heart rate lead to a critical question: Why is low resting heart rate such a robust marker for criminal-related behaviors? One proposed explanation is the sensation seeking theory. Specifically, criminals are chronically underaroused, as evidenced by their lower resting heart rates, which leads them to engage in stimulating activities to increase their arousal level to a more optimal level (Eysenck, 1997; Quay, 1965; Raine, Venables, et al., 1997). These stimulation seeking tendencies may make these individuals more likely to engage in behaviors, such as violence or crime. As support for this theory, a recent meta-analysis of 43 independent effect sizes (total sample of 32,217) found a significant effect size of $d = .19$, demonstrating a relationship between sensation seeking and aggression (Wilson & Scarpa, 2011). Specifically, greater levels of sensation seeking are associated with greater levels of aggression. Moderator analyses revealed that studies including only men had significantly higher effect sizes than studies that included women in their samples. Additionally, studies that included more comprehensive measures of aggression found significantly higher effect sizes than studies that only included behavioral measures of aggression. However, the moderator analyses in the meta-analysis were limited because of the uneven class sizes.

A second common explanation is the fearlessness theory (Raine, 1993; Venables, 1987). Based on this explanation, lower resting heart rate during stressor tasks reflects low levels of fear. This low level of fear results in individuals being less likely to be influenced by social constraints, such as punishment. In terms of development, this chronic low level of arousal and therefore low level of fear may also stunt conscience development. These factors increase the likelihood an individual will engage in criminal behaviors. Both the sensation seeking and fearlessness theories represent not only explanations for the findings presented here, but also the intersection of biological mechanisms, social and personality factors, and criminal behavior.

Skin Conductance

Lorber (2004) also examined resting and task skin conductance in the meta-analysis of studies measuring aggression, psychopathy, and conduct problems. The findings evidenced a significant effect size of psychopathy ($d = -.30$) in relation to resting skin conductance, but not for aggression or conduct problems. Therefore, greater psychopathy was related to lower skin conductance at rest. In terms of task skin conductance, the findings revealed significant effect sizes for psychopathy ($d = -.25$) and conduct problems ($d = -.23$), but not aggression. Thus, greater psychopathy and conduct problems were associated with lower skin conductance during task. When considered in tandem with the heart rate findings presented above, aggression and conduct problems are strongly related to lower arousal, as measured through heart rate. Conversely, psychopathy is strongly related to lower arousal, as measured through skin conductance. Again, these differential findings support these as distinct constructs and psychophysiology provides an instrument through which these differences can be captured.

Autonomic arousal during a crime-related task may be particularly informative for understanding the mechanisms associated with an individual's likelihood to engage in crime. Choi et al. (2011) found that skin conductance levels increased when participants were shown an aggression image, such as a fight scene from a movie, compared to a nonaggression image, such as nature landscapes. Additionally, the findings suggest that the more aggressive a participant was based on self-report, the less increase the participant's skin conductance evidenced when shown the aggression image compared to the nonaggression image. Thus, these findings support a biological marker for the level of aversion to aggression and therefore provide insight into individual differences related to crime.

Given that personality is stable across time (Lynam, 1997) and personality traits (e.g., psychopathy) have been linked to crime, it may prove to be informative to consider biological markers of such influences in adolescence. In fact, a study (Fung et al., 2005) examining skin conductance in adolescence found results comparable to Choi et al. (2011). Specifically, adolescents identified as psychopathy-prone evidenced reduced skin conductance to multiple tasks, including in anticipation of an aversive event. Furthermore, as discussed earlier, Brennan and colleagues (1997) found that higher skin conductance may actually serve as a protective factor in terms of criminal behavior, even in the context of social risk factors (i.e., criminal father). Thus, these findings underscore the importance of psychophysiological risk and protective factors in considering trajectories related to criminality, and may prove informative in terms of prevention and intervention work.

Additional work has supported that skin conductance levels differ depending on whether researchers are examining reactive or proactive aggression. Scarpa, Haden, and Tanaka (2010) found that in a sample of children (ages 6 to 13), proactive aggression was significantly related to increased skin conductance and heart rate variability, whereas reactive aggression was significantly related to decreased heart rate variability and the relationship approached significance for decreased skin conductance. Therefore, these findings suggest that autonomic nervous system profiles may differ depending on the nature of the criminal action (i.e., proactive vs. reactive).

Neurobiology

A considerable amount of research has been dedicated to pinpointing the functional and structural brain differences in individuals who engage in criminal behavior. For example, some of the areas that have been identified as impaired in antisocial populations include the dorsal and ventral regions of the prefrontal cortex, amygdala, hippocampus, angular gyrus, and posterior cingulate (Raine & Yang, 2006). Of note, there is some overlap between the areas that have been identified as impaired in criminal populations and those areas identified as related to moral cognition and emotionality. Specifically, the antisocial, violent, and psychopathic behaviors observed in criminals may in part stem from deficits in the areas of the brain related to moral reasoning and emotions (e.g., dorsal and ventral prefrontal cortex, amygdala).

In a review of neuroimaging studies, Bufkin and Luttrell (2005) found that 100% of the 10 studies using single-photon emission computer tomography (SPECT) or positron emission tomography (PET) demonstrated either prefrontal or frontal deficits in aggressive or antisocial individuals. Among the four studies that used magnetic resonance imaging, two demonstrated reduced gray matter volume in prefrontal or frontal regions.

In a study using functional magnetic resonance imaging, Glenn, Raine, and Schug (2009) found amygdala disruption in psychopathic individuals. Specifically, individuals with greater levels of psychopathy demonstrated reduced amygdala activation during an emotional moral decision-making task. These findings provide further support for structural deficits in a particular brain area and, more specifically, deficits in an area of the brain linked to moral judgment. Given that psychopathy is characterized by a lack of remorse, impulsivity, and poor decision making, brain imaging research provides an inside look at the biological processes behind this construct.

Yang, Raine, Colletti, Toga, and Narr (2009) found significant cortical gray matter thinning in the right frontal and temporal cortex regions of psychopathic participants compared to nonpsychopathic participants. These impairments reflect structural areas associated with emotionality, such as the recognition of facial expressions. This study also confirmed similar findings from previous studies that also demonstrated a reduction of gray matter in psychopathic individuals (e.g., Raine, Lencz, Bihrle, LaCasse, & Colletti, 2000). As a side note, Raine and colleagues (2000) also found the psychopathic participants evidenced reduced autonomic arousal during a social stressor task, as measured through heart rate and skin conductance, in addition to the deficits related to gray matter. Thus these findings support the autonomic arousal literature presented earlier and emphasize that no single biological mechanism accounts for all individual differences.

The study conducted by Raine et al. (2000) also provided valuable support for biological mechanisms as independent risk factors, above and beyond social risk factors. Specifically, even after accounting for 10 social risk factors (e.g., familial social class, parental divorce, parental criminality, abuse experiences), Raine and colleagues (2000) still found significant differences in gray matter volume between the psychopathic and nonpsychopathic groups. Additionally, the 10 social variables were found to account for 41.3% of the variance in psychopathy group membership. By adding the prefrontal gray matter, heart rate, and skin conductance variables there was a significant increase in explained variance, with the social and physiological variables together accounting for an astonishing 76.7% of the variance. As such, this study highlights the importance of considering both psychosocial and physiological factors in criminology research.

Neuroendocrine

Because psychopathy is associated with fearlessness, reduced sensitivity to punishment, reward seeking, and aggression (Hare, 2003), the hormonal axes charged with maintaining the body's response to fear and threatening stimuli have become a focus of empirical attention (Glenn, Raine, Schug, Gao, & Granger, 2011). These two systems are called the hypothalamus-pituitary-adrenal (HPA) and hypothalamus-pituitary-gonadal (HPG) axes. In the few studies that have examined the role of hormone systems and crime-related constructs, such as psychopathy, the findings have been inconsistent. Glenn and colleagues (2011) suggest that these mixed results are due to researchers examining single hormones in isolation. More recently, researchers have begun to stress the importance of examining the hormone systems as interconnected and discourage against breaking these complex systems down into measures of single hormones (Bauer, Quas, & Boyce, 2002; Brown et al., 2008; Glenn et al., 2011; Lovallo & Thomas, 2000).

Brown et al. (2008) reviewed the findings of numerous studies examining the role of multiple biochemical mechanisms in relation to impulsive aggressive behavior.

Of the 15 studies reviewed, inconsistent results were reported for the role of cortisol, with the results including positive, negative, or no correlation depending on the study. Furthermore, studies differed in whether cortisol variability or levels were found to be related to aggression. The most consistent finding across the studies was elevated testosterone levels, with 10 of 15 studies demonstrating this finding. However, there is some debate about whether it is the sole influence of elevated testosterone or the coupled influence of elevated testosterone and an imbalance in another hormone (e.g., cerebrospinal-fluid 5-hydroxyindoleacetic acid). For example, the findings of Brown et al. (2008) suggest that lower cortisol levels and higher testosterone levels in tandem are linked to greater levels of anger. The take-home message is that the hormonal systems are multifaceted and therefore researchers should strive to model the complexities of these mechanisms.

Glenn and colleagues (2011) followed the recommendation of researchers, such as Brown et al. (2008), and jointly examined the HPA and HPG hormone systems through measurements of cortisol and testosterone. The findings suggest that greater levels of psychopathy were characterized by an increased baseline testosterone-to-cortisol reactivity ratio following a stressor. This testosterone-to-cortisol ratio was viewed as a measure of imbalance between the HPA and HPG axes. In further support of examining the multidimensional aspect of these hormonal systems, Glenn et al. (2011) found that neither testosterone nor cortisol independently predicted psychopathy.

Perhaps the neurochemicals that have received the most attention in relation to antisocial behavior are serotonin and the metabolite associated with this neurochemical, called 5-hydroindoleacetic acid (5-HIAA; Asberg, 1994). A meta-analysis of 20 independent effect sizes (total sample of 921) from studies including adult participants yielded a significant mean effect size ($d = -.45$), supporting lower serotonin metabolite levels in antisocial individuals (Moore, Scarpa, & Raine, 2002). Of interest to this article, Moore et al. (2002) included a moderator variable to determine whether the levels of the metabolite 5-HIAA differed based on the type of offense committed (i.e., violent vs. not violent). The findings support lower levels of the metabolite in the antisocial group, regardless of the type of offense committed. Therefore, lower serotonin metabolite levels appear to be a marker for general antisocial behavior.

In support of the importance of examining biosocial interactions in relation to criminal behavior, Haden and Scarpa (2011) found a significant interaction between noradrenergic functioning and factors related to an individual's rearing environment. The noradrenergic system is related to the body's arousal system (e.g., sleep/wake cycle) and a key neurotransmitter associated with this process is norepinephrine (Stanford, 2001). One of the compounds that results from the processing of norepinephrine is called 3-methoxy-4-hydroxyphenyglycol (MHPG). This inactive compound can be measured and provides a measure of noradrenergic functioning. Specifically, Haden and Scarpa (2011) found that as single predictors, physical punishment, parental rejection and baseline MHPG were not related to aggression; however, the findings support a significant interaction between parental rejection and baseline MHPG. The findings suggest that the relationship between parental rejection and greater aggression was strongest in youth with high baseline MHPG. Therefore, parental rejection is a risk factor for aggression, but particularly in the context of quicker processing of norepinephrine into MHPG.

Summary and Implications

Although the findings reported here were not an exhaustive literature review, it is apparent that a large body of research supports the role of psychophysiological variables in regards to understanding risk and protective factors associated with crime and related constructs. For additional information on the psychophysiology of criminal behavior please refer to Scarpa and Raine (2003, 2006, 2007). It should be noted that, just as no single psychosocial risk or protective factor is sufficient to predict criminal behavior, neither is any single biological factor. In addition, biological influences do not exist in a vacuum and the social context must always be taken into account. Therefore, the recommendation that naturally follows from the current article is that criminologists should strive to create an integrative model of criminality that addresses both the more traditional sociological factors, in addition to the biological correlates identified here. The other articles presented in this special issue will provide reviews of additional domains of the literature that should inform criminologists in their work. By including multiple levels of analysis, criminologists will capture a more holistic picture of crime and criminals, and will be more informed in their understanding of crime.

References

American Psychiatric Association. (1994). *Diagnostic and statistical manual of mental disorders* (4th ed.). Washington, DC: Author.

Andrade, J. T. (2008). The inclusion of antisocial behavior in the construct of psychopathy: A review of the research. *Aggression and Violent Behavior, 13*, 328–335.

Asberg, M. (1994). Monoamine neurotransmitters in human aggressiveness and violence: A selective review. *Criminal Behaviour and Mental Health, 4*, 303–327.

Barr, S. J., Harris, L., Fisher, J. K., & Armstrong, A. H. (2010). Successful reentry: What differentiates successful and unsuccessful parolees? *International Journal of Offender Therapy and Comparative Criminology, 54*, 667–692.

Bauer, A. M., Quas, J. A., & Boyce, W. T. (2002). Associations between physiological reactivity and children's behavior: Advantages of a multisystem approach. *Journal of Developmental Behavioral Pediatrics, 23*, 102–113.

Brennan, P. A., Raine, A., Schulsinger, F., Kirkegaard-Sorensen, L., Knopp, J., Hutchings, B., . . . Mednick, S. A. (1997). Psychophysiological protective factors for male subjects at high risk for criminal behavior. *American Journal of Psychiatry, 154*, 853–855.

Brown, G. L., McGarvey, E. L., Shirtcliff, E. A., Keller, A., Granger, D. A., & Flavin, K. (2008). Salivary cortisol, dehydroepiandrosterone, and testosterone interrelationships in healthy young males: A pilot study with implications for studies of aggressive behavior. *Psychiatry Research, 159*, 67–76.

Bufkin, J. L., & Luttrell, V. R. (2005). Neuroimaging studies of aggression and violent behavior: Current findings and implications for criminology and criminal justice. *Trauma, Violence, & Abuse, 6*, 176–191.

Cacioppo, J. T., Tassinary, L. G., & Bernston, G. G. (2000). Psychophysiological science. In J. T. Cacioppo, L. G. Tassinary, & G. G. Bernston (Eds.), *Handbook of psychophysiology* (2nd ed., pp. 3–23). New York, NY: Cambridge University Press.

Cacioppo, J. T., Tassinary, L. G., & Bernston, G. G. (2007). Psychophysiological science: Interdisciplinary approaches to classic questions about the mind. In J. T. Cacioppo, L. G. Tassinary, & G. G. Bernston (Eds.), *Handbook of psychophysiology* (3rd ed., pp. 3–23). New York, NY: Cambridge University Press.

Choi, M. H., Lee, S. J., Yang, J. W., Kim, J. H., Choi, J. H., Kim, H. S., . . . Chung, S. C. (2011). An analysis of the correlation between young males' personal aggression and skin conductance levels during exposure to aggression images. *Psychiatry Research, 186*, 441–442.

Cleckley, H. (1976). *The mask of sanity*. St Louis, MO: Mosby.

Day, C., Kowalenko, S., Ellis, M., Dawe, S., Harnett, P., & Scott, S. (2011). The helping families programme: A new parenting intervention for children with severe and persistent conduct problems. *Child and Adolescent Mental Health, 16*, 167–171.

Eisermann, K. (1992). Long-term heart rate responses to social stress in wild European rabbits: Predominant effect of rank position. *Physiology and Behavior, 52*, 33–36.

Eysenck, H. J. (1997). Personality and the biosocial model of antisocial and criminal behavior. In A. Raine, P. Brennan, D. P. Farrington, & S. A. Mednick (Eds.), *Biosocial bases of violence* (pp. 21–38). New York, NY: Plenum.

Farrington, D. P. (1997). The relationship between low resting heart rate and violence. In A. Raine, P. A. Brennan, D. P. Farrington, & S. A. Mednick (Eds.), *Biosocial bases of violence* (pp. 89–106). New York, NY: Plenum.

Fung, M. T., Raine, A., Loeber, R., Lynam, D. R., Steinhauer, S. R., Venables, P. H., & Stouthamer-Loeber, M. (2005). Reduced electrodermal activity in psychopathy-prone adolescents. *Journal of Abnormal Psychology, 114*, 187–196.

Glenn, A. L., Raine, A., & Schug, R. A. (2009). The neural correlates of moral decision-making in psychopathy. *Molecular Psychiatry, 14*, 5–9.

Glenn, A. L., Raine, A., Schug, R. A., Gao, Y., & Granger, D. A. (2011). Increased testosterone-to-cortisol ratio in psychopathy. *Journal of Abnormal Psychology, 120*, 389–399.

Haden, S. C., & Scarpa, A. (2011). The interactive roles of parental rejection and noradrenergic activation in at-risk youth. In C. Quin & S. Tawse (Eds.), *Handbook of aggressive behavior research* (pp. 397–415). New York, NY: Nova Science.

Hare, D. (2003). *Hare Psychopathy Checklist-Revised (PCL-R)* (2nd ed.). Toronto, Ontario, Canada: Multi-Health Systems.

Kreibig, S. D. (2010). Autonomic nervous system activity in emotion: A review. *Biological Psychology, 84*, 394–421.

Langan, P. A., & Levin, D. J. (2002). *Recidivism of prisoners released in 1994*. Washington, DC: Bureau of Justice Statistics.

Lorber, M. F. (2004). Psychophysiology of aggression, psychopathy, and conduct problems: A meta-analysis. *Psychological Bulletin, 130*, 531–552.

Lovallo, W. R., & Thomas, T. L. (2000). Stress hormones in psychophysiological research: Emotional, behavioral, and cognitive implications. In J. T. Cacioppo, L. G. Tassinar, & G. G. Bernston (Eds.), *Handbook of psychophysiology* (2nd ed, pp. 342–367). New York, NY: Cambridge University Press.

Lynam, D. R. (1997). Pursuing the psychopath: Capturing the fledgling psychopath in a nomological net. *Journal of Abnormal Psychology, 106*, 425–438.

Maliphant, R., Hume, F., & Furnham, A. (1990). Autonomic nervous system (ANS) activity, personality characteristics, and disruptive behaviours in girls. *Journal of Child Psychology and Psychiatry and Allied Disciplines, 31*, 619–628.

Matson, C. T. (2010). *Criminal victimization in the United States, 2007—Statistical tables*. Washington, DC: Bureau of Justice Statistics.

McGuire, J. (2004). *Understanding psychology and crime: Perspectives on theory and action*. Berkshire, UK: Open University Press.

Mednick, S. A. (1977). A bio-social theory of the learning of law-abiding behavior. In S. A. Mednick & K. O. Christiansen (Eds.), *Biosocial basis of criminal behavior*. New York, NY: Gardner Press.

Moffitt, T. E., & Caspi, A. (2001). Childhood predictors of differentiate life-course persistent and adolescent limited pathways among males and females. *Development and Psychopathology, 13*, 355–375.

Moore, T. M., Scarpa, A., & Raine, A. (2002). A meta-analysis of serotonin metabolite 5-HIAA and antisocial behavior. *Aggressive Behavior, 28*, 299–316.

Oritz, J., & Raine, A. (2004). Heart rate level and antisocial behavior in children and adolescents: A meta-analysis. *Journal of the American Academy of Child and Adolescent Psychiatry, 43*, 154–162.

Raine, A. (1993). *The psychopathology of crime: Criminal behavior as a clinical disorder*. San Diego, CA: Academic Press.

Raine, A. (2002). Annotation: The role of prefrontal deficits, low autonomic arousal, and early health factors in the development of antisocial and aggressive behavior in children. *Journal of Child Psychology and Psychiatry, 43*, 417–434.

Raine, A. (2002). Biosocial studies of antisocial and violent behavior in children and adults: A review. *Journal of Abnormal Child Psychology, 30*, 311–326.

Raine, A. (2005). The interaction of biological and social measures in the explanation of antisocial and violent behaviors. In D. M. Stoff & E. J. Susman (Eds.), *Developmental psychobiology of aggression* (pp. 13–42). New York, NY: Cambridge University Press.

Raine, A., Brennan, P. A., & Farrington, D. (1997). Biosocial bases of violence: Conceptual and theoretical issues. In A. Raine, P. A. Brennan, D. P. Farrington, & S. A. Mednick (Eds.), *Biosocial bases of violence* (pp. 1–20). New York, NY: Plenum Press.

Raine, A., Lencz, T., Bihrle, S., LaCasse, L., & Colletti, P. (2000). Reduced prefrontal gray matter volume and reduced autonomic activity in antisocial personality disorder. *Archives of General Psychiatry, 57*, 119–127.

Raine, A., & Venables, P. H. (1981). Classical conditioning and socialization: A biosocial interaction. *Personality and Individual Differences, 2*, 273–283.

Raine, A., & Venables, P. H. (1984). Tonic heart rate levels, social class and antisocial behaviour in adolescents. *Biological Psychology, 18*, 123–132.

Raine, A., Venables, P. H., & Mednick, S. A. (1997). Low resting heart rate at age 3 years predisposes to aggression at age 11 years: Findings from the Mauritius Joint Child Health Project. *Journal of the American Academy of Child and Adolescent Psychiatry, 36*, 1457–1464.

Raine, A., Venables, P. H., & Williams, M. (1990). Relationship between CNS and ANA measures of arousal at age 15 and criminality at age 24. *Archives of General Psychiatry, 47*, 1003–1007.

Raine, A., Venables, P. H., & Williams, M. (1995). High autonomic arousal and electrodermal orienting at age 15 years as protective factors against criminal behavior at age 29 years. *American Journal of Psychiatry, 152*, 1595–1600.

Raine, A., & Yang, Y. (2006). The anatomical bases of psychopathy: A review of brain imaging findings. In C. J. Patrick (Ed.), *Handbook of psychopathy* (pp. 278–295). New York, NY: Guilford.

Scarpa, A., Haden, S. C., & Tanaka, A. (2010). Being hot-tempered: Autonomic, emotional, and behavioral distinctions between childhood reactive and proactive aggression. *Biological Psychology, 84*, 488–496.

Scarpa, A., & Raine, A. (2003). The psychophysiology of antisocial behavior: Interactions with environmental experiences. In A. Walsh & L. Ellis (Eds.), *Biosocial criminology: Challenging environmentalism's supremacy* (pp. 209–226). New York, NY: Nova Science.

Scarpa, A., & Raine, A. (2006). The psychophysiology of human antisocial behavior. In R. J. Nelson (Ed.), *Biology of aggression* (pp. 447–462). Oxford, UK: Oxford University Press.

Scarpa, A., & Raine, A. (2007). Biosocial bases of violence. In D. J. Flannery, A. T. Vazsonyi, & I. Waldman (Eds.), *The Cambridge handbook of violent behavior* (pp. 447–462). Cambridge, UK: Cambridge University Press.

Scarpa, A., Tanaka, A., & Haden, S. C. (2008). Biosocial bases of reactive and proactive aggression: The roles of community violence exposure and heart rate. *Journal of Community Psychology, 36*, 969–988.

Scarpa, A., & Ollendick, T. H. (2003). Community violence exposure in a young adult sample: III. Psychophysiology and victimization interact to affect risk for aggression. *Journal of Community Psychology, 31*, 321–338.

Stanford, S. C. (2001). Noradrenaline. In R. A. Webster (Ed.), *Neurotransmitters, drugs, and brain function* (pp. 163–186). London, UK: Wiley.

Ulmer, J. T. (2001). Intermediate sanctions: A comparative analysis of the probability and severity of recidivism. *Sociological Inquiry, 71*, 164–193.

Venables, P. H. (1987). Autonomic and central nervous system factors in criminal behavior. In S. A. Mednick, T. E. Moffitt, & S. Stack (Eds.), *The causes of crime: New biological approaches* (pp. 110–136). New York, NY: Cambridge University Press.

Warr, M. (2002). *Companions in crime: The social aspects of criminal conduct*. New York, NY: Cambridge University Press.

Wilson, L. C., & Scarpa, A. (2011). The link between sensation seeking and aggression: A meta-analytic review. *Aggressive Behavior, 37*, 81–90.

Yang, Y., Raine, A., Colletti, P., Toga, A. W., & Narr, K. L. (2009). Abnormal temporal and prefrontal cortical gray matter thinning in psychopaths. *Molecular Psychiatry, 14*, 561–562.

Ziherl, S., Travnik, Z. C., Plesnicar, B. K., Tomori, M., & Zalar, B. (2007). Trait aggression and hostility in recovered alcoholics. *European Addiction Research, 13*, 89–93.

/// REVIEW QUESTIONS

1. What do previous studies show regarding resting heart rates between antisocial versus non-antisocial individuals?
2. What do previous studies show regarding skin conductance levels and their link to aggression, conduct problems and other mental or behavioral complications, including criminality?
3. What are the conclusions from neuroimaging studies regarding the structures or regions of the brain that, when trauma has occurred, are key in predicting future antisocial or criminal behavior?
4. What are the findings regarding cortisol and testosterone levels in predicting aggression? What do studies show regarding the levels of neurotransmitters, such as serotonin and dopamine, on criminality?

READING /// 11

In this selection, Jean Marie McGloin, Travis Pratt, and Alex Piquero present a study that examines the nature of the effects of maternal cigarette smoking during pregnancy. They point out the problems of previous studies—namely, concentrating on measures that are not directly based on neuropsychological problems but rather on IQ tests. Furthermore, they base their study on a highly respected and influential model of criminal development presented by Terrie Moffitt, who claimed that the most serious, chronic offenders are those that experience both a disadvantaged environment (bad neighborhood, bad parenting, etc.) and early neuropsychological problems (due to maternal cigarette smoking or intake of other toxins, pregnancy or delivery complications, etc.). Although other studies have supported Moffitt's developmental model (which will be discussed at length in Section XI), this may be the only study that has directly tested and supported her model. While reading this selection, consider that what happens in the womb may have an effect on what happens much later in life.

While reading this piece, consider the following points:

- The distinction of the two types of offenders in Moffitt's theoretical framework as well as what causes each type
- The authors' measure of neuropsychological deficit and their rationale for using that measure
- Any major finding(s) of this study that are inconsistent with Moffitt's theoretical predictions and the potential explanation(s) the authors present for these finding(s)

SOURCE: Jean Marie McGloin, Travis C. Pratt, and Alex R. Piquero, "A Life-Course Analysis of the Criminogenic Effects of Maternal Cigarette Smoking during Pregnancy: A Research Note on the Mediating Impact of Neuropsychological Deficit," *Journal of Research in Crime and Delinquency* 42, no. 4 (2006): 412–26.

A Life-Course Analysis of the Criminogenic Effects of Maternal Cigarette Smoking during Pregnancy

A Research Note on the Mediating Impact of Neuropsychological Deficit

Jean Marie McGloin, Travis C. Pratt, and Alex R. Piquero

Research from a variety of disciplines indicates that maternal cigarette smoking (MCS) during pregnancy is associated with an array of problematic behavioral outcomes in offspring (Cornelius and Day 2000; Wakschlag et al. 2002). Of particular interest to criminologists, this may include such traditional criminological outcomes as violent, persistent, and early-onset offending (Brennan, Grekin, and Mednick 1999; Gibson, Piquero, and Tibbetts 2000; Rasanen et al. 1999). Furthermore, Cotton's (1994) assertion that 20 to 25 percent of pregnant women who smoke continue to do so throughout their pregnancies suggests that this risk factor is worthy of criminologists' attention.

Nevertheless, the question of how MCS risk manifests into criminal behavior still remains. On one hand, some studies have used Moffitt's (1993) developmental taxonomy as a framework for empirical investigation (see Gibson et al. 2000; Gibson and Tibbetts 2000; Piquero et al. 2002). Indeed, MCS fits nicely within the battery of the various congenital risks that serve as the hypothesized roots of life-course-persistent (LCP) offending. Even so, previous investigations that have drawn on Moffitt's framework have not truly tested the developmental pathway specified by her theory. Instead, research has largely focused on the direct relationship between MCS and various measures of LCP offending, which treat MCS as a proxy for neuropsychological deficit (Gibson et al. 2000; Gibson and Tibbetts 2000; Piquero et al. 2002).

The problem with this approach is that Moffitt (1993) did not suggest that MCS is a measure of neuropsychological deficit but rather that MCS is a precursor to such deficits. She specified a mediating relationship in which congenital risks, such as MCS, increase the likelihood of neuropsychological deficits occurring in children, which in turn increase the probability that such youths will eventually engage in LCP offending. Thus, empirical research has yet to be conducted that addresses whether the relationship between MCS and LCP offending is mediated by more direct measures of neuropsychological deficit.

In this research, we addressed this void by determining whether neuropsychological deficit does in fact mediate the connection between MCS and LCP offending. We assessed this relationship while using a number of controls for other early biological risk factors (e.g., low birth weight [LBW]) as well as indicators of social disadvantage at multiple points in time. Our broader purpose, therefore, was to determine whether criminologists should continue to think about MCS in the context of theories that specify neuropsychological deficits—as opposed to, say, parenting effects (i.e., is it simply that mothers who smoke while pregnant also turn out to be inept at shaping prosocial behavior in their kids?)—as a key predictor of criminal behavior.

Despite this goal, we recognize that MCS is, by any reasonable estimation, a distal criminogenic risk factor. To be sure, other variables, such as self-control (Pratt and Cullen 2000), deviant peer influences, and antisocial attitudes (Andrews and Bonta 2001), have all been found to consistently predict antisocial behavior more consistently and robustly than MCS (Wakschlag et al. 2002). Nevertheless, the MCS-crime link provides criminologists with a unique opportunity to examine the relative validity of some of the claims made by the dominant theoretical traditions in the field. Indeed, a complete explanation of the causal processes underlying the link between MCS and crime or deviance may end up telling us a lot about the compatibility, or lack thereof, of theories that specify biological versus social-psychological causes of crime. Again, we took an initial first step in this process by testing the degree to which the link between MCS and LCP offending is mediated by measures of neuropsychological deficit.

Theoretical Context

Moffitt (1993) argued that two offending trajectories with distinct etiologies are obscured within the aggregate age-crime curve. Individuals on the LCP pathway begin offending at an early age and continue throughout the life course, engaging in an array of deviance, including criminal behavior. Individuals on the adolescence-limited trajectory instead start offending at a relatively older age, have a transitory offending time frame typically defined by minor rebellious offending, and desist on the transition to adulthood (Moffitt 1993; Piquero 2000; Piquero et al. 1999). LCP offending occurs in a small proportion of the population and develops out of an evocative interaction between neuropsychological deficits and a disadvantaged environment. Adolescence-limited offending, in contrast, is found in the majority of the population and develops out of social mimicry during the maturational gap of adolescence. Accordingly, when criminologists concentrate on MCS as a risk factor, they typically do so with a focus on the LCP etiological pathway.

According to Moffitt (1993), developmental disturbances of the fetal brain, which can be caused by various pre- and perinatal risk factors, such as exposure to toxins, poor maternal nutrition, and MCS, produce deficits in the central nervous system. Lynam, Moffitt, and Stouthamer-Loeber (1993) stated that "deficits in the neuropsychological abilities referred to as 'executive functions' interfere with a person's ability to monitor and control his or her own behavior" (p. 188). In short, the hypothesis is that congenital, and therefore biological, risks produce neuropsychological deficits, which can manifest behaviorally in a bad temperament and, later, criminal behavior.

Indeed, neuropsychological deficit, which has also been measured through proxies such as low cognitive ability (Denno 1990; Moffitt 1990), has emerged as an important discriminating factor between offenders and nonoffenders (see Hirschi and Hindelang 1977; Wolfgang, Figlio, and Sellin 1972) as well as a predictor of more severe markers of offending within criminal populations (McGloin and Pratt 2003; Piquero and White 2003). Moreover, despite criticism about the validity of articulating only two trajectories (Nagin, Farrington, and Moffitt 1995; White, Bates, and Buyske 2001), the main hypothesis that offenders, especially serious offenders, suffer from neuropsychological and/or biological deficits is well supported empirically (Moffitt, Lynam, and Silva 1994; Piquero 2001; Piquero and White 2003).

Even so, in studying the link between MCS and crime or deviance, existing criminological research has used MCS as a proxy of neuropsychological deficit rather than as a precursor to it. For example, Gibson et al. (2000) found a significant relationship between MCS and age at first police contact net of statistical controls,[1] a finding that was echoed by Gibson and Tibbetts[2] (2000) and by Piquero et al. (2002). Although these studies offered some support for the association between MCS and LCP offending, none of them specified the purported mediating mechanism between MCS and neuropsychological deficit.

A substantial gap in the research therefore continues to exist. To be sure, the precise mechanism whereby MCS operates as a criminogenic risk factor is still unknown. Moffitt (1993) argued that neuropsychological deficit is a result of some injury to, or disturbance of, the proper fetal developmental process. She did not suggest that such risks, in this case MCS during pregnancy, should themselves be treated as a proxy for minimal brain dysfunction but rather that they are assumed to represent, among others, the primary causes of neuropsychological deficits. Accordingly, this research explicitly examined the mechanism whereby MCS produces a criminogenic risk (i.e., through its effect on neuropsychological deficits) for LCP offending.

Methods

Data

Data for this project came from both the original Philadelphia portion of the National Collaborative Perinatal Project (NCPP) and a recent criminal history search conducted on the original cohort of 987 youths born to African American mothers who participated in the NCPP (see Piquero et al. 2002). Moffitt (1997) considered the NCPP data to be particularly well suited to analyses addressing issues associated with neuropsychological deficits, thereby making the use of the NCPP particularly relevant for the questions under investigation in this study. Given the focus on LCP offending, analyses were conducted on the offender subsample (n = 220) of the original 987 subjects.[3]

In the early 1980s, information was collected related to school functioning and criminal histories, including all police contacts through age 17 (see Denno 1990).[4] Adult criminal history data, in the form of convictions, are available through age 36 for those sample members born into the 1962 cohort and through age 39 for those born into the 1959 cohort.[5] Some might suggest that conviction data from the adult follow-up are not as reliable as self-report, police contact, or arrest data. All sources of criminal justice data, however, are subject to limitations (see Hindelang et al. 1981; Lauritsen 1998; Wolfgang et al. 1972), and extant theory does not anticipate that certain relationships would be found only when analyzing certain types of outcome data.[6] Moreover, many empirical investigations have used various sources of criminal history data, including self-report and conviction data (Farrington et al. 1996; Ge, Donnellan, and Wenk 2001; Moffitt et al. 1994). To this end, Farrington (1989) showed that self-reports and official conviction data produce "comparable and complementary results on such important topics as prevalence, continuity, versatility, and specialization in different types of offenses" (p. 418).[7]

Dependent Variable

LCP offending. Individuals who exhibited an early onset (prior to age 14) and accumulated at least two adult convictions during the follow-up period (after age 18) were coded 1, and all other sample members were coded 0 (the same approach with these data was taken by Gibson et al. 2000, Gibson and Tibbetts 2000, McGloin and Pratt 2003, Piquero 2001, and Tibbetts and Piquero 1999; see also Piquero and White 2003).

Independent Variables

Neuropsychological deficit. To measure neuropsychological deficit, we used the total battery score of the California Achievement Test (CAT), a measure that has also been used in past criminological research (see Ge et al. 2001; McGloin and Pratt 2003; Piquero and White 2003). The CAT yields total scores in the academic domain of reading, arithmetic, and language (Tiegs and Clark 1970: 14). The total battery score for Grades 7 and 8 (ages 12 to 14), which we used in this study, reflects a student's standing in terms of total achievement level. The CAT is, in general, highly praised in terms of its validity, comprehensive test and interpretive materials, reliability, and standardization procedure (Denno 1990:173).[8]

We used the CAT because we recognized the potential conceptual, empirical, and ideological concerns with using IQ to assess neuropsychological functioning within a sample of economically disadvantaged African American youth. Moreover, Moffitt (1990) argued that the array of cognitive tests is so highly interrelated that interchanging them is acceptable. One could also argue that research on LCP offending should consider measures other than IQ to establish convergent validity (McGloin and Pratt 2003). This is especially true with this data set, which has been subject to much empirical investigation under Moffitt's (1993) framework and has largely relied on IQ as the measure of neuropsychological deficit. Nevertheless, for those who prefer IQ as a measure, we also estimated the models with the verbal subscale of the Wechsler Intelligence Scale for Children (WISC), which was assessed at ages 7 to 8.[9]

Sex. Sex was coded 1 for male and 2 for female. Of these 220 offenders, approximately 70 percent were male.

Low birth weight. LBW was associated with MCS and has been shown to have a relationship with criminal outcomes (see Gibson et al. 2000; McGloin and Pratt 2003; Tibbetts and Piquero 1999). Following designation made by the World Health Organization and used in past research, LBW is a dichotomous variable indicating its presence (1) or absence (0). The cutoff for LBW is five pounds, eight ounces.[10] Of the 220 offenders, 19 percent were LBW.

Risk at birth. Our risk-at-birth composite was a summed index of three dichotomous items measured at birth from the mother: birth complications, marital status, and age at childbirth. Following Farrington and Loeber (2000), these variables were dichotomized to reflect the risk-factor paradigm. Consistent with Nagin, Farrington, and Pogarsky (1997), mother's age at childbirth was coded 0 (18 and older) or 1 (under 18), and mother's marital status at childbirth was coded 0 (married) or 1 (single).

Finally, birth complications were coded 0 (for no birth complications during pregnancy) or 1 (for one or more birth complications during pregnancy). All of these items have been considered indicators of maternal disadvantage and have been related to important offspring problems, including crime (see Farrington and Loeber 2000; Raine 1993).

Risk at age 7. Socioeconomic status was originally measured in a standardized method by all sites of the NCPP with a single-item score, ranging from 0 to 100, that was a composite measure of three indicators collected at age 7 for each child: education of the head of the household, income of the head of the household, and occupation of the head of the household (Myrianthopoulos and French 1968). Those individuals scoring in the lowest 25th percentile (very low socioeconomic status) were coded 1, and all others were coded 0.

Maternal cigarette smoking. MCS was assessed during pregnancy. Mothers were asked to self-report the average number of cigarettes they smoked each day. Although this variable was originally coded continuously, we followed the coding procedure outlined by Brennan et al. (1999) and replicated by others: 0, 1 to 2, 3 to 10, 11 to 20, and 20 or more. This measure, then, assessed a potential dose-response relationship.[11]

Analytic Strategy

The analysis focused on determining whether neuropsychological deficit mediates the relationship between MCS and LCP offending. Given the dichotomous dependent variable of LCP offending, the main analyses estimated the multivariate models via logistic regression techniques. To establish a mediating relationship, three criteria must be satisfied. First, MCS must predict the mediating mechanism of interest, neuropsychological deficit. Second, it must be established that MCS in fact predicts LCP offending. Finally, the inclusion of the potential mediator, neuropsychological deficit, should eliminate much (if not all) of the significance of MCS in the multivariate model.

With this in mind, the first step in the analysis determined whether MCS predicted neuropsychological deficit, net of statistical controls. This analysis relied on ordinary least squares regression techniques, given the continuous measure of neuropsychological deficit. Next, three models were estimated for the prediction of LCP offending. Model 1 included the MCS measure along with the control variables to gauge the relationship between MCS and LCP offending. Model 2 included the measure of neuropsychological deficit to determine if it stripped MCS of its significance and acted as a mediator. Finally, model 3 included the composite of risk at age 7, which was added separately from the other controls given its temporal distinction.

Table 1 • Slopes and Standard Errors for the Ordinary Least Squares Regression Model Predicting Neuropsychological Deficit (n = 220)

Variable	B	SE
Sex	1.022	2.972
Low birth weight	−2.599	3.642
Risk at birth	2.736	1.660
Maternal cigarette smoking	−2.661**	1.161
Constant	20.399	
F	2.406	
R^2	.044	

**$p < .05$.

Results

Table 1 presents the results from the ordinary least squares regression model predicting neuropsychological deficit. The findings suggest that the offspring of mothers who smoked (many) cigarettes during pregnancy were more likely to experience lower scores on the CAT.[12]

For the next step in the analysis, three logistic regression models predict LCP offending. Model 1 revealed that MCS did predict LCP offending where estimated (not shown), net of statistical controls.[13] In particular, it was the most severe category of smoking that held significance: The offspring of mothers who smoked 20 or more cigarettes per day, compared with mothers who did not smoke, were significantly more likely to manifest LCP offending. This suggests that the damage of MCS exists on a spectrum. Others have also confirmed the importance of allowing for a potential dose-response relationship, finding a growing risk for a certain type of offending as the number of cigarettes a mother smoked during pregnancy increased (Brennan et al. 1999; Gibson et al. 2000; Piquero et al. 2002).

Model 2 included the CAT variable to determine whether introducing an indicator of neuropsychological deficit mediated the effect of the MCS measure. Although the CAT emerged as a significant predictor of LCP offending, it did not affect the significance level of MCS. Thus, neuropsychological deficit did not appear to mediate the relationship between MCS and LCP offending. The same conclusion was reached even with the inclusion of risk at age 7 in model 3, which showed that adding this additional risk factor to the model did not eliminate the significance of the MCS variable.

Discussion

The primary focus of this research was to determine the mechanism whereby MCS manifests itself as a criminogenic risk factor. Despite the fact that previous research has used Moffitt's (1993) theoretical framework, no study has specified this mediating mechanism articulated by Moffitt. The results presented here show that although MCS is a significant precursor to neuropsychological deficit and that neuropsychological deficit significantly predicts LCP offending, this is not the mediating mechanism at work in the relationship between MCS and LCP offending. Indeed, a significant relationship remains between MCS and LCP offending that operates independent of neuropsychological dysfunction.

This finding, although somewhat inconsistent with Moffitt's (1993) theoretical predictions, is not necessarily inconsistent with earlier empirical work. Previous research in this area that has used IQ as a control variable has shown that MCS retained its ability to predict criminal outcomes (Gibson et al. 2000; Piquero et al. 2002). Thus, these models provided a hint that Moffitt's theoretical framework was not explaining the nature of the relationship between MCS and LCP offending. The findings offered here, though in a decidedly more explicit fashion, suggest that the risk of MCS does not operate (solely) through the indirect pathway of neuropsychological deficit. At a minimum, these results call into question using an MCS measure as a proxy for neuropsychological deficit.

The question now, therefore, concerns what is in fact the mediating mechanism between MCS and LCP offending. Accordingly, there are two primary potential mediators that should be addressed in future research. First, parenting may play an important role in explaining the empirical relationship between MCS and offending. A mother who smokes cigarettes during pregnancy, particularly a "high-rate" smoker, may illustrate a "foreshadowing" propensity to put her immediate, hedonistic tendencies and desires before long-term considerations for her child's health. Perhaps it is not the toxins inherent to cigarettes that are so damaging to a child (although such toxins certainly provide no known benefit). Rather, it may be that smoking is predictive of poor parenting practices. To be sure, a variety of criminological perspectives highlight the importance of parenting. For example, social learning theorists argue that parents who serve as models of deviance and/or create reinforcement contingencies supportive of such behavior can essentially mold a delinquent child (Akers 1998). Others note that the probability of delinquency increases when parents fail to consistently provide their children with affirming social support (Cullen 1994; Wright and Cullen 2001). Control perspectives, from Hirschi's (1969) original social-bond perspective to Gottfredson and Hirschi's (1990) self-control theory, also rely heavily on the notion of parental efficacy. Although some researchers have highlighted this potential pathway (Gibson et al. 2000), it still remains a hypothesized rather than an empirically confirmed developmental process.

Second, MCS is a known risk for temperamental and conduct problems in childhood. For example, Sadowski and Parish (2005) noted that MCS consistently predicts attention-deficit hyperactivity disorder (ADHD), even when controlling for other important factors, such as maternal socioeconomic status. When combined with the finding that ADHD predicts delinquency (Pratt et al. 2002), mainly through its influence on self-control (Unnever, Cullen, and Pratt 2003), it becomes clear that this is another potential mediating pathway. It is worth noting that these two mediating mechanisms may also act in concert. Given that low self-control is endogenous to ADHD, and that Gottfredson and Hirschi (1990) allowed for variation in temperament, which makes some youth more vulnerable to ineffective parenting practices, a child born to a mother who engages in MCS may have conduct problems and be subject to poor parenting practices. Thus, future research should also investigate a potential interaction between these two pathways.

It is also worth noting a potential genetic explanation, in which the connection between MCS and ADHD in offspring may reflect inherited biological predispositions. For example, recent research suggests that ADHD is highly heritable, with some estimates claiming that up to 80 percent of the variation in the disorder is genetic or biological (see the discussion by Pratt et al. 2002). Thus, the link between MCS and ADHD may potentially reflect mothers who have ADHD and engage in excessive smoking as self-medication. Given the recent focus on genetics with regard to self-control (Wright and Beaver 2005), it would also be wise to consider the role of heredity as another pathway through which the criminogenic effects of MCS may operate.

In the end, though the scope of the present study was modest, our results highlight some important issues. In particular, it should be recognized that the purported link between MCS and LCP offending has been embedded within the larger assumption that damage to a developing fetus is what starts this developmental pathway. The findings presented here, however, question this assumption and instead indicate that our attention should shift elsewhere, perhaps to parenting and/or self-control. Indeed, it seems that the criminogenic risk of MCS, which was supposedly "owned" by one theory, may belong under the heading of another.

Notes

1. This association disappeared in the female subsample with controls, but Gibson et al. argued that this may have been due to the small sample size, because the odds ratio for the women was actually larger than that for the men.

2. Gibson and Tibbetts (2000) did not simply specify a direct relationship. They also included an interaction term with MCS and the absence of a father or husband in the household to specify the neuropsychological deficit and disadvantage environment interaction of which Moffitt wrote.

3. This subsample was defined as those individuals who had at least one official police contact by the age of 18 years.

4. *Police contact* refers to whether a juvenile had contact with police that resulted in either an official arrest or a remedial disposition. This measure of juvenile offending has also been used in the Philadelphia (see Wolfgang et al. 1972; Tracy, Wolfgang, and Figlio 1990) and Racine (see Shannon 1991) cohort studies. More generally, police contacts are positively and moderately correlated with both self-reported offending estimates and other official records of offending such as arrests and convictions (Hindelang, Hirschi, and Weis 1981). Furthermore, Smith and Gartin (1989) noted that "among the domain of official measures, police contacts provide a closer approximation of the true level of offending than arrests or convictions" (p. 102).

5. The criminal history data included offenses committed and officially processed in Philadelphia only. As was the case in another Philadelphia birth cohort study, Tracy and Kempf-Leonard (1996) knew that the sample members were residents of Philadelphia through age 17 but had to assume that the same was true for the adult period as well. In addition, data for women may have been compromised by the fact that women may have married and changed their surnames. Although the original names and social security numbers of the sample subjects were known in the present study, several women changed both. Thus, the analysis may have underestimated the criminal offending of female sample members.

6. Recall that Moffitt et al. (1994) found neuropsychological scores to be related to police, self-report, and court records in very similar ways.

7. As a practical matter, the city of Philadelphia, following the Pennsylvania Crime Code, expunges all arrests from the criminal history database for all of its citizens if the arrests do not lead to convictions within three years; therefore, the use of arrest data would also be limited in the sense that a true arrest for an offense may have in fact occurred but was deleted from the criminal history database because of the three-year rule.

8. Our use of the CAT as a proxy for neuropsychological deficit, although not necessarily ideal (relative to a more direct

measure), is consistent with Moffitt's (1990) view that measures such as the CAT serve as adequate proxies for neuropsychological deficit. Our interest in this research, therefore, was to be as consistent as possible to Moffitt's work, because we were assessing the relative merits of her explanation of the relationship between MCS and crime or delinquency.

9. It is true that measures of executive functioning would also capture neuropsychological deficit. Even so, Moffitt (1990) argued strongly that verbal IQ is a valid measure of neuropsychological deficit.

10. Because LBW is endogenous to MCS, some may view its inclusion in the models as unnecessary. The two variables did not, however, evidence multicollinearity, and failing to include LBW could have overestimated the impact of MCS. Thus, we erred on the conservative side and retained this measure. Additional analyses illustrated that removing LBW did not substantively alter the findings.

11. There were no indications of multicollinearity among the independent variables.

12. When we reestimated this model with the entire sample ($N = 987$), MCS still predicted neuropsychological deficit. It also was a significant predictor when using the WISC measure rather than the CAT.

13. Given the limited regressor space provided by the relatively small sample size ($n = 220$) with fully specified models, we should note that the significance levels for the MCS variable (the category of 20 or more cigarettes per day) were consistently at $p = .064$, below the .10 cutoff but above the "industry standard" of .05. Because p-level cutoff points are both theoretically arbitrary and highly dependent on sample size (Tabachnick and Fidell 2001), we maintain that the significance levels reported here indicate a substantively meaningful relationship in the multivariate models.

References

Akers, Ronald L. 1998. *Social Learning and Social Structure: A General Theory of Crime and Deviance.* Boston: Northeastern University Press.

Andrews, D. A., and James Bonta. 2001. *The Psychology of Criminal Conduct.* 3rd ed. Cincinnati, OH: Anderson.

Brennan, Patricia A., Emily R. Grekin, and Sarnoff Mednick. 1999. "Maternal Cigarette Smoking during Pregnancy and Adult Male Criminal Outcomes." *Archives of General Psychiatry* 56:215–19.

Cornelius, Marie D., and Nancy Day. 2000. "The Effects of Tobacco Use during and after Pregnancy on Exposed Children." *Alcohol Research and Health* 24:242–49.

Cotton, P. 1994. "Smoking Cigarettes May Do Developing Fetus More Harm Than Ingesting Cocaine, Some Experts Say." *JAMA* 271:576–77.

Cullen, Francis T. 1994. "Social Support as an Organizing Concept for Criminology: Presidential Address to the Academy of Criminal Justice Sciences." *Justice Quarterly* 11:527–59.

Denno, Deborah J. 1990. *Biology and Violence.* Cambridge, UK: Cambridge University Press.

Farrington, David P. 1989. "Self-Reported and Official Offending from Adolescence to Adulthood." Pp. 399–423 in *Cross-National Research in Self-Reported Crime and Delinquency,* edited by M. W. Klein. Boston: Kluwer Academic.

Farrington, David P., and Rolf Loeber. 2000. "Some Benefits of Dichotomization in Psychiatric and Criminological Research." *Criminal Behaviour and Mental Health* 10:100–22.

Farrington, David P., Rolf Loeber, Magda Stouthamer-Loeber, W. B. Van Kammen, and L. Schmidt. 1996. "Self-Report Delinquency and a Combined Seriousness Scale Based on Boys, Mothers, and Teachers: Concurrent and Predictive Validity." *Criminology* 34:493–517.

Ge, Xiaojia, M. Brent Donnellan, and Ernst Wenk. 2001. "The Development of Persistent Criminal Offending in Males." *Criminal Justice and Behavior* 28:731–55.

Gibson, Chris L., Alex R. Piquero, and Stephen G. Tibbetts. 2000. "Assessing the Relationship between Maternal Cigarette Smoking during Pregnancy and Age at First Police Contact." *Justice Quarterly* 17:519–41.

Gibson, Chris L., and Stephen G. Tibbetts. 2000. "A Biosocial Interaction in Predicting Early Onset of Offending." *Psychological Reports* 86:509–18.

Gottfredson, Michael R., and Travis Hirschi. 1990. *A General Theory of Crime.* Stanford, CA: Stanford University Press.

Hindelang, Michael J., Travis Hirschi, and Joseph Weis. 1981. *Measuring Delinquency.* Beverly Hills, CA: Sage.

Hirschi, Travis. 1969. *Causes of Delinquency.* Berkeley: University of California Press.

Hirschi, Travis, and Michael J. Hindelang. 1977. "Intelligence and Delinquency: A Revisionist Review." *American Sociological Review* 42:571–87.

Lauritsen, Janet L. 1998. "The Age-Crime Debate: Assessing the Limits of Longitudinal Self-Report Data." *Social Forces* 77: 127–55.

Lynam, Donald R., Terrie E. Moffitt, and Magda Stouthamer-Loeber. 1993. "Explaining the Relationship Between IQ and Delinquency: Class, Race, Test Motivation, School Failure or Self-Control?" *Journal of Abnormal Psychology* 102: 187–96.

McGloin, Jean M., and Travis C. Pratt. 2003. "Cognitive Ability and Delinquent Behavior among Inner-City Youth: A Life-Course Analysis of Main, Mediating, and Interaction Effects." *International Journal of Offender Therapy and Comparative Criminology* 47:253–71.

Moffitt, Terrie E. 1990. "The Neuropsychology of Juvenile Delinquency: A Critical Review." Pp. 99–170 in *Crime and Justice: A Review of the Research, Vol. 12,* edited by M. Tonry and N. Morris. Chicago: University of Chicago Press.

———. 1993. "Adolescence-Limited and Life-Course-Persistent Antisocial Behavior: A Developmental Taxonomy." *Psychological Review* 100:674–701.

———. 1997. "Neuropsychology, Antisocial Behavior, and Neighborhood Context." Pp. 116–70 in *Violence,* edited by J. McCord. New York: Cambridge University Press.

Moffitt, Terrie E., Donald Lynam, and Phil A. Silva. 1994. "Neuropsychological Tests Predicting Persistent Male Delinquency." *Criminology* 32:277–300.

Myrianthopoulos, Ntinos C., and K. S. French. 1968. "An Application of the U.S. Bureau of the Census Socioeconomic Index to a Large, Diversified Patient Population." *Social Science Medicine* 2:283–99.

Nagin, Daniel S., David P. Farrington, and Terrie E. Moffitt. 1995. "Life-Course Trajectories of Different Types of Offenders." *Criminology* 33:111–39.

Nagin, Daniel, Daniel P. Farrington, and Greg Pogarsky. 1997. "Adolescent Mothers and the Criminal Behavior of Their Children." *Law and Society Review* 31:137–62.

Piquero, Alex R. 2000. "Frequency, Specialization, and Violence in Offending Careers." *Journal of Research in Crime and Delinquency* 37:392–418.

———. 2001. "Testing Moffitt's Neuropsychological Variation Hypothesis for the Prediction of Life-Course Persistent Offending." *Psychology, Crime and Law* 7:193–215.

Piquero, Alex R., Chris L. Gibson, Stephen G. Tibbetts, Michael G. Turner, and Solomon H. Katz. 2002. "Maternal Cigarette Smoking during Pregnancy and Life Course Persistent Offending." *International Journal of Offender Therapy and Comparative Criminology* 46:231–48.

Piquero, Alex R., Raymond Paternoster, Paul Mazerolle, Robert Brame, and Charles W. Dean. 1999. "Onset Age and Offense Specialization." *Journal of Research in Crime and Delinquency* 36:275–99.

Piquero, Alex R., and Norman A. White. 2003. "On the Relationship between Cognitive Abilities and Life Course-Persistent Offending among a Sample of African Americans: A Longitudinal Test of Moffitt's Hypothesis." *Journal of Criminal Justice* 31:399–409.

Pratt, Travis C., and Francis T. Cullen. 2000. "The Empirical Status of Gottfredson and Hirschi's General Theory of Crime: A Meta-Analysis." *Criminology* 38:931–64.

Pratt, Travis C., Francis T. Cullen, Kristie R. Blevins, Leah Daigle, and James D. Unnever. 2002. "The Relationship of Attention Deficit Hyperactivity Disorder to Crime and Delinquency: A Meta-Analysis." *International Journal of Police Science and Management* 4:344–60.

Raine, Adrian. 1993. *The Psychopathology of Crime.* San Diego, CA: Academic Press.

Rasanen, Pirkko, Helina Hakko, Matti Isohanni, Sheilagh Hodgins, Marjo-Ritta Jarvelin, and Jari Tihonen. 1999. "Maternal Smoking during Pregnancy and Risk of Criminal Behavior among Adult Male Offspring in a Northern Finland 1966 Cohort." *American Journal of Psychiatry* 156:857–62.

Sadowski, Kelly, and Thomas G. Parish. 2005. "Maternal Smoking Contributes to the Development of Childhood ADHD." *Internet Journal of Allied Health Sciences and Practice* 3(1). Available at http://ijahsp.nova.edu/articles/v013num1/sadowski.htm

Shannon, Lyle W. 1991. *Changing Patterns of Delinquency and Crime: A Longitudinal Study in Racine.* Boulder, CO: Westview.

Smith, Douglas A., and Patrick R. Gartin. 1989. "Specifying Specific Deterrence: The Influence of Arrest on Future Criminal Activity." *American Sociological Review* 54:94–105.

Tabachnick, Barbara G., and Linda S. Fidell. 2001. *Using Multivariate Statistics.* 4th ed. Boston: Allyn & Bacon.

Tibbetts, Stephen G., and Alex R. Piquero. 1999. "The Influence of Gender, Low Birth Weight, and Disadvantaged Environment in Predicting Early Onset of Offending: A Test of Moffitt's Interactional Hypothesis." *Criminology* 37:843–77.

Tiegs, Ernest W., and Willis W. Clark. 1970. *Examiner's Manual and Test Coordinator's Handbook: California Achievement Tests.* New York: McGraw-Hill.

Tracy, Paul E., and Kimberley Kempf-Leonard. 1996. *Continuity and Discontinuity in Criminal Careers.* New York: Plenum.

Tracy, Paul E., Marvin E. Wolfgang, and Robert M. Figlio. 1990. *Delinquency Career in Two Birth Cohorts.* New York: Plenum.

Unnever, James D., Francis T. Cullen, and Travis C. Pratt. 2003. "Parental Management, ADHD, and Delinquent Involvement: Reassessing Gottfredson and Hirschi's General Theory." *Justice Quarterly* 20:471–500.

Wakschlag, Lauren S., Kate E. Pickett, Edwin Cook, Neal L. Benowitz, and Bennett Leventhal. 2002. "Maternal Smoking during Pregnancy and Severe Antisocial Behavior on Offspring: A Review." *American Journal of Public Health* 92:966–74.

White, Helene R., Marsha E. Bates, and Steven Buyske. 2001. "Adolescence-Limited versus Persistent Delinquency: Extending Moffitt's Hypothesis into Adulthood." *Journal of Abnormal Psychology* 110:600–09.

Wolfgang, Marvin E., Robert Figlio, and Thorstin Sellin. 1972. *Delinquency in a Birth Cohort.* Chicago: University of Chicago Press.

Wright, John P., and Kevin M. Beaver. 2005. "Do Parents Really Matter in Creating Self-Control in Their Children? A Genetically Informed Test of Gottfredson and Hirschi's Theory of Low Self-Control." *Criminology* 43:1169–1202.

Wright, John Paul, and Francis T. Cullen. 2001. "Parental Efficacy and Delinquent Behavior: Do Control and Support Matter?" *Criminology* 39:677–705.

REVIEW QUESTIONS

1. In terms of Moffitt's theoretical framework, name and briefly describe the two distinct offending trajectories as well as what causes each of them.
2. How did McGloin, Pratt, and Piquero measure neuropsychological deficit? Do you agree that this measure is a valid measure of this concept? Why or why not?
3. One of the major findings of this study is inconsistent with Moffitt's theoretical predictions. What finding is this? What potential explanations do the authors present for this finding?

SECTION VI

Early Social Structure and Strain Theories of Crime

This section will review the development of **anomie** or **strain theory**, starting with early social structure theorists, such as Émile Durkheim, then Robert K. Merton, and on to the most modern versions (e.g., general strain theory). We will also examine the empirical research findings on this perspective, which remains one of the dominant theoretical explanations of criminal behavior today. We will finish by discussing the policy implications of this research.

We'll begin with a review of explanations of criminal conduct that emphasize the differences among varying groups in societies, particularly in the United States. Such differences are easy to see in everyday life, and many theoretical models place the blame for crime on observed inequalities and cultural differences between groups. In contrast to the theories presented in previous sections, social structure theories disregard any biological or psychological variations across individuals. Instead, social structure theories assume that crime is caused by the way societies are structurally organized.

These social structure theories vary in many ways—most notably in what they propose as the primary constructs and processes responsible for causing criminal activity. For example, some structural models emphasize variations in economic or academic success, whereas others focus on differences in cultural norms and values. Still others concentrate on the actual breakdown of the social structure in certain neighborhoods and the resulting social disorganization that occurs from this process, a topic we will reserve for Section VII. Regardless of their differences, all of the theories examined in this section emphasize a common theme: Certain groups of individuals are more likely to break the law because of disadvantages or cultural differences resulting from the way a society is structured.

The most important distinction between these theories and those discussed in previous sections is that they emphasize group differences instead of individual differences. Structural models tend to focus on the macro level of analysis as opposed to the micro level. Therefore, it is not surprising that social structure theories are commonly used to explain the propensity of certain racial or ethnic groups for committing crime as well as the overrepresentation of the lower class in criminal activity.

As you will see, these theoretical frameworks were presented as early as the 1800s and reached prominence in the early to mid-1900s, when the political, cultural, and economic climate of society was most conducive to such explanations. Although social structural models of crime have diminished in popularity in recent decades,[1] there is much validity to their propositions in numerous applications to contemporary society.

Early Theories of Social Structure: Early to Mid-1800s

Most criminological and sociological historians trace the origin of social structure theories to the research done in the early to mid-1800s by a number of European researchers—the most important including Auguste Comte, André-Michel Guerry, and Adolphe Quetelet.[2] It is important to understand why structural theories developed in 19th-century Europe. The Industrial Revolution, defined by most historians as beginning in the mid-1700s and ending in the mid-1800s, was in full swing at the turn of the century, so societies were quickly transitioning from primarily agriculturally based economies to industrial based economies. This transition inevitably brought people from rural farmlands to dense urban cities, resulting in an enormous increase in social problems. These social problems ranged from failure to properly dispose of waste and garbage, to constantly losing children and not being able to find them, to much higher rates of crime (which urban areas continue to show today, as compared to suburban and rural areas).

The problems associated with such fast urbanization, as well as the shift in economics, led to drastic changes in the basic social structures in Europe as well as the United States. At the same time, other types of revolutions were also having an effect. Both the American (1776) and French (1789) Revolutions occurred in the last quarter of the 18th century. These two revolutions, inspired by the Enlightenment movement (see Section II), shared an ideology that rejected tyranny and insisted that people should have a voice in how they were governed. Along with the Industrial Revolution, these political revolutions affected intellectual theorizing on social structures, as well as on crime, throughout the 1800s.

Auguste Comte

One of the first important theorists in the area of social structure theory was Auguste Comte (1798–1857), who is widely credited with coining the term *sociology*.[3] Comte distinguished the concepts of **social statics** and **social dynamics.** Social statics are aspects of society that relate to stability and social order; they allow societies to continue and endure. Social dynamics are aspects of social life that alter how societies are structured and pattern the development of societal institutions. Although such conceptualization seems elementary by today's standards, it had a significant influence on sociological thinking at the time. Furthermore, the distinction between static and dynamic societal factors was incorporated into several criminological theories in decades to come.

Between 1851 and 1854, Comte published a four-volume work titled *A System of Positive Polity* that encouraged the use of scientific methods to observe and measure societal factors.[4] Although we tend to take this for granted in modern times, the idea of applying such methods to help explain social processes was rather profound at the time; probably for this reason, Comte is generally considered the founder or father of sociology. Comte's work set the stage for the positivistic perspective, which emphasized social determinism and rejected the notion of free will and individual choice that had been common up until that time.

---

[1]Anthony Walsh and Lee Ellis, "Political Ideology and American Criminologists' Explanations for Criminal Behavior," *The Criminologist* 24, no. 6 (1999): 1, 4; Lee Ellis and Anthony Walsh, "Criminologists' Opinions about Causes and Theories of Crime and Delinquency," *The Criminologist* 24, no. 4 (1999): 1–4.

[2]Much of the discussion of the development of structural theories of the 19th century is drawn from James W. Vander Zanden, *Sociology: The Core*, 2nd ed. (New York: McGraw-Hill, 1990), 8–14.

[3]Vander Zanden, *Sociology: The Core*, 8–9.

[4]Auguste Comte, *A System of Positive Polity*, trans. John Henry Bridges (New York: Franklin, 1875).

André-Michel Guerry and Adolphe Quetelet

After the first modern national crime statistics were published in France in the early 1800s, a French lawyer named André-Michel Guerry (1802–1866) published a report that examined these statistics and concluded that property crimes were higher in wealthy areas, but violent crime was much higher in poor areas.[5] Some experts have claimed that this report likely represents the first study of scientific criminology[6]; it was later expanded and published as a book, titled *Essay on the Moral Statistics of France*, in 1833. Ultimately, Guerry concluded that the explanation was opportunity: The wealthy had more to steal, and that is the primary cause of property crime. Interestingly, this conclusion is supported by recent U.S. Department of Justice (DOJ) statistics, which show that, compared to lower-class households, property crime is just as common—and maybe more so—in middle- to upper-class households, but violent crime is not.[7] As Guerry stated centuries ago, there is more to steal in wealthier areas, and poor individuals take the opportunity to steal goods and currency from these households and establishments.

▲ **Image 6.1** Lambert Adolphe Quetelet (1796–1874), the Belgian astronomer and sociologist, circa 1860.

SOURCE: © Getty Images / Popperfoto / Contributor

Adolphe Quetelet (1796–1874) was a Belgian researcher who, like Guerry, examined French statistics in the mid-1800s. Besides showing relative stability in the trends of crime rates in France, such as in age distribution and female-to-male ratios of offending, Quetelet also showed that certain types of individuals were more likely to commit crime.[8] Specifically, young, male, poor, uneducated, and unemployed individuals were more likely to commit crime than their counterparts,[9] a finding also supported by modern research. Like Guerry, Quetelet concluded that opportunities, in addition to demographic characteristics, had a lot to do with where crime was concentrated.

However, Quetelet added a special component: Greater inequality or gaps between wealth and poverty in the same place tend to excite temptations and passions. This is a concept referred to as **relative deprivation**, a condition quite distinct from simple poverty.

For example, a number of deprived areas in the United States do not have high rates of crime—likely because virtually everyone is poor—so people are generally content with their lives relative to their neighbors. However, in areas of the country where very poor people live in close proximity to very wealthy people, animosity and feelings of

---

[5]For more thorough discussions of Guerry and Quetelet, see the sources from which I have drawn the information presented here: Piers Beirne, *Inventing Criminology* (Albany: SUNY Press, 1993); Thomas J. Bernard, Jeffrey B. Snipes, and Alexander L. Gerould, *Vold's Theoretical Criminology*, 6th ed. (Oxford: Oxford University Press, 2010) (see chap. 2).

[6]Terrence Morris, *The Criminal Area* (New York: Routledge, 1957), 42–53, as cited in Bernard et al., *Vold's Theoretical Criminology*, 22.

[7]U.S. Department of Justice, Bureau of Justice Statistics, *Sourcebook of Criminal Justice Statistics, 2000, NCJ-190251* (Washington, DC: USGPO, 2001), Table 3.26, 202; Table 3.13, 194.

[8]Beirne, *Inventing Criminology*, 78–81.

[9]Bernard et al., *Vold's Theoretical Criminology*, 23–26.

being deprived develop. Studies have supported this hypothesis.[10] It may well explain why Washington, DC, perhaps the most powerful city in the world and one with many neighborhoods that are severely run-down and poor, has a higher crime rate than any other jurisdiction in the country.[11] Modern studies have also shown a clear linear association between higher crime rates and relative deprivation. For example, David Sang-Yoon Lee found that crime rates were far higher in cities that had wider gaps in income: The larger the gap between the 10th and 90th percentiles, the greater the crime levels.[12]

In addition to the concept of relative deprivation, Quetelet also showed that areas with the most rapidly changing economic conditions have high crime rates. He is perhaps best known for commenting that "the crimes . . . committed seem to be a necessary result of our social organization. . . . Society prepares the crime, and the guilty are only the instruments by which it is executed."[13] This statement makes it clear that crime is a result of societal structure and not the result of individual propensities or personal decision making. Thus, it is not surprising that Quetelet's position was controversial at the time in which he wrote, and he was rigorously attacked by critics for removing all decision-making capabilities from his model of behavior. In response, Quetelet argued that his model could help lower crime rates by leading to social reforms that address the inequalities due to the social structure.[14]

One of the essential points of Guerry's and Quetelet's work is the positivistic nature of their conclusions: that the distribution of crime is not random but rather the result of certain types of people committing certain types of crimes in particular places, largely due to the way society is structured and the way it distributes resources. This perspective of criminality strongly supports the tendency of crime to be clustered in certain neighborhoods as well as among certain people. Such findings support a structural, positivistic perspective of criminality, in which criminality is seen as being deterministic and, thus, caused by factors outside of an individual's control. In some ways, early structural theories were a response to the failure of the classical approach to crime control. As the 19th century drew to a close, classical and deterrence-based perspectives of crime fell out of favor, while social structure theories and other positivist theories of crime, such as the structural models of Guerry and Quetelet, attracted far more attention.

Durkheim and the Concept of Anomie

Although influenced by earlier theorists (e.g., Comte, Guerry, and Quetelet), Durkheim (1858–1916) was perhaps the most influential theorist in the area of modern structural perspectives on criminality.[15] Like most other social theorists of the 19th century, he was strongly affected by the American and French Revolutions and the Industrial Revolution. In his doctoral dissertation (1893) at the University of Paris, the first sociological dissertation at that institution, Durkheim developed a general model of societal development largely based on economic and labor distribution in which societies are seen as evolving from a simplistic, mechanical society toward a multilayered, organic society (see Figure 6.1).

---

[10]Velmer Burton and Frank Cullen, "The Empirical Status of Strain Theory," *Journal of Crime and Justice* 15 (1992): 1–30; Nikos Passas, "Continuities in the Anomie Tradition," in *Advances in Criminological Theory, Vol. 6: The Legacy of Anomie Theory*, ed. Freda Adler and William S. Laufer (New Brunswick, NJ: Transaction Press, 1995); Nikos Passas, "Anomie, Reference Groups, and Relative Deprivation," in *The Future of Anomie Theory*, ed. Nikos Passas and Robert Agnew (Boston: Northeastern University Press, 1997).

[11]U.S. Department of Justice, Bureau of Justice Statistics, *Sourcebook*, Table 3.124, 290.

[12]David Sang-Yoon Lee, "An Empirical Investigation of the Economic Incentives for Criminal Behavior" (bachelor's thesis in economics) (Boston: Harvard University, 1993), as cited in Richard B. Freeman, "The Labor Market," in *Crime*, ed. James Q. Wilson and Joan Petersilia (San Francisco: ICS Press, 1995), 171–92.

[13]Beirne, *Inventing Criminology*, 88, as cited in Bernard et al., *Vold's Theoretical Criminology*, 25.

[14]Bernard et al., *Vold's Theoretical Criminology*, 25–26.

[15]Much of this discussion of Durkheim is taken from Bernard et al., *Vold's Theoretical Criminology*, 100–116 as well as Vander Zanden, *Sociology: The Core*, 11–13.

Figure 6.1 • Durkheim's continuum of development from mechanical to organic societies

Mechanical Societies	Organic Societies
⟶	Industrialization ⟶
Primitive	Modern
Rural	Urban
Agricultural-based economy	Industrial-based economy
Simple division of labor (few divisions)	Complex division of labor (many specialized divisions)
Law used to enforce conformity	Law used to regulate interactions among divisions
Typically stronger collective conscience	Typically weaker collective conscience

As outlined in this dissertation, titled *The Division of Labor in Society*, in primitive **mechanical societies**, all members essentially perform the same functions, such as hunting (typically done by males) and gathering (typically done by females). Although there are a few anomalies (e.g., medicine men), virtually everyone experiences essentially the same daily routine. Such similarities in work, as well as constant interaction with like members of the society, leads to a strong uniformity in values, which Durkheim called the **collective conscience**. The collective conscience is the degree to which individuals of a society think alike, or as Durkheim put it, the totality of social likenesses. The similar norms and values among people in these primitive, mechanical societies create *mechanical solidarity*, a very simple social structure with a very strong collective conscience. In mechanical societies, law functions to enforce the **conformity** of the group.

However, as societies progress toward more modern, **organic societies** in the industrial age, the distribution of labor becomes more highly specified. An *organic solidarity* arises in which people tend to depend on other groups because of the highly specified division of labor, and laws have the primary function of regulating interactions and maintaining solidarity among the groups.

For example, modern researchers at universities in the United States tend to be trained in extremely narrow topics—one might be an expert on something as specific as the antennae of certain species of ants. On the other hand, some individuals are still gathering trash from the cans on the same streets every single day. The antennae experts probably have little in common with the garbage collectors and not much interaction with them other than when they pay them. According to Durkheim, moving from the universally shared roles of mechanical societies to the extremely specific roles of organic societal organization results in huge cultural differences and giant contrasts in normative values and attitudes across groups. Thus, the collective conscience in such societies is weak, largely because there is little agreement on moral beliefs or opinions. The preexisting solidarity among members breaks down and the bonds are weakened, which creates a climate for antisocial behavior.

Durkheim was clear in stating that crime is not only normal but necessary in all societies. As a result, his theory is often considered a good representation of structural functionalism. He claimed that all social behaviors, especially crime, provide essential functions in a society. Durkheim thought crime serves several functions. First, it defines the moral boundaries of societies. Few people know or realize what is against societal laws until they see someone punished for a violation. This reinforces their understanding of both what the rules are and what it means to break them. Furthermore, the identification of rule breakers creates a bond among the other members of the society, perhaps through a common sense of self-righteousness or superiority.

In later works, Durkheim said the resultant bonding is what makes crime so necessary in a society. Given a community that has no law violators, he thought, society will change the legal definitions of what constitutes a crime

▲ **Image 6.2** Émile Durkheim (1858–1917).

SOURCE: © Getty Images / Bettmann / Contributor

to define some of its members as criminals. Examples of this are prevalent, but perhaps the most convincing is that of the Salem witch trials wherein hundreds of individuals were accused and tried for an almost laughable offense and more than a dozen were executed. Durkheim would say this was inevitable because crime was so low in the Massachusetts Bay Colony, as historical records confirm, that society had to come up with a fabricated criterion for defining certain members of the population as offenders.

Other examples are common in everyday life. The fastest way to have a group of strangers bond is to give them a common enemy, which often means forming into cliques and ganging up on others in the group. In a group of three or more college roommates, for example, two or more of the individuals will quickly join together and complain about the others. This is an inevitable phenomenon of human interaction and group dynamics that has always existed throughout the world across time and place. As Durkheim said, even in "a society of saints . . . crimes . . . will there be unknown; but faults which appear venial to the layman will create there the same scandal that the ordinary offense does in ordinary consciousnesses. . . . This society . . . will define these acts as criminal and will treat them as such."[16]

Law enforcement should always be cautious in cracking down on gangs, especially during relatively inactive periods, because it may make the gang stronger. Like all societal groups, when a common enemy appears, gang members—even those who do not typically get along—will come together and "circle the wagons" to protect themselves via strength in numbers. This very powerful bonding effect is one that many sociologists, and especially gang researchers, have consistently observed.[17]

Traditional, mostly mechanical societies could count on relative consensus about moral values and norms, and this sometimes led to too much control and a stagnation of creative thought. Durkheim thought that progress in society typically depends on deviating from established moral boundaries, especially if the society is in the mechanical stage. Some of the many examples include virtually all religious icons. Jesus, Buddha, and Mohammed were persecuted as criminals for deviating from societal norms in the times they preached. Political heroes have also been prosecuted and incarcerated as criminals, such as Gandhi in India, Mandela in South Africa, and Dr. King in the United States. In one of the most compelling cases, scientist and astronomer Galileo proposed a theory that Earth was not the center of the universe. Even though he was right, he was persecuted for his belief in a society that strictly adhered to its beliefs. Durkheim was clearly accurate in saying that the normative structure in some societies is so strong that it hinders progress and that crime is the price societies pay for progress.

In contrast to mechanical societies, modern societies do not have such extreme restraint against deviations from established norms. Rather, almost the opposite is true; there are too many differences across groups because the division of labor is highly specialized. Thus, the varying roles in society, such as farmers versus scientific

[16]Émile Durkheim, *The Rules of the Sociological Method*, ed. George E. G. Catlin, trans. Sarah A. Solovay and John H. Mueller (New York: Free Press, 1965), as cited in Bernard et al., *Vold's Theoretical Criminology.*

[17]See discussion in Malcolm Klein, "Street Gang Cycles," in *Crime*, ed. James Q. Wilson and Joan Petersilia (San Francisco: ICS Press, 2002), 217–36.

researchers, lead to extreme differences in the cultural values and norms of each group. There is a breakdown in the collective conscience because there is really no longer a collective nature in society. Therefore, law focuses not on defining the norms of society but on governing the interactions that take place among the different classes. According to Durkheim, law provides a service in regulating such interactions as societies progress toward more organic (more industrial) forms.

Durkheim emphasized that human beings, unlike other animal species who live according to their spontaneous needs, have no internal mechanism to signal when their needs and desires are satiated. Therefore, the selfish desires of humankind are limitless; the more an individual has, the more he or she wants. People are greedy by nature, and without something to tell them what they need and deserve, they will never feel content.[18] According to Durkheim, society provides the mechanism for limiting this insatiable appetite, having the sole power to create laws that set tangible limits.

Durkheim also noted that in times of rapid change, society fails in this role of regulating desires and expectations. Rapid change can be due to numerous factors, such as war or social movements (like the changes seen in the United States in the 1960s). The transitions Durkheim likely had in mind when he wrote were the American and French Revolutions and the Industrial Revolution. When society's ability to serve as a regulatory mechanism breaks down, the selfish, greedy tendencies of individuals are uncontrolled, causing a state Durkheim called *anomie*, or *normlessness.* Societies in such anomic states experience increases in many social problems, particularly criminal activity.

Durkheim was clear that, whether the rapid change was for good or bad, it would have negative effects on society. For example, whether the U.S. economy was improving, as it did during the late 1960s, or quickly tanking, as it did during the Depression of the 1930s, criminal activity would increase due to the lack of stability in regulating human expectations and desires. Interestingly, these two periods experienced the greatest crime waves of the 20th century, particularly for murder.[19] Another fact that supports Durkheim's predictions is that middle- and upper-class individuals have higher suicide rates than those from lower classes. This is consistent with the idea that it is better to have stability, even if it means always being poor, than it is to have instability at higher levels of income. In his best-known work, *Suicide,* Durkheim took an act that would seem to be the ultimate form of free choice or free will and showed that the decision to take one's own life was largely determined by external social factors. He argued that suicide is a *social fact,* a product of meanings and structural aspects that result from interactions among people.

Durkheim showed that the rate of suicide was significantly lower among individuals who were married, younger, and practiced religions that were more interactive and communal (e.g., Jewish). All of these characteristics boil down to one aspect: The more the social interaction and bonding with the community, the less the suicide. Thus, Durkheim concluded that variations in suicide rates are due to differences in social solidarity or bonding to society. Examples of this are still seen today, as in recent reports of high rates of suicide among people who live in remote areas, like Alaska (which has the highest rate of juvenile suicide), Wyoming, Montana, and the northern portions of Nevada. Another way of looking at the implications of Durkheim's conclusions is that social relationships are what make people happy and fulfilled. If they are isolated or have weak bonds to society, they will likely be depressed and discontented with their lives.

Another reason that Durkheim's examination of suicide was important was that he showed that suicide rates increased in times of rapid economic growth or rapid decline. Although researchers later argued that crime rates

---

[18]For more details on these issues, see Émile Durkheim's works: *The Division of Labor in Society* (1893; repr., New York: Free Press, 1965) and *Suicide* (1897; repr., New York: Free Press, 1951).

[19]U.S. Department of Justice, Bureau of Justice Statistics, *Violent Crime in the United States* (Washington, DC: Bureau of Justice Statistics, 1996), as illustrated in Joseph P. Senna and Larry G. Siegel, *Introduction to Criminal Justice*, 8th ed. (Belmont, CA: West/Wadsworth, 1999).

did not always follow this pattern,[20] Durkheim used quantified measures to test his propositions as the positivistic approach recommended. At the least, Durkheim created a prototype of how theory and empirical research could be combined in testing differences across social groups. This theoretical framework was drawn on heavily for one of the most influential and accepted criminological theories of the 20th century: strain theory.

Strain Theories

All forms of strain theory share an emphasis on frustration as a factor in crime causation, hence the name *strain* theories. Although the theories differ regarding what exactly is causing the frustration—and the way individuals cope (or don't cope) with stress and anger—they all hold that strain is the primary causal factor in the development of criminality. Strain theories all trace their origin to Robert K. Merton's seminal theoretical framework.

Merton's Strain Theory

Working in the 1930s, Merton drew heavily on Durkheim's idea of anomie in developing his own theory of structural strain.[21] Although Merton altered the definition of anomie, Durkheim's theoretical framework was a vital influence in the evolution of strain theory. Combining Durkheimian concepts and propositions with an emphasis on American culture, Merton's structural model became one of the most popular perspectives in criminological thought in the early 1900s and remains one of the most cited theories of crime in the criminological literature.

Cultural Context and Assumptions of Strain Theory

Some have claimed that Merton's seminal piece in 1938 was the most influential theoretical formulation in criminological literature, and it is one of the most frequently cited papers in sociology.[22] Although its popularity is partially due to its strong foundation in previous structural theories, Merton's strain theory also benefited from the timing of its publication. Virtually every theory discussed in this book became popular because it was well suited to the political and social climate of the times, fitting perspectives of how the world worked. Perhaps no other theory better represents this phenomenon than strain theory.

Most historians would agree that, in the United States, the most significant social issue of the 1930s was the economy. The influence of the Great Depression, largely a result of a stock market crash in 1929, affected virtually every aspect of life in the United States. Unemployment and extreme poverty soared, along with suicide rates and crime rates, particularly murder rates.[23] American society was fertile ground for a theory of crime that placed virtually all of the blame on the U.S. economic structure.

---

[20]William J. Chambliss, "Functional and Conflict Theories of Crime," in *Whose Law? What Order?*, ed. William J. Chambliss and Milton Mankoff (New York: Wiley, 1976), 11–16.

[21]For reviews of Merton's theory, see both the original and more recent works by Merton himself: Robert K. Merton, "Social Structure and Anomie," *American Sociological Review* 3 (1938): 672–82; Robert K. Merton, *Social Theory and Social Structure* (New York: Free Press, 1968); and Robert K. Merton, "Opportunity Structure: The Emergence, Diffusion, and Differentiation as Sociological Concept, 1930s–1950s," in *Advances in Criminological Theory: The Legacy of Anomie Theory*, Vol. 6, ed. Freda Adler and William Laufer (New Brunswick, NJ: Transaction Press, 1995). For reviews by others, see Ronald L. Akers and Christine S. Sellers, *Criminological Theories: Introduction, Evaluation, and Application*, 6th ed. (Oxford: Oxford University Press, 2012), 164–68; Stephen E. Brown, Finn-Aage Esbensen, and Gilbert Geis, *Criminology: Explaining Crime and Its Context*, 8th ed. (Cincinnati: Anderson, 2013), 297–307; Marshall B. Clinard, "The Theoretical Implications of Anomie and Deviant Behavior," in *Anomie and Deviant Behavior*, ed. Marshall B. Clinard (New York: Free Press, 1964), 1–56; and Thomas J. Bernard, "Testing Structural Strain Theories," *Journal of Research in Crime and Delinquency* 24 (1987): 262–80.

[22]Clinard, "Theoretical Implications." See also the discussion in Brown et al., *Criminology*, 297.

[23]Larry J. Siegel, *Introduction to Criminal Justice*, 12th ed. (Belmont, CA: Wadsworth, 2010), 44.

On the other side of the coin, Merton was highly influenced by what he saw happening to the country during the Depression and how much the economic institution impacted almost all other social factors, particularly crime. He watched how the breakdown of the economic structure drove people to kill themselves or others, not to mention the rise in property crimes such as theft. Many once-successful individuals were now poor, and some felt driven to crime for survival. Notably, Durkheim's hypotheses regarding crime and suicide were supported during this time of rapid change, and Merton apparently realized that the framework simply had to be brought up-to-date and supplemented.

One of the key assumptions that distinguishes strain theory from Durkheim's perspective is that Merton altered his version of what anomie means. Merton focused on the nearly universal socialization of the American Dream in U.S. society—the idea that as long as people work very hard and pay their dues they will achieve their goals in the end. According to Merton, the socialized image of the goal is material wealth, whereas the socialized concept of the means of achieving the goal is hard work (e.g., education, labor). The conventional model of the American Dream was consistent with the Protestant work ethic, which called for working hard for a long time, knowing that you will be paid off in the distant future.

Furthermore, Merton thought that nearly everyone was socialized to believe in the American Dream no matter what economic class he or she was raised in as a child. There is some empirical support for this belief, and it makes sense. Virtually all parents, even if they are poor, want to give their children hope for the future if they are willing to work hard in school and at a job. Parents and society usually use celebrities as examples of this process—individuals who started off poor and rose to become wealthy. Modern examples include former secretary of state Colin Powell, owner of the NBA Dallas Mavericks Mark Cuban, Oscar-winning actress Hilary Swank, and Hollywood director and screenwriter Quentin Tarantino, not to mention Arnold Schwarzenegger and his amazing rise from teenage immigrant to Mr. Olympia and California governor.

These stories epitomize the American Dream, but parents and society do not also teach the reality of the situation. As Merton pointed out, a small percentage of people rise from the lower class to become materially successful, but the vast majority of poor children don't have much chance of ever obtaining such wealth. This near-universal socialization of the American Dream—which turns out not to be true for most people—causes most of the strain and frustration in American society, Merton said. Furthermore, he thought that most of the strain and frustration was due not to the failure to achieve conventional goals (i.e., wealth) but rather to the differential emphasis placed on material goals and the de-emphasizing of the importance of conventional means.

Merton's Concept of Anomie and Strain

Merton claimed that, in an ideal society, there would be an equal emphasis on conventional goals and means. However, in many societies, one is emphasized more than the other. Merton thought the United States epitomized the type of society that emphasized the goals far more than the means. The disequilibrium in emphasis between the goals and means of societies is what Merton called anomie. So, like Durkheim, Merton saw anomie as a negative state of society; however, the two men had very different ideas of how this state of society was caused. Whereas Durkheim believed that anomie was primarily caused by a society's transitioning too fast to maintain its regulatory control over its members, for Merton, anomie represented too much focus on the goals of wealth in the United States at the expense of conventional means.

Hypothetical situations can be used to illustrate Merton's view: Which of the following two men would be more respected by youths (or even adults) in our society: (1) John, who has his PhD in physics and lives in a one-bedroom apartment because his job as a postdoctoral student pays $25,000 a year; or (2) Joe, who is a relatively successful drug dealer and owns a four-bedroom home, drives a Hummer, dropped out of school in the 10th grade, and makes about $90,000 a year? In years of asking such a question to our classes, we have found that the answer is usually Joe, the drug dealer. After all, he appears to have obtained the American Dream, and little emphasis is placed on how he achieved it.

Still another way of supporting Merton's idea that America is too focused on the goal of material success is to ask you, the reader, to think about why you are taking the time to read this book or to attend college. Specifically, the question for you is this: If you knew that studying this book—or earning a college degree—would not lead to a better employment position, would you read it anyway just to increase your own knowledge? In over a decade of putting this question to about 10,000 students in various university courses, one of the authors of this book has found that only about 5% (usually fewer) of respondents say yes. Interestingly, when asked why they put all of this work into attending classes, many of them say it's for the partying or social life. Ultimately, it seems that most college students would not be engaging in the hard work it takes to educate themselves if it weren't for some payoff at the end of the task. In some ways, this supports Merton's claim that there is an emphasis on the goals and little or no intrinsic value placed on the work itself (i.e., the means). This phenomenon is not meant to be a disheartening or a negative statement; it is meant only to exhibit the reality of American culture. It is quite common in our society to emphasize the goal of financial success as opposed to hard work or education.

Merton thought that individuals, particularly those in the lower class, eventually realize that the ideal of the American Dream is a lie or at least a false illusion for the vast majority. This revelation will likely take place when people are in their late teens to mid-20s, and according to Merton, this is when the frustration or strain is evident. That is consistent with the age–crime peak of offending at the approximate age of 17. Learning that hard work won't necessarily provide rewards, some individuals begin to innovate ways that they can achieve material success without the conventional means of getting it. Obviously, this is often through criminal activity. However, not all individuals deal with strain in this way; most people who are poor do not resort to crime. To Merton's credit, he explained that individuals deal with the limited economic structure of society in different ways. He referred to these variations as **adaptations to strain**.

▲ **Image 6.3** Robert K. Merton (1910–2003), the sociologist who first proposed strain theory in the 1930s.

SOURCE: © Getty Images / Pictorial Parade / Staff

Adaptations to Strain

According to Merton, there are five adaptations to strain. The first of these is conformity, in which people buy into the conventional goals of society and the conventional means of working hard in school or at their labor.[24] Like conformists, most readers of this book would probably like to achieve material success and are willing to use conventional means of achieving success through educational efforts and doing a good job at work. Another adaptation to strain is **ritualism**. Ritualists do not pursue the goal of material success—probably because they know they don't have a realistic chance of obtaining it. However, they do buy into the conventional means in the sense that they like to do their jobs or are happy with just making ends meet through their current positions.

[24]Merton, *Social Theory*.

For example, studies have shown that some of the most contented and happy people in society are those who don't hope to become rich; are quite content with their blue-collar jobs; and often have a strong sense of pride in their work, even if it is sometimes quite menial. To these people, work is a type of ritual, performed without a goal in mind; rather, it is a form of intrinsic goal in and of itself. Ultimately, conformists and ritualists tend to be at low risk for offending, which is in contrast to the other adaptations to strain.

The other three adaptations to strain are far more likely to be associated with criminal offending: **innovation**, **retreatism**, and **rebellion**. Perhaps most likely to become predatory street criminals are the innovators, who Merton claimed greatly desire the conventional goals of material success but are not willing to engage in conventional means. Obviously, drug dealers and professional auto thieves, as well as many other variations of chronic property criminals (bank robbers, etc.), would fit this category. They are innovating ways to achieve the goals without the hard work that is usually required. However, innovators are not always criminals. In fact, many of them are the most respected individuals in our society. For example, some entrepreneurs have used the capitalistic system of our society to produce useful products and services (e.g., the men who designed Google for the Internet) and have made a fortune at a very young age without advanced college education or years of work at a company. Other examples are successful athletes who sign multimillion-dollar contracts at age 18. So, it should be clear that not all innovators are criminals.

The fourth adaptation to strain is retreatism. Retreatists do not seek to achieve the goals of society, and they also do not buy into the idea of conventional hard work. There are many varieties of this adaptation: for example, people who become homeless by choice or who isolate themselves in desolate places without human contact. A good example of a retreatist is Ted Kaczynski, the Unabomber, who left a good position as a professor at the University of California, Berkeley, to live in an isolated cabin in Montana that had no running water or electricity; he did not interact with humans for many months at a time. Other types of retreatists, perhaps the most likely to be criminal, are those who are heavy drug users who actively disengage from social life and try to escape via mind-altering drugs. All of these forms of retreatists seek to drop out of society altogether, thus not buying into its means or goals.

Finally, the last adaptation to strain, according to Merton, is rebellion, which is the most complex of the five adaptations. Interestingly, rebels buy into the idea of societal goals and means, but they do not buy into those currently in place. Most true rebels are criminals by definition, largely because they are trying to overthrow the current societal structure. For example, the founders of the United States were all rebels because they actively fought the governing state—English rule—and clearly committed treason in the process. Had they lost or been caught during the American Revolution, they would have been executed as the criminals they were by law. However, because they won the war, they became heroes and presidents. Another example is Karl Marx. He bought into the idea of goals and means of society—just not those of capitalistic societies. Rather, he proposed socialism or communism as a means to the goal of utopia. So, there are many contexts in which rebels can be criminals, but sometimes they end up being heroes.

Merton also noted that one individual can represent more than one adaptation. Perhaps the best example is that of the Unabomber, who obviously started out as a conformist in that he was a respected professor at the University of California, Berkeley, who was well on his way to tenure and promotion. He then seemed to shift to retreatism in that he isolated himself from society. Later, he became a rebel who bombed innocent people in his quest to implement his own goals and means as described in his manifesto, which he coerced several national newspapers to publish. This subsequently resulted in his apprehension when his brother read it and informed authorities that he thought his brother was the author.

Finally, some have applied a sports analogy to these adaptations.[25] Assuming a basketball game is taking place, conformists will play to win, and they will always play by the rules and won't cheat. Ritualists will play the

[25]Bernard et al., *Vold's Theoretical Criminology*, 140.

game just because they like to play; they don't care about winning. Innovators will play to win, and they will break any rules they can to triumph in the game. Retreatists don't like to play and obviously don't care about winning. Finally, rebels won't like the rules on the court, so they will try to steal the ball and go play by their own rules on another court. Although this is a somewhat simplistic analogy, it is likely to help readers remember the adaptations and perhaps enable them to apply these ways of dealing with strain to everyday situations, such as criminal activity.

Case Study: The Black Binder Bandit

A recent news story reported on a jobless man who was arrested for committing a dozen bank robberies across the Phoenix valley. The man, Cristian Alfredo Urquijo, 39, told authorities that he did it to survive and that "desperation was a great motivator." He was accused of robbing at least a dozen banks between 2010 and 2011. The criminal complaint noted that he had been laid off from work, was unable to find employment, and robbed the Phoenix-area banks to survive. He went on to say, "It's pretty simple. It's black and white. I don't have a job, I had to work, and I rob to survive." During his crime spree, authorities called him the "Black Binder Bandit" because he typically hid a revolver in a black binder and also would usually place the stolen money in this binder.

Urquijo pleaded guilty to nine counts of bank robbery, three counts of armed bank robbery, and one count of use of a firearm in a crime of violence, which carries an enhanced sentence. He had originally been charged with 16 counts of bank robbery, but as often happens in plea negotiations, the counts were reduced. He did admit that he had robbed at least 12 banks and also that he had obtained more than $49,000 from these bank robberies.

It is obvious that this man committed these crimes because he wanted to provide for himself in an economic recession. This is just one of many examples of individuals who are strongly motivated to commit crimes—even the major federal crime of bank robbery—to deal with the economic strain or frustration of not being able to "get ahead" or achieve the American Dream of success. This section discusses the evolution of theories that address this concept of trying to provide for oneself or succeed while dealing with societal and economic dynamics in American society. Specifically, this section reviews the development of anomie or strain theory, starting with its origins among early social structure theorists, such as Durkheim, and moving to its further development by Merton. The section also examines the development of various strain models of offending as well as the most modern versions of strain theory (e.g., general strain theory). We will also examine the empirical research findings on this perspective, which reveal that this framework remains one of the dominant theoretical explanations of criminal behavior in modern times. We will finish this section by examining the policy implications suggested by this perspective for explaining criminal behavior, and we will further discuss the case of the Black Binder Bandit toward the end of this section.

"It's pretty simple. It's black and white. I don't have a job, I had to work, and I rob to survive."

It should be noted that the Federal Bureau of Investigation (FBI) typically assigns nicknames (such as the Black Binder Bandit) to serial bank robbers. The FBI does so for a very important reason: The public is more likely to take note of serial bank robbers when there is a catchy moniker or nickname attached to them. Apparently, this strategy is useful, because bank robbery actually has a much higher clearance rate than other types of robbery. Other notable nicknames of serial bank robbers in the past few years are the "Mesh-Mask Bandit" (still at large in Texas; wears a mesh mask), the "Geezer Bandit" (still at large in Southern California; authorities believe that the offender may be a young person disguising himself as an elderly person), and the "Michael Jackson Bandit" (still at large in Southern California; wears one glove during robberies). Although all these bank robbery suspects are still at large, many others have been caught as a result of making their nicknames notable to the public.

Think About It

1. Can you articulate why the Black Binder Bandit seems to be a good example of Merton's strain theory?
2. Based on what he said to the police and his behavior, what adaptation of strain would you say best fits him?
3. Outside of the nicknames already listed in this discussion, do you know of any other robbers the authorities have nicknamed and the reason(s) the robbers were given their monikers?

▲ **Image 6.4** As surveillance photos show, Urquijo typically carried into the bank a black binder in which he hid a revolver and the money he acquired from the bank robbery.

SOURCE: azcentral.com

Evidence and Criticisms of Merton's Strain Theory

Merton's framework, which emphasized the importance of economic structure, had a high degree of face validity during the Great Depression; however, many later scientific studies showed mixed support for strain theory. Although research that examined the effects of poverty on violence and official rates of various crimes has found relatively consistent support for Merton's views (albeit with weaker effects than strain theory implies), a series of studies of self-reported delinquent behavior found little or no relationship between social class and criminality.[26] Furthermore, the idea that unemployment drives people to commit crime has received little support.[27]

[26]For examples and reviews of this research, see F. Ivan Nye, *Family Relationships and Delinquent Behavior* (New York: Wiley, 1958); Ronald L. Akers, "Socio-Economic Status and Delinquent Behavior: A Retest," *Journal of Research in Crime and Delinquency* 1 (1964): 38–46; Charles R. Tittle and Wayne J. Villemez, "Social Class and Criminality," *Social Forces* 56 (1977): 474–503; Charles R. Tittle, Wayne J. Villemez, and Douglas A. Smith, "The Myth of Social Class and Criminality: An Empirical Assessment of the Empirical Evidence," *American Sociological Review* 43 (1978): 643–56; Michael J. Hindelang, Travis Hirschi, and Joseph C. Weis, "Correlates of Delinquency: The Illusion of Discrepancy between Self-Report and Official Measures," *American Sociological Review* 44 (1979): 995–1014; Michael J. Hindelang, *Measuring Delinquency* (Beverly Hills, CA: Sage, 1980); Terence P. Thornberry and Margaret Farnworth, "Social Correlates of Criminal Involvement," *American Sociological Review* 47 (1982): 505–17; and Gregory R. Dunaway et al., "The Myth of Social Class and Crime Revisited: An Examination of Class and Adult Criminality," *Criminology* 38 (2000): 589–632. For one of the most thorough reviews, see Charles R. Tittle and Robert F. Meier, "Specifying the SES/Delinquency Relationship," *Criminology* 28 (1990): 271–99.

[27]Gary Kleck and Ted Chiricos, "Unemployment and Property Crime: A Target-Specific Assessment of Opportunity and Motivation as Mediating Factors," *Criminology* 40 (2000): 649–680.

On the other hand, some experts have argued that Merton's strain theory is primarily a structural model of crime that is more a theory of societal groups, not individual motivations.[28] Therefore, some modern studies have used aggregated group rates (i.e., macro-level measures) to test the effects of deprivation as opposed to using individual (micro-level) rates of inequality and crime. Most of these studies provide some support for the hypothesis that social groups and regions with higher rates of deprivation and inequality have higher rates of criminal activity.[29] In sum, there appears to be some support for Merton's strain theory at the macro level of analysis when official measures are being used to indicate criminality.

However, many critics have claimed that these studies do not directly measure perceptions or feelings of strain, so they are only indirect examinations of Merton's theory. In light of these criticisms, some researchers focused on the disparity between what individuals aspire to in various aspects of life (e.g., school, occupation, social life) and what they realistically expect to achieve.[30] The rationale behind these studies was that if an individual has high aspirations (i.e., goals) but a low expectation of actually achieving the goals due to structural barriers, then that individual is more likely to experience feelings of frustration and strain. Furthermore, it was predicted that the larger the gap between aspirations and expectations, the stronger the sense of strain. Of the studies that examined discrepancies between aspirations and expectations, most did not find evidence to link a large gap between these two levels with criminal activity. In fact, several studies found that for most antisocial respondents there was virtually no gap between aspirations and expectations. Rather, most of the subjects who reported the highest levels of criminal activity (typically young males) tended to report low levels of both aspirations and expectations.

Surprisingly, when aspirations were high, it seemed to inhibit offending, even when expectations to achieve those goals were low. One interpretation of these findings is that individuals who have high goals will not jeopardize their chances even if they are slim. On the other hand, individuals who don't have high goals are likely to be indifferent to their future and, in a sense, have nothing to lose. So, without a stake in conventional society, this predisposes them to crime. While this conclusion supports social control theories, it does not provide support for strain theory.

Some critics have argued that most studies on the discrepancies between aspirations and expectations have not been done correctly. For example, Margaret Farnworth and Michael J. Leiber claimed that it was a mistake to examine differences between educational goals and expectations or differences between occupational goals and expectations, which is what most of these studies did.[31] Rather, they proposed testing the gap between economic aspirations (i.e., goals) and educational expectations (i.e., means of achieving the goals). This makes sense, and Farnworth and Leiber found support for a gap between these two factors and criminality. However, they also found that people who reported low economic aspirations were more likely to be delinquent, which supports the previous studies that they criticized. Another criticism of this type of strain theory study is that simply reporting a gap between expectations and aspirations may not mean that the individuals actually feel strain; rather,

---

[28]Bernard, "Testing Structural Strain Theories"; Steven F. Messner, "Merton's 'Social Structure and Anomie': The Road Not Taken," *Deviant Behavior* 9 (1988): 33–53. See also discussion in Burton and Cullen, "Empirical Status."

[29]For a review of these studies, see Kenneth C. Land, Patricia L. McCall, and Lawrence E. Cohen, "Structural Covariates of Homicide Rates: Are There Any Invariances across Time and Social Space?" *American Journal of Sociology* 95 (1990): 922–63.

[30]For examples and reviews of these types of studies, see Travis Hirschi, *Causes of Delinquency* (Berkeley: University of California Press, 1969), 4–10; Allen E. Liska, "Aspirations, Expectations, and Delinquency: Stress and Additive Models," *Sociological Quarterly* 12 (1971): 99–107; Margaret Farnworth and Michael J. Leiber, "Strain Theory Revisited: Economic Goals, Educational Means, and Delinquency," *American Sociological Review* 54 (1989): 263–74; Burton and Cullen, "Empirical Status"; Velmer S. Burton et al., "Reconsidering Strain Theory: Operationalization, Rival Theories, and Adult Criminality," *Journal of Quantitative Criminology* 10 (1994): 213–39; and Robert F. Agnew et al., "A New Test of Classic Strain Theory," *Justice Quarterly* 13 (1996): 681–704. See also discussion of this issue in Akers and Sellers, *Criminological Theories*, 173–75.

[31]Farnworth and Leiber, "Strain Theory."

researchers have simply, and perhaps wrongfully, assumed that a gap between the two measures indicates feelings of frustration.[32]

Other criticisms of Merton's strain theory include historical evidence and the theory's failure to explain the age–crime curve. Regarding the historical evidence, it is hard to understand why some of the largest increases in crime took place during a period of relative economic prosperity, namely the late 1960s. Between 1965 and 1973, which were generally good economic years in the United States, crime increased more than it had ever done since recording crime rates began. Therefore, if strain theory is presented as the primary explanation for criminal activity, it would probably have a hard time explaining this historical era. On the other hand, the growth in the economy in the 1960s and early 1970s may have caused more disparity between the rich and the poor, thereby producing more relative deprivation.

The other major criticism of strain theory is that it does not explain one of the most established facts in the field: the age–crime curve. In virtually every society in the world, across time and place, predatory street crimes (robbery, rape, murder, burglary, larceny, etc.) tend to peak sharply in the teenage years to early 20s and then drop off very quickly, certainly before age 30. However, most studies show that feelings of stress and frustration tend not to follow this pattern. For example, suicide rates tend to be just as high or higher as one gets older, with middle-aged and elderly people having much higher rates of suicide than those in their teens or early 20s.

On the other hand, it can be argued that crime rates go down even though strain can continue or even increase with age because individuals develop coping mechanisms for dealing with the frustrations they feel. But even if this is true regarding criminal behavior, apparently this doesn't seem to prevent suicidal tendencies. General strain theory emphasized this concept. However, before we cover general strain theory, we will discuss two other variations of Merton's theory that were both developed between 1955 and 1960 to explain gang formation and behavior using a structural strain framework.

Variations of Merton's Strain Theory: Cohen's Model and Cloward and Ohlin's Theory

Cohen's Theory of Lower-Class Status Frustration and Gang Formation

In 1955, Albert Cohen presented a theory of gang formation that used Merton's strain theory as a basis for why individuals resort to such group behavior.[33] In Cohen's model, young, lower-class males are at a disadvantage in school because they lack the normal interaction, socialization, and discipline instituted by educated parents of the middle class. This is in line with Merton's original framework identifying a disadvantage for underclass youth. According to Cohen, such youths are likely to experience failure in school because they are unprepared to conform with middle-class values and fail to meet the middle-class measuring rod, which emphasizes motivation, accountability, responsibility, deferred gratification, long-term planning, respect for authority and property, controlling emotions, and so on.

Like Merton, Cohen emphasized the youths' internalization of the American Dream and the idea that they had a fair chance of success, which would mean that failure to be successful according to this middle-class standard would be very frustrating for them. The strain felt as a result of failure in school performance and lack of respect among peers is often referred to as *status frustration*. It leads youth to develop a system of values opposed to middle-class standards and values. Some have claimed that this represents a Freudian defense mechanism known as **reaction formation**, which involves adopting attitudes or committing behaviors that are opposite of what is expected as a

---

[32]Agnew et al., "A New Test."

[33]Albert Cohen, *Delinquent Boys: The Culture of the Gang* (New York: Free Press, 1955).

form of defiance so as to feel less guilty for not living up to unachievable standards. Specifically, instead of abiding by middle-class norms of obedience to authority, school achievement, and respect for authority, these youths change their normative beliefs to value the opposite characteristics: malicious, negativistic, and nonutilitarian delinquent activity.

Delinquent youths will begin to value destruction of property and skipping school not because these behaviors lead to a payoff or success in the conventional world but simply because they defy the conventional order. In other words, they turn middle-class values upside down and consider activity that violates the conventional norms and laws good, thereby psychologically and physically rejecting the cultural system that has been imposed on them without preparation and fair distribution of resources. Furthermore, Cohen claimed that while these behaviors do not appear to have much utility or value, they are quite valuable and important from the perspective of the strained youths. Specifically, they do these acts to gain respect from their peers.

Cohen stated that he believed that this tendency to reject middle-class values is the primary cause of gangs, a classic example of "birds of a feather flock together." Not all lower-class males resort to crime and join a gang in response to this structural disadvantage. Other variations, beyond that of the **delinquent boy** described previously, include the **college boy** and the **corner boy.** The college boy responds to his disadvantaged situation by dedicating himself to overcoming the odds and competing in middle-class schools despite his unlikely chances for success. The corner boy responds to the situation by accepting his place as a lower-class individual who will somewhat passively make the best of life at the bottom of the social order.

When compared to Merton's original adaptations, Cohen's delinquent boy is probably best seen as similar to a rebel because he rejects the means and goals of conventional society (i.e., middle-class values and success in school), substituting new means and goals (negativistic behaviors and peer respect in the gang). Some would argue that delinquent boys should be seen as innovators because their goals are ultimately the same: peer respect. However, the actual peers involved completely change, so we argue that, through the reaction formation process, the delinquent boy actually creates his own goals and means that go against the conventional, middle-class goals and means. Regarding the college boy, the adaptation that seems to fit the best is that of conformity, because the college boy continues to believe in the conventional goals (i.e., financial success and achievement) and means (hard work via education or labor) of middle-class society. Finally, the corner boy probably best fits the adaptation of ritualism because he knows that he likely will never achieve the goals of society but resigns himself to not obtaining financial success; at the same time, he does not resort to predatory street crime but rather holds a stable, blue-collar job or makes ends meet in other typical, legal ways. Some corner boys end up simply collecting welfare and give up working altogether; they may actually become more like the adaptation of retreatism because they have virtually given up on the conventional means of society (hard work) as well as the goals.

At the time that Cohen developed his theory, official statistics showed that virtually all gang violence, and most violence for that matter, was concentrated among lower-class male youth. However, with the development of self-report studies in the 1960s, Cohen's theory was shown to be somewhat overstated: Middle-class youth were well represented among those who committed delinquent acts.[34] Other studies have also been critical of Cohen's theory, particularly the portions that deal with his proposition that crime rates will increase after youths drop out of school and join gangs. Although the findings are mixed, many studies have found that delinquency is often higher before youths drop out of school and may actually decline once they drop out and

[34]Tittle et al., "Myth of Social Class"; Hindelang et al., "Correlates of Delinquency."

become employed.[35] Some critics have pointed out that such findings discredit Cohen's theory, but this is not necessarily true. After all, delinquency may peak right before the youths drop out because they feel the most frustrated and strained then, whereas delinquency may decrease after they drop out because some are raising their self-esteem by earning wages and taking pride in having jobs.

Still, studies have clearly shown that lower-class youths are far more likely to have problems in school and that school failure is consistently linked to criminality.[36] Furthermore, there is little dispute that much of delinquency represents malicious, negativistic, and nonutilitarian activity. For example, what do individuals have to gain from destroying mailboxes or spraying graffiti on walls? These acts will never earn much money or any payoff other than peer respect. So, ultimately, it appears that there is some face validity to what Cohen proposed in the sense that some youths engage in behavior that has no value other than earning peer respect, even though that behavior is negativistic and nonutilitarian according to the values of conventional society. Regardless of some criticisms of Cohen's model, he provided an important structural strain theory of the development of gangs and lower-class delinquency.

Cloward and Ohlin's Theory of Differential Opportunity

Five years after Cohen published his theory, Richard Cloward and Lloyd Ohlin presented yet another structural strain theory of gang formation and behavior.[37] Like Merton and Cohen, Cloward and Ohlin assumed in their model that all youths, including those in the lower class, are socialized to believe in the American Dream and that when individuals realize that they are blocked from conventional opportunities they become frustrated and strained. What distinguishes Cloward and Ohlin's theory from that of the previous strain theories is that they identified three different types of gangs based on the characteristics of each neighborhood's social structure. They believed the nature of gangs varied according to the availability of illegal opportunities in the social structure. So, whereas previous strain theories focused only on lack of legal opportunities, Cloward and Ohlin's model emphasized both legal and illegal opportunities; the availability or lack of these opportunities largely determined what type of gang would form in that neighborhood, hence the name *differential opportunity theory.* Furthermore, the authors acknowledged Edwin Sutherland's influence on their theory (see Section VIII), and it is evident in their focus on the associations made in the neighborhood.

According to differential opportunity theory, the three types of gangs that form are criminal gangs, conflict gangs, and retreatist gangs. **Criminal gangs** form in lower-class neighborhoods that have an organized structure of adult criminal behavior. Such neighborhoods are so organized and stable that criminal networks are often known and accepted by the conventional individuals in the area. In these neighborhoods, the adult gangsters mentor the youth and take them under their wings. This can pay off for the adult criminals, too, because youths can often be used to do the dirty work for the criminal enterprises in the neighborhood without risk of serious punishment if they are caught. The successful adult offenders supply the youths with the motives and techniques for committing

---

[35]See Bernard, "Testing Structural Strain Theories"; Merton, "Opportunity Structure"; Delbert Elliott and Harwin Voss, *Delinquency and Dropout* (Lexington, MA: D. C. Heath, 1974); Terence P. Thornberry, Melanie Moore, and R. L. Christenson, "The Effect of Dropping Out of High School on Subsequent Criminal Behavior," *Criminology* 23 (1985): 3–18; G. Roger Jarjoura, "Does Dropping Out of School Enhance Delinquent Involvement? Results from a Large-Scale National Probability Sample," *Criminology* 31 (1993): 149–72; and G. Roger Jarjoura, "The Conditional Effect of Social Class on the Dropout Delinquency Relationship," *Journal of Research in Crime and Delinquency* 33 (1996): 232–55. See discussion in Donald J. Shoemaker, *Theories of Delinquency*, 6th ed. (New York: Oxford University Press, 2009).

[36]Alexander Liazos, "School, Alienation, and Delinquency," *Crime and Delinquency* 24 (1978): 355–70; Joseph W. Rogers and G. Larry Mays, *Juvenile Delinquency and Juvenile Justice* (New York: Wiley, 1987); Clarence E. Tygart, "Strain Theory and Public School Vandalism: Academic Tracking, School Social Status, and Students' Academic Achievement," *Youth and Society* 20 (1988): 106–18; Hirschi, *Causes of Delinquency.*

[37]Richard A. Cloward and Lloyd E. Ohlin, *Delinquency and Opportunity: A Theory of Delinquent Gangs* (New York: The Free Press, 1960). For a discussion and theoretical critique of the model, see Bernard, "Testing Structural Strain Theories," and Merton, "Opportunity Structure," respectively.

▲ **Image 6.5** Organized crime syndicates are typically found in neighborhoods with more structured criminal organizations.

SOURCE: © istockphoto.com / mbbirdy

crime. So, while members of criminal gangs are blocked from legal opportunities, they are offered ample opportunities in the illegal realm.

Criminal gangs tend to reflect the strong organization and stability of such neighborhoods. Therefore, criminal gangs primarily commit property or economic crimes with the goal of making a profit through illegal behavior. These crimes can range from running numbers as local bookies to fencing stolen goods to running businesses that are fronts for vice crimes (e.g., prostitution, drug trading). All of these businesses involve making a profit illegally, and there is often a system or structure in which the criminal activity takes place. Furthermore, these criminal gangs most closely follow Merton's adaptation of innovation because the members still want to achieve the goals of conventional society (financial success). Because of their strong organizational structure, these gangs favor members who have self-control and are good at planning over individuals who are highly impulsive or uncontrolled.

Examples of criminal gangs are seen in movies depicting highly organized neighborhoods that often consist primarily of one ethnicity, including *The Godfather, The Godfather Part II, A Bronx Tale, State of Grace, Sleepers, New Jack City, Clockers, GoodFellas, Better Luck Tomorrow*, and many others that were partially based on real events. All of these depictions involve a highly structured hierarchy of a criminal enterprise, which is largely a manifestation of the organization of the neighborhood. Hollywood motion pictures also produce stories about older criminals taking younger males from the neighborhood under their wings and training them in the ways of criminal networks. Furthermore, virtually all ethnic groups offer examples of this type of gang or neighborhood; the list of movies that was just given includes Italian American, Irish American, African American, and Asian American examples. Thus, criminal gangs can be found across the racial and ethnic spectrum, largely because all groups have certain neighborhoods that exhibit strong organization and stability.

Conflict gangs were another type of gang that Cloward and Ohlin identified. Conflict gangs tend to develop in neighborhoods that have weak stability and little or no organization. In fact, the neighborhood often seems to be in a state of flux with people constantly moving in and out. Because the youths in the neighborhood do not have a solid crime network or adult criminal mentors, they tend to form as relatively disorganized gangs, and they typically lack the skills and knowledge to make a profit through criminal activity. Therefore, the primary illegal activity of conflict gangs is violence, which they use to gain prominence and respect among themselves and the neighborhood. Due to the disorganized nature of the neighborhoods as well as the gangs themselves, conflict gangs never quite achieve the respect and stability that criminal gangs typically achieve. The members of conflict gangs tend to be more impulsive and lack self-control compared to members of criminal gangs, largely because there are no adult criminal mentors to control them.

According to Cloward and Ohlin, conflict gangs are blocked from both legitimate and illegitimate opportunities. In applying Merton's adaptations, conflict gangs would probably fit the category of rebellion, largely because none of the other categories fit well, but it can also be argued that conflict gangs have rejected the goals and means of conventional society and implemented their own values, which emphasize violence. Examples of motion pictures that depict this type of breakdown in community structure and a mostly violent gang culture are *Menace II Society*,

Boyz n the Hood, *A Clockwork Orange*, *Colors*, and *The Outsiders*, which all emphasize the chaos and violence that results when neighborhood and family organization is weak.

Finally, if individuals are double failures in both legitimate and illegitimate worlds, meaning that they can't achieve success in school or status in their local gangs, they join together to form **retreatist gangs**. Because members of retreatist gangs are no good at making a profit from crime or using violence to achieve status, the primary form of offending is usually drug usage. Like individuals who choose Merton's retreatist adaptation to strain, the members of retreatist gangs often want simply to escape from reality. Therefore, the primary activity of the gang when they get together is usually just to get high, which is well represented by Hollywood in such movies as *Trainspotting*, *Drugstore Cowboy*, and *The Panic in Needle Park*. In all of these movies, the only true goal of the gangs is getting stoned to escape from the worlds where they have failed.

There are a number of empirical studies and critiques of Cloward and Ohlin's theory, with the criticisms being similar to those of Merton's strain theory. Specifically, the critics argue that there is little evidence that gaps between what lower-class youths aspire to and what they expect to achieve produce frustration and strain, nor do such gaps appear predictive of gang membership or criminality.[38] Another criticism of Cloward and Ohlin's theory is the inability to find empirical evidence that supports their model of the formation of three types of gangs and their specializations in offending. While some research supports the existence of gangs that appear to specialize in certain forms of offending, many studies find that the observed specializations of gangs do not exactly follow the categories that Cloward and Ohlin proposed.[39] Additional studies have shown that many gangs tend not to specialize but rather to engage in a wider variety of offending behaviors.

Despite the criticisms of Cloward and Ohlin's model of gang formation, their theoretical framework inspired policy, largely due to the influence that their work had on Attorney General Robert Kennedy, who had read their book. In fact, Kennedy asked Ohlin to assist in developing federal policies regarding delinquency,[40] which resulted in the Juvenile Delinquency Prevention and Control Act of 1961. Cloward and Ohlin's theory was a major influence on the Mobilization for Youth project in New York City, which, along with the federal legislation, stressed creating education and work opportunities for youths. Although evaluations of this program showed little effect on reducing delinquency, it was impressive that such theorizing about lower-class male youths could have such a large impact on policy interventions.

Ultimately, the variations presented by Cohen, as well as Cloward and Ohlin, provided additional revisions that seemed at the time to advance the validity of strain theory. However, most of these revisions were based on official statistics that showed that lower-class male youth committed most crime, which were later shown by self-reports to be exaggerated.[41] Once scholars realized that most of the earlier models were not empirically valid for most criminal activity, strain theory became unpopular for several decades. But during the 1980s, another version was devised by Robert Agnew, who rejuvenated interest in strain theory by devising a way to make it more general and applicable to a larger variety of crimes and forms of deviance.

---

[38] James F. Short, "Gang Delinquency and Anomie," in *Anomie and Deviant Behavior*, ed. Marshall B. Clinard (New York: Free Press, 1964), 98–127; James F. Short, Ramon Rivera, and Ray A. Tennyson, "Perceived Opportunities, Gang Membership, and Delinquency," *American Sociological Review* 30 (1965): 56–67; James F. Short and Fred L. Strodtbeck, *Group Processes and Gang Delinquency* (Chicago: University of Chicago Press, 1965); Liska, "Aspirations"; and Hirschi, *Causes of Delinquency*. See discussion in Shoemaker, *Theories of Delinquency*, 121–30.

[39] Irving Spergel, *Racketville, Slumtown, and Haulburg: An Exploratory Study of Delinquent Subcultures* (Chicago: University of Chicago Press, 1964); Short and Strodtbeck, *Group Processes*; Paul E. Tracy, Marvin E. Wolfgang, and Robert M. Figlio, *Delinquency Careers in Two Birth Cohorts* (New York: Plenum, 1990).

[40] Lamar T. Empey, *American Delinquency*, 4th ed. (Belmont, CA: Wadsworth, 1999).

[41] Tittle et al., "Myth of Social Class"; Hindelang et al., "Correlates of Delinquency."

▲ **Image 6.6** Individuals experience stressors every day, and general strain theory emphasizes the importance of stress and anger in increasing the likelihood of engaging in criminal behavior.

SOURCE: © istockphoto.com / grinvalds

General Strain Theory

In the 1980s, Robert Agnew proposed **general strain theory**, which covers a much larger range of behavior by not concentrating on simply the lower class but providing a model more applicable to the frustrations that all individuals feel in everyday life.[42] Unlike other strain theories, general strain theory does not rely on assumptions about the frustration arising when people realize that the American Dream is a false promise to those of the lower classes. Rather, this theoretical framework assumes that people of all social classes and economic positions deal with frustrations in routine daily life.

Previous strain theories, such as the models proposed by Merton, Cohen, and Cloward and Ohlin, focused on individuals' failure to achieve positively valued goals that they had been socialized to work to obtain. General strain theory also focuses on this source of strain; however, it identifies two additional categories of strain: *presentation of noxious stimuli* and *removal of positively valued stimuli.* In addition to the failure to achieve one's goals, Agnew claimed that the presentation of noxious stimuli (i.e., bad things) in one's life could cause major stress and frustration. Examples of noxious stimuli would include things like an abusive parent, a critical teacher, or an overly demanding boss. These are just some of the many negative factors that can exist in one's life—the number of examples is endless.

The other strain category Agnew identified was the removal of positive stimuli, which is likely the largest cause of frustration. Examples of removal of positively valued stimuli include the loss of a good job, loss of the use of a car for a period of time, or the loss of a loved one. Such losses, like the other two sources of strain, may have varying degrees of influence depending on the individual. One person may not feel much frustration in losing a job or divorcing a spouse, whereas another person may experience severe anxiety or depression from such events.

Ultimately, general strain theory proposes that these three categories of strain (failure to achieve goals, noxious stimuli, and removal of positive stimuli) will lead to stress and that this results in a propensity to feel anger. Anger can be seen as a primary mediating factor in the causal model of the general strain framework. It is predicted that, to the extent that the three sources of strain cause feelings of anger in an individual, he or she will be predisposed to commit crime and deviance. However, Agnew was clear in stating that if an individual can somehow cope with this anger in a positive way, then such feelings do not necessarily have to result in criminal activity. These coping mechanisms vary widely across individuals; different strategies work for some people better than others. For example, some

[42] For Agnew's works regarding this theory, see Robert Agnew, "A Revised Strain Theory of Delinquency," *Social Forces* 64 (1985): 151–67; Robert Agnew, "Foundation for a General Strain Theory of Crime and Delinquency," *Criminology* 30 (1992): 47–88; Robert Agnew and Helene Raskin White, "An Empirical Test of General Strain Theory," *Criminology* 30 (1992): 475–500; Robert Agnew, "Controlling Delinquency: Recommendations from General Strain Theory," in *Crime and Public Policy: Putting Theory to Work*, ed. Hugh Barlow (Boulder: Westview Press, 1995), 43–70; Agnew et al., "A New Test," 681–704; Robert Agnew, "Building on the Foundation of General Strain Theory: Specifying the Types of Strain Most Likely to Lead to Crime and Delinquency," *Journal of Research in Crime and Delinquency* 38 (2001): 319–61.

people relieve stress by working out or running, whereas others watch television or a movie. One type of activity that has shown relatively consistent success in relieving stress is laughter, which psychologists are now prescribing as a release of tension. Another is yoga, which includes simple breathing techniques such as taking several deep breaths; it has been shown to physiologically enhance release of stress.

Although Agnew did not originally provide details on how coping mechanisms work or explore the extant psychological research on these strategies, he specifically pointed to such mechanisms for dealing with anger in prosocial ways. The primary prediction regarding coping mechanisms is that individuals who find ways to deal with their stress and anger positively will no longer be predisposed to commit crime, whereas individuals who do not find healthy, positive outlets for their anger and frustrations will be far more likely to commit crime. Obviously, the goal is to reduce the use of antisocial and negative coping mechanisms, such as drug usage or aggression, which either are criminal in themselves or increase the likelihood of offending.

Recent research and theoretical development has more fully examined various coping mechanisms and their effectiveness in reducing anger and, thus, preventing criminal activity. Obviously, in focusing on individuals' perceptions of stress and anger as well as on their personal ability to cope with such feelings, general strain theory places more emphasis on the micro level of analysis. Still, due to its origins in structural strain theory, it is included in this section and is typically classified as belonging to the category of strain theories, which include the earlier theories that are more oriented to the macro level. In addition, recent studies and revisions of the theory have attempted to examine the validity of general strain theory propositions at the macro, structural level.[43]

Since it was first proposed in the mid-1980s, there has been a vast amount of research examining various aspects of general strain theory.[44] For the most part, studies have generally supported the model. Most studies find a link between the three categories of strain and higher rates of criminality as well as a link between the sources of strain and feelings of anger or other negative emotions (e.g., anxiety, depression).[45] However, the theory and especially the way it has been tested have also been criticized.

It is important for strain research to measure subjects' perceptions and feelings of frustration, not simply the occurrence of certain events themselves. Unfortunately, some studies have only looked at the latter, and the validity

---

[43]Timothy Brezina, Alex Piquero, and Paul Mazerolle, "Student Anger and Aggressive Behavior in School: An Initial Test of Agnew's Macro-Level Strain Theory," *Journal of Research in Crime and Delinquency* 38 (2001): 362–86.

[44]Agnew and White, "An Empirical Test"; Agnew et al., "A New Test"; Justin W. Patchin and Sameer Hinduja, "Traditional and Nontraditional Bullying among Youth: A Test of General Strain Theory," *Youth and Society* 43 (2011): 727–51; Raymond Paternoster and Paul Mazerolle, "General Strain Theory and Delinquency: A Replication and Extension," *Journal of Research in Crime and Delinquency* 31 (1994): 235–63; Timothy Brezina, "Adapting to Strain: An Examination of Delinquent Coping Responses," *Criminology* 34 (1996): 39–60; John P. Hoffman and Alan S. Miller, "A Latent Variable Analysis of General Strain Theory," *Journal of Quantitative Criminology* 14 (1998): 83–110; John P. Hoffman and Felicia Gray Cerbone, "Stressful Life Events and Delinquency Escalation in Early Adolescence," *Criminology* 37 (1999): 343–74; Paul Mazerolle and Alex Piquero, "Linking Exposure to Strain with Anger: An Investigation of Deviant Adaptations," *Journal of Criminal Justice* 26 (1998): 195–211; Paul Mazerolle, "Gender, General Strain, and Delinquency: An Empirical Examination," *Justice Quarterly* 15 (1998): 65–91; John P. Hoffman and S. Susan Su, "Stressful Life Events and Adolescent Substance Use and Depression: Conditional and Gender Differentiated Effects," *Substance Use and Misuse* 33 (1998): 2219–62; Lisa M. Broidy, "A Test of General Strain Theory," *Criminology* 39 (2001): 9–36; Nicole Leeper Piquero and Miriam Sealock, "Generalizing General Strain Theory: An Examination of an Offending Population," *Justice Quarterly* 17 (2000): 449–84; Paul Mazerolle and Jeff Maahs, "General Strain and Delinquency: An Alternative Examination of Conditioning Influences," *Justice Quarterly* 17 (2000): 753–78; Paul Mazerolle et al., "Strain, Anger, and Delinquent Adaptations: Specifying General Strain Theory," *Journal of Criminal Justice* 28 (2000): 89–101; Stephen W. Baron and Timothy F. Hartnagel, "Street Youth and Labor Market Strain," *Journal of Criminal Justice* 30 (2002): 519–33; Carter Hay, "Family Strain, Gender, and Delinquency," *Sociological Perspectives* 46 (2003): 107–35; Sung Joon Jang and Byron R. Johnson, "Strain, Negative Emotions, and Deviant Coping among African Americans: A Test of General Strain Theory," *Journal of Quantitative Criminology* 19 (2003): 79–105; Paul Mazerolle, Alex Piquero, and George E. Capowich, "Examining the Links between Strain, Situational and Dispositional Anger, and Crime: Further Specifying and Testing General Strain Theory," *Youth and Society* 35 (2003): 131–57; Stephen W. Baron, "General Strain, Street Youth and Crime: A Test of Agnew's Revised Theory," *Criminology* 42 (2004): 457–84.

[45]A recent review of this research can be found in Baron, "General Strain," 457–67.

Figure 6.2 • Model of general strain theory

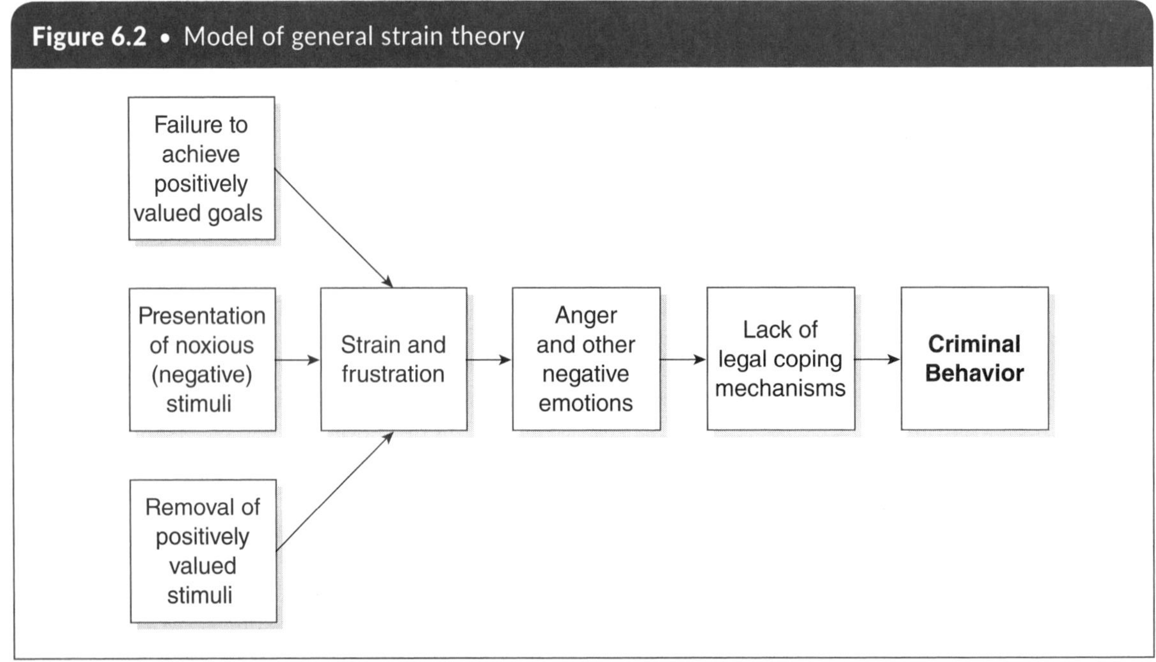

of such findings is questionable.[46] Other studies, however, have directly measured subjective perceptions of frustration as well as personal feelings of anger.[47]

Such studies have found mixed support for the hypothesis that certain events lead to anger[48] but less support for the prediction that anger leads to criminality, and this link is particularly weak for nonviolent offending.[49] On the other hand, the most recent studies have found support for the links between strain and anger as well as anger and criminal behavior, particularly when coping variables are considered.[50] Still, many of the studies that examine the effects of anger use time-stable, trait measures as opposed to incident-specific, state measures that would be more consistent with the situation-specific emphasis of general strain theory.[51] This is similar to the methodological criticism that has been leveled against studies of self-conscious emotions, particularly shame and guilt; when it comes to measuring emotions such as anger and shame, criminologists should choose their measures carefully and make sure the instruments are consistent with the theory they are testing. Thus, future research on general strain theory should employ more effective, subjective measures of straining events and situational states of anger.

---

[46]For examples, see Jean-Louis Van Gelder, Danielle Reynald and Henk Elffers, "Anticipated Emotions and Immediate Affect in Criminal Decision Making: From Shame to Anger," in *Affect and Cognition in Criminal Decision Making*, ed. Jean-Louis Van Gelder, Henk Elffers, Danielle Reynald, and Daniel Nagin (London: Routledge, 2014), 161–78; Paternoster and Mazerolle, "General Strain Theory"; Hoffman and Cerbone, "Stressful Life Events and Delinquency"; and Hoffman and Su, "Stressful Life Events."

[47]Broidy, "A Test"; Baron, "General Strain."

[48]See Brezina, "Adapting to Strain"; Broidy, "A Test"; Mazerolle and Piquero, "Linking Exposure."

[49]Mazerolle and Piquero, "Linking Exposure"; Piquero and Sealock, "Generalizing General Strain Theory"; Mazerolle et al., "Strain, Anger."

[50]Baron, "General Strain"; Mazerolle et al., "Examining the Links."

[51]For examples, see Mazerolle et al., "Strain, Anger"; and Baron, "General Strain." See discussions in Mazerolle et al., "Examining the Links"; and Akers and Sellers, *Criminological Theories*, 180–82.

Regardless of the criticisms of general strain theory, it is hard to deny its face validity. After all, virtually everyone can relate to reacting differently to similar situations based on what kind of day they are having. For example, we all have days in which everything seems to be going great—it's a Friday, you receive accolades at work, and you are looking forward to a nice weekend with your friends or family. If someone says something derogatory to you or cuts you off in traffic, you will probably be inclined to let it go because you're in such a good mood. On the other hand, we also all have days in which everything seems to be going horribly—it's Monday, you get blamed for mishaps at work, and you have a fight with your spouse or significant other. At this time, if someone yells at you or cuts you off in traffic, you may be more inclined to respond aggressively in some way. Or perhaps you will overreact and snap at a loved one or friend when he or she really didn't do much to deserve it; this is often a form of displacement in which a cumulative buildup of stressors results in taking frustration out on another individual. In many ways, this type of behavior, which is prevalent and easy to see in everyday life, supports general strain theory.

Summary of Strain Theories

The common assumption found across all variations of strain theory is that crime is far more common among individuals who are under a great degree of stress and frustration, especially those who can't cope with stress in a positive way. The origin of most variations of strain theory can be traced to Durkheim's and Merton's concepts of anomie, which essentially means a state of chaos, or normlessness, in society due to a breakdown in the ability of societal institutions to regulate human desires, thereby resulting in feelings of strain.

Although different types of strain theories were proposed and gained popularity at various periods throughout the 20th century, they all became accepted during eras that were politically and culturally conducive to such perspectives, especially in terms of the differences across the strain models. For example, Merton's formulation of strain in the 1930s emphasized the importance of the economic institution, which was developed and became very popular during the Great Depression. Then, in the late 1950s, two strain theories that focused on gang formation were developed, by Cohen and by Cloward and Ohlin; they became popular among politicians and society due to a focus on official statistics suggesting that most crime at that time was being committed by lower-class, inner-city male youths—many of whom were gang members. Finally, Agnew developed his general strain model in the mid- to late 1980s, during a time in which a number of general theories of crime were being developed (e.g., Michael Gottfredson and Travis Hirschi's low self-control theory and Rob Sampson and John Laub's developmental theory), so such models were popular at that time, particularly those that emphasized personality traits (such as anger) and experiences of individuals. So, all of the variations of strain, like all of the theories discussed in this book, were manifestations of the period in which they were developed and became widely accepted by academics, politicians, and society.

Policy Implications

Although this section dealt with a wide range of theories regarding social structure, the most applicable policy implications are those suggested by the most recent theoretical models of this genre. Thus, we will focus on the key policy factors in the most modern versions of this perspective. The factors that are most vital for policy implications regarding social structure theories are those regarding educational and vocational opportunities and programs that help people develop healthy coping mechanisms to deal with stress.

Empirical studies have shown that intervention programs are needed for high-risk youths that focus on educational or vocational training and opportunities, because developing motivation for such endeavors can have a significant impact on reducing their offending rates.[52] Providing an individual with a job, or the preparation for one,

[52]John P. Wright, Stephen Tibbetts, and Leah Daigle, *Criminals in the Making: Criminality across the Life Course* (Thousand Oaks, CA: Sage, 2015).

is key to building a more stable life, even if it is not a high-paying position. As a result, the individual is less likely to feel stressed or strained. In modern times, a person is lucky to have a stable job, and this must be communicated to our youths, and hopefully, they will find some intrinsic value in the work they do.

Specifically, in regard to Merton's strain theory, there have been significant attempts to address the more global issues of deprivation that result from poverty in U.S. society. Perhaps the best example is the War on Poverty, a federal program introduced by President Lyndon B. Johnson during the 1960s. Although an enormous amount of money and other resources were spent in trying to aid the poor in order to reduce crime rates in America, crime rates soared during this period. Many experts noted that the federal investment was not efficiently handed out, but the rise in crime during this period still casts doubt on the effectiveness of such a strategy.

Rather, the Maryland Report of "What Works, What Doesn't?" (see Section V) concludes that vocational training for adult male offenders has consistently lowered offending rates, as have intensive residential training programs for at-risk youth (such as Job Corps).[53] This conclusion appears consistent with our previous finding that a focus on certain high-risk individuals is more effective than programs addressing an entire group, such as all types of offenders. Perhaps this is because not all offenders have the target characteristic, but such programs tend to be effective for those who do. For example, some offenders are thrust into drug programs even though they have never used drugs or alcohol. Also, some offenders are coerced into engaging in vocational programs when they already have skills in a certain trade. Thus, it makes sense to focus resources (e.g., vocational programs, drug programs) on the people who are most at risk for the given risk factor.

Another key area of recommendations from this perspective involves developing healthy coping mechanisms. Everyone deals with stress virtually every day. The key is not avoiding stress or strain, because that is inevitable. Rather, the key is to develop healthy, legal ways to cope with such strain. Many programs have been created to train individuals on how to handle stress without resorting to antisocial behavior. There has been some success gained from anger management programs, particularly the ones that take a cognitive behavioral approach and often involve role-playing to teach individuals to think before they act.[54]

Conclusion

This section examined the theories that emphasize inequitable social structure as the primary cause of crime. First, we examined early perspectives, which established that societies vary in the extent to which they are stratified, and looked at the consequences of the inequalities in and complexities of such structures as well as a variety of social concepts that early seminal sociologists noted in the 19th century, such as relative deprivation, collective conscience, and anomie. An important part of this theoretical evolution was the proposition that decisions made by individuals that traditionally were thought to be entirely made by the individual, such as suicide, were actually highly predicted by societal factors.

Our examination of strain theories explored theoretical models proposing that individuals and groups who are not offered equal opportunities for achieving success can develop stress and frustration and, in turn, dispositions for committing criminal behavior. We also examined more modern versions of strain, such as general strain theory, which has shown much support in empirical studies. Finally, we examined the policy recommendations suggested by this theoretical model, which include the need to provide individuals with educational and job opportunities and help them develop healthy coping mechanisms.

---

[53]Lawrence Sherman et al., *Preventing Crime: What Works, What Doesn't, What's Promising: A Report to the United States Congress* (Washington, DC: U.S. Department of Justice, 1997).

[54]Patricia Van Voorhis and Emily Salisbury, *Correctional Counseling and Rehabilitation*, 8th ed. (Cincinnati, OH: Anderson, 2013).

SECTION SUMMARY

- First, we discussed the primary distinction between social structure theories and other types of explanations (e.g., biological or social process theories).
- We examined the importance of the early sociological positivists, particularly Guerry, Quetelet, and Durkheim as well as their contributions to the study of deviance and crime.
- We explored reasons why strain theory was developed and became popular in its time and discussed the primary assumptions and propositions of Merton's strain theory.
- We identified, defined, and examined examples of all five adaptations to strain identified by Merton.
- We discussed the variations of strain theory of groups presented by Cohen as well as by Cloward and Ohlin, who presented models of youth delinquency or gang formation based on a strain perspective.
- Both Cohen and Cloward and Ohlin presented models that had similar categories of offenders based on the ways that individuals deal with the strain or frustration they face; these types of offenders or gangs mimic some of the adaptations that Merton presented in his original strain framework.
- General strain theory was examined with an emphasis on how it is far more robust and general a theory than Merton's original framework, which only focused on economic strain.
- We examined the empirical support of general strain theory, the emphasis that this theory has placed on factors outside of the economy that frustrate individuals, and the importance of coping mechanisms in dealing with such strain.

KEY TERMS

adaptations to strain 238
anomie 229
collective conscience 233
college boy 244
conflict gangs 246
conformity 233
corner boy 244
criminal gangs 245
delinquent boy 244
general strain theory 248
innovation 239
mechanical societies 233
organic societies 233
reaction formation 243
rebellion 239
relative deprivation 231
retreatism 239
retreatist gangs 247
ritualism 239
social dynamics 230
social statics 230
strain theory 229

DISCUSSION QUESTIONS

1. How does sociological positivism differ from biological or psychological positivism?
2. Which of the early sociological positivism theorists do you think contributed most to the evolution of social structure theories of crime? Why? Do you think their ideas still hold up today?
3. Can you think of modern examples of Durkheim's image of mechanical societies? Do you think such societies have more or less crime than modern organic societies?

4. What type of adaptation to strain do you think fits you the best? The least? What adaptation do you think best fits your professor? Your postal delivery worker? Your garbage collector?
5. Do you know school friends who fit Cohen's model of status frustration? What did they do in response to the feelings of strain?
6. How would you describe the neighborhood where you or others you know grew up in terms of Cloward and Ohlin's model of organization or disorganization? Can you relate to the types of gangs they discussed?

WEB RESOURCES

Émile Durkheim

https://kpulawandsociety.wordpress.com/2012/10/22/durkheims-views-crime-as-normal
https://www.thoughtco.com/emile-durkheim-relevance-to-sociology-today-3026482
http://www.azquotes.com/author/4244-Emile_Durkheim

Strain Theory

http://www.umsl.edu/~keelr/200/strain.html
http://www.oxfordbibliographies.com/view/document/obo-9780195396607/obo-9780195396607-0005.xml

READING /// 12

In this selection, Robert Merton, who is one of the most cited and respected sociologists of the 20th century, explains his theory for why individuals commit crime. Specifically, he asserts that the primary cause of crime is the economy. It plays a large part in determining criminal offending as well as the many adaptations to strain that Merton proposes. Although strain theory, particularly Merton's framework, emphasizes the macro or group level of analysis, the theory also describes five stereotypical ways that individuals deal with such frustrations or strain.

While reading this entry, consider the following points:

- When Merton's theory became so popular and why it would happen at that time
- The various types of adaptations to strain and how they are defined or distinguished from each other
- The type(s) of criminal behavior Merton's theory emphasizes and thus would explain best

Social Structure and Anomie

Robert K. Merton

There persists a notable tendency in sociological theory to attribute the malfunctioning of social structure primarily to those of man's imperious biological drives which are not adequately restrained by social control. In this view, the social order is solely a device for "impulse management" and the "social processing" of tensions. These impulses which break through social control, be it noted, are held to be biologically derived. Nonconformity is assumed to be rooted in original nature. Conformity is by implication the result of a utilitarian calculus or unreasoned conditioning. This point of view, whatever its other deficiencies, clearly begs one question. It provides no basis for determining the nonbiological conditions which induce deviations from prescribed patterns of conduct. In this paper, it will be suggested that certain phases of social structure generate the circumstances in which infringement of social codes constitutes a "normal" response.

The conceptual scheme to be outlined is designed to provide a coherent, systematic approach to the study of socio-cultural sources of deviate behavior. Our primary aim lies in discovering how some social structures *exert a definite pressure* upon certain persons in the society to engage in nonconformist rather than conformist conduct. The many ramifications of the scheme cannot all be discussed; the problems mentioned outnumber those explicitly treated.

Among the elements of social and cultural structure, two are important for our purposes. These are analytically separable although they merge imperceptibly in concrete situations. The first consists of culturally defined goals, purposes, and interests. It comprises a frame of aspirational reference. These goals are more or less integrated and involve varying degrees of prestige and sentiment. They constitute a basic, but not the exclusive, component of what Linton aptly has called "designs for group living."

SOURCE: Robert Merton, "Social Structure and Anomie," *American Sociological Review* 3, no. 3 (2002): 672–82. Selection taken from S. Cote, ed., *Criminological Theories: Bridging the Past to the Future* (Thousand Oaks, CA: Sage, 2002), 95–103. (Original publication 1938).

Some of these cultural aspirations are related to the original drives of man, but they are not determined by them. The second phase of the social structure defines, regulates, and controls the acceptable modes of achieving these goals. Every social group invariably couples its scale of desired ends with moral or institutional regulation of permissible and required procedures for attaining these ends. These regulatory norms and moral imperatives do not necessarily coincide with technical or efficiency norms. Many procedures which from the standpoint of particular *individuals* would be most efficient in securing desired values, e.g., illicit oil-stock schemes, theft, fraud, are ruled out of the institutional area of permitted conduct. The choice of expedients is limited by the institutional norms.

To say that these two elements, culture goals and institutional norms, operate jointly is not to say that the ranges of alternative behaviors and aims bear some constant relation to one another. The emphasis upon certain goals may vary independently of the degree of emphasis upon institutional means. There may develop a disproportionate, at times, a virtually exclusive, stress upon the value of specific goals, involving relatively slight concern with the institutionally appropriate modes of attaining these goals. The limiting case in this direction is reached when the range of alternative procedures is limited only by technical rather than institutional considerations. Any and all devices which promise attainment of the all important goal would be permitted in this hypothetical polar case. This constitutes one type of cultural malintegration. A second polar type is found in groups where activities originally conceived as instrumental are transmuted into ends in themselves. The original purposes are forgotten and ritualistic adherence to institutionally prescribed conduct becomes virtually obsessive. Stability is largely ensured while change is flouted. The range of alternative behaviors is severely limited. There develops a tradition-bound, sacred society characterized by neophobia. The occupational psychosis of the bureaucrat may be cited as a case in point. Finally, there are the intermediate types of groups where a balance between culture goals and institutional means is maintained. These are the significantly integrated and relatively stable, though changing groups.

An effective equilibrium between the two phases of the social structure is maintained as long as satisfactions accrue to individuals who conform to both constraints, viz., satisfactions from the achievement of the goals and satisfactions emerging directly from the institutionally canalized modes of striving to attain these ends. Success, in such equilibrated cases, is twofold. Success is reckoned in terms of the product and in terms of the process, in terms of the outcome and in terms of activities. Continuing satisfactions must derive from sheer participation in a competitive order as well as from eclipsing one's competitors if the order itself is to be sustained. The occasional sacrifices involved in institutionalized conduct must be compensated by socialized rewards. The distribution of statuses and roles through competition must be so organized that positive incentives for conformity to roles and adherence to status obligations are provided for every position within the distributive order. Aberrant conduct, therefore, may be viewed as a symptom of dissociation between culturally defined aspirations and socially structured means.

Of the types of groups which result from the independent variation of the two phases of the social structure, we shall be primarily concerned with the first, namely, that involving a disproportionate accent on goals. This statement must be recast in a proper perspective. In no group is there an absence of regulatory codes governing conduct, yet groups do vary in the degree to which these folkways, mores, and institutional controls are effectively integrated with the more diffuse goals which are part of the culture matrix. Emotional convictions may cluster about the complex of socially acclaimed ends, meanwhile shifting their support from the culturally defined implementation of these ends. As we shall see, certain aspects of the social structure may generate countermores and antisocial behavior precisely because of differential emphases on goals and regulations. In the extreme case, the latter may be so vitiated by the goal-emphasis that the range of behavior is limited only by considerations of technical expediency. The sole significant question then becomes, which available means is most efficient in netting the socially approved value? The technically most feasible procedure, whether legitimate or not, is preferred to the institutionally prescribed conduct. As this process continues, the integration of the society becomes tenuous and anomie ensues.

Thus, in competitive athletics, when the aim of victory is shorn of its institutional trappings and success in contests becomes construed as "winning the game" rather than "winning through circumscribed modes of activity," a premium is implicitly set upon the use of illegitimate but technically efficient means. The star of the opposing football team is surreptitiously slugged; the wrestler furtively incapacitates his opponent through ingenious but illicit techniques; university alumni covertly subsidize "students" whose talents are largely confined to the athletic field. The emphasis on the goal has so attenuated the satisfactions deriving from sheer participation in the competitive activity that these satisfactions are virtually confined to a successful outcome. Through the same process, tension generated by the desire to win in a poker game is relieved by successfully dealing oneself four aces, or, when the cult of success has become completely dominant, by sagaciously shuffling the cards in a game of solitaire. The faint twinge of uneasiness in the last instance and the surreptitious nature of public delicts indicate clearly that the institutional rules of the game *are known* to those who evade them, but that the emotional supports of these rules are largely vitiated by cultural exaggeration of the success-goal. They are microcosmic images of the social macrocosm.

Of course, this process is not restricted to the realm of sport. The process whereby exaltation of the end generates a *literal demoralization,* i.e., a deinstitutionalization, of the means is one which characterizes many groups in which the two phases of the social structure are not highly integrated. The extreme emphasis upon the accumulation of wealth as a symbol of success in our own society militates against the completely effective control of institutionally regulated modes of acquiring a fortune. Fraud, corruption, vice, crime, in short, the entire catalogue of proscribed behavior, becomes increasingly common when the emphasis on the *culturally induced* success-goal becomes divorced from a coordinated institutional emphasis. This observation is of crucial theoretical importance in examining the doctrine that antisocial behavior most frequently derives from biological drives breaking through the restraints imposed by society. The difference is one between a strictly utilitarian interpretation which conceives man's ends as random and an analysis which finds these ends deriving from the basic values of the culture.

Our analysis can scarcely stop at this juncture. We must turn to other aspects of the social structure if we are to deal with the social genesis of the varying rates and types of deviate behavior characteristic of different societies. Thus far, we have sketched three ideal types of social orders constituted by distinctive patterns of relations between culture ends and means. Turning from these types of *culture patterning,* we find five logically possible, alternative modes of adjustment or adaptation by *individuals* within the culture-bearing society or group. These are schematically presented in Figure 1, where (+) signifies "acceptance," (−) signifies "elimination" and (±) signifies "rejection and substitution of new goals and standards."

Our discussion of the relation between these alternative responses and other phases of the social structure must be prefaced by the observation that persons may shift from one alternative to another as they engage in different social activities. These categories refer to role adjustments in specific situations, not to personality *in toto.* To treat the development of this process in various spheres of conduct would introduce a complexity

Figure 1

	Culture Goals	Institutionalized Means
I. Conformity	+	+
II. Innovation	+	−
III. Ritualism	−	+
IV. Retreatism	−	−
V. Rebellion	±	±

unmanageable within the confines of this paper. For this reason, we shall be concerned primarily with economic activity in the broad sense, "the production, exchange, distribution and consumption of goods and services" in our competitive society, wherein wealth has taken on a highly symbolic cast. Our task is to search out some of the factors which exert pressure upon individuals to engage in certain of these logically possible alternative responses. This choice, as we shall see, is far from random.

In every society, Adaptation I (conformity to both culture goals and means) is the most common and widely diffused. Were this not so, the stability and continuity of the society could not be maintained. The mesh of expectancies which constitutes every social order is sustained by the modal behavior of its members falling within the first category. Conventional role behavior oriented toward the basic values of the group is the rule rather than the exception. It is this fact alone which permits us to speak of a human aggregate as comprising a group or society.

Conversely, Adaptation IV (rejection of goals and means) is the least common. Persons who "adjust" (or maladjust) in this fashion are, strictly speaking, *in* the society but not *of* it. Sociologically, these constitute the true "aliens." Not sharing the common frame of orientation, they can be included within the societal population merely in a fictional sense. In this category are some of the activities of psychotics, psychoneurotics, chronic autists, pariahs, outcasts, vagrants, vagabonds, tramps, chronic drunkards and drug addicts. These have relinquished, in certain spheres of activity, the culturally defined goals, involving complete aim-inhibition in the polar case, and their adjustments are not in accord with institutional norms. This is not to say that in some cases the source of their behavioral adjustments is not in part the very social structure which they have in effect repudiated nor that their very existence within a social area does not constitute a problem for the socialized population.

This mode of "adjustment" occurs, as far as structural sources are concerned, when both the culture goals and institutionalized procedures have been assimilated thoroughly by the individual and imbued with affect and high positive value, but where those institutionalized procedures which promise a measure of successful attainment of the goals are not available to the individual. In such instances, there results a twofold mental conflict insofar as the moral obligation for adopting institutional means conflicts with the pressure to resort to illegitimate means (which may attain the goal) and inasmuch as the individual is shut off from means which are both legitimate *and* effective. The competitive order is maintained, but the frustrated and handicapped individual who cannot cope with this order drops out.

Defeatism, quietism, and resignation are manifested in escape mechanisms which ultimately lead the individual to "escape" from the requirements of the society. It is an expedient which arises from continued failure to attain the goal by legitimate measures and from an inability to adopt the illegitimate route because of internalized prohibitions and institutionalized compulsives, *during which process the supreme value of the success-goal has as yet not been renounced.* The conflict is resolved by eliminating *both* precipitating elements, the goals and means. The escape is complete, the conflict is eliminated and the individual is asocialized.

Be it noted that where frustration derives from the inaccessibility of effective institutional means for attaining economic or any other type of highly valued "success," that Adaptations II, III, and V (innovation, ritualism and rebellion) are also possible. The result will be determined by the particular personality, and thus, the *particular* cultural background, involved. Inadequate socialization will result in the innovation response whereby the conflict and frustration are eliminated by relinquishing the institutional means and retaining the success-aspiration; an extreme assimilation of institutional demands will lead to ritualism wherein the goal is dropped as beyond one's reach but conformity to the mores persists; and rebellion occurs when emancipation from the reigning standards, due to frustration or to marginalist perspectives, leads to the attempt to introduce a "new social order."

Our major concern is with the illegitimacy adjustment. This involves the use of conventionally proscribed but frequently effective means of attaining at least the simulacrum of culturally defined success—wealth, power, and the like. As we have seen, this adjustment occurs when the individual has assimilated the cultural emphasis on success without equally internalizing the morally prescribed norms governing means for its attainment. The question arises, Which phases of our social structure predispose toward this mode of adjustment? We may examine a concrete instance, effectively analyzed by

Lohman, which provides a clue to the answer. Lohman has shown that specialized areas of vice in the near north side of Chicago constitute a "normal" response to a situation where the cultural emphasis upon pecuniary success has been absorbed, but where there is little access to conventional and legitimate means for attaining such success. The conventional occupational opportunities of persons in this area are almost completely limited to manual labor. Given our cultural stigmatization of manual labor, and its correlate, the prestige of white collar work, it is clear that the result is a strain toward innovational practices. The limitation of opportunity to unskilled labor and the resultant low income cannot compete *in terms of conventional standards of achievement* with the high income from organized vice.

For our purposes, this situation involves two important features. First, such antisocial behavior is in a sense "called forth" by certain conventional values of the culture *and* by the class structure involving differential access to the approved opportunities for legitimate, prestige-bearing pursuit of the culture goals. The lack of high integration between the means-and-end elements of the cultural pattern and the particular class structure combine to favor a heightened frequency of antisocial conduct in such groups. The second consideration is of equal significance. Recourse to the first of the alternative responses, legitimate effort, is limited by the fact that actual advance toward desired success-symbols through conventional channels is, despite our persisting open-class ideology, relatively rare and difficult for those handicapped by little formal education and few economic resources. The dominant pressure of group standards of success is, therefore, on the gradual attenuation of legitimate, but by and large ineffective, strivings and the increasing use of illegitimate, but more or less effective, expedients of vice and crime. The cultural demands made on persons in this situation are incompatible. On the one hand, they are asked to orient their conduct toward the prospect of accumulating wealth and on the other, they are largely denied effective opportunities to do so institutionally. The consequences of such structural inconsistency are psycho-pathological personality, and/or antisocial conduct, and/or revolutionary activities. The equilibrium between culturally designated means and ends becomes highly unstable with the progressive emphasis on attaining the prestige-laden ends by any means whatsoever. Within this context, Capone represents the triumph of amoral intelligence over morally prescribed "failure," when the channels of vertical mobility are closed or narrowed *in a society which places a high premium on economic affluence and social ascent for all its members.*

This last qualification is of primary importance. It suggests that other phases of the social structure besides the extreme emphasis on pecuniary success must be considered if we are to understand the social sources of antisocial behavior. A high frequency of deviate behavior is not generated simply by "lack of opportunity" or by this exaggerated pecuniary emphasis. A comparatively rigidified class structure, a feudalistic or caste order, may limit such opportunities far beyond the point which they are obtained in our society today. It is only when a system of cultural values extols, virtually above all else, certain common symbols of success for the population at large while its social structure rigorously restricts or completely eliminates access to approved modes of acquiring these symbols for a considerable part of the same population, that antisocial behavior ensues on a considerable scale. In other words, our egalitarian ideology denies by implication the existence of noncompeting groups and individuals in the pursuit of pecuniary success. The same body of success-symbols is held to be desirable for all. These goals are held to transcend class lines, not to be bounded by them, yet the actual social organization is such that there exist class differentials in the accessibility of these common success-symbols. Frustration and thwarted aspiration lead to the search for avenues of escape from a culturally induced intolerable situation; or unrelieved ambition may eventuate in illicit attempts to acquire the dominant values. The American stress on pecuniary success and ambitiousness for all thus invites exaggerated anxieties, hostilities, neuroses and antisocial behavior.

This theoretical analysis may go far toward explaining the varying correlations between crime and poverty. Poverty is not an isolated variable. It is one in a complex of interdependent social and cultural variables. When viewed in such a context, it represents quite different states of affairs. Poverty as such, and consequent limitation of opportunity, are not sufficient to induce a conspicuously high rate of criminal behavior. Even the often mentioned "poverty in the midst of plenty" will not necessarily lead to this result. Only insofar as poverty and associated disadvantages in competition for the culture values approved for *all* members of the society is linked with the assimilation of a cultural emphasis on monetary accumulation as a symbol of success is antisocial conduct a "normal" outcome. Thus, poverty is less highly correlated with crime in southeastern Europe than in the United States. The possibilities of vertical mobility in these European areas would seem to be fewer than in this country, so that neither poverty *per se* nor its association with limited opportunity is sufficient to account for the varying correlations. It is only when the full configuration is considered, poverty, limited opportunity and a commonly shared system of success symbols, that we can explain the higher association between poverty and crime in our society than in others where rigidified class structure is coupled with *differential class symbols of achievement.*

In societies such as our own, then, the pressure of prestige-bearing success tends to eliminate the effective social constraint over means employed to this end. "The-end-justifies-the-means" doctrine becomes a guiding tenet for action when the cultural structure unduly exalts the end and the social organization unduly limits possible recourse to approved means. Otherwise put, this notion and associated behavior reflect a lack of cultural coordination. In international relations, the effects of this lack of integration are notoriously apparent. An emphasis upon national power is not readily coordinated with an inept organization of legitimate, i.e., internationally defined and accepted, means for attaining this goal. The result is a tendency toward the abrogation of international law, treaties become scraps of paper, "undeclared warfare" serves as a technical evasion, the bombing of civilian populations is rationalized, just as the same societal situation induces the same sway of illegitimacy among individuals.

The social order we have described necessarily produces this "strain toward dissolution." The pressure of such an order is upon outdoing one's competitors. The choice of means within the ambit of institutional control will persist as long as the sentiments supporting a competitive system, i.e., deriving from the possibility of outranking competitors and hence enjoying the favorable response of others, are distributed throughout the entire system of activities and are not confined merely to the final result. A stable social structure demands a balanced distribution of affect among its various segments. When there occurs a shift of emphasis from the satisfactions deriving from competition itself to almost exclusive concern with successful competition, the resultant stress leads to the breakdown of the regulatory structure. With the resulting attenuation of the institutional imperatives, there occurs an approximation of the situation erroneously held by utilitarians to be typical of society generally wherein calculations of advantage and fear of punishment are the sole regulating agencies. In such situations, as Hobbes observed, force and fraud come to constitute the sole virtues in view of their relative efficiency in attaining goals, which were for him, of course, not culturally derived.

It should be apparent that the foregoing discussion is not pitched on a moralistic plane. Whatever the sentiments of the writer or reader concerning the ethical desirability of coordinating the means-and-goals phases of the social structure, one must agree that lack of such coordination leads to anomie. Insofar as one of the most general functions of social organization is to provide a basis for calculability and regularity of behavior, it is increasingly limited in effectiveness as these elements of the structure become dissociated. At the extreme, predictability virtually disappears and what may be properly termed cultural chaos or anomie intervenes.

This statement, being brief, is also incomplete. It has not included an exhaustive treatment of the various structural elements which predispose toward one rather than another of the alternative responses open to individuals; it has neglected, but not denied the relevance of, the factors determining the specific incidence of these responses; it has not enumerated the various concrete responses which are constituted by combinations of specific values of the analytical variables; it has omitted, or included only by implication, any consideration of the social functions performed by illicit responses; it has not tested the full explanatory power of the analytical scheme by examining a large number of group variations in the frequency of deviate and conformist behavior; it has not adequately dealt with rebellious conduct which seeks to refashion the social framework radically; it has not examined the relevance of cultural conflict for an analysis of culture-goal and institutional-means malintegration. It is suggested that these and related problems may be profitably analyzed by this scheme.

/// REVIEW QUESTIONS

1. Why do you think Merton's theory became so popular when it did?
2. Which adaptation to strain do you most identify with?
3. Which types of criminal behavior does Merton's theory have more difficulty explaining? Which types of offending does it explain best?

READING /// 13

In this study, Olena Antonaccio, William R. Smith, and Feodor A. Gostjev use data from a sample of adolescents in post-Soviet Ukraine to reassess Merton's strain theory. Specifically, the researchers focus on other considerations, such as larger sociocultural environments and external constraints that previous research has not emphasized, thus providing an example of how Merton's theory of anomic strain can be improved by added clarifications.

While reading this article, one should consider the following topics:

- The authors' claim regarding the nature of most American studies of Merton's theory as using samples drawn from individuals that do not experience anomic sociocultural conditions, as does Ukraine, which they give data to support is in a state of upheaval
- The use of multiple measures for operationalizing strain and anomie to include both individual perceptions of blocked economic aspirations and more structural concerns such as relative deprivation compared to other groups in their society
- Findings of the current study regarding the moderating effects of perceptions of formal and informal sanctions as well as the potential influence of other factors, such as social bonds and control variables
- How the influence of the predicting variables varies between the two types of strain measures—economic strain and relative strain—and which type of measure the authors seem to prefer given the results

SOURCE: Olena Antonaccio, William R. Smith, and Feodor A. Gostjev, "Anomic Strain and External Constraints: A Reassessment of Merton's Anomie/Strain Theory Using Data from Ukraine," *International Journal of Offender Therapy and Comparative Criminology* 59, no. 10 (2015): 1079–103.

Anomic Strain and External Constraints

A Reassessment of Merton's Anomie/Strain Theory Using Data from Ukraine

Olena Antonaccio, William R. Smith, and Feodor A. Gostjev

Merton's (1938, 1968) strain/anomie theory of crime and delinquency is considered one of the dominant paradigms in the study of criminal behavior. Over the years, the theory has become a classic work in the criminological tradition of strain theories, inspired much theoretical following (e.g., Agnew, 1992; Cohen, 1965; Messner & Rosenfeld, 1994), and undergone numerous empirical evaluations (see Burton & Cullen, 1992). Nevertheless, the theory also has been criticized for its ambiguity and has been open to differing interpretations of its arguments (e.g., Baumer, 2007; Tittle, 1995). Furthermore, accumulated empirical evidence on a micro-level version of strain/anomie theory has been generally unfavorable to it (Burton & Cullen, 1992).

There are two possible reasons for a weak empirical support of Merton's account of crime. First, as many scholars have noted, the failure of the research to support the theory may have resulted from misinterpretations of the theory such as, for example, neglect of contingencies and inadequate operationalizations of the concept of Merton's anomic strain (Agnew, Cullen, Burton, Evans, & Dunaway, 1996; Baron, 2011; Baumer, 2007; Burton, Cullen, Evans, & Dunaway, 1994). Yet, the research on moderators of anomic strain–crime relationships has been extremely limited, with many likely conditioning factors never considered so far. In addition, almost no studies of Merton's theory have evaluated alternative operationalizations of anomic strain simultaneously. Second, Merton (1938) argued that criminal adaptations to strain caused by the inability of individuals to achieve highly desired materialistic goals through legitimate channels were more likely in more anomic environments. Yet, despite numerous tests, the theory has never been assessed in sociocultural contexts that can be regarded as truly anomic. In fact, most of empirical evaluations of the theory have been conducted with the samples from the United States, perhaps because Merton's original writings portrayed American sociocultural context as especially anomic. The recent research has cast some doubt on such characterization of the United States and actually shown that other countries, especially those from the former Soviet Union, could be more accurately described as anomic (Chamlin & Cochran, 2007). However, to date, there have been no empirical studies on individual-level propositions from Merton's theory using the data from such contexts.

Our study aims to make two important contributions to the extant research on Merton's theory. First, it assesses whether the theoretical structure of classic strain theory may be improved by incorporating external constraint variables such as sanction threats and social bonds as individual-level contingencies to anomic strain–delinquency relationships. Second, using the data from the sample of adolescents in an especially suitable and unusual setting, the city of Lviv in post-Soviet Ukraine, it evaluates predictive powers of anomic strain in such arguably more anomic societal context. In addition, the research also presents a robust test of those issues by considering alternative measures of anomic strain and a wide range of delinquent behaviors.

Merton's Strain/Anomie Theory and the Empirical Research

In his seminal article, Merton (1938) argued that, in unbalanced societies, disparity between the approved success goals and endorsement of legitimate means to achieve them combined with the limited availability of legitimate opportunities produced the state of *anomie*. He further suggested that anomic conditions at the societal level were more likely to induce strain in individuals and individual-level criminal behavioral adaptations. In particular, according to his classic strain/anomie theory, those who have high aspirations for financial success but were not sufficiently regulated by norms of the society may be more likely to "innovate" by resorting to illicit avenues in the absence of legitimate channels to success. Following Merton's original writings regarding those individual-level adaptations, early empirical tests commonly examined the goals-means discrepancy operationalizing anomic strain as the disjunction between individual aspirations and expectations for educational/occupational goals but, overall, found a very weak empirical support (see Burton & Cullen, 1992, for a review). In pursuit of more adequate operationalizations of anomic strain, the scholars have also measured it in terms of monetary dissatisfaction, blocked opportunities, or relative deprivation (e.g., Agnew et al., 1996; Baron, 2006; Burton & Cullen, 1992; Farnworth & Leiber, 1989; Vowell and May, 2000). Whereas those studies generally have been more supportive of Merton's theory, they have shown that the effects of those measures of anomic strain were not robust in the presence of other predictors of crime (e.g., Burton et al., 1994).

Another direction in the contemporary research on classic anomie/strain theory has been exploration of individual-level contingencies in criminogenic effects of anomic strain. As several scholars have pointed out (e.g., Agnew et al., 1996; Baumer, 2007), Merton (1968) did not suggest that involvement in crime was an inevitable adaptation to anomic strain. To the contrary, he clearly stated that, even under anomic conditions, the modal individual response to strain was conformity. Although he briefly mentioned that other factors such as norm commitment might influence the types of behavioral adaptations to strain that individuals select, Merton did not discuss in depth under what conditions strained individuals were most likely to opt for deviant adaptations. However, for classic strain theory to become a more precise explanation of crime, various contingencies should be articulated in more detail (Baumer, 2007; Tittle, 1995). For example, in addition to moral norms, other crime-inhibiting factors such as perceived risk of punishment or social bond may serve as contingencies under which the impact of anomic strain may be more or less pronounced. In particular, individuals who experience anomic strain but have strong social bonds or perceive risks of the imposition of either formal or informal punishment as more certain may be dissuaded from misbehavior. Therefore, the effects of anomic strain on criminal involvement may be amplified at lower levels of perceptions of sanction certainty and social bonds.

To date, the empirical research on conditional effects of anomic strain has been scarce. To our knowledge, only four empirical studies (Agnew et al., 1996; Baron, 2006, 2011; Özbay & Özcan, 2006) have attempted to test any propositions of conditionality of Merton's strain and crime association with mixed results. Two of these studies have found that deviant peer association might magnify the effect of financial strain and relative deprivation on crime and delinquency among street youth and a sample of adolescents (Agnew et al., 1996; Baron, 2006; but see Baron, 2011). Another study has shown significant amplifying effects of monetary dissatisfaction and blocked access to legitimate economic opportunities on the magnitude of association between the monetary goals-commitment to legitimate means interaction and projected property crime (Baron, 2011). However, other studies have revealed no significant moderating effects of cultural support, social modeling, or gender in effects of anomic strain on delinquency (Baron, 2011; Özbay & Özcan, 2006).

Furthermore, the research on interrelationships of anomic strain and external constraints in their effects on crime is practically nonexistent. In general, previous studies have found that some external controls have direct influences on crime and delinquency. Deterrence theory is credited with identifying fear of formal and informal sanctions as a constraint to criminal behavior (Tittle, 1980). According to the most recent meta-analysis of deterrence literature, while the mean effect sizes were modest, measures of perceived certainty of formal sanctions and fear of informal sanctions have been found to be associated with crime (Pratt, Cullen, Blevins, Daigle, & Madensen, 2006). Furthermore, the crime-preventive effects of social bonds (i.e., attachment, commitment, involvement, and belief) are emphasized by social control theory (Hirschi, 1969). A review of research testing it has indicated that the attachment and commitment in two domains, family and school, have the hypothesized direct effects on involvement in misbehavior while the effects of the other two elements of social bond are less consistent (Kempf, 1993). However, only one study (Baron, 2011) has investigated possible moderating impact of those external constraints and found none. It relied only on one indicator of risk perceptions (the threat of getting caught) and one outcome (one type of property crime). No empirical assessment of possible conditioning effects of perceptions of informal sanctions and social bonds on relationships between anomic strain and crime has been conducted so far.

Another understudied area in the research on Merton's theory is possible contextual influences on criminogenic effects of anomic strain. Merton (1938) argued that *anomic macro-level* conditions in any society were likely to produce anomic strain among *individuals* living in these environments and possibly invoke *individual-level* criminal responses. Ideally, testing these ideas would require multilevel data from samples of individuals within many societies with various degree of anomie. In the absence of such data, at least evaluations of individual-level effects of anomic strain in samples of respondents from especially anomic societies could be informative and provide some initial evidence on this argument. However, most studies on individual-level classic strain have been conducted in the United States, perhaps because Merton's original discussion of anomie focused heavily on the American culture and structure as an especially fruitful ground for breeding crime induced by anomie and because in some subsequent writings, the United States was assumed to be exceptional in that sense (Cohen, 1965; Messner & Rosenfeld, 1994). Yet, the more recent research has cast some doubt on this assumption of Merton's theory showing that a contemporary United States might be mislabeled as a truly anomic environment (Chamlin & Cochran, 2007). Instead, it has shown that the emphases on material success goals and overall cultural anomie were much more prominent in other countries of the world such as former Soviet Union republics (Chamlin & Cochran, 2007). Surprisingly, little is known about the applicability of these arguments to various cross-national contexts with only one study conducted using a non-Western sample (school students from Ankara, Turkey), and producing mostly negative findings (Özbay & Özcan, 2006). But, to date, no research on them has been conducted in such arguably more anomic sociocultural contexts as former Soviet countries.

Our research site in post-Soviet Ukraine appears to be an especially suitable locale for collecting individual-level data for an evaluation of Merton's individual-level propositions. Since the break-up of the former Soviet Union, drastic political, economic, and sociocultural changes have taken place in Ukraine and other countries that previously comprised the Union of Soviet Socialist Republics (USSR). Politically, independent Ukraine, though formally considered a democratic state, has been undergoing numerous governmental disputes and political fracturing. Economically, the transition from the socialistic mode of production characterized by the state ownership of the means of production to capitalism marked by the dominance of private ownership has been accompanied by the erosion of the welfare state that was a staple of the socialist state and by dramatic increases in economic inequality and the gap between the rich and the poor (e.g., Foglesong & Solomon, 2001; Kalman, 2002). Other byproducts of those transitions include deterioration in many traditionally strong institutions such as education. Whereas under the communist regime, universal and free access to educational and professional opportunities for youth and benefits of educational and professional growth were taken for granted, young people growing up in new free market conditions face a more uncertain future with more limited legitimate opportunities to advance academically and professionally. For example, in contemporary Ukraine, many professional jobs requiring advanced education are not well paid and cannot satisfy most financial needs. Thus, many Ukrainians in those occupations still have to depend on alternative sources of income such as participation in secondary labor markets, spousal financial support, remittances from relatives abroad, and so on.

Various official indicators of the country's well-being confirm some unfortunate consequences of these societal upheavals. Modern Ukraine is characterized by significantly lower life expectancy than the United States (68 vs. 78), high percentages of population in poverty (29% vs. 12%), low freedom ratings, and is among the most corrupt countries in the world (Central Intelligence Agency, 2008; Transparency International, 2008). Moreover, although national homicide rates are lower than in the mid-90s, they remain significantly higher than in Western countries. For instance, the homicide rate in Ukraine in 2004 was 8.5 per 100,000 residents, compared with 4.8 in the United States (United Nations Office on Drugs and Crime, 2006). In addition, crime victimization studies and other self-report surveys conducted in Ukraine have shown a high level of violent crime (Antonaccio & Tittle, 2008; Kostenko, 1999–2000).

Furthermore, these transitions have also included substantial sociocultural transformations that are pertinent to Merton's account of societal anomie. Whereas, in a socialist totalitarian Ukraine, idealized communitarian values and objectives prevailed and the means of achieving them were rigidly prescribed, in a contemporary Ukraine, value orientations and behavioral regulations accompanying them have undergone significant changes necessary for adapting to a new capitalistic environment (Antonaccio & Tittle, 2008; Kalman, 2002). In particular, achievement of individual financial success has increasingly emerged and is seen as a principal goal desirable by the majority in the country where the economic inequality and the gap between the rich and the poor is now much more visible and where Ukrainian nouveau riche without hesitation demonstrate publicly their newly found wealth. In addition, legitimate means of achieving societally approved goals are clearly de-emphasized in this social context. In fact, laws are often circumvented to benefit individual interests and corruptive practices among governmental officials and ordinary citizens are widespread and virtually go unpunished, undoubtedly, helping promote the idea that wealth and status in Ukraine can be gained through illegal channels (Markovskaya, Pridemore, & Nakajima, 2003; Spector, Winbourne, O'Brien, & Rudenshiold, 2006).

Not surprisingly, in this situation one can hardly refrain from using Mertonian terminology such as "*anomic*" to describe contemporary conditions in Ukraine. Moreover, this characterization of post-Soviet Ukraine has been also supported by recent cross-national research. According to Chamlin and Cochran (2007), more than half of the Ukrainian sample (53%) report that monetary compensation is the most important reason for employment and less than half (49%) agree that less emphasis should be placed on material possessions whereas the corresponding figures for the American respondents are 32% and 69%, respectively. Therefore, if Merton's account is correct and more "anomic" macro-level economic and sociocultural characteristics interact with micro-level strain to increase the probability of criminal behavior (Baumer, 2007), then enhanced criminogenic effects of anomic strain might be found in a more socially disorganized environment like contemporary Ukraine.

Current Study

This study attempts to fill in some gaps in the research on Merton's theory. First, this research is the first empirical attempt to evaluate moderating effects of multiple individual-level constraining factors such as threats of formal and informal sanctioning and several types of social bonds. Second, using unique data on juvenile delinquency from post-Soviet Ukraine, this study provides the first empirical assessment of Merton's individual-level theoretical arguments regarding anomic strain in a sociocultural environment that can be truly described as "anomic." The study will test the following hypotheses:

> **Hypothesis 1:** The levels of anomic strain experienced by individuals are positively associated with involvement in crime and delinquency.
>
> **Hypothesis 2:** Lower perceptions of certainty of formal and informal sanctioning will enhance the effects of anomic strain on involvement in crime and delinquency.
>
> **Hypothesis 3:** Weaker attachment and commitment will magnify the effects of anomic strain on involvement in crime and delinquency.

In addition, all hypotheses will be evaluated using alternative measures of anomic strain and indicators of a wide range of delinquent behaviors.

Method

Data

The data for this study come from a self-report self-administered survey of a random sample of high school students conducted in the city of Lviv, Ukraine, in May 2006. The data collection project was approved by the U.S. university institutional review board and the services of SOCIS, Center for Social and Marketing Research, the leading and largest professional survey organization in Ukraine, were used to perform data collection procedures. The survey sample consisted of the ninth graders in Lviv public schools. The selection of exclusively ninth graders was warranted to obtain a maximally diverse sample of school students because in Ukraine compulsory public education consists of 9 years of schooling and only those who are more academically oriented stay in school after the ninth grade. This age group is also especially suitable for assessing effects of anomic strain because at this point of their lives, Ukrainian adolescents face various stressful decisions and circumstances related to aspirations and expectations emphasized in Merton's theory.

The participating students were randomly chosen using a two-stage sample selection procedure. First, a random sample of schools was selected from the list of all 118 city public schools in six city districts. Second, one class of ninth graders was randomly chosen from each of the selected schools out of the pool of all classes of ninth graders (these classes had 30–35 students in each class). The participants filled in self-administered questionnaires in Ukrainian (back translated and pretested). The response rate was 85% and the final sample is 600 students (297 males and 303 females) in 18 schools.

Variables

Dependent variables. The dependent variables in this study include several measures of respondents' past and projected involvement in delinquent behavior. They are constructed from 27 survey items asking respondents their past and projected likelihood of future involvement in delinquent activities. Most of the items were extracted from the Normative Deviance Scale designed specifically for the purpose of measuring reliably a range of delinquent behaviors in which adolescents are likely to be involved independently of cultural definitions of deviance (see Vazsonyi, Pickering, Junger, & Hessing, 2001, for a detailed discussion of this scale). The original response categories are from 1 to 7 (never, once, twice, 3–5 times, 6–10 times, 11–50 times, more than 50 times) for past delinquency items and from 1 to 4 (from "*very unlikely*" to "*very likely*") for projected delinquency items. Both self-reports of past misbehavior and projections of future deviance have been used by criminologists and the validity of both measures have been supported (e.g., Cantor & Lynch, 2000; Pogarsky, 2004). However, to be more confident in our results, we use the measures of both past and projected future delinquency as dependent variables.

Anomic strain measures: Economic and relative strains. To construct our first measure, anomic economic strain, we directly assess the disparity between financial aspirations and expectations. Following Burton et al. (1994), to calculate it, we subtracted individual scores on the survey item of economic expectations from the scores on the item on economic aspirations (see the appendix for the list of items and response categories). Higher computed scores indicate higher degrees of economic strain. In addition, some scholars emphasize that individual perceptions of their standing on different factors including access to legitimate opportunities relative to that of other important reference groups may be a more salient way of tapping anomic strain (Burton & Dunaway, 1994; Cohen, 1965). Because such anomic experiences may be especially salient in the context of post-Soviet Ukraine characterized by increasing economic inequality, we construct an index of relative anomic strain. Drawing on previous research (Burton et al., 1994), this additive index combines *z* scores of six survey items tapping perceptions of limited opportunities for success and three survey items indicating feelings of relative deprivation. Higher scores on this measure reflect more relative strain experienced by individuals.

Perceptions of sanctions. As perceived certainty of punishment has been shown to be the most effective crime-preventive dimension of sanctioning in Western and non-Western samples (Paternoster, 1987; Tittle, Botchkovar, & Antonaccio, 2011), our research focuses on perceptions of likelihood of punishment. In addition, because the past studies have found perceptions of informal sanctioning to be predictors of offending (Pratt et al., 2006), it includes the indicators of threats of both formal and informal punishment. Drawing on the previous research on deterrence variables (e.g., Jensen, Erickson, & Gibbs, 1978; Tittle, 1980), we construct a general index of perceived risk of formal sanctioning by adding *z* scores on the three items asking about the likelihood of being arrested, imprisoned for breaking the law, and going unpunished for a theft. Likewise, a general index of perceived fear of informal sanctioning is constructed by summing *z* scores on five survey items asking respondents about possibility of losing respect of valued people if they are involved in misconduct. Higher scores on both measures indicate perceptions of higher probabilities of formal and informal sanctioning.

Social bonds. We create three measures of the two established components of the social bond, attachment and commitment (Kempf, 1993). In particular, the indices of two dimensions of parental attachment were constructed by summing the *z* scores. Both indices are based on the individual survey items from the 1979 and 1997 National Longitudinal Survey of Youth that have been used to measure similar concepts (Bureau of Labor Statistics, 2005). The first index taps direct social control (parental supervision) and consists of five survey items. The second index reflects an emotional component of the bond of attachment, parental support, and consists of the average of the sum of the *z* scores on four survey items on maternal support and the four items on paternal support or, in cases where only one parent was available, on support from either parent. Finally, the measure of school commitment was calculated by summing *z* scores on six survey items asking respondents about their school experiences. Higher scores on each measure reflect stronger social bonds.

Control variables. We incorporate into our analyses several variables to control for antecedent influences. These are gender (0 = *male*, 1 = *female*), family intactness (0 = *living with both biological parents*, 1 = *other*), and family socioeconomic status (perceptions of respondents' family income relative to other Ukrainian families on the five-point scale from *"far below average"* to *"far above average"*). We do not control for age as all survey respondents are from the same age group. Finally, to account for other relevant unmeasured prior influences and verify the robustness of the results, the four-offense additive index of past delinquency is utilized as a control in the analyses where projections of future delinquency are a dependent variable. Descriptive statistics for all variables are presented in Table 1.

Table 1 • Descriptive Statistics

Variables	Range	*M*	*SD*	Alphas	*n*
Dependent variables					
Past vandalism	5–25	9.60	4.72	.77	600
Past theft	6–30	7.27	3.37	.86	600
Past violence	4–20	6.22	3.26	.77	599
Past general deviance	8–40	14.17	6.29	.81	597
Past total delinquency	23–110	37.25	14.90	.91	596
Logged total delinquency	3.14–4.70	3.55	0.34		596
Projected 4-offense delinquency	4–19	6.30	2.69	.75	599
Logged projected 4-offense delinquency	1.39–2.94	1.76	0.38		599
Independent variables					
Economic strain	−4–4	1.45	1.36		600
Combined relative strain	−12.45–21.19	0.00	5.16	.74	600
Mediating and conditional variables					
Formal sanctioning	−6.99–3.69	0.00	2.20	.58	600
Informal sanctioning	−7.99–7.75	0.00	3.57	.76	600

(Continued)

Table 1 • (Continued)

Variables	Range	*M*	*SD*	Alphas	*n*
Parental supervision	−9.62–8.44	0.00	3.55	.75	600
Parental attachment	−8.57–5.17	0.00	2.69	.83	600
School commitment	−12.97–9.58	0.00	3.57	.63	600
Control variables					
Male	0–1	0.495	0.505		600
Family intactness	0–1	0.19	0.39		600
Family socioeconomic status	1–5	3.27	0.62		600
Past 4-offense delinquency	4–18	6.35	2.89	.61	599
Logged past 4-offense delinquency	1.39–2.89	1.77	0.39		599

Analysis

A number of alternative analytic techniques are used to evaluate the research hypotheses of this study. We find virtually the same patterns of substantive results using these techniques with the only few differences observed. Therefore, we report the results from the OLS regression models, noting any divergent findings. In addition, conducted diagnostic tests detected no multicollinearity (no Variance Inflation Factors exceeded 2.5) and no undue influential cases (Cook's D_i were well under 1).

Results

Table 2 displays the bivariate correlations between all variables used in the study. First, we explore zero-order associations between economic and relative measures of anomic strain and two dependent variables, logged past total delinquency and logged projected four-offense delinquency. The results of bivariate analyses concerning economic strain are mixed. This operationalization of anomic strain is significantly and positively related to past delinquency (.12), but there is no significant association between it and projected involvement in delinquency. However, relative strain is significantly associated with both dependent variables in the predicted direction (.19 and .18, respectively).

The results of multivariate analyses for past delinquency for projected delinquency bear more evidence regarding Hypothesis 1 on associations between anomic strain and delinquency. Results confirm that the observed bivariate associations are quite robust. Economic strain predicting past delinquency and relative strain predicting both past and projected delinquency continue to exert positive significant effects on misbehavior when all controls are incorporated, even though the sizes of its standardized coefficients are small to moderate. The findings also reveal that variables representing likelihood of formal and informal sanctioning have a negative and significant effect on past and projected delinquency, net of all controls, even though the additional sensitivity analyses show that significant effects of informal sanctions on projected delinquency are not robust once standard errors are adjusted for clustering. Finally, the results demonstrate that two out of three measures of social bonds—parental supervision and school commitment—are negatively and significantly related to past delinquency, although this association holds up only for school commitment in the model predicting projected delinquency.

Table 2 • Correlations Between Variables

		1	2	3	4	5	6	7	8	9	10	11	12	13	14	15
1.	Past total delinquency															
2.	Past total delinquency (ln)	**.98**														
3.	Past 4-offense delinquency	**.86**	**.84**													
4.	Past 4-offense delinquency (ln)	**.83**	**.84**	**.98**												
5.	Project 4-offense delin-quency	**.60**	**.60**	**.56**	**.55**											
6.	Project 4-offense delin-quency (ln)	**.58**	**.60**	**.55**	**.55**	**.98**										
7.	Economic strain	**.12**	**.12**	**.09**	**.09**	.07	.05									
8.	Relative strain	**.19**	**.19**	**.19**	**.19**	**.19**	**.17**	**.23**								
9.	Formal sanctioning	**–.33**	**–.34**	**–.28**	**–.27**	**–.35**	**–.35**	.04	–.10							
10.	Informal sanctioning	**–.25**	**–.26**	**–.19**	**–.19**	**–.23**	**–.23**	.02	**.15**	**.33**						
11.	Parental supervision	**–.33**	**–.36**	**–.33**	**–.35**	**–.26**	**–.27**	–.06	**–.16**	**.27**	**.22**					
12.	Parental attachment	**–.13**	**–.13**	**–.17**	**–.17**	**–.15**	**–.15**	.00	**–.22**	**.18**	**.10**	**.34**				
13.	School commitment	**–.31**	**–.32**	**–.29**	**–.29**	**–.26**	**–.26**	–.08	**–.15**	**.29**	**.27**	**.38**	**.31**			
14.	Gender Female = 0	**–.37**	**–.39**	**–.27**	**–.27**	**–.22**	**–.23**	–.03	.02	**.18**	**.12**	**.25**	**–.10**	**.22**		
15.	Family intactness	.03	.03	.04	.04	.02	.01	.03	–.01	.00	–.05	–.07	**–.17**	–.08	.02	
16.	Family socioeconomic status	.05	.04	–.01	–.01	–.02	–.01	**–.10**	**–.26**	–.02	–.07	.07	**.12**	.01	–.06	**–.09**

NOTE: Bold font coefficients indicate that correlation is statistically significant at $p < .05$ level, two-tailed test.

Notably, the association between economic strain and past delinquency and relative strain and both past and projected delinquency remain statistically significant net of the effects of fear of formal and informal sanctions. No regression coefficients for these measures of anomic strain are attenuated by the inclusions of likelihood of sanctioning. Thus, the effects of economic and relative strains on past and projected delinquency seem to be independent of these external constraint variables. Somewhat similar results are observed in models that consider the effects of economic strain and relative strain on past delinquency, net of the social bond variables. Although slight reductions in the regression coefficients for economic and relative strain occur in those instances, these coefficients, nonetheless, remain significant. Furthermore, in the equation predicting projected delinquency, the inclusion of the measures of social bond renders the regression coefficient for relative strain nonsignificant. However, in the most inclusive that incorporate all control variables as well as both sets of external constraint variable, robustness of effects of anomic strain is further demonstrated as associations between economic strain and past delinquency and associations between relative strain and both past and projected delinquency remain significant. Furthermore, these results are also confirmed in the analyses using all alternative techniques discussed above. Moreover, the comparison of standardized coefficients in those models suggest that the impact of relative strain is, though quite modest, still comparable with some of the other significant predictors of delinquency such as perceptions of risks of sanctioning. Overall, then, the results appear to provide at least partial support for Hypothesis 1 when anomic strain is operationalized as economic strain and stronger support for it when anomic strain is operationalized as relative strain.

Next, concerning Hypothesis 2 on the conditioning effects of fear of formal and informal sanctioning on the link between classic strains and delinquency, the examination of these coefficients reveals that any moderating effects may be limited to one measure of anomic strain and one indicator of fear of sanctioning. One significant interaction term between economic strain and fear of informal sanctioning is found in the equation predicting past juvenile delinquency. As expected, the interaction between economic strain and fear of informal sanctioning is negative, indicating that criminogenic effects of classic strain are more pronounced for those with less fear of informal sanctioning.

We find little consistent evidence of conditioning effects of social bonding variables on the associations between our measures of anomic strains and past and projected delinquency outlined in Hypothesis 3. Only the interaction between relative strain and school commitment in the equations predicting projected delinquency is significant and, as expected, negative, indicating that positive effects of relative strain on projected delinquency are stronger for adolescents with lower school commitment. However, this interaction is quite small and its robustness has not been supported in any additional analyses. Finally, another marginally significant interaction between economic strain and parental supervision is not in the predicted direction and has not been confirmed in any other models or additional analyses.

Discussion

This study has accomplished several goals. First, it has assessed whether criminogenic effects of anomic strain are more pronounced among adolescents with lower perception of certainty of sanctioning and weaker social bonds. Second, it has explored potential influences of a larger macro-level sociocultural context on predictive powers of anomic strain by testing it with unique data from a sample of Ukrainian adolescents. In addition, it has compared several alternative operationalizations of anomic strain and evaluated their impact on a wide range of delinquent behaviors. Overall, several interesting findings emerge from our analysis.

First, with respect to independent effects of anomic strain, the results of our analyses illuminate both strengths and weaknesses of Merton's classic strain/anomie theory. Consistent with Merton's arguments, the concept of anomic strain, especially when it is operationalized in terms of relative strain, arises as a valid predictor of involvement in delinquency in the sample of adolescents from Lviv, Ukraine. This finding is also surprisingly robust. In particular, the significant positive associations between relative strain and adolescent misbehavior persist in the presence of control variables including that of prior delinquency, multiple measures of deterrence and social bonds as well as several other influential predictors of crime that have been investigated in the sensitivity analyses. This quite consistent pattern of results stands in contrast to the mixed findings of the research on anomic strain conducted mostly in Western countries showing not robust or at best conditional effects of similar measures of anomic strain (e.g., Baron, 2011; Burton et al., 1994). Furthermore, corroborating Merton's argument about the applicability of his theory to both utilitarian and nonutilitarian deviance (Merton, 1968, p. 232), criminogenic effects of the more promising measures of classic strain do not seem to be crime-specific and are very similar for such different types of delinquency as assault, theft, vandalism, and general deviance. Thus, in general, as expected, in the arguably more anomic context of post-Soviet Ukraine, some measures of anomic strain are consistently related to delinquency.

The findings of our study also shed more light on predictive powers of various operationalizations of anomic strain. In accord with the findings of most research conducted with Western samples, our investigation confirms that traditional measures of disjunctions between educational and occupational aspirations and expectations are not good predictors of adolescent misbehavior. The results also reveal that the most promising way of conceptualizing anomic strain is by incorporating perceptions of individuals' relative standing on different factors such as opportunities for success or various aspects of financial deprivation as well as negative feelings associated with them. At least, our results suggest that such "relative anomic strain" appears to be particularly salient for adolescents in post-Soviet Ukraine. At the same time, it is also obvious that an overall explanatory power of even the best measures of anomic strain is quite modest, suggesting that the theory needs to be refined to provide a more satisfactory account of juvenile delinquency.

Next, the results of our analyses uncover more direct evidence suggesting that Merton's explication of crime may be too simplistic. Merton's theory clearly failed to incorporate into its explanatory framework in any consistent way several external constraints to crime that have been featured as central variables in such established criminological theories as deterrence and social bond (Hirschi, 1969). However, our findings corroborate the arguments of those theories and indicate that some of their principal concepts such as perceptions of certainty of formal and informal sanctioning and direct social control and school commitment may also play an important role in the etiology of delinquency in Ukraine, independently of anomic strain.

Finally, the results of our analyses speak to the question of whether elaboration of Merton's theory through the introduction of additional individual-level contingencies is promising. Overall, crime-instigating effects of anomic strain do not appear to be conditioned by deterrence or social bond variables as we find little consistent evidence of significant interactions between anomic strain and perceptions of sanctions or social bonds. Although, in a few instances, the results suggest that higher perceptions of certainty of informal sanctioning or higher levels of school commitment may attenuate criminogenic effects of anomic strain, the evidence regarding robustness of those interactions is generally weak. As previous studies have also failed to find a conditioning effect of perceived risk of getting caught on strain and crime relationship (Baron, 2011), it is possible that the effects of anomic strain and external constraints on crime are independent of each other. Yet, we also cannot rule out the possibility that those findings may have been affected by the unique sociocultural context of Ukraine. In a more socially disorganized environment of Ukraine, effects of anomic strain may be more powerful than usual and thus may be able to stand out as potent independent predictors of juvenile delinquency that operate with the same strength at all levels of external constraints experienced by adolescents. Thus, we hesitate to make any decisive conclusions about the existence of possible moderating effects until more research on this issue is conducted and one of those interpretations is substantiated further.

Overall, the findings from the study have several important implications for further research on Merton's theory. First, they confirm that clarifications and elaborations of the concepts and ideas from Merton's theory may prove to be a fruitful theoretical exercise. For example, some promising ways of improving the concept of anomic strain include assessments of individual standing on different factors (such as perceptions of opportunities for success) in comparison with other individuals or relative financial deprivation resulting in frustration and negative feelings. Furthermore, although the findings regarding contingencies involving anomic strain and deterrence and social bond variables are largely negative, the results of this research demonstrate that anomic strain and a number of external constraints have consistent independent influences on adolescent misbehavior. Therefore, empirical evidence seems to point to the necessity of some kind of theoretical integration of the classic strain/anomie account of crime with external control theories considered in this study (deterrence and social bond). As all of these factors appear to be independent pieces of a puzzle of delinquent behavior, the ultimate way of improving Merton's anomie/strain theory (as well as other strain theories) may be to construct a comprehensive theory of "constrained motivation" that includes at minimum strain as a motivational factor and several inhibitory factors as constraint variables. Finally, the last notable finding of this research conducted in a unique sociocultural setting of Ukraine is discovering the importance of contextual influences that may make micro-level effects of anomic strain more criminogenic. In an arguably more anomic context of contemporary Ukraine, effects of anomic strain on adolescent crime and delinquency are found to be persistent and robust, and endure even when other predictors of juvenile delinquency such as fear of sanctions and social bonds are also taken into consideration. Overall, it appears that a larger sociocultural environment also may serve as a contingency for the operation of individual-level processes and affect nature of relationships between theoretical predictors such as anomic strain and misconduct. Therefore, potential differential societal influences and sociocultural effects should also have their place in any adequate strain theory.

Nevertheless, the study has a number of limitations that should be considered. First of all, like any data from self-report surveys, these data may suffer from problems of telescoping, memory losses, attempts at cognitive consistency, and so on. Whereas it is not possible to exclude such biases completely, we are more confident in the reliability of these results because many patterns of the findings are similar to those revealed by other studies. In addition, as any other survey data collected from students attending schools, they are subject to possible attrition bias due to the fact that more delinquent students may be especially likely to skip school and not be present during survey administration. Unfortunately, Ukrainian public schools do not provide any statistics on sociodemographic characteristics of their student bodies making impossible any comparisons between our final sample and the overall body of ninth graders in the public schools of Lviv. Yet, because our survey response rate is comparable or higher than those usually obtained in the U.S. school delinquency surveys such as Add Health or Monitoring the Future (Carolina Population Center, 2013; Office of Juvenile Justice and Delinquency Prevention, 2013), we suspect that the likelihood of such bias is not any higher than in any other comparable research. Furthermore, our sample is age limited and further research with more representative samples is certainly needed to verify our findings. Finally, although we have attempted to establish correct causal sequencing by utilizing retrospective and prospective measures, the cross-sectional character of our data does not permit us to do it unambiguously.

Despite these limitations, our study represents an important first step in evaluating Merton's account of crime in unusual sociocultural contexts of post-Soviet states. It uses interesting data from adolescents who are sampled at the time when they have to make important life-changing decisions and face many uncertainties in an anomic social environment and extends the extant literature by exploring additional individual-level contingencies to relationships between anomic strain and crime. Finally, the results of this study point to several avenues for further research on classic strain theory. In particular, other sources of strain such as those outlined in Agnew's (1992, 2006) general strain theory should be examined in the context of contemporary Ukraine, and internal constraints like self-control and morality should be considered for further elaboration of Merton's account. Finally, the results of this study should be replicated in other sociocultural contexts and with different samples.

References

Agnew, R. (1992). Foundation for a general strain theory of crime and delinquency. *Criminology*, *30*, 47–87.

Agnew, R. (2006). *Pressured into crime: An overview of general strain theory*. Los Angeles, CA: Roxbury.

Agnew, R., Cullen, F., Burton, V., Evans, D., & Dunaway, G. (1996). A new test of classic strain theory. *Justice Quarterly*, *13*, 681–704.

Antonaccio, O., & Tittle, C. R. (2008). Morality, self-control, and crime. *Criminology*, *46*, 801–832.

Baron, S. W. (2006). Street youth, strain theory, and crime. *Journal of Criminal Justice*, *34*, 209–223.

Baron, S. W. (2011). Street youths and the proximate and contingent causes of instrumental crime: Untangling anomie theory. *Justice Quarterly, 28,* 413–436.

Baumer, E. P. (2007). Untangling research puzzles in Merton's multilevel anomie theory. *Theoretical Criminology, 11,* 63–93.

Bureau of Labor Statistics. (2005). *The NLS79 user's guide 2002.* Available from www.bls.gov

Burton, V., & Cullen, F. T. (1992). The empirical status of strain theory. *Crime and Justice, 15,* 1–30.

Burton, V., Cullen, F. T., Evans, D. T., & Dunaway, R. G. (1994). Reconsidering strain theory: Operationalization, rival theories, and adult criminality. *Journal of Quantitative Criminology, 10,* 213–239.

Cantor, D., & Lynch, J. P. (2000). Self-report survey and measures of crime and criminal victimization. In D. Duffee (Ed.), *Criminal justice 2000: Vol. 4. Measurement and analysis of crime and justice* (pp. 85–138). Washington, DC: U.S. Department of Justice Programs, National Institute of Justice.

Carolina Population Center. (2013). *Add health.* Retrieved from http://www.cpc.unc.edu/projects/addhealth

Central Intelligence Agency. (2008). *The world factbook.* Available from https://www.cia.gov

Chamlin, M. B., & Cochran, J. K. (2007). An evaluation of the assumptions that underlie institutional anomie theory. *Theoretical Criminology, 11,* 39–61.

Cohen, A. (1965). The sociology of the deviant act: Anomie theory and beyond. *American Sociological Review, 30,* 5–14.

Farnworth, M., & Leiber, M. J. (1989). Strain theory revisited: Economic goals, educational means, and delinquency. *American Sociological Review, 54,* 263–274.

Foglesong, T. S., & Solomon, P. H. (2001). *Crime, criminal justice, and criminology in post-Soviet Ukraine.* Washington, DC: U.S. Department of Justice.

Hirschi, T. (1969). *Causes of delinquency.* Berkeley: University of California Press.

Jensen, G. F., Erickson, M. L., & Gibbs, J. P. (1978). Perceived risk of punishment and self-reported delinquency. *Social Forces, 57,* 57–78.

Kalman, A. (2002). *Organized economic crime and corruption in Ukraine.* Final report for the National Institute of Justice. Retrieved from www.ojp.usdoj.gov/nij/international/programs/ukraine.html

Kempf, K. L. (1993). The empirical status of Hirschi's control theory. In F. Adler & W. S. Laufer (Eds.), *New directions in criminological theory* (Vol. 4, pp. 143–185). New Brunswick, NJ: Transaction.

Kostenko, N. (1999–2000). Hazardous everyday life: International survey of crime victims in Kiev. *International Journal of Sociology, 29,* 16–32.

Markovskaya, A., Pridemore, W. A., & Nakajima, C. (2003). Laws without teeth: An overview of the problems associated with corruption in Ukraine. *Crime, Law, and Social Change, 39,* 193–213.

Merton, R. (1938). Social structure and anomie. *American Sociological Review, 3,* 672–682.

Merton, R. (1968). *Social theory and social structure.* New York, NY: Free Press.

Messner, S. F., & Rosenfeld, R. (1994). *Crime and the American dream.* Belmont, CA: Wadsworth Publishing.

Office of Juvenile Justice and Delinquency Prevention. (2013). *Monitoring the future: A continuing study of the lifestyles and values of youth.* Retrieved from http://www.ojjdp.gov/ojstatbb/Compendium

Özbay, Ö., & Özcan, Y. Z. (2006). Classic strain theory and gender. *International Journal of Offender Therapy and Comparative Criminology, 50,* 21–38.

Paternoster, R. (1987). The deterrent effect of the perceived certainty and severity of punishment: A review of the evidence and issues. *Justice Quarterly, 4,* 173–218.

Pogarsky, G. (2004). Projected offending and contemporaneous rule-violation: Implications for heterotypic continuity. *Criminology, 42,* 111–135.

Pratt, T. C., Cullen, F. T., Blevins, K. R., Daigle, L. E., & Madensen, T. D. (2006). The empirical status of deterrence theory: A meta-analysis. In F. T. Cullen, J. P. Wright, & K. R. Blevins (Eds.), *Taking stock: The status of criminological theory* (pp. 367–395). New Brunswick, NJ: Transaction Publishers.

Spector, B. I., Winbourne, S., O'Brien, J., & Rudenshiold, E. (2006, February). *Corruption assessment: Ukraine* (Final report). USAID. Available from www.scribd.com/doc/46994371/Anti-Corruption-Assessment-Ukraine-Usaid

Tittle, C. R. (1980). *Sanction and social deviance: The question of deterrence.* New York, NY: Praeger.

Tittle, C. R. (1995). *Control balance: Toward a general theory of deviance.* Boulder, CO: Westview Press.

Tittle, C. R., Botchkovar, E., & Antonaccio, O. (2011). Criminal contemplation, national context, and deterrence. *Journal of Quantitative Criminology, 27,* 225–249.

Transparency International. (2008). *Corruption perceptions index.* Available from www.transparencyinternational.org

United Nations Office on Drugs and Crime. (2006). *United Nations surveys on crime trends and operations of the criminal justice system.* Available from www.unodc.org

Vazsonyi, A. T., Pickering, L. E., Junger, M., & Hessing, D. (2001). An empirical test of a general theory of crime: A four-nation comparative study of self-control and the prediction of deviance. *Journal of Research in Crime & Delinquency, 38,* 91–131.

Vowell, P. R., & May, D. (2000). Another look at classic strain theory: Poverty status, perceived blocked opportunity, and gang membership as predictors of adolescent violent behavior. *Sociological Inquiry, 70,* 42–60.

/// REVIEW QUESTIONS

1. Why do the authors claim post–Soviet Ukraine provides a better region for testing strain or anomie theory? Give facts to say why you agree or disagree.
2. What do the findings indicate regarding the influence of perceived sanctions on the measures of strain? What do the results show regarding the influence of social bonds? Did any control variables stand out as important in their analyses?
3. Given the results, what do the authors conclude regarding the two measures of strain? Do they seem to prefer one over the other?

READING /// 14

In this empirical study, Byongook Moon and Merry Morash use a sample of Korean adolescents to test the effectiveness of general strain theory to explain gender differences in delinquency causation. The authors not only include multiple measures of strain and key variables from other theoretical perspectives but also examine the differential emotional responses of females and males across violent, property, and status offending.

While reading this article, one should consider the following topics:

- What previous studies show regarding gender differences in whether there are differences in how females and males are more likely to internalize or externalize reactions to strain and how this has implications for the types of offending they commit
- What previous findings reveal about gender differences regarding interaction effects between conditioning factors and strain on delinquency
- Characteristics of the Korean culture that the authors claim makes it unique and useful for testing general strain theory
- The findings of the current study regarding gender differences in strain measures, negative emotions related to strain, and other key theoretical factors as well as how such differences influence the types of offending committed

SOURCE: Byongook Moon and Merry Morash, "Gender and General Strain Theory: A Comparison of Strains, Mediating, and Moderating Effects Explaining Three Types of Delinquency," *Youth & Society* 49, no. 4 (2017): 484–504.

Gender and General Strain Theory

A Comparison of Strains, Mediating, and Moderating Effects Explaining Three Types of Delinquency

Byongook Moon and Merry Morash

Introduction

The General Strain Theory (GST) has received considerable research attention for nearly two decades and has developed into a complex explanation of youths' illegal behavior (Agnew & Brezina, 1997; Hoffmann & Su, 1997; Jennings, Piquero, Gover, & Perez, 2009; Kaufman, 2009; Mazerolle & Maahs, 2000; Moon & Morash, 2004; Moon, Morash, McCluskey, & Hwang, 2009; Piquero & Sealock, 2004). According to the theory (Agnew 1992, 2006), various negative social relations/situations (e.g., failure to achieve positively valued goals, removal of positively valued stimuli, and experience of negative stimuli) directly influence delinquency or indirectly influence it by increasing negative emotions. To adapt to strain, individuals use coping strategies that are cognitive (i.e., minimizing the importance of strain and negative outcomes, or accepting responsibility for adversity), emotional (i.e., alleviating negative emotions through physical exercise or meditation), and behavioral (i.e., eliminating the source of strain or engaging in vengeful behavior). Individuals who lack non-delinquent coping strategies and who have a strong disposition to engage in deviance are more likely than others to alleviate strain and negative emotions through delinquent behaviors (Agnew, 1992).

In a seminal piece that sets forth but does not present a new test of the relevance of GST to how gender affects delinquency, Broidy and Agnew (1997) proposed that the theory might explain gender differences in both the etiology and the amount of delinquency. Drawing on research conducted in the traditions of GST, feminist criminology/sociology, and the social-psychological literature on gender and stress, they proposed gender differences in the types of strain experienced, emotional reactions to strain, conditioning factors that moderate the effects of strain, and level and type of delinquency.

Suggesting the need for further study, the many empirical studies to test hypotheses derived from GST's key propositions regarding gender have yielded inconsistent findings (Agnew & Brezina, 1997; Hoffmann & Su, 1997; Jang & Johnson, 2005; Kaufman, 2009; Mazerolle, 1998). Supporting the theory, some studies (Kaufman, 2009; Mazerolle, 1998; Piquero & Sealock, 2004) found significant gender differences in strains and negative emotions and in their effects on delinquency. However, other studies (Agnew & Brezina, 1997; Hoffmann & Su, 1997) revealed limited or no significant gender differences in strains, negative emotions, and conditioning factors.

Research to further understanding of GST's contribution to understanding gender differences in delinquency requires consideration of several general issues relevant to testing the theory. First, empirical tests must include measures of key strains hypothesized to be related to the deviance of both boys and girls (Agnew, 2006). Second, a majority of prior studies (except Lin, Cochran, & Mieczkowski, 2011; Mazerolle & Maahs, 2000) assessed the interaction effect of each of several conditioning factors with strains on the strain-delinquency relationship. However, Agnew (2006) indicates that this approach has a methodological limitation, because it may not matter that a particular conditioning factor interacts with strains to increase or decrease delinquency, as long as *some* conditioning factor has an effect. To overcome this limitation, he suggested that the "overall standing" of these variables should be studied as a moderator of the relationship between strains and delinquency (Agnew, 2006, pp. 109–110). Limited research (Lin et al., 2011; Mazerolle & Maahs, 2000) has examined combined effects of conditioning factors on the strain-delinquency relationship, and we are unaware of any research to examine gender differences in the moderating influence of a composite measure of conditioning factors. Third, most prior studies examined the moderating effects of conditioning factors on the strain-delinquency relationship, but ignored the possible moderating effects of conditioning factors on the negative emotions-delinquency relationship. Fourth, previous empirical findings (Mazerolle, 1998; Morash & Moon, 2007) suggest that gender differences in the effects of strains, negative emotions, and conditioning factors depend on the type of delinquency. Supporting this view, some tests of GST have shown that girls tend to internalize reactions, which leads to status offenses, but boys tend to externalize their reactions by becoming aggressive or committing property offenses (Leadbeater, Blatt, & Quinlan, 1995). Therefore, research to understand gender differences in the effects of strains should separate violent, property, and status offending.

Gender, General Strain Theory, and Empirical Findings

Broidy and Agnew (1997) argue that gender differences in the *types* of strains may explain gender differences in delinquency. As males highly value material success and extrinsic achievement, they are more likely to experience financial strain resulting from the inability to achieve monetary goals. Also, males are more likely to experience peer conflict and criminal victimization because their peer relationships are based on competition and conflict. However, females experience more interpersonal strain due to their greater concern with maintaining close relationships with significant others. They also are expected to report more strain due to gender discrimination.

Broidy and Agnew (1997) also suggested that gender differences in negative emotional reactions to strains produce gender differences in deviant behaviors. In their view, although boys and girls report similar levels of anger in response to strain, girls more often respond to strain with a mix of negative emotions. Because boys are more likely to report that their anger results from moral outrage at being challenged or treated unjustly, they tend to externalize their reactions by becoming aggressive or committing property offenses (Leadbeater et al., 1995). In contrast, angry, frustrated, and depressed girls tend to internalize reactions to strains that may lead to substance abuse, truancy, or running away from home.

Finally, Broidy and Agnew (1997) wrote that girls less than boys respond to strain with delinquent behavior because of moderating influences that affect the connection of strains to delinquency. Parents and friends often expect girls to conform to gender-related expectations that limit their opportunities to break the law, provide them with more supervision and control, and restrict association with delinquent peers, all of which limit serious and aggressive delinquent behaviors. On the contrary, conducive to serious and aggressive delinquent behaviors, boys are more likely to have lower social/parental control and to associate with delinquent peers.

Over the last decade, a number of empirical studies have tested Broidy and Agnew's extension of GST to explaining gender differences in the etiology of delinquency, and some but not all support the theory's key propositions. Studies (Agnew & Brezina, 1997; Jennings et al., 2009; Kaufman, 2009; Mazerolle, 1998) showed that males more often report negative relations with peers, conflict with significant others, and physical punishment and criminal victimization, but females report more problems forming and maintaining positive relationships with family and friends and strain from expectations that they do housework, which suggests perceived gender discrimination. Contradicting these results, Morash and Moon (2007) showed no gender differences for adolescents in financial strain, academic performance related strain, negative life events, and parental physical/emotional punishment.

Researchers (Mazerolle, 1998; Morash & Moon, 2007; Piquero & Sealock, 2004) have also documented significant gender differences in the effects of various strains on delinquent behaviors. Family strains, negative life events, or a composite measure of strain had stronger effects on violent delinquency for males than females. Morash and Moon (2007) found the somewhat different pattern, that negative life events, parental punishment, and financial strains, had significant effects on female violent and status delinquency but not on male delinquent behaviors. Contrary to these findings, Hoffmann and Su (1997), Kaufman (2009), and Jennings et al. (2009) discovered no significant gender differences in the effects of some strains on delinquent behaviors.

Research on gender differences in the interaction effects between conditioning factors and strains on delinquency is especially limited and inconsistent in its findings (see Jang, 2007; Jang & Johnson, 2005; Jennings et al., 2009; Morash & Moon, 2007). Specific to gender differences, Jang (2007) and Jang and Johnson (2005) found that due to their being more religious, strained females were less likely than their male counterparts to commit interpersonal violence. Jennings et al. (2009) similarly showed that females with higher levels of physical/spiritual coping resources and/or peer social support were less likely to engage in interpersonal aggression or property delinquent behaviors. However, Morash and Moon (2007) found that the interaction between teachers' punishment and delinquent peer association significantly, positively affected delinquency regardless of gender.

General Strain Theory in the Context of South Korea

The Korean context provides opportunities to investigate culture-specific childhood strains and the generalizability of GST outside the United States. Strains that are uncommon in the United States but which are pervasive in South Korea and other parts of the world include stressful, highly competitive examinations that strongly affect future success and physical and verbal punishment by teachers and parents. Also unique to Korea and some other countries, after middle school begins, youth spend a significant amount of their time after school in tutoring, and thus away from parental supervision.

Prior empirical studies (see Moon et al., 2009; Morash & Moon, 2007) suggest that core propositions of GST apply to youth in Korea. For example, Moon et al. (2009) found that various strains (i.e., family conflict, parental/teacher punishment, criminal victimization) are significantly and positively related to delinquent behaviors, and that situational anger had positive effects on various delinquent behaviors. Their additional finding that strained Korean youths less often engaged in delinquency when they had positive relationships with parents or had higher problem-solving ability further supported GST.

Only two previous studies (Morash & Moon, 2007; Yun, Kim, & Morris, 2014) examined GST's utility for explaining gender differences in delinquency causation in Korea. Morash and Moon (2007) found that boys more often than girls experienced examination-related strain and physical and emotional punishment by teachers. However, they found no gender differences in levels of financial strain, and teachers' punishment significantly predicted delinquency regardless of gender. Yun et al. (2014) indicate that males and females experience different types of strains, in that male students tend to experience parental physical punishment and peer stress, but female students are more likely to report victimization, health problems, and appearance stress, which have significant effects on deviance through their influence on anger and conditioning factors. These prior studies have limitations. Moon et al. (2009) used gender as a control variable and did not examine the moderation effect of a sum of the conditioning factors on the connection of strain to delinquency or on the connection of negative emotions to delinquency. Morash and Moon (2007) tested only part of the model suggested by GST, failing to examine the mediating/moderating effects of negative emotions and conditioning factors on delinquency. Moreover, Yun et al. (2014) measured limited types of deviant behaviors and only trait-based negative emotions. In a comparison of tests of the GST-derived explanatory models for girls and boys, the present research attempts to address these limitations.

Hypotheses

Based on theory and prior research, we predict that boys are more likely to experience emotional/physical punishment by parents and teachers, criminal victimization, examination-related strain, and financial strain (so-called male strains), but females are more likely to report higher levels of family conflict and gender discrimination (so-called female strains). Second, we expect that male strains are more likely to lead to violent and property-related deviant behaviors, and female strains are more likely to result in status delinquency. Finally, because males are higher in delinquency-promoting conditioning factors, we predict that there will be gender differences in the moderating effects of a combined measure of multiple conditioning factors on the connection of both strains and negative emotions to delinquency.

Method

Sample

Data were collected from middle school students in South Korea in two waves of a longitudinal study. The first and second waves of the longitudinal data were collected from middle school students in South Korea during the summers of 2005 and 2006. To adequately represent middle school students in South Korea, students who attended middle schools were randomly selected in two metropolitan cities (Incheon and Daegu) and one medium-sized city (Cheongju). Incheon and Daegu are metropolitan cities with a population of approximately 2.6 million and 2.5 million, respectively. Cheongju is a medium-sized city with a population of approximately 600,000. A comparison of several social economic status indicators (i.e., poverty, divorce) for these three cities and for other cities/provinces revealed that the three cities are not noticeably different from other population centers in South Korea.

In the summer of 2005, a list of schools in these cities was assembled: There were 90 middle schools in Incheon, 108 middle schools in Daegu, and 30 middle schools in Cheongju. From the list of middle schools in each of the research sites, one school was randomly selected. With the approval of school administrators and teachers, all eighth-grade students in the three selected schools and their parents were informed about the purpose of the research, and youth whose parents provided a signed consent form were asked to voluntarily complete questionnaires. To maximize confidentiality and accuracy of the responses, researchers distributed questionnaires, allowed time for their completion, and collected them after 1 hr. Attendance records for each class indicated low absentee rates at the time of the data collection. Of 900 questionnaires distributed, 817 were collected; however, 30 collected questionnaires with extensive missing data were discarded. Overall, the response rate was 87% (787 out of 900). Approximately 1 year later (summer 2006), students who participated in the first wave of data collection were asked to voluntarily complete the second wave questionnaires in their classrooms. Six hundred sixty-four ninth graders completed the second wave questionnaire, yielding a response rate of 84% (664 out of 787). The attrition rate from the first wave to the second wave data collection was 16%. We conducted a series of *t*-tests on key Wave I variables considered in the present study to compare students who did and did not continue to participate and found no statistically significant differences for variables used in the analysis. For the current study, 659 valid cases were used for analyses after listwise deletion of missing values.

Measurement

Both independent and dependent variables are presented in Table 1. Most items used to operationalize variables were taken from prior research. To clarify time order, independent variables were measured at Wave I, and dependent variables were measured at Wave II. The scales were coded so that a higher score indicates a higher level of each strain, negative emotion, and delinquency. Recoding was used for some measures of conditioning factors so

Table 1 • Comparisons of Key Variables by Gender

	Males (n = 255)		Females (n = 404)		
Variables	*M*	*SD*	*M*	*SD*	*t* **value**
Family C.	2.32	1.97	2.78	2.03	−2.84*
Parental P	2.12	2.87	1.87	2.39	1.16
Teacher P	2.36	3.49	1.24	2.01	4.68*
Exam S	5.94	2.38	6.05	2.08	−0.58
Financial S	2.63	2.20	2.75	2.19	−0.69
Gender D	1.12	2.25	0.82	1.58	1.82
Victim	0.51	1.84	0.20	0.72	2.61*

Variables	Males ($n = 255$)		Females ($n = 404$)		
	M	*SD*	*M*	*SD*	*t* value
Sanger1	1.89	2.26	2.05	2.16	−0.92
Depres1	2.01	2.42	3.08	2.61	−5.24*
Sanger2	1.18	2.03	1.43	2.11	−1.51
Depres2	1.42	2.28	2.21	2.64	−4.05*
Sanger3	1.41	2.49	1.07	2.04	1.83
Depres3	1.07	2.18	1.14	2.17	−0.40
Sanger4	1.92	2.62	1.43	2.15	2.47*
Depres4	2.04	2.84	2.75	2.75	−3.19*
Sanger5	0.84	1.75	0.61	1.42	1.80
Depres5	1.02	1.83	1.38	2.13	−2.29*
Sanger6	0.81	1.91	1.05	2.06	−1.54
Depres6	0.69	1.78	1.24	2.33	−3.39*
Sanger7	0.51	1.74	0.30	1.36	1.60
Depres7	0.35	1.45	0.21	1.02	1.31
N. Parents R	9.85	3.09	8.98	2.92	3.67*
L. Parental C	14.64	3.65	13.35	3.26	4.61*
Legitimacy	9.37	4.09	8.20	3.30	3.85*
Low S.C	53.98	12.31	54.66	9.08	−0.76
T. Conditioning	9.03	1.65	8.39	1.47	5.07*
Violent delinquency at Wave I	0.76	2.47	0.14	0.61	3.91*
Property delinquency at Wave I	0.25	0.85	0.10	0.35	2.69*
Status delinquency at Wave I	0.57	1.90	0.35	0.76	1.81
Violent delinquency at Wave II	0.69	1.62	0.18	1.18	4.37*
Property delinquency at Wave II	1.05	2.63	0.20	1.57	4.67*
Status delinquency at Wave II	0.87	1.97	0.41	1.18	3.33*

NOTE: Due to the space limitation, we abbreviated key variables' names in the Tables throughout the article. Family conflict as Family C; Parental punishment as Parental P; Teacher punishment as Teacher P; Examination-related strain as Exam S; Financial strain as Financial S; Gender discrimination as Gender D; Victimization as Victim; Anger to family conflict as Sanger1; Depression to family conflict as Depres1;Anger to parental punishment as Sanger2; Depression to parental punishment as Depres2; Anger to teacher punishment as Sanger3; Depression to teacher punishment as Depres3; Anger to examination-related strain as Sanger4; Depression to examination-related strain as Depres4; Anger to financial strain as Sanger5; Depression to financial strain as Depres5; Anger to gender discrimination as Sanger6; Depression to gender discrimination as Depres61; Anger to victimization as Sanger7; Depression to victimization as Depres7; Negative relationship with parents as N. Parents R; Low parental control as L. Parental C; Legitimacy of violence as Legitimacy; Low self-control as Low S.C; Composite condition factor as T. Conditioning.

* $p \leq .05$.

that for each, a high score indicated the presence of a variable thought to increase delinquency.

Independent Variables

Seven strains. The family conflict scale was created by combining three items, measuring the frequency of verbal arguments, tensions, and conflicts of a study participant with one or more parents during the last 6 months. The response options ranged from *strongly disagree* (1) to *strongly agree* (4). The parent emotional and physical punishment scale consisted of four items adopted from Piquero and Sealock (2000). The scale measures how often a respondent was emotionally and physically punished by parents through acts such as name calling, negative comparison with others, and hitting. The teachers' emotional and physical punishment scale was created by using a parallel set of the items used for parental punishment. The response options for the punishment scales ranged from 0 (*none*) to 4 (*10 or more times*). The examination-related strain scale consists of the three items: "I feel a lot of stress about studying," "I am not satisfied with my grades," and "My parents stress studying too much." *Strongly disagree* (1) to *strongly agree* (4) ratings were used with these items and for the financial strain items. The financial strain scale combines responses to the three items: "I am not satisfied with the amount of money I have," "My family has too little money for clothing or food," and "My family does not have enough money to support me." Four items adapted from Landrine and Klonoff (1996) comprise the gender discrimination scale. These four items, originally developed to measure racial discrimination, were slightly rephrased to measure respondents' experiences of discrimination because of their gender, specifically that they were treated with less courtesy and respect. Finally, the victimization scale consists of five items, measuring respondents' and family members' experience of being victims of theft, robbery, burglary, sexual assault, and physical assault. We recognize the possibility that a person's own victimization experience is distinct from family members' victimization (a vicarious strain). However, we assume that the measurement does not greatly reduce any effect of victimization on negative emotions and deviant behaviors, as any family member's criminal victimization experience could have a negative effect on other family members, causing high levels of stress and negative emotions (see Agnew, 2002, for more information on the effects of vicarious strains on delinquency), especially in a collective society such as South Korea, which is characterized by strong family ties and interdependency among family members.

Situation-based negative emotions: Anger and depression.[1] For each of the seven strains for which respondents indicated any presence, study participants were asked to report whether they responded with uncontrollable outbursts of temper, urges to beat or harm someone, and urges to break things. These three indicators of anger were combined to reflect situational anger for each strain. The measure of situation-based depression consists of three items reflecting respondents' experience of sadness, worthlessness, and depression in response to any of the seven strains that was reported. Responses to the three items were combined to create measures of situational depression for each type of strain reported. Overall, seven situation-based anger and seven situation-based depression indicators were created; each of them was associated with one of the seven strains. The response options, which ranged from 0 for *never* to 3 for *always*, reflected how often respondents experienced the reaction in response to a specific type of strain.

Four conditioning factors. As suggested by Agnew (2006), we included four conditioning variables hypothesized to increase the likelihood of strained and emotionally distraught adolescents engaging in delinquent behaviors. Four items—measuring respondents' perception of parents' understanding, interest, and openness toward respondents—are combined to create a negative relationship with parents scale. The low parental supervision scale consists of five items, measuring respondents' perception of their parents' knowledge of their whereabouts and deviant behaviors. The scale is coded so that a higher value indicates a low level of parental control. The legitimacy of violence scale included five items, measuring whether violence can be justifiable in various situations, for example, to defend one's rights, achieve respect, and avoid appearing weak. The low self-control scale was created by summing 24 items derived from Grasmick, Tittle, Bursik, and Arneklev (1993), measuring six dimensions of low self-control. For all conditioning variables, four-point Likert-type (from *strongly disagree* to *strongly agree*) ratings were used as response options.

In constructing a composite conditioning index to reflect tendencies toward delinquent coping, because Agnew (2006) did not hypothesize different effect sizes of the conditioning factors affecting deviant behaviors, we assumed equal influence of the four conditioning factors. Thus, first the summed score for each conditioning scale was divided by the number of items (e.g., the self-control measure was divided by 24 and the low parental control measure by 5). Second, the resulting values for the four conditioning influence scales were summed to create the composite measure.

Dependent variables—three types of delinquency. At Wave II, participating students were asked how often they engaged in various types of delinquent behaviors over the last year. The violent delinquency scale consists of six items, measuring the frequency of involvement in behaviors such as "used force or strong-arm methods to get money or things from others" and "hit or threatened to hit fellow students." The property-related delinquency scale was created by summing 11 items such as "broken or tried to break into a building or vehicle to steal something" and "sold or tried to sell a stolen good to others." The status delinquency scale was created by summing responses to four items: "drinking alcohol," "smoking," "running away," and "skipping classes without a reason." The response options for each item were 0 (*never*), 1 (*1 to 3*), 2 (*4 to 6*), 3 (*7 to 9*), and 4 (*10 or more times*).

Analysis

The analysis first compares the males and females on all independent and dependent variables included in the multivariate models to predict delinquency. Then, to see the effect of strains and the direct and mediating effects of composite emotions, separately for each gender group, we (a) regress each type of delinquency on strains, and (b) then regress each type of delinquency on the strains plus composite indices of anger and depression. Finally, we examine gender differences in the interaction effects of the composite measure of the four conditioning factors on the relationship of strain to delinquency as well as the relationship of negative emotions to delinquency. To avoid multicollinearity problems with multiple strains and negative emotions, we used composite measures of total strains, total situational-based anger, and total situational-based depression. These composite variables were created by adding measures of seven strains, anger, and depression, respectively.

Results

The results of *t*-tests for gender differences in all variables included in the present research. Consistent with GST, boys are more likely to experience emotional/physical punishment by teachers and criminal victimization, whereas girls are more likely to report higher levels of family conflict. Unexpectedly, boys report more gender discrimination than girls, though the difference is not significant. For parental punishment, financial, and examination-related strain, the *t*-tests show no significant gender differences.

Regarding gender differences in negative emotions related to each strain, girls are more likely than boys to report significantly higher levels of depression in response to all strains except teacher punishment and criminal victimization, for which there were no gender differences. The only gender difference in anger is that boys score significantly higher than girls on anger in response to examination-related strain.

As expected, there are significant gender differences for most conditioning variables and the composite conditioning index. Boys are more likely than girls to report lower levels of parental control and negative relationships with parents and to have positive attitudes toward the use of violence. However, there is no significant gender difference in self-control. With the exception of status offending at Wave I, compared with girls, boys report significantly more of each type of deviant behavior at Waves I and II.

The findings indicate that family conflict, parental punishment, and examination strain are significant predictors of violent, property, or status delinquent behaviors for males, while gender discrimination has a significant positive effect on violent delinquency for females, after controlling the effects of negative emotions and conditioning factors. Unexpectedly, financial strain is found to have a negative effect on status delinquency for females. Contrary to GST propositions, for both gender groups the composite measures of anger and depression have no significant relationship to delinquent behaviors and no mediating effect on the link of strains to delinquent behaviors. The results of z-statistic comparisons indicate that gender differences in the effects of most strains and composite measurements of anger and depression are non-significant except that examination-related strain has a stronger effect on boys' violent delinquency, but gender discrimination has a statistically stronger effect on girls' violent delinquency.

The tests for moderating effects of the composite conditioning index on the strain-delinquency and on the negative emotions-delinquency relationships. All three interaction terms are significantly related to violent delinquency for males. Strained, angry, or depressed male adolescents are more likely to engage in violent delinquency when they have a higher risk for delinquent coping as indicated by the composite conditioning index. However, none of the three interaction terms involving strain, negative emotions, and a total conditioning index has a significant effect on violent delinquency for females. For property delinquency, no interaction terms are found to be a significant predictor for either males or females. For status offenses there is a tendency for angry males to commit status offenses when they report a higher tendency toward criminal coping. Like males, angry females report more status offending when conditioning factors reflect tendencies toward illegal behavior.

The z-statistic comparisons show significant gender differences in the effects of interactions with conditioning factors on delinquency. Four interaction terms (for violent delinquency, Strain × Conditioning, Anger × Conditioning, and Depression × Conditioning; and for status delinquency, Depression × Conditioning) had significantly stronger effects on violent and status delinquent behaviors for boys.

Discussion and Conclusion

The present study tested hypotheses deduced from key GST propositions by exploring gender differences in strains, negative emotions, and conditioning factors and by showing whether and how these variables relate to delinquent outcomes. The findings provide partial support for the theory's hypothesized gender differences in types of strains that males and females experience. As expected, males are more likely to report higher levels of teachers' physical/emotional punishment and criminal victimization, and females report higher levels of family conflict. However, contrary to the theory's prediction, no significant gender differences in financial strain, examination-related strain, and gender discrimination are found. As Broidy and Agnew (1997) suggested, all contemporary adolescents may be encouraged to succeed financially and academically in an economically developed and consumerist society, and thus they may experience similar levels of financial and examination strain. The finding of no significant gender difference in gender discrimination is unexpected, especially considering that despite girls' equal access to education, Korea is still a highly patriarchal society (Patterson, Bae, & Lim, 2013). It is plausible that in a patriarchal society, adolescent males see themselves as being treated with less courtesy and respect than females. This is consistent with our finding of more severe punishment by teachers being directed at male compared with female students. We also speculate that the young age of study participants may be related to this unexpected finding, since as girls mature, they may face more gender discrimination, for example in the workforce. Also, parents' and teachers' higher level of monitoring and supervision of girls may lead to their spending most of their time at school or home and thus having limited exposure to various situations in which they experience gender discrimination.

Consistent with GST, some strains (parental punishment, examination-related strain, financial strain, and criminal victimization) are significantly related to violent or property delinquency, but only for males, and two strains (family conflict and gender discrimination) have significant effects on violent or status delinquency only for females. Furthermore, examination-related strain has a stronger effect on violent delinquency for males, while gender discrimination is found to have a stronger effect on status delinquency for females. However, variables predictive of boys' delinquency were not always the so-called "male" strains. Notably, family conflict, which is assumed to be a "female strain" and was found to be significantly higher for girls, still significantly predicted boys' violent, property, and status delinquency.

Examination strain appeared to significantly contribute to violence and status delinquency for male adolescents. This is inconsistent with Agnew's (2006) prediction that strains such as failure to achieve educational success goals and excessive demand associated with conventional pursuits are less likely to be related to deviant behaviors because they are less likely to be perceived as unjust and do not create pressure for delinquent coping. To understand why examination-related strain, which studies in the United States do not consider, is related to Korean boys' delinquent behaviors, the college entrance examination system and the importance of being admitted into prestigious universities in South Korea needs to be understood. Quite different from the United States, there is extreme emphasis on preparation for college entrance examinations throughout East Asia, but especially in South Korea. Most high school students are required to remain at school until late evening for self-study or to attend private, after-school academic institutions to improve their test scores. The resulting pressures on Korean students to achieve high examinational grades and succeed academically contribute to their high levels of stress and anxiety (Lee & Larson, 2000). A recent survey (Pang Jong-Hwan Research Center, 2010) of 5,437 Korean schoolchildren found that approximately half reported dissatisfaction with their lives. Compared with youth from the 26 member-countries of the Organization of Economic Cooperation and Development, Korean adolescents were the unhappiest. School-generated strain (i.e., examination pressures, negative interaction with teachers) was one of main causes of their dissatisfaction. Examination-related strain, which may be non-criminogenic in the United States, may become a criminogenic strain when a society and culture over-emphasizes the goal of academic success.

In the present research, negative emotions generally did not significantly mediate the connection of strains to delinquency. These findings are unexpected, especially considering that situation-based negative emotions in response to each strain were measured. Possibly youth's experience of these distressing strains have damaging effects and thus result in delinquent behaviors, regardless of experience of negative emotions (see Moon et al., 2009; Piquero & Sealock, 2004). Alternatively, our use of longitudinal data may account for the findings if it fails to capture the effects of negative emotions on delinquency accurately. GST (Agnew, 1992) presents the relationship among strains, negative emotions, and delinquency as contemporaneous in that angry/depressed youth in response to strains engage in deviant coping within a relatively short period of time.

The tests of models that include the interaction effects of strains and emotions with the composite conditioning index provide limited support for GST. Strained, angry, or depressed boys are more likely to engage in violent delinquency when they report a higher risk for delinquent coping. For females, just one interaction term (Anger × Conditioning index) was significantly related to delinquency (i.e., status offending) in the expected positive direction. The interactions between conditioning factors and both strains and negative emotions are not useful in explaining property delinquency for either gender group. For males, the current study provides some support for the moderating effects of a composite conditioning index on the relationships between strain and violent delinquency, and for females it provides minimal support. These findings (also see Lin et al., 2011) raise a question about Agnew's (2006) argument (p. 110) that "total risk" for criminal coping can better explain strain-delinquency and negative emotions-delinquency relationships. However, we believe that future research would benefit from including more or different conditioning factors (e.g., association with delinquent peers, inadequate conventional coping skills) that may be more likely to condition the effects of strains and negative emotions on delinquency (Agnew, 2006).

Limitations of the research should be considered in interpreting results. First, we measured situational-based anger and depression by combining several items widely used in prior GST research. We recommend the employment of more items measuring these negative emotions, for instance by including the many dimensions contained in the Beck Depression Inventory (Sharp & Lipsky, 2002), to better understand situation-based negative emotions and their effects on deviance. Also, of course it would be useful to have more detailed longitudinal data to sort out the time order of strains, negative emotions, and delinquency. Given the immediacy of emotion in response to a negative event and emotion's effect on deviant coping behaviors, methods like maintaining a diary or frequent interviews (longitudinal data with short time gaps) would be most useful (Agnew, 1992). Third, GST indicates that other forms of negative emotions such as guilt, fear, shame, frustration, and anxiety are important in explaining gender differences in various types of delinquency. It may be that emotions other than anger and depression are relevant to Korean girls' delinquency, and for both gender groups, these should be explored in future study. Fourth, several key conditioning variables (i.e., delinquent peer association and criminal skills/resources) and non-delinquent coping strategies were not measured. We recommend that future research use a comprehensive list of conditioning factors and non-delinquent coping strategies to better understand the interaction effects of conditioning factors on the strain-delinquency relationship.

In conclusion, the current study provides some support for GST's utility in explaining differences in how girls and boys become delinquent (Broidy & Agnew, 1997). Findings also advance the empirical development of Broidy and Agnew's GST explanation of the influence of gender. Moreover, it provides partial evidence of the GST's generalizability in explaining gender differences in pathways to delinquency outside of the Western context in which the theory was initially developed and tested empirically. It also demonstrates the importance of including culturally unique and influential strains, in the case of Korea, teachers' punishment and examination-related strain, as hypothesized influences on delinquency.

Note

1. As overall findings show no significant mediating effects of *each of negative emotions* on the relationship between *each of strains* and deviance, we do not present the findings due to space limitation.

References

Agnew, R. (1992). Foundation for a general strain theory of crime and delinquency. *Criminology, 30*, 47–88.

Agnew, R. (2002). Experienced, vicarious, and anticipated strain: An exploratory study on physical victimization and delinquency. *Justice Quarterly, 19*, 603–632.

Agnew, R. (2006). General strain theory: Current status and directions for further research. In F. T. Cullen, J. P. Wright, & K. Blevins (Eds.), *Taking stock: The status of criminological theory—Advances in criminological theory*, 101–123. New Brunswick, NJ: Transaction.

Agnew, R., & Brezina, T. (1997). Relational problems with peers, gender, and delinquency. *Youth & Society, 29*, 84–111.

Ai, C., & Norton, E. C. (2003). Interaction terms in logit and probit models. *Economics Letters, 80*, 123–129.

Aiken, L. S., & West, S. G. (1991). *Multiple regression: Testing and interpreting interactions*. Newbury Park, CA: Sage.

Broidy, L., & Agnew, R. (1997). Gender and crime: A general strain theory perspective. *Journal of Research in Crime & Delinquency, 34*, 275–306.

Grasmick, H. G., Tittle, C. R., Bursik, R. J., Jr., & Arneklev, B. J. (1993). Testing the core empirical implications of Gottfredson and Hirschi's general theory of crime. *Journal of Research in Crime & Delinquency, 30*, 5–29.

Hoffmann, J. P., & Su, S. S. (1997). The conditional effects of stress on delinquency and drug use: A strain theory assessment of sex differences. *Journal of Research in Crime & Delinquency, 34*, 46–78.

Jang, S. J. (2007). Gender differences in strain, negative emotions, and coping behaviors: A general strain theory approach. *Justice Quarterly, 24*, 523–553.

Jang, S. J., & Johnson, B. R. (2005). Gender, religiosity, and reactions to strain among African Americans. *Sociological Quarterly, 46*, 323–357.

Jennings, W. G., Piquero, N. L., Gover, A. R., & Perez, D. M. (2009). Gender and general strain theory: A replication and exploration of Broidy and Agnew's gender/strain hypothesis among a sample of southwestern Mexican American adolescents. *Journal of Criminal Justice, 37*, 404–417.

Kaufman, J. M. (2009). Gendered responses to serious strain: The arguments for a general strain theory of deviance. *Justice Quarterly, 26*, 410–444.

Landrine, H., & Klonoff, E. A. (1996). The schedule of racist events: A measure of racial discrimination and a study of its negative physical and mental health consequences. *Journal of Black Psychology, 22*, 144–168.

Leadbeater, B. J., Blatt, S. J., & Quinlan, D. M. (1995). Gender-linked vulnerabilities to depressive symptoms, stress, and problem behaviors in adolescents. *Journal of Research on Adolescence, 5*, 1–29.

Lee, M., & Larson, R. (2000). The Korean "Examination Hell": Long hours of studying, distress, and depression. *Journal of Youth and Adolescence, 29*, 249–271.

Lin, W., Cochran, J. K., & Mieczkowski, T. (2011). Direct and vicarious violent victimization and juvenile delinquency: An application of general strain theory. *Sociological Inquiry, 81*, 195–222.

Long, J. S. (1997). *Regression models for categorical and limited dependent variables*. London: Sage.

Mazerolle, P. (1998). Gender, general strain, and delinquency: An empirical examination. *Justice Quarterly, 15*, 65–91.

Mazerolle, P., & Maahs, J. (2000). General strain and delinquency: An alternative examination of conditioning influences. *Justice Quarterly, 17*, 753–777.

Moon, B., & Morash, M. (2004). Adaptation of theory for alternative cultural contexts: Agnew's general strain theory in South Korea. *International Journal of Comparative and Applied Criminal Justice, 28*, 77–104.

Moon, B., Morash, M., McCluskey, C. P., & Hwang, H. (2009). A comprehensive test of general strain theory: Key strains, situational- and trait-based negative emotions, conditioning factors, and delinquency. *Journal of Research in Crime & Delinquency*, *46*, 182–212.

Morash, M., & Moon, B. (2007). Gender differences in the effects of strain on the delinquency of South Korean youth. *Youth & Society*, *38*, 300–321.

Pang Jong-Hwan Research Center. (2010). 한국 어린이 · 청소년 행복지수의 국 제비교 (International comparison of Korean children & adolescents). Seoul, Korea: Author.

Paternoster, R., Brame, R., Mazerolle, P., & Piquero, A. (1998). Using the correct statistical test for the equality of regression coefficients. *Criminology*, *36*, 859–866.

Patterson, L., Bae, S. O., & Lim, J. Y. (2013). Gender equality in Korean firms: Recent evidence from HR practitioners. *Asia Pacific Journal of Human Resources*, *51*, 364–381.

Piquero, N. L., & Sealock, M. D. (2004). Gender and general strain theory: A preliminary test of Broidy and Agnew's gender/GST hypotheses. *Justice Quarterly*, *21*, 125–157.

Piquero, N. L., & Sealock, M. D. (2000). Generalizing general strain theory: An examination of an offending population. *Justice Quarterly*, *17*, 449–484.

Sharp, L., & Lipsky, M. (2002). Screening for depression across the lifespan: A review of measures for the use in primary care settings. *American Family Physician*, *66*, 1001–1008.

Yun, M., Kim, E., & Morris, R. (2014). Gendered pathways to delinquency: An examination of general strain theory among South Korean youth. *Youth Violence and Juvenile Justice*, *12*, 268–292.

/// REVIEW QUESTIONS

1. What do previous studies show regarding gender differences in whether there are differences in how females and males are more likely internalize or externalize reactions to strain? What are some implications for the types of offending they commit?
2. The authors claim that certain characteristics of the Korean culture make it unique and useful for testing general strain theory. Do you agree or disagree, and why?
3. What do the findings of the current study suggest regarding gender differences in strain measures and negative emotions related to strain?
4. What other key theoretical factors showed differential influence on the various types of offending for females as compared to males?

SECTION **VII**

The Chicago School and Cultural and Subcultural Theories of Crime

This section will examine the origin and evolution of the Chicago or Ecological School theory, otherwise known as the ecological perspective or the theory of social disorganization. We will also discuss modern research on this theory, which assumes that the environments people live in determine their behavior. Finally, we will discuss the assumptions and dynamics of cultural and subcultural theory in society, highlighting differences in certain models emphasizing inner-city subcultures and other modern examples of subcultures (e.g., street gangs). We will finish by reviewing the policy implications that have been suggested by this perspective of crime.

The Chicago School evolved during the late 19th and early 20th centuries when the city of Chicago desperately needed answers for its exponentially growing problem of delinquency and crime. This became a primary focus in Chicago, where total chaos prevailed at the time.

A significant portion of the Chicago perspective focused on the transmission of cultural values to peers and even across generations as the older youths relayed their antisocial values and techniques to the younger children. Thus, the cultural and subcultural perspective is also a key area of this theoretical model. This cultural aspect of the Chicago model is also examined in this section, as are other subculture frameworks of offending behaviors.

The Ecological School and the Chicago School of Criminology

Despite the fact that its name specifies one city, the **Chicago School of Criminology** represents one of the most valid and generalizable theories we will discuss in this book in the sense that many of its propositions can be readily applied to the growth and evolution of virtually all cities around the world. The Chicago School, which is often referred to as the **Ecological School** or the theory of **social disorganization**, also represents one of the earliest examples of balancing theorizing with scientific analysis and at the same time guiding important programs and policy implementations that still thrive today. Perhaps most important, the Chicago School of Criminology was the epitome of using theoretical development and scientific testing to help improve conditions in society when it was most needed, which can be appreciated only by understanding the degree of chaos and crime that existed in Chicago in the late 1800s and early 1900s.

▲ **Image 7.1** Virtually all large cities, like Chicago, New York, and Los Angeles, grew the same predictable way, and the formation of certain zones or types of areas follow ecological principles.

SOURCE: © istockphoto.com / marchello74

Cultural Context: Chicago in the 1800s and Early 1900s

Experts have determined that 19th-century Chicago was the fastest-growing city in U.S. history.[1] Census data show that the population went from about 5,000 in the early 1800s to more than 2 million by 1900; put another way, the population more than doubled every decade during the 19th century.[2] This massive rate of growth—much faster than that seen in other large U.S. cities such as Boston, Baltimore, New York, Philadelphia, and San Francisco—was due to Chicago's central geographic position. It was in many ways landlocked because, although it sits on Lake Michigan, there was no water route to the city from the Atlantic Ocean until the Erie Canal opened in 1825, which provided access to the Great Lakes region for shipping and migration of people. Three years later came the first U.S. passenger train, the Baltimore and Ohio Railroad, whose route extended from the mid-Atlantic to central areas of the country. These two transportation advancements created a continual stream of migration to the Chicago area, which increased again when the transcontinental railroad was completed in 1869, linking both coasts with the U.S. Midwest.[3]

It is important to keep in mind that, in the early to mid-1800s, many large U.S. cities had virtually no formal social agencies to handle the problems of urbanization—no social workers, building inspectors, garbage collectors, or even police officers. Once police agencies were introduced, their duties often included finding lost children and collecting the garbage, primarily because there weren't other agencies to perform these tasks. Therefore, communities were largely responsible for solving their own problems, including crime and delinquency. By the late 1800s, however, Chicago was largely made up of citizens who did not speak a common language and did not share each other's cultural values. This phenomenon is consistent with U.S. Census Bureau data from that era, which show that 70% of Chicago residents were foreign born and another 20% were first-generation Americans. It was almost impossible for these citizens to organize themselves to solve community problems because, in most cases, they could not even understand each other.

This resulted in the type of chaos and normlessness that Émile Durkheim predicted would occur when urbanization and industrialization occurred too rapidly; in fact, Chicago represented the archetype of a society in an anomic state, with almost a complete breakdown in control. One of the most notable manifestations of this breakdown in

[1]For an excellent discussion of the early history of Chicago, see Thomas J. Bernard, *The Cycle of Juvenile Justice*, 2nd ed. (New York: Oxford University Press, 2010).

[2]See discussion in Thomas J. Bernard, Jeffrey B. Snipes, and Alexander L. Gerould, *Vold's Theoretical Criminology*, 6th ed. (Oxford: Oxford University Press, 2010), 117–22 (see chap. 1).

[3]These dates were taken from *The World Almanac, 2000*, Millennium Collector's Edition (Mahwah, NJ: Primedia Reference, 2000).

social control was that children were running wild on the streets in gangs, with adults making little attempt to intervene. So, delinquency was soaring, and it appeared that the gangs controlled the streets as much as any other group.

The leaders and people of Chicago needed theoretical guidance to develop solutions to their problems, particularly regarding the high rates of delinquency. This was a key factor in why the Department of Sociology at the University of Chicago became so important and dominant in the early 1900s. Essentially, modern sociology developed in Chicago because this city needed it the most to solve its social problems. Thus, Chicago became a type of laboratory for sociological researchers, and they developed a number of theoretical models of crime and other social ills that are still shown to be empirically valid today.

▲ **Image 7.2** The American buffalo was introduced to Catalina Island in California and destroyed much of the unique plant life there. This is an example of a foreign element creating chaos, such as crime does in residential areas.

SOURCE: © istockphoto.com / dmbaker

Ecological Principles in City Growth and Concentric Circles

In the 1920s and 1930s, several new perspectives of human behavior and city growth were offered by sociologists at the University of Chicago. The first relevant model was proposed by Robert E. Park, who claimed that much of human behavior, especially the way cities grow, follows the basic principles of ecology that had been documented and applied to wildlife for many years at that point.[4] Ecology is essentially the study of the dynamics and processes through which plants and animals interact with the environment. In an application of Darwinian theory, Park proposed that the growth of cities follows a natural pattern and evolution.

Specifically, Park claimed that cities represent a type of complex organism with a sense of unity composed of the interrelations among its citizens and groups. Park applied the ecological principle of symbiosis to explain the dependency of various citizens and units on each other: Everyone is better off working together as a whole. Furthermore, Park claimed that all cities would contain identifiable clusters, which he called **natural areas**, which would take on a life or organic unity of their own. To clarify, many cities have neighborhoods that are made up of primarily one ethnic group or are distinguished by certain features. For example, New York City's Hell's Kitchen, Times Square, and Harlem represent areas of one city that have each taken on unique identities; however, each of them contributes to the whole makeup and identity of the city. The same can be seen in other cities, such as Baltimore, which in a two-mile area has the Inner Harbor, Little Italy, and Fell's Point, with each area complementing the other zones. From Miami to San Francisco to New Orleans, all cities across America, and throughout the world for that matter, contain these identifiable natural areas.

Applying several other ecological principles, Park also noted that some areas (or species) may invade and dominate adjacent areas (species). The dominated area or species can recede, migrate to another location, or die off.

[4]Robert E. Park, "Human Ecology," *American Journal of Sociology* 42 (1936): 158–64; Robert E. Park, *Human Communities* (Glencoe, IL: Free Press, 1952).

▲ **Image 7.3** The Chicago or Ecological model proposed that as factories invaded and dominated residential areas, the residents who could afford to leave did and those left were the poor and deprived, which increased risk of crime.

SOURCE: © istockphoto.com / shaunl

In wildlife, an example is the incredible proliferation of a plant called kudzu, which grows at an amazing pace and has large leaves. It grows on top of other plants, trees, fields, and even houses, seeking to cover everything in its path and steal all the sunlight needed by other plants. Introduced to the United States in the 1800s at a world exposition, this plant was originally used to stop erosion but got out of control, especially in the southeastern region of the United States. Now kudzu costs the government more than $350 million each year because of its destruction of crops and other flora. This is a good example of a species that invades, dominates, and causes the recession of other species in the area.

A similar example can be found in the introduction of bison on Santa Catalina Island off the Southern California coast in the 1930s. About three dozen buffalo were originally imported to the island for a movie shoot, and the producers decided not to spend the money to remove them after the project, so they have remained and multiplied. Had this occurred in other parts of the United States, it would not have caused a problem. However, the largest mammal native to the island before the bison was a 4-pound fox. So, the buffalo—now numbering in the hundreds, to the point where several hundred were recently shipped to their native Western habitat—have destroyed much of the environment, driving to extinction some plants and animals unique to Catalina Island. Like the kudzu, the bison came to dominate the environment; in this case, other species couldn't move off the island and died off.

Park claimed that a similar process occurs in human cities as some areas invade other zones or areas, and the previously dominant area must relocate or die off. This is easy to see in modern times with the growth of what is known as *urban sprawl.* Geographers and urban planners have long acknowledged the detriment to traditionally stable residential areas when businesses move in. Some of the most recent examples involve the battles of longtime homeowners against the introduction of malls, businesses, and other industrial centers in districts previously zoned residential. The media have documented such fights, especially with the proliferation of such establishments as Walmart and Kmart supercenters, which residents perceive, and perhaps rightfully so, as an invasion. Such an invasion can create chaos in a previously stable residential community due to increased traffic; transient populations; and, perhaps most important, crime. Furthermore, some cities are granting power to such development through eminent domain, by which the local government can take land from homeowners to rezone and import businesses.

When Park developed his theory of ecology, he observed a trend in which businesses and factories were invading the traditionally residential areas of Chicago, which caused major chaos and breakdown in the stability of those areas. Readers, especially those who were raised in suburban or rural areas, can likely relate to this; going back to where they grew up, they can often see fast growth. Such development can devastate the informal controls (such as neighborhood networks or family ties) because it promotes invasion by a highly transient group of consumers and residents who do not have strong ties to the area.

This leads to a psychological indifference to the neighborhood in which no one cares about protecting the community any longer. Those who can afford to leave the area do, and those who can't afford to get out remain until they can save enough money to do so. When Park presented his theory of ecology in the 1920s, having factories that moved into the neighborhood often meant having a lot of smoke billowing out of chimneys. No one wanted to live in such a place, particularly at a time when the effects of pollution were not understood and smokestacks had no filters. Certain parts of Chicago and other U.S. cities were perpetually covered by the smog these factories created. In highly industrial areas, the constant and vast coverage of smoke and pollutants made it seem to be snowing or overcast most of the time. It is easy to see how such invasions can completely disrupt the previously dominant and stable residential areas of a community.

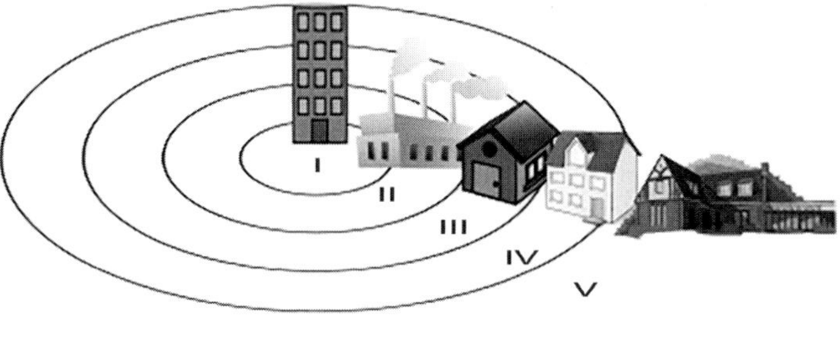

▲ **Image 7.4** Virtually all large cities in the world historically developed and grew with the same basic design of concentric circles.

SOURCE: Zeimusu / Wikimedia Commons

Park's ideas became even more valid and influential with the complementary perspective offered by Ernest W. Burgess,[5] who proposed a theory of city growth in which cities were seen as growing not simply on the edges but from the inside outward. It is easy to observe cities growing on the edges, as in the example of urban sprawl, but Burgess claimed that the source of growth was in the cities' centers. Growth of the inner city puts pressure on adjacent zones, which in turn begin to grow into the adjacent zones, following the ecological principle of *succession* identified by Park. This type of development is referred to as radial growth, meaning beginning on the inside and rippling outward.[6]

An example of this can be seen by watching a drop of water fall into the center of a bucket filled with water. The waves from the impact will form circles that ripple outward. This is exactly how Burgess claimed that cities grow. Although the growth of cities is most visible on the edges, largely due to development of businesses and homes where only trees or barren land existed before, the reason for growth there is the pressure forming at the very heart of the city. Another good analogy is the domino effect, because pressure from the center leads to growing pressure on the next zone, which leads to pressure on the adjacent zones and so forth.

Burgess also specified the primary zones—five pseudodistinctive natural areas in a constant state of flux due to growth—that all cities appear to have. He depicted these zones as a set of concentric circles. The first, innermost circle was called Zone I, or the central business district. This area of a city contained the large business buildings, modern skyscrapers that are home to banks, chambers of commerce, courthouses, and other essential business, and political centers such as police headquarters and post offices.

Just outside the business district was the unnumbered factory zone. It was perhaps the most significant in terms of fostering crime because it invaded the previously stable residential areas in Zone II, which Burgess identified as the **zone in transition**. Zone II was appropriately named because it was truly in a state of transition from residential to industrial, primarily because this was the area of the city in which businesses and factories were invading residential areas. Zone II was the area that was most significantly subjected to the ecological principles Park suggested: invasion, domination, recession, and succession. Subsequent criminological theorists focused on this zone.

According to Burgess's **theory of concentric circles**, Zone III was the workingmen's homes, relatively modest houses and apartment buildings; Zone IV consisted of higher-priced family dwellings and more expensive apartments; and Zone V was the suburban or commuter zone. These outer three zones Burgess identified were of less

[5]Ernest W. Burgess, "The Growth of the City," in *The City*, ed. Robert Park, Ernest W. Burgess, and Roderick D. McKenzie (Chicago: University of Chicago Press, 1928).

[6]See George Vold, *Theoretical Criminology* (New York: Oxford University Press, 1958), 118–21.

importance in terms of crime, primarily because, as a general rule, the farther a family could move out of the city, the better the neighborhood was in terms of social organization and the lower the rate of social ills (e.g., poverty, delinquency). The important point of this theory of concentric circles is that the growth of each inner zone puts pressure on the next zone to grow and push into the next adjacent zone.

It is easy for readers to see examples of concentric circles theory. Wherever you live in the United States, any major city provides real-life evidence of the validity of this perspective. For example, whether people drive on Interstate 95 through Baltimore or Interstate 5 through Los Angeles, they will see the same pattern of city structure. As they approach each of the cities, they see suburban wealth in the homes and buildings, often hidden by trees off the highway. Closer to the cities, they see homes and buildings deteriorating in terms of value. Because parts of the highway systems near Baltimore and Los Angeles are somewhat elevated, drivers entering Zone II can easily see the prevalence of factories and the highly deteriorated nature of the areas. Today, many 20th-century factories have been abandoned or have limited use; these factory zones consist of rusted-out or demolished buildings. Zone II is also often the location of subsidized or public housing. Only the people who can't afford to live anywhere else are forced to live in these neighborhoods. Finally, as drivers enter the inner city of skyscrapers, the conditions improve dramatically because the major businesses have invested their money there. Compared to Zone II, this innermost area is a utopia.

This theory applies around the world, and we challenge readers to find any major city throughout the world that did not develop this way. Nowadays, some attempts have been made to plan community development, and other cities have experienced the convergence of several patterns of concentric circles as central business districts (i.e., Zone Is) are developed in what was previously suburbia (i.e., Zone Vs). However, for the most part, the theoretical framework of concentric circles still has a great deal of support. In fact, even cities found in Eastern cultures have evolved this way. Therefore, Park's application appears to be correct: Cities grow in a natural way across time and place, abiding by the natural principles of ecology.

Case Study: Los Angeles Gangs

Although most case studies we review in this book are about individuals, in this case we concentrate on groups, which is fitting for this section because virtually all the theories we will cover in this section are macro- or group-level theories. A recent scientific study by researchers at the University of California, Los Angeles, showed that when Los Angeles gangs and incidents of gang activities are mapped, the places with the highest frequency of violence are on the borders between two or more rival gangs.[7]

. . . When Los Angeles gangs and incidents of gang activities are mapped, the places with the highest frequency of violence are on the borders between two or more rival gangs.

This 2012 report showed that, contrary to popular belief, the most dangerous places to be in Los Angeles are not the regions deeply within the territory of a dominant gang but rather on the boundaries of gang territories, perhaps due to turf disputes or the increased likelihood of encountering rival factions. We shall see that this recently observed phenomenon among established gang territories was to some extent predicted and explained by Chicago School theories of crime and city growth proposed

[7]Dennis Romero, "Gang Map Study Shows Crime Happens along Borders between Sets in L.A." *LA Weekly*, June 27, 2010, http://blogs.laweekly.com/informer/2012/06/gang_maps_angeles_murder_attacks_borders_ucla_study.php?print=true. See also actual study: P. Jeffrey Brantingham et al., "The Ecology of Gang Territorial Boundaries," *Criminology* 50, no. 3 (2012): 851–885. doi:10.1111/j.1745-9125.2012.00281.x.

more than half a century ago. We will follow up on this case study toward the end of this section.

Think About It

1. Why do you think the most violent areas of Los Angeles are those on the borders of rival gangs as opposed to the regions that are strongly dominated by a single gang?

▲ **Image 7.5** It is on the borders of their territories that gang violence is at a high level, as compared to well within their established home turf where the gangs have entrenched dominance in that region.

SOURCE: © Ted Soqui / Corbis Historical Collection / Getty Images

Shaw and McKay's Theory of Social Disorganization

Clifford Shaw and Henry McKay drew heavily on their colleagues at the University of Chicago in devising their theory of social disorganization, which became known as the Chicago School theory of criminology.[8] Shaw had been producing excellent case studies for years on the individual (i.e., micro) level before he took on theorizing on the macro (i.e., structural) level of crime rates.[9] However, once he began working with McKay, he devised perhaps the most enduring and valid model of why certain neighborhoods have more social problems, such as delinquency, than others.

In this model, Shaw and McKay proposed a framework that began with the assumption that certain neighborhoods in all cities have more crime than other parts of the city, most of them located in Burgess's Zone II, which is the zone in transition from residential to industrial due to the invasion of factories. According to Shaw and McKay, the neighborhoods that have the highest rates of crime typically have at least three common problems (see Figure 7.1): physical dilapidation, poverty, and heterogeneity (which is a fancy way of saying a high cultural mix). There were other common characteristics that Shaw and McKay noted, such as a highly transient population, meaning that people constantly move in and out of the area, as well as unemployment among the residents of the neighborhood.

---

[8]Clifford Shaw and Henry D. McKay, *Juvenile Delinquency and Urban Areas* (Chicago: University of Chicago Press, 1942); Clifford Shaw and Henry D. McKay, *Juvenile Delinquency and Urban Areas*, rev. ed. (Chicago: University of Chicago Press, 1969).

[9]Clifford Shaw, *Brothers in Crime* (Chicago: University of Chicago Press, 1938); Clifford Shaw, *The Jackroller* (Chicago: University of Chicago Press, 1930); Clifford Shaw, *The Natural History of a Delinquent Career* (Chicago: University of Chicago Press, 1931).

Figure 7.1 • Model of Shaw and McKay's theory of social disorganization

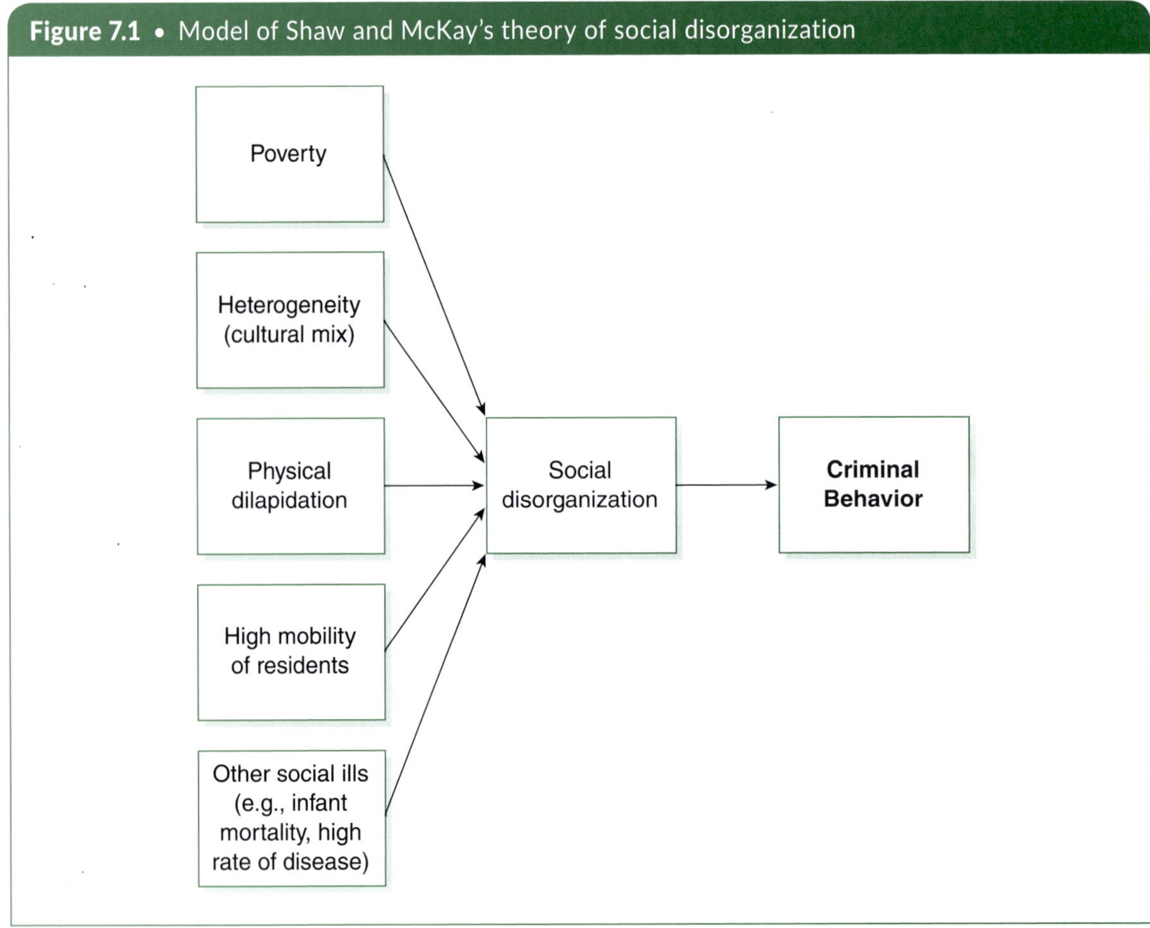

SOURCE: Stephen G. Tibbetts and Craig Hemmens, *Criminological Theory: A Text/Reader*, 2nd ed. (Thousand Oaks, CA: Sage, 2015).

As noted in Figure 7.1, other social ills are included as antecedent factors in the theoretical model. The antecedent social ills tend to lead to a breakdown in social organization, which is why this model is referred to as the theory of social disorganization. Specifically, it is predicted that the antecedent factors of poverty, heterogeneity, and physical dilapidation lead to a state of social disorganization, which in turn leads to crime and delinquency. This means that in a neighborhood that fits the profile of having a high rate of poor, culturally mixed residents in a dilapidated area, people cannot come together to solve problems, such as delinquency among youth.

One of the most significant contributions of Shaw and McKay was that they demonstrated that the prevalence and frequency of various social ills—such as poverty, disease, and low birth weight—tend to overlap with higher delinquency rates. Regardless of what social problem is measured, higher rates are almost always clustered in the zone in transition. Shaw and McKay believed there is a breakdown of informal social controls in these areas and that children begin to learn offending norms from their interactions with peers on the street, through what the researchers call *play activities.*[10] Thus, the breakdown in the conditions of the neighborhood leads to social disorganization, which in turn leads to delinquency in children who learn criminal activities from older youths. Ultimately, the failure of the neighborhood residents to organize themselves allows the older youths to govern the behavior of the younger children. Basically, the older youths in the area provide a system of organization where the neighborhood adults cannot, so younger children follow them.

One of the best things about Shaw and McKay's theoretical model is that they supported their propositions with data from U.S. census and city records, showing that neighborhoods with high rates of poverty and physical dilapidation and high cultural mixes also had the highest rates of delinquency and crime. Furthermore, the high rates of delinquency and other social problems were consistent with Burgess's framework of concentric circles in that the highest rates were observed for the areas that were in Zone II, the zone in transition. There was one exception to the model: The Gold Coast area along the northern coast of Lake Michigan did not have the high rates of social problems, particularly delinquency, even though it was geographically in Zone II according to the otherwise consistent model of concentric circles and neighborhood zones.

Thus, the findings of Shaw and McKay were as predicted in the sense that high delinquency rates occurred in areas where factories were invading residential districts. Furthermore, Shaw and McKay's longitudinal data showed that it did not matter which ethnic groups lived in Zone II; all groups (with the exception of Asians) that lived in that zone had high delinquency rates during their residency. On the other hand, once most of an ethnic group had moved out of Zone II, the delinquency rate among its youths decreased significantly.

This finding rejects the notion of **social Darwinism** because it is clearly not the culture that influences crime and delinquency but rather the criminogenic nature of the environment. If ethnicity or race made a difference, the delinquency rates in Zone II would fluctuate based on who lived there, but the rates continued to be high from one group to the next. Rather, the zone determined the rates of delinquency.

Reaction and Research on Social Disorganization Theory

Over the past few decades, the Chicago School theoretical framework has received an enormous amount of attention from researchers.[11] Virtually all of the research has supported Shaw and McKay's version of social disorganization and the resulting high crime rates in neighborhoods that exhibit such deprived conditions. Modern research has supported the theoretical model proposed by Shaw and McKay, specifically in terms of the high crime rates in disorganized neighborhoods. Also, virtually every city that has an elevated highway (e.g., Richmond, Virginia; Baltimore, Maryland; Los Angeles, California) visually supports Shaw and McKay's model of crime in concentric circles. Drivers entering those cities can see the pattern of dilapidated structures in the zone of transition surrounding the inner-city area. Before and after this layer of dilapidated structures, drivers encounter a layer of houses and residential areas that seem to increase in quality as the driver gets farther away from the inner-city area.

---

[10]Shaw, *Brothers in Crime*, 354–55.

[11]Wouter Steenbeek and John R. Hipp, "A Longitudinal Test of Social Disorganization Theory: Feedback Effects among Cohesion, Social Control, and Disorder," *Criminology* 49 (2011): 833–71; John Laub, "Urbanism, Race, and Crime," *Journal of Research in Crime and Delinquency* 20 (1983): 283–98; Robert Sampson, "Structural Sources of Variation In Race-Age-Specific Rate of Offending across Major U.S. Cities," *Criminology* 23 (1985): 647–73; J. L. Heitgard and Robert J. Bursik, "Extracommunity Dynamics and the Ecology of Delinquency," *American Journal of Sociology* 92 (1987): 775–87; Robert Bursik, "Social Disorganization and Theories of Crime and Delinquency: Problems and Prospects," *Criminology* 26 (1988): 519–51; Ralph Taylor and Jeanette Covington, "Neighborhood Changes in Ecology and Violence," *Criminology* 26 (1988): 553–89; Robert Bursik, "Ecological Stability and the Dynamics of Delinquency," in *Crime and Community*, ed. Albert J. Reiss and Morris H. Tonry (Chicago: University of Chicago Press, 1986), 35–66; Robert Sampson, "Transcending Tradition: New Directions in Community Research, Chicago Style—The American Society of Criminology 2001 Sutherland Address," *Criminology* 40 (2002): 213–30; Robert Sampson, J. D. Morenoff, and T. Gannon-Rowley, "Assessing 'Neighborhood Effects': Social Processes and New Directions in Research," *Annual Review of Sociology* 28 (2002): 443–78; P. O. Wikstrom and Rolf Loeber, "Do Disadvantaged Neighborhoods Cause Well-Adjusted Children to Become Adolescent Delinquents?" *Criminology* 38 (2000): 1109–42.

Figure 7.2 • Zone map of male delinquents in Chicago, 1925–1933

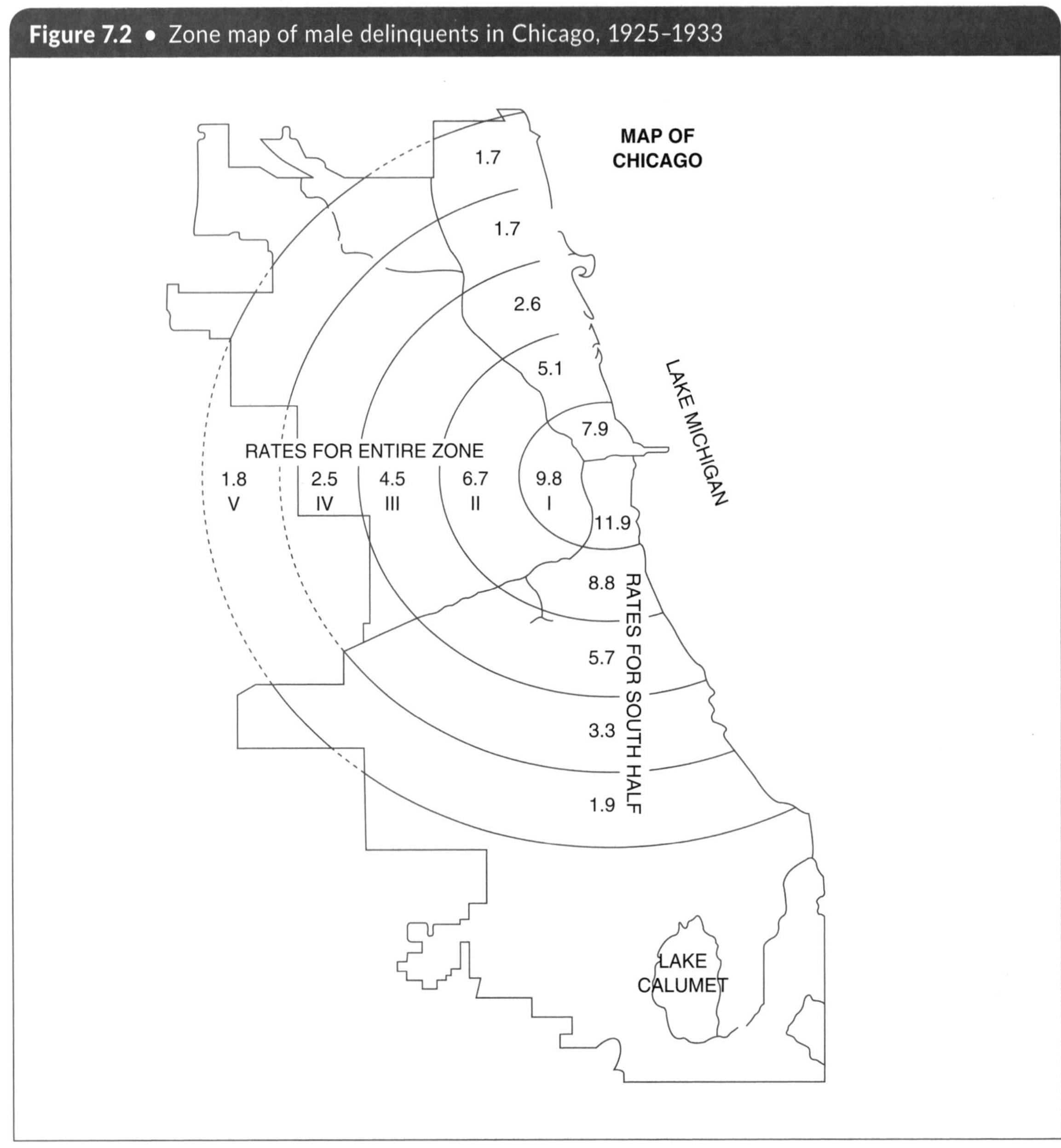

SOURCE: "Delinquency Rates and Community Characteristics," Shaw, Clifford R., and Henry D. McKay, in *Juvenile Delinquency and Urban Areas*, 2nd edition, by C.R. Shaw and H.D. McKay.

Some critics, however, have raised some valid concerns regarding the original model, arguing that Shaw and McKay's original research did not actually measure their primary construct: social disorganization. Although this criticism is accurate, recent research has shown that the model is valid even when valid measures of social disorganization are included.[12] Such measures of social disorganization include simply asking members of the neighborhood how many neighbors they know by name or how often they observe unsupervised peer groups in the area.

Additional criticisms of Shaw and McKay's formulation of social disorganization focus on the emphasis that the theory places on the macro, or aggregate, level of analysis. Although their theory does a good job of predicting which neighborhoods have higher crime rates, the model does not even attempt to explain why most youths in the worst areas do not become offenders. Furthermore, their model does not attempt to explain why some youths—although a very small number of them—in the best neighborhoods (i.e., in Zone V) choose to commit crime. However, the previously cited case studies completed and published by Shaw, such as *The Jackroller* and *Brothers in Crime,* attempted to address the individual (micro) level of offending.

Also, there was one notable exception to Shaw and McKay's proposition that all ethnic and racial groups have high rates of delinquency and crime while they live in Zone II. Evidence showed that when Japanese Americans made up a large portion of residents in this zone in transition, they had very low rates of delinquency. Thus, as in most theoretical models in social science, there was an exception to the rule.

Perhaps the biggest criticism of Shaw and McKay's theory, one that has yet to be adequately addressed, deals with the fact that they blatantly neglected to propose ways to ameliorate the most problematic source of criminality in Zone II neighborhoods. Although they clearly point to the invasion of factories and businesses into residential areas as a problem, they do not recommend how to slow such invasion. This is likely due to political and financial concerns: Owners of factories and businesses partially financed their research and later were the primary funders of implementation of their policies. Neglect is further represented in their failure to explain the exception of the Gold Coast in their results and conclusions.

Despite the criticisms and weaknesses of the Chicago School perspective of criminology, this theory resulted in one of the largest programs to date in attempting to reduce delinquency rates. Shaw was put in charge of establishing the Chicago Area Project (CAP), which created neighborhood centers in the most crime-ridden parts of Chicago. These centers offered activities for youths and tried to establish ties between parents and officials in the neighborhood. Although this program was never scientifically evaluated, it still exists, and many cities have implemented programs based on this model. For example, Boston implemented a very similar program, which was evaluated by Walter Miller.[13] This evaluation showed that, although the project was effective in establishing relationships and interactions between local gangs and community groups and in providing more educational and vocational opportunities, it seemed to fail in reducing delinquent and criminal behavior. Thus, the overall conclusion made by experts was that the Boston project and other similar programs, like the CAP, typically fail to prevent criminal behavior.[14]

---

[12]Robert Sampson and W. Byron Groves, "Community Structure and Crime: Testing Social Disorganization Theory," *American Journal of Sociology* 94 (1989): 774–802.

[13]Walter B. Miller, "The Impact of a 'Total-Community' Delinquency Control Project," *Social Problems* 10 (1962): 168–91.

[14]For a review, see Richard Lundman, *Prevention and Control of Juvenile Delinquency*, 2nd ed. (New York: Oxford University Press, 1993). See also Bernard et al., *Vold's Theoretical Criminology*, 125–26.

Case Study: Whitey Bulger

▲ **Image 7.6** Whitey Bulger (1929–) was the head of one of the most notorious organized crime syndicates in Boston until he was apprehended in Southern California in 2011.

SOURCE: United States Marshals Service, United States Department of Justice, via Wikimedia Commons

Whitey Bulger (James Joseph "Whitey" Bulger Jr.) is perhaps the most notorious gangster from the South Boston area, which is saying a lot given the history and tradition of organized crime in "Southie," as they call it. Bulger was a key figure of a criminal organization from the early 1970s to the mid-1990s and head of this organization for much of that time. Under heat from authorities, he fled in 1994, and for 12 years he was on the Federal Bureau of Investigation (FBI) Ten Most Wanted list. Bulger was apprehended with his long-term girlfriend, Catherine Greig, in Santa Monica, California, in 2011. He was sentenced on November 14, 2013, to two terms of life imprisonment, plus 5 years.

Bulger is believed to have been largely in charge of narcotics distribution and extortion rackets in the Southie area during most of the 1980s and early 1990s, along with the violence inherent to such a position. Interestingly, most sources show that he was also an FBI informant during much of this time period, which allowed him to essentially "get away with murder" and his other illegal activities.

Perhaps most related to this section, Bulger was seen locally as a type of Robin Hood figure, considered by most people on the streets as a sort of guardian protecting the interests of the neighborhood or local area. After all, Bulger had been a key element of organized crime in that area for many years, and this led to a subcultural or cultural climate placing him as an authority for all that happened in that locale. Furthermore, much of his business dealt with narcotics distribution and extortion, so his motives fit the other theories in this section of being largely based on finding criminal opportunities despite the relatively poor and deprived conditions of the South Boston region.

> ***. . . Bulger was seen locally as a type of Robin Hood figure, considered by most people on the streets as a sort of guardian protecting the interests of the neighborhood or local area.***

As alluded to before, Bulger likely saw the draw of organized crime as being his only way to accomplish the higher financial and/or social status that could be obtained in the South Boston area. After all, there were not many legitimate opportunities open to him given his early criminal record, not to mention the deprivation and lack of stable employment in that region. Furthermore, he probably also desired to become an important figure in the subculture or culture of that area, and the only likely way to do that was to become a prominent figure in the organized crime syndicates.

Think About It

1. Can you relate to Bulger's local community's attitude toward him as a type of hero?
2. How do you think such a subculture develops in local communities for such prominent gangsters?

SOURCES: Edward MacKenzie Jr. and Phyllis Karas, *Street Soldier: My Life as an Enforcer for "Whitey" Bulger and the Boston Irish Mob* (Hanover, NH: Steerforth, 2004); Kevin Weeks and Phyllis Karas. *Brutal: My Life Inside Whitey Bulger's Irish Mob* (New York: HarperCollins, 2009).

Cultural and Subcultural Theories of Crime

Cultural and subcultural theories of crime assume that there are unique groups in society that socialize their children to believe that certain activities that violate conventional law are good and positive ways to behave. Although it is rather difficult to find large groups of people or classes who fit this definition, it may be that some subcultures or isolated groups of individuals buy into a different set of norms than the conventional, middle-class set of values.

Early Theoretical Developments and Research in Cultural and Subcultural Theory

One of the key developments of cultural theory is the 1967 work of Franco Ferracuti and Marvin Wolfgang, who examined the violent themes of a group of inner-city youths from Philadelphia.[15] Ferracuti and Wolfgang's primary conclusion was that violence is a culturally learned adaptation to deal with negative life circumstances and that learning such norms occurs in an environment that emphasizes violence over other options.[16] These researchers based their conclusion on an analysis of data that showed great differences in the rates of homicide across racial groups. However, Ferracuti and Wolfgang were clear that their theory was based on subcultural norms. Specifically, they proposed that no subculture can be totally different from or totally in conflict with the society of which it is a part.[17] This brings the distinction of culture and subculture to the forefront.

A culture represents a distinct set of norms and values among an identifiable group of people—values that are distinctly different from those of the mainstream culture. For example, communism is distinctly different from capitalism because it emphasizes equality over competition, and it values utopia (i.e., everyone gets to share all profits) over the idea that the best performer gets the most reward. So, it can be said that communists tend to have a different culture than capitalists. There is also a substantial difference between a culture and a subculture, which is typically only a pocket of individuals who may have a set of norms that deviate from conventional values. Therefore, what Ferracuti and Wolfgang developed is not so much a cultural theory as it is a subcultural theory.

This is also seen in the most prominent (sub)culture theory, which was presented by Miller.[18] Miller's theoretical model proposed that the entire lower class had its own cultural value system. According to this model, virtually everyone in the lower class believes in and has been socialized to the values of six **focal concerns**: fate, autonomy, trouble, toughness, excitement, and smartness. Fate means luck, or whatever life has dealt you; it disregards responsibility and accountability for one's actions. Autonomy is the value of independence from authority. Trouble means staying out of legal problems as well as getting into and out of personal difficulties (e.g., pregnancy). Toughness is maintaining your reputation on the street in many ways. Excitement is engagement in activities, some illegal, that help liven up an otherwise mundane existence of being lower class. Smartness emphasizes street smarts or the ability to con others. Miller thought that members of the lower class teach these six focal concerns as a culture or environment (or "milieu," as stated in the title of his work).

A more recent subculture model, proposed by Elijah Anderson, has received a lot of attention in the past few years.[19] This theory focuses on African Americans; because of the very deprived conditions in inner cities, Black Americans who live there feel a sense of hopelessness, isolation, and despair, Anderson asserted. He clearly noted that, although many African Americans believe in middle-class values, these values have no weight on the street,

---

[15]Bernard et al., *Vold's Theoretical Criminology*, 165–69; Frank Schmalleger, *Criminology Today*, 6th ed. (Upper Saddle River: Prentice Hall, 2011).

[16]Franco Ferracuti and Marvin Wolfgang, *The Subculture of Violence: Toward an Integrated Theory of Criminology* (London: Tavistock, 1967).

[17]As quoted in Schmalleger, *Criminology Today*, 230–31.

[18]Walter B. Miller, "Lower Class Culture as a Generating Milieu of Gang Delinquency," *Journal of Social Issues* 14 (1958): 5–19.

[19]Elijah Anderson, *Code of the Street* (New York: W. W. Norton, 2000).

particularly among young urban males. According to Anderson, the "code of the street," which is the appropriate title of his book, is to maintain one's reputation and demand respect. For example, to be treated with disrespect ("dissed") is considered grounds for a physical attack. Masculinity and control of one's immediate environment are treasured characteristics; the immediate environment is perceived as the only thing people can control, given the harsh conditions (e.g., unemployment, poverty) in which they live.

Criticisms of Cultural Theories of Crime

Studies on cultural theories of crime, at least in the United States, find no large groups that blatantly deny the middle-class norms of society. Miller's model of lower-class focal concerns is not consistent across the entire lower class. Studies show that most adults in the lower class attempt to socialize their children to believe in conventional values, such as respect for authority, hard work, and delayed gratification, and not the focal concerns that Miller specified in his model.[20] Ferracuti and Wolfgang admitted that their research findings led them to conclude that their model had more of a subcultural perspective than one emphasizing a distinctly different culture. There may be small groups or gangs who have subcultural normative values, but that doesn't constitute a completely separate culture in society. Perhaps the best subculture theories are those presented by Cohen or Cloward and Ohlin (see Section VI) in their variations of strain theory that emphasize the formations of gangs among lower-class male youths. A recent example of a specific group that seems to embrace a different normative code is that of adult male bar fighters, which was presented by Heith Copes and his colleagues.[21] So apparently there are subcultural groups in U.S. society; however, they seem to make up a very small percentage of the population, which somewhat negates the cultural and subcultural perspective of criminality, which claims that crime-fostering subcultures make up a large, distinctive portion of the population. Still, this type of perspective may be important regarding the criminality of select subgroups of offenders, such as street gangs.

Policy Implications

Many of the policy implications suggested by the theoretical models proposed in this section are rather ironic. Regarding social disorganization, a paradox exists in the sense that the very neighborhoods most desperately in need of becoming organized to fight crime are the same inner-city ghetto areas where it is, by far, the most difficult to cultivate that organization (e.g., through neighborhood watch or block watch groups). Rather, the neighborhoods that have high levels of organization tend to be those that already have very low levels of crime because the residents naturally police their neighbors' well-being and property; they have a stake in the area's remaining crime free. Although there are some anecdotal examples of success of neighborhood watch programs in high-crime neighborhoods, most of the empirical evidence shows that this approach is "almost uniformly unsupportive" in its ability to reduce crime there.[22] Furthermore, many studies of these neighborhood watch programs find that the groups actually increase the fear of crime in some places, perhaps due to the heightened awareness of crime issues in these areas.[23]

---

[20]Bernard et al., *Vold's Theoretical Criminology.*

[21]Heith Copes, Andy Hochstetler, and Craig Forsyth, "Peaceful Warriors: Codes for Violence among Adult Male Bar Fighters," *Criminology* 51 (2013): 761–94.

[22]John Worrall, *Crime Control in America: What Works?* 2nd ed. (Boston: Allyn & Bacon, 2008), 95.

[23]Ibid.

On the other hand, other types of community crime prevention programs do seem to show some success according to a 2017 systematic review by David Weisburd and his colleagues.[24] Specifically, the study concludes that improving street lighting and adding closed-circuit television cameras can lower crime rates in neighborhoods. The researchers also conclude that the most effective strategies to mobilize communities against crime are programs that involve proactive engagement with the police and other civic partners to enhance social cohension.[25]

Perhaps the most notable programs that resulted from the Chicago School or social disorganization model—the CAP and similar programs—have been dubbed failures in reducing crime rates among the participants. Still, as mentioned previously, there have been some advances in trying to get residents of high-crime areas to become organized in fighting crime. The more specific the goals regarding crime reduction (a specific goal might be careful monitoring of high-level offenders through more intensive supervised probation, repeat victimization prevention programs), the more effective the implementation.[26]

Regarding cultural and subcultural theories, some promising intervention and outreach programs have been suggested by such models. Many programs attempt to build prosocial attitudes among high-risk youths—often young children. For example, a recent evaluation showed that a program called PeaceBuilders, which focuses on children in early grades, was effective in producing gains in conflict resolution, development of prosocial values, and reductions in aggression; a follow-up showed that these attributes were maintained for a long period of time.[27] Another recent anti-aggression training program for boys in foster care showed positive effects in levels of empathy, self-efficacy, and attribution style among boys who had exhibited early-onset aggression.[28] Ultimately, there are effective programs out there that promote prosocial norms and culture. More effort should be given to promoting such programs to help negate the antisocial cultural norms of individuals, especially among high-risk youths.

Conclusion

In this section, we examined theoretical perspectives proposing that the lack of social organization in broken-down and dilapidated neighborhoods leads to the inability to contain delinquency and crime. Furthermore, we discussed how this model of crime was linked to processes derived from ecological principles. This type of approach has been tested numerous times, and virtually all studies show that the distribution of delinquents and crime activity is consistent with this model.

We then discussed the ability of cultural and subcultural theories to explain criminal activity. Empirical evidence shows that cultural values make a contribution to criminal behavior but that the existence of an actual alternative culture in our society has not been found. However, some subcultural pockets, particularly inner-city youth gangs, certainly exist and provide some validity for this perspective of crime. Furthermore, the Chicago School perspective plays a role, because these subcultural groups tend to be found in zones of transition.

---

[24]David Weisburd, David P. Farrington, and Charlotte Gill, "What Works in Crime Prevention and Rehabilitation: An Assessment of Systematic Reviews," *Criminology & Public Policy* 16 (2017): 415–49.

[25]Ibid.

[26]Lundman, *Prevention and Control*; Sampson and Groves, "Community Structure"; Bernard et al., *Vold's Theoretical Criminology*; Weisburd et al., "What Works in Crime Prevention."

[27]Daniel J. Flannery, Mark I. Singer, and Kelly L. Wester, "Violence, Coping, and Mental Health in a Community Sample of Adolescence," *Violence and Victims* 18 (2003): 403–18. For a review of this research, see Stephen G. Tibbetts, "Perinatal and Developmental Determinants of Early Onset of Offending: A Biosocial Approach for Explaining the Two Peaks of Early Antisocial Behavior," in *The Development of Persistent Criminality*, ed. Joanne Savage (New York: Oxford University Press, 2009), 179–201.

[28]Karina Weichold, "Evaluation of an Anti-aggressiveness Training with Antisocial Youth," *Gruppendynamik* 35 (2004): 83–105. For a review, see Tibbetts, "Perinatal and Developmental Determinants."

Finally, we examined policy implications suggested by these theoretical models. Regarding social disorganization, we noted that neighborhood crime-fighting groups are hardest to establish in high-crime neighborhoods and easiest to build in those neighborhoods with an already low rate of crime. Nevertheless, there have been some successes. We also looked at intervention and outreach programs based on cultural and subcultural perspectives.

SECTION SUMMARY

- We examined how principles of ecology were applied to the study of how cities grow, as well as to the study of crime, by researchers at the University of Chicago and how the resultant theories became known as the Chicago (or Ecological) School of Criminology.
- Examples from wildlife were presented as an analogy to illustrate how such ecological principles also apply to criminal elements invading and dominating city areas.
- We learned the history of Chicago and why that history made the city uniquely suited for the development of criminological theory.
- We reviewed the various zones of the concentric circles theory, also a key contribution of the Chicago School of Criminology, and explored which zones are most prone to crime.
- We examined why the findings from the Chicago School of Criminology showed that social Darwinism was not accurate in attributing varying crime rates to ethnicity or race.
- We reviewed much of the empirical evidence regarding the theory of social disorganization and examined the strengths and weaknesses of this theoretical model.
- We discussed the cultural and subcultural model presented by Ferracuti and Wolfgang as well as the cultural model of inner-city urban youths presented by Anderson.
- We discussed Miller's theory of lower-class culture, particularly its six focal concerns.
- We reviewed the strengths and weaknesses of cultural and subcultural theories of crime based on empirical evidence.

KEY TERMS

Chicago School of Criminology 287

cultural and subcultural theories 299

Ecological School 287

focal concerns 299

natural areas 289

social Darwinism 295

social disorganization 287

theory of concentric circles 291

zone in transition 291

DISCUSSION QUESTIONS

1. Identify and discuss an example of the ecological principles of invasion, domination, and succession among animals or plants that was not discussed in this section.

2. Can you see examples of the various zones that Shaw and McKay described in the town or city where you live (or the one nearest you)? Try obtaining a map or sketching a plot of this city or town, and then draw the various concentric circles where you think the zones are located.
3. What forms of organization and disorganization have you observed in your own neighborhood? Try to supply examples of both if possible.
4. Can you provide modern-day examples of different cultures and subcultures in the United States? What regions or parts of the country would you say have cultures that are more conducive to crime?
5. Do you know people who believe most or all of Miller's focal concerns? What are their social classes? What are their other demographic features (age, gender, urban vs. rural, etc.)?
6. Do you know individuals who seem to fit either Ferracuti and Wolfgang's cultural theory or Anderson's model of inner-city youths' street code? Why do you believe they actually fit such a model?

WEB RESOURCES

Chicago School of Criminology

http://study.com/academy/lesson/the-chicago-schools-social-disorganization-theory.html
http://www.encyclopedia.com/law/legal-and-political-magazines/ecology-crime
http://userpages.umbc.edu/~lutters/pubs/1996_SWLNote96-1_Lutters,Ackerman.pdf

Subcultural Theories

http://study.com/academy/lesson/what-is-subculture-theories-definition-examples.html
http://www.umsl.edu/~keelr/200/subcult.html
https://www.slideshare.net/RSJones/crime-and-deviance-subcultural-approach

READING /// 15

In this selection, Clifford Shaw and Henry McKay present a theoretical model of various characteristics of neighborhoods that contribute to higher crime and delinquency rates. Specifically, they examine physical, economic, and population factors that contribute to higher rates of delinquency in certain communities. Such observations of certain neighborhoods provide the basis for the theory of social disorganization (also known as the Chicago or Ecological School of Criminology). Because this theory fits virtually all cities around the world—and because of their methodology—Shaw and McKay are generally considered two of the most prominent criminologists of the 20th century.

While reading this selection, consider the following points:

- The places you have lived or visited that may fit the characteristics of high-risk communities described in this reading
- The types of physical indicators that Shaw and McKay claim are present in neighborhoods that have high delinquency/crime rates
- The conclusion of Shaw and McKay, based on their data, regarding the crime rates of neighborhoods containing a population composition high in minorities or recent immigrants over time

Delinquency Rates and Community Characteristics

Clifford R. Shaw and Henry D. McKay

The question has been asked many times: "What is it, in modern city life that produces delinquency?" Why do relatively large numbers of boys from the inner urban areas appear in court with such striking regularity, year after year, regardless of changing population structure or the ups and downs of the business cycle? [Elsewhere] a different series of male delinquents were presented which closely parallel one another in geographical distribution although widely separated in time, and the close resemblance of all these series to the distribution of truants and of adult criminals was shown. Moreover, many other community characteristics—median rentals, families on relief, infant mortality rates, and so on—reveal similar patterns of variation throughout the city. The next step would be to determine, if possible, the extent to which these two sets of data are related. How consistently do they vary together, if at all, and how high is the degree of association?

Where high zero-order correlations are found to exist uniformly between two variables, with a small probable error, it is possible and valid to consider either series as an approximate index, or indicator, of the other. This holds

SOURCE: "Delinquency Rates and Community Characteristics," Shaw, Clifford R., and Henry D. McKay, in *Juvenile Delinquency and Urban Areas*, 2nd edition, by C. R. Shaw and H. D. McKay.

true for any two variables which are known to be associated or to vary concomitantly. The relationship, of course, may be either direct or inverse. In neither case, however, is there justification in assuming, on this basis alone, that the observed association is of a cause-and-effect nature; it may be, rather, that both variables are similarly affected by some third factor. Further analysis is needed. Controlled experimentation is often useful in establishing the degree to which a change in one variable "causes" or brings about a corresponding change in the other. In the social field, however, experimentation is difficult. Instead, it is often necessary to rely upon refined statistical techniques, such as partial correlation, which, for certain types of data, enable the investigator to measure the effects of one factor while holding others relatively constant. By the method of successive redistribution, also, the influence of one or more variables may be held constant. Thus, it is possible to study the relationship between rates of delinquents and economic status for a single nationality group throughout the city or for various nationality groups in the same area or class of areas. This process may be extended indefinitely, subject only to the limitations of the available data. In the analysis to be presented, both of the latter methods have been used in an attempt to determine how much weight should be given to various more or less influential factors.

Several practical considerations prevent the neat and precise statistical analysis which would be desirable. The characteristics studied represent only a sampling of the myriad forms in which community life and social relationships find expression. The rate of delinquents must itself be thought of as an imperfect enumeration of the delinquents and an index of the larger number of boys engaging in officially proscribed activities. Not only will there be chance fluctuations in the amount of alleged delinquency from year to year, but the policy of the local police officer in referring boys to the Juvenile Court, the focusing of the public eye upon conditions in an area, and numerous other matters may bring about a change in the index without any essential change in the underlying delinquency-producing influences in the community or in the behavior resulting therefrom. If the infant mortality rates or the rates of families on relief are looked upon as indexes of economic status or of the social organization of a community, it is obvious that they can be considered only very crude indicators at best. The perturbing influence of other variables must always be considered.

Certain exceptional conditions are known to limit the value of other variables chosen as indicators of local community differentiation. Median rental has been used widely because of its popularity as an index of economic status, although in Chicago such an index is far from satisfactory when applied to areas of colored population. The Negro is forced to pay considerably higher rents than the whites for comparable housing—thus his economic level is made to appear higher on the basis of rental than it actually is. Similarly, rates of increase or decrease of population are modified in Negro areas by restrictions on free movement placed upon the Negro population. Thus, in certain areas the population is increasing where it normally would be expected to decrease if there were no such barriers. Likewise, the percentage of families owning homes is not entirely satisfactory as an economic index in large urban centers, where many of the well-to-do rent expensive apartments. It is, however, an indication of the relative stability of population in an area.

Correlation of series of rates based on geographical areas is further complicated by the fact that magnitude of the coefficient is influenced by the size of the area selected. This tendency has been noted by several writers, but no satisfactory solution of the problem has been offered. If it be borne in mind that a correlation of area data is an index of geographical association for a particular type of spatial division only, rather than a fixed measure of functional relationship, it will be apparent that a change in area size changes the meaning of the correlation. Thus, an r of .90 or above for two series of rates calculated by square-mile areas indicates a high degree of association between the magnitudes of the two rates in most of the square miles but does not tell us the exact degree of covariance for smaller or larger areas.

With these limitations clearly in mind, a number of correlation coefficients and tables of covariance are presented. The statistical data characterizing and differentiating local urban areas may be grouped under three headings: (1) physical status, (2) economic status, and (3) population composition. These will be considered, in turn, in relation to rates of delinquents.

Indexes of Physical Status in Relation to Rates of Delinquents

The location of major industrial and commercial developments, the distribution of buildings condemned for demolition or repair, and the percentage increase or decrease in population by square-mile areas were presented [elsewhere] as indications of the physical differentiation of areas within the city. Quantitative measures of the first two are not available, but inspection of the distribution maps shows clearly that the highest rates of delinquents are most frequently found in, or adjacent to, areas of heavy industry and commerce. These same neighborhoods have the largest number of condemned buildings. The only notable exception to this generalization, for Chicago, appears in some of the areas south of the central business district.

There is, of course, little reason to postulate a direct relationship between living in proximity to industrial developments and becoming delinquent. While railroads and industrial properties may offer a field for delinquent behavior, they can hardly be regarded as a cause of such activities. Industrial invasion and physical deterioration do, however, make an area less desirable for residential purposes. As a consequence, in time there is found a movement from this area of those people able to afford more attractive surroundings. Further, the decrease in the number of buildings available for residential purposes leads to a decrease in the population of the area.

Population Increase or Decrease. Increase or decrease of population and rates of delinquents, by square-mile areas, do not exhibit a linear relationship. A relatively slight difference in rate of decrease of population, or of rate of increase for areas where the increase is slight, is generally associated with a considerable change in rates of delinquents; while for large differences in rates of increase of population, where increase is great, there is little or no consistent difference in rates of delinquents. Thus, areas increasing more than 70 per cent show no corresponding drop in rates of delinquents, although the relationship is clear up to this point. . . .

[T]here is a similarity between the pattern of distribution of delinquency and that of population growth or decline. The data do not establish a causal relationship between the two variables, however. The fact that the population of an area is decreasing does not impel a boy to become delinquent. It may be said, however, that decreasing population is usually related to industrial invasion of an area and contributes to the development of a general situation conducive to delinquency.

Population Composition in Relation to Rates of Delinquency

In Chicago, as in other northern industrial cities, as has been said, it is the most recent arrivals—persons of foreign birth and those who have migrated from other sections of this country—who find it necessary to make their homes in neighborhoods of low economic level. Thus the newer European immigrants are found concentrated in certain areas, while Negroes from the rural South and Mexicans occupy others of comparable status. Neither of these population categories, considered separately, however, is suitable for correlation with rates of delinquents, since some areas of high rates have a predominantly immigrant population and others are entirely or largely Negro. Both categories, however, refer to groups of low economic status making their adjustment to a complex urban environment. Foreign-born and Negro heads of families will therefore be considered together in order to study this segregation of the newer arrivals, on a city-wide scale.

Percentage of Foreign-Born and Negro Heads of Families.[1] When the rates of delinquents in the 1927–33 series are correlated with the percentage of foreign-born and Negro heads of families as of 1930, by 140 square-mile areas, the coefficient is found to be .60 ± .03. Similarly, when the 1917–23 delinquency data are correlated with percentages of foreign-born and Negro heads of families for 1920, by the 113 areas into which the city was divided for that series, the coefficient is .58 ± .04. When rates of delinquents are calculated for the classes of areas . . . wide variations are found between the rates in the classes where the percentage of foreign-born and Negro heads of families is high and in those where it is low. . . . Since the number of foreign-born heads of families in the population decreased and the number of Negroes increased between 1920 and 1930, the total proportions of foreign-born and Negro heads of families in each class do not correspond. The variation with rates of delinquents, however, remains unchanged.

While it is apparent from these data that the foreign born and the Negroes are concentrated in the areas of high rates of delinquents, the meaning of this association is not easily determined. One might be led to assume that the relatively large number of boys brought into court is due to the presence of certain racial or national groups, were it not for the fact that the population composition of many of these neighborhoods has changed completely, without appreciable change in their rank as to rates of delinquents. Clearly, one must beware of attaching causal significance to race or nativity. For, in the present social and economic system, it is the Negroes and the foreign born, or at least the newest immigrants, who have least access to the necessities of life and who are therefore least prepared for the competitive struggle. It is they who are forced to live in the worst slum areas and who are least able to organize against the effects of such living.

In Chicago three kinds of data are available for the study of nativity, nationality, and race in relation to rates of delinquents. These data concern (1) the succession of nationality groups in the high-rate areas over a period of years; (2) changes in the national and racial backgrounds of children appearing in the Juvenile Court; and (3) rates of delinquents for particular racial, nativity, or nationality groups in different types of areas at any given moment. In evaluating the significance of community characteristics found to be associated with high rates of delinquents, the relative weight of race, nativity, and nationality must be understood. . . .

It appears to be established, then, that each racial, nativity, and nationality group in Chicago displays widely varying rates of delinquents; that rates for immigrant groups in particular show a wide historical fluctuation; that diverse racial, nativity, and national groups possess relatively similar rates of delinquents in similar social areas; and that each of these groups displays the effect of disproportionate concentration in its respective areas at a given time. In the face of these facts it is difficult to sustain the contention that, by themselves, the factors of race, nativity, and nationality are vitally related to the problem of juvenile delinquency. It seems necessary to conclude, rather, that the significantly higher rates of delinquents found among the children of Negroes, the foreign born, and more recent immigrants are closely related to existing differences in their respective patterns of geographical distribution within the city. If these groups were found in the same proportion in all local areas, existing differences in the relative number of boys brought into court from the various groups might be expected to be greatly reduced or to disappear entirely.

It may be that the correlation between rates of delinquents and foreign-born and Negro heads of families is incidental to relationships between rates of delinquents and apparently more basic social and economic characteristics of local communities. Evidence that this is the case is seen in two partial correlation coefficients computed. Selecting the relief rate as a fair measure of economic level, the problem is to determine the relative weight of this and other factors. The partial correlation coefficient between rate of delinquents and percentage of families on relief, holding constant the percentage of foreign-born and Negro heads of families, in the 140 areas, is .76 ± .02. However, the coefficient for rates of delinquents and percentage of foreign-born and Negro heads of families, when percentage of families on relief is held constant, is only .26 ± .05. It is clear from these coefficients, therefore, that the percentage of families on relief is related to rates of delinquents in a more significant way than is the percentage of foreign-born and Negro heads of families.

It should be emphasized that the high degree of association between rates of delinquents and other community characteristics . . . does not mean that these characteristics must be regarded as causes of delinquency, or vice versa. Within certain types of areas differentiated in city growth, these phenomena appear together with such regularity that their rates are highly correlated. Yet the nature of the relationship between types of conduct and given physical, economic, or demographic characteristics is not revealed by the magnitude either of zero-order or partial correlation coefficients, or of other measures of association.

A high degree of association may lead to the uncritical assumption that certain factors are causally related, whereas further analysis shows the existing association to be entirely adventitious. This is apparently the case with the data on nativity, nationality, and race. . . . That, on the whole, the proportion of foreign-born and Negro population is higher in areas with high rates of delinquents there can be little doubt; but the facts furnish ample basis for the further conclusion that the boys brought into court are not delinquent *because* their parents are foreign born or Negro but rather because of other aspects of the total situation in which they live. In the same way, the relationship between rates of delinquents and each associated variable should be explored, either by further analysis, by experimentation, or by the study of negative cases.

Summary

It has been shown that, when rates of delinquents are calculated for classes of areas grouped according to rate of any one of a number of community characteristics studied, a distinct pattern appears—the two sets of rates in each case varying together. When values of these other community characteristics, in turn, are calculated for classes of areas grouped by rate of delinquents, the same consistent trends appear. . . . The data . . . indicate a high degree of association between rates of delinquents and other community characteristics when correlations are computed on the basis of values in square-mile areas or similar subdivisions, and a still closer general association by large zones or classes of areas. . . .

Note

1. The categories "foreign born" and "Negro" are not compatible, since the former group is made up primarily of adults, while the latter includes all members of the race. The classification "heads of families" has been used; therefore, foreign-born and Negro family heads are entirely comparable groupings. The census classification "other races" has been included—a relatively small group, comprising Mexicans, Japanese, Chinese, Filipinos, etc.

/// REVIEW QUESTIONS

1. What do Shaw and McKay have to say about delinquency rates in neighborhoods located in or near heavy industrial areas? What types of physical indicators are present in such areas?
2. What do Shaw and McKay conclude regarding the crime rates of neighborhoods containing a population composition high in minorities or recent immigrants?
3. What do Shaw and McKay claim would happen to delinquency or crime rates if racial or ethnic groups, as well as recent immigrants, were equally distributed across all neighborhoods of a city (such as Chicago)?

READING /// 16

Using georeferenced homicide data and census data from Recife, Brazil, for the years 2009–2013, Débora V. S. Pereira, Caroline M. M. Mota, and Martin A. Andresen test social disorganization theory in that city, which has been one of the most violent regions in Brazil in the past couple of decades, despite a recent relative decrease in homicide. The researchers examine the influence of the key variables in the traditional social disorganization model, such as income, rented houses, inequality, and population density, but also examine the effects of other social ills on homicide.

While reading this article, one should consider the following topics:

- The authors' claim, with supporting data, regarding the contexts specific to Brazil that are quite different from North America, which makes their study of social disorganization unique and important in advancing knowledge about this theoretical framework
- The types of social ills that the researchers included in their analysis that are not commonly found in censuses in North American contexts, such as households with electricity, water supply, garbage collection, open sewage, etc.

- Findings of the current study regarding the impact of the various predicting variables, with an emphasis on the ones that were found to be significant determinants of homicide
- How consistent the findings of the current study are with those of the original proponents of social disorganization, namely Shaw and McKay

Social Disorganization and Homicide in Recife, Brazil

Débora V. S. Pereira, Caroline M. M. Mota, and Martin A. Andresen

Introduction

In Brazil, since 2000, approximately 50,000 people are murdered every year. In a span of 30 years (1980–2010), more than 1 million homicides were registered in Brazil (Waiselfisz, 2012). That is an incredible magnitude of homicides for a country that does not currently have conflicts based on religion, ethnicity, race, or territory. The quantity of homicides in Brazil is so high that this country alone was responsible for 10% of the homicides in the entire world in 2012, while having less than 3% of the world's population (World Health Organization, 2014).

In 2012, the homicide rate in Brazil was 29 homicides per 100,000 inhabitants (Waiselfisz, 2014). However, this rate varies significantly across the country: While a few states are experiencing a homicide drop, other states are experiencing an increase. Rio Grande do Norte and Bahia, for example, more than doubled their homicide rates in the past decade, while São Paulo, Rio de Janeiro, and Pernambuco had significant decreases (Waiselfisz, 2014). Regardless of these decreases in some states, all the Brazilian states exceed the threshold for epidemic established by the World Health Organization of 10 homicides per 100,000 inhabitants (United Nations Development Programme, 2013).

In 2012, research published by the Institute for Applied Economic Research (IAER)—a Brazilian federal public foundation—showed that feelings of personal security in Brazil are low: 62.4% of Brazilians declared to have an intense fear of being murdered, and 23.2% claimed to have some level of fear (IAER, 2012). In the northeast region, however, the situation is the worst in Brazil: 72.9% of the population has an intense fear of being murdered and 19.9% has some level of fear (IAER, 2012). This same research indicates the causes of criminality in Brazil, according to public opinion, to be social and economic inequality (23.8%) and a lack of investment in education (20.5%); these are the greatest problems facing this country (IAER, 2012). As shown in the literature review below, this is generally supported by the empirical research.

Historically, Brazil has been marked by violence, emphasizing the colonization process, the slave market, and the military dictatorship (Oliveira Júnior, 2013). Currently, however, violence is primarily understood through drug trafficking and disputes between criminal factions. Moreover, this unfavorable context is aggravated by unemployment, inequality, and low education. In the context of the state of Pernambuco, de Lima et al. (2002) attributed violence to high illiteracy rates, unemployment,

SOURCE: Débora V. S. Pereira, Caroline M. M. Mota, and Martin A. Andresen, "Social Disorganization and Homicide in Recife, Brazil," *International Journal of Offender Therapy and Comparative Criminology* 21, no. 1 (2016): 21–38.

high-income concentration, and social inequality. This situation developed an atmosphere that was conducive to violence and the consequences continue today. Although Pernambuco experienced an increase in its socioeconomic indicators in the recent years, the homicide rate is still significantly higher than the national average.

Specifically with regard to the capital of Pernambuco, the Metropolitan Region of Recife (MRR), de Lima, Ximenes, de Souza, Luna, and de Albuquerque (2005) highlighted the context of drugs, interpersonal conflict, and the formation of gangs. Minayo and Constantino (2012) conducted qualitative research in one of the municipalities of MRR and the respondents believe violence is related to drug trafficking, with an emphasis on grooming youth, and the conflicts between traffickers and users. In this context, the present article has the purpose of investigating the role of demographic, social, and economic variables that may be associated with homicides. We build on previous research through an updated data set on homicide in Recife as well as greatly expanding the set of potential explanatory variables through the Brazilian census: 28 variables, in total. The analysis was conducted using data from the MRR (Pernambuco, Brazil) that has had national attention because of the notable reduction of homicides between 2006 and 2013, 46%.

Social Disorganization Theory: Theory and Evidence

One of the most common theoretical frameworks to be used to understand the spatial distribution of crime, including homicide, is social disorganization theory. As discussed below, social disorganization theory is particularly instructive for Recife, Brazil, because of the socioeconomic conditions of this city and the developing world, more generally. Though spatial, or ecological, studies of crime date back to the early 1800s in France (Quetelet, 1842), social disorganization theory and its focus on smaller units of analysis, such as neighborhoods, has its roots in the Chicago School of sociology from the early 20th century (Shaw & McKay, 1931, 1942; Shaw, Zorbaugh, McKay, & Cottrell, 1929). In this framework, the level of social organization in an area was directly linked to the level of criminal activity: Less social organization leads to more crime. This is simply because without social organization, a neighborhood cannot come together or organize to prevent criminal activity. The two primary drivers of a lack of social organization during this time were ethnic heterogeneity and population turnover. With the former, the neighborhood residents literally could not speak to one another to discuss common issues and with the latter, very few residents would be willing to invest the time to discuss common issues because they planned to leave the neighborhood as soon as possible. In both cases, social disorganization emerges, as does the corresponding crime. In their own research, Shaw and McKay (1942) found strong support for their theoretical framework.

There have been two tests of social disorganization theory by contemporary researchers that warrant discussion. The first test of social disorganization theory that considered community organization used the British Crime Survey. This research was undertaken by Sampson and Groves (1989) who extended the concepts of Shaw and McKay (1942) to include sparse local friendship networks, unsupervised teenage peer groups, and low organizational (neighborhood) participation. In their causal model, Sampson and Groves found strong support for social disorganization theory. This support for social disorganization theory was critical because through the British Crime Survey these researchers were able to directly measure aspects of social disorganization theory. And, equally important, they were able to show that social disorganization theory was still relevant 60 years later. The second test of social disorganization theory revisited the work of Sampson and Groves, considering subsequent iterations of the British Crime Survey (Lowenkamp, Cullen, & Pratt, 2003). This subsequent research confirmed the results of Sampson and Groves, further showing the relevance of social disorganization theory in a more recent context.

The difficulty with social disorganization theory, however, is operationalizing the primary factors that have a causal link to criminal activity: sparse local friendship networks, unsupervised teenage peer groups, and low organizational (neighborhood) participation. Such information is available through some of the more comprehensive crime victimization surveys but is far from universal. This is why there are so few direct tests of social disorganization in the literature. However, as outlined in the causal model of Sampson and Groves (1989), these three primary factors are influenced by low economic status, ethnic heterogeneity, residential mobility, family disruption, and urbanization. These latter factors affect the primary factors that then affect criminal activity.

In the spatial criminology literature, in particular, those studies that use census-based variables, research that considers social disorganization theory uses these latter factors to represent the primary factors of social disorganization theory: Ethnic heterogeneity represents the ability of residents to form friendship networks because of language and cultural barriers, and low economic status represents the willingness to engage in organizational participation, for example. The research in this area has used census-based variables such as the percentage of recent immigrants, direct measures of ethnic heterogeneity, the unemployment rate, the percentage of people with a university degree, average family income and the standard deviation of average family income, the percentage of single-parent families, and the percentage of rental residences in the spatial unit (see Andresen, 2006, 2011; Cahill & Mulligan, 2003; Linsky & Straus, 1986; Stark, 1996; Tseloni, Osborn, Trickett, & Pease, 2002). It is this literature that informs variable choices for studies in Brazil that consider social disorganization theory, including variables that represent these factors specifically in a Brazilian context.

Recent Research on Homicide in Brazil: Social Disorganization and Spatial Analyses

Gawryszewski and Costa (2005) analyzed homicide rates for the year 2000 across the 96 administrative units in São Paulo City. These authors considered the infant mortality rate, average income, the proportion of adolescent mothers, population density, and the percentage of children not attending school. Using a bivariate correlation analysis, Gawryszewski et al. found that the homicide rate was positively related to the infant mortality rate, the percentage of adolescent mothers, and the percentage of children not attending school, whereas the homicide rate was negatively associated with average income—population density had a positive but statistically insignificant relationship with the homicide rate. However, in a regression context, only the percentage of children not attending school and monthly average income remained statistically significant.

In a spatial analysis of homicide in the districts of the State of Pernambuco, de Lima et al. (2005) analyzed homicide rates considering an index of living conditions, a human development index, per capita family income, the Theil index, the Gini index, the average income of the head of the family, a poverty index, a rate of illiteracy, and population density. Homicide rates were statistically related to all of these independent variables in a correlation analysis, only with the illiteracy rate and poverty index being retained in the final regression models as statistically significant. In a linear regression model, these two variables were able to account for almost 25% of the variation in the homicide rate.

Sachsida, Mendonça, Loureiro, and Gutierrez (2007) analyzed homicide rates across Brazilian states, 1981–1995, considering average family income, law enforcement spending, urbanization, the Gini index, the unemployment rate, schooling, and poverty. These authors undertook a variety of regression models (ordinary least squares, random effects, and fixed effects) and found that income inequality, urbanization, and unemployment were all statistically significant and positively related to state-level homicide rates.

Ceccato, Haining, and Kahn (2007) analyzed the geography of homicide in São Paulo, Brazil, using police districts, standardized homicide ratios, low income, the presence of slum areas, alcohol problems, urban areas, the presence of transportation nodes, the presence of bars and restaurants, and betting houses. Ceccato and colleagues found that homicide was strongly related to low income, the presence of transportation nodes, the availability of weapons, and drug-related activity.

In addition to all these social disorganization theory explanations for homicide in Brazil, Araújo et al. (2010) found that ethnicity played a statistically significant role in the prediction of homicide in Salvador, Brazil. Specifically, Araújo et al. found a positive relationship between the presence of Black males aged 15 to 49 and homicide rates. They explain that this result emerges from a long history and process of social inequality in Brazil. As noted by Kilsztajn, Carmo, Sugahara, and Lopes (2003), there is an overrepresentation of this population who are poor and male; as such, any inference with regard to such a variable must be made with caution.

Most recently, but in an analysis that pools Brazil with other countries that have high homicide rates,

Loureiro and Silva (2012) investigated homicide considering life expectancy, the Gini index (a measure of income inequality), economic growth, the human development index, and the rate of urbanization. Similar to the research that focuses on Brazil, Loureiro and Silva found that income inequality, low human development, and low life expectancy were all associated with higher levels of homicide.

Overall, it should be clear that there is a link between homicide and social disorganization theory (Shaw & McKay, 1942) in the context of Brazilian homicide; this is also a common theme in the previous research in Brazil on homicide (Câmara, Monteiro, Ramos, Sposati, & Koga, 2001; Cardia, Adorno, & Poleto, 2003; Carneiro, 1998). However, all of these studies work with a relatively small set of explanatory variables to explain homicide. In our analysis below, we build on this research associating social disorganization with homicide in Brazil through the use of a spatial regression technique that controls for heteroskedasticity in addition to spatial autocorrelation and incorporates 28 explanatory variables. As shown below, many of these variables are not retained in our final model because of statistical insignificance, but we are able to contribute to this literature through a more nuanced approach to incorporating social disorganization into a Brazilian context.

Data and Method

Recife, Brazil

Recife is located in the state of Pernambuco and is one of the most prominent cities and state capitals in Brazil. In 2010, Recife had 1,537,704 inhabitants and an estimated population of 1,608,488 for 2014 (Brazilian Institute of Geography and Statistics [BIGS], 2013, 2014, 2015). The MRR had an estimated population of almost 4 million people in 2014 and it represents almost 42% of Pernambuco's population. Displaying its geographical location in Brazil in Figure 1, Recife is shown in relation to the two most recognized Brazilian cities, Rio de Janeiro and São Paulo; Recife is situated in the northeast of Brazil. In 2011, the Gross Domestic Product (GDP) of Recife was R$33.15 billion (approximately US$12.5 billion), ranking

Figure 1 • Brazil's map and Recife's location

Recife as the 10th largest economy among the 26 capitals of Brazil and the 15th largest economy among the 5,565 Brazilian municipalities. And in recent years, the state of Pernambuco has had the attention of the entire country because of its homicide drop.

According to Waiselfisz (2014), Pernambuco was the most dangerous Brazilian state in 1998, with a homicide rate of 58.9 homicides per 100,000 inhabitants. This state, however, fell to the 10th position in 2012, with a rate of 31.7. The homicide trends for Brazil, Pernambuco, and Metro Recife between 2000 and 2012 can be seen in Figure 2. As can be seen in Figure 2, the homicide rate in Brazil was effectively constant from 2000 to 2012. Since 2000, the rate ranged between 25 and 30 homicides per 100,000 inhabitants, with a peak of 29 in 2012. However, in the case of Pernambuco and Recife, we can observe a decrease of homicides starting in 2007. Between 2007 and 2012, Pernambuco had a decrease of 30.13% in homicides, while in Recife, the drop was 36.7%. However, even considering the decline, the homicide rates in Recife and Pernambuco are still notably higher than the national average.

When compared with the other Brazilian states in the northeast, Pernambuco is unique. In the northeast, Pernambuco is the only state that had a decrease in homicides between 2002 and 2012. Five of the nine states in the northeast are among those that had the greatest increases of homicide in Brazil between 2002 and 2012: Rio Grande do Norte (increase of 229.1% in its homicide rate), Bahia (221.6%), Maranhão (162.4%), Ceará (136.7%), and

Figure 2 • Homicide rate, Recife, Pernambuco, Brazil, 2000–2012

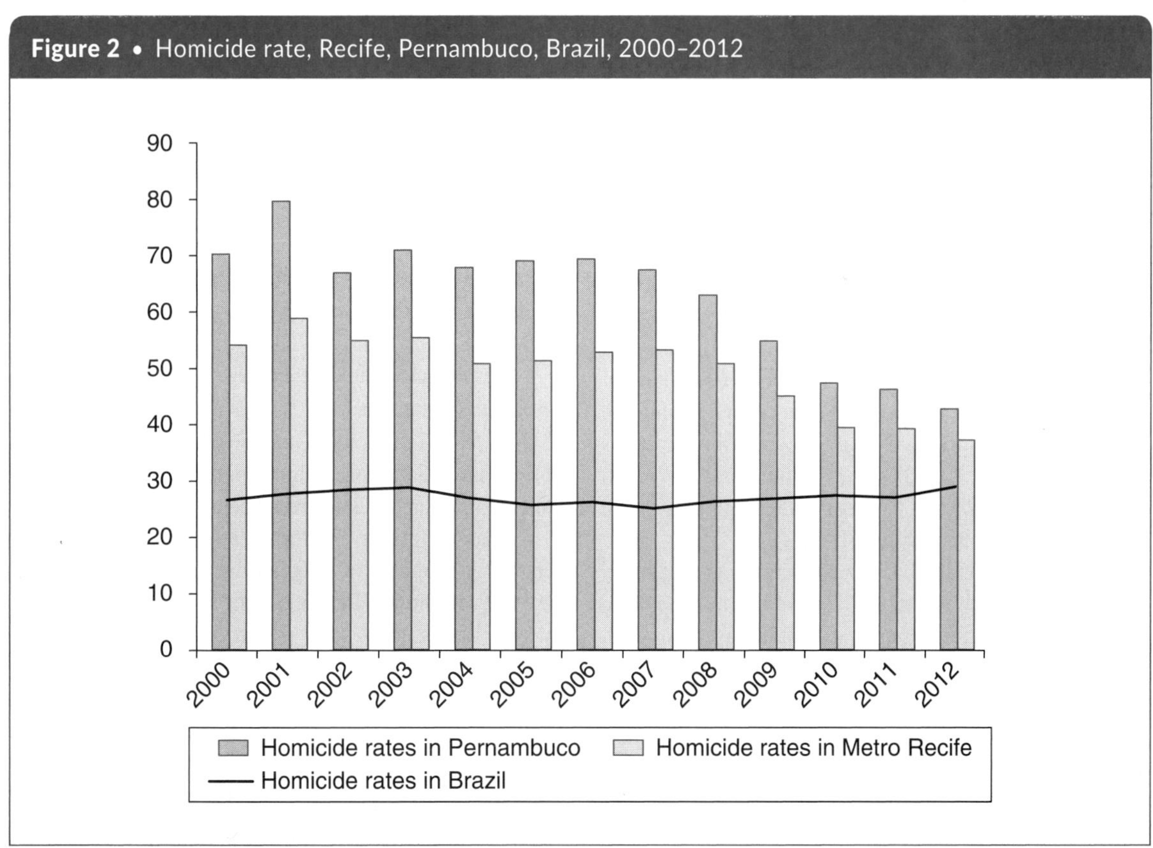

SOURCE. The data for Brazil and Pernambuco between 2000 and 2001 were obtained from Waiselfisz (2012), and the data for 2002–2012 were obtained from Waiselfisz (2014). The data for Metro Recife between 2000 and 2010 were obtained from the Ministry of Health (2015), and for 2011–2012 were obtained from the Secretariat of Social Defense (SSD) (2014).

Paraíba (130.2%; Waiselfisz, 2014). The homicide drop in Pernambuco has been attributed to a project put forth by the state government that began in 2007, the Pact for Life—see Ratton et al. (2014).

Crime Data

In this article, we analyzed homicides that occurred in the MRR from 2009 to 2013. The data were provided by the Secretariat of Social Defense (SSD), an official department that consolidates homicide data from civil police, military police, Institute of Forensic Medicine, and Institute of Criminalistics. Much of the research considering homicides uses data from the Information System of Morbidity (ISM), provided by Ministry of Health. However, we opted for SSD's data because, according to Sauret (2012), SSD is a very reliable database that has been consistently improving since its inception in 2007.

Between 2009 and 2013, the MRR (Recife and its 13 municipalities) had 2,047; 1,733; 1,713; 1,595; and 1,358 homicides, respectively (8,446 events in total). Our analysis began in 2009 because this is the first available complete year for spatial analyses—The collection of geographical coordinates started in the middle of 2008. The last year considered for analysis is 2013 because the data were solicited in 2014. Though our homicide data predate the census year by 1 year (census data are discussed below) and postdate the census year by 3 years, we have chosen to use all available data because we are not forecasting homicide rates, but investigating theoretical relationships. As such, we consider all 5 years for our analysis in an effort to control for any particular aberrant year in the spatial pattern of homicide.

The data provided by SSD contain the geographical coordinates of each occurrence, so we did not require a geocoding process for this analysis. In rare cases, however, it was not possible to obtain the geographical coordinates, for reasons unknown to the authors. There are 10 occurrences without geographic coordinates between 2009 and 2013, representing 0.1184% of the 8,446 homicides. With such a small percentage, there is no reason to be concerned about bias with the representation of spatial points obtained with SSD data—There is no pattern to these few missing points, and our "geocoding hit rate" is well above the 85% threshold set by Ratcliffe (2004).

Census Variables

The demographic, social, and economic variables used in our analysis were obtained from the demographic census of 2010. The BIGS publishes these data every 10 years. We used census tracts as spatial units of analysis, because they are the smallest territorial unit available in the demographic census with reliable data. There are 4,589 census tracts at MRR; however, only 4,494 of them were considered in this analysis—95 census tracts did not have data for all the variables. The reason for the lack of data is unknown in a few cases, but in other cases, it is because the census tract comprises only collective households (local areas containing administrative rules such as pensions, prisons, nursing homes, orphanages, student republics, etc.). Even with this situation, however, we are confident that our analysis and results were not distorted because only 2.07% of census tracts were excluded, and those spatial units of analysis are responsible for only 1.63% of homicides (138 occurrences).

Our selection of explanatory variables is dominantly based on social disorganization theory and based on the literature review above considered the theory in general as well as specifics in Brazil. We consider ethnic heterogeneity, social and economic deprivation, family disruption, population turnover, population characteristics, employment status, income levels, and dwelling values as factors related to social disorganization theory.

To measure ethnic heterogeneity, we used Blau's heterogeneity index (Blau, 1977). In our case, the demographic census takes into account six categories for race (White, Black, Asian, South Asian, Indigenous, and "Other"), with a maximum value for Blau's index being 0.833.

Also in relation to ethnic heterogeneity, we considered Black population. People from different nationalities are not common in Recife, but the racial heterogeneity is strong across the entire country. In this context, we included two variables for the Black population: the percentage of Black people and the percentage of Black males between 15 and 24 years old. In the work of Breetzke (2010), the percentage of Blacks also was utilized to represent ethnic heterogeneity. It is important to note that the presence of these subpopulations does not represent a particularly criminogenic group, but rather social and historical conditions that are not easily represented with other socioeconomic variables. In Recife, the following racial groups are identified in the census: Multiracial (49.1%), White (41.4%), Black (8.3%), Asian (1%), and Amerindian (0.2%) (BIGS, 2015).

We measure social and economic deprivation using variables representing unemployment, education, income, and inequality. Unemployment is not measured at census tract level. However, we included a proxy for unemployment that involves people without income: people without monthly income. Regarding education, two variables are considered: literate people older than 5 years old and literate people older than 15 years old. We used multiple variables when considering income: people with monthly income less than the minimum wage, people with monthly income greater than 10 times the minimum wage, and the natural logarithm of the value of monthly income of household heads. It is important to highlight that in 2010, the minimum wage in Brazil was R$510 per month, approximately US$290, considering the current exchange rate.

As mentioned above, research on public opinion and research in general has identified inequality as an important factor to understand the criminal activity. Though the Gini index is commonly used for a measure of inequality in an area, this indicator is not available at census tract level. In its place, we use the standard deviation of the monthly income of household heads and the Index of Concentration at the Extremes (ICE). The standard deviation of income shows the dispersion between people's income. ICE measures concentrations of wealth and poverty within a neighborhood or area, recognizing that it is the "*proportional* imbalance between affluence [and] poverty within a neighborhood that really matters" (Massey, 2001, p. 44, emphasis in original). The index can be calculated as the difference between the number of families or persons classified as wealthy and the number of families or persons classified as poor in a given neighborhood divided by the population of that neighborhood. ICE can range between −1 and 1: −1 means that all families/persons are poor, 1 means that all of them are wealthy, and 0 means that the number of poor and wealthy is balanced (Massey, 2001). We considered that poor people are those who live at the poverty line or lower; that is, living with less than half of the minimum wage per month or do not have any income. With respect to wealthy people, we considered those who receive at least 10 times minimum wage per month.

With the intent to represent social and economic deprivation, a few variables were included to capture the vulnerability of households or neighborhoods that are not available in censuses within Western contexts. We chose seven variables to consider this vulnerability, a common problem in Brazil and Recife: households with electricity, households with garbage collection, households with water supply, households with an exclusive bathroom, households without open sewage, households with paving, households with public illumination, and the percentage of improvised households. Improvised households are those that are inappropriate for housing, such as slums or homes inside commercial establishments. We decided to not consider an index that could aggregate all these variables because individual variables may affect homicide in a different manner. Finally, we considered family disruption. We considered the percentage of homes headed by women as proxy for single-parent families. Breetzke (2010) used the same variable to represent family disruption in a South African context. In addition, two variables were included to capture the stability (or lack thereof) in the neighborhood: rented households and owned or in acquisition households.

We also considered variables representing population characteristics, employment status, income levels, and dwelling values. In relation to population characteristics, we included the number of residents, population density, and street network density; the population count was included because Boivin (2013) has identified this as a better method than calculating crime rates at the neighborhood level. To obtain population density, we calculated the area within ArcGIS software and then divided the population by the area; we used a similar method to calculate the total length of streets in a census tract, dividing by its total area. The percentage of the population between the ages of 15 and 24 years old and the percentage of males between the ages of 15 and 24 years old was included to control for this most criminogenic subpopulation (Boyd, 2000; Hirschi & Gottfredson, 1983). It is important to mention that homicide was the main cause of death for youths in MRR in 2010 (51.82% for people between 15 and 19 years old, and 44.56% for 20 and 29 years old; Ministry of Health, 2015).

We included the percentage of married people, defined as those people living with spouses or partners (different or the same sex). We considered this variable because married people tend to spend more of their free time at home, resulting in lower levels of victimization (Kennedy & Forde, 1990). Consequently, they are less likely to spend time outside in socially disorganized areas, placing them at risk of criminal victimization, including homicide because of the possibility of being involved in fights or going to bars. Finally, it is important to include a dummy variable to identify whether the census tract is located in a rural or urban space.

Results and Discussion

Descriptive Results

The descriptive statistics for the dependent and independent variables are shown in Table 1. The dependent variable is the sum of homicides for 2009 to 2013 to prevent the analysis of an aberrant year of data. As shown in Table 1, homicides range from 0 to 25 with a mean of 2.14 homicides per census tract. Generally speaking, the table shows how the census tracts of Metro Recife vary significantly in the context of homicide, as well as variables representing social, economic, and demographic factors. The range of all variables indicates that there is little evidence for homogeneity within the city, with only a few exceptions: households with electricity, households with an exclusive bathroom, and urban space. These results show the importance of using the smallest spatial unit as possible, with the intent of capturing the particularities of each area.

Though the ranges of these variables are not often of principal interest in the spatial criminology research, the context of a Brazilian city is particularly interesting.

Table 1 • Descriptive Statistics, Recife, 2010

	Minimum	Maximum	*M*	*SD*
Homicide (count), 2009–2013	0	25	2.1	2.6
Number of residents	16	4,128	818.3	363.4
Population density	1.8	181,643	15,110	12,607
Street network density, km per km sq. area	0.00	1,453.75	2.23	25.47
Young population, %	0	40.5	17.5	2.9
Young male population, %	0	33.2	8.6	1.8
Black population, %	0	50.1	8.3	5.5
Young male Black population, %	0	6.7	0.77	0.67
Index of heterogeneity	0.04	0.73	0.53	0.08
Married population, %	4.8	29.4	18.4	2.3
Households headed by women, %	0	93.1	44.9	11.7
Literate people (5 years old and above), %	40.1	99.4	83.8	8.3
Literate people (15 years old and above), %	23.5	98.6	70.6	9.9
Average income, ln	4.6	9.8	6.7	0.75
Standard deviation, average income, ln	10.2	21.9	13.6	1.7

	Minimum	Maximum	*M*	*SD*
Income lesser than 1 minimum wage, %	0	51.9	26.3	9.4
Income greater than 10 minimum wage, %	0	34.9	1.75	4.7
No income population, %	10.8	84.2	34.9	7.1
Index of Concentration at the Extremes (ICE)	−0.83	0.14	−0.39	0.12
Improvised households, %	0	52.2	0.12	1.06
Households with electricity, %	30.6	100	99.8	1.6
Households with garbage collection, %	0	100	92.9	18.1
Households with water supply, %	0	100	83.8	25.1
Households with exclusive bathroom, %	21.7	100	98.9	4.4
Households without open sewage, %	0	100	57.3	42.2
Households with paving, %	0	100	49.4	40.9
Households with public illumination, %	0	100	70.1	42.7
Rented households, %	0	95.8	19.9	9.7
Own households or in acquisition, %	0	100	74.3	12.5
Urban space (dummy variable)	0	1	0.97	0.18

Regarding total population, we can see that the range is large and, consequently, so is the standard deviation. This can be explained by the agglomeration of residential buildings in Metro Recife, mainly in the richest neighborhoods. The differences of Recife's population can be perceived by the large ranges for young population, young male population, Black population, young male Black population, and married population. For example, there are census tracts without Black people while there are areas where they are more than half of the population, similarly for young population, but with a maximum of 40%.

A large range can be observed in the percentage of households headed by women: This variable ranges from 0 to 93% and a mean of 45%. Regarding education, we can see that in some census tracts almost all the population is educated and the averages are high (almost 84% for 5 years old and above, and approximately 70.5% for 15 years old and above). However, we need to interpret these numbers with caution: For the demographic census, a literate person is able to read and write a simple note. Therefore, being literate does not indicate that the person has many years of education. Perhaps a better variable would be the average of years of schooling, but this is not available in the census. Regarding the schooling time, Pereira and Mota (2014) asserted that few Human Development Units in Recife have satisfactory mean years of schooling: The majority of the Units do not achieve the period indicated as mandated by Brazilian law.

Considering income, there is heterogeneity across census tracts. If we compare the income across the census tracts (average income) and within census tracts (standard deviation of average income), there are disparities/inequalities. Moreover, there are some areas where 50% of the people are living with less than the minimum wage (US$145) per month, while in other census tracts, nobody lives in this situation. We also need to highlight that there are areas where almost 85% of the population do not receive any income. In addition, the inequality indicator has a maximum value of 0.99, confirming that there are extremely unequal areas in Recife. Pereira and Mota (2014) indicated that many areas in Recife have monthly *per capita* income lower than poverty line. According this work, only 16.13% of the Human Development Units in Recife could be classified as high or very high human development areas. Finally, we consider the variables capturing the vulnerability of households and their surroundings. These variables are of particular interest because they simply are not measured in censuses in Western nations that the authors are aware of. Almost all the variables (aside from improvised households, electricity, and exclusive bathroom) have a range between 0% and 100%, indicating diversity within Metro Recife: There are households and surroundings with basic infrastructure, but there are entire neighborhoods (census tracts) that do not have this kind of service. However, we can affirm that almost all the households have electricity and an exclusive bathroom, as noted above. The variables that measure the quantity of rented and owned households also present significant variation.

We expected a very high correlation between some explanatory variables, but we decided to include all of them in the initial model to test which ones would better explain homicides in Recife. We found very high correlations among some variables (>0.8) but as stated above, we consider both individual and joint significance testing to avoid removing relevant variables and avoiding omitted variable bias.

Inferential Results

In the final model, the remaining statistically significant variables are generally supportive of social disorganization theory. It should come as no surprise that many of the original 28 explanatory variables were statistically insignificant, but our final model retains 10 explanatory variables.

Many of the explanatory variables that remain in the final model not only relate to social disorganization theory but do so, most often, in the expected ways. The estimated signs of income, income inequality, literate people, public illumination, households with an exclusive bathroom, and rented households all have their expected relationships with homicide. Only households with electricity are contrary to expectations with a statistically significant and positive estimated parameter. Though inference at the level of the individual cannot be made with census data, by definition, it may be the case that census tracts with households that have electricity are more attractive areas for criminal activity that leads to homicide.

With respect to income, this variable has an inverse relationship with homicides. With income being measured as a natural logarithm, this parameter is interpreted that a 1% increase in income leads to an expected decrease of 0.695 homicides. With the average number of homicides over the period of 4 years being just over 2, this is a significant impact, indicating the importance of income, likely low income. However, it is important to notice that there is not a direct relationship between poverty and criminality. As outlined by Shaw and McKay (1942), those places with the greatest level of delinquency are those in the zone in transition that are, by definition, low income. Why? These are the places with the lowest number of legitimate opportunities potentially leading to violent interactions that can lead to a death, armed robbery, for example. In addition, as highlighted by Sant'Anna, Aerts, and Lopes (2005), crime needs to be analyzed beyond poverty because there is an incorrect conception that poor people are responsible for violence. There is a complex structural and historical context related to this issue.

As discussed above, research on homicide in a Brazilian context has shown a relationship between income and homicide, but only a few have found a statistically significant relationship. For example, the research of Gawryszewski and Costa (2005) and Menezes, Silveira-Neto, Monteiro, and Ratton (2013) have found a negative relationship between income and homicide, but the work of Santos (2009) indicates the opposite. In our analysis, and consistent with the result for income, income inequality has its expected positive relationship with homicide: A 1% increase in the standard deviation of average income (inequality) leads to an increase of 0.132 homicides. Though this is not as strong as a relationship found with income, it is consistent with the previous research on homicide in Brazil. However, there are other studies that have used a more direct measure, the Gini index (Araújo et al., 2010; Loureiro & Silva, 2012; Menezes et al., 2013; Sachsida et al., 2007).

Literacy is found to have its expected inverse relationship with homicide. This is consistent with the research of Santos (2009), but not Araújo et al. (2010) and de Lima et al. (2005) who found a positive relationship. It is expected that positive relationships between homicide and literacy are the result of omitted variable bias and/or rather aggregate spatial units of analysis. Literacy is expected to lead to a decrease in homicide, and other criminal activity, because a more literate population, on average, will be able to secure better employment and greater income. Moreover, we can assume that school keeps the youths busy, lowering the probability of their involvement in criminal activity. Consistent with this assumption, the work of Sant'Anna et al. (2005) reveals that 79% of the murdered youths in Porto Alegre (Brazil) were not attending school when they were killed.

Public illumination and households with an exclusive bathroom were found to have a negative relationship with homicide. The existence of public illumination and households with an exclusive bathroom can represent the presence of other infrastructure elements, such as paving, sewage, or garbage collection. We can consider these variables as a measure for social and economic deprivation, as well as the presence of public power. Moreover, we need to take into account that public illumination can be a demotivating factor to commit murders in such locales. Potential offenders may prefer to commit their crimes in dark public areas to avoid the recognition and detection—see Farrington and Welsh (2002) for a systematic review of the effects of street lighting on crime.

The percentage of rented houses has a positive relationship, as expected. This result is in accordance with social disorganization theory because the greater the quantity of rented houses, the greater is the turnover of the population. In areas with a high turnover, normally there is little social and cultural cohesion that would bring a protective network to the neighborhood because the population is not willing to make the effort to establish local connections.

Population density and street network density both have a negative impact on homicide. There are two possible explanations for these results. First, considering the context of Recife, we can confirm that population density is related to economic patterns. In Recife, some of the wealthier neighborhoods contain large residential buildings, particularly those close to the beach, that increase the density in these areas. These wealthier neighborhoods have fewer homicides. As a second explanation, we can consider the theory of Jane Jacobs (1961): eyes on the street. Jacobs asserts that in areas with greater population density there is more traffic on the streets. Therefore, such areas are less likely to experience criminal activities because the aggressors believe that there is a greater probability of being seen or caught.

The percentage of households with electricity exhibits a positive relationship with homicide: A 1% increase in households with electricity leads to an increase of 0.03 homicides. Though this is not a particularly large magnitude effect, the presence of electricity likely represents census tracts that have more criminal opportunities that can lead to homicide, such as various forms of robbery.

Finally, we can see that the number of residents is positively and significantly related to the number of homicides, as expected: Where there are more people, there are more potential victims for homicides and crimes that may lead to a homicide, such as armed robbery. This shows the importance of controlling for population size.

Overall, we can observe that social disorganization theory can explain homicides in Recife. The spatial regression results indicate that factors related to social disorganization theory are important to understand homicides in Recife. In the context of social disorganization theory, it is important to note the work of Minayo and Constantino (2012) that compares two Brazilian municipalities, one with high and other with low homicide rates. According to these authors, some of the elements that distinguish both places are related to social disorganization theory. In the less-violent municipality, there are factors that contribute positively with the social system and socialization of residents. In this area, "the social relationships and the internal relations that promote social solidarity are internalized by the culture," with the presence of a "communication network to promote the social control and the cohesion among residents," in addition to "more consensus, consistency, and clarity about the common values." On the contrary, the violent municipality is marked by the "dispersion of efforts" and "historical and persistent social inequalities" that "reduced the collective effectiveness to face problems, creating a feeling of withdrawal and impotence in relation to the criminality and the homicide is seen as an inevitable fatality" (Minayo & Constantino, 2012). Minayo and Constantino also cite the example of three successful programs to combat criminality in Brazil. The common point among them is the promotion of social cohesion.

As discussed above, in the context of social disorganization theory more generally, Shaw and McKay (1942) found that the two primary aspects of a neighborhood that lead to social disorganization are population turnover and ethnic heterogeneity. With greater levels of population turnover (usually because of poor economic conditions), fewer people were able to establish a local network that allowed for setting common goals to reduce criminal activity. Ethnic heterogeneity also contributed to this inability of a neighborhood to come together, primarily because people literally could not understand one another: Ethnic heterogeneity at that time in Chicago meant that people came from different countries (most often European countries) and did not share a common language.

In their causal model of social disorganization theory, Sampson and Groves (1989) expanded on the work of Shaw and McKay in the following way: Sparse local friendship networks, unsupervised teenage peer groups, and low organizational (neighborhood) participation led to crime and delinquency. These three factors were influenced by low economic status, ethnic heterogeneity, residential mobility, family disruption, and urbanization. As discussed above, these five factors have been measured in a number of different ways, most often using census data in the geography of crime literature. Our results support the importance of low economic status and residential mobility. Of particular interest to a lack of support is ethnic heterogeneity. Recife has notable levels of ethnic heterogeneity, but none of the variables representing this construct were statistically significant in any of the results.

The most direct measure of population turnover, rented households, supports the hypothesis put forth in the social disorganization literature: more renters, more population, more homicides. Low economic status is also important but in particular ways. With regard to the more traditional measure of economic status, the results here for income and income inequality are supportive of the Western literature. But because of the magnitude of poverty not measured in Western countries, low economic status was measured in Recife considering a host of other neighborhood variables such as public illumination, electricity, and open sewers. Some of these variables proved to be statistically significant and in support of social disorganization theory. As such, not only do we find expected relationships, consistent with the western literature, but also find expected relationships that are consistent with the general concepts of social disorganization theory and relate specifically to Brazil.

Conclusion

In this article, we have investigated the relationship between homicide in the census tracts of Recife, Pernambuco and a set of variables relating to social disorganization theory. Though we did not always find statistically significant relationships with our full set of explanatory variables, the results of the final model were instructive. Of particular note is that variables relating to conditions specific to a Brazilian context are important. Though not all of the explanatory variables that may represent high levels of poverty were statistically significant (open sewers, garbage, improvised housing, and electricity), public illumination and exclusive bathrooms proved to be important in the expected direction. This supports the need to not simply incorporate explanatory variables that represent social disorganization theory (or any theory for that matter) in a Western context. There is definitely some generalizability of these theories, but local conditions matter.

These local results are particularly important in the context of policy implications. The standard policy response to results such as these is to improve factors such as income, income inequality, and literacy. Our results support such policies. However, it is important to note from our results that improvements to infrastructure will also affect homicide in Recife. Specifically, increases in the presence of electricity in households may initially increase homicides and other related crimes because the presence of electricity can represent more criminal opportunities. Future research should investigate this phenomenon as the relationship may turn out to be quadratic: Initial increases in households with electricity may increase homicides and other crimes, but then subsequently decrease as better infrastructure may encourage social organization. Such encouragement can be facilitated through policies that consider multiple initiatives. For example, if households with electricity are increased, public illumination should also be increased in those places to potentially offset any increases in opportunity from the presence of electricity alone. This highlights the importance of understanding the local context for policy implementation.

Despite these promising results, our work is not without its limitations. Though it is common in the spatial criminology literature for research studies to only consider 1 year of data, connected to census variables in a corresponding year, the crime of homicide is a rare event. Consequently, identifying patterns and testing theory may be difficult when dealing with low counts. However, as discussed above, there are a lot of homicides in Recife, Brazil, making such an analysis more feasible. Moreover, we considered 5 years of homicide data that not only add to the count of homicides but also mitigate the use of 1 aberrant year of data. In addition, our analysis only considers one city for analysis. Though we find support for the use of social disorganization theory in a Brazilian context, it is important to note that the generalizability of our results is limited. As such, we encourage researchers to conduct similar analyses in different Brazilian cities to see whether our local (Recife, specific) results are generalizable to other Brazilian contexts.

Regardless of these limitations, we did find some interesting results. Overall, average income and the standard deviation of average income (income inequality) prove to be the most important variables for understanding the distribution of homicide across the census tracts of Recife. This confirms previous research as well as popular opinion in Brazil. However, our analysis extends previous research through our extended set of explanatory variables, a priori, as well as a regression technique that accounts for both spatial autocorrelation and heteroskedasticity.

The investigation of demographic, social, and economic factors that may be associated with homicides is relevant because this information can be useful in the development of crime prevention activities. Crime prevention efforts can be more efficient when the most vulnerable groups and the explanatory factors that affect the dynamics of criminal behavior are known. The benefits of analyses such as this are not confined to testing Western-based theories in other (developing world) contexts. Though the high levels of homicide in a country such as Brazil is both an epidemic according to the World Health Organization and tragic for the country itself, such a situation presents an opportunity to better understand rather rare criminal events in the Western world. Because of the rare nature of homicides in many cities in the Western world, it is difficult to understand their spatial patterns and, therefore, their causes that relate to the distribution of resources in a society. Through the study of homicide in a country such as Brazil, we are able to better understand this phenomenon in hopes of providing prevention in many other contexts.

References

Andresen, M. A. (2006). A spatial analysis of crime in Vancouver, British Columbia: A synthesis of social disorganization and routine activity theory. *Canadian Geographer, 50*, 487–502.

Andresen, M. A. (2011). The ambient population and crime analysis. *Professional Geographer, 63*, 193–212.

Araújo, E. M., Costa, M. C. N., Oliveira, N. F., Santana, F. S., Barreto, M. L., Hogan, V., & Araújo, T. M. (2010). Spatial distribution of mortality by homicide and social inequalities according to race/skin color in an intra-urban Brazilian space. *Revista Brasileira de Epidemiologia, 13*, 549–560.

Blau, P. M. (1977). *Inequality and heterogeneity*. New York, NY: Free Press.

Boivin, R. (2013). On the use of crime rates. *Canadian Journal of Criminology and Criminal Justice, 55*, 263–277.

Boyd, N. (2000). *The beast within: Why men are violent*. Vancouver, British Columbia, Canada: Greystone Books.

Brazilian Institute of Geography and Statistics. (2013). *Produto Interno dos Municípios 2011* [Domestic product of municipalities 2011]. Rio de Janeiro, Brazil: Ministério do Planejamento, Orçamento e Gestão.

Brazilian Institute of Geography and Statistics. (2014). *Cidades: Recife* [Cities: Recife]. Retrieved from http://cidades.ibge.gov.br/xtras/perfil.php?codmun=261160

Brazilian Institute of Geography and Statistics. (2015). *Censo demográfico 2010-Resultados do universo* [Census 2010 – results]. Retrieved from http://censo2010.ibge.gov.br

Breetzke, G. D. (2010). Modeling violent crime rates: A test of social disorganization in the city of Tshwane, South Africa. *Journal of Criminal Justice, 38*, 446–452.

Cahill, M. E., & Mulligan, G. F. (2003). The determinants of crime in Tucson, Arizona. *Urban Geography, 24*, 582–610.

Câmara, G., Monteiro, A. M., Ramos, F. R., Sposati, A., & Koga, D. (2001). *Mapping social exclusion/inclusion in developing countries* (Draft version). Retrieved from http://www. dpi.inpe.br/gilberto/papers/saopaulo_csiss.pdf

Cardia, N., Adorno, S., & Poleto, F. Z. (2003). Homicide rates and human rights violations in São Paulo, Brazil: 1990–2002. *Health and Human Rights, 6*, 15–33.

Carneiro, L. P. (1998). Firearms in Rio de Janeiro: Culture, prevalence and control. In K. der Ghougassian & L. P. Carneiro (Eds.), *Connecting weapons with violence: The South American experience* (Monograph No. 25). Pretoria, South Africa: Institute for Security Studies. Retrieved from http://www.iss.co.za/Pubs/Monographs/No25/Contents.html

Ceccato, V., Haining, R., & Kahn, T. (2007). The geography of homicide in São Paulo, Brazil. *Environment and Planning A, 39*, 1632–1653.

de Lima, M. L., de Souza, E. R., Ximenes, R., de Albuquerque, M. de, F., Bitoun, J., & Barros, M. D. (2002). Homicide progression per geographical area in the State of Pernambuco, Brazil, 1980–1998. *Revista de Saúde Pública, 36*, 462–469.

de Lima, M. L., Ximenes, R. A., de Souza, E. R., Luna, C. F., & de Albuquerque, M. & de, F. (2005). Spatial analysis of socioeconomic determinants of homicide in Brazil. *Revista de Saúde Pública, 39*, 176–182.

Farrington, D. P., & Welsh, B. C. (2002). *Effects of improved street lighting on crime: A systematic review* (Home Office Research Study No. 251). London, England: Home Office.

Gawryszewski, V. P., & Costa, L. S. (2005). Social inequality and homicide rates in São Paulo city, Brazil. *Revista de Saúde Pública, 39*, 191–197.

Hirschi, T., & Gottfredson, M. (1983). Age and the explanation of crime. *American Journal of Sociology, 89*, 552–584.

Institute for Applied Economic Research. (2012). *Sistema de Indicadores de Percepção Social: segurança pública* [System of social perception indicators: Public safety] (2nd ed.). Brasília, Brazil: Secretaria de Assuntos Estratégicos da Presidência da República.

Jacobs, J. (1961). *The death and life of great American cities*. New York, NY: Random House.

Kennedy, L. W., & Forde, D. R. (1990). Routine activities and crime: An analysis of victimization in Canada. *Criminology, 28*, 137–152.

Kilsztajn, S., Carmo, N., Sugahara, L., & Lopes, E. S. (2003). *Vitimas da Cor: Homicidios na Região Metropolitana de São Paulo, 2000* [Victims of color: Homicide in Greater São Paulo]. São Paulo, Brazil: LES/PUCSP.

Linsky, A., & Straus, M. (1986). *Social stress in the United States: Links to regional patterns in crime and illness*. Dover, MA: Auburn House.

Loureiro, P. R. A., & Silva, E. C. D. (2012). What causes intentional homicide? *Journal of International Development, 24*, 287–303.

Lowenkamp, C. T., Cullen, F. T., & Pratt, T. C. (2003). Replicating Sampson and Groves's test of social disorganization theory: Revisiting a criminological classic. *Journal of Research in Crime & Delinquency, 40*, 351–373.

Massey, D. (2001). The prodigal paradigm returns: Ecology comes back to sociology. In A. Booth & A. C. Crouter (Eds.), *Does it take a village? Community effects on children, adolescents, and families* (pp. 41–48). Mahwah, NJ: Lawrence Erlbaum.

Menezes, T., Silveira-Neto, R., Monteiro, C., & Ratton, J. L. (2013). Spatial correlation between homicide rates and inequality: Evidence from urban neighborhoods. *Economics Letters, 120*, 97–99.

Minayo, M. C. D. S., & Constantino, P. (2012). An ecosysthemic vision of homicide. *Ciência & Saúde Coletiva, 17*, 3269–3278.

Ministry of Health. (2015). *Banco de dados do Sistema Único de Saúde—DATASUS* [Database system unified health—DATASUS]. Retrieved from http://www.datasus.gov.br

Oliveira Júnior, F. J. M. (2013). *Trinta anos de homicídios em Pernambuco: Tendência e distribuição espacial no período de 1981 a 2010* [Thirty years of homicides in Pernambuco: Trends and spatial distribution in the 1981–2010 period] (Unpublished thesis). Fundação Oswaldo Cruz, Brazil. Retrieved from http://www.cpqam.fiocruz.br/bibpdf/2011leal-accl.pdf

Pereira, D. V. S., & Mota, C. M. M. (2014). Human development index based on ELECTRE TRI-C multicriteria method: An application in the City of Recife. *Social Indicators Research*. doi:10.1007/s11205-014-0836-y

Quetelet, L. A. J. (1842). *A treatise on man and the development of his faculties*. Edinburgh, UK: W. & R. Chambers.

Ratcliffe, J. H. (2004). Geocoding crime and a first estimate of a minimum acceptable hit rate. *International Journal of Geographical Information Science, 18*, 61–72.

Ratton, J. L., Galvão, C., & Fernandez, M. (2014). Pact for Life and the reduction of homicides in the state of Pernambuco. *Stability: International Journal of Security & Development, 3*, 1–15.

Sachsida, A., Mendonça, M. J. C., Loureiro, P. R. A., & Gutierrez, M. B. S. (2007). Inequality and criminality revisited: Further evidence from Brazil. *Empirical Economics, 39*, 93–109.

Sampson, R. J., & Groves, W. B. (1989). Community structure and crime: Testing social-disorganization theory. *American Journal of Sociology, 94*, 774–802.

Sant'Anna, A., Aerts, D., & Lopes, M. J. (2005). Adolescent homicide victims in Southern Brazil: Situations of vulnerability as reported by families. *Cadernos de Saúde Pública, 21*, 120–129.

Santos, M. J. (2009). Dinâmica temporal da criminalidade: Mais evidências sobre o "efeito inércia" nas taxas de crimes letais nos estados brasileiros [Temporal dynamics of crime: More evidence of the "inertia effect" in lethal crime rates in the Brazilian states]. *Revista Economia, 10*, 169–174.

Sauret, G. (2012). Inovações na contagem de homicídios: Implantação da pulseira de identificação de cadáver [Innovations in the homicide count: Implementation of the corpse identification bracelet]. In G. Sauret (Ed.), *Estatísticas pela vida: A coleta e análise de informações criminais como instrumentos de enfrentamento da violência letal* [Statistics for life: The collection and analysis of criminal intelligence as lethal violence coping instruments) (pp. 20–33). Recife, Brazil: Bargaço Design.

Secretariat of Social Defense. (2014). Base de dados da Secretaria de Defesa Social do Estado de Pernambuco. Fonte de dados primários: números de vítimas de CVLI em Recife e Região Metropolitana de 01 de junho de 2008 a 30 de setembro de 2014 [Database of the social protection department of the State of Pernambuco. Source of primary data: CVLI of casualty figures in Recife and the metropolitan area from 01 June 2008 to September 30, 2014].

Shaw, C. R., & McKay, H. D. (1931). *Social factors in juvenile delinquency*. Washington, DC: U.S. Government Printing Office.

Shaw, C. R., & McKay, H. D. (1942). *Juvenile delinquency and urban areas: A study of rates of delinquency in relation to differential characteristics of local communities in American cities*. Chicago, IL: University of Chicago Press.

Shaw, C. R., Zorbaugh, F., McKay, H. D., & Cottrell, L. S. (1929). *Delinquency areas: A study of the geographic distribution of school truants, juvenile delinquents, and adult offenders in Chicago*. Chicago, IL: University of Chicago Press.

Stark, R. (1996). Deviant places: A theory of the ecology of crime. In P. Cordella & L. J. Seigel (Eds.), *Readings in contemporary criminological theory* (pp. 128–142). Boston, MA: Northeastern University Press.

Tseloni, A., Osborn, D. R., Trickett, A., & Pease, K. (2002). Modelling property crime using the British Crime Survey: What have we learnt? *British Journal of Criminology*, *42*, 109–128.

United Nations Development Programme. (2013). *Regional human development report 2013–2014. Citizen security with a human face: Evidence and proposals for Latin America*. New York, NY: Author.

Waiselfisz, J. J. (2012). *Mapa da violência 2012: Os novos padrões da violência homicida no país* [Map of violence 2012: The new patterns of homicidal violence in the country]. Brasília, Brazil: Secretaria-Geral da Presidência da República.

Waiselfisz, J. J. (2014). *Mapa da violência 2014: Os jovens do Brasil* [Map of violence 2014: Young people of Brazil]. Brasília, Brazil: Secretaria-Geral da Presidência da República.

World Health Organization. (2014). *Global status report on violence prevention 2014*. Geneva, Switzerland: Author.

/// REVIEW QUESTIONS

1. Why do the authors claim Brazil is a unique and important region to test social disorganization theory? Give facts to say why you agree or disagree.
2. What do the findings indicate are the most significant determinants of homicide in Recife, Brazil? Which findings do you find most surprising or least surprising?
3. Given the results, how consistent are the findings of this study with those of Shaw and McKay, the original proponents of social disorganization theory?

READING /// 17

In this piece by Heith Copes, Andy Hochstetler, and Craig Forsyth, we see a type of subcultural normative code applied to the behavior of males who fight in bars. The authors elaborate on a particular code of behavior for honor and order as revealed by their sample of White, working-class males in the southeastern portion of the United States. Interestingly, the authors find that some of the regulations of this normative code actually reduce violent behavior or at least the degree to which it could escalate.

While reading this article, one should consider the following topics:

- The authors' evidence of the participants' statements in this study regarding the need to "verify" or prove their masculinity
- The types of deterrents or key characteristics that prevented some of the participants from committing further violence in their behavior
- The authors' overall summary and conclusions, especially in terms of the theoretical framework of subcultural norms or values for violence

SOURCE: Heith Copes, Andy Hochstetler, and Craig Forsyth, "Peaceful Warriors: Codes for Violence among Adult Male Bar Fighters," *Criminology* 51 (2013): 761–794.

Peaceful Warriors

Codes for Violence among Adult Male Bar Fighters

Heith Copes, Andy Hochstetler, and Craig Forsyth

Understanding Codes of Conduct

The study of subcultures that endorse violence has a long history, and investigators have emphasized different influences on the content and development of codes for violence (Cohen 1955; Miller 1958; Wolfgang and Ferracuti 1967). Whereas theoretical explanations of violence that rely on value systems often have emphasized distinct aspects and origins, investigators have agreed that codes for violence reflect that actors condone, justify, or legitimize violence as a means of grievance resolution or vengeance (Anderson 1999; Berg and Stewart 2013). In deciding to commit violence, actors often draw on portrayals of honor as well as on shared understandings of tolerance of provocation to determine the appropriate response to conflict. Accordingly, far from being senseless and random, aggression is patterned and expectable when considered in light of the subcultural values governing its use.

Wolfgang's (1958) research on the prevalence and incidence of violence paved the way for subcultural interpretations of violence by highlighting variation in the construction of meanings in confrontational situations between groups and subcultures and by nesting these meanings in general values and expectations:

> The significance of a jostle, a slightly derogatory remark, or the appearance of the weapon in the hands of an adversary are stimuli differentially perceived and interpreted.... Social expectations of response in particular types of social interaction result in differential "definitions of the situation." A male is usually expected to defend the name and honor of his mother, the virtue of womanhood ... and to accept no derogation about ... his masculinity. Quick resort to physical combat as a measure of daring, courage or defense of status appears to be a cultural expectation, especially for lower socio-economic class males of both races. (Wolfgang 1958:188–9)

Ethnographers with an interest in codes for violence often have emphasized urban decline, deindustrialization, and inner-city poverty as structural sources of cultural or cognitive landscapes that contribute to high rates of violence in some neighborhoods (Jacobs and Wright 2006; Sanders 1994; Vigil 1988), a finding that also has been borne out in the quantitative research (Piquero et al. 2012). The attitudes and beliefs thought to result from structural disadvantages also seem to influence violent behavior. Those in lower or working classes place greater emphasis on demonstrating courage and the willingness to escalate conflict than those from higher classes (Markowitz 2003). Additionally, those who commit violence endorse some forms of violent crime (Mills, Kroner, and Hemmati 2004), believe that the use of violence serves important purposes (Stewart, Simmons, and Conger 2002), perceive violence as a demonstration of admirable character (Felson et al. 1994), emphasize courage and escalation in the face of conflict (Markowitz and Felson 1998), and endorse a code that calls for violence in the face of disrespect (Berg et al. 2012; Matsueda, Drakulich, and Kubrin 2006).

Methods

We base our findings on the narratives of 23 men who had been in multiple fights with nonfamily members as adults. These individuals lived in or near the city of Lafayette, Louisiana (population 120,623 as of 2010). Like most midsized cities in the southern United States, Lafayette has above average crime rates, especially violent crime. The number of assaults per 100,000 people in Lafayette was 579, whereas across the United States it was 254. The city's population is primarily White (63.5%) and Black (30.9%). The poverty rate is high (19.8% in 2010). The most central industry in the town is oil and gas extraction.

We located interviewees with the help of a lifelong resident who has a history of offenses related to drinking and fighting, and who is known for being a street fighter. He reported being in numerous bar fights (too many to list precisely), and several tavern owners have banned him entry for fighting. Although he has been arrested for disorderly conduct (including fighting), he denied taking part in other illegal activities and had no felony record. The recruiter relied on personal contacts and snowball sampling to locate the sample.

To be eligible, participants had to be White and male, and they had to have been in at least one nondomestic, physical fight within the past 3 months. The reason for restricting the racial composition of the sample was our hope to delve more deeply into how a particular group of persons (i.e., those inhabiting a social sphere of predominantly White, working-class taverns and neighborhoods) thought about fighting and their social world. We did so to act as a counterbalance to the numerous studies that focus on urban, minority youth (see also Jackson-Jacobs 2013). With such a purposive strategy, generalization to other populations is hazardous.

All the individuals we approached agreed to the interview, but one man never could arrange his schedule for a meeting time and was not interviewed. The age range of participants was 22 to 48; the average participant was 33 years of age. All participants feasibly can be classified as working class using their occupations and educational backgrounds at the time of the interview. Twenty were employed. The work these men performed included various labor jobs, such as plumbers' assistants, general contractors, and positions related to oil extraction. Two participants owned businesses (one a small restaurant and the other a screen-print shop). All graduated high school. Six participants graduated college or community college, but none worked in the white-collar workforce, in their major, or had advanced degrees. Eight participants were married. Whereas nearly all participants had been arrested for behaviors they defined as "little things, nothing serious," only one served time in prison. The majority identified with a Cajun ancestry, which is common in the area.

When asked how many fights they had been in as adults, all participants had a hard time providing accurate numbers and most provided ranges or estimates instead, which is common when repeat offenders report their crimes (Shover 1996). The estimated number of fights ranged from 5 to 50. The median range offered by participants was 12 to 15 fights. From their descriptions, participants had a high threshold for counting altercations as fights. They did not consider verbal arguments or quickly interrupted scuffles as fights.

We constructed an interview guide based on a consultation with the recruiter and prior literature on males who engaged in street fights (e.g., Oliver 2001). The recruiter also served as the interviewer. We trained him on proper interviewing techniques, such as probing and active listening. In addition, we listened to each of the first five interviews and offered feedback on how to improve or modify the interviews. Although he followed the same interview guide throughout, we read interviews as they progressed and encouraged him to pursue a few themes that he or we identified.

The interviewer conducted the interviews in private locations such as his home, the home of interviewees, or the homes of others they both knew. When recruiting participants, our contact explained that everything would be kept confidential and that there would be no financial compensation for participation. The interviews lasted between 30 and 45 minutes, and the interviewer recorded them with each participant's permission. We transcribed the interviews verbatim; however, on occasion we edited the text by dropping superfluous filler words and sounds, as well as using punctuation for clarity and readability. We also removed identifying remarks and assigned aliases to each.

To ensure interrater reliability in coding, each of us read the excerpts independently to identify relevant and common themes. We coded using strategies consistent with grounded theory, including open coding and axial coding (Charmaz 2006). We began our open coding by reading electronic versions of the transcripts and marking notes with editing functions in a word processor. We then compared coding and came to agreement on axial codes (theoretical and logical grouping of open codes). On the few cases where we differed on coding, we discussed the discrepancy and reached agreement. We then recoded transcripts using the axial codes we developed, which are reflected in the major themes discussed in the results.

Verifying Masculine Character

Defending and verifying character is a major motivator for violence among urban and rural residents in the United States and abroad (Anderson 1999; Brookman et al., 2011; Nisbett and Cohen 1996). Our participants were not exceptions, and many tied this belief directly to masculinity. When asked why it was important to fight when confronted, Kevin said:

> I think it's important to show who you are as a man, how you feel about yourself, and how you feel about your friends and loved ones. [To show] that you're there to protect them. People, even your friends, need to know that you're there for them, that you're there for yourself, that you have the strength to stand up for yourself and kinda prove you're a man.

David said the willingness to fight allows people to "keep their pride intact. Just sayin' that they're not chumps." Participants asserted that principled individuals know that their character is worth defending physically (Jackson-Jacobs 2013).

They believed that fights were an important part of maintaining self-image. This belief was evident when we asked what they would think of themselves if they did not fight when insulted. In response to this question, David said, "I hate to use the word, but the word pussy comes to mind. . . . That you punked out and you couldn't handle your own business." Similarly, Kevin answered:

> I'd feel guilty. I'd feel weak. I'd feel like I let myself down. I'd feel like I let anybody else that was involved down. I'd feel like the other person involved got the upper hand. I'd feel like I lost something. And most of all I wouldn't feel like a man.

Eric said that if he did not fight he would think:

> That I just wasn't a man, straight and simple. I feel like if I'm tested and I walk away, if I didn't fight that person or prove myself, you know, I'd just feel real down on myself and feel like I'm kind of a coward. They ain't nothin' more that I hate than feelin' like a coward. So, if I'm tested, I'm gonna do what I gotta do to not feel like a coward.

Fighting affirmed a sense of self as a capable and dependable man, but also it fended off powerful negative emotions and shame from refusal to meet the call when provoked.

Being perceived as men who are willing to defend principles was important for participants' sense of self. Using violence was more than saving face; it served internalized and private purposes. A desire to uphold their character led several participants to say that at times they were disappointed deeply in themselves for not fighting. Kevin explained:

> There's times when I kicked myself for days for not hurtin' somebody because I felt they disrespected me in front of people. And just to myself, I felt less of a man. I felt guilty for not doing anything. I felt like a chump. All around it affected me for a while.

Deterrence

There was a pragmatic reason for a firm and unyielding stance in the face of challenge or insult. Fighters believed that by violently responding to affronts they could prevent future insults and deter potential victimizers (Topalli, Wright, and Fornango 2002). Kelly said that, "Without doing it [fighting], you'd just be a sitting duck. You'd be the one getting beaten up. Incidentally, laying the foundation to get beat up again, picked on, taken advantage of, or exploited later." Fred indicated that his latest fight was because, "I didn't want them to think that I was just some pussy. I wanted to show that I could take care of my business." In short, some violence was motivated by the desire to communicate that aggressors had selected the wrong person to confront.

Beaten rivals from the past also show that violence can be an effective specific deterrent. As Dana said:

> [If] you tell somebody not to keep hittin' on your wife, and they're not listenin' there's gotta be consequences. . . . I told him to back off, and he didn't so I knocked him out. After that he never fucked with her again. . . . [The police] wouldn't have solved anything. Really, I solved it. Maybe it wasn't the way everybody wants it to be handled, but it was handled. I got my point across and it never happened again.

Renee emphasized that his violence was a response to an insult, and for him the important thing was to show aggressors that they cannot insult with impunity:

> You give a man a warning, you ask him to respect it, and he doesn't want to listen to you, that's almost a sign of disrespect again. And if he already disrespected you once, he's gonna disrespect you again, and he's gonna always disrespect you. So you almost have to use physical violence, not to say teach him a lesson, but show him that you're not playin' around, and that you are willing to stand your ground and do it every time you see him.
>
> He tried talkin' his way out of it, but I didn't want to hear his talkin'. So, as soon as he was done talkin', I just hit him, and I hit him 'til I cut his eye, and I stopped. I told him, "Take your ass-beatin' like a man," and I walked back to the bar and he left.

By telling his opponent to follow the rule against retaliation for an honorable fight, he affirmed that the contest had ended, that the conflict was settled, and that no future violence should follow.

Conduct in Combat

Equal Combatants

One way to determine a "fair" fight was whether the combatants were matched equally, at least by appearances (see Garot 2010). As Kelly said, "A fair fight is when [they're] equally matched in physical stature, strength, age. Unfair would be age, physical stature, intoxication, outnumbered." Although any touching or attempt to intimidate by invading space during confrontation might set off a fight, participants claimed that they avoided throwing a first blow and would attempt to deescalate conflict when their opponent had lost the chance to win. Exceptions to the dictate to avoid the first blow were when they believed they were far outmatched and the fight was inevitable. They claimed that throwing the first blow in these situations might give a "puncher's chance" to escape unharmed. Still, several participants said that there is little purpose in fighting when there is no chance of winning, such as when a far superior fighter insults you. It is very bad form to bully far outside one's size and fighting ability; if personal pride allows, then there is little shame in letting it go when it happens. As Chris said, "If you're definitely gonna get your ass whipped, there's no point in fightin'. You might as well just walk away." It is possible to walk away from a fight and avoid humiliation when unquestionably outmatched (Garot 2010).

Exceptions to Rules

Although participants articulated rules of combat, they also said that they sometimes abandoned these rules. Several indicated that for some transgressions—a sexual crime or other serious offense against those held close—the injured can cast rules aside. It may be acceptable to approach with stealth, gang up on, blindside, or pull a weapon first when the sole objective is vengeance and inflicting pain on dishonorable and egregious offenders who deserve it, but such events were rare among this group. Departures from the code also occurred for less intentional reasons; these events are much more common and received considerably more attention from participants. Here, we elaborate on the situations and circumstances where the participants did not follow the accepted rules of fighting.

Loyalty

Loyalty to friends or the unprotected can conflict with the imperative that fights be fair. Fighters often recognize that despite the need to let a fight proceed to culmination without interference, they should not let friends be injured severely or humiliated. Louis said that one must assist a friend in the fray "if they need it—if they're getting hurt or losing." David explained that he is sure to intervene in fights if a friend is outnumbered, but he said also that he would aid as a gesture of friendship and unwillingness to watch a compatriot suffer:

> Oh yeah, you jump in to help. Why? Because I guess it's your friend and it all depends, you know, how many friends they got with 'em. But yeah, I'd jump in for a friend of mine just 'cause it's your friend. You don't want to see them get hurt, get beat up.

Onlookers are attentive to how a battle unfolds and whether those with whom they side have the upper hand. If they judge that significant injury to their side is occurring or impending, or that the situation requires a demonstration of loyalty, then they may violate the abstract belief that people should fight their own battles. They cast such violations as reluctant, however. The following dialogue with Sal reflected his decision-making process for determining when to violate the ethic of fighting fair:

Interviewer: Would you jump in even if it was a fair fight?

Sal: Well, I guess it depends. I guess you'd have to be in the situation, see what it calls for.

Interviewer: Let's say it's a fair fight and your friend's winning, would you jump in?

Sal: No, I wouldn't jump in. I'd let him handle his business.

Interviewer: But if he was getting beat up?

Sal: I'd probably jump in, yeah.

Jason relied on loyalty to explain the use of a weapon in a fight where he normally would avoid it. He relayed a story of smashing a glass on an antagonist's head:

> This big dude was harassing a guy I knew, who was pretty small. I told him, "don't worry that dude won't do nothing." Right after I said that, the big dude pushed my friend hard against the wall. I was like, "Fuck man, I just told him nothin' was going to happen to him." I had to do something. So I smashed my drink over the dude's head.

The participants were not blind to conflicting imperatives that shape how they should respond to a fight. Reportedly, it is a complicated decision determining when to intervene in an ongoing fight. The decision requires speedily considering the entirety of the situation; a significant part of the calculation is how much punishment one allows a friend who has lost momentum in a fight to take before intervening to assist. Onlookers should allow fights to proceed in most cases, but at some point, the beating of a friend must stop.

Discussion

Our aims with this research were to explore the content and implementation of codes for fighting among a group of adult, working-class, White males and to determine how they talk about such codes in relation to constructing identities. In describing the content of their code for violence, participants said fighting was a means of constructing an identity as someone deserving respect, but only when conducted acceptably. They emphasized how defending honor, seeking quick conflict resolution, and establishing admirable qualities motivated them to fight. They were proud of their willingness and ability to oppose adversaries with violence when protecting honorable positions or defending character. They thought people should not seek out violence, but they should not back down from it either. They saw value in fighting to defend honor and to establish order. Defending themselves under the right circumstances enhanced self-respect and confidence that they were men of character and good repute. Failure to fight in appropriate circumstances led to self-doubt and regret.

They believed that fighting served functions beyond building a reputation, however. To them, fighting bolstered a confident demeanor, gave advantage in daily nonviolent interactions, and warded off future disrespectful interactions. They portrayed fighting as a reasonable means for dispute resolution because it ended verbal confrontation, brought conflicts to conclusion, and brought grudges out in the open. Completed fights settled disputes that if left untendered could fester and lead to nastier consequences, including shame associated with feeling cowed, gossip and other harmful talk, or sneaky vengeance. For these reasons and because fighting was an intimidating event, many believed it was the better strategy and found it psychologically easier to charge ahead and be done than to wait or act in hesitation.

Analyses of the codes that pertain to violence often contrast subcultural codes, which analysts cast as those that condone or allow violence, with those of the dominant culture, which they presume to proscribe violence. Our interviews imply that codes that are conducive to crime in some ways can be prohibitive in others. In some circumstances, a code for violence dissuades violent responses and limits the insults that lead to them. Therefore, a code may be useful to people who live within the law in general and think about the future; our participants defend it thus. Undoubtedly, few persons endorse codes for violence that condone ruthlessness, brutality, killing, and long-running cycles of escalating retaliation. Certainly, more individuals, like our participants, believe measured violence is appropriate when faced with certain insults and in a narrowly defined range of contexts. Restrictive codes for the use of violence may be enthusiastically perpetuated not only by the down-and-out but also by those rungs above on the class structure—say men who are solidly working class or pursuing college educations. Allowances for violence contained in these codes can contribute to violence, or help rationalize it, in situations clearly defined as appropriate and even in situations where misapplication occurs. Fighters often feel no regret when the former applies, as a code provides neat rationale, but in other cases, they may rest on good intentions, understandable mistakes, and circumstantial complexities. Flexibility in the implementation of codes and as a device for framing diverse violent events surely is one reason that codes for violence endure in so many contexts. For those avoiding callous or criminal reputations, the code may be durable and defensible not for its allowance but because of the restrictions it contains.

References

Agnew, Robert. 2006. "Storylines as a neglected cause of crime". *Journal of Research in Crime and Delinquency* 43:119–47.

Anderson, Elijah. 1999. *Code of the Street: Decency, Violence, and the Moral Life of the Inner City.* New York: Norton.

Athens, Lonnie. 1997. *Violent Criminal Acts and Actors Revisited.* Champaign: University of Illinois Press.

Berg, Mark T., and Eric Stewart. 2013. "Street Culture and Crime". In *Oxford Handbook of Criminological Theory*, eds. Francis T. Cullen and Pamela Wilcox. Oxford, U.K.: Oxford University Press.

Berg, Mark T., Eric Stewart, Christopher Schreck, and Ronald L. Simons. 2012. The victim-offender overlap in context: Examining the role of neighborhood street culture. *Criminology* 50:359–90.

Brezina, Timothy, Robert Agnew, Francis T. Cullen, and John P. Wright. 2004. "The Code of the Street: A Quantitative Assessment of Elijah Anderson's Subculture of Violence Thesis". *Youth Violence and Juvenile Justice* 4:303–28.

Brookman, Fiona, Trevor Bennett, Andy Hochstetler, and Heith Copes. 2011. "The Role of the 'Code of the Street' in the Generation of Street Violence in the UK". *European Journal of Criminology* 8:17–31.

Brookman, Fiona, Heith Copes, and Andy Hochstetler. 2011. "Street Codes, Accounts, and Rationales for Violent Crime". *Journal of Contemporary Ethnography* 40:397–424.

Charmaz, Kathy. 2006. *Constructing Grounded Theory.* Thousand Oaks, CA: Sage.

Cohen, Albert K. 1955. *Delinquent Boys: The Culture of the Gang.* Glencoe, IL: Free Press.

Copes, Heith, Fiona Brookman, and Anastasia Brown. 2013. "Accounting for Violations of the Convict Code". *Deviant Behavior.* In press. DOI: 10.1080/01639625.2013.781444.

DiMaggio, Paul. 1997. "Culture and Cognition". *Annual Review of Sociology* 23:263–87.

Faupel, Charles E. 1991. *Shooting Dope: Career Patterns of Hardcore Heroin Users.* Gainesville: University of Florida Press.

Felson, Richard B., Allen Liska, Scott J. South, and Thomas L. McNulty. 1994. "The Subculture of Violence: Individual vs. School Context Effects". *Social Forces* 73:155–73.

Ferguson, Ann A. 2001. *Bad Boys: Making of Black Masculinity.* Ann Arbor: University of Michigan Press.

Garot, Robert. 2010. *Who You Claim? Performing Gang Identity in School and on the Streets.* New York: New York University Press.

Guest, Greg, Arwen Bunce, and Laura Johnson. 2006. "How Many Interviews Are Enough? An Experiment with Data Saturation and Variability". *Field Methods* 24:59–82.

Harding, David. 2007. "Cultural Context, Sexual Behavior, and Romantic Relationships in Disadvantaged Neighborhoods". *American Sociological Review* 72:341–64.

Harding, David. 2010. *Living the Drama: Community, Conflict, and Culture among Inner-City Boys.* Cambridge, MA: Harvard University Press.

Hochstetler, Andy, Heith Copes, and Patrick Williams. 2010. "That's Not Who I Am: How Offenders Commit Violent Acts and Reject Authentically Violent Selves". *Justice Quarterly* 27:492–516.

Horowitz, Ruth. 1983. *Honor and the American Dream: Culture and Identity in a Chicano Community.* Newark, NJ: Rutgers University Press.

Jackson-Jacobs, Curtis. 2013. "Constructing Physical Fights: An Interactionist Analysis of Violence among Affluent, Suburban Youth". *Qualitative Sociology* 36:23–52.

Jacobs, Bruce A., and Richard Wright. 2006. *Street Justice: Retaliation in the Criminal Underworld.* New York: Cambridge University Press.

Jimerson, Jason B., and Matthew K. Oware. 2006. "Telling the Code: An Ethnomethodological Ethnography". *Journal of Contemporary Ethnography* 35:24–50.

Katz, Jack. 1988. *Seductions of Crime.* New York: Basic Books.

Klenowski, Paul, Heith Copes, and Christopher Mullins. 2011. "Gender, Identity and Accounts: How White Collar Offenders Do Gender When They Make Sense of Their Crimes". *Justice Quarterly* 28:46–69.

Kornhauser, Ruth. 1978. *The Social Sources of Delinquency: An Appraisal of Analytical Methods*. Chicago, IL: University of Chicago Press.

Lee, Matthew, and Edward S. Shihadeh. 2009. "The Spatial Concentration of Southern Whites and Argument-Based Lethal Violence". *Social Forces* 91:1671–94.

Loseke, Donileen R. 2007. "The Study of Identity as Cultural, Institutional, Organizational, and Personal Narratives: Theoretical and Empirical Integrations". *Sociological Quarterly* 48:661–88.

Markowitz, Fred E. 2003. "Socioeconomic Disadvantage and Violence: Recent Research on Culture and Neighborhood Control as Explanatory Mechanisms". *Aggression and Violent Behavior* 8:145–54.

Markowitz, Fred E., and Richard B. Felson. 1998. "Socio-demographic Differences in Attitudes and Violence". *Criminology* 36:117–38.

Maruna, Shadd, and Heith Copes. 2005. "What Have We Learned from Five Decades of Neutralization Research. In *Crime and Justice: A Review of Research*, Vol. 32, ed. Michael H. Tonry. Chicago, IL: University of Chicago Press.

Matsueda, Ross L., Kevin Drakulich, and Charis E. Kubrin. 2006. "Race and Neighborhood Codes of Violence". In *The Many Colors of Crime*, eds. Ruth D. Peterson, Lauren J. Krivo, and John Hagan. New York: New York University Press.

Miller, Walter. 1958. Lower class culture as a generating milieu of gang delinquency. *Journal of Social Issues* 1:5–20.

Mills, Jeremy F., Daryl G. Kroner, and Toni Hemmati. 2004. The measure of criminal attitudes and associates: The prediction of general and violent recidivism. *Criminal Justice and Behavior* 31:717–33.

Nisbett, Richard, and Dov Cohen. 1996. *Culture of Honor: The Psychology of Violence in the South*. Boulder, CO: Westview Press.

Oliver, William. 2001. *The Violent Social World of Black Men*. San Francisco, CA: Jossey-Bass.

Piquero, Alex, Jonathan Intravia, Eric Stewart, Nicole L. Piquero, Mark Gertz, and Jake Bratton. 2012. "Investigating the Determinants of the Street Code and its Relation to Offending Among Adults". *American Journal of Criminal Justice* 37: 19–32.

Presser, Lois. 2010. "Collecting and Analyzing the Stories of Offenders". *Journal of Criminal Justice Education* 21:431–46.

Rosenfeld, Richard, Bruce Jacobs, and Richard Wright. 2003. "Snitching and the Code of the Street". *British Journal of Criminology* 43:291–309.

Sampson, Robert, and Lydia Bean. 2006. "Cultural Mechanisms and Killing Fields: A Revised Theory of Community-Level Racial Inequality". In *The Many Colors of Crime: Inequalities of Race, Ethnicity, and Crime in America*, eds. Ruth Peterson, Lauren Krivo, and John Hagan. New York: New York University Press.

Sampson, Robert, and William J. Wilson. 1995. "Toward a Theory of Race, Crime and Urban Inequality". In *Crime and Inequality*, eds. John Hagan and Ruth Peterson. Palo Alto, CA: Stanford University Press.

Sandberg, Sveinung. 2009a. "A Narrative Search for Respect". *Deviant Behavior* 30:487–510.

Sandberg, Sveinung. 2009b. "Gangster, Victim or Both? The Interdiscursive Construction of Sameness and Difference in Self-Presentations". *British Journal of Sociology* 60: 523–42.

Sandberg, Sveinung. 2010. "What Can "Lies" Tell Us about Life? Notes towards a Framework of Narrative Criminology". *Journal of Criminal Justice Education* 21:447–65.

Sanders, William B. 1994. *Gangbangs and Drive-Bys: Grounded Culture and Juvenile Gang Violence*. New York: Aldine de Gruyter.

Scott, Marvin B., and Scott M. Lyman. 1968. "Accounts". *American Sociological Review* 33:46–62.

Shover, Neal. 1996. *Great Pretenders: Pursuits and Careers of Persistent Thieves*. Boulder, CO: Westview Press.

Spierenburg, Pieter. 1998. "Masculinity, Violence, and Honor". In *Men Violence: Gender, Honor, and Ritual in Modern Europe and America*, ed. Pieter Spierenburg. Athens: The Ohio State University Press.

Stewart, Eric A., and Ronald L. Simons. 2010. "Race, Code of the Street, and Violent Delinquency: A Multilevel Investigation of Neighborhood Street Culture and Individual Norms of Violence". *Criminology* 48:569–605.

Stewart, Eric A., Ronald L. Simons, and Rand Conger. 2002. "Assessing Neighborhood and Social Psychological Influences on Childhood Violence in an African-American Sample". *Criminology* 40:801–30.

Stokes, Randall, and John Hewitt. 1976. "Aligning Action". *American Sociological Review* 41:838–49.

Swidler, Ann. 1986. "Culture in Action: Symbols and Strategies". *American Sociological Review* 51:273–86.

Topalli, Volkan. 2005. "When Being Good Is Bad: An Expansion of Neutralization Theory". *Criminology* 43:797–836.

Topalli, Volkan, Richard Wright, and Robert Fornango. 2002. "Drug Dealers, Robbery, and Retaliation: Vulnerability, Deterrence and the Contagion of Violence". *British Journal of Criminology* 42:337–351.

Vigil, James D. 1988. *Barrio Gangs: Street Life and Identity in Southern California*. Austin: University of Texas Press.

Wacquant, Loic. 2002. "Scrutinizing the Street: Poverty, Morality, and the Pitfalls of Urban Ethnography". *American Journal of Sociology* 107:1468–532.

Wieder, D. Lawrence. 1974. *Language and Social Reality: The Case of Telling the Convict Code*. The Hague, the Netherlands: Mouton.

Wilson, William J. 1996. *When Work Disappears: The World of the New Urban Poor*. New York: Knopf.

Wolfgang, Marvin E. 1958. *Patterns in Criminal Homicide*. Philadelphia: University of Pennsylvania Press.

Wolfgang, Marvin E., and Franco Ferracuti. 1967. *The Subculture of Violence: Towards an Integrated Theory in Criminology*. London, U.K.: Tavistock.

/// REVIEW QUESTIONS

1. What do the participants in this study reveal regarding the need to "verify" their masculinity?
2. What were some of the deterrents that prevented some of the subjects from committing further violence?
3. What was the overall conclusion of this study in terms of subcultural codes for violence?

SECTION VIII

Social Process and Learning Theories of Crime

This section will discuss Edwin Sutherland's development of differential association theory and how this evolved into Ronald Akers's work of differential reinforcement and other social learning theories, such as techniques of neutralization. Then, the modern state of research on these theories will be presented. We will also discuss the evolution of control theories of crime, emphasizing social bonding and the scientific evidence found regarding the key constructs in Travis Hirschi's control theories, which are two of the most highly regarded perspectives according to criminological experts and their studies.[1] Most of the social process theories assume that criminal behavior is learned behavior, which means that criminal activity is actually learned from others through social interaction, much like riding a bike or playing basketball. Namely, people learn criminal activity from significant others, such as family, peers, or coworkers. However, other social process theories, namely control theories, assume that offending is the result of natural tendencies and thus must be controlled by social processes. Social process theories examine how individuals interact with other individuals and groups and how the learning that takes place in these interactions leads to a propensity for criminal activity. This section will explore both of these theoretical frameworks and explain how social processes are vital to both perspectives in determining criminal behavior.

This section begins with social process theories known as **learning theories**. Such learning theories attempt to explain how and why individuals learn from significant others to engage in criminal rather than conventional behavior. Next, we discuss **control theories**, which emphasize personal or socialization factors that prevent individuals from engaging in selfish, antisocial behaviors.

Learning Theories

In this section, we review theories that emphasize how individuals learn criminal behavior through interacting with significant others, people with whom they typically associate. These learning theories assume that people are born with no tendency toward or away from committing crime. This concept is referred to as **tabula rasa**, or blank slate, meaning that all individuals are completely malleable and will believe what they are told by their significant

[1]Anthony Walsh and Lee Ellis, "Political Ideology and American Criminologists' Explanations for Criminal Behavior," *The Criminologist* 24 (1999): 1, 14 (see chap. 1, n. 13).

others and act accordingly. Thus, such theories of learning tend to explain how criminal behavior is learned through cultural norms. One of the main concepts in learning theories is the influence of peers and significant others on an individual's behavior.

Here, three learning theories are discussed: (1) differential association theory, (2) differential identification theory, and (3) differential reinforcement theory. Then we examine techniques of neutralization.

Differential Association Theory

Sutherland introduced his **differential association theory** in the late 1930s.[2] He proposed a theoretical framework that explained how criminal values could be culturally transmitted to individuals from their significant others. Sutherland proposed a theoretical model that included nine principles, but rather than list them all, we will summarize the main points of his theory.

Perhaps the most interesting principle is the first: Criminal behavior is learned. This was a radical departure from previous theories (e.g., Lombroso's "born criminal" theory, Goddard's feeblemindedness theory, Sheldon's body type theory). Sutherland was one of the first to state that criminal behavior is the result of normal social processes, resulting when individuals associate with the wrong type of people, often by no fault on their part. By associating with crime-oriented people, whether parents or peers, an individual will inevitably choose to engage in criminal behavior because that is what he or she has learned, Sutherland thought.

Perhaps the most important of Sutherland's principles, and certainly the most revealing one, was number six in his framework: "A person becomes delinquent because of an excess of definitions favorable to violation of law over definitions unfavorable to violation of law."[3] Sutherland noted that this principle represents the essence of differential association theory. It suggests that people can have associations that favor both criminal and noncriminal behavior patterns. If an individual is receiving more information and values that are pro-crime than anticrime, the individual will inevitably engage in criminal activity. Also, Sutherland claimed that such learning can take place only in interactions with significant others and not via television, movies, radio, or other media.

It is important to understand the cultural context at the time Sutherland was developing his theory. In the early 20th century, most academics, and society for that matter, believed that there was something abnormal or different about criminals. Sheldon's body type theory was popular in the same period, as was the use of IQ to pick out people who were of lower intelligence and supposedly predisposed to crime (both of these theories were covered in Section IV). So, the common assumption when Sutherland created the principles of differential association theory was that there was essentially something wrong with individuals who commit crime.

In light of this common assumption, Sutherland's proposal—that criminality is learned just like any conventional activity—was extremely profound. This suggests that any normal person, when exposed to attitudes favorable to crime, will learn criminal activity and that the processes and mechanisms of learning are the same for crime as for most legal, everyday behaviors—namely, social interaction with family and friends and not reading books or watching movies. How many of us learned to play basketball or other sports by reading a book about it? Virtually no one learns how to play sports this way. Rather, we learn the techniques (e.g., how to do a jump shot) and motivations for playing sports (e.g., it is fun or you might be able to earn a scholarship) through our friends, relatives, coaches, and other people close to us. According to Sutherland, crime is learned the same way; our close associates teach us both the techniques (e.g., how to steal a car) and the motivations (e.g., it is fun; you might be able to sell it or its parts). While most criminologists tend to take it for granted that criminal behavior is learned, the idea was rather unique and bold when Sutherland presented his theory of differential association.

---

[2]Edwin H. Sutherland, *Principles of Criminology*, 3rd ed. (Philadelphia: Lippincott, 1939).

[3]Edwin H. Sutherland and Donald R. Cressey, *Principles of Criminology*, 5th ed. (Chicago: Lippincott, 1950), 78.

It is important to keep in mind that differential association theory is just as positivistic as earlier biological and psychological theories. Sutherland clearly believed that if people were receiving more information that breaking the law was good, then they would inevitably commit crimes. There is virtually no allowance for free will and rational decision making in this model of offending. Rather, people's choices to commit crime are determined through their social interactions with those close to them; they do not actually make the decisions to engage (or not engage) in criminal activities. So, differential association can be seen as a highly positive, deterministic theory, much like Lombroso's "born criminal" and Goddard's feeblemindedness theories (see Section IV), except that instead of biological or psychological traits causing crime, it is social interaction and learning. Furthermore, Sutherland claimed that individual differences in biological and psychological functioning have little to do with criminality; however, this idea has been discounted by modern research, which shows that such variations do in fact affect criminal behavior, largely because such biopsychological factors influence the learning processes of individuals, thereby directly impacting the basic principles of Sutherland's theory (see Sections IV and V).

▲ **Image 8.1** Edwin H. Sutherland (1883–1950), University of Chicago and Indiana University, author of differential association theory.

SOURCE: © The Estate of Donald Cressey

Classical Conditioning: A Learning Theory with Limitations

Sutherland used the dominant psychological theory of learning in his era as the basis for his theory of differential association. This model was **classical conditioning**, which was primarily developed by Ivan Pavlov. Classical conditioning assumes that animals as well as people learn through associations between stimuli and responses.[4] Organisms, animals or people, are somewhat passive actors in this process, meaning that they simply receive and respond in natural ways to various forms of stimuli; over time, they learn to associate certain stimuli with certain responses.

For example, Pavlov showed that dogs, which are naturally afraid of loud noises such as bells, could be quickly conditioned not only to be less afraid of bells but to actually desire and salivate at their sound. A dog naturally salivates when presented with meat, so when this presentation of an unconditioned stimulus (meat) is given, a dog will always salivate (unconditioned response) in anticipation of eating. Pavlov demonstrated through a series of experiments that if a bell (conditioned stimulus) is always rung at the same time the dog is presented with meat then the dog will learn to associate what was previously a negative stimulus with a positive stimulus (food). Thus, the dog will very quickly begin to salivate at the ringing of a bell, even when meat is not presented. When this occurs, it is called a conditioned response because it is not natural; however, it is a very powerful and effective means of learning, and it sometimes takes only a few occurrences of coupling the bell ringing with meat before the conditioned response takes place.

[4] For a discussion, see Thomas J. Bernard, Jeffrey B. Snipes, and Alexander L. Gerould, *Vold's Theoretical Criminology*, 6th ed. (Oxford: Oxford University Press, 2010), 156–57 (see chap. 2).

One modern use of this in humans is the administration of drugs that make people ill when they drink alcohol. Alcoholics are often prescribed drugs that make them very sick, often to the point of vomiting, if they ingest any alcohol. The idea is that they will learn to associate feelings of sickness with drinking and thus stop wanting to consume alcohol. One big problem with this strategy is that alcoholics often do not consistently take the drugs, so they quickly slip back into addiction. Still, if they were to maintain their regimen of drugs, it would likely work, because people do tend to learn through association.

This type of learning model was used in the critically acclaimed 1964 novel (and later motion picture) *A Clockwork Orange*. In this novel, the author, Anthony Burgess, told the story of a juvenile murderer who is "rehabilitated" by doctors who force him to watch hour after hour of violent images while simultaneously giving him drugs that make him sick. In the novel, the protagonist is "cured" after only 2 weeks of this treatment, having learned to consistently associate violence with sickness. However, once he is let out, he lacks the ability to choose violence and other antisocial behavior, which is seen as losing his humanity. Therefore, the ethicists order a reversal treatment and make him back into his former self, a violent predator. Although a fictional piece, *A Clockwork Orange* is probably one of the best illustrations of the use of classical conditioning in relation to criminal offending and rehabilitation.

▲ **Image 8.2** The Russian scientist Ivan Petrovich Pavlov (1849–1936). He is best known for his studies of conditioned reflexes and his theory of classical conditioning.

SOURCE: © Getty Images / Hulton Deutsch / Contributor

Another example of classical conditioning is the associations we make with certain smells and sounds. For example, all of us can relate good times to smells that were present during those occasions. If a loved one or someone we dated wore a certain perfume or cologne, smelling that scent at a later time can bring back memories. When our partner goes out of town, we can smell his or her pillow, and it will remind us of our partner because we associate his or her smell with his or her being. Or perhaps the smell of a turkey cooking in an oven always reminds us of Thanksgiving or another holiday. Regarding associations of sounds, we can all remember songs that remind us of happy and sad times in our lives. Often these songs will play on the radio, and they take us back to those occasions, whether good or bad. People with post-traumatic stress disorder (PTSD) also experience sound associations; war veterans, for example, may hit the deck when a car backfires. These are all clear examples of classical conditioning and associating stimuli with responses.

Since Sutherland's theory was published, many of the principles outlined in his model have come under scrutiny. Follow-up research has shown some flaws in, as well as misinterpretations of, his work.[5] Specifically, Sutherland theorized that crime occurs when associations favorable to violation of the law outweigh associations favorable to conforming to the law. However, measuring this type of ratio is nearly impossible for social scientists.[6]

[5]Edwin H. Sutherland and Donald R. Cressey, *Criminology*, 9th ed. (Philadelphia, PA: Lippincott, 1974).

[6]Ross L. Matsueda and Karen Heimer, "Race, Family Structure, and Delinquency: A Test of Differential Association and Social Control Theories," *American Sociological Review* 47 (1987): 489–504; Charles R. Tittle, M. J. Burke, and E. F. Jackson, "Modeling Sutherland's Theory of Differential Association: Toward an Empirical Clarification," *Social Forces* 65 (1986): 405–32.

Another topic of criticism involves Sutherland's claim that all criminals learn the behavior from others before they engage in such activity. However, many theorists have noted that individuals may engage in criminal activity without being taught such behavior, and then seek out others with attitudes and behavior similar to their own.[7] So, do individuals learn to commit crime after they are taught by delinquent peers, or do they start associating with similar delinquents or criminals once they have initiated their offending career (i.e., "birds of a feather flock together")? This exact debate was examined by researchers, and the most recent studies point to the occurrence of both causal processes: Criminal associations cause more crime, and committing crime causes more criminal associations. Both are key in the causal process, so Sutherland was missing half of this equation.[8]

Another key criticism is that if each individual is born with a blank slate and all criminal behavior is learned, then who committed crime in the first place? Who could expose the first criminal to the definitions favorable to violation of law? Furthermore, what factor(s) caused that individual to do the crime if it was not learned? Obviously, if it were due to any factor(s) other than learning—and it must have been because there was no one to teach it—then it obviously was not explained by learning theories. This criticism cannot be addressed, so it is somewhat ignored in the scientific literature.

Despite the criticisms and flaws, much research supports Sutherland's theory. For example, researchers have found that older criminals teach younger delinquents.[9] In addition, delinquents often associate with criminal peers prior to engaging in criminal activity.[10] Furthermore, research has shown that criminal friends, attitudes, and activity are highly associated.[11] Still, Sutherland's principles are quite vague and elusive in terms of measurement, which renders them difficult for social scientists to test.[12] Related to these issues, perhaps one of the biggest problems with Sutherland's formulation of differential association is that he used primarily one type of learning model—classical conditioning—to formulate most of his principles, and thus he neglected other important ways that we learn attitudes and behavior from others. Ultimately, Sutherland's principles are hard to test; more current versions of his framework have incorporated other learning models and thus are easier to test so that empirical validity can be demonstrated.

Differential Identification Theory

Glaser's Concept of Differential Identification

Another reaction to Sutherland's differential association dealt with the influence of movies and television, as well as other reference groups outside of one's significant others. As stated previously, Sutherland claimed that learning of criminal definitions can take place only through social interactions with significant others as opposed to reading a book or watching movies. However, in 1956, Daniel Glaser proposed the idea of **differential identification theory**, which allows for learning to take place not only through people close to us but also through other reference groups, even distant ones, such as sports heroes or movie stars whom we have never actually met and with whom we have never corresponded.[13] Glaser claimed that it did not matter much whether an individual had a personal relationship

---

[7]Tittle et al., "Modeling Sutherland's Theory."

[8]Terence Thornberry, "Toward an Interactional Theory of Delinquency," *Criminology* 25 (1987): 863–87.

[9]Kenneth Tunnell, "Inside the Drug Trade: Trafficking from the Dealer's Perspective," *Qualitative Sociology* 16 (1993): 361–81.

[10]Douglas Smith, Christy Visher, and G. Roger Jarjoura, "Dimensions of Delinquency: Exploring the Correlates of Participation, Frequency, and Persistence of Delinquent Behavior," *Journal of Research in Crime and Delinquency* 28 (1991): 6–32.

[11]Matthew Ploeger, "Youth Employment and Delinquency: Reconsidering a Problematic Relationship," *Criminology* 35 (1997): 659–75.

[12]Reed Adams, "The Adequacy of Differential Association Theory," *Journal of Research in Crime and Delinquency* 1 (1974): 1–8; James F. Short, "Differential Association as a Hypothesis: Problems of Empirical Testing," *Social Problems* 8 (1960): 14–25.

[13]Daniel Glaser, "Criminality Theories and Behavioral Images," *American Journal of Sociology* 61 (1956): 433–44.

with a reference group; in fact, he argued, a group could be imaginary, such as fictitious characters in a movie or book. The important thing, according to Glaser, was that an individual must identify with a person or character and thus behave in ways that fit the norm set of this reference group or person.

Glaser's proposition has been virtually ignored, with the exception of Kenneth Dawes's study of delinquency in 1973, which found that identification with people other than parents was strong when youths perceived a greater degree of rejection from their parents.[14] Given the profound influence of movies, music, and television on today's youth culture, it is obvious that differential identification was an important addition to Sutherland's framework, and more research should examine the validity of Glaser's theory in contemporary society.

Although Glaser and others modified differential association, the most valid and respected variation is differential reinforcement theory.

Differential Reinforcement Theory

In 1965, C. R. Jeffery provided an extensive critique and reevaluation of Sutherland's differential association theory. He argued that the theory was incomplete without some attention to an updated social psychology of learning (e.g., operant conditioning and modeling theories of learning).[15] He wanted Sutherland to account for the fact that people can be conditioned into behaving in certain ways, such as by being rewarded for conforming behavior. Then, in 1966, Robert Burgess and Akers criticized and responded to Jeffery's criticism by proposing a new theory that incorporated some of these learning models into Sutherland's basic framework.[16] The result was what is now known as **differential reinforcement theory**. Ultimately, Burgess and Akers argued that by integrating Sutherland's work with contributions from the field of social psychology, criminal behavior could be more clearly understood.

In some ways, differential reinforcement theory may appear to be no different than rational choice theory (see Section III). To an extent, this is true, because both models focus on reinforcements and punishments that occur after an individual offends. However, differential reinforcement theory can be distinguished from the rational choice perspective. The latter assumes that humans are born with the capacity for rational decision making, whereas the differential reinforcement perspective assumes people are born with a blank slate and, thus, must be socialized and taught how to behave through various forms of conditioning (e.g., operant and classical) as well as modeling.

Burgess and Akers developed seven propositions to summarize differential reinforcement theory, which largely represent efficient modifications of Sutherland's original nine principles of differential association.[17] The strong influence of social psychologists is illustrated in their first statement as well as throughout the seven principles. Although differential reinforcement incorporates the elements of modeling and classical conditioning learning models in its framework, the first statement clearly states that the essential learning mechanism in social behavior is operant conditioning, so it is important to understand what operant conditioning is and how it is evident throughout life.

---

[14]Kenneth J. Dawes, "Family Relationships, Reference Others, Differential Identification and Their Joint Impact on Juvenile Delinquency" (doctoral dissertation, Ann Arbor, MI: University Mircrofilms, 1973).

[15]C. Ray Jeffery, "Criminal Behavior and Learning Theory," *Journal of Criminal Law, Criminology, and Police Science* 56 (1965): 294–300.

[16]Robert Burgess and Ronald Akers, "A Differential Association-Reinforcement Theory of Criminal Behavior," *Social Problems* 14 (1966): 131.

[17]For a more recent version of these principles, see Ronald Akers, *Deviant Behavior: A Social Learning Approach*, 3rd ed. (Belmont, CA: Wadsworth, 1985). See also Ronald L. Akers and Christine S. Sellers, *Criminological Theories: Introduction, Evaluation, and Application*, 6th ed. (Oxford: Oxford University Press, 2012).

Operant Conditioning

The idea of **operant conditioning** was primarily developed by B. F. Skinner,[18] who ironically was working just across campus from Sutherland when he was developing differential association theory at Indiana University. As in modern times, academia was too intradisciplinary and intradepartmental. Had Sutherland been aware of Skinner's studies and theoretical development, he likely would have included it in his original framework. In his defense, operant conditioning was not well known or researched at the time; as a result, Sutherland incorporated the then-dominant learning model, classical conditioning. Burgess and Akers went on to incorporate operant conditioning into Sutherland's framework.

Operant conditioning concerns how behavior is influenced by reinforcements and punishments. Furthermore, operant conditioning assumes that an animal or human being is a proactive player in seeking out rewards and not just a passive entity that receives stimuli, as classical conditioning assumes. Behavior is strengthened or encouraged through reward (**positive reinforcement**) and avoidance of punishment (**negative reinforcement**). For example, if someone is given a car for graduation from college, that would be a positive reinforcement. On the other hand, if a teenager who has been grounded is allowed to start going out again because he or she has better grades, this would be a negative reinforcement, because he or she is now being rewarded via the avoidance of something negative. Like different types of reinforcement, punishment comes in two forms as well. Behavior is weakened, or discouraged, through adverse stimuli (**positive punishment**) or lack of reward (**negative punishment**). A good example of positive punishment would be a good, old-fashioned spanking, because it is certainly a negative stimulus; anything that directly presents negative sensations or feelings is a positive punishment. On the other hand, if parents take away car privileges from a teenager who broke curfew, that would be an example of negative punishment because the parents are removing a positive aspect or reward.

Some notable examples of operant conditioning include teaching a rat to successfully run a maze. When rats take the correct path and finish the maze quickly, they are either positively reinforced (e.g., rewarded with a piece of cheese) or negatively reinforced (e.g., not zapped with electricity as they were when they chose the wrong path). On the other hand, when rats take wrong turns or do not complete the maze in adequate time, they are either positively punished (e.g., zapped with electricity) or negatively punished (e.g., not given the cheese they expect to receive). The rats, like humans, tend to learn the correct behavior very fast using such consistent implementation of reinforcements and punishments.

In humans, such principles of operant conditioning can be found even at very early ages. In fact, many of us have implemented such techniques (or been subjected to them) without really knowing they were called operant conditioning. For example, during toilet training, children learn to use the bathroom to do their natural duty rather than doing it in their pants. To reinforce the act of going to the bathroom on a toilet, we encourage the correct behavior by presenting positive rewards, which can be as simple as applauding the child or giving him or her a piece of candy for a successful job. While parents (we hope) rarely proactively use spanking in toilet training, there is an inherent positive punishment involved when children go in their pants; namely, they have to be in their dirty diaper for a while, not to mention the embarrassment that most children feel when they do this. Furthermore, negative punishments are present in such situations because the child does not get the applause or candy, so the rewards have been removed.

Of course, this does not apply only to early behavior. An extensive amount of research has shown that humans learn attitudes and behavior best through a mix of reinforcements and punishments throughout life. In terms of criminal offending, studies have clearly shown that the rehabilitative programs that appear to work most effectively in reducing recidivism in offenders are those that provide opportunities for reward as well as threats of punishment. Empirical research has combined the findings from hundreds of such studies of rehab programs, showing that the programs that are most successful in changing the attitudes and behavior of previous offenders are those that offer

[18]B. F. Skinner, *Science and Human Behavior* (New York: Macmillan, 1953).

▲ **Image 8.3** B. F. Skinner (1904–1990) was the key proponent of operant conditioning, which emphasized both rewards and punishments in affecting behavior.

SOURCE: © Getty Images / Bettmann / Contributor

at least four reward opportunities for every one possible punishment.[19] So, whether it is training children to go potty correctly or altering criminals' thinking and behavior, operant conditioning is a well-established form of learning that makes differential reinforcement theory a more valid and specified model of offending than differential association.

Whether deviant or conforming behavior occurs and continues "depends on the past and present rewards or punishment for the behavior, and the rewards and punishment attached to alternative behavior."[20] In contrast to Sutherland's differential association model, which looks only at what happens before an act (i.e., classical conditioning), not at what happens after the act is completed (i.e., operant conditioning), Burgess and Akers's model looks at both. Criminal behavior is likely to occur, Burgess and Akers theorized, when its rewards outweigh the punishments.

Bandura's Theory of Modeling and Imitation

Another learning model that Burgess and Akers emphasized in their formulation of differential reinforcement theory was the element of **modeling and imitation**. Although Sutherland's original formulation of differential association theory was somewhat inspired by Gabriel Tarde's concept of imitation,[21] the nine principles did not adequately emphasize the importance of modeling in the process of learning behavior. Sutherland's failure was likely due to the fact that Albert Bandura's primary work in this area had not occurred when Sutherland was formulating differential association theory.[22]

Through a series of experiments and theoretical development, Bandura demonstrated that a significant amount of learning takes place without any form of conditioning. Specifically, he claimed that individuals can learn even if they are not rewarded or punished for behavior (i.e., operant conditioning) and even if they have not been exposed to associations between stimuli and responses (i.e., classical conditioning). Rather, Bandura proposed that people learn many of their attitudes and behaviors from simply observing the behavior of others, namely through mimicking what others do. This is often referred to as *monkey see, monkey do*, but it is not just monkeys that do this. Like most animal species, humans are biologically hardwired to observe and learn the behavior of others, especially elders, to see what behavior is essential for survival and success.

[19]Patricia Van Voorhis and Emily Salisbury, *Correctional Counseling and Rehabilitation*, 8th ed. (Cincinnati: Anderson, 2013).

[20]Ronald L. Akers, *Deviant Behavior: A Social Learning Approach*, 2nd ed. (Belmont, CA: Wadsworth, 1977), 57.

[21]Gabriel Tarde, *Penal Philosophy*, trans. Rapelje Howell (Boston: Little, Brown, 1912).

[22]See Albert Bandura, *Principles of Behavior Modification* (New York: Holt, Rinehart & Winston, 1969); Albert Bandura, *Aggression: A Social Learning Analysis* (Englewood Cliffs, NJ: Prentice Hall, 1973); Albert Bandura, *Social Learning Theory* (Englewood Cliffs, NJ: Prentice Hall, 1977).

Bandura showed that simply observing the behavior of others, especially adults, can have profound learning effects on the behavior of children. Specifically, he performed experiments in which a randomized experimental group of children watched a video of adults acting aggressively toward Bobo dolls (which are blow-up plastic dolls); the control group of children did not watch such a video. Both groups of children were then sent into a room containing Bobo dolls, and the experimental group, who had seen the adult behavior, mimicked their elders by acting far more aggressively toward the dolls than the children in the control group. The experimental group had no previous associations of more aggressive behavior toward the dolls and no good feelings or motivations, let alone rewards, for such behavior. Rather, the children became more aggressive themselves simply because they were imitating what they had seen older people do.

▲ **Image 8.4** On Thursday, May 19, 2016, in the East Room of the White House, President Barack Obama awarded the National Medal of Science to Dr. Albert Bandura, Stanford University, California. He is considered the key proponent of the learning theory of modeling and imitation affecting human behavior.

SOURCE: © Getty Images / NICHOLAS KAMM / Staff

Bandura's findings have important implications for the modeling behavior of adults (and peers) and for the influence of television, movies, video games, and other factors. Furthermore, the influences demonstrated by Bandura supported a phenomenon commonplace in everyday life. Mimicking is the source of fashion trends—wearing low-slung pants or baseball hats turned a certain way. Styles tend to ebb and flow based on how some respected person (often a celebrity) wears clothing. This can be seen very early in life; parents must be careful what they say and do because their children, as young as 2 years old, imitate what their parents do. This continues throughout life, especially in the teenage years as young persons imitate the cool trends and styles as well as behaviors. Of course, sometimes this behavior is illegal, but individuals are often simply mimicking the way their friends or others are behaving with little regard for potential rewards or punishments. Ultimately, Bandura's theory of modeling and imitation adds a great deal of explanation to a model of learning, and differential reinforcement theory includes such influences, whereas Sutherland's model of differential association does not, largely because the psychological perspective had not yet been developed.

Burgess and Akers's theory of differential reinforcement has also been the target of criticism by theorists and researchers. Perhaps the most important criticism of differential reinforcement theory is that it appears *tautological*, meaning that the variables and measures used to test its validity are true by definition. To clarify, studies testing this theory have been divided into four groups based on variables or factors: associations, reinforcements, definitions, and modeling.

Some critics have noted that if individuals who report that they associate with those who offend are rewarded for offending, believe offending is good, and have seen many of their significant others offend, they will inevitably be more likely to offend. In other words, if your friends and family are doing it, there is little doubt that you will be doing it.[23] For example, critics would argue that a person who primarily hangs out with car thieves knows he will be rewarded for stealing cars, believes stealing cars is good and not immoral, and has observed many respected others stealing cars, will inevitably commit auto theft himself. However, it has been well argued that such criticisms of tautology are not valid because none of these factors necessarily makes offending by the respondent true by definition.[24]

Differential reinforcement theory has also faced the same criticism that was addressed to Sutherland's theory—namely, that delinquent associations may take place after criminal activity rather than before. However, Burgess and Akers's model clearly has this area of criticism covered in the sense that differential reinforcement includes what comes after the activity, not just what happens before it. Specifically, it addresses the rewards or punishments that follow criminal activity and whether those rewards come from friends, parents, or other members or institutions of society.

It is arguable that differential reinforcement theory may have the most empirical validity of any contemporary (nonintegrated) model of criminal offending, especially considering that studies have examined a variety of behaviors, ranging from drug use to property crimes to violence. The theoretical model has also been tested in samples across the United States as well as in other cultures, such as South Korea, with the evidence being quite supportive of the framework. Furthermore, a variety of age groups have been examined, ranging from teenagers to middle-aged adults to the elderly, with all studies providing support for the model.[25]

Specifically, researchers found that the major variables of the theory had a significant effect in explaining marijuana and alcohol use among adolescents.[26] The researchers concluded that the "study demonstrates that central learning concepts are amenable to meaningful questionnaire measurement and that social learning theory can be adequately tested with survey data."[27] Other studies have also supported the theory when attempting to understand delinquency, cigarette smoking, and drug use.[28] Therefore, the inclusion of three psychological learning models—namely, classical conditioning, operant conditioning, and modeling and imitation—appears to have made differential reinforcement one of the most valid theories of human behavior, especially in regard to crime.

[23]Mark Warr, "Parents, Peers, and Delinquency," *Social Forces* 72 (1993): 247–64; Mark Warr and Mark Stafford, "The Influence of Delinquent Peers: What They Think or What They Do?" *Criminology* 29 (1991): 851–66.

[24]Akers and Sellers, *Criminological Theories*, 98–101.

[25]See studies including Ronald Akers and Gang Lee, "A Longitudinal Test of Social Learning Theory: Adolescent Smoking," *Journal of Drug Issues* 26 (1996): 317–43; Ronald Akers and Gang Lee, "Age, Social Learning, and Social Bonding in Adolescent Substance Abuse," *Deviant Behavior* 19 (1999): 1–25; Ronald Akers and Anthony J. La Greca, "Alcohol Use among the Elderly: Social Learning, Community Context, and Life Events," in *Society, Culture, and Drinking Patterns Re-examined*, ed. David J. Pittman and Helene Raskin White (New Brunswick, NJ: Rutgers Center of Alcohol Studies, 1991), 242–62; Sunghyun Hwang, "Substance Use in a Sample of South Korean Adolescents: A Test of Alternative Theories" (doctoral dissertation, Ann Arbor, MI: University Microfilms, 2000); and Sunghyun Hwang and Ronald Akers, "Adolescent Substance Use in South Korea: A Cross-Cultural Test of Three Theories," in *Social Learning Theory and the Explanation of Crime: A Guide for the New Century*, ed. Ronald Akers and Gary F. Jensen (New Brunswick, NJ: Transaction, 2003).

[26]Ronald Akers et al., "Social Learning and Deviant Behavior: A Specific Test of a General Theory," *American Sociological Review* 44 (1979): 638.

[27]Akers et al., "Social Learning and Deviant Behavior," 651.

[28]Richard Lawrence, "School Performance, Peers and Delinquency: Implications for Juvenile Justice," *Juvenile and Family Court Journal* 42 (1991): 59–69; Marvin Krohn et al., "Social Learning Theory and Adolescent Cigarette Smoking: A Longitudinal Study," *Social Problems* 32 (1985): 455–71; L. Thomas Winfree, Christine Sellers, and Dennis Clason, "Social Learning and Adolescent Deviance Abstention: Toward Understanding the Reasons for Initiating, Quitting, and Avoiding Drugs," *Journal of Quantitative Criminology* 9 (1993): 101–23; Akers and Lee, "A Longitudinal Test."

Neutralization Theory

Neutralization theory is associated with Gresham Sykes and David Matza's techniques of neutralization[29] and Matza's drift theory.[30] Like Sutherland, both Sykes and Matza thought that social learning influences delinquent behavior, but they also asserted that most criminals hold conventional beliefs and values. Specifically, Sykes and Matza argued that most criminals are still partially committed to the dominant social order. According to Sykes and Matza, youths are not immersed in a subculture that is committed to either extreme: complete conformity or complete nonconformity. Rather, these individuals vacillate, or drift, between these two extremes and are in a state of *transience.*[31]

While remaining partially committed to the conventional social order, youths can drift into criminal activity, Sykes and Matza claimed, and avoid feelings of guilt for these actions by justifying or rationalizing their behavior. This typically occurs in the teenage years, when social controls (parents, family, etc.) are at their weakest point and peer pressures and associations are at their highest level. Why is this called neutralization theory? The answer is that people justify and rationalize behavior through neutralizing it or making it appear not so serious. They make up situational excuses for behavior that they know is wrong to alleviate the guilt they feel for doing such immoral acts. In many ways, this resembles Freud's defense mechanisms, which allow us to forgive ourselves for the bad things we do even when we know they are wrong. The specific techniques of neutralization outlined by Sykes and Matza in 1957 are much like excuses for inappropriate behavior.

Techniques of Neutralization

Sykes and Matza identified methods or techniques of neutralization[32] that people use to justify their criminal behavior. These techniques allow people to neutralize or rationalize their criminal and delinquent acts by making themselves look as though they are conforming to the rules of conventional society. If individuals can create such rationalizations, then they are free to engage in criminal activities without serious damage to their consciences or self-images. According to Sykes and Matza, there are five common techniques of neutralization:

1. *Denial of responsibility*: Individuals may claim they were influenced by forces outside themselves and that they are not responsible or accountable for their behavior. For example, many youths blame their peers for their own behavior.
2. *Denial of injury*: This is the rationalization that no one was actually hurt by the offender's behavior. For instance, if someone steals from a store, he or she may rationalize this by saying that the store has insurance, so there is no direct victim.
3. *Denial of the victim*: Offenders see themselves as avengers and the victims as the wrongdoers. For example, some offenders believe that a person who disrespects or "disses" them deserves what he or she gets, even if it means serious injury.
4. *Condemnation of the condemners*: Offenders claim that the condemners (usually the authorities who catch them) are hypocrites. For instance, one may claim that police speed on the highway all the time, so everyone else is entitled to drive higher than the speed limit.

---

[29]Gresham M. Sykes and David Matza, "Techniques of Neutralization: A Theory of Delinquency," *American Sociological Review* 22 (1957): 664–70.

[30]David Matza, *Delinquency and Drift* (New York: Wiley, 1964).

[31]Ibid., 28.

[32]Sykes and Matza, "Techniques of Neutralization."

5. *Appeal to higher loyalties*: Offenders often overlook the norms of conventional society in favor of the rules of a belief they have or of a group to which they belong. For example, people who kill doctors who perform abortions tend to see their crimes as above the law because they are serving a higher power.

Although Sykes and Matza specifically labeled only five techniques of neutralization, it should be clear that there may be endless excuses people make up to rationalize behaviors they know are wrong. Techniques of neutralization have been applied to white-collar crime, for example. Several studies have examined the tendency to use such excuses to alleviate guilt for engaging in illegal corporate crime; they point out new types of excuses white-collar criminals use to justify their acts, techniques that were not discussed in Sykes and Matza's original formulation.[33]

Studies that have attempted to empirically test neutralization theory are, at best, inconsistent. For example, Agnew argued that there are essentially two general criticisms of studies that support neutralization theory.[34] First, theorists and researchers have noted that some neutralization techniques are much more difficult to measure than commitment to unconventional attitudes or norms.[35] The second major criticism is the concern that criminals may not use techniques of neutralization prior to committing a criminal offense but rather only after committing a crime. As estimated by previous studies, temporal ordering can be problematic in terms of causal implications when neutralization follows a criminal act.[36] This temporal ordering problem results from research conducted at a single point in time. Some would argue that the temporal ordering problem is not a major criticism because individuals may be predisposed to make up such rationalizations for their behavior regardless of whether they do it before or after the act of offending. Such a propensity may be related to low self-control theory, which we will examine later in this section.

Summary of Learning Theories

Learning theories tend to emphasize the social processes of how and why individuals learn criminal behavior. These theories also focus on the impact of significant others involved in the socialization process, such as family, friends, and teachers. Ultimately, empirical research has shown that learning theories are key in our understanding of criminal behavior, particularly in terms of whether criminal behavior is rewarded or punished. In summary, if individuals are taught and rewarded for performing criminal acts by the people they interact with on a day-to-day basis, they will in all likelihood engage in illegal activity.

Control Theories

The learning theories discussed in the previous section assume that individuals are born with a conforming disposition. By contrast, control theories assume that all people would naturally commit crimes if it weren't for restraints on their innate selfish tendencies. Social control perspectives of criminal behavior thus assume that there is some type

[33]For a review and a study on this topic, see Nicole Piquero, Stephen Tibbetts, and Michael Blankenship, "Examining the Role of Differential Association and Techniques of Neutralization in Explaining Corporate Crime," *Deviant Behavior* 26 (2005): 159–88. See also Lynne Vieraitis et al., "Do Women and Men Differ in Their Neutralizations of Corporate Crime?" *Criminal Justice Review* 37 (2012): 478–93.

[34]Robert Agnew, "The Techniques of Neutralization and Violence," *Criminology* 32 (1994): 563–64.

[35]W. William Minor, "The Neutralization of Criminal Offense," *Criminology* 18 (1980): 116; W. William Minor, "Neutralization as a Hardening Process: Considerations in the Modeling of Change," *Social Forces* 62 (1984): 995–1019. See also Roy L. Austin, "Commitment, Neutralization, and Delinquency," in *Juvenile Delinquency: Little Brother Grows Up*, ed. Theodore N. Ferdinand (Beverly Hills, CA: Sage, 1977); and Quint C. Thurman, "Deviance and the Neutralization of Moral Commitment: An Empirical Analysis," *Deviant Behavior* 5 (1984): 291–304.

[36]Travis Hirschi, *Causes of Delinquency* (Berkeley: University of California Press, 1969), 207. See also Mark Pogrebin, Eric Poole, and Amos Martinez, "Accounts of Professional Misdeeds: The Sexual Exploitation of Clients by Psychotherapists," *Deviant Behavior* 13 (1992): 229–52; and John Hamlin, "The Misplaced Concept of Rational Choice in Neutralization Theory," *Criminology* 26 (1988): 425–38.

Figure 8.1 • Frequencies of hitting, biting, and kicking at ages 2 to 12 years

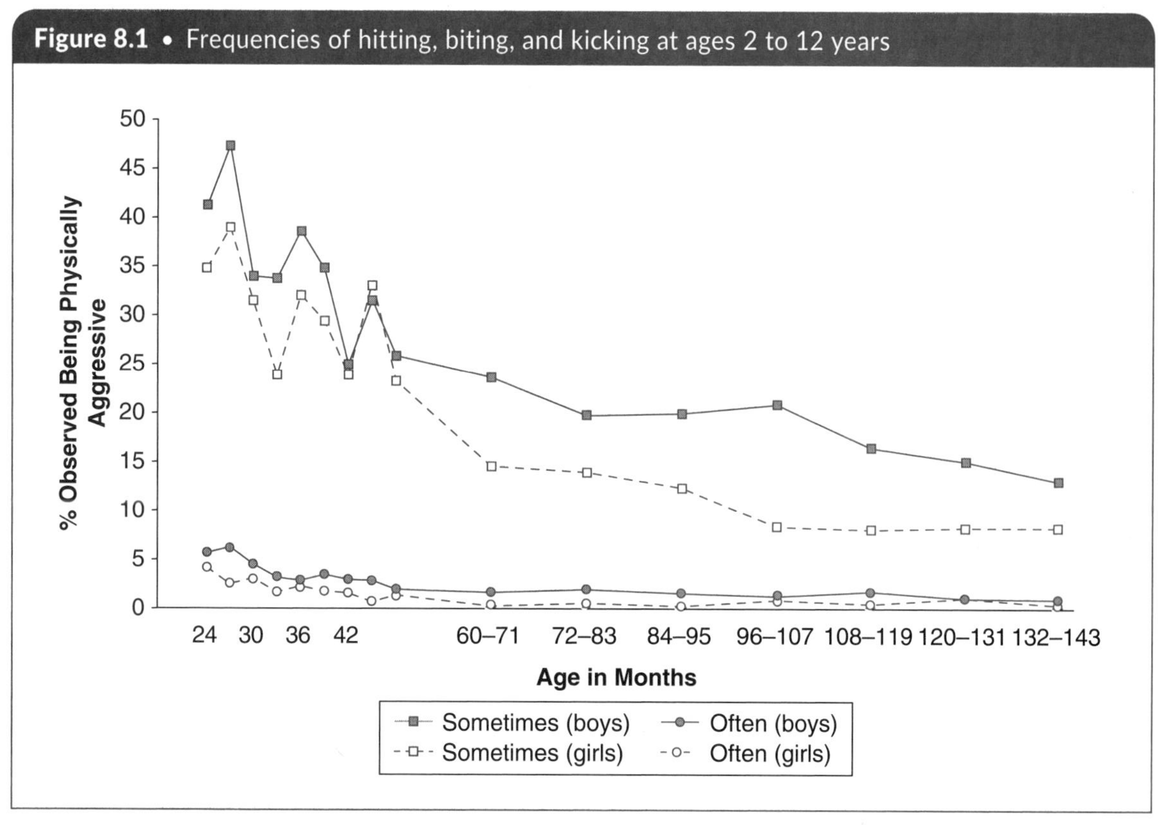

of basic human nature and that all human beings exhibit antisocial tendencies. Such theories are concerned with why individuals don't commit crime or deviant behaviors. Control theorists ask questions like this: What is it about society and human interaction that causes people not to act on their impulses?

The assumption that people have innate antisocial tendencies is a controversial one because it is nearly impossible to test. Nevertheless, some recent evidence supports the idea that human beings are inherently selfish and antisocial by nature. Specifically, researchers have found that most individuals are oriented toward selfish and aggressive behaviors at an early age, with such behaviors peaking at the end of the second year (see Figure 8.1).[37]

An example of antisocial dispositions appearing early in life was reported by Richard Tremblay and David LeMarquand, who found that most young children's (particularly boys') aggressive behaviors peaked at age 27 months. These behaviors included hitting, biting, and kicking others.[38] Their research is not isolated; virtually all developmental experts acknowledge that toddlers exhibit a tendency to show aggressive behavior toward others. This line of research would seem to support the notion that people are predisposed toward antisocial, even criminal, behavior.

---

[37]Michael Lewis, Steven Alessandri, and Margaret Sullivan, "Expectancy, Loss of Control, and Anger in Young Infants," *Developmental Psychology* 25 (1990): 745–51; Albert Restoin et al., "New Data on the Development of Communication Behavior in the Young Child with His Peers," *Recherches de Psychologie Sociale* 5 (1985): 31–56; Richard Tremblay et al., "The Search for the Age of 'Onset' of Physical Aggression: Rousseau and Bandura Revisited," *Criminal Behaviour and Mental Health* 9 (1999): 8–23.

[38]Richard Tremblay and David LeMarquand, "Individual Risk and Protective Factors," in *Child Delinquents: Development, Intervention, and Service Needs*, ed. Rolf Loeber and David Farrington (London: Sage, 2001): 137–64.

Control theorists do not necessarily assume that people are predisposed toward crime in a way that remains constant throughout life. On the contrary, research shows that most individuals begin to desist from such behaviors starting at around age two. This trend continues until approximately age 5, wherein only the most aggressive individuals (i.e., chronic offenders) continue such behavior at higher ages.

It is important to note that, at the same time selfish and aggressive behaviors decline, self-consciousness is formed. In addition, social emotions—such as shame, guilt, empathy, and pride—begin to appear.[39] This observation is critical because it is what separates control theories from the Classical School of criminology and the predispositional theories that we already discussed. According to control theories, without appropriate socialization, people act on their preprogrammed tendency toward crime and deviance.

In short, control theories claim that all individuals have natural tendencies to commit selfish, antisocial, and even criminal behavior. So, what is it that curbs this natural propensity? Many experts believe the best explanation is that individuals are socialized and controlled by social attachments and investments in conventional society. This assumption regarding the vital importance of early socialization is probably the primary reason why control theories are currently the most popular and accepted theories among criminologists.[40] We will now discuss several early examples of these control theories.

Early Control Theories of Human Behavior

Thomas Hobbes

Control theories are found in a variety of disciplines, including biology, psychology, and sociology. Perhaps the earliest significant use of social control in explaining deviant behavior is found in a perspective offered by the 17th-century Enlightenment philosopher Thomas Hobbes (see Section II). Hobbes claimed that the natural state of humanity is one of selfishness and self-centeredness to the point of constant chaos, characterized by a state of warfare between individuals. He stated that all individuals are inherently disposed to take advantage of others in order to improve their own personal well-being.[41]

However, Hobbes also claimed that the constant fear created by such selfishness results in humans rationally coming together to create binding contracts that will keep individuals from violating others' rights. Even with such controlling arrangements, however, Hobbes was clear that the selfish tendencies people exhibit can never be extinguished. In fact, they explain why punishments are necessary to maintain an established social contract among people.

Durkheim's Idea of Awakened Reflection and Collective Conscience

Consistent with Hobbes's view of individuals as naturally selfish, Émile Durkheim later proposed a theory of social control in the late 1800s that suggested that humans have no internal mechanism to let them know when they are fulfilled.[42] To this end, Durkheim coined the terms *automatic spontaneity* and *awakened reflection.* Automatic spontaneity can be understood with reference to animals' eating habits. Specifically, animals stop eating when they are full, and they are content until they are hungry again; they don't start hunting right after they have filled their stomachs with food. In contrast, awakened reflection concerns the fact that humans do not have such an

---

[39]For reviews of supporting studies, see June Price Tangney and K. W. Fischer, *Self-Conscious Emotions: The Psychology of Shame, Guilt, Embarrassment, and Pride* (New York: Guilford Press, 1995); and Michael Lewis, *Shame: The Exposed Self* (New York: Macmillan, 1992).

[40]Walsh and Ellis, "Political Ideology."

[41]Thomas Hobbes, *Leviathan* (1651; repr., Cambridge: Cambridge University Press, 1904).

[42]Émile Durkheim, *The Division of Labor in Society* (1893; repr., New York: Free Press, 1965); Émile Durkheim, *Suicide* (1897; repr., New York: Free Press, 1951) (see chap. 6, n. 18).

internal, regulatory mechanism. That is because people often acquire resources beyond what is immediately required. Durkheim went so far as to say that "our capacity for feeling is in itself an insatiable and bottomless abyss."[43] This is one of the reasons that Durkheim believed crime and deviance are quite normal, even essential, in any society.

Durkheim's awakened reflection has become commonly known as greed. People tend to favor better conditions and additional fulfillment because they apparently have no biological or psychological mechanism to limit such tendencies. As Durkheim noted, the selfish desires of humankind "are unlimited so far as they depend on the individual alone. . . . The more one has, the more one wants."[44] Thus, society must step in and provide the regulative force that keeps humans from acting too selfishly.

One of the primary elements of this regulative force is the *collective conscience*, which is the extent of similarities or likenesses that people share. For example, almost everyone can agree that homicide is a serious and harmful act that should be avoided in any civilized society. The notion of collective conscience can be seen as an early form of the idea of social bonding, which has become one of the dominant theories in criminology.[45]

According to Durkheim, the collective conscience serves many functions in society. One such function is the establishment of rules that keep individuals from following their natural tendencies toward selfish behavior. Durkheim also believed that crime allows people to unite together in opposition against deviants. In other words, crime and deviance allow conforming individuals to be bonded together in opposition against a common enemy, as can be seen in everyday life when groups come together to face opposition. This enemy consists of the deviants who have not internalized the code of the collective conscience.

Many of Durkheim's ideas hold true today. Just recall a traumatic incident you may have experienced with other strangers (e.g., being stuck in an elevator during a power outage, weathering a serious storm, or being involved in a traffic accident). Incidents such as these bring people together and permit a degree of bonding that would not take place in everyday life. Crime, Durkheim argued, serves a similar function.

How is all of this relevant today? Most control theorists claim that individuals commit crime and deviant acts not because they are lacking in any way but because certain controls have been weakened in their development. This assumption is consistent with Durkheim's theory, which we discussed previously (see Section VI).

Freud's Concepts of the Id, Superego, and Ego

Although psychoanalytic theory would seem to have few similarities with sociological positivistic theory, in this case, it is extremely complementary. One of Freud's most essential propositions is that all individuals are born with a tendency toward inherent drives and selfishness due to the **id** domain of the psyche (see Figure 8.2).[46] According to Freud, all people are born with equal amounts of id drives (e.g., libido, food) and motivations toward selfishness and greed. Freud said this inherent selfish tendency must be countered by controls produced from the development of the **superego**, which is the subconscious domain of the psyche that contains our conscience. According to Freud, the superego is formed through the interactions between a young infant or child and his or her significant others. As you can see, the control perspective has a long history in many philosophical and scientific disciplines.

---

[43]Durkheim, *Suicide*, 246–47. Also, much of this discussion is adapted from Raymond Paternoster and Ronet Bachman, *Explaining Criminals and Crime* (Los Angeles: Roxbury, 2001) (see chap. 5, n. 10).

[44]Durkheim, *Suicide*, 254.

[45]A good discussion of Durkheim's concepts, particularly that of the collective conscience, can be found in Bernard et al., *Vold's Theoretical Criminology*, 124–39 (see chap. 2).

[46]Sigmund Freud, "The Ego and the Id," in *The Complete Psychological Works of Sigmund Freud*, Vol. 19, ed. James Strachey (1923; repr., London: Hogarth Press, 1959).

Figure 8.2 • Freud's model of the three domains of the psyche

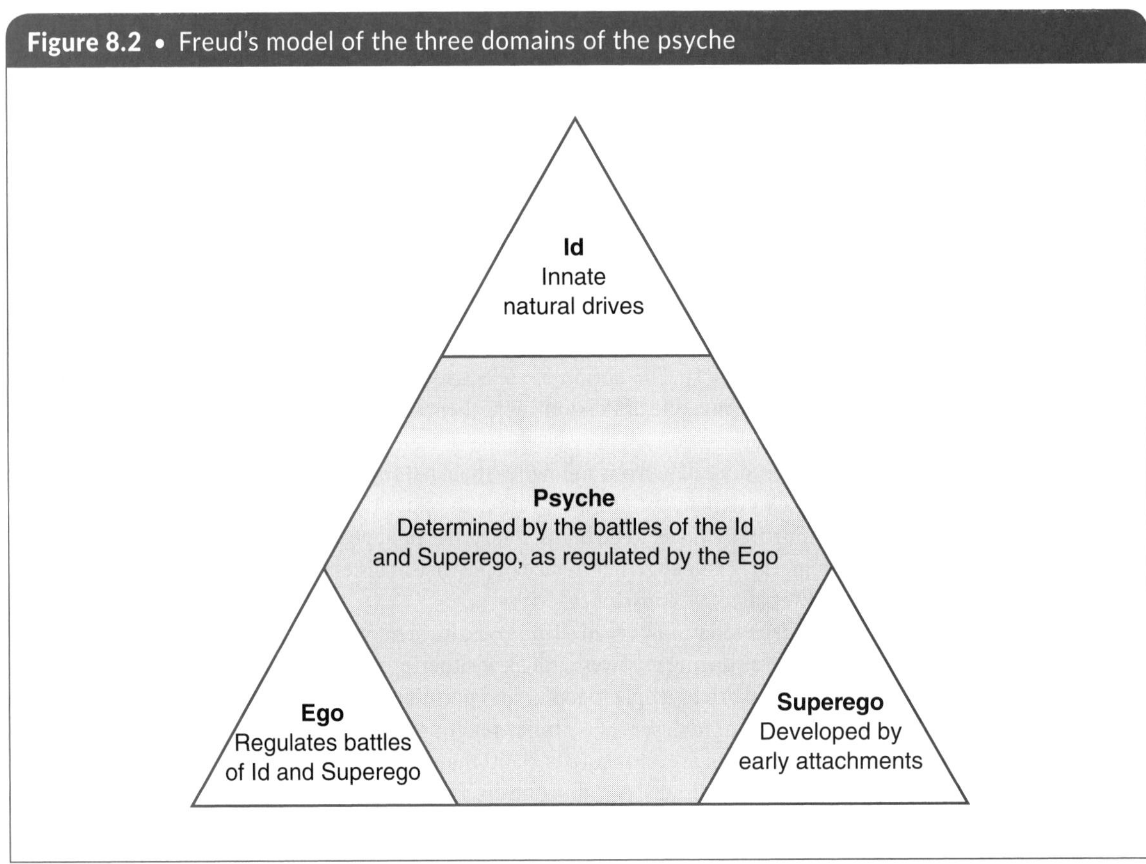

These two drives of the subconscious domains of the id and superego are regulated, Freud thought, by the only conscious domain of the psyche: the **ego**. This ego mediates the battles between our innate drives (id) and our socialized constraints (superego); it represents our personality. There have been a number of applications of Freud's theoretical model to criminality, such as the concept of a deficient superego (due to a lack of early attachments) or a weak ego (which fails to properly regulate the battle between the id and superego). The main point is that Freud was an early control theorist and that his theoretical model was highly influential among psychologists in the early 1900s as they tried to determine why certain individuals committed criminal offenses.[47]

Early Control Theories of Crime

Throughout the 1950s and 1960s, criminologists borrowed and built on some of the ideas just discussed. Until that time, most research in the criminological literature was dominated by the learning theories discussed earlier in this section, or social structure theories such as the Chicago School or Merton's strain theory (see Sections VI and VII). While early control theories may not be particularly popular in this day and age, they were vitally important in the sense that they laid the groundwork for future theoretical development.

[47]Ibid.

Reiss's Control Theory

One of the first control theories of crime was proposed by Albert Reiss in 1951. Reiss claimed that delinquency was a consequence of weak ego or superego controls among juvenile probationers.[48] Reiss found no explicit motivation for delinquent activity. Rather, he thought it would occur in the absence of controls or restraints against such behavior.

Like Freud, Reiss believed that the family was the primary source through which deviant predispositions were discouraged. Furthermore, Reiss claimed that a sound family environment would provide for an individual's needs and the essential emotional bonds that are so important in socializing individuals. Another important factor in Reiss's model was close supervision, not only by the family but also by the community. He said that individuals must be closely monitored for delinquent behavior and adequately disciplined when they break the rules.

Personal factors, such as the ability to restrain one's impulses and delay gratification, were also important in Reiss's framework. These concepts are very similar to later, more modern concepts of control theory, which have been consistently supported by empirical research.[49] For this reason, Reiss was ahead of his time when he first proposed his control theory. Although the direct tests of Reiss's theory have provided only partial support for it, his influence is apparent in many contemporary criminological theories.[50]

Toby's Concept of Stake in Conformity

Soon after Reiss's theory was presented, a similar theory was developed. In 1957, Jackson Toby proposed a theory of delinquency and gangs.[51] He claimed that individuals were more inclined to act on their natural inclinations when the controls on them were weak. Like most other control theorists, Toby claimed that such inclinations toward deviance were distributed equally across all individuals. Furthermore, he emphasized the concept of a **stake in conformity** that supposedly prevents most people from committing crime. The stake in conformity Toby was referring to is the extent to which individuals have investments in conventional society. In other words, how much is a person willing to risk when he or she violates the law?

Studies have shown that stake in conformity is one of the most influential factors in individuals' decisions to offend. People who have nothing to lose are much more likely to take risks and violate others' rights than those who have relatively more invested in social institutions.[52]

One distinguishing feature of Toby's theory is his emphasis on peer influences in terms of both motivating and inhibiting antisocial behavior depending on whether most peers have low or high stakes in conformity. Toby's stake in conformity has been used effectively in subsequent control theories of crime.

Nye's Control Theory

A year after Toby introduced the stake in conformity, F. Ivan Nye proposed a relatively comprehensive control theory that placed a strong focus on the family.[53] Following the assumptions of early control theorists, Nye claimed that

---

[48]Albert Reiss, "Delinquency as the Failure of Personal and Social Controls," *American Sociological Review* 16 (1951): 196–207.

[49]For a comprehensive review of studies of low self-control, see Travis Pratt and Frank Cullen, "The Empirical Status of Gottfredson and Hirschi's General Theory of Crime: A Meta-analysis," *Criminology* 38 (2000): 931–64.

[50]See Bernard et al., *Vold's Theoretical Criminology*, 202–3.

[51]Jackson Toby, "Social Disorganization and Stake in Conformity: Complementary Factors in the Predatory Behavior of Hoodlums," *Journal of Criminal Law, Criminology, and Police Science* 48 (1957): 12–17.

[52]Hirschi, *Causes of Delinquency*; Robert Sampson and John Laub, *Crime in the Making: Pathways and Turning Points in Life* (Cambridge, MA: Harvard University Press, 1993).

[53]F. Ivan Nye, *Family Relationships and Delinquent Behavior* (New York: Wiley, 1958).

there was no significant positive force that caused delinquency because such antisocial tendencies are universal and would be found in virtually everyone if not for certain controls usually found in the home.

Nye's theory consisted of three primary components of control. The first component was internal control, which is formed through social interaction. This socialization, he claimed, assists in the development of a conscience. Nye further claimed that if individuals are not given adequate resources and care, they will follow their natural tendencies toward doing what is necessary to protect their interests.

Nye's second component of control was direct control, which consists of a wide range of constraints on individual propensities to commit deviant acts. Direct control includes numerous types of sanctions, such as jail and ridicule, and the restriction of one's chances to commit criminal activity. Nye's third component of control was indirect control, which occurs when individuals are strongly attached to their early caregivers. For most children, it is through an intense and strong relationship with their parents or guardians that they establish an attachment to conventional society. However, Nye suggested that when the needs of an individual are not met by their caregivers, inappropriate behavior can result.

As shown in Figure 8.3, Nye predicted a U-shaped curve of parental controls in predicting delinquency. Specifically, he argued that either no controls (i.e., complete freedom) or too much control (i.e., no freedom at all) would predict the most chronic delinquency. He believed that a healthy balance of freedom and parental control was the best strategy for inhibiting criminal activity. Some recent research supports Nye's prediction.[54] Contemporary control theories, such as Charles Tittle's control–balance theory, draw heavily on Nye's idea of having a healthy balance of controls and freedom.[55]

Figure 8.3 • Nye's control theory

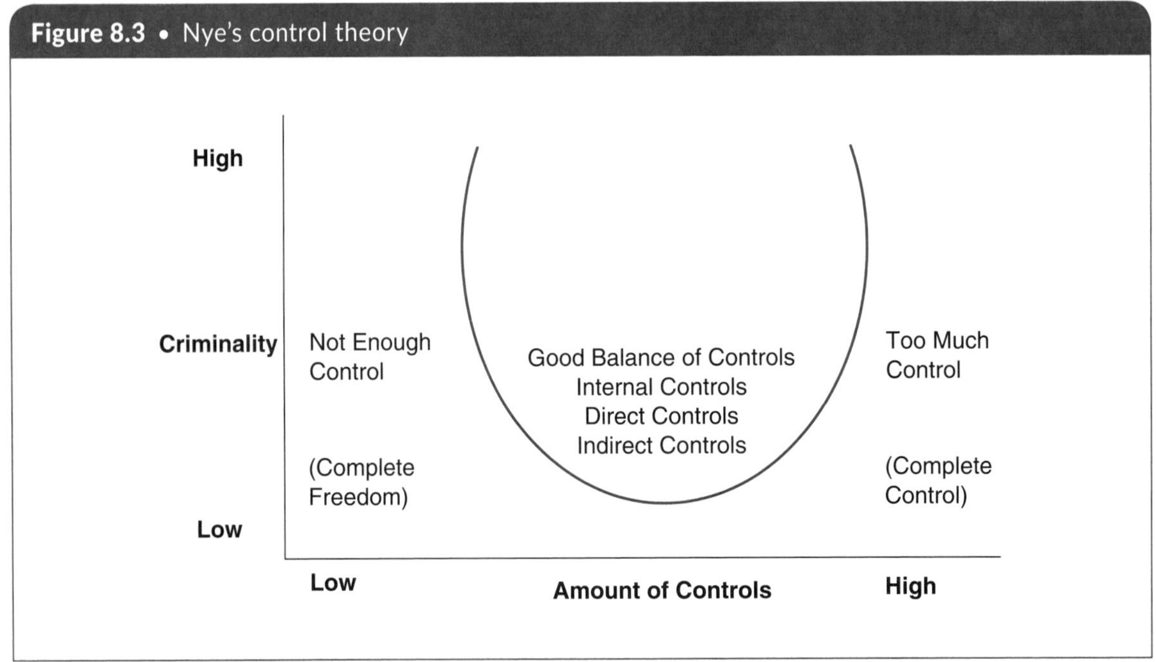

[54]Ruth Seydlitz, "Complexity in the Relationships among Direct and Indirect Parental Controls and Delinquency," *Youth and Society* 24 (1993): 243–75.

[55]Charles Tittle, *Control Balance: Toward a General Theory of Deviance* (Boulder, CO: Westview, 1995).

Reckless's Containment Theory

Another control theory, known as **containment theory**, has been proposed by Walter Reckless.[56] This theory emphasizes both inner containment and outer containment, which can be viewed as internal and external controls. Reckless broke from traditional assumptions of social control theories by identifying predictive factors that push or pull individuals toward antisocial behavior. However, the focus of his theory remained on the controlling elements, which can be seen in the emphasis placed on containment in the theory's name.

Reckless claimed that individuals can be pushed into delinquency by their social environment, such as by a lack of opportunities for education or employment. Furthermore, he pointed out that some individual factors, such as brain disorders or risk-taking personalities, could push some people to commit criminal behavior. Reckless also noted that some individuals could be pulled into criminal activity by hanging out with delinquent peers, watching too much violence on television, and so on. All told, Reckless went beyond the typical control theory assumption of inborn tendencies. In addition to these natural dispositions toward deviant behavior, containment theory proposes that extra pushes and pulls can motivate people to commit crime.

Reckless further claimed that the pushes and pulls toward criminal behavior could be enough to force individuals into criminal activity unless they are sufficiently contained or controlled. Reckless claimed that such containment should be both internal and external. By *internal containment*, he meant building a person's sense of self, which helps the person resist the temptations of criminal activity. According to Reckless, other forms of internal containment include the ability to internalize societal norms. With respect to *external containment*, Reckless claimed that social organizations, such as school, church, and other institutions, are essential in building bonds that inhibit individuals from being pushed or pulled into criminal activity.

Reckless offered a visual image of containment theory, which we present in Figure 8.4. The outer circle (Circle 1) in the figure represents the social realm of pressures and pulls (e.g., peer pressure), whereas the innermost circle (Circle 4) symbolizes a person's individual-level pushes to commit crime, such as predispositions or personality traits that are linked to crime. In between these two circles are the two layers of controls, external containment (Circle 2) and internal containment (Circle 3). The structure of Figure 8.4 and the examples included in each circle are those specifically noted by Reckless.[57]

While some studies have shown general support for containment theory, others offer more support for some components, such as internalization of rules, than for other factors, such as self-perception, in accounting for variations in delinquency.[58] External factors may be more important than internal ones. Furthermore, some studies have noted weaker support for Reckless's theory among minorities and females, who may be more influenced by their peers or other influences. Thus, the model appears to be most valid for White males—at least according to empirical studies.[59]

One of the problems with containment theory is that it does not go far enough toward specifying the factors that are important in predicting criminality, especially regarding specific groups of individuals. For example, an infinite number of concepts could potentially be categorized either as a push or pull toward criminality or as an inner or outer containment of criminality. Thus, the theory could be considered too broad or vague and not specific enough to be of practical value. To Reckless's credit, however, containment theory has increased the exposure of control

---

[56]Walter Reckless, *The Crime Problem*, 4th ed. (New York: Appleton-Century-Crofts, 1967).

[57]Ibid., 479.

[58]Richard Lawrence, "School Performance, Containment Theory, and Delinquent Behavior," *Youth and Society* 7 (1985): 69–95; Richard A. Dodder and Janet R. Long, "Containment Theory Reevaluated: An Empirical Explication," *Criminal Justice Review* 5 (1980): 74–84.

[59]William E. Thompson and Richard A. Dodder, "Containment Theory and Juvenile Delinquency: A Reevaluation through Factor Analysis," *Adolescence* 21 (1986): 365–76.

Figure 8.4 • Reckless's containment theory

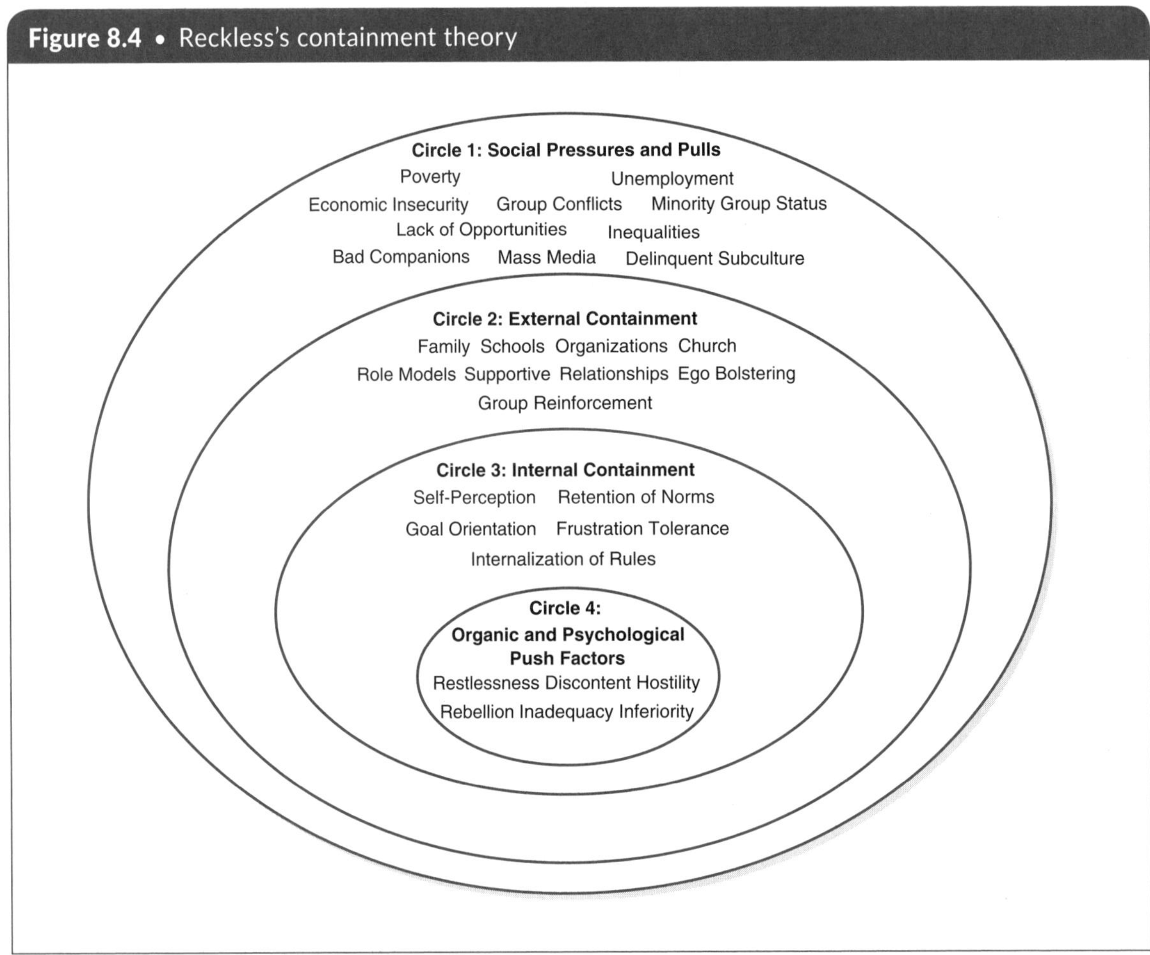

theories of criminal behavior. And although support for containment theory has been mixed, there is no doubt that it has influenced other, more recent control theories.[60]

Modern Social Control Theories

As the previous sections attest, control theory has been around in various forms for some time. Modern social control theories build on these earlier versions and add levels of depth and sophistication. Two modern social control theories are Matza's drift theory and Hirschi's social bonding theory.

Matza's Drift Theory

The theory of drift, or **drift theory**, presented by Matza in 1964, claims that individuals offend at certain times in their lives when social controls—such as parental supervision, employment, and family ties—are weakened.[61]

---

[60]Akers, *Criminological Theories*, 3rd ed., 103–4.

[61]Matza, *Delinquency and Drift.*

Figure 8.5 • Matza's theory of drift

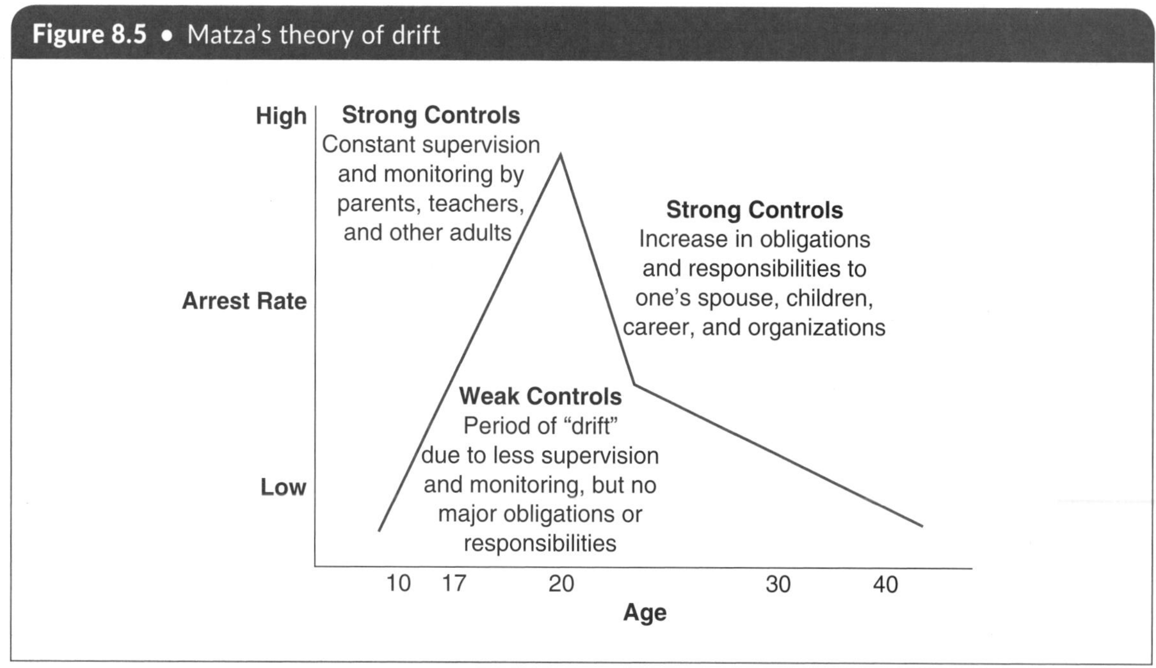

In developing his theory, Matza criticized earlier theories and their tendency to predict too much crime. For example, the Chicago School would incorrectly predict that all individuals in bad neighborhoods will commit crime. Likewise, strain theory predicts that all poor individuals will commit crime. Obviously, this is not true. Thus, Matza claimed, there is a degree of determinism (i.e., Positive School) in human behavior but also a significant amount of free will (i.e., Classical School). He called this perspective **soft determinism**, which is the gray area between free will and determinism. This is illustrated in Figure 8.5.

Returning to the basics of Matza's theory, he claimed that individuals offend at the time in life when social controls are most weakened. As is well known, social controls are most weakened for most individuals during the teenage years. At this time, parents and other caretakers stop having a constant supervisory role, and at the same time, teenagers generally do not have too many responsibilities—such as careers or children—that would inhibit them from experimenting with deviance. This is very consistent with the well-known age–crime relationship; most individuals who are arrested experience this in their teenage years.[62] Once sufficient ties are developed, people tend to mature out of criminal lifestyles.

Matza further claimed that when supervision is absent and ties are minimal, the majority of individuals are the most free to do what they want. Where, then, does the term *drift* come from? During the times when people have few ties and obligations, they will drift in and out of delinquency, Matza proposed. He pointed out that previous theories were unsuccessful in explaining this age–crime relationship:

[62] *OJJDP Statistical Briefing Book.* Unpublished arrest data for 1980–1997 from the Federal Bureau of Investigation for 1998, 1999, and 2000 from *Crime in the United States* reports (Washington, DC: Government Printing Office, 1999, 2000, and 2001, respectively).

> Most theories of delinquency take no account of maturational reform; those that do often do so at the expense of violating their own assumptions regarding the constrained delinquent.[63]

Matza insisted that drifting is not the same as a commitment to a life of crime. Instead, it is experimenting with questionable behavior and then rationalizing it. The way youths rationalize behavior that they know to be wrong is through learning the techniques of neutralization discussed earlier.

Drift theory goes on to say that individuals do not reject the conventional normative structure. On the contrary, much offending is based on neutralizing or adhering to **subterranean values**, which young people have been socialized to use as a means of circumventing conventional values. This is basically the same as asserting one's independence, which tends to occur with a vengeance during the teenage years.

Subterranean values are quite prevalent and underlie many aspects of our culture, which is why Matza's drift theory is also classified as a learning theory. For example, while it is conventional to believe that violence is wrong, boxing matches and sports that commonly lead to injury are some of the most popular spectator activities. Such phenomena create an atmosphere that readily allows neutralization or rationalization of criminal activity.

We will see other forms of subterranean values when we discuss risk-taking and low self-control later in this section. In many contexts, such as business, risk-taking and aggressiveness are seen as desirable characteristics, so many individuals are influenced by such subterranean values. This, according to Matza, adds to individuals' likelihood of drifting into crime and delinquency.

Matza's theory of drift seems sensible on its face, but empirical research examining the theory has shown mixed results.[64] One of the primary criticisms of Matza's theory, which even he acknowledged, is that it does not explain the most chronic offenders, the people who are responsible for the vast majority of serious, violent crimes. Chronic offenders often offend long before and well past their teenage years, which clearly limits the predictive value of Matza's theory.

Despite its shortcomings, Matza's drift theory appears to explain why many people offend exclusively during their teenage and young adult years but then grow out of it. Also, the theory is highly consistent with several of the ideas presented by control theorists, including the assumption that (a) selfish tendencies are universal, (b) these tendencies are inhibited by socialization and social controls, and (c) the selfish tendencies appear at times when controls are weakest. The theory goes beyond previous control theories by adding the concepts of soft determinism, neutralization, and subterranean values as well as the idea that, in many contexts, selfish and aggressive behaviors are not wrong but actually desirable.

Hirschi's Social Bonding Theory

Perhaps the most influential social control theory was presented by Hirschi in 1969.[65] Hirschi's model of **social bonding theory** takes an assumption from Durkheim that "we are all animals, and thus naturally capable of committing criminal acts."[66] However, as Hirschi acknowledged, most humans can be adequately socialized to become tightly bonded to conventional entities, such as families, schools, and communities. Hirschi said that the more strongly a person is bonded to conventional society, the less prone to engaging in crime he or she

[63]"Age-Arrest Rate Curve" is loosely based on data provided by the Federal Bureau of Investigation, *Crime in the United States* report (Washington, DC: Government Printing Office, 1997).

[64]See Bernard et al., *Vold's Theoretical Criminology*, 205–7.

[65]Hirschi, *Causes of Delinquency* (see chap. 6, n. 30).

[66]Ibid., 31, in which Hirschi cites Durkheim.

Figure 8.6 • Hirschi's social bonding theory

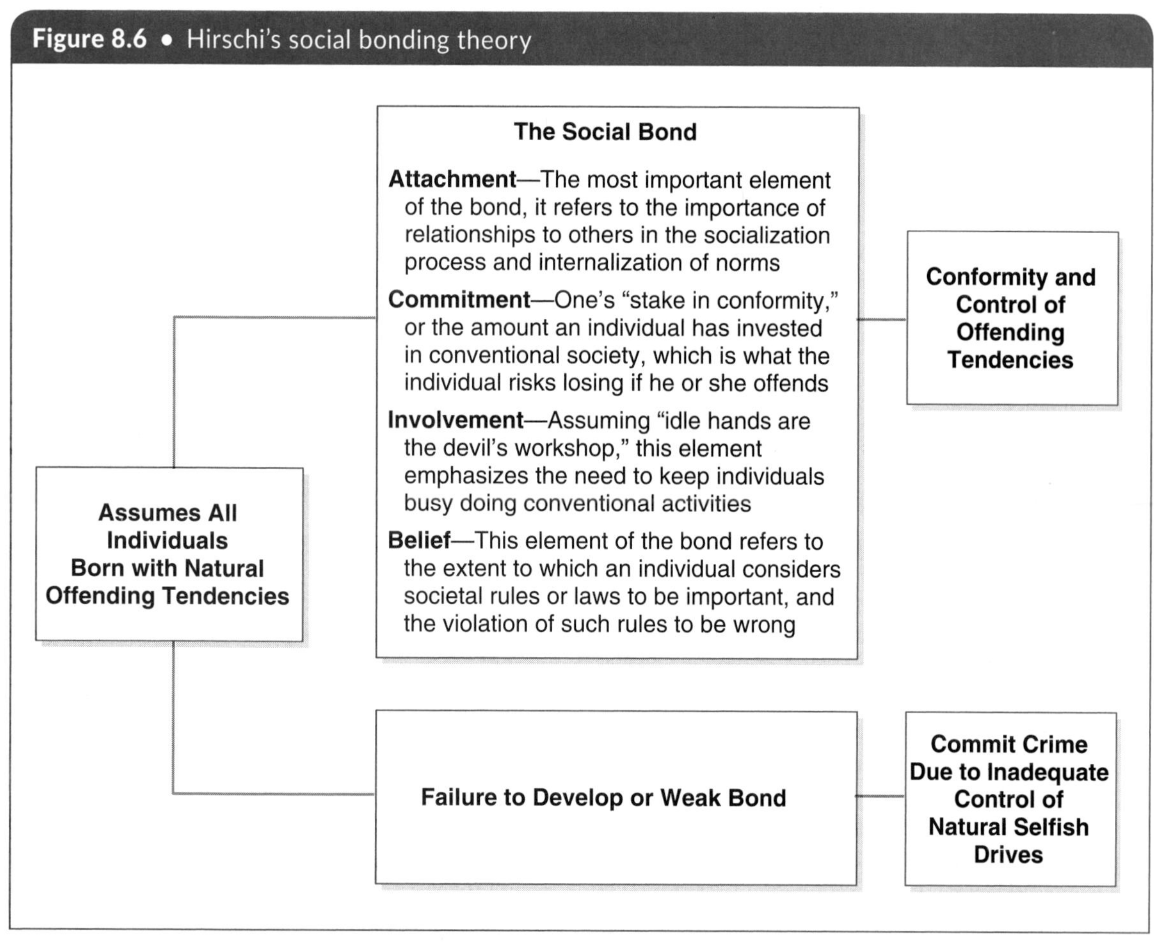

will be. More specifically, the stronger the social bond, the lower the likelihood that an individual will commit criminal offenses.

As shown in Figure 8.6, Hirschi's social bond is made up of four elements: (1) attachment, (2) commitment, (3) involvement, and (4) moral belief. The stronger or more developed the person is in each of the four elements, the lower the likelihood that he or she will commit crime. Let us now consider each element in detail.

The most important factor in the social bond is attachment, which consists of affectionate bonds between an individual and his or her significant others. Attachment is vitally important for the internalization of conventional values. Hirschi said, "The essence of internalization of norms, conscience, or superego thus lies in the attachment of the individual to others."[67] Hirschi made it clear, as did Freud, that strong, early attachments are the most important factor in developing a social bond. The other constructs in the social bond—commitment, involvement, and belief—are contingent on adequate attachment to others, he argued. That is, without healthy attachments, especially early in life, the probability of acting inappropriately increases.

Commitment, the second element of Hirschi's social bond, is the investment a person has in conventional society. This has been explained as one's stake in conformity, or what is at risk of being lost if one gets caught

[67]Ibid., 18.

committing crime. If people feel they have much to lose by committing crime, they will probably not do it. In contrast, if someone has nothing to lose, what is to prevent that person from doing something he or she may be punished for? The answer is, of course, not much. And this, some theorists claim, is why it is difficult to control so-called chronic offenders. Trying to instill a commitment to conventional society in such individuals is extremely difficult.

Another element of the social bond is involvement, which is the time spent in conventional activities. The assumption is that time spent in constructive activities will reduce time devoted to illegal behaviors. This element of the bond goes back to the old adage that "idle hands are the devil's workshop."[68] Hirschi claimed that participating in conventional activities can inhibit delinquent and criminal activity.

The last element of the social bond is beliefs, which have generally been interpreted as moral beliefs concerning the laws and rules of society. This is one of the most examined and consistently supported aspects of the social bond. Basically, individuals who feel that a course of action is against their moral beliefs are much less likely to pursue it than individuals who don't see a breach of morality in such behavior. For example, we all probably know some people who see drunk driving as a very serious offense because of the injury and death it can cause. However, we also probably know individuals who don't see a problem with such behavior. The same can be said about speeding in a car, shoplifting from a store, or using marijuana; people differ in their beliefs about most forms of criminal activity.

Hirschi's theory has been tested by numerous researchers and has, for the most part, been supported.[69] However, one criticism is that the components of the social bond may predict criminality only if they are defined in a certain way. For example, with respect to the involvement element of the bond, studies have shown that not all conventional activities are equal when it comes to preventing delinquency. Only academic or religious activities seem to have consistent effects in inhibiting delinquency. In contrast, many studies show that teenagers who date or play sports actually have an increased risk of committing crime.[70]

Another major criticism of Hirschi's theory is that the effect of attachment on crime depends on to whom one is attached. Studies have clearly and consistently shown that attachment to delinquent peers is a strong predictor of criminal activity.

Finally, some evidence indicates that social bonding theory may better explain why individuals start offending than why they continue or escalate in their offending. One reason for this is that Hirschi's theory does not elaborate on what occurs after an individual commits criminal activity. This is likely the primary reason why some of the more complex, integrated theories of crime often attribute the initiation of delinquency to a breakdown in the social bond. However, other theories (such as differential reinforcement) are typically seen as better predictors of what happens after the initial stages of the criminal career.[71]

Despite the criticism it has received, Hirschi's social bonding theory is still one of the most accepted theories of criminal behavior.[72] It is a relatively convincing explanation for criminality because of the consistent support that it has found among samples of people taken from all over the world.[73]

---

[68]Ibid., 22.

[69]For a review, see Akers, *Criminological Theories*, 3rd ed., 105–10.

[70]Ibid.

[71]Delbert Elliott, David Huizinga, and Suzanne Ageton, *Explaining Delinquency and Drug Use* (Beverly Hills, CA: Sage, 1985).

[72]Walsh and Ellis, "Political Ideology."

[73]Dennis Wong, "Pathways to Delinquency in Hong Kong and Guangzhou, South China," *International Journal of Adolescence and Youth* 10 (2001): 91–115; Alexander Vazsonyi and Martin Killias, "Immigration and Crime among Youth in Switzerland," *Criminal Justice and Behavior* 28 (2001): 329–66; Manuel Eisner, "Crime, Problem Drinking, and Drug Use: Patterns of Problem Behavior in Cross-National Perspective," *Annals of the American Academy of Political and Social Science* 580 (2002): 201–25.

Case Study: Jesse Pomeroy

Jesse Pomeroy

▲ **Image 8.5** Jesse Pomeroy.

SOURCE: © AP Photo

Jesse Pomeroy was born on November 29, 1859, in Charlestown, Massachusetts. His father, Thomas, was a violent alcoholic. He would often go on drinking binges and then proceed to beat his two sons, Charles and Jesse. Jesse's mother, Ruth Ann, eventually divorced Thomas in the 1870s; divorce was extremely uncommon during this time. In fact, Ruth Ann revealed that she divorced her husband after one of these brutal beatings:

> Jesse later admitted to his doctors that his father had made him go to his room and strip totally naked, whereupon Thomas had proceeded to lash out with a leather belt. . . . [Jesse] realized the beatings . . . were not that bad, not nearly as horrific as the relentless pummeling he had received almost four years earlier, when his father had taken Jesse, just eight years old, to an abandoned shed in the woods. There Thomas had become so enraged that the blows from a horsewhip had nearly killed his son.[74]

Ruth Ann realized that Jesse was a strong-willed boy. Jesse was often made fun of at school, primarily because of a deformity in his right eye. Jesse's teacher complained of his problem behavior at school. The teacher noted that he was a loner; he preferred to read cheap "dime novels." During this time, these novels were full of violence, sex, battles, and mayhem. Eventually, Ruth Ann was asked to remove her son from school.

Jesse's problems were not restricted to just school. His mother brought home two yellow canaries; she would come home looking forward to their chirping in the wooden cage. One afternoon, she came home to find the two canaries dead—their heads were twisted off their bodies. Prior to this, a neighbor had told Ruth Ann that her little kitten had gone missing. A few days later, Ruth Ann watched Jesse walking down a nearby street with the dead kitten in one hand and a kitchen knife in the other. In 1871, there were reports that children in the next city over, Chelsea, were being beaten by an older boy. Some of these children were sexually assaulted. The victims reported that this boy would offer them money and treats; then he would suggest they go to a remote locale. There he would abuse the children.[75] The newspapers referred to him as "The Boy Torturer" and "The Red Devil." After reading a description of this boy in the *Boston Globe*, Ruth Ann recognized this was her son; she moved her family to South Boston. In August 1872, a young boy was found tortured in South Boston; a month later, a child was found beaten, assaulted, and tied up to a telephone pole. This victim, however, was able to give a very detailed

(Continued)

[74]Roseanne Montillo, *The Wilderness of Ruin: A Tale of Madness, Fire, and the Hunt for America's Youngest Serial Killer* (New York: William Morrow, 2015), 18.

[75]Ibid.

(Continued)

description. This resulted in Jesse Pomeroy being arrested and sentenced to the State Reform School at Westborough for the remainder of his minor-status years (e.g., six years). Ruth Ann, however, diligently worked to have her son released earlier; Jesse was released months after.[76]

In March 1874, nine-year-old Katie Curran disappeared. During the investigation, it was revealed that the last place she had been seen was at the Pomeroys' shop; Jesse was interrogated, but there was no arrest at that time. In April, the body of four-year-old Horace Millen was found on the beach of Dorchester Bay. His throat had been cut and he had been stabbed 15 times; also, one of his eyes had been torn out. The police recalled the beatings of the other children two years earlier and arrested Jesse Pomeroy; he was 14 years old at the time. In July 1874, Jesse confessed to Horace Millen's murder. Jesse Pomeroy also confessed to the murder of Katie Curran. He had lured her into the basement of his mother's dress shop. He had then cut her throat and buried her body under an ash heap. When he was asked why he committed the murders, he stated, "I couldn't help it."[77] On September 7, 1876, Jesse Pomeroy was sentenced to death. Subsequently, his sentence was commuted to life in prison—solitary confinement. In 1916, he was released from solitary confinement and was allowed to mix with other prisoners at the Charlestown Prison. On September 29, 1932, he died at the age of 73 years.[78]

When he was asked why he committed the murders, he stated, "I couldn't help it."

Think About It

1. So why did he do it? As described by the theories presented in this section, specifically various social control theories (such as Hirschi's theory of social bonding) and socialization theories (e.g., differential association theory, differential reinforcement theory), it appears that Jesse Pomeroy never had much of a chance to form strong social bonds with conventional society, nor was he adequately socialized. To clarify, his father was abusive. He was considered a loner at school. He began early in life to demonstrate cruel behavior to animals. Thus, do you think Jesse Pomeroy engaged in such behaviors out of selfishness and personal satisfaction, and without any empathy for his victims, because that was what his experience in the world taught him to do?
2. If you maintain that Jesse had low self-control and therefore engaged in these behaviors, why did he have such low self-control?
3. What types of things could have been done to improve Jesse's low self-control?

Integrated Social Control Theories

Although we will review integrated theories in detail in Section XI, it is worthwhile to briefly discuss the two integrated models that most incorporate the control perspective into their frameworks. These two integrated

---

[76]"The Story of Jesse Pomeroy, 14-Year-Old Serial Killer," CBS News, March 13, 2015. http://www.cbsnews.com/news/the-story-of-jesse-pomeroy-14-year-old-serial-killer.

[77]"Jesse Pomeroy: The Boy Fiend," CelebrateBoston.com, n.d. http://www.celebrateboston.com/crime/jesse-pomeroy-serial-killer.htm.

[78]Thomas M. McDade, *The Annals of Murder* (Norman: University of Oklahoma Press, 1961).

models are control–balance theory and power–control theory. Both have received considerable attention in the criminological literature. Other integrated theories that incorporate control theory to a lesser extent include John Braithwaite's shaming theory and Sampson and Laub's life-course theory. These will be covered in more detail in Sections XI and XII.

Tittle's Control–Balance Theory

Presented by Tittle in 1995, **control–balance theory** proposes that (a) the amount of control to which one is subjected and (b) the amount of control one can exercise determine the probability that deviance will occur. The balance between these two types of control, he argued, can even predict the type of behavior that is likely to be committed.[79]

Tittle argued that a person is least likely to offend when he or she has a balance of controlling and being controlled. Furthermore, the likelihood of offending increases when these become unbalanced. If individuals are more controlled (Tittle called this *control deficit*), then the theory predicts that they will commit predatory or defiant acts. In contrast, if an individual possesses an excessive level of control (Tittle calls this *control surplus*), then he or she will be more likely to commit acts of exploitation or decadence. Note that excessive control is not the same as excessive self-control. Tittle argued that people who are controlling—that is, who have excessive control over others—will be predisposed toward inappropriate activities.

Initial empirical tests of control–balance theory have reported mixed results with both surpluses and deficits predicting the same types of deviance.[80] In addition, researchers have uncovered differing effects of the control–balance ratio on two types of deviance that are contingent on gender. This finding is consistent with the gender-specific support found for Reckless's containment theory, described earlier in this section.[81]

Hagan's Power–Control Theory

Power–control theory is an integrated theory that was proposed by John Hagan and his colleagues.[82] The primary focus of this theory is on the level of control and patriarchal attitudes, as well as structure in the household, which are influenced by parental positions in the workforce. Power–control theory assumes that mothers will be less likely to exert control on their daughters in households where the mothers and fathers have relatively similar levels of power at work (i.e., balanced households). These balanced households will be less likely to experience gender differences in the criminal offending of the children. However, households in which mothers and fathers have dissimilar levels of power in the workplace (i.e., unbalanced households) are more likely to suppress criminal activity in daughters. In addition, assertiveness and risky activity among the males in the house will be encouraged. This assertiveness and risky activity may be a precursor to crime.

---

[79]Tittle, *Control Balance.*

[80]Alex Piquero and Matthew Hickman, "An Empirical Test of Tittle's Control Balance Theory," *Criminology* 37 (1999): 319–42; Matthew Hickman and Alex Piquero, "Exploring the Relationships between Gender, Control Balance, and Deviance," *Deviant Behavior* 22 (2001): 323–51.

[81]Hickman and Piquero, "Exploring the Relationships," 323–51.

[82]John Hagan, *Structural Criminology* (Newark, NJ: Rutgers University Press, 1989); John Hagan, A. Gillis, and J. Simpson, "The Class Structure of Gender and Delinquency: Toward a Power-Control Theory of Common Delinquent Behavior," *American Journal of Sociology* 90 (1985): 1151–78; John Hagan, A. Gillis, and J. Simpson, "Clarifying and Extending Power-Control Theory," *American Journal of Sociology* 95 (1990): 1024–37; John Hagan, J. Simpson, and A. Gillis, "Class in the Household: A Power-Control Theory of Gender and Delinquency," *American Journal of Sociology* 92 (1987): 788–816.

Most empirical tests of power–control have provided moderate support for the theory, while more recent studies have further specified the validity of the theory in different contexts.[83] For example, one recent study reported that the influence of mothers, not fathers, on sons had the greatest impact on reducing the delinquency of young males.[84] Another researcher found that differences in perceived threats of embarrassment and formal sanctions varied between more patriarchal and less patriarchal households.[85] Finally, studies have also started measuring the effect of patriarchal attitudes on crime and delinquency.[86] Power–control theory is a good example of a social control theory in that it is consistent with the idea that individuals must be socialized and that the gender differences in such socialization make a difference in how people will act throughout life.

A General Theory of Crime: Low Self-Control

In 1990, Hirschi, along with his colleague Michael Gottfredson, proposed a general **theory of low self-control**, which is often referred to as *the general theory of crime.*[87] This theory has led to a significant amount of debate and research in the field since its appearance—more than any other contemporary theory of crime. Like previous control theories of crime, this theory assumes that individuals are born predisposed toward selfish, self-centered activities and that only effective child rearing and socialization can create self-control. Without such adequate socialization (i.e., social controls) and reduction of criminal opportunities, individuals will follow their natural tendencies to become selfish predators. Furthermore, the general theory of crime assumes that self-control must be established by age 10. If it has not formed by that time, then, according to the theory, individuals will forever exhibit low self-control.

Although Gottfredson and Hirschi still attribute the formation of controls to the socialization processes, the distinguishing characteristic of this theory is its emphasis on the individual's ability to control himself or herself. That is, the general theory of crime assumes that people can take a degree of control over their own decisions and, within certain limitations, control themselves.

The general theory of crime is accepted as one of the most valid theories of crime.[88] This is probably because it identifies only one primary factor that causes criminality—low self-control. But low self-control theory may actually implicate a series of personality traits and behavior, including risk-taking, impulsiveness, self-centeredness, short-term orientation, and quick temper. For example, recent research has supported the idea that inadequate child-rearing practices tend to result in lower levels of self-control among children and that these low levels produce various risky behaviors, including criminal activity.[89] Such propensities toward low self-control can manifest in

---

[83]Hagen et al., "Class in the Household," 788–816; B. McCarthy and John Hagan, "Gender, Delinquency, and the Great Depression: A Test of Power-Control Theory," *Canadian Review of Sociology and Anthropology* 24 (1987): 153–77; Merry Morash and Meda Chesney-Lind, "A Reformulation and Partial Test of the Power-Control Theory of Delinquency," *Justice Quarterly* 8 (1991): 347–77; Simon Singer and Murray Levine, "Power-Control Theory, Gender, and Delinquency: A Partial Replication with Additional Evidence on the Effects of Peers," *Criminology* 26 (1988): 627–47.

[84]B. McCarthy, John Hagan, and T. Woodward, "In the Company of Women: Structure and Agency in a Revised Power-Control Theory of Gender and Delinquency," *Criminology* 37 (1999): 761–88.

[85]Brenda Sims Blackwell, "Perceived Sanction Threats, Gender, and Crime: A Test and Elaboration of Power-Control Theory," *Criminology* 38 (2000): 439–88.

[86]Blackwell, "Perceived Sanction Threats," 439–88; Kristin Bates and Chris Bader, "Family Structure, Power-Control Theory, and Deviance: Extending Power-Control Theory to Include Alternate Family Forms," *Western Criminology Review* 4 (2003).

[87]Michael Gottfredson and Travis Hirschi, *A General Theory of Crime* (Palo Alto, CA: Stanford University Press, 1990).

[88]For an excellent review of studies regarding low self-control theory, see Pratt and Cullen, "The Empirical Status," 931–64. For critiques of this theory, see Ronald Akers, "Self-Control as a General Theory of Crime," *Journal of Quantitative Criminology* 7 (1991): 201–11. For a study that demonstrates the high popularity of the theory, see Walsh and Ellis, "Political Ideology."

[89]Carter Hay, "Parenting, Self-Control, and Delinquency: A Test of Self-Control Theory," *Criminology* 39 (2001): 707–36; Karen Hayslett-McCall and Thomas Bernard, "Attachment, Masculinity, and Self-Control: A Theory of Male Crime Rates," *Theoretical Criminology* 6 (2002): 5–33.

varying forms across an individual's life. For example, teenagers with low self-control will likely hit or steal from peers, and as they grow older, they will be more likely to gamble or cheat on taxes.

Psychological Aspects of Low Self-Control

Criminologists have recently claimed that low self-control may be due to the emotional disposition of individuals. For example, one study showed that the effects of low self-control on intentions to commit drunk driving and shoplifting were tied to individuals' perceptions of pleasure and shame. More specifically, the findings of this study showed that individuals who had low self-control had significantly lower levels of anticipated shame but significantly higher levels of perceived pleasure in committing both drunk driving and shoplifting.[90] These results suggest that individuals who lack self-control will be oriented toward gaining pleasure and taking advantage of resources and toward avoiding negative emotional feelings (e.g., shame) that are primarily induced through socialization.

Physiological Aspects of Low Self-Control

Low self-control can also be tied to physiological factors. Interestingly, research has shown that chronic offenders show greater arousal toward danger and risk-taking than toward the possibility of punishment.[91] This arousal has been measured by monitoring brain activity in response to certain stimuli. The research suggests that individuals are encouraged to commit risky behavior due to physiological mechanisms that reward their risk-taking activities by releasing pleasure chemicals in their brains.[92]

In a similar vein, recent studies show that chronic gamblers tend to get a physiological high (such as a sudden, intense release of brain chemicals similar to that following a small dose of cocaine) from the activity of betting, particularly when they are gambling with their own money and risking a personal loss.[93] Undoubtedly, a minority of individuals thrive off of risk-taking behaviors significantly more than others. This suggests that physiological as well as psychological differences may explain why certain individuals favor risky behaviors.

Researchers have also found that criminal offenders generally perceive a significantly lower level of internal sanctions (e.g., shame, guilt, embarrassment) than do nonoffenders.[94] So, in summary, a select group of individuals appear to derive physiological and psychological pleasure from engaging in risky behaviors while simultaneously being less likely to be inhibited by internal emotional sanctions. Such a combination, Gottfredson and Hirschi claimed, is very dangerous and helps explain why impulsive individuals often end up in prison.

Finally, the psychological and physiological aspects of low self-control may help explain the gender differences observed between males and females. Specifically, studies show that females are significantly more likely than males to experience internal emotional sanctioning for offenses they have committed.[95] In other words, there appears to be something innately different about males and females that helps explain the differing levels of self-control each possesses.

---

[90]Alex Piquero and Stephen Tibbetts, "Specifying the Direct and Indirect Effects of Low Self-Control and Situational Factors in Offenders' Decision Making: Toward a More Complete Model of Rational Offending," *Justice Quarterly* 13 (1996): 481–510.

[91]Adrian Raine, *The Psychopathology of Crime* (San Diego, CA: Academic Press, 1993).

[92]Anthony Walsh, *Biosocial Criminology: Introduction and Integration* (Cincinnati, OH: Anderson, 2002).

[93]Christopher D. Fiorillo, Phillippe N. Tobler, and Wolfram Schultz, "Discrete Coding of Reward Probability and Uncertainty by Dopamine Neurons," *Science* 299 (2003): 1898–1902.

[94]Harold Grasmick and Robert Bursik, "Conscience, Significant Others, and Rational Choice: Extending the Deterrence Model," *Law and Society Review* 24 (1990): 837–61; Stephen Tibbetts, "Shame and Rational Choice in Offending Decisions," *Criminal Justice and Behavior* 24 (1997): 234–55.

[95]Stephen Tibbetts and Denise Herz, "Gender Differences in Factors of Social Control and Rational Choice," *Deviant Behavior* 17 (1996): 183–208.

Summary of Control Theories

Control perspectives are among the oldest and most respected explanations of criminal activity. The fundamental assumption that humans have an inborn, selfish disposition that must be controlled through socialization distinguishes control theories from other theories of crime. The control perspective's longevity as one of the most popular criminological theories demonstrates its legitimacy as an explanation of behavior. This is likely due to the dedication and efforts of criminologists who are constantly developing new and improved versions of control theory—many of which we have discussed here.

Policy Implications

Numerous policy implications can be taken from the various types of social learning and control theories presented here. We will concentrate on those that are likely to be most effective and pragmatic in helping to reduce criminal behavior.

A number of policy implications can be drawn from the various learning models. Perhaps their most important suggestion is to supply many opportunities for positive reinforcements, or rewards, for good behavior. Such reinforcements have been found to be far more effective than punishments, especially among criminal offenders.[96] Furthermore, studies show that the most effective rehabilitation programs for offenders should be based on a cognitive behavioral approach, which teaches individuals to think before they act.[97] Furthermore, evaluation studies have shown that simply grouping offenders together for counseling or peer therapy sessions is not an effective strategy; rather, it appears that such programs often show no effect, or actually increase offending among participants, perhaps because they tend to learn more antisocial attitudes from such sessions.[98] Ultimately, offender programs that emphasize positive reinforcements and are based on a cognitive behavioral approach show the greatest success.

Regarding the policy implications of control theories, we will focus on the early social bonding that must take place and the need for more parental supervision to help an individual develop or learn self-control and create healthy, strong bonds to conventional society. Most control theories assume that individuals are predisposed to criminal behavior, so the primary focus of programs should be to reduce this propensity toward such behavior. According to most control perspectives, the most important factor in preventing or controlling this predisposition involves early parenting and building attachments or ties to prosocial aspects of the individual's environment.

According to the Maryland Report of "What Works" (see previous sections), evidence consistently supports programs that involve long-term, frequent home visitation combined with preschool as well as family therapy by clinical staff for at-risk youth.[99] Furthermore, the Maryland Report stressed the success of school programs that aim to clarify and communicate norms for various behaviors by establishing school rules and consistently enforcing them through positive reinforcement and schoolwide campaigns.[100] Other effective school programs focus on various competency skills, such as developing self-control, stress management, responsible decision making, problem solving, and communication skills.[101] On the other hand, the Maryland Report noted some school programs that do

---

[96]Van Voorhis and Salisbury, *Correctional Counseling.*

[97]Ibid.

[98]Ibid. See also reviews of such programs in Richard J. Lundman, *Prevention and Control of Juvenile Delinquency* (New York: Oxford University Press, 1993); and Akers and Sellers, *Criminological Theories*, 101–8.

[99]Ibid.

[100]Ibid.

[101]Ibid.

not reduce delinquent behavior, such as those that counsel students in a peer-group context (see reasoning above), as well as substance use programs that simply rely on information dissemination or fear arousal (such as the traditional D.A.R.E. [Drug Abuse Resistance Education] program).[102]

Consistent with the Maryland Report, in a 2017 study that systematically reviewed the extant literature, David Weisburd and his colleagues claimed that there is "good evidence" for the effectiveness of programs designed to strengthen and restore positive social ties with at-risk youth.[103] These researchers also concluded that the most effective programs target specific risk factors and that the key mechanisms underlying effective programs across all dimensions are efforts to enhance supportive and informal social controls and reintegration into the community by repairing social bonds.[104]

Ultimately, programs that teach youths to develop cognitive or thinking skills are beneficial as opposed to those that simply focus on providing information about drugs or criminal offending. The bottom line for successful programs appears to be that they must instruct youths to deal with everyday influences in a healthy way (according to a cognitive behavioral model) as opposed to just giving them information about crime and drugs.

Thus, perhaps the most important policy recommendation is to increase the ties between early caregivers or parents and their children. A variety of programs try to increase the relationship and bonding that takes place between infants and young children and their parents as well as to monitor the supervision that takes place in this dynamic. Such programs have consistently been shown to be effective in preventing and reducing criminality in high-risk children, especially when such programs involve home visitations by health care providers (e.g., nurses) and social care experts (e.g., social workers).[105] By visiting the homes of high-risk children, workers can provide more direct, personal attention in aiding and counseling parents about how best to nurture, monitor, and discipline their young children.[106] These types of programs may lead to more control over behavior while building stronger bonds to society and developing self-control among these high-risk individuals.

Conclusion

In this section, we have discussed a wide range of theories that may appear to be quite different. However, all of the criminological theories here share an emphasis on social processes as the primary reason why individuals commit crime. This is true of the learning theories, which propose that people are taught to commit crime, as well as the control theories, which claim that people offend naturally and must be taught not to commit crime. Despite their seemingly opposite assumptions of human behavior, the fact is that learning and control theories both identify socialization, or the lack thereof, as the key cause of criminal behavior.

We also examined some of the key policy recommendations that have been suggested by both of these theoretical perspectives. Specifically, we noted that programs that simply group offenders together only seem to reinforce their tendency to offend, whereas programs that take a cognitive behavioral approach and use many reward opportunities appear to have some effect in reducing recidivism. Also, we concluded that programs that involve home visitations by experts (e.g., nurses, counselors) tend to aid in developing more effective parenting and building social bonds among young individuals, which helps them to build strong attachments to society and develop self-control.

---

[102]Ibid.

[103]David Weisburd, David P. Farrington, and Charlotte Gill, "What Works in Crime Prevention and Rehabilitation: An Assessment of Systematic Reviews," *Criminology & Public Policy* 16 (2017): 415–49.

[104]Ibid.

[105]Joycen Carmouche and Joretta Jones, "Her Children, Their Future," *Federal Prisons Journal* 1 (1989): 23, 26–27.

[106]For a review, see Stephen G. Tibbetts, "Perinatal and Developmental Determinants of Early Onset of Offending: A Two-Peak Model Approach," in *The Development of Persistent Criminality*, ed. Johanna Savage (New York: Oxford University Press, 2009), 179–201.

SECTION SUMMARY

- First, we discussed what distinguishes learning theories of crime from other perspectives.
- Then we reviewed Glaser's differential identification theory, which emphasizes the learning that takes place via reference groups or role models.
- We then discussed Sutherland's differential association theory and how this framework was improved by Akers's differential reinforcement theory.
- We examined in depth the psychological learning model of classical conditioning as well as its limitations.
- We then explored two other learning models that formed the basis of differential reinforcement theory—namely, operant conditioning and learning according to modeling and imitation.
- We reviewed the theory of neutralization, including the five original techniques of neutralization presented by Sykes and Matza.
- We also reviewed several early forms of social control theory, such as Hobbes's, Freud's, and Durkheim's.
- Then we examined the early social control theories of crime, presented by Reiss, Toby, and Nye along with Reckless's containment theory.
- We then examined more modern social control theories, such as Matza's drift theory and Hirschi's social bonding theory.
- Integrated social control theories were briefly examined, including Tittle's control–balance theory and Hagan's power–control theory.
- Finally, we reviewed low self-control theory from both a psychological and a physiological perspective.

KEY TERMS

classical conditioning 335
containment theory 351
control–balance theory 359
control theories 333
differential association theory 334
differential identification theory 337
differential reinforcement theory 338
drift theory 352
ego 348
id 347
learning theories 333
modeling and imitation 340
negative punishment 339
negative reinforcement 339
neutralization theory 343
operant conditioning 339
positive punishment 339
positive reinforcement 339
power–control theory 359
social bonding theory 354
soft determinism 353
stake in conformity 349
subterranean values 354
superego 347
tabula rasa 333
theory of low self-control 360

DISCUSSION QUESTIONS

1. What distinguishes learning theories from other criminological theories?
2. What distinguishes differential association from differential reinforcement theory?
3. What did differential identification add to learning theories?
4. Which technique of neutralization do you use or relate to the most? Why?
5. Which technique of neutralization do you find least valid? Why?
6. Which element of Hirschi's social bond do you find you have the highest levels of?
7. Which element of Hirschi's social bond do you find you have the lowest levels of?
8. Can you identify someone you know who fits the profile of a person with low self-control?
9. Which aspects of the low self-control personality do you think you fit?
10. Do you think Matza's theory of drift relates to when you or your friends have committed crime in life? Studies show that most people commit crimes or at least know people who do when they are in their teens or 20s (e.g., drinking under age 21, speeding).

WEB RESOURCES

Differential Association Theory

http://study.com/academy/lesson/differential-association-theory-definition-examples.html
https://www.d.umn.edu/~bmork/2306/Theories/BAMdiffassn.htm

Differential Reinforcement Theory

http://study.com/academy/lesson/differential-reinforcement-theory-definition-quiz.html
http://www.sociologyassignments.com/differential-association-theory-and-differential-reinforcement-theory-4795

Social and Self-Control Theory

http://study.com/academy/lesson/social-control-definition-theory-examples.html
http://forensicpsychology.umwblogs.org/organized-crime/the-social-control-theory
http://www.everydaysociologyblog.com/2008/11/gottfredson-and.html

Techniques of Neutralization

http://study.com/academy/lesson/five-techniques-of-neutralization.html
https://www.britannica.com/biography/Gresham-M-Sykes#ref940804

READING /// 18

This selection may be one of the most important entries in the book, primarily because it is written by Edwin Sutherland, who is generally regarded as the most important criminologist of the 20th century. One of the key reasons that Sutherland is held in such high regard is because of his proposed theoretical model of criminal behavior, which is known as differential association theory. This theory contains nine propositions, which are the focus of this selection. Readers should keep in mind that when these nine propositions were presented in the early to mid-1900s, the primary emphasis of criminological theory and research was on how offenders are physically (e.g., body type theories) or psychologically (e.g., IQ) different from nonoffenders. Although the social learning of criminal behavior is often assumed by modern criminologists, at that time Sutherland's emphasis was seen as a major break from widely accepted theoretical frameworks.

Specifically, Sutherland claims that offenders are no different, physically or psychologically, from nonoffenders. Rather, he concludes that individuals engage in offending because they are exposed to significant others (e.g., family, friends) who teach them the norms and techniques beneficial for committing crime. It is also important to keep in mind that Sutherland's theory is just as deterministic as previous theories (e.g., Cesare Lombroso's theory, Henry H. Goddard's feeblemindedness theory, William Sheldon's body type theory) in the sense that Sutherland claims that people do not have free choice or free will in determining their actions; rather, it all comes down to whom they associate with the most, and their attitudes regarding the violation of law.

While reading this entry, consider the following points:

- Sutherland's first three propositions of his theory regarding what he has to say about how criminal behavior is learned
- The two types of learning Sutherland claims takes place in his fourth proposition
- Sutherland's sixth proposition, which is considered the best summary of his theory, so pay special attention to this one
- The four types of associations identified by Sutherland in his seventh proposition

A Sociological Theory of Criminal Behavior

Edwin H. Sutherland

Explanation of Criminal Behavior

The following statement refers to the process by which a particular person comes to engage in criminal behavior.

1. *Criminal behavior is learned.* Negatively, this means that criminal[ity] is not inherited, as such; also, the person who is not already trained in crime does not invent criminal behavior, just as a person

does not make mechanical inventions unless he has had training in mechanics.

2. *Criminal behavior is learned in interaction with other persons in a process of communication.* This communication is verbal in many respects but includes also "the communication of gestures."

3. *The principal part of the learning of criminal behavior occurs within intimate personal groups.* Negatively, this means that the impersonal agencies of communication, such as movies and newspapers, play a relatively unimportant part in the genesis of criminal behavior.

4. When criminal behavior is learned, the learning includes (a) techniques of committing the crime, which are sometimes very complicated, sometimes very simple; (b) the specific direction of motives, drives, rationalizations, and attitudes.

5. *The specific direction of motives and drives is learned from definitions of the legal codes as favorable or unfavorable.* In some societies an individual is surrounded by persons who invariably define the legal codes as rules to be observed, while in others he is surrounded by persons whose definitions are favorable to the violation of the legal codes. In our American society these definitions are almost always mixed, with the consequences that we have culture conflict in relation to the legal codes.

6. A person becomes delinquent because of an excess of definitions favorable to violation of law over definitions unfavorable to violation of law. This is the principle of differential association. It refers to both criminal and anti-criminal associations and has to do with counteracting forces. When persons become criminal, they do so because of contacts with criminal patterns and also because of isolation from anti-criminal patterns. Any person inevitably assimilates the surrounding culture unless other patterns are in conflict; a Southerner does not pronounce "r" because other Southerners do not pronounce "r." Negatively, this proposition of differential association means that associations which are neutral so far as crime is concerned have little or no effect on the genesis of criminal behavior. Much of the experience of a person is neutral in this sense, e.g., learning to brush one's teeth. This behavior has no negative or positive effect on criminal behavior except as it may be related to associations which are concerned with the legal codes. This neutral behavior is important especially as an occupier of the time of a child so that he is not in contact with criminal behavior during the time he is so engaged in the neutral behavior.

7. *Differential associations may vary in frequency, duration, priority, and intensity.* This means that associations with criminal behavior and also associations with anti-criminal behavior vary in those respects. "Frequency" and "duration" as modalities of associations are obvious and need no explanation. "Priority" is assumed to be important in the sense that lawful behavior developed in early childhood may persist throughout life, and also that delinquent behavior developed in early childhood may persist throughout life. This tendency, however, has not been adequately demonstrated, and priority seems to be important principally through its selective influence. "Intensity" is not precisely defined but it has to do with such things as the prestige of the source of a criminal or anti-criminal pattern and with emotional reactions related to the associations. In a precise description of the criminal behavior of a person these modalities would be stated in quantitative form and a mathematical ratio be reached. A formula in this sense has not been developed, and the development of such a formula would be extremely difficult.

8. The process of learning criminal behavior by association with criminal and anti-criminal patterns involves all of the mechanisms that are involved in any other learning. Negatively, this means that the learning of criminal behavior is not restricted to the process of imitation. A person who is seduced, for instance, learns criminal behavior by association, but this process would not ordinarily be described as imitation.

9. While criminal behavior is an expression of general needs and values, it is not explained by those general needs and values since non-criminal behavior

> is an expression of the same needs and values. Thieves generally steal in order to secure money, but likewise honest laborers work in order to secure money. The attempts by many scholars to explain criminal behavior by general drives and values, such as, the happiness principle, striving for social status, the money motive, or frustration, have been and must continue to be futile since they explain lawful behavior as completely as they explain criminal behavior. They are similar to respiration, which is necessary for any behavior but which does not differentiate criminal from non-criminal behavior.

It is not necessary, at this level of explanation, to explain why a person has the associations which he has; this certainly involves a complex of many things. In an area where the delinquency rate is high a boy who is sociable, gregarious, active, and athletic is very likely to come in contact with the other boys in the neighborhood, learn delinquent behavior from them, and become a gangster; in the same neighborhood the psychopathic boy who is isolated, introvert, and inert may remain at home, not become acquainted with the other boys in the neighborhood, and not become delinquent. In another situation, the sociable, athletic, aggressive boy may become a member of a scout troop and not become involved in delinquent behavior. The person's associations are determined in a general context of social organization. A child is ordinarily reared in a family; the place of residence of the family is determined largely by family income; and the delinquency rate is, in many respects, related to the rental value of the houses. Many other factors enter into this social organization, including many of the small personal group relationships.

The preceding explanation of criminal behavior is stated from the point of view of the person who engages in criminal behavior. As indicated earlier, it is possible, also, to state sociological theories of criminal behavior from the point of view of the community, nation, or other group. The problem, when thus stated, is generally concerned with crime rates and involves a comparison of the crime rates of various groups or the crime rates of a particular group at different times. The explanation of a crime rate must be consistent with the explanation of the criminal behavior of the person, since the crime rate is a summary statement of the number of persons in the group who commit crimes and the frequency with which they commit crimes. One of the best explanations of crime rates from this point of view is that a high crime rate is due to social disorganization. The term "social disorganization" is not entirely satisfactory and it seems preferable to substitute for it the term "differential social organization." The postulate on which this theory is based, regardless of the name, is that crime is rooted in the social organization and is an expression of that social organization. A group may be organized for criminal behavior or organized against criminal behavior. Most communities are organized both for criminal and anti-criminal behavior and in that sense the crime rate is an expression of the differential group organization. Differential group organization as an explanation of variations in crime rates is consistent with the differential association theory of the processes by which persons become criminals. . . .

/// REVIEW QUESTIONS

1. Using Sutherland's first three propositions, how does he claim criminal behavior is learned? What does he have to say about the effect of movies and media on the learning of criminal behavior?
2. What two types of learning does Sutherland claim take place in his fourth proposition? Provide an example of each of these two types.
3. Sutherland's sixth proposition is often considered the best summary of his theory. Explain what this proposition means as if you were trying to tell a person who knows nothing about criminology. Also, do you agree with it? Why or why not?
4. What four types of associations are identified by Sutherland in his seventh proposition? Explain each, and provide your opinion on which of the four types is most important in determining criminal activity.

READING /// 19

In this selection, Ron Akers presents a theoretical model known as differential reinforcement theory. Although some, including Akers himself, often refer to this theory as social learning theory, this label is a bit confusing because there are many social learning theories. We prefer differential reinforcement theory as the name of this framework because when you say this criminologists know exactly which theoretical model you are referring to and also because the term *reinforcement* specifies the key concept that distinguishes this model from all other social learning theories.

Differential reinforcement theory builds on the framework provided by Edwin Sutherland's differential association theory but adds two important models of social learning that were not included in Sutherland's theory. Specifically, Sutherland based his differential association model on only one type of social learning: classical conditioning. While including classical conditioning in its framework, Akers's theory of differential reinforcement adds two additional learning models: operant conditioning and modeling and imitation. Operant conditioning is based on B. F. Skinner's work in psychology, which emphasizes whether punishments or reinforcements (i.e., rewards) occur after a given activity. The other learning model is modeling and imitation, which is largely based on Albert Bandura's psychological model of learning through observation, such as what happens when children watch what adults do and then imitate their behavior—in other words, "monkey see, monkey do." Differential reinforcement theory is an improvement over Sutherland's differential association theory because it takes all three learning processes—classical conditioning, operant conditioning, and modeling and imitation—into account in the theoretical model.

While reading this selection, consider the following points:

- The four main components of the theory of differential reinforcement according to Akers and which of these propositions is primarily based on Sutherland's differential association theory as compared to those that are operant conditioning or modeling and imitation
- The discussion by Akers on the importance of behavioral feedback and reciprocal effects
- Akers's discussion of the concept of definitions and the implications of such

A Social Learning Theory of Crime

Ronald L. Akers

Concise Statement of the Theory

The basic assumption in social learning theory is that the same learning process, operating in a context of social structure, interaction, and situation, produces both conforming and deviant behavior. The difference lies in the direction of the process in which these mechanisms operate. In both, it is seldom an either-or, all-or-nothing process; what is involved, rather, is the balance of influences on behavior. That balance usually exhibits some

SOURCE: "A Social Learning Theory of Crime," in *Social Learning and Social Structure: A General Theory of Crime and Deviance* by Ronald L. Akers.

stability over time, but it can become unstable and change with time or circumstances. Conforming and deviant behavior is learned by all of the mechanisms in this process, but the theory proposes that the principal mechanisms are in that part of the process in which differential reinforcement (instrumental learning through rewards and punishers) and imitation (observational learning) produce both overt behavior and cognitive definitions that function as discriminative (cue) stimuli for the behavior. Always implied, and sometimes made explicit when these concepts are called upon to account for deviant/conforming behavior, is the understanding that the behavioral processes in operant and classical conditioning are in operation (see below). However, social learning theory focuses on four major concepts—differential association, differential reinforcement, imitation, and definitions. The central proposition of the social learning theory of criminal and deviant behavior can be stated as a long sentence proposing that criminal and deviant behavior is more likely when, on balance, the combined effects of these four main sets of variables instigate and strengthen nonconforming over conforming acts:

> The probability that persons will engage in criminal and deviant behavior is increased and the probability of their conforming to the norm is decreased when they differentially associate with others who commit criminal behavior and espouse definitions favorable to it, are relatively more exposed in-person or symbolically to salient criminal/deviant models, define it as desirable or justified in a situation discriminative for the behavior, and have received in the past and anticipate in the current or future situation relatively greater reward than punishment for the behavior.
>
> The probability of conforming behavior is increased and the probability of deviant behavior is decreased when the balance of these variables moves in the reverse direction.

Each of the four main components of this statement can be presented as a separate testable hypothesis. The individual is more likely to commit violations when:

1. He or she differentially associates with other[s] who commit, model, and support violations of social and legal norms.
2. The violative behavior is differentially reinforced over behavior in conformity to the norm.
3. He or she is more exposed to and observes more deviant than conforming models.
4. His or her own learned definitions are favorable toward committing the deviant acts.

General Principles of Social Learning Theory

Since it is a general explanation of crime and deviance of all kinds, social learning is not simply a theory about how novel criminal behavior is learned or a theory only of the positive causes of that behavior. It embraces variables that operate to both motivate and control delinquent and criminal behavior, to both promote and undermine conformity. It answers the questions of why people do and do not violate norms. The probability of criminal or conforming behavior occurring is a function of the variables operating in the underlying social learning process. The main concepts/variables and their respective empirical indicators have been identified and measured, but they can be viewed as indicators of a general latent construct, for which additional indicators can be devised (Akers & La Greca, 1991; Akers & Lee, 1996).

Social learning accounts for the individual becoming prone to deviant or criminal behavior and for stability or change in that propensity. Therefore, the theory is capable of accounting for the development of stable individual differences, as well as changes in the individual's behavioral patterns or tendencies to commit deviant and criminal acts, over time and in different situations. . . . The social learning process operates in each individual's learning history and in the immediate situation in which the opportunity for a crime occurs.

Deviant and criminal behavior is learned and modified (acquired, performed, repeated, maintained, and changed) through all of the same cognitive and behavioral mechanisms as conforming behavior. They differ in the direction, content, and outcome of the behavior learned. Therefore, it is inaccurate to state, for instance, that peer influence does not explain adolescent deviant behavior since conforming behavior is also peer influenced in adolescence. The theory expects peer influences to be implicated in both; it is the content and direction of the influence that is the key.

The primary learning mechanisms are differential reinforcement (instrumental conditioning), in which behavior is a function of the frequency, amount, and probability of experienced and perceived contingent rewards and punishments, and imitation, in which the behavior of others and its consequences are observed and modeled. The process of stimulus discrimination/generalization is another important mechanism; here, overt and covert stimuli, verbal and cognitive, act as cues or signals for behavior to occur. As I point out below, there are other behavioral mechanisms in the learning process, but these are not as important and are usually left implied rather than explicated in the theory.

The content of the learning achieved by these mechanisms includes the simple and complex behavioral sequences and the definitions (beliefs, attitudes, justifications, orientations) that in turn become discriminative for engaging in deviant and criminal behavior. The probability that conforming or norm-violative behavior is learned and performed, and the frequency with which it is committed, are a function of the past, present, and anticipated differential reinforcement for the behavior and the deviant or nondeviant direction of the learned definitions and other discriminative stimuli present in a given situation.

These learning mechanisms operate in a process of differential association—direct and indirect, verbal and nonverbal communication, interaction, and identification with others. The relative frequency, intensity, duration, and priority of associations affect the relative amount, frequency, and probability of reinforcement of conforming or deviant behavior and exposure of individuals to deviant or conforming norms and behavioral models. To the extent that the individual can control with whom she or he associates, the frequency, intensity, and duration of those associations are themselves affected by how rewarding or aversive they are. The principal learning is through differential association with those persons and groups (primary, secondary, reference, and symbolic) that comprise or control the individual's major sources of reinforcement, most salient behavioral models, and most effective definitions and other discriminative stimuli for committing and repeating behavior. The reinforcement and discriminative stimuli are mainly social (such as socially valued rewards and punishers contingent on the behavior), but they are also nonsocial (such as unconditioned physiological reactions to environmental stimuli and physical effects of ingested substances and the physical environment).

Sequence and Reciprocal Effects in the Social Learning Process

Behavioral feedback effects are built into the concept of differential reinforcement—actual or perceived changes in the environment produced by the behavior feed back on that behavior to affect its repetition or extinction, and both prior and anticipated rewards and punishments influence present behavior. Reciprocal effects between the individual's behavior and definitions or differential association are also reflected in the social learning process. This process is one in which the probability of both the initiation and the repetition of a deviant or criminal act (or the initiation and repetition of conforming acts) is a function of the learning history of the individual and the set of reinforcement contingencies and discriminative stimuli in a given situation. The typical process of initiation, continuation, progression, and desistance is hypothesized to be as follows:

1. The balance of past and current associations, definitions, and imitation of deviant models, and the anticipated balance of reinforcement in particular situations, produces or inhibits the initial delinquent or deviant acts.
2. The effects of these variables continue in the repetition of acts, although imitation becomes less important than it was in the first commission of the act.
3. After initiation, the actual social and nonsocial reinforcers and punishers affect the probability that the acts will be or will not be repeated and at what level of frequency.
4. Not only the overt behavior, but also the definitions favorable or unfavorable to it, are affected by the positive and negative consequences of the initial acts. To the extent that they are more rewarded than alternative behavior, the favorable definitions will be strengthened and the unfavorable

definitions will be weakened, and it becomes more likely that the deviant behavior will be repeated under similar circumstances.

5. Progression into more frequent or sustained patterns, rather than cessation or reduction, of criminal and deviant behavior is promoted to the extent that reinforcement, exposure to deviant models, and norm-violating definitions are not offset by negative formal and informal sanctions and norm abiding definitions.

The theory does not hypothesize that definitions favorable to law violation always precede and are unaffected by the commission of criminal acts. Although the probability of a criminal act increases in the presence of favorable definitions, acts in violation of the law do occur (through imitation and reinforcement) in the absence of any thought given to whether the acts are right or wrong. Furthermore, the individual may apply neutralizing definitions retroactively to excuse or justify an act without having contemplated them beforehand. To the extent that such excuses become associated with successfully mitigating others' negative sanctions or one's self-punishment, however, they become cues for the repetition of deviant acts. Such definitions, therefore, precede committing the same acts again or committing similar acts in the future.

Differential association with conforming and nonconforming others typically precedes the individual's committing crimes and delinquent acts. This sequence of events is sometimes disputed in the literature because it is mistakenly believed to apply only to differential peer association in general or to participation in delinquent gangs in particular without reference to family and other group associations. It is true that the theory recognizes peer associations as very important in adolescent deviance and that differential association is most often measured in research by peer associations. But the theory also hypothesizes that the family is a very important primary group in the differential association process, and it plainly stipulates that other primary and secondary groups besides peers are involved (see Sutherland, 1947, pp. 164–65). Accordingly, it is a mistake to interpret differential association as referring only to peer associations. The theoretical stipulation that differential association is causally prior to the commission of delinquent and criminal acts is not confined to the balance of peer associations; rather, it is the balance (as determined by the modalities) of family, peer, and other associations. According to the priority principle, association, reinforcement, modeling, and exposure to conforming and deviant definitions occurring within the family during childhood, and such antisocial conduct as aggressiveness, lying, and cheating learned in early childhood, occur prior to and have both direct and selective effects on later delinquent and criminal behavior and associations. . . .

The socializing behavior of parents, guardians, or caretakers is certainly reciprocally influenced by the deviant and unacceptable behavior of the child. However, it can never be true that the onset of delinquency precedes and initiates interaction in a particular family (except in the unlikely case of the late-stage adoption of a child who is already delinquent or who is drawn to and chosen by deviant parents). Thus, interaction in the family or family surrogate always precedes delinquency.

But this is not true for adolescent peer associations. One may choose to associate with peers based on similarity in deviant behavior that already exists. Some major portion of this behavioral similarity results from previous association with other delinquent peers or from anticipatory socialization undertaken to make one's behavior match more closely that of the deviant associates to whom one is attracted. For some adolescents, gravitation toward delinquent peers occurs after and as a result of the individual's involvement in delinquent behavior. However, peer associations are most often formed initially around interests, friendships, and such circumstances as neighborhood proximity, family similarities, values, beliefs, age, school attended, grade in school, and mutually attractive behavioral patterns that have little to do directly with co-involvement or similarity in specifically law-violating or serious deviant behavior. Many of these factors in peer association are not under the adolescents' control, and some are simply happenstance. The theory does not, contrary to the Gluecks' distorted characterization, propose that "accidental differential association of nondelinquents with delinquents is the basic cause of crime" (Glueck & Glueck, 1950, p. 164). Interaction and socialization in the family precedes and affects choices of both conforming and deviant peer associations.

Those peer associations will affect the nature of models, definitions, and rewards/punishers to which the person is exposed. After the associations have been established, their reinforcing or punishing consequences as well as direct and vicarious consequences of the deviant behavior will affect both the continuation of old and the seeking of new associations (those over which one has any choice). One may choose further interaction with others based on whether they too are involved in deviant or criminal behavior; in such cases, the outcomes of that interaction are more rewarding than aversive and it is anticipated that the associates will more likely approve or be permissive toward one's own deviant behavior. Further interaction with delinquent peers, over which the individual has no choice, may also result from being apprehended and confined by the juvenile or criminal-justice system.

These reciprocal effects would predict that one's own deviant or conforming behavioral patterns can have effects on choice of friends; these are weaker in the earlier years, but should become stronger as one moves through adolescence and gains more control over friendship choices. The typical sequence outlined above would predict that deviant associations precede the onset of delinquent behavior more frequently than the sequence of events in which the delinquent associations begin only after the peers involved have already separately and individually established similar patterns of delinquent behavior. Further, these behavioral tendencies that develop prior to peer association will themselves be the result of previous associations, models, and reinforcement, primarily in the family. Regardless of the sequence in which onset occurs, and whatever the level of the individual's delinquent involvement, its frequency and seriousness will increase after the deviant associations have begun and decrease as the associations are reduced. That is, whatever the temporal ordering, differential association with deviant peers will have a causal effect on one's own delinquent behavior (just as his actions will have an effect on his peers).

Therefore, both "selection," or "flocking" (tendency for persons to choose interaction with others with behavioral similarities), and "socialization," or "feathering" (tendency for persons who interact to have mutual influence on one another's behavior), are part of the same overall social learning process and are explained by the same variables. A peer "socialization" process and a peer "selection" process in deviant behavior are not mutually exclusive, but are simply the social learning process operating at different times. Arguments that social learning posits only the latter, that any evidence of selective mechanisms in deviant interaction run counter to social learning theory (Strictland, 1982; Stafford & Ekland-Olson, 1982), or that social learning theory recognizes only a recursive, one-way causal effect of peers on delinquent behavior (Thornberry et al., 1994; Catalano et al., 1996) are wrong.

Behavioral and Cognitive Mechanisms in Social Learning

The first statement in Sutherland's theory was a simple declarative sentence maintaining that criminal behavior is learned, and the eighth statement declared that this involved all the mechanisms involved in any learning. What little Sutherland added in his (1947, p. 7) commentary downplayed imitation as a possible learning mechanism in criminal behavior. He mentioned "seduction" of a person into criminal behavior as something that is not covered by the concept of imitation. He defined neither imitation nor seduction and offered no further discussion of mechanisms of learning in any of his papers or publications. Recall that filling this major lacuna in Sutherland's theory was the principal goal of the 1966b Burgess-Akers reformulation. To this end we combined Sutherland's first and eighth statements into one: "Criminal behavior is learned according to the principles of operant conditioning." The phrase "principles of operant conditioning" was meant as a shorthand reference to all of the behavioral mechanisms of learning in operant theory that had been empirically validated.

Burgess and I delineated, as much as space allowed, what these specific learning mechanisms were: (1) operant conditioning, differential reinforcement of voluntary behavior through positive and negative reinforcement and punishment; (2) respondent (involuntary reflexes), or "classical," conditioning; (3) unconditioned (primary) and conditioned (secondary) reinforcers and punishers; (4) shaping and response differentiation; (5) stimulus discrimination and generalization, the environmental and internal stimuli that provide cues or signals indicating differences and similarities across situations that help elicit, but do not directly reinforce, behavior; (6) types of reinforcement schedules, the rate and ratio in which rewards and punishers follow behavior; (7) stimulus-response constellations; and (8) stimulus satiation and deprivation. We also reported research showing the applicability of these mechanisms of learning to both conforming and deviant behavior.

Burgess and I used the term "operant conditioning" to emphasize that differential reinforcement (the balance of reward and punishment contingent upon behavioral responses) is the basic mechanism around which the others revolve and by which learning most relevant to conformity or violation of social and legal norms is produced. This was reflected in other statements in the theory in which the only learning mechanisms listed were differential reinforcement and stimulus discrimination.

We also subsumed imitation, or modeling, under these principles and argued that imitation "may be analyzed quite parsimoniously with the principles of modern behavior theory," namely, that it is simply a sub-class of behavioral shaping through operant conditioning (Burgess and Akers, 1966b, p. 138). For this reason we made no specific mention of imitation in any of the seven statements. Later, I became persuaded that the operant principle of gradual shaping of responses through "successive approximations" only incompletely and awkwardly incorporated the processes of observational learning and vicarious reinforcement that Bandura and Walters (1963) had identified. Therefore, without dismissing successive approximation as a way in which some imitative behavior could be shaped, I came to accept Bandura's conceptualization of imitation. That is, imitation is a separate learning mechanism characterized by modeling one's own actions on the observed behavior of others and on the consequences of that behavior (vicarious reinforcement) prior to performing the behavior and experiencing its consequences directly. Whether the observed acts will be performed and repeated depends less on the continuing presence of models and more on the actual or anticipated rewarding or aversive consequences of the behavior. I became satisfied that the principle of "observational learning" could account for the acquisition, and to some extent the performance, of behavior by a process that did not depend on operant conditioning or "instrumental learning." Therefore, in later discussions of the theory, while continuing to posit differential reinforcement as the core behavior-shaping mechanism, I included imitation as another primary mechanism in acquiring behavior. Where appropriate, discriminative stimuli were also specifically invoked as affecting behavior, while I made only general reference to other learning mechanisms.

Note that the term "operant conditioning" in the opening sentence of the Burgess-Akers revision reflected our great reliance on the orthodox behaviorism that assumed the empirical irrelevance of cognitive variables. Social behaviorism, on the other hand, recognizes "cognitive" as well as "behavioral" mechanisms (see Bandura, 1969; 1977a; 1977b; 1986; 1989; Grusec, 1992; Staats, 1975). My social learning theory of criminal behavior retains a strong element of the symbolic interactionism found in Sutherland's theory (Akers, 1985, pp. 39–70). As a result, it is closer to cognitive learning theories, such as Albert Bandura's, than to the radical operant behaviorism of B. F. Skinner with which Burgess and I began. It is for this reason, and the reliance on such concepts as imitation, anticipated reinforcement, and self-reinforcement, that I have described social learning theory as "soft behaviorism" (Akers, 1985, p. 65).

The unmodified term "learning" implies to many that the theory only explains the acquisition of novel behavior by the individual, in contrast to behavior that is committed at a given time and place or the maintenance of behavior over time (Cornish and Clarke, 1986). It has also been interpreted to mean only "positive" learning of novel behavior, with no relevance for inhibition of behavior or of learning failures (Gottfredson and Hirschi, 1990). As I have made clear above, neither of these interpretations is accurate. The phrase that Burgess and I used, "effective and available reinforcers and the existing reinforcement contingencies," and the discussion of reinforcement occurring under given situations (Burgess & Akers, 1966b, pp. 141, 134) make it obvious that we were not proposing a theory only of past reinforcement in the acquisition of a behavioral repertoire with no regard for the reward/cost balance obtaining at a given time and place. There is nothing in the learning principles that restrict[s] them to prior socialization or past history of learning. Social learning encompasses both the acquisition and the performance of the behavior, both facilitation and inhibition of behavior, and both learning successes and learning failures. The learning mechanisms account not only for the initiation of behavior but also for repetition, maintenance and desistance of behavior. They rely not only on prior behavioral processes but also on those operating at a given time in a given situation. . . .

Definitions and Discriminative Stimuli

[In] *The Concept of Definitions,* Sutherland asserted that learning criminal behavior includes "techniques of committing the crime which are sometimes very complicated, sometimes very simple" and the "specific direction of motives, drives, rationalizations and attitudes" (1947, p. 6). I have retained both definitions and techniques in social learning theory, with clarified and modified conceptual meanings and with hypothesized relationships to criminal behavior. The qualification that "techniques" may be simple or complex shows plainly that Sutherland did not mean to include only crime-specific skills learned in order to break the law successfully. Techniques also clearly include ordinary, everyday abilities. This same notion is retained in social learning theory.

By definition, a person must be capable of performing the necessary sequence of actions before he or she can carry out either criminal or conforming behavior—inability to perform the behavior precludes committing the crime. Since many of the behavioral techniques for both conforming and criminal acts are the same, not only the simple but even some of the complex skills involved in carrying out crime are not novel to most or many of us. The required component parts of the complete skill are acquired in essentially conforming or neutral contexts to which we have been exposed—driving a car, shooting a gun, fighting with fists, signing checks, using a computer, and so on. In most white-collar crime, the same skills needed to carry out a job legitimately are put to illegitimate use. Other skills are specific to given deviant acts—safe cracking, counterfeiting, pocket picking, jimmying doors and picking locks, bringing off a con game, and so on. Without tutelage in these crime-specific techniques, most people would not be able to perform them, or at least would be initially very inept.

Sutherland took the concept of "definitions" in his theory from W. I. Thomas's "definition of the situation" (Thomas and Thomas, 1928) and generalized it to orienting attitudes toward different behavior. It is true that "Sutherland did not identify what constitutes a definition 'favorable to' or 'unfavorable to' the violation of law" (Cressey, 1960, p. 53). Nevertheless . . . there is little doubt that "rationalizations" and "attitudes" are subsumed under the general concept of definitions—normative attitudes or evaluative meanings attached to given behavior. Exposure to others' shared definitions is a key (but not the only) part of the process by which the individual acquires or internalizes his or her own definitions. They are orientations, rationalizations, definitions of the situation, and other attitudes that label the commission of an act as right or wrong, good or bad, desirable or undesirable, justified or unjustified.

In social learning theory, these definitions are both general and specific. General beliefs include religious, moral, and other conventional values and norms that are favorable to conforming behavior and unfavorable to committing any of a range of deviant or criminal acts. Specific definitions orient the person to particular acts or series of acts. Thus, there are people who believe that it is morally wrong to steal and that laws against theft should be obeyed, but at the same time see little wrong with smoking marijuana and rationalize that it is all right to violate laws against drug possession. The greater the extent to which one holds attitudes that disapprove of certain acts, the less likely one is to engage in them. Conventional beliefs are negative toward criminal behavior. The more strongly one has learned and personally believes in the ideals of honesty, integrity, civility, kindness, and other general standards of morality that condemn lying, cheating, stealing, and harming others, the less likely he or she is to commit acts that violate social and legal norms. Conversely, the more one's own attitudes approve of, or fail to condemn, a behavior, the greater the chances are that he or she will engage in it. For obvious reasons, the theory would predict that definitions in the form of general beliefs will have less effect than specific definitions on the commission of specific criminal acts.

Definitions that favor criminal or deviant behavior are basically positive or neutralizing. Positive definitions are beliefs or attitudes that make the behavior morally desirable or wholly permissible. They are most likely to be learned through positive reinforcement in a deviant group or subculture that carries values conflicting with those of conventional society. Some of these positive verbalizations may be part of a full-blown ideology of politically dissident, criminal, or deviant groups. Although such ideologies and groups can be identified, the theory does not rest only on this type of definition favorable to deviance; indeed, it proposes that such positive definitions occur less frequently than neutralizing ones.

Neutralizing definitions favor violating the law or other norms not because they take the acts to be positively desirable but because they justify or excuse them. Even those who commit deviant acts are aware that others condemn the behavior and may themselves define the behavior as bad. The neutralizing definitions view the act as something that is probably undesirable but, given the situation, is nonetheless justified, excusable, necessary, all right, or not really bad after all. The process of acquiring neutralizing definitions is more likely to involve negative reinforcement; that is, they are verbalizations that accompany escape or avoidance of negative consequences like disapproval by one's self or by society.

While these definitions may become part of a deviant or criminal subculture, acquiring them does not require participation in such subcultures. They are learned from carriers of conventional culture, including many of those in social control and treatment agencies. The notions of techniques of neutralization and subterranean values (Sykes and Matza, 1957; Matza and Sykes, 1961; Matza, 1964) come from the observation that for nearly every social norm there is a norm of evasion. That is, there are recognized exceptions or ways of getting around the moral imperatives in the norms and the reproach expected for violating them. Thus, the general prohibition "Thou shalt not kill" is accompanied by such implicit or explicit exceptions as "unless in time of war," "unless the victim is the enemy," "unless in self-defense," "unless in the line of duty," "unless to protect others"! The moral injunctions against physical violence are suspended if the victim can be defined as the initial aggressor or is guilty of some transgression and therefore deserves to be attacked.

The concept of neutralizing definitions in social learning theory incorporates not only notions of verbalizations and rationalizations (Cressey, 1953) and techniques of neutralization (Sykes & Matza, 1957) but also conceptually similar if not equivalent notions of "accounts" (Lyman & Scott, 1970), "disclaimers" (Hewitt & Stokes, 1975), and "moral disengagement" (Bandura, 1976, 1990). Neutralizing attitudes include such beliefs as "Everybody has a racket"; "I can't help myself, I was born this way"; "It's not my fault"; "I am not responsible"; "I was drunk and didn't know what I was doing"; "I just blew my top"; "They can afford it"; "He deserved it." Some neutralizations (e.g., nonresponsibility) can be generalized to a wide range of disapproved and criminal behavior. These and other excuses and justifications for committing deviant acts and victimizing others are definitions favorable to criminal and deviant behavior.

Exposure to these rationalizations and excuses may be through after-the-fact justifications for one's own or others' norm violations that help to deflect or lessen punishment that would be expected to follow. The individual then learns the excuses either directly or through imitation and uses them to lessen self-reproach and social disapproval. Therefore, the definitions are themselves behavior that can be imitated and reinforced and then in turn serve as discriminative stimuli accompanying reinforcement of overt behavior. Deviant and criminal acts do occur without being accompanied by positive or neutralizing definitions, but the acts are more likely to occur and recur in situations the same as or similar to those in which the definitions have already been learned and applied. The extent to which one adheres to or rejects the definitions favorable to crime is itself affected by the rewarding or punishing consequences that follow the act.

References

Akers, R. L. (1985). *Deviant behavior: A social learning approach.* Belmont, CA: Wadsworth.

Akers, R. L., & La Greca, A. J. (1991). Alcohol use among the elderly: Social learning, community context, and life events. In D. J. Pittman & H. R. White (Eds.), *Society, culture, and drinking patterns re-examined* (pp. 242–262). New Brunswick, NJ: Rutgers Center of Alcohol Studies.

Akers, R. L., & Lee, G. (1996). A longitudinal test of social learning theory: Adolescent smoking. *Journal of Drug Issues, 26,* 317–343.

Bandura, A. (1969). *Principles of behavior modification.* New York: Holt, Rinehart & Winston.

Bandura, A. (1976). *Analysis of delinquency and aggression.* New York: Lawrence Erlbaum.

Bandura, A. (1977a). Self-efficacy: Toward a unifying theory of behavioral change. *Psychological Review, 84,* 191–215.

Bandura, A. (1977b). *Social learning theory.* Englewood Cliffs, NJ: Prentice Hall.

Bandura, A. (1986). *Social foundations of thought and action: A social cognitive theory.* Englewood Cliffs, NJ: Prentice Hall.

Bandura, A. (1989). Human agency and social cognitive theory. *American Psychologist, 44,* 1175–1184.

Bandura, A. (1990). Selective activation and disengagement of moral control. *Journal of Social Issues, 46,* 27–46.

Bandura, A., & Walters, R. H. (1963). *Social learning and personality development.* New York: Holt, Rinehart & Winston.

Burgess, R. L., & Akers, R. L. (1966b). A different association-reinforcement theory of criminal behavior. *Social Problems, 14,* 128–147.

Catalano, R. F., Kosterman, R., Hawkins, J. D., Newcomb, M. D., & Abbott, R. D. (1996). Modeling the etiology of adolescent substance use: A test of the social development model. *Journal of Drug Issues, 26,* 429–455.

Cornish, D. B., & Clarke, R. V. (1986). *The reasoning criminal: Rational choice perspectives on offending.* New York: Springer-Verlag.

Cressey, D. R. (1953). *Other people's money.* Glencoe, IL: Free Press.

Cressey, D. (1960). Epidemiology and individual conduct. *Pacific Sociological Review, 3,* 47–58.

Glueck, S., & Glueck, E. (1950). *Unraveling juvenile delinquency.* Cambridge, MA: Harvard University Press.

Gottfredson, M., & Hirschi, T. (1990). *A general theory of crime.* Stanford, CA: Stanford University Press.

Grusec, J. E. (1992). Social learning theory and developmental psychology: The legacies of Robert Sears and A. Bandura. *Developmental Psychology, 28,* 776–786.

Hewitt, J. P., & Stokes, R. (1975). Disclaimers. *American Sociological Review, 40,* 1–11.

Lyman, S. M., & Scott, M. B. (1970). *A sociology of the absurd.* New York: Appleton-Century-Crofts.

Matza, D. (1964). *Delinquency and drift.* New York: Wiley.

Matza, D., & Sykes, G. M. (1961). Juvenile delinquency and subterranean values. *American Sociological Review, 26,* 712–719.

Staats, A. (1975). *Social behaviorism.* Homewood, IL: Dorsey.

Stafford, M. C., & Ekland-Olson, S. (1982). On social learning and deviant behavior: A reappraisal of the findings. *American Sociological Review, 47,* 167–169.

Strictland, D. E. (1982). Social learning and deviant behavior: A specific test of a general theory: A comment and critique. *American Sociological Review, 47,* 162–167.

Sutherland, E. H. (1947). *Criminology.* Philadelphia: J. B. Lippincott.

Sykes, G. M., & Matza, D. (1957). Techniques of neutralization: A theory of delinquency. *American Sociological Review, 22,* 664–670.

Thomas, W. I., & Thomas, D. S. (1928). *The child in America: Behavior problems and programs.* New York: Knopf.

Thornberry, T. P., Lizotte, A. J., Krohn, M. D., Farnworth, M., & Jang, S. J. (1994). Delinquent peers, beliefs, and delinquent behavior: A longitudinal test of interactional theory. *Criminology, 32,* 47–83.

/// REVIEW QUESTIONS

1. What are the four main components of the theory of differential reinforcement according to Akers? Which of these propositions is primarily based on Sutherland's differential association theory? Which of these components is based on operant conditioning? Which of these are based on imitation and modeling? Explain your reasons in each case.

2. Akers seems to emphasize the importance of behavioral feedback and reciprocal effects. Explain what these concepts mean and why they are important.

3. What does Akers mean when he talks about the concept of definitions? Provide a thorough explanation and some examples.

READING /// 20

In this selection, Lynne Vieraitis, Nicole and Alex Piquero, Stephen Tibbetts, and Michael Blankenship examine gender differences in the effects of techniques of neutralization in decisions to engage in unethical decision-making in a corporate setting. One very interesting aspect of this study is that their sample is made up of students in a master of business administration (MBA) program, and a significant portion of this group were in an executive MBA program, meaning that they had many years of corporate experience. The students were asked how they would deal with the knowledge that a drug their company sold was found to be harmful to those who take it. Readers will likely find the results quite surprising and insightful.

While reading this entry, consider the following points:

- The new types of neutralization that were added to this study that were not presented by Gresham Sykes and David Matza in their original theoretical framework
- The gender that showed significantly higher intentions to engage in unethical corporate practices and explanations for why given the findings
- The reported results of the split-gender regression models with a focus on whether the estimated model did a better job of explaining unethical decision making by women or men and also which variables seemed to be driving the difference between gender differences

Do Women and Men Differ in Their Neutralizations of Corporate Crime?

Lynne M. Vieraitis, Nicole Leeper Piquero,
Alex R. Piquero, Stephen G. Tibbetts, and Michael Blankenship

Since its publication in 1957, Sykes and Matza's "Techniques of Neutralization: A Theory of Delinquency" has been one of the most influential and most frequently cited articles in the criminological literature—accounting for over 2,800 citations in Google Scholar as of September 2012. Their work was groundbreaking for its divergence from the then current assumption by criminological theorists that most delinquents were "committed" to delinquent values. It also marked a departure from the dominant thinking in psychology that individual behavior was undertaken in response to a series of positive and negative stimuli. In contrast, Sykes and Matza argued that most delinquents were not committed to delinquent values and did not conceive of themselves as delinquents or criminals. To maintain this "noncriminal" self-image, offenders justified their behaviors by employing one or more of the five techniques of neutralization as

SOURCE: Lynne M. Vieraitis, Nicole Leeper Piquero, Alex R. Piquero, Stephen G. Tibbetts, & Michael Blankenship. "Do Women and Men Differ in Their Neutralizations of Corporate Crime?" *Criminal Justice Review* 37 (2012): 478–93.

delineated by Sykes and Matza (1957), including denial of responsibility ("It's not my fault"), denial of injury ("No one got hurt"), denial of victim ("The victim had it coming"), appeal to higher loyalties ("I didn't do it for myself, I did it for my children"), and condemnation of the condemners ("The police are corrupt"). Subsequent studies on neutralization theory have produced additional excuses and justifications, including metaphor of the ledger ("I've done a lot of good things in my life"; Klockars, 1974), the claim of normality ("Everyone else is doing it"; Benson, 1985; Coleman, 2006), the defense of necessity ("I didn't have a choice"; Benson, 1985; Coleman, 2006; Minor, 1981), justification by comparison ("I'm not as bad as others"; Cromwell & Thurman, 2003), and the claim of entitlement ("I deserve this, they owed me"; Coleman, 2006).

Yet despite the number and scope of crimes and criminals examined by researchers, the gender differences among offenders' use of neutralizations are rarely examined and the differences between men and women remain an underexplored area of criminological research (for exceptions, see Copes & Vieraitis, 2012; Daly, 1989; Klenowski et al., 2011; Zietz, 1981).

Background

Current Focus

This article builds on prior research in the application of techniques of neutralization to white-collar/corporate crime by examining the degree to which men and women use specific techniques to account for their corporate offending. To the extent that techniques of neutralization operate as a general theoretical process, then we should find that men and women do or do not use the techniques in the same manner. Such a view does not negate the possibility of differences in the average values of techniques themselves. On the other hand, some gender-specific theoretical models and more gendered theories of crime would suggest that the theoretical processes underlying the gender–corporate crime relationship will evince differences not only in degree but also differences in kind. That is, the techniques men and women rely on to rationalize the same offending behavior should be used in different ways, such that some should matter for one group but not the other.

Data and Method

Data were obtained from a questionnaire administered to a convenience sample of 133 students enrolled in either a traditional MBA program (80%) or the executive MBA program (20%) at a single university.[1] The use of a sample of MBA students for this particular study is justified for at least three reasons. First, MBA students include a cadre of persons with knowledge about the business world and thus find themselves in situations where the opportunity for corporate misbehavior may occur. Second, although on the younger side of a typical business age structure, MBA students are to become future managers and corporate executives over the next few decades of their professional careers and understanding their decision-making styles provides a unique window into the sorts of things that may influence their decision making. Finally, on a practical level, there are very few secondary sources available that permit analyses of corporate malfeasance and none that contain the array of theoretical variables elaborated in neutralization theory with respect to corporate crime decision making.

The survey included a range of questions about attitudes toward business practices and also asked respondents to indicate their purported intentions to engage in a specific behavior after reading a scenario about a hypothetical drug. All 133 students were presented with the purpose of the study, were asked to participate, and all of them gave voluntary consent and completed the full survey. On average, the sample was over 30 years of age (M = 30.70, SD = 7.37, range: 22–55), mostly White (77%), and predominately male (67%).[2]

Dependent Variable

The use of scenarios (or vignettes) has been common in previous white-collar/corporate crime research (Paternoster & Simpson, 1996; N. L. Piquero, 2012; N. L. Piquero et al., 2005; N. L. Piquero, Exum, & Simpson, 2005; Simpson, Paternoster, & Piquero, 1998; Simpson & Piquero, 2002). This methodology presents a scenario to respondents depicting a hypothetical situation in which a character engages in a particular behavior or act. Following each scenario, respondents are typically asked (on a Likert-type scale) whether they would do what the character in the scenario did. The current study presented respondents with a scenario regarding the inhibition or promotion of a hypothetical drug, Panalba, which was banned by the Food and Drug Administration. Serving as the main outcome variable, respondents were asked to report the extent to which they would promote or inhibit the distribution of Panalba, which is known to harm persons. This measure was coded on a scale ranging from 1 to 6 as follows: (1) *recall Panalba immediately and destroy all existing inventories,* (2) *stop production of Panalba immediately but allow existing inventories to be sold,* (3) *stop all advertising and promotion of Panalba, but continue distribution to those physicians who request it,* (4) *continue efforts to effectively market Panalba until its sale is actually banned,* (5) *continue efforts to market Panalba while taking legal, political, and other actions to prevent its banning,* and (6) *continue efforts to market Panalba in other countries after the FDA bans the drug in the U.S.* The average score was 2.57 (SD = 1.70), which suggests that the average respondent chose to either stop production but allow existing inventories to be sold or to stop all advertising and promotion but continue distribution to physicians who request it.[3]

Techniques of Neutralization

Our measures of the techniques of neutralization are informed by the early research on neutralization, where studies used scenarios to assess the degree to which people accepted neutralizing statements under the assumption that delinquents would be more accepting of neutralizing statements than nondelinquents. Maruna and Copes's (2005) review of these studies provides strong validity for the techniques measures, and we use these as the starting point for our measures that are reoriented to the business domain. Specifically, we operationalize Sykes and Matza's five techniques of neutralization with modifications to reflect the context of the workplace environment and workplace decision making (see Hollinger, 1991; N. L. Piquero, Tibbetts, & Blankenship, 2005). All 5 items had response options that ranged from 1 (*strongly disagree*) to 3 (*neutral*) to 5 (*strongly agree*). Higher scores on all 5 items, which did not lead to concerns over multicollinearity as judged by variance inflation factors (VIFs) and the fact that the highest correlation among the five techniques items was $r = .435$, indicate stronger levels of neutralization and should be positively associated with increased intentions to promote and sell Panalba.

Denial of injury (government exaggerates dangers to consumers). Respondents were asked, "The government exaggerates the danger to consumers from most products." According to N. L. Piquero et al. (2005, p. 170), by agreeing with this statement, respondents are able "to deny the injury of the act by claiming that the government is overly cautious in assessing the danger to the public. This belief also relates to denial of responsibility in the sense that it implies that there is minimal danger in the use of marketed products, so the companies that produce such items should not be held responsible if injuries do happen to occur from usage."

Condemnation of the condemners (regulations impede). Respondents were asked: "Government regulations impede business." Here, the blame of the act is deflected to the government and the strict regulations it places on business.

Appeal to higher loyalty (profit most important). Respondents were asked: "Profit is emphasized above everything else at my place of work." By placing the blame onto the organization or company for which the respondent works, he or she is able to deflect feelings of guilt associated with the behavior and its outcomes.

Denial of victim (Caveat emptor motto). Respondents were asked: "'Caveat emptor' (let the buyer beware) is the motto of my employer." By deflecting the blame of the act onto the victim the respondent can claim that the victim should have known better.

Denial of responsibility (anything to make a profit). Respondents were asked: "Where I work, it is all right to do anything to make a profit unless it is against the law." Here, the individual places the responsibility of the act onto the organization (by its rules and culture of how it does its business) in which he or she is employed and thus can deny his or her own individual responsibility for the behavior and its outcomes.

Table 1 presents descriptive statistics for study variables.

Analytic Plan

To examine the extent to which techniques of neutralization relate to the marketing and sale of the unsafe drug Panalba across gender, we begin by examining the extent

Table 1 • Descriptive Statistics

Variable	*M* (*SD*)
Denial of injury	2.82 (1.09)
Condemnation of condemners	2.55 (1.00)
Appeal to higher loyalty	2.90 (1.24)
Denial of victim	2.30 (1.07)
Denial of responsibility	2.42 (1.11)
Gender (1 = *M*, 2 = *F*)	1.33 (0.47)
Age	30.70 (7.37)
Race (1 = *W*, 2 = *NW*)	1.77 (0.42)
Program (1 = *MBA*, 2 = *Exec*)	1.21 (0.41)
Intentions to offend	2.57 (1.67)

to which there are any gender differences with respect to (a) intentions to offend and (b) techniques of neutralization. To presuppose our findings, we do indeed observe some average differences for these two constructs. These preliminary results support the need to examine split-gender models where we examine the extent to which the techniques of neutralization relate to offending intentions in similar or unique ways for males and females using ordinary least squares (OLS) regression models.[4] A series of coefficient comparison tests will also be conducted to examine the equality of regression coefficients across gender (see Paternoster, Brame, Mazerolle, & Piquero, 1998).

Results

Bivariate Analysis

Initial results show that men and women significantly differ on the overall intentions outcome variable, with men ($M = 2.82$) reporting a significantly higher average value compared to women ($M = 2.04$; $t = 2.78$, $p < .05$). Figure 1 provides a graphical portrayal of this relationship. Here, it can be seen that while there are a higher percentage of women at the two lower decision options (recalling Panalba, stopping production of Panalba), at the other end of the continuum there is a higher percentage of men who would impede the ban of Panalba or who would continue to market Panalba outside the United States.

Having established a bivariate relationship between gender and offending intentions, we next examine how men and women responded to the five techniques of neutralization items. As seen in Table 2, there are significant differences on two of the items and no differences on the other three items. With respect to the two items that differ across gender, (a) men are more likely than women to agree that the government exaggerates the danger to consumers from most products (denial of injury) and (b) women are more likely to agree that government regulations impede business (condemnation of the condemners).

Full-Sample Analysis

Next, we estimated a full-sample OLS regression model predicting offending intentions with the five techniques of neutralization measures, gender, and three control variables (age, race, MBA program status). Three of the techniques variables are significantly associated with higher

Figure 1 • Relationship between gender and intentions to inhibit or promote Panalba

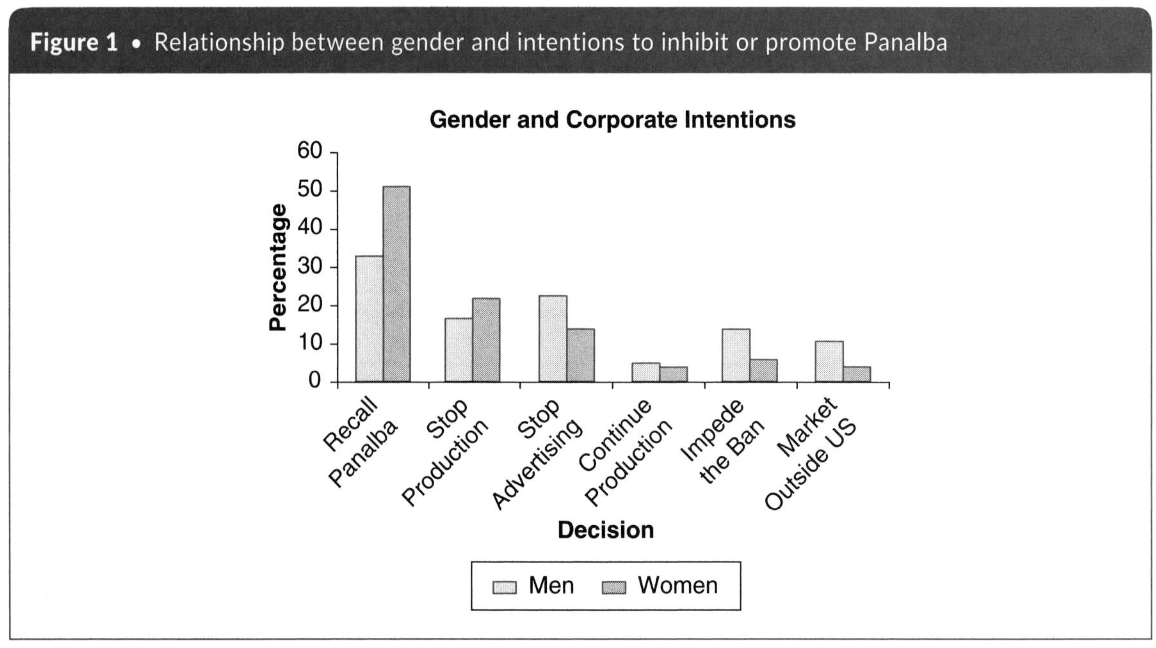

intentions to offend: denial of injury (government exaggerates), condemnation of the condemners (regulations impede), and appeal to higher loyalty (profit is most important), and the model explains almost 20% of the variation in offending intentions.[5] Higher agreement with each of these techniques was associated with continued interest in marketing and selling Panalba. Confirming the bivariate results, we found that women were less likely to market and sell Panalba and instead more likely to recall it or stop its production. Of the control variables, only program status was significant, indicating that executive MBA enrollees were less likely to report affirmative intentions to offend.[6] In short, these findings show that techniques of neutralization relate to corporate misbehavior in some similar ways when compared to how neutralizations have been found to relate to other deviant acts. Yet, we also find some differences in that not all techniques that have been found to relate to deviance in other studies relate similarly to corporate deviance, supporting Sykes and Matza's suggestion that certain techniques are better

Table 2 • Mean Differences for Techniques of Neutralization by Gender

Technique of Neutralization	Men *M* (*SD*)	Women *M* (*SD*)
Denial of injury	3.02 (1.12)	2.41 (0.89)*
Condemnation of condemners	2.36 (0.97)	2.96 (0.96)*
Appeal to higher loyalty	2.93 (1.24)	2.86 (1.25)
Denial of victim	2.28 (1.03)	2.31 (1.14)
Denial of responsibility	2.50 (1.11)	2.24 (1.10)

NOTE: *$p < .05$.

adapted to particular deviant acts than others (p. 670). Further, the results indicate that certain techniques of neutralization appear better adapted to corporate misbehavior than other techniques, but whether this pattern of findings replicates across gender is unknown and becomes the focus of the next set of analyses.

Gender-Specific Models Predicting Offending Intentions

Next, we estimate split-gender models to ascertain the relationship between the techniques of neutralization and offending intentions for men and women (see Table 3).[7] Among men, two of the five techniques were significantly associated with offending intentions: denial of injury (government exaggerates) and appeal to higher loyalties (profit most important). Once again, agreeing with these techniques was associated with continued efforts to impede the ban of Panalba or market the sale of Panalba outside the United States. Among women, two of the five techniques of neutralization were significantly associated with offending intentions. Specifically, women who agreed that the government exaggerates the danger from most products (denial of injury) to consumers were more likely to report affirmative offending intentions. On the other hand, and opposite of the corresponding male coefficient, women who believed that their place of business eschewed the belief that it was acceptable to do anything to make a profit unless it was against the law (denial of responsibility) were more likely to report higher offending intentions. None of the other three techniques of neutralization were significantly related to offending intentions among women. One control variable, MBA program status, had a negative and significant effect on offending intentions among women, with women in the executive MBA program reporting lower offending intentions. However, there were only eight women in the executive MBA program and this effect should be interpreted with caution.[8] In short, we find that some techniques operate in the same way across gender (denial of injury), others are gender-specific (i.e., higher loyalties for males but denial of responsibility for females), and others that are unimportant for either males or females. Thus, some neutralizations appear gender-neutral while others may be gender-specific.

Table 3 • Split-Gender OLS Regressions Predicting Intentions to Inhibit or Promote Panalba

	Men *B (SE)*	Women *B (SE)*
Denial of injury	0.40 (0.17)*	0.62 (0.27)*
Condemnation of condemners	0.22 (0.21)	0.15 (0.24)
Appeal to higher loyalty	0.41 (0.16)*	−0.24 (0.21)
Denial of victim	−0.03 (0.21)	−0.14 (0.19)
Denial of responsibility	−0.08 (0.19)	0.53 (0.24)*
Age	0.04 (0.03)	−0.01 (0.04)
Race (1 = W, 2 = NW)	−0.54 (0.52)	0.33 (0.43)
Program (1 = MBA, 2 = Exec)	−0.70 (0.54)	−1.48 (0.63)*
Constant	0.82 (1.73)	1.49 (2.30)
R^2	.16	.39

NOTE: *$p < .05$, unstandardized coefficient reported.

Discussion

Sykes and Matza's neutralization theory has been applied to a wide variety of offenders. Although a sound empirical knowledge base has accumulated (Maruna & Copes, 2005), the examination of the role of gender has received limited attention. The present study assessed the extent to which techniques of neutralization related to corporate offending decisions varied across gender. In doing so, it sought to contribute to underdeveloped and underexplored research areas in criminology more generally, by focusing on potential gender differences in corporate offending (see N. L. Piquero & Moffitt, 2012). Using a sample of MBA students, four key findings emerged from our analysis.

First, bivariate comparisons showed that men were more likely than women to indicate their intention to commit corporate crime by agreeing to continue to market or sell the banned drug Panalba. Second, men and women differed from one another on two of the five techniques of neutralization: Men were most likely to rely on denial of injury to justify their intention to offend, while women reported greater agreement with condemnation of condemners. Third, regression analyses of the full sample indicated that women were less likely to continue to market and sell Panalba and more likely to recall the drug or stop its production and that three techniques of neutralization (appeal to higher loyalties, condemnation of condemners, and denial of injury) were associated with greater corporate offending intentions. Finally, split-gender analysis indicated that one of the techniques, denial of injury, was significantly associated with greater intentions to offend for both men and women, while appeal to higher loyalties was a significant predictor among men and denial of responsibility was a significant predictor among women. A series of coefficient comparison tests of the relationship between the five techniques of neutralization measures and corporate offending intentions across gender failed to indicate any significant difference between men and women.

In short, our analyses showed gender differences in intentions to offend and minor mean-level differences between men and women for only a few of the techniques of neutralization. Our finding that women were less likely than men to report intentions to engage in corporate crime (by marketing and continuing to sell Panalba) is consistent with what little is known about white-collar offending differences between men and women. Data from convicted white-collar offenders repeatedly suggest that men are more commonly involved in the more complex white-collar crimes (i.e., antitrust and securities fraud), while women are involved in the less complex offenses such as bank embezzlement (Weisburd, Waring, & Chayet, 2001; Weisburd et al., 1991). In fact, Daly (1989) found that the female share of corporate crime was quite low, approximately 1%, and thus, noted that almost all of women's white-collar crimes were petty offenses.

Authors' Note

Michael Blankenship passed away on April 21, 2011. He was responsible for the data collection used in this study and we are indebted to his contribution and friendship.

Declaration of Conflicting Interests

The authors declared no potential conflicts of interest with respect to the research, authorship, and/or publication of this article.

Funding

The authors received no financial support for the research, authorship, and/or publication of this article.

Notes

1. The academic content of the executive MBA program does not significantly differ from that of the traditional MBA program but is designed to accommodate full-time working professionals and business executives. As such, those enrolling in the executive MBA program tend to have much more business or "real-world" experience than their counterparts in the traditional MBA program.

2. As with any sampling frame, the use of university students, even in MBA programs, is limited. Still, given the lack of available data on business decision making within a criminological context (Simpson & Piquero, 2002), the application of techniques of neutralization across gender in the current study provides a baseline to which future studies can be modeled after and results compared against.

3. We recognize that there may be some concerns over the use of the vignette methodology and the solicitation of purported offending intentions. For example, the method has been

criticized because it places individuals in a hypothetical situation that may not be realistic or that such persons may not (now or ever) find themselves in. And while such methods have been routinely used in criminology generally (Nagin & Paternoster, 1993; A. Piquero & Tibbetts, 1996) and the study of white-collar/corporate crime in particular (Simpson et al., 1998; Simpson & Piquero, 2002; N. L. Piquero, 2012; N. L. Piquero, Tibbetts, & Blankenship, 2005), there is the issue about whether purported intentions equate perfectly with actual behavior. Importantly, the survey used in our study was modeled closely after those that have been successfully administered and judged valid and realistic by survey respondents (including our own, who rated the scenario as very believable) and furthermore there are a sizable number of studies showing a strong concordance between projected and actual behavior (Pogarsky, 2004).

4. Although the distribution of the outcome variable did not evince any extreme skew, we also estimated supplemental Ordered Logistic Regression models, the results of which were substantively the same as those reported in the main text with OLS.

5. There were no problems with multicollinearity in this (or subsequent) model estimations.

6. Caution should be exercised with respect to the MBA program status effect as there were only 31 enrollees in the executive MBA program. We nevertheless felt the need to control for program status because there may be a "different kind" of student in the executive compared to traditional program.

7. Since the sample size for female respondents is small, caution should be exercised when interpreting these results.

8. A series of coefficient comparison tests indicated that only one coefficient (denial of responsibility technique: anything to make a profit) approached being significantly different across gender ($z = 1.47$). Although not statistically significant at conventional levels, this is a potentially interesting difference as the effect was negative and insignificant for males but positive and significant for females.

References

Benson, M. L. (1985). Denying the guilty mind: Accounting for involvement in white-collar crime. *Criminology, 23,* 583–608.

Borkowski, S. C., & Ugras, Y. J. (1998). Business students and ethics: A meta-analysis. *Journal of Business Ethics, 17,* 117–127.

Brookman, F., Mullins, C., Bennett, T., & Wright, R. (2007). Gender, motivation and the accomplishment of street robbery in the United Kingdom. *British Journal of Criminology, 47,* 861–884.

Brooks-Gordon, B., & Gelsthorpe, L. (2003). What men say when apprehended for kerb crawling: A model of prostitutes clients' talk. *Psychology, Crime and Law, 9,* 145–171.

Byers, B. D., & Crider, B. W. (2002). Hate crimes against the Amish: A qualitative analysis of bias motivation using routine activities theory. *Deviant Behavior, 23,* 115–148.

Cohen, A. K. (1955). *Delinquent boys: The culture of the gang.* New York, NY: Free Press.

Coleman, J. W. (2006). *The criminal elite: Understanding white-collar crime* (6th ed.). New York, NY: Worth.

Copes, H. (2003). Societal attachments, offending frequency, and techniques of neutralization. *Deviant Behavior, 24,* 101–127.

Copes, H., & Vieraitis, L. M. (2009). Bounded rationality of identity thieves: Using offender-based research to inform policy. *Criminology & Public Policy, 8,* 101–126.

Copes, H., & Vieraitis, L. M. (2012). *Identity thieves: Motives and methods.* Boston, MA: Northeastern University Press.

Copes, H., Vieraitis, L. M., & Jochum, J. (2007). Bridging the gap between research and practice: How neutralization theory can inform Reid interrogations of identity thieves. *Journal of Criminal Justice Education, 18,* 444–459.

Copes, H., & Williams, P. (2007). Techniques of affirmation: Deviant behavior, moral commitment, and resistant subcultural identity. *Deviant Behavior, 28,* 247–272.

Cressey, D. R. (1953). *Other people's money: A study in the social psychology of embezzlement.* Glencoe, IL: Free Press.

Cromwell, P., & Thurman, Q. (2003). The devil made me do it: Use of neutralizations by shoplifters. *Deviant Behavior, 24,* 535–550.

Dabney, D. A. (1995). Neutralization and deviance in the workplace: Theft of supplies and medicines by hospital nurses. *Deviant Behavior, 16,* 313–331.

Daly, K. (1989). Gender and varieties of white collar crime. *Criminology, 27,* 769–794.

DeYoung, M. (1988). The indignant page: Techniques of neutralization in the publications of pedophile organizations. *Child Abuse and Neglect, 12,* 583–591.

Durkin, K. F., & Bryant, C. (1999). Propagandizing pederasty: A thematic analysis of the on-line exculpatory accounts of unrepentant pedophiles. *Deviant Behavior, 20,* 103–127.

Edelhertz, H. (1970). *The nature, impact and prosecution of white-collar crime.* Washington, DC: U.S. Department of Justice.

Eliason, S. L., & Dodder, R. (1999). Techniques of neutralization used by deer poachers in the Western United States. *Deviant Behavior, 20,* 233–252.

Evans, R. D., & Porche, D. A. (2005). The nature and frequency of medicare/medicaid fraud and neutralization techniques among speech, occupational, and physical therapists. *Deviant Behavior, 26,* 253–270.

Ferraro, K. J., & Johnson, J. M. (1983). How women experience battering: The process of victimization. *Social Problems, 30,* 325–339.

Goode, S., & Cruise, S. (2006). What motivates software crackers? *Journal of Business Ethics, 65,* 173–201.

Greenberg, J. (1990). Employee theft as a reaction to underpayment inequity: The hidden cost of pay cuts. *Journal of Applied Psychology, 75,* 561–568.

Higginson, J. G. (1999). Defining, excusing, and justifying deviance: Teen mothers' accounts of statutory rape. *Symbolic Interaction, 22,* 25–44.

Hollinger, R. C. (1991). Neutralizing in the workplace: An empirical analysis of property theft and production deviance. *Deviant Behavior, 12,* 169–202.

Holt, T. J., & Copes, H. (2010). Transferring subcultural knowledge online: Practices and beliefs of persistent digital pirates. *Deviant Behavior, 31,* 625–654.

Holtfreter, K. (2005). Is occupational fraud "typical" white-collar crime? A comparison of individual and organizational characteristics. *Journal of Criminal Justice, 33,* 353–365.

Ingram, J. R., & Hinduja, S. (2008). Neutralizing music piracy: An empirical examination. *Deviant Behavior, 29,* 334–366.

Jesilow, P., Pontell, H. N., & Geis, G. (1993). *Prescription for profit: How doctors defraud Medicaid.* Berkeley: University of California Press.

Klenowski, P. M., Copes, H., & Mullins, C. W. (2011). Gender, identity, and accounts: How white collar offenders do gender when making sense of their crimes. *Justice Quarterly, 28,* 46–69.

Klockars, C. B. 1974. *The professional fence.* New York, NY: Free Press.

Levi, K. 1981. Becoming a hit man: Neutralization in a very deviant career. *Urban Life, 10,* 47–63.

Maruna, S., & Copes, H. (2005). What have we learned from five decades of neutralization research? *Crime and Justice: A Review of Research, 32,* 221–320.

Miller, J. (1998). Up it up: Gender and the accomplishment of street robbery. *Criminology, 36,* 37–66.

Minor, W. W. (1981). Techniques of neutralization: A reconceptualization and empirical examination. *Journal of Research in Crime and Delinquency, 18,* 295–318.

Mullins, C., & Cherbonneau, M. (2011). Establishing connections: Gender, motor vehicle theft, and disposal networks. *Justice Quarterly, 28,* 278–302.

Mullins, C., Wright, R., & Jacobs, B. A. (2004). Gender, streetlife, and criminal retaliation. *Criminology, 42,* 911–940.

Nagin, D. S., & Paternoster, R. (1993). Enduring individual differences and rational choice theories of crime. *Law & Society Review, 27,* 467–469.

Paternoster, R., Brame, R., Mazerolle, P., & Piquero, A. (1998). Using the correct statistical test for the equality of regression coefficients. *Criminology, 36,* 859–866.

Paternoster, R., & Simpson, S. (1996). Sanction threats and appeals to morality: Testing a rational choice model of corporate crime. *Law and Society Review, 30,* 549–583.

Peretti-Watel, P. (2003). Neutralization theory and the denial of risk: Some evidence from cannabis use among French adolescents. *British Journal of Sociology, 54,* 21–42.

Piquero, A., & Tibbetts, S. G. (1996). Specifying the direct and indirect effects of low self-control and situational factors in offender decision making: Toward a more complete model of rational offending. *Justice Quarterly, 13,* 601–631.

Piquero, A. R., Farrington, D. P., & Blumstein, A. (2003). The criminal career paradigm. In M. Tonry (Ed.), *Crime and justice: A review of research (Vol. 30).* Chicago, IL: University of Chicago Press.

Piquero, N. L. (2012). The only thing we have to fear is fear itself: Investigating the relationship between fear of falling and white-collar crime. *Crime and Delinquency, 58,* 362–379.

Piquero, N. L., & Moffitt, T. E. (2012). Can childhood factors explain workplace deviance? *Justice Quarterly,* doi:10.1080/07418825.2012.661446

Piquero, N. L., Exum, M. L., & Simpson, S. S. (2005). Integrating the desire for control and rational choice in a corporate crime context. *Justice Quarterly, 22,* 252–280.

Piquero, N. L., Tibbetts, S. G., & Blankenship, M. B. (2005). Examining the role of differential association and techniques of neutralization in explaining corporate crime. *Deviant Behavior, 26,* 159–188.

Pogarsky, G. (2004). Projected offending and contemporaneous rule violation: Implications for heterotypic continuity. *Criminology, 42,* 111–135.

Pogrebin, M. R., Poole, E. D., & Martinez, A. (1992). Accounts of professional misdeeds: The sexual exploitation of clients by psychotherapists. *Deviant Behavior, 13,* 229–252.

Pogrebin, M. R., Stretesky, P. B., Unnithan, N. P., & Venor, G. (2006). Retrospective accounts of violent events by gun offenders. *Deviant Behavior, 27,* 479–501.

Presser, L. (2003). Remorse and neutralization among violent male offenders. *Justice Quarterly, 20,* 801–825.

Priest, T. B., & McGrath, J. H., III. (1970). Techniques of neutralization: Young adult marijuana smokers. *Criminology, 8,* 185–194.

Ray, M. C., & Simons, R. L. (1987). Convicted murderers' accounts of their crimes: A study of homicide in small communities. *Symbolic Interaction, 10,* 57–70.

Scully, D., & Marolla, J. (1984). Convicted rapists' vocabulary of motive: Excuses and justifications. *Social Problems, 31,* 530–544.

Shapiro, S. P. (1990). Collaring the crime, not the criminal: Reconsidering the concept of white-collar crime. *American Sociological Review, 55,* 346–365.

Shover, N., Coffey, G., & Sanders, C. R. (2004). Dialing for dollars: Opportunities, justifications, and telemarketing fraud. *Qualitative Sociology, 27,* 59–75.

Simpson, S. S., Paternoster, R., & Piquero, N. L. (1998). Exploring the micro-macro link in corporate crime research. In P. A. Bamberger & W. J. Sonnenstuhl (Eds.), *Research in the sociology of organizations* (Vol. 15, pp. 35–68). Stamford, CT: JAI Press.

Simpson, S. S., & Piquero, N. L. (2002). Low self-control, organizational theory, and corporate crime. *Law & Society Review, 36*, 509–547.

Sutherland, E. H. (1983). *White collar crime: The uncut version.* New Haven, CT: Yale University Press.

Sutherland, E. H. (1940). White-collar criminality. *American Sociological Review, 5*, 1–12.

Sykes, G. M., & Matza, D. (1957). Techniques of neutralization: A theory of delinquency. *American Sociological Review, 22*, 664–670.

Thurman, Q. C., St. John, C. & Riggs, L. (1984). Neutralizations and tax evasion: How effective would a moral appeal be in improving compliance to tax laws? *Law and Policy, 6*, 309–328.

Vaughan, D. (1996). *The challenger launch decision: Risky technology, culture and deviance at NASA*. Chicago, IL: University of Chicago Press.

Weisburd, D., Waring, E., & Chayet, E. (2001). *White-collar crime and criminal careers.* New York, NY: Cambridge University Press.

Weisburd, D., Wheeler, S., Waring, E., & Bode, N. (1991). *Crimes of the middle classes.* New Haven, CT: Yale University Press.

Zietz, D. (1981). *Women who embezzle or defraud: A study of convicted felons.* New York, NY: Praeger Publishers.

/// REVIEW QUESTIONS

1. What are some of the additional neutralization techniques that have been added over the years to Sykes and Matza's original five that they presented back in 1957?
2. Which gender showed significantly higher intentions to engage in unethical corporate practices?
3. According to the reported results of the split-gender regression models, did the estimated model do a better job of explaining unethical decision making by women or men?

READING /// 21

This empirical study examines gender differences in the effects of peer influence on delinquency rates of a sample of youth from the Netherlands. Frank M. Weerman and Machteld Hoeve utilize a theoretical framework based on Terrie Moffitt's taxonomy of offenders to examine possible explanations of the gender gap in criminal behavior. The findings also have implications for social learning theories, particularly regarding the sex composition of peer groups in affecting boys' and girls' own delinquent activity.

While reading this article, one should consider the following topics:

- The competing explanations for the gender gap in delinquency between males and females, specifically the "differential exposure hypothesis" versus the "vulnerability hypothesis"
- What previous studies show regarding gender differences in terms of peer influences on youth delinquent behavior
- Findings of the current study regarding the impact of the predicting variables on criminal behavior, especially those of the various peer-related variables between boys and girls
- How the results of the current study align (or differ) from previous studies regarding the influence of peer groups on delinquent activity between males and females

SOURCE: Frank M. Weerman and Machteld Hoeve, "Peers and Delinquency among Girls and Boys: Are Sex Differences in Delinquency Explained by Peer Factors?" *European Journal of Criminology* 9, no. 3 (2012): 228–44.

Peers and Delinquency among Girls and Boys

Are Sex Differences in Delinquency Explained by Peer Factors?

Frank M. Weerman and Machteld Hoeve

Introduction

The relationship between peers and delinquent behaviour is one of the most researched and debated issues in criminology (Warr, 2002). Many studies have found associations between an individual's delinquent behaviour and delinquent behaviour among friends (for example, Elliott et al., 1985; Matsueda and Anderson, 1998; Patterson and Dishion, 1985) or other peer factors, such as time spent with peers (Osgood and Anderson, 2005; Svensson and Oberwittler, 2010). Recently, the use of social network data among youths has provided new insights into the relationship between peers and delinquency (Haynie, 2001; Weerman and Bijleveld, 2007).

Within this still growing body of research, limited attention has been paid to sex differences in the relationship between peer variables and delinquent behaviour. This is unfortunate because various studies have reported that the peer relationships of girls differ in various aspects from those of boys (Erwin, 1998; Rose and Rudolph, 2006; Waldrop and Halverson, 1975). Such differences may imply that the influence of peers on delinquency is different for girls compared with boys. For example, the effects of delinquent peers may be weaker for girls because they are less susceptible to them, or other aspects of peer relations may be more important for girls. It is also possible that the effects are similar for girls and boys but that girls are differentially exposed to criminogenic influences from peers, leading to less delinquent behaviour.

Extensive study of the role of peers among girls and boys can contribute to understanding the so-called 'gender gap' in crime—the finding that, on average, females and girls are less involved in delinquency than are males and boys (see Mears et al., 1998; Moffitt et al., 2001). Studies that have been conducted on sex differences in the relationship between peers and delinquency have not been conclusive. Further, most of these studies have been confined to the United States. European studies focusing on the explanation of sex differences in delinquency are still scarce (for example, Junger-Tas et al., 2004; see, for a systematic review, Wong et al., 2010). Most of them do not include peer factors or employ only one peer measure, peer delinquency (as perceived by the respondents).

In this article, we focus on sex differences and the relationship between peer factors and delinquency. We use data from the School Study from the Netherlands Institute for the Study of Crime and Law Enforcement (NSCR), which included a longitudinal survey and the collection of social network data among secondary school students. The study was aimed specifically at the relationship between peers and delinquency, and rich data about peer factors were collected, including measurements of peer delinquency as reported by the peers themselves, time spent with peers, peer attachment, peer pressure and the sex composition of peer networks. Together with measures of important other correlates of delinquency, these data enable us to investigate in detail the relationship between peers and delinquency among girls and boys.

The 'Gender Gap' in Delinquency and Potential Sex Differences in Peer Relations

Moffitt et al. (2001) addressed several general explanations for the 'gender gap' in crime, in particular the 'differential exposure hypothesis' and the 'vulnerability hypothesis'. The differential exposure hypothesis posits that the causes of delinquency are the same for males and females but that males are more exposed than females to risk factors. According to the vulnerability hypothesis, the aetiology of delinquency may differ for males and females. Males may be more vulnerable than females to certain risk factors (Moffitt et al., 2001).

Applying the differential exposure hypothesis to the relationship between peers and juvenile delinquency, an explanation of the gender gap could be that females simply have fewer peers who engage in delinquent behaviour than do males. This would imply that females are less exposed to the peer influences hypothesized in various criminological theories that are based on principles of social learning (Akers, 1973; Sutherland, 1947; Warr, 2002). Unfortunately, these theories do not provide much information about why these sex differences may exist. One of the explanations they do provide (see Warr, 2002) is that girls may be less exposed to peer influences because they experience higher levels of social control. Studies consistently find that parental supervision and monitoring are less intense for boys than for girls (Svensson, 2003).

Females may also be less exposed than males to deviant peer influences because adolescents tend to become friends with someone of the same sex (Benenson, 1990; Weerman and Smeenk, 2005). Very young girls display a preference to play with someone of the same sex as early as the age of 2; for boys this preference starts a little later. At the age of 6 or 7, both boys and girls play almost exclusively with someone of the same sex and this extends into adolescence (Erwin, 1998). As a consequence, female adolescents will get less exposure than male adolescents to delinquent peers (Moffitt et al., 2001).

Contrary to the differential exposure hypothesis, the differential vulnerability hypothesis suggests that the gender gap might be explained by differences between girls and boys in the relationship between peers and delinquency. According to this reasoning, females would be less influenced than males by their peers, even when they are also exposed to delinquent peers. The literature on peer relationships in adolescence reveals that this may be a plausible hypothesis. Although studies find several similarities between boys' and girls' friendships (for example, they both want to experience trust, authenticity and similar status), they also report substantial gender differences in the nature of friendships. According to Waldrop and Halverson (1975), females tend to concentrate on one or a few best friends more often than do males, and their peer relations tend to be characterized more strongly by intimacy, emotional involvement and confidentiality. Girls have also been found to be more prosocial towards their friends and to feel more empathy for their friends (Rose and Rudolph, 2006). Boys, on the other hand, find it difficult to talk about personal matters and have more friendships in groups. Their peer networks are characterized by more hierarchy (Rose and Rudolph, 2006).

Another reason for females to be less vulnerable to (deviant) peers is that they may be less sensitive to peer influences or group pressures. Male identities seem to place a stronger emphasis on competitiveness, whereas female identities are relatively more concerned with relations to others and dependency (Agnew, 2009). These differences are partly caused by biological differences between the sexes but are enhanced by cultural role patterns and gender-specific social expectations (Eliot, 2010). Further, females' stronger moral beliefs may protect them from the negative influences of peers (Warr, 2002). Boys have a greater tendency to approve of delinquent behaviours in particular circumstances, for example in the context of conflicting loyalties (Agnew, 2009).

In summary, two hypotheses can be formulated about potential gender differences in the relationship between peers and delinquency: (1) delinquent behaviour of girls is influenced by peers in the same way as that of boys, but girls are less exposed than boys to peer influences for several reasons, including a preference for same-sex friendships (differential exposure hypothesis); (2) girls are less vulnerable to the influence of (deviant) peers, because they differ from boys in the quality of their peer relations, sensitivity to peer pressure and moral beliefs (differential vulnerability hypothesis). Separately or in concert, these two hypotheses may contribute to the explanation of why females engage less often in delinquency.

Earlier Studies on Sex Differences in the Relationship between Peers and Delinquency

Several studies have focused on sex differences in peer influences on delinquency. In order to measure delinquency in peers, most of these studies relied on reports by participants on the extent to which their peers engaged in delinquent behaviour (Hartjen and Priyadarsini, 2003; Laird et al., 2005; Mears et al., 1998; Piquero et al., 2005).

Most of these studies report significant and similarly sized correlations between delinquent peers and individual delinquency for boys as well as for girls. Laird et al. (2005), in a longitudinal study, compared reports by almost 400 boys and girls and found relatively similar effects of delinquent peers. Several meta-analyses on gender differences in risk factors of delinquency also report that the effects of peer variables on delinquency in girls are comparable to the effects in boys (Hubbard and Pratt, 2002; Simourd and Andrews, 1994; Wong et al., 2010).

A limitation of the conventional method of measuring peer delinquency by asking respondents about their perception of their peers' behaviour is that adolescents have no full information about their peers and may project their own behaviour on them. Earlier studies (Kandel, 1996; Weerman and Smeenk, 2005) have suggested that respondents often misperceive the delinquency levels of their peers and overestimate similarity to their own behaviour. Until now, only a few studies on gender differences in the relationship between peers and delinquency have used social network methods by which peers report about themselves. Haynie and Osgood (2005) collected data on peer relations in a large sample of almost 9000 adolescents, and found only modest effects of mean levels of peer delinquency on individual delinquency, and these effects were found to be similar for males and females. In a smaller study using social network methods, Brendgen et al. (2000) found that peer delinquency mainly had a short-term effect on individual delinquency, and the findings were similar for males and females.

Whereas most studies report evidence that the influence of delinquent peers is relatively similar for both boys and girls, a few studies found gender differences in the relationship between peer factors and delinquency. A cross-sectional study conducted by Mears et al. (1998) reported that boys were more strongly affected than girls by delinquent peers, and that delinquent peers had an effect only on girls who did not have a negative attitude towards delinquency. Otherwise, moral rejection of offending moderated the influence of peers among females but not among males. Using longitudinal data, Piquero et al. (2005) found that peer factors had stronger effects on delinquency in males than in females. They also found that peer influence was moderated by other factors, including disapproval of delinquency and legal sanctions.

The aforementioned studies on the relationship between peers and delinquency do not take the sex composition of peer relations into account. Recently, a few studies (Haynie et al., 2007; McCarthy et al., 2004) have investigated whether cross-gender peer relations are related to delinquent behaviour. These studies on the sex composition of peer relations revealed that girls seem to be more delinquent when they have a lot of male peers. The risk of delinquency in boys, on the other hand, seems to decrease if they have more friends of the opposite sex. Thus, cross-gender peers seem to have a different effect on males and females.[1]

To summarize, previous studies have shown that the influence of peers on delinquency is relatively similar for males and females. A few studies, however, found that boys' delinquency is more strongly affected than girls' delinquency by peer factors. The vast majority of these studies have been conducted in North America. Only a few European studies exist that focus on explanatory factors for gender differences in delinquency (for a systematic review, see Wong et al., 2010). Most of the previous studies have focused on only one peer measure and used the conventional method of peer delinquency as perceived by the respondents instead of reported by the peers themselves. In the present study, we focus on several peer factors and we use a measurement of peer delinquency derived from the peers themselves. The sex composition of peer groups will also be taken into account. In addition, the study is longitudinal and controls for other important risk factors such as individual, family and school factors in order to analyse the unique contribution of peer factors to delinquency in males and females.

Method

Sample

In the present study, we used data from 1110 respondents, who participated fully in the first and second waves of the NSCR School Study (conducted in spring 2002 and 2003). The respondents were recruited in 10 secondary schools that participated in the full study in both waves.[2] The sampling procedure was intended to obtain a relatively 'high-risk' sample together with substantial variation in contexts. Therefore, students in lower vocational education in a major Dutch city (The Hague) were overrepresented in the sample,[3] but respondents from schools in smaller cities and towns in the region were also included. This procedure implies that the sample is not random, but that it should be considered as a fairly good representation of lower-educated youths in the urbanized southwest region of the Netherlands.

The sample is divided in two age cohorts: a younger cohort of students who were in the first grade of secondary school during the first wave of the study (mostly 13 years old), and an older cohort from students that were in the third grade during the first wave (mostly 15 years old). In total, 1561 respondents from the 10 schools participated in the first wave; in the second wave, 1156 students participated again, of whom 1110 provided usable network information in both study waves. This means that there was a total loss of 28.9 percent of students between the first wave and the second. Attrition analysis shows that respondents who fell out of the sample did not differ significantly in sex or ethnic background. However, they did differ significantly in their level of delinquent behaviour, indicating that relatively delinquent youths participated less often in the second wave. To investigate whether this might influence our conclusions, additional analyses were conducted in which respondents were weighted based on their delinquency level at wave 1. It appeared that results with these weights were similar to those reported in the paper, indicating that there is no reason to believe that the selective attrition biased our findings.

The final sample contained more boys than girls (57 percent versus 43 percent). Ages ranged from 11 to 18 years in the first wave but, owing to the cohort design of the study (first and third grades), respondents aged 13 and 15 years in the first wave dominated (respectively 37 percent and 22 percent; the mean age is 13.9). The majority of respondents (61 percent) went to school in the large city area of The Hague (about 500,000 inhabitants), a substantial number (27 percent) lived in a medium-sized city (about 120,000 inhabitants) and some respondents (12 percent) were recruited in a smaller town (about 15,000 inhabitants). More than one-third of the sample consisted of respondents with an immigrant background,[4] but respondents with parents born in the Netherlands were in the majority (60 percent).

The questionnaires were group administered in the classroom setting during school hours and at least two members of the research team were present during the administration of the questionnaire. Computers were used instead of the usual paper and pencil method, to enhance completion of all questions and facilitate data entry. Parents were informed about the study and could refuse participation by their child (passive consent). Respondents received a reward when they completed the questionnaire (a €5 voucher).

Measures

Delinquent behaviour was measured using self-report questions about 12 different offences, ranging from painting graffiti and stealing small things to burglary and robbery. Respondents were asked whether (and how often) they committed these offences during the past school year, marked by the summer vacation, to provide respondents a reference point. The wordings of the delinquency items were based on existing national and international self-report instruments (such as the International Survey on Self-Reported Delinquency). Item responses were combined into a *total delinquency* scale, constructed by counting the number of offence types. This 'variety scale' of delinquent behaviour was preferred over a 'frequency scale' based on the total number of self-reported offences. The reason is that the 12 offences included in the questionnaire varied greatly in seriousness. Using frequencies would bias the score towards high occurrences of relatively mild offences (for additional reasons to use variety indices instead of frequency ones, see Bendixen et al., 2003). Because self-report questions are retrospective in nature (referring to the previous year), we used delinquency at time 2 as the dependent variable in the present study to ensure the correct temporal ordering of the independent and dependent variables.

A relatively large number of peer-related variables were included. Most were based on reports by the respondents about their peers, but some were based on social network data about peer relations within the schools. To collect these network data, respondents were provided with a numbered list of all students in the same grade in their school. After that, they were asked to fill in the numbers of those fellow students they spend much time with at school, with a maximum of 10 possible nominations (see Weerman and Bijleveld, 2007, for details).

Mean delinquency level of peers was based on the reports by the peers from the school social network themselves. This scale was constructed by linking the social network data to self-reports by the peers themselves who were also participating in the study. We used the average scores of the respondents' peers in wave 1 and wave 2 to ensure that the timing of this variable precedes that of the dependent variable but not that of the other independent variables (which are all focused on the present situation).

Time spent with peers consists of five items indicating how often and how long respondents are in the company of their friends.[5] *Bond with peers* consists of four items providing respondents with statements of their feelings towards their friends.[6] *Deviant peer pressure* was measured by five statements enquiring whether the respondents' friends applied pressure and reinforcement to make them perform dangerous and illegal acts.[7]

Finally, *proportion girls among peers* was measured by counting the number of female friends in the school networks of the respondents and dividing it by the total size of the network (total number of nominated friends).

Four additional control variables, covering major criminological perspectives, were included in the analyses. *Bond with parents* is a scale consisting of five items indicating whether respondents like their parents and have a positive relationship with them.[8] *Bond with school* is a scale consisting of eight items, indicating whether students like school and try their hardest to achieve good results.[9] *Self-control* is a measure that consists of three subscales (impulsivity, risk-seeking, anger) adapted from Grasmick et al. (1993).[10] It contains 12 items.[11] *Moral attitude* consists of four items that indicate to what extent respondents are willing to bend the law.[12]

Analytical Strategy

Our analyses were conducted in five steps. First, we analysed to what extent there actually is a 'gender gap' in our data by comparing the prevalence of various offending types among girls and boys in the present study. Second, we used ANOVA analyses to explore whether girls and boys differ in their peer relations (and the investigated control variables). Third, we used simple correlations to explore whether peer variables are differentially associated with delinquency among girls and boys. Fourth, we employed multivariate regression analyses to investigate whether the independent effects of peer variables were significant and similar or different among girls and boys. These analyses were conducted in two models, with and without the inclusion of previous levels of delinquency as an independent variable. To determine whether independent peer effects significantly differed between boys and girls, we accounted for the standard errors of coefficients in the regression analyses, using the formula provided in Paternoster et al. (1998). Finally, stepwise regression analyses were conducted to investigate to what extent the 'gender gap' in delinquency is mediated by peer (and other) variables.

Results

Table 1 compares involvement in delinquent behaviours among girls and boys in the sample. The first two rows of Table 1 show that a modest sex difference exists at a general level: more boys (47 percent) than girls (37.5 percent) reported at least one of the 12 investigated offences during the school year preceding wave 2, and also the average delinquency score of boys (1.04) is significantly higher

Table 1 • Delinquent behaviour at T2 among girls and boys (n = 1110)

	Girls (n = 493)	Boys (n = 617)	Significance (χ^2 or F)
Percent any of the 12 offences	37.5	47.0	**
Average delinquency score	0.75	1.04	**
Percent writing on walls, graffiti	17.2	11.8	*
Percent destroying things	6.9	16.0	***
Percent shoplifting < €5	14.6	10.2	*
Percent shoplifting > €5	4.7	3.6	n.s.
Percent buying stolen goods	7.5	12.3	*

	Girls (n = 493)	Boys (n = 617)	Significance (χ^2 or F)
Percent stealing bike or moped	1.0	8.9	***
Percent stealing a car	0.2	1.9	**
Percent burglary	0.2	1.0	n.s.
Percent stealing in other ways	1.4	3.2	n.s
Percent hitting or fighting	15.4	25.0	***
Percent wounding someone	3.9	8.4	**
Percent robbing someone	0.2	0.6	n.s.

n.s. not significant, $*p < .05$, $**p < .01$, $***p < .001$

than that of girls (0.75). The next 12 rows specify these differences. It appears that boys are more involved in aggressive acts (fighting and wounding someone) and vandalism and in certain property offences (stealing bikes/mopeds or cars; buying stolen goods). Girls, on the other hand, are certainly not absent among the offenders. They are actually more often involved in shoplifting and graffiti or writing on walls than boys.

Table 2 shows that there are many sex differences in mean scores on peer and control variables. There is a modest but strongly significant difference between the mean delinquency scores of peers nominated by the girls and those of peers nominated by the boys. The table further shows that boys spend somewhat more time with peers than do girls. Girls, on the other hand, report a stronger bond with their peers than do boys and substantially less deviant peer pressure. Girls and boys also differ with regard to the sex composition of their school networks. Not surprisingly, girls have many more girls than boys among their school friends.[13]

Table 2 further reveals that, on average, boys have a stronger bond than girls with parents, but the bond with school is relatively similar for both sexes. It appears that girls' level of self-control is higher than that of boys and that they have stronger conventional moral attitudes than boys. The mean level of delinquency appears to be higher among boys than among girls in both the first and the second wave.

Table 3 explores whether the investigated peer and other variables are differentially associated with delinquency among girls and boys. Most of the reported correlations are significant for girls as well as for boys and are

Table 2 • Mean differences between girls and boys (n = 1110)

	Girls	Boys	F
Mean delinquency level of peers	0.93 (0.64)	1.14 (0.79)	23.35***
Time spent with peers	5.64 (2.59)	5.96 (2.59)	4.09*
Bond with peers	13.74 (2.60)	13.07 (2.69)	16.57***
Deviant peer pressure total	4.34 (4.19)	5.85 (4.84)	24.91***

(Continued)

Table 2 • (Continued)

	Girls	Boys	*F*
Proportion girls among peers	0.86 (0.21)	0.07 (0.16)	5217.17***
Bond with parents	27.97 (4.93)	28.89 (3.81)	12.09**
Bond with school	21.62 (5.86)	21.28 (6.01)	0.79 n.s.
Self-control	21.67 (8.43)	20.09 (8.64)	9.43**
Moral attitude	11.60 (3.20)	10.52 (3.67)	27.10***
Delinquency score at T1	0.81 (1.32)	1.07 (1.70)	7.72**
Delinquency score at T2	0.75 (1.30)	1.04 (1.58)	10.81**

n.s. not significant, $*p < .05$, $**p < .01$, $***p < .001$

Table 3 • Correlations between delinquency and peer and other variables among boys and girls (n = 1110)

	Girls	Boys
Delinquency score at T1	.528***	.519***
Mean delinquency of peers	.296***	.219***
Time spent with peers	.296***	.273***
Bond with peers	.033 n.s.	.085*
Deviant peer pressure total	.168***	.133**
Proportion girls among peers	–.096*	.046 n.s.
Bond with parents	–.133**	–.110**
Bond with school	–.276***	–.221***
Self-control	–.318***	–.264***
Moral attitude	–.298***	–.270***

n.s. not significant, $*p < .05$, $**p < .01$, $***p < .001$

of similar magnitude, but some interesting differences can be detected. First of all, mean peer delinquency appears to be more strongly correlated with delinquency for girls than for boys. There are also differences with regard to time spent with peers, bond with peers (significantly correlated for boys but not for girls) and deviant peer pressure, but these differences are relatively small. The proportion of girls in the network is significantly related to less delinquency among girls, but not among boys. Further, the associations between all four control variables and delinquency are somewhat higher among girls than among boys.

Regression analysis reveals that there are many similarities between girls and boys in the multivariate effects of peer and other variables. For both girls and boys, mean peer delinquency and time spent with peers have substantial and significant effects on delinquency. For girls, the effect of delinquent peers seems to be somewhat higher. However, although this difference is substantial, it appears to be only one-sided significant (according to the formula provided in Paternoster et al., 1998). For girls, but not for boys, deviant peer pressure is significantly related to delinquency; the difference in magnitude between the coefficients is, however, non-significant. Unlike the bivariate correlations suggest, bond with peers and proportion of girls among peers do not have a significant multivariate effect for both sexes. Three of the control variables have significant effects for both sexes: bond with school (though only one-sided significant for girls), level of self-control and conventional moral attitude. Bond with parents does not have a significant independent effect for either sex. Neither of the differences between girls' and boys' effect sizes appears to be statistically significant.

Delinquency at time 1 is strongly related to delinquent behaviour in the second wave, indicating continuity in delinquent behaviour. In this longitudinal model, many of the other effects disappear. The effect of mean peer delinquency remains for girls but not for boys. This difference in effect between girls and boys is one-sided significant. Time spent with peers has a significant effect on the delinquent behaviour of boys but not of girls (although the difference between the coefficients is not significant). Finally, there is a one-sided significant effect of deviant peer pressure for girls, but the effect size does not differ significantly from the effect size among boys. The other peer variables again have no significant effects on delinquency. Of the control variables, only self-control appears to remain related to delinquency, once controlled for earlier delinquency. The effect is significant only for girls (although the effects do not differ significantly in magnitude between boys and girls).

The results of a stepwise regression analysis exploring whether the effect of the respondent's sex is mediated by the included peer and other variables, and shows the univariate effect of sex: being a girl has a significant and substantial negative effect on delinquency. When the peer variables are added to the model, three of them appear to have significant effects: mean peer delinquency level, time spent with peers and deviant peer pressures. Interestingly, the effect of sex has decreased by more than one-third and is no longer statistically significant. This is an indication that peer variables are partly mediating the effect of sex on delinquent behaviour.

Discussion

Summary of the Main Findings

Despite many investigations into peers and delinquency, limited attention has been paid to differences in the relationship between peers and delinquency among males and females. Focusing on potential sex differences in the influence of peers on delinquent behaviour is important because it may offer insights into the gender gap in crime. The current study investigated sex differences in delinquency and the relationship between delinquency and peer variables, using detailed data on peers in a Dutch school sample.

Modest sex differences in delinquency were found. We found that boys had higher levels of violent and serious offending than girls. However, girls had higher levels of shoplifting and graffiti and, moreover, the sex differences in delinquency that were found in the present study are smaller than those usually found in police data (Zahn, 2009). This may be owing to the less serious nature of most self-reported offences in comparison with those leading to arrest, but it may also be related to the earlier maturation of girls, which temporarily decreases sex differences in delinquency during early adolescence (Moffitt et al., 2001) and explains this finding by the fact that females mature slightly earlier than males. The relatively small differences in delinquency levels between boys and girls in this study (ages 13 and 15) are in accordance with other studies (for example, Van der Laan and Blom, 2006).

We found many sex differences in mean scores on peer variables. For example, boys' peers reported higher levels of delinquency than did girls' peers, and boys spent more time with peers than did girls. In addition, the quality of girls' bonds with peers seems to be on average higher than that of boys: girls report a stronger bond with peers and less peer pressure. This is in accordance with literature suggesting that the quality of relations with peers is different for girls, in particular being less competitive and more focused on communication and intimacy (Eliot, 2010; Rose and Rudolph, 2006). Our findings suggest that the peer relations of girls are relatively less 'riskfull' (or more protective) compared with those of boys.

Most peer variables were correlated with delinquency for both girls and boys, indicating that peer factors can be important in explaining delinquency in both sexes. The effects of several peer variables remained significant in multivariate analyses controlling for established etiological correlates of delinquency. Mean peer delinquency seems to be an important peer variable for both sexes. This finding is in line with studies showing relatively similar effects of peer delinquency on boys' and girls' own delinquency (Brendgen et al., 2000; Hartjen and Priyadarsini, 2003; Haynie and Osgood, 2005; Heinze et al., 2004; Hubbard and Pratt, 2002; Laird et al., 2005; Liu and Kaplan, 1999; Moffitt et al., 2001; Simourd and Andrews, 1994). It is remarkable that we found a significant effect of mean peer delinquency in the longitudinal model for girls only and not for boys, although the difference between the estimates was only one-sided significant. It may be that friends outside school still have an effect for boys—note that the mean peer delinquency variable relates only to the school friend network.

Adding to mean peer delinquency, time spent with peers also seems to be an important peer variable for boys as well as for girls: it has relatively strong multivariate effects for both sexes. Controlling for previous delinquency, the effect estimates were larger for boys, but the difference from girls is not significant. Deviant peer pressure seems to be less important, in particular for boys, which might be seen as surprising.

The sex composition of peer groups is correlated with less delinquency among girls but not among boys. This is only partly in line with previous studies, as several found that having girls as friends is related to less delinquency among boys as well (Haynie et al., 2007; McCarthy et al., 2004). The sex composition of peer groups, however, does not seem to have an effect on delinquent behaviour, once other variables are taken into account. Thus, from our study it seems that in the end the amount of time spent with peers and the behaviour of peers are what matters, not whether they are boys or girls.

The effect of the respondent's sex on delinquency is reduced by one-third once peer variables are added to the analyses. This suggests that peer factors explain at least part of the (modest) 'gender gap' in delinquency. Other variables also reduce the effect of sex, but do not diminish the effects of peer delinquency, time spent with peers and peer pressure.

With regard to the different perspectives on explaining the 'gender gap' in delinquency, our findings do not support the 'differential vulnerability' hypothesis with regard to peers. Although our results clearly suggest that the relation with peers has a different quality for girls than for boys, the effects of peers are at least similar in size and stronger rather than weaker. Our results do provide evidence for the 'differential exposure' hypothesis. Girls seem to be less exposed to delinquent peers, spend less time with them and experience less pressure. At the same time, these peer variables seem to be mediating the effects of sex on delinquent behaviour.

Limitations

Several limitations of the present study may be noted. First, although we had many peer variables, measures were not perfect. Actual peer delinquency was related only to school friends, and it is possible that friends outside school have additional effects on delinquency, which may differ between boys and girls. Second, this study consisted of two measurement moments only. Given that the peak in girls' delinquency differs from the peak for boys, it would be interesting to investigate whether links between peer factors and the delinquency of boys and girls change over time. Third, we did not explicitly investigate the time ordering of peer variables and delinquency. In criminology, a longstanding debate concerns whether the association between peers and delinquency is explained by the influence of peers or by the selection of peers who are similar in behaviour to the respondent (see, for example, Matsueda and Anderson, 1998; Warr, 2002).

Analysis of this issue would require specialized social network analysis that goes beyond the scope of this article (see, for example, Weerman, 2011). Fourth, although we included many control variables, we may have missed some that are also important in explaining the 'gender gap'. Wong et al. (2010), in a European review, found some evidence to suggest that females were more at risk of criminal behaviour if they were affected by negative life events and physical abuse by parents. Furthermore, females were found to have more internalizing problems. Fifth, we did not distinguish between boys and girls from different ethnic backgrounds in the study. It is known that sex differences in delinquency are not similar across ethnic groups. For example, a Dutch study has reported that boys and girls of Antillean and Cape Verdean descent differ less in their level of delinquency than boys and girls in other ethnic categories (Junger-Tas et al., 2004). It remains a pending question to what extent boys and girls from different ethnic backgrounds are differentially exposed and vulnerable to criminogenic peer contexts. Future studies based on large enough mixed samples within each ethnic category are needed to shed more light on this issue. Sixth, it is possible that the role of peers differs over age periods or that peers have different meanings for boys and girls in different countries. Wong et al. (2010) noted that findings about risk factors of delinquency in girls from studies in the US could not be generalized to Europe, and this may apply to the relationship between peers and delinquency among girls and boys.

Conclusion

Despite its limitations, our study has demonstrated that peer variables offer a promising avenue for explaining sex differences in delinquency during adolescence. It also suggests that girls are as sensitive to peers as are boys during the age period we investigated. This implies that policy makers and practitioners should consider peer influences for both boys and girls when designing prevention and intervention strategies.

Notes

1. This is also in line with studies on the effect of romantic relationships on adolescent delinquency (for example, Haynie et al., 2005; Lonardo et al., 2009).

2. Originally, two more schools participated in the first wave. One school was left out because it was so large that it was not possible to study complete school year networks in this school (only a few classes). The other school was left out because it moved to a different location in wave 2, and the new head of the school refused further participation.

3. In the Netherlands as a whole, 60 percent of young people attend this type of school.

4. A substantial number of respondents of Turkish (9 percent), Surinamese (12 percent) and Moroccan (6 percent) origin were represented in the sample, together with respondents from a wide range of other ethnic backgrounds.

5. For example, 'How often do you spend time with your friends after school?'

6. For example, 'I feel good being with my friends' and 'I would like to have other friends'.

7. For example, 'My friends would ridicule me if I was afraid of something' and 'My friends would find it funny if I did something illegal'.

8. For example, 'My parents are nice to me', 'I don't like being with my parents' (reverse coded).

9. For example, 'I like going to school', 'I try hard to get high grades'.

10. The wording of the items was slightly adapted to enhance comprehension and understanding for Dutch students following lower levels of education.

11. Examples of items are: 'I say what I think immediately', 'I like to try out scary things', 'People better stay away from me when I am angry'.

12. For example, 'It's all right to do something that is illegal now and then, as long as you don't get caught'.

13. However, it also appears that girls nominate relatively more (almost twice as many) peers from the other sex than boys do. They also nominate slightly more fellow students as peers (on average about 7, boys on average about 6).

References

Agnew R (2009) The contribution of 'mainstream' theories to the explanation of female delinquency. In: Zahn MA (ed.) *The Delinquent Girl*. Philadelphia: Temple University Press.

Akers RL (1973) *Deviant Behavior: A Social Learning Approach*. Belmont, CA: Wadsworth Publishing Company.

Bendixen M, Endresen IM and Olweus D (2003) Variety and frequency scales of antisocial involvement: Which one is better? *Legal and Criminological Psychology* 8: 135–150.

Benenson JF (1990) Gender differences in social networks. *Journal of Early Adolescence* 10: 472–495.

Brendgen M, Vitaro F and Bukowski WM (2000) Stability and variability of adolescents' affiliation with delinquent friends: Predictors and consequences. *Social Development* 9: 205–225.

Eliot L (2010) Closing opportunity gaps: The myth of pink and blue brains. *Educational Leadership* 68: 32–36.

Elliott DS, Huizinga D and Ageton SS (1985) *Explaining Delinquency and Drug Use*. Beverly Hills, CA: Sage.

Erwin P (1998) *Friendship in Childhood and Adolescence*. London: Routledge.

Grasmick HG, Tittle CR, Bursik RJ and Arneklev BJ (1993) Testing the core empirical implications of Gottfredson and Hirschi's *General Theory of Crime*. *Journal of Research in Crime and Delinquency* 30: 5–29.

Hartjen AC and Priyadarsini S (2003) Gender, peers, and delinquency: A study of boys and girls in rural France. *Youth and Society* 34: 387–414.

Haynie DL (2001) Delinquent peers revisited: Does network structure matter? *American Journal of Sociology* 104: 1013–1057.

Haynie DL and Osgood DW (2005) Reconsidering peers and delinquency: How do peers matter? *Social Forces* 84: 1109–1130.

Haynie DL, Steffensmeier D and Bell KE (2007) Gender and serious violence: Untangling the role of friendship sex composition and peer violence. *Youth Violence and Juvenile Justice* 5: 235–253.

Haynie DL, Giordano PC, Manning WD and Longmore MA (2005) Adolescent romantic relationships and delinquency involvement. *Criminology* 43: 177–210.

Heinze HJ, Toro PA and Urberg KA (2004) Antisocial behavior and affiliation with deviant peers. *Journal of Clinical Child and Adolescent Psychology* 33: 336–346.

Hubbard DJ and Pratt TC (2002) A meta-analysis of the predictors of delinquency among girls. *Journal of Offender Rehabilitation* 34: 1–13.

Junger-Tas J, Ribeaud D and Cruyff MJLF (2004) Juvenile delinquency and gender. *European Journal of Criminology* 1: 333–375.

Kandel DB (1996) The parental and peer contexts of adolescent deviance: An algebra of interpersonal influences. *Journal of Drug Issues* 26: 289–315.

Laird RD, Pettit GS, Dodge KA and Bates JE (2005) Peer relationship antecedents of delinquent behaviour in late adolescence: Is there evidence of demographic group differences in developmental processes? *Development and Psychopathology* 17: 127–144.

Liu X and Kaplan HB (1999) Explaining the gender difference in adolescent delinquent behavior: A longitudinal test of mediating mechanisms. *Criminology* 37: 195–215.

Lonardo RA, Giordano PC, Longmore MA and Manning WD (2009) Parents, friends, and romantic partners: Enmeshment in deviant networks and adolescent delinquency involvement. *Journal of Youth and Adolescence* 38: 367–383.

Long JS (1997) *Regression Models for Categorical and Limited Dependent Variables*. Thousand Oaks, CA: Sage.

McCarthy B, Felmlee D and Hagan J (2004) Girls friends are better: Gender, friends, and crime among school and street youth. *Criminology* 42: 805–835.

Matsueda RL and Anderson K (1998) The dynamics of delinquent peers and delinquent behavior. *Criminology* 36: 269–308.

Mears DP, Ploeger M and Warr M (1998) Explaining the gender gap in delinquency: Peer influence and moral evaluations of behavior. *Journal of Research in Crime and Delinquency* 35: 251–266.

Moffitt TE, Caspi A, Rutter M and Silva PA (2001) *Sex differences in antisocial behaviour: Conduct disorder, delinquency, and violence in the Dunedin Longitudinal Study*. New York: Cambridge University Press.

Osgood DW and Anderson AL (2005) Unstructured socializing and rates of delinquency. *Criminology* 42: 519–550.

Paternoster R, Brame R, Mazerolle P and Piquero A (1998) Using the correct statistical test for the equality of regression coefficients. *Criminology* 36: 859–866.

Patterson GR and Dishion TJ (1985) Contributions of families and peers to delinquency. *Criminology* 23: 63–79.

Piquero NL, Gover AR, MacDonald JM and Piquero AR (2005) The influence of delinquent peers on delinquency: Does gender matter? *Youth and Society* 36: 251–275.

Rose AJ and Rudolph KD (2006) A review of sex differences in peer relationship processes: Potential trade-offs for the emotional and behavioral development of girls and boys. *Psychological Bulletin* 132: 98–131.

Simourd L and Andrews DA (1994) A look at gender differences. *Forum on Corrections Research* 6: 21–31.

Sutherland EH (1947) *Principles of Criminology*. Philadelphia: J.B. Lippincott.

Svensson R (2003) Gender differences in adolescent drug use: The impact of parental monitoring and peer deviance. *Youth and Society* 34: 300–329.

Svensson R and Oberwittler D (2010) It's not the time they spend, it's what they do. The interaction between delinquent friends and unstructured routine activity on delinquency: Findings from two countries. *Journal of Criminal Justice* 38: 1006–1014.

Van der Laan AM and Blom M (2006) *Jeugddelinquentie: Risico's en bescherming* [Juvenile delinquency: Risks and protection]. The Hague: Boom Juridische Uitgevers.

Waldrop MF and Halverson CF (1975) Intensive and extensive peer behavior: Longitudinal and cross-sectional analysis. *Child Development* 46: 19–26.

Warr M (2002) *Companions in Crime: The Social Aspects of Criminal Conduct*. Cambridge: Cambridge University Press.

Weerman FM (2011) Delinquent peers in context: A longitudinal network analysis of selection and influence effects. *Criminology* 49: 253–286.

Weerman FM and Bijleveld CC (2007) Birds of different feathers: School networks of serious delinquent, minor delinquent and non-delinquent boys and girls. *European Journal of Criminology* 4: 357–383.

Weerman FM and Smeenk WH (2005) Peer similarity in delinquency for different types of friends: A comparison using two measurement methods. *Criminology* 43: 499–524.

Wong TM, Slotboom A-M and Bijleveld CC (2010) Risk factors for delinquency in adolescent and young adult females: A European review. *European Journal of Criminology* 7: 266–284.

Zahn MA (2009) *The Delinquent Girl.* Philadelphia, PA: Temple University Press.

REVIEW QUESTIONS

1. Given the findings of the current study, do you believe that the "differential exposure hypothesis" or the "vulnerability hypothesis" is more valid in explaining the gender gap in youth delinquency rates between males and females?
2. Which types of peer-related variables seem to show the most differences and/or have the most differential influences on criminal activity between boys and girls in this sample?
3. To what extent do sex differences in peer group compositions account for or mediate the differences in delinquency rates across gender?

SECTION IX

Social Reaction and Critical Models of Crime

This section will discuss the evolution of social reaction and labeling theory, reviewing contributions made by early theorists as well as modern developments in this area. We will then discuss social conflict and reaction models of criminal behavior, emphasizing the foundational assumptions and principles of Karl Marx as well as the more criminological applications of Marxist and conflict theory by Willem Bonger, Austin Turk, George Vold, and others. During the 1960s and early 1970s, social reaction and labeling theories as well as various critical and conflict theories became popular. At the time, society was looking for theories that placed the blame for criminal offending on government authorities—either the police or societal institutions like economic or class structures. Here, we explore these various theories with a special emphasis on how they radically altered the way that crime and law were viewed as well as how these perspectives highly represented the overall climate in the United States at that time. Specifically, many groups of people—particularly the lower class, minorities, and women—were fighting for their rights during this period, and this manifested itself in criminological theory and research.

Labeling and Social Reaction Theory

Social reaction theory, otherwise referred to as **labeling theory**, is primarily concerned with how individuals' personal identities are highly influenced by the way that society or authorities tend to categorize them as offenders. With such categorization or labeling, an offender becomes a self-fulfilling prophecy, from this perspective, and results in individuals confirming their status as criminals or delinquents by increasing the frequency or seriousness of their illegal activity. Furthermore, this perspective assumes that there is a tendency to put negative labels on lower-class individuals or minorities as offenders significantly more often than on middle- or upper-class White people.[1]

This perspective assumes that people who are labeled offenders have virtually no choice but to conform to the role that they have been "assigned" by society. Thus, social reaction theory claims that recidivism can be reduced by limiting stigmatization by authorities (e.g., law enforcement) and society. This is referred to as the *hands-off policy*,

---

[1]Thomas J. Bernard, Jeffrey B. Snipes, and Alexander L. Gerould, *Vold's Theoretical Criminology*, 6th ed. (Oxford: Oxford University Press, 2010) (see chap. 2).

and it became very popular in the 1960s and early 1970s.[2] Policies that became popular during this period were diversion, decriminalization, and deinstitutionalization (known as the *Ds*). All of these attempted to get youthful or first-time offenders out of the formal justice system as soon as possible to avoid stigmatizing or labeling them as offenders. Today, these very policies have led critics to dismiss labeling theory by claiming that it promotes lenient and ineffective sentencing.[3]

Labeling theory was based on seminal work by George Mead and Charles Cooley, which emphasized the importance of the extreme ways that individuals react to and are influenced by the social reaction to their roles and behavior. Mead, who was a member of the Chicago School (see Section VII), said that a person's sense of self is constantly constructed and reconstructed through the various social interactions a person has on a daily basis.[4] Every person is constantly aware of how she or he is judged by others through social interactions.

Readers can probably relate to this in the sense that they have experienced how differently they are treated in stores or restaurants if they are dressed nicely as opposed to being less well dressed; as you have observed, there is a significant difference in the way one is treated. Also, when growing up, you probably heard your parents or guardians warn that you should not hang out with Johnny or Sally because they were "bad" kids. Or perhaps you were a Johnny or Sally at some point. Either way, you can see how certain individuals can be labeled by authorities or society and then ostracized by mainstream groups. This can lead to isolation and typically results in a person having only other bad kids or adults to hang out with. This results in a type of feedback system in which the person begins associating with others who will only increase their propensity for illegal activity.[5]

Many strain theorists claim that certain demographic factors, such as social class or the neighborhood where a certain offense took place, may make it more likely that the offender will be caught and labeled by authorities. This claim is quite likely to be true, especially given recent policing strategies that target areas or neighborhoods that have high rates of crime. This is the side of social reaction and labeling theory that deals with the disproportionate rate at which members of the lower class and minorities are labeled as offenders.

Some of the earliest labeling theorists laid the groundwork for this perspective long before it became popular in the 1960s. For example, in the 1930s, Frank Tannenbaum noted the **dramatization of evil** that occurred when youth were arrested and charged with their first offense.[6] Later, other theorists such as Edwin Lemert contributed a highly important causal sequence to how labeling affects criminality among those who are labeled. Lemert said that individuals, typically youths, commit **primary deviance**, which is not serious (i.e., it is nonviolent) and not frequent, but they happen to be caught by police and are subsequently labeled.[7] The stigma of the label makes them think of themselves as offenders and forces them to associate only with other offenders. This results in what Lemert referred to as **secondary deviance** in which offending is more serious (often violent) and far more frequent. Thus, the causal model that Lemert describes is illustrated as follows:

Primary Deviance → Caught and Labeled → Secondary Deviance

---

[2]Edwin Schur, *Radical Nonintervention: Rethinking the Delinquency Problem* (Englewood Cliffs, NJ: Prentice Hall, 1973).

[3]Ronald L. Akers and Christine S. Sellers, *Criminological Theories: Introduction, Evaluation, and Application*, 6th ed. (Oxford: Oxford University Press, 2012) (see chap. 8).

[4]George H. Mead, *Mind, Self, and Society* (Chicago: University of Chicago, 1934).

[5]Howard S. Becker, *Outsiders: Studies in the Sociology of Deviance* (New York: Free Press, 1963).

[6]Frank Tannenbaum, *Crime and the Community* (Boston: Ginn, 1938).

[7]Edwin Lemert, *Human Deviance, Social Problems, and Social Control*, 2nd ed. (Englewood Cliffs, NJ: Prentice Hall, 1972).

According to Lemert's model, if the label or stigma is not placed on a young or first-time offender, then the more serious and more frequent offending of secondary deviance will not take place. Therefore, Lemert's model is highly consistent with the labeling approach's hands-off policies, such as diversion, decriminalization, and deinstitutionalization. If you ignore such behavior, Lemert reasoned, it will tend to go away. However, since the mid-1970s, the get-tough approach has become highly dominant, so such policies are not emphasized by society or policy makers today.

▲ **Image 9.1** California Sociologist Dr. Edwin M. Lemert (1912–1996), key proponent of labeling theory, offered a better solution to help delinquents and claimed attempts to rehabilitate juvenile delinquents by putting them in large institutions have failed. He was a consultant to the President's Commission on Law Enforcement and Administration of Justice.

SOURCE: © Getty Images / Ed Maker / Contributor

Research on labeling theory suffered a significant blow in the 1970s and 1980s when empirical findings consistently showed that formal arrests and sanctions did not tend to have results that supported traditional labeling theory.[8] In fact, most people who are arrested once are never arrested again, which tends to support deterrence theory and does not support labeling theory. In addition, some experts have concluded that "the preponderance of research finds no or very weak evidence of [formal] labeling effects. . . . The soundest conclusion is that official sanctions by themselves have neither strong deterrent nor a substantial labeling effect."[9] Furthermore, some theorists have questioned the basic assumptions of labeling theory, pointing out that the label does not cause the initial (or primary) offending and that labeling theorists largely ignore the issue of what is causing individuals to engage in illegal activity in the first place. Also, labeling theorists do not recognize the fact that offenders who are caught tend to be the ones who are committing more crimes than those who are not caught; in fact, there tends to be a strong relationship between being caught and committing multiple offenses.[10]

However, more contemporary research and theorizing have emphasized more informal forms of labeling, such as labeling by the community, parents, or friends. Studies have shown more support for the influence of this informal labeling on individuals' behavior.[11] After all, it only makes sense that informal labeling by people with whom you interact on a daily basis (i.e., parents, friends, neighbors, employers) will have more impact in terms of how you feel about yourself than labeling by police or other authorities, which tends to be temporary or situational.

Marxist Theories of Crime

Based on the writings of Marx, Marxist theories of crime focus on the fact that people from the lower classes (i.e., the poor) are arrested and charged with crimes at a disproportionate rate. Like conflict criminology, Marxist

[8]Marvin Wolfgang, Robert Figlio, and Thorsten Sellin, *Delinquency in a Birth Cohort* (Chicago: University of Chicago Press, 1972).

[9]Akers and Sellers, *Criminological Theories*, 142.

[10]Charles Wellford, "Labeling Theory and Criminology," *Social Problems* 22 (1975): 313–32.

[11]Lening Zhang, "Informal Reactions and Delinquency," *Criminal Justice and Behavior* 24 (1997): 129–50.

▲ **Image 9.2** Karl Marx (1818–1883), German social theorist and revolutionary, who founded Marxism theory.

SOURCE: © Getty Images / Roger Viollet / Contributor

theories emphasize the effects of a capitalistic society on how justice is administered, describing how society is divided by money and power.[12] Marx said the law is the tool by which the **bourgeoisie** (the ruling class in a country without a ruling aristocracy, e.g., industrialists and financiers in Western industrialized countries) controls the lower classes (the **proletariat** and the lowest group, the *lumpenproletariat*) and keeps them in a disadvantaged position. In other words, the law is used as a mechanism by which the middle or upper class maintains its dominance over the lower classes. More specifically, Marx claimed that law is used as a tool to protect the economic interests and holdings of the bourgeoisie, as well as to prevent the lower classes from gaining access to financial resources.[13] Thus, Marxist theories propose that economic power can be translated into legal or political power and substantially accounts for the general disempowerment of the majority.

Willem Bonger

One early key theorist who applied Marxist theory to crime was Bonger, who emphasized the relationship between economy and crime but did not believe simply being poor would cause criminal activity. Rather, he thought crime came about because capitalism caused a difference in the way individuals felt about society and their place in it. In the early 1900s, Bonger said that the contemporary economic structure, particularly capitalism, was the cause of crime in the sense that it promoted a system based on selfishness and greed.[14] Such selfishness manifests itself in competition among individuals, which is obvious in interactions and dealings carried out for the purpose of obtaining goods and resources. This competition and selfishness led to more isolation, individualism, and egoistic tendencies, which promote a strong focus on self-interests at the expense of communitarianism and societal well-being. Bonger believed that this strong focus on the individual leads to criminal behavior.[15] He also stressed the association between social conditions (largely the result of economic systems) and criminal offending; because of cultural differences, crime can be a normal, adaptive response to social and economic problems, he argued. The poor often develop a strong feeling of injustice, which also contributes to their entering into illegal activity.[16]

Richard Quinney

Although Bonger's theory did not become popular in the early 1900s, when his book was originally published, his ideas received a lot of attention when a neo-Marxist period began in the early 1970s. This renewed interest in Marxist theory was coupled with harsh criticisms leveled at the existing theoretical frameworks, which is why these neo-Marxist theories are often referred to as critical theories. This time, Marxist theories

---

[12]Karl Marx, *Selected Works of Karl Marx and Frederick Engels* (Moscow: Foreign Languages Publishing House, 1962).

[13]Bernard et al., *Vold's Theoretical Criminology.*

[14]Willem Bonger, *Criminality and Economic Conditions* (1905; repr., Bloomington: Indiana University Press, 1969).

[15]Bernard et al., *Vold's Theoretical Criminology*; Akers and Sellers, *Criminological Theories.*

[16]Bonger, *Criminality and Economic Conditions.*

of crime became quite popular, largely because the social climate desired such perspectives. Whereas notable European theorists in this vein include Ian Taylor, Paul Walton, and Jock Young,[17] one of the key figures in this neo-Marxist perspective in the United States was Richard Quinney.[18]

Like Bonger, Quinney claimed that crime was caused by the capitalistic economic structure and the emphasis on materials that this system produced. One way that Quinney's theory goes beyond Bonger is that Quinney further proposed that even the crimes committed by the upper classes are caused by capitalism. To clarify, Quinney claimed that such acts are crimes of "domination and repression" committed by the elite to keep the lower classes down or to protect their property, wealth, and power.[19] A good example is white-collar crimes, which almost always involve raising profits or income, whether for individual or company advantage; such crimes often result in losses to the relatively lower-income clients or customers.

▲ **Image 9.3** Richard Quinney, a renowned American sociologist who is best known for his philosophical and critical approach to crime and social justice.

SOURCE: Courtesy of Richard Quinney.

Evidence regarding Marxist Theories of Crime

Many critics noted that these seminal Marxist theories of crime were too simplistic as well as somewhat naive in the sense that they seemed to claim that the capitalistic economic system was the only reason for crime and that socialism or communism was the only sure way to reduce crime in the United States.[20] Now, even most Marxist theorists reject this proposition. Thus, more modern frameworks have been presented that place more emphasis on factors that stem from capitalism. For example, Mark Colvin and John Pauly presented a theoretical model that claims that delinquency and crime are the result of problematic parenting, which results from the degrading and manipulative treatment that parents of lower-class children get in the workplace.[21] However, the empirical tests of this more modern Marxist theory have demonstrated rather weak effects regarding the importance of capitalism (or parenting practices resulting from employment positions or social class).[22] Thus, there does not seem to be much empirical support for Marxist or neo-Marxist theories of crime, which is perhaps why this theoretical framework is not one of the primary models currently accepted by most criminologists.[23]

---

[17]Ian Taylor, Paul Walton, and Jock Young, *The New Criminology: For a Social Theory of Deviance* (New York: Harper & Row, 1973).

[18]Richard Quinney, *Critique of Legal Order: Crime Control in Capitalist Society* (Boston: Little, Brown, 1974).

[19]Quinney, *Critique of Legal Order.* See also Akers and Sellers, *Criminological Theories*, 224–26, for a discussion.

[20]For a discussion, see Akers and Sellers, *Criminological Theories*, 226–31.

[21]Mark Colvin and John Pauly, "A Critique of Criminology: Toward an Integrated Structural Marxist Theory of Delinquency Production," *American Journal of Sociology* 89 (1983): 513–51.

[22]See Sally Simpson and Lori Elis, "Is Gender Subordinate to Class? An Empirical Assessment of Colvin and Pauly's Structural Marxist Theory of Delinquency," *Journal of Criminal Law and Criminology* 85 (1994): 453–80. See further discussion in Akers and Sellers, *Criminological Theories.*

[23]Lee Ellis and Anthony Walsh, "Criminologists' Opinions about the Causes and Theories of Crime and Delinquency," *The Criminologist* 24 (1999): 1–4.

▲ **Image 9.4** Thorsten Sellin (1896–1994) was a Swedish American sociologist at the University of Pennsylvania, a penologist, and one of the pioneers of scientific criminology, especially in the area of conflict and subcultural theory.

SOURCE: Courtesy of Thorsten Sellin

Conflict Theories of Crime

Conflict theories of crime assume that all societies are in a process of constant change and that this dynamic process inevitably creates conflicts among various groups.[24] Much of the conflict is due to the competition to have each group's interests promoted, protected, and often put into law. If all groups were equally powerful and had the same amount of resources, such battles would involve much negotiation and compromise; however, groups tend to differ significantly in the amount of power or resources that they have. Thus, laws can be created and enforced such that powerful groups can exert dominance over the weaker groups. So, as in Marxist theories, law is seen as a tool by which some groups gain and maintain dominance over less powerful groups. Furthermore, this state of inequality and resulting oppression creates a sense of injustice and unfairness among members of the less powerful groups, and such feelings are a primary cause of crime.[25]

There are several types of conflict theory, and fittingly, for this framework (as well as inherently supportive of the model), theorists of varying types often give scathing reviews of the other types of conflict theory. Marxist theories are one example. Critics have noted that many communistic countries (e.g., Cuba, Russia) have high rates of crime, whereas some countries that have capitalistic economic structures have very low crime rates, such as Sweden.

Another type of conflict theory is referred to as *pluralistic*; it argues that, instead of one or a few groups holding power over all the other groups, a multitude of groups must compete on a relatively fair playing field.[26] However, this latter type of conflict theory is not one of the more popular versions among critical theorists because it is sometimes seen as rather naive and idealistic.[27] Some of the key theorists in the **pluralistic (conflict) perspective** are Thorsten Sellin, Vold, and Turk.

Thorsten Sellin

Sellin applied Marxist and conflict perspectives, as well as numerous other types of models, to studying the state of cultural diversity in industrial societies. Sellin claimed that separate cultures will diverge from a unitary, mainstream set of norms and values held by the dominant group in society.[28] Thus, these minority groups that break off from the mainstream will establish their own norms. Furthermore, when laws are enacted, they will reflect only the values and interests of the dominant group, which causes what Sellin referred to as *border culture conflict*. This conflict of values, which manifests itself when different cultures interact, can cause a backlash by the weaker groups,

[24]William Chambliss and Robert Seidman, *Law, Order, and Power* (Reading, PA: Addison-Wesley, 1971).

[25]Bernard et al., *Vold's Theoretical Criminology.*

[26]Akers and Sellers, *Criminological Theories.*

[27]Quinney, *Critique of Legal Order.*

[28]Thorsten Sellin, *Culture Conflict and Crime* (New York: Social Science Research Council, 1938).

which tend to react defiantly or defensively. According to Sellin, the more unequal the balance of power, the worse the conflict tends to be.[29]

George Vold

Another key conflict theorist was Vold, who presented his model in his widely used textbook, *Theoretical Criminology.*[30] Vold claimed that people are naturally social and inevitably form groups out of shared needs, values, and interests. Because various groups compete with each other for power and to promote their values and interests, each group competes for control of political processes, including the power to create and enforce laws that can suppress the other groups. Some critics have argued that Vold put too much emphasis on the battle for creation of laws as opposed to the power to enforce laws.[31]

Austin Turk

Like the other conflict theorists, Turk assumed that the competition for power among various groups in society is the primary cause of crime.[32] Turk emphasized the idea that a certain level of conflict among groups can be very beneficial because it reminds citizens to consider whether the status quo or conventional standards can be improved. This type of idea is very similar to Émile Durkheim's proposition that a certain level of crime is healthy for society because it defines moral boundaries and sometimes leads to progress (see Section VI). Another aspect of Turk's theorizing, which separates him from other conflict theorists, is that he saw conflict among the various components of the criminal justice system. For example, the police often are at odds with the courts and district attorney's office. Such tension or conflict among formal agencies that should be on the same side of the playing field leads to even more frustration and inefficiency when it comes to fighting crime and ensuring that justice is served.

Case Study: Ted "the Unabomber" Kaczynski

Ted Kaczynski

In 1978, the explosion of what was considered a primitive homemade bomb sent to a Chicago university started Theodore Kaczynski's "reign of terror." Over the next 17 years, these bombs were either hand-delivered or mailed, resulting in three deaths and 24 injuries. In 1979, a Federal Bureau of Investigation (FBI) task force, including the Bureau of Alcohol, Tobacco, Firearms, and Explosives and the U.S. Postal Inspection Service, was formed to investigate what was designated as the UNABOM (university and airline bombing targets) case. This task force, which grew to more than 150 full-time investigators, analysts, and others, attempted to recover bomb components and examined the lives of the victims in an effort to identify the bomber.[33]

(Continued)

[29]Ibid.

[30]George Vold, *Theoretical Criminology* (New York: Oxford University Press, 1958).

[31]Akers and Sellers, *Criminological Theories.*

[32]Austin Turk, *Criminality and Legal Order* (Chicago: Rand McNally, 1969).

[33]"FBI 100: The Unabomber," FBI.gov, April 24, 2008, http://www.fbi.gov/news/stories/2008/april/unabomber_042408.

(Continued)

In 1995, the unidentified "Unabomber" sent the FBI a 35,000-word essay that explained, from his perspective, the reasons for these bombs as well as his views on the ills of modern society. The following is just one item among the 232 listed in the manifesto:

> 4. We therefore advocate a revolution against the industrial system. This revolution may or may not make use of violence; it may be sudden or it may be a relatively gradual process spanning a few decades. We can't predict any of that. But we do outline in a very general way the measures that those who hate the industrial system should take in order to prepare the way for a revolution against that form of society. This is not to be a POLITICAL revolution. Its object will be to overthrow not governments but the economic and technological basis of the present society.[34]

Its object will be to overthrow not governments but the economic and technological basis of the present society.

FBI director Louis Freeh and Attorney General Janet Reno agreed with the task force's recommendation to publish the essay, hoping that a reader could identify the author. This manifesto was printed in the *Washington Post* and the *New York Times*.

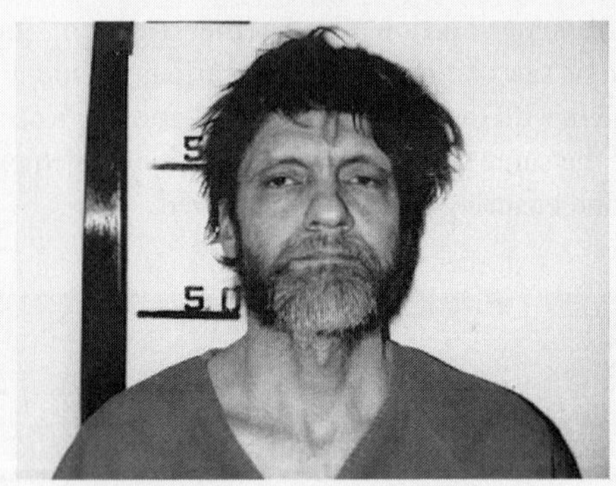

▲ **Image 9.5** Mug shot of Theodore "Ted" Kaczynski. Federal Bureau of Investigation.

SOURCE: Federal Bureau of Investigation, via Wikimedia Commons

While thousands of people offered various suspects, one stood out. In January 1996, in his family home in Illinois, David Kaczynski found papers, written by his brother Theodore (Ted), that contained Unabomber-like rhetoric. David Kaczynski notified the FBI. Linguistic analysis revealed that the author of these documents was most likely the author of the manifesto as well. On April 3, 1996, Ted Kaczynski was arrested in his remote mountain cabin in Stemple Pass, Montana. During the search of his cabin, investigators found a large number of bomb components, 40,000 handwritten journal pages, descriptions of Unabomber crimes, and one live bomb ready for mailing. Following his guilty plea in January of 1998, Ted Kaczynski was incarcerated in an isolated cell in a Colorado supermax prison.[35]

Think About It

1. Are any features of this type of offense reflected in the various theories that have been discussed?

[34]See "The Unabomber Trial: The Manifesto," *Washington Post*, 1997, http://www.washingtonpost.com/wp-srv/national/longterm/unabomber/manifesto.text.htm.

[35]"FBI 100."

Evidence regarding Conflict Theories of Crime

Empirical tests of conflict theories are rare, likely because of the nature of the framework, which lends itself to a global view of societal structure and a perhaps infinite number of interest groups who are constantly in play for power.[36]

However, one notable study found evidence of a relationship between U.S. states that had large numbers of interest groups and violent crime but not property crime.[37] The authors concluded that these findings demonstrated the need for more discussion about how competitiveness in the United States affects criminal behavior, but no other studies have examined the influence of political interest groups on criminal behavior. It is rather difficult to test conflict theory in other ways. Perhaps conflict theory researchers should build an agenda of more rigorous ways to test the propositions of their theoretical perspective; as it stands, it remains quite vague. The few studies there are do not seem rigorous enough to persuade other criminologists or readers toward accepting the validity of this model.[38]

Despite the lack of empirical research supporting the conflict (and Marxist or critical) theories of crime, there is little doubt that such perspectives have contributed much to the theorizing and empirical studies of criminologists regarding this framework. In fact, the American Society of Criminology (ASC)—which is probably the largest and best-known professional society in the discipline—has a special division made up of experts devoted to this area of study. Thus, it is likely that theorizing and empirical research will be greatly enhanced in the near future. Furthermore, it is clear that criminologists have acknowledged the need to explore the various issues presented by the conflict and Marxist perspectives in research in criminal justice and offending.

Policy Implications

A variety of policy implications have come from the theoretical perspectives reviewed in this section. Regarding social reaction and labeling theory, several policies have evolved, known as the *Ds*: diversion, decriminalization, and deinstitutionalization. **Diversion**, which is now commonly used, involves trying to get cases out of the formal justice system as soon as possible. Courts try to get many juvenile cases and, in recent times, drug possession cases diverted to a less formal, more administrative process (e.g., drug courts, youth accountability boards or teams). Such diversion programs appear to have saved many billions of dollars, since the offenders would otherwise have been incarcerated, while providing a way for first-time or relatively nonserious offenders not to experience the stigmatizing effects of being incarcerated. Although empirical evaluations of such diversion programs are mixed and suffer from methodological problems (i.e., the individuals who volunteer or qualify for such programs are likely the better cases among the sample population), some studies have shown their potential promise.[39]

There have also been numerous examples of **decriminalization**, which refers to reducing the criminality of certain illegal activities. A good example is the legal approach to marijuana possession in California. Unlike other jurisdictions, California does not incarcerate individuals for possessing less than an ounce of marijuana; rather, they receive a citation, similar to a parking ticket. There are many other forms of decriminalization (which is distinguished from legalization, which makes an act completely legal and not subject to legal sanction). The purpose of decriminalization is to de-emphasize less dangerous crimes and decrease the resources devoted to offenders who

[36]See discussion by Akers and Sellers, *Criminological Theories*, 210–12.

[37]Gregory G. Brunk and Laura A. Wilson, "Interest Groups and Criminal Behavior," *Journal of Research in Crime and Delinquency* 28 (1991): 157–73.

[38]Ellis and Walsh, "Criminologists' Opinions."

[39]For a review, see John Worrall, *Crime Control in America: What Works?* 2nd ed. (Boston: Allyn & Bacon, 2008): 228–29.

pose less danger to society. In terms of social reaction and labeling theory, decriminalization also reduces the stigmatization of individuals who are relatively minor offenders but would likely become more serious offenders if they were incarcerated with more chronic offenders.

Another policy implication of this section is **deinstitutionalization**. In the early 1970s, federal laws were passed that ordered all youth status offenders to be removed from incarceration facilities. This has not been accomplished; some are still being placed in such facilities. However, the number and rate of status offenders being placed in incarceration facilities has declined, avoiding any further stigmatization and integration into further criminality. Overall, this deinstitutionalization has kept relatively minor, often first-time offenders from experiencing the ordeals of incarceration.

Additional policy implications that can be inferred from this section involve providing more economic and employment opportunities to those who do not typically have access to such options. From a historical perspective, such as the New Deal, which was meant to deal with the effects of the Great Depression of the 1930s, providing more employment opportunities can greatly enhance the well-being of the population, and in that period, there was a very significant decrease in crime and homicide rates (see Section I). Today, perhaps nothing could be more important in our nation than creating jobs; the ability to do this will largely determine future crime rates.

The bulk of policies that have been derived from conflict theories have emphasized attempting to make laws, enforcement, and processing through the justice system more equitable in terms of social class. For example, the federal sentencing guidelines were recently reviewed for drug possession because it became clear that they were unfair in how they punished drug possession offenders. Specifically, according to the 1980s guidelines, possession of an ounce of crack cocaine earned a defendant a sentence 100 times longer than an offender who possessed an ounce of powder cocaine. Not surprisingly, crack cocaine is typically used and sold by lower-class minorities, whereas cocaine powder is typically used and sold by upper- or middle-class Whites. The disparity in this form of sentencing, which clearly penalizes a certain group of people more than another, has recently become a target for reform by the Obama administration, so there are current efforts to address this issue. This is just one example of how laws and processing are significantly disproportionate in the sense that certain groups (typically lower-class minorities) are arrested, punished, and locked up far more than well-to-do offenders. Studies showing higher conviction rates and longer sentences for offenders who must rely on public defenders to represent them consistently support the high degree of disparities in the criminal justice system, which policies derived from conflict theory attempt to address.

Recently, these hands-off policies have been less attractive to authorities and politicians who want to be seen as hard on criminal offenders so they will be elected or retained in office. Still, due to recent economic crises in many state and local communities, it is likely that many jurisdictions will reconsider these approaches and find alternative strategies for dealing with nonviolent offenders.

Conclusion

This section examined the theories that place responsibility for individuals' criminal behavior on societal factors, particularly factors that are unjust or discriminatory. Specifically, this section discussed theories of social reaction or labeling as well as critical perspectives of criminal behavior. All of these theories have a common theme: They emphasize the use of legal or criminal justice systems to target or label certain groups of people (the poor, women, etc.) as criminals while protecting the interests of those who have power (typically White males). Given the evidence discussed here, you will have enough evidence to make objective conclusions about whether this perspective is valid as well as which aspects of these theories are more supported by empirical research and which are more in question.

We also examined Marxist perspectives of society as explanations of crime. Other theories were examined that are similar to Marxist theory but also include other types of group conflict than those just based on economic factors, such as cultural and political. Most of these latter types of group conflict theories claim that there are a multitude of groups constantly competing for power and influence over the other groups, especially by trying to enact or enforce laws favorable to their group.

/// SECTION SUMMARY

- First, we explored the basic assumptions of social reaction and labeling theory.
- We then reviewed the primary theoretical concepts and propositions of labeling theory, especially the importance of distinguishing primary deviance from secondary deviance.
- We discussed the current state of labeling theory, which emphasizes informal sources of social reaction, not just the formal sources as in traditional models.
- Then we examined Marx's perspective on reasons for class conflict, particularly the conflict between the bourgeoisie and the proletariat.
- We then discussed numerous subsequent versions of Marxist theory that attempted to directly explain crime.
- One of these was developed by Bonger, who claimed that the contemporary economic structure, particularly capitalism, was the cause of crime in the sense that it promoted a system based on selfishness, individualism, and greed rather than more communitarian values and goals.
- Another Marxist perspective of crime was presented by Quinney, who went a bit further than Bonger in proposing that even the crimes committed by the upper classes are caused by capitalism, such as crimes of "domination and repression" committed by the elite to keep the lower classes down or to protect their property, wealth, and power.
- We also examined conflict theories that were not based only on Marxist principles or limited to economic factors but rather emphasize that there are multiple groups that are constantly competing for influence and power, which results in crime.
- One key culture conflict theory was proposed by Sellin, who claimed that when laws are enacted, they will reflect only the cultural values and interests of the dominant group, which can cause a backlash by the weaker groups that tend to react defiantly or defensively.
- Vold presented a theory that various groups compete with each other for power and to promote their values and interests via control of political processes and enacting laws that can suppress the other groups.
- Also, Turk proposed a theory that emphasized the idea that a certain level of conflict among groups can be very beneficial because it reminds citizens to consider whether the status quo or conventional standards can be improved and also applied group conflict to the various agencies in the criminal justice system.

/// KEY TERMS

bourgeoisie 404

decriminalization 409

deinstitutionalization 410

diversion 409

dramatization of evil 402

labeling theory 401

pluralistic (conflict) perspective 406

primary deviance 402

proletariat 404

secondary deviance 402

DISCUSSION QUESTIONS

1. What are the major assumptions of labeling and social reaction theory, and how do they differ significantly from other traditional theories of crime?
2. According to Lemert, what is the difference between primary deviance and secondary deviance?
3. How can you relate personally to being labeled, even if not for offending?
4. How do Marx's ideas relate to the study of crime? Provide some examples.
5. Which conflict theory do you buy into the most? The least? Why?

WEB RESOURCES

Conflict Theories

https://www.khanacademy.org/test-prep/mcat/society-and-culture/social-structures/v/conflict-theory
https://www.thoughtco.com/conflict-theory-3026622
http://study.com/academy/lesson/social-conflict-theory-in-sociology-definition-lesson-quiz.html

Labeling Theory

http://study.com/academy/lesson/labeling-theory-of-deviance-definition-examples-quiz.html
https://www.thoughtco.com/labeling-theory-3026627
https://www.youtube.com/watch?v=lrQ454s0mgo

Marxist Theory

http://law.jrank.org/pages/819/Crime-Causation-Sociological-Theories-Critical-theories.html
http://www.allaboutphilosophy.org/what-is-marxism-faq.htm
https://www.nyu.edu/projects/ollman/docs/what_is_marxism.php

READING /// 22

In this selection, Lening Zhang provides a brief review of the history of labeling theory, discussing its prominence in the 1960s and the declaration in 1985 that labeling theory was "dead," largely because the tests of the theory up to that time had been based solely on formal labeling, such as that given by law enforcement, courts, or corrections, that showed little or no effect for the labeling perspective. Then Zhang reviews the various studies and perspectives that revitalized labeling theory in the 1990s, largely by introducing the informal labeling process by significant others (peers, parents, employers, etc.)—in other words, the labeling that takes place during interactions with people or agencies who are not part of the formal justice system (i.e., police, courts, and corrections).

Zhang then presents a test of this informal labeling process. Specifically, Zhang uses a national sample of youths, called the National Youth Survey (NYS), to test his predictions that delinquency produces informal labeling, that such informal labeling by parents produces social isolation, and that this social isolation increases the likelihood of recidivism or subsequent delinquency.

While reading this entry, carefully consider the following points:

- The way Zhang measures informal labeling, the child's perceptions of informal labels, and other parental measures
- The key findings from this study regarding parents' labeling and which types of the youths' perceptions of labeling had the greatest effect on their subsequent delinquency
- The findings of this study with special emphasis on the influence of informal labeling on recidivism or reoffending by youths who have been labeled "bad" kids.

Informal Reactions and Delinquency

Lening Zhang

In formulating a symbolic interaction theory of delinquency, Matsueda (1992) recently developed a model of reflected appraisals and behavior based on Felson's (1985, 1989) and Kinch's (1963) work. A reflected appraisal is how one perceives the way others see one. Matsueda's model predicts that actual delinquent acts affect both actual and reflected appraisals by significant others. In turn, both actual and reflected appraisals influence subsequent delinquent behavior. Also, actual appraisals by significant others have an effect on reflected appraisals of others, and prior delinquent behavior directly affects subsequent delinquency.[1] Drawing on labeling theory, Matsueda also argued that these predictions derived from the model implied the role of informal labeling in accounting for subsequent delinquency. Youths who have engaged in delinquent behavior should be more likely to be labeled delinquent by significant others. Significant others' labeling increases the probability of further delinquency. Although his

SOURCE: Lening Zhang, "Informal Reactions and Delinquency." *Criminal Justice and Behavior* 24, no. 1 (1997): 129–50.

study shed light on the relationship between informal labeling processes and subsequent life and behavioral adjustments, Matsueda did not fully address the issue because the focus of his study was not on this issue. Using Matsueda's basic framework, the present research specified a comprehensive theoretical model of the informal labeling process and tested this model with data from the National Youth Survey (NYS; Elliott & Ageton 1980), a longitudinal study of delinquency and drug use.

The labeling perspective on deviance has undergone an uneven development. During the 1960s, labeling, or reaction, theory emerged as a new and dominant perspective in criminology. In the mid-1970s, the perspective was subjected to serious critiques (Gibbs, 1966, 1972; Gove, 1980; Hagan, 1974; Tittle, 1975, 1980a; Wellford, 1975) and by 1985 was pronounced "dead" (Paternoster & Iovanni, 1989, p. 359). After its unpopular position in the study of crime for several years, the perspective has been revitalized since the late 1980s and the early 1990s (Berk, Campell, Klap, & Western, 1992; Farrell, 1989; Gove & Hughes, 1989; Hagan & Palloni, 1990; Heimer & Matsueda, 1994; Link, 1982, 1987; Link & Cullen, 1983; Link, Cullen, Frank, & Wozniak, 1987; Link, Cullen, Struening, Shrout, & Dohrenwend, 1989; Matsueda, 1992; Palamara, Cullen, & Gersten, 1986; Pate & Hamilton, 1992; Paternoster & Iovanni, 1989; Sampson, 1986; Sherman & Smith, 1992; Tittle, 1988; Tittle & Curran, 1988; Triplett & Jarjoura, 1994).

This revitalization reflects new theoretical and research interests in labeling theory, which indicate the potential power and capacity of the theory for explaining deviance and crime. However, the new developments do not represent a simple return to the traditional version of labeling theory. They entail new attempts to elaborate, to specify, and to expand the theory in a new context of studies in criminology. As Paternoster and Iovanni (1989) pointed out, the above-mentioned efforts suggested some of the components that might constitute a *neolabeling theory.*

Consistent with these new research interests in the labeling perspective, the present study addressed an important but relatively neglected issue—the informal labeling process and delinquency.

Despite this relative neglect, a few scattered early studies (Alvarez, 1968; Black, 1970; Black & Reiss, 1970; DeLamater, 1968; Orcutt, 1973; Swigert & Farrell, 1978; Tittle, 1975) involved attempts to explore the issues of informal reactions. A notable example was Orcutt's (1973) research, in which he differentiated between formal and informal reactions on the basis of the labeling perspective and noted the underemphasis on informal reactions. He argued that studies of the labeling perspective must pay greater attention to informal reactions.

According to Swigert and Farrell (1978), the evaluations and views of social audiences, such as parents and close friends, might have significant effects on the self-evaluations of labeled deviants. Hence informal groups may be crucial for self-identity and behavioral adjustment of labeled individuals. A similar argument was offered by Tittle (1975). He suggested that cultural patterns in different communities might serve as important variables that could interact with official formal reactions and affect the outcome of formal reactions. However, Tittle observed, these effects of cultural patterns had not yet been addressed theoretically and empirically.

In addition, several early studies dealt with family reactions to drinking problems and mental disorders (Jackson, 1954, 1962; Sampson, Messinger, & Towne, 1962; Yarrow, Schartz, Murphy, & Deasy, 1955). These studies indicated how family reactions change in response to drinking and mental problems from "inclusive" to "exclusive" reactions (Orcutt, 1973). Although these early studies appealed for attention to informal reactions to deviance, studies of labeling phenomena have focused primarily on formal official reactions.

Recently, in the resurgence of labeling theory, some scholars (Braithwaite, 1989; Heimer & Matsueda, 1994; Matsueda, 1992; Pate & Hamilton, 1992; Paternoster & Iovanni, 1989; Tittle, 1988; Triplett & Jarjoura, 1994) again have called attention to informal reactions to deviance. An interesting formulation of this issue was Braithwaite's (1989) specification of informal reactions associated with "reintegrative shaming." He argued that

> if the labeling perspective is to be the stimulus to testable propositions with any hope of consistent empirical support, then a strategy is required for predicting the circumstances where labeling will be counterproductive and where it will actually reduce crime. (p. 20)

To meet this challenge, he identified two types of shaming: reintegrative and disintegrative (stigmatization) shaming. Reintegrative shaming refers to expressions of community disapproval with gestures of reacceptance into the community of law-abiding citizens. Such informal labeling reduces crime. In contrast, disintegrative shaming divides the community by creating a class of outcasts. It is conceived of as criminogenic labeling.

In discussing the secondary deviance hypothesis of labeling theory, Paternoster and Iovanni (1989) similarly called for more attention to informal rather than official reactions, whereas Triplett and Jarjoura (1994) formulated an integrated model of the labeling perspective and social learning theory. In their model, (a) parents' labeling of their child and (b) the youth's interpretation that parents are labeling him or her as delinquent are treated as key variables that may predict parental attachment, school attachment, and subsequent delinquency. Their findings indicate that both objective and subjective labels are factors in accounting for a child's relationship with major socialization sources, such as school and friends and subsequent delinquency. Thus they concluded that the labeling perspective could contribute more to criminological theory and research than it did in the past.

In the deterrence literature, informal sanctions have been demonstrated to have much stronger effects on deviance than do formal sanctions, and they significantly mediate the relationship between formal sanctions and deviance. As Tittle (1980b) observed,

> Social control as a general process seems to be rooted almost completely in informal sanctioning. Perceptions of formal sanction probabilities or severities do not appear to have much of an effect, and those effects that are evident turn out to be dependent upon perceptions of informal sanctions. (p. 241)

For a review of the deterrence literature, see Braithwaite (1989) and Williams and Hawkins (1986). Recently, on the basis of the Dade County spouse assault experiment, Pate and Hamilton (1992) examined the interaction effects between formal and informal deterrents on domestic violence. They found that formal arrest had no independent effect on the occurrence of a subsequent domestic assault. Its effect was contingent on employment status, with formal arrest more likely to exhibit a significant deterrent effect for employed suspects than for unemployed suspects. These observations in the deterrence literature also may be valuable and useful in exploring the role of informal reactions in the labeling process.

All of these studies suggest that informal reactions play an important role in explaining deviant behavior. Following this general line of studies, the present study attempted to further clarify some conceptual issues by specifying informal reactions as a dependent variable, an independent variable, and an intervening variable in the labeling process.

Treating informal reactions as a dependent variable is concerned with explaining why some people come to be labeled deviant by significant others, such as parents, friends, and neighbors or the public (for a general discussion of societal reaction as a dependent variable, see Gove, 1980; Orcutt, 1973). The explanation involves three analytic dimensions: (a) Informal labeling is caused by formal labeling such as police arrest and court hearings; (b) actual deviant behavior leads to informal reactions; and (c) status characteristics of individuals, including those of both labelee and labeler (e.g., race, sex, social status) are relevant to informal reactions.

Viewing informal reaction as an independent variable focuses on the consequences that follow if a person is labeled deviant by significant others or the public. Four possible consequences can be specified. First, informal reactions may lead to formal (official) reactions. For instance, neighbors' complaints of someone's behavior may lead to formal actions by official agencies (Black, 1970; Black & Reiss, 1970). Second, informal reactions may push the labeled person to commit further deviance. Third, informal reactions may have negative consequences in other areas of the labeled person's life, such as interpersonal relationships. Finally, as deterrence theory predicts, informal reactions may be important factors in deterring further deviance.

In considering informal reactions as an intervening variable, the major concerns are with the mediating role of informal reactions in explaining the effects of formal reactions and actual deviant behavior on further deviance and other areas of a person's life. The role can be specified in two possibly opposite directions underlying efforts at social control. If informal labeling following and accompanying formal labeling or actual deviant behavior comes with reintegrative shaming, it may play an important and positive role in rehabilitating a rule breaker. This is a positive direction expected by a society. For example, Braithwaite (1989) emphasized the contributions of the informal mechanisms to low crime rate in Japanese society. In contrast, informal reactions may reinforce the stigma imposed by official agencies and thereby become a significant factor leading to further deviance.

These conceptual specifications suggest a framework for examining the relationship of informal labeling processes to delinquency. On the basis of available data from the NYS, the author developed a specific model focused on this relationship (see Figure 1). The model uses Matsueda's (1992) symbolic interactionist framework and extends his study to reflect the conceptual specifications proposed in the present study. The key extension is that the present study introduces an important variable—social isolation—into the model. First, in the model, social isolation from significant others is treated as a dependent variable caused by informal labeling. As previously specified, informal reactions may have negative consequences for other areas of the labeled person's life, one of which is negative change in interpersonal relations. Recently, an important dimension of the trend to revitalize labeling theory has involved efforts to focus on the effect of formal reactions on other areas of a person's life rather than just on subsequent deviance. Specifically, in the research areas of labeling theory and mental illness, Link and his colleagues (Link, 1982, 1987; Link et al., 1987, 1989) noted the previous overemphasis on the effect of formal labeling on subsequent mental disorders in comparison with the neglect of specifying the direct effect of formal labeling on problems of life adjustment, such as marriage and job problems, experienced by ex-mental patients. Their studies provided evidence for the relationship between formal labeling and life adjustment. Similarly, it is reasonable to speculate that informal labeling not only increases the possibility of further delinquency involvement but also has negative consequences for other areas of the labeled person's life, such as interpersonal relationships.

Second, social isolation is also treated as an intervening variable between informal reactions and subsequent delinquency. The theoretical hypothesis is that informal reactions result in social isolation from significant others, and, in turn, such isolation increases the probability of further delinquency. It is possible that a negative label, through a series of reinforcing conditions, such as rejection by significant others, increases the probability of further deviance. Link (1982) pointed out that if this were demonstrated by further research, the eventual results of such a program of research offered the genuine possibility of developing a theory that assigned a partial role to labeling in the etiology of deviance. Similarly, Liska (1987) proposed a clear diagram regarding the association of labeling with further deviance. His diagram assumed that the effect of societal reaction on further deviance was through its effect on self-concept, interpersonal networks, and structured opportunities. Therefore, the present model posits that social isolation has a mediating role for the effect of informal labeling on subsequent delinquency

Figure 1 • A causal model for informal reactions and delinquency

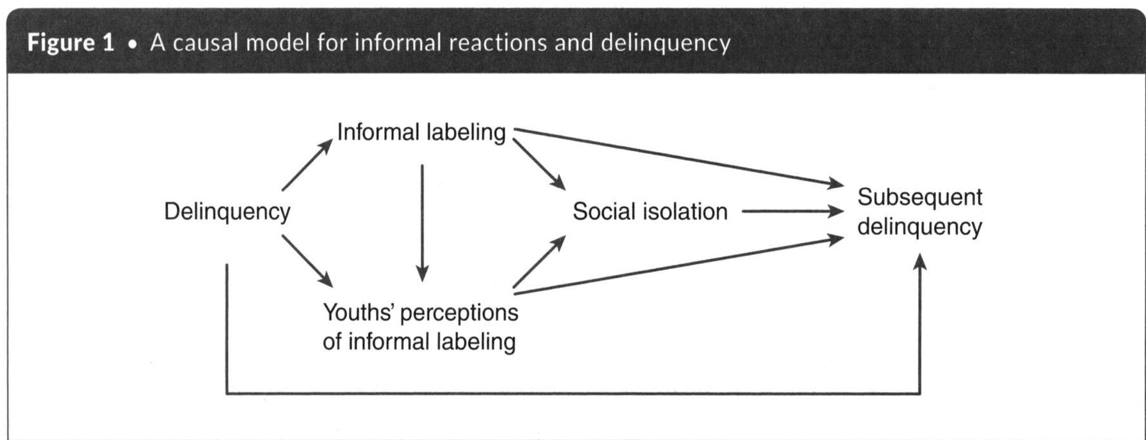

NOTE: Controls for gender, race, age, parent education, and family income are included in all regressions but are not shown in the diagram.

involvement, even though this mediating role may be only partial.

In summary, the predictions from this model are as follows:

1. Delinquent acts are a significant predictor of informal labeling.
2. Both delinquent acts and informal labeling positively affect youths' perceptions of informal labeling.
3. Both informal labeling and youths' perceptions of informal labeling lead to two possible consequences: social isolation from significant others experienced by the labeled youths and subsequent delinquency.
4. Social isolation, in turn, increases the likelihood of subsequent delinquency.

Finally, as previous studies (see Gibbons & Krohn, 1991, for a review) have indicated, stable delinquent patterns exist. Therefore, a path included in the model predicts that prior delinquency is a significant predictor of subsequent delinquency.

An additional dimension of efforts to revitalize labeling theory involves attempts to specify a variety of contingencies that potentially influence the effect of official labeling on subsequent deviance (Berk et al., 1992; Palamara et al., 1986; Ray & Downs, 1986; Sherman & Smith, 1992). Studies have demonstrated that official reactions do affect the likelihood of subsequent deviance but that the effects are contingent on specific circumstances, such as gender, marital status, and employment status. The effect of official punishment on subsequent deviance is not uniform across different individual characteristics and different social contexts. In this vein, the present study, hypothesizing that women are more vulnerable to informal reactions than are men, assessed gender differences with the model. In addition, the present study also speculated that youth's perceptions of different kinds of informal labeling by different significant others (e.g., parents, friends, and teachers) may have differential associations with preceding variables such as delinquent behavior and subsequent variables such as social isolation. Therefore, the present study assessed the model with respect to youths' perceptions of different kinds of informal labeling.

Method

Sample

The data used for the present study came from the NYS, conducted by Elliott and his colleagues (Elliott & Ageton, 1980; Elliott, Huizinga, & Ageton, 1985; Elliott, Huizinga, & Menard, 1989). The original sample size of 1,725 youths was obtained from a national probability sample of households by employing a multistage cluster sample frame. The age range of these youths at the first wave was 11 to 17 years.

The data from the first two waves of the NYS were used for the present study. The first wave survey was conducted in early 1977 and the second in early 1978.

Measurement

The NYS used personal interview to collect self-reports of delinquent acts; parents' labeling of their child; the child's perceptions of parents', friends', and teachers' labeling; and the child's perceptions of social isolation from family, from friends, and at school. The variables included in the model presented above were measured as follows:

Informal labeling. Because only data concerning parents' attitudes toward their child were available in the NYS, the informal labeling was reflected in parents' labeling. The parents' labeling consisted of a set of four measures, including "bad kid," "gets into trouble," 'breaks rules," and "does things against the law." These measures reflected the extent to which parents labeled their child as deviant, with a 5-point scale ranging from 1 (*strongly disagree*) to 5 (*strongly agree*).

Child's perceptions of informal labeling. Youth respondents were asked to indicate the extent to which their parents, their friends, and their teachers labeled them as deviant. The items and scoring for youth responses were the same as those for parents' labeling.

Social isolation. Youth respondents reported their perceptions of interpersonal relationships with their families, their friends, and at school. Each type of relationship was assessed by five items. A 5-point scale ranging from 1 (*strongly disagree*) to 5 (*strongly agree*) was used for each item. The scoring for these items was rearranged by the present investigator so that high scores represented high isolation. For isolation related to family, the items were as follows: "outsider with family," "feel lonely with family," "family not interested in problems," "family listens to problems," and "feel close to family." For isolation from friends, the five items were the following: "don't fit with friends," "friends don't take interest," "feel lonely with friends," "feel close to friends," and "friends listen to problems." Similarly, five items reflected isolation at school: 'Teachers don't call on me," "nobody at school cares," "don't belong at school," "feel lonely at school," and "teachers don't ask me to work on projects."

Delinquent acts. The NYS included a delinquency inventory to represent the entire range of delinquent acts. Each of the self-reported delinquent acts was coded in two parts: (a) absolute frequency and (b) categorical responses, ranging from 1 (*never*) to 9 (*two to three times per day*). Following Elliott et al. (1985) and Matsueda (1992), the present study used a 24-item scale of general delinquency with the categorical responses because the categorical responses have less skewed distributions. The delinquency items included auto theft, $5 theft, $5 to $50 theft, buying stolen goods, runaway, concealed weapon, aggravated assault, prostitution, sexual intercourse, gang fights, sold marijuana, hit parents, hit teachers, hit students, disorderly conduct, sold drugs, joyriding, sexual assault, strong-armed students, strong-armed teachers, strong-armed others, breaking and entering, panhandled.

The present study created several additive indexes to represent these variables in the model (i.e., indexes for parents' labeling; youths' perceptions of parents', friends', and teachers' labeling; social isolation from family, from friends, and at school; and delinquency) by using the above items. The standardized reliability coefficient for each index ranged from .65 to .75.

In addition to these key variables in the model, the present study included the following control variables that may be related to the informal labeling process: race; age; family income, measured by a 10-point scale ranging from 1 (*$6,000 or less*) to 10 (*$38,001 or more*); and parental education, measured by a 7-point scale ranging from 1 (*some grade school*) to 7 (*graduate degree*).

Based on time and logical order, self-reported delinquency in the first wave of the NYS consisted of delinquent acts prior to parents' labeling and youths' perceptions of informal labeling. In the first wave, the adolescent respondents reported their delinquency during the previous year. Also, in the first wave, parents were interviewed to report their current attitudes toward their child, and youths reported their current perceptions of parents', friends', and teachers' labeling and their perceptions of isolation from family, from friends, and at school. Thus parents' labeling, youths' perceptions of informal labeling, and social isolation were measured in the first wave. In addition, race, age, family income, and parental education were measured in the first wave. The measure of subsequent self-reported delinquency occurred in the second wave.

Ordinary least squares regression (OLS) was employed to assess the model. In addition, the present study examined the interactions between gender and each of the primary independent variables to assess the possible role of gender differences in the informal labeling process.

Results

The present study begins its analysis with the effect of delinquency on parents' labeling (see Table 1). Delinquency significantly and positively affected parents' labeling of their child (β = 23). Also, there were significant associations between race, age, and parental education and parents' labeling, which indicated that younger and non-White youths and youths whose parents' education was lower were more likely to be labeled as deviant by their parents. These results supported the predictions of labeling theory that individual and social disadvantages are related to the labeling process.

Table 2 presents the effects of delinquency and parents' labeling on youths' perceptions of parents', friends', and teachers' labeling. Three equations are included in Table 2 for the three dependent variables—perceived parents', friends', and teachers' labeling. Both parents' labeling and delinquency had significant effects on youths' perceptions of parents' labeling (β = .29 and .25, respectively), friends' labeling (β = .22 and .35, respectively), and teachers' labeling (β = .23 and .36, respectively).

In addition to the direct effect of delinquency on youths' perceptions of significant others' labeling, delinquency had indirect effects on these youths' perceptions through parents' labeling. However, these indirect effects

Table 1 • Regression for Effects of Delinquency on Parents' Labeling, with Control Variables Included

Independent Variable	β	T
Delinquency	.23	9.54*
Gender	.04	1.72
Race	–.13	–4.96*
Age	–.07	–2.93*
Parent education	–.13	–4.83*
Family income	–.03	–1.21

NOTE: Beta (β) = Standardized regression coefficient. $R^2 = .12$.

*$p < .05$.

were fairly small. On the basis of the direction of these indirect effects, they increased the amount of total positive effects of delinquency on youths' perceptions of in formal labeling.

Furthermore, both gender and parent education were significantly associated with youths' perceptions of parents', friends', and teachers' labeling, whereas family income exhibited significant effects on youths' perceptions of parents' and friends' labeling. Men and youths whose parental education was lower were more likely to perceive labeling by parents, friends, and teachers. Youths who came from families with lower

Table 2 • Regression for Effects of Delinquency and Parents' Labeling on Youths' Perceptions of Informal Labeling by Parents, Friends, and Teachers, with Control Variables Included

	Youths' Perceptions of Informal Labeling					
	Parents		Friends		Teachers	
Independent Variable	β	T	β	T	β	T
Parents' labeling	.29	12.00*	.22	9.28*	.23	10.04*
Delinquency	.25	10.57*	.35	15.19*	.36	15.41*
Gender	.05	2.19*	.11	4.68*	.09	4.05*
Race	.02	0.02	–.01	–0.71	–.01	–0.31
Age	–.04	–1.86	.03	1.53	–.01	–0.62
Parent education	–.06	–2.54*	–.08	–3.17*	–.08	–3.32*
Family income	–.05	–1.97*	.06	2.37*	.03	1.18

NOTE: Beta (β) = Standardized regression coefficient. $R^2 = .22$ for parents, .25 for friends, and .26 for teachers.

*$p < .05$.

income were more likely to perceive labeling by parents and friends.

Table 3 presents the results of regressions of social isolation on parents' labeling and youths' perceptions of significant others' labeling. Similar to Table 2, Table 3 includes three equations for the three dependent variables—isolation from family, from friends, and at school. First, youths' perceptions of parents' labeling were a significant predictor of isolation from family (β = .31), from friends (β = .20), and at school (β = .24). The greater the youths' perceptions of parents' labeling, the greater were their perceptions of isolation from all three kinds of significant others. Second, youths' perceptions of friends' labeling had a positive effect only on isolation from friends (β = .18), and youths' perceptions of teachers' labeling had a positive effect only on isolation at school (β = .13). Third, parents' labeling significantly affected isolation from family (β = .05). Furthermore, on the basis of the causal order, parents' labeling had indirect effects on isolation from significant others through youths' perceptions of significant others' labeling. All of these findings were consistent with propositions of labeling theory. Informal labeling appears to lead to negative changes in interpersonal relationships, as assessed by degree of isolation.

Finally, the results in Table 3 also show that delinquency was negatively related to youths' perceptions of friends' isolation (β = –11). This may imply that delinquency is an important factor leading to closer group association. In addition, non-White youths were more likely to perceive isolation from family, from friends, and at school. Older and female youths were more likely to perceive isolation from family, whereas younger and male youths were more likely to perceive isolation from friends. Family income was significantly and negatively related to isolation from friends.

Table 3 • Regression for Effects of Delinquency; Parents' Labeling; Youths' Perceptions of Informal Labeling by Parents, Friends, and Teachers on Youths' Perceptions of Social Isolation from Family, Friends, and at School, with Control Variables Included

	Youths' Perceptions of Informal Labeling					
	Family		Friends		School	
Independent Variable	β	*T*	β	*T*	β	*T*
Parents' labeling	.05	2.10*	–.01	–0.33	.01	0.43
Delinquency	.04	1.38	–.11	–3.81*	.01	0.25
Youths' perceptions of parents' labeling	.31	9.43*	.20	5.84*	.24	7.05*
Youths' perceptions of friends' labeling	.05	1.30	.18	4.32*	.03	0.77
Youths' perceptions of teachers' labeling	.06	1.60	–.06	–1.34	.13	3.10*
Gender	–.12	–4.97*	.07	2.81*	–.03	–1.41
Race	–.07	–2.77*	–.12	–4.51*	–.05	–2.04*
Age	.13	5.69*	–.07	–2.84*	–.04	–1.86
Parent education	–.04	–0.02	.02	0.89	–.04	–1.42
Family income	–.02	–0.56	–.06	–2.24*	–.04	–1.31

NOTE: Beta (β) = Standardized regression coefficient. R^2 = .22 for isolation from family, .13 for isolation from friends, and .16 for isolation at school.

*$p < .05$.

The results of a full regression equation predicting subsequent delinquency are reported in Table 4. Consistent with labeling theory, parents' labeling and youths' perceptions of teachers' labeling yielded significantly positive coefficients (β = .08 and .08, respectively). They predicted an increased possibility of subsequent delinquency. Also, parents' labeling had an indirect effect on subsequent delinquency via perceived teachers' labeling. Inconsistent with labeling theory, social isolation from family, from friends, and at school evidenced no significant positive effects on subsequent delinquency. Thus social isolation had no mediating role for the relationship between informal labeling and subsequent delinquency.[2]

The results in Table 4 also revealed that, as predicted, prior delinquency was significantly and positively related to subsequent delinquency (β = .50). Furthermore, consistent with labeling theory, part of the total effect of prior delinquency on subsequent delinquency was positively mediated by parents' labeling and youths' perceptions of teachers' labeling. Finally, the significant coefficients for gender (β = .09) and age (β = .09) indicated that older and male youths were more likely to be involved in delinquency.

The present study also examined possible interactions between gender and the primary variables. The results revealed three kinds of significant interaction effects. First, there was a significant interaction of delinquency and gender on parents' labeling (β = –.56), which indicated that delinquency exerted a greater effect on parents' labeling for women than for men. This was consistent with the hypothesis that women are more likely to suffer informal labeling. Second, parents' labeling and gender had an interaction effect on subsequent delinquency (β = .20), which indicated that parents' labeling was more likely to increase the probability of delinquency involvement for men than for women. This was at odds with the hypothesis proposed in the present study. Third,

Table 4 • Regression for Effects Hypothesized Predictors on Subsequent Delinquency

Independent Variable	β	*T*
Parents' labeling	.08	3.66*
Prior delinquency	.50	21.17*
Youths' perceptions of parents' labeling	–.01	–0.26
Youths' perceptions of friends' labeling	.03	0.93
Youths' perceptions of teachers' labeling	.08	2.41*
Family isolation	–.02	–0.94
Friends' isolation	–.01	–0.06
School isolation	–.02	–0.81
Gender	.09	4.18*
Race	.01	0.52
Age	.09	4.04*
Parent education	–.01	–0.11
Family income	–.03	–1.10

NOTE: Beta (β) = Standardized regression coefficient. $R^2 = .39$.

*$p < .05$.

there was a significant interaction effect between prior delinquency and gender on subsequent delinquency ($\beta = .57$). Consistent with previous research, prior delinquency exhibited a greater effect on further delinquency for men than for women. That is, a stable delinquent pattern was more likely to exist among men than women.

Discussion

There were several noteworthy findings in the present study. First, delinquent behavior significantly increased the probability of parents' labeling of their child, with the probability greater for women than men. Also, as Matsueda (1992) reported, some demographic variables exhibited significant effects on parents' labeling of their children as deviant. Non-White, younger youths and youths whose parents had lower education were more likely to be labeled as deviant by their parents. These findings were consistent with the propositions of labeling theory, which predict that individual and social disadvantages are related to the labeling process.

Second, delinquent behavior and parents' labeling exerted significant effects on youths' perceptions of labeling by significant others, including parents, friends, and teachers. This implies that delinquent behavior and informal labeling may damage youths' previous conventional self-identity through their self-perceptions of their own delinquent acts and significant others' labeling, thereby increasing the probability of their self-degradation and self-labeling. This finding was also consistent with the labeling perspective.

Third, youths' perceptions of parents' labeling were significantly and positively related to their perceptions of isolation from family, from friends, and at school. Parents' labeling was more likely to increase the probability of family isolation, and youths' perceptions of friends' and teachers' labeling exerted, respectively, positive and significant effects on isolation from friends and at school. Thus labeling by significant others and perceptions of the labeling were more likely to lead to feelings of social rejection. Although youths' perceptions of parents' labeling were a source of feelings of isolation from all three kinds of significant others (i.e., family, friends, and school), specificity of effects also existed, in that (a) parents' labeling led to feelings of isolation from family, (b) youths' perceptions of friends' labeling led to feelings of isolation from friends, and (c) youths' perceptions of teachers' labeling led to feelings of isolation from school. These findings were consistent with the hypothesis that informal labeling has direct and negative consequences for other areas of a person's life.

Fourth, prior delinquency significantly affected subsequent delinquency, with the effect greater for male youths than female youths. This was consistent with previous findings of stable delinquent patterns among youths and among male youths in particular. Furthermore, parents' labeling and youths' perceptions of teachers' labeling were significantly and positively related to subsequent delinquency. Also, a gender difference was uncovered, indicating that parents' labeling was more likely to be a negative factor leading to subsequent delinquency for male youths than for female youths. Again, these results were in agreement with the prediction of labeling theory that deviant labels increase the likelihood of further delinquency involvement, and they reaffirmed the importance of recent efforts to specify the variety of contingencies that may influence the effect of a deviant label on further deviant behavior.

Fifth, youths' perceptions of social isolation from significant others had no direct and significant effect on subsequent delinquency and thus had no mediating role for the effect of informal labeling on subsequent delinquency. This was at odds with the hypothesis derived from labeling theory.

Finally, some indirect effects were found in the present study. For instance, part of the total effect of delinquency on social isolation from significant others was mediated by parents' labeling and youths' perceptions of parents', friends', and teachers' labeling. These findings were consistent with recent studies of labeling theory, which have adopted a "softer" rather than a "harder" stance by specifying a variety of intervening variables that may, in part, account for the association of labeling with delinquency. As Paternoster and Iovanni (1989) pointed out, this softer stance, compared with a deterministic one, can represent more plausibly the classic implication of labeling theory.

In addition to these major results related to the predictions derived from the model, an unanticipated but important finding was the negative relationship between delinquency and youths' perceptions of isolation from their friends. This finding may have two implications. First, delinquency may be a medium or vehicle that ties youths together, even though their relationships are not close and intimate. Second, according to self-derogation theory (Kaplan, 1975, 1980), adolescents are motivated to commit delinquency in order to enhance their self-esteem, and, thus, appreciative companionship is necessary to satisfy the motivation. Therefore, delinquency and peer companionship may be positively correlated.

The informal labeling process appears to play an important role in explaining youths' life and behavioral adjustments. Elaborations and specifications of this informal labeling process should be valuable in the development of "neolabeling" theory. Second, in some important aspects, such as parents' labeling, the informal labeling process is not uniform across gender. This reaffirms the trend of revitalizing labeling theory by specifying a variety of contingencies. Such specifications of contingencies should be an important requirement for any attempts to develop a neolabeling theory. Third, social isolation from significant others appears to have no significant effect on further delinquency. This challenges the proposition derived from labeling theory that social rejection caused by deviant labels necessarily results in further deviance. It may be that any such relationship, if it exists, depends on the nature and type of social rejection and deviant behavior. Future research is needed to address these important issues. Such research would contribute to the further development of neolabeling theory.

Notes

1. More recent work by Heimer and Matsueda (1994) has extended Matsueda's study by adding some variables of social control, such as attachment to family and friends. This social control model, based on Matsueda's (1992) model of reflected appraisals, has been tested by Heimer and Matsueda.

2. Tests for multicollinearity among youths' perceptions of parents', friends', and teachers' labeling and among youths' perceptions of isolation from family, from friends, and at school indicated no multicollinearity problems in each equation.

References

Alvarez, R. (1968). Informal reactions to deviance in simulated work organizations: A laboratory experiment. *American Sociological Review, 33,* 895–912.

Berk, R. A., Campell, A., Klap, R., & Western, B. (1992). The deterrent effect of arrest: A Bayesian analysis of four field experiments. *American Sociological Review, 57,* 689–708.

Black, D. J. (1970). Production of crime rates. *American Sociological Review, 35,* 733–748.

Black, D. J., & Reiss. A. J. (1970). Police control of juveniles. *American Sociological Review, 35,* 63–47.

Braithwaite, J. (1989). *Crime, shame, and reintegration.* Cambridge, England: Cambridge University Press.

DeLamater, J. (1968). On the nature of deviance. *Social Forces, 46,* 445–455.

Elliott, D. S., & Ageton, S. S. (1980). Reconciling race and class differences in self-reported and official estimates of delinquency. *American Sociological Review, 40,* 95–110.

Elliott, D. S., Huizinga, D., & Ageton, S. S. (1985). *Explaining delinquency and drug use.* Beverly Hills, CA: Sage.

Elliott, D. S., Huizinga. D., & Menard, S. (1989). *Multiple problem youth: Delinquency, substance use, and mental health problems.* New York: Springer-Verlag.

Farrell, R. A. (1989). Cognitive consistency in deviance causation: A psychological elaboration of an integrated system model. In S. F. Messner, M. D. Krohn, & A. E. Liska (Eds.), *Theoretical integration in the study of deviance and crime: Problems and prospects* (pp. 77–92). Albany: State University of New York Press.

Felson, R. B. (1985). Reflected appraisal and the development of self. *Social Psychology Quarterly, 48,* 71–77.

Felson, R. B. (1989). Parents and reflected appraisal process: A longitudinal analysis. *Journal of Personality and Social Psychology, 56,* 965–971.

Gibbons, D. C., & Krohn, M. D. (1991). *Delinquent behavior* (5th ed.). Englewood Cliffs, NJ: Prentice Hall.

Gibbs, J. P. (1966). Conception of deviant behavior: The old and the new. *Pacific Sociological Review, 9,* 9–14.

Gibbs, J. P. (1972). Issues in defining deviant behavior. In R. A. Scott & J. D. Douglas (Eds.), *Theoretical perspectives on deviance* (pp. 39–68). New York: Basic Books.

Gove, W. R. (1980). The labeling perspective: An overview. In W. R. Gove (Ed.), *The labeling of deviance: Evaluating a perspective* (2nd ed., pp. 9–33). Beverly Hills, CA: Sage.

Gove, W. R., & Hughes, M. (1989). A theory of mental illness: An attempted integration of biological, psychological, and social variables. In S. F. Messner, M. D. Krohn, & A. E. Liska (Eds.), *Theoretical integration in the study of deviance and crime: Problems and prospects* (pp. 61–76). Albany: State University of New York Press.

Hagan, J. (1974). Extra-legal attitudes and criminal sanctioning: An assessment and a sociological view. *Law and Society Review, 8,* 357–383.

Hagan, J., & Palloni, A. (1990). The social reproduction of a criminal class in working-class London. *American Journal of Sociology, 96,* 265–299.

Heimer, K., & Matsueda, R. L. (1994). Role-taking, role commitment, and delinquency: A theory of differential social control. *American Sociological Review, 59,* 356–390.

Jackson, J. K. (1954). The adjustment of the family to the crisis of alcoholism. *Quarterly Journal of Studies on Alcohol, 15,* 564–586.

Jackson, J. K. (1962). Alcoholism and the family. In D. J. Pittman & C. R. Snyder (Eds.), *Society, culture, and drinking patterns* (pp. 472–479). New York: Wiley.

Kaplan, H. B. (1975). Increase in self-rejection as an antecedent of deviant responses. *Journal of Youth and Adolescence, 4,* 438–458.

Kaplan, H. B. (1980). *Deviant behavior in defense of self.* New York: Academic Press.

Kinch, J. W. (1963). A formalized theory of the self-concept. *American Journal of Sociology, 68,* 481–486.

Link, B. (1982). Mental patient status, and income: An examination of the effects of a psychiatric label. *American Sociological Review, 47,* 456–478.

Link, B. (1987). Understanding labeling effects in the area of mental disorders: An assessment of the effects of expectations of rejection. *American Sociological Review, 52,* 1004–1081.

Link, B., & Cullen, F. T. (1983). Reconsidering the social rejection of external patients: Levels of attitudinal response. *American Journal of Community Psychology, 11,* 261–273.

Link, B., Cullen, F. T., Frank, J., & Wozniak, J. F. (1987). The social rejection of former mental patients: Understanding why labels matter. *American Journal of Sociology, 92,* 1461–1500.

Link, B., Cullen, F. T., Struening, E., Shrout, P. E., & Dohrenwend, B. P. (1989). A modified labeling theory approach to mental disorders: An empirical assessment. *American Sociological Review, 54,* 400–423.

Liska, A. E. (1987). *Perspectives on deviance.* Englewood Cliffs, NJ: Prentice Hall.

Matsueda, R. L. (1992). Reflected appraisals, parental labeling, and delinquency: Specifying a symbolic interactionist theory. *American Journal of Sociology, 97,* 1577–1611.

Orcutt, J. D. (1973). Social reaction and the response to deviation in small groups. *Social Forces, 52,* 259–267.

Palamara, F., Cullen, F. T., & Gersten, J. C. (1986). The effect of police and mental health intervention on juvenile delinquency: Specifying contingencies in the impact of formal reaction. *Journal of Health and Social Behavior, 27,* 90–105.

Pate, A. M., & Hamilton, E. E. (1992). Formal and informal deterrents to domestic violence: The Dade County spouse assault experiment. *American Sociological Review, 57,* 691–697.

Paternoster, R., & Iovanni, L. (1989). The labeling perspective and delinquency: An elaboration of the theory and an assessment of the evidence. *Justice Quarterly, 6,* 359–394.

Ray, M. C., & Downs, W. R. (1986). An empirical test of labeling theory using longitudinal data. *Journal of Research in Crime and Delinquency, 23,* 169–194.

Sampson, H., Messinger, S. L., & Towne, R. D. (1962). Family processes and becoming a mental patient. *American Journal of Sociology, 68,* 88–96.

Sampson, R. J. (1986). Effects of socioeconomic context on social reaction to juvenile delinquency. *American Sociological Review, 51,* 876–885.

Sherman, L. W., & Smith, D. A. (1992). Crime, punishment, and stake in community: Legal and informal control of domestic violence. *American Sociological Review, 57,* 680–690.

Swigert, L. V., & Farrell, R. A. (1978). Referent others and deviance causation: A neglected dimension in labeling research. In M. D. Krohn & R. L. Akers (Eds.), *Crime, law, and sanctions: theoretical perspectives* (pp. 59–72). Beverly Hills, CA: Sage.

Tittle, C. R. (1975). Deterrence or labeling? *Social Forces, 53,* 399–410.

Tittle, C. R. (1980a). Labeling and crime: An empirical evaluation. In W. R. Gove (Ed.), *The labeling of deviance: Evaluating a perspective* (2nd ed., pp. 241–263). Beverly Hills, CA: Sage.

Tittle, C. R. (1980b). *Sanctions and social deviance: The question of deterrence.* New York: Praeger.

Tittle, C. R. (1988). Two empirical regularities (maybe) in search of an explanation: Commentary on the age/crime debate. *Criminology, 26,* 75–86.

Tittle, C. R., & Curran, D. A. (1988). Contingencies for dispositional disparities in juvenile justice. *Social Forces, 67,* 23–58.

Triplett, R. A., & Jarjoura, G. R. (1994). Theoretical and empirical specification of a model of informal labeling. *Journal of Quantitative Criminology, 10,* 241–276.

Wellford, G. F. (1975). Labeling theory and criminology: An assessment. *Social Problems, 22,* 332–345.

Williams, K. R., & Hawkins, R. (1986). Perceptual research on general deterrence: A critical review. *Law and Society Review, 20,* 545–547.

Yarrow, M. R., Schartz, C. G., Murphy, H. S., & Deasy, L. C. (1955). The psychological meaning of mental illness in the family. *Journal of Social Issues, 11,* 12–24.

/// REVIEW QUESTIONS

1. How does Zhang measure informal labeling, the child's perceptions of informal labeling, and social isolation? Do you agree that such measures are valid? How would you improve such measures?

2. What did findings from this study show regarding parents' labeling? Which types of the youths' perceptions of labeling had the greatest effect on their subsequent delinquency? Explain these findings.

3. Given the findings of this study, do you believe that informal labeling has an important impact on recidivism or reoffending by youths who have been labeled "bad" kids? What types of policies would you advise based on these findings?

READING /// 23

In this study, Brian C. Renauer examines consensus and conflict approaches to explaining police stops and searches in 94 neighborhoods in Portland, Oregon, from 2004 to 2008 using police data collected from onboard or handheld computers. The data analyzed come from an impressive amount of more than 206,000 police stops and more than 38,000 searches with a focus on racial or ethnic makeup of suspects and level of disadvantage in the areas where such stops and searches were performed.

While reading this article, one should consider the following topics:

- What the consensus approach is, which the author refers to as the "police deployment" perspective and others have referred to as "differential exposure"
- What the conflict approach is, which includes several types of perspectives, such as racial threat, race out of place, and social conditioning
- Findings of the current study regarding the impact of the various predicting variables on decisions to stop and/or search with an emphasis on the ones that were found to support (or not support) the consensus or conflict perspectives
- The extent to which the level of disorder or disadvantage of a given area influences police decisions to stop and/or search suspects

Neighborhood Variation in Police Stops and Searches

A Test of Consensus and Conflict Perspectives

Brian C. Renauer

Introduction

Concerns over racial profiling in law enforcement have led to the proliferation of data collection by law enforcement agencies on the race and ethnicity of drivers in traffic stops and after stop outcomes. A common critique of aggregate jurisdictional studies of traffic stop and search disparities is their lack of control for variation in social demographics and police deployment across neighborhoods or beats (Fagan, Geller, Davis, & West, 2010; Gaines, 2006; Ridgeway, 2006; Schell, Ridgeway, Dixon, Turner, & Riley, 2007). A small number of studies have examined neighborhood or police beat variation in traffic stops and searches. These studies have generally applied consensus and conflict theory perspectives to explain variation in stops and searches. This study examines the application of these two theoretical perspectives to inform a new study of traffic stops and searches across

SOURCE: Brian C. Renauer, "Neighborhood Variation in Police Stops and Searches: A Test of Consensus and Conflict Perspectives," *Police Quarterly* 15, no. 3 (2012): 219–40.

neighborhoods in an urban setting. The consensus and conflict perspectives highlight a core justice concern in the application of social control in democratic societies: Are patterns in macro social control by law enforcement related to community desires to have police maintain safety through proactive law enforcement or is law enforcement targeted toward certain groups and strata identified as dangerous and threatening?

Consensus and Conflict Theory

The consensus perspective, also referred to as structural functionalism, assumes a general consensus over societal goals and values exists and the structure of crime control is to "maintain society's values-goals-needs" (Liska, 1987, p. 71). Under this framework, law enforcement behavior, like stopping motorists and searching vehicles, is a response to society's uniform desire for police to control crime and disorder. Police actions are a response to the violational behavior of citizens regardless of officers' or citizens' ascribed and achieved statuses. Chamlin (2009, p. 554) notes that "consensus theories maintain that the police, as well as other agencies of social control, function to meet the defense needs of society as a whole rather than any subdivision within it." In certain neighborhoods police are regularly called by citizens to respond to disturbances, heightening police presence and proactivity and increasing the likelihood *of all motorists* who drive through these neighborhoods of being observed for traffic violations. In sum, motorists who frequently drive through high crime and calls for service neighborhoods have a "differential exposure" (Schell et al., 2007) to police, increasing their chances of being stopped and searched (Gaines, 2006; Novak & Chamlin, 2008; Ousey & Lee, 2008; Withrow, 2004). This consensus theory framework for examining spatial patterns in police stops and searches will be referred to as the "police deployment" perspective (see also Roh & Robinson, 2009).

The police deployment perspective is race-neutral. In other words, a legal factor like citizen calls for police services should explain traffic stops and searches *equally across race/ethnicity*, and racial/ethnic composition of neighborhoods should not be related to stops and searches. Roh and Robinson (2009, p. 163) suggest that targeted, proactive policing does not bring up a discrimination issue as long as it is based on legal factors. Deploying police resources according to localized needs through problem-oriented policing methods or hot spot enforcement is generally regarded as a best practice (Gaines, 2006; Roh & Robinson, 2009; Sherman, 1996).

The conflict perspective, on the other hand, does not view police as neutral actors equally applying social control in all cases of law violation (Liska, 1987). A common conflict perspective theme is that crime control institutions tend to focus their social control functions on "dangerous groups and strata, rather than the mere suppression of illegal activities" (Novak & Chamlin, 2008, p. 5). Studies of neighborhood police stops and searches have applied three types of conflict perspectives: racial threat, race out of place, and social conditioning. All three of these perspectives explain in different ways the uneven distribution of crime control based on group status.

The racial threat perspective has a long history of being used to explain macro law enforcement behavior (e.g., resources, arrests, police shootings; Liska, 1987; Parker, Stults, & Rice, 2005; Petrocelli, Piquero, & Smith, 2003). The theory proposes minority population growth may pose an economic or political competition threat to a privileged or ruling class, which police represent, and police in turn "use the crime control apparatus of the state to restrain and limit those who threaten their interests" (Petrocelli et al., 2003, p. 2). Accordingly, police stops and searches should occur in places with greater percentages of non-White citizens.

Drawing from a theory of contextual attentiveness, the "race out of place" perspective recognizes that police officer attention and suspiciousness is raised toward individuals and groups that do not fit what is usual, customary, or expected (Withrow, 2004). Blacks in predominately White neighborhoods may draw police suspicion while Whites in predominately Black neighborhoods may be equally considered out of place by police (Novak & Chamlin, 2008; Withrow, 2004). For example, the percentage of the neighborhood population that is Black should be negatively related to Black stop rates because the presence of Black drivers in predominately Black neighborhoods is not an unusual social feature; however, percent Black should be positively related to White stops and searches where White drivers may be considered suspiciously out of place (Novak & Chamlin, 2008).

The "social conditioning" perspective describes how societal subgroups can become linked to criminal activity creating stereotypes that guide police suspicion and behavior (Smith & Alpert, 2007). By internalizing beliefs about subgroup criminality that are transmitted through overt racism, racial stereotypes, or media portrayals, police "adopt unconscious profiles regarding specific demographic groups in society" (Tillyer & Engel, 2010, p. 5). Negative experiences and constant exposure to criminal suspects on the job may exasperate the problem by reinforcing group beliefs and profiles (Tillyer & Engel, 2010). A seemingly benign institutional decision to focus patrol in high crime neighborhoods may influence officer decision making by stigmatizing certain neighborhoods as high crime, disorderly, or dangerous and "skewing how officers perceive and interpret the actions of citizens" (Fagan et al., 2010, p. 317). Thus legitimate crime control efforts may turn into an "abuse of discretion" (Roh & Robinson, 2009, p. 164). Both racial threat and social conditioning perspectives are concerned about threatening subgroups, but the former focuses on perceived economic, cultural, or social status threats and the latter on public safety threats.

Disorder and Disadvantage

Disorder/incivilities and urban disadvantage theories have also been applied to ecological studies of police stops and searches. The description and application of these theories does not neatly fit into either the consensus or conflict classification. Fagan et al. (2010) describe how the incivilities thesis (i.e., broken windows) has received both a consensus and conflict spin by different sources. For example, the traditional broken windows thesis advocates proactive police responses in disorderly neighborhoods to halt a "contagious spread" of crime (Fagan et al., 2010, p. 313). Similarly, reduced informal social control due to economic and familial disadvantages would necessitate more proactive crime control approaches to reestablish order (Parker, Lane, & Alpert, 2010). This interpretation of disorder and disadvantage theories views crime control as a functional response to deteriorating structural conditions, not an attempt to target subgroups or motivated by self-interests.

Conversely, others have argued that concentrated disadvantage, particularly for Blacks, is due to historical housing discrimination practices, racial segregation, and White "flight" (Logan & Molotch, 1987; Parker et al., 2005; Wilson, 1987). As a consequence, concentrated disadvantage and its relationship with reduced informal social control and heightened violence is in part related to historical episodes of racial conflict, threat, and economic control by White power elites (Parker et al., 2005). Furthermore, neighborhoods with pronounced levels of disorder and disadvantage can be stigmatized by officers, similar to the social conditioning approach, drawing increased attention and suspicion of local residents who tend to be racial minorities (Fagan et al., 2010).

Ecological Studies of Police Stops and Searches

The following literature review examines the application of consensus and conflict perspectives in the police stop and search literature. Only studies that have empirically examined *neighborhood* (or police beat) *variation* in traffic stops or after stop searches are reviewed.

Consensus Theory Findings

The term "consensus theory" is typically not mentioned in ecological studies of police stops and searches. The existing research uses terms like "police deployment" or "workload" to essentially represent a consensus framework. The consensus perspective is typically applied as a statistical control against the more common conflict theory framework. UCR Part 1 crime or arrest rates have been the most common consensus variables utilized. The basic consensus hypothesis applied to police stops and searches is that neighborhood crime or calls for services should increase police deployment and subsequently increase stops and searches (Gaines, 2006; Novak & Chamlin, 2009; Roh & Robinson, 2009).

Whether measured through crime rates, arrest rates, number of deployments, or calls for service, the police deployment perspective helps to explain variation in neighborhood police behavior. Five studies find police deployment measures are positively related to neighborhood stop rates. Petrocelli et al. (2003) found that neighborhood crime was positively related to neighborhood stop rates in Richmond, VA. Withrow (2004) found that reported crimes per 1,000 residents had a significant, positive relationship to patrol stops in 36 Wichita police beats, controlling for race, population size, and income.

Gaines (2006) found that citizen calls for service, Part I violent and property crimes, and drug calls exhibited strong positive correlations to neighborhood stops of African Americans, Hispanics, and Whites across 133 police districts in Riverside, CA. Roh and Robinson (2009) measured the average number of police-initiated deployments per shift for each beat to examine a police deployment perspective in 121 police beats in Houston. Police deployment was positively related to neighborhood stops. Fagan et al. (2010) included a lagged measure of homicide arrests to control for a police deployment perspective in 55 New York precincts. They found homicide arrests in the prior year were significantly related to increased neighborhood stop rates across all the models. Only Novak and Chamlin (2008) found an insignificant relationship between police deployment, using a combined factor variable of calls for service and UCR Part I crimes, with stop rates in 70 Kansas City police beats.

The relationship between police deployment measures and neighborhood search rates is more mixed; two studies show positive relationships between police deployment and searches, one study shows a variable relationship, and one study shows no relationship. The police workload measure in the Novak and Chamlin (2008) study exhibited a positive relationship to total, Black, and White search rates. Roh and Robinson (2009) found that neighborhood police deployments were related to neighborhood searches. Parker et al. (2010) used a homicide rate per 10,000 to control for a police deployment perspective in 249 to 327 Miami-Dade census tracts. Miami-Dade census tract homicide rates were positively related to Hispanic search rates, but not Black or White search rates. Petrocelli et al. (2003) did not find that neighborhood crime was related to neighborhood search rates in Richmond, VA. These less consistent findings for search rates may be related to the complexity of after stop search decisions wherein unique contextual factors (e.g., suspect demeanor, time of day) are missing from aggregate data collection (Engel & Johnson, 2006).

This current study seeks to differentiate itself from prior studies of police stops and searches by highlighting citizen calls for service as an important measure of the consensus theory perspective. Only two studies have used calls for service as a variable and only one was a multivariate study. Neighborhood variation in citizen calls for service provides a robust approximation of traditional consensus theory. Neighborhoods with higher concentrations of citizen calls for police services, particularly calls that are deemed high priority, would appear to be a vital signal for police that community consensus over crime and disorder problems exists and social control responses are warranted. If traffic stops and searches are more likely in neighborhoods where citizens are requesting police presence at higher rates, then differential enforcement appears to be more democratically based.

Conflict Theory Findings

Racial threat. Only two studies, Petrocelli et al. (2003) and Novak and Chamlin (2008), specifically set out to test a racial threat theory perspective of neighborhood variation in traffic stops and searches and both did not find strong support. Percent of the neighborhood population that is Black was the key racial threat variable although both studies examined economic measures of class threat too. Petrocelli et al.'s (2003) study of Richmond neighborhoods found that percent of the population that is Black was not related to neighborhood stop rates but was positively related to neighborhood search rates. The authors concluded their results offer mixed support for a conflict theory framework. Novak and Chamlin (2008) found that the percentage of the population that was Black and economic inequality indicators were not significantly related to total or Black neighborhood stop rates in Kansas City neighborhoods.

Three additional studies controlled for percentage of neighborhood population that is Black but did not specifically develop hypotheses related to racial threat or conflict theory. Withrow (2004) found that the percentage of the patrol beat that was Black was significantly correlated with Black stops but was not a significant predictor of total beat stops when controlling for other factors like reported crime. Roh and Robinson (2009) found that areas with larger Black populations also experienced more drivers being stopped and subjected to consent searches, consistent with racial threat and profiling claims. However, percent Black was positively related to higher rates of finding contraband in searches; a result inconsistent with racial profiling claims. Roh and Robinson (2009) concluded with a cautionary policy statement, "more effective police practices at the community level (e.g., a higher hit rate to detect contraband) may generate a greater likelihood of becoming subject to more frequent and more intensive police practices at the individual level." Fagan et al. (2010) found an opposite pattern in New York: predominately Black neighborhoods had higher stop rates but significantly lower arrest rates. Fagan et al. (2010) believed New York's order maintenance police style increased enforcement contacts in Black neighborhoods over time, despite evidence of declining or stagnant crime trends, and appeared to provide less return in crime detection (i.e., arrests; Fagan et al., 2010). Overall, the findings supportive of racial threat theory are more mixed in comparison to the police deployment perspective.

Race out of place. Examining the race out of place argument requires using race-specific stop and search data, which only one study has examined using multivariate analysis. Race-specific stop and search data can discern whether the effect of neighborhood racial composition on stops and search rates is conditioned by the racial characteristics of drivers (Novak & Chamlin, 2008). Novak and Chamlin (2008) claim their results provide substantial support for the "race out of place" perspective. They found that White stop, search, and citation rates were positively and significantly related to the percentage of the population that was Black. Percent Black was also negatively related to Black stop, search, and citation rates. In other words, the presence of White drivers in increasingly Black neighborhoods looked unusual to police, subsequently raising their suspicions and leading to increased stop, search, and arrest rates for Whites, but Black drivers in increasingly Black neighborhoods was normal.

Social conditioning. Although not touted as a test of social conditioning, Parker et al.'s (2010) examination of Hispanic immigration and foreign-born populations in Miami-Dade census tracts is related. They found that Hispanic immigration was not related to search rates and percent foreign-born population was negatively related to Black, Hispanic, and White search rates. Parker et al. (2010, p. 358) apply social conditioning language in their conclusion: "the negative association . . . might suggest that police officers do not equate immigrants . . . with those responsible for criminal activity in those areas." Fagan et al. (2010) found no significant relationship between foreign-born population and police stops and arrests in New York precincts.

Disorder and Disadvantage Findings

Most of the studies that have used disorder or disadvantage measures have found insignificant or mixed results. Measures of poverty and unemployment were not significantly related to neighborhood stop, search, and arrest rates in Petrocelli et al.'s (2003) Richmond study. Fagan et al.'s (2010) study of New York precincts did not find a strong relationship between precinct disorder (i.e., residential mobility, vacancy rate, and physical disorder) with police stop and arrest rates per precinct controlling for race and lagged homicide arrest rates. Similarly, their measures of neighborhood disadvantage (i.e., % receiving public assistance, % foreign-born, and racial entropy) showed weak relationships to stop and arrest rates. Novak and Chamlin (2008) found mixed results for disorder and disadvantage control variables. Population mobility and percent renters were positively related to total, Black, and White stop rates but were not related to neighborhood search rates. Novak and Chamlin's (2008) social disorganization measure (i.e., single-parent households, % poverty) was not related to stop rates but was positively related to total and White search rates. Parker et al. (2010) also found mixed support. Percentage of housing units that were vacant was negatively related to Black and White search rates in Miami-Dade census tracts. Residential mobility was positively related to White search rates, but not Black or Hispanic. Race-specific measures of concentrated disadvantage were related to Hispanic and White search rates, but not Black. To explain the negative relationship in Black neighborhoods Parker et al. (2010, p. 358) reason it is the result of more severe disadvantages creating a "benign-neglect" phenomenon and leading police to be less active in such socially isolated places.

Status of Empirical Literature

Each of the above studies utilized different methodologies for examining the relationship between neighborhood structural conditions and traffic stops and searches. The most consistent finding is the positive relationship between police deployment measures and neighborhood stops; some studies also found support for racial threat and race out of place perspectives. Given this small and diverse pool of ecological studies, some of which were descriptive rather than inferential with multivariate models, it is important to improve on the application of consensus and conflict perspectives to macro-level patterns in stops and searches. There are five deficiencies in the extant empirical literature this study will address. First, the consensus perspective has received less theoretical attention leading to a variety of measurement approaches. This study argues that the use of citizen calls for service, which has been underutilized, represents a more theoretically pertinent variable for measuring a community consensus that police presence and action is required within neighborhoods. Second, the social conditioning perspective has not been directly examined in ecological studies of traffic stops and searches. This study proposes to examine ecological social conditioning using a race-specific measure of *lagged violent crime suspects* per 1,000 in the population. As police investigate violent crimes they discover, or visually observe, the race/ethnicity of alleged suspects. Racial/ethnic concentrations of violent crime suspects that persist in some neighborhoods over time could influence future deployment strategies and negative stereotypes, leading to increased pretext stops and search rates (Gelman, Fagan, & Kiss, 2007; Ridgeway, 2007). Officers could be "socially conditioned" to view racial/ethnic concentrations of suspects with heightened suspicion. The perception of the common violent suspect, whether accurate or not, may have a stronger influence on cognitive scripts of who is dangerous compared to actual arrests and convictions. Third, previous studies have examined one or two aspects of the conflict perspective, whereas this study will examine the three conflict perspectives reviewed above: racial threat, race out of place, and social conditioning. Fourth, Withrow (2004) and Novak and Chamlin (2008) noted that aggregating stops and searches can mask unique neighborhood context and race dynamics. Using race-specific measures of neighborhood populations, stops, and searches will allow for testing of the race out of place perspective, which only one multivariate study has accomplished. Fifth, the models in this study are more conservative than prior studies by controlling for spatial autocorrelation in stops and searches and the proportion of stops made after sunset, an important contextual feature potentially related to search rates.

Method

Stop and Search Data

Data for the study come from all traffic stops recorded by the Portland Police Bureau (Oregon) from January 1, 2004, through June 30, 2008, using onboard or handheld computers (N = 354,771). Each stop record could be linked to a CAD record that provided data on the time and location of the stop. Stop locations were then mapped into 94 official neighborhood boundaries. There were 88,009 stops that did not contain addresses, were unreadable, or outside of official Portland neighborhoods and were excluded from the analysis. Examination of the unmapped stops revealed virtually identical race/ethnicity breakdowns to mapped stops, thus the missing data appears random. The final data set only included neighborhood traffic stops conducted by regular patrol units. Stops made by traffic enforcement units were excluded from analysis because their deployment is focused on high traffic intersections, they do not respond to general calls for service, and typically utilize techniques that reduce officer discretion (e.g., radar and sting operations). The regular patrol units travel throughout neighborhoods, respond to calls for service, and have broader discretionary powers to engage in investigative or pretext stop situations. The race-specific analyses focused on stops where the driver was identified as Black, Hispanic, or White. The final sample of stops aggregated to the 94 neighborhood boundaries was 206,083. There were 38,493 searches (any type) connected to these stops (18.7%).

Dependent Variables

Stop Rate. Total and race-specific stop rates measured the number of total, Black, Hispanic, and White traffic stops (2004–2008) per neighborhood and were offset by the natural log of total, Black, Hispanic, or White persons aged 15 and older in the neighborhood.[1]

Search Rate. Total and race-specific search rates measured the number of total, Black, Hispanic, and White searches following a traffic stop (2004–2008) per neighborhood. Neighborhood search counts were also offset by the natural log of total, Black, Hispanic, or White persons aged 15 and older in the neighborhood. The search rate measure contains all search types; the data collection system allowed officers only two search codes, inventory or noninventory search.[2]

Independent Variables

% Black and %Hispanic (Census 2000). The percentage of the population that is Black or Hispanic was used to test for the racial threat perspective. As neighborhood racial populations increase, more social control should be applied to all drivers. Alternatively, the race out of place perspective argues that the effect of racial composition is conditioned by the neighborhood racial context. Thus percent Black and Hispanic should be negatively related to Black and Hispanic stop and search rates but positively related to White stop and search rates where Whites are perceived as more unusual/suspicious given the neighborhood context (Novak & Chamlin, 2008; Withrow, 2004).

Disadvantage (Census 2000). As noted earlier, the literature has applied both consensus and conflict interpretations to the hypothesized impact of neighborhood disadvantage and disorder on formal social control. This study utilized a social disorganization measure of disadvantage and interpretation of its effect on social control. Neighborhood disadvantage can reduce informal social control increasing criminal opportunities and events (Morenoff, Sampson, & Raudenbush, 2001), which often leads to police saturation and enhanced officer suspicion in disadvantaged neighborhoods (Parker et al., 2010). Three race-specific economic disadvantage indexes for each neighborhood were created (Black disadvantage, Hispanic disadvantage, and White disadvantage). The race-specific index was based on the percentage unemployed, percentage of families below poverty level, and percentage of female-headed households with children. Exploratory factor analysis found the measures for each index loaded onto single factors. Measures of unemployment, poverty, and female-headed households were *z*-scored and combined into an index.

Priority Calls for Service. The police deployment perspective and consensus theory was represented by the neighborhood rate of high-priority citizen calls for service (2004–2008). Higher rates of calls for service are likely to increase police presence, provide more opportunities for observing traffic infractions and suspicious behaviors, and motivate proactive enforcement. Citizen calls for service come from the city's Bureau of Emergency Communications (BOEC). Calls were classified from low priority (e.g., telephone report unit, routine, expedite) to high-priority (High-emergency, High-immediate, High-urgent). High-priority calls for service represented 42% of all citizen calls. High priority calls were aggregated by neighborhood and converted into a rate per 1,000 households.[3] If priority calls for service rates represent a community consensus over crime and public safety, it should explain stop and search rates for all race/ethnicity groups controlling for other factors.

Violent Crime Suspects. A lagged rate of total and race-specific violent crime suspects per 1,000 in the population was used to test the social conditioning perspective. Neighborhoods where there are historic concentrations of violent crime suspects are likely to draw increased police resources and officers may be "socially conditioned" to view racial/ethnic concentrations of suspects with heightened suspicion (Gelman et al., 2007; Ridgeway, 2007). Since the analysis controls for citizen calls for service, the lagged measure of violent crime suspects *expresses the portion of prior violent crime suspect rates that is not related to future calls for service.* A significant finding tells us there is something about prior rates of violent crime suspects that helps explain future police stops and searches above and beyond what can be explained by rates of citizen calls for service. That "something else" could be stereotyping and social conditioning. The suspect database only includes persons of interest who were positively identified from police report information (i.e., name matches prior criminal record, driver's license, other ID) or arrested at the scene of the crime. The data set included 16,814 suspects and their race/ethnicity for homicide, robbery, rape, aggravated assault, simple assault, and weapons offenses from 2000 to 2003. The suspect data was aggregated to the neighborhood where the alleged violent crime occurred, not where the suspect resided.

Nighttime Stops. The percentage of neighborhood stops that occurred after sunset and before sunrise was used to represent nighttime stops. Nighttime stop percentage was used in the search rate models only. Officers are likely to approach traffic stops at night with greater suspicion increasing the likelihood that a search may result in any stop (Dunham, Alpert, Stroshine, & Bennett, 2005; Ridgeway, 2006). Neighborhoods with a greater proportion of nighttime traffic stops should have higher search rates. The effect of nighttime on neighborhood search rates should be consistent across race and ethnicity. Sunrise and sunset data from the United States Naval Observatory was matched to the date and time of the stop to create the measure.

Results

The descriptive statistics of the key variables used in the study are shown in Table 1. The average number of stops per 94 neighborhoods was 2,192, 342 Black stops, 201 Hispanic stops, and 1,392 White stops. The average number of searches per neighborhood was 409, 94 for Black, 56 for Hispanic, and 221 for White drivers. Both Black and Hispanic drivers are overrepresented in stop and search percentages. For example, 17% of the total traffic stops in the data set were of Black drivers who comprise 6% of the population aged 15 and older and 10% of stops are attributed to Hispanic drivers who comprise 6% of the population aged 15 and over. Black and Hispanic drivers were also 16% more likely to be searched than White drivers.

Results for the total and race-specific stop rate models show neighborhood citizen calls for service rates were significant and positively related to total, Black, Hispanic, and White stop rates. For a standard deviation increase in neighborhood calls for service rate the number of police stops per 1,000 persons aged 15 and older increases 136% holding other variables constant. A standard deviation increase in neighborhood calls for service rate increases the Black stop rate by 32%, the Hispanic stop rate 105%, and the White stop rate 132% holding other variables constant. These findings offer strong support for the consensus perspective that citizen calls for service represent a general public desire for police action, which increases neighborhood social control of all persons regardless of race/ethnicity.

The neighborhood racial composition variables showed patterns indicative of the race out of place perspective, similar to Novak and Chamlin's (2008) findings. The percentage of the population that is Black was positively related to total and White stop rates. The percentage of the population that is Black or Hispanic was negatively related to Black and Hispanic stop rates. Thus Black and Hispanic drivers are not out of place in increasingly Black and Hispanic neighborhoods but expected and are negatively related to stop rates (Novak & Chamlin, 2008). The positive relationship between percent Black and total stop rates is due principally to its positive relationship to the White stop rate, thus White drivers may be perceived as out of place in increasingly Black neighborhoods drawing more law enforcement attention.

Prior neighborhood violent suspect rates, used to measure the social conditioning perspective, were only significant in the Black stop rate model. The prior Black violent suspect rate was significant ($p < .01$) and positively related to Black stop rates. Neighborhood disadvantage was insignificant in all four models.

Table 2 shows the results for the total and race-specific search rate models. The strongest predictors of neighborhood search rates were the percentage of neighborhood stops conducted at night and citizen calls for service rate. The percentage of stops occurring at night exhibited a significant ($p < .05$) and positive relationship to total, Black, and White search rates. Citizen calls for service rate was significant ($p < .05$) and positively related to total, Black, and White search rates, and close to significance for Hispanic search rates ($p = .09$). Similar to the stop rate models, total, Hispanic, and White violent suspect rates were not significantly related to search rates. The Black violent suspect rate was significant ($p < .01$) and positively related to Black search rates. The racial composition measures also showed patterns consistent with the race out of place perspective as in the stop rate models. Both percent Black and Hispanic were negatively related to Black and Hispanic search rates respectively, whereas percent Hispanic was significant ($p < .05$) and positively related to White search rates.

Discussion

The most consistent support in the above models was for the police deployment and race out of place perspectives. Police deployment, a consensus theory variable based on neighborhood rates of citizen calls for service, was positively related to stop and search rates across race/ethnicity in all of the models, except the Hispanic search rate. In the

Table 1 • Descriptive Statistics

	Total		Black		Hispanic		White	
	Mean	*SD*	Mean	*SD*	Mean	*SD*	Mean	*SD*
Dependent variables								
Traffic stops[a]	2192.4	(2292.8)	342.2	(519.2)	201.3	(272.1)	1392.0	(1459.6)
Searches[a]	409.5	(484.7)	94.9	(137.4)	56.5	(86.57)	221.3	(274.99)
Offset variable								
Population 15 and older[a]	4106.1	(3115.9)	263.8	(396.3)	269.0	(328.4)	3573.4	(2800.7)
Independent variables								
% of population[a]	NA	NA	6.8	(10.0)	5.7	(4.1)	NA	NA
Disadvantage[a]	0	(.9)	0	(0.7)	0	(0.7)	0.0	(0.8)
Violent suspect rate[a]	45.4	(87.38)	318.6	(661.6)	60.5	(133.7)	28.7	(46.2)
Priority calls for service	1127.1	(1825.6)						
% of stops at night	66.71	(12.5)						

NOTE: $N = 94$ (except Black suspect rate = 92).

[a]Denotes a race or ethnic specific indicator, except in the total column.

Table 2 • Negative Binomial Regression of Race-specific Search Rates Controlling for Neighborhood Police Deployment and Social Structure

	Total search rate		Black search rate		Hispanic search rate		White search rate	
	b	*SE*	*b*	*SE*	*b*	*SE*	*b*	*SE*
% Black	.0111	.0078	−.0487**	.0112			.0064	.0072
% Hispanic	.0467	.0256			−.0893*	.0439	.0536*	.0270
Disadvantage[a]	.0676	.1522	.1852	.0956	.0792	.2931	.0743	.1610
Calls for service rate	.0004**	.0001	.0001*	.0000	.0003	.0002	.0004**	.0001
Violent suspect rate[a]	−.0022	.0023	.0007**	.0001	.0005	.0021	−.0047	.0040
% stops at night	.0229**	.0087	.0281**	.0097	.0186	.0115	.0197*	
Spatial lag_stops[a]	.3806**	.0787	.3830**	.1114	.3645**	.0856	.3427**	.0885
Constant	−5.212		−3.142		−2.945		−5.339	
Log Likelihood	−576.415		−413.025		−404.042		−528.015	
N	94		92		94		94	

NOTE: Negative binomial models with robust standard errors.

[a]Denotes a race or ethnic specific indicator, except in the total search rate model.

$*p < .05$. $**p < .01$.

race-specific models neighborhood racial composition showed patterns consistent with the race out of place perspective and Novak and Chamlin's (2008) findings. Percent Black and Hispanic were negatively related to Black and Hispanic stops and search rates. Percent Black was significantly related to increased White stop rates and percent Hispanic was significantly related to increased White search rates. These findings indicate that Black and Hispanic drivers were less likely to be stopped and searched in increasingly Black and Hispanic neighborhoods, whereas White drivers were more at risk.

Examination of the correlation matrix in the appendix shows that the relationship between percent Black and Hispanic with the log of Black and Hispanic stop and search rates is insignificant. What caused the change in significance in the regression models? Using a step-wise approach to enter variables revealed that both percent Black and Hispanic only became significant when the spatial autocorrelation variable of Black or Hispanic stops and searches was entered. Percent Black and Hispanic were also highly correlated with the spatial autocorrelation variable for Black and Hispanic stops and searches. In short, Black and Hispanic stops, searches, and population centers are highly clustered making their stop rates normal in such areas, but unusual elsewhere.

The correlations in the appendix also show that White economic disadvantage and the prior White violent crime suspect rate exhibit stronger correlations with White stop and search rates than percent Black and Hispanic. White economic disadvantage and violent suspect rates were insignificant in the negative binomial models however. Given the strong intercorrelations among the variables in the White stop and search models, it is hard to say whether the relationships between racial/ethnic populations and White stop and search rates represent a "pure" race out of place phenomenon. It appears that Whites are also more likely to be stopped and searched in economically disadvantaged communities where there are more citizen calls for service, historically higher rates of violent crime, and a more diverse population.

The study results offered less consistent findings for the social conditioning perspective. Prior violent crime suspect rates were used to measure the social conditioning perspective. Neighborhood concentrations in violent crime suspects may come to represent a type of cognitive script identifying common dangerous offenders in neighborhoods. Neighborhoods with historically higher rates of Black violent crime suspects, based on rates 5 years prior to stop data collection, had significantly higher Black stop and search rates, controlling for other factors. On the other hand, neighborhood rates of total, Hispanic, or White violent crimes suspects were not significantly related to future stop and search rates for these groups. Neighborhood calls for service rates were strongly correlated with prior total, Hispanic, and White violent crime suspect rates (see appendix), but less so for Black violent crime suspect rates. This racial difference in the relationship between violent crime suspect concentrations and calls for service rates led to the difference in the multivariate regression findings. There was something about prior Black violent crime suspect rates that predicted future Black stop and search rates above and beyond what could be explained by high rates of citizen calls for service. Racial stereotypes and social conditioning regarding dangerousness may explain this relationship, but another possible explanation is that the relationship between prior Black violent suspect rates and future Black stops and searches represents deliberate enforcement tactics (e.g., hot spot missions, gang enforcement units) concentrated in certain neighborhoods. For example, gang enforcement units may be more active in certain neighborhoods known for gun crimes that are not necessarily the highest calls for service rate neighborhoods.

The results did not support the neighborhood disadvantage or racial threat perspectives. Neighborhood disadvantage, which was conceptualized under a consensus theory framework, was not significantly related to stop and search rates in any of the models. Both percent Black and Hispanic were not positively related to total search rates nor Black and Hispanic stop/search rates, inconsistent with the racial threat hypothesis. Percent Black was related to total stop rates but that was mostly explained by its relationship to increased White stop rates, thus lending supporting for the race out of place rather than racial threat perspective.

There are some important methodological limitations to consider with this study. The most significant limitation, common to macro-level studies of this nature, is the difficulty of accurately representing both consensus and conflict theories with aggregate measures. For example, the concepts of racial threat, suspiciousness, and dangerous stereotypes that underlie the racial threat, race out of place, and social conditioning perspectives are difficult to operationalize and measure, particularly at an aggregate level (Chamlin, 2009; Liska, 1987). Individual, multilevel, and experimental research is needed to thoroughly examine the link between the contextual factors of stop incidents and neighborhoods with officer perceptions and behavior (Chamlin, 2009; Novak & Chamlin, 2008; Smith & Alpert, 2007). This study also makes the assumption that calls for service rates accurately assess community consensus regarding public safety and desires for police presence and proactivity (Liska, 1987). Although the findings presented here are generally consistent with previous research, the results are based on one city and the findings may not be generalizable to other places. Every city can offer a unique mix of neighborhood demographics and geography requiring special consideration. The police deployment perspective may only have relevance to understanding urban variation in police services and may not be applicable to state highway patrol and smaller towns where there may not be enough spatial variation in deployment. Offsetting stop and search counts by the driving aged population creates more conservative rates compared to using the entire population, but may still over or underestimate the actual population that is at risk for being stopped or searched in the neighborhood (Roh & Robinson, 2009). Distinguishing Hispanic ethnicity can be difficult for officers, thus the measure of Hispanic stops, searches, and suspects may not be reliable (Roh & Robinson, 2009). The Census 2000 data may not adequately reflect neighborhood changes in race/ethnicity and social class between 2000 and 2004–2008 when the stop data was recorded. Finally, search codes did not allow for a more finite examination of different search types, like consent searches, which could have produced more idiosyncratic findings in the search models.

Conclusion

Police scholars have noted that aggregate or jurisdictional level studies of police stops and searches can overlook important contextual differences in stop and search patterns. It remains critical to understand the ecological contexts wherein stops and searches are concentrated to inform debates over stop and search disparities, police bias, and racial profiling. Consensus and conflict theories have been the primary perspectives used to explain neighborhood differences in stop and search patterns. The consensus perspective hypothesizes variation in police services is a response to differential community needs and desires for protection wherein social control is equally applied to all transgressors of the law regardless of race or class. In contrast, the conflict perspective hypothesizes that social control is differentially applied to certain groups and social strata. The findings in this study support both the police deployment and race out of place perspectives, thus both consensus and conflict perspectives appear relevant. Citizen calls for service were positively related to police stop or search rates controlling for other explanations and consistent with prior studies that have generally found a similar effect using different measures of police deployment (e.g., crime rates, arrest rates, calls for service, or number of deployments; Fagan et al., 2010; Gaines, 2006; Novak & Chamlin, 2008; Parker et al., 2010; Petrocelli et al., 2003; Roh & Robinson, 2009). After controlling for spatial autocorrelation in stops and searches, the racial composition variables showed patterns supportive of the race out of place perspective similar to Novak and Chamlin (2008). Black and Hispanic drivers were significantly less likely to be stopped and searched in increasingly Black and Hispanic neighborhoods and White drivers were more at risk for social control.

Empirical support for the social conditioning perspective was inconsistent. Black violent crime suspect rates were significantly related to Black stop and search rates. Total, Hispanic, and White violent crime suspect rates, although exhibiting significant bivariate correlations to stop and search rates, were not significant in the regression models. There was something about prior Black violent suspect rates, above and beyond the other variables, that was unique to predicting an increased future risk of Black drivers being stopped and searched in certain neighborhoods. The exact nature of this relationship is not clear; it could be some form of social conditioning, but an alternative explanation may entail concentrations of gang enforcement unit activity and hot spot mission tactics focused on drug and gun crimes in certain neighborhoods. Future research should attempt to obtain deployment measures of gang and drug tactical team activity across neighborhoods.

Appendix

Correlation Matrix

	LN Stoprt	LN Black stoprt	LN Hispanic stoprt	LN white stoprt	LN Searchrt	LN black searchr	LN Hispanic searchrt	LN White searchrt	%Black	%Hispanic
LN stoprt	1	.744**	.780**	.994**	.931**	.652**	.705**	.927**	.350**	.365**
LN black stoprt	.744**	1	.696**	.737**	.702**	.939**	.650**	.728**	−.058	.133
LN Hispanic stoprt	.780**	.696**	1	.759**	.683**	.606**	.921**	.660**	.056	−.075
LN white stoprt	.994**	.737**	.759**	1	.909**	.632**	.670**	.919**	.321**	.338**
LN searchrt	.931**	.702**	.683**	.909**	1	.693**	.682**	.981**	.388**	.484**
LN black searchrt	.652**	.939**	.606**	.632**	.693**	1	.630**	.712**	−.123	.125
LN Hispanic searchrt	.705**	.650**	.921**	.670**	.682**	.630**	1	.657**	.006	−.088
LN white searchrt	.927**	.728**	.660**	.919**	.981**	.712**	.657**	1	.285**	.446**
% Black	.350**	−.058	.056	.321**	.388**	−.123	.006	.285**	1	.460**
% Hispanic	.365**	.133	−.075	.338**	.484**	.125	−.088	.446**	.460**	1
Disadv	.573**	.208*	.156	.560**	.632**	.183	.125	.598**	.629**	.690**
Black disadv	.476**	.370**	.275**	.469**	.471**	.317**	.265*	.468**	.102	.272**
Hispanic disadv	.397**	.064	.172	.377**	.450**	−.013	.140	.409**	.439**	.452**
White disadv	.535**	.270**	.187	.531**	.590**	.274*	.174	.599**	.289**	.555**
calls for service	.634**	.469**	.480**	.647**	.537**	.416**	.435**	.560**	.133	.101
Suspectrt	.549**	.366**	.346**	.557**	.496**	.342**	.325**	.498**	.269**	.198
Black sus-pectrt	.302**	.536**	.215**	.320**	.272**	.543**	.202	.304**	−.063	−.047
Hispanic suspectrt	.499**	.379**	.355**	.505**	.453**	.368**	.388**	.469**	.118	.073
White suspectrt	.574**	.409**	.370**	.586**	.527**	.392**	.349**	.545**	.162	.216*
% of stops at night	.299**	.239*	.278**	.254*	.528**	.269*	.222*	.393**	.397**	.324**

NOTE: Pairwise deletion (N = 89 to 94).

*$p < .05$. **$p < .01$.

Disadv	Black disadv	Hispanic disadv	White disadv	Calls for service	Suspectrt	Black suspectrt	Hispanic suspectrt	White suspectrt	% of stops at night
.573**	.476**	.397**	.535**	.634**	.549**	.302**	.499**	.574**	.299**
.208*	.370**	.064	.270**	.469**	.366**	.536**	.379**	.409**	.239*
.156	.275**	.172	.187	.480**	.346**	.215*	.355**	.370**	.278**
.560**	.469**	.377**	.531**	.647**	.557**	.320**	.505**	.586**	.254*
.632**	.471**	.450**	.590**	.537**	.496**	.272**	.453**	.527**	.528**
.183	.317**	–.013	.274*	.416**	.342**	.543**	.368**	.392**	.269*
.125	.265*	.140	.174	.435**	.325**	.202	.388**	.349**	.222*
.598**	.468**	.409**	.599**	.560**	.498**	.304**	.469**	.545**	.393**
.629**	.102	.439**	.289**	.133	.269**	–.063	.118	.162	.397**
.690**	.272**	.452**	.555**	.101	.198	–.047	.073	.216**	.324**
1	.412**	.619**	.843**	.329**	.347**	–.016	.172	.370**	.363**
.412**	1	.285**	.414**	.291**	.187	.271*	.137	.237*	.228*
.619**	.285**	1	.503**	.157	.193	–.129	.042	.202	.282**
.843**	.414**	.503**	1	.383**	.293**	–.005	.165	.386**	.260*
.329**	.291**	.157	.383**	1	.851**	.428**	.790**	.891**	.152
.347**	.187	.193	.293**	.851**	1	.444**	.900**	.976**	.208*
–.016	.271**	–.129	–.005	.428**	.444**	1	.463**	.446**	.095
.172	.137	.042	.165	.790**	.900**	.463**	1	.871**	.187
.370**	.237*	.202	.386**	.891**	.976**	.446**	.871**	1	.198
.363**	.228*	.282**	.260*	.152	.208*	.095	.187	.198	1

The primary question posed by this study in the introduction is whether patterns in macro social control by law enforcement appear related to community desires to have police maintain safety through proactive law enforcement or is social control targeted toward certain groups and strata identified as dangerous and threatening? Scholars have noted that contrasting consensus and conflict theories as two polarizing perspectives limits theoretical development (Bernard & Engel, 2001). Duffee, Worden, and Maguire (2007, p. 303) suggest that consensus and conflict "may be operating at different levels in the same place and same time." The results of this study support this contention, the strength of consensus and conflict perspective variables in explaining social control fluctuated according to the dependent variable (stops or searches), and race/ethnicity.

The policy relevance of this study is that both police and communities need to fully understand consensus and conflict perspectives and mutually agree on their relevance. Polarization at the policy level between these two perspectives will lead to a stalemate and disengagement in dialogue. For example, police departments routinely make available information on neighborhood variation in crime and arrests to the public, but rarely is neighborhood variation in citizen calls for service presented to community members or at public forums. One of the important theoretical contributions of this study is the use of citizen calls for service. Calls for service rates measure a community consensus that police presence and action is desired within neighborhoods, or at the very least provides an invitation for police proactivity. Efforts on behalf of police, community, and government to address concerns over racial profiling and overrepresentation should entail discussion and analysis of citizen calls for service. Examining the connection between neighborhood calls for service and police outputs like stops, searches, and arrests can illustrate for police administrators and the public whether police outputs appear more democratically based and less arbitrary than perceived. Attempting to understand whether some portion of racial/ethnic disparity in police stops and searches is related to citizen calls for service will help communities recognize the complexity of the issue and highlight the important service functions police provide. In short, police administrators should regularly analyze citizen calls for service data, measure police-initiated deployments and tactical missions, and report to the public on neighborhood variations in calls for service and deployment along with stop, search, and crime data. As police and communities grapple with concerns over police bias and overrepresentation issues, their discussion should ideally be informed by examining the efficacy of both the crime control and due process functions of police. It is therefore equally important for police administrators and the public to agree that police actions have the possibility to be influenced by cultural and contextual stereotypes and biases. This study supports the contention that neighborhood variation in police stops and searches are potentially influenced by unique contexts and situations related to race/ethnicity that officers find unusual and suspicious. Ongoing police training is still needed to reinforce how stereotypes based on race/ethnicity and presumptions about the unusualness of a context may be unethical, illegal, or lead to unintended consequences.[4]

In conclusion, both police and community will benefit when they feel confident that the balance between crime control and due process is thoroughly assessed and weighed.

Declaration of Conflicting Interests

The author declared no potential conflicts of interest with respect to the research, authorship, and/or publication of this article.

Funding

The author received no financial support for the research, authorship, and/or publication of this article.

Notes

1. Most of the findings remained the same when using an alternative offset based on race-specific households per 1,000 as used by Fagan et al. (2010). The impact of calls for service on stop and search rates was even stronger, but the significant relationship between Black violent suspect rate and stops and searches was no longer significant.

2. The ability to disaggregate more discretionary search types (e.g., consent search) from less discretionary (e.g., incident to arrest) was not possible. Without such finite coding it

made sense to combine all search types similar to Parker et al. (2010).

3. Analyses using all calls for service produced weaker models but did not change the overall substantive results.

4. One such training being implemented throughout Oregon and California is Perspectives on Profiling© developed by the Simon Wiesenthal Museum of Tolerance.

References

Akins, S., Rumbaut, R., & Stansfield, R. (2009). Immigration, economic disadvantage, and homicide: A community-level analysis of Austin, Texas. *Homicide Studies, 13*, 307–314.

Anselin, L. (2005). *Exploring spatial data with GeoDa™: A workbook*. Urbana, IL: Center for Spatially Integrated Social Science.

Berk, R., & MacDonald, J. (2007). *Overdispersion and Poisson Regression*. Philadelphia: University of Pennsylvania.

Bernard, T., & Engel, R. (2001). Conceptualizing criminal justice theory. *Justice Quarterly, 18*, 1–30.

Chamlin, M. B. (2009). Threat to whom? Conflict, consensus, and social control. *Deviant Behavior, 30*, 539–559.

Duffee, D., Worden, A., & Maguire, E. (2007). Directions for theory and theorizing in criminal justice. In D. E. Duffee & E. R. Maguire (Eds.), *Criminal justice theory: Explaining the nature and behavior of criminal justice* (pp. 291–320). New York, NY: Routledge Taylor & Francis Group.

Dunham, R. G., Alpert, G. P., Stroshine, M. S., & Bennett, K. (2005). Transforming citizens into suspects: Factors that influence the formation of police suspicion. *Police Quarterly, 8*, 366–393.

Engel, R., & Johnson, R. (2006). Toward a better understanding of racial and ethnic disparities in search and seizure rates. *Journal of Criminal Justice, 34*, 605–617.

Fagan, J. A., Geller, A., Davis, G., & West, V. (2010). Street stops and broken windows revisted: The demography and logic of proactive policing in a safe and changing city. In S. K. Rice & M. D. White (Eds.), *Race, ethnicity, and policing: New and essential readings* (pp. 309–348). New York: New York University Press.

Gaines, L. K. (2006). An analysis of traffic stop data in Riverside, California. *Police Quarterly, 9*, 210–233.

Gelman, A., Fagan, J., & Kiss, A. (2007). An analysis of the New York City police department "stop-and-frisk" policy in the context of claims of racial bias. *Journal of the American Statistical Association, 102*, 813–823.

Hagan, J. (1989). Why is there so little criminal justice theory? Neglected macro and micro-level links between organization and power. *Journal of Research in Crime and Delinquency, 26*, 116–135.

Lee, M., & Stevenson, G. (2006). Gender-specific homicide offending in rural areas. *Homicide Studies, 10*, 55–73.

Liska, A. (1987). A critical examination of macro perspectives on crime control. *Annual Review of Sociology, 13*, 67–88.

Logan, J., & Molotch, H. (1987). *Urban fortunes: The political economy of place*. Berkeley, CA: University of California Press.

Long, J. S., & Freese, J. (2006). *Regression models for categorical dependent variables using Stata* (2nd ed.). College Station, TX: Stata Press.

Morenoff, J. D., Sampson, R. J., & Raudenbush, S. W. (2001). Neighborhood inequality, collective efficacy, and the spatial dynamics of urban violence. *Criminology, 39*, 517–558.

Nielsen, A. L., Lee, M. T., & Martínez, R. (2005). Integrating race, place, and motive in social disorganization theory: Lessons from a comparison of Black and Latino homicide types in two immigrant destination cities. *Criminology, 43*, 837–865.

Novak, K. J., & Chamlin, M. B. (2008). Racial threat, suspicion, and police behavior: The impact of race and place in traffic enforcement. *Crime & Delinquency*. Advance online publication. doi:10.1177/0011128708322943

Osgood, D. W. (2000). Poisson-based regression analysis of aggregate crime rates. *Journal of Quantitative Criminology, 16*, 21–44.

Ousey, G., & Lee, M. (2008). Racial disparity in formal social control: An investigation of alternative explanations of arrest rate inequality. *Journal of Research in Crime and Delinquency, 45*, 322–355.

Parker, K. F., Stults, B. J., & Rice, S. K. (2005). Racial threat, concentrated disadvantage and social control: Considering the macro-level sources of variation in arrests. *Criminology, 43*, 1111–1134.

Parker, K. F., Lane, E. C., & Alpert, G. P. (2010). Community characteristics and police search rates: Accounting for the ethnic diversity of urban areas in the study of Black, White, and Hispanic searches. In S. K. Rice & M. D. White (Eds.), *Race, ethnicity, and policing: New and essential readings* (pp. 349–367). New York: New York University Press.

Petrocelli, M., Piquero, A. R., & Smith, M. R. (2003). Conflict theory and racial profiling: An empirical analysis of police traffic stop data. *Journal of Criminal Justice, 31*, 1–11.

Ridgeway, G. (2006). Assessing the effect of race bias in post-traffic stop outcomes using propensity scores. *Journal of Quantitative Criminology, 22*, 1–29.

Ridgeway, G. (2007). *Analysis of racial disparities in the New York Police department's stop, question, and frisk practices*. Santa Monica, CA: RAND Corporation.

Roh, S., & Robinson, M. (2009). A geographical approach to racial profiling: The microanalysis and macroanalysis of racial disparity in traffic stops. *Police Quarterly, 12*, 137–169.

Schell, T., Ridgeway, G., Dixon, T. L., Turner, S., & Riley, J. (2007). *Police-community relations in Cincinnati: Year three evaluation report*. Santa Monica, CA: RAND Corporation.

Sherman, L. (1996). Policing for crime prevention. In L. Sherman, D. Gottfredson, D. MacKenzie, J. Eck, P. Reuter, & S. Bushway (Eds.), *Preventing crime: What works, what doesn't, what's promising*. College Park, MD: Department of Criminology and Criminal Justice, University of Maryland.

Smith, M. R., & Alpert, G. P. (2007). Explaining police bias: A theory of social conditioning and illusory correlation. *Criminal Justice and Behavior, 34*, 1262–1283.

Spohn, R. E., & Kurtz, D. L. (2011). Family structure as a social context for family conflict: Unjust strain and serious delinquency. *Criminal Justice Review, 36*, 332–356.

Tillyer, R., & Engel, R. S. (2010). The impact of drivers' race, gender, and age during traffic stops: Assessing the interaction terms and the social conditioning model. *Crime & Delinquency*. Advance online publication. doi:10.1177/0011128711421652

Wilson, W. J. (1987). *The truly disadvantaged: The inner city, the underclass, and public policy*. Chicago, IL: University of Chicago Press.

Withrow, B. L. (2004). Driving while different: A potential theoretical explanation for race-based policing. *Criminal Justice Policy Review, 15*, 344–364.

REVIEW QUESTIONS

1. What does the author mean when he refers to the "police deployment" perspective?
2. What is meant by the conflict approach? Provide several examples of this approach.
3. What are the findings of the current study regarding the impact of the various predicting variables on decisions to stop and/or search?
4. To what extent do the results regarding level of disorder or disadvantage of a given area have an influence on police decisions to stop and/or search suspects?

SECTION X

Feminist Models of Crime

In this section, we will examine the importance of feminist perspectives of crime. Feminist criminology evolved when various assumptions and stereotypes about women in criminal justice were being questioned. Such questions included women as both offenders and victims. It is important to note up front that there is no single feminist perspective, and they often seem to be at odds with each other. However, the overall goal of this perspective is agreed on: to further advance the importance of understanding and furthering research regarding females in the realm of crime and criminal justice. After all, given that far fewer females commit serious violence than males, if we could better explain why women have much lower rates of criminality, then perhaps we could apply this in order to significantly reduce male offending. We will also review feminist critiques of previous research as well as policy implications of feminist perspectives of crime.

Feminist Theories of Crime

About the same time that Marxist theories of crime were becoming popular in the early 1970s, the feminist perspective began to receive attention; this was a key period in the women's rights movement. The Feminist School of criminology began largely as a reaction to the lack of rational theorizing about why females commit crime and why they tend to be treated far differently by the criminal justice system.[1] Prior to the 1970s, theories of why girls and women engage in illegal activities were primarily based on false stereotypes.

Key Terms in the Feminist Perspective

Before discussing the various feminist perspectives, it is essential for readers to appreciate key terms associated with these perspectives. A few of these key terms are *chivalry*, *paternalism*, and *patriarchy*.

Chivalry pertains to behaviors and attitudes toward certain individuals that treat them as though they are on a pedestal.[2] Chivalrous behavior is more complex than just preferential treatment. Engaging in a chivalrous

[1]Meda Chesney-Lind and Lisa Pasko, *The Female Offender: Girls, Women, and Crime* (Thousand Oaks, CA: Sage, 2004).

[2]Joanne Belknap, *The Invisible Woman: Gender, Crime, and Justice*, 3rd ed. (Belmont, CA: Wadsworth, 2007), 150–51; Elizabeth F. Moulds, "Chivalry and Paternalism: Disparities of Treatment in the Criminal Justice System," in *Women, Crime, and Justice*, ed. Susan K. Datesman and Frank R. Scarpitti (New York: Oxford University Press, 1980), 279.

relationship usually entails a bartering system in which men hold a more powerful status than do women. Social class and race or ethnicity are also intertwined with such treatment. Women of certain social classes and racial or ethnic backgrounds are considered more worthy of chivalrous treatment than other women. This is best illustrated by Sojourner Truth's speech "Ain't I a Woman?" The idea of **paternalism** denotes that women need to be protected for their own good. In a broader social context, paternalism implies independence for men and dependence for women. Both chivalry and paternalism suggest that certain individuals or groups need protection because they are weak and helpless. This protection can also lead to various types of control.

The Latin word *pater* refers to the social role of a father as opposed to the biological role of a father. Patriarchal societies exclude women from the exercise of political responsibilities; **patriarchy** refers to the subordinate role of women and male dominance.[3] Thus, patriarchy is a social, legal, and political climate based on male dominance and hierarchy. A key aspect to this ideology is that women's nature is biologically, not culturally, determined.[4]

Key Issues in Research on Gender Differences in Offending

Much of the attention of theorists in the feminist area can be broken into two categories: the *gender ratio* issue and the *generalizability* issue. The gender ratio issue refers to theorizing and research that examines why females so often commit less serious, less violent offenses than males. Some experts feel that this does not matter; however, if we understood why females commit far less violence, then perhaps we could apply such knowledge to reducing male offending.[5] The generalizability argument is consistent with the ideas some have about the gender ratio issue; specifically, many of the same critics argue that theorists should simply take the findings found for male offending and generalize them to females. However, given the numerous differences found between males and females in what predicts their offending patterns, simply generalizing across gender is not a wise thing to do.[6] It is far more complicated than that.

Another important issue in feminist research on crime is that women today have more freedom and rights than those in past generations. Seminal theories of female crime in the 1970s predicted that this would result in far higher offending rates for women.[7] However, this has not been seen in serious, violent crimes. Rather, increases have been observed in property and public order crimes, but they are typically committed by girls or women who have not benefited from such freedom and rights—for example, those who do not have much education, are poor, or who lack strong employment records.

Types of Feminism

Also, there are numerous forms of feminism and, thus, many types of feminist theories of crime, as pointed out by Daly and Chesney-Lind.[8] One of the earliest was **liberal feminism**, which assumed that differences between males and females in offending were due to the lack of opportunities for females in education and employment and that,

---

[3]Janet K. Boles and Diane Long Hoeveler, *Historical Dictionary of Feminism* (Lanham, MD: Scarecrow Press, 2004), 253.

[4]Belknap, *The Invisible Woman*, 10; see also Anne Edwards, "Male Violence in Feminist Theory: An Analysis of the Changing Conception of Sex/Gender Violence and Male Dominance," in *Women, Violence, and Social Control*, ed. Jalna Hanmer and Mary Maynard (Atlantic Highlands, NJ: Humanities Press International, 1987), 13–29.

[5]For a discussion, see Stephen Tibbetts and Denise Herz, "Gender Differences in Factors of Social Control and Rational Choice," *Deviant Behavior* 17 (1996): 183–208.

[6]Tibbetts and Herz, "Gender Differences."

[7]Freda Adler, *Sisters in Crime: The Rise of the New Female Criminal* (New York: McGraw-Hill, 1975).

[8]Kathleen Daly and Meda Chesney-Lind, "Feminism and Criminology," *Justice Quarterly* 5 (1988): 536–58.

as more females were given such opportunities, they would come to resemble males in terms of offending. Liberal feminism, also termed *mainstream feminism*, is founded on political liberalism, which holds a positive view of human nature as well as the ideals of liberty, equality, justice, dignity, and individual rights. A major feature of liberal feminism is that women should receive the same rights and treatment as men.[9] This perspective purports that gender inequality is due to women's blocked opportunities to participate in various aspects of the public sphere, such as education, employment, and political activity.[10] Strategies for social change are devised to free women from oppressive gender roles—for instance, performing only those jobs associated with the traditional feminine personality (e.g., nursing, teaching, child care).[11]

There are generally two types of liberal feminists: classical and welfare. Both approaches rely a great deal on legal remedies to address gender inequality. Classical liberal feminists support limited government and a free market as well as political and legal rights. Central facets of this approach are freedom of expression, religion, and conscience. Welfare liberal feminists favor government involvement in providing citizens, particularly underprivileged individuals, with housing, education, health care, and social security. They also maintain that the market should be limited through significant taxes and restricting profits.[12]

A major criticism of the liberal feminist perspective is that it primarily focuses "on the interests of white, middle-class, heterosexual women."[13] Specifically, within the area of feminist criminology, some argue that the liberal perspective poses "men as the criminal yardstick." This results in equating justice with equality and not considering other influential standpoints such as race/ethnicity and social class.[14] Joanne Belknap maintains this:

> Prison reform for women would not be nearly as effective in achieving equality with men's prisons if the only goal was to allow the same access to health care, vocational, educational, legal, and treatment programs. While these would be significant advances, it is also necessary to request reforms that address women prisoners' experiences, needs, and histories that differ from male prisoners.[15]

Another area where the "equal treatment" doctrine is problematic is in sentencing. Specifically, sentencing reforms aimed at reducing race- and class-based disparities in sentencing for male offenders "may yield equality with a vengeance" for female offenders.[16] Thus, "equality defined as equal treatment of men and women . . . forestalls more fundamental change and in some instances may worsen women's circumstances."[17]

Another major feminist perspective of crime is **critical feminism** or **radical feminism**, which emphasizes the idea that many societies (such as the United States) are based on a structure of patriarchy wherein males dominate virtually every aspect of society, including politics, family structure, and the economy. Radical feminism evolved from the women's liberation movement of the 1960s. This perspective emphasizes the

---

[9]Boles and Hoeveler, *Historical Dictionary of Feminism*, 192.

[10]Daly and Chesney-Lind, "Feminism and Criminology," 537.

[11]Rosemarie Tong, *Feminist Thought: A More Comprehensive Introduction*, 3rd ed. (Boulder, CO: Westview Press, 2009), 34.

[12]Ibid., 35.

[13]Ibid., 43.

[14]Dana M. Britton, "Feminism in Criminology: Engendering the Outlaw," *Annals of the American Academy of Political and Social Science* 571 (2000): 57–76.

[15]Belknap, *The Invisible Woman*, 13.

[16]Daly and Chesney-Lind, "Feminism and Criminology," 525.

[17]Ibid., 526.

▲ **Image 10.1** Female gang member.

SOURCE: © istockphoto.com / Bluberries

importance of personal feelings, experiences, and relationships. Gender is a system of male dominance, and women's biology is the main cause of patriarchy.[18]

The cause of gender inequality, according to this perspective, is based on men's need or desire to control women's sexuality and reproductive potential. Further, the process of gender formation is founded on the power relations between men and women wherein boys and men view themselves as superior to and having a right to control girls and women. These relations are further intensified through heterosexual sexuality, as defined by men.[19]

Radical feminists maintain, in principle, that sexism is the first, most widespread form of human oppression. They do not, however, agree on the nature or function of this sexism or on what strategies are needed for social change. Rosemarie Tong identified two types of radical feminism: libertarian and cultural.[20] Radical-libertarian feminists assert that an exclusively feminine gender identity will most often limit a woman's development as a full human person. They encourage women to become androgynous individuals who embody both (good) masculine and (good) feminine characteristics. Radical-cultural feminists argue that women should be strictly female or feminine. They should not try to be like men. Women should emphasize such values and virtues as interdependence, community, connection, sharing, emotion, body, trust, absence of hierarchy, nature, immanence, process, joy, peace, and life. Alternatively, women should not emphasize such values as independence, autonomy, intellect, will, wariness, hierarchy, domination, culture, transcendence, product, asceticism, war, and death.

Tong noted that this distinction, while not perfect, does the following:

> [It] helps explain not only why some radical feminists embrace the concept of androgyny and others eschew it, but also why some radical feminists view both sex and reproduction as oppressive, even dangerous for women and why others view these aspects as liberating, even empowering for women. . . . *Radical feminists are not afraid to take exception to each other's views* [emphasis added].[21]

Suggested strategies for social change among some radical feminists include overthrowing patriarchal relations, developing methods of biological reproduction to permit women's sexual autonomy, and establishing women-centered social institutions and women-only organizations. Other radical feminists celebrate gender differences, particularly women's special capacities or talents; however, these feminists do not pose gender differences in the framework of power relations.[22]

One of the criticisms of radical-libertarian and radical-cultural feminism is that they need to reconcile the split between themselves in an effort to avoid polarization, particularly in the area of sexuality. Even though radical-libertarian feminists are hesitant about consensual heterosexuality, they maintain that these relationships can be pleasurable for women. Radical-cultural feminists warn against the dangers of heterosexuality and have implied

[18]Boles and Hoeveler, *Historical Dictionary of Feminism*, 270–71.

[19]Daly and Chesney-Lind, "Feminism and Criminology," 538.

[20]Tong, *Feminist Thought*, 48–51.

[21]Ibid., 51.

[22]Daly and Chesney-Lind, "Feminism and Criminology," 538.

that there is no such thing as consensual heterosexuality. Thus, according to this view, "only lesbians are capable of consensual sex in a patriarchal society."[23] Citing Ann Ferguson, a socialist feminist, Tong noted that there is no one universal "function" for human sexuality.[24]

It is hard to contest the primary assumption of this theory. Despite the fact that more women than ever hold professional, white-collar jobs, men still get paid a significant amount more than women for the same positions, on average. Furthermore, the U.S. Senate and House of Representatives—and other high political offices, such as president, vice president, cabinet posts, and U.S. Supreme Court justices—are still held primarily (or exclusively) by men. So the United States, like most other countries in the world, appears to be based in patriarchy.

The extent to which this model explains female criminality, however, remains to be seen. Regarding serious crimes, it is not clear why this perspective would expect higher or lower rates of female criminal behavior. Regarding some delinquent offenses, it may partially explain the greater tendency to arrest females. For example, virtually every self-report study ever conducted shows that males run away far more than females; however, Federal Bureau of Investigation (FBI) data show that female juveniles are arrested for running away far more often than males. Critical feminism may provide the best explanation for this difference. Females are more protected—that is, reported and arrested for running away—because they are considered to be more like property in our patriarchal society. This is just one explanation, but it appears to be somewhat valid.

Similar to critical or radical feminism is **Marxist feminism**, which emphasizes men's ownership and control of the means of economic production, thus focusing solely on the economic structure. Marxist feminists point out that men control economic success in our country—as well as in virtually every country in the world—and that this flows from capitalism. One of the primary assumptions of capitalism is *survival of the fittest* or *the best person for the job*, which would seem to favor women. Studies have found that women in the United States do far better, despite our capitalistic system, than those in most other countries. Furthermore, women in countries based on Marxism have a less favorable lifestyle and are no better off economically than those in the United States. Whether or not one believes in a Marxist economic structure, it does not readily explain female criminality.

Another feminist perspective is that of **socialist feminism**, which moved away from focusing on economic structure (e.g., Marxism) as the primary detriment for females and instead emphasized control of reproductive systems. This model believes that women should take control of their own bodies and their reproductive functions in order to control their criminality. It is not entirely clear how females' taking charge of their reproductive destinies can increase or reduce their crime rates. Although no one can deny that data show that females who reproduce frequently, especially in inner-city, poor environments, tend to offend more often than other females, it appears that other factors mediate these effects. Women who want good futures tend to take more precautions against becoming pregnant; on the other hand, the very females who most need to take precautions against getting pregnant are the least likely to do so, despite the availability of numerous forms of contraception. This is one of the many paradoxes in our field. It is unclear how much socialist feminism has contributed to an understanding of female criminality.

Some scholars maintain that while it is possible to distinguish between Marxist feminism and socialist feminism, it is difficult, particularly because these two perspectives' differences are more an issue of emphasis than of substance.[25] Marxist feminism places gender in the context of production methods. The burdens of physical and social reproduction in the home are operated and reinforced in a male-dominated economic and political order.[26]

---

[23]Tong, *Feminist Thought*, 92–93; see also Ann Ferguson, "Sex War: The Debate between Radical and Libertarian Feminists," *Signs: The Journal of Women in Culture and Society* 10 (1984): 106–12.

[24]Tong, *Feminist Thought*, 93.

[25]Ibid., 96.

[26]Boles and Hoeveler, *Historical Dictionary of Feminism*, 204–5.

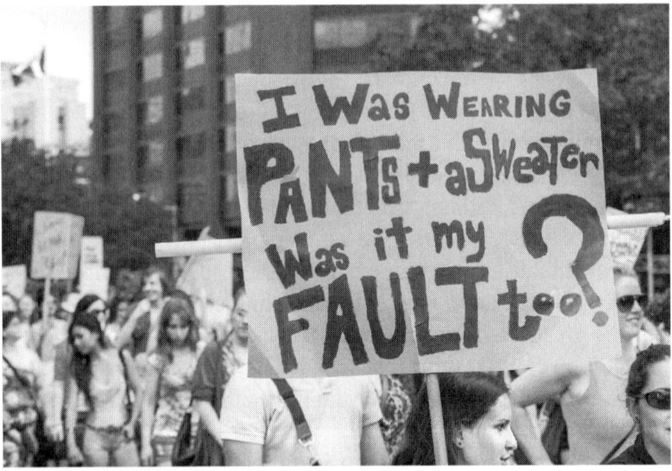

▲ **Image 10.2** Feminist protests and influence have done much to alter how females are viewed and valued in our traditional patriarchal society as well as in most other developed countries around the world.

SOURCE: © istockphoto.com / Jen Grantham

The causes of gender inequality are due to hierarchical relations of control with the increase of private property and ownership among men. Class relations are primary, and gender relations are secondary.[27] An insightful example of such gender and class relations is housework. Traditionally, housework has been delegated to women; however, housework does not produce surplus value or profit. Thus, some do not consider this labor. Jenny van Hooff conducted semistructured interviews to examine dual-career heterosexual couples' explanations and justifications for the division of housework that followed more traditional gender roles. Marxist feminism focuses essentially on work-related inequalities as well as enhancing our understanding of the trivialization of women's work in the home (e.g., raising children, doing housework) and the tedious, poorly paid jobs predominately occupied by women.[28] The General Social Survey reveals that when asking males and females regarding their perceptions as to who does most of the cleaning in the household, there is an overwhelming response of either "always female" or "usually female."

Socialist feminism attempts to synthesize radical and Marxist feminism. This perspective attempts to integrate concepts such as male domination and political–economic relations. Social feminists focus on gender, class, and racial relations of domination. They differ from Marxist feminists in that both class and gender relations are deemed primary.[29] Within the socialist feminism perspective, there are two general themes: (1) two-system explanations of women's oppression and (2) interactive-system explanations of women's oppression. Under the two-system explanations, these emphases are less committed to the Marxist-founded framework. Rather, they maintain that patriarchy, not capitalism, may be women's ultimate worst enemy.[30] The interactive-system explanations attempt to illustrate that both capitalism and patriarchy are equal contributors to women's oppression; they are interdependent. These feminists use terms such as *capitalist patriarchy* or *patriarchal capitalism*.[31]

An additional perspective of feminist criminology is that of**postmodern feminism**, which holds that an understanding of women as a group, even by other women, is impossible because every person's experience is unique. If this is true, we should give up discussing female criminal theory and theories of criminality in general—along with all studies of medicine, astronomy, psychology, and so on—because every person interprets each observation

[27]Daly and Chesney-Lind, "Feminism and Criminology," 537.

[28]Belknap, *The Invisible Woman*, 13; see also Sandra Harding, "Can Men Be Subjects of Feminist Thought?," in *Feminist Perspectives on Social Research*, ed. Sharlene Hesse-Biber and Michelle Y. Yaiser (New York: Oxford University Press, 2004); Heidi I. Hartmann, "The Family as the Locus of Gender, Class, and Political Struggle: The Example of Housework," in *Feminism and Methodology*, ed. Sandra Harding (Bloomington: Indiana University Press, 1987), 109–134.

[29]Belknap, *The Invisible Woman*, 538.

[30]Tong, *Feminist Thought*, 111.

[31]Ibid., 115.

subjectively. This perspective rejects the traditional assumptions about truth and reality; the emphasis is more on the plurality, diversity, and multiplicity of women as distinct from men.[32] Tong argued that the relationship between postmodernists and feminists is "uneasy."[33] For instance, similar to all postmodernists, postmodern feminists reject ideas centered on an absolute world that is "male" in style (i.e., phallogocentric). They also reject any attempts to provide a single explanation or steps women must take to achieve liberation (i.e., a feminist "to-do list"). Those who identify themselves as postmodern feminists "invite each woman who reflects on their writings to become the kind of feminist she wants to be. There is, in their estimation, no single formula for being a 'good feminist.'"[34] The bottom line is that, according to postmodern feminists, there is no point in measuring anything. Thus, this model is based on anti-science and has contributed very little to the study of understanding or explaining female criminality or gaining some useful information about females as victims.

In all these variations of feminist perspectives, it is interesting that little emphasis is placed on parental differences in how children are disciplined and raised. Studies have clearly and consistently shown that parents, often without realizing it, tend to globally reward young boys for completing a task (e.g., "You are such a good boy"), whereas they tend to tell a young girl that she did a good job. On the other hand, when young boys do not successfully complete a task, most parents tend to excuse the failure (e.g., "It was a hard thing to do; don't worry"), whereas for young girls, the parents will often globally evaluate them for the task (e.g., "Why couldn't you do it?").[35] Although numerous psychological studies have found this tendency, it has yet to make it into the mainstream criminological theories of crime.

Case Study: Gertrude Baniszewski

When the police arrived at the home of Gertrude Baniszewski in October 1965, they found the lifeless body of 16-year-old Sylvia Likens. Sylvia's parents had found employment as carnival workers. This required them to move around, so Gertrude Baniszewski agreed to board Sylvia and her sister Jenny for $20 a week. When one of the checks arrived late, Baniszewski lashed out at the two girls. This was followed by 3 weeks of violent and sadistic attacks, especially on Sylvia. A number of Baniszewski's seven children, along with some neighborhood children, watched or actually joined in the torture. This was all done under the supervision of Baniszewski. No one reported the abuse.[36]

Sylvia's emaciated corpse was covered with more than 150 wounds ranging from burns to cuts. Sylvia was burned with cigarettes numerous times, was forced to dance naked in front of the other children, took baths in scalding water, and was constantly beaten and starved. On one horrible night, Baniszewski took a sewing needle and carved an "I" in Sylvia's abdomen.

Do we as a society perceive such offenses committed by a mother differently than similar offenses committed by a father?

(Continued)

[32]Boles and Hoeveler, *Historical Dictionary of Feminism*, 262–63.

[33]Tong, *Feminist Thought*; see also Toril Moi, *Sexual/Textual Politics* (London: Methuen, 1985).

[34]Tong, *Feminist Thought*, 270.

[35]June Price Tangney and Kurt W. Fischer, *Self-Conscious Emotions: The Psychology of Shame, Guilt, Embarrassment, and Pride* (New York: Guilford Press, 1995).

[36]Sam Stall, "Looking Back on Indiana's Most Infamous Crime, 50 Years Later," Indianapolis Monthly, October 21, 2015, http://www.indianapolismonthly.com/features/looking-back-indianas-infamous-crime-50-years-later.

(Continued)

▲ **Image 10.3** A 1965 photograph of Sylvia Likens.

SOURCE: © INDIANAPOLIS STAR / ASSOCIATED PRESS

She then gave the needle to a neighbor boy and instructed him to spell the word *prostitute.*

After this incident, Sylvia was dead, and Baniszewski was arrested along with eight youthful offenders ranging in age from 11 to 17 years. The children stated that they participated in the torture of Sylvia because "Gertie" told them to. In 1966, Gertrude Baniszewski was convicted of first-degree murder; her daughter, Paula, was convicted of second-degree murder; and the remaining offenders were found guilty of lesser homicide charges.[37]

Think About It

1. After reading this case, one may ask, How could a mother do that to another child? How could a mother ask her children to engage in torturing another child? Do we as a society perceive such offenses committed by a mother differently than similar offenses committed by a father?
2. If so, we need to explore how gender influences our attitudes about criminal behavior as well as criminal offenders.

Evidence regarding Feminist Theories of Crime

As discussed previously, there is no doubt that female offenders were highly neglected by traditional models of criminological theory, and given that females make up at least 50% of the population of the world, it is important that they be covered and explained by such theories. Furthermore, we also discussed the fact that if we knew why females everywhere commit far less violence than men, it would likely go a long way toward devising policies to reduce the extremely higher rates of violence among males. However, in other ways, the feminist theories of crime have not been supported.

For instance, as noted previously, the seminal feminist crime theories specifically proposed that, as women became liberated, their rates of crime would become consistent with the rates of male offending.[38] Not only did this fail to occur, but the evidence actually supports the opposite trend; specifically, the females who were given the most opportunities (e.g., education, employment, status) were the *least* likely to offend, whereas the women who were not liberated or given such opportunities were the *most* likely to engage in criminal behavior.[39]

On the other hand, one major strength of feminist theories of crime is that they have led to a number of studies showing that the factors causing crime in males are different than those for females. For example, females appear

[37] Mara Bovsun, "Teen Girl Fatally Bullied in Indiana House of Horrors," *New York Daily News,* April 6, 2013, http://www.nydailynews.com/news/justice-story/teen-girl-fatally-bullied-indiana-house-horrors-article-1.1309751.

[38] Adler, *Sisters in Crime.*

[39] For a discussion, see Ronald L. Akers and Christine S. Sellers, *Criminological Theories: Introduction, Evaluation, and Application,* 6th ed. (Oxford: Oxford University Press, 2012). See also the discussion in Thomas J. Bernard, Jeffrey B. Snipes, and Alexander L. Gerould, *Vold's Theoretical Criminology,* 6th ed. (Oxford: Oxford University Press, 2010), 117–22 (see chap. 1).

to be far more influenced by internal, emotional factors; they are more inhibited by moral emotions, such as shame, guilt, and embarrassment.[40] Ultimately, there is no doubt that feminist theories of crime have contributed much to the discourse and empirical research regarding why females (as well as males) commit crime. In fact, some highly respected criminology and criminal justice journals have been created to deal with that very subject. So, in that sense, the field has recognized and accepted the need to examine feminist theorizing and research on offending and the justice system and explore the various issues involved.

▲ **Image 10.4** Female delinquency has become more common in recent decades.

SOURCE: © istockphoto.com / Daxus

Feminist criminology evolved, primarily from liberal feminists, with the realization and objection that gender was essentially ignored and excluded from criminological theory.[41] This exclusion was difficult to understand given that gender was such a strong predictor of criminal behavior.[42] Further, feminists recognized the limitations of critical and radical criminological perspectives given the primary focus on economic disparities without examining the issues of race and gender. Thus, "early feminist criminologists demanded that analyses of crime include consideration of gender in ways that had not occurred before."[43] Twenty years after her essay on female crime, Dorie Klein included an afterword; she maintained that feminist criminologists need to address three major challenges: They must (1) continue to search for the scientific basis of theories of men's and women's criminal behavior, (2) reexamine gender and racial/ethnic biases in the social sciences, and (3) develop a new definition of crime.[44] Joanne Belknap gave an overview of the potential of various traditional criminological theories to provide insight in examining gender differences and similarities in understanding criminal behavior. Some of the traditional criminological theories that do have some promise in this area of understanding include differential association theory and strain and general strain theory.[45]

---

[40]For a review, see Tibbetts and Herz, "Gender Differences."

[41]Amanda Burgess-Proctor, "Intersections of Race, Class, Gender, and Crime: Future Directions for Feminist Criminology," *Feminist Criminology* 1 (2006): 30.

[42]Ibid.; see also Alfred Blumstein et al., "Introduction: Studying Criminal Careers," in *Criminal Careers and "Career Criminals,"* ed. Alfred Blumstein et al. (Washington, DC: National Academy Press, 1986), 12–30; Darrell Steffensmeier and Emilie Allan, "Gender and Crime: Toward a Gendered Theory of Female Offending," *Annual Review of Sociology* 22 (2006): 459–87.

[43]Burgess-Proctor, "Intersections of Race, Class, Gender, and Crime," 31.

[44]Dorie Klein, "The Etiology of Female Crime: A Review of the Literature," in *The Criminal Justice System and Women: Offenders, Victims, and Workers*, 2nd ed., ed. Barbara Raffel Price and Natalie Sokoloff (New York: McGraw-Hill, 1995), 48–52.

[45]Belknap, *The Invisible Woman*, 36–56.

Kathleen Daly and Meda Chesney-Lind identified the following five elements that distinguish feminist thought from other forms of social and political thought:

1. Gender is not a natural fact but a complex social, historical, and cultural product; it is related to but not simply derived from biological sex differences and reproductive capacities.
2. Gender and gender relations order social life and social institutions in fundamental ways.
3. Gender relations are constructs of masculinity and femininity and are not symmetrical but are based on an organizing principle of men's superiority and social and political–economic dominance over women.
4. Systems of knowledge reflect men's views of the natural and social world; the production of knowledge is gendered.
5. Women should be at the center of intellectual inquiry, not peripheral, invisible, or appendages to men.[46]

When addressing whether there can be a feminist criminology, Daly and Chesney-Lind maintained that feminist theories and research should be incorporated in any criminologist's study of crime. Incorporating such perspectives entails more than just a focus on women or sexism. Rather, these approaches provide an opportunity to study unexplored aspects of men's crime and forms of justice as well as forms of theory construction and verification. Thus, they argued that the promise of feminist thought has barely been realized.[47]

Almost 20 years after Daly and Chesney-Lind's article on feminist criminology, Amanda Burgess-Proctor argued that for contemporary third-wave feminist criminologists, it is essential to build on the foundation laid by previous feminist criminologists.[48] Specifically, she maintained that feminist criminology needs to embrace all sources of oppression without prioritizing gender. Thus, feminist criminology should incorporate an intersectional framework, informed by multiracial feminism, which includes such defining social characteristics as race, class, gender, sexuality, nationality, and age.[49]

One feminist framework that has been used to explore the experiences of women in the criminal justice system is pathways research:

> A feminist approach to understanding the etiology of females' (and sometimes males') offending is termed by some as "pathways to crime." . . . [T]his approach attempts to determine life experiences, particularly childhood ones, that place one at risk of offending. The pathways research indicates that traumas such as physical and sexual abuse and child neglect are not only defining features in the lives of many female offenders, but also these traumas are often related to one's likelihood of committing crimes.[50]

Critiques of Feminist Theories

A number of criticisms concerning feminist theories have been raised by feminist scholars. In the 1960s, women of color challenged feminism by arguing that these perspectives essentially focused on the experiences

---

[46]Daly and Chesney-Lind, "Feminism and Criminology," 504.

[47]Ibid., 504.

[48]Burgess-Proctor, "Intersections of Race, Class, Gender, and Crime," 27–47.

[49]Ibid., 43.

[50]Emily Gaarder and Joanne Belknap, "Tenuous Borders: Girls Transferred to Adult Court," *Criminology* 40 (2002): 484.

of White middle-class women.[51] After reviewing feminist theory in sociology, Janet Saltzman Chafetz argued that the current topic among feminist scholars is the intersection of race, class, and gender.[52] A number of feminist scholars maintain that examining difference, rather than equality, is a major emphasis of current feminist studies.

While some feminist scholars maintain that this shift in focus has revitalized feminist theory,[53] others assert that it has introduced new conflicts in feminist studies.[54] Maxine Baca Zinn and Bonnie Thornton Dill stressed, however, that while there may be problems when focusing on difference,

> our perspectives take their bearings from social relations. Race and class difference are crucial, we argue, not as individual characteristics . . . but insofar as they are primary organizing principles of a society which locates and positions groups within that society's opportunity structures.[55]

Some feminist scholars emphasize the importance of examining the interlocking, or intersection, of race, class, and gender.[56] The development of an intersectional perspective on gender and race is rooted in the work of scholars focusing on women of color.[57]

Burgess-Proctor identified key conceptual factors that distinguish multiracial feminism from other feminist perspectives.[58] First, multiracial feminism claims that gender relations do not exist in a vacuum; rather, men and women are also characterized by their race, class, sexuality, age, physical ability, and other social locations of inequality. Second, multiracial feminism stresses the importance of recognizing the ways intersecting systems of power and privilege interact on all social–structural levels. Third, multiracial feminism is founded on the concept of *relationality*; this "assumes that groups of people are socially situated in relation to other groups of people based on their differences."[59] Other key conceptual facets to multiracial feminism include appreciating the interaction of social structure and women's agency, implementing various methodological approaches, and an emphasis on understandings founded on the lived experiences of women. This evolving perspective uses various terms such as *multiracial feminism*, *multicultural feminism*, and *U.S. Third World feminism*.[60] Another issue that has been raised by feminist scholars is that, when conducting research on women, it is essential that one avoid placing these women as *either* offenders *or* victims. This has been referred to as the "blurred boundaries" theory of victimization and criminalization. As Mary Gilfus noted, "Criminalization is connected to women's subordinate position in society where victimization by violence coupled with economic marginality related to race, class, and gender all too often blur the boundaries between victims and

---

[51]Maxine Baca Zinn and Bonnie Thornton Dill, "Theorizing Difference from Multiracial Feminism," *Feminist Studies* 22 (2006): 321–31.

[52]Janet Saltzman Chafetz, "Feminist Theory and Sociology: Underutilized Contributions for Mainstream Theory," *Annual Review of Sociology* 23 (1997): 97–120. See also Burgess-Proctor, "Intersections of Race, Class, Gender, and Crime."

[53]Faye Ginsberg and Anna Lowenhaupt Tsing, "Introduction," in *Uncertain Terms, Negotiating Gender in American Culture*, ed. Faye Ginsberg and Anna Lowenhaupt Tsing (Boston: Beacon Press, 1990), 1–32.

[54]Susan E. Martin, "Outsider within" the Station House: The Impact of Race and Gender on Black Women Police," *Social Problems* 41 (1994): 383–400.

[55]Zinn and Thornton Dill, "Theorizing Difference from Multiracial Feminism."

[56]Patricia Hill Collins, *Black Feminist Thought: Knowledge, Consciousness and the Politics of Empowerment*, 2nd ed. (London: HarperCollins, 1999).

[57]Irene Browne and Joya Misra, "The Intersection of Gender and Race in the Labor Market," *Annual Review of Sociology* 29 (2003): 487–513.

[58]Burgess-Proctor, "Intersections of Race, Class, Gender, and Crime," 36–7.

[59]Ibid., p. 37.

[60]See Alison M. Jaggar and Paula S. Rothenberg, *Feminist Frameworks: Alternative Theoretical Accounts of the Relations between Women and Men*, 3rd ed. (New York: McGraw-Hill, 1993); Chela Sandoval, "U.S. Third World Feminism: The Theory and Method of Oppositional Consciousness in the Postmodern World," *Genders* 10 (Spring 1991): 1–24; Zinn and Thornton Dill, "Theorizing Difference from Multiracial Feminism."

offenders."[61] This false categorization of women as *either* offenders *or* victims does not provide an enhanced understanding about women who commit crime.

Policy Implications

There are numerous policy implications regarding feminist theory and feminist perspectives of crime. A key aspect to understanding policies based on feminist theories of crime is that some policies are not always directly related to crime. Rather, feminist perspectives also incorporate broader social issues that are connected to criminal behavior.[62] Thus, aspects of policies related to feminist theories of crime are reflected in broader concepts of feminism. For instance, feminist researchers emphasize the importance of *reflexivity*.[63] This is when research empowers women; this form of research takes women's experiences seriously and centers on the idea that "the personal is the political":

> Feminist work has demonstrated that even the most apparently private interactions have political consequences and motivations. The inextricable connections between the personal and the political means that what happens to "the individual" is not merely the result of individual processes. As a consequence, it is unsatisfactory to treat individuals as if they were isolated from society—at the very least because this cannot give an accurate picture of people and their lives.[64]

This phrase—"The personal is the political"—refers to the notion that the "private sphere" (e.g., sexuality and domestic life) is as structured by power relations involving gender, sexuality, race, class, and age as the "public sphere" (e.g., waged work outside the home, party politics, and state institutions).[65]

Another aspect related to feminism is praxis. According to Josephine Donovan, praxis does not refer just to consciousness raising. Rather, praxis also refers to "the development of alternative arrangements that will themselves provide models for change and will in the process change consciousness."[66] Praxis also implies building alternative institutions, such as the establishment of rape crisis centers and shelters as well as changes in personal relationships. Generally, praxis is when theory translates into action. One of the most essential opportunities for praxis centers on the pursuit of social justice.[67]

Influenced by the women's movement (i.e., the second wave of feminism), our understanding of and the legal response to rape have undergone substantial changes.[68] For instance, Julia and Herman Schwendinger theorized how rape myths have pervaded the legal sphere of society, as exemplified by the belief that if a rape victim did not "fight back" or resist, as well as demonstrate physical evidence of such a confrontation, then she must have initially

---

[61] Mary E. Gilfus, "From Victims to Survivors to Offenders: Women's Routes of Entry and Immersion into Street Crime," *Women and Criminal Justice* 4 (1992): 86.

[62] Franklin P. Williams and Marilyn D. McShane, *Criminological Theory*, 3rd ed. (Upper Saddle River, NJ: Prentice Hall, 1999), 260.

[63] Christine Griffin and Ann Phoenix, "The Relationship between Qualitative and Quantitative Research: Lessons from Feminist Psychology," *Journal of Community & Applied Social Psychology* 4 (1994): 290.

[64] Ibid.

[65] Ibid.

[66] Josephine Donovan, *Feminist Theory: The Intellectual Traditions of American Feminism* (New York: Frederick Ungar, 1985), 88.

[67] Burgess-Proctor, "Intersections of Race, Class, Gender, and Crime," 42. See also Margaret L. Andersen and Patricia Hill Collins, *Race, Class, and Gender*, 5th ed. (Belmont, CA: Wadsworth, 2004); Lynn Weber, *Understanding Race, Class, Gender, and Sexuality: A Conceptual Framework* (Boston: McGraw-Hill, 2001).

[68] Katherine van Wormer and Clemens Bartollas, *Women and the Criminal Justice System* (Boston: Allyn & Bacon, 2000).

given her consent and afterward "changed her mind."[69] In the past, this myth has been significant in laws that required a demonstration of resistance. However, the Schwendingers provided the following analogy to elucidate the misconceptions associated with this myth:

> Businessmen may forcibly resist theft of their property. But no law *demands* this kind of personal resistance as a condition for the lawful protection of his property rights. Women's rights, on the other hand, seem to be another matter [italics in original].[70]

Legislative reforms were enacted in an effort to modify state rape statutes. Patricia Searles and Ronald Berger asserted that the five major goals of the legislative reforms included (1) increasing the reporting of rape and enhancing the prosecution and conviction in rape cases, (2) improving the treatment of rape victims involved in the criminal justice process, (3) achieving comparability between the legal treatment of rape and other violent offenses, (4) prohibiting a broader range of coercive sexual conduct, and (5) expanding the range of persons protected by the law.[71] Four major types of legislative reforms were identified: (1) redefinition of the offense, (2) evidentiary reforms, (3) statutory offenses, and (4) penal structure.[72]

Another example of how feminist criminologists have informed policies is in the area of gender-specific programming. The Office of Juvenile Justice and Delinquency Prevention established a funding opportunity to enhance programs specifically targeted to juvenile girls.[73] Such programming gives females an increased sense of community. This sense of community has been associated with juveniles developing and integrating a healthy identity.[74]

There have been efforts to incorporate these key factors of gender-specific services for female juvenile offenders. For instance, Lisa Bond-Maupin and her colleagues argued that intake officials recognized an appreciation of how gender, class, and race influence the lives of female juveniles.[75] Other studies have also recommended that agencies providing services to female juveniles incorporate gender-specific or gender-responsive programs.[76] Such programming has also been recommended for adult female offenders with substance abuse problems[77] as well as for adult female prisoners.[78]

---

[69]Julia R. Schwendinger and Herman Schwendinger, "Rape Myths: In Legal, Theoretical, and Everyday Practice," *Crime and Social Justice* 1 (1974): 18–26.

[70]Ibid., 21.

[71]Patricia Searles and Ronald J. Berger, "The Current Status of Rape Reform Legislation: An Examination of State Statutes," *Women's Rights Law Reporter* 10 (1987): 25.

[72]Ibid., 25–27.

[73]Donna Bownes and Rodney L. Albert, "State Challenge Activities," in *OJJDP Juvenile Justice Bulletin* (Washington, DC: Office of Juvenile Justice and Delinquency Prevention, September 1996); Kimberly Kempf-Leonard and Lisa L. Sample, "Disparity Based on Sex: Is Gender-Specific Treatment Warranted?" *Justice Quarterly* 17 (2000): 89–128.

[74]Paula Smith and William A. Smith, "Experiencing Community through the Eyes of Young Female Offenders," *Journal of Contemporary Criminal Justice* 21 (2005): 364–85.

[75]Lisa Bond-Maupin, James R. Maupin, and Amy Leisenring, "Girls' Delinquency and the Justice Implications of Intake Workers' Perspectives," *Women & Criminal Justice* 13 (2002): 51–77.

[76]Suman Kakar, Marie-Luse Friedemann, and Linda Peck, "Girls in Detention: The Results of Focus Group Discussion Interviews and Official Records Review," *Journal of Contemporary Criminal Justice* 18 (2002): 57–73; Wansley Walters, "The Miami-Dade Juvenile Assessment Center National Demonstration Project: An Overview," *Journal of Offender Rehabilitation* 41 (2005): 1–37.

[77]Michael Fendrich, Amy Hubbell, and Arthur J. Lurigio, "Providers' Perceptions of Gender-Specific Drug Treatment," *Journal of Drug Issues* 36 (2006): 667–86.

[78]Katherine van Wormer and Laura E. Kaplan, "Results of a National Survey of Wardens in Women's Prisons: The Case for Gender Specific Treatment," *Women and Therapy* 29 (2006): 133–51.

Conclusion

In this section introduction, we discussed the reasons for why it is so very important to examine the feminist perspective of crime. Importantly, we examined a wide variety of types of feminist perspectives and the factors that each of them focus on. We also examined the evidence that empirical research has shown for the feminist perspectives as well as the critiques of such theories in this realm. We also discussed some of the policy implications that can be derived from these models. Ultimately, it is of primary importance to include such feminist perspectives in future research and theoretical developments. Furthermore, it is important to realize that females offend far less than males; if criminologists could figure out why, this could be a landmark finding in efforts to reduce crime, especially if we could apply some of the findings of research on this perspective to chronic male offending.

SECTION SUMMARY

- An emphasis on the feminist perspective on crime grew out of a long history of females being neglected in the history of criminological research as well as concern for them as victims in the criminal justice system.
- Various concepts are key in the feminist perspective, such as chivalry, patriarchy, and paternalism—all essentially diminish the status of females in society.
- One primary research question in this area is about why females are universally less likely to commit serious violent crime than males, called the gender-ratio issue.
- The other primary research area deals with whether or not the same key factors (e.g., peers, unemployment, poverty) apply in the same way for females as they do for males, which is referred to as the generalizability issue.
- We examined five different key types of feminism and what each of them focus on regarding why females are discriminated against and what leads them to commit crime.
- Evidence regarding feminist models of crime are mixed with some showing clear support and others showing the opposite of what was predicted.
- Daly and Chesney-Lind's list of the elements of feminist thought were discussed and presented as one of the key propositions of the feminist perspective on not just criminology but also society and social life.
- Critiques of feminist theories showed that many women take issue with what other feminist scholars have proposed, particularly by neglecting the issues of race and social class and focusing only on gender.
- It is notable that the critiques mentioned led to much research and discussion on the intersection of these various classes of people, which has advanced the understanding of feminism, racism, classism, etc., across the board.
- Policy implications based on the feminist perspective were also examined with the ultimate conclusion that if we could truly understand and explain why females commit so many fewer serious violent crimes, then we could likely reduce our crime rate dramatically by applying such knowledge to males.

KEY TERMS

chivalry 441
critical feminism 443
liberal feminism 442
Marxist feminism 445
paternalism 442
patriarchy 442
postmodern feminism 447
radical feminism 443
socialist feminism 445

DISCUSSION QUESTIONS

1. What are some of the key concepts of the feminist perspective?
2. What are the key assumptions and features of the various types of feminist perspectives?
3. Which type of feminist theory do you believe is the most helpful for explaining crime?
4. Do you believe the "generalizability" hypothesis is accurate and that key factors or causes of crime are the same for males and females? In other words, do the same factors (e.g., unemployment, peers, emotions) have the same influence across gender?
5. What are the primary critiques of feminist criminological theories?
6. Which of the policy implications based on the feminist perspective do you most agree with? Least agree with?

WEB RESOURCES

Feminist Theories of Crime

http://www.youtube.com/watch?v=wIdzD8kpYwk
http://faculty.washington.edu/matsueda/courses/517/Readings/Daly%20Chesney-Lind%20Feminism%201988.pdf
http://now.org
http://www.historylearningsite.co.uk/sociology/crime-and-deviance/feminism-and-crime
https://www.google.com/#q=feminist+theories+of+crime
http://www.oxfordbibliographies.com/view/document/obo-9780195396607/obo-9780195396607-0013.xml

READING /// 24

In this selection, Meda Chesney-Lind discusses feminist criminology as an outgrowth of the second wave of feminism and argues for combining racial factors with the feminist perspective as a dual focus for research. The author promotes this combined approach as the best method to advance the emphasis on both of these factors for future criminological research. She asserts that this combination of factors will lead to more research attention and that examinations of both race and feminism will be more likely to foster an understanding of criminality and criminal justice processing for both.

While reading this selection, readers are encouraged to consider the following points:

- The author's meaning when she claims there is a contemporary "backlash" against feminist criminology
- The primary reasons why the author believes that combining gender with race will lead to a better understanding of criminality as well as more fairness in handling by the criminal justice system
- The author's meaning of the term *vengeful equity*
- The unique needs of certain populations (e.g., women, especially single mothers) that are not adequately addressed by the criminal justice system, particularly in cases of incarceration

Patriarchy, Crime, and Justice

Feminist Criminology in an Era of Backlash

Meda Chesney-Lind

A product of the second wave of the women's movement, feminist criminology has been in existence now for more than three decades. Although any starting point is arbitrary, certainly one could point to the publication of key journal issues and books in the 1970s,[1] and it is clear that a signal event was the founding of the Women and Crime Division of the American Society of Criminology in 1982 (Rafter, 2000, p. 9). Since that time, the field has grown exponentially, which makes it increasingly impossible to do justice to all its dimensions in the space of an article. This article, instead, focuses on the challenges facing our important field as we enter a millennium characterized by a deepening backlash against feminism and other progressive movements and perspectives.

Feminist Criminology in the 20th Century: Looking Backward, Looking Forward

The feminist criminology of the 20th century clearly challenged the overall masculinist nature of theories of crime, deviance, and social control by calling attention to the repeated omission and misrepresentation of women in criminological theory and research (Belknap, 2001;

SOURCE: Meda Chesney-Lind, "Patriarchy, Crime, and Justice: Feminist Criminology in an Era of Backlash," *Feminist Criminology* 1, no. 1 (2006): 6–26.

Cain, 1990; Daly & Chesney-Lind, 1988). Turning back the clock, one can recall that prior to path-breaking feminist works on sexual assault, sexual harassment, and wife abuse, these forms of gender violence were ignored, minimized, and trivialized. Likewise, girls and women in conflict with the law were overlooked or excluded in mainstream works while demonized, masculinized, and sexualized in the marginalized literature that brooded on their venality. Stunning gender discrimination, such as the failure of most law schools to admit women, the routine exclusion of women from juries, and the practice of giving male and female "offenders" different sentences for the same crimes went largely unchallenged (see Rafter, 2000, for a good overview of the history in each of these areas).

The enormity of girls' and women's victimization meant that the silence on the role of violence in women's lives was the first to attract the attention of feminist activists and scholars. Because of this, excellent work exists on the problem of women's victimization—especially in the areas of sexual assault, sexual harassment, sexual abuse, and wife battery (see, e.g., Buzawa & Buzawa, 1990; Dziech & Weiner, 1984; Estrich, 1987; D. Martin, 1977; Rush, 1980; Russell, 1986; Schechter, 1982; Scully, 1990). In retrospect, the naming of the types and dimensions of female victimization had a significant impact on public policy, and it is arguably the most tangible accomplishment of both feminist criminology and grassroots feminists concerned about gender, crime, and justice. The impact on the field of criminology and particularly criminological theory was mixed, however, in part because these offenses did not initially seem to challenge androcentric criminology per se. Instead, the concepts of "domestic violence" and "victimology," although pivotal in the development of feminist criminology, also supplied mainstream criminologists and some criminal justice practitioners with a new area in which to publish, "new" crimes to study (and opportunities to secure funding), and new men to jail (particularly men of color and other marginalized men). More recent, the field of domestic violence has even been home to a number of scholars who have argued that women are as violent as men (for critical reviews, see DeKeseredy, Sanders, Schwartz, & Alvi, 1997; DeKeseredy & Schwartz, 1998; S. Miller, 2005). In part because of these trends, the focus on girls' and women's victimization has produced a range of challenges for feminist criminology and for feminist activists that have become even more urgent as we move into the new century.

Compared to the wealth of literature on women's victimization, interest in girls and women who are labeled, tried, and jailed as "delinquent" or "criminal" was slower to fully develop[2] in part because scholars of "criminalized" women and girls had to contend early on with the masculinization (or "emancipation") hypothesis of women's crime, which argues in part that "in the same way that women are demanding equal opportunity in the fields of legitimate endeavor, a similar number of determined women are forcing their way into the world of major crimes" (Adler, 1975, p. 3; see also Simon, 1975). Feminist criminologists, as well as mainstream criminologists, debated the nature of that relationship for the next decade and ultimately concluded it was not correct (Chesney-Lind, 1989; Steffensmeier, 1980; Weis, 1976), but this was a costly intellectual detour (and also a harbinger of things to come, as it turned out).

The 1980s and 1990s, however, would see breakthrough research on the lives of criminalized girls and women. Rich documentation of girls' participation in gangs, as an example, challenges earlier gang research that focuses almost exclusively on boys (see Chesney-Lind & Hagedorn, 1999; Moore, 1991). Important work on the role of sexual and physical victimization in girls' and women's pathways into women's crime (see Arnold, 1995; Chesney-Lind & Rodriquez, 1983; Chesney-Lind & Shelden, 1992; Gilfus, 1992) began to appear, along with work that suggests unique ways in which gender and race create unique pathways for girl and women offenders into criminal behavior, particularly in communities ravaged by drugs and overincarceration (Bourgois & Dunlap, 1993; Joe, 1995; Maher & Curtis, 1992; Richie, 1996). Needless to say, the focus on girls' and women's gender also highlights the fact that masculinity and crime need to be both theorized and researched (Bowker, 1998; Messerschmidt, 2000).

Instead of the "add women and stir" (Chesney-Lind, 1988) approach to crime theorizing of the past century (which often introduces gender solely as a "variable" if at all), new important work on the gender/crime nexus *theorizes gender*. This means, for example, drawing extensively on sociological notions of "doing gender" (West & Zimmerman, 1987) and examining the role of "gender regimes" (Williams, 2002) in the production of girls' and women's behavior. Contemporary approaches to gender and crime (see Messerschmidt, 2000; J. Miller, 2001) tend to avoid the problems of reductionism and determinism that characterize early discussions of gender and gender relations, stressing instead the complexity, tentativeness, and variability with which individuals, particularly youth, negotiate (and resist) gender identity (see Kelly, 1993; Thorne, 1993). J. Miller and Mullins (2005), in particular, have argued for the crafting of "theories of the middle range" that recognize that although society and social life are patterned on the basis of gender, it is also the case that the *gender order* (Connell, 2002) is "complex and shifting" (J. Miller & Mullins, 2005, p. 7).

Feminist Criminology and the Backlash

Feminist criminology in the 21st century, particularly in the United States, finds itself in a political and social milieu that is heavily affected by the backlash politics of a sophisticated and energized right wing—a context quite different from the field's early years when the initial intellectual agenda of the field evolved. Political backlash eras have long been a fixture of American public life, from reconstruction after the Civil War to the McCarthy era of the 1950s. Most of these have certain common characteristics, including a repression of dissent, imperialistic adventure, a grim record of racism, and "resistance to extending full rights to women" (Hardisty, 2000, p. 10).

The current backlash era, however, uses crime and criminal justice policies as central rather than facilitating elements of political agenda—a pattern clearly of relevance to feminist criminology. The right-wing intent to use the "crime problem" became evident very early. Consider Barry Goldwater's 1964 unsuccessful presidential campaign where he repeatedly used phrases such as *civil disorder* and *violence in the streets* in a "covertly racist campaign" to attack the civil rights movement (Chambliss, 1999, p. 14). Both Richard Nixon and Ronald Reagan refined the approach as the crime problem became a centerpiece of the Republican Party's efforts to wrest electoral control of southern states away from the Democratic Party. Nixon's emphasis on *law and order* and Reagan's *war on drugs* were both built on "white fear of black street crime" (Chambliss, 1999, p. 19). With time, crime would come to be understood as a code word for race in U.S. political life, and it became a staple in the Republican attacks on Democratic rivals. When Reagan's former vice president, George Bush Sr., ran for office, he successfully used the Willie Horton incident (where an African American on a prison furlough raped and murdered a woman) to derail the candidacy of Michael Dukakis in 1988 (Chambliss, 1999).

His son, George W. Bush, would gain the presidency as a direct result of backlash criminal justice policies, because felony disenfranchisement of largely African American voters in Florida was crucial to his political strategy in that state (Lantigua, 2001). In Bush's second election campaign, however, another feature would be added to the Republican mix: an appeal to "moral values." Included in the moral values agenda, designed to appeal to right-wing Christians, is the rolling back of the gains of the women's movement of the past century, including the recriminalization of abortion and the denial of civil rights to gay and lesbian Americans. Bush's nominee to the Supreme Court, John Roberts, has even questioned "whether encouraging homemakers to become lawyers contributes to the public good" (Goldstein, Smith, & Becker, 2005).

The centrality of both crime and gender in the current backlash politics means that feminist criminology is uniquely positioned to challenge right-wing initiatives. To do this effectively, however, the field must put an even greater priority on *theorizing patriarchy and crime*, which means focusing on the ways in which the definition of the crime problem and criminal justice practices support patriarchal practices and worldviews.

To briefly review, patriarchy is a sex/gender system[3] in which men dominate women and what is considered masculine is more highly valued than what is considered feminine. Patriarchy is a system of social stratification, which means that it uses a wide array of social control policies and practices to ratify male power and to keep girls and women subordinate to men (Renzetti & Curran, 1999, p. 3). Often, the systems of control that women experience are explicitly or implicitly focused on controlling female sexuality (such as the sexual double standard; Renzetti & Curran, 1999, p. 3). Not infrequently, patriarchal interests overlap with systems that also reinforce class and race privilege, hence, the unique need for feminist criminology to maintain the focus on intersectionality that characterizes recent research and theorizing on gender and race in particular (see Crenshaw, 1994).

Again, in this era of backlash, the formal system of social control (the law and criminal justice policies) play key roles in eroding the rights of both women and people of color, particularly African Americans but increasingly, other ethnic groups as well. Feminist criminology is, again, uniquely positioned to both document and respond to these efforts. To theorize patriarchy effectively means that we have done cutting-edge research on the interface between patriarchal and criminal justice systems of control and that we are strategic about how to get our findings out to the widest audience possible, issues to which this article now turns.

Race, Gender, and Crime

If feminist criminology is to fully understand the interface between patriarchal control mechanisms and criminal justice practices in the United States, we must center our analysis on the race/gender/punishment nexus. Specifically, America's long and sordid history of racism and its equally disturbing enthusiasm for imprisonment must be understood as intertwined, and both of these have had a dramatic effect on African American women in particular (Bush-Baskette, 1998; Horton & Horton, 2005; Johnson, 2003; Mauer, 1999).

More than a century ago, W. E. B. Du Bois saw the linkage between the criminal justice system and race-based systems of social control very clearly. Commenting on the dismal failure of "reconstruction," he concluded,

> Despite compromise, war, and struggle, the Negro is not free. In well-nigh the whole rural South the black farmers are peons, bound by law and custom to an economic slavery from which the only escape is death or the penitentiary. (as quoted in Johnson, 2003, p. 284)

Although the role of race and penal policy has received increased attention in recent years, virtually all of the public discussion of the issues has focused on African American males (see, e.g., Human Rights Watch, 2000). More recent, the significant impact of mass incarceration on African American and Hispanic women has received the attention it deserves. Current data show that African American women account for "almost half (48 percent)" of all the women we incarcerate (Johnson, 2003, p. 34). Mauer and Huling's (1995) earlier research adds an important perspective here; they noted that the imprisonment of African American women grew by more than 828% between 1986 and 1991, whereas that of White women grew by 241% and of Black men by 429% (see also Bush-Baskette, 1998; Gilbert, 2001). Something is going on, and it is not just about race or gender; it is about both—a sinister synergy that clearly needs to be carefully documented and challenged.

Feminist criminologist Paula Johnson (2003), among others, advocated a "Black Feminist analysis of the criminal justice system." An examination of Black women's history from slavery through the Civil War and the post-war period certainly justifies a clear focus on the role that the criminal justice system played in the oppression of African American women and the role of prison in that system (Rafter, 1990). And the focus is certainly still relevant because although women sometimes appear to be the unintended victims of the war on drugs, this "war" is so heavily racialized that the result can hardly be viewed as accidental. African American women have always been seen through the "distorted lens of otherness," constructed as "subservient, inept, oversexed and undeserving" (Johnson, 2003, pp. 9–10), in short, just the "sort" of women that belong in jail and prison. Hence, any good work on criminalized women must also examine the ways in which misogyny and racism have long been intertwined themes in the control of women of color (as well as other women) in the United States, as the next section demonstrates.

Media Demonization and the Masculinization of Female Offenders

As noted earlier, the second wave of feminism had, by the 1980s, triggered an array of conservative political, policy, and media responses. In her book *Backlash: The Undeclared War Against American Women*, Susan Faludi (1991), a journalist, was quick to see that the media in particular were central, not peripheral, to the process of discrediting and dismissing feminism and feminist gains. She focused specific attention on mainstream journalism's efforts to locate and publicize those "female trends" of the 1980s that would undermine and indict the feminist agenda. Stories about "the failure to get husbands, get pregnant, or properly bond with their children" were suddenly everywhere, as were the very first stories on "bad girls"; Faludi noted that "NBC, for instance, devoted an entire evening news special to the pseudo trend of 'bad girls' yet ignored the real trends of bad boys: the crime rate among boys was climbing twice as fast as for girls" (p. 80).

Faludi's (1991) recognition of the media fascination with bad girls was prescient. The 1990s would produce a steady stream of media stories about violent and bad girls that continues unabated in the new millennium. Although the focus would shift from the "gangsta girl," to the "violent girl," to the "mean girl" (Chesney-Lind & Irwin, 2004), the message is the same: Girls are bad in ways that they never used to be. As an example, the Scelfo (2005) article titled "Bad Girls Go Wild," published in the June 13, 2005, issue of *Newsweek*, describes "the significant rise in violent behavior among girls" as a "burgeoning national crisis" (p. 1).

Media-driven constructions such as these generally rely on commonsense notions that girls are becoming more like boys on both the soccer field and the killing fields.[4] Implicit in what might be called the "masculinization" theory (Chesney-Lind & Eliason, in press; Pollock, 1999) of women's violence is the idea that contemporary theories of violence (and crime more broadly) need not attend to gender but can, again, simply add women and stir. The theory assumes that the same forces that propel men into violence will increasingly produce violence in girls and women once they are freed from the constraints of their gender. The masculinization framework also lays the foundation for simplistic notions of "good" and "bad" femininity, standards that will permit the demonization of some girls and women if they stray from the path of "true" (passive, controlled, and constrained) womanhood.

Ever since the first wave of feminism, there has been no shortage of scholars and political commentators issuing dire warnings that women's demand for equality would result in a dramatic change in the character and frequency of women's crime (Pollak, 1950; Pollock, 1999; Smart, 1976). As noted earlier, in the 1970s, the notion that the women's movement was causing changes in women's crime was the subject of extensive media and scholarly attention (Adler, 1975; Chesney-Lind, 1989; Simon, 1975). Again, although this perspective was definitely refuted by the feminist criminology of the era (see Gora, 1982; Steffensmeier & Steffensmeier, 1980; Weis, 1976), media enthusiasm about the idea that feminism encourages women to become more like men and, hence, their "equals" in crime, remains undiminished (see Chesney-Lind & Eliason, in press).

As examples, *Boston Globe Magazine* proclaimed in an article as well as on the issue's cover, over the words *BAD GIRLS* in huge red letters, that "girls are moving into the world of violence that once belonged to boys" (Ford, 1998). And from *San Jose Mercury News* came a story titled "In a New Twist on Equality, Girls' Crimes Resemble Boys'" that features an opening paragraph arguing that

> juvenile crime experts have spotted a disturbing nationwide pattern of teenage girls becoming more sophisticated and independent criminals. In the past, girls would almost always commit crimes with boys or men. But now, more than ever, they're calling the shots. (Guido, 1998, p. 1B)

In virtually all the stories on this topic (including the Scelfo, 2005, article appearing in *Newsweek*), the issue is framed as follows. A specific and egregious example of female violence is described, usually with considerable, graphic detail about the injury suffered by the victim—a pattern that has been dubbed "forensic journalism" (Websdale & Alvarez, 1997, p. 123). In the *Mercury News* article, for example, the reader hears how a 17-year-old girl, Linna Adams, "lured" the victim into a car where her boyfriend "pointed a .357 magnum revolver at him, and the gun went off. Rodrigues was shot in the cheek, and according to coroner's reports, the bullet exited the back of his head" (Guido, 1998, p. 1B). Websdale and Alvarez (1997) noted that this narrative style, while compelling and even lurid reading, actually gives the reader "more and more information about less and less" and stresses "individualistic explanations that ignore or de-emphasize the importance of wider social structural patterns of disadvantage" (p. 125).

These forensic details are then followed by a quick review of the Federal Bureau of Investigation's arrest statistics showing what appear to be large increases in the number of girls arrested for violent offenses. Finally, there are quotes from "experts," usually police officers, teachers, or other social service workers, but occasionally criminologists, interpreting the narrative in ways consistent with the desired outcome: to stress that girls, particularly African American and Hispanic girls whose pictures often illustrate these stories, are getting more and more like their already demonized male counterparts and, hence, becoming more violent (Chesney-Lind & Irwin, 2005).

There are two problems with this now familiar frame: One, there are considerable reasons to suspect that it is demonstrably wrong (i.e., that girls' violence is not increasing) and two, it has created a "self-fulfilling prophecy" that has had dramatic and racialized effects on girls' arrests, detentions, and referrals to juvenile courts across our country.

Although arrest data consistently show dramatic increases in girls' arrests for "violent" crimes (e.g., arrests of girls for assault climbed an astonishing 40.9%, whereas boys' arrests climbed by only 4.3% in the past decade; Federal Bureau of Investigation, 2004), other data sets, particularly those relying on self-reported delinquency, show no such trend (indeed they show a decline; Chesney-Lind, 2004; Chesney-Lind & Belknap, 2004; Steffensmeier, Schwartz, Zhong, & Ackerman, 2005). It seems increasingly clear that forces other than changes in girls' behavior have caused shifts in girls' arrests (including such forces as zero-tolerance policies in schools and mandatory arrests for domestic violence; Chesney-Lind & Belknap, 2004). There are also indications that although the hype about bad girls seems to encompass all girls, the effects of enforcement policies aimed at reducing "youth violence" weigh heaviest on girls of color whose families lack the resources to challenge such policies (Chesney-Lind & Irwin, 2005).

Take juvenile detention, a focus of three decades of deinstitutionalization efforts. Between 1989 and 1998, girls' detentions increased by 56% compared to a 20% increase seen in boys' detentions, and the "large increase was tied to the growth in the number of delinquency cases involving females charged with person offenses (157%)" (Harms, 2002, p. 1). At least one study of girls in detention suggests that "nearly half" the girls in detention are African American girls, and Latinas constitute 13%; Caucasian girls, who constitute 65% of the girl population, account for only 35% of those in detention (American Bar Association & National Bar Association, 2001, pp. 20–21).

It is clear that two decades of the media demonization of girls, complete with often racialized images of girls seemingly embracing the violent street culture of their male counterparts (see Chesney-Lind & Irwin, 2004), coupled with increased concerns about youth violence and images of "girls gone wild," have entered the self-fulfilling prophecy stage. It is essential that feminist criminology understand that in a world governed by those who self-consciously manipulate corporate media for their own purposes, newspapers and television may have moved from simply covering the police beat to constructing crime "stories" that serve as a "nonconspiratorial source of dominant ideology" (Websdale & Alvarez, 1997, p. 125). Feminist criminology's agenda must consciously challenge these backlash media narratives, as well as engage in "newsmaking criminology" (Barak, 1988), particularly with regard to constructions of girl and women offenders. The question of how to do this is one that must also engage the field. As a start on such a discussion, consider the advice of Bertold Brecht (1966):

> One must have the courage to write the truth when the truth is everywhere opposed; the keenness to recognize it, although it is everywhere concealed; the skill to manipulate it as a weapon; the judgment to select in whose hands it will be effective, and the cunning to spread the truth among such persons. (p. 133)

The advocacy work coupled with excellent research that one sees with reports issued by The Sentencing Project and the Center for Juvenile and Criminal Justice provide models of how this work might be done. It certainly requires that we work more closely with progressive journalists than many academics are used to, but given the success of these agencies in doing just that, feminist criminologists should consider this a priority and use our national and regional meetings, as a start, to develop strategies toward this end.

Criminalizing Victimization

Many feminist criminologists have approached the issue of mandatory arrest in incidents of domestic assault with considerable ambivalence (see Ferraro, 2001). On one hand, as noted earlier, the criminalization of sexual assault and domestic violence was in one sense a huge symbolic victory for feminist activists and criminologists alike. After centuries of ignoring the private victimizations of women, police and courts were called to account by those who founded rape crisis centers and shelters for battered women and those whose path-breaking research laid the foundation for major policy and legal changes in the area of violence against women (see Schecter, 1982).

On the other hand, the insistence that violence against women be handled as a criminal matter threw victim advocates into an uneasy alliance with police and prosecutors—professions that feminists had long distrusted and with good reason (see Buzawa & Buzawa, 1990; Heidensohn, 1995; S. Martin, 1980). The criminal justice approach, however, was bolstered in the mid-1980s by what appeared to be overwhelming evidence that arrest decreased violence against women (Sherman & Berk, 1984). Although subsequent research would find that arrest was far less effective than originally thought (see Ferraro, 2001; Maxwell, Garner, & Fagan, 2002), for the policy world, the dramatic early research results seemed to ratify the wisdom of a law enforcement–centered approach to the problem of domestic violence. Ultimately, the combined effects of the early scientific evidence; political pressure from the attorney general of the United States, the American Bar Association, and others; and the threat of lawsuits against departments who failed to protect women from batterers "produced nearly unanimous agreement that arrest was the best policy for domestic violence" (Ferraro, 2001, p. 146).

As the academic debate about the effectiveness of arrest in domestic violence situations continued unabated, the policy of "mandatory arrest" became routinized into normal policing and quite quickly, other unanticipated effects began to emerge. When arrests of adult women for assault increased by 30.8% in the past decade (1994 to 2003), whereas male arrests for this offense fell by about 5.8% (Federal Bureau of Investigation, 2004, p. 275), just about everybody from the research community to the general public began to wonder what was happening. Although some, such as criminologist Kenneth Land, quoted in a story titled "Women Making Gains in Dubious Profession: Crime," attributed the increase to "role change over the past decades" that presumably created more females as "motivated offenders" (Anderson, 2003, p. 1), others were not so sure. Even the Bureau of Justice Statistics looked at a similar trend (increasing numbers of women convicted in state courts for "aggravated assault") and suggested the numbers might be "reflecting increased prosecution of women for domestic violence" (Greenfeld & Snell, 1999, pp. 5–6).

Much like the increases seen in girls' assaults, this trend requires critical review, a process that takes the reader through the looking glass to a place that the feminists who worked hard to force the criminal justice system and the general public to take wife battery seriously could never have imagined. In this world, as in California recently, the female share of domestic violence arrests tripled (from 5% in 1987 to 17% in 1999; S. Miller, 2005, p. 21); and as it turned out, it was not just a California phenomenon.

Despite the power of the stereotypical scenario of the violent husband and the victimized wife, the reality of mandatory arrest practices has always been more complicated. Early on, the problem of "mutual" arrests—the practice of arresting both the man and the woman in a domestic violence incident if it is not clear who is the "primary" aggressor—surfaced as a concern (Buzawa & Buzawa, 1990). Nor has the problem gone away, despite efforts to clarify procedures (Bible, 1998; Brown, 1997); indeed, many jurisdictions report similar figures. In Wichita, Kansas, for example, women were 27% of those arrested for domestic violence in 2001 (Wichita Police Department, 2002). Prince William County, Maryland, saw the number of women arrested for domestic violence triple in a 3-year period, with women going from 12.9% of those arrested in 1992 to 21% in 1996 (Smith, 1996). In Sacramento, California, even greater increases were observed; there the number of women arrested for domestic violence rose by 91% between 1991 and 1996, whereas arrests of men fell 7% (Brown, 1997).

A Canadian study (Comack, Chopyk, & Wood, 2000) provides an even closer look at the impact of mandatory arrest on arrests of women for crimes of violence. Examining the gender dynamics in a random sample of 1,002 cases (501 men and 501 women) involving charges filed by the Winnipeg, Manitoba, police services for violent crimes during the period 1991 through 1995, the researchers found that the "zero-tolerance" policy implemented by the police force in 1993 had a dramatic effect on women's arrest patterns. Although the policy resulted in more arrests of both men and women for domestic violence, the impact on women's arrests was most dramatic. In 1991, domestic violence charges represented 23% of all charges of violence against women; by 1995, 58% of all violent crime charges against women were for partner violence (Comack et al., 2000, p. ii). Most significant, the researchers found that in 35% of the domestic violence cases involving women, the accused woman had actually called the police for help (only 5% of male cases showed this pattern; Comack et al., 2000, p. 15).

Susan Miller's (2005) study of mandatory arrest practices in the state of Delaware adds an important dimension to this discussion. Based on data from police ride alongs, interviews with criminal justice practitioners, and observations of groups run for women who were arrested as offenders in domestic violence situations, Miller's study comes to some important conclusions about the effects of mandatory arrest on women.

According to beat officers S. Miller (2005) and her students rode with, in Delaware, they do not have a "pro-arrest policy, we have a pro-paper policy" (p. 100) developed in large part to avoid lawsuits. What initially surfaces as a seemingly minor, and familiar, lament begins to take on far more meaning. It emerges that at least in Delaware (but one suspects elsewhere), police departments, often in response to threatened or real lawsuits, have developed an "expansive definition" (S. Miller, 2005, p. 89) of domestic violence, including a wide range of family disturbances. As a consequence, although the officers "did not believe there was an increase in women's use of violence" (S. Miller, 2005, p. 105), "her fighting back now gets attention too" (S. Miller, 2005, p. 107) because of this sort of broad interpretation of what constitutes domestic violence.

Another significant theme in police comments reflects male batterers' increased skill in deploying the criminal justice system to further intimidate and control their wives. Officers reported that men are now more willing to report violence committed by their wives and more willing to use "cross-filings" in securing protective orders against their wives and girlfriends. Police particularly resent what they regard as "bogus" violations of protective orders that are actually just harassment (S. Miller, 2005, p. 90).

None of the social service providers and criminal justice professionals S. Miller (2005) spoke with felt women had become more aggressively violent; instead, they routinely called the women "victims." They noted that at least in Delaware, as the "legislation aged," the name of the game began to be "get to the phone first" (S. Miller, 2005, p. 127). Social service workers noted that male batterers tended to use their knowledge of the criminal justice system and process as a way to threaten their wives with the loss of the children, particularly if they had managed to get the woman placed on probation for abuse. Workers echoed the police complaints about paperwork, noting it takes 8 hours to do the paperwork if an arrest is made, but then they made a crucial link to the arrest of women, noting that police, weary of being told they were the problem, have channeled at least some of their resentment into making arrests of women who act out violently (regardless of context or injury) because "according to police policy," they have to make an arrest.

Essentially, it appears that many mandatory arrest policies have been interpreted on the ground to make an arrest if any violent "incident" occurs, rather than considering the context within which the incident occurs (Bible, 1998). Like problematic measures of violence that simply count violent events without providing information on the meaning and motivation, this definition of *domestic violence* fails to distinguish aggressive and instigating violence from self-defensive and retaliatory violence. According to S. Miller (2005) and other critics of this approach, these methods tend to produce results showing "intimate violence is committed by women at an equal or higher rate than by men" (p. 35). Although these findings ignited a firestorm of media attention about the "problem" of "battered men" in the United States (Ferraro, 2001, p. 137), the larger question of how to define *domestic violence* in the context of patriarchy is vital. Specifically, much feminist research of the sort showcased here is needed on routine police and justice practices concerning girls' and women's "violence." In particularly short supply are studies of girls' arrests, particularly those of girls of color (who are often detained for "assault"), although indirect evidence certainly suggests this is happening (see Chesney-Lind & Irwin, 2005). The evidence to date suggests the distinct possibility that in addition to the well-documented race and class problems, with draconian criminal justice approaches to domestic violence (S. Miller, 1989; Richie, 1996), we have a gender issue: Are these policies criminalizing women's (and girls') attempts to protect themselves?

Women's Imprisonment and the Emergence of Vengeful Equity

When the United States embarked on a policy that might well be described as mass incarceration (Mauer & Chesney-Lind, 2002), few considered the impact that this correctional course change would have on women. Yet the number of women in jail and prison continues to soar (outstripping male increases for most of the past decade), completely untethered from women's crime rate, which has not increased by nearly the same amount (Bloom & Chesney-Lind, 2003). The dimensions of this shift are staggering: For most of the 20th century, we imprisoned about 5,000 to 10,000 women. At the turn of the new century, we now have more than 100,000 women doing time in U.S. prisons (Harrison & Beck, 2004, p. 1). Women's incarceration in the United States not only grew during the past century but also increased tenfold; and virtually all of that increase occurred in the final two decades of the century.

The number of women sentenced to jail and prison began to soar at precisely the same time that prison systems in the United States moved into an era that abandoned any pretense of rehabilitation in favor of punishment. As noted earlier, decades of efforts by conservative politicians to fashion a crime policy that would challenge the gains of the civil rights movement as well as other progressive movements in the 1960s and 1970s had, by the 1980s, born fruit (Chambliss, 1999). Exploiting the public fear of crime, particularly crime committed by "the poor, mostly nonwhite, young, male inner-city dwellers" (Irwin, 2005, p. 8), all manner of mean-spirited crime policies where adopted. The end of the past century saw the war on drugs and a host of other "get tough" sentencing policies, all of which fueled mass imprisonment (see Mauer, 1999). The period also saw the development of what Irwin (2005) has called "warehouse prisons," a correctional regime that focuses on a physical plant designed to control (not reform), rigid enforcement of extensive rules, and easy transfer of unruly prisoners to even more draconian settings.

Although feminist legal scholars can and do debate whether equality under the law is necessarily good for women (see Chesney-Lind & Pollock-Byrne, 1995), a careful look at what has happened to women in U.S. prisons might serve as a disturbing case study of how correctional equity is implemented in practice. Such a critical review is particularly vital in an era where decontextualized notions of gender and race "dis-crimination" are increasingly and successfully deployed against the achievements of both the civil rights and women's movements (Pincus, 2001/2002).

Consider the account of Martha Sierra's experience of childbirth. As she

> writhed in pain at a Riverside hospital, laboring to push her baby into the world, Sierra faced a challenge not covered in the childbirth books: her wrists were shackled to the bed. Unable to roll on her side or even sit straight up, Sierra managed as best she could. The reward was fleeting . . . she watched as her daughter, hollering and flapping her arms, was taken from the room. (Warren, 2005, p. A1)

As difficult as it was to talk about giving birth while serving time in prison, Sierra was particularly "distressed and puzzled" by her medical treatment: "Did they think I was going to get up and run away?" asked the 28-year-old California prisoner (Warren, 2005, p. A1).

Sierra's story is unfortunately all too familiar to anyone who examines gender themes in modern correctional responses to women inmates. In fact, her experience is less horrific than the case of Michelle T., a former prisoner from Michigan who told Human Rights Watch (1996) that she was accompanied by two male correctional officers into the delivery room:

> According to Michelle T., the officers handcuffed her to the bed while she was in labor and positioned themselves where they could view her genital area while giving birth. She told [Human Rights Watch] they made derogatory comments about her throughout the delivery. (p. 249)

Basically, male prisoners have long used visits to hospitals as opportunities to escape, so correctional regimes have generated extensive security precautions to assure that escapes do not occur, including shackling prisoners to hospital beds (Amnesty International, 1999, p. 63). This is the dark side of the equity or parity model of justice—one which emphasizes treating women offenders as though they were men, particularly when the outcome is punitive, in the name of equal justice—a pattern that could be called vengeful equity.

Vengeful equity could have no better spokesperson than Sheriff Joe Arpaio who, when he defended his controversial chain gang for women in Maricopa County, Arizona, proclaimed himself an "equal opportunity incarcerator" and went on to explain his controversial move by saying,

> If women can fight for their country, and bless them for that, if they can walk a beat, if they can protect the people and arrest violators of the law, then they should have no problem with picking up trash in 120 degrees. (Kim, 1996, p. A1)

Other examples of vengeful equity can be found in the creation of women's boot camps, often modeled on the gender regimes found in military basic training. These regimes, complete with uniforms, shorn hair, humiliation, exhausting physical training, and harsh punishment for even minor misconduct have been traditionally devised to "make men out of boys." As such, feminist researchers who have examined them contended, they "have more to do with the rites of manhood" than the needs of the typical woman in prison (Morash & Rucker, 1990).

Although these examples might be seen as extreme, legal readings by correctional administrators and others that define any attention to legitimate gender differences as "illegal" have clearly produced troubling outcomes. It is obviously misguided to treat women as if they were men with reference to cross-gender supervision, strip searches, and other correctional regimes while ignoring the ways in which women's imprisonment has unique features (such as pregnancy and vulnerability to sexual assault). Recently, this approach has been correctly identified by Human Rights Watch (1996) as a major contributing factor to the sexual abuse of women inmates.

Reviewing the situation of women incarcerated in five states (California, Georgia, Michigan, Illinois, and New York) and the District of Columbia, Human Rights Watch (1996) concluded,

> Our findings indicate that being a woman prisoner in U.S. state prisons can be a terrifying experience. If you are sexually abused, you cannot escape from your abuser. Grievance or investigatory procedures where they exist, are often ineffectual, and correctional employees continue to engage in abuse because they believe they will rarely be held accountable, administratively or criminally. Few people outside the prison walls know what is going on or care if they do know. Fewer still do anything to address the problem. (p. 1)
>
> Human Rights Watch also noted that their investigators were "concerned that states' adherence to U.S. anti-discrimination laws, in the absence of strong safeguards against custodial sexual misconduct, has often come at the fundamental rights of prisoners." (p. 2)

Institutional subcultures in women's prisons, which encourage correctional officers to "cover" for each other, coupled with inadequate protection accorded women who file complaints, make it unlikely that many women prisoners will formally complain about abuse. In addition, the public stereotype of women in prison as bad makes it difficult for a woman inmate to support her case against a correctional officer in court. Finally, what little progress has been made is now threatened by recent legislation that curtails the ability of prisoners and advocates to commence a legal action concerning prison conditions (Stein, 1996, p. 24).

Finally, it appears that women in prison today are also recipients of some of the worst of the more traditional, separate-spheres approach to women offenders (which tends to emphasize gender difference and the need to focus on "saving" women by policing even minor behaviors, particularly sexual behaviors; Rafter, 1990). Correctional officers often count on the fact that women prisoners will complain, not riot, and as a result, often punish women inmates for offenses that would be ignored in male prisons. McClellan (1994) found this pattern quite clearly in her examined disciplinary practices in Texas prisons. Following up two cohorts of prisoners (one male and one female), she found most men in her sample (63.5%) but only a handful of women (17.1%) had no citation or only one citation for a rule violation. McClellan found that women prisoners not only received numerous citations but also were charged with different infractions than men. Most frequent, women were cited for "violating posted rules," whereas males were cited most often for "refusing to work" (McClellan, 1994, p. 77). Women were more likely than men to receive the most severe sanctions.

McClellan (1994) noted that the wardens of the women's prisons in her study stated quite frankly that they demand total compliance with every rule on the books and punish violations through official mechanisms. McClellan concluded by observing that there exists

> two distinct institutional forms of surveillance and control operating at the male and female facilities. . . . This policy not only imposes extreme constraints on adult women but also costs the people of the State of Texas a great deal of money. (p. 87)

Much good, early feminist criminology focuses on the conditions of girls and women in training schools, jails, and prisons (see Burkhart, 1976; Carlen, 1983; Faith, 1993; Freedman, 1981). Unfortunately, that work is now made much harder by a savvy correctional system that is extremely reluctant to admit researchers, unless the focus of the research is clearly the woman prisoner and not the institution. That said, there is much more need for this sort of criminology in the era of mass punishment, and the work that is being done in this vein (see Bloom, 2003; Owen, 1998) points to the need for much of the same. Huge numbers of imprisoned girls and women are targeted by male-based systems of "risk" and "classification" (Hannah-Moffat & Shaw, 2003) and then subjected to male-based interventions such as "cognitive behaviorism" to address their "criminal" thinking as though they were men (Kendall & Pollack, 2003). Good work has also been done on the overuse of "chemical restraints" with women offenders (Auerhahn & Leonard, 2000; Leonard, 2002). In short, as difficult as it might be to do, in this era of mass imprisonment, feminist criminology needs to find creative ways to continue to engage core issues in girls' and women's carceral control as a central part of our intellectual and activist agenda. As Adrian Howe (1994) put it, "Academics must not let 'theoretical rectitude' deter them from committing themselves as *academics* and *feminists* to campaigns on behalf of women lawbreakers" (p. 214).

Theorizing Patriarchy: Concluding Thoughts

In 1899, Jane Addams was asked to address the American Academy of Political and Social Science. She took the occasion to reflect on the role of the social science of her day:

> As the college changed from teaching theology to teaching secular knowledge the test of its success should have shifted from the power to save men's souls to the power to adjust them in healthful relations to nature and their fellow men. But the college failed to do this, and made the test of its success the mere collecting and dissemination of knowledge, elevating the means unto an end and falling in love with its own achievement. (Addams, 1899, pp. 339–340)

Perhaps Addams's use of the generic *he* to describe the universities of her day was more a simple convention. Recall that when Addams worked in Chicago, criminology as a discipline was taking shape at the University of Chicago, whose researchers often relied heavily on contacts made at Hull House while systematically excluding women from its faculty ranks and distancing themselves from the female-dominated field of social work (see Deegan, 1988).

How do we avoid the pitfalls Addams (1899) observed in the male-dominated criminology of her day? This article argues that although feminist criminology has made a clear contribution to what might be described as the criminological project, it is positioned to play an even more central role in the era of political backlash. Certainly, we, as feminist scholars, shoulder many burdens, but perhaps the most daunting is the one articulated by

Liz Kelly (as quoted in Heidensohn, 1995): "Feminist research investigates aspects of women's oppression while seeking at the same time to be a part of the struggle against it" (p. 71).

For feminist criminology to remain true to its progressive origins in very difficult times, we must seek ways to blend activism with our scholarship (and senior scholars, in particular, need to make the academy safe for their junior colleagues to do just that by redefining tenure criteria to make this work a part of "scholarship"). We must discuss the many tensions and difficulties with this work, again in an era of backlash when the right is actively patrolling faculty behavior (Horowitz & Collier, 1994), and be honest about the many challenges ahead. We must create venues for feminist criminology, including peer-reviewed journals (such as *Critical Criminology*, *Feminist Criminology*, and *Women & Criminal Justice*) while also writing for broader audiences, particularly practitioners and policy makers (see *Women, Girls & Criminal Justice*). We must engage in continued activism on the part of girls and women who are the victims of crimes and whose very experiences are being trivialized by well-funded backlash research (Hoff Sommers, 1994) while also documenting the problems those same girls and women have when they take their cases to court (see Estrich, 1987; Matoesian, 1993). It means close attention and continued vigilance about the situations of women working in various aspects of the criminal justice system, particularly as the right wing cynically appropriates concepts such as discrimination. Finally, and most important, it means activism on behalf of criminalized girls and women, the least powerful and most marginalized of all those we study.

Again, given the focus of the backlash, this article argues that feminist criminology is uniquely positioned to do important work to challenge the current political backlash. To do so effectively, however, it is vital that in addition to documenting that gender matters in the lives of criminalized women, we engage in exploration of the interface between systems of oppression based on gender, race, and class. This work will allow us to make sense of current crime-control practices, particularly in an era of mass incarceration, so that we can explain the consequences to a society that might well be ready to hear other perspectives on crime control if given them (consider the success of drug courts and some initiatives that encourage alternatives to incarceration; Mauer, 2002). Researching as well as theorizing both patriarchy and gender is crucial to feminist criminology so that we can craft work, as the right wing does so effectively, that speaks to backlash initiatives in smart, media-savvy ways. To do this well means foregrounding the role of race and class in our work on gender and crime, as the work showcased here makes clear. There is simply no other way to make sense of key trends in both the media construction of women offenders and the criminal justice response that increasingly awaits them, particularly once they arrive in prison.

Finally, we must also do work that will document and challenge the policy and research backlash aimed at the hard fought and vitally important feminist and civil rights victories of the past century. To do any less would be unthinkable to those who fought so long to get us where we are today, and so it must be for us.

Notes

1. One might cite the appearance of the classic special issue on women and crime of *Issues in Criminology*, edited by Dorie Klein and June Kress (1973); two important books on the topic of women and crime by Rita Simon (1975) and Freda Adler (1975); and the publication of Del Martin's (1977) *Battered Wives* and Carol Smart's (1976) *Women, Crime and Criminology*.

2. Early but important exceptions to this generalization are Klein and Kress (1973), Smart (1976), Crites (1976), Bowker, Chesney-Lind, and Pollock (1978), Chapman (1980), and Jones (1980). There has also been an encouraging outpouring of more recent work on women offenders in the past decade. See Belknap (2001), Chesney-Lind and Pasko (2004), and DeKeseredy (1999) for reviews of this recent work.

3. Sex-gender systems include the following elements: (a) the social construction of gender categories on the basis of biological sex, (b) a sexual division of labor in which specific tasks are allocated on the basis of sex, and (c) the social regulation of sexuality, in which particular forms of sexual expression are positively and negatively sanctioned (Renzetti & Curran, 1999, p. 3).

4. I owe this analogy to Frank Zimring who, in response to a question from a reporter, quipped, "Women's liberation didn't turn girls into boys—violence is still particularly male. There has been much more diversification of gender roles on the soccer field than the killing field" (Ryan, 2003, p. 2).

References

Addams, J. (1899). A function of the social settlement. *Annals of the Academy of Political and Social Science, 13*, 323–345.

Adler, F. (1975). *Sisters in crime*. New York: McGraw-Hill.

American Bar Association and the National Bar Association. (2001, May 1). *Justice by gender: The lack of appropriate prevention, diversion and treatment alternatives for girls in the justice system*. Retrieved from http://www.abanet.org/crimjust/juvjus/justicebygenderweb.pdf

Amnesty International. (1999). *Not part of my sentence: Violations of the human rights of women in custody*. Washington, DC: Author.

Anderson, C. (2003, October 28). Women making gains in dubious profession: Crime. *Arizona Star*, p. A1.

Arnold, R. (1995). Processes of criminalization: From girlhood to womanhood. In M. B. Zinn & B. T. Dill (Eds.), *Women of color in American society* (pp. 136–146). Philadelphia: Temple University Press.

Auerhahn, K., & Leonard, E. (2000). Docile bodies? Chemical restraints and the female inmate. *The Journal of Criminal Law and Criminology, 90*(2), 599–634.

Barak, G. (1988). Newsmaking criminology: Reflections on the media, intellectuals, and crime. *Justice Quarterly, 5*(4), 565–587.

Belknap, J. (2001). *The invisible woman: Gender, crime and justice* (2nd ed.). Belmont, CA: Wadsworth.

Bible, A. (1998). When battered women are charged with assault. *Double-Time, 6*(1/2), 8–10.

Bloom, B. (Ed.). (2003). *Gendered justice*. Durham, NC: Carolina Academic Press.

Bloom, B., & Chesney-Lind, M. (2003). Women in prison: Vengeful equity. In R. Muraskin (Ed.), *It's a crime: Women and the criminal justice system* (pp. 175–195). New Jersey: Prentice Hall.

Bourgois, P., & Dunlap, E. (1993). Exorcising sex–for crack: An ethnographic perspective from Harlem. In M. Ratner (Ed.), *The crack pipe as pimp* (pp. 97–132). New York: Lexington Books.

Bowker, L. (Ed.). (1998). *Masculinities and violence*. Thousand Oaks, CA: Sage.

Bowker, L., Chesney-Lind, M., & Pollock, J. (1978). *Women, crime, and the criminal justice system*. Lexington, MA: D. C. Heath.

Brecht, B. (1966). *Galileo* (E. Bentley, Ed., C. Laughton, Trans.). New York: Grove.

Brown, M. (1997, December 7). Arrests of women soar in domestic assault cases. *Sacramento Bee*. Retrieved July 31, 2005, from http://www.sacbee.com/static/archive/news/projects/violence/part12.html

Burkhart, K. W. (1976). *Women in prison*. New York: Popular Library.

Bush-Baskette, S. (1998). The war on drugs as a war against Black women. In S. L. Miller (Ed.), *Crime control and women* (pp. 113–129). Thousand Oaks, CA: Sage.

Buzawa, E., & Buzawa, C. G. (1990). *Domestic violence: The criminal justice response*. Newbury Park, CA: Sage.

Cain, M. (1990). Realist philosophy and standpoint epistemologies or feminist criminology as a successor science. In L. Gelsthorpe & A. Morris (Eds.), *Feminist perspectives in criminology* (pp. 124–140). Buckingham, UK: Open University Press.

Carlen, P. (1983). *Women's imprisonment: A study in social control*. London: Routledge.

Chambliss, W. (1999). *Power, politics and crime*. Boulder, CO: Westview.

Chapman, J. R. (1980). *Economic realities and the female offender*. Lexington: Lexington Books.

Chesney-Lind, M. (1988, July–August). Doing feminist criminology. *The Criminologist, 13*, 16–17.

Chesney-Lind, M. (1989). Girls' crime and woman's place: Toward a feminist model of female delinquency. *Crime & Delinquency, 35*(10), 5–29.

Chesney-Lind, M. (2004, August). Girls and violence: Is the gender gap closing? *National Electronic Network on Violence Against Women*. Retrieved from http://www.vawnet.org/DomesticViolence/Research/VAWnetDocs/ARGirlsViolence.php

Chesney-Lind, M., & Belknap, J. (2004). Trends in delinquent girls' aggression and violent behavior: A review of the evidence. In M. Putallaz & P. Bierman (Eds.), *Aggression, antisocial behavior and violence among girls: A development perspective* (pp. 203–222). New York: Guilford.

Chesney-Lind, M., & Eliason, M. (in press). From invisible to incorrigible: The demonization of marginalized women and girls. *Crime, Media, Culture: An International Journal.*

Chesney-Lind, M., & Hagedorn, J. M. (Eds.). (1999). *Female gangs in America: Essays on gender and gangs*. Chicago: Lakeview Press.

Chesney-Lind, M., & Irwin, K. (2004). From badness to meanness: Popular constructions of contemporary girlhood. In A. Harris (Ed.), *All about the girl: Culture, power, and identity* (pp. 45–56). New York: Routledge.

Chesney-Lind, M., & Irwin, K. (2005). Still "the best place to conquer girls": Gender and juvenile justice. In J. Pollock-Byrne & A. Merlo (Eds.), *Women, law, and social control* (pp. 271–291). Boston: Allyn & Bacon.

Chesney-Lind, M., & Pasko, L. (2004). *The female offender*. Thousand Oaks, CA: Sage.

Chesney-Lind, M., & Pollock-Byrne, J. (1995). Women's prisons: Equality with a vengeance. In J. Pollock-Byrne & A. Merlo (Eds.), *Women, law, and social control* (pp. 155–176). Boston: Allyn & Bacon.

Chesney-Lind, M., & Rodriguez, N. (1983). Women under lock and key. *The Prison Journal, 63*, 47–65.

Chesney-Lind, M., & Shelden, R. G. (1992). *Girls, delinquency and juvenile justice*. Belmont, CA: Wadsworth.

Comack, E., Chopyk, V., & Wood, L. (2000). *Mean streets? The social locations, gender dynamics, and patterns of violent crime in Winnipeg*. Ottawa, Ontario: Canadian Centre for Policy Alternatives.

Connell, R. W. (2002). *Gender*. Cambridge, UK: Polity.

Crenshaw, H. (1994). Mapping the margins: Intersectionality, identity politics, and violence against women of color. In M. A. Fineman & R. Mykitiuk (Eds.), *The public nature of private violence* (pp. 93–118). New York: Routledge.

Crites, L. (Ed.). (1976). *The female offender*. Lexington, MA: Lexington Books.

Daly, K., & Chesney-Lind, M. (1988). Feminism and criminology. *Justice Quarterly*, *5*(4), 497–538.

Deegan, M. J. (1988). *Jane Addams and the men of the Chicago School, 1892–1918*. New Brunswick, NJ: Transaction Books.

DeKeseredy, W. (1999). *Women, crime, and the Canadian criminal justice system*. Cincinnati, OH: Anderson.

DeKeseredy, W., Sanders, D., Schwartz, M., & Alvi, S. (1997). The meanings and motives for women's use of violence in Canadian college dating relationships. *Sociological Spectrum*, *17*, 199–222.

DeKeseredy, W., & Schwartz, M. (1998, February). *Measuring the extent of woman abuse in intimate heterosexual relationships: A critique of the conflict tactics scales*. Retrieved from VAWnet Web site: http://www.vawnet.org/DomesticViolence/Research/VAWnetDocs/AR_ctscrit.php

Dziech, B. W., & Weiner, L. (1984). *The lecherous professor*. Boston: Beacon.

Estrich, S. (1987). *Real rape*. Cambridge, MA: Harvard University Press.

Faith, K. (1993). *Unruly women: The politics of confinement & resistance*. Vancouver, British Columbia, Canada: Press Gang.

Faludi, S. (1991). *Backlash: The undeclared war against American women*. New York: Anchor Doubleday.

Federal Bureau of Investigation. (2004). *Crime in the United States, 2003*. Washington, DC: Government Printing Office.

Ferraro, K. (2001). Women battering: More than a family problem. In C. Renzetti & L. Goodstein (Eds.), *Women, crime and criminal justice* (pp. 135–153). Los Angeles: Roxbury.

Ford, R. (1998, May 24). The razor's edge. *Boston Globe Magazine*, pp. 3, 22–28.

Freedman, E. (1981). *Their sisters' keepers: Women and prison reform, 1830–1930*. Ann Arbor: University of Michigan Press.

Gilbert, E. (2001). Women, race, and criminal justice processing. In C. Renzetti & L. Goodstein (Eds.), *Women, crime and criminal justice* (pp. 222–231). Los Angeles: Roxbury.

Gilfus, M. (1992). From victims to survivors to offenders: Women's routes of entry into street crime. *Women & Criminal Justice*, *4*(1), 63–89.

Goldstein, A., Smith, J., & Becker, J. (2005, August 19). Roberts resisted women's rights. *Washington Post*, p. A1.

Gora, J. (1982). *The new female criminal: Empirical reality or social myth*. New York: Praeger.

Greenfeld, A., & Snell, T. (1999). *Women offenders: Bureau of Justice Statistics, special report*. Washington, DC: U.S. Department of Justice.

Guido, M. (1998, June 4). In a new twist on equality, girls' crimes resemble boys'. *San Jose Mercury News*, p. 1B-4B.

Hannah-Moffat, K., & Shaw, M. (2003). The meaning of "risk" in women's prisons: A critique. In B. Bloom (Ed.), *Gendered justice* (pp. 25–44). Durham, NC: Carolina Academic Press.

Hardisty, J. V. (2000). *Mobilizing resentment*. Boston: Beacon.

Harms, P. (2002, January). *Detention in delinquency cases, 1989-1998* (OJJDP Fact Sheet No. 1). Washington, DC: U.S. Department of Justice.

Harrison, P. M., & Beck, A. J. (2004). *Prisoners in 2003*. Washington, DC: U.S. Department of Justice, Bureau of Justice Statistics.

Heidensohn, F. (1995). Feminist perspectives and their impact on criminology and criminal justice in Britain. In N. H. Rafter & F. Heidensohn (Eds.), *International feminist perspectives in criminology* (pp. 63–85). Buckingham, UK: Open University Press.

Hoff Sommers, C. (1994). *Who stole feminism? How women have betrayed women*. New York: Simon & Schuster.

Horowitz, D., & Collier, P. (1994). *The heterodoxy handbook: How to survive the PC campus*. Lanham, MD: National Book Network.

Horton, J. O., & Horton, L. (2005). *Slavery and the making of America*. Oxford, UK: Oxford University Press.

Howe, A. (1994). *Punish and critique: Towards a feminist analysis of penality*. London: Routledge.

Human Rights Watch. (1996). *All too familiar: Sexual abuse of women in U.S. state prisons*. New York: Human Rights Watch.

Human Rights Watch. (2000, May). Punishment and prejudice: Racial disparities in the war on drugs. *Human Rights Watch Reports*, *12*(2). Available from http://www.hrw.org/reports/2000/usa

Irwin, J. (2005). *The warehouse prison*. Los Angeles: Roxbury.

Joe, K. (1995). Ice is strong enough for a man but made for a woman: A social cultural analysis of methamphetamine use among Asian Pacific Americans. *Crime, Law and Social Change*, *22*, 269–289.

Johnson, P. (2003). *Inner lives: Voices of African American women in prison*. New York: New York University Press.

Jones, A. (1980). *Women who kill*. New York: Fawcett Columbine.

Kelly, D. M. (1993). *Last chance high: How girls and boys drop in and out of alternative schools*. New Haven, CT: Yale University Press.

Kendall, K., & Pollack, S. (2003). Cognitive behaviorism in women's prisons. In B. Bloom (Ed.), *Gendered justice* (pp. 69–96). Durham, NC: Carolina Academic Press.

Kim, E.-K. (1996, August 26). Sheriff says he'll have chain gangs for women. *Tuscaloosa News*, p. A1.

Klein, D., & Kress, J. (Eds.). (1973). Women, crime and criminology [Special issue]. *Issues in Criminology, 8*(3).

Lantigua, J. (2001, April 30). How the GOP gamed the system in Florida. *The Nation*, pp. 1–8.

Leonard, E. (2002). *Convicted survivors: The imprisonment of battered women.* New York: New York University Press.

Maher, L., & Curtis, R. (1992). Women on the edge: Crack cocaine and the changing contexts of street-level sex work in New York City. *Crime, Law and Social Change, 18*, 221–258.

Martin, D. (1977). *Battered wives.* New York: Pocket Books.

Martin, S. (1980). *Breaking and entering: Police women on patrol.* Berkeley: University of California Press.

Matoesian, G. (1993). *Reproducing rape domination through talk in the courtroom.* Chicago: University of Chicago Press.

Mauer, M. (1999). *Race to incarcerate.* New York: New Press.

Mauer, M. (2002). State sentencing reforms: Is the "get tough" era coming to a close. *Federal Sentencing Reporter, 15*, 50–52.

Mauer, M., & Chesney-Lind, M. (Eds.). (2002). *Invisible punishment: The collateral consequences of mass imprisonment.* New York: New Press.

Mauer, M., & Huling, T. (1995). *Young Black Americans and the criminal justice system: Five years later.* Washington, DC: The Sentencing Project.

Maxwell, C., Garner, J. H., & Fagan, J. A. (2002). The preventive effects of arrest on intimate partner violence: Research, policy and theory. *Criminology & Public Policy, 2*(1), 51–80.

McClellan, D. S. (1994). Disparity in the discipline of male and female inmates in Texas prisons. *Women & Criminal Justice, 5*(20), 71–97.

Messerschmidt, J. W. (2000). *Nine lives: Adolescent masculinities, the body, and violence.* Boulder, CO: Westview.

Miller, J. (2001). *One of the guys: Girls, gangs, and gender.* New York: Oxford University Press.

Miller, J., & Mullins, C. (2005). *Taking stock: The status of feminist theories in criminology.* Unpublished manuscript.

Miller, S. (1989). Unintended side effects of pro-arrest policies and their race and class implications for battered women: A cautionary note. *Criminal Justice Policy Review, 3*, 299–317.

Miller, S. (2005). *Victims as offenders: Women's use of violence in relationships.* New Brunswick, NJ: Rutgers University Press.

Moore, J. (1991). *Going down to the barrio: Homeboys and homegirls in change.* Philadelphia: Temple University Press.

Morash, M., & Rucker, L. (1990). A critical look at the idea of boot camp as a correctional reform. *Crime & Delinquency, 36*(2), 204–222.

Owen, B. (1998). *"In the mix": Struggle and survival in a women's prison.* Albany: State University of New York Press.

Pincus, F. (2001/2002). The social construction of reverse discrimination: The impact of affirmative action on Whites. *Journal of Inter-Group Relations, 38*(4), 33–44.

Pollak, O. (1950). *The criminality of women.* Philadelphia: University of Pennsylvania Press.

Pollock, J. (1999). *Criminal women.* Cincinnati, OH: Anderson.

Rafter, N. H. (1990). *Partial justice: Women, prisons and social control.* New Brunswick, NJ: Transaction Books.

Rafter, N. H. (Ed.). (2000). *Encyclopedia of women and crime.* Phoenix, AZ: Oryx Press.

Renzetti, C., & Curran, D. J. (1999). *Women, men and society.* Boston: Allyn & Bacon.

Richie, B. (1996). *Compelled to crime: The gender entrapment of battered Black women.* New York: Routledge.

Rush, F. (1980). *The best kept secret: Sexual abuse of children.* New York: McGraw-Hill.

Russell, D. (1986). *The secret trauma.* New York: Basic Books.

Ryan, J. (2003, September 5). Girl gang stirs up false gender issue: Data show no surge in female violence. *San Francisco Chronicle*, p. 2.

Scelfo, J. (2005, June 13). Bad girls go wild. *Newsweek.* Retrieved July 31, 2005, from http://www.msnbcnsn.com/id.8101517/site/newsweek/page/2

Schecter, S. (1982). *Women and male violence: The visions and struggles of the battered women's movement.* Boston: South End.

Scully, D. (1990). *Understanding sexual violence.* Boston: Unwin Hyman.

Sherman, L. W., & Berk, R. A. (1984). The specific deterrent effects of arrest for domestic assault. *American Sociological Review, 49*(1), 261–272.

Simon, R. (1975). *Women and crime.* Lexington, MA: Lexington Books.

Smart, C. (1976). *Women, crime and criminology: A feminist critique.* London: Routledge Kegan Paul.

Smith, L. (1996, November 18). Increasingly, abuse shows a female side: More women accused of domestic violence. *Washington Post*, p. B1.

Steffensmeier, D. J. (1980). Sex differences in patterns of adult crime, 1965–1977. *Social Forces, 58*, 1080–1108.

Steffensmeier, D. J., Schwartz, J., Zhong, H., & Ackerman, J. (2005). An assessment of recent trends in girls' violence using diverse longitudinal sources. *Criminology, 43*, 355–406.

Steffensmeier, D. J., & Steffensmeier, R. H. (1980). Trends in female delinquency: An examination of arrest, juvenile court, self-report, and field data. *Criminology, 18*, 62–85.

Stein, B. (1996, July). Life in prison: Sexual abuse. *The Progressive*, 23–24.

Thorne, B. (1993). *Gender play.* New Brunswick, NJ: Rutgers University Press.

Warren, J. (2005, June 19). Rethinking treatment of female prisoners. *Los Angeles Times*, p. A1.

Websdale, N., & Alvarez, A. (1997). Forensic journalism as patriarchal ideology: The newspaper construction of homicide-suicide. In D. Hale & F. Bailey (Eds.), *Popular culture, crime and justice* (pp. 123–141). Belmont, CA: Wadsworth.

Weis, J. G. (1976). "Liberation and crime": The invention of the new female criminal. *Crime and Social Justice, 6*, 17–27.

West, C., & Zimmerman, D. H. (1987). Doing gender. *Gender & Society, 1*, 125–151.

Wichita Police Department. (2002). *Domestic violence statistics: 2001.* Retrieved from http://wichitapolice.com/DV/DV_statistics.htm

Williams, L. S. (2002). Trying on gender, gender regimes, and the process of becoming women. *Gender & Society, 16*, 29–52.

REVIEW QUESTIONS

1. What does the author mean when she claims there is a contemporary "backlash" against feminist criminology?
2. What are the primary reasons the author believes that combining gender with race will lead to a better understanding of criminality as well as more fairness in handling by the criminal justice system?
3. What does the author mean when she discusses the term *vengeful equity*?
4. What are some of the unique needs of certain populations (e.g., women, especially single mothers) that are not adequately addressed by the criminal justice system, particularly in cases of incarceration?

READING /// 25

This qualitative piece examines female criminality with an emphasis on an intimate understanding of the intersections of systems of oppression that emanate from power structures that uniquely shape the life of females, particularly those that have been criminals. This reading also includes a specific case study of a woman who engaged in criminal activity and examines the specific factors that contributed to her decisions to engage in such activity.

While reading this article, one should consider the following points:

- The author's emphasis on examining "differential identity"
- The author's use of Merton's strain theory as the framework for examining female criminal activity in this reading
- Regarding the case study in this article, the types of factors that the author focuses on in explaining female criminality, and the author's claim of the most significant differences from explaining male offending behavior

The Intersectional Alternative

Explaining Female Criminality

April Bernard

Introduction

Female criminality has been explained from a variety of feminist perspectives; marginalization from conventional institutions, disrupted family and personal relationships, and institutionalized racism, sexism, and economic disadvantage have all been explored as explanations for the involvement of women in crime (Broidy & Agnew, 1997; Chesney-Lind, 1986, 1997; Daly & Chesney-Lind, 1988; Owen, 1998; Ritchie, 2004). Marginalized women involved in crimes tend to be young, poor, non-white, high school dropouts, unmarried mothers, un-/under-employed and educated, with a history of drug problems, family violence, and sexual abuse. The vulnerabilities that color the

SOURCE: April Bernard, "The Intersectional Alternative: Explaining Female Criminality," *Feminist Criminology* 8, no. 1 (2013): 3–19.

lives of marginalized women can be difficult to measure due to the overlapping influence or intersectionality of multiple forms of subjugation such as ingrained racism, sexism, economic disadvantage, abuse, exploitation, and the historical undervaluation of women in society (Collins, 2000; Kelly, 1994).

The need for grounding theorizing about women's criminality in an understanding of intersecting identities that emerge from cross-cutting systems of oppression has been emphasized in Black and multiracial feminist and criminology analyses (Baca Zinn & Thornton Dill, 1996; Barak, 1998; Beale, 1995; Belknap, 2001; Britton, 2004; Brown, 2010; Burgess-Proctor, 2006; Collins, 2000; Daly & Stephens, 1995; Gordon, 1987; King, 1988; Potter, 2006; Ritchie, 1996; Wing, 2003). Collins describes this intersectionality as functioning within matrices of domination that represent amalgamations of micro- through macro-level power structures and interrelated systems of oppression. The historically and socially specific ways in which these power structures are constructed and systems of oppression are blended create different kinds of social realities, identities, and experiences. This analysis uses an intersectional approach to provide an explanation of women's criminality in that it seeks to be grounded in an intimate understanding of the multiplicative, overlapping, and cumulative effects of the simultaneous intersections of oppressions that affect women's decisions to engage in crime.

This article begins by challenging aspects of malestream theorizing on crime that fail to capture the multiple forces that serve to construct gender realities (Carlen, 1985; Dekeseredy & Perry, 2006; Maidment, 2006). The significance of the intersectional approach is discussed as a viable alternative paradigm that recognizes the influence of multiple constraining factors on women's criminality. The concept of *doing identity* is then introduced to describe the unique attempts of individuals, particularly marginalized women, to navigate through power structures and multiple systems of oppression that shape their life experiences. A case study consisting of an exploration of factors contributing to one woman's decision to engage in criminal activity as a means of doing identity is presented. The importance of this intersectional model for feminist criminology is underscored through a discussion of implications and recommendations for theoretical praxis, policy, and programmatic provisions.

Alternative Theorizing: Strained or Constrained Realities

The primary tenet underlying this alternative approach is that counter to malestream perspectives on crime, women's criminality may be best understood as an adverse response to a lack of legitimate means for women to demonstrate an authentic and efficacious identity that is unfettered by the constraining effects of intersecting systems of oppression. Although my critique seeks to offer an alternative to the malestreaming of mainstream criminal justice research in general, the intention is not to diminish the significance of any of these contributions.

This work should be understood as an attempt to encourage the extension of malestream theorizing on crime by acknowledging the potential of the intersectional approach to encompass the complexities of the realities that are faced by marginalized women. In this vein, an analysis of Merton's strain theory using an alternative intersectional perspective is provided as one, but not the only, example of the limitations of malestream theorizing in general on women's criminality. This application of an intersectional perspective on Merton's strain theory is one demonstration of the need for more in-depth analyses of the underlying causes and complexities that influence women's decisions to engage in crime that hopefully will encourage further intersectional analyses of this and other theories in the future.

According to Merton (1968) deviance is an adaptive response to a lack of legitimate means to achieve shared cultural goals. A commitment to the cultural goals and institutionalized means for success results in conformity, yet when access to the institutionalized means for success is strained or limited (typically due to differences in class), innovative attempts to achieve and retain shared cultural goals are forwarded. Deviance and crime increase in society when the option to conform is not accepted and this innovation results in illegitimate means to achieve success.

Merton viewed the rejection of cultural goals and/or institutional means as an innovative or adaptive response that occurs within an anomic context in which incongruence between shared cultural goals and institutional means for success exists. Strain, frustration, and stress result where goals exceed means. The alternative intersectional paradigm suggests that women's criminality may be more an expression of constrained rather than strained realities. This alternative approach de-emphasizes individual frustrations and pathologies and instead stresses the ways in which power structures and systems of oppression work to circumscribe the life experiences of persons socially located at the intersections of multiple vulnerabilities.

The proposed alternative framework also suggests that although there may exist agreement on the general nature of the cultural goals that are shared among the population in a society (such as obtaining an education, a job, a house, and a car in Westernized capitalist societies) as described by Merton, the specifics of each individual's desired goals and opportunities may differ in regard to quality and quantity. The intersections that shape unique experiences of privilege/oppression in turn foster the development of multiple realities in which one person's specific goals and opportunities to obtain a particular type of house, number of cars, or quality of education may be very distinct in comparison to another's. Having an understanding of an individual's specific desired goals and opportunities is therefore suggested as taking precedence over having knowledge of shared cultural goals and institutionalized means for success in explaining decisions to engage in criminal activity.

This alternative framework also reconstructs Merton's concept of a class differential and suggests that the disparities that influence access to opportunities and life outcomes represent the cumulative impact of the intersections of multiple inequalities/privileges including (but not limited to) race, class, and gender on the life experiences of individuals. The differential advantage some have over others is less a reflection of their individual merit and propensity toward conformity than of differences in power. The social, economic, and political place and space individuals hold within society relative to the legitimate means, resources, and opportunities for achieving some measure of success may be more or less constrained depending on the ways in which they affect and are affected by existing power structures and systems of oppression. Embedded within the concept of a matrix of domination is the recognition that to achieve the ideals of social justice and equality would require the reduction of the differential advantage of some over others through the restructuring of the domains of power (law, bureaucracy, culture and relationships/interactions) and the dismantling and eradication of their interconnections that function to maintain (and are maintained by) ideologies and systems of oppression that foster multiple and overlapping inequalities, including, but not limited to, race, class, and gender.

What affects an individual's access to legitimate means for success is not just about social capital, social networks, or other class indicators, but encompasses the micro- through macro-level social, sexual, national, economic, political, and other socially inherited and ascribed histories, norms, and social spaces an individual represents and encounters (Collins, 2000; Harding, 2004). This intersectional approach claims that social location, or the combination of micro- though macro-level social identities and social roles and relationships, is a primary contributing factor to decisions about criminality. The decision to engage in crime is influenced by the unique combination of factors that represent a particular social location regardless of an individual or group's relationship to income-generating resources and assets or differences in class as postulated by Merton. Social location can be described as the cumulative impact of intersections of oppression/privilege and represents the intercorrelation of multiple factors and conditions that are unique to each individual that influence his or her experiences, opportunities, and choices.

The significance of Merton's concept of institutionalized means is minimized in this alternative framework due to its ambiguity and the pejorative implications for developing policies that respond to the variety of social and economic conditions affecting marginalized populations. From this alternative perspective, the belief in the existence of omnipresent functional, normal, stable, fixed, and solid social structures, institutions, communities, families, opportunities, or *institutional means* (to which individuals can choose to conform, accept, or reject) requires rethinking to acknowledge the particular matrix of domination and systems of oppression and the fluidity of associated factors that characterize an individual's social and economic condition. The fluidity of relationships, norms, cultures, and institutions in global and modern societies has been identified as a key contributor to the growing sense of social isolation, decay, risk, and insecurity that depict the challenges of late modernity (Bauman, 2000; Beck, 1992). Instead of institutionalized means, emphasis in the proposed paradigm is placed on the acknowledgment of existing social contradictions (the limitations of capitalist ideology and the erosion of the American Dream), risk (the potential for victimization, exploitation, subjugation) and uncertainty (various forms of insecurity) within contemporary society that function to further disadvantage members of vulnerable populations.

This alternative theoretical framework challenges the assumption that the social contradictions, risk, and uncertainty that are evident in late modernity can be effectively managed through equal opportunity and antidiscrimination legislation, social control, and punitive reforms. The assumption that the impact of these factors on the ability of all individuals to cope with the challenge of navigating through the complexity of their vulnerabilities and inequalities toward achieving success can be mitigated through obedience to the law and conformity to dominant social norms is also challenged. This alternative framework acknowledges the relativity of deviance and rejects paradigms built upon the premise that deviance and conformity are dichotomous states rather than overlapping spheres of potential responses that can be differentially interpreted depending on the circumstances or context (Curra, 2000). What is deemed deviant in one community (fighting among youth, for example) may be viewed as good common sense in another.

Not all marginalized women resort to crime, and some affluent women seek illegitimate means to achieve their goals. Conformity in an intersectional context can be defined as individuals actively engaged in the process of constantly assessing and reassessing their goals and resigning themselves to accept those that can be achieved given their social location in relation to opportunities (means) amidst multiple inequalities, risks, and uncertainty that exist in society. For marginalized women, if the consequences of conformity may require an acceptance of a life that is less than their goals prescribe then crime may become an innovative response. What may distinguish the affluent female criminal from another of less wealth is that though both choose an illegitimate response to their circumstances, their opportunities and agency to commit crimes differ in regard to quality and consequences (Reiman, 2003).

When combined, the concepts of individual (rather than shared) goals for success, social location (as opposed to a class differential), and societal contradictions, insecurity, and risk (instead of institutionalized means) result in a differential means for "doing" identity (navigating through multiple inequalities to achieve a particular or individual-specific measure of success), which leads to an adaptive response that is more or less legitimate depending on the context. Doing identity can be described as a process of producing unique biographical solutions to systemic contradictions (Beck, 1992). This concept of "doing" identity is based on the work conducted by Carlen (1988) and Messerschmidt (1993) and their perspectives on crime for marginalized populations as an adaptive response to societal circumstances.

Pat Carlen (1988) addresses the issues of conformity, identity, and criminality among underclass women. Based on her study of 39 convicted women between the ages of 15 and 46, Carlen suggests that the cultural goals for success that govern the lives of women are influenced by two social compromises or deals related to gender and class. The *class deal* stipulates that women's conformity is motivated by the opportunity for them to earn their own wages and ultimately achieve financial success, or the "good life" as defined by the society, through their work in the public domain. The *gender deal* is motivated by the promise of a happy and fulfilling family life that is to result from the woman's labor for and love of a man who is the primary breadwinner. The gender deal breaks down when women are unable to obtain or maintain successful relationships with a male breadwinner, are abused, and/or socially isolated, and the class deal is compromised when women are unable to achieve financial success through work. Carlen's thesis is that women resort to crime when the class and/or gender deals break down.

Although Carlen's thesis is convincing, the question remains whether class and gender are the only socially relevant aspects of women's existence upon which deals can be made and whether there are other aspects of women's identities or social locations that significantly factor into their responses to adversity and potential criminality. The following analysis will also seek to reveal additional factors as well as consider Carlen's description of the class and gender deals as significant factors that influence women's adaptive responses to risk and contradictions in society.

Messerschmidt (1993) provides a gendered approach to the development of criminological theory to describe the relationship between masculinity and crime.

Messerschmidt suggests that to understand male behavior, including crime, one must begin by acknowledging the historical and social structural conditions that construct hegemonic masculine ideologies and social actions. He argues, "Hegemonic masculinity emphasizes practices toward authority, control, competitive individualism, independence, aggressiveness, and the capacity for violence" (p. 82). Crime, he observes, may be one way of "doing gender" or demonstrating one's masculinity, when legitimate means of demonstrating one's identity are stifled.

Messerschmidt's thesis is that crime as a means of "doing gender" becomes a form of social action or a practical response to structured opportunities and constraints in society that are related to class, race, and gender relationships. Although Messerschmidt's analysis does not involve women and emphasizes the construct of masculinity, I argue that it is not simply "doing masculinity" or "doing femininity" or "doing race" that is the issue, but rather "doing identity." How one navigates through multiple oppressions to achieve his or her desired goals and ultimately find space and place for self in contemporary capitalist society is a complex process of which an individual's sex, age, gender, sexual identity, race, nationality, class, level of education, and a host of other factors are significant components.

This alternative paradigm suggests that the issue of crime and women (and perhaps men) with multiple vulnerabilities can be explained based on an understanding of the process of *doing identity* or the process of becoming somebody (self-defined) while navigating through multiple social contradictions and inequalities. Becoming somebody requires individuals to draw upon complex and advanced decision-making capabilities that can be employed at life's perpetual crossroads to assess the vulnerabilities of their social location amidst the solid and liquid aspects of their reality. Here at the crossroads individuals are challenged with the task of identifying among the plethora of ends the ones that are reasonable and feasible given their social location, circumstances, and context (Bauman, 2000). Establishing priorities in a world that appears to be full of possibilities adds complexity to the challenge, and the uncertainty of life's comparative objectives is all the more perplexing to persons facing multiple vulnerabilities in the process of doing identity.

Method

The primary aim of the methodology was to utilize a feminist and interpretive approach to the data collection, interpretation, and analysis of the life stories and reflections of incarcerated women who have committed drug-related crimes (Denzin, 1989; Lynch, 1996; Oakley, 1981). Rather than seeking results that can be generalized to broader populations, the purpose of the methodology is to ground the findings in the standpoint of the women interviewed, and ultimately, to demystify and humanize their lived experiences and perspectives while providing a range of practical explanations of the choices and behavior of women involved in drug-related crimes. This preliminary analysis focuses on the life story of one young Afro-Caribbean woman who was incarcerated in 2010 due to a drug-related crime. This analysis begins with this single case of one woman as an intentional means of avoiding conundrums inherent in (a) positivists' research that tends to quantify experiences rather than validating nuances, difference, and the production of knowledge based on a single case, and (b) androcentric approaches that reinforce the "malestream" nature of criminology that often omit or misrepresent the experiences of women due to an emphasis on male crime (Belknap, 2001). The intention of this article is not to ignore men or avoid the rigors of scientific study involving multiple cases (both will be considered in future analysis), but simply to begin with the experiences of women, and in this case, one woman as the unit of analysis. The single case that was selected for this analysis is of a Jamaican female in her early 20s serving 2 years for attempting to transport marijuana from Jamaica to St. Maarten with the hope of earning US$900. For the purpose of telling her story, the pseudonym Angelique will be used when referring to the respondent.

The use of a single case as the unit of analysis also provides an opportunity to explore the unique ways in which the conceptual categories that make up the theoretical framework fit the particular case and allows the researcher to assess whether the constructs need further refinement before being applied to a broader set of cases. This process is purposefully iterative in nature and intends to reveal and refine conceptual categories that can be used to further feminist theorizing on the topic of women (and perhaps men) and crime.

In writing this analysis, a difficult methodological consideration I had to make was whether or not to point to a specific theory as an example of malestream criminological theorizing. I was initially uncomfortable with using Merton's strain theory directly as a means to demonstrate the significance of the intersectional approach for examining women's criminality, and I tried to avoid doing so by looking at "Strain Theories" in general, but the distractions were apparent. I then considered focusing on a single aspect of one strain theory, but that did not allow me to demonstrate the potential breadth and depth of the intersectional analytical approach. To more accurately describe Angelique's circumstances as *constrained* rather than *strained,* I felt strongly that I wanted to compare and contrast the intersectional approach with an existing theoretical framework as a means to develop salient alternative concepts in relation to the findings. With this as my motivation, I felt compelled to maintain a focus on Merton's strain theory, not as a critique of the significance of the theory, but as a means to encourage continued articulation and solidification of the intersectional approach as something distinct from, yet useful within existing theoretical traditions. The following analysis briefly describes one woman's process of navigating through multiple oppressions within a high-risk context and incorporates the concepts of (a) individual goals for success; (b) social location; (c) social contradictions, risk, and uncertainty; and (d) adaptive responses that include legitimate (legally sanctioned by dominant culture) versus illegitimate (illegal, yet sanctioned by subculture) means to achieve desired success. Together these concepts will be used to describe a unique attempt at *doing identity.*

Findings: There Is No Safe Place

A safe space, prison is not, but a correction facility may be the only environment where the extent to which inequality, deprivation, and the randomness of uncertainty that affect the lives of marginalized women is to some degree leveled, controlled, or restricted. In prison, there exists no class or gender deal that requires work or marriage to be successful, social location within the dominant social structure has limited significance, and the cultural goals for success are redefined to fit a new (although typically temporary) reality. Angelique's story will be discussed without a particular beginning or ending, using the concepts from the theoretical framework as a guide to explaining her journey toward crime.

Goals

Angelique states that she had her aspirations set on achieving her dream of "the good life," which for her meant "becoming somebody" and consisted of obtaining an education, a job, a house, and a future for her children:

> I wanted to better my life. I wanted to give my sons a future, a good life, an education—something I never get.
>
> I wanted to own a business—be a hair dresser and own a house. I had the dream. I went to cosmetology school and got a certificate. If my sister no die we would finish school together, save our money together and open a [beauty] parlor and buy a house together.

Angelique shared the socially sanctioned belief that all are entitled to seek an array of possibilities toward achieving the good life. She believed in the class deal that if she could only find a job and work hard that she could obtain financial prosperity. Her specific goals for success included becoming a hairdresser and working in collaboration with her sister to combine the resources necessary to start a business and buy a house. Although her goals seemed reasonable and feasible, Angelique's dream of owning a salon and a home was formally disrupted when her sister died. In time her commitment to finding legitimate means to achieve her dream of becoming somebody began to wane. She describes how she began to lose faith in her ability to achieve her goals:

> When I started college my sister died [her sister was killed by a distant relative]. From that time my life went down. We went to the same school, we were very close. After she died I lived care free.

Social Location

Unfortunately, Angelique's unique combination of social factors and conditions that influenced her reality included a history of sexual and physical abuse, family disruption, and marginalization from social, educational, and economic resources and support. Her environment was imbued with images that included men who distributed guns to young boys, young girls that danced at strip clubs, and adults and children struggling to survive by selling chicken on the roadside while others were selling drugs. She states, "In my area, people do what they can to survive." For Angelique these were the only examples and opportunities that were available, and it was within this limited and restricted reality that Angelique sought to achieve success.

Angelique's reality contradicted with her dream of becoming somebody. As a victim of ongoing abuse by her mother and her mother's boyfriend, Angelique found it difficult to reconcile to the fate she seemed to have inherited. Her attempts to try to find a solution to her circumstances were met with disdain; repeatedly, she was silenced or ignored:

> I lived with mother, my mother's boyfriend and six siblings in one bedroom house. My mother beat me all the while. I had to wash for she, her man, and my brothers and sisters. One time after she gave me lunch money, I put it down and her boyfriend took my lunch money and gone. So I asked someone in my yard (a neighbor) for lunch money and my mom chopped me with a knife.
>
> The worst of the abuse was at night. I slept on the ground and my mom, she boyfriend and my brother and sister slept in the bed. Him (the boyfriend) come down and abuse me every night. Me tell her and she never believe me. She love him more than me. He come on the ground and force my foot open every night. The first time I was 9 and this continued until I was 12. I continued to tell my mother what happened. One time she threw hot porridge on me to burn me and I ran. Then I start to runaway.

Compiled upon her experience of being repeatedly silenced at home was her feeling of being socially excluded at school. Angelique describes the first time she contemplated suicide:

> I felt like I was not human. Me don't feel like me loved. I tried to commit suicide when I was 10. My mom abuse me, he abuse me. I felt left out at school. My friends had a good life, and me no have none. She was at work and I tried to do it, then I say why kill myself. I said I will reach my goal and show my mother I can be somebody.

Angelique was not a good student academically and often got into fights at school. She stated she often felt angry at school due to her inability to discuss the victimization she experienced at home. She responded to her feelings of being excluded in school by dropping out and seeking the type of wage-paying employment that was available to young undereducated women in her neighborhood:

> I dropped out of school at age 16 and started to dance at a strip club. I made $600 JA [Jamaican dollars] a night plus tips, and I danced every day. I was able to pay some of my school fees and got in contact with my father and he helped pay my fees for me to start college [to become a hair dresser]. I danced naked freelance to make money. I had to take care of my children.

Angelique's early introduction into adulthood was void of legitimate opportunities to demonstrate the identity she sought to achieve. The abuse she suffered, the death of her sister, and the social exclusion she faced at school were a harsh introduction into the reality of the combined effects of multiple oppressions that shaped her social location and their unique impact on her ability to achieve her goals.

Contradiction and Risk

As a young adult, the only guides through the maze of uncertainty available to Angelique were the local examples of success that she befriended and others to whom she was related. All of them were engaged in socially deviant behavior. Angelique's first child was born when she was 15, and she describes the child's father as worthless because, as she states, "Him no want work, I don't want that life so I move out." Angelique's observation of the father of her first child suggests that she initially sought to conform to the gender deal, by seeking a male primary breadwinner to assist her in achieving her desired reality, yet he was unable to fulfill her expectations and hope of achieving her ideal of the "good life," and therefore, the relationship ended.

A subsequent boyfriend was a drug dealer. This boyfriend offered Angelique an alternative means to achieve the good life and an opportunity to achieve her dreams. Life with this boyfriend meant that Angelique would have to relinquish her desire to conform to the promises of the class deal through her notion of legitimate institutionalized means and adapt to an environment in which the rules that sanctioned behavior deviated from those of the dominant society. Angelique's new reality included the indulgence in drugs, and although this boyfriend could function as the primary breadwinner, his methods for achieving wealth required her to engage in crime:

> My friends set me up with a youth who was a bad man. They had money and things. They would drink, do drugs and gamble for fun. They would rob too. If they want me to carry a gun I say I would do it, for him. With my friends I felt happy, stress free. When I smoke, things just gone. They were kind of like a family. I prefer to be with them than my own. I always felt burdened when I came home [to my mother], but I never felt like that with them. I would rob, but mainly with my boyfriend.

For Angelique, her new family allowed her the freedom to combine the class and gender deals, albeit through illegitimate means, and to adopt an acceptable (if not desired) reality (identity). Unfortunately, this new reality did not free Angelique from risk, as the abuse she suffered from her mother was replaced by exploitation.

> [When I went to England to live with my boyfriend] I had to send money two times a week to my mother because she was taking care of my children. My mother cravin' [is greedy]. She wanted to carry it [drugs] up [from Jamaica to England]. I told her she was not ready, but she neva stop. She wanted to come to England. So we gave her ganja [marijuana] in a tin and some coke [cocaine]. She get catch [arrested] in Jamaica. I flew down and my boyfriend too. She was in jail and we had to put $100,000 [Jamaican dollars to post bond].

Adaptive Response

Disruption in Angelique's life continued as her boyfriend was also arrested after returning to England. With her primary source of income gone, Angelique adapted to this change by relying on her own income-earning abilities to obtain the means to maintain her mother's now abandoned children as well as her own. With the bulk of her experience, networks, and opportunities concentrated around her boyfriend's illegal endeavors, Angelique inherited his business and began to engage in the transportation of drugs:

> My boyfriend got 17 years. He got caught with drugs and guns in the house. I had to start to carry drugs to small islands in a suitcase. The drugs were built into the suitcase. I traveled every week carrying ganja from Jamaica [to England] and coke [from England] back to Jamaica, Grenada, St. Maarten and Panama. With 3–4 pounds of weed I could make $800 US and with 1 kilo of coke, $900 US for myself. My boss would send money to immigration to clear my way and collect the money, but I don't know his name.

Upon reflection, Angelique says she realizes that she could have made better choices. She stated that she could have obviously continued to go to school to be a hairdresser and potential salon owner after her sister died as an example, yet with an understanding of her social location and history of risks and contradictions, she may have had little faith that her conformity to the class deal would have resulted in the trappings of the good life she imagined. In Angelique's quest to become somebody, the lack of available legitimate examples, means, and opportunities to help augment her ability to navigate through the complexities of multiple subjugations, uncertainties, risks, and contradictions she encountered was compensated by adaptive responses characterized by increasing levels of deviance.

As an ex-offender, upon her release, Angelique may find her options for access to education and the formal labor market further restricted. When pressed to specify the choices she plans to make in the future upon her release from prison, as if acknowledging the high degree of uncertainty she will face given the addition of the label of "ex-offender" to the other vulnerabilities that characterize her social location, Angelique spoke with ambiguity and then with resolve:

> I want to get a job and go to [cosmetology] school in England, but me don't know what me may do [when I get out of prison]. I don't know my situation. I may go back into it [carrying drugs].

For Angelique, the American Dream has been replaced by a reality that reflects her limitations and the constraints, circumscription, and contradictions within society. For Angelique and other vulnerable men and women the process of *doing identity* is wrought with constraints and barriers that place their reach just short of their aspirations. Angelique attempts to define herself, achieve her dreams, and possibly benefit from the class and gender deals ascribed for women in society, yet her attempts are met with a dearth of feasible and legitimate options that are compensated by illicit ones. A life of crime, for Angelique, becomes the practical solution to social and economic conditions that are ripe with uncertainty and contradictions.

Angelique's profile of vulnerabilities and inequalities fits those of other women who may turn to crime as a solution to life's limitations. She is young, poor, nonwhite, a high school dropout, an unmarried mother, and unemployed and has a history of family violence, sexual abuse, and some drug use. Throughout her life, the impact of the combination of these factors remained virtually ignored by all but one social institution (the prison) and the "family of friends" that she adopted as a refuge and escape from her own. Her new family provided her with an example of how to obtain the tokens and semblance of the good life that could be acquired through illegal means. Due to the random and incremental accumulation of loss and lack in addition to the deprived conditions she inherited, in time Angelique became removed from her vision of being somebody and achieving her goals through legitimate means and decided to join her new family in search of some remnant of a dream. Eventually she ends up in prison, with little hope of finding alternative means to navigate through the inequalities and social contradictions that face her upon release.

One of the unanticipated findings this analysis revealed is the extent to which motherhood factors into women's decisions to commit crime or continue to pursue their dreams through legitimate means while confronting adversity. Angelique described how her children were the source of her motivation for achieving her goals and her sole inspiration in difficult times; here she states how her children give her the will to live despite continued abuse and challenges:

> I tried to commit suicide again. A girl told me what to buy, and I tried to kill myself. I drink some, but not enough, and then I vomit, vomit, vomit. I got weak, and pale and my mother took me to the hospital. During the drive to the hospital my mother told me I was wicked. I spent weeks in the hospital. In the hospital I was thinking about my son. He so bad loves me, and I said I would never do that again. When I came out, I got involved with a youth [a young boy] and got pregnant again. My children give me the strength to move, they make me want to live.

For Angelique, like many mothers, her children function as a tremendous source of encouragement in the midst of uncertainty. Despite the option to forfeit parental responsibilities due to strained social and economic conditions, many mothers continue to try to care for their children. Perhaps this phenomenon of commitment despite uncertainty can be described as another deal that can be added to Carlen's class and gender deals. The mother deal can be found at the intersection between the class and gender deals where the belief that the good life (as defined in noneconomic and more affective terms) results from a mother's dedication to her children. Crime results when illegitimate options for mothers to meet the needs of their children as well as their own are more readily available than those that are legitimate. Tapping into this bond between some mothers and their children as a way to guide and nurture their progress toward the achievement of their goals through legitimate means may lead to innovative policy and programmatic responses to female criminality.

Conclusion: Policy Implications

Although Adler (1975) contends that women's liberation resulted in increasing levels of women's willful criminality, her thesis fails to explain the higher likelihood of young, poor, non-white, high school dropouts, unmarried mothers, un-/under-employed or educated, with a history of drug problems, family violence, and sexual abuse, to be represented among incarcerated women. If a correlation between women's liberation and an increase in women's criminality exists perhaps this is due to the increased vulnerability of marginalized women to being criminalized as a result of punitive polices that blame them for the same conditions that constrain their progress.

The state through its promotion of policy, norms, and ideology contributes to the illusion that the financial prosperity of the affluent is somehow justified due to their hard work, integrity, and good choices. The consequence of upholding this belief is that it supports the claim that a life of less for others is often attributed to their own individual pathologies, deficiencies, and lack of conformity, and therefore, should the less affluent become deviant, they should be removed from society and punished. To effectively remove the constraints that limit access to *legitimate* options for the vulnerable to achieve an equitable reality would mean breaking the illusion of justified position or class in society and creating a new ideology, norms, institutions (safe places), and social policies that have the notions of interdependency and collective responsibility at the core. Rather than advocating the need for a revolution to combat crime, Left Realists would recommend, and I agree, that the focus of policy and interventions must be on creating communities of care that rebuild neighborhoods and encourage social responsibility and community cohesion as strategies to mitigate against the relative deprivation that affects the life outcomes of vulnerable individuals. Left Realist criminologists are critical of conservative policies that seek to build more prisons and lengthen sentences to deal with crime and are supportive of realistic solutions that fit within the existing social framework (Young, 1997). The increasing incarceration rate for women due to drug-related crimes suggests a need to revisit short-sighted legislative policies and to develop opportunities to prevent women's criminality through intervention at the micro (individual and family) and mezzo (groups and community) levels of society. One example of an innovative intervention that seeks to reduce social isolation and capitalizes on the potential bond between mothers and their children is the creation of women-centered kinship networks consisting of a community of fictive and biological mothers, aunts, grandmothers, and nonparents, some of whom may be education and social service providers who can function as sources of support, examples, guidance, and communal childcare for young mothers who may be at risk of dropping out of school, engaging in crime, or other forms of deviance (Collins, 2000; Mullins, 1997; White, 1985).

Nonresponsive policies and programs have resulted from a lack of understanding of the complex influence of multiple forms of oppression on women's lives and have rendered many marginalized women virtually invisible (Belknap, 2001). Addressing the problem of women and crime requires society to be willing to confront its failures, including its core ideologies, institutions, norms, and policies that justify a war on marginalized women (and men) under the guise of a war on drugs (Chesney-Lind, 1991). The challenge is for theorizing on female criminality to complicate malestream perspectives on women's criminality by including more empirical studies that seek to deconstruct one-dimensional and essentialist understandings of women's lives while intentionally exploring the interconnected, constraining, and multiple, yet unique, manifestations of power and oppression. The praxis of feminist criminology serves as a reminder that alternative theorizing, policy, and programmatic provisions in support of innovative interventions designed to nurture the development of each member of society are needed. An intersectional approach to feminist criminology functions to confront the collective culpability of all members of society in perpetuating oppressive ideologies and structures that favor the progress of the elite over those who, like Angelique, have limited means to escape the margins.

References

Adler, F. (1975). *Sisters in crime.* New York, NY: McGraw-Hill.

Baca Zinn, M., & Thornton Dill, B. (1996). Theorizing difference from multiracial feminism. *Feminist Studies, 22*(2), 321–331.

Barak, G. (1998). *Integrating criminologies.* Boston, MA: Allyn & Bacon.

Bauman, Z. (2000). *Liquid modernity.* Cambridge, UK: Polity.

Beale, F. (1995). Double jeopardy: To be Black and female. In B. Guy-Sheftall (Ed.), *Words of fire: An anthology of African-American feminist thought* (pp. 146–155). New York, NY: New Press. (Original work published 1970)

Beck, U. (1992). *Risk society: Towards a new modernity.* New Delhi, India: Sage.

Belknap, J. (2001). *The invisible woman: Gender, crime and justice.* Belmont, CA: Wadsworth.

Britton, D. M. (2004). Feminism in criminology: Engendering the outlaw. In P. J. Schram & B. Koons-Witt (Eds.), *Gendered (in) justice: Theory and practice in feminist criminology* (pp. 49–67). Long Grove, IL: Waveland.

Broidy, L., & Agnew, R. (1997). Gender and crime: A general strain theory perspective. *Journal of Research in Crime and Delinquency, 34*(3), 275–306.

Brown, G. (2010). *The intersectionality of race, gender, and reentry: Challenges for African-American women* (Issue Brief: 1–18). Washington, DC: American Constitution Society for Law and Policy.

Burgess-Proctor, A. (2006). Intersections of race, class, gender, and crime: Future directions for feminist criminology. *Feminist Criminology, 1*(1), 24–47.

Carlen, P. (1985). *Criminal woman.* Cambridge, UK: Polity.

Carlen, P. (1988). *Women, crime and poverty.* London: Open University Press.

Chesney-Lind, M. (1986). Women and crime: The female offender. *Signs, 12*(1), 78–96.

Chesney-Lind, M. (1991). Patriarchy, prisons and jails: A critical look at trends in women's incarceration. *The Prison Journal, 51*(11), 51–67.

Chesney-Lind, M. (1997). *The female offender: Girls, women and crime.* Thousand Oaks, CA: Sage.

Collins, P. H. (2000). *Black feminist thought: Knowledge, consciousness, and the politics of empowerment* (2nd ed.). New York, NY: Routledge.

Curra, J. (2000). *The relativity of deviance.* Thousand Oaks, CA: Sage.

Daly, K., & Chesney-Lind, M. (1988). Feminism and criminology. *Justice Quarterly, 5*(4), 497–535.

Daly, K., & Stephens, D. J. (1995). The "dark figure" of criminology: Towards a Black and multi-ethnic feminist agenda for theory and research. In N. Hahn Rafter & F. Heidensohn (Eds.), *International feminist perspectives in criminology: Engendering a discipline* (pp. 189–215). Philadelphia: Open University Press.

Dekeseredy, W., & Perry, B. (2006). *Advancing critical criminology: Theory and application.* Lanham, MD: Lexington Books.

Denzin, N. K. (1989). *Interpretive interactionism.* Thousand Oaks, CA: Sage.

Gordon, V. V. (1987). *Black women, feminism and Black liberation: Which way?* Chicago, IL: Third World Press.

Harding, S. (Ed.). (2004). *The feminist standpoint theory reader.* London: Routledge.

Kelly, M. (1994). *Critique and power: Recasting the Foucault/Habermas debate.* Boston, MA: MIT Press.

King, D. K. (1988). Multiple jeopardy, multiple consciousness: The context of Black feminist ideology. *Signs: Journal of Women in Culture and Society, 14*(1), 42–72.

Lynch, M. J. (1996). Class, race, gender and criminology: Structured choices and the life course. In D. Milovanovic & M. D. Schwartz (Eds.), *Race, gender, and class in criminology: The intersections* (pp. 3–28). New York, NY: Garland.

Maidment, M. (2006). Transgressing boundaries: Feminist perspectives in criminology. In W. DeKeseredy & B. Perry (Eds.), *Advancing critical criminology: Theory and application* (pp. 43–62). Lanham, MD: Lexington Books.

Merton, R. (1968). *Social theory and social structure,* enlarged edition. New York, NY: Free Press.

Messerschmidt, J. (1993). *Masculinities and crime: Critique and reconceptualization of theory.* Lantham, MD: Rowman and Littlefield.

Mullins, L. (1997). *On our own terms: Race, class and gender in the lives of African American women.* New York, NY: Routledge.

Oakley, A. (1981). Interviewing women: A contradiction in terms. In H. Roberts (Ed.), *Doing feminist research* (pp. 30–62). London: Routledge & Kegan Paul.

Owen, B. (1998). *"In the mix": Struggle and survival in a women's prison.* Albany, NY: SUNY Press.

Potter, H. (2006). An argument for Black feminist criminology: Understanding African American women's experiences with intimate partner abuse using an integrated approach. *Feminist Criminology, 1*(2), 106–124.

Reiman, J. (2003) *The rich get richer and the poor get prison: Ideology, class, and criminal justice* (7th ed.). Boston, MA: Allyn & Bacon.

Ritchie, B. E. (1996). *Compelled to crime: The gender entrapment of battered Black women.* New York, NY: Routledge.

Ritchie, B. E. (2004). Feminist ethnographies of women in prison. *Feminist Studies, 30*(2), 438–450.

White, D. (1985). *Ar'n't I a woman? Female slaves in the Plantation South.* New York, NY: Norton.

Wing, A. K. (Ed.). (2003). *Critical race feminism: A reader* (2nd ed.). New York: New York University Press.

Young, J. (1997). Left realist criminology: Radical in its analysis, realist in its policy. In M. Maguire (Ed.), *The Oxford handbook of criminology* (pp. 473–498). Oxford, UK: Oxford University Press.

REVIEW QUESTIONS

1. What does the author mean by examining "differential identity"?
2. Why does the author use Merton's strain theory as the framework for examining female criminal activity? Do you agree or think other theories would be a better model for explaining criminal activity for women?
3. Given the case study in this article, which types of factors do you think are most important in explaining female criminality? What are the most significant differences from explaining male offending behavior?

SECTION XI

Life-Course Perspectives of Criminality

This section will discuss the development of the life-course perspective in the late 1970s and its influence on modern research on criminal trajectories. We will explain the various concepts in the life-course perspective, such as onset, desistence, and frequency as well as the arguments against this perspective. Finally, we will review the current state of research regarding this perspective.

This section will present one of the most current and progressive approaches to explaining why individuals engage in criminal activity—namely, **developmental theories** of criminal behavior. Developmental theories are explanatory models of criminal behavior that follow individuals throughout their life courses of offending, thus explaining the development of offending over time. Such developmental theories represent a break with traditional theoretical frameworks, which typically focused on the effects of constructs and variables on behavior at a given point in time. Virtually no theories attempted to explain the various stages (e.g., onset, desistence) of individuals' criminal careers, and certainly no models differentiated the varying factors that are important at each stage. Developmental theories have been prominent in modern times, and we believe that readers will agree that developmental theories have added a great deal to our understanding of and thinking about why people commit criminal behavior.

Developmental Theories

Developmental theories, which are also to some extent integrated, are distinguished by their emphasis on the evolution of individuals' criminality over time. Developmental theories tend to look at the individual as the unit of analysis, and such models focus on the onset, frequency, seriousness or intensity, duration, persistence or consistency, desistence, and other aspects of the individual's criminal career. The onset of offending is when the offender first begins offending, and desistence is when an individual stops committing crime. Frequency refers to how often the individual offends, whereas intensity is the degree of seriousness of the offenses he or she commits. Persistence is the concept of how consistent the individual's offending rate is over time. Finally, duration is the length of an individual's criminal career.[1]

---

[1]Matt DeLisi and Kevin M. Beaver, eds., *Criminological Theory: A Life-Course Approach*, 2nd ed. (Burlington, MA: Jones & Bartlett, 2014). See also Alex R. Piquero, David P. Farrington, and Alfred Blumstein, "Criminal Career Paradigm: Background, Recent Developments, and the Way Forward," *International Annals of Criminology* 41 (2003): 243–69; and Brame et al., "Cumulative Prevalence of Arrest."

Experts have long debated and examined these various aspects of the development of criminal behavior. For example, virtually all studies show an escalation from minor status offending (e.g., truancy, underage drinking, tobacco use) to petty crimes (e.g., shoplifting, smoking marijuana) to far more serious criminal activity, such as robbery and aggravated assault, and then murder and rape. This development of criminality is shown across every study that has ever been performed and demonstrates that, with very few exceptions, people begin with relatively minor offending and progress toward more serious, violent offenses.

Although this trend is undisputed, other issues are not yet resolved. For example, studies have not yet determined when police contact or an arrest becomes **early onset**. Most empirical studies draw the line at age 14, so that any arrest or contact prior to this time is considered early onset.[2] However, other experts would disagree and say that this line should be drawn earlier (say, 12 years old) or even later (such as 16 years old). Still, however it is defined, early onset is one of the most important predictors of any of the measures we have in determining who is most at risk for developing serious, violent offending behavior.

Perhaps the most discussed and researched aspect of developmental theory is *offender frequency*, which has been referred to as **lambda**. Estimates of lambda (or λ), or average frequency of offending by criminals over a year's time, vary greatly.[3] Some estimates of lambda are in the high single digits, and some are in the triple digits. Given this large range, it does not do much good to estimate what the frequency of most offenders is. Rather, the frequency depends on many, many variables, such as what type of offenses the individual commits. Perhaps if we were studying only drug users or rapists, it would make sense to determine lambda, but given the general nature of most examinations of crime, such estimates are not useful. Even within the same crime type, the frequency of offending varies so widely across individuals that we question its use in understanding criminal careers.

Before we discuss the dominant models of developmental theory, it is important to discuss the opposing viewpoint, which is that of complete stability in offending. Such counterpoint views assume that the developmental approach is a waste of time because the same individuals who show antisocial behavior at early ages (before age 10) are those who will exhibit the most criminality in their teenage years, 20s, 30s, 40s, and so on. This framework is most notably represented by the theoretical perspective proposed by Michael Gottfredson and Travis Hirschi in their model of low self-control.

Case Study: Henry Earl

Henry Earl is, according to all available sources, the most arrested individual on record, at least in recent times. Hailing from the area of Lexington, Kentucky (Fayette County), Earl was born in 1949 and has since done quite an impressive job of getting himself arrested, especially after he turned 21. Specifically, Earl is on record for being arrested well over 1,300 times since 1970. Although the actual number is disputed, and likely growing every month, recent official reports from the local jurisdictions show that Earl has been arrested for more than 1,352 offenses and has spent more than 15 years in jail. Despite being jailed for much of his life, Earl appears to make up for lost time when he is not incarcerated, as the data show.

---

[2]For more discussion, see Stephen G. Tibbetts, "Perinatal and Developmental Determinants of Early Onset of Offending: A Biosocial Approach for Explaining the Two Peaks of Early Antisocial Behavior," in *The Development of Persistent Criminality*, ed., Joanne Savage (New York: Oxford University Press, 2009), 179–201; Matt DeLisi, "Zeroing In on Early Arrest Onset: Results from a Population of Extreme Career Criminals," *Journal of Criminal Justice* 34 (2006): 17–26; Stephen Tibbetts and Alex Piquero, "The Influence of Gender, Low Birth Weight, and Disadvantaged Environment in Predicting Early Onset of Offending: A Test of Moffitt's Interactional Hypothesis," *Criminology* 37 (1999): 843–78; and Chris L. Gibson and Stephen Tibbetts, "A Biosocial Interaction in Predicting Early Onset of Offending," *Psychological Reports* 86 (2000): 509–18.

[3]For a review, see Samuel Walker, *Sense and Nonsense about Crime and Drugs: A Policy Guide*, 7th ed. (Belmont, CA: Cengage, 2011). See also Piquero et al., "Criminal Career Paradigm."

Although many of his arrests were for public intoxication, he also had a number of more serious charges, including third-degree trespassing and various charges of disorderly conduct. Readers are probably wondering how this man could still be on the streets, but the most likely explanation is that virtually all his arrests were for nonviolent, nontheft, and nondrug (except alcohol) violations, which tend not to get much jail time. However, one would think that after the first hundred arrests, not to mention the first thousand, the judges would try to put this public nuisance away for a long time. Apparently, that is not the case. Earl's last publicly documented arrest was in November 2013, so he is seemingly still active and perhaps trying to achieve a record of arrests that may be hard for anyone to beat. According to developmental theory, he clearly is the "poster child" for the definition of persistent or consistency in offending.

... If someone is highly motivated to commit crime, he or she can easily find ways to do so.

This goes to show a couple of things that relate to this section. First, if someone is highly motivated to commit crime, he or she can easily find ways to do so. After all, anyone can simply leave the house and commit numerous felonies against neighbors, people driving by on the street, and so forth—not to mention what that person is capable of outside of his or her neighborhood. Second, there is virtually no way to deter or stop a person from committing a crime he or she is highly motivated to commit, especially if that person has nothing to lose. Obviously, Earl has nothing at stake in terms of conventional society.

▲ **Image 11.1** Henry Earl, arrested more than 1,300 times, is widely considered the most arrested individual in U.S. history.

SOURCE: Lexington-Fayette Urban County Government Community Corrections / United States Department of Justice

This case is notable in the context of developmental/life-course criminology. Although a highly extreme case study, it reveals that normal development, such as key transitions in life, as noted by Robert Sampson and John Laub's theory, clearly don't apply in this case. Some individuals have an extremely high predisposition to offend, an even higher predisposition than Gottfredson and Hirschi's theory of low self-control may have imagined possible. Regardless, this amazingly strong predisposition toward such antisocial behavior is likely due to major failures in all areas of development throughout Earl's life course, beginning with his genetics, early development, and adolescence.

Think About It

1. Can you apply the life-course persistent label from Terrie Moffitt's theory to Henry Earl?
2. Can you think of any intervention or policy that would help Mr. Earl reduce his consistent arrests?

SOURCES: "Henry Earl: Setting the Record Straight," SmokingGun.com, September 25, 2008, http://www.thesmokinggun.com/documents/crime/henry-earl-setting-record-straight; Lexington-Fayette Urban County Government, Division of Community Corrections, JailWebsite.com, n.d., http://jail.lfucg.com/Secure/Account/Login.aspx?ReturnUrl=%2fQueryProfile.aspx%3foid%3d137&oid=137. "Henry Earl, Arrested More than 1500 Times, in Jail Again," *HuffPost*, November 27, 2013, http://www.huffingtonpost.com/2013/11/27/henry-earl-arrest-1500-thanksgiving-in-jail_n_4352833.html.

Antidevelopmental Theory: Low Self-Control Theory

In 1990, Hirschi, along with his colleague Gottfredson, proposed a general theory of low self-control as the primary cause of all crime and deviance (see prior discussion in Section VIII); this is often referred to as *the general theory of crime*.[4] This theory has led to a significant amount of debate and research in the field since its appearance, more than any other contemporary theory of crime.

Like other control theories of crime, this theory (see Figure 11.1) assumes that individuals are born predisposed toward selfish, self-centered activities and that only effective child rearing and socialization can create self-control. Without such adequate socialization (i.e., social controls) and reduction of criminal opportunities, individuals will follow their natural tendencies to become selfish predators. The general theory of crime assumes that self-control must be established by age 10. If it has not formed by that time, then according to the theory, individuals will forever exhibit low self-control. The assumption that self-control must be formed by age 10 is the feature of this theory that opposes the developmental perspective. The authors assert that once low self-control is set by age 10, there is no way to develop it afterward. In contrast, developmental theory assumes that people can indeed change over time.

Like others, Gottfredson and Hirschi attribute the formation of controls to socialization processes in the first years of life; the distinguishing characteristic of this theory is its emphasis on the individual's ability to control himself or herself. That is, the general theory of crime assumes that people can take a degree of control over their own decisions and, within certain limitations, control themselves. The general theory of crime is accepted as one of the most valid theories of crime.[5] This is probably due to the parsimony, or simplicity, of the theory, as it identifies only one primary cause of criminality—low self-control. However, low self-control may actually consist of a series of personality traits, including risk-taking, impulsiveness, self-centeredness, short-term orientation, and quick temper. Recent research has supported the idea that inadequate child-rearing practices tend to result in lower levels of self-control among children and that these low levels produce various risky behaviors, including criminal activity.[6] It is important to note that this theory has a developmental component in the sense that it proposes that self-control develops during early years from parenting practices; thus, even this most notable antidevelopment theory actually includes a strong developmental aspect.

In contrast to Gottfredson and Hirschi's model, one of the most dominant and researched frameworks of the past 20 years, another sound theoretical model shows that individuals can change their life trajectories in terms of crime. Research shows that events or realizations can occur that lead people to alter their frequency or incidence of offending, sometimes to zero. To account for such extreme **transitions**, we must turn to the dominant life-course model of offending, which is **Sampson and Laub's developmental model**.

---

[4]Michael Gottfredson and Travis Hirschi, *A General Theory of Crime* (Palo Alto, CA: Stanford University Press, 1990).

[5]For reviews of studies regarding low self-control theory, see John P. Wright, Stephen G. Tibbetts, and Leah Daigle, *Criminals in the Making: Criminality across the Life Course*, 2nd ed. (Thousand Oaks, CA: Sage, 2015) (see chap. 1); George E. Higgins and Margaret Mahoney, "Self-Control Theory and Antisocial Behavior," in *Criminological Theory: A Life-Course Approach*, 2nd ed., ed. Matt DeLisi and Kevin M. Beaver (Burlington, MA: Jones & Bartlett, 2014), 249–60; and Travis Pratt and Frank Cullen, "The Empirical Status of Gottfredson and Hirschi's General Theory of Crime: A Meta-analysis," *Criminology* 38 (2000): 931–64. For critiques of this theory, see Ronald Akers, "Self-Control as a General Theory of Crime," *Journal of Quantitative Criminology* 7 (1991): 201–11. For a study that demonstrates the high popularity of the theory, see Anthony Walsh and Lee Ellis, "Political Ideology and American Criminologists' Explanations for Criminal Behavior," *The Criminologist* 24 (1999): 1, 14 (see chap. 1, n. 13).

[6]Carter Hay, "Parenting, Self-Control, and Delinquency: A Test of Self-Control Theory," *Criminology* 39 (2001): 707–36; K. Hayslett-McCall and T. Bernard, "Attachment, Masculinity, and Self-Control: A Theory of Male Crime Rates," *Theoretical Criminology* 6 (2002): 5–33.

Figure 11.1 • Gottfredson and Hirschi's theory of low self-control

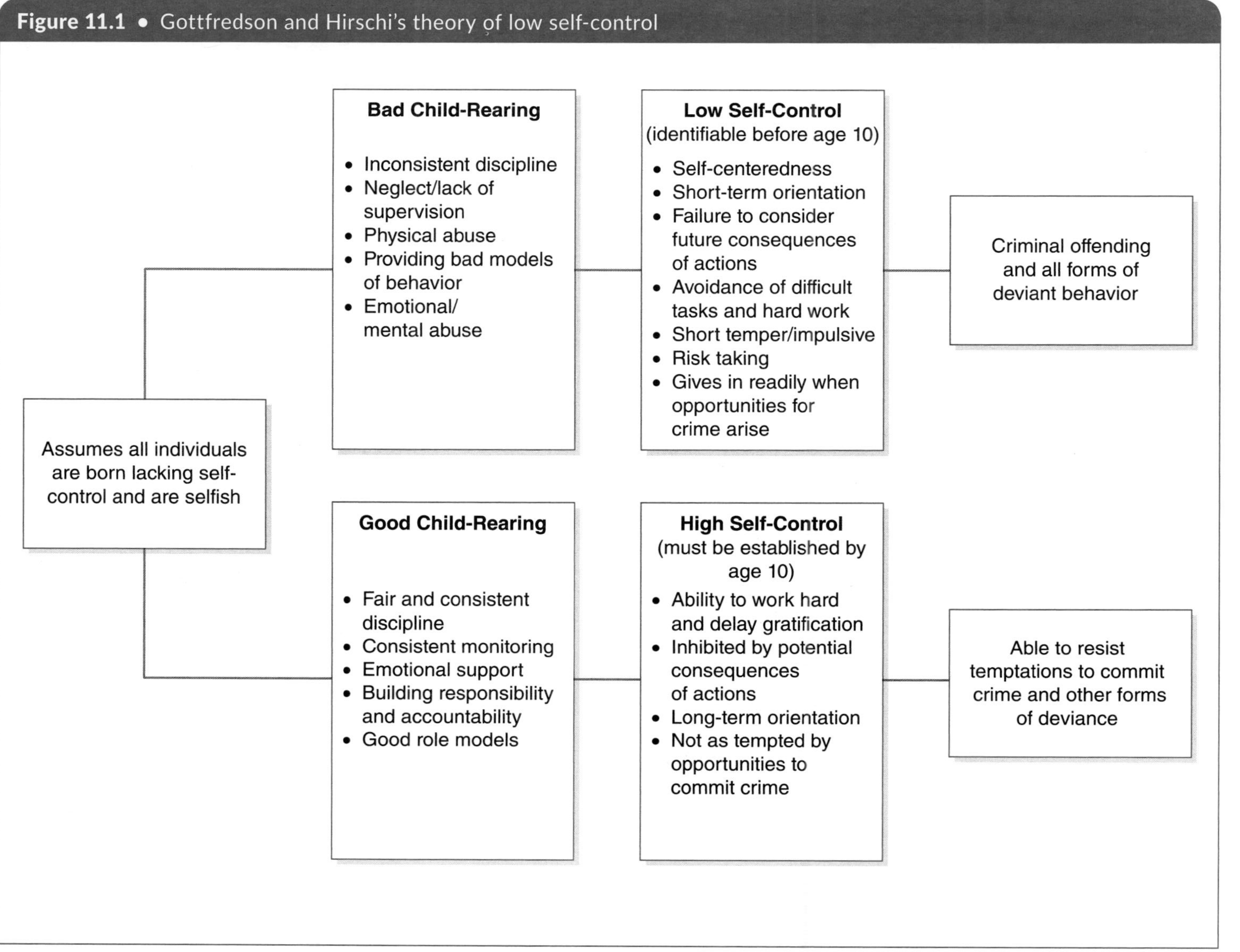

Sampson and Laub's Developmental Model

Perhaps the best-known and best-researched developmental theoretical model to date is that of Sampson and Laub.[7] Sampson and Laub have proposed a developmental framework that is largely based on a reanalysis of original data collected by Sheldon and Eleanor Glueck in the 1940s. As a prototypical developmental model, this theoretical perspective focuses primarily on individual stability and change.

Most significantly, Sampson and Laub emphasized the importance of certain events and life changes, which can alter an individual's decisions to commit (or not commit) criminal activity. Although based on a social control framework, this model contains elements of other theoretical perspectives. First, Sampson and Laub's model assumes, like other developmental perspectives, that early antisocial tendencies among individuals, regardless of social variables, are often linked to later adult criminal offending. Furthermore, some social structure factors (e.g., family structure, poverty) also tend to lead to problems in social and educational development, which then lead to crime. Another key factor in this development of criminality is the influence of delinquent peers or siblings, which further increases an individual's likelihood for delinquency.

▲ **Image 11.2** Robert Sampson (1956–) and John Laub (1954–), who proposed one of the most researched theoretical frameworks, largely based on transitions and trajectories in life.

SOURCE: Courtesy of Robert Sampson and John Laub

However, Sampson and Laub also strongly emphasized the importance of transitions, or events that are important in altering life trajectories, such as marriage, employment, or military service, drastically changing a person's criminal career. Sampson and Laub showed sound evidence that many individuals who were once on a path toward a consistent form of behavior—in this case, serious, violent crime—suddenly (or gradually) halted due to such a transition or series of transitions. In some ways, this model is a more specified form of David Matza's theory of drift, which we discussed in Section VIII, in which individuals tend to grow out of crime and deviance due to the social controls imposed by marriage, employment, and so on. Still, Sampson and Laub's framework contributed much to the knowledge of criminal offending by providing a more specified and grounded framework that identified the ability of individuals to change their criminal trajectories via life-altering transitions. In fact, recent research has consistently shown that marriage and full-time employment significantly reduce the recidivism of California parolees, and other recent studies have shown similar results from employment in later years.[8]

---

[7]Robert Sampson and John Laub, "Crime and Deviance over the Life Course: The Salience of Adult Social Bonds," *American Sociological Review* 55 (1990): 609–27; Robert Sampson and John Laub, "Turning Points in the Life Course: Why Change Matters to the Study of Crime," *Criminology* 31 (1993): 301–26; Robert Sampson and John Laub, *Crime in the Making: Pathways and Turning Points through Life* (Cambridge: Harvard University Press, 1993).

[8]Alex Piquero, Robert Brame, Paul Mazzerole, and Rudy Haapanen, "Crime in Emerging Adulthood," *Criminology* 40 (2002): 137–70; Chris Uggen, "Work as a Turning Point in the Life Course of Criminals: A Duration Model of Age, Employment, and Recidivism," *American Sociological Review* 65 (2000): 529–46.

Case Study: Teen Burglar

The Teen Burglar

A news story from the spring of 2012 reported that a 14-year-old boy had been arrested in Tennessee in connection with nearly 100 burglaries in the north Nashville area of Tennessee.[9] Officers said the teen was linked to these burglaries over the previous 2 years (making him 12 when he started offending). According to police, he had a specific and consistent modus operandi, or method of operation (MO). Specifically, he would kick in back doors, enter, and steal whatever he could grab quickly, such as flat-screen TVs or video games. Officers noted his creativity and innovation, which included using a go-kart as his getaway vehicle, driving from house to house through back alleys. The police also mentioned that he had lost both parents and likely didn't have much guidance or anyone looking out for him. They had evidence tying him to the burglaries, such as fingerprints and items found inside his home, which likely is the reason he admitted to many of the break-ins. It is unfortunate that this boy had such a poor family life and so little parental supervision, but one must wonder what inspired him to commit more than 100 residential burglaries, starting when he was 12 years old! We will revisit this case in our conclusion, with additional insight into why he may have committed these crimes.

. . . One must wonder what inspired him to commit more than 100 residential burglaries, starting when he was 12 years old!

Think About It

1. Have you ever met or known about a child this young in your neighborhood doing so many crimes before the age of 14? If so, what do you think were the causes?
2. How much do you think having poor parental supervision contributed to his crimes? Do you think he would have been prevented, or do you think he was driven to commit these crimes regardless of family supervision?
3. What do you think of his MO in how he committed his burglaries? Do you see some intellectual skill in how he did it, given that he wasn't caught for 2 years?

Moffitt's Developmental Taxonomy

Another primary developmental model that has had a profound effect on the current state of criminological thought and theorizing is **Moffitt's developmental theory (taxonomy)**, proposed in 1993.[10] Moffitt's framework distinguishes two types of offenders: **adolescence-limited offenders** and **life-course-persistent offenders.** Adolescence-limited offenders make up most of the general public and include all persons who committed offenses when they were teenagers or young adults. Their offending is largely caused by association with peers and a desire to engage in activities exhibited by the adults that they are trying to be. Such activities are a type of rite of passage and quite normal among all people who have normal social interactions with their peers in their teenage or

[9] "14-Year-Old Suspected in Nearly 100 Nashville Burglaries," WSMV.com, May 18, 2012, http://www.wsmv.com/story/18151966/14-year-old-suspected-in-north-nashville-burglaries.

[10] Terrie Moffitt, "Adolescence Limited and Life Course Persistent Antisocial Behavioral: A Developmental Taxonomy," *Psychological Review* 100 (1993): 674–701. For a review, see Savage, *Development of Persistent Criminality*.

▲ **Image 11.3** Life-course theories attempt to uncover points of desistence, critical events that may change a person's life path from deviant behavior back to law-abiding status. Getting married and being employed are considered some of the most significant events. Once one is married or gains steady employment, free time to hang out with one's friends tends to disappear.

SOURCE: © istockphoto.com / simonkr

young adult years. It should be noted that a very small percentage of the population (about 1% to 3%) are nonoffenders who quite frankly do not have normal relations with their peers and therefore do not offend at all, even in adolescence.

On the other hand, there exists another small group of offenders, referred to in this model as life-course-persistent offenders. This small group, estimated to be 4% to 8% of offenders—albeit the most violent and chronic—commit the vast majority of the serious, violent offenses in any society, such as murder, rape, and armed robbery. In contrast to the adolescence-limited offenders, the disposition of life-course-persistent offenders toward offending is caused by an entirely different model: an interaction between neurological problems and the disadvantaged or criminological environments in which they are raised.

For example, if an individual has only neurological problems or only a poor, disadvantaged environment, then that individual will be unlikely to develop a life-course-persistent **trajectory** toward crime. However, if a person has both neurological problems and a disadvantaged environment, then that individual will have a very high likelihood of becoming a chronic, serious, violent offender. This proposition, which has been supported by empirical studies,[11] suggests that it is important to pay attention to what happens early in life. Because illegal behaviors are normal among teenagers or young adults, more insight can be gained by looking at the years prior to age 12 to determine who is most likely to become a chronic, violent offender. Life-course-persistent offenders begin offending very early in life and continue to commit crime far into adulthood, even to middle age, whereas adolescence-limited offenders tend to engage in criminal activity only during their teenage and young adult years. Moffitt's model suggests that more than one type of development explains criminality. Furthermore, this framework shows that different types of offenders commit crime due to entirely different causes and factors.

Policy Implications

There are many, perhaps an infinite number of, policy implications that can be derived from developmental theories of criminality. In a 2017 systematic review of the extant literature on developmental programs, David Weisburd and his colleagues concluded that there are positive findings for a wide range of prevention strategies, including individual and family programs as well as school-based programs.[12] Thus, we will focus on one of the most important,

[11]See Tibbetts and Piquero, "Influence of Gender." For a recent review of such studies, see Wright et al., *Criminals in the Making* (see chap. 1). See also Savage, *Development of Persistent Criminality*.

[12]David Weisburd, David P. Farrington, and Charlotte Gill, "What Works in Crime Prevention and Rehabilitation: An Assessment of Systematic Reviews," *Criminology & Public Policy* 16 (2017): 415–49.

which concerns the prenatal and perinatal stages of life, because the most significant and effective interventions can occur during this time. If policy makers hope to reduce early risk factors for criminality, they must insist on universal health care for pregnant women as well as their newborn infants through the first few years of life. The United States is one of the few developed nations that does not guarantee this type of maternal and infant medical care and supervision. Doing so would go a long way toward avoiding the costly (in many ways) damages of criminal behavior among youths at risk.[13]

▲ **Image 11.4** Terrie Moffitt (1955–), who proposed one of the most researched frameworks in developmental criminology.

SOURCE: Courtesy of Terrie Moffitt

Furthermore, there should be legally mandated interventions for pregnant women who are addicted to drugs or alcohol. Although this is a highly controversial topic, it appears to be a no-brainer that women who suffer from such addictions may become highly toxic to the child(ren) they carry and should receive closer supervision and more health care. There may be no policy implementation that would have as much influence on reducing future criminality in children as making sure their mothers do not take toxic substances while they are pregnant.[14]

Other policy implications include assigning special caseworkers to high-risk infants, such as those with low birth weight or low Apgar scores. Another advised intervention would be to have a centralized medical system that provides a flag for high-risk infants who have numerous birth or delivery complications so that the doctors who are seeing them for the first time are aware of their vulnerabilities.[15] Finally, universal preschool should be funded and provided to all young children; studies have shown that this leads to better performance once they enter school, both academically and socially.[16]

Ultimately, as the many developmental theories have shown, there are many concepts and stages of life that can have a profound effect on the criminological trajectories that lives can take. However, virtually all of these models propose that the earlier stages of life are likely the most important in determining whether an individual will engage in criminal activity throughout life or not. Therefore, policy makers should focus their efforts on providing care and interventions in this time period.

Conclusion

This section presented a brief discussion of the importance of developmental or life-course theories of criminal behavior. This perspective, having become popular in the 1970s, is relatively new compared to other traditional theories explored in this text. Ultimately, this is one of the most cutting-edge areas of theoretical development,

[13] Wright et al., *Criminals in the Making*, 260–62.

[14] Ibid., 184–86, 258.

[15] Ibid., 259–62.

[16] Ibid.

and life-course theories are likely to be the most important frameworks in the future of the field of criminological theory.

We discussed the various concepts of developmental theory, including those of offending onset, frequency, seriousness, duration, and desistance. We also examined the importance of early onset and how it is considered one of the most important predictors of any of the measures we have in determining who is most at risk for developing serious, violent offending behavior yet has issues regarding where researchers draw the line in what constitutes "early" onset versus normal or late onset. Additionally, we discussed frequency of offending, often presented as an estimate called lambda (or λ), and the problematic issue of making such estimates—especially for different types of offenders.

Then we examined the policy implications of this developmental approach, emphasizing the need to provide universal care for pregnant mothers as well as their newborn children. Other policy implications include legally mandated interventions for mothers who are addicted to toxic substances (e.g., alcohol, drugs) and assignment of caseworkers to high-risk infants and children, such as those with a history of complications at birth. Such interventions would go a long way toward saving society the many problems (e.g., financial difficulties, victimization) that will persist without such interventions. Ultimately, a focus on the earliest stages of intervention will provide "the biggest bang for the buck."

SECTION SUMMARY

- Developmental or life-course theory focuses on the individual, following people throughout life to examine their offending careers. In-depth consideration of changes during the life course are of highest concern, especially regarding general conclusions that can be made about the factors that tend to increase or decrease the risk that individuals will continue offending.
- Life-course perspectives emphasize onset of offending, frequency of offending, duration of offending, seriousness of offending, persistence or consistency in offending rate, desistence of offending, and other factors that play key roles in when individuals offend and why they do so—or don't do so—at certain times of their lives.
- Early onset is one of the most important predictors of any of the measures we have in determining who is most at risk for developing serious, violent offending behavior.
- The criteria of determining what early onset is varies much based on the researchers making the decision, the type of offense(s) being studied, and the type of data being used in the study (e.g., self-reports vs. official police data).
- Lambda (or λ) is used to represent the average rate of offending by offenders in a given period of time, typically a year.
- Problems exist with using estimates of lambda, given how drastically different the estimates are across studies of various types of offenses as well as across different types of measures (e.g., official arrest data as compared to self-report data [SRD]).
- There are many critics of the developmental or life-course perspective, particularly those who buy into the low self-control model, which is antidevelopmental in the sense that it assumes that propensities for crime do not change over time but rather remain unchanged across life.

- One of the developmental models that has received the most attention is that of Sampson and Laub, which emphasizes transitions in life (e.g., marriage, military service, employment) that alter trajectories either toward or away from crime.
- Moffitt's developmental theory of chronic offenders (whom she labeled *life-course-persistent offenders*) versus more normal offenders (whom she labeled *adolescence-limited offenders*) is the developmental model that has received the most attention over the last decade, and much of this research is supportive of the interactive effects of biology and environment that combine to create chronic, habitual offenders.

KEY TERMS

adolescence-limited offenders 489

developmental theories 483

early onset 484

lambda (offender frequency) 484

life-course-persistent offenders 489

Moffitt's developmental theory (taxonomy) 489

Sampson and Laub's developmental model 486

trajectory 490

transitions 486

DISCUSSION QUESTIONS

1. What characteristic distinguishes developmental theories from traditional theoretical frameworks?
2. What aspects of a criminal career do experts consider important in such a model? Describe all of the aspects they look at in a person's criminal career.
3. Discuss the primary criticisms of the developmental perspective, particularly as it was presented by Gottfredson and Hirschi. Which theoretical paradigm do you consider most valid? Why?
4. What transitions or trajectories have you seen in your life or your friends' lives that support Sampson and Laub's developmental model? What events encouraged offending or inhibited it?
5. Given Moffitt's dichotomy of life-course-persistent offenders and adolescence-limited offenders, which of these should be given more attention by research? Why do you feel this way?
6. Do you think the use of lambda as an estimate of offending rates is useful for comparison across studies, given the large range and differences in the estimates that have been reported for different types of offenses and different types of measures?

WEB RESOURCES

Developmental Theories of Crime

https://quizlet.com/15249226/flashcards
http://www.cram.com/flashcards/criminology-chapter-9-developmental-theories-life-course-latent-trait-and-trajectory-3470365
https://benthamopen.com/contents/pdf/TOCRIJ/TOCRIJ-4-13.pdf

Sampson and Laub's Model

http://www.everydaysociologyblog.com/2008/12/sampson-laubs-a.html
https://scholar.harvard.edu/sampson/content/crime-and-life-course
http://harvardmagazine.com/2004/03/twigs-bent-trees-go-stra.html

Moffitt's Theory

http://www.colorado.edu/ibs/jessor/psych7536-805/readings/moffitt-1993_674-701.pdf
https://www.ncbi.nlm.nih.gov/pmc/articles/PMC4465023
http://www.wpic.pitt.edu/research/famhist/PDF_Articles/APA/BF16.pdf

READING /// 26

In this selection, Alex Piquero, David Farrington, and Alfred Blumstein provide a comprehensive review of the concepts, issues, and propositions presented by the criminal career framework on which developmental theories are based. The developmental paradigm is, by definition, based on following the criminal activity of individuals over time and exploring the reasons why they offend when they do, as well as why these individuals don't offend at certain times. The authors explore the history of the criminal career perspective, as well as the key concepts of participation, offending frequency, duration, and co-offending patterns. Piquero et al. also explore the policy implications that can be gathered, given the current state of research on these various dimensions.

Then the authors explore the issues related to chronic offenders, who are the small percentage of society (approximately 5% to 8% of the population) who commit the vast majority of violent and serious offenses. Piquero et al. also provide policy recommendations, especially regarding incarceration policies. Finally, the authors review the extant research on career length and desistence (or the ceasing of offending in an individual's life) as well as prescribing issues that future research should examine.

While reading this selection, readers should consider the following points:

- The key concepts of the career criminal paradigm according to Piquero et al., such as offending frequency and duration, and the concepts that seem most important in determining which individuals pose the greatest danger to society
- The policy implications suggested by Piquero et al. that are logical given the criminal career framework
- The criteria that distinguish individuals as chronic offenders and some of the primary causes for their chronic offending

Criminal Career Paradigm

Background, Recent Developments, and the Way Forward

Alex R. Piquero, David P. Farrington, and Alfred Blumstein

Researchers have long been interested in the patterning of criminal activity throughout the course of criminal careers. Early on, Quetelet (1831) recognized that the age was closely related to the propensity for crime. Using data on crimes committed against persons and property in France from 1826 to 1829, Quetelet found that crimes peaked in the late teens through the mid twenties. Since Quetelet's findings, a number of researchers have pursued the relationship between age and crime, across cultures and historical periods, and for a number of different crime types (Hirschi and Gottfredson 1983). Research on the relationship between age and crime has been one of the most studied issues within criminology (Farrington 1986; Steffensmeier et al. 1989; Tittle and Grasmick 1993).

The relationship between age and crime raises the question of the degree to which the aggregate pattern displayed in the age/crime curve is similar to—or different from—the pattern of individual careers and whether conclusions about individuals can be validly drawn from aggregate data. For example, how far does the observed peak of the aggregate age/crime curve reflect changes within individuals as opposed to changes in the composition of offenders? In other words, is the peak in the age/crime curve a function of active offenders committing more crime, or is it a function of more individuals actively offending during those peak years?

Within individuals, to what extent is the slowing past the peak age a function of deceleration in continued criminal activity or stopping by some of the individuals? Across individuals, how much of the age/crime curve can be attributed to the arrival/initiation and departure/termination of different individuals? How about the role of co-offending? How much of the continuation of offending by lone/solo offenders is attributable to identifying theirs as the key criminal careers of long duration, with their co-offenders serving merely as transients with shorter careers? How much of the age/crime curve for any particular crime type is a consequence of individuals persisting in offending, but switching from less serious crime types early in the career to more serious crime types as they get older? What about the relationship between past and future offending? Is it due to some causal factors or changes in causal factors (state dependence), unobserved individual differences (persistent heterogeneity), or some combination?

These questions are central to theory, as well as policy, especially those policies that are geared toward incapacitative effects of criminal sanctions, as well as to changes in the criminal career (e.g., rehabilitation or criminalization patterns as a result of actions by the criminal justice system). For example, if crime commission and arrest rates differ significantly among offenders and over the career, the effect of sentence length on overall crime will depend on who is incarcerated, and for how long (Petersilia 1980:325). Addressing these and related issues requires knowledge about individual criminal careers, their initiation, their termination and the dynamic changes between these end points (Blumstein et al. 1986).

In 1983, a Panel on Research on Criminal Careers was convened by the National Academy of Science at the request of the U. S. National Institute of Justice and was charged with evaluating the feasibility of predicting the future course of criminal careers, assessing the effects of prediction instruments in reducing crime through incapacitation, and reviewing the contribution of research on criminal careers to the development of fundamental knowledge about crime and criminals. This report outlined a novel approach of asking questions regarding the longitudinal patterning of criminal activity over the life course, i.e., the criminal career paradigm (Blumstein et al. 1986).

Since publication of the report, numerous theoretical, empirical, and policy issues have surfaced regarding the longitudinal patterning of criminal careers. One concerned the relevance (or lack thereof) of criminal career research for criminology generally, and public policy in particular. Gottfredson and Hirschi (1990) levied a series of critiques against the criminal career approach in which they claimed that attempts to identify career criminals and other types of offenders were doomed to failure. Perhaps the most important issue they raised concerns causality. Although the criminal career paradigm necessitates a longitudinal focus in order to study both the between- and within-individual patterning of criminal activity, Gottfredson and Hirschi questioned whether longitudinal research designs could actually resolve questions of causal order. They also argued that, since correlations with offending were relatively stable over the life-course, cross-sectional designs were suitable for studying the causes of crime.

This paper summarizes background and recent developments regarding the criminal career paradigm. Section I provides a brief review of the criminal career paradigm, as well as an overview of the empirical findings generated by criminal careers research, with a concentration on the dimensions of criminal careers. Section II presents a discussion of selected policy implications including the identification of career criminals and policies associated with sentence duration. Section III offers an agenda for future theoretical, empirical, and methodological research. The full conclusion of our report may be found in the essay "The Criminal Career Paradigm," published in *Crime and Justice: A Review of Research, Volume 30* (Piquero, Farrington, and Blumstein 2003).

I. The Criminal Career Paradigm

At its most basic level, a criminal career is the "characterization of the longitudinal sequence of crimes committed by an individual offender" (Blumstein et al. 1986:12). This definition helps to focus researchers' attention on entry into a career when or before the first crime is committed and dropout from the career when or after the last crime is committed. The criminal career paradigm recognizes that individuals start their criminal activity at some age, engage in crime at some individual crime rate, commit a mixture of crimes, and eventually stop. Hence, the criminal career approach emphasizes the need to investigate issues related to why and when people start offending (onset), why and how they continue offending (persistence), why and if offending becomes more frequent or serious (escalation) or specialized, and why and when people stop offending (desistance). The study of criminal careers does not imply that offenders necessarily derive their livelihood exclusively or even predominantly from crime; instead, the concept is intended only as a means of structuring the longitudinal sequence of criminal events associated with an individual in a systematic way (Blumstein et al. 1982:5). In sum, the criminal career approach focuses on both between- and within-individual changes in criminal activity over time.

A. Dimensions of a Criminal Career

1. Participation

The criminal career approach partitions the aggregate crime rate into two primary components: "participation," the distinction between those who commit crime and those who do not; and "frequency," the rate of offending among active offenders, commonly denoted by the Greek letter λ (Blumstein et al. 1986:12). Participation is measured by the fraction of a population ever committing at least one crime before some age or currently active during some particular observation period. In any period, active offenders include both new offenders whose first offense occurs during the observation period, and persisting offenders who began criminal activity in an earlier period and continue to be active during the observation period. Importantly, the longer the average duration of offending, the greater the contribution of persisters to measured participation in successive observation periods.

Estimates of ever-participation in criminal activity vary across reporting method (they tend to be much higher with self-report than with official records which are a filtered subset of self-reports), the crimes in which participation is being measured (there is more participation in less serious criminal activity), the level of threshold of involvement (police contact, arrest, conviction), and the characteristics and representativeness of the sample (high school students, college students, general population, offender-based, etc.). In general, ever-participation estimates are fairly common across data sets and consistent with most criminological findings.

There is a relatively high rate of participation among males in criminal activity (Elliott et al. 1987:502). Blumstein et al. (1986) reported that about 15 percent of urban males are arrested for an index offense by age eighteen, and about 25 to 45 percent of urban males are arrested for a non-traffic offense by age eighteen. Visher and Roth's (1986) overview of several longitudinal studies employing police and court records indicates a lifetime prevalence estimate of 40 to 50 percent, with slightly higher rates for blacks and much lower rates among females. Stattin et al.'s (1989) longitudinal study of Swedish males and females revealed that by age 30, 37.7% of Swedish males and 9% of Swedish females were registered for a criminal offense. The cumulative prevalence of self-reported offenses is even more striking. For example, in the Cambridge study, Farrington (2003) found that 96 percent of the males had reported committing at least one of ten specified offenses (including burglary, theft, assault, vandalism, and drug abuse) up to age thirty-two. Kelley et al. (1997) used self-reported data on serious violence from three longitudinal studies funded by the Office of Juvenile Justice and Delinquency Prevention, the Causes and Correlates studies, and found that 39 percent of Denver males, 41 percent of Pittsburgh males, 40 percent of Rochester males, 16 percent of Denver females, and 32 percent of Rochester females reported committing at least one serious violent act by age sixteen.

Regardless of whether official or self-report records are used to study prevalence, three main conclusions emerge. First, male participation rates are typically higher than those for females, and especially so for the more serious offenses. Second, black participation rates are typically higher than those for whites, especially when participation is examined via official records as opposed to self-reports (Hindelang et al. 1981). In self-reports, blacks have also been found to report continuing their violent offending at higher rates than whites (Elliott 1994). Third, there is a strong relationship between age and participation. In particular, the probability of initiating a criminal career at a given age is highest between thirteen and eighteen, on the lower end for self-report estimates and on the higher end for arrest and conviction records, with little to no gender difference (Moffitt et al. 2001). Also, evidence on the probability of committing an offense at a given age is mixed, with some research indicating a consistent increase through the mid-teens to a peak at age nineteen and then subsequent decline, while other research indicates a decline in self-reported participation through the teens (Elliott et al. 1983; Lauritsen 1998; Thornberry 1989). Studying demographic differences in prevalence remains controversial. For example, Hindelang et al. (1981) argued that there is a race difference in the validity of self-reported delinquency measures, which leads to a serious underestimation of black males' prevalence rates.

2. Key Dimensions of Active Criminal Careers

The criminal career paradigm encompasses several dimensions of active criminal careers including offending frequency, duration, crime type mix and seriousness, and co-offending patterns.

a. Offending Frequency. The offending rate for individual offenders, λ, reflects the frequency of offending by individuals who are actively engaged in crime (Blumstein et al. 1986:55). Much criminal career research has been concerned with estimating the individual offending frequency of active offenders during their criminal careers (Blumstein and Cohen 1979; Cohen 1986; Loeber and Snyder 1990).

Blumstein et al. (1986) summarized variation in λ for active offenders by gender, age, and race. Regarding gender, they found little variation in frequency across males and females (i.e., the ratios are generally 2:1 or less) for most crimes (Blumstein et al. 1986:67–68). Thus, if active in a crime type, females commit crimes at rates similar to those of males (for an exception see Wikström 1985). Regarding age, Blumstein et al. reported little change with age in offense-specific frequency rates for active offenders, but when all offense types are combined, there tended to be an increase during the juvenile years and a decrease during the adult years. In the Rand Inmate surveys, there appeared to be some evidence of general stability of λ over age (Chaiken and Chaiken 1982). The number of active crime types declined with age in the Rand survey, but crime-specific frequencies tended to be stable (Peterson and Braiker 1980). Finally, although research based on official records tends to indicate that there is not a strong relationship between offending frequency and demographic characteristics, some recent self-report data on serious violence tends to indicate otherwise (Elliott 1994).

Spelman (1994) summarized current knowledge on offending frequencies. First, there are different values for the average offense frequencies across studies because researchers provide different definitions and operationalizations of the offense rate. Second, most of the variation in offense rates can be attributed to differences in the populations sampled and especially where in the criminal justice system they are sampled. Third, the average offender commits around eight crimes per year, while offenders who are incarcerated at some point in their lives commit thirty to fifty crimes per year, and the average member of an incoming prison cohort commits between sixty and 100 crimes per year. Fourth, criminals do not commit crimes all the time; in other words, there is evidence that many offenders spend long periods of time in which they commit no crimes. Fifth, the distribution of offending frequencies is highly skewed, with a few offenders committing crimes at much higher than average rates.

b. Duration, the Interval between Initiation and Termination. One aspect of the criminal career paradigm that has received a great deal of research attention is initiation, or the onset of antisocial and criminal activity (Farrington et al. 1990). Several studies have reported higher recidivism rates among offenders with records of early criminal activity as juveniles (Blumstein et al. 1986). Although many researchers argue that individuals who begin offending early will desist later, and thus have lengthy careers (Hamparian et al. 1978; Krohn et al. 2001), there has been much less research on the duration of criminal careers, or an individual's criminal career (Piquero, Brame, and Lynam 2003). It is more tenable, however, to measure a rate of desistance for an identified group of offenders (Bushway et al. 2001). Research on desistance, or the termination of a criminal career, has received even less attention because of difficulties in measurement and operationalization (Laub and Sampson 2001).

The two most common approaches for studying career termination have been through providing estimates of termination probabilities after each arrest, and estimating the time between the first and last crimes committed. Regarding termination probabilities, Blumstein et al. (1986) calculated persistence probabilities for six different data sets and found that after each subsequent event (i.e., police contact, arrest, conviction, etc.), the persistence probability increases, reaching a plateau of .7 to .9 by the fourth event across all data sets. Farrington, Lambert, and West (1998) used conviction data to calculate recidivism probabilities for Cambridge study males through age thirty-two and found that after the third offense, the recidivism probability ranged from .79 to .91 through the tenth offense.

A number of studies have attempted to derive estimates of career duration, typically measured as career length in years. Three major studies conducted in the 1970s estimated career lengths to be between five and fifteen years (Greenberg 1975; Greene 1977; Shinnar and Shinnar 1975). In 1982, Blumstein, Cohen, and Hsieh conducted the most detailed study of criminal career duration and used data on arrests rather than on arrestees to estimate career lengths, and concluded that criminal careers are relatively short, averaging about five years for offenders who are active in index offenses as young adults. Residual careers, or the length of time still remaining in careers, increase to an expected ten years for index offenders still active in their thirties. Persistent offenders who begin their adult careers at age eighteen or earlier and who are still active in their thirties are most likely to be persistent offenders and are likely to continue to commit crimes for about another ten years (Visher 2000).

Spelman (1994) studied career lengths with data from the three-state Rand Inmate Survey, and developed estimates of total career lengths of about six or seven years (Spelman 1994). Spelman showed that young and inexperienced offenders, those in the first five years of their career, were more likely than older offenders to drop out each year, but after five years the rate of dropout leveled off, rising only after the twentieth year as an active offender. Farrington (2003) examined the duration of criminal careers in the Cambridge study using conviction data to age forty and found that the average duration of criminal careers was 7.1 years. Excluding one-time offenders, whose duration was zero, the average duration of criminal careers was 10.4 years. Piquero et al. (2003) studied the length of criminal careers using data from a sample of serious offenders paroled from California Youth Authority institutions in the 1970s and found that the average career length was 17.27 years, with little difference between white (16.7 years) and non-white parolees (17.7 years).

c. Crime Type Mix and Seriousness. The mix of different offense types among active offenders is another important criminal career dimension. The study of crime-type mix involves studying seriousness (the tendency to commit serious crimes throughout one's criminal career), escalations (the tendency to move toward more serious crimes as one's career progresses), specialization (the tendency to repeat the same offense type on successive crimes), and crime-type switching (the tendency to switch types of crimes and/or crime categories on successive crimes).

Diverse methodological techniques have been employed to investigate specialization, or the tendency to repeat the same offense type on successive crimes. Using official records, some research provides evidence in favor of some small degree of specialization (Bursik 1980; Rojek and Erickson 1982; Smith and Smith 1984), but most find that generality is the norm throughout offending careers (Farrington et al. 1988; Wolfgang et al. 1972; Nevares et al. 1990; Tracy et al. 1990). At the same time, important differences in specialization are observed between adults and juveniles such that specialization appears to be stronger in magnitude for adult rather than for juvenile offenders (Le Blanc and Fréchette 1989; Piquero et al. 1999). On the other hand, self-report data from the Rand studies suggest that, although there is some evidence of property specialization (Spelman 1994), incarcerated offenders tend to report much more generality than speciality (Petersilia et al. 1978; Peterson and Braiker 1980; Chaiken and Chaiken 1982).

Some scholars have investigated specialization in violence. Using official records, Farrington (1989) and Piquero (2000) reported little evidence of specialization in violence in the Cambridge study or the Philadelphia perinatal cohort, and that the commission of a violent offense in a criminal career is a function of offending frequency: frequent offenders are more likely to accumulate a violent offense in their career. Similar results have been obtained by Capaldi and Patterson (1996) with self-report data from the Oregon Youth Study.

Directly related to the specialization issue is the switching that occurs across clusters of crime types. Clusters represent natural groupings of offense types (violence, property, other), and research indicates that adult offenders display a stronger tendency to switch among offense types within a cluster and a weaker tendency to switch to offense types outside a cluster, but the strong partitioning is not as sharp among juveniles (Blumstein et al. 1986; Cohen 1986). Adult offenders and incarcerated juveniles are more likely to commit offenses within a cluster than to switch to offenses outside a cluster (Rojek and Erickson 1982; Blumstein et al. 1988). Drug offenders, however, do not tend to switch to either violent or property offenses.

d. Co-offending Patterns. Another important criminal career feature is whether a person commits on offense alone or with others (Reiss 1986). Little empirical work has been completed on co-offending, and even less information exists regarding the group criminal behavior of youths in transition to adult status or of adult offenders at different ages. In the Cambridge Study, Reiss and Farrington (1991) report that the incidence of co-offending is greatest for burglary and robbery, and that juvenile offenders primarily commit their crimes with others, whereas adult offenders primarily commit their crimes alone. Although the decline in co-offending may, at first glance, be attributed to co-offenders dropping out, it seems to occur because males change from co-offending in their teenage years to lone offending in their twenties. In the Swedish Borlänge study, Sarnecki (1990) found that 45 percent of all youths suspected of offense at some stage during the six-year study period could be linked together in a single large network that accounted for most offenses. Recently, Sarnecki (2001) used data from all individuals aged twenty or less who were suspected of one or more offenses in Stockholm during 1991–1995 to study the extent and role of co-offending and uncovered that 60 percent of the individuals had a co-offender at some point. Interestingly, he also found that males tended to co-offend primarily with other males, but among females, the proportion of girls choosing other females was lower than the proportion of boys choosing other males as co-offenders. Conway and McCord (2002) conducted the first co-offending study designed to track patterns of violent criminal behavior over an eighteen-year period (1976–1994) among a random sample of 400 urban offenders and their accomplices in Philadelphia. Using crime data collected from court records and "rap sheets," they found that nonviolent offenders who committed their first co-offense with a violent accomplice were at increased risk for subsequent serious violent crime, independent of the effects of age and gender.

B. Policy Issues

The criminal career paradigm suggests three general orientations for crime control strategies: prevention, career modification, and incapacitation. Knowledge concerning the patterning of criminal careers is intimately related to these policy issues. Prevention strategies, including general deterrence, are intended to reduce the number of nonoffenders who become offenders. Career modification strategies, including individual deterrence and rehabilitation, are focused on persons already known to be criminals and seek to reduce the frequency or seriousness of their crimes. In addition, these strategies encourage the termination of ongoing criminal careers through mechanisms such as job training and drug treatment. Incapacitative strategies focus on the crimes reduced as a result of removing offenders from society during their criminal careers. Two types of incapacitation are general, or collective, and selective, which focuses on the highest frequency offenders. These three crime control strategies are intimately related to specific laws, including habitual offender statutes, truth-in-sentencing laws, three-strikes laws, and mandatory minimum sentences laws.

1. Crime Control Strategies

Of all crime control strategies, the criminal career paradigm has focused extensive attention on incapacitation. General or collective incapacitation strategies aim to reduce criminal activity as a consequence of increasing the total level of incarceration while selective incapacitation policies focus primarily on offenders who represent the greatest risk of future offending. The former approach is consistent with the equal treatment concerns of a just-deserts sentencing policy while the latter focuses as much on the offenders as the offense. Importantly, the degree to which selective incapacitation policies are effective depends on the ability to distinguish high- and low-risk offenders, and to identify them early enough before they are about to terminate criminal activity. Three related issues arise: the ability to classify individual offenders in terms of their projected criminal activity; the quality of the classification rules; and the legitimacy of basing punishment of an individual on the possibility of future crimes rather than only on the crimes already committed (and the consequent level of disparity that is considered acceptable).

Regarding collective incapacitation, Blumstein et al. (1986) suggest that achieving a 10 percent reduction in crime may require more than doubling the existing inmate population. However, under selective incapacitation policies, long prison terms would be reserved primarily for offenders identified as most likely to continue committing serious crimes at high rates. Blumstein et al. conclude that selective incapacitation policies could achieve 5 to 10 percent reductions in robbery with 10 to 20 percent increases in the population of robbers in prison, while much larger increases in prison populations are required for collective incapacitation policies.

2. Relationship to Laws

Both collective and selective incapacitation policies are directly influenced by laws and policies that govern criminal justice decisions regarding the punishment of offenders. For example, habitual offender statutes give special options to prosecutors for dealing with repeat offenders. Truth-in-sentencing laws are intended to increase incapacitation by requiring offenders, particularly violent offenders, to serve a substantial portion of their prison sentence, and parole eligibility and good-time credits are restricted or eliminated. Three-strikes laws provide that any person convicted of three, typically violent, felony offenses, must serve a lengthy prison term, usually a minimum term of twenty-five-years-to-life. Mandatory-minimum sentence laws require a specified sentence and prohibit offenders convicted of certain crimes from being placed on probation, while other statutes prohibit certain offenders from being considered for parole. Mandatory-minimum sentence laws can also serve as sentencing enhancement measures, requiring that offenders spend additional time in prison if they commit particular crimes in a particular manner (e.g., committing a felony with a gun). The net effect of these laws is to increase prison populations by incarcerating certain kinds of offenders or increasing the sentence length of those offenders convicted for certain types of crimes.

C. "Chronic" Offenders

Criminologists have long recognized that a small group of individuals is responsible for a majority of criminal activity. Wolfgang et al. (1972) focused attention on the chronic offender by applying that label to the small group of 627 delinquents in the 1945 Philadelphia birth cohort who committed five or more offenses by age seventeen (hereafter five-plus). This group constituted just 6 percent of the full cohort of 9,945 males and 18 percent of the delinquent subset of 3,475, but was responsible for 5,305 offenses, or 52 percent of all delinquency in the cohort through age seventeen. The chronic offenders were responsible for an even larger percentage of the more serious, violent offenses. The finding that a small subset of sample members are responsible for a majority of criminal activity is supported by data from other longitudinal data sets, including the second 1958 Philadelphia birth cohort (Tracy et al., 1990), the Puerto Rico Birth Cohort Study (Nevares et al., 1990), the Dunedin New Zealand Multidisciplinary Health Study (Moffitt et al. 2001), the Philadelphia (Piquero 2000) and Providence (Piquero and Buka 2002) perinatal projects, the Racine, WI, birth cohorts (Shannon 1982), the Cambridge study (Farrington 2003), and also by cohort studies in Sweden (Wikström 1985), Finland (Pulkkinen 1988), and Denmark (Guttridge et al. 1983). The finding is also replicated across gender and race (Moffitt et al. 2001; Piquero and Buka 2002), and emerges from both official and self-report data. Research also indicates that chronic offenders exhibit an early onset, a longer career duration, and involvement in serious offenses—including person/violent-oriented offenses—than other offenders (Loeber and Farrington 1998).

The five-plus cutoff advanced by Wolfgang et al. (1972) has been employed in several studies; however, since theoretical and empirical definitions of chronicity have yet to be established, questions have been raised about the extent to which similar definitions of chronicity should be used across gender (Farrington and Loeber 1998; Piquero 2000), as well as the relatively arbitrary designation of five-plus offenses as characteristic of chronicity (Blumstein et al. 1985). Blumstein et al. (1985) raised other concerns with the use of five-plus as the chronicity cut point. They argued that the chronic offender calculation, which was based on the full cohort, overestimates the chronic offender effect because many cohort members will never be arrested. Instead, they urge that the ever-arrested subjects should be the base used to calculate the chronic offender effect. With the base, the 627 chronics with five-plus arrests represented 18 percent of those arrested, as opposed to 6 percent of the cohort. Blumstein and colleagues also argued that the proportion of chronic offenders observed by Wolfgang et al. (1972) could have resulted from a homogenous population of persisters. Blumstein et al. (1985) tested the hypothesis that all persisters (those with more than three arrests) could be viewed as having the same rearrest probability. Such an assumption could not be rejected. Although those with five-plus arrests accounted for the majority of arrests among the persisters, such a result could have occurred even if all subjects with three or more arrests had identical recidivism probabilities. Thus, the chronic offenders who were identified retrospectively as those with five or more arrests could not have been distinguished prospectively from nonchronics with three or four arrests.

II. Policy Implications

Research on criminal careers has direct import for decision-making in the criminal justice system. In this section, we address four implications of criminal career research: the role of criminal career research in policy and individual decision-making, individual prediction of offending frequencies (λ), sentence duration, and research on career length and desistance and its relation to intelligent sentencing policy.

A. Role of Criminal Career Research in Policy and Individual Decision-Making

A principal example of the importance of criminal career research for criminal justice policy is criminal career length. Three-strikes and selective incapacitation philosophies assume that high-rate offenders will continue to offend at high rates and for long periods of time if they are not incarcerated. From an incapacitative perspective, incarceration is only effective in averting crimes when it is applied during an active criminal career. Thus, incarceration after the career ends or when a career is abating, is wasted for incapacitation purposes (Blumstein et al. 1982:70). By identifying career lengths, especially residual career lengths, policymakers can better target incarceration on offenders whose expected remaining careers are longest. Incarceration policies should be based on career duration distribution information. The more hardcore committed offenders with the longest remaining careers are identifiable only after an offender has remained active for several years (Blumstein et al. 1982). Earlier and later in criminal careers, sanctions will be applied to many offenders who are likely to drop out shortly anyway (Blumstein et al. 1982:71). The benefits derived from incapacitation will vary depending on an individual's crime rate and the length of his or her remaining criminal career. Continuing to incarcerate an offender after his/her career ends limits the usefulness of incarceration.

B. Individual Prediction of λ

Rand's second inmate survey highlighted the extreme skewness of the distribution of λ for a sample of serious criminals (Chaiken and Chaiken 1982; Visher 1986). Naturally, the identification of a small number of inmates who reported committing several hundred crimes per year led to the search for a method to identify these offenders in advance. If high-rate offenders cannot be identified prospectively, then crime control efforts will be hampered (Visher 1987). In this section, we highlight two related issues: the difficulty in identifying high-λ individuals, and the alleviation of the concern over prediction by "stochastic selectivity."

1. Difficulty in Identifying High-λ Individuals

Although high-λ individuals emerge in the aggregate, it has been difficult to identify specific individuals. Greenwood and Turner (1987) used data consisting of follow-up criminal history information on the California inmates who were included in the original Rand survey and who had been out of prison for two years to examine the extent to which Greenwood's seven-item prediction scale succeeded in predicting recidivism. The scale was not very effective in predicting post-release criminal activity when the recidivism measure was arrest. The majority of released inmates, regardless of whether they were predicted to be low- or high-rate offenders, were rearrested within two years. Greenwood and Turner also created a measure of the offender's annual arrest rate (i.e., the number of arrests per year of street time) for the follow-up sample and defined high-rate offenders as those inmates who had an actual arrest rate greater than 0.78. They found that the seven-item scale was less accurate in predicting annual arrest rates than it was in predicting re-incarceration.

There are also concerns related to the false positive prediction problem in identifying high-λ individuals. For example, Visher (1986:204–5) reanalyzed the Rand second inmate survey and found that not only were the estimates of λ for robbery and burglary sensitive to choices in computation (i.e., handling missing data, street time, etc.), but also that some inmates reported annual rates of 1,000 or more robberies or burglaries, thus strongly affecting the distribution of λ, and especially its mean. Finally, Visher's analysis of the Greenwood scale for identifying high-rate offenders indicated that 55 percent of the classified high-rate group (27 percent of the total sample) were false positives who did not commit crimes at high rates. In fact, the prediction scale worked better in identifying low-rate offenders. Recently, Auerhahn (1999) replicated Greenwood and Abrahams's (1982) selective incapacitation study with a representative sample of California state prison inmates, and found that the scale's overall predictive accuracy was 60 percent, indicating a great deal of error in identifying serious, high-rate offenders.

2. Concern and Need for Prediction Alleviated by "Stochastic Selectivity"

Many analyses of the crime control potential of increasing incarceration rely on a single estimate of mean λ derived from prison inmates and applying it indiscriminately to all related populations of offenders (Canela-Cacho et al. 1997). This assumes that all offenders engage in the same amount (λ) of criminal behavior—regardless of whether they are in prison or jail, or free in the community—and that the probability of their detection and incarceration is equal. However, measures of λ derived from arrestee/convictee populations display a strong selection bias because individuals who have gone through the criminal justice process are unlikely to be representative of the total offender population. This selection bias could be because samples of arrestees have a higher propensity for arrest or different offending frequencies. A highly heterogeneous distribution of offending frequency in the total population of offenders combines with relatively low imprisonment levels to lead to substantial selectivity of high-λ offenders among resident inmates and a correspondingly low mean value of λ among those offenders who remain free (Canela-Cacho et al. 1997). "Stochastic selectivity," then, draws into prison new inmates disproportionately from the high end of the λ distribution of free offenders. Further, the higher the incarceration probability following a crime, the deeper into the offender pool incarceration will reach, and the lower will be the incapacitation effect associated with the incoming cohorts (Canela-Cacho et al. 1997).

Using data from the second Rand inmate survey, Canela-Cacho et al. (1997) studied the issue of stochastic selectivity and found that the proportion of low-λ burglars and robbers among free offenders was much larger than among resident inmates, while at the high end of the offending frequency distribution there was a larger proportion of high-λ burglars and robbers among resident inmates than among free offenders. Thus, selectivity occurred naturally as high-λ offenders experienced greater opportunities for incarceration through the greater number of crimes they committed (Canela-Cacho et al. 1997:142), thereby obviating the need for efforts to explicitly identify individual high-λ offenders.

C. Sentence Duration

Information about crime rates and career lengths is particularly useful for incapacitation and incarceration decisions and policies, and such knowledge can also provide useful information regarding the intelligent use of incapacitation and may even provide powerful arguments against lengthy incapacitation policies. Principal among these is the decision regarding sentence length. Many current sentencing policies are based on the assumption that high-rate offenders will continue committing crimes at high rates and for lengthy periods, and thus prescribe lengthy incarceration stints. The extent to which this policy is effective, however, is contingent on the duration of a criminal career.

Much debate regarding sentence length has centered on three-strikes policies. These policies severely limit judges' discretion because they prescribe a mandatory prison sentence of (typically) twenty-five-years-to-life. The incapacitation effectiveness of three-strikes laws, however, depends on the duration of criminal careers. To the extent that sentencing decisions incarcerate individuals with short residual career lengths, a three-strikes law will waste incarceration resources (Stolzenberg and D'Alessio 1997:466).

Stolzenberg and D'Alessio (1997) used aggregate data drawn from the ten largest cities in California to examine the impact of California's three-strikes law on serious crime rates and found that the three-strikes law did not decrease serious crime or petty theft rates below the level expected on the basis of preexisting trends. Zimring et al. (1999) obtained a sample of felony arrests (and relevant criminal records) in Los Angeles, San Francisco, and San Diego, both before and after the California law went into effect to study the three-strikes issue. Two key findings emerged from their study. First, the mean age at arrest for two strikes and above was 34.6 years. This is particularly important because: "[O]n average the two or more strikes defendant has an almost 40 percent longer criminal adult career behind him (estimated at 16.6 years) than does the no-strikes felony defendant. All other things being equal, this means that the twenty-five-years-to-life mandatory prison sentence will prevent fewer crimes among the third-strike group than it would in the general population of felons because the group eligible for it is somewhat older" (Zimring et al. 1999:34). Second, when comparing crime trends in the three cities before and after the law, Zimring et al. found that there was no decline in the crimes committed by those targeted by the new law. In particular, the lower crime rates in 1994 and 1995 (just immediately after the three-strikes law went into effect) were evenly spread among targeted and non-targeted populations, suggesting that the decline in crime observed after the law went into effect was not due to the law.

D. Research on Career Length and Desistance

Sentencing practices involving lengthy sentence durations assume that affected offenders will continue to commit crime at a high rate and for a long period. To the extent that this is the case, incapacitation policies will avert crimes and thwart continued careers. However, to the extent that offenders retire before the expiration of a lengthy sentence, shorter career durations will reduce the effects of lengthy sentences. Using data from Florida, Schmertmann et al. (1998) concluded that the aging of prison populations under three-strikes policies in that state will undermine their long-run effectiveness. In particular, they noted that the policies will cause increases in prison populations due to the addition of large numbers of older inmates who are unlikely to commit future offenses.

The key to the sentence duration issue, and why estimates of criminal career duration are so important, rests on the characteristics of the person years—not the people—that are removed from free society as a result of such policies (Schmertmann et al. 1998:458). Such policies will be effective only to the extent that they incarcerate offenders during the early stages of their criminal careers when they are committing crimes at a high-rate.

Unfortunately, research on career duration and desistance is in its infancy. Knowledge on this subject will be important for furthering criminal justice policy and the cost-effective use of criminal justice resources.

III. Directions for Future Criminal Career Research

Evidence on criminal career issues cuts to the heart of theory and policy. On the theoretical side, knowledge on the correlates of criminal career dimensions is relevant to the necessity for general versus typological models. If research indicates that the correlates of one offending dimension are similar to another offending dimension, then more general and non-dimension-specific theories are warranted. If the correlates of one offending dimension are different from another offending dimension, then the causal process(es) underlying these two particular dimensions are probably different and different explanations and theories are required.

Better knowledge on various criminal career dimensions would aid policy initiatives designed to prevent initial involvement, curtail current offending, and accelerate the desistance process. If research suggests that poor parental socialization is related to early initiation, then prevention efforts should include parent-training efforts. Similarly, if drug use is associated with continued involvement in delinquent and criminal behavior, then intervention efforts should include drug treatment. Finally, if some set of correlates is associated with desistance, then policy efforts may wish to provide for specific prevention and intervention efforts.

Knowledge on career length and residual career length could best inform criminal justice policies because it deals directly with sentencing and incapacitation policies that are now driven more by ideology than by empirical knowledge. For example, if residual criminal career lengths average around five years, criminal justice policies advocating multi-decade sentences waste scarce resources. Similarly, if offenders are incarcerated in late adulthood when their residual career lengths have diminished, incarceration space will be wasted, and health care costs will increase, thereby further straining scarce resources.

Empirical study of criminal careers requires data collection for large samples of individuals beginning early in life and continuing for a lengthy period into adulthood. Such data are needed if questions surrounding initiation, continuation, and desistance are to be adequately addressed, and this is especially the case among serious offenders for which little longitudinal data exists (Laub and Sampson 2001; Piquero et al. 2002). The use of such longitudinal data, of course, brings with it several potential problems that need to be considered including methodological issues such as street time (Piquero et al. 2001), mortality (Eggleston, Laub, and Sampson 2003) and sample attrition (Brame and Piquero 2003), as well as statistical issues that deal with various modeling strategies and assumptions (Bushway et al. 1999; Nagin 1999; Raudenbush 2001). Nevertheless, continued data collection and research are important to identify and study unaddressed and unresolved criminal career issues, and to update thirty-year-old estimates.

Information derived from criminal career research is important to advance fundamental knowledge about offending and to assist criminal justice decision-makers in dealing with offenders. Much more important criminal career research lies on the horizon nationally and internationally, and we look forward to seeing this research emerge.

References

Auerhahn, Kathleen. 1999. "Selective Incapacitation and the Problem of Prediction." *Criminology* 37: 703–34.

Blumstein, Alfred, and Jacqueline Cohen. 1979. "Estimation of Individual Crime Rates from Arrest Records." *Journal of Criminal Law and Criminology* 70: 561–85.

Blumstein, Alfred, Jacqueline Cohen, Somnath Das, and Soumyo D. Moitra. 1988. "Specialization and Seriousness during Adult Criminal Careers." *Journal of Quantitative Criminology* 4: 303–45.

Blumstein, Alfred, Jacqueline Cohen, and Paul Hsieh. 1982. *The Duration of Adult Criminal Careers.* Final report submitted to National Institute of Justice, August 1982. Pittsburgh, PA: School of Urban and Public Affairs, Carnegie-Mellon University.

Blumstein, Alfred, Jacqueline Cohen, Jeffrey A. Roth, and Christy A. Visher, eds. 1986. *Criminal Careers and "Career Criminal."* 2 vols. Panel on Research on Criminal Careers, Committee on Research on Law Enforcement and the Administration of Justice. Commission on Behavioral and Social Sciences and Education, National Research Council. Washington, DC: National Academy Press.

Blumstein, Alfred, David P. Farrington, and Soumyo Moitra. 1985. "Delinquency Careers: Innocents, Desisters, and Persisters." In *Crime and Justice: An Annual Review of Research,* Vol. 6, ed. Michael Tonry and Norval Morris. Chicago: University of Chicago Press.

Brame. Robert, and Alex R. Piquero. 2003. "The Role of Sample Attrition in Studying the Longitudinal Relationship between Age and Crime." *Journal of Quantitative Criminology.*

Bursik, Robert J., Jr. 1980. "The Dynamics of Specialization in Juvenile Offenses." *Social Forces* 58: 851–64.

Bushway, Shawn, Robert Brame, and Raymond Paternoster. 1999. "Assessing Stability and Change in Criminal Offending: A Comparison of Random Effects, Semiparametric, and Fixed Effects Modeling Strategies." *Journal of Quantitative Criminology* 15: 23–64.

Bushway, Shawn D., Alex R. Piquero, Lisa M. Broidy, Elizabeth Cauffman, and Paul Mazerolle. 2001. "An Empirical Framework for Studying Desistance as a Process." *Criminology* 39: 491–515.

Canela-Cacho, José E., Alfred Blumstein, and Jacqueline Cohen. 1997. "Relationship between the Offending Frequency (λ) of Imprisoned and Free Offenders." *Criminology* 35: 133–76.

Capaldi, Deborah N., and Gerald R. Patterson. 1996. "Can Violent Offenders Be Distinguished from Frequent Offenders: Prediction from Childhood to Adolescence." *Journal of Research in Crime and Delinquency* 33: 206–31.

Chaiken, Jan M., and Marcia R. Chaiken. 1982. *Varieties of Criminal Behavior.* Rand Report R-2814-NIJ. Santa Monica, CA: Rand Corporation.

Cohen, Jacqueline. 1986. "Research on Criminal Careers: Individual Frequency Rates and Offense Seriousness." In *Criminal Careers and "Career Criminals,"* Vol. 1, ed. Alfred Blumstein, Jacqueline Cohen, Jeffrey A. Roth, and Christy A. Visher. Washington, DC: National Academy Press.

Conway, Kevin P., and Joan McCord. 2002. "A Longitudinal Examination of the Relation between Co-offending with Violent Accomplices and Violent Crime." *Aggressive Behavior* 28: 97–108.

Eggleston, Eliane, John H. Laub, and Robert J. Sampson. 2003. "Examining Long-term Trajectories of Criminal Offending: The Glueck Delinquents from Age 7 to 80." *Journal of Quantitative Criminology*, forthcoming.

Elliott, Delbert S. 1994. "1993 Presidential Address—Serious Violent Offenders: Onset, Developmental Course, and Termination." *Criminology* 32: 1–22.

Elliott, Delbert S., Suzanne S. Ageton, David Huizinga, Barbara Knowles, and R. Canter. 1983. *The Prevalence and Incidence of Delinquent Behavior: 1976–1980.* National Youth Survey, Report No. 26. Boulder, CO: Behavioral Research Institute.

Elliott, Delbert S., David Huizinga, and Barbara Morse. 1987. "Self-Reported Violent Offending: A Descriptive Analysis of Juvenile Violent Offenders and Their Offending Careers." *Journal of Interpersonal Violence* 1: 472–514.

Farrington, David P. 1986. "Age and Crime." In *Crime and Justice: An Annual Review of Research,* Vol. 7, ed. Michael Tonry and Norval Morris. Chicago: University of Chicago Press.

———. 1989. "Self-Reported and Official Offending from Adolescence to Adulthood." In *Cross-National Research in Self-Reported Crime and Delinquency,* ed. Malcolm W. Klein. Dordrecht: Kluwer.

———. 2003. "Key Results from the First Forty Years of the Cambridge Study in Delinquent Development." In *Taking Stock of Delinquency: An Overview of Findings from Contemporary Longitudinal Studies,* ed. Terence P. Thornberry and Marvin D. Krohn. New York: Kluwer/Plenum.

Farrington, David P., Sandra Lambert, and Donald J. West. 1998. "Criminal Careers of Two Generations of Family Members in the Cambridge Study in Delinquent Development." *Studies on Crime and Crime Prevention* 7: 85–106.

Farrington, David P., and Rolf Loeber. 1998. "Major Aims of This Book." In *Serious & Violent Juvenile Offenders: Risk Factors and Successful Interventions,* ed. Rolf Loeber and David P. Farrington. Thousand Oaks, CA: Sage.

Farrington, David P., Rolf Loeber, Delbert S. Elliott, J. David Hawkins, Denise Kandel, Malcolm Klein, Joan McCord, David Rowe, and Richard Tremblay. 1990. "Advancing Knowledge about the Onset of Delinquency and Crime." In *Advances in Clinical and Child Psychology,* ed. Bernard Lahey and A. Kazdin. New York: Plenum.

Farrington, David P., Howard N. Snyder, and Terrence A. Finnegan. 1988. "Specialization in Juvenile Court Careers." *Criminology* 26: 461–87.

Gottfredson, Michael R., and Travis Hirschi. 1990. *A General Theory of Crime.* Stanford, CA: Stanford University Press.

Greenberg, David F. 1975. "The Incapacitative Effect of Imprisonment: Some Estimates." *Law and Society Review* 9: 541–80.

Greene, M. A. 1977. The Incapacitative Effect of Imprisonment on Policies of Crime. Unpublished PhD thesis, School of Urban and Public Affairs, Carnegie-Mellon University, Pittsburgh, PA (University Microfilms, Ann Arbor, MI).

Greenwood, Peter W., and Allan Abrahams. 1982. *Selective Incapacitation.* Rand Report R-2815-NIJ. Santa Monica, CA: Rand.

Greenwood, Peter W., and Susan Turner. 1987. *Selective Incapacitation Revisited: Why the High-Rate Offenders Are Hard to Predict.* Rand Report R-3397-NIJ. Santa Monica, CA: Rand.

Guttridge, P., W. F. Gabrielli, Jr., Sarnoff A. Mednick, and Katherine T. Van Dusen. 1983. "Criminal Violence in a Birth Cohort." In *Prospective Studies of Crime and Delinquency,* ed. Katherine T. Van Dusen and Sarnoff A. Mednick. Boston: Kluwer-Nijhoff.

Hamparian, D. M., R. Schuster, S. Dinitz, and J. Conrad. 1978. *The Violent Few: A Study of Dangerous Juvenile Offenders.* Lexington, MA: Lexington Books.

Hindelang, Michael, Travis Hirschi, and Joseph Weis. 1981. *Measuring Delinquency.* Beverly Hills, CA: Sage.

Hirschi, Travis, and Michael G. Gottfredson. 1983. "Age and the Explanation of Crime." *American Journal of Sociology* 89: 552–84.

Kelley, Barbara Tatem, David Huizinga, Terence P. Thornberry, and Rolf Loeber. 1997. *Epidemiology of Serious Violence.* Office of Juvenile Justice Bulletin. Washington, DC: U.S. Department of Justice, Office of Juvenile Justice and Delinquency Prevention.

Krohn, Marvin D., Terence P. Thornberry, Craig Rivera, and Marc Le Blanc. 2001. "Later Delinquency Careers." In *Child Delinquents: Development, Intervention, and Service Needs,* ed. Rolf Loeber and David P. Farrington. Thousand Oaks, CA: Sage.

Laub, John H., and Robert J. Sampson. 2001. "Understanding Desistance from Crime." In *Crime and Justice: A Review of Research,* Vol. 28, ed. Michael Tonry. Chicago: University of Chicago Press.

Lauritsen, Janet. 1998. "The Age-Crime Debate: Assessing the Limits of Longitudinal Self-Report Data." *Social Forces* 77: 127–55.

Le Blanc, Marc, and Marcel Fréchette. 1989. *Male Criminal Activity from Childhood through Youth: Multilevel and Developmental Perspectives.* New York: Springer-Verlag.

Loeber, Rolf, and David P. Farrington, eds. 1998. *Serious & Violent Juvenile Offenders: Risk Factors and Successful Interventions.* Thousand Oaks, CA: Sage.

Loeber, Rolf, and Howard N. Snyder. 1990. "Rate of Offending in Juvenile Careers: Findings of Constancy and Change in Lambda." *Criminology* 28: 97–110.

Moffitt, Terrie E., Avshalom Caspi, Michael Rutter, and Phil A. Silva. 2001. *Sex Differences in Antisocial Behaviour: Conduct Disorder, Delinquency, and Violence in the Dunedin Longitudinal Study.* Cambridge, UK: Cambridge University Press.

Nagin, Daniel S. 1999. "Analyzing Developmental Trajectories: A Semi-Parametric, Group-Based Approach." *Psychological Methods* 4: 139–77.

Nevares, Dora, Marvin E. Wolfgang, and Paul E. Tracy. 1990. *Delinquency in Puerto Rico: The 1970 Birth Cohort Study.* New York: Greenwood Press.

Petersilia, Joan. 1980. "Criminal Career Research: A Review of Recent Evidence." In *Crime and Justice: An Annual Review of Research,* Vol. 2, ed. Norval Morris and Michael Tonry. Chicago: University of Chicago Press.

Petersilia, Joan, Peter W. Greenwood, and Marvin Lavin. 1978. *Criminal Careers of Habitual Felons.* Washington, DC: National Institute of Law Enforcement and Criminal Justice, Law Enforcement Assistance Administration, U.S. Government Printing Office.

Peterson, Mark A., and Harriet B. Braiker. 1980. *Doing Crime: A Survey of California Prison Inmates.* Report R-2200-DOJ. Santa Monica, CA: Rand.

Piquero, Alex R. 2000. "Assessing the Relationships between Gender, Chronicity, Seriousness, and Offense Skewness in Criminal Offending." *Journal of Criminal Justice* 28: 103–16.

Piquero, Alex R., Alfred Blumstein, Robert Brame, Rudy Haapanen, Edward P. Mulvey, and Daniel S. Nagin. 2001. "Assessing the Impact of Exposure Time and Incapacitation on Longitudinal Trajectories of Criminal Offending." *Journal of Adolescent Research* 16: 54–74.

Piquero, Alex R., Robert Brame, and Donald Lynam. 2003. "Do the Factors Associated with Life-Course-Persistent Offending Relate to Career Length?" *Crime and Delinquency,* forthcoming.

Piquero, Alex R., David P. Farrington, and Alfred Blumstein. 2003. "The Criminal Career Paradigm." In *Crime and Justice: A Review of Research,* Vol. 30, ed. Michael Tonry. Chicago: University of Chicago Press.

Piquero, Alex R., Robert Brame, Paul Mazerolle, and Rudy Haapanen. 2002. "Crime in Emerging Adulthood." *Criminology* 40: 137–70.

Piquero, Alex R., and Stephen L. Buka. 2002. "Linking Juvenile and Adult Patterns of Criminal Activity in the Providence Cohort of the National Collaborative Perinatal Project." *Journal of Criminal Justice* 30: 1–14.

Piquero, Alex R., Raymond Paternoster, Paul Mazerolle, Robert Brame, and Charles W. Dean. 1999. "Onset Age and Offense Specialization." *Journal of Research in Crime and Delinquency* 36: 275–99.

Pulkkinen, L. 1988. "Delinquent Development: Theoretical and Empirical Considerations." In *Studies of Psychosocial Risk: The Power of Longitudinal Data,* ed. Michael Rutter. Cambridge, UK: Cambridge University Press.

Quetelet, Adolphe. 1831. *Research on the Propensity for Crime at Different Ages.* 1984 edition translated by Sawyer F. Sylvester. Cincinnati, OH: Anderson Publishing Company.

Raudenbush, Stephen W. 2001. "Toward a Coherent Framework for Comparing Trajectories of Individual Change." In *New Methods for the Analysis of Change,* ed. Linda M. Collins and Aline G. Sayers. Washington, DC: American Psychological Association.

Reiss, Albert J., Jr. 1986. "Co-Offender Influences on Criminal Careers." In *Criminal Careers and "Career Criminals,"* ed. Alfred Blumstein, Jacqueline Cohen, Jeffrey A. Roth, and Christy A. Visher. Washington, DC: National Academy Press.

Reiss, Albert J., Jr., and David P. Farrington. 1991. "Advancing Knowledge about Co-Offending: Results from a Prospective Longitudinal Survey of London Males." *Journal of Criminal Law and Criminology* 82: 360–95.

Rojek, D. G., and M. L. Erickson. 1982. "Delinquent Careers: A Test of the Career Escalation Model." *Criminology* 20: 5–28.

Sarnecki, Jerzy. 1990. "Delinquent Networks in Sweden." *Journal of Quantitative Criminology* 6: 31–51.

———. 2001. *Delinquent Networks. Youth Co-Offending in Stockholm.* Cambridge, UK: Cambridge University Press.

Schmertmann, Carl P., Adansi A. Amankwaa, and Robert D. Long. 1998. "Three Strikes and You're Out: Demographic Analysis of Mandatory Prison Sentencing." *Demography* 35: 445–63.

Shannon, Lyle. 1982. *Assessing the Relationship of Adult Criminal Careers to Juvenile Careers.* Washington, DC: U.S. Department of Justice, Office of Juvenile Justice and Delinquency Prevention.

Shinnar, Shlomo, and Reuel Shinnar. 1975. "The Effects of the Criminal Justice System on the Control of Crime: A Quantitative Approach." *Law and Society Review* 9: 581–611.

Smith, D. Randall, and William R. Smith. 1984. "Patterns of Delinquent Careers: An Assessment of Three Perspectives." *Social Science Research* 13: 129–58.

Spelman, William. 1994. *Criminal Incapacitation.* New York: Plenum.

Stattin, Håkan, David Magnusson, and Howard Reichel. 1989. "Criminal Activity at Different Ages: A Study Based on a

Swedish Longitudinal Research Population." *British Journal of Criminology* 29: 368–85.

Steffensmeier, Darrell J., Emilie Andersen Allan, Miles D. Harer, and Cathy Streifel. 1989. "Age and the Distribution of Crime." *American Journal of Sociology* 94: 803–31.

Stolzenberg, Lisa, and Stewart J. D'Alessio. 1997. "'Three Strikes and You're Out': The Impact of California's New Mandatory Sentencing Law on Serious Crime Rates." *Crime and Delinquency* 43: 457–69.

Thornberry, Terence P. 1989. "Panel Effects and the Use of Self-Reported Measures of Delinquency in Longitudinal Studies." In *Cross-National Research in Self-Reported Crime and Delinquency,* ed. Malcolm W. Klein. Dordrecht: Kluwer Academic.

Tittle, Charles R., and Harold G. Grasmick. 1993. "Criminal Behavior and Age: A Test of Three Provocative Hypotheses." *Journal of Criminal Law and Criminology* 88: 309–42.

Tracy, Paul E., Marvin E. Wolfgang, and Robert M. Figlio. 1990. *Delinquency Careers in Two Birth Cohorts.* New York: Plenum.

Visher, Christy A. 1986. "The Rand Inmate Survey: A Re-Analysis." In *Criminal Careers and "Career Criminals,"* Vol. 2, ed. Alfred Blumstein, Jacqueline Cohen, Jeffrey A. Roth, and Christy A. Visher. Washington, DC: National Academy Press.

———. 1987. "Incapacitation and Crime Control: Does a 'Lock 'em Up' Strategy Reduce Crime?" *Justice Quarterly* 4: 513–43.

———. 2000. "Career Criminals and Crime Control." In *Criminology: A Contemporary Handbook,* ed. Joseph F. Sheley. 3rd ed. Belmont, CA: Wadsworth.

Visher, Christy A., and Jeffrey A. Roth. 1986. "Participation in Criminal Careers." In *Criminal Careers and "Career Criminals,"* Vol. 1, ed. Alfred Blumstein, Jacqueline Cohen, Jeffrey A. Roth, and Christy A. Visher. Washington, DC: National Academy Press.

Wikström, Per-Olof H. 1985. *Everyday Violence in Contemporary Sweden: Situational and Ecological Aspects.* Stockholm: National Council for Crime Prevention, Sweden, Research Division.

Wolfgang, Marvin E., Robert M. Figlio, and Thorsten Sellin. 1972. *Delinquency in a Birth Cohort.* Chicago: University of Chicago Press.

Zimring, Franklin E., Sam Kamin, and Gordon Hawkins. 1999. *Crime and Punishment in California: The Impact of Three Strikes and You're Out.* Berkeley, CA: Institute of Governmental Studies Press, University of California.

REVIEW QUESTIONS

1. Explain in your own words some of the concepts that Piquero et al. point out as key concepts of the career criminal paradigm, such as offending frequency and duration. Which of the concepts do you feel are most important in determining which individuals pose the greatest danger to society?

2. Which policy implications suggested by Piquero et al. do you feel make the most sense? Which make the least sense to you, and why?

3. Do you know any individuals in your life whom you would classify as chronic offenders? (If not, consider stories in the media.) What do you think caused them to become such habitual offenders? What do you think are the primary causes for their chronic offending, and what types of policies would you implement to prevent others from becoming such persistent offenders?

READING /// 27

In this empirical study, Fleur A. Souverein, Catherine L. Ward, Ingmar Visser, and Patrick Burton examine the distinctions between life-course-persistent offenders and other offenders based on a sample of 395 individuals in South Africa. Using the theoretical framework based on Moffitt's taxonomy of offenders, this study looks at the degree to which various types of variables, such as gender, violence at home and school, school performance, alcohol abuse, gang membership, and victimization distinguish life-course-persistent offenders from others, specifically the more common adolescence-limited offenders.

While reading this article, one should consider the following topics:

- To what extent the contexts specific to South Africa are quite different from those in North America, which makes this study of life-course-persistent offenders unique and important in advancing knowledge about Moffitt's theoretical framework
- The types of predicting factors that the authors claim constitute "snares" that diminish the probability of breaking away from a criminal trajectory
- Findings of the current study regarding the impact of the various predicting variables with an emphasis on the ones that were found to be significant determinants of life-course-persistent offending

Serious, Violent Young Offenders in South Africa

Are They Life-Course Persistent Offenders?

Fleur A. Souverein, Catherine L. Ward, Ingmar Visser, and Patrick Burton

South Africa has a very high rate of violence. One index of this is the homicide rate: In 2012 to 2013, there were 31.1 murders, and 355.6 assaults with intent to commit grievous bodily harm, per 100,000 population (South African Police Service, 2013). By contrast, Germany had a homicide rate of only 0.7 per 100,000 in 2012 (Bundesministerium des Innern, 2013), and New Zealand a rate of 0.009 per 100,000 (New Zealand Police National Headquarters, 2013). In addition, of the 31,177 non-natural deaths recorded in South Africa in 2008, 31.5% (9,831) were as a result of violence (National Injury Mortality Surveillance System [NIMSS], 2010). Moreover, it seems that children are often caught in the cross fire and the rates of (severe) child injuries as a result of violence are extremely high (Fieggen et al., 2004).

Clearly, violence prevention initiatives are urgently needed in South Africa. A particular concern should be offenders who are on what Moffitt (1993) described as a "life-course persistent" trajectory because, by definition, life-course persistent offenders will continue to offend throughout their life span unless their trajectories of offending are interrupted, committing serious violence

SOURCE: Fleur A. Souverein et al., "Serious, Violent Offenders in South Africa: Are They Life-Course Persistent Offenders?" *Journal of Interpersonal Violence* 31, no. 10 (2016): 1859–82.

offenses. Two concerns arise in terms of prevention and life-course persistent offending: First, efforts should be made to prevent young people from taking this course in the first place (primary prevention), and second, if young people are arrested, prevention efforts should focus on interrupting their criminal path so that their trajectories are not those of life-course persistent offenders (secondary prevention).

In the current study, we therefore explored two questions: First, "Is there a cohort of young South African offenders who may be identified as being on a life-course persistent trajectory?" Second, "Which risk factors identify this group (and therefore might be targets for prevention initiatives)?"

Patterns of Offending in Life-Course Persistent Groups

Moffitt's (1993) typology of offending, which distinguishes adolescent-limited offenders from life-course persistent offenders, has been supported in repeated studies by a number of different countries (Moffitt, 2006). The adolescence-limited offender and life-course persistent offender are two qualitatively distinct types of offenders, each with a unique history, etiology, and prognosis: adolescence-limited offenders and life-course persistent offenders. For the adolescence-limited offender, the causal factors are proximal and specific to the period of adolescent development. They engage in temporary and situational antisocial behavior during adolescence and they desist from crime as they mature out of adolescence. In contrast, for the life-course persistent offender, causal factors originate early in their lives and interact cumulatively with their environment across development, leading to stable and persistent antisocial behavior throughout the life span. Antisocial behavior in this regard constitutes all behavior that harms or lacks consideration for the well-being of others: biting and hitting at age 3, stealing and lying at age 10, drug dealing and car theft at age 16, armed robbery and rape at age 21, and fraud and domestic violence at age 30 (Moffitt, 1993).

Life-course persistent offenders have been shown, in those countries where the typology has been investigated, to constitute approximately 5% of the male population, but they commit the bulk of serious violent offenses in that country (Moffitt, 2006). Serious offenses are regarded as significant violations of the law that typically carry more than a 6-month punishment (Reuters, 2014).

An early onset of antisocial behavior, combined with continued, serious offending, are hallmarks of life-course persistent offending (Moffitt, Caspi, Harrington, & Milne, 2002), and this has been demonstrated in a number of cohorts of offenders. In the California Youth Authority Study, which followed 4,000 inmates into their 30s, significantly more offenders with an early onset continued offending past ages 21, 25, and 31 (Ge, Donellan, & Wenk, 2001). Similarly, in a Philadelphia, United States, birth cohort, young people who had their first contact with police between ages 7 and 12 subsequently averaged more serious crimes than those who were first in contact with police between ages 13 and 16 (Wolfgang, Figlio, & Sellin, 1972). And when the Dunedin, New Zealand, cohort (in which the typology was first identified) reached age 18, the life-course persistent offenders were differentially associated with conviction for violent crimes (Moffitt, Caspi, Dickson, Silva, & Stanton, 1996), and at age 26 this difference persisted (Moffitt et al., 2002). Furthermore, chronic delinquents are antisocial in more than one setting and display a higher variety of antisocial behaviors (Loeber, 1982). Children who show antisocial behavior in more than one setting are more likely to persist than those who show this behavior only in one setting (Schachar, Rutter, & Smith, 1981).

Life-course persistent antisocial behavior is thus distinguishable from adolescent-limited antisocial behavior through an early start to offending, antisocial behavior in multiple domains, and the commission of more serious and violent crimes than other offenders.

Risk Factors Influencing Life-Course Persistent Offending

The troubled lives of life-course persistent offenders start with biological risk factors that predispose them to antisocial behavior (Moffitt, 1990b; Moffitt & Henry, 1991; Raine, 2002). Neuropsychological deficits, as indicated by observables such as inattention, hyperactivity, and under-controlled temperament, are necessary (but not sufficient) for the development of life-course persistent antisocial behavior (Aguilar, Sroufe, Egeland, & Carlson, 2000).

The likelihood of entry into, and persistence in, antisocial lifestyles is increased when these biological risk factors cumulatively interact with children's environments. Family environments that include harsh and inconsistent parenting, violence, single parenting, and family members involved in crime, and school environments, which make it difficult for young people to attach to school, both increase the risk of offending (Herrenkohl et al., 2000; Sampson & Laub, 1997). These person–environment interactions set in motion a downhill snowball of consequences that cut off options for change (Moffitt, 1993). Addiction to drugs or alcohol, school dropout, teen parenthood, injuries, truncated educational opportunities, and incarceration all constitute "snares" (Moffitt, 1993) that diminish the probability of breaking away from a criminal trajectory (Wilson & Herrnstein, 1985). Moreover, young people facing these risks are more likely to miss out on opportunities to learn a conventional prosocial behavioral repertoire as they lack resources to access other options. Problems at school, for example, place a limit on the variety of job skills that can be obtained and thereby cut off options to pursue legitimate employment (Maughan, Gray, & Rutter, 1985; Moffitt, 1990a).

As the number of risk factors increases, so does the likelihood of becoming a life-course persistent offender (Herrenkohl et al., 2000). As asserted by the Cumulative Risk Hypothesis, the greater the number of risk factors, the greater the deleterious effect on later developmental outcomes (Appleyard, Egeland, Van Dulmen, & Sroufe, 2005; Rutter, 1979; Sameroff, 2000). The higher the number of risks, particularly in early childhood, the greater the likelihood of behavior problems in adolescence (Appleyard et al., 2005).

For instance, in the Cambridge study of delinquent development, a vulnerability score was developed on the basis of 5 risk factors (low family income, convicted parent, large family size, low intelligence, and poor parental rearing behavior). The percentage of boys convicted for violence increased from 3% of those with none of these risk factors to 31% of those with four or five (Farrington, 1997). Similarly, in a Finnish study, Räsänen and colleagues (1999) found a 2-fold increase in violent offending at age 26 in the offspring of mothers who smoked during pregnancy. But prenatal nicotine exposure—a risk factor for neuropsychological deficits linked with aggression—led to a 12-fold increase in recidivistic violence when combined with single household families and a 14-fold increase when combined with teenage pregnancy, unwanted pregnancy, single household families, and developmental motor lags (Räsänen et al., 1999).

Risk Factors for Life-Course Persistent Trajectories in South Africa

Moffitt's typology has only been investigated in high-income countries, where contexts may present a different profile of risk from low- and middle-income countries (Moffitt, 2006). For instance, the typology was developed in New Zealand (Moffitt, 1993), a high-income country with a very low rate of offending (New Zealand Police National Headquarters, 2013) compared with South Africa's much higher rates (South African Police Service, 2013). Understanding offending, and the risk factors that drive it in countries such as South Africa, are therefore critical issues for primary prevention. It is equally important to identify whether serious, violent offending is widespread among offenders, or whether there is an identifiable subgroup more at risk of perpetrating such crimes across the life span, and who might therefore benefit from specifically targeted correctional services.

It seems that South African children are at high risk of exposure to environments considered aggressogenic (Herrenkohl et al., 2000; Sampson & Laub, 1997). In the family, for example, children are at high risk of being exposed to harsh and inconsistent parenting, violence in the home, single parenting, and criminality of family members. While no national data on parenting practices is yet available in South Africa, rates of child maltreatment (the extreme end of harsh and inconsistent parenting) are high (Richter & Dawes, 2008). In a national survey, 33% of parents admitted to beating their children (Dawes, Long, Alexander, & Ward, 2004). Moreover, in a nationally representative youth victimization survey, 21.8% of the children reported that they had witnessed aggressive disputes between family members, and 16% reported that someone in their family had been imprisoned (Leoschut & Burton, 2006). Furthermore, another nationally representative study found that only 40.1% of young people aged 12 to 22 years lived with both parents (Leoschut, 2009).

School is another important area for child socialization and can serve as a protective factor against offending. However, many South African schools are chaotic rather than ameliorating environments; teacher time is limited by many other functions, school management is often unable to fulfill its functions, the majority of students fail, and dropout rates are high (Ward, 2007). Furthermore, despite the fact that it is illegal, corporal punishment is still used in many schools and the levels of violence and crime in schools are very high (Burton & Leoschut, 2013; McConnell, Mutongwizo, & Anderson, 2009). In South Africa, violence and crime are serious concerns in both primary and secondary schools, across school categories, and across gender, age, and race (Jefthas & Artz, 2007).

It thus seems that current conditions in South Africa are replete with opportunities in social environments for young people to learn violent behavior, and deficient in opportunities for young people to learn prosocial behavior and achieve their goals. An important question in this context, therefore, is the extent to which these conditions lead to life-course persistent offending, and which risk factors are the most likely to be associated with this serious, violent, and persistent trajectory. Because these risk factors appear to occur at very high rates, higher than the rates at which they occur in the mostly high-income countries in which the typology has thus far been investigated (Moffitt, 2006), it may well be that life-course persistent offenders form a far larger group in South Africa than they do in other countries. Alternatively, it may be that these risk factors are unable to distinguish life-course persistent offenders from others, because so many young people experience these risks.

We took advantage of the Centre for Justice and Crime Prevention's young offender study to explore some preliminary questions related to the development of life-course persistent offending in South Africa: whether we can distinguish a serious, violent offender group that is at risk of life-course persistence, and which risk factors are associated with this group. These questions have important implications for both primary prevention and for services offered in prisons.

Method

Sample

This study uses data from the National Youth Offending and Resilience Study (Leoschut & Bonora, 2007), conducted by the Centre for Justice and Crime Prevention, a South African civil society organization that promotes evidence-based crime prevention. Offenders aged 12 to 25 years ($N = 395$) were selected from eight different correctional facilities in four provinces of South Africa; the offender sample was stratified by urban and rural prison setting, and by offense type (violent or non-violent; Burton, Leoschut, & Bonora, 2009).

The ultimate sample of offenders was 94.7% male, and the majority (72%) were Black African; the remainder were colored (24.9%), White (1.8%), and Indian (1.3%). (Note that four race categories were identified by the Apartheid regime in South Africa: Black African, White, Colored, and Indian/Asian; the sample is identified by these categories as they continue to have impact today on a range of outcomes and opportunities, including health and education; Coovadia, Jewkes, Barron, Sanders, & McIntyre, 2009.) The majority (53.7%) were aged between 19 and 21 years, with 23.6% aged 16 to 18 years, 21.7% aged 22 to 25 years, and only 1% aged 12 to 15 years. The crime for which most offenders were incarcerated was armed robbery, followed by housebreaking, rape, and murder. Table 1 describes the sample in terms of the variables investigated in this study.

Procedure

The young offenders were interviewed by trained interviewers using structured questionnaires in a private setting. All interviews were conducted in the language in which the respondent felt most comfortable conversing. Respondents were assured of confidentiality and anonymity and informed consent was obtained from all respondents (Leoschut & Bonora, 2007).

Measures of Risk Factors

We constructed measurements for the following risk factors from the questionnaire administered to the youth: violence and abuse at home (single, binary

Table 1 • Sample Characteristics (*N* = 394)

	Percentage (*n*)		
Crime for which offender was incarcerated			
Armed robbery	30.9% (122)		
Housebreaking	23.5% (93)		
Rape	10.6% (42)		
Murder	9.9% (39)		
Theft	6.8% (27)		
Assault	4.6% (18)		
Attempted crimes	3.8% (15)		
Car theft	3.5% (14)		
Possession of illegal substances	3.0% (12)		
Fraud	0.8% (3)		
Other	2.3% (9)		
Other categorical descriptive variables			
Offenders who experienced violence/abuse at home	25% (98)		
Offenders who experienced violence/abuse at school	25.9% (101)		
Offenders who had a family member who had gone to jail	41.8% (165)		
Offenders with hyperactivity/attention deficits	30.3% (70)		
Continuous Descriptive Variables	**Range**	***M***	***SD***
School performance and motivation	0–3	1.97	0.55
Victimization	0–6	1.50	1.32
Support from parents	0–5	1.95	1.47
Harsh parental discipline	0–2.2	1.65	0.42
Parental monitoring and control	0–3.2	2.3	0.65
Severity of offending	0–11	4.50	2.90
Age at which offender first did something that could have got them sent to prison	0–20	16.12	2.65

item), violence and abuse at school (single, binary item), victimization (8 items), familial crime (single, binary item), support from caregivers (5 items), and school motivation and performance (4 items). Table 2 shows how the risk factors have been operationalized.

Table 2 • Risk Factors and the Corresponding Items

Risk Factor	Item
Violence and abuse at home[a]	Has anybody threatened to hurt you, scare you, or harm you in any way, or actually hurt you when you have been at home?
Violence and abuse at school[a]	Has anybody threatened to hurt you, scare you, or harm you in any way, or actually hurt you when you were at school?
Familial crime[a]	Has anyone in your family have ever been in prison?
Victimization[a] ($\alpha = .95$)	Have you ever personally experienced assault?
	Have you ever personally experienced robbery?
	Have you ever personally experienced home burglary?
	Have you ever personally experienced theft of vehicle or bicycle?
	Have you ever personally experienced theft of personal property/crops/livestock?
	Have you ever personally experienced hijacking of a vehicle or bicycle?
	Have you ever personally experienced sexual assault/rape?
	Have you ever personally experienced deliberate damage to property?
Support from parents[b] ($\alpha = .83$)	During the course of your lifetime, have you spent a lot of time with your father?
	During the course of your lifetime, have you spent a lot of time with your mother?
	During the course of your lifetime, have you received financial support from your father?
	During the course of your lifetime, have you received financial support from your mother?
	During the course of your lifetime, have you received emotional support from your father?
School motivation/performance[c] ($\alpha = .85$)	At school, my marks were better than the marks of most of the other children in my class
	I tried hard to work at school
	It was/is important to me to get good marks at school
	I want(ed) very much to go to university or technikon when I left/leave my school

[a]Item response code; *no* = 0; *yes* = 1.

[b]Item response code; *yes* = 0; *no* = 1.

[c]Item response code; *strongly agree* = 1; *agree* = 2; *disagree* = 3; *strongly disagree* = 4.

Snares

In addition, we explored the role that ensnaring factors may play in the development of the life-course persistent offender. Teen parenthood, addiction to drugs or alcohol, gang membership, and time spent incarcerated can act as "snares": Snares prevent those who may, under other circumstances, have been adolescence-limited offenders from desisting from their criminal careers, so that in effect they become life-course persistent offenders (Moffitt, 1993). Using this data set, we were able to operationalize two of these snares, namely, alcohol abuse and gang membership.

Alcohol abuse was operationalized using the question, "Have you ever tried and failed to control, cut down or stop using alcohol?" We recoded the original response ("no never," "yes in the past 12 months," "yes but not in the past 12 months") into a binary response set: The responses "yes in the past 12 months" and "yes but not in the past 12 months" were both recoded as "yes" and "no never" was coded as "no." Gang membership was measured with the question, "Can you tell me if you belong(ed) to a gang, or any other group of people that might be considered a gang, before your incarceration?" The response was binary and a positive response was used as an indicator for gang membership.

Data Analyses

Distinguishing life-course persistent from adolescence-limited offenders. To identify the offenders in this sample who were most likely to be life-course persistent offenders, we used three variables: two assessing age of onset and one assessing diversity of offending (a scale that included items on theft, weapon carrying, property damage, burglary, robbery, and fighting). The two variables indicating the age of onset were responses to the questions "What age did you first do something that could have got you sent to prison?" to which a continuous response option was allowed; and "What age did you first do something that could have got you into trouble with the law?" where the response item was categorized into four categories: "9 and younger," "10 to 15," "16 to 18," and "19 to 25." Table 3 provides the correlations between these variables within the offender group; all correlations are significant with $p < .001$. As expected, severity was negatively correlated with age of onset; early starters commit more and more serious crimes.

We then used latent class modeling to try to distinguish those likely to be life-course persistent offenders from those likely to be adolescence-limited offenders. Latent class modeling constructs homogeneous latent groups on the basis of observed variables such that correlation between the observed variables is explained by the latent groups (McCutcheon, 1987). In criminology, latent class modeling has been used to identify different criminal careers (Bartolucci, Pennoni, & Brain, 2007) and to discriminate recidivists from one-time offenders (Bijleveld & Mooijaart, 2003).

Latent class models with two through four classes were fitted to these three variables together. The three-class model was the best-fitting and most parsimonious model, as determined by the Bayesian Information Criterion (BIC; Schwarz, 1978); lower BIC values indicate a better trade-off between goodness-of-fit and parsimony of

Table 3 • Correlations Between Categories of Age of Onset and Severity of Offending

	First Did Something That Could Get You Into Trouble With the Law?	First Did Something That Meant You Could Have Been Sent to Prison?	Severity of Offending
First Did Something That Could Get You Into Trouble With the Law?	1.00		
First Did Something That Meant You Could Have Been Sent to Prison?	0.70	1.00	
Severity of Offending	−0.49	−0.43	1.00

the model. BIC values were 4,130, 4,043, and 4,048, respectively, for the two-, three-, and four-class models, and hence the three-class model was optimal. The main difference between the two-class and three-class model was that Classes 1 and 2 from the three-class model merged into a single class in the two-class model. Using posterior probabilities, offenders were assigned to classes in the two- and three-class models respectively. Table 4 gives the cross-classification of class memberships between the two- and three-class models. As can be seen, everyone in Class 3 in the three-class model is in Class 2 in the two-class model. Hence, according to both the two- and three-class models, there is a homogeneous group of severe offenders containing 164 (41.5%) of the 395 offenders.

The unconditional probabilities and means for the three-class model are reported in Table 5. The unconditional probabilities are 0.204, 0.406, and 0.390; these are the a priori probabilities for the young offenders to belong to each of the three classes. The typical offender in Class 3 of the three-class model has a high probability (0.948) of committing his first crime (that could have put him in contact with the law) between the ages of 10 and 15 years. Typical Class 3 offenders committed their first crime that could have got them into prison at age 14, and they have a mean severity score of 6.48.

Based on this latent class analysis, we concluded that we had identified a homogeneous group of 164 offenders (41.5% of the sample) who all had an early age of onset and displayed severe antisocial behavior, and who were clearly distinguished from other offenders; we classified offenders in this group as likely to be life-course persistent offenders.

Risk Factor Analysis

We had several questions we wished to test: First, "Which of the risk factors was associated with age of onset (the age at which the offenders first did something that could have got them sent to prison)?" Second, "Which of the risk factors was associated with severity of offending?" Third, "Which risk factors discriminated our class of likely

Table 4 • Cross Classification Two-Class and Three-Class Model (*n* in Each Group)

	Class	Two-Class Model	
		1	2
Three-class model	1	81	1
	2	144	5
	3	0	164

NOTE: In both the two- and three-class models, there are 164 offenders classified into the most severe category.

Table 5 • Class-Specific Parameters for the Three Classes of Offender

Class of Offender	Probability for an Offender in This Class First Doing Something That Could Have Got Him or Her Into Trouble With the Law at a Certain Age				Age at Which First Imprisoned		Severity of Offending	
	Age 9	Age 11	Age 17	Age 22	*M*	*SD*	*M*	*SD*
1	.03	.03	.04	.90	20	1.32	2.04	1.97
2	.00	.01	.88	.00	17	1.14	3.84	2.63
3	.05	.95	.00	.00	14	2.36	6.48	2.16

life-course persistent offenders from the other offenders?" Finally, "How were the snares of alcohol abuse and gang membership associated with age of onset, severity scores, and life-course persistent offending?"

We used linear regression to explore the relationship between the risk factors and the age of onset, and between risk factors and severity of antisocial behavior. We used logistic regression to explore the relationship between the risk factors and our binary measure for life-course persistent offending. Throughout these analyses, missing data were handled by listwise deletion.

Results

The results of our regression analyses are summarized below.

Age of Onset

The age of onset (age at which the young offender first did something that might have resulted in imprisonment) was significantly associated with violence and abuse at home: Violent home environments were associated with a lower age of onset.

Severity

Severity of offending was significantly associated with victimization, familial crime, violence and abuse at home, school performance and motivation, and violence and abuse at school. Also, males had significantly higher severity scores.

Life-Course Persistent Offending

Serious, violent offending with an early age of onset—offending we identified as likely to be life-course persistent—was significantly associated with violence and abuse at home, violence and abuse at school, and familial crime.

Snares

Alcohol abuse was significantly associated with severity; offenders who had a problem with the use of alcohol had significantly higher severity scores. Moreover, gang membership yielded significant results in all models: The offenders who belonged to a gang had a significantly younger age of onset, a significantly higher severity score, and were more than 5 times more likely to be in our life-course persistent offender group.

Discussion

We had two aims with this study. First, we were curious as to whether we could identify a homogeneous group of offenders likely to be on a life-course persistent trajectory in South Africa, a group that would be significantly distinguished from other offenders by early onset and severe antisocial behavior. Second, we wished to identify risk factors associated, in South Africa, with offending that may be life-course persistent.

Using latent class modeling, we indeed identified a homogeneous group of offenders that was clearly discriminated from the other offenders by an early age of onset (before age 14) and severe antisocial behavior, and who therefore may possibly be on a life-course persistent trajectory of offending. This group constituted 164 offenders (41.5% of the 395 offenders). This is a proportion markedly higher than the proportions identified in other studies. In a Dutch cohort study of offenders, for example, 7.3% of their sample was identified as those who were on a life-course persistent trajectory of offending (Blokland, Nagin, & Nieuwbeerta, 2005).

In terms of risk factors associated with life-course persistent offending, it seems that the family risk factors identified in other countries for offending may also play an important role in South Africa. Children reporting violence and abuse in their families had a significantly younger age of onset and displayed more violent and severe antisocial behavior. Results further showed that children coming from families in which one or more adults had been in prison showed more violent and severe antisocial behavior and they were almost twice as likely to be in the group we identified as possible life-course persistent offenders. Numerous studies consistently find the same differentiating familial risk factors for life-course persistent offending (Moffitt, 2006).

School factors were also found to be associated with membership in our life-course persistent group; poor performance and lack of motivation at school were associated with more severe antisocial behavior. Again, this is consonant with the literature on life-course persistent offending (Moffitt, 2006).

More strikingly, youth indicating that they had experienced violence and abuse at school displayed more violent and severe behavior and were almost twice as likely to fall into the serious, violent offending group. School violence is seldom investigated as a stand-alone risk factor; most often, violence in the family is included in risk factors studies and the school included for risk factors such as the child's performance and motivation—see, for instance, Dahlberg and Potter (2001), and Herrenkohl and colleagues (2000). Our models—in which we control for family violence when exploring school violence—suggest that it makes an important and independent contribution, over and above exposure to family violence.

Where school violence has been investigated, there are similar results to ours. For instance, in a study conducted in Los Angeles, school and community violence both contributed to the aggression of boys, but only school violence to the aggression of girls (O'Keefe, 1997)—findings that also highlight the importance of school violence as a risk factor separate from exposure to violence in other locations. Clearly, important information is lost in studies if exposure to violence is not disaggregated by location (for instance, if it is conflated into a "community violence" category). Given the small literature that does exist on school violence specifically, and our findings, future studies should investigate violence at school as a unique risk factor for offending.

In addition, if violence at school is independent of other risk factors in its association with offending, it suggests a very specific locale for preventive interventions.

Our results further showed that victimization is significantly associated with the severity of offending; being the victim of a crime led to more severe antisocial behavior, again in accord with the literature on offending (Sherman et al., 1998).

We further investigated the role of snares. Alcohol abuse was significantly associated with severity: Offenders who had problems with alcohol abuse had significantly higher severity scores. Gang involvement was more broadly associated with younger age of onset, a significantly higher severity score, and a 5 times greater likelihood of becoming a serious, violent offender. While children involved in gangs are both more likely to be victims and perpetrators of violent crime around the world, the extent to which gangs affect young male South Africans (Walsh & Mitchell, 2006) and are associated with crime in South Africa (Hough, 2000) raises cause for great concern. Some sense of the scale of the problem is provided by an estimate that in Cape Town alone (then a city of 2.9 million people; Statistics South Africa, 2001), by the late 1990s, there were 100,000 gang members (Standing, 2005).

Limitations

Our study yielded interesting and important results; however, there are a few limitations to our study that need to be considered. First, this was not a representative sample of all offenders in South Africa, but a limited sample of young offenders. In addition, the bulk of our sample (94.7%) was male, and thus the findings regarding the association between male gender and life-course persistent offending should be treated with caution. Future studies should include a larger sample of female offenders and explore whether there is a difference in risk factors associated with offending by gender.

Nor are we able, in this study, to identify persistence in criminal behavior beyond the age of 25. We were not able to follow the offenders over the life course, and so we have in effect identified a group of serious, violent offenders who are likely to be (rather than certainly) on a life-course persistent trajectory. Nonetheless, that a very high proportion of young offenders in this sample was identified as early-onset, serious, violent offenders is cause for concern, as these are highly likely to be the young people who are on a life-course persistent trajectory of offending (Moffitt, 1993). Future studies should investigate whether this proportion is reflected in the full age range of offenders, both in South Africa and elsewhere, and should follow offenders over the full course of their lives. Estimating the proportion of possible life-course persistent offenders is important particularly for the kinds of services that are provided by correctional services institutions, as this group is likely to need intensive services.

In addition, the best-fitting model in the latent class analysis identified three groups of offenders. We were most interested in the group with early onset of offending and the most serious scores, but future studies may also wish to identify whether the other two classes are perhaps adolescence-limited offenders and whether the two groups are distinguishable in terms of risk factors and the correctional services interventions they may require.

Given the quantity of literature identifying biological risk factors that predispose children to antisocial behavior (Moffitt, 1990b; Moffitt & Henry, 1991; Raine, 2002), future studies should also attempt to follow children from very early in the life course. This is particularly important in South Africa, where there is a great deal of research suggesting that the biological risk factors for life-course persistent antisocial behavior may be found at an elevated rate in South Africa. For instance, in terms of prenatal risks to fetal neurodevelopment, tobacco is widely used among South African women (Sitas et al., 2004) and the prevalence of Fetal Alcohol Syndrome is the highest recorded in the world with rates, in high-prevalence areas, 33 to 148 times higher than estimates for children in the United States (Viljoen et al., 2005). Furthermore, rates for stunting, an indicator of chronic malnutrition, are significantly higher than in European and North American countries (Labadarios, 2007). Each of these risk factors has been associated with aggression and/or hyperactivity (Hōōk, 2006; Liu & Raine, 2006). However, in this study we were unable to explore these risk factors as caregivers for the majority of our sample could not be traced. Future studies should certainly explore the prevalence and role of these early risk factors for life-course persistent offending.

Finally, this is a cross-sectional study, and prospective longitudinal designs are essential for identifying causal factors. Future longitudinal studies should seek to identify whether the risk factors we identified are in fact playing a causal role in serious, violent offending in South Africa (and other low- and middle-income countries with similar conditions, such as high levels of poverty and violence).

Implications

Despite these limitations, the study demonstrates that, within a sample of young South African offenders, a large proportion can be identified as serious, violent offenders who are distinguishable from other offenders on the basis of their age of onset and severity of offending, and who fit a risk pattern for life-course persistent offending. This in and of itself is concerning, because these offenders are likely to recidivate, which has important implications for correctional services. Effective treatments for such offenders have been identified and include cognitive and cognitive-behavioral psychotherapy, and treatments that take a multifocal approach (working simultaneously in different areas of offenders' lives; Garrido & Morales, 2007). These programs should be implemented in correctional facilities to prevent recidivism.

However, these interventions rely on highly skilled personnel, as they are typically the domain of at least a master's-level clinical psychologist. In low- and middle-income countries (such as South Africa), it is unlikely that there will be sufficient professionals capable of delivering these services to such a large number of offenders. For instance, at the end of 2011, the South African Department of Correctional Services reported that, of 162,162 inmates in their facilities, 31,678 were youth aged 14 to 25 years who had been sentenced (Department of Correctional Services, 2012); if 41.5% of these are likely to be life-course persistent offenders, there were then 13,146 young offenders in need of this kind of intensive treatment. Yet there were only 50 psychologists employed in South Africa's correctional services in 2011 (Department of Correctional Services, 2012). Alternative modes of delivery (perhaps by paraprofessionals working under the supervision of a professional) should urgently be identified and tested.

On a more hopeful note, however, our study identified key factors that appear to play a role in increasing risk for offending and which may therefore be targets for early preventive intervention. Longitudinal studies should explore whether these are in fact playing a causal role in this context, and intervention studies should explore whether offending could be prevented through intervening with these risk factors. In addition, future studies should explore other variables as potential moderators (for instance, children who receive warm, consistent parenting may be less likely to become aggressive even when victimized than those who receive harsh, inconsistent parenting; Gorman-Smith, Henry, & Tolan, 2010). This would also allow more accurate targeting of interventions.

Preventing child abuse should be a high priority for intervention studies. Parenting programs, such as home visiting programs and group parent training interventions, have been demonstrated to do so effectively (Barlow, Johnston, Kendrick, Polnay, & Stewart-Brown, 2006; Mikton & Butchart, 2009), and the possibility of making these widely and freely available should be explored.

Prevention of intimate partner violence should also receive attention. Although the evidence base for programs to prevent intimate partner violence is not as strong as for child maltreatment, there are promising programs available (Feder & Sardinha, 2015; Heise, 2015).

Prevention of violence at schools is another key priority. Teacher training to provide alternatives to corporal punishment, such as the Incredible Years teacher programs assisting teachers to learn effective, non-violent forms of classroom management, should form a critical part of national crime and violence prevention initiatives (Webster-Stratton, Reid, & Stoolmiller, 2008). Wider school programs to prevent violence between students (Ttofi & Farrington, 2011; Vreeman & Carroll, 2007) must likewise form part of national approaches to crime prevention. In addition, support for children who are struggling academically should not be neglected: As a part of other, broader school programs, academic support has a role to play in promoting attachment to school and improving children's outcomes (Catalano, Haggerty, Oesterle, Fleming, & Hawkins, 2004; Gottfredson, 1986).

Our findings also suggest that young people who have recently been victimized are at risk of offending. Although the evidence base for interventions to reduce poor outcomes for those who have recently had a traumatic experience is not yet strong, there are promising models (Gray & Litz, 2005). These should be made widely available and be tested further for their effectiveness in reducing aggression and offending.

As alcohol abuse also played significant roles in the seriousness of young people's criminal behavior, this too needs attention as a possible part of a broad crime prevention strategy. Substance abuse treatment is not widely available in South Africa, particularly to young people of color (Myers, Louw, & Pasche, 2010). Efforts to expand treatment accessibility, as well as other efforts to reduce alcohol use and the flow of illegal drugs within the country are also essential elements of crime prevention (Parry & Dewing, 2006).

Addressing these risk factors should also reduce the likelihood of young people's joining gangs, as there is a great deal of overlap between the risk factors for delinquency in general and gang membership specifically (Herrenkohl et al., 2000). However, specific strategies both for limiting gang involvement and for limiting gang violence should also be implemented. These may include a range of programs intended to reduce the likelihood of young people's joining gangs, such as the Gang Resistance Education and Training program, a school-based gang-prevention curriculum with evidence of effectiveness (Esbensen et al., 2011), as well other approaches to assisting existing members to detach from gangs and reducing the violent activities of the gangs themselves (Cooper & Ward, 2012).

Conclusion

Crime prevention initiatives in South Africa must, as matters of priority, attend to specific interventions targeting serious, violent young offenders who are incarcerated. Good use of the opportunity presented by incarceration could reduce recidivism and prevent young offenders from taking the life-course persistent offending path. Primary prevention is also crucial, and our study suggests a number of points of intervention to reduce young people's chance of becoming offenders in the first place. Attention should be paid to reducing violence at home and at school, providing treatment to those who have recently been victimized, reducing access to alcohol and providing substance abuse treatment for young people who need it, and reducing both the numbers of young people who join gangs and gang violence itself. All of these are critical for improving outcomes for South African youth.

References

Aguilar, B., Sroufe, A. L., Egeland, B., & Carlson, E. (2000). Distinguishing the early-onset/persistent and adolescence-onset antisocial behaviour types: From birth to 16 years. *Development and Psychopathology, 12*, 109–132.

Appleyard, K., Egeland, B., Van Dulmen, M. H. M., & Sroufe, L. A. (2005). When more is not better: The role of cumulative risk in child behaviour outcomes. *Journal of Child Psychology and Psychiatry, 46*, 235–245.

Barlow, J., Johnston, I., Kendrick, D., Polnay, L., & Stewart-Brown, S. (2006). Individual and group-based parenting programmes for the treatment of physical child abuse and neglect. *Cochrane Database of Systematic Reviews*, Issue 3, CD005463. doi:10.1002/14651858.CD005463.pub2

Bartolucci, F., Pennoni, F., & Brain, F. (2007). A latent Markov model for detecting patterns of criminal activity. *Journal of the Royal Statistical Society: Series A, 170*, 115–132.

Bijleveld, C. C. J. H., & Mooijaart, A. (2003). Latent Markov Modelling of Recidivism Data. *Statistica Neerlandica, 57*, 305–320. doi:10.1111/1467-9574.00233

Blokland, A. A., Nagin, D., & Nieuwbeerta, P. (2005). Life-span offending trajectories of a Dutch conviction cohort. *Criminology, 43,* 919–954.

Bundesministerium des Innern. (2013). *Polizeiliche Kriminalstatistik 2012* [Police Crime Statistics 2012]. Berlin, Germany: Author.

Burton, P., & Leoschut, L. (2013). *School violence in South Africa: Results of the 2012 National School Violence Study.* Cape Town, South Africa: Centre for Justice and Crime Prevention.

Burton, P., Leoschut, L., & Bonora, A. (2009). *Walking the tightrope: Youth resilience to crime in South Africa.* Cape Town, South Africa: Centre for Justice and Crime Prevention.

Catalano, R. F., Haggerty, K. P., Oesterle, S., Fleming, C. B., & Hawkins, J. D. (2004). The importance of bonding to school for healthy development: Findings from the Social Development Research Group. *Journal of School Health, 74,* 252–261.

Cooper, A., & Ward, C. L. (2012). Intervening with youth in gangs. In C. L. Ward, A. Van der Merwe, & A. R. L. Dawes (Eds.), *Youth violence in South Africa: Sources and solutions* (pp. 241–273). Cape Town, South Africa: University of Cape Town.

Coovadia, H., Jewkes, R., Barron, P., Sanders, D., & McIntyre, D. (2009). The health and health system of South Africa: Historical roots of current public health challenges. *The Lancet, 374,* 817–834. Retrieved from http://dx.doi.org.ezproxy.uct.ac.za/10.1016/S0140-6736(09)60951-X

Dahlberg, L. L., & Potter, L. B. (2001). Youth violence: Developmental pathways and prevention challenges. *American Journal of Preventive Medicine, 20*(Suppl. 1), 3–14.

Dawes, A., Long, W., Alexander, L., & Ward, C. L. (2004). *Partner violence, attitudes to child discipline and the use of corporal punishment.* Cape Town, South Africa: Human Sciences Research Council.

Department of Correctional Services. (2012). *Department of correctional services: Annual report 2011/2012.* Pretoria, South Africa: Department of Correctional Services.

Esbensen, F.-A., Peterson, D., Taylor, T. J., Freng, A., Osgood, D. W., Carson, D. C., & Matsuda, K. N. (2011). Evaluation and evolution of the Gang Resistance Education and Training (GREAT) program. *Journal of School Violence, 10*(1), 53–70.

Farrington, D. (1997). Early prediction of violent and non-violent youthful offending. *European Journal on Criminal Policy and Research, 5*(2), 51–66. doi:10.1007/BF02677607

Feder, G., & Sardinha, L. (2015). Preventing intimate partner violence through advocacy and support programmes. In P. D. Donnelly & C. L. Ward (Eds.), *Oxford textbook of violence prevention: Epidemiology, evidence and policy* (pp. 193–200). Oxford, UK: Oxford University Press.

Fieggen, A. G., Wiemann, M., Brown, C., Van As, A. B., Swingler, G. H., & Peter, J. C. (2004). Inhuman shields—Children caught in the crossfire of domestic violence. *South African Medical Journal, 94,* 293–296.

Garrido, V., & Morales, L. A. (2007). Serious (violent or chronic) juvenile offenders: A systematic review of treatment effectiveness in secure corrections. *Campbell Systematic Reviews,* 3(7). doi:10.4073/csr.2007.7

Ge, X., Donellan, M. B., & Wenk, E. (2001). The development of persistent criminal offending in males. *Criminal Justice and Behavior, 28,* 731–755.

Gorman-Smith, D., Henry, D. B., & Tolan, P. H. (2010). Exposure to community violence and violence perpetration: The protective effects of family functioning. *Journal of Clinical Child & Adolescent Psychology, 33,* 439–449.

Gottfredson, D. (1986). An empirical test of school-based environmental and individual interventions to reduce the risk of delinquent behavior. *Criminology, 24,* 705–731.

Gray, M. J., & Litz, B. T. (2005). Behavioral interventions for recent trauma: Empirically informed practice guidelines. *Behavior Modification, 29,* 189–215. doi:10.1177/0145445504270884

Heise, L. (2015). Preventing intimate partner violence. In P. D. Donnelly & C. L. Ward (Eds.), *Oxford textbook of violence prevention: Epidemiology, evidence and policy* (pp. 185–189). Oxford, UK: Oxford University Press.

Herrenkohl, T. I., Maguin, E., Hill, K. G., Hawkins, J. D., Abbott, R. D., & Catalano, R. F. (2000). Developmental risk factors for youth violence. *Journal of Adolescent* Health, 26, 176–186. Retrieved from http://dx.doi.org.ezproxy.uct.ac.za/10.1016/S1054-139X(99)00065-8

Hōōk, B. (2006). Prenatal and postnatal maternal smoking as risk factors for preschool children's mental health. *Acta Paediatrica, 95,* 671–677.

Hough, M. (2000). Urban terror in South Africa: A new wave? *Terrorism & Political Violence, 12*(2), 67–75.

Jefthas, D., & Artz, L. (2007). Youth violence: A gendered perspective. In P. Burton (Ed.), *Someone stole my smile: An exploration into the causes of youth violence in South Africa* (pp. 37–56). Cape Town, South Africa: Centre for Justice and Crime Prevention.

Labadarios, D. (2007). *The National Food Consumption Survey: The knowledge, attitude, behaviour and procurement regarding fortified foods, a measure of hunger and the anthropometric and selected micronutrient status of children aged 1–9 years and women of child-bearing age: South Africa, 2005.* Pretoria, South Africa: Human Sciences Research Council.

Leoschut, L. (2009). *Running nowhere fast: Results of the 2008 National Youth Lifestyle Study.* Cape Town, South Africa: Centre for Justice and Crime Prevention.

Leoschut, L., & Bonora, A. (2007). Offender perspectives on violent crime. In P. Burton (Ed.), *Someone stole my smile: An exploration into the causes of youth violence in South Africa* (pp. 89–112). Cape Town, South Africa: Centre for Justice and Crime Prevention.

Leoschut, L., & Burton, P. (2006). *How rich the rewards? Results of the 2005 National Youth Victimisation Survey.* Cape Town, South Africa: Centre for Justice and Crime Prevention.

Liu, J., & Raine, A. (2006). The effect of childhood malnutrition on externalizing behavior. *Current Opinion in Pediatrics, 18,* 565–570.

Loeber, R. (1982). The stability of antisocial and delinquent child behaviour: A review. *Child Development, 53*, 1431–1446.

Maughan, B., Gray, G., & Rutter, M. (1985). Reading retardation and antisocial behaviour: A follow-up into employment. *Journal of Child Psychology and Psychiatry and Allied Disciplines, 26*, 741–758. doi:10.1111/1469-7610.ep11655074

McConnell, J., Mutongwizo, T., & Anderson, K. (2009). *Corporal punishment in South Africa: Experiences at home and at school*. Cape Town, South Africa: Centre for Justice and Crime Prevention.

McCutcheon, A. L. (1987). *Latent class analysis* (Vol. 07-064). Newbury Park, CA: Sage.

Mikton, C., & Butchart, R. A. (2009). Child maltreatment prevention: A systematic review of reviews. *Bulletin of the World Health Organisation, 87*, 353–361.

Moffitt, T. E. (1990a). Juvenile delinquency and attention-deficit disorder: Developmental trajectories from age 3 to 15. *Child Development, 61*, 893–910.

Moffitt, T. E. (1990b). The neuropsychology of delinquency: A critical review of theory and research. In N. Morris & M. Tonry (Eds.), *Crime and justice* (pp. 99–169). Chicago, IL: University of Chicago Press.

Moffitt, T. E. (1993). Adolescence-limited and life-course persistent antisocial behavior: A developmental taxonomy. *Psychological Review, 100*, 674–701.

Moffitt, T. E. (2006). Life-course persistent versus adolescence-limited antisocial behaviour. In D. Cicchetti & D. J. Cohen (Eds.), *Developmental psychopathology* (pp. 571–598). New York, NY: Wiley.

Moffitt, T. E., Caspi, A., Dickson, N., Silva, P. A., & Stanton, W. (1996). Childhood-onset versus adolescent-onset antisocial conduct in males: Natural history from age 3 to 18. *Development and Psychopathology, 8*, 399–424.

Moffitt, T. E., Caspi, A., Harrington, H., & Milne, B. J. (2002). Males on the life-course persistent and adolescence-limited antisocial pathways: Follow-up at age 26 years. *Development and Psychopathology, 14*, 179–207.

Moffitt, T. E., & Henry, B. (1991). Neuropsychological studies of juvenile delinquency and violence: A review. In J. Milner (Ed.), *The neuropsychology of aggression* (pp. 67–91). Norwell, MA: Kluwer Academic.

Myers, B. J., Louw, J., & Pasche, S. C. (2010). Inequitable access to substance abuse treatment services in Cape Town, South Africa. *Substance Abuse Treatment, Prevention, and Policy, 5*, Article 28. doi:10.1186/1747-597X-5-28

National Injury Mortality Surveillance System. (2010). *A profile of fatal injuries in South Africa; 10th Annual Report 2008*. Cape Town, South Africa: Medical Research Council.

New Zealand Police National Headquarters. (2013). *New Zealand Crime Statistics 2012: A summary of recorded and resolved offence statistics*. Wellington, New Zealand: New Zealand Police National Headquarters.

O'Keefe, M. (1997). Adolescents' exposure to community and school violence: Prevalence and behavioral correlates. *Journal of Adolescent Health, 20*, 368–376.

Parry, C. D., & Dewing, S. (2006). A public health approach to addressing alcohol-related crime in South Africa. *African Journal of Drug and Alcohol Studies, 5*, 41–56.

Raine, A. (2002). Biosocial studies of antisocial and violent behavior in children and adults: A review. *Journal of Abnormal Child Psychology, 30*, 311–326.

Räsänen, P., Hakko, H., Isohanni, M., Hodgins, S., Järvelin, M.-R., & Tiihonen, J. (1999). Maternal smoking during pregnancy and risk of criminal behaviour among adult male offspring in the northern Finland 1966 birth cohort. *American Journal of Psychiatry, 156*, 857–862.

Reuters, T. (2014). *Black's law dictionary* (10th ed.). Eagan, MN: Thomson West.

Richter, L. M., & Dawes, A. R. L. (2008). Child abuse in South Africa: Rights and wrongs. *Child Abuse Review, 17*, 79–93. doi:10.1002/car.1004

Rutter, M. (1979). Protective factors in children's responses to stress and disadvantage. In M. W. Kent & J. E. Rolf (Eds.), *Primary prevention of psychopathology* (pp. 49–74). Hanover, NH: University of New England Press.

Sameroff, A. J. (2000). Dialectical processes in developmental psychopathology. In A. Sameroff, M. Lewis, & S. Miller (Eds.), *Handbook of developmental psychopathology* (pp. 23–40). New York, NY: Kluwer Academic.

Sampson, R. J., & Laub, J. H. (1997). A life-course theory of cumulative disadvantage and the stability of delinquency. In T. P. Thornberry (Ed.), *Developmental theories of crime and delinquency: Advances in criminological theory* (Vol. 7, pp. 133–161). New Brunswick, NJ: Transaction Publishers.

Schachar, R., Rutter, M., & Smith, A. (1981). The characteristics of situationally and pervasively hyperactive children: Implications for syndrome definition. *Journal of Child Psychology and Psychiatry, 22*, 375–392.

Schwarz, G. (1978). Estimating the dimensions of a model. *The Annals of Statistics, 6*, 461–464.

Sherman, L. W., Gottfredson, D. C., Mackenzie, D. L., Eck, J., Reuter, P., & Bushway, S. D. (1998). *Preventing crime: What works, what doesn't, what's promising*. Washington, DC: National Institute of Justice.

Sitas, F., Urban, M., Bradshaw, D., Kielkowski, D., Bah, S., & Peto, R. (2004). Tobacco attributable deaths in South Africa. *Tobacco Control, 13*, 396–399.

South African Police Service. (2013). *An analysis of the national crime statistics: Addendum to the Annual report 2012/13*. Pretoria, South Africa: SAPS Strategic Management.

Standing, A. (2005). *The threat of gangs and anti-gangs policy: Policy discussion paper*. Pretoria, South Africa: Institute for Security Studies.

Statistics South Africa. (2001). Census 2001, City of Cape Town. Retrieved from http://www.capetown.gov.za/en/stats/2001census/Documents/suburb%20index.htm

Ttofi, M. M., & Farrington, D. (2011). Effectiveness of school-based programs to reduce bullying: A systematic and meta-analytic review. *Journal of Experimental Criminology, 7*, 27–56.

Viljoen, D. L., Gossage, P., Brooke, L., Adnams, C. M., Jones, K. L., Robinson, L. K., . . . May, P. A. (2005). Fetal Alcohol Syndrome epidemiology in a South African community: A second study of a very high prevalence area. *Journal of Studies on Alcohol, 66*, 593–604.

Vreeman, R. C., & Carroll, A. E. (2007). A systematic review of school-based interventions to prevent bullying. *Archives of Pediatric and Adolescent Medicine, 161*, 78–88.

Walsh, S., & Mitchell, C. (2006). I'm too young to die: HIV, masculinity, danger and desire in urban South Africa. *Gender & Development, 14*, 57–68.

Ward, C. L. (2007). Young people's violent behaviour: Social learning in context. In P. Burton (Ed.), *Someone stole my smile: An exploration into the causes of youth violence in South Africa* (pp. 9–36). Cape Town, South Africa: Centre for Justice and Crime Prevention.

Webster-Stratton, C., Reid, M. J., & Stoolmiller, M. (2008). Preventing conduct problems and improving school readiness: Evaluation of the Incredible Year Teacher and Child Training Programs in high-risk schools. *Journal of Child Psychiatry and Psychology, 49*, 471–488. doi:10.1111/j.1469-7610.2007.01861.x

Wilson, J. Q., & Herrnstein, R. J. (1985). *Crime and human nature.* New York, NY: Simon & Schuster.

Wolfgang, M. E., Figlio, R. M., & Sellin, T. (1972). *Delinquency in a birth cohort.* Chicago, IL: University of Chicago Press.

/// REVIEW QUESTIONS

1. Do you think the sample being from South Africa influenced the findings of this study? If yes, then how?
2. What do the findings of the current study show are significant determinants of life-course persistent offending as compared to adolescence-limited offending?
3. Given the results of this study, how much does it support Moffitt's theoretical framework? Which parts of her theory are most (and least) supported by these findings?

READING /// 28

In this entry, Christy A. Visher presents a critical review of the implications of the National Research Council regarding criminal careers and career criminals, which was done more than 30 years ago. Visher was part of the panel that prepared the report. The panel included some of the world's most prestigious criminologists, and their goal was to to assess the effects of prediction instruments in reducing crime as well as to examine the contribution of research on criminal careers. This reading presents a 30-year retrospective on the policy implications that were likely influenced by this report.

While reading this article, one should consider the following topics:

- The major emphases of the report
- The effects of the era of the 1980s influencing the report
- The key policy implications that seemed to come out of this report
- The future directions that are proposed by the author

SOURCE: Christy A. Visher, "Unintended Consequences: Policy Implications of the NAS Report on Criminal Careers and Career Criminals," *Journal of Research in Crime and Delinquency* 53, no. 3 (2016): 306–20.

Unintended Consequences

Policy Implications of the NAS Report on Criminal Careers and Career Criminals

Christy A. Visher

Introduction

In 1986, the National Research Council of the National Academy of Sciences (NAS) released *Criminal Careers and "Career Criminals."* The Panel on Criminal Careers was a veritable "Who's Who" of social and behavioral scientists, legal scholars, and practitioners, including a practicing prosecutor, judge, and police chief. The Panel members included James Q. Wilson, Albert Reiss, Norval Morris, Delbert Elliott, David Farrington, and Charles Manski. The distinguished Chair of the Panel, Alfred Blumstein, had directed several such panels at the National Research Council and had decades of experience in criminal justice research and policy. Jeffrey Roth, an economist, was the senior staff officer to the Panel. Jacqueline Cohen, Consultant to the Panel, brought a background in quantitative methods and incapacitation to the study. Finally, during this author's last year as a PhD student at Indiana University, I had heard about the possibility of a panel on criminal careers while attending an annual meeting of the American Society of Criminology. I applied to the postdoctoral fellows program at NAS and once the Panel funding was secured, I was selected as an NAS Fellow and assigned to work with the Panel.

The Panel had been convened in 1983 at the request of the National Institute of Justice (NIJ) to "evaluate the feasibility of predicting the future course of criminal careers, to assess the effects of prediction instruments in reducing crime through incapacitation, and to review the contribution of research on criminal careers to the development of knowledge about crime and criminals" (Blumstein et al. 1986:x). In some respects, the Panel was a follow-on to the Panel on Deterrent and Incapacitative Effects (Blumstein et al. 1978). That panel's report noted that accurate appraisals of the deterrent and incapacitative effects of criminal justice sanctions on crime rates require better estimates of individual offending rates, that is, the number of crimes committed by an individual offender in a given time period. Thus, the panel called for a better understanding of criminal careers—individual offending patterns over time—which led NIJ to request a review of current research on criminal careers.

This article provides a 30-year retrospective on the policy implications of the NAS Criminal Careers report. First, the article briefly reviews the primary findings of the report and its intended audience. Second, the social and political context in which the report was released is presented in order to frame the discussion of short- and long-term policy impact. Third, opinions about the policy implications of the 1986 report are offered and debated. In particular, the report may have led to a focus on narrower offender-focused criminal justice responses to the nation's crime problems rather than broader social and community strategies, and other unintended policy consequences. Finally, the article concludes with some thoughts about future policy directions for research on criminal careers.

Topics in the Criminal Careers Report

To set the stage for a discussion of the report's policy implications, it is helpful to review the report's major topics and themes. For readers unfamiliar with the NAS report, it essentially summarized what little was known about criminal careers and generated a research agenda for criminology. Research on criminal careers had never been systematically reviewed and the wide-reaching implications of such research for criminal justice policy decisions had not been debated in academic circles.[1]

It should be noted that the term "career criminal" was not a new one. At the time of the report's release, Congress had just passed legislation entitled the *Armed Career Criminal Act*, which provided sentence enhancements for repeat felons convicted of crime with a firearm.

And terms such as "habitual offender" and criminal career actually had a long history in research and policy discussions (e.g., Gibbons 1973; Morris 1951; Shaw 1951). Nonetheless, the memorable title of the Panel's report signaled an important shift in both research on crime and criminal justice responses that would come to dominate the field for decades.

The primary focus of the report was the introduction of the criminal career approach to understanding individual criminal behavior, including the characteristics of those who participate in crime (i.e., age, sex, race/ethnicity), how much crime individuals commit (i.e., frequency), the seriousness of those crimes, and the length of individuals' criminal careers. Contemporary research on criminal careers likely originated with the 1977 Rand Corporation's report, *Criminal Careers of Habitual Felons* (Petersilia, Greenwood, and Lavin 1977), which was a systematic analysis of interviews with 49 felons. The Rand Corporation followed this report with a series of studies on criminal careers that were reviewed by the Panel.

A second major focus was a review of research knowledge about how information on criminal careers could shape major crime control strategies: prevention, career modification, and incapacitation. The Panel concluded that in the mid-1980s limited reliable evidence existed to identify effective preventive and modification interventions, such as programs to prevent high-risk children or teenagers from engaging in crime, or behavioral or substance abuse treatment programs. Further, attempts to quantify the impact of incarceration on criminal careers suffered from a lack of knowledge about offending patterns such as offending frequency and career duration.

The third focus of the Panel's report was the use of criminal career information in criminal justice decision making. Of particular interest to the Panel was a focus on whether information about an individual's criminal career, such as the instant offense type, record of prior offenses, including any juvenile record, and other information, such as serious drug use, should be used in determining criminal sanctions. The Panel debated the methodological, operational, and ethical challenges involved in using predictions about criminal careers in criminal justice decision making. Also, the Panel paid special attention to the controversial conclusion of a report from The Rand Corporation on *Selective Incapacitation* which examined whether the selective use of incarceration for the most active offenders—the career criminals—might significantly reduce crime rates (Greenwood and Abrahamse 1982).

Although the framework adopted by the Panel and the Panel's conclusions were derived from policy concerns, the Panel's report was essentially intended as a research agenda. All of its recommendations were directed toward developing knowledge about patterns of criminal offending over the life course and conducting rigorous research on intervention strategies. Perhaps prompted by the panel's primary recommendation, several large-scale, longitudinal studies commenced in the late 1980s, including three studies funded by the Office of Juvenile Justice and Delinquency Prevention and the Project on Human Development in Chicago Neighborhoods funded by the National Institute of Justice and the John D. and Catherine T. MacArthur Foundation (see Piquero, Farrington, and Blumstein 2003). And indeed, in the last two decades, developmental and life-course criminology has emerged as a central focus of criminological research (Piquero et al. 2003).

The Panel's report actually had no direct policy recommendations except for a call for more funding of one of the research programs at NIJ, which had previously funded studies on prediction, measurement, deterrence, and incapacitation. In fact, the Panel's report provides a decidedly reserved analysis of whether the use of information about criminal careers would yield more effective crime control strategies and crime reductions. Indeed, a follow-up study to assess the predictive utility of the risk assessment scale used in *Selective Incapacitation* concluded that the instrument was ineffective in predicting future risk (Greenwood and Turner 1987), confirming the Panel's stated cautions about prediction. Yet despite the Panel's restrained conclusions regarding the possible crime control benefits of targeted incapacitation, the past three decades have witnessed a threefold rise in the U.S. imprisonment rate.

The Social and Political Context of Crime Control in 1986

The Panel on Criminal Careers faced a tough challenge. The two-volume report culminating almost four years of work advocated the use of better knowledge about individual offenders and their crime patterns as a means to a more effective crime control policy. Yet, the 1980s was a period of intensive social and political focus on the rising crime rate and how to respond to it. In 1980, violent crime was at an all-time high with more than 23,000 homicides and almost 600 violent crimes per 100,000 persons, up from just over 400 in the early 1970s. Also, the Republicans took control of the U.S. House of Representatives in 1980 and immediately set an agenda for crime policy that can only be described as "getting tough on criminals" (see Gest 2001:43).[2]

In 1981, President Reagan created a task force on violent crime which proposed increasing the federal role in the prosecution of violent crime, and other far-reaching changes in federal law including abolishing parole, expanding prisons, and restrictions on sentencing discretion. Many of these proposals were incorporated into the *Comprehensive Crime Control Act of 1984*. This sweeping federal anticrime legislation included sentence enhancements for armed career criminals, creation of a new U.S. Sentencing Commission, expansion of the federal death penalty, and new regulations regarding civil asset forfeiture. Gest (2001:64) describes this period as an era of "creeping federalization of local crime prosecutions."

The mid-1980s was also the height of the crack cocaine epidemic in U.S. cities, fueling drug-related violence as drug sales led to disputes among dealers with devastating effects on neighborhoods. Politicians quickly associated crack cocaine with violence, and the U.S. Congress debated Federal involvement in drug enforcement. Then, in June 1986, University of Maryland's basketball star Len Bias died of a cocaine overdose at the age of 22, the night after being selected by the Boston Celtics. Eight days after Bias' death, Don Rogers of the Cleveland Browns died of a similar overdose at the age of 23. Shortly thereafter, the Congress passed the *Anti-Drug Abuse Act of 1986* which enacted mandatory minimum sentences for federal drug crimes and instituted a minimum sentence of five years without parole for possession of five grams of crack cocaine, but the same sentence for possession of 500 grams of powder cocaine—the now infamous 100 to 1 ratio (Gest 2001).

In the midst of this national discussion on rising violent crime, crack cocaine, and punitive sentences for drug crimes, the Panel on Criminal Careers released its report.

At a symposium to highlight the report and its utility for policy discussion, Attorney General Edwin Meese provided opening remarks. Just two years later, additional federal legislation was passed, creating the Office of National Drug Control Policy and a national "drug czar," and establishing a federal death penalty for drug-related killings. Violent crime continued to rise through the end of the decade, reaching a peak in 1991.[3]

Thus, the 1980s witnessed a major shift in federal response to local violent crime, and as violent crime continued to escalate, the decade ended with violent crime being designated as a priority area for the Federal Bureau of Investigation in 1989, reprogramming agents from "Cold War" counterintelligence duty to serve on federal–state task forces. The political and social climate of the 1980s virtually precluded any rational discussion about crime policy. The cautious conclusions of the Panel regarding the difficulty of identifying career criminals and using incapacitation as a principal means of crime control would seem to have fallen on deaf ears.

Unintended Policy Consequences

U.S. crime policy continued its "tough-on-crime" focus in the early 1990s. Several high-profile mass shootings occurred including the 1989 schoolyard massacre in Stockton, California, and the shooting at Luby's Cafeteria in Killeen, Texas, in 1991 which killed 23 people. Opinion polls placed crime as a central issue among the public and by the early 1990s, Democrats were determined to regain credibility on the crime issue (Chernoff, Kelly, and Kroger 1996). Candidate Bill Clinton campaigned as an enforcer of the death penalty in Arkansas, advocated a new program to put 100,000 cops on the street, and a ban on semiautomatic weapons.

After Clinton was elected, the Democrats and Republicans went through several years of behind-the-scenes wrangling before finally enacting the *Violent Crime Control and Law Enforcement Act of 1994* (Crime Act). None of the accounts of how the Crime Act was written mention any reliance on research or scientific recommendations in drafting the bill (Chernoff et al. 1996; Gest 2001; Simon 2007). In fact, several policymakers interviewed for the Vera Institute of Justice's Crime Act @20 initiative, including former Assistant Attorney General Laurie Robinson and Representative Bobby Scott (D-Va), explicitly said that research was not considered (Vera Institute of Justice 2015).

Yet, the Panel's report could have been used to inform several aspects of the Crime Act. Most of the crime prevention provisions of the Act were eventually cut in final deliberations, having been labeled as "pork" by the Republicans. However, funding was included for prevention programming with no research basis such as millions of dollars for "operating or coordinating recreation programs and services," which were derided by Republicans as support for "midnight basketball." Indeed, the Panel's report explicitly concluded that "most of the evaluative research on prevention interventions is nondefinitive" (p. 114). As another example, a significant component of the Crime Act was its provisions on prison construction and "truth-in-sentencing" (TIS). Billions of dollars were authorized to be spent on new state prison construction, provided that the state would certify that convicted offenders would serve at least 85 percent of their sentence for qualifying offenses.[4] But the Panel's report had expressed doubt that large increases in incarceration would significantly reduce crime rates stating that "even very large increases in inmate populations [would] lead to only modest percentage reductions in crime" (p. 129).

Another common legislative response to rising crime rates after the Panel's report was released were "three strikes and you're out" laws, which were endorsed by President Clinton during his 1994 State of the Union address. This type of statute emerged in 1993 following a murder in the state of Washington by a paroled rapist and gained even more attention after the murder of Polly Klaas in California (see Austin et al. 2000; Gest 2001). Only a few years earlier, the Panel's report had noted that the effectiveness of habitual offender statutes in reducing crime "depends on the residual length of these offenders' criminal careers compared to their total time served" with life sentences likely representing a "waste of prison space" because most careers do not even approach 20 years (p. 128). Finally, other tough-on-crime provisions in the Crime Act such as waiving juveniles to adult courts, enhanced penalties for certain drug and gun crimes, and new death penalty statutes were not supported by research on criminal careers.

Thus, it is clear that the Panel's report and its conclusions regarding the lack of research about whether various crime control strategies would reduce crime rates certainly had no impact on anticrime legislation in the decade following the report's release. But perhaps one of the unintended consequences of the Panel's report and its catchy title was to cement language such as career criminals and "habitual offenders" into the everyday lexicon. The use of inflammatory language about possible crime dangers continued into the 1990s. In 1996, John DiIulio warned of a new type of young criminals he called "super-predators." According to DiIulio's thesis, a large increase in the number of young black male teenagers who were living in seriously disadvantaged circumstances would lead to an unprecedented crime wave. Criminologist James Fox spoke of a forthcoming "bloodbath" of teenage violence due to the intersection of demographic trends and social factors such as single parenthood, drug abuse, and jobless urban neighborhoods (1995). Yet, at the same time as DiIulio and Fox were getting extraordinary media (and Congressional) attention for their ominous predictions, violent crime had already started its historic decline.

A more significant unintended consequence of the Panel's report likely lies in opportunities lost. It is fair to say that throughout the 1980s, policymakers, practitioners, and even criminologists (e.g., Hirschi and Gottfredson 1990; Wilson and Herrnstein 1985) shared a view of crime that stressed individual responsibility over social influences. Theories that invoked "the root causes of crime" (i.e., poverty, joblessness, inequality) were dismissed outright and the phrase became shorthand for soft-on-crime approaches. Unfortunately, the Panel's report did not provide a counterpoint to these arguments and may have delayed opportunities to develop crime control strategies that focused on the role of social conditions and related interventions[5] or postponed opportunities to consider the intersection between individuals and their social environments as a context for delinquency and criminal behavior and foster strategies that incorporated this interaction. Thus, opportunities were lost to avoid the mass incarceration experience and its consequences that gripped the United States for more than a decade.

Ten years after the release of the Panel's report, Alfred Blumstein (1996) astutely observed that the 1980s was a period of "overt politicization" (p. 350) of criminal justice policy with little regard for research knowledge. Indeed, he noted that crime policy "seems to have ignored research findings that counseled against certain policies" (p. 358), citing examples such as mandatory sentences, three-strikes laws, and drug law enforcement. And, in a prescient statement about crime policy in the mid-1990s and beyond, Blumstein remarked:

> The potentially emerging coalition of fiscal conservatives and those concerned with effective government may lead to a more aggressive search for alternative means of dealing with nonviolent convicted offenders. (p. 360)

Ironically, the foundation for these crime control alternatives was laid in the Panel's report that had been ignored for a decade.

Future Policy Directions

As mentioned earlier, the Panel's research agenda called for longitudinal and life-course studies of criminal behavior. These longitudinal studies, particularly the Project on Human Development in Chicago Neighborhoods (PHDCN), have broadened theories of crime and delinquency beyond perspectives that focused solely on individual responsibility, although their original intent was to focus on individual trajectories. PHDCN was launched in 1991 and its seminal article examined the relationship between neighborhood cohesion and control (i.e., "collective efficacy") and violent crime (Sampson, Raudenbush, and Earls 1997).[6] Another influential report that helped launch life-course criminology was *Crime in the Making* (Sampson and Laub 1993). Culminating five years of study, the book presented a detailed reanalysis of data gathered by Sheldon and Eleanor Glueck about 1,000 disadvantaged boys with an explicit focus on the social factors that affected their life pathways and turning points.

These theoretical directions have opened doors to the alternative crime policies that Blumstein pondered. Today, there is bipartisan recognition at both the state and federal level that our overreliance on incarceration is in need of recalibration. The imperative to maintain low crime rates without imposing unnecessary burdens on communities or taxpayers is pronounced. We have witnessed the reversal of many get-tough crime policies that were enacted in the 1980s and 1990s, including modification of federal sentencing guidelines, changes in sentencing for drug offenses involving crack versus powder cocaine, reform of civil asset forfeiture statutes, and roll back of the death penalty in many states.

In their place, we have seen attention to a broad array of preventive and career modification strategies such as family-based interventions for high-risk youth (Greenwood and Welsh 2012), specialty courts (i.e., drug and mental health courts), diversion to substance abuse treatment (e.g., California Proposition 36; see Hser et al. 2007), and cognitive behavioral therapy (Landenberger and Lipsey 2005). These alternative strategies have been bolstered by the rigorous research designs called for by the Panel to document their effectiveness. In addition, states are experimenting with broader crime control strategies such as justice reinvestment initiatives (Bureau of Justice Assistance 2015) and greater use of graduated sanctions for individuals on probation.

The fairly recent attention to offender risk assessment as a component of comprehensive crime control strategies is difficult to trace to the Panel's report. The widespread use of third-generation instruments that combine actuarial and dynamic risk factors such as the Level of Service Inventory, extensive use of pretrial risk assessment, and even hot spots policing have origins apart from the Panel.[7] The Panel commissioned three papers on the substantive, methodological, and ethical challenges of prediction, all of which cited weak evidence of its utility, and then explicitly called for "developing better information on the strength and validity of various candidate predictors" (1986:198). These issues remain important today and have yet to be fully resolved. However, the Panel's findings about the variability of offending rates between offenders may have provided some impetus for greater attention to incorporating dynamic risk factors in the newest generation of assessment tools which took hold as part of emerging crime control strategies in the 1990s.

Michael Tonry argues that to substantially alter sentencing and incarceration policies in the United States will require moral arguments pointing out that laws in the 1980s and 1990s were unjust (2014). These laws have unfairly affected large segments of our population including millions of children of incarcerated parents (Travis, Western, and Redburn 2014). Research needs to play a role in these conversations and the criminal career paradigm can help focus both the research and policy communities on evidence-based crime control strategies. First, understanding criminal career trajectories helps to identify plausible interventions and the timing of those interventions. Second, primary and secondary preventive interventions for adolescence and young adulthood need to incorporate individual, family, and community risk factors. Third, any discussion of rational sentencing policies needs to take account of criminal career dimensions, such as length of typical criminal careers. Finally, desistance and reentry interventions could benefit from a close examination of how individual, family, and community factors interact to create the conditions conducive to desistance.

Conclusions

In the 1980s and 1990s, research had little influence on the tough-on-crime policies enacted at federal, state, and local levels, and the report of the Panel on Criminal Careers was not a part of those discussions. Jonathan Simon (2007) remarked that these policies were meant to reassure the public and demonstrate state control in the face of rising crime rates and extraordinary media attention to crime problems. As crime has declined, there has been less pressure on policymakers to return to tough-on-crime legislation. Indeed, the United States has seen a "normative change of heart" and we may be ready to begin "unwinding mass incarceration" (Tonry 2014:525–27). Nonetheless, media reports of serious crimes continue to attract substantial attention and reactionary policies often follow (e.g., the recent attention to sexual assault crimes on college campuses).

Thus, the challenge is to make research a regular element in crime policy debates. Evidence-based policymaking has been slow to appear in discussions about crime control strategies. However, the last decade has witnessed increasing attention to rigorous evaluation and evidence-based research to guide social policy decisions. Part of this new focus can be attributed to the work of Jon Baron and the Coalition for Evidence-Based Policy (see Herk 2009; Wallace 2011). The Coalition has been an influential voice in efforts to use evidence from randomized experiments to make federal budget decisions. Moreover, the Obama Administration has consistently cited the use of science in policymaking. During Obama's first term, Assistant Attorney General Laurie Robinson created a Science Advisory Board and launched www.crimesolutions.gov, a website that provides research-based information about the effectiveness of programs and policies.

Additionally, the increasing emphasis by scholars on rigorous research designs has become a major focus of the evidence-based movement in criminology and criminal justice (e.g., Mears 2007). Research organizations such as the Center for Evidence-Based Crime Policy at George Mason University and the Jerry Lee Center of Criminology at the University of Pennsylvania have emphasized the importance of using rigorous research to guide criminal justice policy and practice. Moreover, in 2014, the American Society of Criminology together with the Academy of Criminal Justice Sciences created the Criminal Justice Research Alliance, which is designed to improve the visibility of research on crime issues in the U.S. Congress.

The report of the Panel on Criminal Careers was released in a difficult social and political climate. The historic crime decline in the past two decades has provided a window for scientific discourse to partner with policymaking to permit more emphasis on evidence-based crime control strategies. Such coordination between research and policy should be the goal for the next decade.

Notes

1. Possibly, the first contemporary review of research on criminal careers and career criminals appeared in an appendix to the Rand Corporation report, *Criminal Careers of Habitual Felons* (Petersilia et al. 1977).

2. The historical perspective on crime and politics briefly outlined in this article benefited greatly from the detailed history chronicled in *Crime & Politics* (Gest 2001) and an article recounting the politics of crime control at the federal level from 1968 through 1994 (Chernoff et al. 1996).

3. See United States Crime Rates, 1960 to 2013. Accessed at www.disastercenter.com.

4. The catchy truth-in-sentencing language was developed by Representative Dan Lungren (R-Calif) for C-SPAN to gain public support for tough-on-crime policies favored by Republicans, although he did not create the phrase (Gest 2001).

5. In the late 1980s and early 1990s, a public health approach to violence prevention and control emerged through a recommendation from another NAS report, *Injury in America: A Continuing Public Health Problem* (see http://www.cdc.gov/violenceprevention/pdf/history_violence-a.pdf). The Division of Violence Prevention at the Centers for Disease Control and

Prevention was created in 1993; much of its focus has been on youth violence.

6. In *Great American City*, Sampson (2012:chapter 4) describes the history of the Project on Human Development in Chicago Neighborhoods, which was originally conceived as a longitudinal study of individuals to identify the origins and patterns of criminal behavior with a focus on individual development. The original title of the project was actually the Project on Human Development and Criminal Behavior. With the appointment of Professor Albert Reiss to the steering group and the involvement of Professor Sampson, a revised project design was eventually conceived that embedded the study of individuals within communities.

7. The origin of the Level of Service Inventory (LSI) traces to Canadian psychologists, Donald Andrews and James Bonta. Their initial work on offender risk and needs assessment that led to the development of the LSI was published in the early 1980s, but was not cited in the Panel's report. Pretrial risk assessment originated in the 1960s with early work by the Vera Institute of Justice. Lawrence Sherman's "criminal careers of places" concept borrowed the language of the Panel's report but was much more concerned with places as the unit of analysis rather than individual offenders.

References

Austin, James, John Clark, Patricia Hardyman, and D. Alan Henry. 2000. Three Strikes and You're Out: The Implementation and Impact of Strike Laws. NJC 181297. Washington, DC: National Institute of Justice, U.S. Department of Justice.

Blumstein, Alfred. 1996. "Interaction of Criminological Theory and Public Policy." *Journal of Quantitative Criminology* 12: 349–61.

Blumstein, Alfred, Jacqueline Cohen, and Daniel S. Nagin, eds. 1978. *Deterrence and Incapacitation*. Washington, DC: Committee on Deterrent and Incapacitative Effects, National Research Council, National Academies Press.

Blumstein, Alfred, Jacqueline Cohen, Jeffrey Roth, and Christy Visher, eds. 1986. *Criminal Careers and Career Criminals*. Washington, DC: Panel on Research on Criminal Careers, Committee on Law and Justice, National Research Council, National Academies Press.

Bureau of Justice Assistance. 2015. *Justice Reinvestment Initiative*. U.S. Department of Justice. Retrieved August 25, 2015 (https://www.bja.gov/programs/justi cereinvestment/index.html).

Chernoff, Harry A., Christopher M. Kelly, and John R. Kroger. 1996. "The Politics of Crime." *Harvard Journal on Legislation* 33:527–79.

DiIulio, John J. 1996. "Fill Churches, Not Jails: Youth Crime and 'Superpredators.'" Testimony before the United States Senate Subcommittee on Youth Violence, U.S. Senate, Washington, DC, February 28. Retrieved August 25, 2015 (http://www. brookings institution.org/dybdocroot/views/testimony/DIIULIO/19960228.htm).

Fox, James A. 1995. "A Disturbing Trend in Youth Crime." Presentation at the Annual Meeting of the American Association for the Advancement of Science, Boston, MA.

Gest, Ted. 2001. *Crime & Politics: Big Government's Erratic Campaign for Law and Order*. Oxford, UK: Oxford University Press.

Gibbons, Donald C. 1973. *Society, Crime, and Criminal Careers*. 2nd ed. Englewood Cliffs, NJ: Prentice-Hall.

Greenwood, Peter W. and Allan Abrahamse. 1982. *Selective Incapacitation*. Santa Monica, CA: The Rand Corporation.

Greenwood, Peter W. and Brandon C. Welsh. 2012. "Promoting Evidence-Based Practice in Delinquency Prevention at the State Level." *Criminology and Public Policy* 11:493–513.

Greenwood, Peter W. and Susan Turner. 1987. *Selective Incapacitation Revisited: Why High Rate Offenders Are Hard to Identify*. Santa Monica, CA: The Rand Corporation.

Herk, Monica. 2009. *The Coalition for Evidence-based Policy: Its Role in Advancing Evidence-based Reform, 2004–2009*. New York: William T. Grant Foundation.

Hser, Yih-Ing, Cheryl Teruya, Alison H. Brown, David Huang, Elizabeth Evans, and M. Douglas Anglin. 2007. "Impact of California's Proposition 36 on the Drug Treatment System: Treatment Capacity and Displacement." *American Journal of Public Health* 97:104–9.

Hirschi, Travis and Michael Gottfredson. 1990. *A General Theory of Crime*. Stanford, CA: Stanford University Press.

Landenberger, Nana A. and Mark Lipsey. 2005. "The Positive Effects of Cognitive-behavioral Programs for Offenders: A Meta-analysis of Factors Associated with Effective Treatment." *Journal of Experimental Criminology* 1: 451–76.

Mears, Daniel P. 2007. "Towards Rational and Evidence-based Crime Policy." *Journal of Criminal Justice* 35:667–82.

Morris, Norval. 1951. *The Habitual Criminal*. London, UK: Longmans Green.

Petersilia, Joan, Peter W. Greenwood, and Marvin Lavin. 1977. *Criminal Careers of Habitual Felons*. Santa Monica, CA: The Rand Corporation.

Piquero, Alex R., David P. Farrington, and Alfred Blumstein. 2003. "The Criminal Career Paradigm." Pp. 359–506 in *Crime and Justice*, vol. 30, edited by M. Tonry. Chicago: University of Chicago Press.

Shaw, Clifford R. 1951. *The Natural History of a Delinquent Career*. Philadelphia, PA: Albert Saifer.

Sampson, Robert J. 2012. *Great American City: Chicago and the Enduring Neighborhood Effect*. Chicago, IL: University of Chicago Press.

Sampson, Robert J., Steven W. Raudenbush, and Felton Earls. 1997. "Neighborhoods and Violent Crime: A Multilevel Study of Collective Efficacy." *Science* 277:918–24.

Sampson, Robert J. and John H. Laub. 1993. *Crime in the Making: Pathways and Turning Points through Life*. Cambridge, MA: Harvard University Press.

Simon, Jonathan. 2007. *Governing through Crime*. New York: Oxford University Press.

Tonry, Michael. 2014. "Remodeling American Sentencing." *Criminology & Public Policy* 13:503–34.

Travis, Jeremy, Bruce Western, and Steven Redburn, eds. 2014. *The Growth of Incarceration in the United States*. Committee on Causes and Consequences of High Rates of Incarceration. National Research Council. Washington, DC: National Academies Press.

Vera Institute of Justice. 2015. *Crime Bill @20*. Retrieved August 25, 2015 (http://crimebill20.vera.org/justiceinfocus).

Wallace, John W. 2011. *Review of the Coalition for Evidence-based Policy*. New York: MDRC.

Wilson, James Q. and Richard Herrnstein. 1985. *Crime and Human Nature*. New York: Simon & Schuster.

REVIEW QUESTIONS

1. What types of topics were emphasized in the original NAS report in 1986?
2. What does the author conclude were the most significant "unintended policy consequences" that came out of the original report?
3. What future policy directions does the author advise? Which do you agree with, or disagree with?

SECTION XII

Integrated Theoretical Models and New Perspectives of Crime

This section will introduce **integrated theories**: those in which two or more traditional theories are merged into one cohesive model. We will then discuss the pros and cons of integrating theories and explain the various ways theories can be integrated. A review of integrated theories will demonstrate the many ways different theories have been merged to form more empirically valid explanations for criminal behavior.

This section examines relatively recent changes in criminological development; virtually all of these advances have taken place in the past few decades. Specifically, we discuss the types of models that modern explanatory formulations seem to have adopted, namely integrated theories. Of course, other unique theoretical frameworks have been presented in the past 30 years, but most of the dominant models presented during this time fall into the category of integrated theories.

Integrated theories attempt to put together two or more traditionally separate models of offending to form one unified explanatory theory. Given the empirical validity of most of the theories discussed in previous sections, as well as the failure of these previously examined theories to explain all variation in offending behavior, it makes sense that theorists would try to combine the best of several theories while disregarding or de-emphasizing the concepts and propositions that don't seem to be as scientifically valid. Furthermore, some forms of theoretical integration deal with only concepts or propositions, while others vary by level of analysis (micro vs. macro, or both). Although such integrated formulations sound attractive and appear to be surefire ways to develop sounder explanatory models of behavior, they have a number of weaknesses and criticisms. Here, we explore these issues as well as the best-known and most accepted integrated theories that are currently being examined and tested in the criminological literature.

Integrated Theories

About 30 years ago at a conference at the State University of New York at Albany, leading scholars in criminological theory development and research came together to discuss the most important issues in the growing area of theoretical integration.[1] Some integrated theories go well beyond formulating relationships between two or more

[1] For a compilation of the papers presented at this conference, see Steven F. Messner, Marvin D. Krohn, and Allen E. Liska, eds., *Theoretical Integration in the Study of Deviance and Crime: Problems and Prospects* (Albany: State University of New York Press, 1989).

traditionally separate explanatory models; they actually fuse the theories into one all-encompassing framework. The following sections will examine why integrated theories became popular over the past several decades while discussing different types of integrated theories, the strengths and weaknesses of theoretical integration, and several of the better-known and better-respected integrated theories.

The Need for Integrated Theories in Criminology

The emphasis on theoretical integration is a relatively recent development that has evolved due to the need to improve the empirical validity of traditional theories, which suffer from lack of input from various disciplines.[2] This was the result of the history of criminological theory, which we discussed in prior sections of this book. Specifically, most 19th-century theories of criminal behavior are best described as based on single-factor (e.g., intelligence quotient, or IQ) or limited-factor (e.g., stigmata) reductionism. Later, in the early 1900s, a second stage of theoretical development involved the examination of various social, biological, and psychological factors, which became known as the multiple-factor approach and is most commonly linked with the work of Sheldon and Eleanor Glueck.

Finally, in the latter half of the 20th century, a third stage of theoretical development and research in criminology became dominant, which represented a backlash against the multiple-factor approach. This stage has been called *systemic reductionism*, which refers to pervasive attempts to explain criminal behavior in terms of a particular system of knowledge.[3] For example, a biologist who examines only individuals' genotypes will likely not be able to explain much criminal behavior because he is missing a lot of information about the environment in which the people live, such as their levels of poverty or unemployment. For the past 60 years, the criminological discipline in the United States has been dominated by sociologists, which is largely due to the efforts and influence of Edwin Sutherland (see Section VIII). Thus, as one expert has observed,

> It is not surprising to find that most current explanations of criminal behavior are sociologically based and are attempts to explain variations in the rates of criminal behavior as opposed to individual instances of that behavior. . . . Even when the effort is to explain individual behavior, the attempt is to use exposure to or belief in cultural or social factors to explain individual instances or patterns of criminal behavior. . . . We find ourselves at the stage of development in criminology where a variety of sociological systemic reductionistic explanations dominate, all of which have proven to be relatively inadequate (to the standard of total explanation, prediction, or control) in explaining the individual occurrence or the distribution of crime through time or space.[4]

Other criminologists have also noted this sociological dominance, with some going as far to claim that

> Sutherland and the sociologists were intent on turning the study of crime into an exclusively sociological enterprise and . . . they overreacted to the efforts of potential intruders to capture some of what they regarded as their intellectual turf.[5]

---

[2] This discussion is largely drawn from Charles F. Wellford, "Towards an Integrated Theory of Criminal Behavior," in Messner et al., *Theoretical Integration*, 119–27.

[3] Ibid., 120.

[4] Ibid., 120–21.

[5] This quote is taken from Stephen E. Brown, Finn-Aage Esbensen, and Gilbert Geis, *Criminology: Explaining Crime and Its Context*, 8th ed. (Cincinnati: Anderson, 2013), 251 (see chap. 6), regarding claims made by Robert Sampson and John Laub, "Crime and Deviance over the Life Course: The Salience of Adult Social Bonds," *American Sociological Review* 55 (1990): 609–27. See also discussion in Richard A. Wright, "Edwin H. Sutherland," *Encyclopedia of Criminology*, Vol. 1, ed. Richard A. Wright and J. Mitchell Miller (New York: Routledge, 2005).

This dominance of sociology over the discipline is manifested in many obvious ways. For example, virtually all professors of criminology have doctorates of philosophy (PhDs) in sociology or criminal justice, and virtually no professors have a degree in biology, neuropsychology, or other fields that obviously have important influence on human behavior. Furthermore, virtually no undergraduate (or even graduate) programs in criminal justice and criminology currently require students to take a course that covers principles in biology, psychology, anthropology, or economics; rather, virtually all the training is sociology based. In fact, most criminal justice programs in the United States do not even offer a course in biopsychological approaches to understanding criminal behavior, despite the obvious need for and relevance of such perspectives.

Many modern criminologists now acknowledge the limitations of this state of systemic reductionism, which limits theories to only one system of knowledge, in this case sociology.[6] What resulted is a period of relative stagnation in theoretical development; experts regarded the 1970s as "one of the least creative periods in criminological history."[7] In addition, the mainstream theories that were introduced for most of the 1900s (such as differential association, strain, social bonding, and labeling, which we reviewed in previous sections) received limited empirical support, which should not be too much of a surprise given that they were based on principles of only one discipline—namely, sociology. Thus, it has been proposed that integrated theories evolved as a response to such limitations and the need to revitalize progress in the area of criminological theory building.[8] After reviewing some of the many integrated theories that have been proposed in the past two decades, we think readers will agree that combining explanatory models has indeed helped stimulate much growth in the area of criminological theory development. But, before examining these theories, it is important to discuss the varying forms they take.

Different Forms of Integrated Theories

There are several different types of integrated theories, which are typically categorized by the way that their creators propose that the theories should be fused together. The three most common forms of propositional theoretical integration, meaning synthesis of theories based on their postulates, are known as end-to-end, side-by-side, and up-and-down integration.[9] We will first explore each of these types before discussing a few more variations of combining theoretical concepts and propositions.

End-to-End Integration

The first type, **end-to-end (or sequential) integration**, typically is used when theorists expect that one theory will come before or after another in terms of temporal ordering of causal factors. This type of integration is more developmental in the sense that it tends to propose a certain ordering of the component theories that are being merged. For example, an integrated theory may claim that most paths toward delinquency and crime have their early roots in the breakdown of social attachments and controls (i.e., social bonding theory), but later, the influence of negative peers (i.e., differential association) becomes more emphasized. Thus, such a model would look like this:

Weak Social Bond → Negative Peer Associations → Crime

---

[6] Wellford, "Towards an Integrated Theory"; Sampson and Laub, "Crime and Deviance."

[7] Wellford, "Towards an Integrated Theory," 120, citing Frank P. Williams III, "The Demise of Criminological Imagination: A Critique of Recent Criminology," *Justice Quarterly* 1 (1984): 91–106.

[8] Wellford, "Towards an Integrated Theory."

[9] This typology is largely based on Travis Hirschi, "Separate and Unequal Is Better," *Journal of Research in Crime and Delinquency* 16 (1979): 34–37.

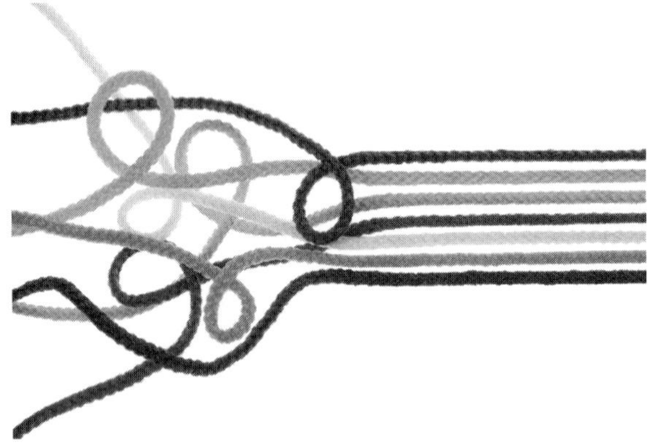

▲ **Image 12.1** This image of very different and unique threads coming together forms a much stronger fabric, which similarly mimics how various different strands (i.e., theories) come together to form a more unified, stronger piece. Integrated theories are the same in the sense that the combining of various different strands of theoretical frameworks can come together to form a much stronger, more robust understanding of criminal behavior.

SOURCE: © istockphoto.com / JamesBrey

Such an integrated model is referred to as an end-to-end (or sequential) integration, which is appropriately named because it conveys the linkage of the theories based on the temporal ordering of two or more theories in their causal timing.[10] Specifically, the breakdown of social bonds comes first, followed by the negative peer relations. Another way of saying this is that the breakdown of social bonds is expected to have a more remote or indirect influence on crime, which is mediated by differential peer influences; on the other hand, according to this model, peer influences are expected to have a more immediate or direct effect on crime, with no mediating influences of other variables. This model is hypothetical and presented to illustrate the end-to-end form of integration, but we will see that some established frameworks have incorporated similar propositions regarding social bonding and differential association and reinforcement theories.

Many of the traditionally separate theories that we have examined in previous sections tend to differ in their focus on either remote or immediate causal factors.[11] For instance, one of the assumptions of differential association theory is that psychological learning of crime is based on day-to-day (or even moment-to-moment) learning, so the emphasis is on more immediate causes of crime—namely, interactions with peers and significant others. On the other hand, other theories tend to focus more on remote causes of crime, such as social disorganization and strain theory, which place the emphasis on social structure factors (e.g., relative deprivation or industrialization) that most experts would agree are typically not directly implicated in situational decisions to engage in an actual criminal act but are extremely important nonetheless.

This situation seems conducive to the use of end-to-end integration, and often, the theories seem to complement each other quite well, as in our hypothetical example in which social control theory proposes the remote cause (i.e., weakened bonds) and differential association theory contributes the more direct, proximate cause (i.e., negative peer influence). On the other hand, two or more theories that focus only on more immediate causes of crime would be harder to combine because they both claim they are working at the same time, each in a sense competing against the other for being the primary direct cause of criminal activity; thus, they would be unlikely to fuse together as nicely and would not complement one another. Also, some theorists have argued that end-to-end integration is simply a form of **theoretical elaboration**, which we will discuss later. Another major limitation of end-to-end integration is the issue of whether the basic assumptions of the included theories are consistent with one another. We will investigate this in the following section, which discusses criticism of integration. But first, we must examine the other forms of theoretical integration.

---

[10] Allen E. Liska, Marvin D. Krohn, and Steven F. Messner, "Strategies and Requisites for Theoretical Integration in the Study of Crime and Deviance," in Messner et al., *Theoretical Integration*, 1–19.

[11] Much of our discussion of these forms of integration is taken from Liska et al., "Strategies and Requisites.".

Side-by-Side Integration

Another type of integrated theory is called **side-by-side (or horizontal) integration**. In the most common form of side-by-side integration, cases are classified by a certain criterion (e.g., impulsive vs. planned), and two or more theories are considered parallel explanations depending on what type of case is being considered. So, when the assumptions or target offenses of two or more theories are different, a side-by-side integration is often the most natural way to integrate them. For example, low self-control theory may be used to explain impulsive criminal activity, whereas rational choice theory may be used to explain criminal behavior that involves planning, such as white-collar crime. Traditionally, many theorists would likely argue that low self-control and rational choice theory are quite different, almost inherently opposing perspectives of crime. However, contemporary studies and theorizing have shown that the two models complement and fill gaps in each other.[12] Specifically, the rational choice and deterrence framework has always had a rather hard time explaining and predicting why individuals often do very stupid things for which there is little payoff and a high likelihood of getting in serious trouble, so the low self-control perspective helps fill in this gap by explaining that some individuals are far more impulsive and are more concerned about the immediate payoff (albeit often small) than they are about any long-term consequences.

An illustration of side-by-side integration of these two theories might thus look something like this:

For most typical individuals

High Self-Control → Consideration of Potential Negative Consequences →
Deterred from Committing Crime

For more impulsive individuals or activities

Low Self-Control → Desire for Immediate Payoff → Failure to Consider Consequences →
Decision to Commit Criminal Act

This side-by-side integration shows how two different theories can each be accurate, depending on what type of individual or criminal activity is being considered. As some scholars have concluded, rational choice theory is likely not a good explanation for homicides between intimates (which tend to be spontaneous acts), but it may be very applicable to corporate crime.[13]

---

[12] Daniel Nagin and Raymond Paternoster, "Enduring Individual Differences and Rational Choice Theories of Crime," *Law and Society Review* 27 (1993): 467–96; Alex Piquero and Stephen Tibbetts, "Specifying the Direct and Indirect Effects of Low Self-Control and Situational Factors in Offenders' Decision Making: Toward a More Complete Model of Rational Offending," *Justice Quarterly* 13 (1996): 481–510; Stephen Tibbetts and Denise Herz, "Gender Differences in Factors of Social Control and Rational Choice," *Deviant Behavior* 17 (1996): 183–208 (chap. 8, n. 90); Stephen Tibbetts and David Myers, "Low Self-Control, Rational Choice, and Student Test Cheating," *American Journal of Criminal Justice* 23 (1999): 179–200; Bradley Wright, Avshalom Caspi, and Terrie Moffitt, "Does the Perceived Risk of Punishment Deter Criminally Prone Individuals? Rational Choice, Self-Control, and Crime," *Journal of Research in Crime and Delinquency* 41 (2004): 180–213. For a review, see Stephen Tibbetts, "Individual Propensities and Rational Decision-Making: Recent Findings and Promising Approaches," in *Rational Choice and Criminal Behavior: Recent Research and Future Challenges*, ed. Alex Piquero and Stephen Tibbetts (New York: Routledge, 2002), 3–24.

[13] Liska et al., "Strategies and Requisites." For a review, see Brown et al., *Criminology: Explaining Crime*. For a recent study of rational choice applied to corporate crime, see Nicole Leeper Piquero, M. Lyn Exum, and Sally S. Simpson, "Integrating the Desire-for-Control and Rational Choice in a Corporate Crime Context," *Justice Quarterly* 22 (2005): 252–81.

Up-and-Down Integration

Another way of combining two or more theories is referred to as **up-and-down (or deductive) integration**. It is generally considered the classic form of theoretical integration because it has been done relatively often in the history of criminological theory development—even before it was considered integration. It often involves increasing the level of abstraction of a single theory so that postulates seem to follow from a conceptually broader theory. Up-and-down integration can take two prevalent forms: (1) theoretical reduction and (2) theoretical synthesis.

Theoretical reduction is typically done when it becomes evident "that theory A contains more abstract or general assumptions than theory B and, therefore, that key parts of theory B can be accommodated within the structure of theory A."[14] We have discussed this form of integration previously in this book without actually calling it by name. For example, in Section VIII, we discussed how differential reinforcement theory subsumed Sutherland's differential association theory. By equating concepts contained in both theories, the authors of differential reinforcement argued somewhat effectively that the learning that takes place through interactions with primary groups is one type of conditioning.[15] As you will recall, the main point is that the concepts and propositions of differential reinforcement theory are more general than—but entirely consistent with—those of differential association theory, such that the latter is typically a specific form of the former model. In other words, differential reinforcement is a much more broad, general theory, which accounts for not only differential association (i.e., classical conditioning) but also many other theoretical concepts and propositions (operant conditioning, modeling, or imitation).

This same type of theoretical reduction was also discussed in Section VI when we noted that general strain theory subsumed Robert Merton's traditional strain theory. Specifically, traditional strain theory focused on only one type of strain: failure to achieve positively valued goals. While general strain theory also places an emphasis on failure to achieve positively valued goals, it is more general and broader because it also focuses on two other forms of strain: loss of positively valued stimuli and exposure to noxious stimuli. Therefore, it seems to make sense that general strain theory would subsume traditional strain theory, because the concepts and principles of traditional strain appear to simply represent a specific type of general strain and can be fully accounted for by the more general version of the theory.[16]

Despite the obvious efficiency in theoretical reduction, many theorists have criticized such subsuming of theories by another. Specifically, many experts in the social sciences view such reduction as a form of theoretical imperialism, because the theory being reduced essentially loses its unique identity.[17] Therefore, the very phrase *theoretical reduction* generally has a negative connotation among scholars. In fact, one of the most accepted reductions in 20th-century criminological literature, the differential association-differential reinforcement synthesis we referred to previously, has been condemned as a "revisionist takeover . . . a travesty of Sutherland's position."[18] So, even the most widely known and cited forms of theoretical reduction have been harshly criticized, which gives readers some idea of how much social scientists can frown upon the subsuming of one theory by another.

The other form of up-and-down integration is referred to as *theoretical synthesis*, which is "done by abstracting more general assumptions from theories A and B, allowing parts of both theories to be incorporated in a new

---

[14] Liska et al., "Strategies and Requisites," 10.

[15] Liska et al., "Strategies and Requisites," 13; Robert L. Burgess and Ronald Akers, "Differential Association-Reinforcement Theory of Criminal Behavior," *Social Problems* 14 (1966): 128–46; Ronald Akers, *Deviant Behavior: A Social Learning Approach*, 3rd ed. (Belmont, CA: Wadsworth, 1985) (see chap. 8).

[16] Robert Agnew, "Foundation for a General Strain Theory of Crime and Delinquency," *Criminology* 30 (1992): 47–87; Robert Agnew and Helen R. White, "An Empirical Test of General Strain Theory," *Criminology* 30 (1992): 475–99.

[17] Liska et al., "Strategies and Requisites."

[18] This quote is from Ian Taylor, Paul Walton, and Jock Young, *The New Criminology* (New York: Harper & Row, 1973), 131–32. See discussion in Liska et al., "Strategies and Requisites," 13.

theory C."[19] This form of up-and-down integration is more uncommon in social science than theoretical reduction, perhaps because it is more difficult to achieve successfully, since by definition it requires the formulation of a new theory with new concepts or hypotheses that are not already found in the original component models. Furthermore, if the constituent theories are competing explanations, then it is quite likely that new terminology will have to be created or incorporated to resolve these differences.[20] However, if theoretical synthesis can be done correctly, it is perhaps the type of integration that provides the most advancement of theory development because, in addition to bringing together previously independent models, it also results in a new theory with predictions and propositions that go beyond the original frameworks.

One of the best-known and most accepted (despite its critics) examples of theoretical synthesis is **Elliott's integrated model**, which we review in detail later in this section.[21] For our purposes here, it is important only to understand why Delbert Elliott's model is considered theoretical synthesis. This is because Elliott's model integrates the concepts and propositions of various theories (e.g., social control and differential association) and contributes additional propositions that did not exist in the component theories.

Levels of Analysis of Integrated Theories

Beyond the variation in types of propositional theoretical integration discussed previously, such synthesis of explanatory models also differs in terms of the level of analysis that is being considered. Specifically, the integrated models can include component theories of micro–micro, macro–macro, or even micro–macro (called *cross-level*) combinations. For example, Elliott's integrated theory is a micro–micro level theory, which means that all of the component theories that make up the synthesized model refer to the individual as the unit of analysis. Although these models can provide sound understanding for why certain individuals behave in certain ways, they typically do not account for differences in criminality across groups (gender, socioeconomic groups, etc.).

On the other hand, some integrated models include theories from only macro levels. A good example of this type of integration is seen in Robert Bursik's synthesis of conflict theory and the social disorganization framework.[22] Both of these component theories focus only on the macro (group) level of analysis, thus neglecting the individual level; for example, they would fail to explain why some individuals do or do not commit crime even in the same structural environment.

The most complicated integrated theories, at least in terms of levels of analysis, are those that include both micro and macro models. Such models are likely the most difficult to synthesize successfully because this involves bringing together rather unnatural relationships between individual-based propositions and group-level postulates. However, when done effectively, such a model can be rather profound in terms of explanation of crime. After all, one of the primary objectives of a good theory is to explain behavior across as many circumstances as possible. Thus, a theory that can effectively explain why crime occurs in certain individuals as well as certain groups would be better than a theory that explains crime across only individuals or only groups.

---

[19] Liska et al., "Strategies and Requisites," 10.

[20] David Wagner and Joseph Berger, "Do Sociological Theories Grow?" *American Journal of Sociology* 90 (1985): 697–728.

[21] Delbert Elliott, Suzanne S. Ageton, and Rachelle J. Canter, "An Integrated Theoretical Perspective on Delinquent Behavior," *Journal of Research in Crime and Delinquency* 16 (1979): 3–27. See also discussion in Delbert Elliott, "The Assumption That Theories Can Be Combined with Increased Explanatory Power: Theoretical Integrations," in *Theoretical Methods in Criminology*, ed. Robert F. Meier (Beverly Hills, CA: Sage, 1985), 123–49. Discussion of Elliott's model as an example of theoretical synthesis can be found in Charles R. Tittle, "Prospects for Synthetic Theory: A Consideration of Macrolevel Criminological Activity," in Messner et al., *Theoretical Integration*, 161–78.

[22] Robert J. Bursik, "Political Decision Making and Ecological Models of Delinquency, Conflict and Consensus," in Messner et al., *Theoretical Integration*, 105–18.

An example of such a theory is **Braithwaite's reintegrative shaming theory**, which begins with an individual (or micro) level theory of social control and bonding—which he refers to as **interdependency**—and then relates levels of this concept to a group or community (or macro) level theory of bonding—which he refers to as **communitarianism**.[23] This theory will be discussed in far more detail later, but it is important here to acknowledge the advantages of explaining both the micro (individual) and macro (group) level of analysis in explanations of criminal behavior, such as in the theory of reintegrative shaming.

Ultimately, the levels of analysis of any component theories are important considerations in the creation of integrated models of crime. It is particularly important to ensure that the merging of certain theories from within or across particular levels makes rational sense and, most important, advances our knowledge and understanding of the causes of crime.

Additional Considerations regarding Types of Integration

Beyond the basic forms of propositional integration models and levels of analysis, there are two additional types of integration—conceptual integration and theoretical elaboration—that are quite common, perhaps even more common than the traditional forms discussed previously. **Conceptual integration** involves the synthesis of models in which "the theorist equates concepts in different theories, arguing that while the words and terms are different, the theoretical meanings and operations of measurement are similar."[24] Essentially, the goal in such a formulation is to take the primary constructs of two or more theories and merge them into a more general framework that aids understanding in explaining behavior by unifying terms that represent fundamentally similar phenomena or issues. Such formulations are considered less intrusive on the component theories than the propositional integrations we discussed previously.

One of the first and most cited examples of conceptual integration was provided by Frank Pearson and Neil Weiner in 1985.[25] As shown in Table 12.1, Pearson and Weiner attempted to map the various concepts of numerous criminological theories. This was done by creating categories that numerous concepts from various theories would appear to fit into through their inclusion in explanatory models of criminal behavior and across levels of explanation. Although based on a social learning and differential reinforcement perspective, Pearson and Weiner's model attempts to include concepts of virtually all existing theories of crime and delinquency. A particular strength is that this model includes feedback or behavioral consequence elements as well as classifying each model by unit of measurement and analysis.

For example, as illustrated in Table 12.1, the conceptual model shows that differential association theory has concepts that apply to all internal aspects and one of the two concepts under consequences or feedback at the micro level but none of the aspects under the external micro level or any of the four macro-level concepts. On the other hand, Marxist-critical theory is shown to apply to three of the internal micro and one of the consequences or feedback level concepts and to most of the macro-level concepts as well. Although only some of the theories that we have discussed in this book are included, largely because Pearson and Weiner's conceptual integration was done in the mid-1980s, this model includes most of the dominant theoretical frameworks that were prevalent in the criminological literature at the time of their formulation. Thus, this conceptual model remains as a sort of prototype for future attempts to conceptually integrate established theories explaining criminal conduct.

---

[23] John Braithwaite, *Crime, Shame and Reintegration* (Cambridge: Cambridge University, 1989).

[24] Liska et al., "Strategies and Requisites," 15; definition adapted from Frank S. Pearson and Neil Alan Weiner, "Toward an Integration of Criminological Theories," *Journal of Criminal Law and Criminology* 76 (1985): 116–50.

[25] Pearson and Weiner, "Toward an Integration." See review in Thomas J. Bernard and Jeffrey B. Snipes, "Theoretical Integration in Criminology," in *Crime and Justice Review*, Vol. 20, ed. Michael Tonry (Chicago: University of Chicago Press, 1996), 301–48.

Table 12.1 • Mapping of the Selected Criminological Theories into the Integrative Structure

	INTEGRATIVE CONSTRUCTS											
	Micro Level						Macro Level					
	Antecedent											
	Internal				External		Consequences or Feedback		Social Structural Production and Distribution of:			
Selected Criminological Theories	**Utility Demand (Deprivation)**	**Behavioral Skill**	**Rules of Expedience**	**Rules of Morality**	**Signs of Favorable Opportunities (Descriminative Stimuli)**	**Behavioral Resources**	**Utility Reception**	**Information Acquisition**	**Utilities**	**Opportunities**	**Rules of Expedience and Morality**	**Belief about Sanctioning Practices**
Differential association	✓	✓	✓	✓			✓					
Negative labeling	✓	✓		✓			✓					
Social control:												
1. Attachment	✓		✓				✓					
2. Commitment	✓		✓		✓			✓				
3. Involvement					✓			✓				
4. Belief				✓								
Deterrence	✓		✓		✓		✓	✓				✓
Economic	✓		✓		✓		✓	✓	✓		✓	
Routine activities	✓	✓	✓		✓	✓			✓	✓		
Neutralization		✓		✓							✓	
Relative deprivation	✓		✓	✓			✓		✓	✓		
Strain	✓	✓	✓	✓	✓		✓	✓	✓	✓	✓	
Normative (culture) conflict				✓							✓	
Generalized strain and normative (culture) conflict	✓	✓	✓	✓	✓	✓	✓	✓	✓	✓	✓	
Marxist-critical/ group conflict	✓		✓	✓			✓		✓	✓	✓	

SOURCE: Frank S. Pearson and Neil Alan Weiner, "Toward an Integration of Criminological Theories," *Journal of Criminal Law and Criminology* 76 (1985): 116–50 (table p. 130).

One notable strength of Pearson and Weiner's conceptual integration is the inclusion of most mainstream theories—differential association, labeling, social control, deterrence, economic, routine activities, neutralization, strain, normative (culture) conflict, generalized strain, and Marxist-critical group conflict—in existence at the time in which they created their integrated framework. Another strength of their integrated framework is the fact that they account for concepts at different levels of analysis, namely the micro (individual) and macro (group) levels, as shown in Table 12.1. So, the framework clearly does a good job at creating links between the most prominent theories in terms of the concepts they propose as the primary causes of crime.

However, Pearson and Weiner's conceptually integrated framework does have several notable weaknesses. One of the most prominent criticisms of the conceptual model is that it is based on a single theory, specifically social learning theory (tied to Akers's differential reinforcement and social learning theory, discussed in Section VIII), and the authors never really provide a strong argument for why they chose this particular base framework for their model. Another major weakness of this conceptual framework is that it completely neglects many biological and biosocial factors—hormones, neurotransmitters, toxins—that have been consistently shown to have profound effects on human behavior. Still, despite the criticisms of this integrated framework, respected theorists have noted that Pearson and Weiner's "integration of these concepts into a consistent, coherent framework is impressive," but the model has never received much attention in the criminological literature.[26]

However, despite the obvious tendency to simplify formulations through conceptual integration, many critics have claimed that such attempts are simply a means toward propositional integration. Thus, despite its categorization as conceptual, this type of integration is not necessarily seen as such, and it may be seen by many as a form of deductive integration. However, many experts have noted that conceptual integration is actually not a form of side-by-side integration, nor is it end-to-end integration. Rather, it is what it says it is: conceptual integration. It is nothing more and nothing less.[27] Therefore, it appears that conceptual integration is a distinct derivative form of integration and that it can and should occur independently if it helps to advance understanding of why people commit crime. As the most knowledgeable experts recently concluded, "establishing some conceptual equivalence is necessary for deductive integration."[28]

An additional variation of integration is theoretical elaboration, which is a strategy that takes an existing theory that is arguably underdeveloped and then further develops it by adding concepts and propositions from other theories. Many critics of traditional theoretical integration have argued that theoretical elaboration is a more attractive strategy because existing theories of offending are not developed enough to fully integrate them.[29] An example of theoretical integration can be seen in the expansion of rational choice theory, which had traditionally focused on ratios of perceived costs and benefits, to include deontological constructs, such as moral beliefs. Specifically, studies have consistently shown that ethical constraints condition the influence of expected consequences on criminal behavior ranging from violence to academic dishonesty to white-collar crime.[30] Although they are not without critics, most rational choice scholars appear to agree that such elaboration advanced the theoretical framework and

---

[26] Ronald L. Akers and Christine S. Sellers, *Criminological Theories: Introduction, Evaluation, and Application*, 6th ed. (Oxford: Oxford University Press, 2012), 288 (see chap. 8).

[27] Liska et al., "Strategies and Requisites," 15.

[28] Ibid., 16.

[29] Liska et al., "Strategies and Requisites," 16; Travis Hirschi, "Exploring Alternatives to Integrated Theory," in Messner et al., *Theoretical Integration*, 37–50; Terence P. Thornberry, "Reflections on the Advantages and Disadvantages of Theoretical Integration," in Messner et al., *Theoretical Integration*, 51–60; Robert F. Meier, "Deviance and Differentiation," in Messner et al., *Theoretical Integration*, 199–212.

[30] Amitai Etzioni, *The Moral Dimension: Toward a New Economics* (New York: Free Press, 1988); Ronet Bachman, Raymond Paternoster, and Sally Ward, "The Rationality of Sexual Offending: Testing a Deterrence/Rational Choice Conception of Sexual Assault," *Law and Society Review* 26 (1992): 401–19; Raymond Paternoster and Sally Simpson, "Sanction Threats and Appeals to Morality: Testing a Rational Choice Model of Corporate Crime," *Law and Society Review* 30 (1996): 378–99; Stephen G. Tibbetts, "College Student Perceptions of Utility and Intentions of Test Cheating," doctoral dissertation, University of Maryland–College Park (Ann Arbor: UMI, 1997). For a review and discussion, see Sally Simpson, Nicole Leeper Piquero, and Raymond Paternoster, "Rationality and Corporate Offending Decisions," in Piquero and Tibbetts, *Rational Choice*, 25–40.

made it a more accurate explanation of human behavior. In sum, theoretical integration, like conceptual integration, is an option for merging and improving theoretical models without completely synthesizing two or more entire paradigms.

Criticisms and Weaknesses of Integrated Theories

A number of criticisms have been leveled at theoretical integration. Perhaps one of the most obvious and prevalent, not to mention extremely valid, criticisms is the argument that caution should be taken in attempting to integrate theories that have apparent contradictions or inconsistencies in their postulates.[31] As we have seen, different theories are based on varying, often opposite, perspectives of human nature. While most versions of strain theory (e.g., Merton's theory) assume that human beings are born with a natural tendency toward being good, most variations of control theory (e.g., Hirschi's social bonding and self-control theories) assume that humans are innately selfish and hedonistic. At the same time, most versions of learning theory (e.g., Sutherland's theory of differential association and Akers's differential reinforcement theory) assume that humans are born with a blank slate; in other words, people are born with neither good nor bad tendencies but rather learn their morality moment to moment from social interaction.

Obviously, attempts to integrate these theories face the hurdles of dealing with such obvious contradictions, and many formulations that do merge some of these perspectives simply do not deal with this issue. The failure to acknowledge, let alone explain, such inconsistencies is likely to result in regression of theoretical development instead of leading to progress in understanding, which is the primary goal of integrating theories in the first place.

Other experts have argued that any attempts to integrate theories must unite three different levels of analysis, including individual (micro), group (macro), and microsituational, which merges the micro level with the spontaneous context.[32] While we agree that this would be the ideal for theory formulation, we know of no theory that does so. Therefore, this proposition is more of an ideal that has not yet been attempted. Thus, we are inclined to go with the best that has been offered by expert theorists. Still, it is hoped that in the future, such an integrated model will be offered that addresses all of these aspects in an explanatory model.

Another argument against theoretical integration is the stance that explanatory perspectives of crime are meant to stand alone. This is the position taken by Travis Hirschi, who has been one of the most cited and respected scholars in criminology over the last 40 years.[33] As others have noted, Hirschi confirmed his position on this debate unequivocally when he stated that "separate and unequal is better" than integrating traditionally independent theoretical models.[34]

This type of perspective is also called *oppositional tradition* or *theoretical competition*, because the separate theories are essentially pitted against one another in a form of battle or opposition. Although scientists are trained to always be skeptical of their own beliefs and open to other possibilities, especially the desire to refine theoretical models that are shown to be invalid, it is surprising that such a position exists. Despite the rather unscientific nature of this stance, such a position of oppositional tradition has many supporters. Specifically, one of the most respected and cited criminologists, Hirschi, claimed the following:

> The first purpose of oppositional theory construction is to make the world safe for a theory contrary to currently accepted views. Unless this task is accomplished, there will be little hope for the survival of the theory and less hope for its development. Therefore, oppositional theorists should not make

[31] Much of this discussion is taken from Brown et al., *Criminology: Explaining Crime*; and Messner et al., *Theoretical Integration*.

[32] James Short, "The Level of Explanation Problem in Criminology," in *Theoretical Methods in Criminology*, ed. Robert Meier (Beverly Hills, CA: Sage, 1985), 42–71. See also James Short, "On the Etiology of Delinquent Behavior," *Journal of Research in Crime and Delinquency* 16 (1979): 28–33.

[33] Bernard and Snipes, "Theoretical Integration"; Hirschi, "Exploring Alternatives."

[34] Hirschi, "Separate but Unequal."

> life easy for those interested in preserving the status quo. They should instead remain at all times blind to the weaknesses of their own position and stubborn in its defense. Finally, they should never smile.[35]

Unfortunately, this position against theoretical integration is presented in a very unscientific tone. After all, scientists should always be critical of their own views and theories. By stating that theorists should be "blind" to opposing viewpoints and "stubborn" in their own perspective's defense, Hirschi advocates a position that is absolutely against science. Still, this statement, albeit flawed, demonstrates the extreme position against theoretical integration that is favorable toward having each independent theory standing opposed to others. It is our position that this stand does not have much defense, which is shown by Hirschi's lack of rational argument. Furthermore, it is generally acceptable to smile when presenting any theoretical or empirical conclusions, even when they involve opposition to or acceptance of integrated theoretical models of criminal behavior.

Perhaps one of the most important criticisms against Hirschi's and others' criticisms of integrated models is that most traditional models alone explain only a limited amount of variation in criminal activity. Elliott and colleagues have claimed the following:

> Stated simply, the level of explained variance attributable to separate theories is embarrassingly low, and, if sociological explanations for crime and delinquency are to have any significant impact upon future planning and policy, they must be able to demonstrate greater predictive power.[36]

While some put this estimate at 10% to 20% of the variance in illegal activities, this is simply an average across different theories and various forms of deviant behavior.[37] However, this range is an overestimate based on many studies investigating the accuracy of separate theories, which tend to show weak support (explaining well under 10% of the variation in offending), particularly social bonding and strain models.[38]

On the other hand, this estimated range of explained variance underestimates the empirical validity of some theoretical frameworks that consistently show high levels of explained variation in certain criminal behaviors. For example, a large number of studies investigating Akers's differential reinforcement and social learning theory (discussed in Section VIII), which examine not only a wide range of samples (in terms of age, nationality, and other demographic characteristics) but also a large range of deviant activities (e.g., cigarette smoking, drug usage, violent sexual crimes), consistently account for more than 20% of variation in such behaviors.[39] Specifically, most of these

---

[35] Hirschi, "Exploring Alternatives," 45.

[36] Delbert Elliott, David Huizinga, and Suzanne Ageton, *Explaining Delinquency and Drug Use* (Beverly Hills, CA: Sage, 1985), 125, as quoted in Bernard and Snipes, "Theoretical Integration," 306.

[37] This estimate can be found in Bernard and Snipes, "Theoretical Integration," 306, but is based on the estimates of others, as discussed in this work.

[38] See review in Akers and Sellers, *Criminological Theories.*

[39] Ronald Akers et al., "Social Learning and Deviant Behavior: A Specific Test of a General Theory," *American Sociological Review* 44 (1979): 635–55; Marvin Krohn and Lonn Lanza-Kaduce, "Community Context and Theories of Deviant Behavior: An Examination of Social Learning and Social Bonding Theories," *Sociological Quarterly* 25 (1984): 353–71; Lonn Lanza-Kaduce et al., "Cessation of Alcohol and Drug Use among Adolescents: A Social Learning Model," *Deviant Behavior* 5 (1984): 79–96; Ronald Akers and John Cochran, "Adolescent Marijuana Use: A Test of Three Theories of Deviant Behavior," *Deviant Behavior* 6 (1985): 323–46; Ronald Akers and Gang Lee, "Age, Social Learning, and Social Bonding in Adolescent Substance Use," *Deviant Behavior* 19 (1999): 1–25; Marvin Krohn et al., "Social Learning Theory and Adolescent Cigarette Smoking: A Longitudinal Study," *Social Problems* 32 (1985): 455–73; Ronald Akers and Gang Lee, "A Longitudinal Test of Social Learning Theory: Adolescent Smoking," *Journal of Drug Issues* 26 (1996): 317–43; Ronald Akers et al., "Social Learning Theory and Alcohol Behavior among the Elderly," *Sociological Quarterly* 30 (1989): 625–38; Scot Boeringer, Constance Shehan, and Ronald Akers, "Social Contexts and Social Learning in Sexual Coercion and Aggression: Assessing the Contribution of Fraternity Membership," *Family Relations* 40 (1991): 558–64; Sunghyun Hwang and Ronald Akers, "Adolescent Substance Use in South Korea: A Cross-Cultural Test of Three Theories," in *Social Learning Theory and the Explanation of Crime: A Guide for the New Century*, ed. Ronald Akers and Gary Jensen (New Brunswick, NJ: Transaction, 2003), 39–64.

studies estimate that Akers's social learning model explains up to 68% or more of the variation in certain deviant behaviors, with the lowest estimate being around 30%.

Obviously, not all independent theories of crime lack empirical validity, so this does not support critics' claims that traditionally separate theories of crime do not do a good job of explaining criminal behavior. However, it is also true that many of the theories that do the best job in empirical tests for validity are those that are somewhat integrated in the sense that they often have been formed by merging traditional theories with other constructs and propositions, much like Akers's differential reinforcement theory, which added more modern psychological concepts and principles (e.g., operant conditioning and modeling) to Sutherland's traditional theory of differential association (see Section VIII). So, in a sense, an argument can be made that theoretical integration (or at least theoretical elaboration) had already occurred, which made this theory far more empirically valid than the earlier model.

Another example of the high level of empirical validity of existing models of offending can be found in some models of rational choice, which have been revised through theoretical elaboration and have explained more than 60% of the explained variation in deviant behavior.[40] However, much of the explanatory power of such frameworks relies on incorporating the constructs and principles of other theoretical models, which is what science is based on; specifically, they revise and improve theory based on what is evident from empirical testing. After all, even some of the harshest critics of theoretical integration admit that traditional theories do not own variables or constructs.[41] For example, Hirschi claimed the following:

Integrationists somehow conclude that variables appear . . . with opposition theory labels attached to them. This allows them to list variables by the theory that owns them. Social disorganization theory . . . might own economic status, cultural heterogeneity, and mobility. . . . Each of the many variables is measured and . . . the theories are ranked in terms of the success of their variables in explaining variation in delinquency . . . such that integration is in effect *required* by the evidence and surprisingly easily accomplished.[42]

This is the way that science and theoretical development and revision are supposed to work, so in our opinion, this is exactly as it should be. All scientists and theoreticians should constantly be seeking to improve their explanatory models and be open to ways to do so as opposed to being staunch supporters of one position and blind to existing evidence.

Despite the criticisms against theoretical integration, a strong argument has been made that theoretical competition and oppositional tradition are generally pointless.[43] A big reason for this belief among proponents of theoretical integration is that various theories tend to explain different types of crime and varying portions of the causal processes for behavior. For example, some theories focus more on property crimes while others focus on violent crimes, and some theories emphasize the antecedent or root causes of crime (e.g., genetics, poverty) while others emphasize more immediate causes (e.g., current social context at the scene). Given that there are multiple factors that contribute to crime and that different factors are more important for different types of crime, it only makes sense that a synthesis of traditionally separate theories must come together to explain the wide range of criminal activity that occurs in the real world.

Ultimately, there are both pros and cons of integrating theories. It is our belief that theoretical integration is generally a good thing as long as there is caution and attention given to merging models that have opposing assumptions, such as those regarding the natural state of human beings (e.g., good vs. bad vs. blank slate). But only

---

[40] For example, see Tibbetts, "College Student Perceptions," which showed that an elaborated rational choice model explained more than 60% of variation in test cheating among college students.

[41] See discussion in Bernard and Snipes, "Theoretical Integration," 306–7.

[42] Hirschi, "Exploring Alternatives," 41, as cited (revised) in Bernard and Snipes, "Theoretical Integration," 307.

[43] Bernard and Snipes, "Theoretical Integration," 306, based on the rationale provided by Elliott et al., *Explaining Delinquency.*

▲ **Image 12.2** Delbert Elliott proposed one of the most widely known and researched integrated theories, which combines elements of strain, social disorganization, bonding or control, and learning or socialization theories into one causal model of offending.

SOURCE: Courtesy of Delbert Elliott.

after considerable empirical research will the true validity of integrated models be tested, and many have already been put to the test. We will now examine a handful of integrated theories that have been proposed over the past couple of decades as well as the studies that have examined their empirical validity. Not surprisingly, some integrated and elaborated theories appear to be more valid than others—with most adding considerably to our understanding of human behavior and contributing to explaining the reasons why certain individuals or groups commit criminal behavior more than others.

Examples of Integrated Criminological Theory

We have already discussed the advantages and disadvantages of theoretical integration as well as the ways in which traditionally separate explanatory models are combined to form new, synthesized frameworks. We will now review a number of the most prominent examples of theoretical integration that have been proposed in the past 35 years, which is largely the time period when most attempts at integration have been presented. We hope that readers will critique each theory based on the criteria that we have already discussed, particularly noting the empirical validity of each model based on scientific observation and the logical consistency of its propositions.

Elliott's Integrated Model

Perhaps the first and certainly the most prominent integrated model is that proposed by Elliott and his colleagues in 1979, which has become known as Elliott's integrated model.[44] In fact, this model "opened the current round of debate on integration," because it was essentially the first major perspective proposed that clearly attempted to merge various traditionally separate theories of crime.[45] Elliott's integrated framework attempts to merge strain, social disorganization, control, and social learning and differential association-reinforcement perspectives for the purpose of explaining delinquency, particularly in terms of drug use but also for other forms of deviant behavior (see Figure 12.1).

As can be seen in Figure 12.1, the concepts and propositions of strain and social disorganization, as well as inadequate socialization, are considered antecedent (or root) causes of delinquency. In other words, failing to achieve one's goals (i.e., strain theory) and coming from a disadvantaged neighborhood (i.e., social disorganization) are key factors predisposing people to criminal behavior. Furthermore, the fact that many low-income households tend to lack adequate socialization, such as when a single parent has to work two or three jobs to make ends meet, is also a major root cause of delinquency.

Because this model clearly shows some constructs that lead to criminality as coming first (e.g., strain, social disorganization) and others as coming later (e.g., weak bonding and then affiliations with delinquents), this is a good example of end-to-end theoretical integration. In other words, this is an end-to-end form of integration

[44] Elliott et al., "An Integrated Theoretical Perspective." For further elaboration and refinement of this theory, see Elliott et al., *Explaining Delinquency.*

[45] Bernard and Snipes, "Theoretical Integration," 310.

Figure 12.1 • Elliott et al.'s integrated theoretical model

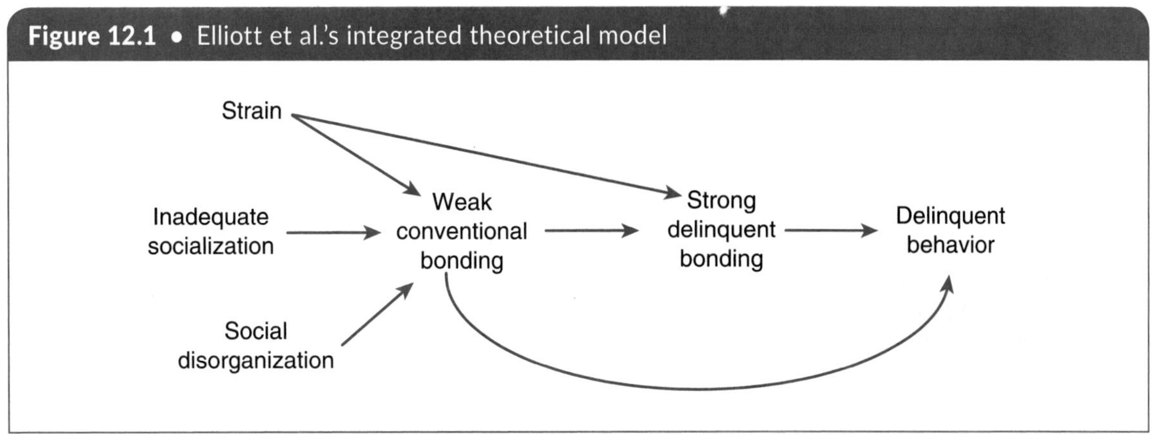

SOURCE: Delbert S. Elliott, David Huizinga, and Suzanne S. Ageton, *Explaining Delinquency and Drug Use* (Beverly Hills, CA: SAGE, 1985), pg. 66. Copyright © 1985 SAGE Publications, Inc. Reprinted by permission of SAGE Publications, Inc.

because some models or concepts, such as strain, occur first, which then lead chronologically to other models and concepts, such as weak conventional bonding or strong delinquent bonding, which then lead to crime.

The notable ways in which this perspective becomes a true integrated model is seen in the mediating or intervening variables. Although some antecedent variables (such as strain) can lead directly to delinquent activity, most of the criminal activity is theoretically predicted through a process that would include a breakdown of conventional bonding (i.e., social control and bonding theory), which occurs in many individuals who experience strain or social disorganization in their neighborhoods along with inadequate socialization. Furthermore, individuals who have such a breakdown in conventional bonding tend to be more highly influenced by the associations that they make in the streets among their peers (i.e., differential association-reinforcement and social learning theory). According to Elliott's integrated theory, this factor—strong delinquent bonding—most directly results in delinquent behavior among most juvenile offenders.

One of the notable features of this theoretical model is that it allows for various types of individuals to become criminal. In other words, unlike traditionally separate frameworks that assume that offenders expect not to achieve their goals (e.g., strain theory) or come from bad neighborhoods (e.g., Chicago or social disorganization theory), Elliott's integrated theory allows for a variety of possibilities when it comes to causal paths that explain how crime and delinquency develop in certain people and groups. This is what makes integrated models so much more powerful; namely, they bring several valid explanations together and allow for various possibilities to occur, all of which explain some criminality. Whereas traditional theories largely provide for only one causal process, Elliott and his colleagues showed right from the first major integrated theory that different types of trajectories, or paths to crime, are possible.

One of the major criticisms of merging such theories, particularly strain (which assumes individuals are born relatively good) and control or social bonding (which clearly assumes that people are born relatively bad [i.e., selfish, greedy, aggressive]), is that they tend to have extremely different, even opposite, assumptions of human behavior. As a recent review of theoretical integration noted, Elliott and his colleagues attempted to circumvent this obvious contrast in basic assumptions by claiming that the model allows for variation in individual motivations for why people engage in delinquency and crime.[46] For example, they claimed that failure to achieve one's goals (i.e., strain theory) is not always the motivation for crime; rather, crime can result from inadequate socialization or from coming from a disadvantaged neighborhood.

[46] Ibid.

Furthermore, Elliott's integrated model allows for different forms of control or social bonding with not all of the delinquents being required to have weak social bonds with conventional society. For instance, as can be seen in Figure 12.1, a person who has experienced strain (or failure to achieve her or his goals) can move directly to the social learning and differential association-reinforcement variables of strong delinquent bonding so that the weak conventional bonding construct is not a required causal process in this theoretical model. So, while some critics claim that Elliott and his colleagues have combined theories that simply cannot be synthesized due to contrasting assumptions, we believe that this integrated theory did, in fact, find a logical and consistent way of showing how both models can be merged in a way that makes a lot of sense in the real world. On the other hand, the model does indeed claim that strain directly causes weak conventional bonding, and the theoretical framework implies that the probability of delinquency is highest when an individual experiences both strain and weak conventional bonding, so to some extent, the critics make an important point regarding the logical consistency of the full model, which Elliott and his colleagues have not adequately addressed.[47]

Despite the presence of elements of four traditionally separate theories (strain, social disorganization, social control or bonding, and social learning or differential association-reinforcement), Elliott and his colleagues identified this integrated theory with social control, as opposed to any of the other perspectives, which they argue is a more general theory and can explain crime and delinquency across different levels of explanation. They also noted that the social control perspective is more sociological in the sense that it places more importance on the role of institutional structures in controlling criminal behavior.[48] Perhaps another reason why they identified their model with social control or bonding theory was because both intervening constructs represent types of bonds formed or not formed with others: weak conventional bonding and strong delinquent bonding. However, it is important to keep in mind that these constructs actually represent two traditionally separate theories—namely, social bonding theory and differential association-reinforcement or social learning, respectively.

The authors of this textbook believe that when an integrated theory (which claims to be such an integrated model) chooses a primary or dominant theory as its basis, this does not help in selling it to the scientific community, let alone others. A similar problem was seen in Pearson and Weiner's conceptual integration in their identifying a single traditionally separate theory—social learning or differential association-reinforcement—as the foundation or basis for their framework. Obviously, the first reaction by many theorists, even those that are not inherently against theoretical integration, would be somewhat cautious or even resistant. After all, why would a theory that claims to be integrated outright claim a single explanatory framework as its basis?

Rather, such models may be seen more as examples of theoretical elaboration, which tends to start with the assumptions and concepts of one theory and draw from other models to improve the base model. Still, despite the criticisms against identifying a single model as a basis for developing an integrated framework for explaining criminality, it is apparent that latitude has been granted. It is important to note that Elliott's model is considered the first true attempt at theoretical integration and is still widely respected as the prototype and example of what an integrated model could and should be.

Much of the empirical evidence supporting Elliott's integrated model has been provided by Elliott and his colleagues themselves through their testing of the theory. Specifically, much of the testing they have done has been via the National Youth Survey (NYS), a national survey collected and synthesized by criminologists at the University of Colorado Boulder, which is where Elliott and most of the colleagues with whom he works are professors. This longitudinal measure of delinquency has been administered and analyzed for several decades, and it represents perhaps the most systematic collection of information from youths regarding key developmental variables and delinquency rates that has ever existed.

---

[47] Ibid.

[48] Ibid., 311–12.

Most of the evidence from the NYS shows general strong support for Elliott's model.[49] However, some evidence has shown few direct effects of the strain and social control concepts, which is surprising given that the basis of the model was the social control and bonding elements of the theory.[50] In fact, the original hypothesis in the model—that strain and social control or bonding would have a direct effect on delinquency—was not observed.[51] Rather, only bonding to delinquent peers had a significant and strong effect on future criminality, which supports social learning and differential association-reinforcement theory. This strongly supports the social learning variables in the model and diminishes the claim made by Elliott and his colleagues about the fundamental theoretical perspective of social control and bonding.

Furthermore, a critical review of Elliott's framework, as presented in his 1985 book (with David Huizinga and Suzanne Ageton), noted that a major problem is that its "most puzzling feature . . . is the inclusion of social disorganization in it as a causal factor, in the absence of any attempt to measure or test the importance of this factor. Presumably, the authors wished to claim that their theory was 'more sociological than psychological.'"[52]

This point is particularly important, given that virtually none of the tests of Elliott's integrated model have included social disorganization factors in their studies, even after this critical review was published more than 25 years ago. So, Elliott and his colleagues should either drop this portion from consideration in the model or provide an adequate test of it in relation to the rest of the framework. Although we would opt for the latter, one of these two alternatives must be chosen.

However, from the presentation that Elliott gave as his presidential address to the American Society of Criminology (ASC) in 1993, it appears that the former alternative was chosen. Specifically, in his model of the onset of serious violent offending, all of the antecedent variables could be explained by the other traditionally separate theoretical models in his framework. He included two bonding constructs (family and school), parental sanctions, stressful life events (i.e., strain), and early exposure to crime and victimization. Perhaps the last factor could be construed as related to social disorganization theory, but it is probably regarded more as a social learning and differential association-reinforcement variable, as is suggested from the original model.

In addition, this critique noted that the existing evidence shows that most delinquent activity is committed among groups of juveniles, and, thus, youths who tend to commit illegal acts naturally associate with delinquents. Yet, the affiliation with delinquent peers is not considered the basic foundation of the theory—as tests of this model demonstrated—but rather an intervening variable in the model. The author of this critique claims that Elliott's model does not emphasize this point strongly enough and thereby does not provide convincing evidence that delinquent peers cause or facilitate offending.[53]

In light of these findings, even Elliott and his colleagues acknowledged that their integrated model best fit the data as a social learning and differential association-reinforcement framework of delinquency.[54] However, they chose to retain social control and bonding theory as the primary foundation of their integrated model, stating that "it is not clear that a social learning model would have predicted a conditional relationship between conventional bonding . . . and deviant bonding."[55] Elliott and colleagues went on to say that they did not attribute most of the explained variation in the model to social learning and differential reinforcement as being the most important

---

[49] See review in Akers and Sellers, *Criminological Theories*, 273–76.

[50] Elliott et al., *Explaining Delinquency.*

[51] Akers and Sellers, *Criminological Theories*, 275.

[52] David Farrington, book review of *Explaining Delinquency*, by Elliott et al., *British Journal of Addiction* 81 (1986): 433; embedded quote taken from p. 67 in Elliott et al.'s book.

[53] Farrington, book review, 433.

[54] Ibid.

[55] Ibid., based on a quote from Elliott et al., *Explaining Delinquency*, 137.

construct because they claimed that such variables did not play a strong enough part in the indirect effects that were seen in the estimated models.

This is actually a logical position, given the fact that their integrated framework would, in fact, predict that social learning and differential association-reinforcement variables were the primary direct effects on delinquency, and social control, strain, and social disorganization variables were considered primarily indirect all along, according to their model. However, some critics, especially the proponents of social learning and differential reinforcement theory, have claimed the following:

> Even with the addition of the interactive effects of conventional bonding, the final model reported by Elliott et al. is more of a variation on social learning theory (with bonding modifications) than it is a variation on social bonding theory (with learning modifications).[56]

After all, the measures of delinquent peer bonds used by Elliott and his colleagues are essentially measures that have been used by theorists and researchers of social learning theory over the past few decades regarding differential associations, reinforcements, and modeling.[57]

Additional analyses using the NYS have tended to agree with the critics regarding the importance of social learning and differential reinforcement variables in predicting crime and delinquency. Specifically, one relatively recent reanalysis of NYS data showed that social learning variables appeared to predict more variation in deviance than did the other models or constructs in the model.[58] The assumption that strong attachments to others, regardless of who they are, reduces offending, has been shown by empirical research to be false (see Section VIII). This is true, and all future integrated models must address this issue if they include social control or bonding propositions or constructs in their models.

Despite these criticisms and empirical observations, it appears that Elliott's integrated model has contributed to our understanding of the development of delinquent behavior. In the least, it inspired other theoretical frameworks, some of which we review here. However, it should also be obvious that there are some valid criticisms of this model, such as the claim that it is based on social control and bonding theory while depending heavily on the strong delinquent bonding that takes place in most cases of criminality, clearly implicating social learning and differential reinforcement theory. Again, we want to stress that a true integrated model should not place any emphasis on a particular theory; otherwise, the critics will have a sound argument when findings show that one theory is more influential than another.

Thornberry's Interactional Theory

After Elliott's integrated model, presented in 1979, the next major integrated framework was that of Terrence Thornberry in 1987.[59] This model incorporated empirical evidence drawn since Elliott's presentation to create a unique and insightful model of criminality, which addressed an extremely important aspect that had never been

---

[56] Akers and Sellers, *Criminological Theories*, 275.

[57] Ibid., 276.

[58] Robert Agnew, "Why Do They Do It? An Examination of the Intervening Mechanisms between 'Social Control' Variables and Delinquency," *Journal of Research in Crime and Delinquency* 30 (1993): 245–66.

[59] Terrence Thornberry, "Toward an Interactional Theory of Delinquency," *Criminology* 25 (1987): 863–87. See also Thornberry, "Reflections"; Terrence Thornberry et al., "Testing Interactional Theory: An Examination of Reciprocal Causal Relationships among Family, School and Delinquency," *Journal of Criminal Law and Criminology* 82 (1991): 3–35; Terrence Thornberry et al., "Delinquent Peers, Beliefs, and Delinquent Behavior: A Longitudinal Test of Interactional Theory," *Criminology* 32 (1994): 47–83.

addressed previously in criminological theory. Specifically, Thornberry's interactional theory was the first to emphasize reciprocal, or feedback, effects in the causal modeling of the theoretical framework.

As a basis for his model, Thornberry combined social control and social learning models. According to Thornberry, both of these theories try to explain criminality in a straightforward, causal process and are largely targeted toward a certain age population.[60] Thornberry uniquely claimed that the processes of both social control and social learning theory affect each other in a type of feedback process.

Thornberry's integrated model incorporates five primary theoretical constructs, which are synthesized in a comprehensive framework to explain criminal behavior. These five concepts include the following: (1) commitment to school, (2) attachment to parents, (3) belief in conventional values (these first three are taken from social control and bonding theory), (4) adoption of delinquent values, and (5) association with delinquent peers (these last two are drawn from social learning and differential association-reinforcement theory). These five constructs, which most criminologists would agree are important in the development of criminality, are obviously important in a rational model of crime, so at first it does not appear that Thornberry has added much to our understanding of criminal behavior. Furthermore, Thornberry's model clearly points out that different variables will have greater effects at certain times; for example, he claims that association with delinquent peers will have more effect in the midteenage years than at other ages.

What Thornberry adds beyond other theories is the idea of reciprocity or feedback loops, which no previous theory had mentioned, much less emphasized. In fact, much of the previous criminological literature had spent much time debating whether individuals become delinquent and then start hanging out with similar peers or whether individuals start hanging out with delinquent peers and then begin engaging in criminal activity. This has been the traditional chicken-or-egg question in criminology for most of the 20th century; namely, which came first, delinquency or bad friends? It has often been referred to as the *self-selection* versus *social learning* debate; in other words, do certain individuals decide to hang out with delinquents based on their own previous behavior, or do they learn criminality from delinquents with whom they start associating? One of the major contributions of **Thornberry's interactional model** is that he directly answered this question.

Specifically, Thornberry noted that most, if not all, contributors to delinquency (and criminal behavior itself) are related reciprocally. Thus, Thornberry postulated that engaging in crime leads to hanging out with other delinquents and that hanging out with delinquents leads to committing crimes. It is quite common for individuals to commit crime and then start hanging out with other peers who are doing the same, and it is also quite common for people to start hanging out with delinquent peers and then start committing offenses. Furthermore, it is perhaps the most likely scenario for a person who is offending to be dealing with both the influences of past experiences and peer effects as well.

As mentioned previously, Thornberry considered the social control and bonding constructs, such as attachment to parents and commitment to school, the most essential predictors of delinquency. Like previous theoretical models of social bonding and control, Thornberry's model puts the level of attachment and commitment to conventional society ahead of the degree of moral beliefs that individuals have regarding criminal offending. However, lack of such moral beliefs leads to delinquent behavior, which in turn negatively affects the level of commitment or attachments an individual may have built in her or his development. Thornberry claimed the following:

> While the weakening of the bond to conventional society may be an initial cause of delinquency, delinquency eventually becomes its own indirect cause precisely because of its ability to weaken further the person's bonds to family, school, and conventional beliefs.[61]

---

[60] Much of this discussion is taken from Bernard and Snipes, "Theoretical Integration," 314–16; and also Akers and Sellers, *Criminological Theories*, 278.

[61] Thornberry, "Toward an Interactional Theory," 876, as quoted by Bernard and Snipes, "Theoretical Integration," 315.

Thus, the implications of this model are that variables relating to social control or bonding and other sources cause delinquency, which then becomes, in itself, a predictor and cause for the breakdown of other important causes of delinquency and crime.

Such a model, although complex and hard to measure, is logically consistent, and the postulates are sound. However, the value of any theory has to be determined by the empirical evidence that is found regarding its validity. Much of the scientific evidence regarding Thornberry's empirical model has been contributed by Thornberry and his colleagues.

Although the full model has yet to be tested, the researchers "have found general support for the reciprocal relationships between both control concepts and learning concepts with delinquent behavior."[62] One test of Thornberry's model used the longitudinal Rochester Youth Development Study to test its postulates.[63] This study found that the estimates of previous unidirectional models (nonreciprocal models) did not adequately explain the variation in the data. Rather, the results supported the interactional model, with delinquent associations leading to increases in delinquency, delinquency leading to reinforcing peer networks, and both directional processes working through the social environment. In fact, this longitudinal study demonstrated that, once the participants had acquired delinquent beliefs from their peers, the effects of these beliefs had further effects on their future behavior and associations, which is exactly what Thornberry's theory predicts (see Figure 12.2).[64]

Case Study: Thornberry's Interactional Model

As an example, consider a person we shall call Johnny who has an absent father and a mother who uses inconsistent discipline and sometimes harsh physical abuse of her son. He sees his mother's state of constant neglect and abuse as proof that belief in conventional values is wrong, and he becomes indifferent toward governmental laws; after all, his main goal is to survive and be successful. Because of his mother's psychological and physical neglect, Johnny pays no attention to school and rather turns to his older peers for guidance and support. These peers guide him toward behavior that gives him both financial reward (selling what they steal) and status in their group (respect for performing well in illegal acts). At some point, Johnny gets caught, and this makes the peers who taught him how to engage in crime very proud, while alienating him from the previous bonds he had with his school, from which he is suspended, and with his mother, who further distances herself from him. This creates a reciprocal effect or feedback loop to the previous factors, which were lack of attachment to his mother and lack of commitment to school. The lowered level of social bonding and control with conventional institutions and factors (mother, school) and increased influence by delinquent peers then leads Johnny to commit more frequent and more serious crimes.

The lowered level of social bonding and control with conventional institutions and factors (mother, school) and increased influence by delinquent peers then leads Johnny to commit more frequent and more serious crimes.

[62] Bernard and Snipes, "Theoretical Integration," 316.

[63] Thornberry et al., "Delinquent Peers."

[64] Ibid.

Figure 12.2 • Thornberry's interactional model of delinquent involvement at middle adolescence

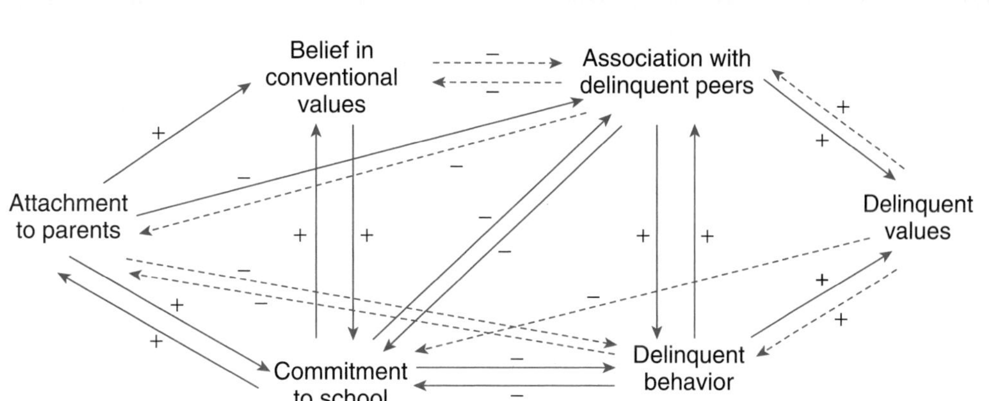

Thornberry's theoretical model is based on reciprocal effects, meaning that what is an outcome variable (e.g., association with delinquent peers) also becomes a predictive variable in that it influences previous variables (e.g., commitment to school). This figure shows how such relationships function with negative signs (–) meaning that there is an inverse relationship between the two variables (e.g., more association with delinquent peers is associated with less commitment to school) or positive (+) signs meaning that there is a direct positive association between two variables (e.g., belief in conventional values is associated with commitment to school). These variables tend to have a feedback loop, as represented in the figure.

Perhaps the most recent test of Thornberry's interactional model examined the age-varying effects of the theory.[65] This study incorporated hierarchical linear modeling in investigating a sample of the NYS. The results showed that, while the effects of delinquent peers were relatively close to predictions, peaking in the midteenage years, the predictions regarding the effects of family on delinquency were not found to be significant in the periods that were expected although family was important during adolescence.

Unlike other authors of integrated theories, Thornberry specifically noted that he prefers to see his approach as theoretical elaboration and not full theoretical integration. While we commend Thornberry for addressing this concern, virtually all criminologists still consider his framework a fully integrated model. And, in many ways, Thornberry's interactional model is far more integrated than others discussed here because it gives equal weight to the traditionally separate theoretical frameworks that are combined into his model in the sense that both are considered antecedent and reciprocal in their effects on criminal behavior.

Braithwaite's Theory of Reintegrative Shaming

A unique integrated model that proposed the synthesis of several traditionally separate theories was presented in 1989 in a book titled *Crime, Shame and Reintegration.*[66] The theory of reintegrative shaming merges constructs and

[65] Sung Joon Jang, "Age-Varying Effects of Family, School, and Peers on Delinquency: A Multilevel Modeling Test of Interactional Theory," *Criminology* 37 (1999): 643–85.

[66] Braithwaite, *Crime, Shame and Reintegration.*

principles from several theories, primarily social control or bonding theory and labeling theory with elements of strain theory, subculture and gang theory, and differential association theory. All of these theories are synthesized in a clear and coherent framework that is presented in both descriptive and graphic form. We will spend extra time discussing John Braithwaite's theory because it addresses not only U.S. culture but also cultural and justice tendencies in Japanese culture.

Braithwaite's idea for the theory was obviously inspired by the cultural differences he observed in Eastern (particularly Japanese) culture, in terms of both socialization practices and the justice system, as compared to the Western world. (Note that Braithwaite is from Australia, which uses the same Western practices as England and the United States.) Specifically, he emphasized the Japanese focus on the aggregate, such as the family, school, or business, to which the individual belongs. In contrast, in many Western cultures, epitomized by U.S. culture, the emphasis is clearly placed on the individual.

This contrast has often been referred to as the *we* culture versus the *me* culture (Eastern vs. Western emphases, respectively). Although this is seen in virtually all aspects of culture and policy practices, it is quite evident in people's names. In most Eastern cultures, people are known by their family name, which is placed first in the ordering. This shows the importance that is placed on the group to which they belong. In contrast, Western societies list individual names first, implying a focus on the individual herself or himself. These naming practices are a manifestation of a virtually all-encompassing cultural difference regarding group dynamics and social expectations across societies, especially in their justice systems. For example, it is quite common in Japan to receive a sentence of apologizing in public, even for the most serious violent crimes.[67] In his book, Braithwaite pointed out that, after World War II, Japan was the only highly industrialized society that showed a dramatic decrease in its crime rate.

Criminological theory would predict an increasing crime rate in Japan, given the extremely high density of urban areas due to rapid industrialization, especially on such a small amount of land—Japan being a large island. As Braithwaite described it, the Japanese suffered from anomie after the war in the sense of a general breakdown of cultural norms, but the nation was able to deal with this anomic state despite the odds. Japan definitively decided not to follow the Western model of justice after the war; rather, it rejected the Western system of stigmatizing convicted felons. Instead, the Japanese implemented a system in which offenders are reintroduced (hence *reintegration*) via a formal ceremony in which citizens accept the offenders back into conventional society. In contrast, in the United States, we typically give our ex-cons about $200 on average and make them promise always to identify themselves as felons on legal documents.

Japan is also extremely lenient in sentencing offenders to prison. In contrast, by rate of incarceration, the United States is the most punitive developed nation. In Japan, Braithwaite noted the following:

> Prosecution only proceeds in major cases . . . where the normal process of apology, compensation, and forgiveness by the victim breaks down. Fewer than 10 percent of those offenders who are convicted receive prison sentences, and for two-thirds of these, prison sentences are suspended. Whereas 45 percent of those convicted of a crime serve a jail sentence in the U.S., in Japan the percentage is under two.[68]

Public apology is the most common punishment among the Japanese, which strongly reflects the nature of honor in Japanese society, as well as pointing out the fundamental differences between how we deal with offenders. Braithwaite claimed that this cultural and political difference has a huge impact on why crime rates in both nations have experienced such different trends.

---

[67] Ibid., 62.

[68] Ibid., citing findings from J. Haley, "Sheathing the Sword of Justice in Japan: An Essay on Law without Sanctions," *Journal of Japanese Studies* 8 (1982): 265–81.

Most developing Western nations, including the United States, experienced a rising crime rate in the 1950s, 1960s, and 1970s. Braithwaite argued that this was likely due to culture and the differential treatment of its offenders:

> It might be argued that this [the downward trend in crime rates after World War II in Japan] was a result of the re-establishment of cultural traditions of shaming wrongdoers, including the effective coupling of shame and punishment. . . . One contention . . . is that the uncoupling of shame and punishment manifested in a wide variety of ways in many Western countries is an important factor in explaining the rising crime rates in those countries.[69]

Furthermore, in contrast to American society, the Japanese are typically less confrontational with authority. For example, some scholars have noted that the Japanese accept the authority of law, and police officers are considered similar to "elder brothers" who rely "on positive rather than negative reinforcement" when it comes to crime control.[70] This difference in the way officers and other authority figures are considered is likely due to the way that the Japanese view society in terms of neighborhood, community, school, and work—the informal institutions of control that we have mentioned earlier in this book as having more effect on the crime rate than formal institutions (i.e., police, courts, prisons).

Beyond discussing the cultural differences, Braithwaite's integrated theory addresses some of the most notable scientific observations regarding which types of individuals and groups are likely to commit crime. Specifically, Braithwaite stated that most crime is committed by young, poor, single males who live in urban communities that have high levels of residential mobility; they are likely to be unattached to or to do poorly in school, have low educational or occupational aspirations, are not strongly attached to their parents, associate with delinquent peers, and do not have moral beliefs against violating the law.[71]

It is obvious from this list that Braithwaite incorporated some of the major theories and corresponding variables into his theoretical perspective. The emphasis on poor people who do not have high educational or occupational aspirations obviously supports strain theory, whereas the inclusion of urban individuals who live in communities with high residential mobility reflects the Chicago School or social disorganization theory. At the same time, Braithwaite clearly highlighted the predisposition of people who have limited moral beliefs and weak attachments, which conjures up images of social bonding and control theory; individuals having delinquent peers obviously supports differential association and reinforcement theory. Thus, a handful of theories are important in the construction of Braithwaite's integrated theory.

Braithwaite noted that much of the effectiveness of the Japanese system of crime control depends on two constructs: (1) interdependency and (2) communitarianism. Interdependency is the level of bonding of an individual to conventional society, such as the degree to which she or he is involved with or attached to conventional groups in society, which would include employment, family, church, and organizations. According to Braithwaite, interdependency is the building block of the other major theoretical construct in his integrated model: communitarianism. Communitarianism is the macro (group) level of interdependency, meaning that it is the cumulative degree of the bonds that individuals have with conventional groups and institutions (e.g., family, employment, organizations, church) in a given society. Obviously, these theoretical constructs are mostly based on the theory of social bonding and control in the sense that they are based on attachments, commitment, and involvement in conventional society.

---

[69] Braithwaite, *Crime, Shame and Reintegration*, 61; brackets are authors' paraphrasing.

[70] David H. Bayley, *Forces of Order: Police Behavior in Japan and the United States* (Berkeley: University of California Press, 1976).

[71] Braithwaite, *Crime, Shame and Reintegration*, 44–53.

▲ **Image 12.3** John Braithwaite, a highly respected scholar, proposed the theory of reintegrative shaming, which has led to many successful policy implementations, especially regarding the use of restorative programs for more minor offenders.

SOURCE: Courtesy of John Braithwaite

Braithwaite's model has a causal ordering that starts with largely demographic variables, such as age, gender, marital status, employment, and aspirations, on the individual level and urbanization and residential mobility on the macro (group) level. All of these factors are predicted to influence the level of interdependency and communitarianism in the model, which, as we previously discussed, is largely based on social control and bonding theory. Depending on which type of culture is considered, or what forms of shaming are used in a given jurisdiction, the various types of shaming that are administered are key in this integrated model.

According to Braithwaite, societies that emphasize reintegrative shaming, such as Japan, will reduce the rates of crime in their societies. When an offender in Japan completes her or his sentence or punishment for committing a crime, the government will often sponsor a formal ceremony in which the offender is reintroduced or reintegrated into conventional society. According to Braithwaite, we in the United States do not reintegrate offenders into our society after shaming them but rather stigmatize them, which leads them to associate only with people from criminal subcultures (e.g., drug users, gang members). Braithwaite claimed that this leads to the formation of criminal groups and the grasping of illegitimate opportunities offered in the local community. Ultimately, this means that people who are not reintegrated into conventional society will inevitably be stigmatized and labeled as offenders, preventing them from becoming productive members of the community, even if their intentions are to do such.

Most empirical studies of Braithwaite's theory show mixed results, with most being in favor of this theory, especially regarding its implementation for policy. Some tests have shown that reintegrative ideology regarding violations of law can have a positive impact on future compliance with the law; others have found that high levels of shaming in parental practices do not increase offending.[72] Studies in other countries, such as China and Iceland, show partial support for Braithwaite's theory.[73] While some studies have found encouraging results,[74] other recent studies have also found weak or no support for the theory.[75]

---

[72] Toni Makkai and John Braithwaite, "Reintegrative Shaming and Compliance with Regulatory Standards," *Criminology* 32 (1994): 361–86; Carter Hay, "An Exploratory Test of Braithwaite's Reintegrative Shaming Theory," *Journal of Research in Crime and Delinquency* 38 (2001): 132–53.

[73] Lu Hong, Zhang Lening, and Terance Miethe, "Interdependency, Communitarianism, and Reintegrative Shaming in China," *Social Science Journal* 39 (2002): 189–202; Eric Baumer et al., "Crime, Shame, and Recidivism: The Case of Iceland," *British Journal of Criminology* 42 (2002): 40–60.

[74] Nathan Harris, Lode Walgrave, and John Braithwaite, "Emotional Dynamics in Restorative Conferences," *Theoretical Criminology* 8 (2004): 191–210; Eliza Ahmed and Valerie Braithwaite, "'What, Me Ashamed'? Shame Management and School Bullying," *Journal of Research in Crime and Delinquency* 41 (2004): 269–94.

[75] Bas Van Stokkom, "Moral Emotions in Restorative Justice Conferences: Managing Shame, Designing Empathy," *Theoretical Criminology* 6 (2002): 339–61; Charles Tittle, Jason Bratton, and Marc Gertz, "A Test of a Microlevel Application of Shaming Theory," *Social Problems* 50 (2003): 592–617; Lening Zhang and Sheldon Zhang, "Reintegrative Shaming and Predatory Delinquency," *Journal of Research in Crime and Delinquency* 41 (2004): 433–53.

The most recent reports regarding the effects of shame show that outcomes largely depend on how shame is measured, which Braithwaite's theory largely ignores. There are, for example, episodic or situational shame states as well as long-term shame traits or propensities. Recent reviews of the literature and studies of how different types of shame are measured show that certain forms of shame are positively correlated with offending, whereas other forms of shame tend to inhibit criminal behavior.[76] If individuals persistently feel shame, they are more likely to commit criminal activity, but if persons who are not predisposed to feel shame perceive that they would feel shame for doing a given illegal activity, then they would be strongly inhibited from engaging in such activity.[77] This is consistent with findings from another recent study that demonstrated that the effect of reintegrative shaming had an interactive effect on delinquency.[78]

Furthermore, Braithwaite's theory does not take into account other important self-conscious emotions, such as guilt, pride, embarrassment, and empathy, that are important when individuals are deciding whether to commit criminal behavior. Although some theorists claim that shame is the key social emotion, studies show that they are clearly wrong. Rather, many emotions, such as guilt and embarrassment, are based on social interaction and self-consciousness; in many ways, they are just as inhibitory or rehabilitating as shame.[79] The literature examining rational choice theory is also an indication of the effects of emotions other than shame in influencing decisions on offending.[80]

Still, Braithwaite's reintegrative theory provides an important step ahead in theoretical development, particularly in terms of combining explanatory models to address crime rates, as well as correctional policies and philosophies, across various cultures. Specifically, Braithwaite's theory makes a strong argument that Eastern (particularly Japanese) policies of reintegration and apology for convicted offenders are beneficial for that culture. Would this system work in Western culture, especially the United States? The answer is definitely unknown, but it is unlikely that such a model would work well in the United States. After all, most of the chronic, serious offenders in the United States would not be highly deterred by having to apologize to the public, and many might consider such an apology or reintegration ceremony an honor, or a way to show that they really hadn't been punished. This may not be true, but we would not know this until such policies were implemented fully in our system. However, programs along these lines have been implemented in our country, and some of these programs will be reviewed later in this book.

Tittle's Control–Balance Theory

One of the more recently proposed models of theoretical integration is Charles **Tittle's control–balance theory**. Presented by Tittle in 1995, control–balance integrated theory proposes that (a) the amount of control to which one is subjected and (b) the amount of control that one can exercise determine the probability of deviance occurring.

---

[76] Stephen Tibbetts, "Shame and Rational Choice in Offending Decisions," *Criminal Justice and Behavior* 24 (1996): 234–55.

[77] Stephen Tibbetts, "Self-Conscious Emotions and Criminal Offending," *Psychological Reports* 93 (2003): 201–31; Stephen G. Tibbetts, "Traits and States of Self-Conscious Emotions in Criminal Decision Making," in *Affect and Cognition in Criminal Decision Making*, ed. Jean-Louis Van Gelder et al. (London: Routledge, 2014), 221–38.

[78] Hay, "An Exploratory Test."

[79] For an excellent review, see June Price Tangney and Kurt Fischer, *Self-Conscious Emotions: The Psychology of Shame, Guilt, Embarrassment, and Pride* (New York: Guilford Press, 1995).

[80] See Harold Grasmick, Brenda Sims Blackwell, and Robert Bursik, "Changes over Time in Gender Differences in Perceived Risk of Sanctions," *Law and Society Review* 27 (1993): 679–705; Harold Grasmick, Robert Bursik, and Bruce Arneklev, "Reduction in Drunk Driving as a Response to Increased Threats of Shame, Embarrassment, and Legal Sanctions," *Criminology* 31 (1993): 41–67; and Tibbetts, "College Student Perceptions."

In other words, the balance between these two types of control, he argued, can predict the type of behavior that is likely to be committed.[81]

In this integrated theoretical framework, Tittle claimed that a person is least likely to offend when she or he has a balance of controlling and being controlled. On the other hand, the likelihood of offending will increase when these become unbalanced. If individuals are more controlled by external forces, which Tittle calls *control deficit*, then the theory predicts that they will commit predatory or defiant criminal behavior. In contrast, if an individual possesses an excessive level of control by external forces, which Tittle refers to as *control surplus*, then that individual will be more likely to commit acts of exploitation or decadence. It is important to realize that this excessive control is not the same as excessive self-control, which would be covered by other theories examined in this section. Rather, Tittle argued that people who are controlling—that is, who have excessive control over others—will be predisposed toward inappropriate activities.

Early empirical tests of control–balance theory have reported mixed results with both surpluses and deficits predicting the same types of deviance.[82] Furthermore, researchers have uncovered differing effects of the control–balance ratio on two types of deviance that are contingent on gender. This finding is consistent with the gender-specific support found for Walter Reckless's containment theory and with the gender differences found in other theoretical models.[83] Despite the mixed findings for Tittle's control–balance theory of crime, this model of criminal offending still gets a lot of attention, and most of the empirical evidence has been in favor of this theory.

Hagan's Power–Control Theory

The final integrated theory that we will cover in this section deals with the influence of familial control and how this relates to criminality across gender. Power–control theory is another integrated theory that was proposed by John Hagan and his colleagues.[84] The primary focus of this theory is on the level of patriarchal attitudes and structure in the household, which are influenced by parental positions in the workforce.

Power–control theory assumes that, in households where the mother and father have relatively similar levels of power at work (i.e., balanced households), mothers will be less likely to exert control on their daughters. These balanced households will be less likely to experience gender differences in the criminal offending of the children. However, households in which mothers and fathers have dissimilar levels of power in the workplace (i.e., unbalanced households) are more likely to suppress criminal activity in daughters. In such families, it is assumed that daughters will be taught to be less risk-taking than the males in the family. In addition, assertiveness and risky activity among the males in the house will be encouraged. This assertiveness and risky activity may be precursors to crime, which is highly consistent with the empirical evidence regarding

---

[81] Charles Tittle, *Control Balance: Toward a General Theory of Deviance* (Boulder, CO: Westview, 1995) (see chap. 8, n. 55).

[82] Alex Piquero and Matthew Hickman, "An Empirical Test of Tittle's Control Balance Theory," *Criminology* 37 (1999): 319–42 (see chap. 8, n. 75); Matthew Hickman and Alex Piquero, "Exploring the Relationships between Gender, Control Balance, and Deviance," *Deviant Behavior* 22 (2001): 323–51 (see chap. 8, n. 75).

[83] Hickman and Piquero, "Exploring the Relationships." For contrast and comparison, see Grasmick et al., "Changes over Time"; Grasmick et al., "Reduction in Drunk Driving"; and Tibbetts, "College Student Perceptions."

[84] John Hagan, *Structural Criminology* (Newark, NJ: Rutgers University Press, 1989) (see chap. 8, n. 77); John Hagan, A. Gillis, and J. Simpson, "The Class Structure of Gender and Delinquency: Toward a Power-Control Theory of Common Delinquent Behavior," *American Journal of Sociology* 90 (1985): 1151–78 (see chap. 8, n. 77); John Hagan, A. Gillis, and J. Simpson, "Clarifying and Extending Power-Control Theory," *American Journal of Sociology* 95 (1990): 1024–37 (see chap. 8, n. 77); John Hagan, J. Simpson, and A. Gillis, "Class in the Household: A Power-Control Theory of Gender and Delinquency," *American Journal of Sociology* 92 (1987): 788–816 (see chap. 8, n. 77).

trends in crime related to gender. Thus, Hagan's integrated theory seems to have a considerable amount of face validity.

Most empirical tests of power–control theory have provided moderate support, while more recent studies have further specified the validity of the theory in different contexts.[85] For example, one recent study reported that the influence of mothers, not fathers, on sons had the greatest impact on reducing the delinquency of young males.[86] Another researcher has found that differences in perceived threats of embarrassment and formal sanctions vary between more patriarchal and less patriarchal households.[87] Finally, studies have also started measuring the effect of patriarchal attitudes on crime and delinquency.[88] However, most of the empirical studies that have shown support for the theory have been done by Hagan or his colleagues. Still, power–control theory is a good example of a social control theory in that it is consistent with the idea that individuals must be socialized and that the gender differences in such socialization make a difference in how people will act throughout life.

Policy Implications

Few policy strategies have actually been derived from integrated or developmental theories, probably because most policy makers are either unaware of such theoretical frameworks or because the theories are so complicated that it is difficult for practitioners to apply them. However, one exception to this rule is Braithwaite's theory of shaming and reintegration. Braithwaite and others have gone to great lengths to apply his theory in Australia, and some evaluations of this approach have shown promise, even if not commonly incorporated in the United States (see Kim and Gerber reading later in this section). Interventions stress the restorative concepts of his theory, particularly the idea of reintegrating offenders into society as opposed to stigmatizing them.[89]

This strategy emphasizes holding offenders accountable, yet it tries to bring them back into conventional society as quickly and efficiently as possible. In contrast, the U.S. system typically gives prisoners a nominal sum of money (in most jurisdictions, about $200), and they must report themselves as convicted felons for the rest of their lives on all job applications. Would Braithwaite's model work here in the United States? We don't know yet, but it seems that there could be a better way to incorporate offenders back into society in such a way that they are not automatically set up to fail.

Other policy implications can be drawn from the various integrated theoretical models that we have discussed in this section. We will focus on the concepts that were most prominent, which are parenting and peer influences. Regarding the former, numerous empirical studies have examined programs for improving the ability of parents and

[85] Hagan et al., "Class in the Household"; B. McCarthy and John Hagan, "Gender, Delinquency, and the Great Depression: A Test of Power-Control Theory," *Canadian Review of Sociology and Anthropology* 24 (1987): 153–77 (see chap. 8, n. 78); Merry Morash and Meda Chesney-Lind, "A Reformulation and Partial Test of the Power-Control Theory of Delinquency," *Justice Quarterly* 8 (1991): 347–77 (see chap. 8, n. 78); Simon Singer and Murray Levine, "Power-Control Theory, Gender, and Delinquency: A Partial Replication with Additional Evidence on the Effects of Peers," *Criminology* 26 (1988): 627–47 (see chap. 8, n. 78).

[86] B. McCarthy, John Hagan, and T. Woodward, "In the Company of Women: Structure and Agency in a Revised Power-Control Theory of Gender and Delinquency," *Criminology* 37 (1999): 761–88 (see chap. 8, n. 79).

[87] Brenda Sims Blackwell, "Perceived Sanction Threats, Gender, and Crime: A Test and Elaboration of Power-Control Theory," *Criminology* 38 (2000): 439–88 (see chap. 8, n. 80).

[88] Blackwell, "Perceived Sanction Threats"; Kristin Bates and Chris Bader, "Family Structure, Power-Control Theory, and Deviance: Extending Power-Control Theory to Include Alternate Family Forms," *Western Criminology Review* 4 (2003): 170–90 (see chap. 8, n. 81).

[89] John Braithwaite, "Restorative Justice: Assessing Optimistic and Pessimistic Accounts," in *Crime and Justice: A Review of Research*, Vol. 25, ed. Michael Tonry (Chicago: University of Chicago Press, 1999), 1–27.

expecting parents to be effective.[90] Such programs typically involve training high school students—or individuals or couples who are already parents—on how to be better parents. Additional programs include Head Start and other preschool programs that attempt to prepare high-risk youth for starting school; these have been found to be effective in reducing disciplinary problems.[91]

Regarding peer influences, numerous programs and evaluations have examined the effects of reducing negative peer influences regarding crime.[92] Programs that emphasize prosocial peer groups are often successful, whereas others show little or no success.[93] The conclusion from most of these studies is that the most successful programs of this type are those that focus on learning life skills and prosocial skills and use a curriculum based on a cognitive behavioral approach.[94] This strategy includes reinforcing positive behavior; clarifying rules of behavior in social settings; teaching life and thinking skills; and, perhaps most important, thinking about the consequences of a given behavior before acting (hence, the cognitive behavioral approach). Studies consistently show that programs using a cognitive behavioral approach (i.e., think before you act) are far more successful than programs that emphasize interactions among peers or use psychoanalysis or other forms of therapy.[95]

Many other policy implications can be derived from integrated theories explaining criminal behavior, but parenting practices and peer influences are the primary constructs in most integrated models. Thus, these are the two areas that should be targeted for policy interventions, but this must be done correctly. For a start, policy makers could review the findings from empirical studies and evaluations and see that the earlier parenting programs start, particularly for high-risk children, the more effective they can be. Regarding the peer influence programs, a combination of cognitive behavioral therapy and training in life skills appears to be more effective than other approaches.

Conclusion

In this section, we have reviewed which factors determine the types of integrated theories and which criteria make an integrated theory a good explanation of human behavior. We have also examined examples of integrated theories that have been proposed in the criminological literature in the past 30 years. All of the examples represent the most researched and discussed integrated theories, and they demonstrate both the advantages and disadvantages of theoretical integration or elaboration. We hope that readers will be able to determine for themselves which of these integrated theories are the best in explaining criminal activity.

In this section, we have examined the various ways in which theoretical integration can be done, including forms of conceptual integration and theoretical elaboration. Furthermore, the criticisms of the different variations of integration and elaboration have been discussed. In addition, numerous examples of theoretical integration have been presented along with the empirical studies that have been performed to examine their validity. Such examples included Elliott's seminal integrated theory as well as Pearson and Weiner's conceptual integration framework. We also examined other integrated theoretical models, such as Braithwaite's theory of reintegration, Tittle's model of control balance, and **Hagan's power–control theory**. All have received much attention and research in order to test the propositions proposed by each integrated perspective—with mixed results.

---

[90] See review in Brown et al., *Criminology: Explaining Crime*, 425.

[91] Ibid.

[92] For a review, see Akers and Sellers, *Criminological Theories*, 102–8.

[93] Ibid.

[94] Ibid., 108.

[95] Ibid.

Finally, we discussed the policy implications that can be recommended from such integrated theories. Specifically, we concluded that early parenting and peer influences are the two most important influences across these theoretical models. Furthermore, we concluded that when it comes to parenting programs, the earlier, the better. We also concluded that a cognitive behavioral approach that includes the teaching of life skills is most effective for peer influence programs.

SECTION SUMMARY

- Theoretical integration is one of the more contemporary developments in criminological theorizing.
- This approach brings with it many criticisms yet arguably many advantages because these models tend to merge separate theories that have very different assumptions about criminal behavior.
- Types of theoretical integration include end-to-end, side-by-side, and up-and-down, which vary greatly and are typically based on the types of theories they are merging or integrating.
- Conceptual integration appears to be a useful, albeit rarely explored, form of theoretical integration.
- Pearson and Weiner presented what is considered the most comprehensive and detailed framework regarding conceptual integration.
- Theoretical elaboration is another form of integration, which involves using one theory as the base or primary model and then incorporating concepts and propositions from other theories to make the primary model stronger.
- A number of seminal integrated theories have been examined using empirical evidence and appear to have enhanced our understanding of criminal behavior.
- Some of the theoretical models that have been proposed, such as the first notable model by Elliott et al., have been supported by empirical research.
- Thornberry's interactive model of criminality was unique in claiming that certain causal variables act as both predictive and consequential variables, which give feedback to other predictive variables and create a type of feedback loop in which the cumulative effects are difficult to measure because variables are acting cumulatively over time as both a consequence and then as a predictor in affecting other key variables as an individual ages over time.
- We also discussed following integrated frameworks, such as Braithwaite's reintegrative model, Tittle's control-balance theory, and Hagan's power-control model of criminality.
- Theoretical integration models have many critics who claim that the assumptions, concepts, and propositions of the mixed theories are counterintuitive.
- Despite the criticisms, integrated theoretical models of crime provide more understanding about criminal activity of individuals because human behavior is highly complex, and the combination of theories is likely more robust and valid than more simple, separate theories on their own.

KEY TERMS

Braithwaite's reintegrative shaming theory 540

communitarianism 540

conceptual integration 540

Elliott's integrated model 539

end-to-end (or sequential) integration 535

Hagan's power-control theory 561

integrated theories 533

interdependency 540

side-by-side (or horizontal) integration 537

theoretical elaboration 536

Thornberry's interactional model 551

Tittle's control–balance theory 558

up-and-down (or deductive) integration 538

DISCUSSION QUESTIONS

1. What is the definition of theoretical integration, and why can such theories be beneficial?
2. Describe what end-to-end theoretical integration is, and provide an example of such integration.
3. Describe what side-by-side theoretical integration is, and provide an example of such integration.
4. Describe what up-and-down theoretical integration is, and provide an example of such integration.
5. Discuss the differences among theoretical elaboration, theoretical integration, and conceptual integration.
6. What are the major strengths and weaknesses of theoretical integration?
7. In your opinion, what is the best of the integrated models? Why do you believe this is the best integrated model?
8. What do you believe is the weakest integrated model? Why?

WEB RESOURCES

Integrated Theories of Crime

http://onlinelibrary.wiley.com/doi/10.1002/9781118517390.wbetc028/full
http://law.jrank.org/pages/821/Crime-Causation-Sociological-Theories-Integrated-theories.html

John Braithwaite/Reintegrative Theory

https://www.anu.edu.au/fellows/jbraithwaite/_documents/Chapters/Shame_Restorative_2005.pdf
https://learn.bu.edu/bbcswebdav/pid-1942479-dt-content-rid-6162758_1/courses/14sprgmetcj602_ol/week06/metcj602_W06L01T04_Reintegrative.html

Hagan's Power–Control Theory

http://www.westerncriminology.org/documents/WCR/v04n3/article_pdfs/bates.pdf

READING /// 29

In this selection, Delbert Elliott, Suzanne Ageton, and Rachelle Canter provide one of the earliest, and still one of the best-known and best-respected, examples of theoretical integration. We shall see that Elliott and his colleagues merge various concepts and propositions from at least three traditional theoretical perspectives, namely, strain theory, social control theory, and various social learning theories.

One of the beneficial aspects of Elliott and his colleagues' integrated theory is that it attempts to merge various versions of each of these perspectives into a cohesive, unitary explanation of delinquency and criminal behavior. For example, the authors go beyond the original strain theory proposed by Robert Merton in 1938 and also take into consideration the subsequent versions of strain theory that appeared in later decades (such as Richard Cloward and Lloyd Ohlin's theory of differential opportunities, as well as Cohen's ideas regarding the formation of gang subcultures). Also, when explaining how control theories were integrated into Elliott and his colleagues' model, the authors do not simply rely on Travis Hirschi's version of social bonding but also consider some of the other versions of control theory (such as control theories by Albert Reiss, F. Ivan Nye, and Walter Reckless as well as David Matza's theory of drift). Finally, the authors don't simply merge Edwin Sutherland's theory of differential association but also take into account the more modern versions of social learning theory, such as Ronald Akers's model of differential reinforcement and Albert Bandura's model of imitation and modeling. Although even more modern versions of each of these theoretical perspectives have been introduced (e.g., general strain theory) since Elliott and his colleagues proposed this model in 1979, it is obvious from this selection that the authors did their best to integrate these three major perspectives using the most recent scientific evidence they had in the late 1970s.

While reading this selection, readers are encouraged to consider the following points:

- The validity of the model by considering themselves or others they grew up with and examining whether the development of the various stages proposed by Elliott and his colleagues seems to fit with the delinquents or criminals they have known
- In the integrated model proposed by Elliott and his colleagues, which theoretical perspective is considered to be antecedent, or most important in the early stages, for developing delinquent or criminal tendencies
- The rationale to merge theoretical perspectives that have opposing basic assumptions, such as merging strain theory, which claims that individuals are born good, with perspectives such as control theory, which claims that people are born bad and must be taught or controlled to be good, as well as merging them with learning theories, such as differential association/reinforcement, that assume individuals are born neither good nor bad

SOURCE: Delbert Elliott, Suzanne S. Ageton, and Rachelle J. Canter, "An Integrated Theoretical Perspective on Delinquent Behavior," *Journal of Research in Crime and Delinquency* 16 (1979): 3–27.

An Integrated Theoretical Perspective on Delinquent Behavior

Delbert S. Elliott, Suzanne S. Ageton, and Rachelle J. Canter

Previous Theories: Strain and Control

Anomie/Strain Perspective

. . . Strain theory has become the most influential and widely used contemporary formulation in the sociology of delinquent behavior. A specific application of strain theory to delinquency has been proposed by Cloward and Ohlin (1960) and, more recently, by Elliott and Voss (1974). Cloward and Ohlin's work is of particular interest to us because their formulation, like that proposed here, represents an attempt to integrate and extend current theoretical positions. Although their theory has been viewed primarily as an extension of the earlier work of Durkheim and Merton, it is equally an extension of the differential association perspective and the prior work of Sutherland (1947). Indeed, much of its significance lies in the fact that it successfully integrated these two traditional perspectives on the etiology of delinquent behavior. Cloward and Ohlin maintain that limited opportunity for achieving conventional goals is the motivational stimulus for delinquent behavior. The specific form and pattern of delinquent behavior are acquired through normal learning processes within delinquent groups. Experiences of limited or blocked opportunities (a result of structural limitations on success) thus lead to alienation (perceived anomie) and an active seeking out of alternative groups and settings in which particular patterns of delinquent behavior are acquired and reinforced (social learning).

Merton, Cloward, and Ohlin have conceptualized the condition leading to anomie in terms of differential opportunities for achieving socially valued goals. Differential access to opportunity creates strain; this is postulated to occur primarily among disadvantaged, low-SES [socioeconomic status] youths, resulting in the concentration of delinquent subcultures in low-SES neighborhoods. It is important to note, however, that Cloward and Ohlin have changed the level of explanation from the macrosociological level which characterized Durkheim's work to an individual level. It is the *perception* of limited access to conventional goals that motivates the *individual* to explore deviant means. This change in level of explanation was essential for the integration of strain and learning perspectives.

Elliott and Voss's more recent work (1974) has attempted to deal with the class-bound assumptions inherent in strain theory. Their formulation extends Cloward and Ohlin's classic statement in the following three ways: (1) The focus on limited opportunities was extended to a wider range of conventional goals. (2) The goal-means disjunction was modified to be logically independent of social class. (3) The role of social learning in the development of delinquent behavior was further emphasized. Elliott and Voss have proposed a sequential, or developmental, model of delinquency: (1) Limited opportunities or failure to achieve conventional goals serves to (2) attenuate one's initial commitment to the normative order and (3) results in a particular form of alienation (normlessness), which serves as a "permitter" for delinquency, and (4) exposure to delinquent groups, which provides learning and rewards for delinquent behavior for those whose bonds have undergone the attenuation process.

From this perspective, aspiration-opportunity disjunctions provide motivation for delinquent behavior. As compared with Merton and Cloward and Ohlin, Elliott and Voss view *both* goals and opportunities as variables. They postulate that middle-class youths are just as likely to aspire beyond their means as are low-SES youths. While the absolute levels of aspirations and opportunities may vary by class, the discrepancies between personal goals and opportunities for realizing these goals need not vary systematically by class. Given Durkheim's (1897/1951, p. 254) view that poverty restrains aspirations, Elliott and Voss have postulated that aspiration-opportunity disjunctions would be at least as great, if not greater, among middle-class youths. In any case, the motivational stimulus for delinquent behavior in the form of aspiration-opportunity discrepancies or goal failure is viewed as logically independent of social class.

Normlessness, the expectation that one must employ illegitimate means to achieve socially valued goals (Seeman, 1959), is postulated to result from perceived aspiration-opportunity disjunctions. When a person cannot reach his or her goals by conventional means, deviant or illegitimate means become rational and functional alternatives. When the source of failure or blockage is perceived as external—resulting from institutional practices and policies—the individual has some justification for withdrawing his or her moral commitment to these conventional norms. In this manner, a sense of injustice mitigates ties to conventional norms and generates normlessness.

Once at this point in the developmental sequence, the relative presence or absence of specific delinquent learning and performance structures accounts for the likelihood of one's behavior. The time-ordering of the exposure to delinquency variable is not explicit. It may predate failure or it may be the result of seeking a social context in which one can achieve some success. While the exposure may result in the acquisition of delinquent behavior patterns, actual delinquent behavior (performance) will not result until one's attachment to the social order is neutralized through real or anticipated failure, and the delinquent behavior has been reinforced. The results of research relative to this set of propositions have been generally encouraging. . . .

While considerable empirical support for an integrated strain-learning approach to delinquency has been amassed, most of the variance in delinquency remains unexplained. If the power of this theoretical formulation is to be improved, some basic modification is required. One avenue is suggested by the weak predictive power of the aspiration-opportunity discrepancy variables. . . . [In some studies], limited academic success at school and failure in one's relationship with parents were predictive, but only weakly. To some extent, the low strength of these predictors might be anticipated, since they are the initial variables in the causal sequence and are tied to delinquency only through a set of other conditional variables. On the other hand, the strong emphasis placed on these specific variables in strain theories seems questionable, given the available data. It might be argued that the difficulty lies in the operationalization or measurement of the relevant goal-opportunity disjunctions. However, we are inclined to reject this position because previous findings as to this postulated relationship have been generally weak and inconclusive (Brennan, 1974; Elliot, 1962; Hirschi, 1969; Jessor et al., 1968; Liska, 1971; Short, 1964; Short, Rivera, & Tennyson, 1965; Spergel, 1967). Furthermore, there is substantial evidence in the above-mentioned studies that many adolescents engaging in significant amounts of delinquent behavior experience no discrepancies between aspirations and perceived opportunities. The lack of consistent support for this relationship suggests that failure or anticipated failure constitutes only one possible path to an involvement in delinquency.

The Control Perspective

The different assumptions of strain and control theories are significant. Strain formulations assume a positively socialized individual who violates conventional norms only when his or her attachment and commitment are attenuated. Norm violation occurs only after the individual perceives that opportunities for socially valued goals are blocked. Strain theory focuses on this attenuation process. Control theories, on the other hand, treat the socialization process and commitment to conventional norms and values as problematic. Persons differ with respect to their commitment to and integration into the conventional social order. . . .

From a control perspective, delinquency is viewed as a consequence of (1) lack of internalized normative controls, (2) breakdown in previously established controls, and/or (3) conflict or inconsistency in rules or social controls. Strain formulations of delinquency appear to be focusing on those variables and processes which account for the second condition identified by Reiss (1951): attenuation or breakdown in previously established controls. On the other hand, most control theorists direct their attention to the first and third conditions, exploring such variables as inadequate socialization (failure to internalize conventional norms) and integration into conventional groups or institutions which provide strong external or social controls on behavior. From our perspective, these need not be viewed as contradictory explanations. On the contrary, they may be viewed as alternative processes, depending on the outcome of one's early socialization experience.

For example, Hirschi (1969) has argued that high aspirations involve a commitment to conventional lines of action that functions as a positive control or bond to the social order. Strain theories, on the other hand, view high aspirations (in the face of limited opportunities) as a source of attenuation of attachment to the conventional order. Recognizing this difference, Hirschi suggested that the examination of this relationship would constitute a crucial test of the two theories. Empirically, the evidence is inconsistent and far from conclusive. One possible interpretation is that both hypotheses are correct and are part of different etiological sequences leading to delinquent behavior.

Empirical studies using the control perspective have focused almost exclusively on the static relation of weak internal and external controls to delinquency without considering the longer developmental processes. These processes may involve an initially strong commitment to and integration into society, which becomes attenuated over time, with the attenuation eventually resulting in delinquency. The source of this difficulty may lie in the infrequent use of longitudinal designs. Without a repeated measure design, youths with strong bonds which subsequently become attenuated may be indistinguishable from those who never developed strong bonds.

An Integrated Strain-Control Perspective

Our proposed integrated theoretical paradigm begins with the assumption that different youths have different early socialization experiences, which result in variable degrees of commitment to and integration into conventional social groups. The effect of failure to achieve conventional goals on subsequent delinquency is related to the strength of one's initial bonds. Limited opportunities to achieve conventional goals constitute a source of strain and thus a motivational stimulus for delinquency only if one is committed to these goals. In contrast, limited opportunities to achieve such goals should have little or no impact on those with weak ties and commitments to the conventional social order.

Limited opportunities to achieve conventional goals are not the only experiences which weaken or break initially strong ties to the social order. Labeling theorists have argued that the experience of being apprehended and publicly labeled delinquent initiates social processes which limit one's access to conventional social roles and statuses, isolating one from participation in these activities and relationships and forcing one to assume a delinquent role (Ageton & Elliott; Becker, 1963; Goldman, 1963; Kitsuse, 1962; Rubington & Weinberg, 1968; Schur, 1971). It has also been argued that the effects of social disorganization or crisis in the home (divorce, parental strife and discord, death of a parent) and/or community (high rates of mobility, economic depression, unemployment) attenuate or break one's ties to society (Andry, 1962; Glueck & Glueck, 1970; Monahan, 1957; Rosen, 1970; Savitz, 1970; Shaw, 1931; Thomas & Znaniecki, 1927; Toby, 1957).

In sum, we postulate that limited opportunities, failure to achieve valued goals, negative labeling experiences, and social disorganization at home and in the community are all experiences which may attenuate one's ties to the conventional social order and may thus be causal factors in the developmental sequence leading to delinquent behavior for those whose early socialization experiences produced strong bonds to society. For those whose attachments to the conventional social order are already weak, such factors may further weaken ties to society but are not necessary factors in the etiological sequence leading to delinquency.

Our basic conceptual framework comes from control theory, with a slightly different emphasis placed on participation in and commitment to delinquent groups. Further, it identifies a set of attenuating/bonding experiences which weaken or strengthen ties to the conventional social order over time. Our focus is on experiences and social contexts which are relevant to adolescents. A diagram of our proposed theoretical scheme is shown in Figure 1. The rows in Figure 1 indicate the direction and sequence of the hypothesized relationships. While the time order designated in Figure 1 is unidirectional, the actual relationships between initial socialization, bonding/attenuation processes, normative orientations of groups, and behavior are often reciprocal and reinforcing. We have also presented the variables in dichotomized form to simplify the model and the discussion of its major elements.

Figure 1 • Integrated Strain-Control Paradigm

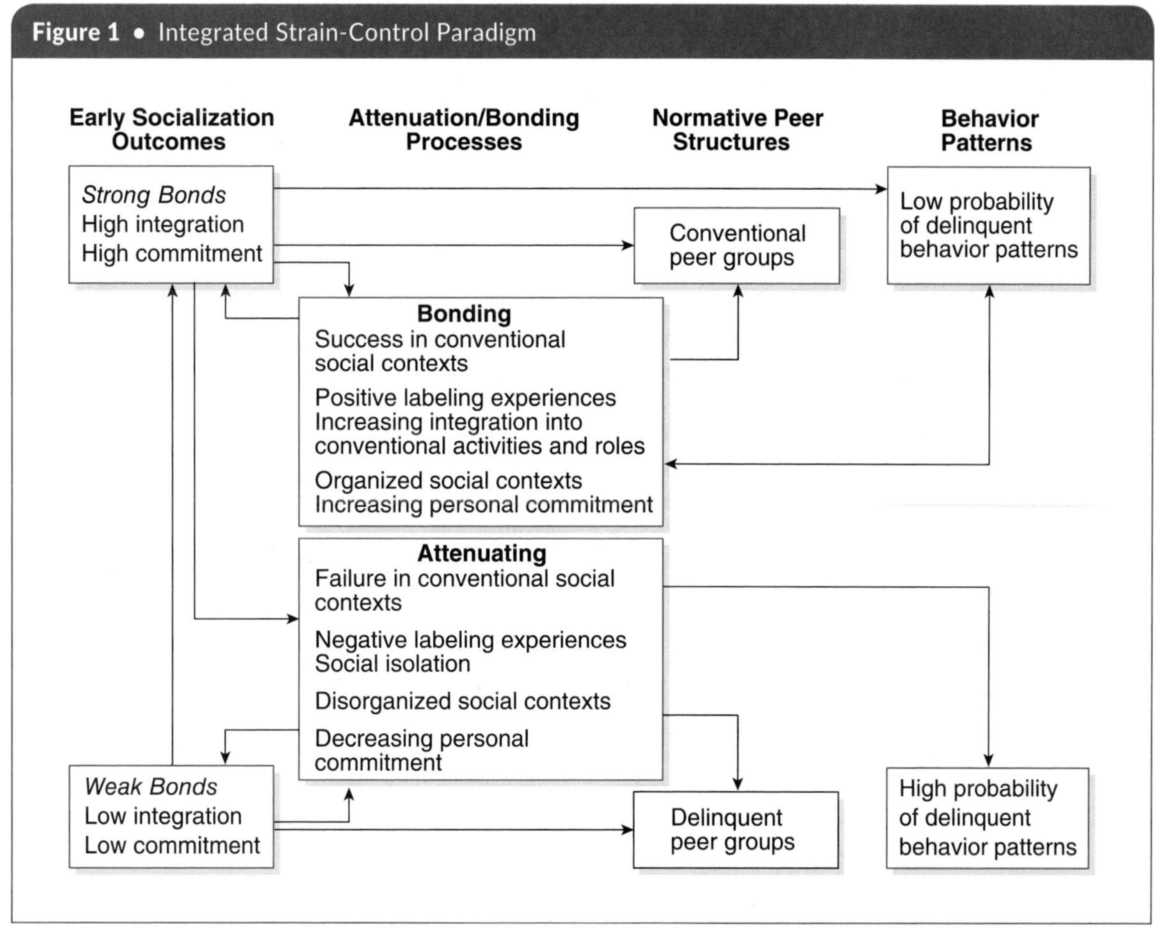

Bonds

Control theorists disagree about sources of control, but they all accept the central proposition that delinquent behavior is a direct result of weak ties to the conventional normative order. In operationalizing control theory, major emphasis has been placed on the bond(s) which tie a person to society. Hirschi (1969) conceptualized four elements of this bond. First, attachment implies a moral link to other people and encompasses such concepts as conscience, superego, and internalization of norms. Commitment, the second factor, is the rational element in the bond. Hirschi views commitment to conformity as an investment in conventional lines of action, such as an educational or occupational career. Other theorists have tied the concept of commitment to such notions as "stake in conformity" (Goode, 1960) and "side bets" (Becker, 1960). Involvement is the time and energy dimension of the bond for Hirschi. Given the limits of time and energy, involvement in conventional activities acts as a social constraint on delinquent behavior. The final bond, *belief,* refers to one's acceptance of the moral validity of social rules and norms. According to Hirschi, this psychological element of the bond is effective as long as a person accepts the validity of the rules. If one denies or depreciates the validity of the rules, one source of control is neutralized.

Other control theorists, such as Reiss (1951), Nye (1958), and Reckless (1967), use a more general classification of bonds as internal (personal) and external (social) controls. Hirschi's dimensions are not easily placed into these two general categories, although Hirschi identifies attachment as an internal and involvement as an external element of the bond (1969, p. 19). We believe that distinguishing internal controls, whose locus is within the person (beliefs, commitment, attitudes, perceptions), from external controls, whose locus is in the surrounding social and physical milieu, poses fewer difficulties and produces greater conceptual clarity than is found in Hirschi's four concepts.

The external, or social, bond we have defined as *integration*. By this, we refer to involvement in and attachment to conventional groups and institutions, such as the family, school, peer networks, and so on. Those persons who occupy and are actively involved in conventional social roles are, by this definition, highly integrated. Group controls exist in the form of sanctioning networks (the formal and informal rules and regulations by which the behavior of social role occupants or group members is regulated). This conceptualization of integration is akin to Hirschi's concepts of involvement and commitment.

The internal, or personal, bond is defined as *commitment*. Commitment involves personal attachment to conventional roles, groups, and institutions. At another level, it reflects the extent to which one feels morally bound by the social norms and rules and the degree to which one internalizes or adopts those norms as directives for action. Our notion of commitment is akin to Hirschi's concepts of attachment and belief. Integration and commitment together constitute the bonds which tie an individual to the prevailing social order. High levels of integration and commitment imply strong bonds and general insulation from delinquent behavior. Conversely, low social integration and commitment presuppose weak bonds and a susceptibility to delinquent behavior. All gradations of integration and commitment are possible.

Building Social Control: The Bonding/Attenuation Processes

The inclusion of the bonding/attenuation process in the model suggests that, throughout adolescence, youths are involved in experiences and processes which attenuate or reinforce their childhood bonds to the conventional social order. Adolescence is a critical life period, both psychologically and socially. As youths make the transition from childhood to adulthood, the level of involvement in the immediate family declines and they move into new and more complex social settings at school and in the community. For one who developed strong childhood bonds, such factors as (1) success experiences at school and in the larger community, (2) positive labeling in these new settings, and (3) a continuous, stable, harmonious home life constitute positive reinforcements of initially strong bonds and continuing insulation from delinquency. For some, the transition is not as smooth, and failure, negative labeling, isolation, and rejection occur in these new social settings; these, in turn, may create difficulties in the youth's relationship with his family. The net effect of these new experiences may be a weakening of one's integration into . . . these social groups and institutions and an increasing likelihood of involvement in delinquent behavior. Finally, for those who never developed strong bonds during childhood, bonding/attenuation experiences will either strengthen the weak bonds, thus reducing the likelihood of delinquency, or further attenuate them, thus maintaining or increasing the probability of delinquent behavior.

We do not propose that this specific set of variables exhausts the possible experiences or conditions which might attenuate or reinforce one's bonds to society during adolescence. Rather, we have purposely selected those conditions and experiences which prior theory and research have suggested as critical variables to illustrate the major dimensions of the paradigm.

Delinquent Learning and Performance Structures

A major criticism of control theory has been that weak bonds and the implied absence of restraints cannot alone account for the specific form or content of the behavior which results. They may account for a state of "drift," as described by Matza (1964), but they do not explain why some youths in this state turn to delinquency, drug use, and various unconventional subcultures, while others maintain an essentially conforming pattern of behavior; nor can they account for emerging patterns of delinquency which may be unique to particular ages or birth cohorts. We therefore postulate that access to and involvement in delinquent learning and performance structures is a necessary (but not sufficient) variable in the etiology of delinquent behavior. Following Sutherland (1947), we maintain that delinquent behavior, like conforming behavior, presupposes a pattern of social relationships through which motives, rationalizations, techniques, and rewards can be learned and maintained (Akers, 1977; Bandura, 1969, 1973; Burgess & Akers, 1966a, 1966b; Mischel, 1968). Delinquent behavior is thus viewed as behavior which has social meaning and must be supported and rewarded by social groups if it is to persist.

By the time children enter adolescence, virtually all have been sufficiently exposed to criminal forms of behavior to have "learned" or acquired some potential for such acts. The more critical issue for any theory of delinquency is why and how this universal potential is transformed into delinquent acts for some youths and not others. For most learning theorists, a distinction is made between learning and performance and the latter is directly tied to reinforcements (Bandura, 1969; Bandura & Walters, 1963; Mischel, 1968; Rotter, 1954). . . .

According to the present social learning formulation, learning or acquisition of novel responses is regulated by sensory and cognitive processes; learning may be facilitated by reinforcement but does not depend on it (e.g., Bandura & Walters, 1963; Hebb, 1966). Direct and vicarious reinforcements are, however, important determinants of response selection in performance.

The delinquent peer group thus provides a positive social setting that is essential for the performance and maintenance of delinquent patterns of behavior over time. Those committed to conventional goals, although they may have been exposed to and learned some delinquent behaviors, should not establish patterns of such behavior unless (1) their ties to the conventional social order are neutralized through some attenuating experiences and (2) they are participating in a social context in which delinquent behavior is rewarded. In social learning terms, they may have acquired or learned delinquent behavior patterns, but the actual performance and maintenance of such behavior are contingent on attenuation of their commitment to conventional norms and their participation in a social context supportive of delinquent acts. Alternatively, for those with weak ties and commitments to the conventional social order, there is no reason for a delay between acquisition and performance of delinquent acts.

In the causal sequence described by strain theory, the individual holds conventional goals but is unable to attain them by conventional means. If attachment to the goals is strong enough, it may support delinquent behavior without participation in delinquent groups, for attaining these goals may provide sufficient reinforcement to maintain the behavior. Therefore, our model shows one direct route to delinquent behavior from attenuating experiences, without mediating group support for delinquency. We view this as the atypical case, however, and postulate that it is difficult to sustain this causal sequence for extended periods of time.

Involvement in a delinquent group is a necessary condition for sustained patterns of delinquency among persons who do not subscribe to conventional goals (the weakly socialized person described by control theory). Individual patterns of delinquency (without group support) are more viable for those committed to conventional goals because there are generally shared expectations and social supports for achievement of those goals. For youths with weak bonds, involvement in a delinquent peer group serves this support function. Cohen (1966) has observed that delinquency often involves a desire for recognition and social acceptance, and, therefore, requires group visibility and support. Maintenance of delinquent behavior patterns should require some exposure to and participation in groups supporting delinquent activities. Though not a necessary condition for delinquent behavior among those with initially strong bonds, contact with delinquent groups should, nevertheless, increase the likelihood of sustained delinquent behavior.

Delineation of the delinquent peer group as a necessary condition for maintenance of delinquent behavior patterns represents an extension of previous statements of control theory. . . . It is one thing to be a social isolate with weak bonds to conventional peer groups and another to be highly committed to and integrated into a delinquent peer group. Both persons may be characterized as having weak bonds to the social order, with few conventional restraints on their behavior; but those committed to and participating in delinquent peer groups have some incentive and social support for specifically delinquent forms of behavior. We agree with Hirschi's (1969) and Hepburn's (1976) argument that those with a large stake in conformity (strong bonds) are relatively immune to delinquent peer group influence. However, we postulate that, in addition to weak bonding and an absence of restraints, some positive motivation is necessary for sustained involvement in delinquent behavior. In the absence of positive motivation, we would not predict significant involvement in delinquency across time even for those with weak bonds, for there is no apparent mechanism for maintaining such behavior (Brennan, Huizinga, & Elliott, 1978). It may be that some exploratory, "primary" forms of delinquency (Lemert, 1951) may occur without group support, or that this constitutes a pathological path to delinquency, but the maintenance of delinquent behavior patterns usually requires some exposure to and participation in groups supporting delinquent activity.

In sum, we postulate that bonding to conventional groups and institutions insulates one from involvement in delinquent patterns of behavior and that bonding to deviant groups or subcultures facilitates and sustains delinquent behavior. When examining the influence of social bonds, it is critical that the normative orientation of particular groups be taken into account. This focus on the normative orientations of groups is the central theme in subcultural theories of delinquency (Cloward & Ohlin, 1960; Cohen, 1955; Miller, 1958) and constitutes an important qualification to a simple interpretation of the relationship between social bonds and delinquency. This position has an empirical as well as a theoretical base. . . .

Delinquent Behavior

Delinquent behavior is viewed as a special subclass of deviant behavior. While deviance includes all violations of all prevailing norms, delinquent behavior includes only violations of statutory proscriptive norms, or, as they are usually called, laws. Thus, delinquent behavior takes on special meaning because (1) there is generally broad community consensus for these norms, (2) virtually all persons are aware that these specific proscriptions are enforced by official sanctions, and (3) the risk of detection and punishment influences the performance of delinquent acts.

We are not concerned here with the isolated delinquent act. Our focus is on sustained patterns of delinquent behavior, whether the person involved is socially or self-defined as a delinquent or nondelinquent person. Although our definition of delinquency subsumes one characteristic of a delinquent role (sustained patterns of delinquent behavior), it is our view that continuing involvement in delinquency may not necessarily involve the enactment of a delinquent role (Becker, 1963). There is empirical evidence that many embezzlers, auto thieves, check forgers, shoplifters, and persons involved in violent assaults against persons (including rape) do not view themselves as criminal or delinquent (Cameron, 1964; Gauthier, 1959; Gebhard et al., 1965; Lemert, 1951, 1953; Robin, 1974). Furthermore, many adolescents involved in sustained patterns of delinquent behavior are never apprehended and publicly labeled as delinquent persons, and have neither a public nor a self-definition as a delinquent or criminal person (Cameron, 1964; Hirschi, 1969; Jensen, 1972; Kelly, 1977; Reiss, 1961; Sykes & Matza, 1957). Thus, our conceptualization of delinquency focuses on sustained patterns of illegal behavior and is logically independent of the concept of delinquent role.

Etiological Paths to Delinquency

There are two dominant etiological paths to delinquency in the paradigm shown in Figure 1. The first involves an integration of traditional control theory and social-learning theory. Weak integration into and commitment to the social order, absence of conventional restraints on behavior, and high vulnerability to the influence of delinquent peer groups during adolescence characterize the socialization experiences related to the first path. Depending on the presence and accessibility of conventional and delinquent peer groups, some weakly bonded youths turn to delinquency while others maintain an essentially conforming pattern of behavior or a legal, but unconventional, lifestyle. The crucial element in this path is the delinquent peer group. Weakly bonded youths may not hold conventional aspirations (as for academic success), but they do share in more general aspirations for friendship and acceptance, as well as status and material rewards, which may be offered through participation in a group. Given an absence of conventional restraints and access to delinquent groups, the reasons for involvement are not unlike those for involvement in more conventional peer groups during adolescence.

The second path represents an integration of traditional strain and social-learning perspectives. Youths who follow this path develop strong bonds to the conventional social order through their socialization experiences. The crucial element in this sequence is the attenuation, or weakening, of these bonds. Attenuating experiences during adolescence involve personal failure to achieve conventional goals and/or threats to the stability and cohesion of one's conventional social groups. Once one's bonds are effectively weakened, like those who never developed strong bonds, one is free to explore alternative means for goal achievement and to participate in delinquent or unconventional groups.

In most instances, this path also involves participation in peer groups which tolerate or encourage delinquent forms of behavior. It is our view that truly individual adaptations to this situation are unlikely to survive long enough to generate detectable patterns of delinquent behavior. However, two possible subtypes deserve mention. The diagram of this integrated paradigm shows a direct causal path from initially strong bonds and subsequent attenuation experiences to delinquent behavior patterns. Under some circumstances, participation in groups providing reinforcements for delinquent acts is unnecessary. Attenuating experiences are sufficient to motivate repeated acts of delinquency, which are attempts to regain conventional rewards through unconventional means. This pattern involves the classic strain model, in which the person retains a strong commitment to conventional goals and values and uses illegal means as a temporary expedient. The attenuation process is only partial, and these youths retain some commitment to and integration into conventional groups. We anticipate such patterns to be of relatively short duration and to involve highly instrumental forms of delinquent behavior. Patterns of theft may characterize this etiological path.

A second subtype corresponds to that described generally by Simon and Gagnon (1976) in their article on the anomie of affluence. This path involves those whose commitments to conventional goals are attenuated by a decreasing gratification derived from goal achievement. Unlike the previously described subtype, which involved failure to achieve conventional success goals because of limited means or abilities, this type has ability and a ready access to legitimate means and is successful by conventional standards. The failure to derive personal gratification from "success" results in an attenuation of the commitment to these success goals and sets in motion a search for alternative goals whose attainment will provide a greater measure of personal gratification. This path to delinquency clearly requires participation in social groups in which delinquent behavior patterns can be learned and reinforced. This pattern of delinquency is characterized by a search for new experiences, which frequently involves illegal forms of behavior, such as illicit drug use and sex-related offenses.

At a more tentative level, we postulate that the two major paths (1) typically involve different forms of personal alienation and (2) result in different self-images and social labels. Conceptually, alienation plays a slightly different role within strain and control perspectives. From a control perspective, alienation, in the form of powerlessness, societal estrangement, and social isolation, directly reflects a weak personal commitment to conventional groups and norms. For strain theory, however, alienation represents a crucial intervening variable linking failure to delinquency. It is evidence of the attenuation of one's commitment bond or, in Hirschi's (1969) terms, the neutralization of "moral obstacles" to delinquency. In the form of alienation described by Cloward and Ohlin (1960), the neutralization is achieved through a blaming process in which failure is attributed to others or to general societal injustice. These same elements are present in Sykes and Matza's (1957) techniques of neutralization. Cartwright et al. (1966) and Cartwright (1971) identify four types of alienation which provide this direct encouragement, justification, or permission for delinquency: normlessness, futility, lack of trust, and perceived indifference. If we assume some relationship between the two causal paths and social class, there is some indirect empirical support for the hypothesis that the form of alienation is tied to the strength of one's initial commitment bond. . . .

We also hypothesize that those with initially strong bonds are less likely to view themselves as delinquent, even when they are involved in sustained patterns of delinquent behavior. Such persons are more likely to come from advantaged backgrounds and to have prosocial self-images. Consequently, they are likely to view their delinquent acts as temporary expedients, retaining at least a partial commitment to conventional goals. The probability of apprehension and public labeling by the police and courts is also much lower for such youths. In contrast, those who never developed strong bonds to the social order are more vulnerable to labeling processes and thus more likely to be viewed as delinquents by themselves and by others (Jensen, 1972). This may account, in part, for the persistent view among law enforcement officials and the general public that most delinquents are poor and/or nonwhite, in spite of the compelling evidence that the incidence of delinquent behavior is unrelated to these variables.

Summary and Discussion

. . . We believe the synthesis of traditional strain, social control, and social-learning perspectives into a single paradigm has several advantages over a conceptualization which treats each theory as separate and independent. First, the provision for multiple etiological paths to delinquency in a single paradigm presents a more comprehensive view. The integration of strain and control perspectives assumes that these two paths are independent and additive and that their integration will account for more variance in sustained patterns of delinquent behavior than either can explain independently. Independent tests of these traditional perspectives in the past have often failed to include the variables necessary to test alternative explanations, and even when such variables were available, the alternative explanations were assumed to be competitive and were thus evaluated with respect to the relative strengths of the two competing hypotheses (Eve, 1977; Hirschi, 1969). Such an approach misses the possibility that both hypotheses are correct and are accounting for different portions of the variance in delinquency. We have also suggested that different patterns of delinquency may be tied to alternative etiological paths; for example, we postulated that one of the strain paths (limited means/goal failure) should produce forms of delinquency which are considered very instrumental by conventional values. The alternative strain path (attenuated commitment to conventional goals) should result in less instrumental forms of delinquency, since it characteristically involves a search for new experiences (e.g., drug use) rather than attempts to achieve conventional goals.

Second, we believe that our integrated paradigm is consistent with previous empirical findings and offers some insight into contradictory findings. Previous research using the social control perspective has established a relationship between the strength of one's bonds and social class, with low-SES and minority youths characterized by weaker bonds (Gold, 1963; Hirschi, 1969; McKinley, 1964; Nye, 1958). In contrast, the attenuated commitment strain path has been associated with affluence, and the limited means-strain path seems most relevant to working-class youths. The combined effect seems consistent with the observed class distribution of self-reported delinquent behavior. Our assumption that weakly bonded youths run the greatest risk of official processing (because of greater surveillance in their neighborhoods, more traditional forms of delinquent behavior, and limited resources with which to avoid processing in the justice system) would account for the observed class distribution of official measures of delinquency. . . .

References

Ageton, S., & Elliott, D. S. (1974). The effects of legal processing on delinquent orientations. *Social Problems, 22,* 87–100.

Akers, R. (1977). *Deviant behavior: A social learning perspective.* Belmont, CA: Wadsworth.

Andry, R. G. (1962). Parental affection and delinquency. In M. E. Wolfgang, L. Savitz, & N. Johnston (Eds.), *The sociology of crime and delinquency* (pp. 342–352). New York: Wiley.

Bandura, A. (1969). *Principles of behavior modification.* New York: Holt, Rinehart & Winston.

Bandura, A. (1973). *Aggression: A social learning analysis.* Englewood Cliffs, NJ: Prentice Hall.

Bandura, A., & Walters, R. H. (1963). *Social learning and personality development.* New York: Holt, Rinehart & Winston.

Becker, H. S. (1960). Notes on the concept of commitment. *American Journal of Sociology, 66,* 32–40.

Becker, H. S. (1963). *Outsiders.* New York: Free Press.

Brennan, T. (1974). *Evaluation and validation regarding the National Strategy for Youth Development: A review of findings* (Report submitted to the Office of Youth Development). Boulder, CO: Behavioral Research and Evaluation Corporation.

Brennan, T., Huizinga, D., & Elliott, D. S. (1978). *The social psychology of runaways.* Lexington, MA: D. C. Heath.

Burgess, R. L., & Akers, R. L. (1966a). Are operant principles tautological? *Psychological Record, 16,* 305–312.

Burgess, R. L., & Akers, R. L. (1966b). A different association-reinforcement theory of criminal behavior. *Social Problems, 14,* 128–147.

Cameron, M. O. (1964). *The booster and the snitch.* New York: Free Press.

Cartwright, D. S. (1971). *Summary of conceptual issues in the National Strategy for Delinquency Prevention* (Document No. 34 in Center for Action Research). Boulder, CO: University of Colorado, Bureau of Sociological Research.

Cartwright, D. S., Reuterman, N. A., & Vandiver, R. I. (1966). *Multiple-factor approach to delinquency.* Boulder: Department of Psychology, University of Colorado.

Cloward, R. A., & Ohlin, L. E. (1960). *Delinquency and opportunity—A theory of delinquent gangs.* New York: Free Press.

Cohen, A. K. (1955). *Delinquent boys: The culture of the gang.* Glencoe, IL: Free Press.

Cohen, A. (1966). *Deviance and control.* Englewood Cliffs, NJ: Prentice Hall.

Durkheim, E. (1951). *Suicide: A study of sociology.* Glencoe, IL: Free Press. (Original work published 1897)

Elliott, D. S. (1962). Delinquency and perceived opportunity. *Sociological Inquiry, 32,* 216–227.

Elliott, D. S., & Voss, H. (1974). *Delinquency and dropout.* Lexington, MA: D. C. Heath.

Eve, R. (1977). *The efficacy of strain, culture conflict and social control theories for explaining rebelliousness among high school students.* Unpublished manuscript, University of Texas at Arlington.

Gauthier, M. (1959). The psychology of the compulsive forger. *Canadian Journal of Corrections, 1,* 62–69.

Gebhard, P. H., et al. (1965). *Sex offenders.* New York: Harper & Row.

Gibbons, D. C. (1977). *Society, crime and criminal careers* (3rd ed.). Englewood Cliffs, NJ: Prentice Hall.

Glueck, S., & Glueck, E. (1950). *Unraveling juvenile delinquency.* Cambridge, MA: Harvard University Press.

Gold, M. (1963). *Status forces in delinquent boys.* Ann Arbor: University of Michigan, Institute for Social Research.

Goldman, N. (1963). *The differential selection of juvenile offenders for court appearance.* Washington, DC: National Council on Crime and Delinquency.

Goode, W. J. (1960). Norm commitment and conformity to role status obligation. *American Journal of Sociology, 64,* 246–258.

Hebb, D. O. (1966). *Psychology.* Philadelphia: Saunders.

Hepburn, J. R. (1976). Testing alternative models of delinquency causation. *Journal of Criminal Law and Criminology, 67,* 450–460.

Hirschi, T. (1969). *Causes of delinquency.* Berkeley: University of California Press.

Jensen, G. F. (1972). Delinquency and adolescent self-conceptions: A study of the personal relevance of infraction. *Social Problems, 20,* 84–103.

Jessor, R., et al. (1968). *Society, personality and deviant behavior: A study of a tri-ethnic community.* New York: Holt, Rinehart & Winston.

Kelly, D. H. (1977). The effects of legal processing upon a delinquent's public identity: An analytical and empirical critique. *Education, 97,* 280–289.

Kitsuse, J. I. (1962). Societal reaction to deviant behavior: Problems of theory and method. *Social Problems, 9*(Winter), 247–256.

Lemert, E. M. (1951). *Social pathology.* New York: McGraw-Hill.

Lemert, E. M. (1953). An isolation and closure theory of naive check forgery. *Journal of Criminal Law, Criminology and Police Science, 44,* 296–307.

Liska, A. E. (1971). Aspirations, expectations and delinquency: Stress and additive models. *Sociological Quarterly, 12,* 99–107.

Matza, D. (1964). *Delinquency and drift.* New York: Wiley.

McKinley, D. G. (1964). *Social class and family life.* New York: Free Press.

Miller, W. B. (1958). Lower class culture as a generating milieu of gang delinquency. *Journal of Social Issues, 14*(3), 5–19.

Mischel, W. (1968). *Personality and assessment.* New York: Wiley.

Monahan, T. P. (1957). Family status and the delinquent child: A reappraisal and some new findings. *Social Forces, 35,* 250–258.

Nye, F. I. (1958). *Family relationships and delinquent behavior.* New York: Wiley.

Reckless, Walter. (1967). *The crime problem* (4th ed.). New York: Appleton-Century-Crofts.

Reiss, A. J., Jr. (1951). Delinquency as the failure of personal and social controls. *American Sociological Review, 16,* 196–207.

Reiss, A. J., Jr. (1961). The social integration of queers and peers. *Social Problems, 9,* 102–120.

Robin, G. (1974). The American customer: Shopper or shoplifter? *Police, 8,* 6–14.

Rosen, L. (1970). The broken home and male delinquency. In M. E. Wolfgang, L. Savitz, & N. Johnston (Eds.), *The sociology of crime and delinquency* (2nd ed., pp. 484–495). New York: Wiley.

Rotter, J. B. (1954). *Social learning and clinical psychology.* Englewood Cliffs, NJ: Prentice Hall.

Rubington, E. R., & Weinberg, M. S. (Eds.). (1968). *Deviance: The interactionist perspective.* New York: Macmillan.

Savitz, L. (1970). Delinquency and migration. In M. E. Wolfgang, L. Savitz, & N. Johnston (Eds.), *The sociology of crime and delinquency* (2nd ed., pp. 473–480). New York: Wiley.

Schur, E. M. (1971). *Labeling deviant behavior.* New York: Harper & Row.

Seeman, M. (1959). On the meaning of alienation. *American Sociological Review, 24,* 783–791.

Shaw, G. (1931). *Delinquency areas.* Chicago: University of Chicago Press.

Short, J. F., Jr. (1964). Gang delinquency and anomie. In M. B. Clinard (Ed.), *Anomie and deviant behavior* (pp. 98–127). New York: Free Press.

Short, J. F., Jr., Rivera, R., & Tennyson, R. A. (1965). Perceived opportunities, gang membership and delinquency. *American Sociological Review, 30,* 56–67.

Simon, W., & Gagnon, J. H. (1976). The anomie of affluence: A post Mertonian conception. *American Journal of Sociology, 82,* 356–378.

Spergel, I. (1967). Deviant patterns and opportunities of pre-adolescent Negro boys in three Chicago neighborhoods. In M. W. Klein (Ed.), *Juvenile gangs in context: Theory, research and action* (pp. 38–54). Englewood Cliffs, NJ: Prentice Hall.

Sutherland, E. H. (1947). *Criminology.* Philadelphia: J. B. Lippincott.

Sykes, G. M., & Matza, D. (1957). Techniques of neutralization: A theory of delinquency. *American Sociological Review, 22,* 664–670.

Thomas, W. I., & Znaniecki, F. (1927). *The Polish peasant in Europe and America.* New York: Knopf.

Toby, J. (1957). The differential impact of family disorganization. *American Sociological Review, 22,* 505–512.

/// REVIEW QUESTIONS

1. In the integrated model proposed by Elliott and his colleagues, which theoretical perspective is considered to be antecedent, or most important in the early stages, for developing delinquent or criminal tendencies? Do you agree with this portion of the model?

2. Do you think it is rational to merge theoretical perspectives that have opposing basic assumptions, such as merging strain theory, which claims that individuals are born good, with perspectives such as control theory, which claims that people are born bad and must be taught or controlled to be good? Or to merge them with learning theories, such as differential association or reinforcement, that assume individuals are born neither good nor bad, but rather as a "blank slate"? If you agree with such integration, explain your reasoning. If not, why?

3. Ultimately, what do you think of Elliott and his colleagues' model? Do you think it was a good early attempt at an integrated theory, or do you think it was rather weak given the information they had at that time (1979)?

READING /// 30

This reading presents an evaluation of the effectiveness of reintegrative shaming and restorative justice conferences in reforming juvenile offenders in Australia. Specifically, Hee Joo Kim and Jurg Gerber examine the use of reintegrative shaming experiments (RISE), based on John Braithwaite's reintegrative shaming theory, among a sample of youths that participated in the program in the late 1990s. This study focuses on the juveniles' perceptions on repaying the victims, their degree of repentance, and preventing their reoffending.

While reading this article, one should consider the following topics:

- The types of concepts or propositions that distinguish Braithwaite's theory of reintegrative shaming from other theoretical approaches to reducing crime, especially as compared to deterrence theory
- What previous studies have shown regarding the effectiveness of restorative justice conferences on reducing criminal activity and other factors, such as perceptions of accountability and making amends to the victims
- What the current study found regarding the four hypotheses they present, regarding the influence of restorative justice conferences on perceptions of reoffending, repaying the victim, repaying society, and/or repentance for their offense

SOURCE: Hee Joo Kim and Jurg Gerber, "The Effectiveness of Reintegrative Shaming and Restorative Justice Conferences: Focusing on Juvenile Offenders' Perceptions in Australian Reintegrative Shaming Experiments," *International Journal of Offender Therapy and Comparative Criminology* 56, no. 7 (2012): 1063–79.

The Effectiveness of Reintegrative Shaming and Restorative Justice Conferences

Focusing on Juvenile Offenders' Perceptions in Australian Reintegrative Shaming Experiments

Hee Joo Kim and Jurg Gerber

Introduction

Sociological explanations of juvenile delinquency include control, subcultural, learning, and labeling theories, and these theories have successfully been explored by many scholars. For example, labeling theory has been developed by Lemert, who defined primary and secondary deviance, and Becker's attempts to conceptualize three situations of delinquents: the pure deviant, the falsely accused deviant, and the secret deviant (Shoemaker, 2005). In his integrated form of these popular theories, Braithwaite found that societal labeling and shaming effectively deter delinquents, but the deterrent effect is influenced by several other factors, such as differences in culture. Attempting to integrate the insights of control, subcultural, learning, and labeling theories of crime, Braithwaite's reintegrative shaming theory suggested that reintegrative shaming can result in lower crime rates. This theory has received considerable attention in the context of common crimes, especially in juvenile crimes, such as predatory delinquency (Zhang & Zhang, 2004) and school bullying (Ahmed & Braithwaite, 2004); most of the studies found that reintegrative shaming can be an effective deterrent to juvenile crimes (Levi, 2002).

The developed and applied forms of Braithwaite's theory are the focus in restorative justice (RJ) conferences and have received considerable attention from many scholars and public policy makers. The purpose of the conference is to confront offenders with the consequences of their actions and encourage them to take personal responsibility for complying with the law in the future. Some jurisdictions in the United States use RJ conferences for various kinds of offenses. Many studies found that RJ conferences were particularly appropriate for very young offenders (McGarrell, 2001).

The police-run conferences in Bethlehem, Pennsylvania, the first formal conferences in the United States, showed a high level of victim satisfaction and reduced recidivism rates for offenses against the person but not for property offenses (McCold & Wachtel, 1998). Australian Reintegrative Shaming Experiments (RISE) is the second implementation of such conferences and are celebrated as a major advance in the evaluation of the effectiveness of diversionary RJ conferences on repeat offending (Tyler, Sherman, Strang, Barnes, & Woods, 2007). RISE also reported high levels of victim satisfaction and showed positive changes in the attitudes of offenders (Strang, Barnes, Braithwaite, & Sherman, 1999) without mentioning the offenders' own perceptions of the experiment. Moreover, a study that examined the effectiveness of RISE found that this program affected offenders charged with different kinds of offenses differently (Sherman, Strang, & Woods, 2000). According to their study, it was found that the dynamics of each type of offense may create a dissimilar emotional climate and basis for legitimacy of legal intervention using court or conference processes. Most previous studies defined the impact and effectiveness of RJ conferences very narrowly usually limiting only to perceptions of fairness and satisfaction, and have only focused on general effects of RJ conferences, such as victim satisfaction, recidivism rates, and changes in the attitudes of offenders. Studies exploring the impact of the offenders' own perceptions have rarely been conducted. Therefore, the purpose of this study is to evaluate the effectiveness of the Australian RISE using original data gathered from the experiment focusing on juvenile offenders' perceptions.

Literature Review

Empirical evidence for Braithwaite's reintegrative shaming theory has been found in a variety of contexts. Mostly, it has been used in the study of blue-collar crimes, including street crimes, juvenile delinquency, and drug offenders. Moreover, this theory has been used in the study of white-collar crimes (Benson, 1990; Elis & Simpson, 1995; Levi & Suddle, 1989; Makkai & Braithwaite, 1994; Murphy & Harris, 2007).

Braithwaite's Reintegrative Shaming Theory

Braithwaite's theory of reintegrative shaming is different from other theories in the way in which it addresses crime control, and his theory has received considerable attention due to its focus on the effect of shaming. Unlike many other traditions of crime control policy, which focus on the offenders' punishment or isolation from society, Braithwaite emphasized the importance of cultural integration and argued that the key factor to "crime control is cultural commitments" (Braithwaite, 1989, p. 1) to shaming. To control crime, society has to provide appropriate reintegrative shaming to people, according to Braithwaite, who recommended that society has to create an environment in which accepting an individual accepted back into society should be the primary goal, rather than labeling offenders to isolate them from society. The rate of offending will be lower especially when society exercises reintegrative shaming with more serious offenses, and the moral educational function of punishment is more important than the deterrent function (Braithwaite, 1989).

Suggesting the reason why some societies have higher crime rates than others, Braithwaite presented two types of shaming: reintegrative and disintegrative. Although disintegrative shaming (stigmatization) creates a class of outcasts and thus prevents offenders from rejoining the society, societies with reintegrative shaming retain bonds of respect or love and sharply terminate disapproval with forgiveness, instead of amplifying deviance by stigmatizing (Braithwaite, 1989). Braithwaite focused on the shaming process, as an explanation for variations in crime rates and as a normative approach to crime control, which he argued should partly replace imprisonment and other severe formal sanctions (Levi, 2002). Furthermore, integrating with the currently popular criminological theories, there are two major concepts in Braithwaite's theory: interdependency and communitarianism. Interdependency and communitarianism were represented as individual and social factors, respectively, to achieve crime control. At the individualistic (interdependency) level, he used individual factors which were taken from the traditional literature that predict increased likelihood to commit crimes, such as being young, male, unmarried, unemployed, and having little education. He used the variables urbanization and residential mobility at the social (communitarianism) level (Braithwaite, 1989). For individual factors that influenced the commission of crime, his theory is influenced by control theory, which emphasizes the importance of positive attachment to institutions such as the family, school, and work. He pointed out that if a strong positive relationship exists, and there is support to help each other not to be involved in deviant behavior, crime intervention would be effective.

Braithwaite cited the culture of Japan as an example of the reintegrative shaming process and pointed out that the shaming process and the role of an apology have an important place in interdependency and communitarianism (Braithwaite, 1989). In Japan, when an individual commits a crime, it affects the offender's social environment, such as family, school, and company (Braithwaite, 1989). Making the group to which an offender belongs take the responsibility for the member's deviant behavior is the idea behind intense collectivism. To make reintegrative shaming work in society, Braithwaite insisted that members of the society should have the "repentant role" (Braithwaite, 1989, p. 162). In other instances of social conflict, such as an airplane crash or collapse of a bridge or public building, which produces many victims, as in criminal cases, the responsible person in organizations needs to apologize for the negative consequences to the people.

Unlike Japan, the United States has multiple ethnic groups with various cultural backgrounds. Thus, it can be argued that the shaming process would not work well if applied in the United States. However, there are a number of studies that have successfully supported the effect of reintegrative shaming in the context of many crimes not only in the United States but also in many other countries (Ahmed & Braithwaite, 2004; Ferdinand & McDermott, 2002; Harris, 2006; Hosser, Windzio, & Greve, 2008; Rodriguez, 2007; Sherman et al., 2000; Tyler et al., 2007; Zhang & Zhang, 2004).

Ahmed and Braithwaite (2005) conducted research to examine the effectiveness of reintegrative shaming on school bullying. This study focuses on the prediction of self-initiated bullying from family, school, personality, and shame management variables. For the sample of juveniles (n = 1,401) and their parents (n = 978), the *Management of Shame State: Shame Acknowledgement and Shame Displacement* instrument was developed to test the importance of shame management in relation to bullying. Their study showed that shame acknowledgment reduced the likelihood of bullying, whereas shame displacement increased it, and shame management partially mediated the effects of family, school, and personality variables on bullying (Ahmed & Braithwaite, 2004).

Harris (2006) conducted research that tested the implication of reintegrative shaming theory that social disapproval has an effect on the emotions offenders have. Using interviews with 720 participants who had been apprehended for driving while intoxicated and had recently attended a court proceeding or family group conference in the Australian Capital Territory (ACT), Harris found that shame-related emotions were predicted by perceptions of social disapproval. Moreover, comparisons between the court cases and family group conferences were not only consistent with expectations that RJ interventions would be more reintegrative but also showed that they were not perceived as less stigmatizing.

RJ Conferences: The Australian RISE

RJ conferences are designed to repair damage between the offender, the victim, and the community. These programs provide an environment in which offenders can be reintegrated into their communities and victims can return to their daily lives without fear. Therefore, the ultimate goal is to create a more cohesive community (Stickle, Connell, Wilson, & Gottfredson, 2008). More specifically, RJ programs repair the harm caused to victims and the community through a process of negotiation, mediation, victim empowerment, and reparation (Rodriguez, 2007). RJ programs are more closely related to the philosophy of the juvenile court than to the retributive philosophy that guides the adult criminal justice processing when the rehabilitation of not only juvenile but adult offenders is also the goal (Rodriguez, 2007).

According to Zehr (1990), the RJ paradigm begins with the assumption that "crime is a violation of people and relationships rather than merely a violation of law" (p. 181). Therefore, the most appropriate reaction to criminal behaviors is to repair the harm caused by the wrongful action (Newell, 2007). The criminal justice system should provide an opportunity for those who are most affected by the crime, such as the victim, the offender, and the community, to come together to discuss the act committed and attempt to understand what can be done to provide appropriate reparation (Latimer, Dowden, & Muise, 2001).

Although RJ programs have received considerable attention from many scholars, the concept still remains problematic in definitional terms (Newell, 2007). However, key elements of RJ programs are as follows:

1. All parties with a stake in a particular conflict or offense come together to collectively resolve how to deal with the aftermath of the conflict or offense and its implications for the future and
2. Offenders have the opportunity to acknowledge the impact of what they have done and to make reparation, and victims have the opportunity to have their harm acknowledged and amends made (Restorative Justice Consortium, 2006).

Australia and New Zealand have implemented RJ conferences as one form of early intervention, and they are being used increasingly throughout the world (McGarrell, 2001). In such conferences, all involved parties, including the juvenile offender, the victim, families of offenders and victims as supporters, and other supporting groups, are brought together. Trained facilitators are present to discuss the incident and the harm it has brought to the victim and the group of supporters (Tyler et al., 2007). During the conference, victims and supporters of offenders or victims have an opportunity to explain how they have been affected and harmed by the incident. After the conference, all participants reach agreement on how the juvenile offender can repay the victim and society, and they sign a reparation agreement, typically including an apology or, more often, community service (McGarrell, 2001).

Sherman et al. (2000) studied the levels of effectiveness of standard court processing and RISE. Using 1,300 cases of drunk driving, juvenile property crimes, juvenile shoplifting, and juvenile violent crimes, they found that diversionary conferences reduced juvenile violent offending rates by about 38 crimes per 100 offenders per year but found no differences in property and shoplifting offending rates between court and conference group. From this study, they concluded that RJ leads to lower recidivism or crime reducing effects on offenders charged with different kinds of offenses. The dynamics of each type of offense may create a different emotional climate and basis for legitimacy of legal intervention using court or conference processes.

However, one study found no significant differences in effects for various types of offenses. Comparing juveniles in an RJ program with juveniles having undergone regular court processing, Rodriguez (2007) measured the influence of an RJ program on recidivism in Maricopa County, Arizona, and found that juveniles in the RJ program showed lower rates of recidivism than those in the court proceeding. Although there were no significant effects between offense type/race and RJ, the study indicated that there were significant effects of the RJ program and gender and criminal records. For example, girls and offenders with minimal criminal histories were the most successful participants in the RJ program.

Arguing for the reform of our criminal justice system, Ferdinand and McDermott (2002) asserted that we need more variability in the manner in which offenders are sentenced and treated in terms of their offense and their needs. According to their study, "If we differentiate civic, social, and criminal offenders, we can also distinguish offenders who will respond to reintegrative shaming, focused professional treatment, secure custody, and specific social, moral, and psychological guidance" (Ferdinand & McDermott, 2002, p. 110). They advocated treating and punishing differently according to each offender's offenses and needs, and that this perspective may be effective with all kinds of offenders.

Moreover, because early involvement in status offenses and delinquency can be a predictor of serious, violent, and chronic offending, McGarrell (2001) emphasized the importance of early interventions for very young offenders. In an evaluation of The Indianapolis Restorative Justice Experiment, an Australian-style RJ conference as an alternative response to juvenile offending, he tried to identify the effects of the RJ conferences and argued that they "can be successfully implemented in an urban U.S. setting" (McGarrell, 2001, p. 9). On the question of the participants' attitudes toward the RJ conferencing as an alternative form to traditional court proceeding, it showed high level of offender and victim satisfaction, but offenders and parents in the traditional court proceedings were slightly more likely to express satisfaction (McGarrell, 2001). In terms of recidivism, juveniles who completed the RJ conference were found to be less likely to be rearrested than those who went through the traditional court proceedings. Males and females in the conference showed lower recidivism rates than those who went through court proceedings, but the difference was greater for females than for males (McGarrell, 2001).

Present Study

Most studies have supported the effectiveness of reintegrative shaming and RJ conferences in the United States (Ahmed & Braithwaite, 2004; Harris, 2006; Hosser et al., 2008; McGarrell, 2001; Rodriguez, 2007; Sherman et al., 2000), and the question regarding juvenile offenders' own perceptions of RJ conferences has been raised. The purpose of this study is to examine the effectiveness of the RISE program by using different aspects from previous literatures. Most previous studies showed significant effects of RJ conferences, including RISE, particularly on preventing recidivism (McGarrell, 2001; Rodriguez, 2007; Sherman et al., 2000). Therefore, juvenile offenders' own perceptions on this effect, preventing future offending, will be addressed in the present study. Moreover, one of the main purposes of RJ conferences is to repair damages between offenders, victims, and the community, so the variables, repaying the victim and society, were included to examine juvenile offenders' own perceptions on this purpose (Stickle et al., 2008). Braithwaite's reintegrative shaming theory (1989) has been the most influential theory, emphasizing that reintegrative shaming reduces reoffending by encouraging offenders to feel ashamed. Citing an example of a shaming process in Japan, he argued that apology is one of the important factors in interdependency and communitarianism, specific social conditions conducive to reintegrative shaming. Feeling repentance can be the predictor conducive to generate reintegrative shaming, so the variable, degree of feeling repentance, was included.

As one of the most popular RJ conferences, RISE bases itself on Braithwaite's theory of reintegrative shaming, and it is known as a major effort to conduct an experimental evaluation of the effectiveness of RJ conferences on repeat offending. During 1995 to 1999, Sherman, Braithwaite, Strang, and Barnes conducted a RISE in Australia consisting of four separate experiments: adult drinking and driving offenders, juvenile personal property criminals, juvenile shoplifters, and violent crime committed by offenders up to age 29. Individuals who committed offenses of drunk driving over .08 blood alcohol content included offenders of any age, juvenile property offenders with personal victims, juvenile shoplifters detected by store security officers, and youth violent criminals (below age 30) in the ACT, which participated in the Australian RISE. However, only three experiments including juvenile offenses were used in this study because of focusing on juvenile offenders.

Therefore, research hypotheses for the current study are as follows:

Hypothesis 1: Offenders who experienced RJ conferences will be more likely to perceive that this treatment will prevent future offenses than those who experienced traditional court processing.

Hypothesis 2: Offenders who experienced RJ conferences will be more likely to perceive that this treatment allowed them to repay the victim of the crime than were those who experienced traditional court processing.

Hypothesis 3: Offenders who experienced RJ conferences will be more likely to perceive that this treatment allowed them to repay society than those who experienced traditional court processing.

Hypothesis 4: Offenders who experienced RJ conferences will be more likely to perceive repentance for their crime than those who experienced traditional court processing.

Data and Method

Data/Sample

In this article, the data set Reintegrative Shaming Experiments (RISE) in Australia, 1995-1999 (ICPSR 2993) was used. Cases were sent to RISE from officers throughout the Australian Federal Police in the ACT region. This included uniformed patrol officers from each of the four Canberra police stations and its special "City Beat" officer in the center of the city and also from the Traffic Division and the Crime Branch. It also tried to include "middle-range offenses" in the conference, which are neither so trivial that they would be dealt with by a simple warning nor so serious that police would be reluctant to bypass the court system in favor of an experimental alternative. Initially, it was proposed that there were 150 cases in each of the two juvenile property experiments and 300 in the youth violence experiment. However, the research design was subsequently amended on the basis of case availability after data collection had commenced. It was difficult to find juvenile offenders in this data set. For example, in many juvenile offense cases, there was no information about the victims who were brought to the conference, sometimes offenders rejected conferencing, offenders reoffended immediately after being assigned to conference, or offenders repeatedly failed to show up for the conference.

The data are from RISE comparing the effects of court and conferences for a select group of offenders. A total of 249 juveniles were randomly assigned to RISE or standard court processing. Data were then taken from interviews with the juvenile offenders to measure their perceptions after the court or conference proceedings. Variables that were investigated included whether the respondents thought the court or conference would prevent future offenses, how much the offenders should repay the victim and society, whether the respondents would accept responsibilities for their acts, whether the respondent would perceive any repentance, and how much the court and conference made the respondents perceive fairness during the proceeding and respect for the justice system.

Demographic variables in this data collection included offenders' country of birth, age, gender, years of education, income, and employment. Among the sample of 249 juvenile offenders, 12 were excluded from the analysis because of missing values, 49.8% were assigned to the standard court, and 50.2% were assigned to the conference. The sample of 249 juvenile offenders included juvenile property offenders (44.6%), juvenile shoplifters (34.5%), and juvenile violent offenders (20.9%).

In addition, the variables income and employment status could not be used as predictors that explain juvenile offenders' perceptions on prevention, repayment, and feeling repentance due to large number of missing values. Among a total of 249 juvenile offenders, more than 161 (65%) of them were unemployed as full-time students and did not have any incomes. In this data set, juvenile property offending was classified into two groups, one focusing on personal victims and the other on shoplifting. There were no significant differences in demographic characteristics between the juvenile offenders who were assigned to RISE and those who went through court processing. Therefore, using these 249 juvenile offenders, including offenders who were randomly assigned either to RISE or court processing, to evaluate their perceptions of RISE would not be problematic.

In our research, comparisons will be made between the effects of standard court processing with the effects of a RJ intervention known as diversionary conferencing for several juvenile offenses. Using four separate multiple regressions, the study will determine whether participation in RISE can explain juveniles' perceptions on preventing future offending, repaying the victim, repaying the society, and the degree of the offenders' feelings of repentance. In addition, the variables gender, age, offense type, and years of education of the juvenile offenders were added because there have been numerous studies which found differential effects of RJ in terms of gender, age, offense type, and education levels (McGarrell, 2001; Rodriguez, 2007).

Dependent Variables

1. Preventing future offense (The conference/court will help prevent you from breaking the law in the future.)
2. Repaying the victim (The conference/court allowed you to repay the victim of your crime for harm that you caused them.)
3. Repaying the society (The conference/court allowed you to repay society for your offense.)
4. The degree of feeling repentance (You regret putting other people at risk as a result of your offense.)

The data were taken from interviews with juvenile offenders to measure their perceptions after the court or conference processing. All the dependent variables (Table 1) were measured by Likert-type scales; 1 = *strongly disagree*, 2 = *disagree*, 3 = *neither*, 4 = *agree*, and 5 = *strongly agree*. All the dependent variables are the same in that they have a positive scale value; 1 means usually negative perception for the conference or court processing and 5 means positive perception for the conference or court processing.

Independent Variables

All independent variables (Table 1) are either dummy or continuous variables. The variable observed treatment was recoded into a dummy variable (0 = *court*, 1 = *conference*). The variables gender, age, years of offenders' education, and offense types were added as characteristic

Table 1 • Variables Used in the Analysis

Metric variables	Values	Average	*SD*	Valid cases
Preventing future offenses	1~5	3.96	0.927	237
Repaying the victim	1~5	3.35	1.172	237
Repaying society	1~5	3.35	1.114	237
Feeling repentance	1~5	3.56	1.029	237
Years of education	0~12	9.09	1.783	249
Age	11~26	16.46	2.272	249

Dummy variables	Values	*n*	%	Valid cases
Treatment	Court	124	49.8	249
	Conference	125	50.2	
Gender	Males	189	75.9	249
	Females	60	24.1	
Offense type	Violent	52	20.9	249
	Nonviolent	197	79.1	

NOTE: Dependent variables are preventing future offenses, repaying the victim, repaying society, and feeling repentance. Independent variables are years of education, age, treatment, gender, and offense type.

variables for the juvenile offenders. The mean years of education was 9.09 (median = 9.00, range = 0~12), 16.46 for offenders' age. A total of 75.9% of the juveniles were males, whereas 24.1% were females, and 79.1% of the offenders committed nonviolent offenses (property and shoplifting offense), whereas 20.9% committed violent offenses.

Results

Beginning with an assessment of the degree of overlap in preventing future offenses and contrasting the standard court processing with the RJ conference processing, attending an RJ conference, instead of attending a standard court, appeared to be more effective on all the variables, including preventing future offenses, repaying the victim, repaying society, and the degree of feeling repentance. The respondents who attended an RJ conference reported more positive perceptions on preventing future offenses than did the respondents who attended standard court processing. Nearly 43.5% of the respondents in RJ conferences stated that conference processing can prevent future offending as compared with 38.4% of the respondents who attended standard court processing. Moreover, more than 36% of the respondents who participated in RJ conferences said that conference processing can make them repay the victim and society as compared with less than 20% of the respondents in standard court processing. In addition, the respondents who attended RJ conferences had a greater degree of a feeling of repentance compared with the respondents who attended standard court processing.

The associations between the dependent variables (the perceptions on preventing future offense, repaying the victim, repaying society, and the degree of feeling repentance) and a treatment (RISE or standard court processing) that the juvenile offenders went through are also examined. According to Pearson chi-square and gamma values, the relationships between the juvenile offenders' perceptions and attending RJ conference were statistically significant, except for the perceptions on preventing future offense. Except for the juvenile offenders' perceptions on preventing future offense, the perceptions on others were indicated as positive associations, meaning that if the offenders participated in the RJ conference instead of standard court processing, the perceptions regarding repaying the victim and society and the degree of feeling repentance would be increased.

As a preliminary analysis, an independent sample *t* test was conducted to see the differences between juveniles who were assigned to courts and RISE in terms of the perceptions on their future offenses, repaying the victim/society, and the degree of feeling repentance. The two groups of juvenile offenders who were randomly assigned to either court or RISE were matched along with their demographic conditions. The mean of juvenile offenders' age in RISE group was 16.61 years, and 16.29 years for juvenile offenders in the court group. The mean of educational level for RISE groups was 9.10, and 9.07 for court group. The gender and offense type of two groups were also matched. RISE group included 80% of males and 20% of females, and 70% of males and 30% females were included in court group. In the RISE group, 22.4% of juveniles were involved in violent offense and 77.6% of them were involved in nonviolent offense, whereas 19.4% of offense type was violent and 80.6% was nonviolent for the court group.

For the perception of preventing future offense, juvenile offenders who were processed by the courts had a mean of 3.92 and who were processed on the RISE had a mean of 4.01. The mean difference was not statistically significant. However, the perceptions of repaying the victim (M = 2.96, for the court group; M = 3.75, for RISE group)/society (M = 2.90, for the court group; M = 3.81, for RISE group) and the degree of feeling repentance (M = 3.40, for the court group; M = 3.71, for RISE group) were significantly different between juveniles in the court and RISE. An independent sample t test also showed significant differences in the perceptions of repaying the victim (t = 5.549, p = .000)/society (t = 6.831, p = .000) and the degree of feeling repentance (t = 2.346, p = .020) between the two groups. Therefore, juvenile offenders in RISE were more likely to perceive that RISE allowed them to repay the victim/society and express repentance for their crime. There were no significant differences in those perceptions in terms of offenders' gender, but we found significant differences along with offense types. Juveniles who committed nonviolent offenses were more likely to perceive that RISE will prevent future offense (t = −2.913, p = .005) and allowed them to repay the victim (t = −2.715, p = .007). Standard multiple regression was conducted to determine the ability of the independent variables (treatment, gender, age, offense type, and years of education) to explain variation in the positive perceptions on preventing future offense, repaying the victim, repaying society, and the degree of feeling repentance. Four separate multiple regression analyses were conducted.

Using the *enter* method, a multiple regression was conducted to determine which independent variables (treatment, gender, age, offense type, and years of education) were predictors for the dependent variables. *Enter* method means entering all independent variables, one at a time, into the model regardless of significant contribution (Mertler & Vannatta, 2005). Because there have been no theoretical models yet, and this data set has a relatively low number of cases, the *enter* method, the simultaneous method, would be the safest one to use (Brace, Kemp, & Snelgar, 2000).

The correlation between the juvenile offenders' perceptions on preventing future offense (Pearson correlation = .125, p = .048), repaying the victim (Pearson correlation = .399, p = .000), repaying society (Pearson correlation = .450, p = .000), and feeling repentance (Pearson correlation = .114, p = .061) and the participation in RISE showed statistically significant relationship. The model summary and the ANOVA table indicate that the overall model of the five independent variables (treatment, gender, age, offense type, and years of education) significantly predict positive perceptions on preventing future offenses, adjusted R^2 = .063, $F(5, 233)$ = 3.352, p = .006. Moreover, it shows that the overall model of the five independent variables significantly generated positive perceptions on repaying the victim, adjusted R^2 = .193, $F(5, 233)$ = 9.394, p = .000, and repaying society, adjusted R^2 = .229, $F(5, 233)$ = 11.442, p = .000. However, the overall model of the five independent variables moderately generated offenders' feelings of repentance, adjusted R^2 = .026, $F(5, 233)$ = 1.975, p = .084. The variance in explaining positive perceptions on each variable is small. In this data set, 249 juveniles were randomly selected to participate in either RISE or the standard court processing, but only 237 juveniles were used in the analysis. Moreover, respondents were interviewed just after the court or conference processing. Therefore, if the interview had been conducted after 2 or 3 years, the variance in explaining positive perceptions on each variable might have been increased and the long-term effects of the RJ conference could have been identified.

Table 2 provides the multiple regression results. A summary of regression coefficients indicates that the five independent variables (treatment, gender, age, offense type, year of education) significantly contribute to the positive perceptions on preventing future offending. However, rather than participating RISE, offenders' age and level of education contributed to the positive perceptions on preventing future offending. Those who were younger and had higher educational levels were more likely to perceive that this treatment will prevent future offending.

Table 2 • Multiple Regression Results for Preventing Future Offenses, Repaying the Victim, Repaying the Society, and the Degree of Feeling Repentance

	DVs			
IVs	**Preventing future offenses**	**Repaying the victim**	**Repaying the society**	**The degree of feeling repentance**
Treatment	.110	.409***	.476***	.142*
Gender	.114	–.039	–.118	–.066
Years of education	.248*	.183	.116	.128
Age	–.284*	–.270*	–.236*	–.268*
Offense type	.110	.095	.016	–.089
F	3.352**	9.394***	11.442***	1.975*
df	236	236	236	236
Adjusted R^2	.063	.193	.229	.026

NOTE: IV = independent variable; DV = dependent variable. The numbers shown are standardized regression coefficients.

*$p < .05$. **$p < .01$. ***$p < .001$.

The multiple regression results indicated that RISE significantly contributed to positive perceptions regarding repayment of the victim and society. Those who experienced RJ conferences were more likely to perceive that this treatment allowed them to repay the victim and society for the crime than those who had experienced traditional court processing. Moreover, it was also found that younger offenders were more likely to perceive the repayment of the victim and society. The multiple regression results demonstrated that treatment significantly contributed to the degree of feelings of repentance. Those who experienced RJ conferences and younger offenders were more likely to express repentance for their crimes than those who had experienced traditional court processing. The overall results about offenders' age are somewhat consistent with McGarrell's (2001) study that RJ programs are particularly appropriate for very young offenders.

Conclusion and Discussion

The important issue addressed in this article is whether those who experienced RJ conferences were more likely to perceive that their future offending was reduced compared with those who went through regular court processing. The results indicate that RJ conferences do not have a significant influence on the juvenile offenders' perceptions of future offending. However, it was found that the participation in RJ conference is a significant predictor of positive perceptions on repaying regarding repaying the victim, repaying the society, and the degree of feeling repentance. Simply put, those who experienced RJ conferences are significantly more likely to perceive that they were able to repay the victim and repay society than those who had experienced traditional court processing. Moreover, those who experienced RJ conferences were significantly more likely to perceive repentance for their crime. Another interesting finding from this study is that juvenile offenders' positive perceptions on preventing future offending, repaying the victim/society, and the degree of feeling repentance is correlated with their age. Similar to McGarrell's (2001) study, emphasizing the importance of early interventions for very young offenders, younger offenders were more likely to perceive positive effects on preventing future offending, repaying the victim/society, and the degree of feeling repentance compared with the older offenders. Especially for the perception on preventing future offending and the degree of feeling repentance, offenders' age was the most significant predictor. Examining the consistency with Sherman et al.'s (2000) study that juveniles charged with different kinds of offense would be affected differently however, there were no differential effects based on the type of offense for the positive perceptions.

There are many appealing features of the RJ conference. For example, they are found to be more satisfying for victims of crime (Strang & Sherman, 2006), and they have many positive psychological effects on offenders (Barnes, 1999; Poulson, 2003). Therefore, even if the RJ conference did not lead to more positive effects than traditional court processing, they might have social value and therefore would be publicly popular (Roberts & Stalans, 2004), provided they did not actually increase reoffending. It should be noted that the effectiveness of RJ programs has to be tested in terms of not only their general effects but also the perceptions of offenders. Focusing on general effects such as victim satisfaction or recidivism rate, many researchers have found support for RJ programs (Ahmed & Braithwaite, 2004; Harris, 2006; Hosser et al., 2008; McGarrell, 2001; Rodriguez, 2007; Sherman et al., 2000). However, the studies exploring the impact of offenders' own perceptions have rarely been conducted. Examining the effects of RJ programs, recidivism rate was the most commonly tested aspect of the general effects (McGarrell, 2001; Rodriguez, 2007; Sherman et al., 2000). Other features that have been explored include victim satisfaction and changes in the attitude of the offenders (Sherman et al., 2000). Using different facets from previous studies to explore the effects of RJ program is necessary because one of the main purposes of an RJ program is to repair damages between all involved parties, including offenders, victims, and the community. Furthermore, scrutinizing offenders' own perceptions of an RJ program, addressing the prevention effect of repaying victims, and discovering how repentance may change the offender's view of society are also important to unveil undiscovered effects of RJ programs.

Some limitations of this article are that this study focused only on three types of juvenile offenders, such as juvenile property criminals, shoplifters, and youth violent criminals, so it cannot be said that the results in this study represent all juvenile offenders' perceptions. Moreover, we examined differential effects based on their criminal history or offenders' race, but there were no variables for representing juvenile offenders' prior records and race in the original raw data. Focusing on the recidivism rate, there is a study that measured the influence of an RJ program along with juvenile offenders' race, offense type, gender, and criminal records (Rodriguez, 2007) and found that there were effects of gender and criminal records, whereas there were no significant program effects in terms of offense type and race. Therefore, for further research, it is necessary to examine the differential perceptions of RJ in terms of offenders' prior record or race. Another limitation of this study will be about data collecting procedure. Respondents were interviewed directly after the court or conference processing. Therefore, if the interview had been conducted after 2 or 3 years, the long-term effects of the RJ conference on the offenders' perceptions could have been identified.

Drawing on the works of Braithwaite (1989) and Sherman (2000), there are other facets that can be tested. Future research should examine other sides of the effectiveness of the RJ conference as compared with traditional court processing. This study tested the utility of one particular aspect of reintegrative shaming theory and the RJ conference, focusing on the juvenile offenders' own perceptions about RISE. Rather than examining the effectiveness of RISE in terms of recidivism rates, the present study explored undiscovered impacts of RISE programs in terms of the juvenile offenders' perceptions. Braithwaite's theory focused on the emotional dynamics, emphasizing that "conscience is a much more powerful weapon to control misbehavior than punishment" (Braithwaite, 1989, p. 71) and that it is the conscience-building effects of shaming that give it superiority over control strategies that are based on changing the rewards and costs of crime. Thus, reintegrative shaming implies that "emotions like shame or guilt" play a critical role, and RJ programs, including RISE, have adopted these theoretical perspectives. Therefore, research findings from this study, what specific conditions signified the offenders' positive perceptions on prevention/repayment issues and feeling repentance, may assist scholars who are studying RJ and RJ program administrators and can provide a greater understanding of the processes and emotional dynamics in RJ programs.

Braithwaite's reintegrative shaming has been one of the most influential criminological theories, with emphasis on the fact that reintegrative shaming reduces reoffending by encouraging offenders to feel ashamed. According to Braithwaite,

> By increasing the capacity of societies to shame, we will increase the extent to which the power of shaming can be harnessed for both good and ill. Shaming can be used to stultify diversity which is the stuff of intellectual, political, and artistic debate and progress, or simply to oppress diversity which is harmless.
>
> Shaming is rough-and-ready justice which runs great risk for wronging the innocent, and that the most important safeguard is for shaming to be reintegrative so that communication channels remain open to learning of injustice, and social bonds remain intact to facilitate apology and recompense. Reintegrative shaming is not only more effective than stigmatization; it is also more just. (Braithwaite, 1989, pp. 159–161)

Examining the relationship between formal sanctions and crime becomes especially important in the current period of expanding alternatives to straight probation and incarceration, such as diversion programs or specialized drug courts (Miethe, Lu, & Reese, 2000). These kinds of formal sanctions are influenced by Braithwaite's theory of reintegrative shaming.

However, because reintegrative shaming or experiencing the RJ conference may not always be effective, it is necessary to conduct more research on reintegrative shaming in terms of various variables. The potential benefits of an RJ program remain to be fully realized in the United States, even though many scholars have argued that RJ provides an appropriate alternative to existing mechanisms found within the juvenile court (Bazemore & Umbreit, 1995). Although many studies have examined the actual effectiveness of the RJ program focusing on recidivism (Sherman et al., 2000; Tyler et al., 2007), we continue to need to address the particular circumstances such as which RJ can be most effective or which type of offenders are most likely to be affected after experiencing the programs. Moreover, more detailed comparisons between the RJ conference and the standard court processing will be needed.

References

Ahmed, E., & Braithwaite, V. (2004). "What, me ashamed?" Shame management and school bullying. *Journal of Research in Crime and Delinquency, 41*, 269–294.

Ahmed, E., & Braithwaite, J. (2005). Forgiveness, shaming, shame and bullying. *Australian and New Zealand Journal of Criminology, 38*, 298–323.

Barnes, G. C. (1999). *Procedural justice in two contexts: Testing the fairness of diversionary conferencing for intoxicated drivers* (Unpublished doctoral dissertation). Department of Criminology and Criminal Justice, University of Pennsylvania.

Bazemore, G., & Umbreit, M. S. (1995). Rethinking the sanctioning function in juvenile court: Retributive or restorative responses to youth crime. *Crime & Delinquency, 41*, 296–316.

Benson, M. (1990). Emotions and adjudication: Status degradation among white-collar criminals. *Justice Quarterly, 7*, 515–528.

Brace, N., Kemp, R., & Snelgar, R. (2000). *SPSS for psychologists: A guide to data analysis using SPSS for windows* (2nd ed.). Mahwah, NJ: Lawrence Erlbaum.

Braithwaite, J. (1989). *Crime, shame and reintegration*. New York, NY: Cambridge University Press.

Elis, L., & Simpson, S. (1995). Informal sanction threats and corporate crime: Additive versus multiplicative models. *Journal of Research in Crime & Delinquency, 32*, 399–424.

Ferdinand, T. N., & McDermott, M. J. (2002). Joining punishment and treatment in substantive equality. *Criminal Justice Policy Review, 13*, 87–116.

Harris, N. (2006). Reintegrative shaming, shame, and criminal justice. *Journal of Social Issues, 62*, 327–346.

Hosser, D., Windzio, M., & Greve, W. (2008). Guilt and shame as predictors of recidivism: A longitudinal study with young prisoners. *Criminal Justice and Behavior, 35*, 138–152.

Latimer, J., Dowden, C., & Muise, D. (2001). *The effectiveness of restorative justice practices: A meta-analysis* (Research and Statistics Division Methodological Series). Ottawa, Ontario: Canadian Department of Justice.

Levi, M. (2002). Suite justice or sweet charity? Some explorations of shaming and incapacitating business fraudsters. *Punishment and Society, 4*, 147–163.

Levi, M., & Suddle, M. (1989). White-collar crime, shamelessness, and disintegration: The control of tax evasion in Pakistan. *Journal of Law and Society, 61*, 489–505.

Makkai, T., & Braithwaite, J. (1994). The dialectics of corporate deterrence. *Journal of Research in Crime and Delinquency, 31*, 347–373.

McCold, P., & Wachtel, B. (1998). *Restorative policing experiment: The Bethlehem Pennsylvania police family group conferencing project*. Pipersville, PA: Community Service Foundation.

McGarrell, E. F. (2001). Restorative justice conferences as an early response to young offenders. *Juvenile Justice Bulletin*. Washington, DC: U.S. Department of Justice, Office of Justice

Programs, Office of Juvenile Justice and Delinquency Prevention.

Mertler, C. A., & Vannatta, R. A. (2005). *Advanced and multivariate statistical methods: Practical application and interpretation* (3rd ed.). Glendale, CA: Pyrczak Publishing.

Miethe, T. D., Lu, H., & Reese, E. (2000). Reintegrative shaming and recidivism risks in drug court: Explanations for some unexpected findings. *Crime & Delinquency, 46*, 522–541.

Murphy, K., & Harris, N. (2007). Shaming, shame and recidivism: A test of reintegrative shaming theory in the white-collar crime context. *British Journal of Criminology, 47*, 900–917.

Newell, T. (2007). Face to face with violence and its effect: Restorative justice practice at work. *Journal of Community and Criminal Justice, 54*, 227–238.

Poulson, B. (2003). A third voice: A review of empirical research on the psychological outcomes of restorative justice. *Utah Law Review, 01*, 167–203.

Restorative Justice Consortium. (2006). Available from http://www.restorativejustice.org.uk

Roberts, J. V., & Stalans, L. J. (2004). Restorative sentencing: Exploring the views of the public. *Social Justice Research, 17*, 315–334.

Rodriguez, N. (2007). Restorative justice at work: Examining the impact of restorative justice resolutions on juvenile recidivism. *Crime & Delinquency, 53*, 355–379.

Sherman, L. W., Strang, H., & Woods, D. J. (2000). *Recidivism patterns in the Canberra Reintegrative Shaming Experiments (RISE)*. Canberra: Center for Restorative Justice, Research School of Social Sciences, Australian National University.

Shoemaker, D. J. (2005). *Theories of delinquency: An examination of explanations of delinquent behavior* (5th ed.). New York, NY: Oxford University Press.

Stickle, W. P., Connell, N. M., Wilson, D. M., & Gottfredson, D. (2008). An experimental evaluation of teen courts. *Journal of Experimental Criminology, 4*, 137–163.

Strang, H., Barnes, G. C., Braithwaite, J., & Sherman, L. W. (1999). *Experiments in restorative policing: A progress report on the Canberra Reintegrative Shaming Experiments (RISE)*. Canberra: Australian National University.

Strang, H., & Sherman, L. W. (2006). Restorative justice to reduce victimization. In B. C. Walsh & D. P. Farrington (Eds.), *Preventing crime: What works for children, offenders, victims and places* (pp. 147–160). Dordrecht, Netherlands: Springer.

Tyler, T. R., Sherman, L., Strang, H., Barnes, G. C., & Woods, D. (2007). Reintegrative shaming, procedural justice, and recidivism: The engagement of offenders' psychological mechanism in the Canberra RISE drinking-and-driving experiment. *Law and Society Review, 41*, 553–585.

Zehr, H. (1990). *Changing lenses: A new focus for crime and justice*. Scottdale, PA: Herald Press.

Zhang, L., & Zhang, S. (2004). Reintegrative shaming and predatory delinquency. *Journal of Research in Crime and Delinquency, 41*, 433–453.

/// REVIEW QUESTIONS

1. What types of Braithwaite's reintegrative shaming theoretical framework makes it unique from most models of criminal offending? Why does he use Japan as a model for this approach?

2. How effective have such restorative justice conferences worked so far, according to past studies, both in the United States and abroad?

3. What did the current study find regarding the effectiveness in influencing young offenders in their perceptions of reoffending, repaying the victim, repaying society, and/or repentance for their offense(s)? Which were significant, and which were not?

READING /// 31

In this selection, Terence Thornberry presents an integrated model that primarily merges two theoretical perspectives, specifically control theory and differential reinforcement or social learning theory. However, the primary distinction between previous integrated frameworks and Thornberry's model is that Thornberry takes into account the reciprocal, or feedback, effects that certain variables may have on the increase of delinquent or criminal behavior.

For example, Thornberry claims that weak bonds to parents (a control concept) may lead to association with delinquent peers (a differential association or social learning concept), which is likely to lead to parents having even weaker bonds with the individual or youth. So it is proposed that a youth's getting in trouble is likely to lead to more alienation or weaker bonds with the youth's parents, which is quite likely in reality. Such an effect is a good example of a reciprocal effect or feedback effect, and this is just one of the many reciprocal effects that are proposed in this model. Thornberry's integrated model of offending is full of such reciprocal (or feedback) effects, and this is what distinguishes his model from previous integrated frameworks or any of the traditional theoretical models that attempted to explain offending.

While reading this selection, readers should consider the following points:

- Your own experience or those of others you know who were caught once (and maybe arrested) for a relatively minor charge. The social "fallout" from this initial arrest may have resulted in more adverse reactions from parents (or others), and that may have made the other factors, such as delinquent peers, more prominent. What is meant by reciprocal (or feedback) effects in Thornberry's model, and how do such effects on causal factors work in such a model in contributing as both a consequential and predictive factor?
- Concepts or theoretical models that Thornberry could or should have incorporated into his integrated feedback model of crime

Toward an Interactional Theory of Delinquency

Terence P. Thornberry

Origins and Assumptions

The basic premise of the model proposed here is that human behavior occurs in social interaction and can therefore best be explained by models that focus on interactive processes. Rather than viewing adolescents as propelled along a unidirectional pathway to one or another outcome—that is, delinquency or conformity—it argues that adolescents interact with other people and institutions and that behavioral outcomes are formed by that interactive process. For example, the delinquent behavior of an adolescent is formed in part by how he and his parents *interact* over time, not simply by the child's perceived, and presumably invariant, *level* of attachment to parents. Moreover, since it is an interactive system, the behaviors of others—for example, parents and school officials—are influenced both by each other and by the adolescent, including his or her delinquent behavior. If this view is correct, then interactional effects have to be modeled explicitly if we are to understand the social and psychological processes involved with initiation into delinquency, the maintenance of such behavior, and its eventual reduction.

Interactional theory develops from the same intellectual tradition as the theories mentioned above, especially the Durkheimian tradition of social control. It asserts that the fundamental cause of delinquency lies in the weakening of social constraints over the conduct of the individual. Unlike classical control theory, however, it does not assume that the attenuation of controls leads directly to delinquency. The weakening of controls simply allows for a much wider array of behavior, including continued conventional action, failure as indicated by school dropout and sporadic employment histories, alcoholism, mental illness, delinquent and criminal careers, or some combination of these outcomes. For the freedom resulting from weakened bonds to be channeled into delinquency, especially serious prolonged delinquency, requires an interactive setting in which delinquency is learned, performed, and reinforced. This view is similar to Cullen's structuring perspective which draws attention to the [indeterminacy] of deviant behavior. "It can thus be argued that there is an *indeterminate* and not a determinate or etiologically specific relationship between motivational variables on the one hand and any particular form of deviant behavior on the other hand" (Cullen, 1984, p. 5).

Although heavily influenced by control and learning theories, and to a lesser extent by strain and culture conflict theories, this is not an effort at theoretical integration as that term is usually used (Elliott, 1985). Rather, this paper is guided by what we have elsewhere called theoretical elaboration (Thornberry, 1987a). In this instance, a basic control theory is extended, or elaborated upon, using available theoretical perspectives and empirical findings to provide a more accurate model of the causes of delinquency. In the process of elaboration, there is no requirement to resolve disputes among other theories—for example, their different assumptions about the origins of deviance (Thornberry, 1987a, pp. 15–18); all that is required is that the propositions of the model developed here be consistent with one another and with the assumptions about deviance stated above.

Organization

The presentation of the interactional model begins by identifying the central concepts to be included in the model. Next, the underlying theoretical structure of the proposed model is examined and the rationale for moving from unidirectional to reciprocal causal models is developed. The reciprocal model is then extended to include a developmental perspective, examining the theoretical saliency of different variables at different developmental stages. Finally, the influence of the person's position in the social structure is explored. Although in some senses the last issue is logically prior to the others, since it is concerned with sources of initial variation in the causal variables, it is discussed last so that the reciprocal relationships among the concepts—the heart of an interactional perspective—can be more fully developed.

Theoretical Concepts

Given these basic premises, an interactional model must respond to two overriding issues. First, how are traditional social constraints over behavior weakened and, second, once weakened, how is the resulting freedom channeled into delinquent patterns? To address these issues, the present paper presents an initial version of an interactional model, focusing on the interrelationships among six concepts: attachment to parents, commitment to school, belief in conventional values, associations with delinquent peers, adopting delinquent values, and engaging in delinquent behavior. These concepts form the core of the theoretical model since they are central to social psychological theories of delinquency and since they have been shown in numerous studies to be strongly related to subsequent delinquent behavior (see Elliott et al., 1985, Chs. 1–3, for an excellent review of this literature).

The first three derive from Hirschi's version of control theory (1969) and represent the primary mechanisms by which adolescents are bonded to conventional middle-class society. When those elements of the bond are weakened, behavioral freedom increases considerably. For that freedom to lead to delinquent behavior, however, interactive settings that reinforce delinquency are required. In the model, those settings are represented by two concepts: associations with delinquent peers and the formation of delinquent values which derive primarily from social learning theory. For the purpose of explicating the overall theoretical perspective, each of these concepts is defined quite broadly. Attachment to parents includes the affective relationship between parent and child, communication patterns, parenting skills such as monitoring and discipline, parent-child conflict, and the like. Commitment to school refers to the stake in conformity the adolescent has developed and includes such factors as success in school, perceived importance of education, attachment to teachers, and involvement in school activities. Belief in conventional values represents the granting of legitimacy to such middle-class values as education, personal industry, financial success, deferral of gratification, and the like.

Three delinquency variables are included in the model. Association with delinquent peers includes the level of attachment to peers, the delinquent behavior and values of peers, and their reinforcing reactions to the adolescent's own delinquent or conforming behavior. It is a continuous measure that can vary from groups that are heavily delinquent to those that are almost entirely nondelinquent. Delinquent values refer to the granting of legitimacy to delinquent activities as acceptable modes of behavior as well as a general willingness to violate the law to achieve other ends. Delinquent behavior, the primary outcome variable, refers to acts that place the youth at risk for adjudication; it ranges from status offenses to serious violent activities. Since the present model is an interactional one, interested not only in explaining delinquency but in explaining the effects of delinquency on other variables, particular attention is paid to prolonged involvement in serious delinquency. . . .

Model Specification

A causal model allowing for reciprocal relationships among the six concepts of interest—attachment to parents, commitment to school, belief in conventional values, association with delinquent peers, delinquent values, and delinquent behavior—is presented in Figure 1. This model refers to the period of early adolescence, from about ages 11 to 13, when delinquent careers are beginning, but prior to the period at which delinquency reaches its apex in terms of seriousness and frequency. In the following sections the model is extended to later ages.

The specification of causal effects begins by examining the three concepts that form the heart of social learning theories of delinquency—delinquent peers, delinquent values, and delinquent behavior. For now we focus on the reciprocal nature of the relationships, ignoring until later variations in the strength of the relationships. Traditional social learning theory specifies a causal order among these variables in which delinquent associations affect delinquent values and, in turn, both produce delinquent

Figure 1 • A reciprocal model of delinquent involvement at early adolescence

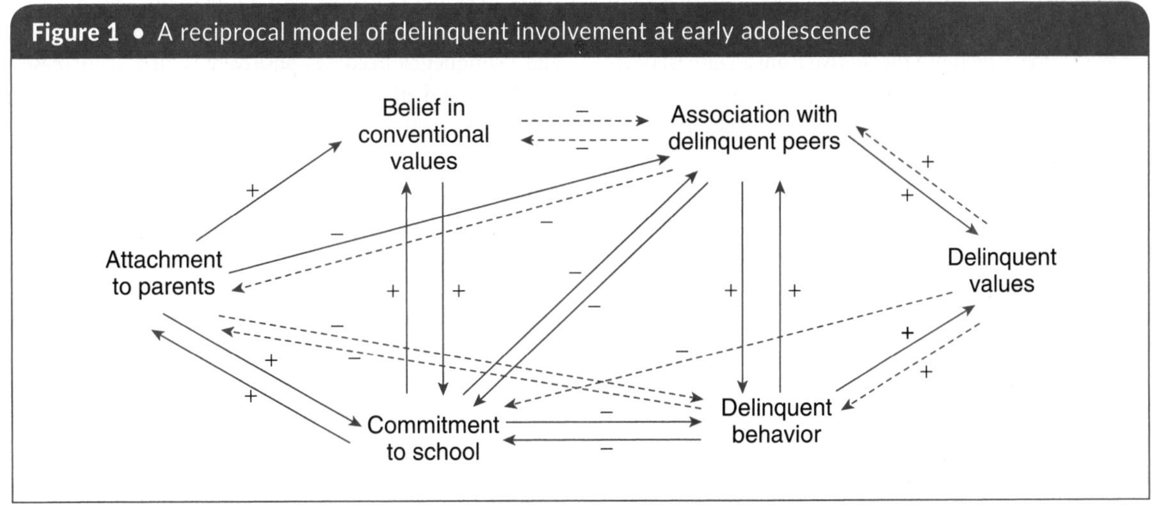

behavior (Akers, Krohn, Lanza-Kaduce, & Radosevich, 1979; Matsueda, 1982). Yet, for each of the dyadic relationships involving these variables, other theoretical perspectives and much empirical evidence suggest the appropriateness of reversing this causal order. For example, social learning theory proposes that associating with delinquents, or more precisely, people who hold and reinforce delinquent values, increases the chances of delinquent behavior (Akers, 1977). Yet, as far back as the work of the Gluecks (1950) this specification has been challenged. Arguing that "birds of a feather flock together," the Gluecks propose that youths who are delinquent seek out and associate with others who share those tendencies. From this perspective, rather than being a cause of delinquency, associations are the result of delinquents seeking out and associating with like-minded peers.

An attempt to resolve the somewhat tedious argument over the temporal priority of associations and behavior is less productive theoretically than capitalizing on the interactive nature of human behavior and treating the relationship as it probably is: a reciprocal one. People often take on the behavioral repertoire of their associates but, at the same time, they often seek out associates who share their behavioral interests. Individuals clearly behave this way in conventional settings, and there is no reason to assume that deviant activities, such as delinquency, are substantially different in this regard.

Similar arguments can be made for the other two relationships among the delinquency variables. Most recent theories of delinquency, following the lead of social learning theory, posit that delinquent associations lead to the formation of delinquent values. Subcultural theories, however, especially those that derive from a cultural deviance perspective (Miller, 1958) suggest that values precede the formation of peer groups. Indeed, it is the socialization of adolescents into the "lower-class culture" and its particular value system that leads them to associate with delinquent peers in the first place. This specification can also be derived from a social control perspective as demonstrated in Weis and Sederstrom's social development model (1981) and Burkett and Warren's social selection model (1987).

Finally, the link between delinquent values and delinquent behavior restates, in many ways, the basic social psychological question of the relationship between attitudes and behavior. Do attitudes form behavior patterns or does behavior lead to attitude formation? Social psychological research, especially in cognitive psychology and balance models (for example, Festinger, 1957; Brehm and Cohen, 1962), points to the reciprocal nature of this relationship. It suggests that people indeed behave in a manner consistent with their attitudes, but also that behavior is one of the most persuasive forces in the formation and maintenance of attitudes.

Such a view of the relationship between delinquent values and behavior is consistent with Hindelang's findings: this general pattern of results indicates that one can "predict" a respondent's self approval [of illegal behaviors] from knowledge of that respondent's involvement/non-involvement [in delinquency] with fewer errors than vice-versa (1974, p. 382). It is also consistent with recent deterrence research which demonstrates that the "experiential effect," in which behavior affects attitudes, is much stronger than the deterrent effect, in which attitudes affect behavior (Paternoster, Saltzman, Waldo, & Chiricos, 1982; Paternoster, Saltzman, Chiricos, & Waldo, 1983).

Although each of these relationships appears to be reciprocal, the predicted strengths of the associations are not of equal strength during the early adolescent period (see Figure 1). Beliefs that delinquent conduct is acceptable [and] positively valued may be emerging, but such beliefs are not fully articulated for 11- to 13-year-olds. Because of their emerging quality, they are viewed as more effect than cause, produced by delinquent behavior and associations with delinquent peers. As these values emerge, however, they have feedback effects, albeit relatively weak ones at these ages, on behavior and associations. That is, as the values become more fully articulated and delinquency becomes positively valued, it increases the likelihood of such behavior and further reinforces associations with like-minded peers.

Summary. When attention is focused on the interrelationships among associations with delinquent peers, delinquent values, and delinquent behavior, it appears that they are, in fact, reciprocally related. The world of human behavior is far more complex than a simple recursive one in which a temporal order can be imposed on interactional variables of this nature. Interactional theory sees these three concepts as embedded in a causal loop, each reinforcing the others over time. Regardless of where the individual enters the loop the following obtains: delinquency increases associations with delinquent peers and delinquent values; delinquent values increase delinquent behavior and associations with delinquent peers; and associations with delinquent peers increase delinquent behavior and delinquent values. The question now concerns the identification of factors that lead some youth, but not others, into this spiral of increasing delinquency.

Social Control Effects

As indicated at the outset of this reading, the promise of interactional theory is that the fundamental cause of delinquency is the attenuation of social controls over the person's conduct. Whenever bonds to the conventional world are substantially weakened, the individual is freed from moral constraints and is at risk for a wide array of deviant activities, including delinquency. The primary mechanisms that bind adolescents to the conventional world are attachment to parents, commitment to school, and belief in conventional values, and their role in the model can now be examined.

During the early adolescent years, the family is the most salient arena for social interaction and involvement and, because of this, attachment to parents has a stronger influence on other aspects of the youth's life at this stage than it does at later stages of development. With this in mind, attachment to parents is predicted to affect four other variables. Since youths who are attached to their parents are sensitive to their wishes (Hirschi, 1969, pp. 16–19), and, since parents are almost universally supportive of the conventional world, these children are likely to be strongly committed to school and to espouse conventional values. In addition, youths who are attached to their parents, again because of their sensitivity to parental wishes, are unlikely to associate with delinquent peers or to engage in delinquent behavior.

In brief, parental influence is seen as central to controlling the behavior of youths at these relatively early ages. Parents who have a strong affective bond with their children, who communicate with them, who exercise appropriate parenting skills, and so forth, are likely to lead their children towards conventional actions and beliefs and away from delinquent friends and actions.

On the other hand, attachment to parents is not seen as an immutable trait, impervious to the effects of other variables. Indeed, associating with delinquent peers, not being committed to school, and engaging in delinquent behavior are so contradictory to parental expectations that they tend to diminish the level of attachment between parent and child. Adolescents who fail at school, who associate with delinquent peers, and who engage in delinquent conduct are, as a consequence, likely to jeopardize their affective bond with their parents, precisely because these behaviors suggest that the "person does not care about the wishes and expectations of other people" (Hirschi, 1969, p. 18), in this instance, his or her parents.

Turning next to belief in conventional values, this concept is involved in two different causal loops. First, it strongly affects commitment to school and in turn is affected by commitment to school. In essence, this loop posits a behavioral and attitudinal consistency in the conventional realm. Second, a weaker loop is posited between belief in conventional values and associations with delinquent peers. Youths who do not grant legitimacy to conventional values are more apt to associate with delinquent friends who share those views, and those friendships are likely to attenuate further their beliefs in conventional values. This reciprocal specification is supported by Burkett and Warren's findings concerning religious beliefs and peer associations (1987). Finally, youths who believe in conventional values are seen as somewhat less likely to engage in delinquent behavior.

Although belief in conventional values plays some role in the genesis of delinquency, its impact is not particularly strong. For example, it is not affected by delinquent behavior, nor is it related to delinquent values. This is primarily because belief in conventional values appears to be quite invariant; regardless of class of origin or delinquency status, for example, most people strongly assert conventional values (Short & Strodtbeck, 1965, Ch. 3). Nevertheless, these beliefs do exert some influence in the model, especially with respect to reinforcing commitment to school.

Finally, the impact of commitment to school is considered. This variable is involved in reciprocal loops with both of the other bonding variables. Youngsters who are attached to their parents are likely to be committed to and succeed in school, and that success is likely to reinforce the close ties to their parents. Similarly, youths who believe in conventional values are likely to be committed to school, the primary arena in which they can act in accordance with those values, and, in turn, success in that arena is likely to reinforce the beliefs.

In addition to its relationships with the other control variables, commitment to school also has direct effects on two of the delinquency variables. Students who are committed to succeeding in school are unlikely to associate with delinquents or to engage in substantial amounts of serious, repetitive delinquent behavior. These youths have built up a stake in conformity and should be unwilling to jeopardize that investment by either engaging in delinquent behavior or by associating with those who do. Low commitment to school is not seen as leading directly to the formation of delinquent values, however. Its primary effect on delinquent values is indirect, via associations with delinquent peers and delinquent behavior (Conger, 1980, p. 137). While school failure may lead to a reduced commitment to conventional values, it does not follow that it directly increases the acceptance of values that support delinquency.

Commitment to school, on the other hand, is affected by each of the delinquency variables in the model. Youths who accept values that are consistent with delinquent behavior, who associate with other delinquents, and who engage in delinquent behavior are simply unlikely candidates to maintain an active commitment to school and the conventional world that school symbolizes.

Summary. Attachment to parents, commitment to school, and belief in conventional values reduce delinquency by cementing the person to conventional institutions and people. When these elements of the bond to conventional society are strong, delinquency is unlikely, but when they are weak the individual is placed at much greater risk for delinquency. When viewed from an interactional perspective, two additional qualities of these concepts become increasingly evident.

First, attachment to parents, commitment to school, and belief in conventional values are not static attributes of the person, invariant over time. These concepts interact with one another during the developmental process. For some youths the levels of attachment, commitment, and belief increase as these elements reinforce one another, while for other youths the interlocking nature of these relationships suggests a greater and greater attenuation of the bond will develop over time.

Second, the bonding variables appear to be reciprocally linked to delinquency, exerting a causal impact on associations with delinquent peers and delinquent behavior; they also are causally affected by these variables. As the youth engages in more and more delinquent conduct and increasingly associates with delinquent peers, the level of his bond to the conventional world is further weakened. Thus, while the weakening of the bond to conventional society may be an initial cause of delinquency, delinquency eventually becomes its own indirect cause precisely because of its ability to weaken further the person's bonds to family, school, and conventional beliefs. The implications of this amplifying causal structure [are] examined below. First, however, the available support for reciprocal models is reviewed and the basic model is extended to later developmental stages. . . .

Developmental Extensions

The previous section developed a strategy for addressing one of the three major limitations of delinquency theories mentioned in the introduction, namely, their unidirectional causal structure. A second limitation is the non-developmental posture of most theories which tend to provide a cross sectional picture of the factors associated with delinquency at one age, but which do not provide a rationale for understanding how delinquent behavior develops over time. The present section offers a developmental extension of the basic model.

Middle Adolescence

First, a model for middle adolescence, when the youths are approximately 15 or 16 years of age is presented (Figure 2). This period represents the highest rates of involvement in delinquency and is the reference period, either implicitly or explicitly, for most theories of delinquent involvement. Since the models for the early and middle adolescent periods have essentially the same structure and causal relationships (Figures 1 and 2), discussion focuses on the differences between them and does not repeat the rationale for individual causal effects.

Perhaps the most important difference concerns attachment to parents which is involved in relatively few strong relationships. By this point in the life cycle, the most salient variables involved in the production of delinquency are likely to be external to the home, associated with the youth's activities in school and peer networks. This specification is consistent with empirical results for

Figure 2 • A reciprocal model of delinquent involvement at middle adolescence

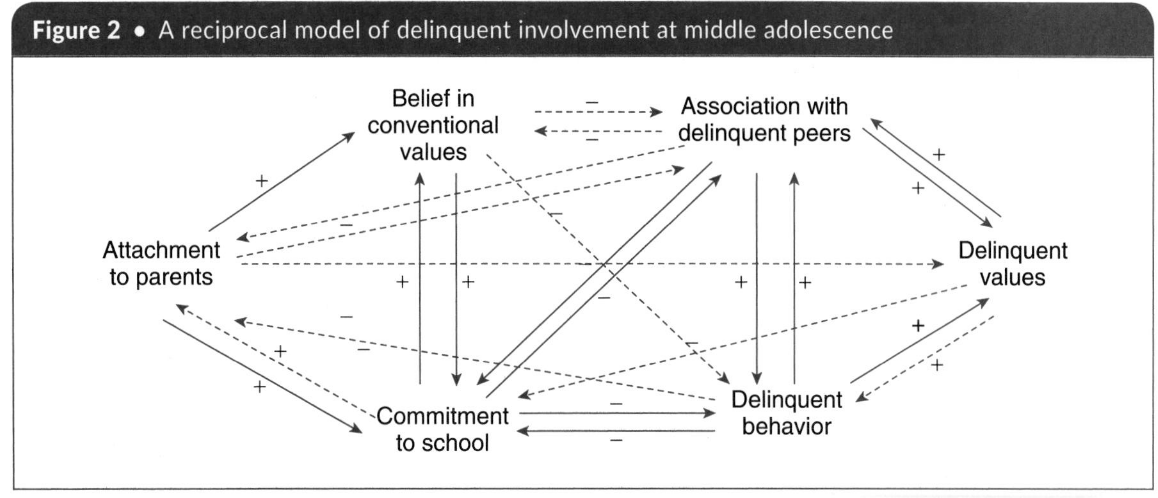

subjects in this age range (Johnson, 1979, p. 105; and Schoenberg, 1975, quoted in Johnson). Indeed, Johnson concludes that "an adolescent's public life has as much or more to do with his or her deviance or conformity than do 'under-the-roof' experiences" (1979, p. 116).

This is not to say that attachment to parents is irrelevant; such attachments are involved in enhancing commitment to school and belief in conventional values, and in preventing associations with delinquent peers. It is just that the overall strength of parental effects [is] weaker than at earlier ages when the salience of the family as a locus of interaction and control was greater. The second major change concerns the increased importance of delinquent values as a causal factor. It is still embedded in the causal loop with the other two delinquency variables, but now it is as much cause as effect. Recall that at the younger ages delinquent values were seen as emerging, produced by associations with delinquent peers and delinquent behavior. Given their emergent nature, they were not seen as primary causes of other variables. At mid-adolescence, however, when delinquency is at its apex, these values are more fully articulated and have stronger effects on other variables. First, delinquent values are seen as major reinforcers of both delinquent associations and delinquent behavior. In general, espousing values supportive of delinquency tends to increase the potency of this causal loop. Second, since delinquent values are antithetical to the conventional settings of school and family, youths who espouse them are less likely to be committed to school and attached to parents. Consistent with the reduced saliency of family at these ages, the feedback effect to school is seen as stronger than the feedback effect to parents.

By and large, the other concepts in the model play the same role at these ages as they do at the earlier ones. Thus, the major change from early to middle adolescence concerns the changing saliency of some of the theoretical concepts. The family declines in relative importance while the adolescent's own world of school and peers takes on increasing significance. While these changes occur, the overall structure of the theory remains constant. These interactive variables are still seen as mutually reinforcing over time.

Later Adolescence

Finally, the causes of delinquency during the transition from adolescence to adulthood, about ages 18 to 20, can be examined (Figure 3). At these ages one should more properly speak of crime than delinquency, but for consistency we will continue to use the term delinquency in the causal diagrams and employ the terms delinquency and crime interchangeably in the text.

Two new variables are added to the model to reflect the changing life circumstances at this stage of development. The more important of these is commitment to conventional activities which includes employment, attending college, and military service. Along with the transition to the world of work, there is a parallel

Figure 3 • A reciprocal model of delinquent involvement at later adolescence

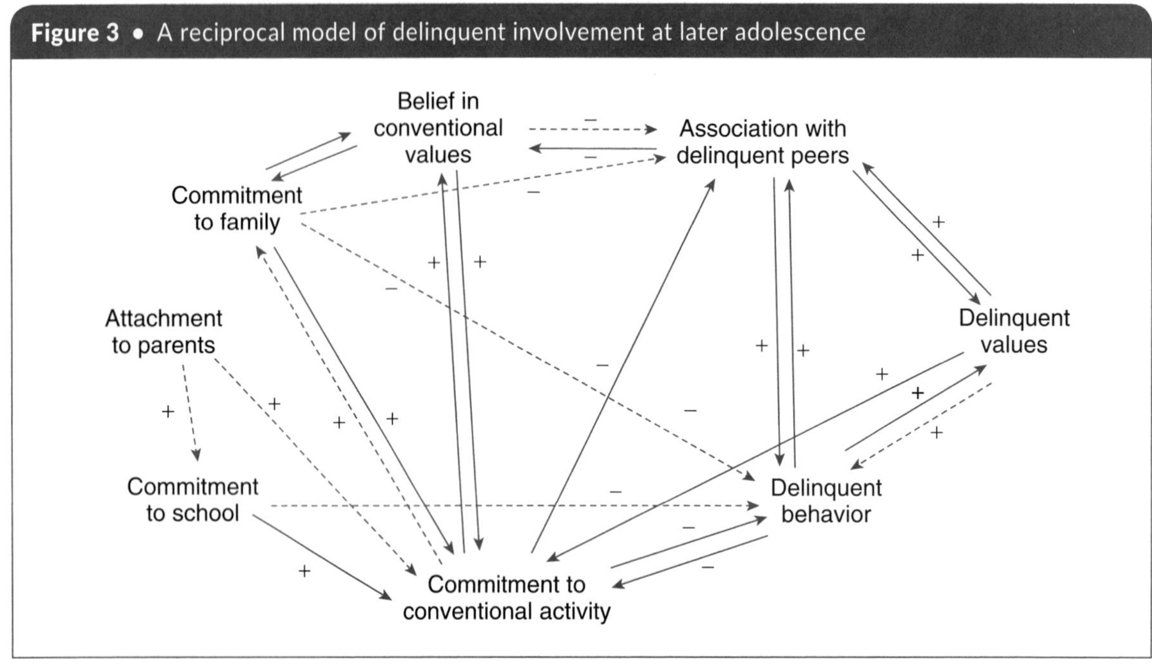

transition from the family of origin to one's own family. Although this transition does not peak until the early 20s, for many people its influence is beginning at this stage. Included in this concept are marriage, plans for marriage, and plans for childrearing. These new variables largely replace attachment to parents and commitment to school in the theoretical scheme; they represent the major sources of bonds to conventional society for young adults. Both attachment to parents and commitment to school remain in the model but take on the cast of exogenous variables. Attachment to parents has only a minor effect on commitment to school, and commitment to school is proposed to affect only commitment to conventional activities and, more weakly, delinquent behavior.

The other three variables considered in the previous models—association with delinquent peers, delinquent values, and delinquent behavior—are still hypothesized to be embedded in an amplifying causal loop. As indicated above, this loop is most likely to occur among adolescents who, at earlier ages, were freed from the controlling influence of parents and school. Moreover, via the feedback paths delinquent peers, delinquent values, and delinquent behavior further alienate the youth from parents and diminish commitment to school. Once this spiral begins, the probability of sustained delinquency increases.

This situation, if it continued uninterrupted, would yield higher and higher rates of crime as the subjects matured. Such an outcome is inconsistent with the desistance that has been observed during this age period (Wolfgang, Thornberry, and Figlio, 1987). Rates of delinquency and crime begin to subside by the late teenage years, a phenomenon often attributed to "maturational reform." Such an explanation, however, is tautological since it claims that crime stops when adolescents get older, because they get older. It is also uninformative since the concept of maturational reform is theoretically undefined. A developmental approach, however, offers an explanation for desistance. As the developmental process unfolds, life circumstances change, developmental milestones are met (or, for some, missed), new social roles are created, and new networks of attachments and commitments emerge. The effects of these changes enter the processual model to explain new and often dramatically different behavioral patterns. In the present model, these changes are represented by commitment to conventional activity and commitment to family.

Commitment to conventional activity is influenced by a number of variables, including earlier attachment to parents, commitment to school, and belief in conventional values. And once the transition to the world of work is made, tremendous opportunities are afforded for new and different effects in the delinquency model. Becoming committed to conventional activities, work, college, military service, and so on—reduces the likelihood of delinquent behavior and associations with delinquent peers because it builds up a stake in conformity that is antithetical to delinquency. Moreover, since the delinquency variables are still embedded in a causal loop, the effect of commitment to conventional activities tends to resonate throughout the system. But, because of the increased saliency of a new variable, commitment to conventional activities, the reinforcing loop is now set in motion to *reduce* rather than increase delinquent and criminal involvement. The variable of commitment to family has similar, albeit weaker, effects since the transition to the family is only beginning at these ages. Nevertheless, commitment to family is proposed to reduce both delinquent associations and delinquent values and to increase commitment to conventional activity. In general, as the individual takes on the responsibilities of family, the bond to conventional society increases, placing additional constraints on behavior and precluding further delinquency.

These changes do not occur in all cases, however, nor should they be expected to since many delinquents continue on to careers in adult crime. In the Philadelphia cohort of 1945, 51% of the juvenile delinquents were also adult offenders, and the more serious and prolonged the delinquent careers were, the greater the odds of an adult career (Wolfgang et al., 1987, Ch. 4). The continuation of criminal careers can also be explained by the nature of the reciprocal effects included in this model. In general, extensive involvement in delinquency at earlier ages feeds back upon and weakens attachment to parents and commitment to school (see Figures 1 and 2). These variables, as well as involvement in delinquency itself, weaken later commitment to family and to conventional activities (Figure 3). Thus, these new variables, commitment to conventional activities and to family, are affected by the person's situation at earlier stages and do not "automatically" alter the probability of continued criminal involvement. If the initial bonds are extremely weak, the chances of new bonding variables being established to break the cycle towards criminal careers are low and it is likely that criminal behavior will continue. . . .

Structural Effects

Structural variables, including race, class, sex, and community of residence, refer to the person's location in the structure of social roles and statuses. The manner in which they are incorporated in the interactional model is illustrated here by examining only one of them, social class of origin. Although social class is often measured continuously, a categorical approach is more consistent with the present model and with most theories of delinquency that incorporate class as a major explanatory variable—for example, strain and social disorganization theories. For our purposes, the most important categories are the lower class, the working lower class, and the middle class.

The lower class is composed of those who are chronically or sporadically unemployed, receive welfare, and subsist at or below the poverty level. They are similar to Johnson's "underclass" (1979). The working lower class is composed of those with more stable work patterns, training for semiskilled jobs, and incomes that allow for some economic stability. For these families, however, the hold on even a marginal level of occupational and economic security is always tenuous. Finally, the middle class refers to all families above these lower levels. Middle-class families have achieved some degree of economic success and stability and can reasonably expect to remain at that level or improve their standing over time.

The manner in which the social class of origin affects the interactional variables and the behavioral trajectories can be demonstrated by comparing the life expectancies of children from lower- and middle-class families. As compared to children from a middle-class background, children from a lower class background are more apt to have (1) disrupted family processes and environments (Conger, McCarty, Wang, Lahey, & Kroop, 1984; Wahler, 1980); (2) poorer preparation for school (Cloward and Ohlin, 1960); (3) belief structures influenced by the traditions of the American lower class (Miller, 1958); and (4) greater exposure to neighborhoods with high rates of crime (Shaw & McKay, 1942; Braithwaite, 1981). The direction of all these effects is such that we would expect children from lower-class families to be initially less bonded to conventional society and more exposed to delinquent values, friends, and behaviors.

As one moves towards the working lower class, both the likelihood and the potency of the factors just listed decrease. As a result, the initial values of the interactional variables improve but, because of the tenuous nature of economic and social stability for these families, both the bonding variables and the delinquency variables are still apt to lead to considerable amounts of delinquent conduct. Finally, youths from middle-class families, given their greater stability and economic security, are likely to start with a stronger family structure, greater stakes in conformity, and higher chances of success, and all of these factors are likely to reduce the likelihood of initial delinquent involvement.

In brief, the initial values of the interactional variables are systematically related to the social class of origin. Moreover, since these variables are reciprocally related, it follows logically that social class is systematically related to the behavioral trajectories described above. Youngsters from the lowest classes have the highest probability of moving forward on a trajectory of increasing delinquency. Starting from a position of low bonding to conventional institutions and a high delinquency environment, the reciprocal nature of the interrelationships leads inexorably towards extremely high rates of delinquent and criminal involvement. Such a view is consistent with prevalence data which show that by age 18, 50%, and by age 30, 70% of low SES minority males have an official police record (Wolfgang et al., 1987).

On the other hand, the expected trajectory of middle-class youths suggests that they will move toward an essentially conforming lifestyle, in which their stakes in conformity increase and more and more preclude serious and prolonged involvement in delinquency. Finally, because the initial values of the interactional variables are mixed and indecisive for children from lower working-class homes, their behavioral trajectories are much more volatile and the outcome much less certain.

Summary. Interactional theory asserts that both the initial values of the process variables and their development over time are systematically related to the social class of origin. Moreover, parallel arguments can be made for other structural variables, especially those associated with class, such as race, ethnicity, and the social disorganization of the neighborhood. Like class of origin, these variables are systematically related to variables such as commitment to school and involvement in delinquent behavior, and therefore, as a group, these structural variables set the stage on which the reciprocal effects develop across the life cycle....

References

Akers, R. (1977). *Deviant behavior: A social learning perspective.* Belmont, CA: Wadsworth.

Akers, R. L., Krohn, M. D., Lanza-Kaduce, L., & Radosevich, M. (1979). Social learning theory and deviant behavior. *American Sociological Review, 44,* 635–655.

Braithwaite, J. (1981). The myth of social class and criminality reconsidered. *American Sociological Review, 46,* 36–58.

Brehm, J. W., & Cohen, A. R. (1962). *Explorations in cognitive dissonance.* New York: Wiley.

Burkett, S. R., & Warren, B. O. (1987). Religiosity, peer influence, and adolescent marijuana use: A panel study of underlying causal structures. *Criminology, 25,* 109–131.

Cloward, R. A., & Ohlin, L. E. (1960). *Delinquency and opportunity—A theory of delinquent gangs.* New York: Free Press.

Conger, R. D. (1980). Juvenile delinquency: Behavior restraint or behavior facilitation? In T. Hirschi & M. Gottfredson (Eds.), *Understanding crime.* Beverly Hills, CA: Sage.

Conger, R. D., McCarty, J. A., Wang, R. K., Lahey, B. B., & Kroop, J. P. (1984). Perception of child, child-rearing values, and emotional distress as mediating links between environmental stressors and observed maternal behavior. *Child Development, 55,* 2234–2247.

Cullen, F. T. (1984). *Rethinking crime and deviance theory: The emergence of a structuring tradition.* Totowa, NJ: Rowman and Allanheld.

Elliott, D. S. (1985). The assumption that theories can be combined with increased explanatory power: Theoretical integrations. In R. F. Meier (Ed.), *Theoretical methods in criminology.* Beverly Hills, CA: Sage.

Elliott, D. S., Huizinga, D., & Ageton, S. S. (1985). *Explaining delinquency and drug use.* Beverly Hills, CA: Sage.

Festinger, L. (1957). *A theory of cognitive dissonance.* Stanford, CA: Stanford University Press.

Glueck, S., & Glueck, E. (1950). *Unraveling juvenile delinquency.* Cambridge, MA: Harvard University Press.

Hindelang, M. J. (1974). Moral evaluations of illegal behaviors. *Social Problems, 21,* 370–384.

Hirschi, T. (1969). Causes of delinquency. Berkeley: University of California Press.

Johnson, R. E. (1979). *Juvenile delinquency and its origins.* Cambridge, UK: Cambridge University Press.

Matsueda, R. (1982). Testing social control theory and differential association. *American Sociological Review, 47,* 489–504.

Miller, W. B. (1958). Lower class culture as a generating milieu of gang delinquency. *Journal of Social Issues, 14*(3), 5–19.

Paternoster, R., Saltzman, L. E., Chiricos, T. G., & Waldo, G. P. (1983). Perceived risk and social control: Do sanctions really deter? *Law and Society Review, 17,* 457–479.

Paternoster, R., Saltzman, L. E., Waldo, G. P., & Chiricos, T. G. (1982). Perceived risk and deterrence: Methodological artifacts in perceptual deterrence research. *Journal of Criminal Law and Criminology, 73,* 1238–1258.

Shaw, C., & McKay, H. D. (1942). *Juvenile delinquency and urban areas.* Chicago: University of Chicago Press.

Short, J. F., Jr., & Strodtbeck, F. L. (1965). *Group process and gang delinquency.* Chicago: University of Chicago Press.

Thornberry, T. P. (1987a). *Reflections on the advantages and disadvantages of theoretical integration.* Paper presented at the Albany Conference on Theoretical Integration in the Study of Crime and Deviance.

Thornberry, T. P. (1987b). Towards an interactional theory of delinquency. *Criminology, 25,* 863–891.

Wahler, R. (1980). The insular mother: Her problems in parent-child treatment. *Journal of Applied Behavior Analysis, 13,* 207–219.

Weis, J. G., & Sederstrom, J. (1981). *The prevention of serious delinquency: What to do?* Washington, DC: U.S. Department of Justice.

Wolfgang, M. E., Thornberry, T. P., & Figlio, R. M. (1987). *From boy to man—From delinquency to crime: Followup to the Philadelphia Birth Cohort of 1945.* Chicago: University of Chicago Press.

REVIEW QUESTIONS

1. Explain what is meant by reciprocal (or feedback) effects. Use a noncrime example to explain such effects.
2. Can you think of concepts or theoretical models other than labeling that Thornberry could or should have incorporated into his integrated model of crime? Explain your rationale for including such concepts or models.
3. Using your own life, or others you know, give an example of someone who follows the causal model proposed by Thornberry. If you can't come up with one, explore the media for someone who does.

Glossary

***actus reus*:** In legal terms, this is whether the offender actually engaged in a given criminal act. This concept can be contrasted with *mens rea,* which is a concept regarding whether the offender had the intent to commit a given act. This concept is important, especially in situations in which juveniles or mentally disabled individuals engage in offending.

adaptations to strain: As proposed by Robert Merton, these are the five ways that individuals deal with feelings of strain; see *conformity, innovation, rebellion, retreatism,* and *ritualism*.

adolescence-limited offenders: These types of offenders are labeled in Terrie Moffitt's developmental theory; such offenders commit crimes only during adolescence and desist from offending once they reach their 20s or adulthood.

adoption studies: Adoption studies examine the criminality of adoptees as compared to the criminality of their biological and adoptive parents; such studies consistently show that biological parents have more influence on children's criminal behavior than the adoptive parents who raised them.

Age of Enlightenment: This was a period of the late 17th to 18th century in which philosophers and scholars began to emphasize the rights of individuals in society. This movement emphasized the rights of individuals to have a voice in their government and to exercise free choice; it also included the idea of the social contract and other important assumptions that influenced our current government and criminal justice system.

anomie: This is a concept originally proposed by Émile Durkheim, which meant "normlessness" or the chaos that takes place when a society (e.g., economic structure) changes very rapidly. This concept was later used by Robert Merton in his strain theory of crime, where he redefined it as a disjunction between the emphasis placed on conventional goals and the conventional means used to achieve such goals.

atavism: This is the belief that certain characteristics or behaviors of a person are a throwback to an earlier stage of evolutionary development.

autonomic nervous system (ANS): This is the portion of the nervous system that consists of our anxiety levels, such as the fight or flight response, as well as our involuntary motor activities (e.g., heart rate). Studies consistently show that lower levels of ANS functioning are linked to criminality.

bourgeoisie: This is a class or status that Karl Marx assigned to the dominant, oppressing owners of production, who are considered the elite class due to ownership of companies, factories, and so on. Marx proposed that this group created and implemented laws that helped retain the dominance of this class over the proletariat or working class.

Braithwaite's reintegrative shaming theory: This integrated theoretical model merges constructs and principles from several theories, primarily social control or bonding theory and labeling theory with elements of strain theory, subculture or gang theory, and differential association theory.

brutalization effect: This is the predicted tendency of homicides to increase after an execution, particularly after high-profile executions.

central nervous system (CNS): This is the portion of the nervous system that largely consists of the brain and spinal column and is responsible for our voluntary motor activities; studies consistently show that low functioning of the CNS (e.g., slower brain wave patterns) is linked to criminal behavior.

cerebrotonic: This is the type of temperament or personality associated with an ectomorphic (thin) body type; these people tend to be introverted and shy.

certainty of punishment: Certainty of punishment is one of the key elements of deterrence; the assumption is that when people commit a crime, they will perceive a high likelihood of being caught and punished.

Chicago School of Criminology: This is a theoretical framework of criminal behavior that is often referred to as the Ecological School or the theory of social disorganization; it emphasizes the environmental impact of living in a high-crime neighborhood and asserts that this increases criminal activity. This model applies ecological principles of invasion, domination, and succession in explaining how cities grow and the implications this has on crime rates. Also, this model emphasizes the level of organization (or lack thereof) in explaining crime rates in a given neighborhood.

classical conditioning: This is a learning model that assumes that animals as well as people learn through associations between stimuli and responses; this model was primarily promoted by Ivan Pavlov.

Classical School: The Classical School of criminological theory is a perspective that is considered the first rational model of crime, one that was based on logic rather than supernatural or demonic factors. It assumes that crime occurs after a rational individual mentally weighs the potential good and bad consequences of crime and then makes a decision about whether or not to engage in a given behavior. This model is directly tied to the formation of deterrence theory and assumes that people have free will to control their behavior

clearance rate: This is the percentage of crimes reported to police that result in an arrest or an identification of a suspect who cannot be apprehended (due to death of suspect, or fleeing, etc.). In other words, the authorities essentially have a very good idea of who committed the crime, so it is considered "solved." The clearance rate can be seen as a rough estimate of the rate at which crimes are solved.

collective conscience: According to Émile Durkheim, this is the extent of similarities or likeness that people in a society share. The theory assumes that the stronger the collective conscience, the less crime in that community.

college boy: This is a type of lower-class male youth identified by Albert Cohen who has experienced the same strains and status frustration as his peers but responds to his disadvantaged situation by dedicating himself to overcoming the odds and competing in the middle-class schools despite his unlikely chances for success.

communitarianism: This is a concept in John Braithwaite's theory of reintegration, which is a macro-level measure of the degree to which the individuals are connected or interdependent on mainstream society (via organizations or groups).

conceptual integration: This is a type of theoretical integration in which a theoretical perspective consumes or uses concepts from many other theoretical models.

concordance rates: Concordance rates are rates at which twin pairs either share a trait (e.g., criminality) or the lack of the trait. For example, either both twins are criminal or neither is criminal; discordant would be if one of the pair is criminal, and the other is not.

conflict gangs: This is a type of gang identified by Richard Cloward and Lloyd Ohlin that tends to develop in neighborhoods with weak stability and little or no organization. Gangs are typically relatively disorganized and lack the skills and knowledge to make a profit through criminal activity; thus, their primary illegal activity is violence, which is used to gain prominence and respect among themselves and the neighborhood.

conflict theories: These are theories of criminal behavior that assume that most people disagree on what the law should be and/or that law is used as a tool by those in power to keep down other groups.

conformity: In strain theory, this is an adaptation to strain in which an individual buys into the conventional means of success and also buys into the conventional goals.

consensual perspective: Consensual perspective encompasses theories that assume virtually everyone is in agreement on the laws and therefore assume no conflict in attitudes regarding the laws/rules of society.

containment theory: Containment theory is a control theory proposed by Walter Reckless in the 1960s. It presented a model that emphasized internal and social pressures to commit crime, which range from personality predispositions to peer influences as well as internal and external constraints, ranging from personal self-control to parental control, that determine whether an individual will engage in criminal activity. This theory is often criticized as being too vague or general, but it advanced criminological theory by providing a framework in which many internal and external factors were emphasized.

control–balance theory: An integrated theory originally presented by Charles Tittle, it assumes that the amount of control to which one is subjected, as compared to the amount of control that one can exercise, determines the probability of deviant behavior and the types of deviance that are committed by that individual. In other words, the balance or imbalance between these two types of control can predict the amount and type of behavior likely to be committed.

control theories: These are a group of theories of criminal behavior that emphasize the assumption that humans are born selfish and have tendencies to be aggressive and offend and that individuals must be controlled typically by socialization and discipline or from internalized self-control that has been developed in their upbringing.

corner boy: This is a type of lower-class male youth identified by Albert Cohen who has experienced the same strains and status frustration as others but responds to his disadvantaged situation by accepting his place in society as someone who will somewhat passively make the best of life at the bottom of the social order. As the label describes, they often "hang out" on corners.

correlation, or covariation: This is a criterion of causality that requires a change in a predictor variable (*X*) to be consistently associated with some change (either positive or negative) in the explanatory variable (*Y*). An example would be unemployment (*X*) being related to criminal activity (*Y*).

craniometry: This is the field of study that emphasized the belief that the size of the brain or skull reflected superiority or inferiority, with larger brains or skulls being considered superior.

criminal gangs: This is a type of gang identified by Richard Cloward and Lloyd Ohlin that forms in lower-class neighborhoods with an organized structure of adult criminal behavior. Such neighborhoods are so organized and stable that their criminal networks are often known and accepted by the conventional citizens. In these neighborhoods, the adult gangsters mentor neighborhood youth and take them under their wing. Such gangs tend to be highly organized and stable.

criminology: Criminology is the scientific study of crime and the reasons why people engage (or don't engage) in criminal behavior as well as the study of why certain trends occur or groups of people seem to engage in criminal behavior more than others.

cross-sectional studies: This is a form of research design modeling in which a collection of data is taken at one point in time (often in survey format).

cultural and subcultural theories: This is a perspective of criminal offending that assumes that many offenders believe in a normative system that is distinctly different than, and often at odds with, the norms accepted by conventional society.

cytogenetic studies: These are studies of crime that focus on the genetic makeup of individuals, having a specific focus on abnormalities in their chromosomal makeup. An example is XYY instead of the normal XX (females) and normal XY (males).

dark figure: This is the vast majority of major crime incidents that never get reported to police due to the failure of victims to file a police report; covers most criminal offending, with the exception of homicide and motor vehicle theft, which are almost always reported to police.

decriminalization: This is a policy related to labeling theory, which proposes less harsh punishments for some minor offenses, such as the possession of small amounts of marijuana; for example, in California, an offender gets a ticket or fine for this offense rather than being officially charged and prosecuted.

deinstitutionalization: This is a policy related to labeling theory. It proposes that juveniles or those accused of relatively minor offenses should not be locked up in jail or prison.

delinquent boy: Identified by Albert Cohen, this is a type of lower-class male youth who responds to strains and status frustration by joining with similar others in a group to commit a crime.

determinism: Determinism is the assumption that human behavior is caused by factors outside of free will and rational decision making (e.g., biology, peer influence, poverty, bad parenting). It is the distinctive, primary assumption of positivism (as opposed to the Classical School of criminological theory, which assumes free will/free choice).

deterrence theory: The theory of crime associated with the Classical School, it proposes that individuals will make rational decisions regarding their behavior. This theory focuses on three concepts: the individual's perception of (1) swiftness of punishment, (2) certainty of punishment, and (3) severity of punishment.

developmental theories: Developmental theories are perspectives of criminal behavior that are also to some extent integrated but are distinguished by their emphasis on the evolution of individuals' criminality over time. Specifically, developmental theories tend to look at the individual as the unit of analysis, and such models focus on the various aspects of the onset, frequency, intensity, duration, desistence, and other aspects of the individual's criminal career.

deviance: Deviance involves behaviors that are not normal. It includes many illegal acts as well as activities that are not necessarily criminal but are unusual and often violate social norms, such as burping loudly at a formal dinner or wearing inappropriate clothing.

differential association theory: This is a theory of criminal behavior that emphasizes the association with significant others (peers, parents, etc.) in learning criminal behavior. This theory was originally presented by Edwin Sutherland.

differential identification theory: This is a theory of criminal behavior that is very similar to differential association theory; the major difference is that differential identification theory takes into account associations with persons or images that are presented in the media (e.g., movies, TV, sports). This model was originally proposed by Daniel Glaser.

differential reinforcement theory: This is a theory of criminal behavior that emphasizes various types of social learning, specifically classical conditioning, operant conditioning, and imitation or modeling. This theory was originally presented by Robert Burgess and Ronald Akers and is one of the most supported theories according to empirical studies.

diversion: Diversion is a set of policies related to labeling theory that attempt to get an offender out of the formal justice system as quickly as possible; an offender might perform a service or enter a rehabilitation program instead of serving time in jail or prison. Often, if an offender successfully completes the contract, the official charge or conviction for the crime is expunged or eliminated from the official record.

dizygotic (DZ) twins: Also referred to as fraternal or nonidentical twins, these are twin pairs that come from two separate eggs (zygotes) and thus share only 50% of the genetic makeup that can vary.

dopamine: This is a neurotransmitter that is largely responsible for "good feelings" in the brain; it is increased by many illicit drugs (e.g., cocaine).

dramatization of evil: A concept proposed by Frank Tannenbaum in relation to labeling theory, it states that often when relatively minor laws are broken, the community tends to overreact and make a rather large deal out of it ("dramatizing" it). A good example is when a very young offender sprays graffiti on a street sign, and the neighborhood ostracizes that youth.

drift theory: This is a theory of criminal behavior in which the lack of social controls in the teenage years allows for individuals to experiment in various criminal offending, often due to peer influence, without the individuals buying into a criminal lifestyle; this theory was introduced by David Matza.

early onset: This is a key criterion that developmental researchers use as a vital predictor of which individuals are most likely to become chronic, persistent offenders throughout life; despite this criterion varying by study or offense, most researchers mark early onset as an arrest occurring before age 14.

Ecological School: See *Chicago School of Criminology*.

ectoderm: This is a medical term for the outer layer of tissue in our bodies (e.g., skin, nervous system).

ectomorphic: This is the type of body shape associated with an emphasis on the outer layer of tissue (ectoderm) during development; these people are disposed to be thin.

ego: This is the only conscious domain of the psyche; according to Sigmund Freud, it functions to mediate the battle between id and superego.

Elliott's integrated model: This is perhaps the first major integrated perspective proposed that clearly attempted to merge various traditionally separate theories of crime. Delbert Elliott's integrated framework attempts to merge strain, social disorganization, control, and social learning or differential association–reinforcement perspectives for the purpose of explaining delinquency, particularly in terms of drug use, as well as other forms of deviant behavior.

empirical validity: This refers to the extent to which a theoretical model is supported by scientific research. Empirical research has consistently supported a number of theories and consistently refuted others.

endoderm: This is the medical term for the inner layer of tissue in our bodies (e.g., digestive organs).

endomorphic: This is the type of body shape associated with an emphasis on the inner layer of tissue (endoderm) during development. These people are disposed to be obese.

end-to-end (or sequential) integration: This is a type of theoretical integration that conveys the linkage of the theories based on the temporal ordering of two or more theories in their causal timing. This means that one theory (or concepts from one theory) precedes another theory (or concepts from another theory) in terms of causal ordering or timing.

equivalency hypothesis: This is a "mirror-image" tendency, which is the observed phenomenon that virtually all studies have shown. The characteristics, such as young, male, urban, poor, or minority, tend to have the highest rates of criminal offending *and* the highest rates of victimization. One important exception is, namely, lower-class offenders tend to have higher rates of theft against middle- to upper-class households/individuals.

eugenics: This is the study of and policies related to the improvement of the human race via discriminatory control over reproduction.

experiential effect: This is the extent to which individuals' previous experience has an effect on their perceptions of how certain or severe criminal punishment will be when they are deciding whether or not to offend again.

family studies: Studies that examine the clustering of criminality in a given family.

feeblemindedness: This was a technical, scientific term in the early 1900s meaning those who had significantly below average levels of intelligence.

focal concerns: This is the primary concept of Walter Miller's theory, which asserts that all members of the lower class focus on a number of concepts they deem important: fate, autonomy, trouble, toughness, excitement, and smartness.

formal controls: These are factors that involve the official aspects of criminal justice, such as police, courts, and corrections (e.g., prisons, parole, probation)

frontal lobes: This is a region of the brain that is, as its name suggests, located in the frontal portion of the brain; most of the "executive functions" of the brain, such as problem solving, take place here, so it is perhaps the most vital portion of the brain and what makes us human.

general deterrence: Punishments given to an individual that are meant to prevent or deter other potential offenders from engaging in such criminal activity in the future.

general strain theory: Although derived from traditional strain theory, this theoretical framework assumes that people of all social classes and economic positions deal with frustrations in routine daily life to which virtually everyone can relate; it includes more sources of strain than traditional strain theory.

Hagan's power–control theory: This integrated theory deals with the influence of familial control and how this relates to criminality across gender; the primary focus of this theory is on the level of patriarchal attitudes and structure in the household, which are influenced by parental positions in the workforce.

hot spots: These are specific locations, such as businesses, residences, or parks, that experience a high concentration of crime incidents. This is a key concept in routine activities theory.

hypotheses: Hypotheses are specific predictions that are based on a scientific theoretical framework and tested via observation.

id: This is a subconscious domain of the psyche, according to Sigmund Freud, with which we are all born; it is responsible for our innate desires and drives (such as libido [sex drive]); it battles the moral conscience of the superego.

index offenses: Also known as Part I offenses, according to the Federal Bureau of Investigation (FBI) Uniform Crime Report (UCR), these are eight common offenses: murder, forcible rape, aggravated assault, robbery, burglary, motor vehicle theft, larceny, and arson. All reports of these crimes, even when they do not result in an arrest, are recorded to estimate crime in the nation and various states or regions.

informal controls: Informal controls are factors like family, church, or friends that do not involve official aspects of criminal justice, such as police, courts, and corrections (e.g., prisons).

innovation: In strain theory, this is an adaptation to strain in which an individual buys into the conventional goals of success but does not buy into the conventional means for getting to the goals.

integrated theories: Integrated theories combine two or more traditional theories into one combined model.

interdependency: A concept in John Braithwaite's theory of reintegration, it is a micro-level measure of the degree to which the individuals are connected or interdependent on mainstream society (via organizations or groups).

interracial: This is a description of when an occurrence (such as a crime event) involves people of a different race or ethnicity, such as a White person committing crime against a Black person.

intraracial: This is when an occurrence (such as a crime event) involves people of the same race or ethnicity, such as a White person committing crime against another White person.

labeling theory: Labeling theory is a theoretical perspective that assumes that criminal behavior increases because certain individuals are caught and labeled as offenders; their offending increases because they have been stigmatized as "offenders." Most versions of this perspective also assume that certain people (e.g., lower class or minorities) are more likely to be caught and punished. Another assumption of most versions is that if such labeling did not occur, the behavior would stop; this assumption led to numerous policy implications, such as diversion, decriminalization, and deinstitutionalization.

lambda (offender frequency): The Greek letter lambda is used by developmental perspective researchers to denote offending frequency by one individual or an average offending rate by a group of offenders, typically over the period of 1 year; the estimate of lambda ranges drastically across estimates for different individuals or groups, especially regarding the type of offense and whether based on self-reports or official data.

learning theories: Learning theories are theoretical models that assume criminal behavior of individuals due to a process of learning from others the motivations and techniques for engaging in such behavior. Virtually all of the variations of the learning perspective propose that the processes involved in a person learning how and why to commit crimes are the same as those involved in learning to engage in conventional activities (e.g., riding a bike, playing basketball).

legalistic approach: A way of defining behaviors as crime, it includes only acts that are specifically against the legal codes of a given jurisdiction. The problem with such a definition is that what is a crime in one jurisdiction is not necessarily a crime in other jurisdictions.

life-course-persistent offenders: These types of offenders, as labeled by Terrie Moffitt's developmental theory, start offending early and persist in offending through adulthood.

logical consistency: This refers to the extent to which concepts and propositions of a theoretical model make sense both in terms of face value and regarding the extent to which the model is consistent with what is readily known about crime rates or trends.

macro level of analysis: These are theories that focus on group or aggregated scores and measures as the unit of analysis, as opposed to individual rates.

***mala in se*:** These are acts that are considered inherently evil and that virtually all societies consider to be serious crimes; an example is murder.

***mala prohibita*:** These are the many acts that are considered crimes primarily because they have been declared bad by the legal codes in that jurisdiction. In other places and times, they are not illegal; examples are gambling, prostitution, and drug usage.

mechanical societies: In Émile Durkheim's theory, these societies were rather primitive with a simple distribution of labor (e.g., hunters and gatherers) and thus a high level of agreement regarding social norms and rules because nearly everyone is engaged in the same roles.

***mens rea*:** In legal terms, this means "guilty mind" or intent. This concept involves whether or not offenders actually knew what they were doing and meant to do it.

mesoderm: This is the medical term for the middle layer of tissue in our bodies (e.g., muscles, tendons, bone structure).

mesomorphic: This is the type of body shape associated with an emphasis on the middle layer of tissue (mesoderm) during development. These people are disposed to be athletic or muscular.

micro level of analysis: This encompasses theories that focus on individual scores and measures as the unit of analysis, as opposed to group or aggregate rates.

minor physical anomalies (MPAs): MPAs are physical features, such as asymmetrical or low-seated ears, which are believed to indicate developmental problems—typically problems in the prenatal stage in the womb.

modeling and imitation: A major factor in differential reinforcement theory, modeling and imitation propose that much social learning takes place via imitation or modeling of behavior; for example, when adults or parents say "bad" words, their children begin using those words.

Moffitt's developmental theory (taxonomy): In this theoretical perspective proposed by Terrie Moffitt, criminal behavior is believed to be caused by two different causal paths: (1) adolescence-limited offenders commit their crimes during their teenage years due to peer pressure, whereas (2) life-course-persistent offenders commit antisocial behavior throughout life, starting very early and continuing on throughout their lives, because of the interaction between their neuropsychological deficits and criminogenic environments in their upbringing.

monozygotic (MZ) twins: Also referred to as identical twins, these are twin pairs that come from a single egg (zygote) and thus share 100% of their genetic makeup.

National Crime Victimization Survey (NCVS): The NCVS is one of the primary measures of crime in the United States collected by the U.S. Department of Justice (DOJ) and the U.S. Census Bureau based on interviews with victims of crime. This measure started in the early 1970s.

natural areas: This is the Chicago School's idea that all cities naturally contain identifiable clusters, such as a Chinatown or Little Italy, and neighborhoods that have low or high crime rates.

negative punishment: This is a concept in social learning in which people are given a punishment by removing something that they enjoy or like (e.g., taking away driving privileges for a teenager).

negative reinforcement: This is a concept in social learning in which people are given a reward by removing something that they dislike (e.g., not being on curfew or not having to do their "chores").

Neoclassical School: The Neoclassical School of criminological theory is virtually identical to the Classical School (both assume free will, rationality, the social contract, deterrence, etc.) except that it assumes that aggravating and mitigating circumstances should be taken into account for purposes of sentencing or punishing an offender.

neurotransmitters: These are nervous system chemicals in the brain and body that help transmit electric signals from one neuron to another, thus allowing healthy communication in the brain and to the body.

neutralization theory: This is a theory of criminal behavior that emphasizes the excuses or neutralization techniques that are used by offenders to alleviate their guilt or to excuse their behavior, when they know that their behavior is immoral; this theory was originally presented by Gresham Sykes and David Matza. In their theory, they presented five key "techniques"—ways that offenders alleviate their guilt or excuse their behavior, which they know is wrong; since they presented this idea in the 1960s, other techniques have been added, especially regarding white-collar crime.

nonindex offenses: Also known as Part II offenses, these are more than two dozen crimes that are considered relatively less serious than index crimes and must result in an arrest to be recorded by the Federal Bureau of Investigation (FBI). Therefore, the data on such results are far less reliable because the vast majority of reports of these crimes do not result in an arrest and are not in the annual FBI report.

operant conditioning: This is the learning model that takes place in organisms (such as humans) based on association between an action and feedback that occurs after it has taken place; for example, a rat running a maze can be trained to run the maze faster based on rewards (reinforcement), such as cheese, as well as punishments, such as electric shocks; introduced and promoted by B. F. Skinner.

organic societies: In the Durkheimian model, those societies have a high division of labor and thus a low level of agreement about societal norms, largely because everyone has such different roles in society, leading to very different attitudes about the rules and norms of behavior.

paradigms: A unique perspective of a phenomenon, it has an essential set of assumptions that significantly oppose those of other existing paradigms or explanations of the same phenomenon.

parsimony: Essentially meaning "simple," this is a characteristic of a good theory, meaning that it explains a certain phenomenon, in our case criminal behavior, with the fewest possible propositions or concepts.

phenotype: A phenotype is an observed manifestation of the interaction of genotypical traits with the environment, such as height (which depends largely on genetic disposition and diet, as exhibited by Asians or Mexicans who are raised in the United States and thus grow taller).

phrenology: This is the science of determining human dispositions based on distinctions (e.g., bumps) in the skull, which was believed to conform to the shape of the brain.

physiognomy: This is the study of facial and other bodily aspects to identify developmental problems, such as criminality.

pluralistic (conflict) perspective: This is a theoretical assumption that instead of one dominant and other inferior groups in society, there are a variety of groups that lobby and compete to influence changes in law; most are linked to George Vold's theoretical model.

policy implications: Policy implications are the extent to which a theory can be used to inform authorities about how to address a given phenomenon—in this case, ways to help law enforcement, court, and prison officials reduce crime or recidivism.

positive punishment: Positive punishment is a concept in social learning in which an individual is given a punishment by doing something he or she dislikes (e.g., spanking, sending to time-out, grounding).

positive reinforcement: Positive reinforcement is a concept in social learning in which an individual is given a reward by providing something he or she likes (e.g., money, curfew extended).

Positive School: The Positive School of criminological theory is a perspective that assumes individuals have no free will to control their behavior. Rather, the theories of the Positive School assume that criminal behavior is "determined" by factors outside of free choices made by the individual, such as peers, bad parenting, poverty, or biology.

power–control theory: Power–control theory is an integrated theory of crime that assumes that in households where the mother and father have relatively similar levels of power at work (i.e., balanced households), the mothers will be less likely to exert control on their daughters. These balanced households will be less likely to experience gender differences in the criminal offending of their children. However, households in which mothers and fathers have dissimilar levels of power in the workplace (i.e., unbalanced households) are more likely to suppress criminal activity in daughters, but more criminal activity is likely in the boys of the household.

primary deviance: A concept in labeling theory originally presented by Edwin Lemert, this is the type of minor, infrequent offending that people commit before they are caught and labeled as offenders. Most normal individuals commit this type of offending due to peer pressure and normal social behavior in their teenage years.

proletariat: In Karl Marx's conflict theory, the proletariat is the oppressed group of workers who are exploited by the bourgeoisie, an elite class that owns the means of production. According to Marx, the proletariat will never truly profit from their efforts because the upper class owns and controls the means of production.

rational choice theory (or lifestyle theory): This is a modern, Classical School–based framework for explaining crime that includes the traditional formal deterrence aspects, such as police, courts, and corrections and adds other informal factors that studies show consistently and strongly influence behavior, specifically informal deterrence factors (such as friends, family, community, etc.) and also the benefits of offending, whether they be monetary, peer status, or physiological (the "rush" of engaging in deviance).

reaction formation: A Freudian defense mechanism applied to Albert Cohen's theory of youth offending, it involves adopting attitudes or committing behaviors that are opposite of what is expected, for example, by engaging in malicious behavior as a form of defiance. Youth buy into this antinormative belief system so that they will feel less guilt for not living up to the standards they are failing to achieve and so they can achieve status among their delinquent peers.

rebellion: In strain theory, this is an adaptation to strain in which an individual buys into the idea of conventional means and goals of success but does not buy into the current conventional means or goals.

relative deprivation: This perception results when relatively poor people live in close proximity to relatively wealthy people. This concept is distinct from poverty in the sense that a poor area could mean that nearly everyone is poor, but relative deprivation inherently suggests that there is a notable amount of wealth and poor in a given area.

retreatism: In strain theory, this is an adaptation to strain in which an individual does not buy into the conventional goals of success and also does not buy into the conventional means.

retreatist gangs: This type of gang identified by Richard Cloward and Lloyd Ohlin tends to attract individuals who have failed to succeed in both the conventional world and the criminal or conflict gangs of their neighborhoods. Members of retreatist gangs are no good at making a profit from crime, nor are they good at using violence to achieve status, so the primary form of offending in retreatist gangs is usually drug usage.

ritualism: In strain theory, this is an adaptation to strain in which an individual buys into the conventional means of success (e.g., work, school) but does not buy into the conventional goals.

routine activities theory: This is an explanation of crime that assumes that most crimes are committed during the normal daily activities of people's lives. It assumes that crime or victimization is highest in places where three factors come together in time and place: motivated offenders, suitable or attractive targets, and absence of guardian. This perspective assumes a rational offender who picks targets due to opportunity.

Sampson and Laub's developmental model: One of the most known and researched developmental frameworks, this model focuses on the various life transitions (e.g., marriage, stable employment) in influencing the long-term trajectory of an individual and whether that trajectory makes him or her more or less likely to commit crime.

scenario (vignette) research: These are studies that involve providing participants with specific hypothetical scenarios and then asking them what they would do in that situation. Typically, they are also asked about their perceptions of punishment and other factors related to that particular situation.

scientific method: This is the method used in all scientific fields to determine the most objective results and conclusions regarding empirical observations. This method involves testing hypotheses via observation or data collection and then making conclusions based on the findings.

scope: Scope refers to the range of criminal behavior that a theory attempts to explain, which in our case can be seen as the amount of criminal activity a theory can account for, such as only violent crime or only property crime, or only drug usage. If a theory has a very large scope, it would attempt to explain all types of offending.

secondary deviance: A concept in labeling theory originally presented by Edwin Lemert, it is the type of more serious, frequent offending that people commit after they get caught and are labeled offenders. Individuals commit this type of offending because they have internalized their status as offenders and often have resorted to hanging out with other offenders.

selective placement: This is a criticism of adoption studies, arguing that adoptees tend to be placed in households that resemble those of their biological parents; thus, adoptees from rich biological parents are placed in rich adoptive households.

self-report data (SRD): This is one of the primary ways that crime data are collected, typically by asking offenders about their own offending; the most useful data for examining key causal factors in explaining crime (e.g., personality, attitudes).

serotonin: It is a neurotransmitter that is key in information processing; low levels are linked to depression and other mental illnesses. This is the neurotransmitter most consistently linked to criminal behavior in its deficiency.

severity of punishment: One of the key elements of deterrence, the assumption is that a given punishment must be serious enough to outweigh any potential benefits gained from a crime (but not too severe, so that it causes people to commit far more severe offenses to avoid apprehension). In other words, this theoretical concept advises graded penalties that increase as the offender recidivates or reoffends.

side-by-side (or horizontal) integration: This is a type of theoretical integration in which cases are classified by a certain criteria (e.g., impulsive vs. planned), and two or more theories are considered parallel explanations based on what type of case is being considered. Thus, there are two different paths in which a case is predicted to go, typically based on an initial variable (such as low or high self-control).

social bonding theory: This control theory proposed by Travis Hirschi in 1969 assumes that individuals are predisposed to commit crime and that the conventional bond that is formed with the individual prevents or reduces his or her offending. This bond is made up of four constructs: attachments, commitment, involvement, and moral beliefs regarding committing crime.

social contract: This is an Enlightenment ideal or assumption that stipulates there is an unspecified arrangement among citizens of a society in which they promise the state or government not to commit offenses against other citizens (to follow the rules of a society), and in turn, they gain protection from being violated by other citizens; violators will be punished.

social Darwinism: This is the belief that only the beneficial (or "fittest") societal institutions or groups of people survive or thrive in society.

social disorganization: See *Chicago School of Criminology*.

social dynamics: This is a concept proposed by Auguste Comte that describes aspects of social life that alter how societies are structured and that pattern the development of societal institutions.

social sciences: This is a category of scientific disciplines or fields of study that focus on various aspects of human behavior, such as criminology, psychology, economics, sociology, or anthropology. The scientific method is typically used for gaining knowledge.

social statics: This concept was proposed by Auguste Comte to describe aspects of society that relate to stability and social order, which allow societies to continue and endure.

soft determinism: This is the assumption that both determinism (the fundamental assumption of the Positive School of criminology) and free will or free choice (the fundamental assumption of the Classical School) play a role in offenders' decisions to engage in criminal behavior. This perspective can be seen as a type of compromise or "middle-road" concept.

somatotyping: This is the area of study, primarily linked to William Sheldon, that links body type to risk for delinquent or criminal behavior. Also, as a methodology, it is a way of ranking body types based on three categories: ectomorphic, endomorphic, and mesomorphic (see other entries).

somotonic: This is the type of temperament or personality associated with a mesomorphic (muscular) body type. These people tend to be risk-taking and aggressive.

specific deterrence: Punishments given to an individual that are meant to prevent or deter that particular individual from committing crime in the future.

spuriousness: This is when other factors (often referred to as *Z* factors) are actually causing two variables (*X* and *Y*) to occur at the same time; it may appear as if *X* causes *Y* when in fact they are both being caused by (an)other *Z* factor(s). To account for spuriousness, which is required for determining causality, researchers must ensure that no other factors are causing the observed correlation between *X* and *Y*. An example is when ice cream sales (*X*) are related to crime rates (*Y*); the *Z* variable is warm weather, which increases the opportunity for crime because more people and offenders are interacting.

stake in conformity: This significant portion of Jackson Toby's control theory applies to virtually all control theories, which refers to the extent to which individuals have investments in conventional society. It is believed—and supported by empirical studies—that the higher the stake in conformity an individual has, the less likely he or she will engage in criminal offending.

stigmata: The physical manifestations of atavism (biological inferiority); according to Lombroso, if a person had more than 5, he or she was a born criminal, meaning that a person or feature of an individual is a throwback to an earlier stage of evolutionary development and inevitably would be a chronic offender. An example is very large ears or very small ears.

strain theory: This is a category of theories of criminal behavior in which the emphasis is placed on a sense of frustration (e.g., economy) in crime causation—hence, "strain" theories.

subterranean values: These are the norms that individuals have been socialized to accept (e.g., violence) in certain contexts in a given society; an example would be the popularity of boxing or Ultimate Fighting Championship events in American society, even though violence is generally viewed negatively. Another example is the romanticized nature and popularity of crime movies, such as *The Godfather* and *Pulp Fiction*.

superego: This is a subconscious domain of the psyche, according to Sigmund Freud; it is not part of our nature but must be developed through early social attachments. It is responsible for our morality and conscience and battles the subconscious drives of the id.

swiftness of punishment: Swiftness of punishment is one of the key elements of deterrence. The assumption is that the faster punishment occurs after a crime is committed, the more an individual will be deterred in the future.

tabula rasa: This is the assumption that when people are born, they have a "blank slate" regarding morality and that every portion of their ethical or moral beliefs is determined by the interactions that occur in the way they are raised and socialized. This is a key assumption of virtually all learning theories.

telescoping: This is a human tendency in which events are perceived to occur much more recently in the past than they actually did, causing estimates of crime events to be overreported. In the National Crime Victimization Survey (NCVS) measure asking respondents to estimate their victimization over the past 6 months, respondents often report victimization that happened before the 6-month cutoff date.

temporal lobes: This is the region of the brain located above our ears, which is responsible for a variety of functions. It is located right above many primary limbic structures, which govern our emotional and memory functions.

temporal ordering: The criterion for determining causality, it requires that the predictor variable (*X*) precede the explanatory variable (*Y*) in time.

testability: This refers to the extent to which a theoretical model can be empirically or scientifically tested through observation and empirical research.

theoretical elaboration: This is a form of theoretical integration that uses a traditional theory as the framework for the theoretical model but also adds concepts or propositions from other theories.

theory: This is a set of concepts linked together by a series of propositions in an organized way to explain a phenomenon.

theory of concentric circles: This is a model proposed by Chicago School theorists; it assumes that all cities grow in a natural way that universally has the same five zones (or circles or areas). For example, all cities have a central Zone I, which contains basic government buildings, as well as a Zone II, which was once residential but is being "invaded" by factories. The outer three zones involve various forms of residential areas.

theory of low self-control: This is a theory that proposes that individuals either develop self-control by the time they are about age 10 or do not. Those who do not develop self-control will manifest criminal or deviant behaviors throughout life. This perspective was originally proposed by Michael Gottfredson and Travis Hirschi.

Thornberry's interactional model: This integrated model of crime was the first major perspective to emphasize reciprocal, or feedback, effects in the causal modeling of the theoretical framework.

Tittle's control–balance theory: This integrated theory was proposed in 1995; it claims (a) the amount of control to which one is subjected and (b) the amount of control that one can exercise determine the probability of deviance occurring. This theory proposes that the balance between these two types of control can predict the type of behavior that is likely to be committed.

trajectory: This is the path that someone takes in life, often due to the transitions (see *transitions*).

transitions: These are events that are important in altering trajectories toward or against crime, such as marriage, employment, or military service.

twins-separated-at-birth studies: These are studies that examine the similarities between identical twins who are separated in infancy; research indicates that such twins are often extremely similar even though they grew up in completely different environments.

twin studies: These are studies that examine the relative concordance rates for monozygotic (MZ) versus dizygotic (DZ) twins with virtually every study showing that identical twins (MZ) tend to be far more concordant for criminality than fraternal (DZ) twins.

Uniform Crime Report (UCR): This is an annual report published by the Federal Bureau of Investigation (FBI) in the U.S. Department of Justice (DOJ), which is meant to estimate most of the major street crimes in the United States. It is based on police reports or arrests throughout the nation, and started in the 1930s.

up-and-down (or deductive) integration: This type of theoretical integration is generally considered the classic form of theoretical integration because it has been done relatively often in the history of criminological theory development. This often involves increasing the level of abstraction of a single theory so that postulates seem to follow from a conceptually broader theory, such as differential reinforcement theory assuming virtually all of the concepts and assumptions of differential association theory.

utilitarianism: This is a philosophical concept that is often applied to social policies of the Classical School of criminology, which relates to the "greatest good for the greatest number."

viscerotonic: This is the type of temperament or personality associated with an endomorphic (obese) body type. These people tend to be jolly, lazy, and happy-go-lucky.

zone in transition: In the Chicago School or social disorganization theory, this zone (labeled Zone II) was once residential but is becoming more industrial because it is being invaded by the factories; this area of a city tends to have the highest crime rates due to the chaotic effect that the invasion of factories has on the area.

Index

About the Authors

Stephen G. Tibbetts has been pursuing an understanding of criminal offending for the past two decades. He has attempted to discover the extent to which individuals' inherent dispositions and attitudinal traits contribute to their offending decisions, especially in relation to other factors, such as demographic, developmental, and situational considerations. Dr. Tibbetts's research has included work on the differences between men and women in their decisions to commit deviant behavior, as well as their perceptions of risk and consequences of getting caught. His additional research interests include the effects of perinatal disorders as an influence in future criminality, the etiology of white-collar crime, gang intervention, and citizens' attitudes regarding various forms of pornography. Dr. Tibbetts has published nine books and more than 50 scholarly papers examining various issues in criminology. He received the annual Outstanding Professor Award at California State University, San Bernardino (CSUSB), in 2011. Dr. Tibbetts taught at East Tennessee State University for four years prior to coming to CSUSB. He served as a court-appointed special advocate in Washington County, Tennessee, for several years, where he directed the disposition of numerous juvenile court cases. He continued this work as a child advocate in San Bernardino County from 2000 to 2006.

Craig Hemmens is chair and professor in the Department of Criminal Justice and Criminology at Washington State University. He holds a JD from North Carolina Central University School of Law and a PhD in criminal justice from Sam Houston State University. He previously served as chair of the Department of Criminology and Criminal Justice at Missouri State University and as chair of the Department of Criminal Justice, director of the Paralegal Studies Program, and director of the Honors College at Boise State University. Professor Hemmens has published more than 20 books and 200 articles and other writings on a variety of criminal justice topics. He has also served as the editor of the *Journal of Criminal Justice Education*.